ASSEMBLER LANGUAGE PROGRAMMING
For IBM and IBM-Compatible Computers

TO THE STUDENT: A Study Guide for the textbook is available through your college bookstore under the title Study Guide to accompany Assembler Language Programming For IBM and IBM-Compatible Computers by Hamilton A. Sager. The Study Guide can help you with course material by acting as a tutorial, review and study aid. If the Study Guide is not in stock, ask the bookstore manager to order a copy for you.

ASSEMBLER LANGUAGE PROGRAMMING

For IBM and IBM-Compatible Computers

(FORMERLY 370/360
ASSEMBLER LANGUAGE PROGRAMMING)

NANCY STERN

Hofstra University

ALDEN SAGER

Nassau Community College

ROBERT A. STERN

Nassau Community College

JOHN WILEY & SONS

New York   Chichester   Brisbane   Toronto   Singapore

Cover: Painting by Edward A. Burke
Senior Designer: Ann Renzi
Copy Editor: Barbara Heaney
Production Manager: David Smith
Illustrations coordinated by Viga Jesionowski, Blaise Zito Associates

Library of Congress Cataloging in Publication Data:

Stern, Nancy B.
  Assembler language programming for IBM and
IBM-compatible computers.

  Rev. ed. of: 370/360 assembler language programming.
1979.
  Includes indexes.
  1. Assembler language (Computer program language)
2. IBM computers—Programming. I. Sager, Alden.
II. Stern, Robert A. III. Stern, Nancy B. 370/360
assembler language programming. IV. Title.
QA76.73.A8S85 1986   005.13′6   85-22763
ISBN 0-471-88657-2

Printed in the United States of America

Printed and bound by Courier Companies, Inc.

13   14   15   16   17   18

To
Flora Dusing
Joseph Perlman
Lori Anne Stern
Melanie Mara Stern

Preface

OBJECTIVES

Assembler language programming is a relatively complex programming language that requires the student to learn machine architecture and structure. For this reason the textbooks in this field are generally inadequate. Computer language books, in general, typically suffer from a reference manual approach, which concentrates on rules rather than applications. This approach is particularly distressing in assembler textbooks because this subject requires far more explanation and illustration than do other languages.

We have abandoned the reference manual approach for a simple, step-by-step introduction that includes numerous examples, self-tests, and questions designed to introduce students to the kind of approach they need to program realistic problems in this language. The book enables students to write simple programs very early and in general, simplifies a difficult subject.

We have provided numerous programs with sample input and output to illustrate not only the mechanics of the language but also the actual operation of the computer. Similarly, we have integrated many problems that emphasize programming logic rather than rules in an effort to teach the techniques of efficient programming as well as the basics of the language.

ORGANIZATION

This book integrates the advantages of both a reference manual and a programmed instruction guide. The result is a combined textbook-workbook. Complementing the explanations of each topic are numerous questions and answers. In addition, each chapter reinforces previously learned material with computer-run illustrations and self-evaluating practice programs that have sample input and output.

The student will benefit from this book's organization. The fragmented approach of many texts makes it extremely difficult for students to understand how to organize a program effectively. They may understand each individual instruction, but the relationship of each program step may remain difficult to conceptualize. In an effort to provide insight into these relationships, this text enables the reader to write complete assembler language programs, however simple, after the first few lessons. Not only are segments of programs provided in each chapter, but at all points previous learning is reinforced and interrelationships among segments are emphasized by illustrating programs in their entirety.

STUDENT MARKET

This book has been written for the junior-college or four-year college student. It is anticipated that the reader will have had some previous exposure to computer concepts. Although it is not essential that the reader be familiar with programming concepts, an understanding of the fundamental operations of a computer system is necessary. The material covered in an introductory computer course would normally be adequate for this purpose.

This textbook has been written primarily for IBM and IBM-compatible computers that run DOS, OS, MUSIC, or some other operating system. ASSIST is also explained.

UNIQUE FEATURES OF THIS TEXT

1. Pedagogic Approach

We have *not* attempted to be complete. Instead, we present material that can be effectively covered in a one- or two-semester college course on assembler language. Moreover, we present the instructions that are most frequently used by programmers; approximately 60 are instructions emphasized throughout the book.

After completing the text, the student should be able to code simple and intermediate-level programs. In short, assembler language is introduced in much the same way as are higher-level programming languages such as COBOL, BASIC, and FORTRAN.

For students who have had some previous exposure to programming, this text provides an understanding of the fundamental differences between high-level and low-level programming.

The book is divided into units, each of which represents a cohesive entity. Each chapter in a unit not only presents new data but reinforces previous concepts. It begins with a chapter outline that indicates how the chapter has been organized. A list of chapter objectives follows.

There are numerous self-evaluating quizzes throughout each chapter and one comprehensive chapter quiz at the end of each chapter. These will assist students in testing their understanding of concepts; hence, solutions are supplied. Page numbers are also provided with the solutions for the chapter quiz so that students can more easily review the material covered by each question.

A complete, tested program with sample input and output is provided at the end of each chapter to illustrate all the concepts presented in that chapter. This program reinforces the topics in the current chapter as well as those from previous chapters.

At the end of each chapter is a list of key terms used in that chapter. In addition, all key terms used throughout the book have been compiled in the glossary in Appendix A. Also at the end of most chapters are review questions and programming assignments to be coded. These may be assigned by the instructor as homework. A chapter summary is also provided.

2. Business Orientation

From the very beginning, this book emphasizes simplified business applications. It is organized so that the instructions most typically used for business applications appear early in the text. The move statement, arithmetic statements, and logical statements provide the framework for an entire unit in which business problems are emphasized. Once students have mastered these basic concepts, we introduce the more complex instruction formats.

3. Housekeeping

We have introduced a method for housekeeping and I/O routines that we believe is very effective. We present them, at the very beginning, as a program *shell*. All of the concepts are briefly explained and references provided to indicate where further explanations may be found. This shell becomes the foundation for all illustrative programs in the text. The student can then use this shell to write programs in their entirety from the *very beginning*. This is in sharp distinction to the manner in which most books cover the typical housekeeping and I/O routines. Generally, these concepts are left to the end of the book. The major disadvantage of the traditional approach is that students will not be able to run full programs in their entirety until the book has been almost completed.

4. Two Levels of Debugging

Debugging in assembler language is a somewhat complex task. To guide the student through those complexities, we present debugging on two levels. First, Unit III presents it on a simplified level, both to reinforce the material presented in Unit II and to introduce the student, in an elementary way, to debugging techniques. Unit V then presents the more sophisticated steps involved in debugging programs.

5. Attention to Structured Programming

Structured programming, an exceedingly important programming technique, has been included in an effort to enhance the efficiency and organization of students' programs. Program logic is highlighted with the use of pseudocode and flowcharts.

MAJOR CHANGES IN THIS REVISED EDITION

1. The following chapters have been added to the text:
   a. Macros.
   b. Tape and disk programming, including sequential processing, ISAM, and VSAM processing.

2. The following topics have been added or expanded in the text:
   a. Floating-point operations: An overview.
   b. Test Under Mask.
   c. Translate/Translate and Test: An overview.
   d. Flowcharting and pseudocode.
   e. More emphasis on structured concepts.
   f. Programming with ASSIST and MUSIC.
   g. Control break processing.
   h. Emphasis on desk checking.

3. All chapters now have a more or less fixed format:
   a. They begin with a chapter outline and objectives.
   b. They include a Practice Program with sample input and output.
   c. They include Debugging Exercises to debug syntax and logic errors.
   d. They include a chapter summary.
   e. They have expanded use of review questions and programming assignments.

4. Three additional supplements have been added:
   a. A student Study Guide that contains:
      (1) Expanded chapter outlines.

      (2) A checklist of knowledge and skills to be gained from each chapter.

      (3) Commentary on programming style relating to each chapter.

      (4) Additional questions with answers.

      (5) Additional programs with sample input and output for debugging exercises—with answers.

  b. Software that contains:

      (1) Data sets for all programming assignments in the text, and

      (2) Debugging exercises for students to find and correct syntax and logic errors.

  c. Transparency Masters

NOTES TO INSTRUCTORS

1. Some chapters have "HELPFUL HINTS" or "NOTES" after specified sections, as well as optional topics designated by two asterisks(**). These sections provide students with techniques that can be used to apply in more advanced ways the concepts presented. They are not intended for all students, just for those who enjoy a challenge.

2. The section on Job Control Language (JCL) was placed in Appendix B so that instructors can assign it with the first problem program to be run on the computer. Because each teacher decides when that point is reached, we decided to separate the topic from the main body of the text. It should be noted that the appendix simply provides an introduction to the topic. The actual JCL required for any particular installation may vary, depending on how the system was generated.

3. If the course is being taught in one semester, a recommended syllabus would include Chapters 1 to 7, selected topics from Chapters 8 to 10, and Chapters 11, 12, and 15. For a two-semester course, the student can get into the more advanced topics discussed in Chapters 13, 14, and 16 to 22.

The reviewers who provided valuable input during the preparation of the manuscript are acknowledged on the next page. We thank them for their effort. We also thank Nancy Johnke, Chris Hammel, Al Magrella, and Bill Smalling for their assistance in the preparation of computer printouts: We would also like to thank John Impagliazzo for his contributions on the MUSIC operating system. Carol L. Eisen, our assistant, has proven invaluable in typing and editing the manuscript. Our special thanks go to Gene Davenport, Senior Editor at Wiley, for his efforts in bringing this project to fruition, and to Ed Burke, Design Director, David Smith, Production Manager, and Barbara Heaney, Senior Copy Editor.

Acknowledgments

We would like to take this opportunity to thank the following reviewers for their extremely helpful suggestions and comments throughout the development of this project.

Professor Joseph Cebula
Community College of Philadelphia
Philadelphia, PA

Professor Andre de Korvin
Indiana University at Indianapolis
Indianapolis, IN

Mr. Jeffrey W. Klein
Chemical Bank
New York, NY

Professor A. J. Michalewicz
Sacred Heart University
Fairfield, CT

Professor Carl Naeher
SUNY, Buffalo
Buffalo, NY

Professor Steven Sheratofsky
Community College of Philadelphia
Philadelphia, PA

Professor Jay Singlemann
William Rainey Harper College
Palatine, IL

Professor Kathleen M. Swigger
North Texas State University
Denton, TX

Professor Jim Van Speybroeck
St. Ambrose College
Davenport, IA

Contents

UNIT

1

AN OVERVIEW OF ASSEMBLER LANGUAGE

1 Introduction to Assembler Language Programming

OBJECTIVES

To familiarize you with:
1. *What a program is.*
2. *Types of programming languages.*
3. *The characteristics of assembler language.*
4. *The basic rules for coding programs in assembler language.*

I. COMPUTER PROGRAMMING

A. What Is a Program?

No matter how complex a **computer system** may be, its actions are directed by individual computer instructions designed and tested by a computer programmer. The **program** consists of a set of instructions that operate on input data and convert it to output. A computer, then, can function only as efficiently and effectively as it is programmed.

1. Machine Language Programs

Programs must be in **machine language** to be run or **executed.** To write instructions using this machine code is difficult and cumbersome because one must keep track of actual storage locations and complex computer codes.

2. Symbolic Language Programs

Because programming in machine language is so difficult, **symbolic programming languages** have been devised that are easier to code and debug. Note that programs written in a symbolic programming language are *not* executable; they must be *translated* into machine language before they can be run. The computer performs this translation process under the control of a special program called a **translator.**

Programmers, then, rarely write instructions in the machine's own language because of the complexity involved. Rather, they write a set of instructions called a **source program** in one of many symbolic programming languages. This source program cannot be executed directly or operated upon by the computer until it has been translated into machine language. The translation process uses the source program as input and produces a machine language equivalent called an **object program** that is then executable (see Figure 1.1).

B. Programming Errors

While the computer is performing this translation process, any errors detected by the translator program will be listed. That is, any violation of a programming rule will be designated as a **syntax error.** For example, if the instruction to add two numbers in storage should be coded as AP in a symbolic language and instead was erroneously coded as A, then the computer will print an error message called a **diagnostic** that identifies the syntax error. If the errors that result are of considerable magnitude, the translation process will be terminated.

Note that syntax errors detected during the translation process are simply rule violations. **Logic errors,** which occur when the sequence of programming steps has not been coded properly, cannot be detected during this process. During translation, the machine cannot judge the logic in a program. This can be tested only by executing or running the program in a trial run.

If there are no syntax errors in the source program, the translation process

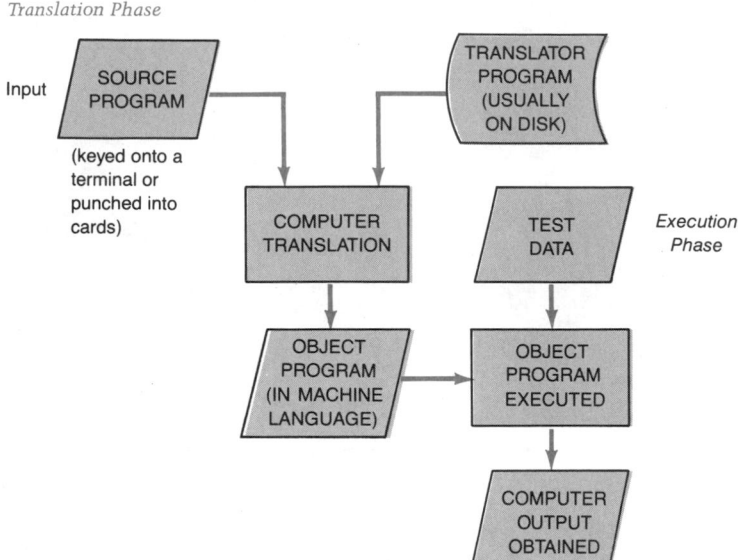

Translation Phase

Input

Figure 1.1
Translating and executing a program.

will convert all symbolic instructions to their machine language equivalent. The object program can then be executed or tested, or it can be stored on disk, tape, or cards for future processing.

II. ASSEMBLER LANGUAGE PROGRAMMING CONTRASTED WITH HIGH-LEVEL PROGRAMMING

A. High-Level Languages

Although there are numerous programming languages, they may be categorized in the following two ways:

TYPES OF PROGRAMMING LANGUAGES

	Type	*Examples*		*Features*
1.	High-level	COBOL FORTRAN BASIC PL/1	a. b. c. d.	Easy to code Least like the machine's own language Requires a complex translation process One-to-many conversion process
2.	Low-level	Assembler language	a. b. c. d.	More difficult to code Most like the machine's own language Requires a relatively simple translation process One-to-one conversion process

High-level languages such as COBOL, FORTRAN, BASIC, and PL/1 are designed to simplify the programmer's task by using instructions that are either English-like or that contain common mathematical expressions. These languages require complex translation processes because they use codes that are very different from the machine's codes. This complex translation process is called a **compilation.** The special program that takes a source program written in a high-level language and converts it to an object program in machine language is called a **compiler.**

A compiler program performs a translation or compilation by taking each symbolic instruction and generating numerous machine language instructions from it. The COBOL instruction COMPUTE A = B + C - D, for example, will translate into several machine language instructions. Because each symbolic instruction is equivalent to many machine language instructions, we call the compilation a **one-to-many conversion process.** The complexity of this compilation results in a translation process that usually takes a good deal of computer time to complete.

B. Low-Level Languages

An assembler or **low-level language** is more difficult for the programmer to code because it is very similar to the machine's own language. The translation process required for low-level languages is called an **assembly,** and the program that performs this translation is called an **assembler.**

In general, for each assembler language instruction, only one machine language instruction is generated. Hence, **assembler language** involves a **one-to-one conversion process.** Later on, you will find that there are several high-level instructions called **macros** that can be coded in the assembler language and that generate numerous machine language instructions. However, the bulk of the instructions coded in this language produce only one object statement for each source statement.

Because the assembly process is not nearly as complex a translation as the compilation, it is a more efficient procedure.

C. Machine Language

1. Uniqueness of Machine Languages

Each computer system has its own unique machine language. Hence, a Digital Equipment Corporation (DEC) computer will have a machine language different from an IBM computer. Because each computer's machine language is unique and because assembler languages are very similar to machine languages, assembler language formats vary depending upon the computer used.

Whereas high-level languages have become standardized so that they can be run on a wide variety of computer systems, assembler languages are much more machine-dependent.

The assembler language that will be described in this text is applicable to a number of computer systems, all of which have very similar machine language codes. The IBM family of **mainframes** (360, 370, 303X, 4300) and numerous IBM-compatible mainframes (Amdahl, UNIVAC, etc.) use the assembler language presented here.

Self-Evaluating Quiz

The questions in these exercises will be followed by the solutions, and are to be used for testing yourself.

1. The set of instructions that operates on input data and converts it to output is called a _____ .
2. The programmer writes a program in a _____ language.
3. To be executed or run, each program must be in _____ language.
4. Programs are rarely written in machine language because _____ .
5. The process used to convert a symbolic program to machine language is called a _____ .

6. The program written in a symbolic language by the programmer is called the _____ .
7. The program translated into machine language is called the _____ .
8. State the names of the *two* processes required to obtain output from a program.
9. What types of languages make programming easier but require more computer time for translation?
10. What types of languages help one understand how the computer actually operates, and result in more efficient translation processes?

SOLUTIONS

1. Program
2. Symbolic programming
3. Machine
4. The codes and addresses that must be used are complex and cumbersome
5. Translation (assembly)
6. Source program
7. Object program
8. Translation or assembly; Execution
9. High-level or compiler languages
10. Low-level or assembler languages

2. Why Study Assembler Language?

For students who have knowledge of high-level programming languages such as COBOL, FORTRAN, BASIC, and PL/1 (and even for students who have not), assembler language programming will be a truly unique experience. Unlike high-level coding, assembler language programming provides you with an understanding of how the machine actually operates on data. This understanding will enable you to program with the utmost efficiency and to code routines that would be difficult to write in other programming languages.

Many of the mysteries of computer processing will be unveiled when studying assembler language. Those who have programmed in a high-level language may have experienced (1) the frustration of encountering a processing error that you were unable to understand because you were unfamiliar with the machine's method of operation, and (2) the desire to learn more about how the computer actually operates on data.

3. Purpose of the Text

The objectives of this text are (1) to reduce the symbolism inherent in other programming languages, and (2) to emphasize, instead, how the computer actually operates. Such objectives will add a dimension to your understanding of computer processing that is simply not possible when studying high-level languages.

Note that this introduction is not meant to diminish the value of high-level programming. High-level languages are extremely useful and important methods of communicating with computers. Accomplishing sophisticated and complex tasks is often not feasible without the use of such languages. These languages, however, sacrifice efficiency and a clear understanding of how the computer actually operates on data. By studying assembler language we will emphasize these two objectives.

III. FEATURES OF A COMPUTER SYSTEM

We will review several features of a computer system that will be relevant to our discussion.

A. Computer System

A computer system consists of a series of devices that interact to read input data, process it, and produce output (see Figure 1.2). The units that comprise this system typically are:

1. Input devices.
2. Output devices.
3. Console typewriter for communicating with the system.
4. **Central processing unit (CPU).**

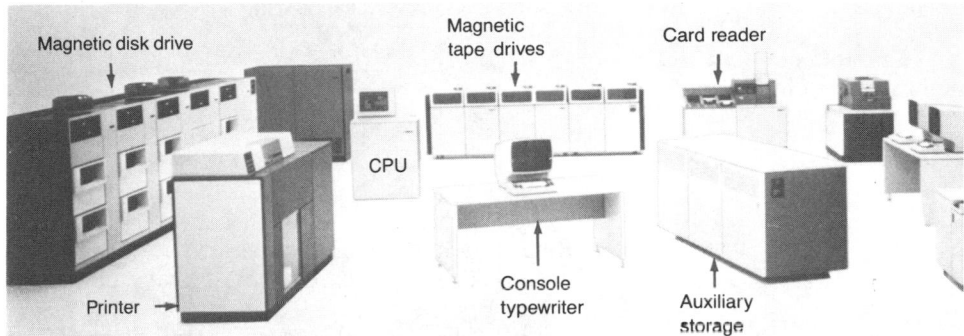

Figure 1.2
IBM 4341 computer system.
(Courtesy IBM)

Magnetic tape and disk drives can serve as either input or output devices. A card reader is an input device and a printer is an output device. We will focus on large computer systems called mainframes, as opposed to microcomputers that most often use other types of assembler languages.

B. Central Processing Unit

The CPU is the "brain" of the computer system, controlling all the operations to be performed.

A mainframe typically consists of hundreds of thousands or millions of storage positions. The following are stored in these positions:

---

1. Data that has been read: located in an input area.
2. Work areas: used for processing data.
3. Actual instructions.
4. Processed data that will serve as output: in an output area.

A position of storage is referred to as a **byte**, and each byte is generally used to store one **character** of data. A character may be a letter, digit, or special symbol such as a $ or an *. One million bytes is called a **megabyte.**

Each byte is analogous to a cell or slot that stores a character of data. The actual method of representing characters within storage will be discussed in Chapters 2 and 3.

Many computers utilize the concept of **virtual storage,** which is a technique of treating the CPU as if it had more storage capacity than it actually has. For example, a computer with a CPU of 256,000 bytes can be made to function as if it has, instead, several million bytes.[1]

Each byte, or storage position, in the CPU has its own **address.** The illustration in Figure 1.3 shows a CPU with a storage capacity, or **memory size,** of

---

[1]See Appendix H for a detailed discussion of how a virtual storage system operates.

256,000 bytes. Notice that the address of the first byte is usually designated as 0, the second byte as 1, and so on.

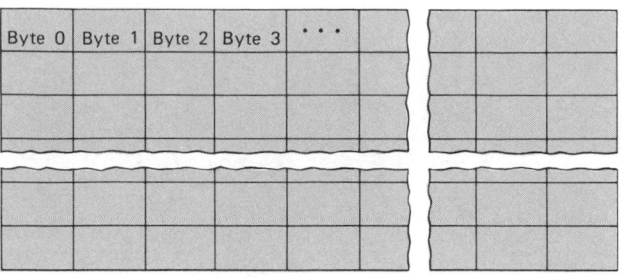

Figure 1.3
Example of a CPU with a
memory size of 256,000 bytes.

C. General Registers

Registers are specific areas of the CPU that may be used for particular purposes. For example, registers may be used as high-speed accumulators in arithmetic operations.

The CPU contains *16* general purpose registers numbered 0 to 15, each *4* bytes long. Registers 2 through 12 are the only ones available for normal assembler language processing; the others are used for special purposes. Throughout this text, but particularly in Units IV through VI, we will explore how registers may be used for processing data.

D. The Supervisor

The operations of the computer system are controlled by a monitor or control program commonly called a **supervisor.** The supervisor, which is usually supplied by a vendor as part of the operating system, controls the operations performed by the system. It must be loaded into the CPU before any programs can be processed.

When an assembler language program is entered as input for translation, for example, the supervisor:

1. Calls for the assembler program to produce an object program.
2. Transfers control to the object program for execution.

Note that the supervisor, as well as the input to be processed and the programs to be executed, is stored in the central processing unit, or CPU, in actual storage locations called addresses. Computer systems are said to utilize the **stored program concept,** which means that instructions, like data, are stored in these actual locations.

The computer system can thus be pictured in general terms as shown in Figure 1.4.

E. Types of Computer Operations

1. Instructions That Operate on Data in Storage: Decimal Operations

Decimal instructions operate on data in main storage. These instructions are discussed in Unit 2 of this text. They include, for example, data transfer or move instructions, and decimal arithmetic operations.

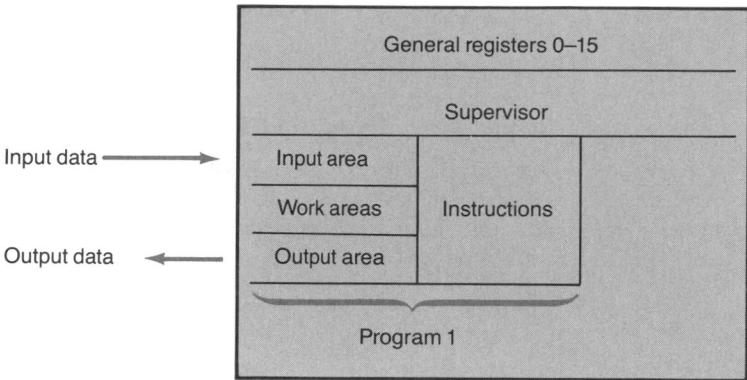

Figure 1.4
Schematic of a CPU.

2. Instructions That Use Registers: Binary Operations

Binary instructions operate on data contained in registers. These can be instructions utilizing registers only, or utilizing both registers and main storage.

Binary operations are performed on data in registers. Binary operations are faster than decimal operations because (1) the computer actually operates on data in binary form, and (2) registers serving as accumulators result in an efficient method of processing data. In Units IV and V we consider this type of instruction.

Floating-point instructions also use registers. Because they are complex to code and not necessary for simple or intermediate-level programs, they are discussed later, in Chapter 20.

Self-Evaluating Quiz

1. Each storage position in a computer is referred to as a _____ .
2. Associated with each byte of storage is a(n) _____ by which we can locate that position.
3. Computer operations are under the control of a monitor program called a

   _____
4. In addition to locations in main storage, there are 16 _____ numbered _____ to _____ that may be used for processing data.
5. (T or F) Binary operations utilize registers.
6. (T or F) The supervisor is part of the operating system.
7. (T or F) The supervisor must be loaded into the CPU before processing can occur.
8. (T or F) A computer system consists of only one unit called a CPU.
9. (T or F) Registers must be used for arithmetic operations in assembler language programs.
10. (T or F) A program, as well as input records, is loaded into actual storage locations.

SOLUTIONS

1. Byte or address
2. Address
3. Supervisor
4. General registers; 0; 15
5. T
6. T
7. T
8. F: there are input and output units as well
9. F: they *may* be used, but they are not always necessary
10. T

IV. CODING ASSEMBLER LANGUAGE PROGRAMS

A. The Coding Sheet

1. Keying a Program from Coding Sheets

Assembler language programs are generally written on **coding** or **program sheets** as shown in Figure 1.5. The coding sheet has space for 80 columns of information. Each *line* of a coding sheet will be keypunched into one punched card, or keyed as one line on a terminal. The entire program keyed from the coding sheets is called the source program.

LABEL	OPERATION	OPERAND	COMMENTS
1	10 16		72

Figure 1.5
Main body of an assembler coding sheet.

Let us examine the coding sheet more closely. The main body of the form is subdivided into columns 1–72 that will be keyed into columns or positions 1–72 respectively of a card or a line on a terminal.

2. Convention: Slashing Zeros

Before discussing entries themselves, note that zeros will contain slashes through them. Because it is very common for programmers and data entry operators mistakenly to key a zero for the letter O and vice versa, computer centers usually establish conventions where either zero or letter O's are slashed. For illustrations in this text, we have adopted the convention of slashing zeros to distinguish them from the letter O.

B. Identification Sequence: Positions 73–80

1. Purpose

There is a provision for an optional program identification number called "Identification Sequence," which references positions 73–80. This field is used to identify a program and to indicate the sequence of instructions. It makes it easier for the programmer to keep track of the sequence of instructions in the program in case resequencing is necessary.

Here are typical entries in positions 73–80 of the first few instructions in a program:

```
STERN010
STERN020
STERN030
     ⋮
```

2. Coding the Identification Sequence

STERN identifies the program; the numbers are used for sequencing. The first instruction generally has number 010, the second 020, etc. They are numbered by tens so that insertions may be made easily. If an entry is inadvertently omitted and must be inserted between numbers 030 and 040, it may be keyed as 035. Note that this Identification Sequence is used to prevent errors and to assist the programmer in organizing the program. It is *not* used by the computer during translation or execution.

C. Continuation: Position 72

If an instruction requires more than one line of coding, it may be continued on the next line. In such cases, a nonblank character is coded in position 72 of the line *to be continued.* That is, if two lines are required for an instruction, only the first one will contain a character in position 72. For all instructions that are coded on a single line, position 72 must be blank.

D. Body of Form: Positions 1–71

Positions 1–71 are used to code each statement. By examining the coding sheet in Figure 1.5, we can see that each statement can consist of from one to four entries.

NAME or LABEL
OPERATION
OPERAND
COMMENTS

The coding sheet is designed so that these entries for each instruction are *always* placed in the same positions in a uniform manner. This facilitates keying and reading of the program. The programmer can, if desired, write instructions free-form without using the suggested positions for each entry. If the free-form style is used, all that is required is that each entry be separated by a blank. When programs are entered using a terminal, this free-form format is typically used. Operating systems such as MUSIC use an ASMFIX command to align the entries automatically.

A brief description of each entry will provide insight into the nature of assembler language instructions.

1. LABEL (Positions 1–8)

This optional entry is used to identify a statement. It may consist of an entry point or **symbolic address** so that another instruction can branch to it:

Example 1.1

LABEL	OPERATION	OPERAND	COMMENTS	
1	10	16		72
STEP1	AR	3,4	THIS IS A TYPE OF ADD INSTRUCTION	
	•		ADDITIONAL	
	•		INSTRUCTIONS FOLLOW	
	•			
	B	STEP1	THIS IS A BRANCH–RETURNS CONTROL TO STEP1	

The LABEL field is also used to assign a name to a storage area.

Example 1.2

LABEL	OPERATION	OPERAND	COMMENTS	
1	10	16		72
HOLD	DS	CL5		

HOLD, which is coded in the LABEL field, becomes the symbolic address by which the field is referenced.

Because instructions and data are placed in actual storage locations, they can both be referenced by a symbolic address called a NAME.

RULES FOR FORMING LABELS (OR NAMES)

1. From 1 to 8 characters.
2. Must start in position 1.
3. The first character must be alphabetic (A–Z, @, #, or $).
4. No blanks or special characters other than @, #, $ allowed within the name.

Notice that for assembler language, alphabetic characters include not only letters, but also the symbols @, #, and $. We will see in Chapter 4 that names for identifying input and output files are also assigned in accordance with these rules.

2. OPERATION Entry (Positions 10–14)

This entry is used to specify the actual operation to be performed, such as adding and moving. This is called an **operation** or **op code.** The term **mnemonic** refers to the symbolic operation that is coded in assembler language. Beginning in Unit 2, we will discuss many of the op codes that may be used in this language.

3. OPERAND Entry (Beginning in Position 16)

This field identifies and describes the data fields to be operated on. Depending upon the instruction format, there may be one or two **operands** associated with each instruction. Most instructions utilize two operands, separated by a comma (no space after the comma).

Example 1.3   1. Add AMT to TOTAL is coded as follows:

LABEL	OPERATION	OPERAND	COMMENTS	
1	10 16			72
	AP	TOTAL,AMT		

2. Add register 3 to register 7 is coded as follows:

LABEL	OPERATION	OPERAND	COMMENTS	
1	10 16			72
	AR	7,3		

RULES FOR FORMING OPERAND NAMES

1. From 1 to 8 characters.
2. The first character must be alphabetic (A–Z, @, #, or $).
3. No blanks or special characters except @, #, or $.

Each symbolic operand specified in the OPERAND field normally will be defined elsewhere in the program in the NAME field. Hence, the rules for forming such names are the same.

Example 1.4

LABEL	OPERATION		OPERAND	COMMENTS	
1	10	16			72
	AP		TOTAL,AMT		
	.				
	.				
	.				
TOTAL	DS		PL5		
AMT	DS		PL3		

4. COMMENT Entry

This entry is used to supply explanatory or descriptive information about a particular instruction. The COMMENT appears in the OPERAND section of the coding sheet and is separated from the last operand by at least one space.

Example 1.5

	LABEL	OPERATION		OPERAND	COMMENTS	
	1	10	16			72
(1)		AP		TOTAL,AMT	TOTAL = SUM OF ALL AMTS	
(2)		AR		7,3	REGISTER3 = QTY, REGISTER7 = SUM	

Note that the COMMENT entry is strictly optional and does not affect the execution of the program in any way. It may, however, be enormously helpful to the programmer by providing brief reminders of the purpose of specific instructions.

The comment included along with an instruction may not extend beyond position 71 of any line. If more comprehensive comments are desired, whole lines may be used exclusively for comments. By coding an asterisk (*) in position 1, the entire line, from positions 1–71, is treated as a comment:

Example 1.6

LABEL	OPERATION		OPERAND	COMMENTS	
1	10	16			72
* THIS PROGRAM WILL READ SALARY RECORDS AND					
* PROVIDE EACH EMPLOYEE WITH A 20% BONUS					
BEGIN	GET				
	.				
	.				
	.				

CHAPTER SUMMARY

I. Computer Programming
  A. A program is a set of instructions that operates on input data and converts it to output.
    1. Programs must be in machine language to be run.
    2. Machine language is a difficult language in which to program.
    3. Symbolic language programs.
      a. Easier to code than machine language.
      b. Require a translation process before being executed.
      c. Symbolic program equals source program. Source program translated into machine language equals object program.
  B. Programming errors.
    1. Syntax errors: rule violations—found during translation.
    2. Logic errors: sequence of steps is wrong—found during execution.
II. Assembler Language Programming Contrasted with High-Level Programming
  A. High-level languages.
    1. Easy to code.
    2. Least like machine language.
    3. Requires a complex translation process.
  B. Low-level languages.
    1. More difficult to code.
    2. Most like machine language.
    3. Efficient because of simplified translation process.
III. Features of a Computer System
  A. General registers.
    Assembler language uses registers as accumulators and for other purposes.
  B. Types of computer operations.
    1. Decimal operations: operate on data in main storage.
    2. Binary operations: operate on data in registers.
    Both are performed in assembler language.
IV. Coding Assembler Language Programs
    The rules provided in this chapter for labels, operation codes, operands, and comments should be learned thoroughly.

CHAPTER SELF-EVALUATING QUIZ

At the end of each chapter there is a self-evaluating quiz that covers the material in the entire chapter. The solutions that are provided after the quiz include page references where explanations of the answers can be found.

1. Assembler language programs are written on _____ sheets.
2. Each line of a coding sheet will be keyed into one _____ .
3. The program keyed from the coding sheets is called the _____ .
4. Optional entries on the coding sheet include _____ , _____ , and _____ .
5. The rules for forming operand names are _____ .
6. Indicate the two ways in which comments may be specified.
7. Column 72 is called a _____ column and is used to _____ .

Indicate what, if anything, is wrong with the following labels:

8. NO GO
9. DISCT%
10. SALESAMOUNT
11. 1A
12. SAM

SOLUTIONS

		Page
1.	Coding or program	10
2.	Card or line on a terminal	10
3.	Source program	10
4.	Name or label; comment; identification sequence (positions 73–80)	10
5.	1–8 characters; no blanks or special characters except $, @, #; the first character must be alphabetic (A–Z, $, @, or #)	12
6.	Leave a blank after the last operand and continue until position 71; code * in position 1 of any line—this makes the entire line a comment	13
7.	Continuation; indicate that the instruction is too long for a given line and will be continued on the next line	11
8.	Embedded blanks are not permitted.	12
9.	% is not permitted.	12
10.	The label is too long.	12
11.	The label must begin with an alphabetic character.	12
12.	Okay.	12

KEY TERMS

Address
Assembler language
Assembly (assembler)
Binary instructions
Byte
Central processing unit (CPU)
Character
Coding sheet
Compilation (compiler)
Computer system
Decimal instructions
Diagnostic
Execution
High-level programming language
Logic error
Low-level programming language
Machine language
Macro
Mainframe

Megabyte
Memory size
Mnemonic
Object program
One-to-many conversion process
One-to-one conversion process
Operand
Operation code
Program
Program sheet
Register
Source program
Stored program concept
Supervisor
Symbolic address
Symbolic programming language
Syntax error
Translator
Virtual storage

[2]All key terms are defined in the glossary.

REVIEW QUESTIONS

1. Programs in machine language are called
   a. Source programs.
   b. Symbolic programs.
   c. Object programs.
   d. Both a and b.

2. Which of the following statements is false?
   a. The object program must be tested to determine if it is correct.
   b. A program written in a symbolic language is not directly executable on a computer.
   c. The assembly process checks for syntax errors in the source program.
   d. The assembly program checks for logic errors in the source program.

3. Which of the following names are valid?
   a. $AMT
   b. X9Y
   c. GROSS PAY
   d. DEPENDENTS

4. Which of the following statements is false?
   a. Symbolic names used as operands must be defined elsewhere in the program.
   b. Operands in a single instruction must be separated by commas.
   c. An operand describes the data or storage area to be operated on by the instruction.
   d. Machine instructions do not require operands.

5. (T or F) The entries on a coding sheet may be separated by one or more blanks.

6. Comments are coded in assembler language by coding
   a. C in position 1.
   b. an * in position 4.
   c. an * in position 1.
   d. a blank in position 1.
   e. None of the above.

7. (T or F) The supervisor program is another name for an assembler program.

8. (T or F) When a machine language program is being executed, the supervisor must be in main storage.

2 Numbering Systems and Data Representation

OBJECTIVES

To familiarize you with:
1. *The representation of numbers in binary form.*
2. *Procedures to be used in converting binary numbers to decimal form, and decimal numbers to binary form.*
3. *Ways in which binary numbers are added and subtracted internally by the computer.*
4. *The actual computer code on IBM and IBM-compatible computers that makes use of binary numbers: the hexadecimal system.*
5. *The internal computer code, called EBCDIC, which represents numbers, letters, and special characters using a form of the binary numbering system.*

I. NUMBERING SYSTEMS

A. Review of Decimal Numbers

1. Introduction

Data is entered into a computer in normal alphanumeric or alphameric form as letters, digits, and special characters. Similarly, information or output from the computer is in the same readable, alphanumeric form. Internally, however, data is represented by a computer code. Although this computer code varies from computer to computer, certain features are standard and independent of any specific system. It is the purpose of this chapter to discuss how data is represented and manipulated by computer systems in general.

All computer codes use the **binary numbering system** in some form or another. We will discuss this system in detail in the following section. The binary numbering system uses two digits, 0 and 1, to represent every possible number, and is ideally suited to computers for one important reason. The 0s are represented internally in the computer as an off-state and the 1s as an on-state. Hence, computer circuits are on or off depending upon the binary representation of numbers. For integrated circuits used in computers, the "1" state means a circuit is on or closed, and a "0" state means a circuit is off or open.

Let us begin by reviewing some features of our own decimal numbering system that also apply to the binary numbering system.

The decimal system, like the binary system, is a **positional numbering system.** This implies that each digit has a different significance or value depending on its position in a sequence of numbers. The decimal system utilizes ten distinct digits, 0 to 9. We sometimes refer to it as a *base 10* system. Each position can contain one of ten digits and, in addition, each position can be expressed as a factor of 10. The following is a schematic of the positional values in the decimal or base 10 system.

Value of Each Position Expressed as Integers	1000	100	10	1
Value of Each Position Expressed as a Power of 10	10^3	10^2	10^1	10^0

Using this schematic, we can see that the fifth position in the base 10 system indicates the number of 10,000s or 10^4, and so on. The 4 in 10^4 is called an exponent or power. 10^4 represents $10 \times 10 \times 10 \times 10$.

2. Explanation of Powers of 10

Hence, in base 10 the first position has unit or 10^0 value. (Any number with exponent of zero is equal to 1.) The second position has value 10, or 10 raised to the first power. The third position has value 100, or 10 raised to the second power, or 10×10. The fourth position has value 1000, or 10 raised to the third power, or $10 \times 10 \times 10$.

Thus, the number 384 may be expressed as

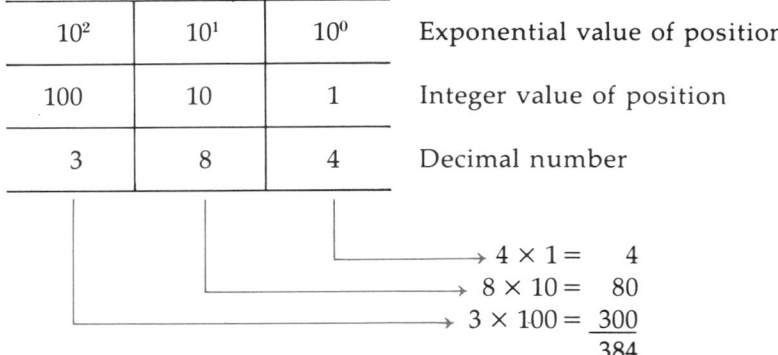

10^2	10^1	10^0	Exponential value of position
100	10	1	Integer value of position
3	8	4	Decimal number

$$4 \times 1 = 4$$
$$8 \times 10 = 80$$
$$3 \times 100 = \underline{300}$$
$$384$$

To obtain the value 384 from the 3 digits 3, 8, and 4, we multiply each digit by its positional value. This method of multiplying any digit by its positional value to determine the value of the entire number is the method we will be using to determine the decimal equivalent of binary numbers.

The decimal numbering system, as indicated, has 10 unique digits, 0 to 9. To represent the numbers 0 to 9 we merely use the digits 0 to 9. To represent the next number, however, we cannot use an additional digit, because no additional single digits exist. Instead, we proceed with the next position (10s position) by putting a 1 there and initializing the units position at zero. Thus we have

```
0
1
2
•
•
•
9
――  → Initialize units position; add 1 to tens position.
10
11
•
•
•
19
```

To represent 1 more than 19, we initialize the units position at zero again and add 1 to the 10s position. Thus we have

```
19
――  → Initialize units position; add 1 to tens position.
20
•
•
•
29
――  → Initialize units position; add 1 to tens position.
30
•
•
•
99
――  → Initialize units and tens positions; add 1 to hundreds position.
100
```

When we have used all digits in the units and tens positions (99), we proceed to the next position, the hundreds, and begin again by initializing units and tens at zero (100).

Although this entire introduction may seem trite and obvious, we will see that all positional numbering systems share basic elements.

B. Binary Numbers

The binary numbering system is a *base 2* system that uses only the digits 0 and 1. This is ideally suited to computer processing, where 0 represents an off-state and 1 represents an on-state.

Using the binary numbering system, all numbers are represented by a series of 0s and 1s. Let us first consider the logical manner in which numbers are incremented using this system, and then we will proceed to the positional representation of binary numbers.

1. Numeric Representation

With only 2 digits, we can only represent the numbers 0 and 1 using a single, or unit, digit. To represent a 2 we must use the next position and initialize the units position at 0. Thus 2 in decimal, or base 10, is a 10 in binary, or base 2. A 3 would be 11; to represent a 4 we must initialize these two first positions and place a 1 in the third position. Thus, a 4 in decimal is 100 in binary. A 5 would be 101. Notice that the sequence is 0, 1, then proceed to the next position and initialize (10, 11, 100, and so on).

Binary	*Decimal*
0	0
1	1
10	2
11	3
100	4
101	5
110	6
111	7
1000	8
⋮	⋮

Notice that any decimal number can be represented by a sequence of 0s and 1s in the binary system. Note, too, that it generally takes far more digits in the binary system to represent a number than in the decimal system.

Let us now consider the *positional* attribute of binary numbers. You will recall that the decimal or base 10 system has these positional values:

. . .	10^3	10^2	10^1	10^0	Exponential value of position
. . .	1000	100	10	1	Integer value of position

That is, a 1 in the tens position and a 0 in the units position (10) is the number after 9. When the largest single digit has been reached, we proceed to the next position, initializing the first position with 0.

Because this system has a base 10, each position has a value that is a factor of 10. The first position is 10^0 or 1, the second is 10^1 or 10, . . . , the seventh position would be 10^6 or 1,000,000.

The binary numbering system has a base of 2. Thus, each position has a value that is a factor of 2. We have then:

. . .	2^4	2^3	2^2	2^1	2^0	Exponential value of position
. . .	16	8	4	2	1	Integer value of position

Recall that any number raised to the zero power is 1; 2^1 is 2; 2^2 is 2×2 or 4; 2^3 is $2 \times 2 \times 2$ or 8, and so on. The two binary digits are 0 and 1. To represent the number 2, we must use the next position. Thus, 10 in binary is 2 in decimal. That is:

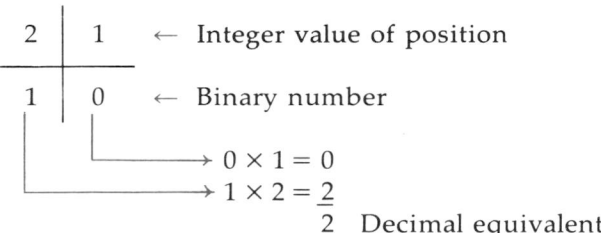

We say, then, $10_2 = 2_{10}$ (10 in base 2 = 2 in base 10).

2. Determining the Decimal Equivalent of a Binary Number

Thus, all positional numbering systems are similar. To obtain the decimal equivalent of a number in any base, multiply the digits by their positional values and add the results.

Example 2.1 $1001_2 = (?)_{10}$

Find the decimal equivalent of 1001 in binary (represented as 1001_2, where the subscript denotes the base).

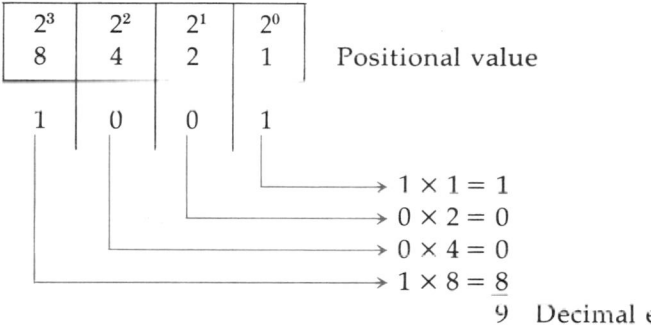

Thus, $1001_2 = 9_{10}$. We can simplify this calculation by eliminating all multiplications where 0 is a factor. Thus we have:

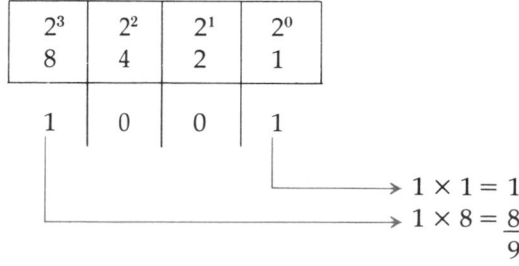

In short, the binary digit 8 and the binary digit 1 are "on," the others are "off." That is, the 8-bit and the 1-bit are on, where **bit** is an abbreviation for *bi*nary di*git*.

Example 2.2 $1110_2 = (?)_{10}$

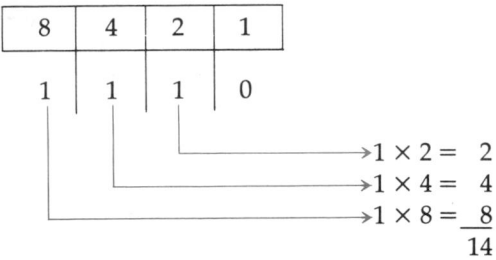

ANS: $(14)_{10}$

Example 2.3 $11101_2 = (?)_{10}$

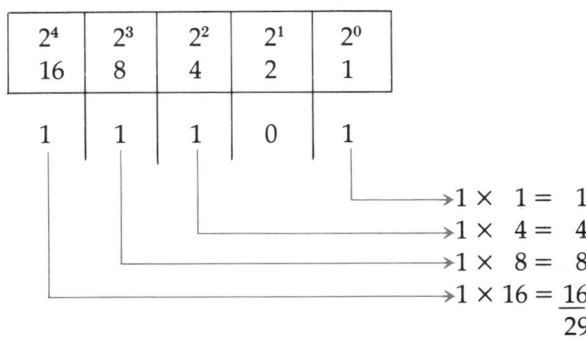

Solution: $(29)_{10}$

Thus, given any binary number we can find its decimal equivalent by the following technique.

RULES FOR FINDING THE DECIMAL EQUIVALENT OF A BINARY NUMBER

1. Determine positional value of each digit.
2. Add the positional values for all positions that contain a 1.

Self-Evaluating Quiz

1. The decimal system has a base of __(no.)__ whereas the binary system has a base of __(no.)__.
2. Because numbers are frequently represented within the computer as a series of on–off switches, the _____ numbering system is well-suited to computer processing.
3. (T or F) All numbers must be entered into the computer in binary form.
4. (T or F) There are numbers that can be expressed in base 2 that cannot be expressed in base 10.
5. (T or F) In general, more digits are necessary to represent a number in binary form than in decimal form.
6. $2^2 =$ _____ .
7. $2^5 =$ _____ .
8. $2^0 =$ _____ .
9. $10^0 =$ _____ .

10. Find the decimal equivalent for each of the following.
    a. 11011_2
    b. 1101_2
    c. 1111_2
    d. 11001_2
    e. 11111_2

SOLUTIONS
1. 10; 2
2. Binary or base 2
3. F: decimal numbers as well as binary numbers can be entered as input.
4. F
5. T
6. $2^2 = 2 \times 2 = 4$
7. $2^5 = 2 \times 2 \times 2 \times 2 \times 2 = 32$
8. 1: any number raised to the zero power is 1
9. 1

10. a. $11011_2 =$

2^4	2^3	2^2	2^1	2^0
16	8	4	2	1

$= 16 + 8 + 2 + 1 = 27_{10}$

```
 1    1    0    1    1
                     │
                     ↓
                  1 × 1 =  1
                  2 × 1 =  2
                  8 × 1 =  8
                 16 × 1 = 16
                          ──
                          27
```

b. $1101_2 =$

8	4	2	1
1	1	0	1

$= 8 + 4 + 1 = 13_{10}$

c. $1111_2 =$

8	4	2	1
1	1	1	1

$= 8 + 4 + 2 + 1 = 15_{10}$

d. $11001_2 =$

16	8	4	2	1
1	1	0	0	1

$= 16 + 8 + 1 = 25_{10}$

e. $11111_2 =$

16	8	4	2	1
1	1	1	1	1

$= 16 + 8 + 4 + 2 + 1 = 31_{10}$

3. Determining the Binary Equivalent of a Decimal Number

Computers generally represent numeric data in binary form or in a variation of this form where digits are indicated by a series of on–off circuits. Keep in mind that numeric data is entered, as input, in standard decimal form and then converted by the computer to a binary representation. Before the data is produced as output it is reconverted to decimal form.

Thus far, we have some idea of the way in which binary numbers are converted into decimal numbers. In this section, we will learn the manner in which the binary equivalent of a decimal number may be determined.

This conversion process is a relatively simple task when small numbers are used. That is, we merely employ the positional values of binary numbers to find the right combination of digits.

Example 2.4 $10_{10} = (?)_2$

For this example, we must determine what combination of 1, 2, 4, 8, 16, 32, will equal 10.

Note that we do not need to use more than four binary digits to represent 10_{10}, because the fifth positional value is 16, which is greater than 10_{10}. Hence, we must determine what combination of 8, 4, 2, 1, will equal 10.

There is only one such combination. The numbers $8 + 2 = 10$. Thus, our binary equivalent is

8	4	2	1	Integer value of position
1	0	1	0	Binary number

To represent the decimal number 10 in binary form, the 8-bit and the 2-bit are on while the others are off. Bit is an abbreviation for binary digit.

Thus, $10_{10} = 1010_2$.

Example 2.5 $(14)_{10} = (?)_2$

Here again, we use 4 binary digits because the next position has a value of 16, which exceeds the required quantity. Again, we must determine what combination of 8, 4, 2, 1 will produce 14.

There is only one such combination: the 8, 4, 2 bits are on $(8 + 4 + 2 = 14)$, while the 1-bit is off.

Thus $(14)_{10} = (1110)_2$.

Example 2.6 $(23)_{10} = (?)_2$

Here, we must use a combination of the numbers 16, 8, 4, 2, 1 that will produce 23. We must determine which bits are "on." The 16-bit must be on, because 8, 4, 2, 1 bits can produce a maximum decimal number of 15. This means that the 16-bit must be on to obtain a number larger than 15. The 8-bit is off because 16-8 produces 24, which exceeds the required number. Thus, the 16-4-2-1 bits are on and only the 8-bit is off. We have, then:

$(23)_{10} = (10111)_2$

This method of determining the combination of positional values that produces the required number is only useful with small numbers. Consider the task of finding the combination of binary numbers for the decimal number 1087, for example. That is, the above method is too cumbersome for larger decimal numbers.

There is a technique called the **remainder method** that may be used to convert a decimal number to any other numbering system. The technique is as follows:

REMAINDER METHOD FOR CONVERTING DECIMAL NUMBERS INTO ANY OTHER BASE

1. Divide the decimal number by the base (for a binary number, divide by 2).
2. Indicate the remainder, which will be either 0 or 1 in the case of binary numbers.
3. Continue dividing into each quotient (result of previous division) until the divide operation produces a zero.
4. The equivalent number in the base desired is the numeric remainders reading from the last division to the first.

These rules are best interpreted by examples.

Example 2.7 $(38)_{10} = (?)_2$

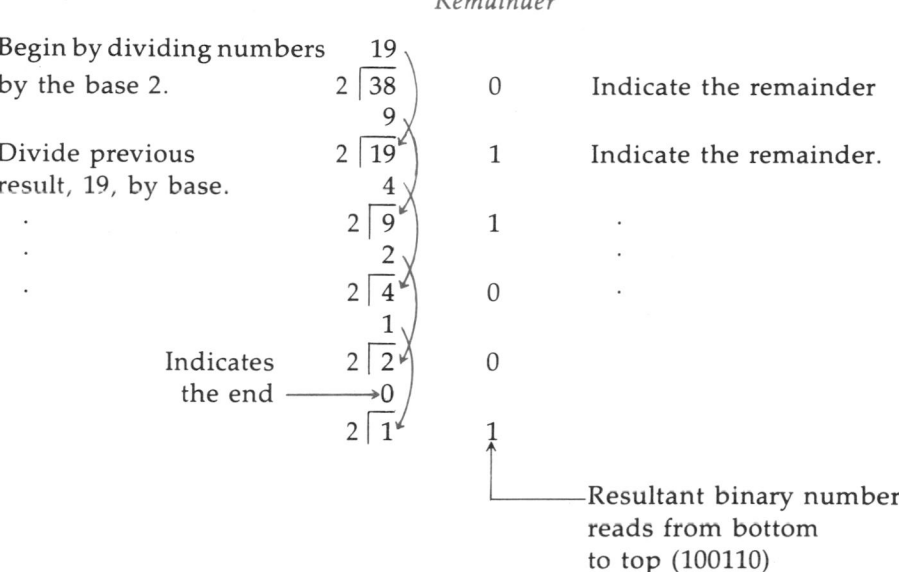

Remainder

Begin by dividing numbers by the base 2.

Divide previous result, 19, by base.

Indicates the end

Indicate the remainder

Indicate the remainder.

Resultant binary number reads from bottom to top (100110)

When the divide operation produces a quotient or result of zero, then the process is terminated. The binary equivalent, reading from the last division to the first is:

$(38)_{10} = (100110)_2$

We should check our result to insure that it is correct.

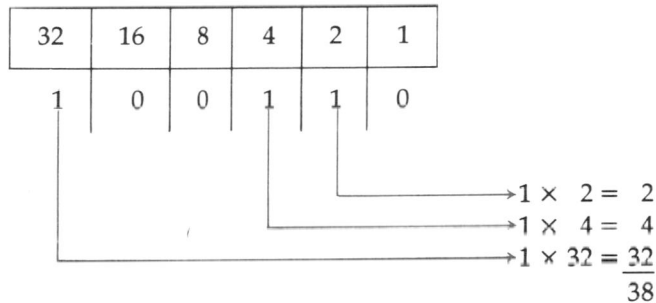

32	16	8	4	2	1
1	0	0	1	1	0

$1 \times 2 = 2$
$1 \times 4 = 4$
$1 \times 32 = \underline{32}$
38

When using the remainder method for converting from decimal to binary, it is better to perform the first divide operation at the bottom of the work sheet and work up.

The following is exactly equivalent to the previous example and is easier to read.

Remainder

```
        0
      2 1      1
      2 2      0
      2 4      0
      2 9      1
    2 19      1
    2 38      0
```

In this case, the result is read from top to bottom : $(100110)_2$.

Example 2.8 $(67)_{10} = (?)_2$

To find the binary equivalent by determining the combination of positional values can be a long and arduous procedure where the numbers are large. Instead, we may use the remainder method.

Remainder

```
        0
      2⌐1      1
  ↑   2⌐2      0
      2⌐4      0
      2⌐8      0
  �下  2⌐16     0
      2⌐33     1
      2⌐67     1
```

Thus the result, reading from top to bottom is: $(1000011)_2 = (67)_{10}$. All operations should be checked for accuracy. Let us make certain that $(1000011)_2$ is indeed equivalent to $(67)_{10}$.

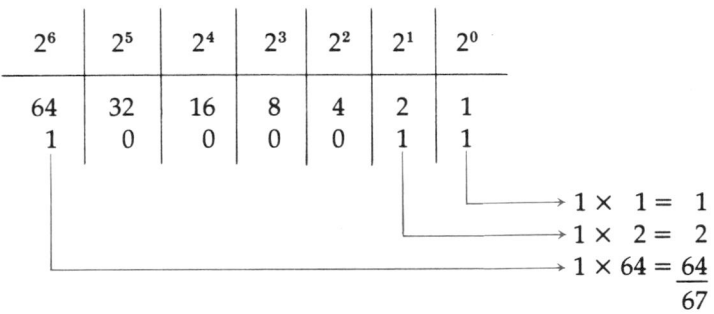

2^6	2^5	2^4	2^3	2^2	2^1	2^0
64	32	16	8	4	2	1
1	0	0	0	0	1	1

$1 \times 1 = 1$
$1 \times 2 = 2$
$1 \times 64 = 64$
$\overline{67}$

Self-Evaluating Quiz

1. The binary numbering system uses __(no.)__ digits.
2. The digits used in the binary numbering system are _____ and _____ .
3. The binary numbering system is ideally suited to computer processing because the digit _____ represents the _____-state and the digit _____ represents the _____-state.
4. The term bit is an abbreviation for _____ _____ .
5. The decimal and binary numbering systems are called _____ numbering systems because the location or position of each digit is significant.
6. The binary numbering system has a base of _____ .
7. The binary number 1011 is equivalent to the decimal number _____ .
8. The binary number 110110 is equivalent to the decimal number _____ .
9. The binary number 11101 is equivalent to the decimal number _____ .
10. The largest decimal number that can be represented by 4 binary digits is _____ .
11. The binary equivalent of the decimal number 86 is _____ .
12. The binary equivalent of the decimal number 101 is _____ .
13. The method used to convert a decimal number to a number in another system is called the _____ _____ .

SOLUTIONS
1. two
2. 0; 1

3. 0; "off"; 1; "on"
4. *Binary digit*
5. Positional
6. 2

7. 11:

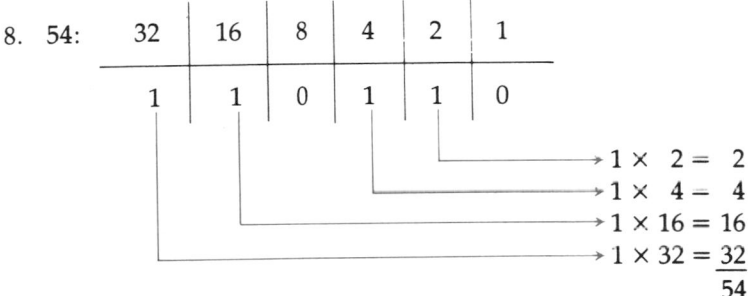

8	4	2	1
1	0	1	1

$$1 \times 1 = 1$$
$$1 \times 2 = 2$$
$$1 \times 8 = 8$$
$$\overline{11}$$

8. 54:

32	16	8	4	2	1
1	1	0	1	1	0

$$1 \times 2 = 2$$
$$1 \times 4 = 4$$
$$1 \times 16 = 16$$
$$1 \times 32 = 32$$
$$\overline{54}$$

9. 29:

16	8	4	2	1
1	1	1	0	1

$$16 + 8 + 4 + 1 = 29$$

10. 15

11. $(1010110)_2$ *Remainder*

```
         0
      2 |1       1
      2 |2       0
      2 |5       1
      2 |10      0
      2 |21      1
      2 |43      1
      2 |86      0
```

12. $(1100101)_2$ *Remainder*

```
         0
      2 |1       1
      2 |3       1
      2 |6       0
      2 |12      0
      2 |25      1
      2 |50      0
      2 |101     1
```

13. remainder method

4. Addition and Subtraction of Binary Numbers

Thus far, we have seen that binary numbers are ideally suited to computer processing because they can be used to represent the on and off circuits. An "on" condition in storage can be indicated by a 1; an "off" condition by a 0.

We have learned to convert numbers from binary to decimal by utilizing the positional values, and to convert from decimal to binary by using the remainder method.

This section will consider the addition and subtraction of binary numbers and how they are performed by the computer.

Addition of binary numbers has a few simple rules.

RULES FOR ADDING BINARY NUMBERS

For Each Position

1. $1 + 0 = 1$
2. $0 + 1 = 1$
3. $0 + 0 = 0$
4. $1 + 1 = 0$ with a carry of 1 to the next position.

Example 2.9 $10_2 + 11_2 = (?)_2$

Binary	Decimal
10	2
+ 11	+3
101	5

Units' position: $0 + 1 = 1$
Two's position: $1 + 1 = 0$ with carry of 1
Four's position: carry of 1 + zero (nothing) = 1

Thus, we have 101 as the sum.

Example 2.10 $1101_2 + 1010_2 = (?)_2$

Binary	Decimal
1101	13
+ 1010	+ 10
10111	23

Notice that, in each example, we checked our solution by converting the binary numbers to decimal and then determining if the decimal sum was equal to the binary total. If not, then an error was made in the binary addition.

The process of binary subtraction is somewhat more complicated than addition. A computer does not perform simple subtraction in the manner that we customarily perform it. It performs subtraction by a series of negative additions. In this way, the same addition rules can be used for subtraction as well.

GENERAL RULES FOR SUBTRACTING BINARY NUMBERS

1. Complement the subtrahend (number to be subtracted) by converting all 1s to 0s and all 0s to 1s.
2. Proceed as in addition.
3. Cross off the high-order or leftmost digit (a 1 when the sum of the addition is positive), and add a 1 to the total.

Example 2.11 $1101_2 - 1000_2 = (?)_2$

Binary	*Decimal*	
1101	13	Minuend
-1000	$-\ 8$	$-$ Subtrahend
	5	Difference

1. Complement the subtrahend or number to be subtracted. To complement a binary number, convert all 0s to 1s and all 1s to 0s. Thus, the complement of 1000 is 0111.
2. Proceed as in addition using the complemented value as the number to be added.

$$
\begin{array}{r}
1101 \\
+0111 \\
\hline
10100
\end{array}
$$

3. Cross off the high-order 1 and add it to result.

$$
\begin{array}{r}
\cancel{1}0100 \\
+\ \ \ \ \ \ 1 \\
\hline
0101
\end{array}
$$

The answer is 0101_2, which is the same as 101_2 because the leftmost zero has no value.

Because $101_2 = 5_{10}$, the difference of 13 minus 8, the solution is correct. This last procedure is called **end-around-carry**.

Example 2.12 $11101_2 - 11000_2 = (?)_2$

Binary	*Decimal*	
11101	29	Minuend
-11000	-24	$-$ Subtrahend
	5	Difference

1. Complement the subtrahend.
   Complement of 11000 — 00111
2. Proceed as in addition.

$$
\begin{array}{r}
11101 \\
+00111 \\
\hline
100100
\end{array}
$$

3. Perform an end-around-carry.

$$
\begin{array}{r}
\cancel{1}00100 \\
+\ \ \ \ \ \ 1 \\
\hline
101
\end{array}
$$

This procedure for subtraction, which is the method used by the computer, is called **complementation and end-around carry**.

In the previous examples, notice that the subtrahend, or number to be subtracted, was always smaller than the minuend, the number from which it was subtracted. However, if the subtrahend is larger than the minuend, the result will be negative. We must modify Step 3 in the rules for subtraction to obtain the correct results.

RULES FOR SUBTRACTING BINARY NUMBERS
(IF SUBTRAHEND IS LARGER THAN MINUEND)

1. Complement the subtrahend (number to be subtracted) by converting all 1s to 0s and all 0s to 1s.
2. Proceed as in addition.
3. Complement the result and place a negative sign in front of the answer.

Example 2.13

Binary	*Decimal*	
11000	24	Minuend
−11101	−29 −	Subtrahend
	−5	Difference

1. Complement the subtrahend.
   Complement of 11101 = 00010
2. Proceed as in addition.

   $$\begin{array}{r} 11000 \\ +00010 \\ \hline 11010 \end{array}$$

3. Complement the result and add negative sign to it.
   Complement of 11010 = 00101

Answer = −00101 or -5_{10}

Example 2.14

Binary	*Decimal*	
1101	13	Minuend
−11001	−25 −	Subtrahend
	−12	Difference

1. Complement the subtrahend.
   Complement of 11001 = 00110
2. Proceed as in addition.

   $$\begin{array}{r} 1101 \\ +00110 \\ \hline 10011 \end{array}$$

3. Complement the result and add negative sign.
   Complement of 10011 = 01100

Answer = -1100_2 or -12_{10}

5. Representing Negative Numbers in Binary Form

The following steps illustrate how a negative number can be represented in binary form.

STEPS FOR FINDING BINARY EQUIVALENT
OF A NEGATIVE NUMBER

1. Represent the number as a positive value in binary form.
2. Replace all 0s by 1s and all 1s by 0s. This is known as *complementation.*
3. Add 1 to the result.

Example 2.15   Represent -5 in binary using 16 bits.

1. Represent the number as a positive value in binary form.
   0000000000000101
2. Complement the number.
   1111111111111010
3. Add 1 to the result.
   $(1111111111111011)_2 = (-5)_{10}$

It should be noted that a negative number in binary always has a 1 in the
high-order (leftmost) bit of the field. A zero means the number is *positive.*

    1111111111111011   0000000000000101

Designates number   Designates number
as negative   as positive

Example 2.16   Represent -10 in binary using 16 bits.

1. Represent the number as a positive value in binary form.
   0000000000001010
2. Complement the number.
   1111111111110101
3. Add 1 to the result.
   $(1111111111110110)_2 = (-10)_{10}$

Self-Evaluating Quiz

1. The addition of 1 + 0 or 0 + 1, in binary, results in _____ .
2. The addition of 1 + 1, in binary, results in _____ .
3. The method used by the computer for subtraction of binary numbers is called
   _____ .
4.   11011
   $+10011$
5.   11111
   $+11011$
6.   111
   $+101$
       110
7.   11011
   -10011
8.   111011
   -110001
9.   010110
   -110001
10. $(-8)_{10} = (?)_2$ (Use 16 bits.)
11. $(-14)_{10} = (?)_2$ (Use 16 bits.)

SOLUTIONS

1. 1
2. 0 with a carry of 1
3. Complementation and end-around-carry
4. 101110 (27 + 19 = 46)
5. 111010 (31 + 27 = 58)

6. 10010 (7 + 5 + 6 = 18)

7.
$$
\begin{array}{r}
11011 \\
+01100 \\
\hline
\cancel{1}00111 \\
\hline
1000
\end{array}
$$
    27 − 19 = 8

8.
$$
\begin{array}{r}
111011 \\
+001110 \\
\hline
\cancel{1}001001 \\
\hline
1010
\end{array}
$$
    59 − 49 = 10

9.
$$
\begin{array}{r}
010110 \\
+001110 \\
\hline
100100
\end{array}
$$
    complement = 011011

    Answer = −11011; (22 − 49 = −27)

10. 1111111111111000

11. 1111111111110010

C. Hexadecimal Numbers

1. Representing Numeric Data with Hexadecimal Numbers

We have seen that a computer uses binary numbers, rather than decimal numbers, to perform arithmetic operations. This is because the 2 binary numbers 1 and 0 can be made to correspond to the on-off state of computer circuits.

However, because binary numbers require many positions to represent relatively small numbers, it would be inefficient for the computer to utilize an entire storage position to represent one binary digit. Although the decimal number 23 would use 2 storage positions, one for the 2 and one for the 3, its binary equivalent 10111 would occupy 5 storage positions if each position represented 1 binary digit. Thus, to have the computer store a single binary digit in one storage position would make inefficient use of large storage capability.

In this section, we see that 4 binary digits can be grouped together to produce one digit in the base 16 or **hexadecimal numbering system**. In computers that represent data in base 16, such as IBM and IBM-compatible mainframes, each storage position can be used to store 2 hexadecimal digits, with each such digit corresponding to 4 binary digits.

In base 10, there are 10 unique digits, 0 to 9. In base 2, there are 2 unique digits, 0 and 1. In base 16, as you might expect, there are 16 unique digits. Because only the 10 individual digits 0–9 are available, 10–15 are represented by letters A to F.

Hexadecimal	Decimal
0	0
.	.
.	.
.	.
9	9
A	10
B	11
C	12
D	13
E	14
F	15

2. Determining the Decimal Equivalent of a Hexadecimal Number

In summary, although the decimal numbering system has only the 10 digits 0 to 9, the hexadecimal numbering system requires 6 more individual characters to represent numbers 10 to 15. The letters A to F represent these numbers.

To determine the next number after F in the hexadecimal system (or 15 in decimal) we must utilize the next position. That is, $(10)_{16} = (16)_{10}$. Because the hexadecimal numbering system has a base of 16, each positional value can be expressed as a factor of 16.

$\cdots$	16^3	16^2	16^1	16^0
$\cdots$	4096	256	16	1

To determine, then, $(10)_{16}$ in base 10 we have:

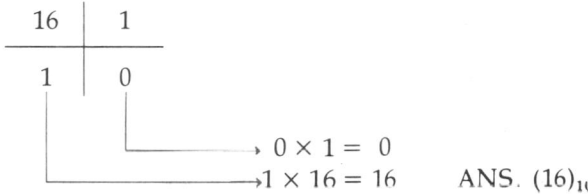

We use the same method as previously discussed to convert from any numbering system to the decimal system: multiply each digit by its positional value and and then obtain the sum or total. Do not become confused by the use of hexadecimal digits A to F. When performing any arithmetic operation, merely convert them to their decimal counterpart (10 to 15, respectively.)

Example 2.17 $(AF)_{16} = (?)_{10}$

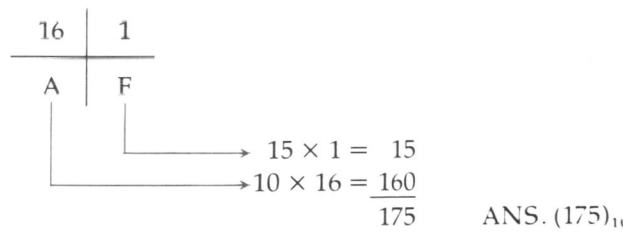

Example 2.18 $(B6A)_{16} = (?)_{10}$

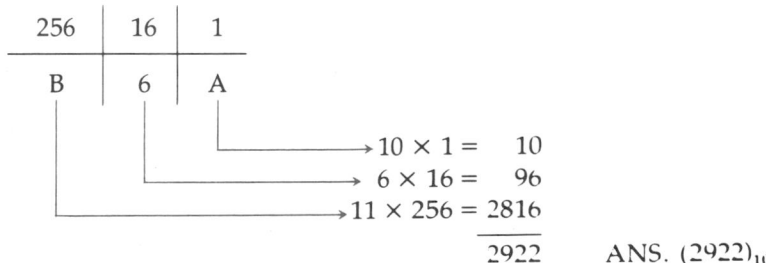

Self-Evaluating Quiz Find the decimal equivalent of the following hexadecimal numbers.

1. $(2E)_{16} = (?)_{10}$
2. $(A23)_{16} = (?)_{10}$

SOLUTIONS

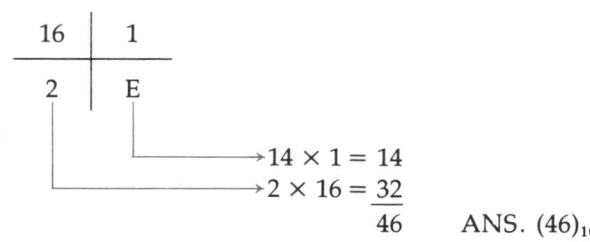

$$14 \times 1 = 14$$
$$2 \times 16 = \underline{32}$$
$$46 \qquad \text{ANS. } (46)_{10}$$

2.

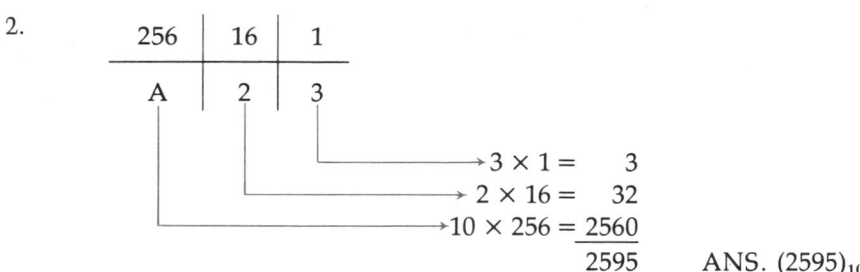

$$3 \times 1 = \qquad 3$$
$$2 \times 16 = \qquad 32$$
$$10 \times 256 = \underline{2560}$$
$$2595 \qquad \text{ANS. } (2595)_{10}$$

3. Determining the Hexadecimal Equivalent of a Decimal Number

To convert from the decimal numbering system to the hexadecimal system we use the remainder method, dividing by 16.

Example 2.19 $(382)_{10} = (?)_{16}$

Remainder in Hex.

```
          0          1
   16 | 1          7
   16 | 23         E
   16 | 382
```

Reading from top to bottom

ANS. $(17E)_{16}$

Example 2.20 $(1583)_{10} = (?)_{16}$

Remainder in Hex.

```
          0          6
   16 | 6          2
   16 | 98         F
   16 | 1583
```

ANS. $(62F)_{16}$

Self-Evaluating Quiz   Find the hexadecimal equivalent of the following decimal numbers.

1. $(132)_{10} = (?)_{16}$
2. $(214)_{10} = (?)_{16}$

SOLUTIONS   1.

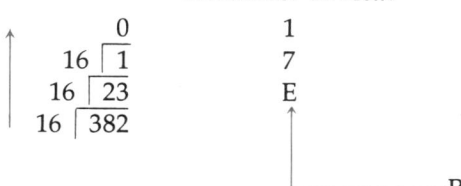

```
          0     8
   16 | 8     4
   16 | 132
```

ANS. $(84)_{16}$

2.
$$16 \overline{)13} \quad\quad \begin{matrix} 0 & D \\ & 6 \end{matrix}$$
$$16 \overline{)214}$$

ANS. $(D6)_{16}$

4. Use of a Table for Conversion from One Numbering System to Another

To simplify the conversion of decimal numbers to their hexadecimal equivalents, and hexadecimal numbers to their decimal equivalents, we can use the following conversion table.

Decimal Value

Hex Digit	Position 6	Position 5	Position 4	Position 3	Position 2	Position 1
0	0	0	0	0	0	0
1	1,048,576	65,536	4,096	256	16	1
2	2,097,152	131,072	8,192	512	32	2
3	3,145,728	196,608	12,288	768	48	3
4	4,194,304	262,144	16,384	1024	64	4
5	5,242,880	327,680	20,480	1280	80	5
6	6,291,456	393,216	24,576	1536	96	6
7	7,340,032	458,752	28,672	1792	112	7
8	8,388,608	524,288	32,768	2048	128	8
9	9,437,184	589,824	36,864	2304	144	9
A	10,485,760	655,360	40,960	2560	160	10
B	11,534,336	720,896	45,056	2816	176	11
C	12,582,912	786,432	49,152	3072	192	12
D	13,631,488	851,968	53,248	3328	208	13
E	14,680,064	917,504	57,344	3584	224	14
F	15,728,640	983,040	61,440	3840	240	15

a. Converting a Hexadecimal Number to Its Decimal Equivalent   Each hex digit is converted, one at a time, into its decimal equivalent. This is accomplished by locating the value of that digit in the column of the table that corresponds to that digit's place in the number. The sum of all the converted digits is the decimal equivalent of the hexadecimal number. The following example illustrates these steps.

Example 2.21 $(5AC)_{16} = (?)_{10}$

1. Locate the digit C in the *first* (rightmost) column, since it is the rightmost digit in the number. Its value is 12.
2. Locate the digit A in the *second* column. Its value is 160.
3. Locate the digit 5 in the *third* column. Its value is 1280.
4. Add the values together.
   $12 + 160 + 1280 = 1452$

Thus, $(5AC)_{16} = (1452)_{10}$

b. Converting a Decimal Number to Its Hexadecimal Equivalent   To convert a decimal number into its hexadecimal equivalent, we use the following procedure.

1. Find an entry in the table that is *closest* to the decimal number being converted *without exceeding* it. The hex digit to be used for that position in the hexadecimal number is found at the left of the table.

2. To find the *next* digit in the hexadecimal number, subtract the closest value previously found from the number that was being converted. Take this *remainder* and repeat step 1.

The following example will clarify this procedure.

Example 2.22 $(1627)_{10} = (?)_{16}$

1. The closet number to 1627 in the table is 1536 in the *third* column from the right. The hexadecimal equivalent therefore has 3 digits in it. The leftmost digit will be a 6, which is the hex digit that corresponds to the number 1536.
2. The remainder at this point is 91 $(1627 - 1536)$.
3. The closest number to 91 is 80. Therefore, the next hex digit will be a 5.
4. The remainder at this point is 11 $(91 - 80)$. This is a B in hex, which is found by looking at the left of the table.

Because there is no remainder at this point, all the conversions have been made. We therefore have this result:

$(1627)_{10} = (65B)_{16}$

5. Addition and Subtraction of Hexadecimal Numbers

Arithmetic operations in hexadecimal are similar to those in other numbering systems. Perform the operation on each column decimally, convert the decimal number to hexadecimal, and proceed.

Example 2.23 $(BAD)_{16} + (431)_{16} = (?)_{16}$

$$
\begin{array}{ccc}
B & A & D \\
4 & 3 & 1 \\
\hline
F & D & E
\end{array}
$$

$11 + 4 = 15 \qquad\qquad 13 + 1 = 14$
$\quad = F \qquad 10 + 3 = 13 \qquad = E$
$\qquad\qquad\quad = D$

ANS. $(FDE)_{16}$

Example 2.24 $(CBA)_{16} + (627)_{16} = (?)_{16}$

$$
\begin{array}{ccc}
C & B & A \\
+\,6 & 2 & 7 \\
\hline
1\,2 & E & 1
\end{array}
$$

$12 + 6 = 18_{10}\qquad\qquad 10 + 7 = 17_{10} = 11_{16}$ (carry 1)
$\quad = 12_{16} \qquad 11 + 2 + 1$ (carry) $= 14_{10} = E_{16}$

ANS. $(12E1)_{16}$

Keep in mind that carrying hexadecimal numbers to the next position is performed exactly as in the decimal numbering system. Note, however, that a sum of 16 results in a carry of 1 $(10_{16} = 16_{10})$.

Example 2.25 $(83E)_{16} + (F6F)_{16} = (?)_{16}$

$$
\begin{array}{ccc}
8 & 3 & E \\
F & 6 & F \\
\hline
1\ 7 & A & D \\
\end{array}
$$

$$\rightarrow 14 + 15 = (29)_{10} = (1D)_{16}\ (\text{carry } 1)$$

ANS. $(17\ AD)_{16}$

We can subtract hexadecimal numbers by again converting each digit to decimal and then converting the difference obtained back to hexadecimal. Note that the system of borrowing from or exchanging with the next position results in an exchange of 16 rather than 10.

Example 2.26 $(26)_{16} - (7)_{16} = (?)_{16}$

$$
\begin{array}{cccc}
26 & & 1 & (16 + 6) \\
-7 = - & & & 7 \\
\hline
& & 1 & F \\
\end{array}
$$

(16 borrowed from 2nd position)

ANS. $(1F)_{16}$

On some computers, specifically on IBM and IBM-compatible ones, computer printouts of storage locations and their contents are printed in hexadecimal. Whereas normal program output is printed decimally, internal representations are indicated in hexadecimal. Thus, it is important to understand positional numbering theory to debug programs.

When errors or "bugs" exist in a program, or when the contents of specific storage locations must be pinpointed for testing purposes, you must be able to perform hexadecimal arithmetic. This is because **storage dumps**, or displays of storage contents, may be in hexadecimal notation. A programmer may be advised that a program began at hexadecimal location 28E6 and that an error occurred at location 3EF2. The program listing, however, only has the address of each instruction *relative* to where the program began. Consequently, to obtain the absolute error point and to find the corresponding instruction, the starting point, 28E6, must be subtracted from 3EF2 to obtain the absolute error point.[1]

To extract items from storage, then, you must understand hexadecimal arithmetic.

$$
\begin{array}{l}
3EF2 \\
-28E6 \\
\hline
160C \quad \text{Absolute error point} \\
\end{array}
$$

6. Converting from Hexadecimal to Binary, and from Binary to Hexadecimal

At the start of this section, we indicated that hexadecimal numbers are used by some computers because they effectively reduce 4 binary digits to a single digit in base 16. That is, we can represent any 4 binary digits by a single hexadecimal digit.

Any binary number, regardless of its size, can be converted to a hexadecimal number by dividing it into groups of 4 digits and representing each group with a single hexadecimal digit.

---

[1] If you are using the ASSIST Educational Assembler, you will not need to perform this type of conversion.

Example 2.27 $(1101001101110111)_2 = (?)_{16}$

8421	8421	8421	8421
1101	0011	0111	0111
D	3	7	7

ANS. $(D377)_{16}$

Example 2.28 $(101101111)_2 = (?)_{16}$

0001	0110	1111
1	6	F

ANS. $(16F)_{16}$

Note that when the binary number does not consist of a multiple of 4 digits, it can be enlarged by using high-order or insignificant zeros. That is, 11 is the same as 0011, which has 4 digits. Because of the simple relation between binary and hexadecimal digits, the computer can represent data in hexadecimal, by still maintaining the binary (on-off state) configuration.

Notice also that it is sometimes easier to determine the *decimal* equivalent of a *binary* number by first finding its hexadecimal equivalent. A large binary number requires numerous calculations to determine the positional values, and then to convert to decimal. The conversion process is easier from hexadecimal to decimal and because we can easily represent binary numbers as hexadecimal numbers, the double conversion often simplifies the operations.

Consider the binary number in the foregoing example—$(101101111)_2$.

Suppose we wish to find its decimal equivalent. We can use the standard method by determining each positional value and then adding all "on" positions. Or, we can convert the number to hexadecimal and obtain 16F as in the example. Then we can convert.

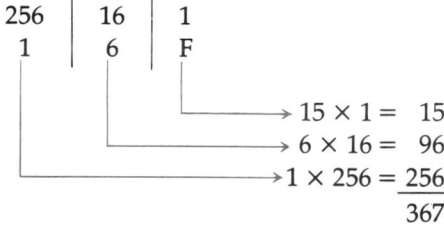

$$
\begin{array}{ccc}
256 & 16 & 1 \\
1 & 6 & F
\end{array}
$$

$$15 \times 1 = 15$$
$$6 \times 16 = 96$$
$$1 \times 256 = \underline{256}$$
$$367$$

ANS. $(367)_{10}$

Often we find that the time it takes to convert large binary numbers to the decimal numbering system is significantly reduced by performing the intermediate conversion to hexadecimal.

Self-Evaluating Quiz

1. $(8E6)_{16} = (?)_{10}$
2. $(9FC)_{16} = (?)_{10}$
3. $(1387)_{10} = (?)_{16}$
4. $(8365)_{10} = (?)_{16}$
5.   8EC
   $$+DE2$$

6.   9CC
   $$+DEE$$

7.   9CE
    − 8DF

8.   AEC
    − 932

9. $(110111111110111)_2 = (?)_{16}$
10. $(111111101111)_2 = (?)_{16}$

SOLUTIONS

1. $(8E6)_{16} = (?)_{10}$

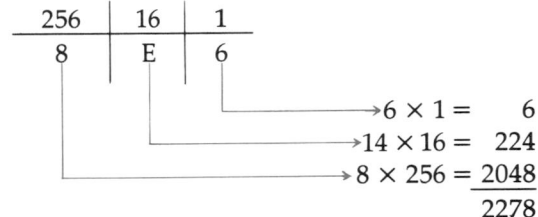

256	16	1
8	E	6

$6 \times 1 = 6$
$14 \times 16 = 224$
$8 \times 256 = \underline{2048}$
2278

ANS. 2278

2. $(9FC)_{16} = (?)_{10}$

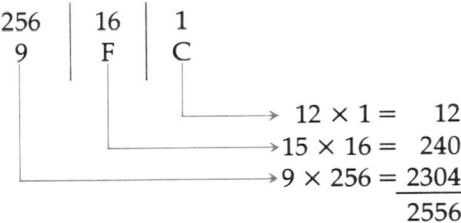

256	16	1
9	F	C

$12 \times 1 = 12$
$15 \times 16 = 240$
$9 \times 256 = \underline{2304}$
2556

ANS. 2556

3. $(1387)_{10} = (?)_{16}$

Remainder in Hex

$$\begin{array}{ll}
0 & 5 \\
16\,\overline{\rceil\,5} & 6 \\
16\,\overline{\rceil\,86} & \text{B} \\
16\,\overline{\rceil\,1387} & \\
\end{array}$$
ANS. 56B

4. $(8365)_{10} = (?)_{16}$

Remainder in Hex

$$\begin{array}{ll}
0 & 2 \\
16\,\overline{\rceil\,2} & 0 \\
16\,\overline{\rceil\,32} & \text{A} \\
16\,\overline{\rceil\,522} & \text{D} \\
16\,\overline{\rceil\,8365} & \\
\end{array}$$
ANS. 20AD

5.   8EC
    DE2

    16CE

6. $$\begin{array}{r} 9CC \\ \underline{DEE} \\ 17BA \end{array}$$

7. $$\begin{array}{r} 9CE \\ \underline{-8DF} \\ EF \end{array}$$

8. $$\begin{array}{r} AEC \\ \underline{-932} \\ 1BA \end{array}$$

9. $(11011111110111)_2$

0011	0111	1111	0111
3	7	F	7

ANS. $(37F7)_{16}$

10. $(111111101111)_2$

1111	1110	1111
F	E	F

ANS. $(FEF)_{16}$

II. REPRESENTATION OF CHARACTERS IN STORAGE

A. The EBCDIC Code

We have seen that through a combination of on-off bits, or binary digits, it is possible to represent any number. Many computers group binary numbers in sets of four in an effort to conserve storage so that data may be represented internally in the hexadecimal numbering system.

Most computer systems use some variation of the binary representation to store all characters including letters and special symbols. We will now discuss in detail the internal computer code used on IBM and IBM-compatible computers. This code is called **EBCDIC** (pronounced eb-ce-dick), which represents *Extended Binary Coded Decimal Interchange Code*. Using EBCDIC, it is possible to represent 256 characters. The characters that can be represented in EBCDIC include numbers, letters (lowercase and uppercase or capital letters), special symbols, and control characters. Lowercase letters have a different bit configuration than uppercase letters.

Using the EBCDIC code, each storage position consists of 8 bits. On many machines, including IBM and IBM-compatible systems, a single storage position consisting of 8 bits is called a **byte**.

Each byte is divided into a zone portion consisting of 4 bits and a digit portion consisting of 4 bits, producing what is referred to as the **zoned-decimal format**.

Zone	Digit

Byte

The zone portion of the byte is represented in exactly the same manner as the digit portion. Each portion consists of 4 *binary* circuits, with the following positional values:

Byte

Zone				Digit			
8	4	2	1	8	4	2	1

The *digit* portion of the byte consists of 4 bits with positional values of 8-4-2-1 or 2^3-2^2-2^1-2^0. Each decimal digit 0-9 can be represented by some combination of 8-4-2-1 "on" bits. The decimal number 9, for example, can be represented as 1001, where 1 means an "on" state and 0 means an "off" state.

The *zone* portion of the byte uses 4 bits with positional values 8-4-2-1 to represent the Hollerith zones 12, 11, and 0. You will recall that the Hollerith zones are used as follows:

12 + digit = A–I   (12 − 1 = A; 12 − 2 = B; ... 12 − 9 = I)
11 + digit = J–R   (11 − 1 = J; 11 − 2 = K; ... 11 − 9 = R)
 0 + digit = S–Z   (0 − 2 = S; 0 − 3 = T; ... 0 − 9 − Z)

For the zone portion, the Hollerith zones are represented as follows.

Hollerith zone	EBCDIC Equivalent
12	1100
11	1101
0	1110

Note that the 11 and 0-zones do *not* have EBCDIC codes of 11 and 0.
Thus the letter A in Hollerith, a 12-zone and a 1-digit is

	Zone (12-zone)				Digit (1-digit)				
	8	4	2	1	8	4	2	1	Positional value
	1	1	0	0	0	0	0	1	Bits

Byte

The 12-zone corresponds to 1100, a 12 in binary, and the 1 is 0001. A hexadecimal printout of this byte would be C1 (8 + 4 in the hexadecimal system is a C). That is, the zone and digit portions are treated independently for printout purposes.

The letter T corresponding to 0–3 in Hollerith is represented as

	Zone (0-zone)				Digit (3-digit)				
Hex Printout	8	4	2	1	8	4	2	1	Character
E3	1	1	1	0	0	0	1	1	T

In a hexadecimal printout, the T would be represented as E3. Numeric characters are also represented in this form. For *unsigned* numbers, all zone bits are on. Thus we have 1111 as the zone portion of all unsigned numbers. The number 8 then is represented in a byte as

	Zone				Digit			
	8	4	2	1	8	4	2	1
	1	1	1	1	1	0	0	0

Actual value   8
Hexadecimal representation   F   8

The 1111 in the zone portion of a byte is used to denote an unsigned number that is assumed to be positive. The number 1111 was selected because it would make unsigned numbers the highest in the collating or sorting sequence. Note that an unsigned 5 in a hexadecimal printout of storage would read as F5.

A definitive positive sign is denoted by 1100 (hex C) and a minus sign by 1101 (hex D).

The following chart summarizes the representation of the zone portion of characters in EBCDIC and hexadecimal.

Summary of Zone Representation

Hollerith	EBCDIC	Hexadecimal
12	1100	C
11	1101	D
0	1110	E
No zone	1111	F
(used for unsigned numbers)		

Note that, as indicated in the previous section, each group of 4 bits or binary digits can be used to represent a single hexadecimal digit. Thus, a shorthand method for representing characters in EBCDIC is to represent them as 2 hexadecimal digits. Because each hexadecimal digit is used to represent 4 binary digits, 2 hexadecimal digits are needed to represent 1 byte or 8 bits.

E6 in hexadecimal represents the EBCDIC code for W.

Zone (0-zone)	Digit (6-digit)
1 1 1 0	0 1 1 0
E	6

This is equivalent to 0–6 in Hollerith or the letter W.

F5 in hexadecimal represents the zoned-decimal format in EBCDIC for a positive 5.

Zone	Digit
F	5
1111	0101

All unsigned numbers in zoned-decimal format are represented hexadecimally with an F followed by a digit.

The following table shows the EBCDIC, Hollerith, and hexadecimal codes for uppercase (capital) letters and numbers.

Character	EBCDIC Zone	EBCDIC Digit	Hollerith	Hexadecimal
A	1100	0001	12-1	C1
B	1100	0010	12-2	C2
C	1100	0011	12-3	C3
D	1100	0100	12-4	C4
E	1100	0101	12-5	C5
F	1100	0110	12-6	C6
G	1100	0111	12-7	C7
H	1100	1000	12-8	C8
I	1100	1001	12-9	C9
J	1101	0001	11-1	D1
K	1101	0010	11-2	D2

L	1101	0011	11-3	D3
M	1101	0100	11-4	D4
N	1101	0101	11-5	D5
O	1101	0110	11-6	D6
P	1101	0111	11-7	D7
Q	1101	1000	11-8	D8
R	1101	1001	11-9	D9
S	1110	0010	0-2	E2
T	1110	0011	0-3	E3
U	1110	0100	0-4	E4
V	1110	0101	0-5	E5
W	1110	0110	0-6	E6
X	1110	0111	0-7	E7
Y	1110	1000	0-8	E8
Z	1110	1001	0-9	E9
0	1111	0000	0	F0
1	1111	0001	1	F1
2	1111	0010	2	F2
3	1111	0011	3	F3
4	1111	0100	4	F4
5	1111	0101	5	F5
6	1111	0110	6	F6
7	1111	0111	7	F7
8	1111	1000	8	F8
9	1111	1001	9	F9

B. Packed Format

Thus far, we have seen how data may be represented in zoned-decimal format using one byte of storage for each character.

For numeric items, we have seen how a byte can store one digit, where the zone portion is equivalent to all bits on, a hexadecimal F, and the digit portion is the binary equivalent of decimal numbers 0 to 9.

Consider the number 68254. Using zoned-decimal format, it would take 5 bytes to represent this number in storage, one for each digit. The zone portion of each byte would indicate all bits on, as shown in the following section.

It really is unnecessary to represent a zone for each digit within the number. That is, one zone for the entire field to indicate that the number is in fact positive would suffice. A method can be employed so that the computer eliminates or strips the zone of all digits except one to indicate the sign. Thus the zone portion of each byte can be employed to represent *another digit*. In this way, 2 digits can be represented by a single byte. This technique is called **packing**, and is a main advantage of using the EBCDIC configuration.

It operates as follows.

1. The zone and digit portions of the **low-order** or rightmost digit are switched; this designates the field as packed.
2. All other zones are stripped and 2 digits are *packed* into 1 byte.

Example 2.29   Zoned-Decimal Representation of the Number 68254 (5 bytes)

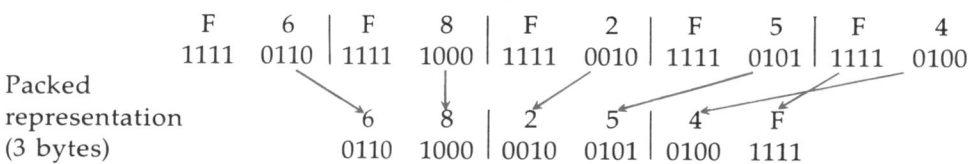

Example 2.30   Representation of 835674 in Zoned-Decimal Format (6 Bytes)

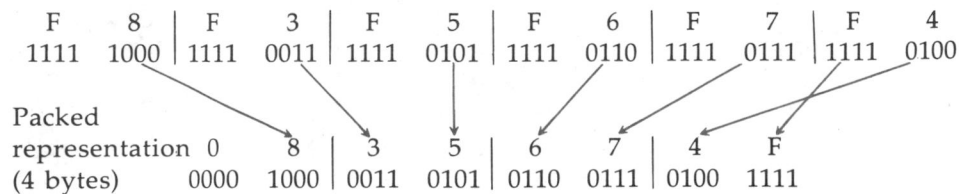

Thus all 1s or a hexadecimal F in the low-order 4 bits of a byte indicate that the byte contains a packed number. (All 1s could not be used to represent any single digit.)

In Example 2.29, the number in zoned-decimal format utilizes 5 bytes while in packed format it utilizes only 3 bytes. A major advantage of packing numbers, then, is to conserve storage.

In Example 2.30, to complete or "fill up" the high-order byte, we add 4 zero bits at the beginning of the field.

Thus, for numeric fields, we can save considerable storage space by using the packed format. In addition, the computer *requires* numeric fields to be packed to perform arithmetic operations. To print out or display numeric fields, however, they must be in zoned-decimal format.

Self-Evaluating Quiz

1. In the hexadecimal numbering system, (no.) binary digits are grouped to represent a single hexadecimal digit.
2. A single storage position consisting of (no.) bits is called a _____ .
3. Each byte is divided into a _____ portion and a _____ portion, each of which consists of (no.) bits.
4. The letter C is represented in a byte as _____ .
5. The letter M is represented in a byte as _____ .
6. The *unsigned* number 8 is represented in a byte as _____ .
7. The *signed* number +8 is represented in a byte as _____ .
8. Four 1s in the zone portion of a byte are used to denote _____ .
9. How would the letter D appear in a hexadecimal printout?
10. How would the unsigned number 7 (in one byte) appear in a hexadecimal printout?
11. Using zoned-decimal format, how many bytes are required to store the unsigned number 118753?
12. In packed format, the above number would require (no.) bytes.
13. (T or F) Numeric fields must be packed to perform arithmetic operations.

		Page
SOLUTIONS	1. 4	32
	2. 8; byte	40
	3. zone; digit; 4	40
	4. 1100 0011 or C3 in hex	42
	zone digit	
	5. 1101 0100 or D4 in hex	43
	zone digit	
	6. 1111 1000 or F8 in hex	43
	zone digit	
	7. 1100 1000 or C8 in hex	42
	zone digit	
	8. an unsigned number that is assumed to be positive	41

9.	binary	<u>1100</u>	<u>0100</u>		42
	hexadecimal	C	4		
10.	binary	<u>1111</u>	<u>0111</u>		43
	hexadecimal	F	7		
11.	6 (one for each digit)				43
12.	4 (01 18 75 3F)				44
13.	T				44

CHAPTER SUMMARY

I. Numbering Systems
  A. All computer codes use some form of the binary or base 2 numbering system.
  B. The Binary or Base 2 Numbering System.
    1. Positional numbering system; each digit has a different value depending on its position in a sequence of numbers.
      a. Each position has a value that is a factor of 2.
      b. The positional values are:
        ... 16 8 4 2 1
    2. Ideally suited to computers.
      a. 0s are represented internally in the computer as an off-state.
      b. 1s are represented as an on-state.
    3. Bit is a shortened form of binary digit.
    4. Rules for Adding Binary Numbers.
    For each position:
      a. 1 + 0 = 1
      b. 0 + 1 = 1
      c. 0 + 0 = 0
      d. 1 + 1 = 0 with a carry of 1 to the next position.
    5. Rules for Subtracting Binary Numbers.
      a. If the subtrahend (number to be subtracted) is smaller than the minuend (number being subtracted from), use the complementation and end-around-carry method.
      b. If the subtrahend is larger than the minuend:
        (1) Complement the subtrahend by converting all 1s to 0s and all 0s to 1s.
        (2) Proceed as in addition.
        (3) Complement the result.
        (4) Place a negative sign in front of the answer.
    6. Rules for Finding the Binary Equivalent of a Negative Number.
      a. Represent the number as a positive value in binary form.
      b. Find the complement of the number (convert all 1s to 0s and all 0s to 1s).
      c. Add 1 to the result.
  C. The Hexadecimal or Base 16 Numbering System.
    1. The 16 digits in base 16 are represented by numbers 0–9 and letters A–F.
    2. Arithmetic operations in base 16 are similar to those in other numbering systems:
      a. Perform the operation on each column decimally.
      b. Convert the decimal number to hexadecimal.
      c. Note that a sum of 16 results in a carry of 1.
II. Representation of Characters in Storage
  A. The EBCDIC Code.
    1. The internal code used on IBM and IBM-compatible computers.
    2. Each storage position or byte consists of eight bits.

  3. Zoned-decimal format:
    a. Each byte is divided into a zone and a digit portion.
    b. The digit portion of the byte consists of four bits with positional values of 8-4-2-1.
    c. The zone portion of the byte uses four bits with positional values of 8-4-2-1 to represent the zone.

Hollerith	*EBCDIC*	*Hexadecimal*
12	1100	C
11	1101	D
0	1110	E
No zone (for unsigned numbers)	1111	F

  B. Packed Format.
    1. Used for numeric items to represent two digits by a single byte.
    2. The zone and digit portions of the low-order or rightmost digit are switched.
    3. All other zones are stripped and two digits are packed into one byte.

KEY TERMS

Binary numbering system

Bit

Byte

Complementation and end-around-carry

Extended Binary Coded Decimal Interchange Code (EBCDIC)

Hexadecimal numbering system

High-order position

Low-order position

Packed format

Positional numbering system

Remainder method

Storage dump

Zoned-decimal format

REVIEW QUESTIONS

1. Determine the decimal equivalents of the following binary numbers.
   a. 10011111
   b. 11100
   c. 110011

2. Determine the binary equivalents of the following decimal numbers.
   a. 234
   b. 435
   c. 333

3. Add the following binary numbers and indicate the sum in binary form. Check your work by converting each number back into decimal form.
   a. 11101111 + 1111101111
   b. 111111011101 + 1111011
   c. 1110111 + 111111

4. Determine the decimal equivalents of the following hexadecimal numbers.
   a. 6FFE
   b. 70FD
   c. 67EE

5. Determine the hexadecimal equivalents of the following decimal numbers.
   a. 10678
   b. 16745
   c. 2345

6. How are the following decimal numbers represented in binary form in 16 bits?
   a. -18
   b. $+20$
   c. 35

7. Indicate how the following characters would appear in a hexadecimal printout.
   a. E
   b. 5
   c. -7

Defining Storage Areas and Constants

<table>
<tr><td></td><td>To familiarize you with:</td></tr>
</table>

OBJECTIVES

To familiarize you with:
1. *How storage is reserved for data.*
2. *The numerous ways in which data can be stored.*
3. *The distinctions between variable and constant data.*
4. *How to store a constant.*

I. THE DEFINE STORAGE ⟨DS⟩ STATEMENT

A. How Storage Is Used

All data to be processed by the computer, as well as all instructions, are placed in main storage in addressable locations called **bytes**. Machine language instructions refer to these storage locations by their actual numeric address. Assembler language instructions may refer to them by symbolic addresses called LABELS or names. For example, if a TOTAL field is to contain the sum of all input amount fields, it may occupy storage positions 1000–1003 when assembled. The programmer, however, need not keep track of such actual addresses but can refer to a field by its symbolic name. The add instruction

LABEL	OPERATION	OPERAND	COMMENTS
1	10 16		72
	AP	TOTAL,AMT	

for example, adds the field called AMT to the field TOTAL. AMT and TOTAL refer to two symbolic storage areas that must be converted to actual machine addresses during the assembly process.

SUMMARY
1. All data processed by the computer, as well as all instructions, are placed in addressable storage locations called *bytes.*
2. The assembler language programmer may refer to these locations by *symbolic names,* but the computer assigns actual storage locations to them during the assembly process.

B. Types of Storage Areas

All data processed by the computer may be categorized as either variable or constant data.

1. Variable Data

Variable data is data that changes during the processing of the program. For most programs, storage must be reserved for the following three types of variable data areas.

a. Input Areas   When an input record is read, the data is automatically transmitted to main storage. The programmer must define and describe an input area that will receive this data. Because the contents of data fields within the input area change each time a record is read, such fields are said to contain *variable* data.

b. Output Areas After data has been processed, it is used to create output information. An area in storage must be reserved for data to be produced as output. Because output data also changes during execution of a program, the fields defined in this area are considered variable.

c. Work Areas During program coding, intermediate fields are defined that are neither part of input nor part of output but are nonetheless necessary for processing. Such fields may be used, for example, to store some intermediate result of an arithmetic operation, or to hold some code for comparison purposes.

In summary, these work areas are used to store variable data that does not remain constant but that changes during the execution of the program.

2. Constant Data

Constant data is data that remains the same during the execution of the program.

Suppose, for example, we wish to multiply each input amount field by 0.05, the tax rate. This tax rate is *not* a value that is entered as input but is nevertheless required for processing. We call 0.05 a *constant*, because it is a form of data required for processing that is *not* dependent upon the input to the system.

Similarly, suppose we wish to edit input records and print the message "INVALID RECORD" for any erroneous record. The message "INVALID RECORD" will be part of output, but it is not entered as input to the system. Rather, it is a constant field, defined within the program and required for processing.

C. Establishing Storage Areas and Constants

Both variable data and constants must be established or defined in an area of the program reserved for such entries. The following statements may be used.

ESTABLISHING STORAGE AREAS AND CONSTANTS

DS reserves storage for variable data
DC defines a constant within storage

Note that all input areas, work areas, and output areas are defined and described with a DS statement. All constants to be used within the program are defined and described by DC statements. All DS and DC statements will be coded at the *end* of each program after the end-of-job routines.

D. DS Statement

All variable data entered or produced as output must be defined with a DS statement. This includes record descriptions and field descriptions within each record.

1. The Record Description

A **record** is a unit of information of a specific nature. A debit record, for example, is a group of related items that together form a unit of information. A print record or header record defines the format for a printed line. Input and output areas are usually defined by one or more DS statements that describe each record layout.

2. Field Descriptions Within Records

A group of consecutive positions that together represent a specific kind of data is called a **field**. Fields within records and fields used by the program as work areas must be defined with a DS statement.

Format of DS Statement

Field or record name	Define storage	Item description
Name	DS	Operand

Note again, that the DS statement does not cause any actual data to be generated. Rather, it simply reserves storage and assigns a name to that storage area.

Example 3.1

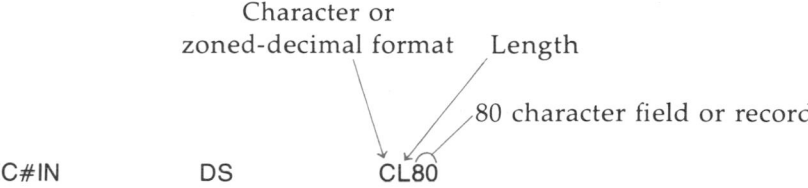

Character or zoned-decimal format   Length

80 character field or record

REC#IN   DS   CL80

This statement defines an 80-position, zoned-decimal area called REC#IN.

Example 3.2

	LABEL	OPERATION		OPERAND	COMMENTS	
1		10	16			72
	AMT	DS	CL5			

This statement defines a 5-position storage area called AMT that will contain data in zoned-decimal form.

E. Specifications of DS Statements

1. Name Field

The field or record name conforms to the rules for forming operands.

```
              RULES FOR FORMING NAMES OR LABELS: REVIEW

    1.  From 1 to 8 characters.
    2.  Letters, digits, $, #, @ may be used.
    3.  No blanks or other special characters.
    4.  Must begin in position 1 of the coding sheet.
```

2. Operand or Item Description

NAME   DS   *OPERAND*
                *dt*L*n*
                d   = duplication factor
                        number of fields to be defined by this entry
                t   = type of data[1]
                        C = character or zoned-decimal format
                        X = hexadecimal format
                        P = packed format
                        B = binary format

[1]Floating-point data is discussed in Chapter 20.

L   = length
it is coded on the form as L
n = number of bytes in the field

Example 3.3

LABEL	OPERATION	OPERAND	COMMENTS
1	10	16	72
INAREA	DS	5CL80	

This entry defines 5 80-position fields that will be filled with zoned-decimal data.

> NOTE: If the operand field or item description does not begin with a duplication factor, the number of fields is assumed to be one (that is, one field is defined).

Example 3.4

LABEL	OPERATION	OPERAND	COMMENTS
1	10	16	72
HEXNUM	DS	XL15	

defines *one* 15-position hexadecimal field.

> NOTE: A zero as duplication factor is used when a field or record is to be subdivided.

Example 3.5

LABEL	OPERATION	OPERAND	COMMENTS
1	10	16	72
REC#IN	DS	0CL80	
AMT1	DS	CL5	
AMT2	DS	CL5	
REST	DS	CL70	

REC#IN is subdivided into three fields.

It should be noted that REC#IN and AMT1 are labels that refer to the same address, as shown in the following illustration.

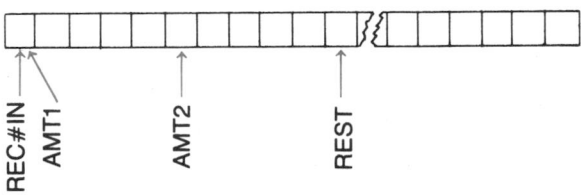

> NOTE: If a DS entry contains no name, then storage will be reserved but the item will not be accessed by name by the program.

Example 3.6   The following record is to be defined.

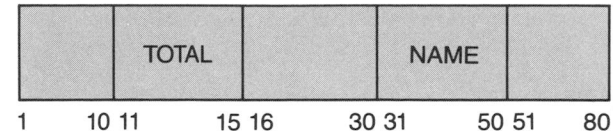

		TOTAL		NAME	
1	10 11	15 16	30 31	50 51	80

Only the TOTAL and NAME fields are to be accessed by the program. To define these two fields, with no entries between them, would cause the computer to assume that they are consecutive fields, which they are not. Hence the following could be coded:

LABEL	OPERATION	OPERAND	COMMENTS
1	10	16	72
REC#IN	DS	ØCL8Ø	
	DS	CL1Ø	
TOTAL	DS	CL5	
	DS	CL15	
NAME	DS	CL2Ø	
	DS	CL3Ø	

This coding aligns the data properly and makes available for processing both the TOTAL and NAME fields. Output print areas are frequently defined in this manner because they usually contain blank areas between data fields for ease of reading.

> NOTE: When using a duplication factor of 0, which indicates that a field or record is to be subdivided, all bytes must be accounted for.

VALID:

LABEL	OPERATION	OPERAND	COMMENTS
1	10	16	72
REC#IN	DS	ØCL8Ø	
AMT	DS	CL5	
DESCRIPT	DS	CL25	
	DS	CL5Ø	

INCORRECT: The entire record has not been defined.

LABEL	OPERATION	OPERAND	COMMENTS
1	10	16	72
REC#IN	DS	ØCL8Ø	
AMT	DS	CL5	
DESCRIPT	DS	CL25	

F. How the Computer Defines Storage Areas

Fields defined by DS statements are assigned storage locations in the precise order in which they are coded. A **location counter** assigns an address to each storage area defined by a DS as each DS is encountered. The address references the **high-order** or *leftmost* position of each field or record.

Example 3.7 Assume the location counter is ready to begin assembling storage areas at hexadecimal location 1000. The following indicates how location counters are assigned.

Location Counter	Name	Operation	Operand
1000	READIN	DS	0CL80
1000	MANNO	DS	CL4
1004	HRSWKD	DS	CL6
100A	DATE	DS	CL6
1010	GROSS	DS	CL6
1016	FEDTAX	DS	CL6
101C		DS	CL52

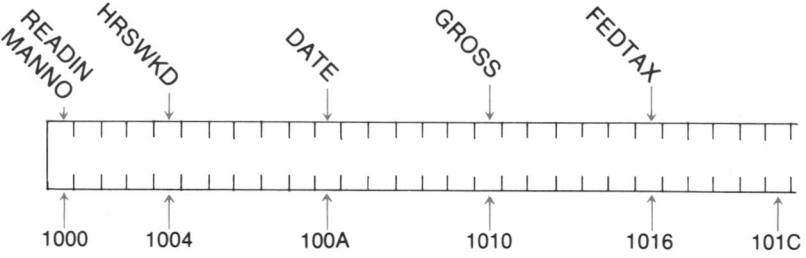

READIN refers to storage position 1000, but it also references the full 80-position area. MANNO, then, is a 4-byte field beginning in storage position 1000, HRSWKD is a 6-byte field beginning in storage position 1004, and so on.

Recall that any storage area, as well as any record, can be subdivided by using a duplication factor of 0. Thus, we could substitute the following for DATE.

LABEL	OPERATION	OPERAND	COMMENTS
DATE	DS	0CL6	
MONTH	DS	CL2	
DAY	DS	CL2	
YEAR	DS	CL2	

In this way we can access the full six-position date as needed or any subfield within it as well.

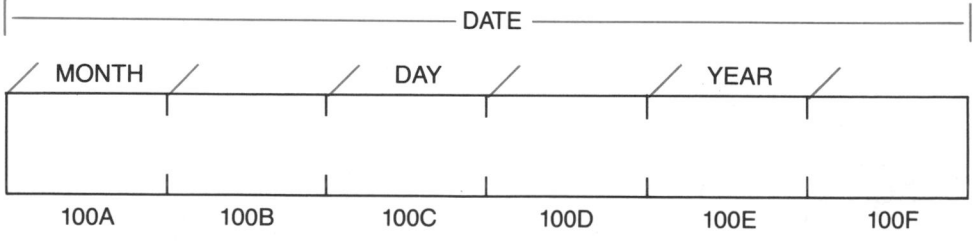

G. Additional Formats for DS Statements

Certain instructions in assembler language require that the data being operated on be a specific length and that it be defined on specific **boundaries**. For example, binary operations sometimes require a data field to consist of 4 bytes and to be placed in a storage address that is divisible by four. Four bytes of storage are called a **fullword** and an instruction that requires a data field to be placed in an address divisible by four is said to require a *fullword boundary*. Binary operations operate on the following types of data fields.

Formats for Fields Used in Binary Operations

Type	Number of Bytes	Boundary Requirements
Halfword	2	Storage address must be divisible by 2.
Fullword	4	Storage address must be divisible by 4.
Doubleword	8	Storage address must be divisible by 8.

In addition to defining data fields as containing zoned-decimal (character), hexadecimal, or packed data, it is also possible to use a DS statement to define halfword, fullword, or doubleword fields. The operand used with the DS would specify a type of H, F, or D, respectively. The use of H, F, or D locates data at addresses divisible by 2, 4, or 8, respectively. Because halfword, fullword, and doubleword fields are used in binary operations, data entered in such fields is usually in binary form.

Example 3.8

1. The following establishes one 4-byte or fullword storage area on a full-word boundary (address divisible by 4).

LABEL	OPERATION	OPERAND	COMMENTS
1	10	16	72
TOTAL	DS	F	

2. The following establishes five 2-byte or halfword storage locations, each on a halfword boundary (address divisible by two).

LABEL	OPERATION	OPERAND	COMMENTS
1	10	16	72
AMT	DS	5H	

3. The following reserves storage for a field to be subdivided and begins the location counter on a doubleword boundary (address divisible by eight).

LABEL	OPERATION	OPERAND	COMMENTS
1	10	16	72
RESULT	DS	ØD	

It is assumed that RESULT will be further subdivided as follows.

LABEL	OPERATION	OPERAND	COMMENTS
1	10	16	72
RESULT	DS	ØD	
QUOTIENT	DS	BL4	
REMAINDR	DS	BL4	

The full format for DS follows.

Full Format for DS

NAME	DS	Operand
1–8 Characters: Letters, digits, $, @, # No blanks or other special characters		dtLn where: d = duplication factor t = type

	C = character
	X = hexadecimal
	P = packed
	B = binary
	F = fullword
	H = halfword
	D = doubleword

Not used with F , H or D $\begin{cases} L = \text{length} \\ n = \text{number of bytes reserved} \end{cases}$

Storage areas are printed on a source listing in hexadecimal form. To determine whether a field has been placed in an address divisible by 2, 4, or 8, it is necessary to convert the rightmost or **low-order** hexadecimal digit in the address to binary.

To determine the boundary alignment, convert the low-order hexadecimal digit to binary. Using the binary number,

1. A low-order or rightmost binary zero ensures halfword alignment.
2. Two low-order or rightmost binary zeros ensure fullword alignment.
3. Three low-order or rightmost binary zeros ensure doubleword alignment.

Example 3.9

1. LOCATION
   68A ☐2☐
   This digit is used to determine the boundary.
   It converts to 001☐0☐ in binary.
   There is only one low-order zero.
   Thus the address is on a halfword boundary.

2. LOCATION
   68A ☐C☐
   This digit is used to determine the boundary.
   It converts to 1100 in binary.
   There are two low-order zeros.
   Thus the address is on a fullword boundary.

3. LOCATION
   68A ☐0☐
   This digit is used to determine the boundary.
   It converts to 0000 in binary.
   There are three low-order zeros.
   Thus the address is on a doubleword boundary.

Self-Evaluating Quiz

1. (T or F) A DS causes data to be stored at a symbolic address.

Indicate what, if anything, is wrong with the following DS statements: (2–5)

2. DS   C3
3. DS   CLX'80'
4. DS   PL4
5. DS   FP
6. (T or F) A DS statement must have a label or name associated with it.
7. The symbolic name refers to the (high-order/low-order) byte of a field.

8. (T or F) In the statement:
   ```
   DS      0CL5
   ```
   the 0 means that the field will be further subdivided.
9. The statement:
   ```
   DS      F
   ```
   actually achieves two results. Name them.
10. A fullword consists of (**no.**) bytes.
11. Each byte consists of (**no.**) bits.
12. Each byte can be expressed as (**no.**) hexadecimal digits.
13. Indicate the location counter for each of the following:

Location Counter	Name	Operation	Operand
2000	OUTAREA	DS	0CL132
		DS	CL20
	NAME	DS	CL20
		DS	CL20
	ADDRESS	DS	CL40
		DS	CL10
		DS	CL22
	TOTAL	DS	D
	DATE	DS	0CL4
	MONTH	DS	CL2
	YEAR	DS	CL2

14. Indicate what is wrong with the following.
    ```
    a.  AOK        DS  CL4
    b.  NO GO      DS  CL10
    c.     COLUMN1 DS  CL5
    d.  7UP        DS  CL7
    e.  SPL*CHAR   DS  CL1
    f.  SOVRYLONG  DS  CL10
    g.  WRONGOP    SD  CL15
    h.  NOTYPE     DS  L15
    ```
15. Indicate the location counter for each of the following.

Location Counter	Name	Operation	Operand
1010	ITEM1	DS	CL20
	AMT2	DS	F
	AMT3	DS	CL5
	AMT4	DS	D
	AMT5	DS	CL2

SOLUTIONS
1. F: DS statements simply reserve storage; they do not place data in the fields.
2. DS CL3
3. X or C but not both; 80 is coded without quotes.
4. Okay
5. F not consistent with P; fullword will contain binary data.
6. F
7. High-order
8. T
9. Four bytes of storage are reserved; the address of the field is divisible by four
10. Four
11. Eight
12. Two

13. Note that the location counter is specified in hex in the problem.

Location Counter	Name	Operation	Operand
Hex			
2000	OUTAREA	DS	0CL132
2000		DS	CL20
2014	NAME	DS	CL20
2028		DS	CL20
203C	ADDRESS	DS	CL40
2064		DS	CL10
206E		DS	CL22
2088	TOTAL	DS	D
2090	DATE	DS	0CL4
2090	MONTH	DS	CL2
2092	YEAR	DS	CL2

Note

OUTAREA occupies hex positions 2000-2083; TOTAL cannot begin in the next storage position, however, because its address must be divisible by 8 and 2084 is not. The next address divisible by 8 is 2088.

14. a. okay
    See the listing in Figure 3-1 for the remaining entries.

```
*           INVALID DEFINE STORAGE INSTRUCTIONS
*
NO GO     DS    CL10          BLANKS NOT PERMITTED
 COLUMN1  DS    CL5           MUST BEGIN IN COLUMN 1, NOT 2
7UP       DS    CL7           BEGINS WITH A NUMBER
SPL*CHAR  DS    CL1           CONTAINS SPECIAL CHARACTER *
SOVRYLONG DS    CL10          TOO LONG
WRONGOP   SD    CL15          INVALID OPERATION FIELD
NOTYPE    DS    L15           INVALID TYPE SPECIFICATION
          END
```

Figure 3.1
Answers to Questions 14(b)–(h).

15. The location counter is shown in hex.

Location Counter	Name	Operation	Operand
101A	ITEM1	DS	CL20
1030	AMT2	DS	F
1034	AMT3	DS	CL5
1040	AMT4	DS	D
1048	AMT5	DS	CL2

II. DEFINING CONSTANTS

A. Format

In summary, the DS statement is specifically used for reserving storage in which variable data will be entered. A DC statement not only specifies the size and type of field but the *actual contents* of the field as well.

DC statements contain the same specifications as DS statements but can also indicate actual data.

Format
NAME   DC   dtLn 'c'
                                       ↓ Actual contents of the storage area
                             Optional

The actual contents to be placed in the field are specified with single quote marks.

Example 3.10

LABEL	OPERATION	OPERAND	COMMENTS
MESSAGE	DC	CL1Ø'DISK ERROR'	
PTOT	DC	PL3'12345'	
TOTAL	DC	F'1Ø46'	

(Data defined by H, F, or D types will be converted to binary by the computer.)

B. Object Codes Generated by DC Statements

1. Zoned-Decimal Format

For each DC statement specified in your program, an area of storage is defined (as with a DS). In addition, actual contents are placed in the field according to the specifications provided.

To ensure the proper value in your DCs make certain that the length specification conforms to the actual contents placed in the field.

If the specification for a field is *not* the same as the contents assigned, then the computer will make certain adjustments, but not necessarily the ones intended by the programmer.

Suppose a field contains more positions than are defined by the constant. Consider the following.

Example 3.11

LABEL	OPERATION	OPERAND	COMMENTS
NAME	DC	CL4'AB'	

In this instance, a 4-position field is defined and only 2 characters are specified. In such a case, low-order or rightmost positions are filled with spaces. Note that this occurs only when the DC is used with a C type (character or zoned-decimal) code.

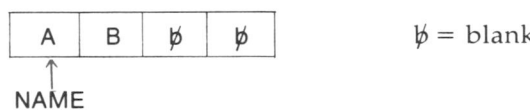

NAME

ƀ = blank

In EBCDIC this would appear as

C 1	C 2	4 0	4 0	*Hexadecimal representation*
A	B	ƀ	ƀ	*Character representation*

RULE

Zoned-decimal data is placed in the field from left to right; low-order or rightmost positions that are unfilled will be replaced with spaces.

Suppose a defined constant is larger than the specified length of the field. Consider the following.

Example 3.12

LABEL	OPERATION		OPERAND	COMMENTS	
1	10	16			72
CODE	DC		CL3'ABCD'		

In this instance, the machine will establish a three-position area in storage; thus, only three characters of data will actually be stored. Because zoned-decimal data is moved from left to right, the "D" will be *truncated* or lost. The following will be stored.

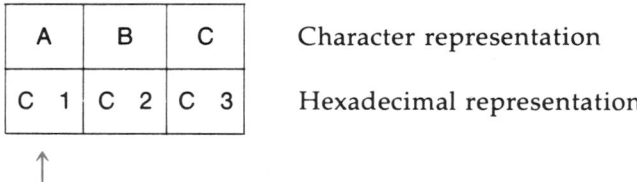

A	B	C
C 1	C 2	C 3

Character representation

Hexadecimal representation

↑
CODE

In summary, to ensure the proper values in your DC statements, make certain that the length of the field assigned is exactly the same as the number of characters in your constant. This applies to all formats.

2. Hexadecimal Format

If X is designated as the type of the DC, the constant must be specified in hexadecimal form. To specify hexadecimal constants for the above two entries, we would have

a.

LABEL	OPERATION		OPERAND	COMMENTS	
1	10	16			72
NAME	DC		XL4'C1C24040'		

b.

LABEL	OPERATION		OPERAND	COMMENTS	
1	10	16			72
CODE	DC		XL4'C1C2C3C4'		

RULE

Hexadecimal data is placed in the field from right to left; *high-order* or leftmost positions that are unfilled will be replaced with zeros.

Consider the following constant.

LABEL	OPERATION	OPERAND	COMMENTS
AMT	DC	XL4'4C'	

It will generate the following for `AMT`.

0 0	0 0	0 0	4 C

The specification `XL4'123456C'` for `CODE` above results in

01	23	45	6C

3. H , F , or D

The constant is defined in decimal and automatically converted by the computer to binary form.

Example 3.13

LABEL	OPERATION	OPERAND	COMMENTS
AMT	DC	F'120'	

Review of Truncation and Padding The programmer must make certain that the number of bytes assigned to a field is large enough to accommodate the result. If not, truncation will occur. The type of truncation depends upon the field specification. If the field is larger than required, padding will take place. The following table summarizes the types of truncation and padding.

Field	Truncation	Padding
C	Right	Blanks
X	Left	Zeros
P	Left	Zeros
B	Left	Zeros
F	Left	Zeros
H	Left	Zeros
D	Left	Zeros

High-order digits will be truncated from all fields that are too short to accommodate the entire results *except* where character specification is indicated. For a field defined as zoned-decimal or type C, rightmost characters will be truncated if the field is not large enough to accommodate the entire constant.

Example 3.14 Consider the following DC where the length is not large enough to accommodate the entire constant.

LABEL	OPERATION	OPERAND	COMMENTS
AMT1	DC	PL3'+123456'	

Truncation of high-order digits in the P field will result. Thus, AMT1 will contain

The high-order 1 was truncated. The plus sign is denoted by hex C.

All fields except those designated as zoned-decimal (type of C) would result in high-order truncation as in the foregoing example, if the constant were too large to be contained within the field.

Example 3.15   Consider the following zoned-decimal DC.

LABEL	OPERATION	OPERAND	COMMENTS
1	10 16		72
CODE	DC	CL4'ABCDE'	

Truncation of low-order characters in the C field will occur resulting in the following in CODE.

$$\boxed{A} \boxed{B} \boxed{C} \boxed{D}$$
CODE

That is, the low order "E" was truncated.

Similarly, if a field is larger than the number of characters specified, high-order bytes will be zero-filled in all cases except for character fields. In character fields, data is placed beginning in the leftmost bytes. Then rightmost unfilled bytes would be padded with blanks.

Example 3.16   Consider the following DC.

LABEL	OPERATION	OPERAND	COMMENTS
1	10 16		72
AMT2	DC	PL3'12'	

Padding of zeros in the P field will result. AMT2 will contain the following.

$$\boxed{0\ 0} \boxed{0\ 1} \boxed{2\ C} \qquad C = +$$
AMT2

High-order zeros are said to *pad* the field.

> **Note**
> All fields are aligned as in this example. That is, the symbolic name addresses the high-order or leftmost byte.

Example 3.17

LABEL	OPERATION	OPERAND	COMMENTS
1	10 16		72
CODE2	DC	CL6'ABCDE'	

will result in

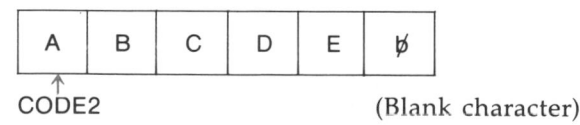

(Blank character)

C. Additional Considerations

1. Relationship Between DSs and DCs

NOTE: If you inadvertently use a DS instead of a DC to define a constant in storage, *no* error messages will be generated.

Instead, the appropriate storage area will be reserved but the value specified will be ignored. This is a common error that you should try to avoid.

Common Error Consider the following use of DS.

LABEL	OPERATION	OPERAND	COMMENTS	72
1	10 16			
CODE	DS	CL4'ABCD'		

The DS should have been coded instead as

LABEL	OPERATION	OPERAND	COMMENTS	72
1	10 16			
CODE	DC	CL4'ABCD'		

In the former, a 4-position area will be reserved for CODE, but the value 'ABCD' will *not* be entered. DS statements simply reserve storage. On the other hand, you may use a DC to define a storage area without specifying a value. The following, then, is a valid statement.

LABEL	OPERATION	OPERAND	COMMENTS	72
1	10 16			
CTR	DC	XL4		

Although a DC may be used in this way, it is a good idea to develop the technique of using DS for storage definitions and DC for constants. Later on, this will make debugging easier.

2. Length of a Constant

A DC can define a zoned-decimal or hexadecimal constant that contains as many as 256 characters. Defining a constant of this size would require several lines of code.

RULES FOR EXTENDING A DC TO TWO OR MORE LINES

1. Name, operation, and operand of first line are exactly the same as in previous examples. Because the constant has not been completely defined by the end of the line, *no end quote is specified* on line 1.
2. A C (or any other character) is placed in position 72 of the first line to indicate that the line is continued.
3. The constant continues in position 16 of the next line; the constant ends with a quote mark.

Example 3.18 Two-Line Constant:

LABEL	OPERATION	OPERAND	COMMENTS
1	10 16		72
VERYLONG	DC	C'THIS IS A CONSTANT WHICH IS C	
		VERY LONG'	

Example 3.19 Three-Line Constant:

LABEL	OPERATION	OPERAND	COMMENTS
1	10 16		72
LONGER	DC	C'THIS IS AN	
		EVEN LONGER	
		CONSTANT'	

CHAPTER SUMMARY

I. The Define Storage (DS) Statement
   A. Reserves storage for variable data.
   B. Format for the DS:

Name	DS	Operand

1–8 Characters:
Letters, digits, $, @, #
No blanks or other
special characters
		dtLn
		where:
		d = duplication factor
		t = type
		  C = character
		  X = hexadecimal
		  P = packed
		  B = binary
		  F = fullword
		  H = halfword
		  D = doubleword
		Not used with F, H or D { L = length
		  n = number of bytes reserved

   C. A zero duplication factor is used when a field or record is to be subdivided.
   D. If a DS entry contains no name, then storage will be reserved but the item will not be accessed by name by the program.
   E. A location counter assigns an address to each storage area defined by a DS as each DS is encountered.
   F. The address assigned by the location counter references the high-order or left-most position of each storage area defined.
   G. The use of H, F, or D locates data at addresses divisible by 2, 4, or 8, respectively.
II. The Define Constant (DC) Statement
   A. Specifies the size and type of the field, as well as the contents.
   B. The specifications are the same as for DS statements. In addition, the actual contents to be placed in the field are specified with single quote marks.
   C. Data defined by H, F, or D types will be converted to binary by the computer.

D. The following is a summary of types of constants and their characteristics.

Summary of Characteristics of Constants

Type	Maximum Length (bytes)	Stored as	Left or Right Truncation or Padding
C	256	Characters	Right
X	256	Hexadecimal Digits	Left
B	256	Binary Digits	Left
F	4	Binary Digits	Left
H	2	Binary Digits	Left
D	8	Binary Digits	Left
P	16	Packed Decimal Digits	Left

E. Rules for extending a DC to two or more lines.
   a. No end quote is specified on line 1.
   b. A C (or any other character) is placed in position 72 of the first line.
   c. The constant continues in position 16 of the next line; the constant ends with a quote mark.

CHAPTER SELF-EVALUATING QUIZ

1. What would be the contents of SAM if the following were coded?
   ```
   SAM     DC      CL2'THINK'
   ```
2. The F-, H-, or D-type DC contains a constant that is specified in (binary/decimal) format but that is converted by the computer to (binary/decimal) format.
3. Indicate the contents in hexadecimal and character form of the following fields.
   a. DC F'0'
   b. DC XL3'C1C3C5'
   c. DC CL6'ABC'

   Indicate the actual number of bytes required for the following constants.
4. C'12345'
5. X'123456'
6. X'1234567890'
7. F'23'
8. H'14'
9. The number +2 stored in a word of memory using a packed-decimal format would be represented in hexadecimal as
   a. F2F0F0F0
   b. 00000002
   c. 0000002C
   d. F0F0F0C2
   e. None of the above
10. Which of the following represents the instruction necessary to reserve a doubleword of memory labeled TEST, which will begin on a doubleword boundary?
    a. TEST DS CL8
    b. TEST DC CL8
    c. TEST DS F
    d. TEST DS D
    e. a and d above

Show how each of the following items of data is stored within the computer's memory. If any of the data will not fit in the size locations provided, indicate the *type* of error. Give your answers in hexadecimal, being sure to indicate what is in every byte.

11. 98: in zoned-decimal format in 2 bytes of memory.
12. +98: in packed-decimal format in a doubleword of memory.
13. −30: in packed-decimal format in a word of memory
14. 3,000,000,000: in a word, packed-decimal format
15. SNAP: in EBCDIC in 4 bytes of memory
16. 205: in EBCDIC in 3 bytes of memory
17. 205: in packed-decimal in a word of memory

Page

SOLUTIONS

1. TH (INK would be truncated because of the length specification   60
2. Decimal; binary   61

3. a.

00	00	00	00

Hexadecimal representation   61

b.

C 1	C 3	C 5

Hexadecimal representation   60

A	C	E

Character representation

c.

C 1	C 2	C 3	4 0	4 0	4 0

Hexadecimal representation   59

A	B	C	ƀ	ƀ	ƀ

Character representation

4. 5 bytes   59
5. 3 bytes; no sign generated

12	34	56

   61

6. 5 bytes

12	34	56	78	90

   61

7. 4 bytes; F defines a fullword   55
8. 2 bytes   55
9. c   62
10. d   55

11.

F 9	F 8

   60

12.

0 0	0 0	0 0	0 0	0 0	0 0	0 9	8 C

   62

13.

0 0	0 0	0 3	0 D

   62

14. constant is too long; truncation will occur; all zeros are placed in the field.   61

15.

E 2	D 5	C 1	D 7

   60

16.

F 2	F 0	F 5

   60

17.

00	00	20	5F

   62

KEY TERMS

Boundary	Halfword
Byte	High-order
Constant data	Location counter
Doubleword	Low-order
Field	Record
Fullword	Variable data

REVIEW QUESTIONS

1. Show how each of the following constants would be stored.

    ```
    ITEM1    DC    F'432'
    ITEM2    DC    P'23'
    ITEM3    DC    X'F3'
    ITEM4    DC    CL4'12AB'
    ```

2. Write DC statements for
    a. 5 fullwords containing zeros.
    b. a halfword whose binary representation is 1111000100011110.
    c. a 5-byte field with value 'NANCY'.
    d. a 3-byte field with each byte containing F3.
    e. a packed decimal field containing −123.

3. Provide a pictorial representation of the storage areas generated by the following.

    ```
    1002    DC    CL4'ABC'
            DC    3PL3'-12'
            DC    XL6'F3F2F5F0F3F1'
            DC    3F'0'
            DS    2F
            DS    H
            DS    D
    ```

4. The DS instruction
    a. generates blanks in a field.
    b. generates zeros in a field.
    c. reserves storage.
    d. reserves storage and places data in the field.

5. Labels or names of data fields are coded
    a. in any column.
    b. in any column after column 8.
    c. starting in column one.
    d. following an asterisk.
    e. none of the above.

6. The instruction

LABEL	OPERATION	OPERAND	COMMENTS	
1	10	16		72
BLANK	DS	CL1' '		

   a. stores a space in the printout area.
   b. stores a hex 40 in the location called BLANK.
   c. reserves one byte of storage.
   d. may cause a problem at execution time.
   e. c and d.

7. The letter C is represented in storage
   a. using the Hollerith code.
   b. in the hex format by C1.
   c. by a decimal 194.
   d. all of the above.
   e. none of the above.

8. If a word is stored in the computer's memory, the byte addressed is the
   a. high-order.
   b. low-order.
   c. rightmost.
   d. least significant.
   e. none of these.

9. A word consists of _____ hex digits.
   a. 2
   b. 4
   c. 8
   d. 16
   e. 32

10. Alphanumeric data is stored in an IBM or IBM-compatible computer's memory in a code called _____ .
    a. BCD
    b. Hollerith
    c. EBCDIC
    d. ANSI
    e. none of the above

UNIT 2

PROGRAMMING BUSINESS PROBLEMS IN ASSEMBLER LANGUAGE

 **Program Shell**

OBJECTIVES

To familiarize you with the procedures to:
1. *Perform necessary "housekeeping" or initializing routines.*
2. *Access input and output files or data sets.*
3. *Read and write information.*
4. *Perform necessary end-of-job operations.*

I. INTRODUCTION

We will explain some fundamental instructions that are used in most assembler language programs. Once you understand them, you can simply incorporate them, line-by-line, in all your programs. We will provide coding sheets at the end of this chapter and at the end of the book that already contain these instructions. So, it will be a simple matter to use them as a standard *shell* of instructions for all of your programs. Your job will be to supply the specific logic needed for each program, using this standard shell as a base.

A. Sample Program

We begin by considering a sample program that will illustrate the structure of assembler language. The object of this program is simply to read in records with the format shown in Figure 4.1 and list them out on the printer as shown. Note that the input records can be on disk, tape, or cards; they are essentially device-independent.

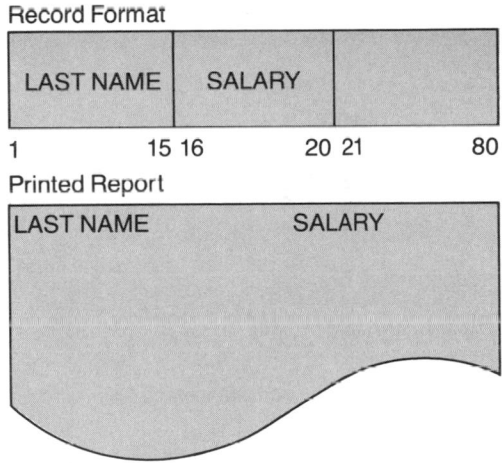

Figure 4.1
Input and output formats for
the sample program.

B. A Note on Operating Systems

You will recall that assembler language programs are typically run either under **OS** (*Operating System*) or **DOS** (*Disk Operating System*), depending on the computer being used. It should be noted that most instructions in assembler language programs are identical, regardless of which system (OS or DOS) is being used. However, because there are some differences, we will illustrate the above program under both OS and DOS to demonstrate that with little difficulty, a program written for one system can be modified easily to run on another. Even if you will be running under DOS, it is recommended that you examine the following OS program to familiarize yourself with the basic concepts and the distinctions.[1]

---

[1]If you are using the ASSIST Educational Assembler, some of the complexities associated with both OS and DOS have been eliminated for you. See Appendix K.

II. OS SAMPLE PROGRAM

Figure 4.2 illustrates an OS program that will read in 80-character data records and print them out. For your convenience, explanatory comments have been added to key instructions to explain their purpose. However, only that part of the program within the box must be supplied as instructions to the computer.

We will now examine the program in detail. Do not be confused by the seeming complexity. As noted, most of the instructions will be included line-by-line in *all* OS programs you will write to read in cards and print out information.

A. Analysis of the Instructions

> NOTE: These instructions will be considered standard for our programs thoughout the text. Most of them are required for proper assembly and execution. Because of their seeming complexity, they will be treated as *precoded* entries. The following explanation has been included for reference only.

	INSTRUCTIONS		OPTIONAL COMMENTS

LOC	OBJECT CODE	ADDR1	ADDR2	STMT	SOURCE STATEMENT			OPTIONAL COMMENTS
				1		PRINT	NOGEN	SUPPRESS GENERATED INSTRUCTIONS
000000				2	PRINTOUT	START		
000000	90EC D00C	0000C		3		STM	14,12,12(13)	
000004	05C0			4		BALR	12,0	ESTABLISH BASE REGISTER AS 12
			00006	5		USING	*,12	ADDRESS OF FIRST INSTRUCTION IN REG.12
000006	50D0 C066	0006C		6		ST	13,SAVEAREA+4	
00000A	41D0 C062	00068		7		LA	13,SAVEAREA	
				8		OPEN	(INFILE,INPUT,OUTFILE,OUTPUT)	ACCESS THE FILES
00001E	D283 C1BB C1BA	001C1	001C0	16	CLEAR	MVC	OUTAREA,SPACES	CLEAR THE PRINT AREA
				17		GET	INFILE,RECORD	READ AND STORE THE INPUT RECORD
000032	D20E C1C0 C16A	001C6	00170	22		MVC	LNAME,LAST	
000038	D204 C1E3 C179	001E9	0017F	23		MVC	SALOUT,SALARY	
				24		PUT	OUTFILE,OUTAREA	PRINT A LINE FROM OUTAREA
00004C	47F0 C018	0001E		29		B	CLEAR	GO BACK TO PROCESS NEXT INPUT RECORD
				30	EOF	CLOSE	(INFILE,,OUTFILE)	RELEASE FILES
00005E	58D0 C066	0006C		38		L	13,SAVEAREA+4	
000062	98EC D00C	0000C		39		LM	14,12,12(13)	
000066	07FE			40		BR	14	
000068				41	SAVEAREA	DS	18F	
				42	*			
				43	INFILE	DCB	DDNAME=INFILE,	
							MACRF=GM,	
							BLKSIZE=80,	
							LRECL=80,	
							DSORG=PS,	
							EODAD=EOF	
				97	*			
				98	OUTFILE	DCB	DDNAME=OUTFILE,	CHARACTERISTICS OF OUTFILE
							MACRF=PM,	
							BLKSIZE=132,	
							LRECL=132,	
							DSORG=PS	
000170				152	RECORD	DS	0CL80	SET UP INPUT AREA & SUBDIVIDE
000170				153	LAST	DS	CL15	INTO LAST NAME
00017F				154	SALARY	DS	CL5	AND SALARY
000184				155		DS	CL60	FIELDS
0001C0	40			156	SPACES	DC	CL1' '	BLANK FOR CLEARING PRINT AREA
0001C1				157	OUTAREA	DS	0CL132	SET UP PRINT AREA & SUBDIVIDE
0001C1				158		DS	CL5	INTO
0001C6				159	LNAME	DS	CL15	LAST NAME
0001D5				160		DS	CL20	AND
0001E9				161	SALOUT	DS	CL5	SALARY
0001EE				162		DS	CL87	FIELDS
				163		END		

Figure 4.2 OS sample program.

B. Housekeeping Instructions

The instructions shown in the boxed areas in Figure 4.3 are *standard* for every OS program. They are necessary for efficient assembly and execution. We will refer to these instructions as **"housekeeping,"** or initializing, **instructions**. Although they are not part of the program logic, they still must be routinely included in each program.

Figure 4.3
Housekeeping instructions (boxed) in OS sample program.

Line	Instruction	Explanation
1	PRINT NOGEN	TERMS: PRINT NOGEN INSTRUCTION MEANING: Suppresses the printing of all instructions generated for each macro. This simplifies the appearance of the listing and the debugging process. The following example illustrates the instructions that would be printed for a macro when PRINT NOGEN is not used.

```
16          GET     INFILE,RECORD
17+         LA      1,INFILE
18+         LA      0,RECORD
19+         L       15,48(0,1)
20+         BALR    14,15
```

REFERENCE: See Chapter 10.

Line	Instruction	Explanation
2	PRINTOUT START	TERMS: PRINTOUT—Name of program INSTRUCTION MEANING: Tells computer where program called PRINTOUT starts. REFERENCE: See Chapter 18.

3, 6, 7, 19		STM	14,12,12(13)	TERMS: STM—Store Multiple
			⋮	ST—Store
		ST	13,SAVEAREA+4	LA—Load Address
		LA	13,SAVEAREA	DS—Define Storage
			⋮	INSTRUCTION MEANING: These four instructions save addresses stored in registers so that processing can continue even if a system interrupt occurs.
	SAVEAREA	DS	18F	REFERENCE: See Appendix D.

4, 5	BALR	12,0	TERMS: BALR—Branch and Link Register
	USING	*,12	INSTRUCTION MEANING: The BALR instruction establishes register 12 as the **base register**. The USING instruction tells the computer that the address of the first instruction in the program will be found in register 12.
			REFERENCE: See Chapter 18 and Appendix F.

16, 17, 18	L	13,SAVEAREA+4	TERMS: L—Load
	LM	14,12,12(13)	LM—Load Multiple
	BR	14	BR—Branch to Register
			INSTRUCTION MEANING: These three instructions are necessary to return control to the operating system after the program has been run.
			REFERENCE: See Chapters 11, 12, 18, and Appendix D.

43	END		TERMS: END
			INSTRUCTION MEANING: This must be the last instruction in the program. It terminates the assembly process. (It tells the assembler where the end of the program is located.)[a]
			REFERENCE: See Chapter 10.

[a]By examining Figure 4.3, you can see that we have adopted the convention of placing file descriptions called DCBs, as well as record and field descriptions (DSs), at the *end* of the program. If we were to locate these entries at the beginning of the program, we would have to add an operand to the END statement. This operand would consist of the label of the first *executable* instruction. In Figure 4.3, that instruction would be the STM.

C. The Access and I/O Macros

The instructions shown in the boxed areas in Figure 4.4 are typical access and **I/O macros** to provide input and output operations. Here again, you will need to include them, as illustrated, in your programs. The explanation that follows is for your information only.

Line	Instruction	Explanation
8	OPEN (INFILE,INPUT,OUTFILE,OUTPUT)	TERMS: INFILE—Name assigned by programmer to the incoming file
		INPUT—Designates INFILE as an input file
		OUTFILE—Name assigned to the print file by programmer
		OUTPUT—Designates OUTFILE as an output file (Note that a file name can consist of 1 to 8 characters—letters, digits, and/or $, @, # although the first must be alphabetic (A–Z, $, @, #).)
		INSTRUCTION MEANING: Accesses the I/O devices associated with the files named. When a computer accesses a device, it determines if the I/O unit is ready to be used. If not, execution is suspended. In addition, certain checking functions regarding header labels are performed when a tape or disk device is accessed.

10	`GET    INFILE,RECORD`	TERMS: `INFILE`—Name assigned to the incoming file `RECORD`—Area in storage where input data is temporarily stored INSTRUCTION MEANING: This **macro** instructs the computer to read in or `GET` one physical record from `INFILE` and store it in the storage area called `RECORD`.
13	`PUT   OUTFILE,OUTAREA`	TERMS: `OUTFILE`—Name assigned to the print file `OUTAREA`—Area in storage from which a line will be printed INSTRUCTION MEANING: This macro instructs the computer to transmit the information from the storage area `OUTAREA` to the output device associated with `OUTFILE`, in this case, the printer. Thus, one line will be printed.
15	`EOF  CLOSE (INFILE,,OUTFILE)`	TERMS: `EOF`—Label of the instruction (abbreviation for end of file) `INFILE`—Name of the input file `OUTFILE`—Name of the print file INSTRUCTION MEANING: When the end-of-data condition is reached for the input file called `INFILE`, the computer automatically branches to this instruction, as discussed in the following section. The `CLOSE` macro closes or releases the files named.

```
               PRINT  NOGEN              SUPPRESS GENERATED INSTRUCTIONS
      PRINTOUT START
               STM    14,12,12(13)
               BALR   12,0               ESTABLISH BASE REGISTER AS 12
               USING  *,12               ADDRESS OF FIRST INSTRUCTION IN REG.12
               ST     13,SAVEAREA+4
               LA     13,SAVEAREA
   8           OPEN   (INFILE,INPUT,OUTFILE,OUTPUT)    ACCESS THE FILES
      CLEAR    MVC    OUTAREA,SPACES                   CLEAR THE PRINT AREA
  10           GET    INFILE,RECORD      READ AND STORE THE INPUT RECORD
               MVC    LNAME,LAST
               MVC    SALOUT,SALARY
  13           PUT    OUTFILE,OUTAREA    PRINT A LINE FROM OUTAREA
               B      CLEAR              GO BACK TO PROCESS NEXT INPUT RECORD
  15  EOF      CLOSE  (INFILE,,OUTFILE)  RELEASE FILES
               L      13,SAVEAREA+4
               LM     14,12,12(13)
               BR     14
      SAVEAREA DS     18F
      *
      INFILE   DCB    DDNAME=INFILE,                                     *
                      MACRF=GM,                                          *
                      BLKSIZE=80,                                        *
                      LRECL=80,                                          *
                      DSORG=PS,                                          *
                      EODAD=EOF
      *                                  CHARACTERISTICS OF OUTFILE
      OUTFILE  DCB    DDNAME=OUTFILE,                                    *
                      MACRF=PM,                                          *
                      BLKSIZE=132,                                       *
                      LRECL=132,                                         *
                      DSORG=PS
      RECORD   DS     0CL80              SET UP INPUT AREA & SUBDIVIDE
      LAST     DS     CL15                      INTO LAST NAME
      SALARY   DS     CL5                       AND SALARY
               DS     CL60                      FIELDS
      SPACES   DC     CL1' '             BLANK FOR CLEARING PRINT AREA
      OUTAREA  DS     0CL132             SET UP PRINT AREA & SUBDIVIDE
               DS     CL5                       INTO
      LNAME    DS     CL15                      LAST NAME
               DS     CL20                      AND
      SALOUT   DS     CL5                       SALARY
               DS     CL87                      FIELDS
               END
```

Figure 4.4
Access and I/O macros (boxed)
in OS sample program.

D. File, Record, and Field Descriptions

The computer must be supplied with detailed descriptions of the characteristics of each file being used and the layouts of the I/O records. These details are essential so that when the access and I/O macros discussed previously (OPEN, GET, PUT, CLOSE) are executed, the computer knows the devices to be used and the precise format of the data being read in or printed out. The instructions shown in the boxed areas in Figure 4.5 illustrate the **file**, **record**, and **field** definitions used in this program.

```
               PRINT  NOGEN                          SUPPRESS GENERATED INSTRUCTIONS
      PRINTOUT START
               STM    14,12,12(13)
               BALR   12,0                            ESTABLISH BASE REGISTER AS 12
               USING  *,12                            ADDRESS OF FIRST INSTRUCTION IN REG.12
               ST     13,SAVEAREA+4
               LA     13,SAVEAREA
               OPEN   (INFILE,INPUT,OUTFILE,OUTPUT)        ACCESS THE FILES
      CLEAR    MVC    OUTAREA,SPACES                            CLEAR THE PRINT AREA
               GET    INFILE,RECORD             READ AND STORE THE INPUT RECORD
               MVC    LNAME,LAST
               MVC    SALOUT,SALARY
               PUT    OUTFILE,OUTAREA           PRINT A LINE FROM OUTAREA
               B      CLEAR                     GO BACK TO PROCESS NEXT INPUT RECORD
      EOF      CLOSE  (INFILE,,OUTFILE)         RELEASE FILES
               L      13,SAVEAREA+4
               LM     14,12,12(13)
               BR     14
      SAVEAREA DS     18F
      *
   21 INFILE   DCB    DDNAME=INFILE,                                           *
   22                 MACRF=GM,                                                *
   23                 BLKSIZE=80,                                              *
   24                 LRECL=80,                                                *
   25                 DSORG=PS,                                                *
   26                 EODAD=EOF
      *                                        CHARACTERISTICS OF OUTFILE
   28 OUTFILE  DCB    DDNAME=OUTFILE,                                          *
   29                 MACRF=PM,                                                *
   30                 BLKSIZE=132,                                             *
   31                 LRECL=132,                                               *
   32                 DSORG=PS
   33 RECORD   DS     0CL80                     SET UP INPUT AREA & SUBDIVIDE
   34 LAST     DS     CL15                              INTO LAST NAME
   35 SALARY   DS     CL5                               AND SALARY
   36          DS     CL60                              FIELDS
   37 SPACES   DC     CL1' '                    BLANK FOR CLEARING PRINT AREA
   38 OUTAREA  DS     0CL132                    SET UP PRINT AREA & SUBDIVIDE
   39          DS     CL5                               INTO
   40 LNAME    DS     CL15                              LAST NAME
   41          DS     CL20                              AND
   42 SALOUT   DS     CL5                               SALARY
   43          DS     CL87                              FIELDS
               END
```

Figure 4.5
File, record, and field descriptions (boxed) in OS sample program.

Line	Instruction	Explanation
21–26	INFILE DCB DDNAME=INFILE, MACRF=GM, BLKSIZE=80, LRECL=80, DSORG=PS, EODAD=EOF	TERMS: DCB—Data Control Block DDNAME—Data Definition Name MACRF—Macro Form BLKSIZE—Block Size LRECL—Logical Record Length DSORG—Data Set Organization EODAD—End-of-Data Address (These entries may appear in any sequence.) INSTRUCTION MEANING: The DCB macro describes the characteristics of the file INFILE as follows: 1. The DDNAME specifies the symbolic names that will be used in a **JCL (Job Control Language)** statement to assign an actual I/O device to the file named INFILE.

2. The MACRF operand indicates that a GET (G) macro will be used to read in records from the file. The "M" indicates that the data is to be moved (M) to the area specified in the GET macro, which in this program is RECORD.
3. The BLKSIZE (**block size)** operand tells the computer that each **physical record** contains 80 bytes.
4. LRECL operand specifies that each **logical record** contains 80 bytes.
5. The DSORG operand indicates that the records are in physical sequential (PS) order. That is, the computer is processing records in sequence.
6. The EODAD operand instructs the computer to branch to the instruction labeled EOF when there is no more input data, so that the end-of-job routine can be performed.

These entries may be coded as individual items on separate lines (with a character in position 72) or in paragraph form across the page.

| 28–32 | OUTFILE | DCB | DDNAME=OUTFILE,
MACRF=PM,
BLKSIZE=132,
LRECL=132,
DSORG=PS | TERMS: DDNAME—Data Definition Name
MACRF—Macro Form
BLKSIZE—Block Size
LRECL—Logical Record Length
DSORG—Data Set Organization |

(These entries may appear in any sequence.)

INSTRUCTION MEANING: This DCB macro describes the characteristics of the file OUTFILE. The operands have the same meaning as those discussed previously for the INFILE DCB. Notice the following, however:

1. The MACRF operand indicates that a PUT (P) macro will be used to write out or transmit information from storage to the output device associated with OUTFILE. The "M" indicates that the data is to be moved (M) from the area specified in the PUT macro. In this program, that area is called OUTAREA.
2. We are using a printer with 132 print positions per line, as indicated by the BLKSIZE and LRECL operands. We will see in Chapter 9 that 133 positions will be defined when we want to incorporate carriage control characters.
3. The DSORG operand specifies that the output will be physical sequential (PS), because we are dealing with a printer.
4. Notice that there is no EODAD entry, because we only test for the end-of-data condition on an *input* file.

These entries may be coded as individual items on separate lines (with a character in position 72) or in paragraph form across the page.

| 33–36 | RECORD
LAST
SALARY
 | DS
DS
DS
DS | 0CL80
CL15
CL5
CL60 | TERMS: DS—Define Storage
CL—Character Length
RECORD—Name of input area |

The DSs and DCs are coded after the end-of-job routines.

INSTRUCTION MEANING: The first DS instruction defines the storage area RECORD that will be used to store 1 input record. The first 0 in 0CL80 specifies that the area, which will hold 80 bytes of data or 80 characters, will be subdivided into the fields defined by the following DS instructions. Thus, RECORD is subdivided into 3 fields: LAST (for last name), consisting of 15 bytes; SALARY, consisting of 5 bytes; and, an unlabeled area of 60 bytes to complete the description of an 80-byte record.

REFERENCE: See Chapter 3.

| 38–42 | OUTAREA

LNAME | DS
DS
DS | 0CL132
CL5
CL15 | TERMS: DS—Define Storage
CL—Character Length
OUTAREA—Name of output area |

```
          DS    CL20
SALOUT    DS    CL5
          DS    CL87
```

INSTRUCTION MEANING: The first DS instruction defines the storage area OUTAREA that will be used to accumulate the information to be printed on each line. The O in front of CL132 indicates that this area will be subdivided into the fields specified by the following DS instructions. The first field (5 bytes long) has no name. The second field in OUTAREA will be the field LNAME (for last name), consisting of 15 bytes. The next field has no name but is defined as 20 bytes long. This area will provide for spacing between the first field printed out, LNAME, and the next field SALOUT (for salary out). Notice that the last DS (unlabeled) is 87 bytes long so that all the fields will add up to the 132 positions in OUTAREA.
REFERENCE: See Chapter 3.

---

37 SPACES DC CL1' '

TERMS: DC—Define Constant
c—Character
L1—Length of one byte
SPACES—Name of constant
INSTRUCTION MEANING: This constant, consisting of a one-position blank, is located *immediately before* the output area OUTAREA, and will be used to clear that area, as discussed in the following section.
REFERENCE: See Chapter 3.

The following summary reviews some of the commonly used DCB operands discussed so far.

SUMMARY OF COMMONLY USED DCB OPERANDS

Format: **dcbname   DCB   operands**

Operand	*Meaning*
DDNAME=ddname	ddname specifies the symbolic file name that will be used in a JCL statement to assign an actual I/O device to this file.
DSORG={ PS Physical Sequential / IS Indexed Sequential / DA Direct Access }	Specifies the data set's organization.
MACRF={ GM / PM }	Specifies the I/O macro to be used and indicates that the data is to be moved to or from the area listed in that macro; G = GET, P = PUT, M = move.
BLKSIZE=	Specifies the block size or length in bytes of each physical record.
LRECL=	Specifies the logical record length in bytes.
EODAD=	Specifies the instruction to branch to when the end-of-file condition is reached.

Chapter 9 (Print Options and Control Break Processing) discusses various techniques that can be used to have the printer space the paper.

E. Logic Instructions

Thus far, we have discussed housekeeping instructions, access and I/O macros, and file, record, and field descriptions. Although record and field descriptions will change from one program to another, the other items are basically standard, with only minor variations from one system to another.[2] Note that the illustrated program prints information from input records in a sequential file. To utilize different formats or I/O media, only slight modifications would be required.

We will now discuss the logic instructions in this program that are shown in the boxed area in Figure 4.6. This is the key part of the program. It includes instructions that will vary depending on the specific program logic.

Line	Instruction			Explanation
9	CLEAR	MVC	OUTAREA,SPACES	TERMS: CLEAR—Label of instruction MVC—Move Character OUTAREA—Name of output area SPACES—Constant INSTRUCTION MEANING: Move the constant SPACES to OUTAREA. This will clear the area by putting blanks in all the bytes. REFERENCE: See Chapter 5.
11, 12		MVC MVC	LNAME,LAST SALOUT,SALARY	TERMS: MVC—Move Character LAST—Input field SALARY—Input field LNAME—Output field SALOUT—Output field INSTRUCTION MEANING: These instructions move the input fields LAST and SALARY from the input area (RECORD) to the output fields LNAME and SALOUT in the output area (OUTAREA). REFERENCE: See Chapter 5.
14		B	CLEAR	TERMS: B—Branch CLEAR—Label of instruction to branch to INSTRUCTION MEANING: Go to the instruction labeled CLEAR. In this manner, we will repeat the sequence of reading a record and processing it. However, before we get the next record (if there is one) we want to clear the output area so that it will be ready to accept a new line of information to be printed out. REFERENCE: See Chapter 8.

By examining the preceding program, you should note that most OS programs that read input and print output will simply require this shell in addition to whatever logic is required between the GET and PUT macros. This shell of instructions will remain basically the same unless the input is entered on disk or tape, in which case a few changes may be required.

---

[2]Examples of these variations are discussed later in this chapter and in Appendix K.

```
                   PRINT  NOGEN                    SUPPRESS GENERATED INSTRUCTIONS
          PRINTOUT START
                   STM    14,12,12(13)
                   BALR   12,0                      ESTABLISH BASE REGISTER AS 12
                   USING  *,12                      ADDRESS OF FIRST INSTRUCTION IN REG.12
                   ST     13,SAVEAREA+4
                   LA     13,SAVEAREA
                   OPEN   (INFILE,INPUT,OUTFILE,OUTPUT)     ACCESS THE FILES
  9       CLEAR    MVC    OUTAREA,SPACES                    CLEAR THE PRINT AREA
 10                GET    INFILE,RECORD     READ AND STORE THE INPUT RECORD
 11                MVC    LNAME,LAST
 12                MVC    SALOUT,SALARY
 13                PUT    OUTFILE,OUTAREA   PRINT A LINE FROM OUTAREA
 14                B      CLEAR             GO BACK TO PROCESS NEXT INPUT RECORD
          EOF      CLOSE  (INFILE,,OUTFILE)  RELEASE FILES
                   L      13,SAVEAREA+4
                   LM     14,12,12(13)
                   BR     14
          SAVEAREA DS     18F
          *
          INFILE   DCB    DDNAME=INFILE,                                          *
                          MACRF=GM,                                               *
                          BLKSIZE=80,                                             *
                          LRECL=80,                                               *
                          DSORG=PS,                                               *
                          EODAD=EOF
          *                                  CHARACTERISTICS OF OUTFILE
          OUTFILE  DCB    DDNAME=OUTFILE,                                         *
                          MACRF=PM,                                               *
                          BLKSIZE=132,                                            *
                          LRECL=132,                                              *
                          DSORG=PS
          RECORD   DS     0CL80             SET UP INPUT AREA & SUBDIVIDE
          LAST     DS     CL15                        INTO LAST NAME
          SALARY   DS     CL5                         AND SALARY
                   DS     CL60                        FIELDS
          SPACES   DC     CL1' '            BLANK FOR CLEARING PRINT AREA
          OUTAREA  DS     0CL132            SET UP PRINT AREA & SUBDIVIDE
                   DS     CL5                         INTO
          LNAME    DS     CL15                        LAST NAME
                   DS     CL20                        AND
          SALOUT   DS     CL5                         SALARY
                   DS     CL87                        FIELDS
                   END
```

Figure 4.6
Logic instructions (boxed) in
OS sample program.

III. DOS SAMPLE PROGRAM

Now that we have examined an OS program, we will look at a sample DOS program. You will see that the instructions are very similar to those used under OS. Although the housekeeping instructions and file descriptions will require some modification, the I/O macros, logic instructions, and record and field descriptions will be *identical*. The access macros will simply require a different format. Thus, if you have followed the discussion of a sample OS program, you should have little difficulty in understanding the sample DOS program in Figure 4.7. For the sake of comparison, this program accomplishes the same tasks as the OS program discussed earlier in this chapter.

A. Housekeeping Instructions

The housekeeping instructions, or those instructions that will appear in every DOS program for proper assembly and execution, are shown in the boxed areas in Figure 4.8.

You will notice that all of these housekeeping instructions were used in the sample OS program except for the EOJ macro. The purpose of the EOJ macro is simply to indicate to the computer that the program has been executed and that control can be returned to the operating system.

B. Access and I/O Macros

The access and I/O macros for this program are shown in the boxed areas in Figure 4.9.

```
        PRINT NOGEN                    SUPPRESS GENERATED INSTRUCTIONS
PRINTOUT START
        BALR  12,0                     ESTABLISH REG 12 AS BASE REGISTER
        USING *,12                     ADDRESS OF FIRST INSTRUCTION IN REG 12
        OPEN  INFILE,OUTFILE           ACCESS THE FILES
CLEAR   MVC   OUTAREA,SPACES           CLEAR THE PRINT AREA
        GET   INFILE,RECORD            READ A RECORD AND STORE
        MVC   LNAME,LAST
        MVC   SALOUT,SALARY
        PUT   OUTFILE,OUTAREA          PRINT A LINE FROM OUTAREA
        B     CLEAR                    GO BACK TO PROCESS NEXT RECORD
EOF     CLOSE INFILE,OUTFILE           RELEASE FILES
        EOJ                            STOP THE PROGRAM
*                                      CHARACTERISTICS OF INFILE
INFILE  DTFCD DEVADDR=SYSIPT,                                              *
              BLKSIZE=80,                                                  *
              IOAREA1=BUFFRIN,                                             *
              WORKA=YES,                                                   *
              DEVICE=2501,                                                 *
              TYPEFLE=INPUT,                                               *
              EOFADDR=EOF
*                                      CHARACTERISTICS OF OUTFILE
OUTFILE DTFPR DEVADDR=SYSLST,                                              *
              BLKSIZE=132,                                                 *
              IOAREA1=BUFFROUT,                                            *
              WORKA=YES,                                                   *
              DEVICE=3203
BUFFRIN  DS   CL80
BUFFROUT DS   CL132
RECORD   DS   0CL80                    SET UP INPUT AREA & SUBDIVIDE
LAST     DS   CL15                           INTO LAST NAME
SALARY   DS   CL5                            AND SALARY
         DS   CL60
SPACES   DC   CL1' '                   BLANK FOR CLEARING PRINT AREA
OUTAREA  DS   0CL132                   SET UP PRINT AREA & SUBDIVIDE
         DS   CL5                            INTO
LNAME    DS   CL15                           LAST NAME
         DS   CL20                           AND
SALOUT   DS   CL5                            SALARY FIELD
         DS   CL87
         END
```

Figure 4.7
DOS sample program.

```
        PRINT NOGEN                    SUPPRESS GENERATED INSTRUCTIONS
PRINTOUT START
        BALR  12,0                     ESTABLISH REG 12 AS BASE REGISTER
        USING *,12                     ADDRESS OF FIRST INSTRUCTION IN REG 12
        OPEN  INFILE,OUTFILE           ACCESS THE FILES
CLEAR   MVC   OUTAREA,SPACES           CLEAR THE PRINT AREA
        GET   INFILE,RECORD            READ A RECORD AND STORE
        MVC   LNAME,LAST
        MVC   SALOUT,SALARY
        PUT   OUTFILE,OUTAREA          PRINT A LINE FROM OUTAREA
        B     CLEAR                    GO BACK TO PROCESS NEXT RECORD
EOF     CLOSE INFILE,OUTFILE           RELEASE FILES
        EOJ                            STOP THE PROGRAM
*                                      CHARACTERISTICS OF INFILE
INFILE  DTFCD DEVADDR=SYSIPT,                                              *
              BLKSIZE=80,                                                  *
              IOAREA1=BUFFRIN,                                             *
              WORKA=YES,                                                   *
              DEVICE=2501,                                                 *
              TYPEFLE=INPUT,                                               *
              EOFADDR=EOF
*                                      CHARACTERISTICS OF OUTFILE
OUTFILE DTFPR DEVADDR=SYSLST,                                              *
              BLKSIZE=132,                                                 *
              IOAREA1=BUFFROUT,                                            *
              WORKA=YES,                                                   *
              DEVICE=3203
BUFFRIN  DS   CL80
BUFFROUT DS   CL132
RECORD   DS   0CL80                    SET UP INPUT AREA & SUBDIVIDE
LAST     DS   CL15                           INTO LAST NAME
SALARY   DS   CL5                            AND SALARY
         DS   CL60
SPACES   DC   CL1' '                   BLANK FOR CLEARING PRINT AREA
OUTAREA  DS   0CL132                   SET UP PRINT AREA & SUBDIVIDE
         DS   CL5                            INTO
LNAME    DS   CL15                           LAST NAME
         DS   CL20                           AND
SALOUT   DS   CL5                            SALARY FIELD
         DS   CL87
         END
```

Figure 4.8
Housekeeping instructions
(boxed) in DOS sample
program.

Notice that the I/O macros (GET and PUT) are identical to those used in the OS program. Notice also that while the OPEN and CLOSE macros serve the same purpose as under OS, their formats are slightly different under DOS. In DOS, the names of the files to be opened or closed are simply listed, *without* the use of parentheses. In addition, the OPEN macro does *not* include a designation as to whether a particular file is input or output. We will see in the following section how this problem is handled in the file description.

```
                PRINT NOGEN                  SUPPRESS GENERATED INSTRUCTIONS
        PRINTOUT START
                BALR  12,0                   ESTABLISH REG 12 AS BASE REGISTER
                USING *,12                   ADDRESS OF FIRST INSTRUCTION IN REG 12
                OPEN  INFILE,OUTFILE         ACCESS THE FILES
        CLEAR   MVC   OUTAREA,SPACES         CLEAR THE PRINT AREA
                GET   INFILE,RECORD          READ A RECORD AND STORE
                MVC   LNAME,LAST
                MVC   SALOUT,SALARY
                PUT   OUTFILE,OUTAREA        PRINT A LINE FROM OUTAREA
                B     CLEAR                  GO BACK TO PROCESS NEXT RECORD
        EOF     CLOSE INFILE,OUTFILE         RELEASE FILES
                EOJ   STOP THE PROGRAM
        *                                    CHARACTERISTICS OF INFILE
        INFILE  DTFCD DEVADDR=SYSIPT,                                        *
                      BLKSIZE=80,                                           *
                      IOAREA1=BUFFRIN,                                      *
                      WORKA=YES,                                            *
                      DEVICE=2501,                                          *
                      TYPEFLE=INPUT,                                        *
                      EOFADDR=EOF
        *                                    CHARACTERISTICS OF OUTFILE
        OUTFILE DTFPR DEVADDR=SYSLST,                                       *
                      BLKSIZE=132,                                          *
                      IOAREA1=BUFFROUT,                                     *
                      WORKA=YES,                                            *
                      DEVICE=3203
        BUFFRIN  DS   CL80
        BUFFROUT DS   CL132
        RECORD   DS   OCL80                   SET UP INPUT AREA & SUBDIVIDE
        LAST     DS   CL15                           INTO LAST NAME
        SALARY   DS   CL5                            AND SALARY
                 DS   CL60
        SPACES   DC   CL1' '                  BLANK FOR CLEARING PRINT AREA
        OUTAREA  DS   OCL132                  SET UP PRINT AREA & SUBDIVIDE
                 DS   CL5                            INTO
        LNAME    DS   CL15                           LAST NAME
                 DS   CL20                           AND
        SALOUT   DS   CL5                            SALARY FIELD
                 DS   CL87
                 END
```

Figure 4.9
Access and I/O macros (boxed) in DOS sample program.

C. File, Record, and Field Descriptions

The instructions that define the characteristics of the files, records, and fields are shown in the boxed areas on page 84.[3]

Notice that the descriptions of the input and output areas, RECORD and OUTAREA, are identical to those used in the OS program.

Line	Instruction		Explanation
15–21	INFILE	DTFCD DEVADDR=SYSIPT, BLKSIZE=80, IOAREA1=BUFFRIN, WORKA=YES,	TERMS: INFILE—Name of input file DTFCD—Define the File on Card Reader DEVADDR—Device Address BLKSIZE—Block Size

[3]Some computer systems do not have certain IOCS (Input/Output Control System) routines available in their relocatable libraries. If you receive an error message when executing your program that indicates an *unresolved external reference,* see Appendix E for the required additions to your program.

```
             DEVICE=2501,
             TYPEFLE=INPUT,
             EOFADDR=EOF
```

IOAREA1—Name of input buffer
WORKA—Work Area
TYPEFLE—Type of File
EOFADDR—End-of-File Address

(These entries can appear in any sequence.)

INSTRUCTION MEANING: This DTF macro describes the characteristics of the input file called INFILE:

1. The symbolic unit name of the input device to be used is SYSIPT, which is short for *system input* and is the name for the card reader or terminal for most systems.

2. The operand BLKSIZE specifies that each input record will contain 80 bytes.

3. The IOAREA1 operand specifies that we want one *buffer* (or I/O area) to be used with this file. We have arbitrarily called the buffer BUFFRIN (for *buffer in*), which must be defined by a DS instruction as 80 bytes long.

4. The WORKA operand indicates that we want a work area in storage. This will increase the efficiency of handling input records.

5. The file will be on the IBM 2501 card reader, as specified by the DEVICE operand.

6. The TYPEFLE operand designates this file as input.

7. The EOFADDR operand indicates the instruction to be branched to when the end-of-file condition is reached. EOF, then, is the label of the end-of-file routine.

These entries may appear as individual items on separate lines (with a character in position 72) or in paragraph form across the page.

23–27	OUTFILE	DTFPR	DEVADDR=SYSLST,
			BLKSIZE=132,
			IOAREA1=BUFFROUT,
			WORKA=YES,
			DEVICE=3203

TERMS: OUTFILE—Name of the print file
DTFPR—Define the File on the Printer
DEVADDR—Device Address
BLKSIZE—Block Size
IOAREA1—Name of the output buffer
WORKA—Work Area

(These entries may appear in any sequence.)

INSTRUCTION MEANING: This DTF macro describes the characteristics of the output file OUTFILE as follows:

1. The symbolic unit name of the output device to be used is SYSLST, which is short for *system list*. This is a symbolic name for the "printer" on most systems.

2. The operand BLKSIZE specifies that each output record will contain 132 bytes, because we are using a printer with 132 print positions per line. We will see in Chapter 9 that 133 positions will be defined when we want to incorporate carriage control characters.

3. The IOAREA1 operand specifies that we want one **buffer** (or I/O area) to be used with this file. We have arbitrarily called the buffer BUFFROUT (for *buffer out*), which must be defined by a DS instruction as 132 bytes long.

4. The WORKA operand indicates that we want a work area in storage to increase the efficiency of handling output records.

5. The DEVICE associated with this file is the IBM 3203 printer.

These entries may appear as individual items on separate lines (with a character in position 72) or they may appear in paragraph form across the page.

28	BUFFRIN	DS	CL80	TERMS: DS—Define Storage
				C—Character
				L80—Length 80
				INSTRUCTION MEANING: This instruction sets up an area in storage 80 bytes long that will serve as the *input* buffer.
				REFERENCE: See Chapter 3.
29	BUFFROUT	DS	CL132	TERMS: DS—Define Storage
				C—Character
				L132—Length 132
				INSTRUCTION MEANING: This instruction sets up an area in storage 132 bytes long that will serve as the *output* buffer.
				REFERENCE: See Chapter 3.

```
                    PRINT NOGEN                     SUPPRESS GENERATED INSTRUCTIONS
          PRINTOUT  START
                    BALR  12,0                       ESTABLISH REG 12 AS BASE REGISTER
                    USING *,12                       ADDRESS OF FIRST INSTRUCTION IN REG 12
                    OPEN  INFILE,OUTFILE             ACCESS THE FILES
          CLEAR     MVC   OUTAREA,SPACES             CLEAR THE PRINT AREA
                    GET   INFILE,RECORD              READ A RECORD AND STORE
                    MVC   LNAME,LAST
                    MVC   SALOUT,SALARY
                    PUT   OUTFILE,OUTAREA            PRINT A LINE FROM OUTAREA
                    B     CLEAR                      GO BACK TO PROCESS NEXT RECORD
          EOF       CLOSE INFILE,OUTFILE            RELEASE FILES
                    EOJ   STOP THE PROGRAM
          *                                          CHARACTERISTICS OF INFILE
    15    INFILE    DTFCD DEVADDR=SYSIPT,                                              *
    16                    BLKSIZE=80,                                                 *
    17                    IOAREA1=BUFFRIN,                                            *
    18                    WORKA=YES,                                                  *
    19                    DEVICE=2501,                                                *
    20                    TYPEFLE=INPUT,                                              *
    21                    EOFADDR=EOF
          *                                          CHARACTERISTICS OF OUTFILE
    23    OUTFILE   DTFPR DEVADDR=SYSLST,                                             *
    24                    BLKSIZE=132,                                                *
    25                    IOAREA1=BUFFROUT,                                           *
    26                    WORKA=YES,                                                  *
    27                    DEVICE=3203
    28    BUFFRIN   DS    CL80
    29    BUFFROUT  DS    CL132
    30    RECORD    DS    0CL80                      SET UP INPUT AREA & SUBDIVIDE
          LAST      DS    CL15                            INTO LAST NAME
          SALARY    DS    CL5                             AND SALARY
                    DS    CL60
          SPACES    DC    CLI' '                     BLANK FOR CLEARING PRINT AREA
          OUTAREA   DS    0CL132                     SET UP PRINT AREA & SUBDIVIDE
                    DS    CL5                             INTO
          LNAME     DS    CL15                            LAST NAME
                    DS    CL20                            AND
          SALOUT    DS    CL5                             SALARY FIELD
                    DS    CL87
                    END
```

Figure 4.10
File, record, and field descriptions (boxed) in DOS sample program.

DTFs typically indicate the specific devices being used. In Figure 4.7 we assume card input so that DTFCD (Define The File on CarDs) is used. Similarly, we assume printed output so that DTFPR (Define The File on the PRinter) is used.

The following are the main DTFs typically used:

DTFCD	for cards
DTFPR	for printed output
DTFMT	for magnetic tape
DTFSD	for sequential disk

DTFIS   for indexed sequential disk
DTFDU   for diskette (floppy disk)
DTFCN   for console unit typewriter

Also, DTFDI may be used for a device-independent file.

An 80-column input record, as described in this chapter, can be on cards, disk, tape, or entered on a terminal. The DTFxx entry and the DEVICE number are the only items that need to be changed.

The following summary reviews some of the commonly used DTF operands.

SUMMARY OF COMMONLY USED DTF OPERANDS

Format: **filename**   DTF**xx**   **operands**

Operand	*Meaning*
DEVADDR=	Specifies the symbolic unit name for the I/O (input/output) device.
IOAREA1=	Specifies the name of the buffer (or I/O area) to be used with the file; the buffer area must be defined by a DS instruction.
WORKA=YES	Indicates that a work area in storage is wanted.
DEVICE-	Specifies the unit number of the particular I/O device to be associated with the file.
EOFADDR=	Specifies the instruction to be branched to when the end-of-file condition is reached.
TYPEFLE= $\begin{Bmatrix} \text{INPUT} \\ \text{OUTPUT} \\ \text{INOUT} \end{Bmatrix}$	Specifies the type of file.
BLKSIZE=	Specifies the block size or length in bytes of a physical record.

The following sample DTFs illustrate how files can be defined for other media, such as magnetic disk and tape. In Unit VII we will see additional operands that can be used with DTFs for magnetic disk and tape.

Example 4.1:   DTFSD—For Sequential Processing of a Disk File
The RECSIZE operand specifies the number of bytes in a logical record.

```
LABEL    OPERATION   OPERAND                          COMMENTS              72
MASTER   DTFSD       DEVADDR=SYS008,
                     DEVICE=3330,
                     TYPEFLE=OUTPUT,
                     WORKA=YES,
                     RECSIZE=100,
                     BLKSIZE=200,
                     IOAREA1=BUFFROUT
```

Example 4.2:   DTFMT—For Defining a Magnetic Tape File

LABEL	OPERATION	OPERAND	COMMENTS	
1	10	16		72
MASTER	DTFMT	BLKSIZE=200,		*
		DEVADDR=SYS009,		*
		WORKA=YES,		*
		IOAREA1=BUFFRIN,		*
		RECSIZE=75,		*
		EOFADDR=EOF		

Example 4.3:   DTFCN—For Defining a File to be Processed on a Console Unit

LABEL	OPERATION	OPERAND	COMMENTS	
1	10	16		72
CONFILE	DTFCN	BLKSIZE=100,		*
		DEVADDR=SYS003,		*
		IOAREA1=CONBUF,		*
		TYPEFLE=INPUT,		*
		WORKA=YES		

D. Logic Instructions

You will notice in Figure 4.10 that the logic instructions from the OPEN macro through the CLOSE macro are *identical* to those used in the OS program.

We have seen that a program written to be run under OS contains virtually the same instructions used under DOS. Essentially, it is the housekeeping instructions and file descriptions (DTFs or DCBs) that will vary slightly. Note that the shell of instructions used in the above DOS program will remain basically the same, unless the input is entered on disk or tape, in which case a few changes may be required.

IV. MUSIC AND ASSIST: A FOCUS ON SYSTEM EFFICIENCY

We have seen in the previous sections how macros such as OPEN, CLOSE, GET, PUT, DCB, and DTF are used in OS and DOS assembler language programs. Depending on the system being used, programs that include macros such as these frequently take a relatively long time to assemble. To provide for more efficient utilization of the system, many college computer centers use MUSIC and/or ASSIST.

MUSIC, an acronym for McGill University System for Interactive Computing, is an operating system developed at McGill University in Montreal, Canada. The system supports OS compilers and assemblers and facilitates the use of terminals to enter and/or modify programs. For assembler language programs, many computer centers provide alternative macros to the standard access, I/O, and DCB macros that are generally more efficient and take less time to assemble. The program in Figure 4.11 illustrates how the program in Figure 4.2 can be modified to run more efficiently under MUSIC using sample macros that have been defined as MOPEN, MCLOSE, MGET, MPUT, MDCBIN, and MDCBOUT. The instructions that comprise each of these macros are provided in Appendix K.

ASSIST, an acronym for Assembler System for Student Instruction and Sys-

```
                PRINT NOGEN
      PRINTOUT  START
                STM   14,12,12(13)
                BALR  12,0
                USING *,12
                ST    13,SAVEAREA+4
                LA    13,SAVEAREA
                MOPEN (INFILE,(INPUT))
                MOPEN (OUTFILE,(OUTPUT))
      CLEAR     MVC   OUTAREA,SPACES
                MGET  INFILE,RECORD
                MVC   LNAME,LAST
                MVC   SALOUT,SALARY
                MPUT  OUTFILE,OUTAREA
                B     CLEAR
      EOF       MCLOSE (INFILE)
                MCLOSE (OUTFILE)
                L     13,SAVEAREA+4
                LM    14,12,12(13)
                BR    14
      SAVEAREA DS     18F
      *
      INFILE    MDCBIN EOF=EOF
      OUTFILE   MDCBOUT
      *
      RECORD    DS    0CL80
      LAST      DS    CL15
      SALARY    DS    CL5
                DS    CL60
      SPACES    DC    CL1' '
      OUTAREA   DS    0CL132
                DS    CL5
      LNAME     DS    CL15
                DS    CL20
      SALOUT    DS    CL5
                DS    CL87
                END
```

Figure 4.11
OS sample program modified
to be run under MUSIC.

tems Teaching, is an assembler that was developed at Pennsylvania State University. ASSIST can be run under OS as well as DOS. In addition to the standard assembler instructions, there are "pseudo-instructions" or macros designed to facilitate certain operations such as input and output. The major pseudo-instructions are XREAD, XPRNT, XDECI, XDECO, and XDUMP. These and other features of ASSIST that greatly simplify the debugging process and decrease execution time will be discussed throughout the book and in Appendix K.

V. STRUCTURED TECHNIQUES FOR IMPROVING PROGRAM DESIGN

A. Structured Programming

When programming became a major profession in the 1960s and 1970s, the primary goal of programmers was getting programs to work. Although this is still a programmer's main objective, writing programs that are easy to read, debug, and modify is also an important factor today. That is, more and more attention is being given currently to programming style and technique, and to making programs as efficient as possible.

A technique for improving the design of a program in any programming language is called **structured programming.** In general, structured programs are easier to read than nonstructured programs. They are also easier to debug and modify if changes are required. Moreover, they are easier to evaluate and allow programming managers to assess programmers' skills better.

Those of you who have had some previous programming experience may have noticed that most nonstructured programs include numerous branch points.

These often make it difficult to follow the logic and to debug a program when an error occurs. One major purpose of structured programming, then, is to simplify debugging by reducing the number of entry and exit points in a program. For that reason, structured programming is sometimes referred to as GO TO-less programming, where a GO TO statement is the code for an unconditional branch in many programming languages. Using the techniques of structured programming, the **branch** statement is avoided where possible. We shall see in Chapter 18 that fully structured programs in assembler language are coded with the use of a BAL (branch and link) instruction. Using the structured technique, each section of a program can be written and even debugged independently without too much concern for where it enters the logic flow.

The typical structured program is subdivided into **modules,** where a main module calls in other modules as needed. That is, the programmer codes one main routine, and when some other routine is required, this routine will appear elsewhere in the program. The terms module and routine can be used interchangeably. With a modularized concept, it is possible to test routines independently. Moreover, it is feasible for different programmers to code different modules or sections of a large and complex program. The main routine simply calls for the execution of the other modules or sections as needed.

Chapter 18 provides an in-depth view of the types of logical control sequences used in structured programs.

B. The Top-Down Approach

Another common technique for making programs easier to read and more efficient is called **top-down programming.** The term implies that proper program design is best achieved by designing major modules or procedures before minor ones. Thus, in top-down programs the first series of instructions represents the main routine that is followed by intermediate and then minor ones.

By arranging modules using this top-down approach, it is unnecessary to skip around a source program listing to find the modules to be executed. This standardized approach provides an excellent complement to the structured approach for achieving efficient program design.

In this text we will use a basic structured technique in all our programs. In addition, we will code in a top-down format with the main module first so that you will learn to program in a standard and effective style.

C. Program Preparation and Debugging

1. Program Specifications

Before a programmer begins to code, he or she is given a set of **program specifications,** usually by the systems analyst who is responsible for the overall design of a computerized business application.

Typically the program specifications consist of:

1. **Record layout forms** to describe the formats of the input and output data on disk, tape, or cards. Figure 4.12 illustrates a sample record layout. It indicates:
   a. The data items or fields within each record.
   b. The location of each data item within the record.
   c. The size of each data item.
   d. For numeric data items, the number of decimal positions. For example, XXX.XX is a 5-digit field with 3 integer and 2 decimal places. (Two decimal places are typically used in dollars and cents fields.)
   e. In some organizations, standard names of the fields to be used in a program. (In other organizations, names of fields are assigned by the programmer.)

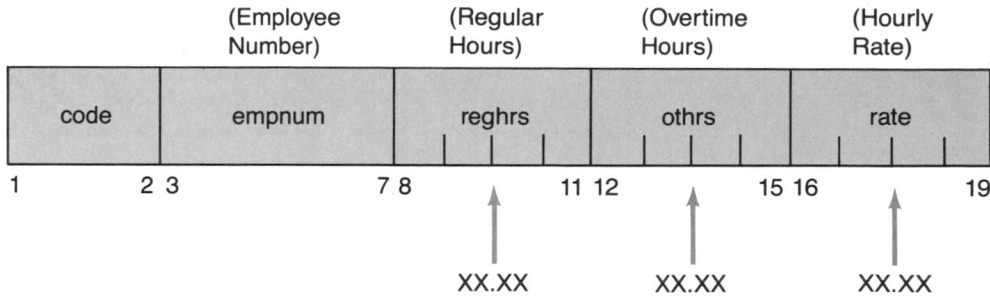

Figure 4.12
Sample record layout.

2. **Printer Spacing Charts** for printed output. Printed output has the following special requirements not typically needed for other types of output.
   a. Headings are usually printed.
   b. Data must be spaced neatly across the page, allowing for margins.
   c. Sometimes, additional lines such as error messages or total lines are required.

A Printer Spacing Chart, as illustrated in Figure 4.13, is a tool used for mapping out the proper spacing of printed output. It specifies the print positions to be used in the output and includes all data items to be printed and their formats.

Thus, a programmer typically receives record layout forms and/or a Printer Spacing Chart to indicate the precise format of the input and output. Along with these layout forms, a set of notes is typically provided by the systems analyst indicating the specific requirements of the program.

Illustrative programs and problems assigned in this text will include these same program specifications so that you will become very familiar with them as you read through the book.

2. Planning Tools

Before a programmer begins to code a program, he or she should plan the logic to be used in the program. Just as an architect draws a blueprint before construction of a building begins, a programmer should use a planning tool before program coding starts.

Two planning tools frequently used by programmers are flowcharts and pseudocode. A **flowchart** is a conventional block diagram providing a pictorial

```
          H    6        PAYROLL  LIST      XX/XX/XX      PAGE  XX

          H    9     EMPLOYEE  REGULAR   OVERTIME     GROSS
          H   10      NUMBER    HOURS     HOURS        PAY
          D   12      XXXXX     XX.XX     XX.XX     $X,XXX.XX
                        .                            .
                        .                            .
                        .                            .
          T   17        TOTAL  GROSS  PAY   $XX,XXX.XX
```

H = Heading line
D = Detail line
T = Total line

Figure 4.13 Sample Printer Spacing Chart.

representation of the logic to be used in a program. **Pseudocode** uses written English-like expressions rather than diagrams and is specifically suited for depicting logic in a structured program. Appendix J provides an in-depth discussion of how flowcharts and pseudocode are used as planning tools. You should review this Appendix if you have had little or no exposure to planning tools. In many of our illustrations, we will depict the logic flow used in a program with one of these tools.

3. Debugging Techniques

After a program has been planned and coded, it must be compiled and executed with test data. Frequently, errors occur during either compilation or execution. Eliminating these errors is called debugging.

There are several levels of debugging that a programmer should perform.

a. Desk Checking. Programmers should carefully review their programs *before* and after they have them keyed in. **Desk checking** will minimize computer time and reduce the time it takes to debug a program. Frequently, programmers fail to see the need for this phase, on the assumption that it is better to let the computer find errors. However, omitting the desk-checking phase can result in undetected logic errors that could take hours—or even days—to debug. Efficient programmers carefully review their programs before keying and compiling them.

b. Correcting Syntax Errors. After a program has been translated or compiled, the computer will print a source listing along with diagnostic messages that point to any rule violations or **syntax errors.** The programmer must then correct the errors and recompile the program before it can be run with test data.

c. Program Walkthroughs. After a program has been listed by the computer in a source listing, programmers test the logic by executing the program with test data. It is best, however, to "walk through" the program first to see if it will produce the desired results. In a **program walkthrough,** the programmer manually steps through the logic of the program using the test data to see if the correct results will be obtained. This is done prior to machine execution. Walkthroughs can help the programmer find logic errors without wasting machine time.

Sometimes, structured walkthroughs are performed directly from pseudocode, *prior to* the actual coding of a program. This procedure also minimizes the need for future program changes.

Frequently, programming teams work together to test the logic in their programs using the walkthrough approach. This method of debugging can save considerable computer time and make the entire debugging phase more efficient.

d. Detecting Logic Errors After Program Execution. In many ways, detecting logic errors after program execution is the most difficult and time-consuming aspect of debugging. If desk checking and program walkthroughs are performed, they will minimize the number of logic errors that might be encountered during program execution. Chapter 10 focuses on techniques used for finding and correcting logic errors in assembler programs.

The preparation of test data is an extremely critical aspect of this phase. It is imperative that the programmer prepare data that will test every possible condition that the program is likely to encounter under normal operating conditions. It is not uncommon for a program, which supposedly has been fully tested and running for some time, suddenly to experience problems. Most often, these problems arise because a specific condition not previously encountered has occurred and the program has not been written to handle the situation.

D. Coding Structured Programs in Assembler Language

Fully structured programs are coded in COBOL with the use of PERFORM statements, in FORTRAN with DO ... WHILE statements, and in assembler with BAL (branch and link) statements, as discussed in Chapter 18.

The basic assembler program fundamentally conforms to a structured approach. That is, the main module of an assembler program

1. Starts the program.
2. Opens files.
3. Initializes fields and record areas.
4. Reads and processes records until there is no more data.

In the programs illustrated so far, the following assembler instructions have constituted the main module.

```
          START
          BALR
          USING
          OPEN
CLEAR MVC
          .
          .                  INITIALIZES, READS, AND
          .                  PROCESSES ALL DATA
          B CLEAR
```

This module can be flowcharted as in Figure 4.14.

The following flowcharting symbols are equivalent to a PERFORM ...
UNTIL sequence.

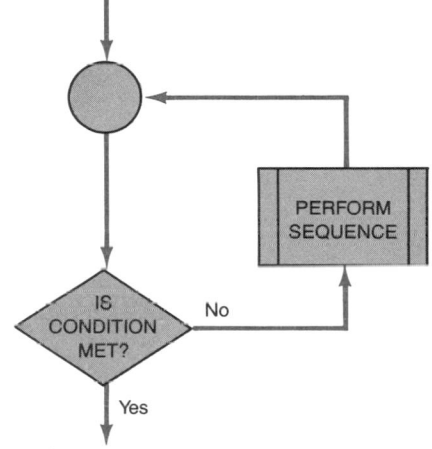

The CLEAR module is executed until there is no more data. Then EOJ is executed. The pseudocode for this illustration uses PERFORM ... UNTIL NO MORE DATA for logical control.

```
HOUSEKEEPING
OPEN FILES
PERFORM UNTIL NO MORE DATA
     INITIALIZE
     READ
     PROCESS
     WRITE
ENDPERFORM
CLOSE FILES
STOP
```

All of our assembler language programs will use this basic structured approach. Other logical control sequences in addition to PERFORM ... UNTIL are discussed in Chapter 6 and in Chapter 18.

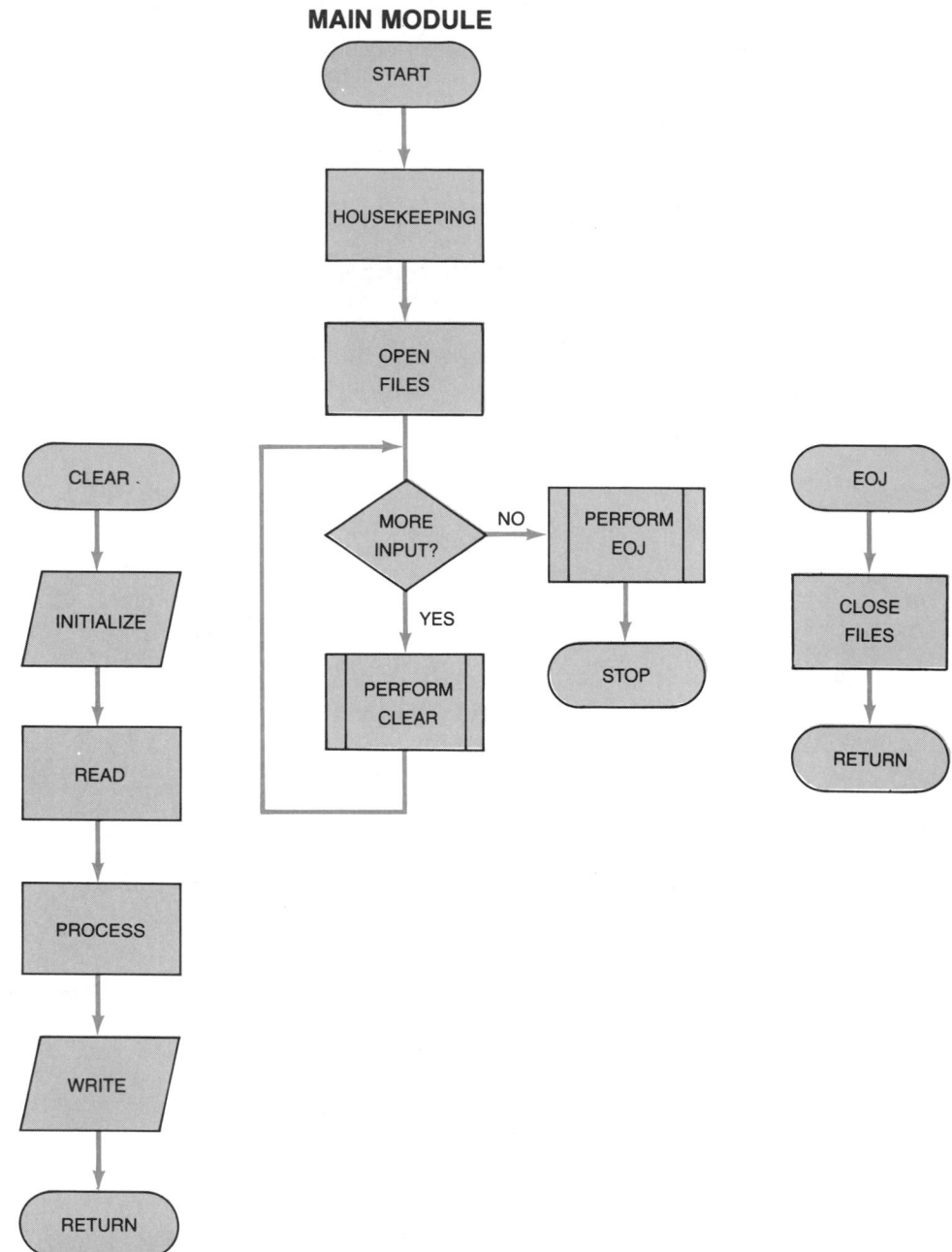

Figure 4.14
Flowchart of the main module
of an assembler program.

CHAPTER SUMMARY

I. Operating Systems
  A. Assembler language programs are typically run either under OS (Operating System) or DOS (Disk Operating System).

B. Most instructions in assembler language programs are identical, regardless of which system is being used.

II. Rules for File Names
   A. Can consist of 1 to 8 characters—letters, digits, and/or $, @, #.
   B. The first character must be alphabetic (A–Z, $, @, #).

III. OS Programs
   Most OS programs that read input and print output will include the shell of instructions shown in Figure 4.15. This shell of instructions, which is designed to read in 80-character records, will require minor changes when the input is entered on disk or tape, and/or when the input records are not 80 bytes long.

```
       LABEL      OPERATION        OPERAND                              COMMENTS
  1                10        16                                                                          72

                  PRINT    NOGEN
                  START             [PLACE NAME OF PROGRAM IN COLS 1-8]
                  STM      14,12,12(13)
                  BALR     12,Ø
                  USING    *,12
                  ST       13,SAVEAREA+4
                  LA       13,SAVEAREA
                  OPEN     (INFILE,INPUT,OUTFILE,OUTPUT)
  CLEAR           MVC      OUTAREA,SPACES
                  GET      INFILE,RECORD
  ** LOGIC GOES HERE
  **             ;
                  PUT      OUTFILE,OUTAREA
                  B        CLEAR
  ** INCLUDE END-OF-JOB ROUTINES HERE,THEN CLOSE;IF NO EOJ ROUTINE  INCL:
  EOF             CLOSE    (INFILE,,OUTFILE)
                  L        13,SAVEAREA+4
                  LM       14,12,12(13)
                  BR       14
  SAVEAREA  DS    18F
  RECORD    DS    ØCL8Ø
  ** PLACE DS'S FOR FIELDS IN INPUT RECORD HERE
  SPACES    DC    CL1' '
  OUTAREA   DS    ØCL132
  ** PLACE DS'S FOR FIELDS IN OUTPUT RECORD HERE- INCLUDING BLANK AREAS
  INFILE    DCB   DDNAME=INFILE,MACRF=GM,BLKSIZE=8Ø,LRECL=8Ø,DSORG=PS,      *
                  EODAD=EOF
  OUTFILE   DCB   DDNAME=OUTFILE,MACRF=PM,BLKSIZE=132,LRECL=132,DSORG=PS
            END
```

Figure 4.15
Sample shell of instructions for an OS program.

IV. DOS Programs
   Most DOS programs that read input and print output will include the shell of instructions shown in Figure 4.16. This shell of instructions, which is designed to read in 80-character records, will require minor changes when the input is entered on disk or tape, and/or when the input records are not 80 bytes long.

```
    LABEL         OPERATION        OPERAND                              COMMENTS
1                 10        16                                                                      72
              PRINT  NOGEN
              START       [PLACE NAME OF PROGRAM IN COLS 1-8]
              BALR   12,0
              USING  *,12
              OPEN   INFILE,OUTFILE
CLEAR         MVC    OUTAREA,SPACES
              GET    INFILE,RECORD
** LOGIC GOES HERE
**       :
              PUT    OUTFILE,OUTAREA
              B      CLEAR
** INCLUDE END OF JOB ROUTINES HERE,THEN CLOSE;IF NO EOJ ROUTINE INCL:
EOF           CLOSE  INFILE,OUTFILE
              EOJ
INFILE        DTFCD  DEVADDR=SYSIPT,BLKSIZE=80,IOAREA1=BUFFRIN,WORKA=YES,    *
                     DEVICE=2501,TYPEFLE=INPUT,EOFADDR=EOF
OUTFILE       DTFPR  DEVADDR=SYSLST,BLKSIZE=132,IOAREA1=BUFFROUT,WORKA=YES,  *
                     DEVICE=3203
BUFFRIN       DS     CL80
BUFFROUT      DS     CL132
RECORD        DS     0CL80
** PLACE DS'S FOR FIELDS IN INPUT RECORD HERE
SPACES        DC     CL1' '
OUTAREA       DS     0CL132
** PLACE DS'S FOR FIELDS IN OUTPUT RECORD HERE-INCLUDING BLANK AREAS
** ALL OTHER DS'S AND DC'S NECESSAY FOR PROCESSING GO HERE
              END
```

Figure 4.16
Sample shell of instructions for a DOS program.

CHAPTER SELF-EVALUATING QUIZ

1. The instructions coded in this chapter are relatively (standard, nonstandard).
2. A housekeeping routine is one that _____ .
3. (T or F) I/O macros are different depending on whether a program is being assembled on a DOS or OS system.
4. Indicate the meaning of the first zero (0) in the following.
   ```
   RECIN  DS  0CL80
   ```
5. BLKSIZE for input from a terminal will typically be _____ and BLKSIZE for printed output will usually be _____ .
6. An EOF condition is reached when _____ .
7. A PRINT NOGEN instruction will suppress the printing of the _____ .
8. An assembler language instruction that generates several machine language instructions is called a(n) _____ .
9. (T or F) An example of a macro is an I/O instruction.
10. Labels are used in programs to provide _____ .

11. The last instruction in every assembler language program must be a(n) _____ statement.
12. The main purpose of the OPEN macro is to _____ .
13. A(n) _____ macro instructs the computer to read in one physical record from the file indicated and to store it in a designated storage area.
14. A(n) _____ macro instructs the computer to transmit information from a designated storage area to the appropriate output device.
15. The purpose of a DCB macro (OS) or DTF macro (DOS) is to _____ .
16. (T or F) The print area typically includes unlabeled areas such as DS CL10.
17. The purpose of the instruction in Question 16 is to _____ .
18. One way of clearing an output area is to _____ .
19. (T or F) Structured programming is sometimes called GO TO-less programming.
20. A buffer is a(n) _____ .

SOLUTIONS

		Page
1.	Standard	71
2.	Is required for efficient assembly and execution of all programs (similar to an initializing routine)	73
3.	F	82
4.	The record will be further subdivided	77
5.	80; 132	85
6.	An end-of-file is sensed—there are no more input records	75
7.	Machine language equivalents of a macro	73
8.	Macro	73
9.	T	74
10.	Branch points	75
11.	END	74
12.	Determine if the required I/O devices are ready to be used	74
13.	GET	75
14.	PUT	75
15.	Describe the characteristics of a particular file	76
16.	T	78
17.	Provide spacing between output fields	78
18.	Move (MVC) a constant, defined as a one-position blank located immediately before the output area, to the output area	79
19.	T	88
20.	I/O area	83

KEY TERMS

ASSIST	I/O macro
Base register	JCL (Job Control Language)
Block Size	Logical record
Branch	Macro
Buffer	Module
Desk checking	MUSIC
DOS (Disk Operating System)	OS (Operating System)
Field	Physical record
File	Printer Spacing Chart
Flowchart	Program walkthrough
Housekeeping instructions	Pseudocode

Record   Syntax error
Structured programming   Top-down programming

DEBUGGING EXERCISES

1. *OS Debugging Exercise*
   Consider the following OS program. What errors, if any, exist?

```
*                                                                          *
*                                    HOUSEKEEPING INSTRUCTIONS GO HERE      *
*                                                                          *
          OPEN    (INFILE,INPUT,OUTFILE,OUTPUT)
READ      MVC     OUTAREA,SPACES
          GET     CARDFILE,RECORD
          MVC     LNAME,LAST
          MVC     FNAME,FIRST
          MVC     SALOUT,SALARY
          PUT     OUTFILE,OUTAREA
          B       READRTN
EOF       CLOSE   (INFILE,OUTFILE)
*
RECORD    DS      ØCL80
SPACES    DC      CL1' '
OUTAREA   DS      ØCL132
          DS      CL5
LNAME     DS      CL15
          DS      CL20
FNAME     DS      CL10
          DS      CL20
SALOUT    DS      CL5
BLANK     DS      CL50
SAVEAREA  DS      18F
INFILE    DCB     DDNAME=INFILE,MACRF=GM,BLKSIZE=80,
                  LRECL=80,DSORG=PS,EODAD=EOF
PRTFILE   DCB     DDNAME=OUTFILE,MACRF=PM,BLKSIZE=132,LRECL=132,DSORG=PS
          END
```

2. *DOS Debugging Exercise*
   Consider the following DOS program. What errors, if any, exist?

```
*         HOUSEKEEPING INSTRUCTIONS GO HERE
*
          OPEN    (INFILE,INPUT,OUTFILE,OUTPUT)
1STRTN    MVC     OUTAREA,SPACES
          GET     INFILE,RECORDIN
          MVC     NAMEIN, NAMEOUT
          PUT     OUTFILE,OUTAREA
          B       1STRTN
EOF       CLOSE   INFILE,OUTFILE
          EOJ
*         DTFS GO HERE
BUFFRIN   DS      CL80
BUFFROUT  DS      CL132
RECORDIN  DS      CL80
NAMEIN    DS      CL20
          DS      CL60
SPACES    DS      CL1' '
OUTAREA   DS      CL132
          DS      CL5
NAMEOUT   DS      CL20
          DS      CL107
          END
```

SOLUTIONS 1.
```
*              SHOULD BE                                    *
*                INFILE              HOUSEKEEPING INSTRUCTIONS GO HERE    *
*                                                                        *
        OPEN    (INFILE,INPUT,OUTFILE,OUTPUT)
READ    MVC     OUTAREA,SPACES
        GET     CARDFILE,RECORD
        MVC     LNAME,LAST
        MVC     FNAME,FIRST        } NOT DEFINED
        MVC     SALOUT,SALARY
        PUT     OUTFILE,OUTAREA
        B       READRTN    ←——— SHOULD BE READ
EOF     CLOSE   (INFILE,OUTFILE)   ——— SHOULD HAVE 2 COMMAS
*
RECORD   DS     ØCL80
SPACES   DC     CL1' '   ←——— INSERT:  LAST  DS CL15
OUTAREA  DS     ØCL132                 FIRST DS CLIØ
         DS     CL5                    SALARY DS CL5
LNAME    DS     CL15                        DS CL50
         DS     CL20
FNAME    DS     CL10                 MISSING CONTINUATION
         DS     CL20                 CHARACTER IN COLUMN 72
SALOUT   DS     CL5                          ↓
BLANK    DS     CL50  ←——— SHOULD BE 57 SO
SAVEAREA DS     18F          THAT OUTAREA ADDS UP TO 132   ◯
INFILE   DCB    DDNAME=INFILE,MACRF=GM,BLKSIZE=80,
                LRECL=8Ø,DSORG=PS,EODAD=EOF
PRTFILE  DCB    DDNAME=OUTFILE,MACRF=PM,BLKSIZE=132,LRECL=132,DSORG=PS
         END
    ↳ SHOULD BE OUTFILE
```

```
*              HOUSEKEEPING INSTRUCTIONS GO HERE
*
        OPEN    (INFILE,INPUT,OUTFILE,OUTPUT)]—— SHOULD BE
1STRTN  MVC     OUTAREA,SPACES               OPEN INFILE,OUTFILE
        GET     INFILE,RECORDIN
        MVC     NAMEIN, NAMEOUT——— SHOULD BE NAMEOUT, NAMEIN
        PUT     OUTFILE,OUTAREA
        B       1STRTN
EOF     CLOSE   INFILE,OUTFILE
        EOJ
*               DTFS GO HERE
BUFFRIN  DS     CL8Ø
BUFFROUT DS     CL132
RECORDIN DS     CL8Ø ]——— SHOULD BE ØCL8Ø
NAMEIN   DS     CL2Ø
         DS     CL6Ø
SPACES   DS     CL1' '  ——— SHOULD BE ØCL132
OUTAREA  DS     CL132]
         DS     CL5
NAMEOUT  DS     CL2Ø
         DS     CL1Ø7
         END    ——— SHOULD BE DC
```

Move Statements

1. *To familiarize you with character move instructions.*
2. *To indicate how a move differs depending on the length of the operands.*
3. *To provide a comparison between* MVC *and* MVI *instructions.*
4. *To provide a comparison between implicit and explicit move instructions.*
5. *To introduce the concept of relative addressing.*

I. STORAGE-TO-STORAGE MOVE INSTRUCTION: MVC

A. Description

When writing programs it is frequently necessary to move data from one storage location to another. Sometimes only a single character is moved, but most often groups of characters, called **fields**, are moved. Because the data movement occurs entirely within main storage, the instruction is classified as a **storage-to-storage instruction**. The Move Character, or MVC, instruction may appear as follows.

Operation 10	Operand 16
MVC	FIELD1,FIELD2

Instruction:	MVC
Meaning:	Move Characters
Operand 1:	The receiving field (FIELD1 in the preceding chart) refers to a storage location or address
Operand 2:	The sending field (FIELD2 in the preceding chart) refers to a storage location or address
Result:	a. The contents of the second operand (sending field) are duplicated at the first operand
	b. The sending field remains unchanged

Example 5.1

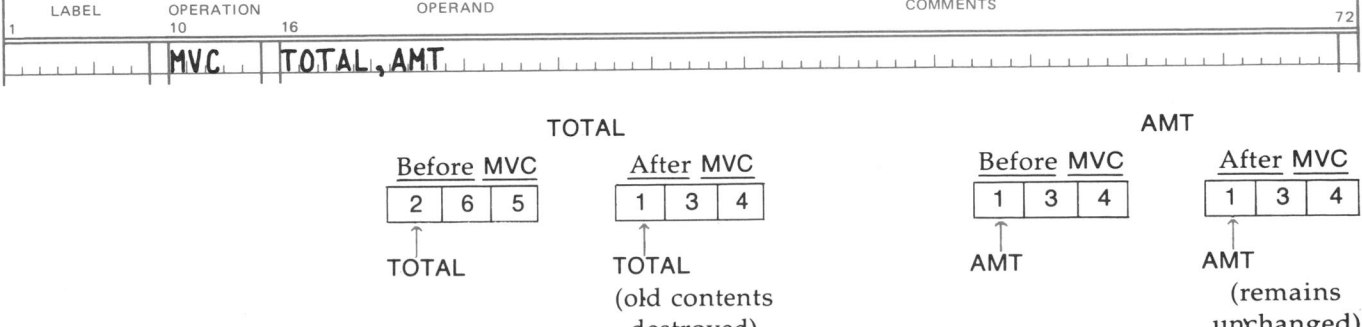

Note that although the MVC is referred to as a move instruction, this is really a misnomer. As the preceding example demonstrates, the operation really involves a duplication. After the instruction is executed, the contents of the sending field are the same as before the execution.

TOTAL and AMT are the names of fields in storage. When the MVC is translated, TOTAL and AMT will refer to actual storage addresses. The contents of these storage locations depends on the data that has been moved or read into these fields.

B. Applications

The MVC or Move Character instruction is generally used by the programmer to transmit data from an input area to an output area. It is used most often to move data in character or EBCDIC form, as opposed to data in packed or binary form. Because input and output areas usually contain data in EBCDIC form, the MVC instruction is ideally suited for data transfers of I/O fields.

The MVC instruction can also be used to move data from an input area to a work area established by a DS, where it will be processed (used in calculations, edited, and so on) and later moved to the output area.

Another common use of the MVC instruction is to allow the programmer to move page and column headings from one area of storage to the output area. After moving all the data to be printed to the output area, a PUT (output) command normally can be issued to transfer the output data to the printing device. Report and column headings and end-of-job messages usually are produced in this manner.

An important use of the MVC instruction is to clear the output area by filling it with spaces or blanks. This is necessary to ensure that a new line of printed data is produced on a blank line, thereby removing or erasing the characters printed in the preceding print operation. You will recall that data remains in a storage location until other data replaces it. The clearing of the output may take place at any time, but this action is usually performed immediately before each GET command.

The following chart summarizes the uses of the MVC instruction.

APPLICATIONS OF THE MVC (MOVE CHARACTER)
INSTRUCTION

Purpose: Move data, usually in EBCDIC form, from one location in storage to another

Use:
1. Move data between I/O areas.
2. Move data to and from work areas.
3. Move headings and titles to the output area.
4. Clear the output area.

C. Rules for Storage-to-Storage Move Instructions

1. MVC on Fields of Equal Length

Consider the following example.

Example 5.2

LABEL	OPERATION	OPERAND	COMMENTS
	MVC	ACCTOUT, ACCTIN	

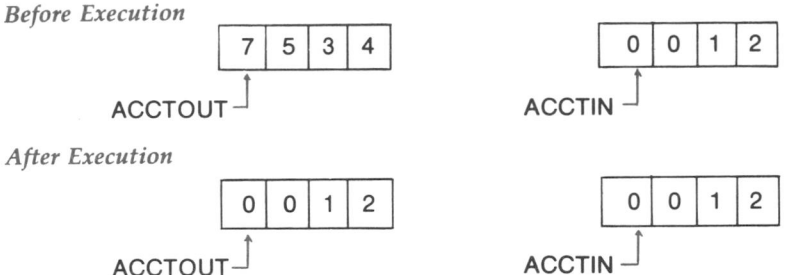

The symbolic names ACCTOUT and ACCTIN, refer to the **high-order position,** or the first (leftmost) byte of the named locations. The second operand is the **sending field** and the first operand is the **receiving field.** The data in the second operand replaces the previous contents of the first operand. After execution of the instruction, the first operand contains an exact copy of the second operand. The second operand remains unchanged. Movement of the data is from left to right, from **high order** to **low order,** within each operand. Each byte of data is moved until the receiving field is filled. The computer requires four steps to move the four bytes as illustrated, because one byte is moved at each step.

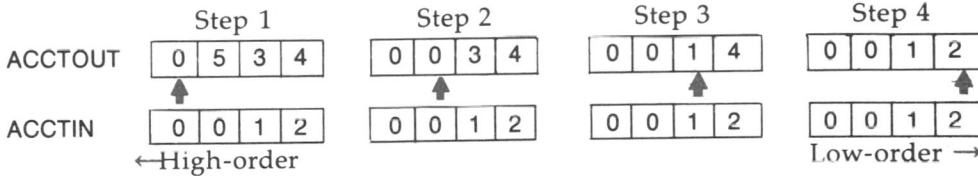

The number of bytes moved depends upon the length of the fields, which may vary from 1 to 256 bytes. The data is always moved 1 byte at a time from left to right. Movement continues until the number of bytes specified in the *first* operand, the receiving field, have all been filled. The computer will assume that the second operand is the same length.

Example 5.3

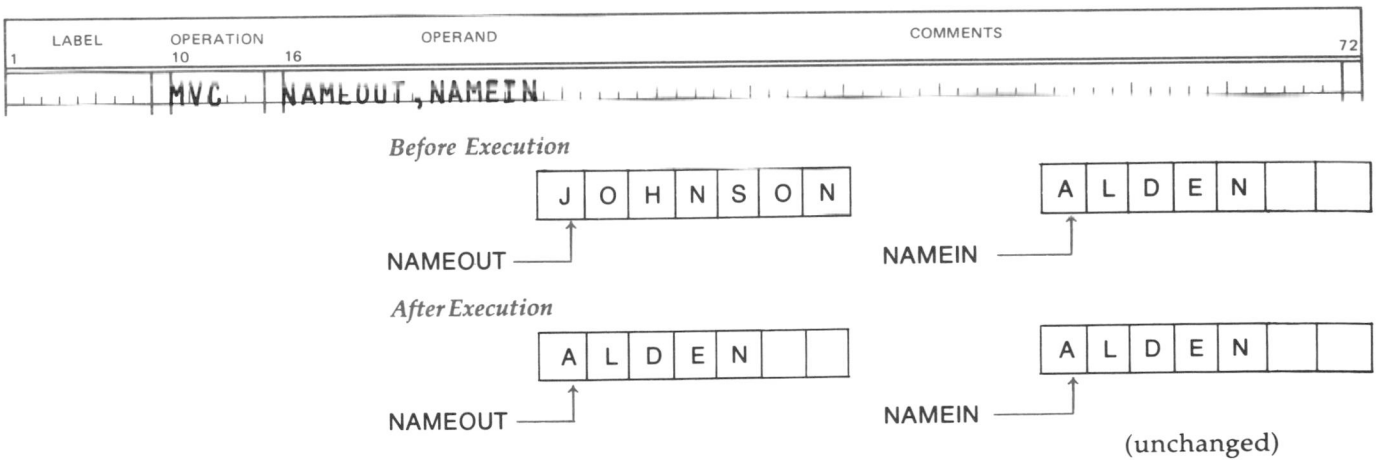

In this example, both the sending and receiving fields are 7 bytes in length and, therefore, the computer will require 7 steps, 1 per byte, to complete the move. Note that the blanks in the 2 low-order positions of the sending field are treated as characters; that is, they overlay characters in the receiving field in the ordinary way.

In the examples given so far, the entire sending field was transmitted to the receiving field. Hence, the MVC produced the same results at the receiving field as appeared at the sending field.

2. MVC on Fields of Unequal Length

Let us now consider a different case.

a. MVC *Where Operand 1 has fewer bytes than Operand 2.*

Example 5.4

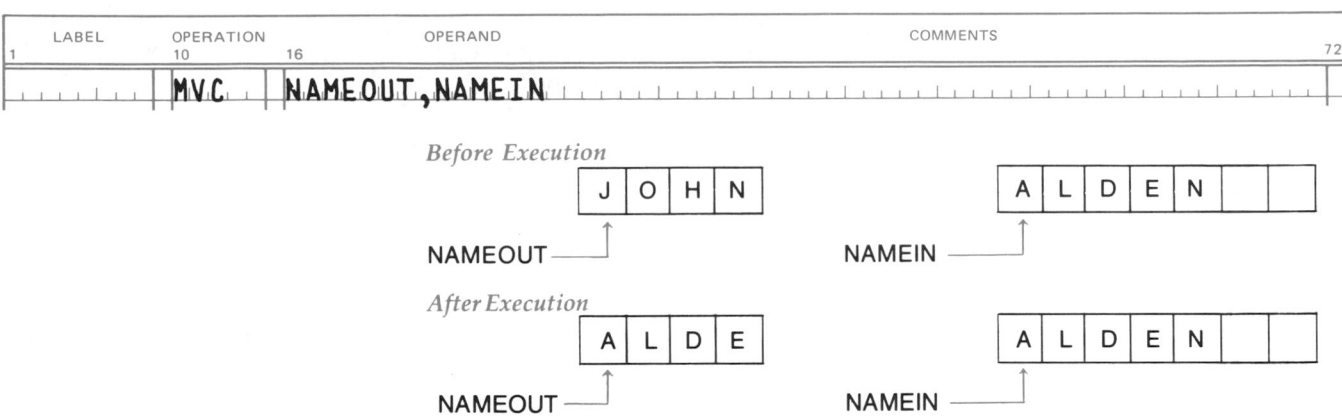

When data fields are not the same size, the length of the move is strictly determined by the *length* of the first operand, unless otherwise specified.[1]

In the above case, the 4-position NAMEOUT field caused a 4-position move. Low-order characters of data in the sending field were *not* moved. Clearly, the programmer must make certain that the receiving field in an MVC operation is large enough to accommodate the results.

> RULE: Unless otherwise specified, the number of characters moved by an MVC instruction is determined by the length of the receiving field.

The following examples will serve as a review.

Example 5.5

LABEL	OPERATION 10 16	OPERAND	COMMENTS	72
	MVC	FIELD2,FIELD1		

	Before		After	
FIELD2:	1 2 3	FIELD2:	8 7 6
FIELD1:	8 7 6	FIELD1:	8 7 6

When fields are the same length, the MVC results in the duplication of the contents of Operand 2 at Operand 1.

---

[1]We will see later in this chapter how we can explicitly indicate the number of bytes to be moved by indicating a length specifier along with Operand 1, *not* Operand 2.

Example 5.6

LABEL	OPERATION	OPERAND	COMMENTS	
1	10 16			72
	MVC	FIELD4,FIELD3		

	Before		*After*	
FIELD4:	A | B | C	FIELD4:	D | E | F
FIELD3:	D | E | F | G	FIELD3:	D | E | F | G

Example 5.7

LABEL	OPERATION	OPERAND	COMMENTS	
1	10 16			72
	MVC	FIELD6,FIELD5		

	Before		*After*	
FIELD6:	6 | 7 | A | B	FIELD6:	1 | 2 | 3 | 5
FIELD5:	1 | 2 | 3 | 5 | 6	FIELD5:	1 | 2 | 3 | 5 | 6

b. MVC *Where Operand 2 has fewer bytes than Operand 1.* If the receiving field is longer than the sending field, movement proceeds past the contents of the sending field, moving consecutive positions from adjacent fields. This could cause erroneous results in a program. Consider the following example.

Example 5.8 Suppose we establish the following 3 storage fields.

LABEL	OPERATION	OPERAND	COMMENTS	
1	10 16			72
AMT1	DC	CL3'123'		
AMT2	DC	CL2'45'		
AMT3	DC	CL2'67'		

These fields will appear in storage consecutively because they are assembled in the same order as they are coded.

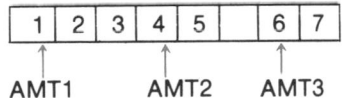

The instruction MVC AMT1, AMT2 will result in a 3-position move because AMT1, the receiving field, is three positions long. Whereas AMT2 contains only 2 positions with contents 45, the move will continue transmitting data from the *next* position of the adjacent field. Hence, the result would be:

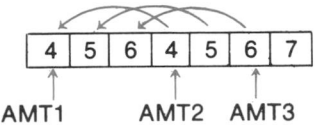

If that instruction was meant to transmit one field to another, as it usually is, the MVC resulted in the movement of too many characters. One method to alleviate the problem is to define AMT2 as a 3-position field.

LABEL	OPERATION	OPERAND	COMMENTS
AMT1	DC	CL3'123'	
AMT2	DC	CL3'45 '	ONE BLANK BYTE EXTRA
AMT3	DC	CL2'67'	

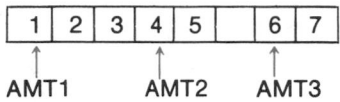

The instruction MVC AMT1,AMT2 would then produce:

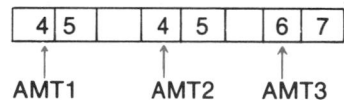

REVIEW—MVC

RULE: Number of characters moved is determined by receiving field.
1. When the sending and receiving fields are the same size, the receiving field will duplicate the sending field.
2. When the receiving field is shorter than the sending field, **truncation** of low-order characters will occur.
3. When the receiving field is longer than the sending field, additional characters from positions adjacent to the sending field will be moved to the receiving field.

Figure 5.1 illustrates a program that prints one line for each set of 2 input records read. Figure 5.2 shows a sample report produced by this program.

In Figure 5.3, we have a program that prints 3 lines for each record read. Sample output is shown in Figure 5.4.

Self-Evaluating Quiz

1. The operation code of a move character instruction is _____ .
2. In an MVC instruction, the first operand is called the _____ field and the second operand is called the _____ field.
3. Movement of data in an MVC instruction is from (left/right) to (left/right).
4. The field name specified for any operand refers to the (high/low)-order position.
5. (T or F) If the sending field is larger than the receiving field, the MVC will result in the truncation of sending-field characters.
6. (T or F) If the receiving field is larger than the sending field, the MVC will fill the receiving field with blanks.
7. Fill in the missing blanks.

	MVC	CODE1,CODE2	
	CODE1		CODE2	
	Before	*After*	*Before*	*After*
a.	124		463	
b.	4920		73268	
c.	127		13	

```
*                                              *
*                     HOUSEKEEPING INSTRUCTIONS GO HERE  *
*                                              *
CLEAR    MVC    OUTAREA,SPACES
         GET    INFILE,REC1
         MVC    LNAME,LAST
         MVC    FNAME,FIRST
         GET    INFILE,REC2
         MVC    STRTOUT,STREET
         MVC    CITYOUT,CITY
         MVC    STATEOUT,STATE
         PUT    OUTFILE,OUTAREA
         B      CLEAR
*                                              *
*                     HOUSEKEEPING INSTRUCTIONS GO HERE  *
*                     ALONG WITH DCB OR DTF MACROS       *
*                                              *
REC1     DS     0CL80        RECORD NO. 1
SOCSEC   DS     CL9              *
LAST     DS     CL15             *
FIRST    DS     CL10             *
         DS     CL46             *
REC2     DS     0CL80        RECORD NO. 2
SSNO     DS     CL9              *
STREET   DS     CL20             *
CITY     DS     CL10             *
STATE    DS     CL2              *
         DS     CL39             *
SPACES   DC     CL1' '
OUTAREA  DS     0CL132
         DS     CL10
LNAME    DS     CL15
         DS     CL5
FNAME    DS     CL10
         DS     CL5
STRTOUT  DS     CL20
         DS     CL5
CITYOUT  DS     CL10
         DS     CL1
STATEOUT DS     CL2
         DS     CL49
         END
```

Figure 5.1
Program to print one line for each set of two input records.

Figure 5.2
Sample output for the program in Figure 5.1.

```
BROWN          LEROY        1 MAIN ST.      BROOKLYN    NY
NEWMAN         PAUL         35 E. 83 ST.    NEW YORK    NY
DEAN           JAMES        2 LAKE DR.      SETAUKET    NJ
```

8. Assume the following DC coding.

```
FLD1    DC    CL3'42A'
FLD2    DC    CL2'61'
FLD3    DC    CL3'411'
```

The fields will appear in storage as follows.

```
4 2 A 6 1 4 1 1
↑     ↑   ↑
F     F   F
L     L   L
D     D   D
1     2   3
```

Indicate the results of the following instructions. Treat each instruction independently using the data provided in the preceding DCs.
a. MVC   FLD1,FLD2
b. MVC   FLD2,FLD3

```
*                                                                      *
*                                      HOUSEKEEPING INSTRUCTIONS GO HERE   *
*                                                                      *
CLEAR      MVC    LINE1,SPACES1
           MVC    LINE2,SPACES2
           MVC    LINE3,SPACES3
           GET    INFILE,RECORD
           MVC    LNAME,LAST
           MVC    FNAME,FIRST
           PUT    OUTFILE,LINE1
           MVC    STRTOUT,STREET
           PUT    OUTFILE,LINE2
           MVC    CITYOUT,CITY
           MVC    STATEOUT,STATE
           PUT    OUTFILE,LINE3
           MVC    LINE1,SPACES1
           PUT    OUTFILE,LINE1
           B      CLEAR
*                                                                      *
*                                      HOUSEKEEPING INSTRUCTIONS GO HERE   *
*                                      ALONG WITH DCB OR DTF MACROS        *
*                                                                      *
RECORD     DS     0CL80
LAST       DS     CL15
FIRST      DS     CL10
           DS     CL11
STREET     DS     CL20
CITY       DS     CL10
STATE      DS     CL2
           DS     CL12
SPACES1    DC     CL1' '
LINE1      DS     0CL132          NAME LINE
           DS     CL10            *
LNAME      DS     CL15            *
           DS     CL5             *
FNAME      DS     CL10            *
           DS     CL92            *
SPACES2    DC     CL1' '
LINE2      DS     0CL132          ADDRESS LINE
           DS     CL10            *
STRTOUT    DS     CL20            *
           DS     CL102           *
SPACES3    DC     CL1' '
LINE3      DS     0CL132          CITY & STATE LINE
           DS     CL10            *
CITYOUT    DS     CL10            *
           DS     CL1             *
STATEOUT   DS     CL2             *
           DS     CL109           *
           END
```

Figure 5.3
**Program to print three lines for
each record read.**

```
BROWN                LEROY
1 MAIN ST.
BROOKLYN    NY


DERNBY               JOYCE
57 WAYNE DR.
SETAUKET    NY


WATSON               RICHARD
129 ROCHESTER LA.
QUEENS      NY
```

Figure 5.4
**Sample output for the program
in Figure 5.3.**

SOLUTIONS 1. MVC
2. Receiving; Sending
3. Left; right
4. High or leftmost
5. T
6. F: movement will continue with adjacent positions in storage until the receiving field is filled.

7. a. CODE1 `[4][6][3]`   CODE2 (remains unchanged) `[4][6][3]`

   b. `[7][3][2][6]`   `[7][3][2][6][8]`

   c. `[1][3][ ]`   `[1][3][ ]`

8. a. `[6][1][4][6][1][4][1][1]`

   F↑ F↑ F↑
   L L L
   D D D
   1 2 3

   b. `[4][2][A][4][1][4][1][1]`

   F↑ F↑ F↑
   L L L
   D D D
   1 2 3

D. Types of Move Operations

1. Defining Implicit and Explicit Moves

The move character instruction may be of two types: **implicit** and **explicit.** Implicit moves are those we discussed in the previous section where the length of the move is strictly determined by the length of the first operand.

An explicit move instruction contains a length specifier that allows the programmer to indicate the precise number of bytes to be moved.

Examples

LABEL	OPERATION	OPERAND	COMMENTS
1	10	16	72
(1)	MVC	ACCTOUT(4),ACCTIN	
(2)	MVC	NAMEOUT(10),NAMEIN	

In Example 1, the number of characters moved will be *4* regardless of the size of the operands; similarly, Example 2 specifies a 10-byte move.

Explicit moves result in fewer programming errors because the programmer can more easily determine the number of characters moved.

It is strongly recommended that the implied MVC be avoided because programming errors may occur if the receiving and sending fields are not the same size. However, when the programmer clearly understands the MVC operation, or when the receiving and sending fields are the same length, the use of the explicit MVC is unnecessary.

2. Comparing Implicit and Explicit Moves

For the following example, OUTAREA is defined as having a length of 10 bytes; in this specific case, it initially contains spaces or blanks. ACCTIN is defined as an input area of four bytes and contains the number 0012. The consecutive positions following ACCTIN are identified to explain the result of the operation.

LABEL	OPERATION	OPERAND	COMMENTS
1	10	16	72
	MVC	OUTAREA,ACCTIN	

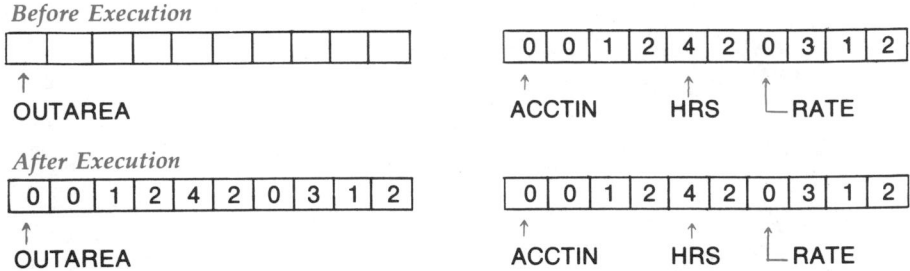

The first operand or receiving field is 10 bytes in length. Therefore, 10 bytes will be moved because the explicit length was not specified. The consecutive positions following ACCTIN will be moved even if this was *not* the programmer's intent. We identified these areas as HRS and RATE to illustrate that the CPU will continue to move the data, one byte at a time until the number of bytes implied by the first operand has been moved. If, however, only the contents of ACCTIN are to be duplicated at OUTAREA, the following explicit move can be used.

LABEL	OPERATION	OPERAND	COMMENTS
	MVC	OUTAREA(4),ACCTIN	

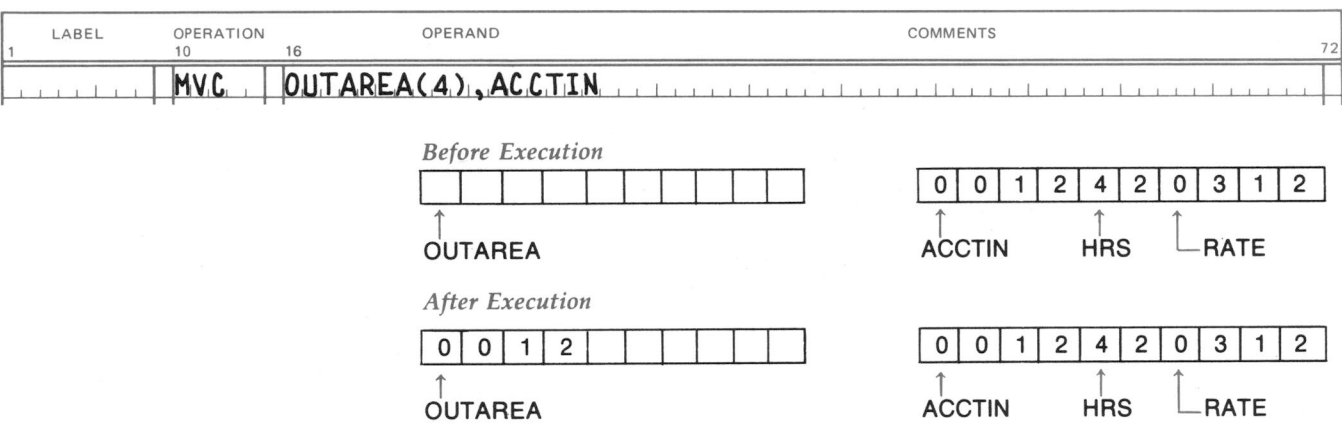

To test your understanding of the MVC instruction carefully examine the examples below. Where an explicit length is not given, the length of the first operand is equal to the number of characters shown in the illustration.

Examples

LABEL	OPERATION	OPERAND	COMMENTS
	MVC	SSOUT,SSIN	

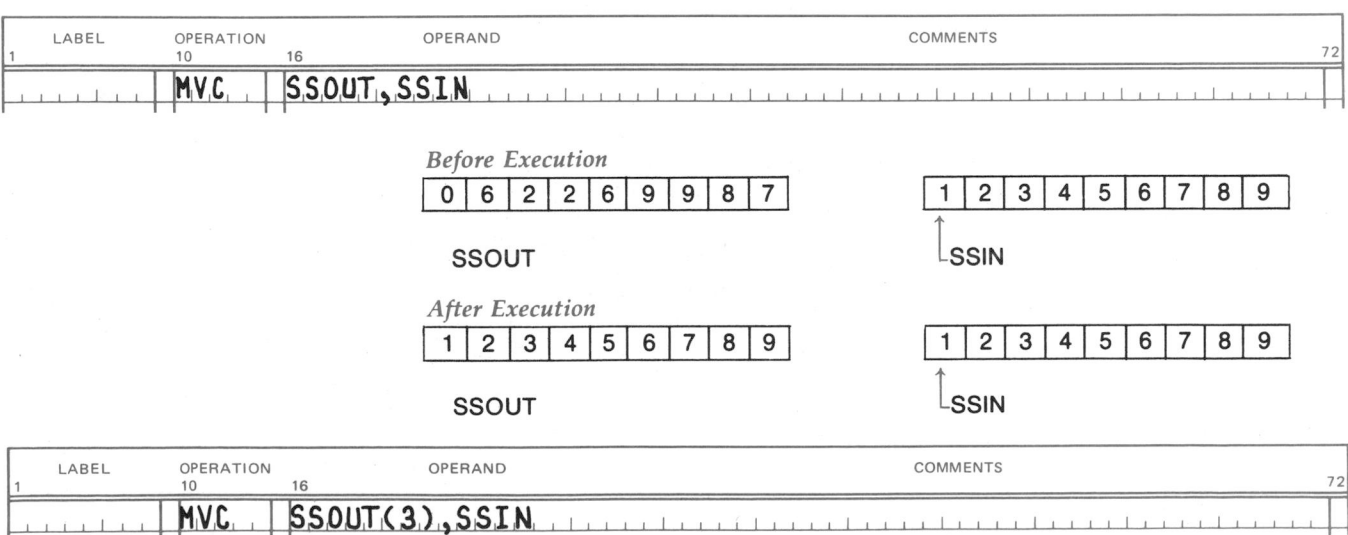

LABEL	OPERATION	OPERAND	COMMENTS
	MVC	SSOUT(3),SSIN	

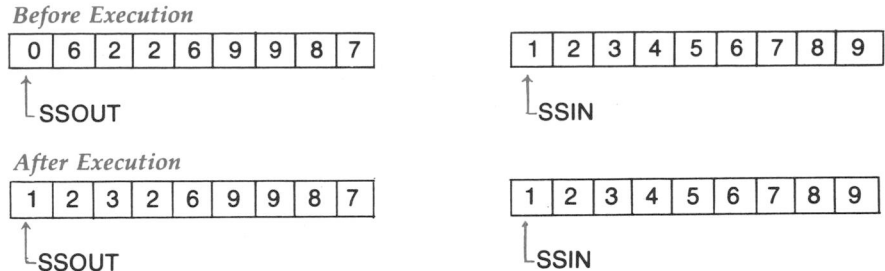

Before Execution

| 0 | 6 | 2 | 2 | 6 | 9 | 9 | 8 | 7 |

└ SSOUT

| 1 | 2 | 3 | 4 | 5 | 6 | 7 | 8 | 9 |

└ SSIN

After Execution

| 1 | 2 | 3 | 2 | 6 | 9 | 9 | 8 | 7 |

└ SSOUT

| 1 | 2 | 3 | 4 | 5 | 6 | 7 | 8 | 9 |

└ SSIN

We will now summarize the rules of the MVC instruction.

RULE SUMMARY

Move Character Instruction (MVC)

1. First Operand—receiving field, contents change.
2. Second Operand—sending field, contents remain the same.[2]
3. Data is moved one byte at a time from left to right.
4. From 1 to 256 bytes may be moved with a single MVC instruction.
5. Contents of the first operand are replaced by the contents of the second.
6. The number of bytes moved depends on whether an explicit or implicit MVC is used.
   a. Explicit—length of the move in digits is specified in first operand.
   b. Implicit—length of first operand determines number of characters moved.

Self-Evaluating Quiz

1. The MVC instruction is classified as a (storage-to-storage/register) type instruction.
2. An instruction that may be used to clear the output area or set up headings is called _____ .
3. In clearing the output areas the programmer moves _____ to the area defined as output.
4. Two operands are used with the MVC instruction. The first operand is the _____ field while the second is the _____ field
5. A symbolic name can be used as an operand only if it is defined as a(n) _____ or a(n) _____ .
6. A single MVC instruction allows from (no.) to (no.) characters to be moved.
7. Indicate the results of the following instruction.

    MVC   EMPNO,INDATA
    Before

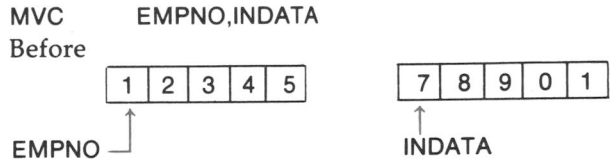

| 1 | 2 | 3 | 4 | 5 |

| 7 | 8 | 9 | 0 | 1 |

EMPNO ┘   INDATA

8. How many steps would be required to complete the MVC instruction given in Question 7?
9. The MVC instruction moves _____ byte(s) at a time, starting with the high/low)-order position.

---

[2]When the sending and receiving fields overlap, the second operand may change. This topic is discussed later in the chapter.

10. When the number of bytes to be moved is not stated explicitly, then the move is said to be _____ , meaning that the number of bytes moved depends on the length of the (first/second) operand.

11. As a precaution, it is advisable that all MVC instructions be of the (implicit/explicit) type.

12. The instruction MVC NAME(10),TITLE is of the (implicit/explicit) type and would move (no.) bytes of data.

13. Let us assume that areas in storage have the following length specifications.

    DESC (7)   TOTAL (4)   PRICE (4)   PART (12)

    These storage areas appear as shown below. Indicate the results in storage after each of the following operations is performed. Treat each problem independently; that is, assume the original contents for each problem.

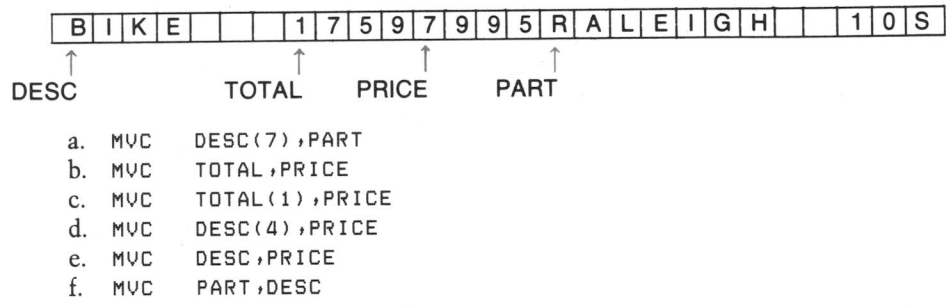

a.	MVC	DESC(7),PART
b.	MVC	TOTAL,PRICE
c.	MVC	TOTAL(1),PRICE
d.	MVC	DESC(4),PRICE
e.	MVC	DESC,PRICE
f.	MVC	PART,DESC

SOLUTIONS

1. Storage-to-storage
2. Move character (MVC)
3. Spaces or blanks
4. Receiving; sending
5. DS (define storage); DC (define constant)
6. 1; 256
7.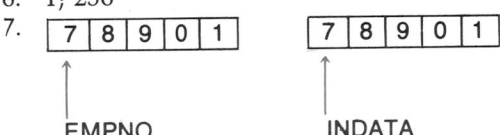
8. 5 steps—it is a 5-byte move
9. 1; high
10. Implicit; First (receiving)
11. Explicit
12. Explicit; 10
13.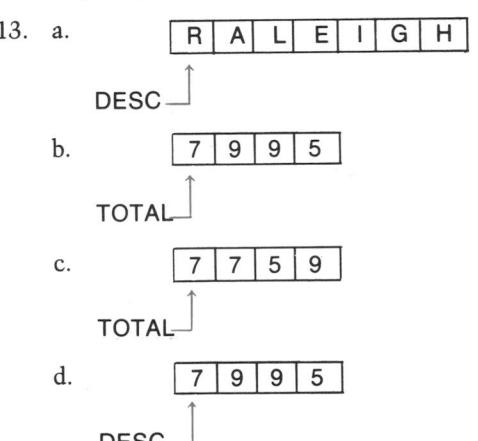

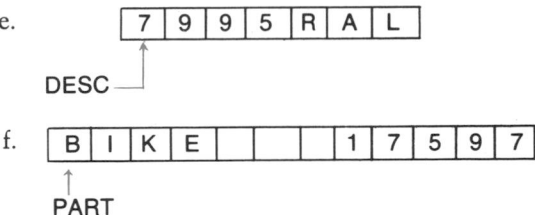

e.

| 7 | 9 | 9 | 5 | R | A | L |

DESC ⌐

f.

| B | I | K | E | | | 1 | 7 | 5 | 9 | 7 |

↑
PART

E. Self-Defining Operands in MVC Instructions

1. Examples

It is possible in assembler language to define a constant as the second operand in an MVC or any storage-to-storage instruction. In such a case, the sending field is called a **self-defining operand.** For example, a message such as "END OF JOB" could be included in the sending field of a move instruction, thereby eliminating the usual DC (define constant) used to define the characters in storage. Consider the following instruction.

LABEL	OPERATION 10	16	OPERAND	COMMENTS	72
	MVC	LINEOUT(10),=C'END OF JOB'			

This MVC would first create a character string containing the message "END OF JOB." This 10-byte message would then be moved to the storage area called LINEOUT.

For the assembler to identify the self-defining operand, it is necessary to begin the operand with an equal sign, followed by the constant as shown in the preceding instruction. The rules for establishing self-defining operands are essentially the same as for specifying constants (DCs). In the MVC, the length specifier should be used in the first operand to ensure correct results. Examples of self-defining operands in MVC instructions follow.

LABEL	OPERATION 10	16	OPERAND	COMMENTS	72
	MVC	MSSG(5),=C'ERROR'			
	MVC	MSSG(5),=X'C5D9D9D6D9'	THIS IS EBCDIC FOR 'ERROR'		
	MVC	MSSG(4),=C'7 UP'			
	MVC	MSSG(4),=X'F740E4D7'	THIS IS EBCDIC FOR '7 UP'		

Self-defining constants can be established in character, hexadecimal, or binary form. The equal sign (=) is the first position of the second operand and signals the computer that a constant is to be defined.

The following summarizes self-defining operands.

SELF-DEFINING OPERANDS

1. A self-defining operand must begin with an equal sign.
2. The next character must be a valid descriptor such as C (character), X (hexadecimal), B (binary), or P (packed).
3. The data is defined in the same manner as a DC (define constant).
4. Self-defining data may appear only in the second operand, which is the sending field of a storage-to-storage instruction.

For programming efficiency, only use self-defining operands for one-of-a-kind messages. Frequently referenced messages or texts are more efficiently programmed using the conventional define constants.

2. Length of Moves When Using a Self-Defining Operand

The self-defining operand to be transmitted should be the same length as

1. The length specified in an explicit move; or
2. The length of the receiving field in an implicit move.

If the self-defining operand is longer than the first operand, then truncation will occur. If the self-defining operand is shorter, then the first operand will continue receiving data from additional storage positions. Because, at this point, we have no way of knowing where the self-defining operand was stored, the additional contents of the receiving field cannot be predicted. (The self-defining constants are placed in a "literal pool" at the end of the program.)

The following examples will illustrate the point.

Examples   *Objective*

To observe how data is moved when the self-defining operand is a different length than the receiving field.

LABEL	OPERATION		OPERAND	COMMENTS	
1	10	16			72
	MVC		FORT,=C'1250'		

We will assume that FORT has been defined as DS CL3 for the first example and as DS CL5 for the second.

	Before MVC		*After* MVC	
1.	FORT—3 bytes	4 5 6	1 2 5	Unpredictable
2.	FORT—5 bytes	9 2 5 3 6	1 2 5 0	

Self-Evaluating Quiz

1. Code a statement to move the constant 'OUT OF LUCK' to an 11-byte storage area called HASH.
2. Code a statement to move the constant 'ERR102' to a 10-byte storage area called MESH.
3. Code a statement to move the constant 'MEA CULPA' to a 6-byte storage area called CHECKIT.
4. In each of the above cases, the second operand in the MVC instruction is called a _____ .
5. (T or F) A constant may be set up as a DC or may appear as a self-defining operand in a storage-to-storage instruction.
6. The MVC instruction
    a. moves one character at a time
    b. moves the entire field as a block
    c. pads blanks at the right
    d. a and c
    e. none of these

SOLUTIONS

1. MVC   HASH,=C'OUT OF LUCK' (*Note* Either implicit or explicit move may be used.)
2. MVC   MESH(6),=C'ERR102' (*Note* You must use an explicit move because MESH is longer than the constant.)
3. The constant will be truncated unless CHECKIT is made longer:
    MVC   CHECKIT,=C'MEA CULPA'
4. Self-defining operand
5. T
6. a

II. MOVE IMMEDIATE INSTRUCTION: MVI

A. Purpose of the MVI

Often, there is a need to move *one byte* of data into a particular storage area where that data has not been defined in the program. The programmer may elect to (a) assign a symbolic name to a defined constant (DC) and code an MVC instruction; (b) use a self-defining operand; or (c) simply use the move immediate (MVI) instruction. With the MVI instruction, the programmer accomplishes the following two tasks at once.

1. Defines one byte of data in the sending field (second operand).
2. Moves that data to the receiving field, which is the first operand.

Typical applications of this instruction include moving dollar signs ($) or other special characters to the output to improve the readability of a report.

B. Format for the MVI

We learned previously that the MVC instruction moves data from one location in storage to another; hence, the MVC is classified as a storage-to-storage instruction. In contrast, the move immediate instruction is of the storage immediate (SI) type.[3] The data to be moved is *defined* in the second operand and therefore is referred to as **immediate** data. *One* byte, and *only* one byte, of data is moved from the second operand to the high-order byte of the first operand. All of the following examples produce the identical results; the only difference is the format used to define the immediate data. In all three instructions, a dollar sign is defined and moved to the storage location called AMT.

left byte

LABEL	OPERATION		OPERAND	COMMENTS	
1	10	16			72
	MVI		AMT,C'$'	CHARACTER DATA	
	MVI		AMT,X'5B'	HEXADECIMAL DATA	
	MVI		AMT,B'01011011'	BINARY DATA	

Character Representation

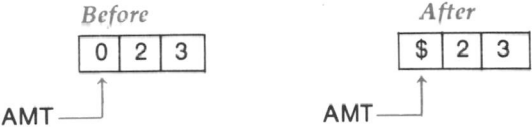

Hexadecimal Representation

Binary Representation

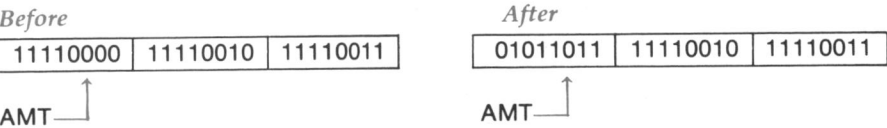

[3]The instruction type is an extremely important concept that is specifically used for debugging purposes. See Chapter 14.

If the MVI instruction had not been used, the following instructions could have been substituted.

LABEL	OPERATION	OPERAND	COMMENTS
1	10	16	72
	MVC	AMT(1),DOLLAR	
	.		
	.		
	.		
DOLLAR	DC	C'$'	

Or, a self-defining operand could have been used.

LABEL	OPERATION	OPERAND	COMMENTS
1	10	16	72
	MVC	AMT(1),=C'$'	

Note that we use an equal sign when coding a self-defining operand, but that no equal sign is used for a single-character immediate operand.

As shown, the programmer can code the one byte of data using any of the three formats illustrated. For example, if it is necessary to move the EBCDIC representation of the number one to an area called NUMB, any one of the following immediate instructions can be used.

LABEL	OPERATION	OPERAND	COMMENTS
1	10	16	72
	MVI	NUMB,C'1'	
*			
	MVI	NUMB,X'F1' EBCDIC FOR NO. 1	
*			
	MVI	NUMB,B'11110001' BINARY FOR NO. 1	

The final choice is usually a simple matter of preference. However, there are limitations.

	REVIEW
Character data	One character must be specified and enclosed in single quotes ' '..
Hexadecimal data	Two hexadecimal digits must be specified and enclosed in single quotes.
Binary data	Eight binary digits must be specified and enclosed in single quotes.

Remember that the storage immediate instruction does not have a length specifier and that the implied length is one byte of data only. The following examples will serve as a further review.

LABEL	OPERATION	OPERAND	COMMENTS
1	10	16	72
	MVI	FLD1,C'%'	

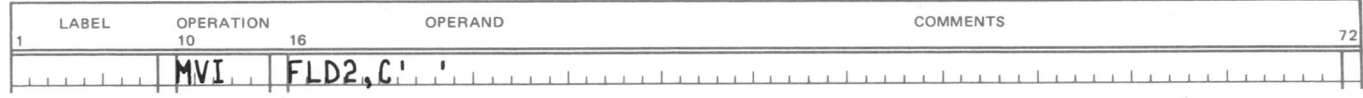

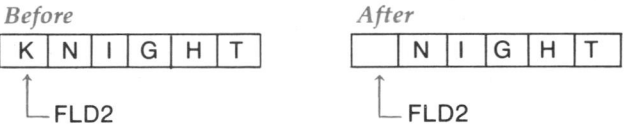

Self-Evaluating Quiz

1. The MVI instruction is of the _____ type.
2. How many bytes are moved with a single MVI instruction? How many hex digits? Bits?
3. An immediate operand is the (**sending/receiving**) field or the (**first/second**) operand.
4. When using the hexadecimal immediate format, how many digits must be specified?
5. The immediate operand does not begin with an equal sign but is followed by the letter _____ when specifying character data.
6. Blanks (**may/may not**) be embedded between the quote marks when using the MVI instruction.
7. Which of the following self-defining operands are not valid in an MVI instruction:

a. X'40'	d. XF1	g. C'THE'	j. C'
b. C'F0	c. C'4'	h. B'12001111'	
c. B'1111'	f. J'3'	i. X'G3'	

8. The difference between a self-defining operand in an MVC instruction and an MVI instruction is _____ .

SOLUTIONS

1. Storage immediate (SI)
2. 1; 2; 8
3. Sending; second
4. 2; that is, X'5B', for example
5. C
6. May not; only *one* character is permitted
7. b. 1 character permitted
   c. 8 bits must be specified
   d. Missing quote marks
   f. J is not a valid type
   g. Too many characters
   h. 2 is not a binary digit
   i. G is not a hex number
   j. Only 1 quote mark
8. MVI—only one character; MVC—any number of characters; also equal sign used in self-defining operand and not used in immediate operand

III. RELATIVE ADDRESSING AND THE MVC INSTRUCTION

A typical problem facing the programmer is referencing data within a record or area that does not contain a symbolic name. For example, assume the following data:

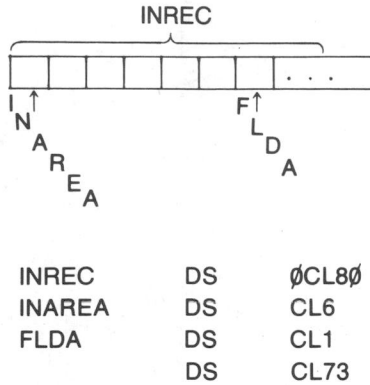

INREC	DS	ØCL8Ø
INAREA	DS	CL6
FLDA	DS	CL1
	DS	CL73

The data resides in storage and the programmer is required to reference the sixth position of INAREA. This data can only be referenced using relative addressing or by assigning a symbolic name to the area. With **relative addressing,** we use a symbolic name near the data and count from there the number of bytes needed to reach the desired storage location. Therefore, the sixth position of INREC can be referenced by INAREA+5 or by FLDA-1. When using relative addressing note that the operand contains three parts in the following sequence:

1. A symbolic address near the required data is referenced.
2. A + or − sign to indicate if displacement is to the right (+) or to the left (−).
3. An integer representing the displacement from the symbolic address.

Note that embedded blanks are *not* permitted in the operand. Consider the following example.

LABEL	OPERATION	OPERAND	COMMENTS
1	10 16		72
	MVC	GENDER(1),INAREA+5	
*			
*	OR		
*			
	MVC	GENDER(1),FLDA-1	

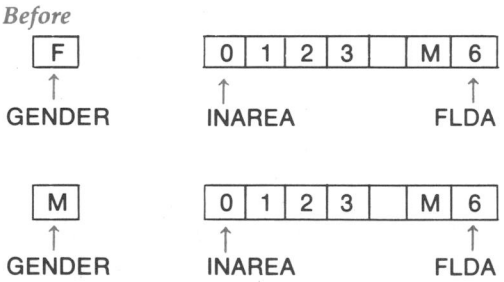

Before

This illustrates how data can be moved to a storage location called GENDER, by either of the MVC instructions shown that use relative addressing. Examining the instructions, we find

1. The receiving field is GENDER.
2. The sending field is INAREA+5 or FLDA-1.
3. The length is explicitly specified as one byte *by the first operand.*

For the next example, assume the programmer desires to move the digits 175 from the storage area illustrated below to an area named WT.

Before

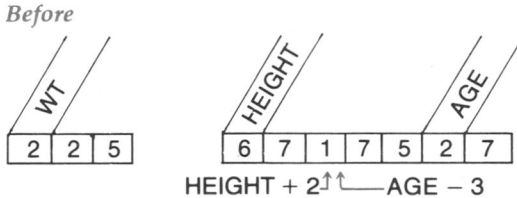

HEIGHT + 2↑↑—AGE − 3

LABEL	OPERATION	OPERAND	COMMENTS	
1	10	16		72
	MVC	WT(3),HEIGHT+2		
*				
*	OR			
*				
	MVC	WT(3),AGE-3		

After

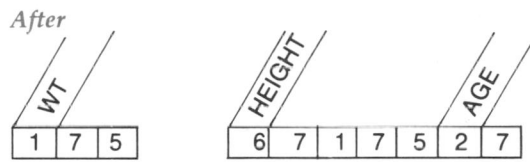

The instructions demonstrate how relative addressing can be used. Notice that the length specifier is critical in controlling the number of bytes to be moved.

Relative addressing may also be used to reference data in *both* operands of a move instruction. This is illustrated in the following example where 4 bytes of data are to be moved from the fourth position of IN to the second position of OUT:

Before

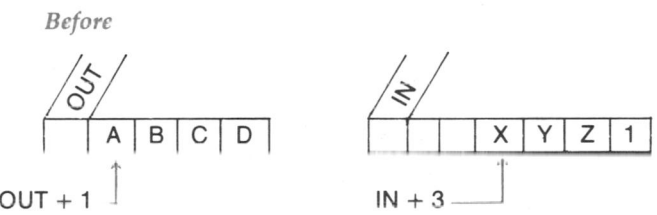

OUT + 1   IN + 3

LABEL	OPERATION	OPERAND	COMMENTS	
1	10	16		72
	MVC	OUT+1(4),IN+3		

After

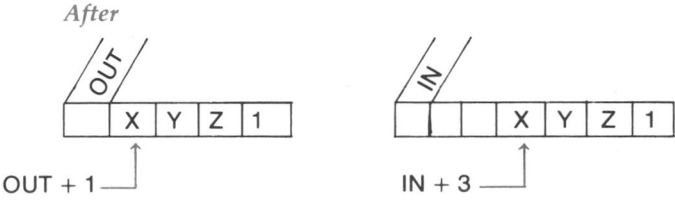

OUT + 1   IN + 3

We observe that

1.   The receiving field begins in OUT+1.

2. The sending field begins in IN+3.
3. The length specifier is four bytes in the first operand.

If the length specifier had been omitted, the number of bytes contained in the DS statement for OUT would have been implied. Relative addressing is very important when referencing overlapped fields or data locations, as we will subsequently see.

IV. OVERLAPPED FIELDS AND THE MVC INSTRUCTION

A. Format

As already noted, the arrangement of data fields in storage is established by the order of the define constant (DC) and/or define storage (DS) instructions. Because the storage areas are assigned sequentially, the following shows how a block of data would be set up by the instructions given.

Name	Operation	Operand
FLDA	DS	CL1
FLDB	DS	CL2
FLDC	DS	CL3

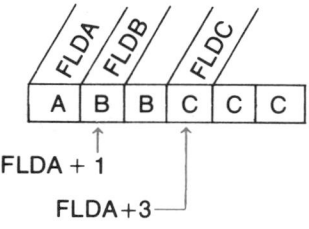

In this example, FLDB can be considered the second position in FLDA; that is, it can be accessed as FLDA+1 as well as FLDB. Similarly, FLDC is the fourth position in FLDA and can be specified as FLDA+3. It can also be specified as the third position in FLDB, or as FLDB+2. This is the manner in which fields are said to *overlap*. The significance of **overlapped fields** is especially important when moving data.

When the sending field is shorter than the receiving field, the data next to the shorter sending field will be included in the move. For example, using the preceding data, consider the following.

Instruction

LABEL	OPERATION		OPERAND	COMMENTS	
1	10	16			72
	MVC		FLDC,FLDA		

Results

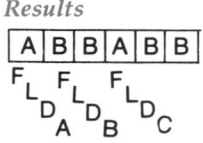

The instruction would generate the characters ABB in FLDC because a length of 3 bytes was implied by the move instruction.

We will now analyze the effects of overlapped fields with the following instruction:

LABEL	OPERATION	OPERAND	COMMENTS	72
	MVC	FLDC,FLDB		

Before

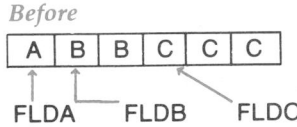

| A | B | B | C | C | C |

FLDA   FLDB   FLDC

FLDC is 3 bytes; hence a 3-byte move follows.

							Byte Moved	
							From	To
	FLDB			FLDC				
1.	A	B	B	¢ B	C	C	FLDB	FLDC
2.	A	B	B	B	¢ B	C	FLDB+1	FLDC+1
3.	A	B	B	B	B	¢ B	FLDB+2 (FLDC)	FLDC+2

After

FLDA   FLDB   FLDC

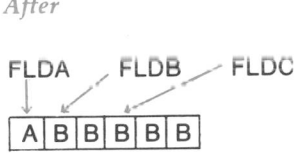

| A | B | B | B | B |

The byte-by-byte movement does not produce what you may have expected. Note that the 3 bytes starting at FLDB initially contained the characters BBC but, as a result of the move instruction, both the sending field FLDB, and the receiving field, FLDC, were filled with Bs. The filling of a field with a particular character from an adjoining area is referred to as **propagation.** The next example further illustrates this concept.

LABEL	OPERATION	OPERAND	COMMENTS	72
	MVC	FLDB(5),FLDA		

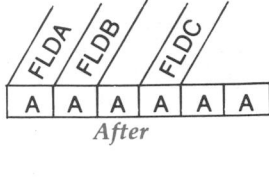

Byte Moved	
From	To
FLDA	FLDB
FLDA+1	FLDB+1
FLDA+2	FLDB+2
FLDA+3	FLDB+3
FLDA+4	FLDB+4

The instruction will propagate the letter A throughout the entire data area. The key to this concept is realizing that the character to be propagated (A) is located immediately before the receiving field. *It is only when this condition prevails that propagation will take place.*

B. An Application: Clearing the Output Area

The programmer cannot assume automatically that an output print area is cleared when execution begins. Rather, one of the first programming requirements is to clear this area to insure that data from a previous program does not affect the next output record. This is best accomplished by an MVC operation that propagates spaces or blanks throughout the output area. For propagation, remember to define the desired character (space) *immediately before* the field to receive the propagated characters. Therefore, the following instructions would be coded.

LABEL	OPERATION	OPERAND	COMMENTS
	MVC	LINEOUT(132),SPACES	
	.		
	.		
	.		
SPACES	DC	CL1' '	
LINEOUT	DS	CL132	
	.		
	.		

Spaces are propagated throughout the area called LINEOUT, thereby clearing that area in preparation for the layout of the next line of print.

There is another method of clearing the output area in which the storage area named SPACES need not be defined. The concept is essentially the same as the previous example, except that we initially place a space in the first position of LINEOUT and then propagate the space throughout the area. The instruction to accomplish this would be coded as follows:

LABEL	OPERATION	OPERAND	COMMENTS
	MVI	LINEOUT,X'40'	
	MVC	LINEOUT+1(131),LINEOUT	

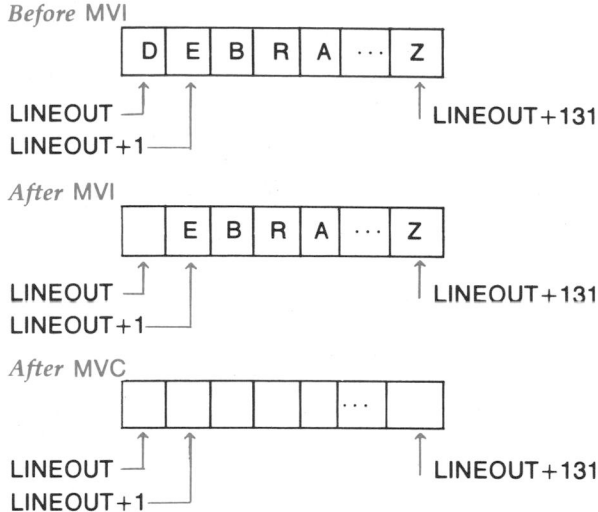

Before MVI

After MVI

After MVC

Note that the MVI instruction places a space in the first byte of LINEOUT, and the MVC instruction is then used to propagate spaces throughout the output area LINEOUT. Also note that the length of the MVC is 131 bytes and not 132, because the move (MVC) begins in LINEOUT+1.

CHAPTER SUMMARY

I. Storage-to-Storage Move Instruction: MVC
   A. Format: MVC FIELD1,FIELD2
      1. To move data, usually in EBCDIC form, from one location in storage to another.
      2. FIELD1 (Operand 1) is referred to as the receiving field.
      3. FIELD2 (Operand 2) is referred to as the sending field.
      4. FIELD1 and FIELD2 are symbolic names that refer to the high-order position, or the first (leftmost) byte, of the named locations.
      5. From 1 to 256 bytes may be moved with a single MVC instruction.
   B. Rules for the MVC Instruction
      1. Data is moved one byte at a time from left to right.
      2. Movement continues until the number of bytes specified in the first operand—the receiving field—have all been filled.
      3. Unless the length of the move is explicitly stated, the number of characters moved is determined by the length of the receiving field.
         a. When the sending and receiving fields are the same size, the receiving field will duplicate the sending field.
         b. When the receiving field is shorter than the sending field, truncation of low-order characters will occur.
         c. When the receiving field is longer than the sending field, additional characters from positions adjacent to the sending field will be moved.
         d. An explicit move instruction contains a length specifier in the first operand that indicates the precise number of bytes to be moved. For example, the instruction MVC FIELD1(4),FIELD2 indicates that 4 bytes are to be moved from FIELD2 to FIELD1.
   C. Self-Defining Operands in MVC Instructions
      1. Definition: When the second operand in an MVC or any storage-to-storage instruction is defined as a constant.
      2. For example, MVC LINEOUT(13),=C'ERROR IN DATA'.

3. Self-defining constants can be established in character (C), hexadecimal (X), binary (B), and packed (P) form.
4. Self-defining constants are typically used only for one-of-a-kind messages.

II. Move Immediate Instruction: MVI
   A. Purpose: To move one byte of data that has not been defined elsewhere in the program into a particular storage area.
   B. The Move Immediate instruction is of the storage immediate type.
   C. The data to be moved is defined in the second operand. For example, MVI AMT,C'$'.
   D. One byte of data is moved from the second operand to the high-order byte of the first operand.

III. Relative Addressing and the MVC Instruction
   A. A symbolic address near the required data is referenced.
   B. A + or − sign indicates whether the displacement of the data is to the right (+) or to the left (−) of the symbolic address.
   C. An integer represents the displacement from the symbolic address.
   D. For example, MVC LINEOUT+19(5),RESULT moves five bytes of RESULT to the receiving field, which begins in LINEOUT+19, or the 20th position of LINEOUT.

IV. Overlapped Fields and the MVC Instruction
   A. The filling of an entire field with a character located immediately before the receiving field is referred to as propagation.
   B. For example, the following MVC can be used to propagate spaces or blanks throughout the output area.

LABEL	OPERATION	OPERAND	COMMENTS
1	10	16	72
	MVC	LINEOUT(132),SPACES	
	.		
	.		
	.		
SPACES	DC	CL1' '	
LINEOUT	DS	CL132	

CHAPTER SELF-EVALUATING QUIZ

1. The method used to reference data that has not been assigned a symbolic name is called _____ .

2. (T or F) The following is a valid instruction using relative addressing.

   ```
   MVC    AGEOUT,PDATA+5(2)
   ```

3. (T or F) The displacement must be positive (+) when using relative addressing.

4. (T or F) Blanks are not permitted before or after the displacement sign in an operand when relative addressing is performed.

5. If the input record area is called IN, how could the programmer reference record position 80?

6. Identify the invalid relative addresses.
   a. LINE+7   e. OUT+3,
   b. IN+K   f. 6+TEMP
   c. OFF*2   g. OUTAREA+100
   d. INDY-5   h. DATA+0

7. Code the instruction to move the digits 78 in the following example to an area called QTY.

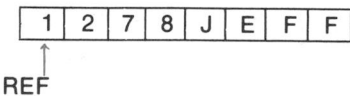

8. Write the two move instructions necessary to fill a 6-byte field called CREDIT with asterisks (*).
9. To clear the output area by propagating spaces, what must the relationship be between the defined constant (SPACE) and the output area (OUTAREA)?
10. Code the instruction to move the message THE END to the fifth position of LINEOUT. Use a self-defining operand.

For each of the following instructions, specify whether its *format* is valid or invalid.

	LABEL	OPERATION	OPERAND	COMMENTS
11.		MVC	FLDA+8Ø,FLDB-3	
12.		MVC	FLDC(1Ø),FLDA(7)	
13.		MVC	FLDA+1Ø,C='ERROR'	
14.		MVI	FLDA,FLDB	
15.		MVC	=C'ERROR,FLDA	
16.		MVI	FLDA,=C'*'	
17.		MVC	FLDB-1Ø(13),=C'ERROR IN DATA'	
18.		MVI	FLDA+25,X'F1'	
19.		MVC	FLDB,FLDA-7	

20. If FLDA = 12345 (5 bytes) and FLDB = 173 (3 bytes), what is the result of the following?

```
MVC    FLDA,FLDB
```

a. 00173
b. 173ƀƀ (ƀ means a blank)
c. 12173
d. 123
e. None of these

Note:
Explain your answer.

SOLUTIONS

		Page
1.	Relative addressing	116
2.	F: The length specifier is used with the *first* operand	109

```
MVC    AGEOUT(2),PDATA+5.
```

3. F: Negative displacements are also permissible — 116
4. T — 116
5. IN+79 — 116
6. b. K is not a decimal number — 116
   c. * is not permitted — 116
   e. , is not permitted — 116
   f. incorrect order — 116

Note
Answer *h* is valid but is the same as DATA

7. MVC   QTY(2),REF+2 — 116

8. ```
   MVI   CREDIT,C'*' (or MVI   CREDIT(1),=C'*')
   MVC   CREDIT+1(5),CREDIT
   ```                                                                    119
   Be sure *never* to use the = sign with the MVI instruction

9. The space must precede OUTAREA.   120

   ```
   SPACE      DC   C' '
   OUTAREA    DS   CL132
   ```

10. ```
    MVC   LINEOUT+4(7),=C'THE END'
    ```                                                                   111

11. Valid   117

12. Invalid; only one operand may have an explicit length   109

13. Invalid; should read MVC   FLDA+10,=C'ERROR'   111
    (Second operand invalid in the question)

14. Invalid; when using the MVI instruction, the second operand must be a 113
    one-byte immediate operand

15. Invalid; the first operand is the receiving field and may not be a self- 111
    defining operand

16. Invalid; the second operand in an MVI instruction is not a self-defining 113
    operand but an immediate operand; no = in the second operand:

    ```
    MVI   FLDA,C'*'
    ```

17. Valid   116

18. Valid   113

19. Valid   116

20. e; The results of the operation cannot be determined with the informa- 109
    tion given. Because the receiving field determines the length of the
    move, 5 bytes of data will be transferred. The first 3 bytes of FLDA will
    be replaced with '173' of FLDB; the low-order 2 bytes of FLDA will be
    replaced with whatever data appears in the 2 positions following FLDB,
    that is, FLDB+3 and FLDB+4.

PRACTICE PROGRAM

Consider the problem definition shown in Figure 5.5. Write a program using relative
addressing to produce the desired results. See Figure 5.6 for a solution.

a. Input Record Layout

Figure 5.5
**Problem definition for the
Practice Program.**

b. Printer Spacing Chart for Printed Output

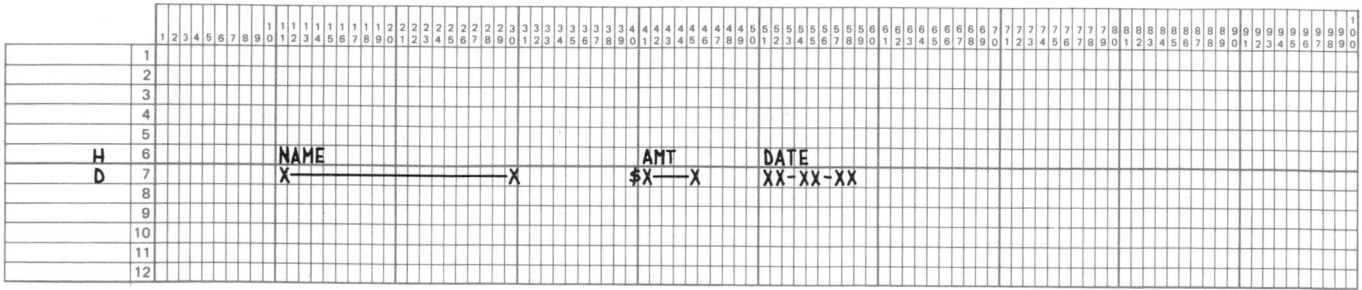

c. Sample Input Data

```
AL ABLE              76325
BETTY BAKER          58109
CARRIE COOK          34116
DENNIS DOWNS         62895
```

d. Sample Output

```
NAME                        AMT        DATE
AL ABLE                     $76325     12-11-87
BETTY BAKER                 $58109     12-11-87
CARRIE COOK                 $34116     12-11-87
DENNIS DOWNS                $62895     12-11-87
```

Figure 5.5
(continued)

```
*                                                                     *
*                                  HOUSEKEEPING INSTRUCTIONS GO HERE  *
*                                                                     *
          MVC     OUTAREA,SPACES
          MVC     OUTAREA+10(4),=C'NAME'
          MVC     OUTAREA+40(3),=C'AMT'
          MVC     OUTAREA+50(4),=C'DATE'
          PUT     OUTFILE,OUTAREA
CLEAR     MVC     OUTAREA,SPACES          CLEAR THE PRINT AREA
          GET     INFILE,RECORD          READ INPUT AND STORE IN RECORD
          MVI     OUTAREA+39,C'$'
          MVC     OUTAREA+10(20),RECORD
          MVC     OUTAREA+40(5),RECORD+20
          MVC     OUTAREA+50(8),=C'12-11-87'
          PUT     OUTFILE,OUTAREA        PRINT A LINE FROM OUTAREA
          B       CLEAR                  GO BACK TO PROCESS NEXT RECORD
*                                                                     *
*                                  HOUSEKEEPING INSTRUCTIONS GO HERE  *
*                                  ALONG WITH DCB OR DTF MACROS       *
*                                                                     *
RECORD    DS      CL80
SPACES    DC      CL1' '
OUTAREA   DS      CL132
          END
```

Figure 5.6
Solution to the Practice
Program.

KEY TERMS

Explicit operation	Propagation
Field	Receiving field
High-order position	Relative addressing
Immediate instruction	Self-defining operand
Implicit operation	Sending field
Low-order position	Storage-to-storage instruction
Overlapped fields	Truncation

REVIEW QUESTIONS

Consider the following for Questions 1–4.

```
FIELDA    DC      CL4'ABCD'
FIELDB    DC      CL3'EFG'
FIELDC    DC      CL4'HIJK'
```

1. Indicate how these fields would appear in storage in hexadecimal.

2. What character is contained in each of the following positions?
   a. `FIELDA+2`
   b. `FIELDB-3`
   c. `FIELDC+1`

3. Indicate the result of the following.
   a. `MVC     FIELDC,FIELDA`
   b. `MVC     FIELDB,FIELDC`
   c. `MVC     FIELDA,FIELDB`

4. Alter the above instructions so that three characters are moved each time.

5. Using a self-defining operand as the sending field
   a. Move 2 zeros to a field called `SUM`.
   b. Move `'A-OK'` to a field called `MESSAGE`.
   c. Move `'123'` to a field called `CODE`.

6. Will the following series of instructions properly clear the print area? Explain your answer.

```
        MVC     PRINT,BLANKS
        :
        :
PRINT   DS      0CL132
BLANKS  DC      CL1' '
```

7. Indicate the result of the following instructions, assuming `AX` to be a 3-position field, with contents `ABC`.
   a. `MVI     AX,C'3'`
   b. `MVI     AX+2,C'4'`

8. Indicate the results of the following operations, assuming `TIME` is a 4-position field.
   a. `MVC     TIME,=C'1123'`
   b. `MVC     TIME,=C'123'`
   c. `MVC     TIME,=C'12345'`
   d. `MVC     TIME,=C'12'`
   e. `MVC     TIME,=C'1'`

9. (T or F) An explicit move with a length specifier always produces the same results as an implied move.

10. Indicate what, if anything, is wrong with the following statements.
    a. `MVI     OUT,C'43'`
    b. `MVC     OUT,C'233'`
    c. `MVC     IN,OUT(2)`
    d. `MVC     IN(4),OUT(3)`
    e. `MVC     IN(280),OUT`
    f. `MVC     IN+7,OUT-3`

DEBUGGING EXERCISES

1. Examine the program excerpt in Figure 5.7. Indicate what errors, if any, exist in the instructions shown.

2. Examine the program in Figure 5.8. Indicate what errors, if any, exist in the instructions shown.

SOLUTIONS

1. See Figure 5.9.

2. The second `MVC` should have an explicit length specified. An implicit length of 132 is indicated. Because `RECIN` is only 80 bytes long, the `MVC` will cause 52 characters of unwanted data to be moved to `LINEOUT`. The instruction should be written as

```
MVC     LINEOUT(80),RECIN
```

```
            NEXT-10   MVC     OUTAREA,SPACES
                      GET     INFILE,RECORD
                      MVC     LNAME,LAST
                      MVC     FNAME,FIRST
                      MVC     SALOUT, SALARY
                      MVI     DOLLAR,X'$'
                      PUT     OUTFILE,OUTAREA
                      B       NEXT-10
                      .
                      .
            RECORD    DS      0CL80           INPUT FORMAT
            LAST      DS      CL15                  *
            FIRST     DS      CL10                  *
            SALARY    DC      CL5                   *
                      DS      CL50                  *
            SPACES    DC      CL1' '
            OUTAREA   DS      0CL132          PRINT FORMAT
                      DS      CL5                   *
            LNAME     DS      CL15                  *
                      DS      CL20                  *
            FNAME     DS      CL10                  *
                      DS      CL19                  *
            DOLLAR    DS      CL1                   *
            SALOUT    DS      CL5                   *
            BLANK     DS      CL57                  *
```

Figure 5.7
Program excerpt for Debugging
Exercise 1.

```
            *
            *
            *                                 HOUSEKEEPING INSTRUCTIONS GO HERE
            READ      GET     INFILE,RECIN
                      MVC     LINEOUT,SPACES
                      MVC     LINEOUT,RECIN
                      PUT     OUTFILE,LINEOUT
                      B       READ
            *
            *                                 HOUSEKEEPING INSTRUCTIONS GO HERE
            *                                 ALONG WITH DTF OR DCB MACROS
            RECIN     DS      CL80
            SPACES    DC      CL1' '
            LINEOUT   DS      CL132
                      END
```

Figure 5.8
Program for Debugging
Exercise 2.

INVALID LABEL

```
            (NEXT-10) MVC     OUTAREA,SPACES
                      GET     INFILE,RECORD
                      MVC     LNAME,LAST
                      MVC     FNAME,FIRST          — NO SPACE ALLOWED
                      MVC     SALOUT, SALARY       — SHOULD BE C FOR
                      MVI     DOLLAR,X'$'            CHARACTER
                      PUT     OUTFILE,OUTAREA
                      B       (NEXT-10)    ←—— INVALID LABEL
                      .                         BECAUSE OF HYPHEN
                      .
            RECORD    DS      0CL80           INPUT FORMAT
            LAST      DS      CL15                  *
            FIRST     DS      CL10                  *
            SALARY    (DC)    CL5    — SHOULD BE DS *
                      DS      CL50                  *
            SPACES    DC      CL1' '
            OUTAREA   DS      0CL132          PRINT FORMAT
                      DS      CL5                   *
            LNAME     DS      CL15                  *
                      DS      CL20                  *
            FNAME     DS      CL10                  *
                      DS      CL19                  *
            DOLLAR    DS      CL1                   *
            SALOUT    DS      CL5                   *
            BLANK     DS      CL57                  *
```

Figure 5.9
Solution to Debugging
Exercise 1.

PROGRAMMING ASSIGNMENTS

1. Write a program to print data from input records. The input is as follows:

CUSTOMER NAME	AMT OF PURCHASE (in dollars)	
1 20	21 25	26 80

Output should appear as follows:

NAME (customer name)	AMT (amt of purchase)	DATE (date of run—entered as a constant)

There will be one line of data for each input record read.

Print positions: customer name   11–30
                         amt of purchase   41–45
                         date (xx-xx-xx)   51–58

With every amount, print a $ in print position 40.

2. Consider the following input record.

NAME	STREET	CITY AND STATE	ZIP	
1 20	21 40	41 60	61 65	80

For each input record, print three lines of data, as follows:

Print positions 31–50   NAME
Print positions 31–50   STREET
Print positions 31–55   CITY, STATE, and ZIP

3. Write a program to create one printed line for every group of two input records. The input consists of two types of records:

Credit Record		*Debit Record*	
1–20	Customer name	1–20	Customer Name
21–25	Amt of Credit ($)	21–40	Address
26–80	Not Used	41–45	Amt of Debit
		46–80	Not Used

4. Redo Programming Assignment 2 using only *one* storage area for the print line. Thus, all output instructions would have the following form: PUT OUTFILE, LINEOUT.

Compare Instructions for Data in Character Form

OBJECTIVES

To familiarize you with:
1. *How conditional statements are used for testing, looping, and logical control.*
2. *The variety of formats and options available with compare instructions.*
3. *The use of flowcharts and pseudocode for planning logical control procedures in programs.*

I. PROGRAM LOGIC DEFINED

Statements in a program are executed in the sequence in which they appear unless the computer is instructed to branch to another routine or sequence of instructions. Frequently, branch instructions are coded to direct the computer to change the sequence of instructions to be executed by proceeding to another point in the program.

II. FLOWCHARTS AND PSEUDOCODE: TOOLS FOR DEPICTING PROGRAM LOGIC

A program is a set of instructions that must be executed in a specific sequence to function properly. When the logic of a program is complex, there are two planning tools that are frequently used to help plan the logic to be used: (1) program flowcharts, and (2) pseudocode.

A **program flowchart** is a pictorial representation of the logic to be used in a program. Advantages of a flowchart include the following:

1. It is a relatively standard planning tool with universally recognized symbols.
2. It is a diagram or illustration frequently helpful in developing the logic to be used in a program.
3. It helps the user to verify that procedures to be incorporated in a program are correct.

But, despite these advantages, program flowcharts have been the subject of considerable controversy in recent years, mainly for the following reasons:

1. Program flowcharts are cumbersome to draw.
2. The newer concepts of structured programming and top-down design have necessitated changes in the traditional format of a flowchart.

To compensate for some of the shortcomings of program flowcharts, another tool is frequently used to depict program logic. This tool is called **pseudocode** and is widely used to depict the logic of a *structured program*. Structured programming is discussed in depth in Chapter 18.

The term pseudocode indicates that this tool uses a code, similar to program code. The prefix "pseudo" implies that although this is a code it is not really a language itself.

In this chapter we will illustrate program logic with the use of flowcharts and pseudocode. For a complete description of these tools and of the structured programming technique, see Appendix J.

The flowchart sequence that corresponds to a simple condition follows.

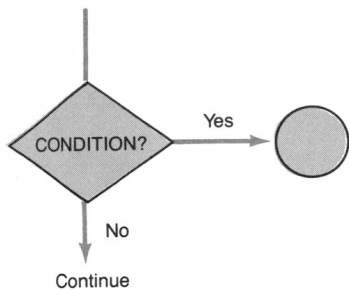

The pseudocode for this condition is:

```
IF   condition
     :
     :
ENDIF
```

Consider the following.

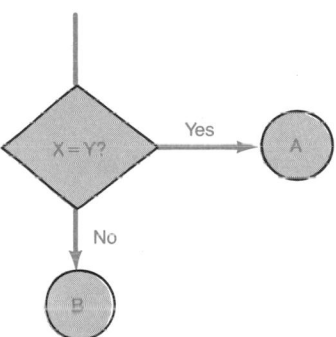

If the condition is met (X = Y), a branch to A occurs; if the condition is not met (X ≠ Y), a branch to B occurs. This is an IFTHENELSE sequence that means that IF X = Y, THEN a branch to A occurs; if X ≠ Y, the ELSE sequence, or a branch to B occurs. The pseudocode for this follows.

```
IF   X = Y
     THEN GO TO A
ELSE
     GO TO B.
```

The logical control procedure called IFTHENELSE is referred to as "Selection." Its full format is:

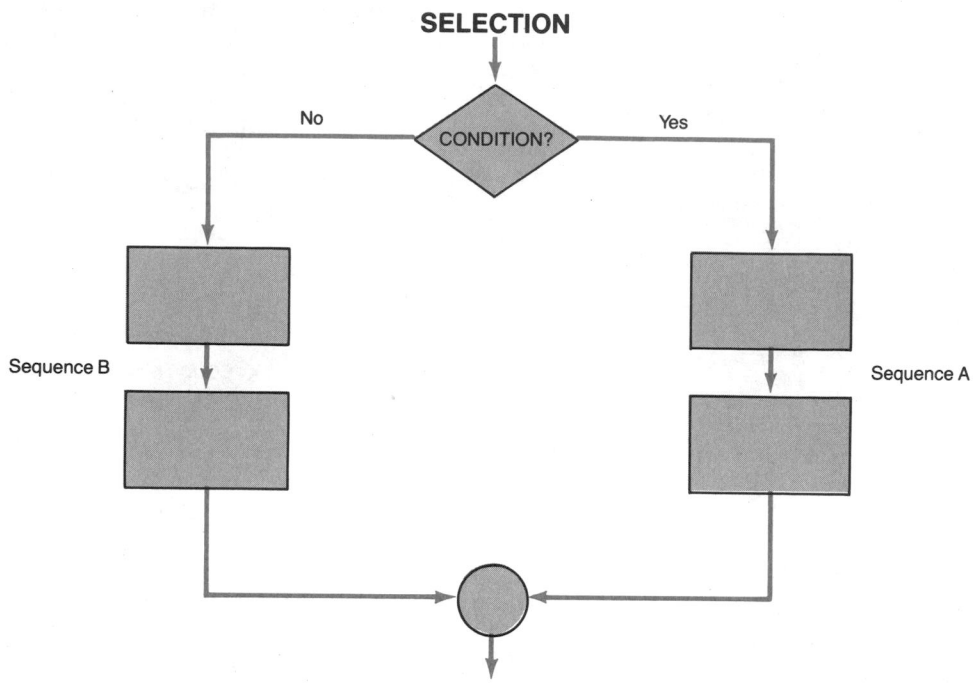

This logical control procedure is used to test a condition. If statements are in a sequence, we use a logical control procedure referred to as "Sequence":

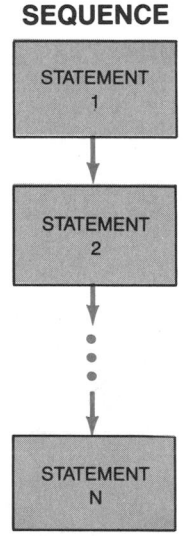

Iteration is a logical control procedure that corresponds to looping, that is, performing a sequence of steps a fixed number of times.

ITERATION

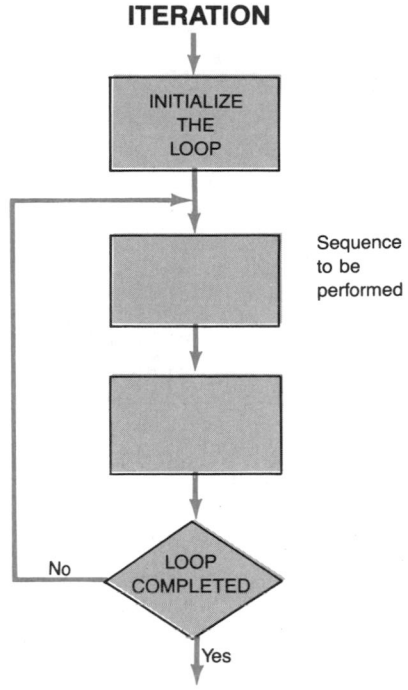

This process involves **branching.** Branching may be one of two types, conditional or unconditional. As the term implies, an unconditional branch will *always* cause a branch to a particular instruction regardless of existing conditions, whereas a conditional branch requires certain conditions to be met within the program for the branch to take place. In high-level languages, these branches appear as GO TO and IF-THEN instructions.

III. TYPES OF LOGICAL CONTROL PROCEDURES

A. Unconditional Branches

An **unconditional branch** will *always* alter the path of a program. Unconditional branching is the method used to instruct the computer to return to the beginning of a program and start processing over again. This repeated execution of a series of instructions is referred to as **looping.** Examine the flowchart excerpt and the corresponding pseudocode in Figure 6.1. An unconditional branch to the read instruction is required to process the next set of data. The instruction for this branch could be written as follows.

Operation 10 14	Operand 16
B	READRTN

where B is the operation code for branch. READRTN is a label that identifies the GET instruction. It appears in the NAME field of the GET statement.

Hence, an excerpt of the program coded from the flowchart would appear as follows.

LABEL	OPERATION		OPERAND	COMMENTS	
1	10	16			72
READRTN	GET		INFILE,RECORD		
	MVC		OUTAREA(80),RECORD		
	.				
	.				
	.				
	B		READRTN		

Unlike other instructions, the unconditional branch has only one operand. A symbolic name used as an operand in a branch instruction *must* appear in the name field of some instruction in the program. Because these names are used to identify a statement, they are frequently referred to as **labels.** The branch instruction transfers control to the instruction with the label or name indicated. At some point in the program, there must be a statement with the specified NAME field or LABEL, as shown in Figure 6.1. Hence, B READRTN is only valid if there is a statement called READRTN in the program. A label is assigned to an instruction by placing the name in the NAME field of the coding sheet (columns 1 through 8), as illustrated. *Labels are not assigned to each instruction*, only to instructions that will serve as branch points. When branching to some **routine** or sequence of instructions, the first instruction of that routine must have a label. The label should also be descriptive and meaningful so it can document the program. The label READRTN, for example, is more descriptive than R, although the latter is an equally valid label.

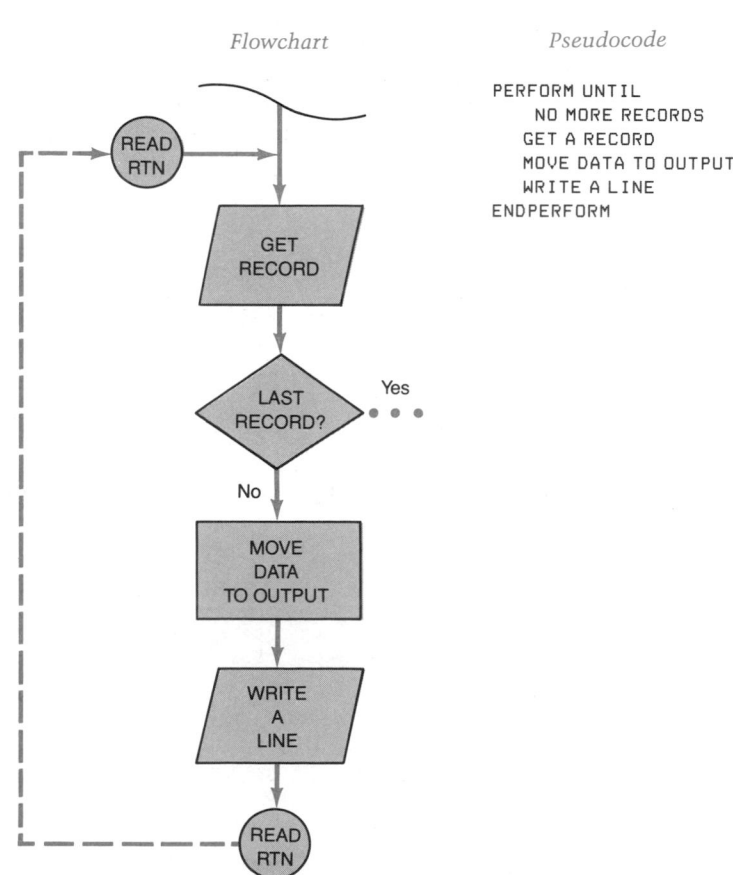

Flowchart

Pseudocode

```
PERFORM UNTIL
    NO MORE RECORDS
    GET A RECORD
    MOVE DATA TO OUTPUT
    WRITE A LINE
ENDPERFORM
```

Figure 6.1
Flowchart excerpt and corresponding pseudocode that illustrate looping.

RULES FOR FORMING LABELS (REVIEW)

1. Begins in position one: 1–8 characters long.
2. First character must be alphabetic (A–Z, @, #, or $).
3. Remaining characters may be any combination of letters (A–Z), numbers (0–9), or @, #, or $.
4. No spaces or special characters other than @, #, $ are permitted.
5. There are *no* reserved words with special meaning.

The following examples illustrate valid and invalid labels. If the label is invalid, the reason for the error is noted.

Label	Valid	Invalid	Reason for Error
XRAY	X		
7UP		X	Label must start with a letter
EMP-NO		X	Hyphen is a special character
B147UP	X		
HAMILTON	X		
CHK RTN		X	No spaces in a label
OUTPUTRTN		X	Too long
U.S.A.		X	Periods are special characters

Self-Evaluating Quiz

1. (T or F) Every instruction should be assigned a label.
2. The two types of branches are _____ and _____ .
3. Program statements are usually executed in _____ .
4. To alter the normal program flow, a(n) _____ instruction must be used.
5. A series of instructions executed repeatedly is called a(n) _____ .
6. The operation code for an unconditional branch is written as _____ .
7. The operand for an unconditional branch must identify the first instruction of a routine and would also therefore appear in the _____ field of the coding form.
8. What, if anything, is wrong with the following labels?

LABEL	OPERATION	OPERAND	COMMENTS	72
1	10 16			
a. STEP5				
b. 1STCLASS				
c. TOTAL12				
d. NAME-IN				
e. SUM%				
f. CHECKIT12				

1. F: Only those branched to
2. Conditional; unconditional
3. Sequence
4. Branch
5. Loop
6. B
7. Name or label
8. a. Embedded blank not permitted
   b. Label must begin with alphabetic character.
   c. Okay
   d. No hyphens in a label
   e. No % in label
   f. Too long

B. Conditional Branches

We define a conditional statement as any statement that tests for the existence of some condition and causes a branch to be made if that condition is found.

A **simple conditional** tests for a specific relation or condition. The following symbols are used to express simple relational conditions.

Symbol	Meaning
<	Less than
>	Greater than
=	Equal to

If the condition is met, a **conditional branch** occurs. If not, the program proceeds to the next sequential step.

A few examples will illustrate simple conditional tests and branches. See Figure 6.2.

To program effectively, it is not enough simply to learn the rules of a programming language. You must be able to apply these rules to solve logic problems. The conditional statement, as illustrated, is of prime importance in solving these logic problems and is, therefore, an integral part of all programming languages.

In high-level languages, the conditional is generally coded by a single IF . . . THEN statement. In assembler language, however, this task requires the following two instructions:

THE CONDITIONAL BRANCH

1. *Compare* two fields.
   The result of the comparison sets a condition code.
2. *Branch* depending upon the condition code.

IV. THE COMPARE INSTRUCTION AND THE CONDITION CODE

A. The Compare Instruction Defined

The purpose of the compare instruction is to compare two operands. This instruction automatically sets an internal **condition code** that can then be

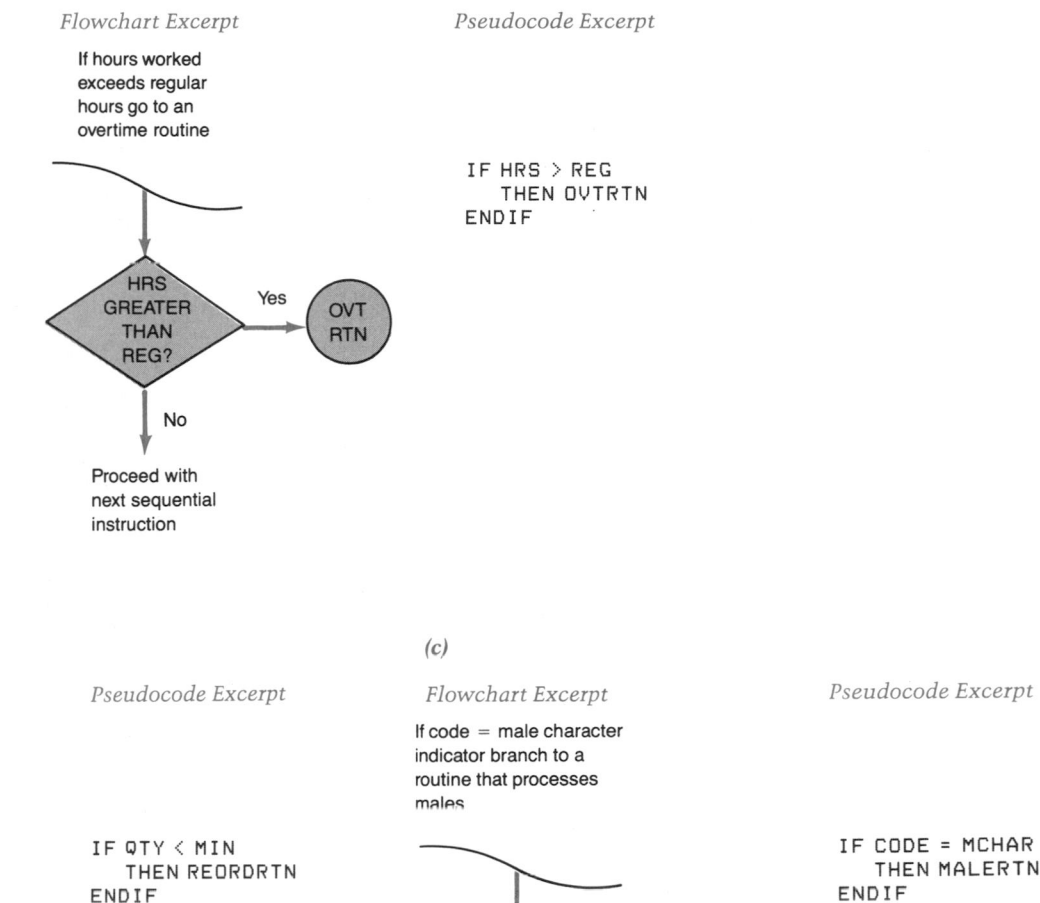

(a)

Flowchart Excerpt

If hours worked exceeds regular hours go to an overtime routine

Pseudocode Excerpt

```
IF HRS > REG
    THEN OVTRTN
ENDIF
```

HRS GREATER THAN REG?

Yes → OVT RTN

No

Proceed with next sequential instruction

(b)

Flowchart Excerpt

If quantity on hand is less than some minimum level branch to reorder routine

Pseudocode Excerpt

```
IF QTY < MIN
    THEN REORDRTN
ENDIF
```

QTY LESS THAN MIN?

Yes → REORD RTN

No

Proceed with next sequential instruction

(c)

Flowchart Excerpt

If code = male character indicator branch to a routine that processes males

Pseudocode Excerpt

```
IF CODE = MCHAR
    THEN MALERTN
ENDIF
```

IS CODE = MCHAR?

Yes → MALE RTN

No

Proceed with next sequential instruction

Figure 6.2 Examples of conditional branches.

tested. A branch is then executed depending upon the status of the code. Note however, that compare instructions do not alter the contents of either operand.

B. The Compare Logical Character ⟨CLC⟩ Instruction

1. Format

The Compare Logical Character ⟨CLC⟩ instruction is classified as a storage-to-storage instruction and is used to set the condition code when comparing two fields in main storage. While two operands being tested may be in any format, the CLC instruction is most commonly used with EBCDIC data. We will see that the field having the *higher binary (bit-by-bit) value* will be considered the greater field.

Format

Operation 10 14	Operand 16
CLC	OP1,OP2

Instruction:	CLC
Meaning:	Compare logical character: storage-to-storage. (Both operands are storage areas.)
Result:	Condition code is set to high, low, or equal depending upon the compare: high—Operand 1 is greater than Operand 2 low—Operand 1 is less than Operand 2 equal—Operand 1 = Operand 2
Operands:	May be in any format; most commonly EBCDIC May be explicit or implicit Operand 2 may be a self-defining operand
Length:	Maximum—256-byte comparison Length of comparison is determined by specification of first operand
Limitation:	The CLC is best used for alphanumeric comparisons and comparisons of *unsigned* numbers.

2. Explicit and Implicit Comparisons

As with the MVC instruction, the CLC instruction may be of two types, explicit or implicit. An **explicit compare** includes a length specifier. In an **implicit compare,** the length of the first operand determines the length of the comparison. An example of both types follows.

Examples

	LABEL	OPERATION 10 16	OPERAND	COMMENTS
1.		CLC	HRS(2),TIME	EXPLICIT COMPARE
2.		CLC	HRS,TIME	IMPLICIT COMPARE

CLC is the operation code.
HRS is the first operand and a symbolic address or location in storage.
TIME is the second operand and a symbolic address or location in storage.

In Example 1, the (2) is the explicit length specifier. A two-position compare will result regardless of the length of the fields. In Example 2, the length of HRS will determine the number of positions compared.

In a CLC instruction, the *first* operand is compared to the *second* operand.

The comparison begins in the high-order position and thereafter proceeds from left to right, one character at a time. As we will see, this left-to-right comparison makes the CLC particularly useful for comparing alphanumeric, as opposed to numeric, data.

The comparison is terminated in one of two ways.
1. An unequal condition occurs. At this point,
   a. if the character in Operand 1 is less than the character in Operand 2, a *low condition* occurs.
   b. if the character in Operand 1 is greater than the character in Operand 2, a *high condition* occurs.
2. The end of the first operand is reached by either:
   a. the implicit length of the first operand, or
   b. the length specifier indicated in the first operand.

---

3. Collating Sequence

The number of bytes to be compared may vary from 1 to 256. As a result of the comparison, the condition code will be set to equal, low, or high depending on the contents compared. Review the collating sequence or the relative weights of each character in EBCDIC because this is the basis for all CLC comparisons. See Figure 6.3.

In the following examples, assume that the length of the first operand implies the length of the comparison, and that the data is in EBCDIC form.

Operand 1	Operand 2	Number of Characters Compared	Result
712	699	1	High (Operand 1 greater than Operand 2)
72	72	2	Equal
1446	1447	4	Low (Operand 1 less than Operand 2)
− 007	+ 007	3	High

The last example clearly illustrates that the CLC instruction does not compare characters on an *algebraic* basis but, instead, performs a *binary* comparison of the EBCDIC characters (F0 F0 D7 > F0 F0 C7). There are instructions to compare packed data *algebraically*, but they will be treated in the next chapter.

When using the CLC instruction for comparing numeric fields, you must be careful, because the results of comparisons are not always what one might ordinarily expect. Signed fields and fields that contain blanks or high-order zeros have binary representations that can result in illogical comparisons. The following table is a list of values in descending sequence.

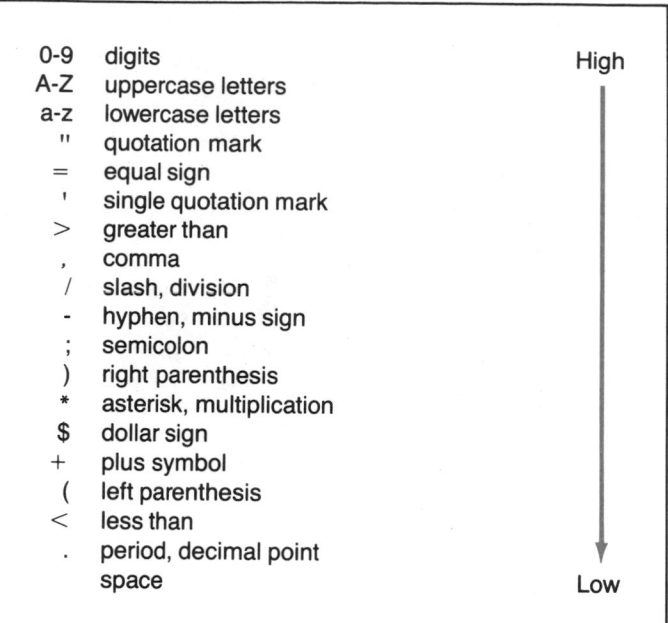

Figure 6.3
The EBCDIC collating
sequence.

0-9	digits	High
A-Z	uppercase letters	
a-z	lowercase letters	
"	quotation mark	
=	equal sign	
'	single quotation mark	
>	greater than	
,	comma	
/	slash, division	
-	hyphen, minus sign	
;	semicolon	
)	right parenthesis	
*	asterisk, multiplication	
$	dollar sign	
+	plus symbol	
(	left parenthesis	
<	less than	
.	period, decimal point	
	space	Low

Values in Descending Sequence

Number	Hex Representation	Binary Representation
12	F1F2	F 1 F 2 — 1111 0001 1111 0010
−12	F1D2	F 1 D 2 — 1111 0001 1101 0010
+12	F1C2	F 1 C 2 — 1111 0001 1100 0010
012	F0F1F2	F 0 F 1 F 2 — 1111 0000 1111 0001 1111 0010
ƀ12	40F1F2	4 0 F 1 F 2 — 0100 0000 1111 0001 1111 0010

Note that the bits are compared, one-by-one, until an inequality occurs or until the first operand is terminated. When 12 is compared to −12, for example, we have:

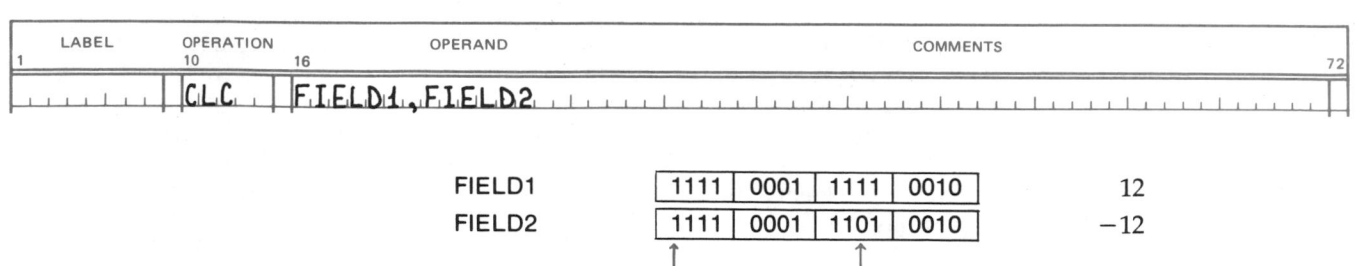

| | | FIELD1 | 1111 | 0001 | 1111 | 0010 | 12 |
| | | FIELD2 | 1111 | 0001 | 1101 | 0010 | −12 |

Compare begins here — Compare will stop at this point.
FIELD1, containing (12), will compare high.

To compare -12 to $+12$, we have:

LABEL	OPERATION		OPERAND	COMMENTS	
1	10	16			72
	CLC		FIELD2,FIELD3		

FIELD2	1111	0001	1101	0010	-12
FIELD3	1111	0001	1100	0010	$+12$

Compare begins here   Compare will stop here.

FIELD2 (-12) will compare high. Despite the fact that -12 is, in reality, less than $+12$, the binary representation is deceptive. To compare signed numbers, then, you should use the compare as noted in the next chapter.

Using the CLC,

    12 is greater than -12

-12 is greater than $+12$

$+12$ is greater than 012

 012 is greater than Ь12

When comparing alphanumeric fields, the normal collating sequence is followed. For example,

ABCD is less than BBCD

BBCD is less than ZBCD

ZBCD is less than 1BCD

ABCD is less than ACCD

ЬBDC is less than ABCD

ABCD is less than ABCE

Note that the CLC instruction is best used for normal alphanumeric comparisons and comparisons of *unsigned* numbers.

4. Examples

Now that the basis for comparison has been explained, we will examine the CLC instruction through a few examples. For the sake of simplicity, the data is shown in character or EBCDIC form rather than in hex form.

Example 1

LABEL	OPERATION		OPERAND	COMMENTS	
1	10	16			72
	CLC		HRS(2),TIME		

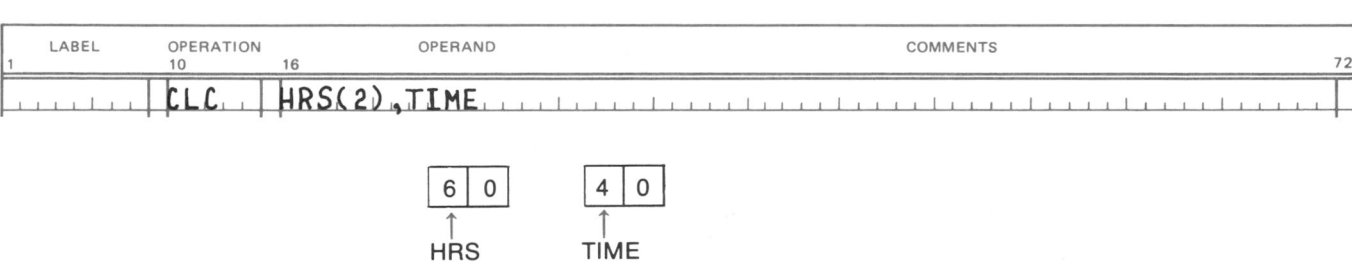

Results

Number of bytes actually compared   ◄————— 1

Condition   ◄————————————— high

(Operand 1 is greater than operand 2.)

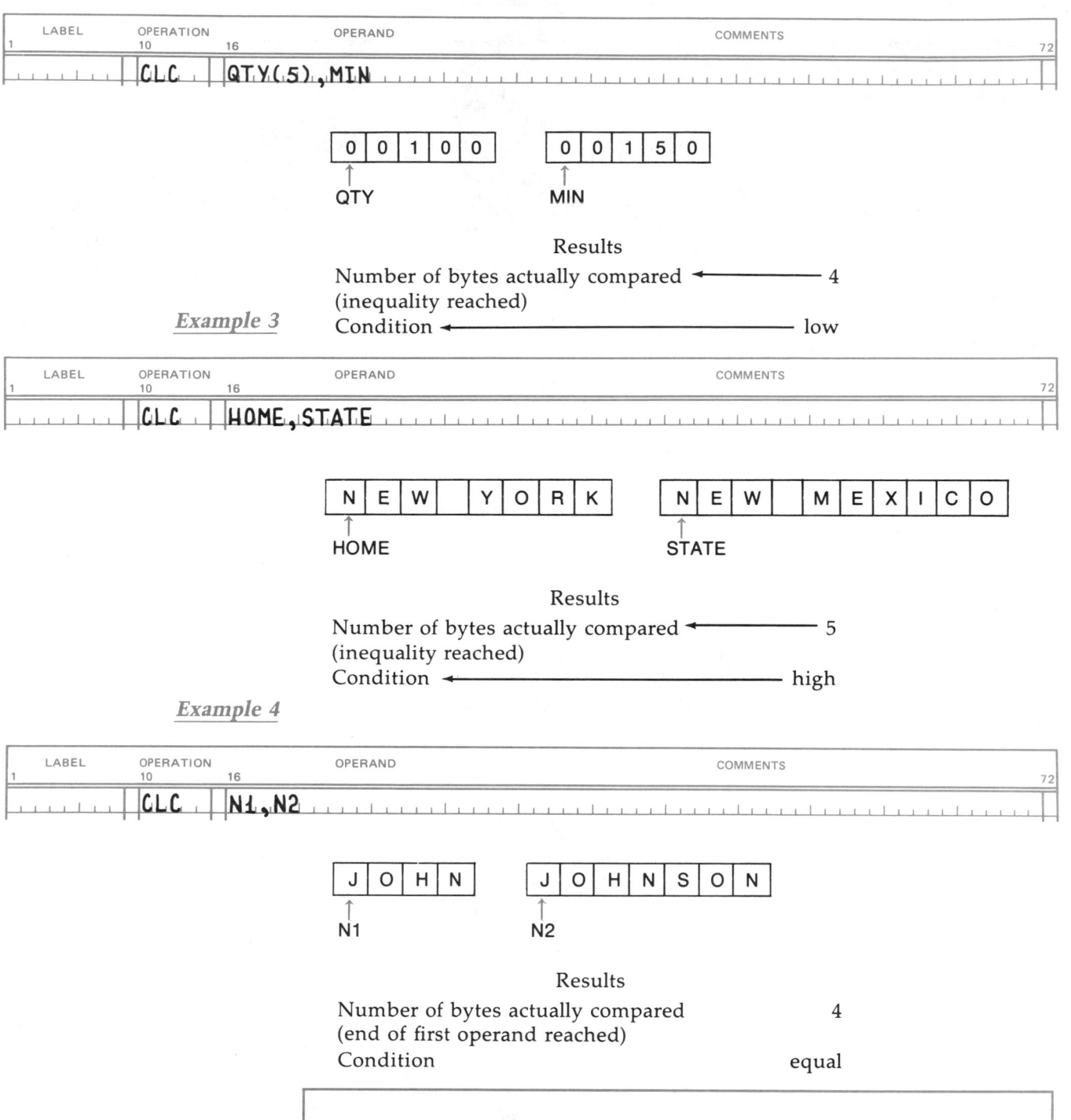

Example 2

LABEL	OPERATION	OPERAND	COMMENTS
	CLC	QTY(5),MIN	

QTY: 0 0 1 0 0   MIN: 0 0 1 5 0

Results

Number of bytes actually compared ← 4
(inequality reached)
Condition ← low

Example 3

LABEL	OPERATION	OPERAND	COMMENTS
	CLC	HOME,STATE	

HOME: N E W   Y O R K   STATE: N E W   M E X I C O

Results

Number of bytes actually compared ← 5
(inequality reached)
Condition ← high

Example 4

LABEL	OPERATION	OPERAND	COMMENTS
	CLC	N1,N2	

N1: J O H N   N2: J O H N S O N

Results

Number of bytes actually compared   4
(end of first operand reached)
Condition   equal

RULES FOR THE COMPARE LOGICAL CHARACTER

1. The data contained in the operands may be in any format; however, the EBCDIC form is most common.
2. The first operand is compared to the second.
3. A bit-by-bit comparison is performed from left to right, one character at a time, until an inequality occurs or until the end of the first operand is reached.
4. The length of the comparison depends on whether an explicit or implicit compare is used.

Self-Evaluating Quiz

Given the following data in storage, determine the number of bytes compared and the setting of the condition code for each instruction executed.

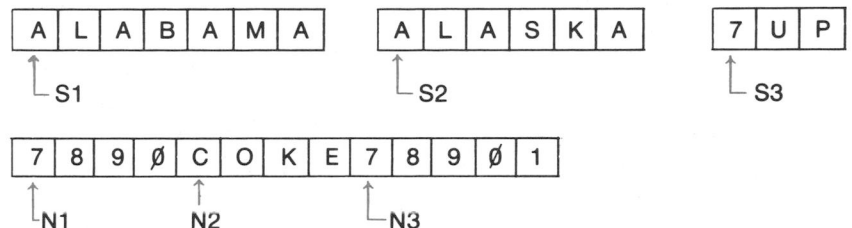

Instruction	Resulting Condition	Number of Bytes Compared	Explanation of Result
1. CLC S1,S2			
2. CLC S3,S1			
3. CLC S2(3),S1			
4. CLC S3(3),N1			
5. CLC N2,S2			
6. CLC N1,N3			
7. CLC N3,N1			
8. CLC S3(1),N3			

SOLUTIONS

Instruction	Resulting Condition	Number of Bytes Compared	Explanation of Result
1. CLC S1,S2	Low	4	Letter B is less than the letter S
2. CLC S3,S1	High	1	The number 7 is greater than the letter A
3. CLC S2(3),S1	Equal	3	
4. CLC S3(3),N1	Low	2	The letter U is less than the number 8
5. CLC N2,S2	High	1	C is greater than A
6. CLC N1,N3	Equal	4	N1 contains 4 bytes-7890 equals 7890
7. CLC N3,N1	High	5	N3 contains 5 bytes-78901 compares high to 7890C
8. CLC S3(1),N3	Equal	1	Explicit one-byte comparison

V. USE OF CONDITION CODES

A. Branch on Condition

Once the condition code has been set by a compare instruction, a conditional branch statement can be used to alter the flow of logic, depending on an existing condition.

As with unconditional branch instructions, the operand field contains the name or label of an instruction. To code the unconditional branch B STEP5 means that STEP5 is the name of a statement within the program.

LABEL	OPERATION	OPERAND	COMMENTS
1	10 16		72
STEP5	MVC	LINEOUT,MSSG	

The conditional branch instructions use operation codes, as follows.

Summary: Branch on Condition

Operation	Meaning	Operand Condition	Numeric Setting of Internal Condition Code
BH	Branch on high	First greater than second ($>$)	2
BL	Branch on low	First less than second ($<$)	1
BE	Branch on equal	First $=$ second	0
BNE	Branch not equal	First not equal second ($\neq$)	1 or 2
BNH	Branch not high	First less than or equal to second ($\leq$)	0 or 1
BNL	Branch not low	First greater than or equal to second ($\geq$)	0 or 2

B. Setting the Condition Code

The compare instruction automatically sets the condition code to 0, 1, or 2 depending on whether the first operand is equal to, less than, or greater than the second operand. In coding the branch instruction, the programmer need not use these codes. To cause a branch to STEP6 if the first operand equals the second operand, for example, you code:

```
BE     STEP6
```

The BE instruction causes the computer to test for a condition code of 0. Condition codes are included here for reference purposes only, because the programmer need not know the corresponding numeric values except for debugging purposes.

Example 1   The conditional branch instructions can be coded as follows.

Pseudocode

```
IF A > B
   THEN GO TO RTN1
ENDIF
```

Flowchart

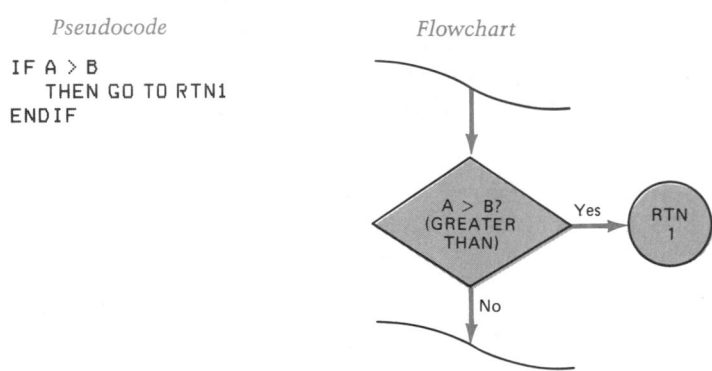

LABEL	OPERATION	OPERAND	COMMENTS
	CLC	A,B	
	BH	RTN1	

If the condition code is High (A > B), then branch to RTN1.

Example 2   *Pseudocode*

IF A < B
    THEN GO TO RTN2
ENDIF

Flowchart

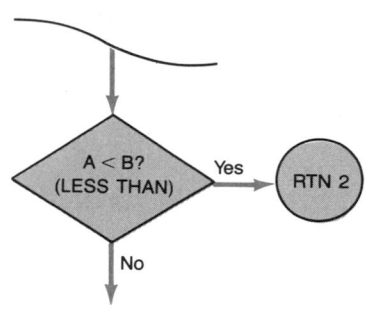

	LABEL	OPERATION		OPERAND	COMMENTS	
1		10	16			72
		CLC	A,B			
		BL	RTN2			

Example 3   *Pseudocode*

IF A = B
    THEN GO TO RTN3
ENDIF

Flowchart

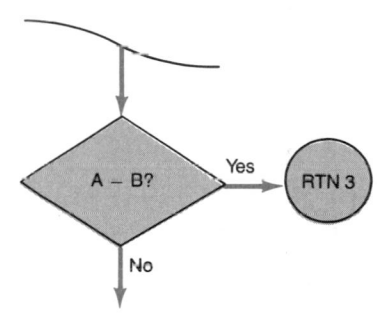

	LABEL	OPERATION		OPERAND	COMMENTS	
1		10	16			72
		CLC	A,B			
		BE	RTN3			

Example 4   *Pseudocode*

IF A NOT EQUAL B
    THEN GO TO RTN4
ENDIF

Flowchart

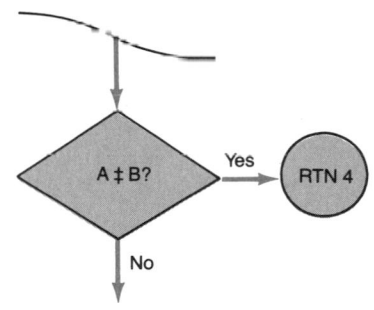

	LABEL	OPERATION		OPERAND	COMMENTS	
1		10	16			72
		CLC	A,B			
		BNE	RTN4			

For any given condition there are several ways to flowchart and to code the conditional branch. For example, the following two illustrations result in the same logic.

Method 1

Flowchart

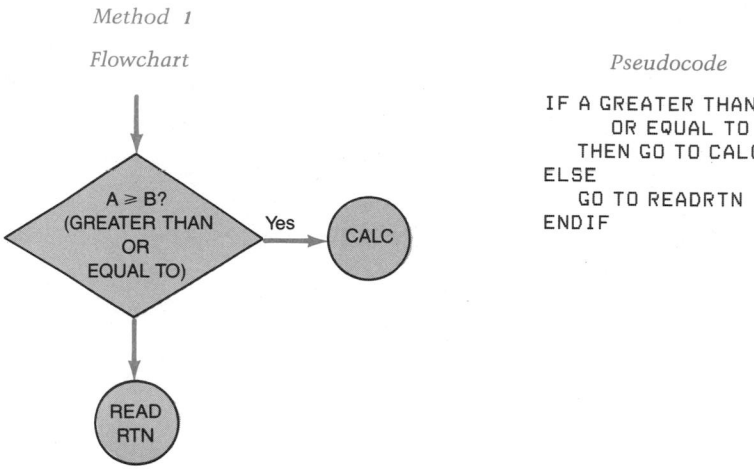

Pseudocode

```
IF A GREATER THAN B
     OR EQUAL TO B
   THEN GO TO CALC
ELSE
   GO TO READRTN
ENDIF
```

LABEL	OPERATION	OPERAND	COMMENTS
	CLC	A,B	
	BNL	CALC	
	B	READRTN	

Method 2

Flowchart

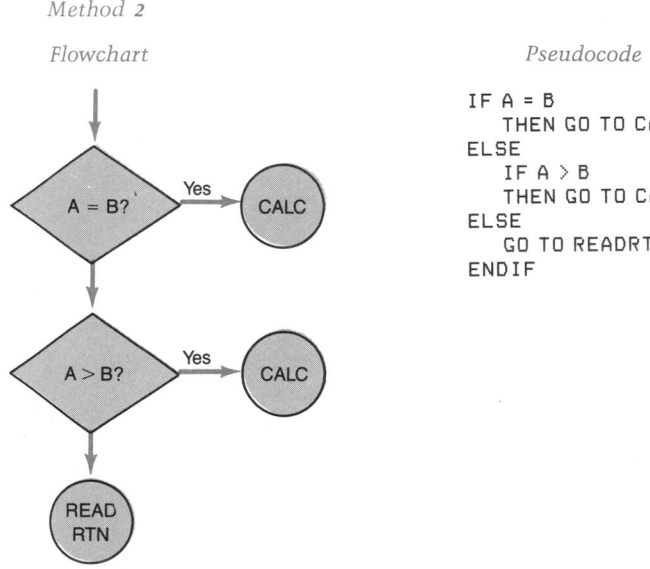

Pseudocode

```
IF A = B
   THEN GO TO CALC
ELSE
   IF A > B
   THEN GO TO CALC
ELSE
   GO TO READRTN
ENDIF
```

LABEL	OPERATION	OPERAND	COMMENTS
	CLC	A,B	
	BE	CALC	
	BH	CALC	
	B	READRTN	

A third method of coding follows.

LABEL	OPERATION	OPERAND	COMMENTS
	CLC	A,B	
	BL	READRTN	
	B	CALC	

The efficient programmer writes a program with a minimum number of steps. Therefore, the preceding Method 1 and Method 3 would be preferable.

Self-Evaluating Quiz

Convert the following flowchart symbols and pseudocode to assembler language coding.

1.   *Flowchart*   *Pseudocode*

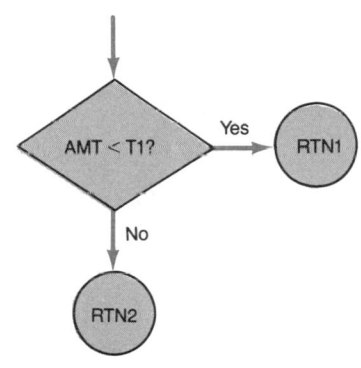

```
IF AMT < T1
    THEN GO TO RTN1
ELSE
    GO TO RTN2
ENDIF
```

2.   *Flowchart*   *Pseudocode*

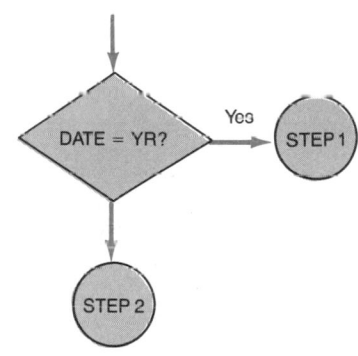

```
IF DATE = YR
    THEN GO TO STEP1
ELSE
    GO TO STEP2
ENDIF
```

3.   *Flowchart*   *Pseudocode*

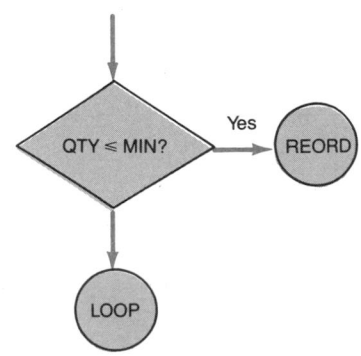

```
IF QTY < MIN OR = MIN
    THEN GO TO REORD
ELSE
    GO TO LOOP
ENDIF
```

4.   *Flowchart*   *Pseudocode*

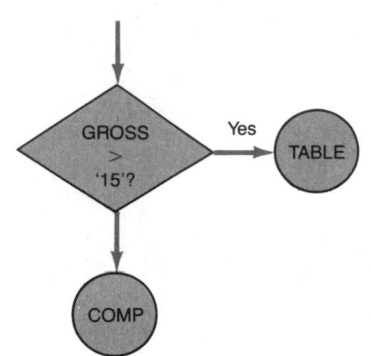

```
IF GROSS > '15'
    THEN GO TO TABLE
ELSE
    GO TO COMP
ENDIF
```

5. For each of the program excerpts (a) to (g) that follows, indicate which branch will occur for the conditions specified below.

```
a.  CLC   X,Y        e.  CLC   Y,X
    BE    ERROR          BL    ERROR
    B     BEGIN          B     BEGIN
b.  CLC   X,Y        f.  CLC   Y,X
    BNE   BEGIN          BNL   BEGIN
    B     ERROR          B     ERROR
c.  CLC   Y,X        g.  CLC   X,Y
    BH    BEGIN          BNH   BEGIN
    B     ERROR          B     ERROR
d.  CLC   X,Y
    B     ERROR
    BNE   BEGIN
```

Condition	a	b	c	d	e	f	g
X < Y							
X = Y							
X > Y							

One of the series of instructions above contains a logic error. Can you find it?

6. For each of the following program excerpts listed below indicate:
   1. The condition code setting.
   2. The number of bytes compared.
   3. Whether or not a branch occurs (yes or no).

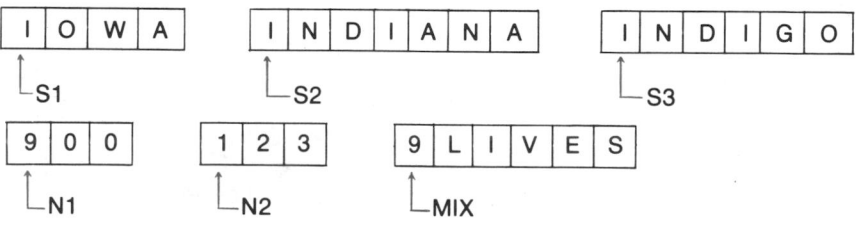

	Coding	Condition	Number of Bytes Compared	Does Branch Occur?
a.	CLC S1,S2			
	BL RTN1			

b.   CLC   S3,S2
       BH   RTN2

c.   CLC   S2(4),S3
       BE   RTN3

d.   CLC   S1,S3
       BNL   RTN4

e.   CLC   N1,N2
       BNE   RTN5

f.   CLC   N1,MIX
       BL   RTN6

SOLUTIONS 1.

```
        CLC   AMT,T1
        BL    RTN1
        B     RTN2
*
*       ALTERNATE METHOD
*
        CLC   AMT,T1
        BNL   RTN2
        B     RTN1
```

2.

```
        CLC   DATE,YR
        BE    STEP1
        B     STEP2
*
*       ALTERNATE METHOD
*
        CLC   DATE,YR
        BNE   STEP2
        B     STEP1
```

3.

```
        CLC   QTY,MIN
        BNH   REORD
        B     LOOP
*
*       ALTERNATE METHOD
*
        CLC   QTY,MIN
        BH    LOOP
        B     REORD
```

4.

LABEL	OPERATION	OPERAND	COMMENTS
	CLC	GROSS,=C'15'	
	BH	TABLE	
	B	COMP	
*			
*	ALTERNATE METHOD		
*			
	CLC	GROSS,=C'15'	
	BNH	COMP	
	B	TABLE	

5.

Condition	a	b	c	d	e	f	g
X < Y	BEGIN	BEGIN	BEGIN	ERROR	BEGIN	BEGIN	BEGIN
X = Y	ERROR	ERROR	ERROR	ERROR	BEGIN	BEGIN	BEGIN
X > Y	BEGIN	BEGIN	ERROR	ERROR	ERROR	ERROR	ERROR

d. The unconditional branch to ERROR precedes the conditional branch. Hence, the unconditional branch always occurs, regardless of the condition. The BNE instruction is never executed.

6.

	Coding		Condition	Number of bytes compared	Does branch occur?
a.	CLC	S1,S2			
	BL	RTN1	High	2	No
b.	CLC	S3,S2			
	BH	RTN2	High	5	Yes
c.	CLC	S2(4),S3			
	BE	RTN3	Equal	4	Yes
d.	CLC	S1,S3			
	BNL	RTN4	High	2	Yes
e.	CLC	N1,N2			
	BNE	RTN5	High	1	Yes
f.	CLC	N1,MIX			
	BL	RTN6	High	2	No

C. Performing a Sign Test

Suppose we wish to determine if a one-byte field called AMT1 is positive, negative, or zero. We could compare the field to an unsigned zero and branch accordingly.

```
CLC     AMT1,=C'0'
BH      POSRTN
BL      NEGRTN
BE      ZERORTN
```

Similarly, we could compare AMT1 to the hex configuration for an unsigned zero as follows.

```
CLC     AMT1,=X'F0'
```

To compare a 5-byte AMT2 field to 0, code the following.

```
CLC     AMT2,=C'00000'
```

D. Determining if a Field is Blank

Before performing arithmetic operations on numeric fields you should ensure that they do not erroneously contain blanks. That is, if you attempt to perform an arithmetic operation on a blank field, the program could reach an **abend** or *ab*normal *end* condition. One common data validation procedure is to compare a field to spaces before performing an arithmetic operation. If the field is equal to spaces, it should not be used in an arithmetic operation as demonstrated here:

```
CLC   FLD1,=C' '
BE    ERRTN
```

E. Testing a Coded Field for Valid Entries

Suppose we wish to select a routine to perform that depends on the contents of a coded input field. The input is a payroll record with a NAME, SAL, and CODE. If CODE = 1, branch to a SALARIED routine; if CODE = 2 branch to an HOURLY routine; otherwise, branch to an error routine.

```
CLC   CODE,=C'1'
BE    SALARIED
CLC   CODE,=C'2'
BE    HOURLY
B     ERRTN
```

Coded fields are frequently used in this way.

F. Inclusive and Exclusive Comparisons

Testing if the contents of a field is between two endpoints is sometimes confusing to programmers. For example, suppose we wish to branch to PRINTRTN if FIELDA is between 4 and 9. Are we to branch to PRINTRTN if FIELDA equals 4 or only if PRINTRTN is greater than 4? Similarly, are we to branch to PRINTRTN if FIELDA equals 9 or only if it is less than 9? To phrase these questions a different way, should the comparison be **inclusive** or **exclusive** of endpoints?

Example 1 Branch to PRINTRTN if FIELDA is between 4 and 9, inclusive of the endpoints. Otherwise, branch to BEGIN. A branch to PRINTRTN occurs if FIELDA is:

(a) = 4;

or

(b) is greater than 4 and less than 9
    (FIELDA > 4 and FIELDA < 9);

or

(c) = 9;

This can be simply stated as:

Branch to PRINTRTN if $4 \le \text{FIELDA} \le 9$

The term "inclusive of endpoints" indicates that the branch is to be performed if FIELDA is between the values 4 and 9, or equal to the values 4 or 9.
This can be programmed as

LABEL	OPERATION		OPERAND	COMMENTS	
1	10	16			72
	CLC		FIELDA,=C'4'		
	BL		BEGIN		
	CLC		FIELDA,=C'9'		
	BH		BEGIN		
	B		PRINTRTN		

The preceding causes a branch to BEGIN if FIELDA is less than 4 or more than 9. Thus, a branch to PRINTRTN will occur if FIELDA is between 4 and 9 inclusive. Note that there are several correct methods that may be used to code this problem. The following is also correct.

LABEL	OPERATION	OPERAND	COMMENTS
*		ALTERNATE METHOD FOR BRANCHING TO PRINTRTN	
*		IF FIELDA IS BETWEEN 4 AND 9 INCLUSIVE	
*			
	CLC	FIELDA,=C'4'	
	BNL	NEXTTEST	
	B	BEGIN	
NEXTTEST	CLC	FIELDA,=C'9'	
	BNH	PRINTRTN	
	B	BEGIN	

Example 2   Branch to PRINTRTN if FIELDA is between 4 and 9, *exclusive* of the endpoints. Otherwise, branch to BEGIN.

A branch to PRINTRTN is to occur if FIELDA:

(a) is greater than 4 (FIELDA > 4)

and

(b) is less than 9 (FIELDA < 9)

"Exclusive of endpoints" means not to branch if FIELDA equals 4 or 9, only if it is between these points.

This can be simply stated as

Branch to PRINTRTN if $4 <$ FIELDA < 9

One method of programming this is:

LABEL	OPERATION	OPERAND	COMMENTS
	CLC	FIELDA,=C'4'	
	BNH	BEGIN	BRANCH ON = OR LESS THAN 4
	CLC	FIELDA,=C'9'	
	BNL	BEGIN	BRANCH ON = OR GREATER THAN 9
	B	PRINTRTN	

The foregoing causes a branch to BEGIN if FIELDA is less than or equal to 4. A branch to BEGIN also occurs if FIELDA is greater than or equal to 9. Hence, a branch to PRINTRTN will occur if FIELDA is greater than 4 and less than 9. An alternate method of coding this is:

LABEL	OPERATION	OPERAND	COMMENTS
	CLC	FIELDA,=C'4'	
	BH	NEXTTEST	
	B	BEGIN	
NEXTTEST	CLC	FIELDA,=C'9'	
	BL	PRINTRTN	
	B	BEGIN	

Unless otherwise noted, the use of the term "between" in this text will mean *inclusive* of the endpoints. Hence, to branch to STEP1 if X is between 10 and 100 can be represented as:

If $10 \le X \le 100$ branch to STEP1.

Self-Evaluating Quiz

Indicate, in each of the following, the condition(s) that cause a branch to ERROR.

```
1.  CLC    IN,=C'1234'
    BNH    ERROR
    B      STEP1
2.  CLC    OUT,=C'222'
    BL     STEP5
    B      ERROR
3.  CLC    FLDA,=C'236'
    BL     STEP2
    CLC    FLDA,=C'923'
    BH     STEP6
    B      ERROR
4.  CLC    FLDB,=C'ABC'
    B      STEP2
    BH     ERROR
```

SOLUTIONS

1. A branch to ERROR occurs when IN is less than or equal to 1234 (≤ 1234).
2. A branch to ERROR occurs when OUT is greater than or equal to 222 (≥ 222).
3. A branch to ERROR occurs when FLDA is between 236 and 923, inclusive ($236 \le$ FLDA ≤ 923).
4. A branch to ERROR *never* occurs; unconditional branch to STEP2 *precedes* the branch on condition and, hence, the computer automatically transfers control to STEP2, regardless of the comparison. Such programming is normally invalid.

VI. COMPARE LOGICAL IMMEDIATE (CLI)

Instruction:	CLI
Meaning:	Compare logical immediate
Operand 1:	Storage area
Operand 2:	One-byte constant expressed in zoned-decimal, hexadecimal, or binary form
	Note *No* = sign precedes the constant.
Result:	Condition codes are set depending upon how Operand 1 compares to Operand 2.
Limitations:	Only a *one*-byte comparison can be made.

Branches coded immediately after a CLI instruction will be executed as follows.

TYPES OF BRANCHES THAT CAN
BE EXECUTED FOLLOWING CLI

Op Code	Instruction	Meaning
BE	Branch equal	Branch if Operand 1 of CLI Instruction = Operand 2
BH	Branch high	Operand 1 > Operand 2
BL	Branch low	Operand 1 < Operand 2
BNE	Branch not equal	Operand 1 ≠ Operand 2
BNH	Branch not high	Operand 1 = Operand 2, or Operand 1 < Operand 2
BNL	Branch not low	Operand 1 = Operand 2, or Operand 1 > Operand 2

Example 1

LABEL	OPERATION	OPERAND	COMMENTS
	CLI	CTR,C'Ø'	
	BH	ERR	

Comparison: | 5 | 1 | 2 | | 0 |

⌐CTR   Operand 2

Only the high-order byte is compared. A branch to ERR will occur because 5 > 0.

Example 2

LABEL	OPERATION	OPERAND	COMMENTS
	CLI	RECIN+79,C'Z'	
	BE	NEXT	

| | | ... | Z | | Z |

↑   ↑
RECIN   RECIN+79   Operand 2

Only one byte is compared. A branch to NEXT will occur.

Example 3

LABEL	OPERATION	OPERAND	COMMENTS
	CLI	CTR,B'11000001'	
	BE	STEP1	

Note that 11000001 is equivalent to hex C1, which is an A in EBCDIC.

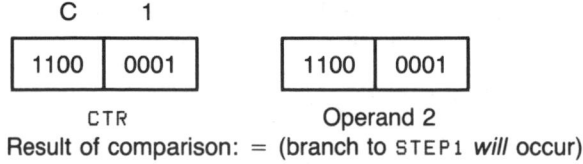

C   1
| 1100 | 0001 | | 1100 | 0001 |

CTR   Operand 2
Result of comparison: = (branch to STEP1 *will* occur)

```
*                                                                        *
*                                         HOUSEKEEPING INSTRUCTIONS GO HERE    *
*                                                                        *
           MVC    OUTAREA,SPACES
           MVC    OUTAREA+20(15),=C'LIST OF FEMALES'
           PUT    OUTFILE,OUTAREA
           MVC    OUTAREA,SPACES
           MVC    FNAME(10),=C'FIRST NAME'
           MVC    LNAME(9),=C'LAST NAME'
           PUT    OUTFILE,OUTAREA
READ       MVC    OUTAREA,SPACES
           GET    INFILE,RECORD
           CLI    CODE,C'2'
           BE     READ
           MVC    LNAME,LAST
           MVC    FNAME,FIRST
           PUT    OUTFILE,OUTAREA
           B      READ
*                                                                        *
*                                         HOUSEKEEPING INSTRUCTIONS GO HERE    *
*                                         ALONG WITH DCB OR DTF MACROS         *
*                                                                        *
RECORD     DS     0CL80
LAST       DS     CL15
FIRST      DS     CL10
CODE       DS     CL1
           DS     CL54
SPACES     DC     CL1' '
OUTAREA    DS     0CL132
           DS     CL5
FNAME      DS     CL10
           DS     CL20
LNAME      DS     CL15
           DS     CL82
           END
```

Figure 6.4
Program to print only the names of females in a file.

Figure 6.4 illustrates a program that reads in records and prints out only the names of the females. A female has a 1 in column 26; a male has a code of 2.

CHAPTER SUMMARY

1. Simple Relational
   A. Types of relations.
      Compare Operand 1 to Operand 2
      The following branches can be executed:
      1. BE   Branch equal
      2. BNE   Branch not equal ($<$ or $>$)
      3. BL   Branch low
      4. BH   Branch high
      5. BNL   Branch not low ($\geq$)
      6. BNH   Branch not high ($\leq$)

   B. If the comparison results in a condition that is met, a branch occurs; otherwise, the next sequential step is executed.

   C. The EBCDIC collating sequence is used for comparison.
      High
            numbers
            uppercase letters
            lowercase letters
            special characters
      Low

II. Types of Logical Control Procedures
    A. Sequence

    B. Selection

    C. Iteration

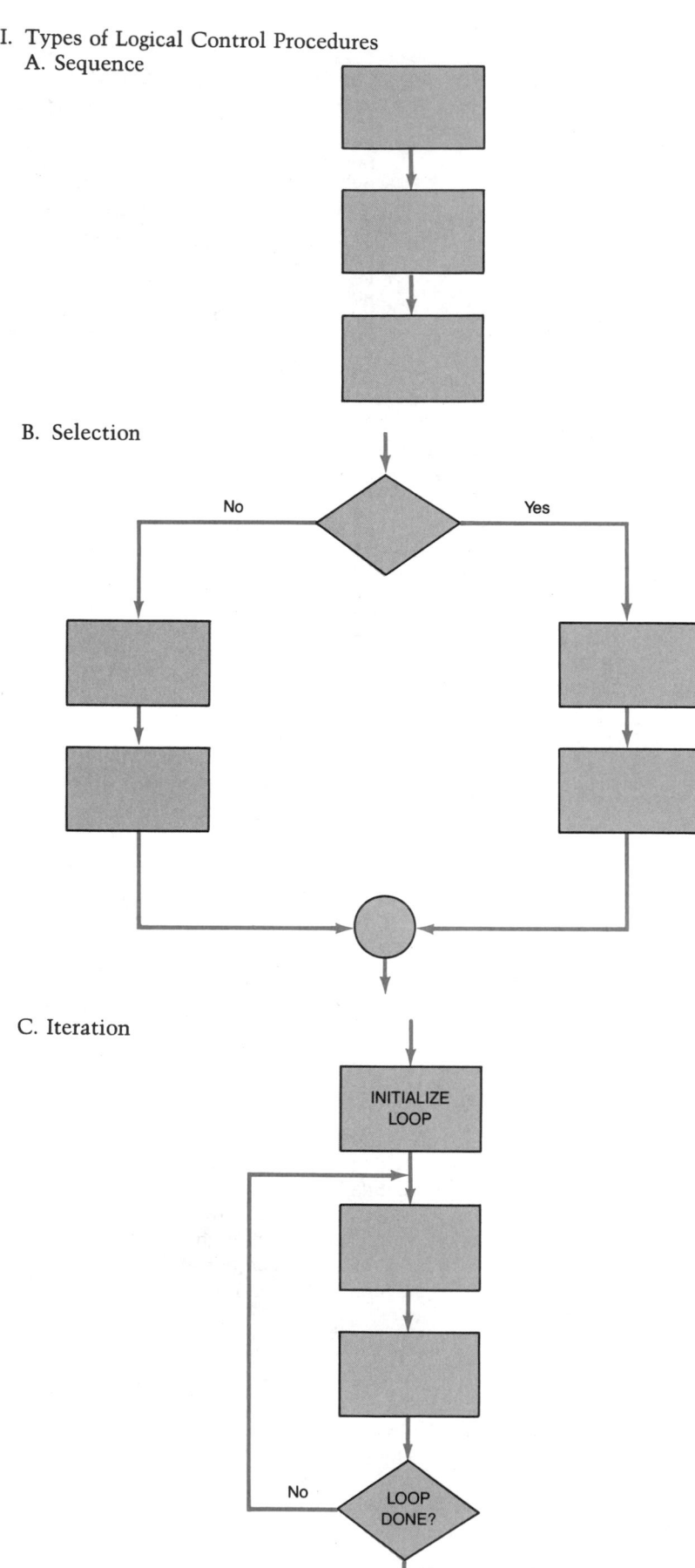

Iteration is used for looping.

CHAPTER SELF-EVALUATING QUIZ

1. A compare instruction automatically sets a(n) _____ code.
2. (T or F) The CLC instruction is most commonly used with data in EBCDIC form.
3. If FLDA contains −9 and FLDB contains +9, the instruction CLC FLDA, FLDB will result in the condition code being set to (high/low/equal).
4. (T or F) The CLC instruction is best used for alphanumeric comparisons and comparisons of signed numbers.
5. (T or F) The following two sets of instructions are equivalent.

     a.
     ```
     CLC   FLDA,FLDB
     BNH   RTN1
     B     RTN2
     ```

     b.
     ```
     CLC   FLDA,FLDB
     BL    RTN1
     B     RTN2
     ```

6. The CLI instruction may be used to compare up to (no.) bytes of data.
7. Determine the values of AMT1, AMT2 and AMT3 after execution of the following instructions. The three fields have the following values before execution.

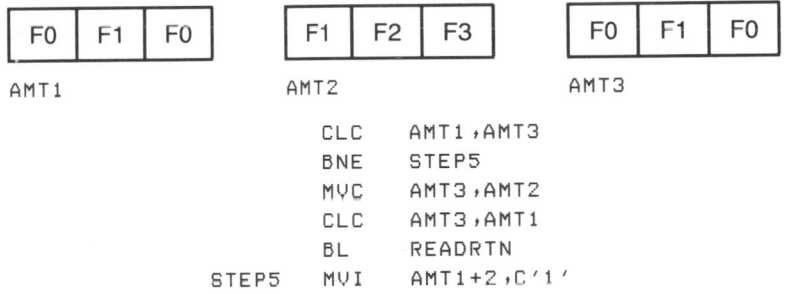

| F0 | F1 | F0 | | F1 | F2 | F3 | | F0 | F1 | F0 |
AMT1   AMT2   AMT3

```
          CLC   AMT1,AMT3
          BNE   STEP5
          MVC   AMT3,AMT2
          CLC   AMT3,AMT1
          BL    READRTN
STEP5     MVI   AMT1+2,C'1'
```

8. Code a routine to branch to PRINT if a field called WEIGHT is between 110 and 125 pounds. Otherwise, branch to READRTN. Assume WEIGHT is defined as follows:

```
WEIGHT   DS   CL3
```

9. Code a routine to branch to PRINT for input records that contain data on blue-eyed, blonde females. Otherwise, branch to READRTN. Records have the following format:

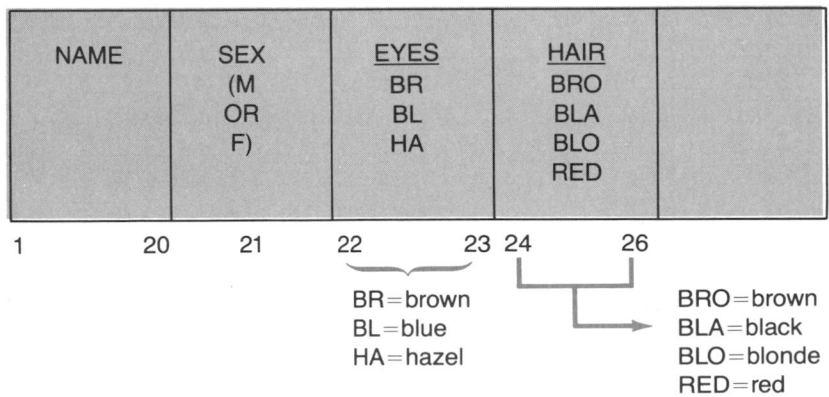

| NAME | SEX (M OR F) | EYES BR BL HA | HAIR BRO BLA BLO RED | |

1   20 21   22   23 24   26

```
BR=brown
BL=blue
HA=hazel

BRO=brown
BLA=black
BLO=blonde
RED=red
```

10. Code a routine to branch to TOTALRTN for insurance records representing male, New York State residents between 18 and 25 years old. Otherwise, branch to READRTN. The input format follows.

NAME	SEX (M OR F)	STATE (NY NJ MA ⋮)	AGE (IN YRS)	

1   20 21 22   23 24   25 26   80

SOLUTIONS

Page

1. Condition   136
2. T   137
3. High (D9 > C9)   141
4. F: (*un*signed numbers and alphanumeric data)   141
5. F: for (a), a branch to RTN2 occurs if FLDA is greater than FLDB, whereas in (b), a branch to RTN2 occurs if FLDA is greater than *or equal* to FLDB.   144
6. one   153
7.

F0	F1	F1

AMT1

F1	F2	F3

AMT2

F1	F2	F3

AMT3   144

8.   151

```
        LABEL      OPERATION   OPERAND                                    COMMENTS
1                  10          16                                                            72
                   CLC         WEIGHT,=C'11Ø'
                   BNL         NEXTTEST
                   B           READRTN
NEXTTEST           CLC         WEIGHT,=C'125'
                   BNH         PRINT
                   B           READRTN
*
*                  NOTE: WE ASSUMED THAT 'BETWEEN' MEANT INCLUSIVE
```

9.   149

```
        LABEL      OPERATION   OPERAND                                    COMMENTS
1                  10          16                                                            72
READRTN            GET         INAREA,RECORD
                   CLC         SEX,=C'F'
                   BNE         READRTN
                   CLC         EYES,=C'BL'
                   BNE         READRTN
                   CLC         HAIR,=C'BLO'
                   BNE         READRTN
                   B           PRINT
*
RECORD             DS          ØCL8Ø
NAME               DS          CL2Ø
SEX                DS          CL1
EYES               DS          CL2
HAIR               DS          CL3
                   DS          CL54
```

LABEL	OPERATION	OPERAND	COMMENTS
1	10	16	72
READRTN	GET	INAREA,RECORD	
	CLC	TESTAREA,=C'FBLBLO'	COMPARE SEX,EYES,HAIR AS A GROUP
	BNE	READRTN	
	B	PRINT	
*			
RECORD	DS	0CL80	
NAME	DS	CL20	
TESTAREA	DS	CL6	
	DS	CL54	

10.   151

LABEL	OPERATION	OPERAND	COMMENTS
1	10	16	72
READRTN	GET	INAREA,RECORD	
	CLC	SEX,=C'M'	
	BNE	READRTN	
	CLC	STATE,=C'NY'	
	BNE	READRTN	
	CLC	AGE,=C'18'	
	BL	READRTN	
	CLC	AGE,=C'25'	
	BH	READRTN	
	B	TOTALRTN	
*			
RECORD	DS	0CL80	
NAME	DS	CL20	
SEX	DS	CL1	
STATE	DS	CL2	
AGE	DS	CL2	
	DS	CL55	

PRACTICE PROGRAM

Consider the problem definition in Figure 6.5. Write a program to list the names and salaries of those people who earn over $15,000. See Figure 6.6 for a solution.

KEY TERMS

Abend	Label
Branching	Loop
Condition code	Program flowchart
Conditional branch	Pseudocode
Exclusive comparison	Routine
Inclusive comparison	Simple conditional
Iteration	Unconditional branch

a. Input Record Layout

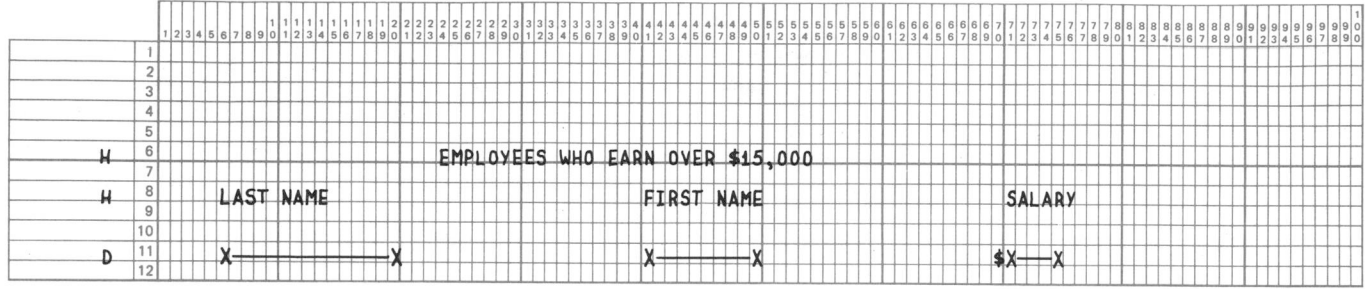

LAST NAME	FIRST NAME	SALARY	
1	15 16	25 26	30 31	80

b. Printer Spacing Chart for Printed Output

```
H          EMPLOYEES WHO EARN OVER $15,000
H    LAST NAME                FIRST NAME                SALARY
D    X————————X              X———————X                $X——X
```

c. Sample Input Data

```
BAGLEY        JOAN        14750
BREWSTER      WESLEY      38950
JOHNSON       SUSAN       21500
MARTIN        HAROLD      13925
WILLIAMS      JAMES       27950
```

d. Sample Output

```
                    EMPLOYEES WHO EARN OVER $15,000

LAST NAME                    FIRST NAME                SALARY

BREWSTER                     WESLEY                    $38950
JOHNSON                      SUSAN                     $21500
WILLIAMS                     JAMES                     $27950
```

Figure 6.5
Problem definition for the Practice Program.

REVIEW QUESTIONS

State whether FIELDA is equal to, less than or greater than FIELDB.

	FIELDA	FIELDB
1.	012	12ƀ
2.	120	12ƀ
3.	−89	+89
4.	ABC	ABCƀ
5.	43	+43

Note
The comparison is performed as follows:

```
CLC    FIELDA,FIELDB
```

Convert each of the above to EBCDIC form to determine the answer.

6. Write a routine to branch to NOTEMP if C is between 98 and 100, inclusive.
7. Write a routine to branch to NOTEMP is C is between 98 and 100, exclusive.
8. For each of the following, indicate:
   a. The condition code setting.
   b. Number of bytes actually compared.
   c. If the branch occurs.

```
*                                                           *
*                           HOUSEKEEPING INSTRUCTIONS GO HERE  *
*                                                           *
        MVC    OUTAREA,SPACES
        MVC    OUTAREA+23(31),=C'EMPLOYEES WHO EARN OVER $15,000'
        PUT    OUTFILE,OUTAREA
        MVC    OUTAREA,SPACES
        PUT    OUTFILE,OUTAREA          PRINT BLANK LINE
        MVC    LNAME(9),=C'LAST NAME'
        MVC    FNAME(10),=C'FIRST NAME'
        MVC    SALOUT(6),=C'SALARY'
        PUT    OUTFILE,OUTAREA
        MVC    OUTAREA,SPACES
        PUT    OUTFILE,OUTAREA          PRINT BLANK LINE
READ    MVC    OUTAREA,SPACES
        GET    INFILE,RECORD
        CLC    SALARY,=C'15000'
        BNH    READ
        MVC    LNAME,LAST
        MVC    FNAME,FIRST
        MVC    SALOUT,SALARY
        MVI    SALOUT-1,C'$'
        PUT    OUTFILE,OUTAREA
        B      READ
*                                                           *
*                           HOUSEKEEPING INSTRUCTIONS GO HERE  *
*                           ALONG WITH DCB OR DTF MACROS       *
*                                                           *
RECORD  DS     0CL80                    INPUT FORMAT
LAST    DS     CL15                        *
FIRST   DS     CL10                        *
SALARY  DS     CL5                         *
        DS     CL50                        *
SPACES  DC     CL1' '
OUTAREA DS     0CL132                   PRINT FORMAT
        DS     CL5                         *
LNAME   DS     CL15                        *
        DS     CL20                        *
FNAME   DS     CL10                        *
        DS     CL20                        *
SALOUT  DS     CL5                         *
        DS     CL57                        *
        END
```

Figure 6.6 Solution to the Practice Program.

The contents of each data field are specified as follows.

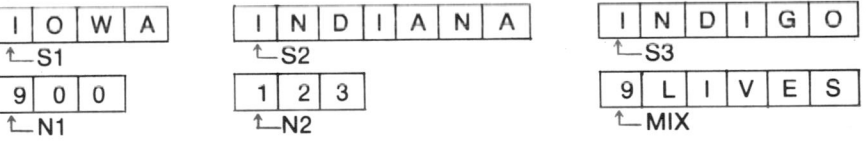

	Coding	Condition	Number of Bytes Compared	Does Branch Occur?
a.	CLC MIX(1),N1			
	BNH RTNA			
b.	CLC N1,MIX			
	BNH RTN7			
c.	CLC S1,N1			
	BNE RTN8			
d.	CLC S2,N2			
	BNE RTNB			
e.	CLC S3,N1			
	BNH RTNC			

9. Write a routine to read in 3 numbers in each input record. Print the largest of these numbers from each record.

10. Code a program excerpt to perform the following pseudocode procedure.

```
IF  A < B
    MOVE A TO OUTPUT
ELSE
    MOVE B TO OUTPUT
ENDIF
WRITE OUTPUT
```

DEBUGGING EXERCISES

The following program excerpt checks the quantity-on-hand (QOH) of an inventory system. If the quantity on hand is greater than the minimum and less than or equal to the maximum, then no action is taken and the program branches to CLEAR. However, if QOH > MAX, then branch to SURPLUS, or if QOH <= MIN then proceed to REORDER. Note the length of MIN is less than QOH, but by referring to PAD a 4-byte field may be accessed. Identify the errors, if any in this program.

```
******************************************************************
*          D E B U G   P R O G R A M     C H A P T E R   6
******************************************************************
CLEAR      MVC    LINEOUT,SPACES
READ       GET    INFILE,RECORD
           CLC    QOH,MAX             QOH DENOTES QUANTITY ON HAND
           BH     SURPLUS
NEXTEST    CLC    MIN,QOH
           BH     CLEAR
REORDER    MVC    LINEOUT+10(80),RECORD
             .
             .
             .
RECORD     DS     CL80
PARTNO     DS     CL5
DESCR      DS     CL20
PAD        DS     CL1
MIN        DS     CL3
MAX        DS     CL4
QOH        DS     CL4
           DS     CL43
*
SPACES     DC     X'40'
LINEOUT    DS     CL133
```

SOLUTIONS

1. RECORD is to be subdivided.

```
RECORD   DS   0CL80
```

2. Note that a zero should be moved to PAD, the byte that precedes MIN, so a comparison can be made of two 4-byte fields. Also note that the second branch should be BL CLEAR.

```
         BH     SURPLUS
         MVI    PAD,C'0'
TEST     CLC    PAD(4),QOH
         BL     CLEAR
```

3. Note that the following is incorrect

```
         BH       REORDER
REORDER  MVC
```

because the program proceeds to REORDER under all circumstances.

PROGRAMMING ASSIGNMENTS

1. Consider the following record format.

LAST NAME	FIRST NAME	CODE 1=FEMALE 2=MALE	SALARY (integers)	WEIGHT (in pounds)	HEIGHT (in inches)	

| 1 | 15 16 | 25 26 | 27 | 31 32 | 34 35 | 36 |

Print the names of all
a. males taller than 6 feet (72 inches) and weighing more than 200 pounds. Also print the message 'RUGGED'.
b. females weighing between 105 and 125 pounds and between 60 inches and 67 inches. Also print the message 'JUST RIGHT'.

2. Write a program to read in records as shown and print the smallest of the three numbers in each record.

NO1	NO2	NO3	

| 1 | 3 4 | 6 7 | 9 |

3. Write a program to print out patient name and diagnosis for each of the following input medical records:

    1–20 Patient name
    21 Lung infection   1—if found
                                       0–if not found
    22 Temperature   1–high
                                         0—normal
    23 Sniffles   1–present
                                         0–absent
    24 Sore throat   1–present
                                         0–absent
    25–80 Not used

    Notes
    a. Output is a printed report with heading DIAGNOSIS REPORT.
    b. If the patient has lung infection and temperature, diagnosis is PNEUMONIA.
    c. If the patient has a combination of two or more symptoms (except the combination of lung infection and temperature), the diagnosis is COLD.
    d. If the patient has any single abnormal symptom, the diagnosis is PHONY.
    e. If the patient has no symptoms, the diagnosis is HEALTHY.

    HINT
    Compare the symptoms in pairs. For example, if CLC SYMPT,=C'11' then branch to PNEURTN.

4. Consider the following input records.

    Record 1

      1–5   ITEM NUMBER
    11–15 DESCRIPTION
    21–25 UNIT COST
    26–28 UNIT OF ISSUE
              EA/BOX/CTN/CSE
    75–76 MONTH OF PURCHASE
    77–78 DAY OF PURCHASE
    79–80 YEAR OF PURCHASE

    Record 2

      1–5   Not Used
    31–33 MINIMUM
    34–36 MAXIMUM
    37–39 QTY ON HAND
    75–80 Same as record 1

An inventory exception report is to be generated when the balance is less than or equal to the minimum or greater than the maximum. The output must contain a heading, column titles, and the message "REORDER" or "OVERSUPPLY," as illustrated in the following sample output.

```
INVENTORY EXCEPTION REPORT

DATE OF                 ITEM                    QUANTITY
PURCHASE    ITEM NO.    DESCRIPTION   PROBLEM   ON HAND    UNITS

02/01/86    12343       WIDGET        REORDER     100      CTN

03/01/86    67812       POOL TABLE    OVERSUPPLY  250      EA
```

Remember, to save an input record it must be moved to another area because the following record overlays the first.

 # Introduction to Decimal Arithmetic Operations

To familiarize you with:
1. *The basic arithmetic operations of addition and subtraction.*
2. *The use of counters in programs.*
3. *The concept of program looping.*
4. *The ways signed numbers may be prepared for printing.*

I. AN OVERVIEW OF BASIC ARITHMETIC

A. Requirements of Storage-to-Storage Arithmetic Operations

Up to this point, our processing has been limited simply to moving data from one location in storage to another, and comparing fields in character form. In this chapter we will consider simple arithmetic operations.

Input data, as we already know, is typically entered in **EBCDIC** or **zoned-decimal format,** and as such cannot be used as is for calculations. To carry out storage-to-storage arithmetic, numeric data must be converted to a form called packed decimal. You will recall that packed-decimal data uses less storage than the conventional zoned-decimal format.

Input data fields must, then, be converted to the **packed-decimal format** by a PACK instruction before it can be used in an arithmetic operation. That is, we assume that numeric fields entered in the zoned-decimal format must be packed first. Note that numeric fields should *not* contain blanks. Blank characters are invalid in numeric data fields. When blanks are packed and later used in arithmetic operations, a **data exception** will occur causing the program to reach an **abend** or *ab*normal *end* condition. Programmers frequently say that a program that reached an abend condition has "bombed" or "hung up."

B. Review of Packed-Data Format

We will now briefly review the packed-data format. A 5–digit number is stored internally in unpacked and packed format as follows:

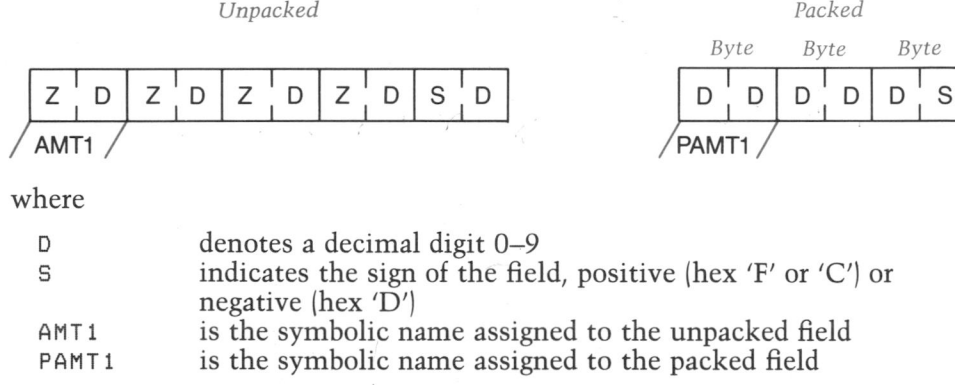

where

D	denotes a decimal digit 0–9
S	indicates the sign of the field, positive (hex 'F' or 'C') or negative (hex 'D')
AMT1	is the symbolic name assigned to the unpacked field
PAMT1	is the symbolic name assigned to the packed field

You will recall that two decimal digits are packed into each byte, except for the low-order byte that contains the sign and one digit. To convert EBCDIC input data to this packed-decimal format, a PACK instruction is used. For example, if card data was read into an area named RECIN, and the first five positions contained the number 12345, the data would be read into the computer and stored in zoned-decimal format as follows:

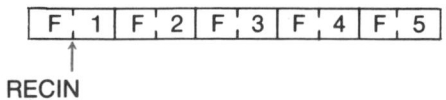

For this data to be used in decimal arithmetic calculations, it must be packed. It would then be represented as follows:

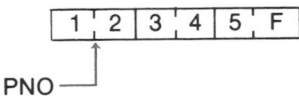

We will now examine the PACK instruction.

Operation 10	Operand 16
PACK	OP1,OP2

Instruction: PACK

Meaning: Before an arithmetic operation can be performed, numeric fields must be in packed format.

Operands: The second operand is packed into the first operand.

Result: In the first operand.

Length: Determined by the first operand, which can be implicit or explicit.
Maximum length—16 bytes.

Limitation:
1. When constants are used in arithmetic operations, they must be in packed-decimal format.
2. Zoned-decimal data that is to be packed should not contain any blanks, or other non-numeric data.

A. Format

Before *any* arithmetic operation can be performed in assembler language, numeric fields must be **packed**. All assembler instructions reference the leftmost or high-order position of each operand. The actual execution of the PACK instruction, however, proceeds from *right* to *left* within the operands.

The PACK instruction converts EBCDIC or zoned-decimal data from the second operand, the sending field, into packed data in the first operand, the receiving field. It is a storage-to-storage instruction, which means that both operands are storage addresses; that is, neither indicates a general register.

Example 7.1

	LABEL	OPERATION 10 16	OPERAND	COMMENTS	72
1		PACK	PNO,ZDNO		

Before

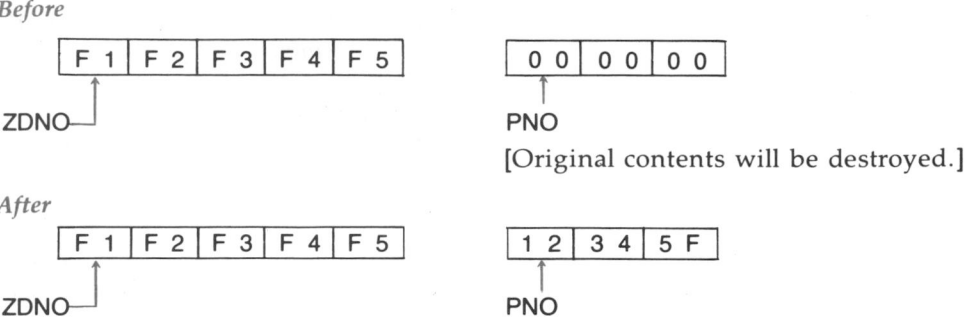

ZDNO would be defined as a character or zoned-decimal field.

LABEL	OPERATION	OPERAND	COMMENTS	
1	10	16		72
ZDNO	DS	CL5 THE VALUE '12345' IS ENTERED BY SOME INSTRUCTION		
*				
*	ZDNO	COULD ALSO BE DEFINED AS FOLLOWS:		
*				
ZDNO	DC	CL5'12345'		

PNO would be defined as a packed field.

LABEL	OPERATION	OPERAND	COMMENTS	
1	10	16		72
PNO	DS	PL3 THE VALUE 'Ø' IS ENTERED BY SOME INSTRUCTION		

PNO could also be defined as follows:

LABEL	OPERATION	OPERAND	COMMENTS	
1	10	16		72
PNO	DC	PL3'Ø'		

The zoned-decimal data in the second operand is packed into the first operand by proceeding one byte at a time from right to left in the step sequence indicated.

Unlike an MVC, for example, the operation proceeds from right to left. That is, F5 is converted to 5F first, then F4 and F3 are placed in the second byte as 34, and so on. The sign and digits are moved from the second operand (sending field) to the first operand (receiving field) and are *not* checked for validity. This is why the packing of blanks or spaces (hex 40) can result in an invalid sign digit. An illustration follows of what happens if there is a blank in the low-order byte of a field that is packed.

Invalid Operand

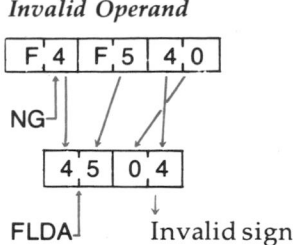

If FLDA were to be used later for decimal arithmetic, a data exception would occur because the sign (4) is invalid. The sign of a packed field must be an F or C for +, or D for −.

B. Implicit Pack

The maximum length for either operand in a PACK instruction is 16 bytes. When a length is not explicitly specified, the length of the first operand determines the length of the pack operation. The previously discussed example 7.1 illustrates an **implicit pack** where the receiving field determines the length of the pack.

C. Explicit Pack

The length may be **explicitly** stated in one or both operands as

LABEL	OPERATION 10	16	OPERAND	COMMENTS	72
	PACK		PNO(3),ZDNO		

or

LABEL	OPERATION 10	16	OPERAND	COMMENTS	72
	PACK		PNO(3),ZDNO(5)		

and the result would be identical to that shown in Example 7.1.

We will now analyze the results when the receiving field in a PACK instruction is either larger or smaller than necessary.

D. Sizing the Fields

1. What if the Receiving Field is Larger Than Necessary for Storing Packed Results?

Example 7.2

LABEL	OPERATION 10	16	OPERAND	COMMENTS	72
	PACK		SAME,NO		

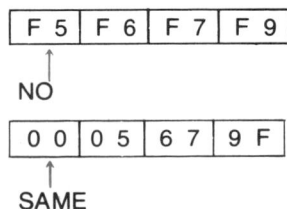

When packing a 4-byte field into a 4-byte area, the high-order positions of the receiving field are filled with zeros. The following example again illustrates a PACK instruction where the receiving field, Operand 1, is larger than necessary.

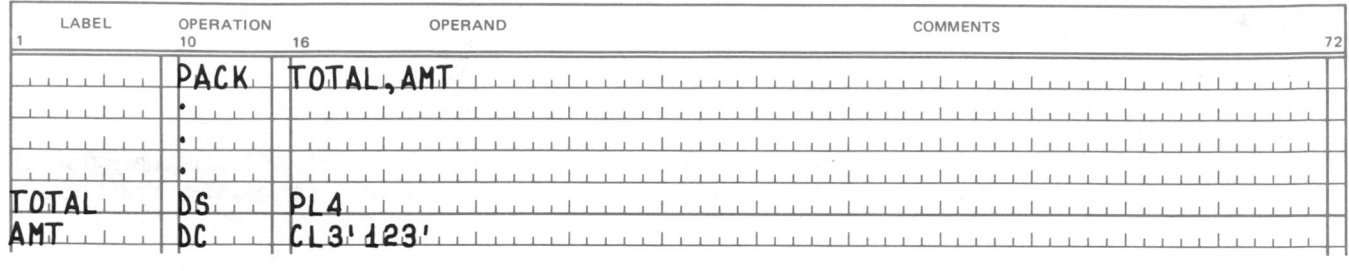

Note that a field may be packed into itself, as in the following:

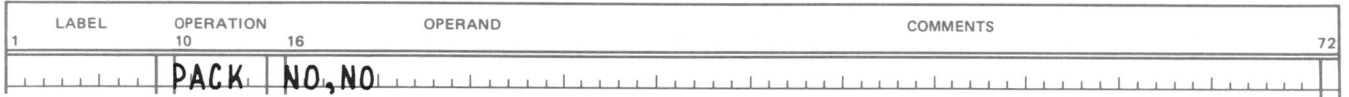

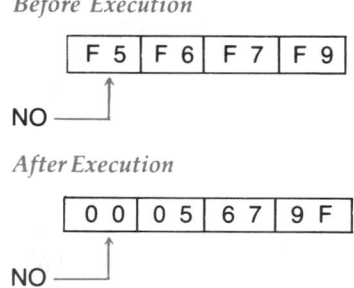

By packing a field into itself, the programmer need not establish an additional storage area for the packed results. If, however, the original EBCDIC format of the data is necessary for printing, it should be moved to the output area *before* it is packed.

> NOTE: Packed data, if inadvertently printed, will not be in a readable form.

2. What if the Receiving Field is Smaller Than Necessary for Storing Packed Results?

If the receiving field is too small to contain the packed data, the high-order positions are **truncated**.

LABEL	OPERATION	OPERAND	COMMENTS
	PACK	SMALL,BIG	

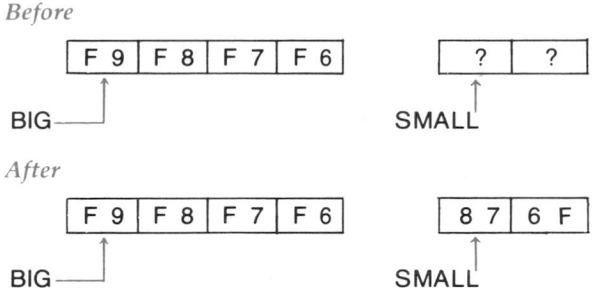

To accommodate the entire result, the length of a packed field may be calculated as follows.

$$\text{Packed length} = \frac{\text{length in zoned–decimal}}{2} + 1$$

For the preceding illustration, SMALL must be at least 3 bytes long:

$$\frac{4}{2} + 1 = 3$$

When the zoned-decimal field contains an odd number of digits, the packed length based on the formula will not be a whole number. For example,

Length in zoned-decimal = 3

$$\text{Packed length} = \frac{3}{2} + 1 = 2.5$$

In such cases, the packed length is computed as the whole number, *without* the fractional part. In the foregoing case, the packed length would be 2.

3. Relative Addressing with Packed Fields

Consider the following PACK instruction.

PACK   CKDIGIT,ZD + 4(1)

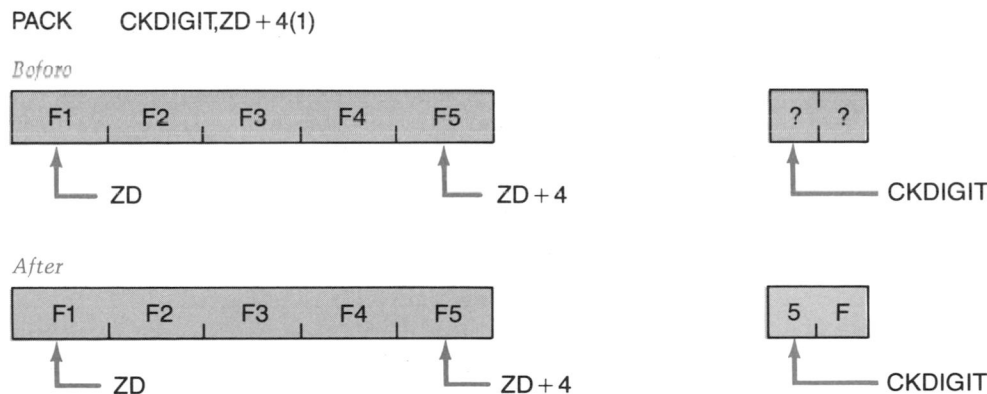

Relative addressing has many pitfalls and should be approached carefully. This example presents the valid use of relative addressing. If a length of one (1) byte in the second operand was not explicitly coded, then the system would have assumed a length of 5 bytes, the length of ZD. Packing would have begun in ZD+9, thereby producing incorrect results.

E. Packed Constants

Data may be established in storage in packed format for use in arithmetic operations. The following illustrate the packed format.

1. Constants Defined with Implicit Lengths

LABEL	OPERATION	OPERAND	COMMENTS
AMT1	DC	P'Ø25'	
AMT2	DC	P'-246'	

Field

0 2	5	C

2 4	6	D

2. Constants Defined with Explicit Lengths

LABEL	OPERATION	OPERAND	COMMENTS
AMT3	DC	PL2'Ø25'	
AMT4	DC	PL3'Ø25'	RESULT: HIGH-ORDER Ø'S
AMT5	DC	PL3'4732687'	RESULT: TRUNCATION

Field

0 2	5	C

0 0	0 2	5	C

3 2	6 8	7	C

SUMMARY OF PACK INSTRUCTION

1. The second operand contains zoned-decimal numbers to be packed and stored in the first operand.
2. Each operand is referenced by the symbolic name assigned to its high-order position.
3. The operands are processed one byte at a time, from right to left.
4. The maximum size of either operand is 16 bytes.
5. The number of digits packed depends on the first operand that may be explicitly or implicitly defined.
6. If the first operand is too long, high-order zeros will be inserted.
7. If the first operand is too short, high-order digits in the second operand will be truncated.
8. Fields are not checked for valid sign or digit representation during the pack operation.
9. A field may be packed into itself.

Self-Evaluating Quiz

1. To perform decimal arithmetic, the data must be in **(no.)** form.
2. Only _____ are permitted in fields that are going to be packed.
3. The sign in a packed-data field is located in the rightmost position of the **(low/high)**-order byte.
4. A zoned-decimal field of 7 bytes could be stored in an area of **(no.)** bytes in length when packed.
5. A pack instruction is of what type?
6. (T or F) Once a field is packed, it may again be packed to save storage.
7. The zoned-decimal data that is to be packed appears in the **(first/second)** operand.
8. The length of the pack operation is dependent upon the **(first/second)** operand.
9. (T or F) The length of the pack may be explicitly or implicitly defined.
10. (T or F) When an invalid sign is generated in the packed field, the programmer is notified by an error message and a program interrupt.
11. If the first operand of a PACK instruction contained 2 bytes and the second operand contained the number 1234 in zoned-decimal format, the result produced would be _____ .
12. When the first operand is larger than the second, the high-order position(s) of the field is/are filled with **(spaces/zeros/nothing)**.
13. (T or F) In executing a PACK instruction, the operation proceeds from left to right.
14. Indicate the results in each of the following.

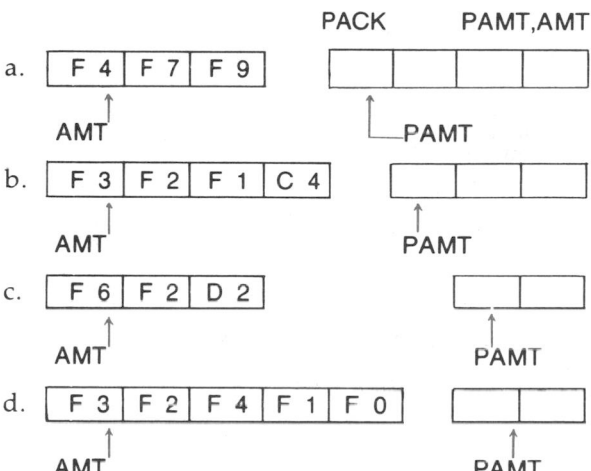

SOLUTIONS

1. Packed-decimal
2. Digits 0–9, along with a sign (no blanks or special characters)
3. Low
4. 4
5. Storage-to-storage (SS)
6. F
7. Second
8. First
9. T
10. F: the sign is not checked; however, an arithmetic operation performed on a field with an invalid sign will cause a program interrupt.
11. 234F; truncation will occur.
12. Zeros
13. F: right to left

14.

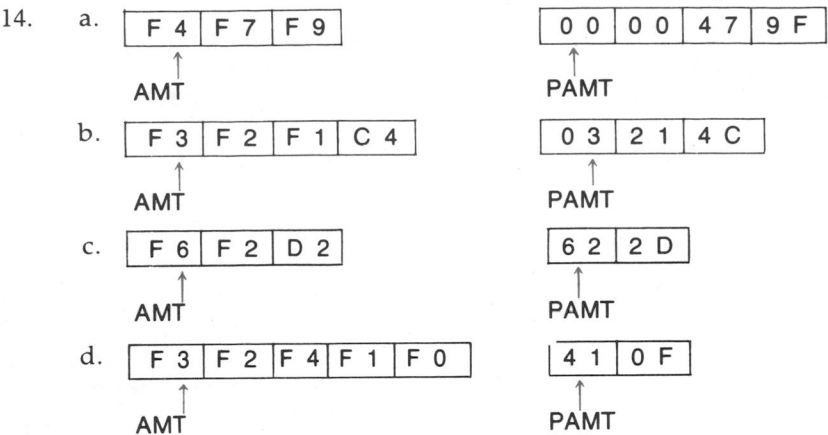

a. | F 4 | F 7 | F 9 | AMT | 0 0 | 0 0 | 4 7 | 9 F | PAMT

b. | F 3 | F 2 | F 1 | C 4 | AMT | 0 3 | 2 1 | 4 C | PAMT

c. | F 6 | F 2 | D 2 | AMT | 6 2 | 2 D | PAMT

d. | F 3 | F 2 | F 4 | F 1 | F 0 | AMT | 4 1 | 0 F | PAMT

III. DECIMAL ADDITION: THE ADD PACKED INSTRUCTION (AP)

A. Format

Operation 10	Operand 16
AP	OP1,OP2

ADD PACKED

Instruction:	AP
Meaning:	Add Packed decimal numbers
Operands:	Second operand added to first; second operand can be literal of form: =P' '
Result:	In first operand; second operand unchanged (second operand may be self-defining)
Lengths:	Both fields may be implicit or explicit; 16-byte limit
Limitation:	Make certain receiving field is large enough for answer

---

The Add Packed instruction is a storage-to-storage instruction that adds *two packed-decimal fields*. The contents of the second operand are added to the contents of the first operand one byte at a time from right to left, that is, from low-order to high-order. The result of the addition is placed in the first operand. An example of the Add Packed (AP) instruction is:

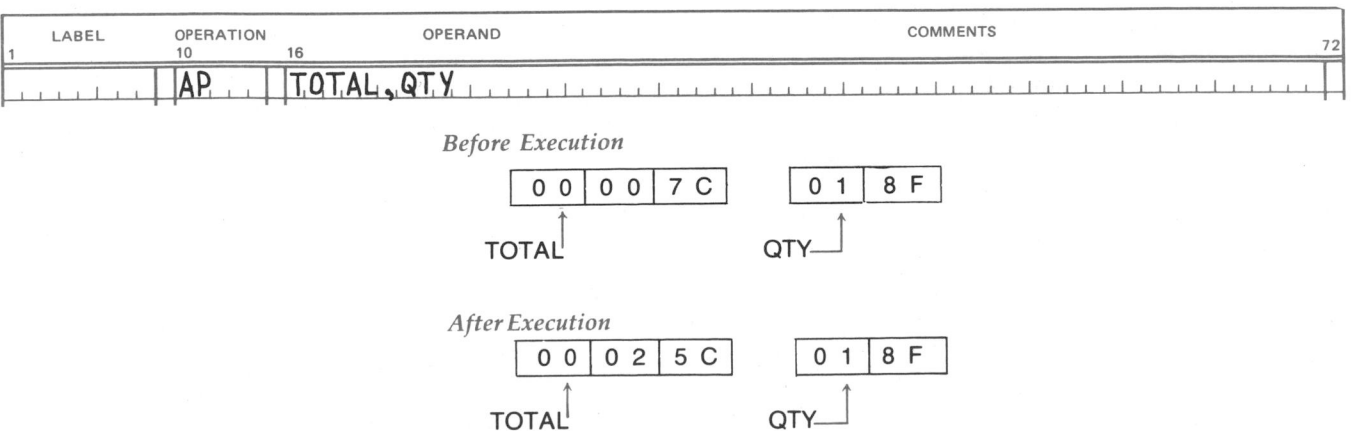

LABEL	OPERATION 10 16	OPERAND	COMMENTS 72
	AP	TOTAL,QTY	

Before Execution

| 0 0 | 0 0 | 7 C | | 0 1 | 8 F |

TOTAL   QTY

After Execution

| 0 0 | 0 2 | 5 C | | 0 1 | 8 F |

TOTAL   QTY

In this example, the first operand (TOTAL) is larger than the second (QTY) and the high-order positions (TOTAL) are filled with zeros. The first operand must always contain enough bytes to hold the largest result anticipated by the programmer.

THE AP INSTRUCTION FOLLOWS
THE NORMAL RULES OF ADDITION

1. If both operands are signed positive (C or F), or both are signed negative (D), addition is performed and the corresponding sign, C or D, is placed in the field. The CPU changes the sign of a positive field from a hex F to a hex C whenever decimal arithmetic operations are performed. The sign of a negative field is represented by a hex D.
2. If one operand is signed positive (C or F) and the other is signed negative, (D), subtraction is performed and the sign of the larger (C or D) is placed in the field.

    Example: $+15 + (-10) = 15 - 10 = +5$

B. Examples

LABEL	OPERATION	OPERAND	COMMENTS
	AP	PAMT1,PAMT2	

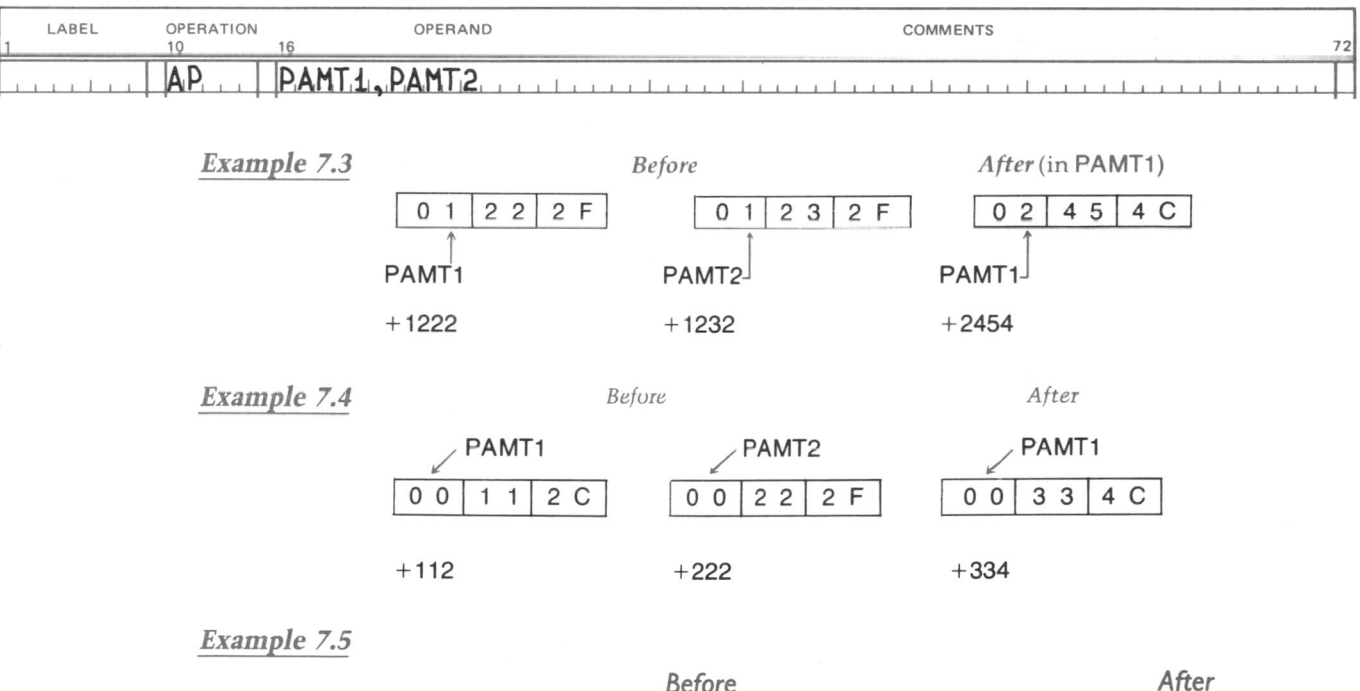

Example 7.3

Before

PAMT1: 0 1 2 2 2 F → PAMT1 +1222

PAMT2: 0 1 2 3 2 F → PAMT2 +1232

After (in PAMT1)

0 2 4 5 4 C → PAMT1 +2454

Example 7.4

Before

PAMT1: 0 0 1 1 2 C +112

PAMT2: 0 0 2 2 2 F +222

After

PAMT1: 0 0 3 3 4 C +334

Example 7.5

Before

PAMT1: 0 0 1 1 2 D −112

PAMT2: 0 0 1 1 2 D −112

After

PAMT1: 0 0 2 2 4 D −224

Example 7.5 leads us to an additional rule.

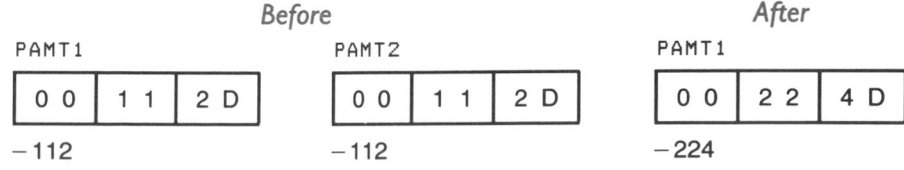

RULE: Adding two negative numbers produces a negative result.

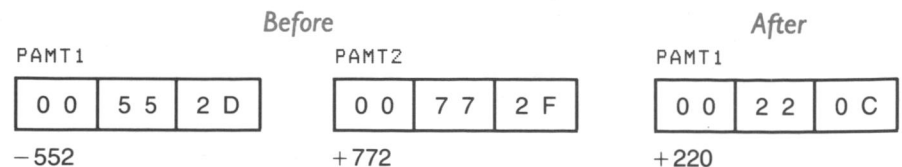

Before		*After*

PAMT1
| 0 0 | 5 5 | 2 D |
−552

PAMT2
| 0 0 | 7 7 | 2 F |
+772

PAMT1
| 0 0 | 2 2 | 0 C |
+220

> RULE: Adding one negative to one positive number: subtract smaller from larger and use sign of larger.

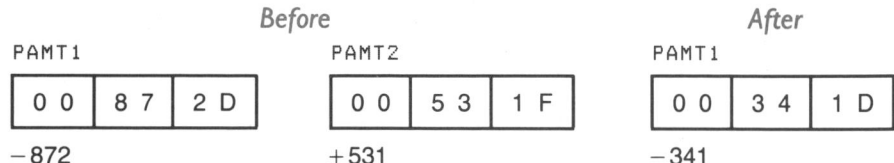

PAMT1
| 0 0 | 8 7 | 2 D |
−872

PAMT2
| 0 0 | 5 3 | 1 F |
+531

PAMT1
| 0 0 | 3 4 | 1 D |
−341

With the AP instruction, length specifiers may be omitted as illustrated, or included in *both* the first and second operands. When omitted, the first operand determines the number of bytes to be added. The previous instruction may be written in explicit form as follows.

LABEL	OPERATION	OPERAND	COMMENTS
	AP	PAMT1(3),PAMT2(3)	

C. Explicit Add

In using the explicit form of the AP instruction, the length specifiers should be the same as those prescribed in the defined storage (DS) instructions. If this practice is not followed, an error may occur because of an invalid sign. For example, consider the following instruction that would result in an error.

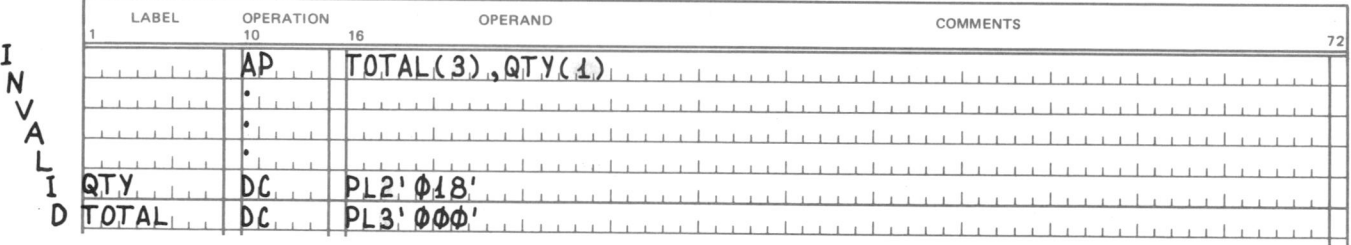

LABEL	OPERATION	OPERAND	COMMENTS
	AP	TOTAL(3),QTY(1)	
	.		
	.		
	.		
QTY	DC	PL2'018'	
TOTAL	DC	PL3'000'	

(INVALID)

Whereas QTY is defined as 2 bytes, this would create an error since the second operand, QTY(1), references *only* the high-order byte that contains the digits 01. The field QTY appears in storage as follows:

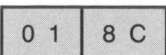

| 0 1 | 8 C |

Note no sign digit is present in QTY(1). The second operand in the AP instruction is therefore invalid. It is thus advisable for the programmer to recheck the defined lengths of the fields when using the explicit form of the AP instruction to ensure that the length indicated includes the sign bits. This checking practice will also serve to ensure that the receiving field is defined larger than the sending field.

A few examples of valid explicit AP instructions are:

LABEL	OPERATION	OPERAND	COMMENTS
	AP	FLD1(3),FLD2(2)	
	AP	FLD1(2),FLD2(1)	
	AP	FLD1(2),FLD2(2)	
	AP	FLD1(2),FLD2+1(1)	

Contents of FLD1	Contents of FLD2	Results Stored in FLD1
07134C	066C	07200C
097C	5D	092C
097C	098D	001D
097C	013C	100C

Note in the last example that only 3 is added to 97.

D. Arithmetic Overflow

The first operand or receiving field must be large enough to hold the result of the addition or else an error condition called an **arithmetic overflow** may result. Consider the following instruction.

Overflow and loss of the digit 1 occur.

LABEL	OPERATION	OPERAND	COMMENTS
** EXAMPLE OF ARITHMETIC OVERFLOW			
*			
	AP	SUM,TOOMUCH	

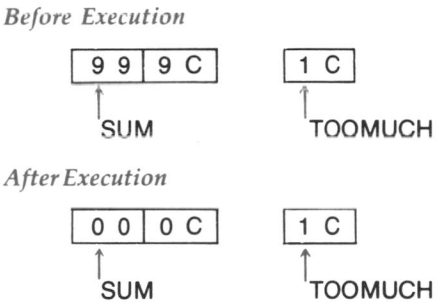

Before Execution

After Execution

In the above, an overflow condition occurs that may result in an interrupt which terminates processing.

In all arithmetic operations, both operands must contain packed data with valid signs; otherwise, another type of error, a data exception, may occur. Unlike the PACK instruction that packs a result without checking for the validity of the sign, the AP instruction results in a "data exception" error if the sign of either operand is invalid.

The following instructions will produce a data exception because the signs are invalid. Invalid signs are circled for ease of identification.

Symbolic Instruction	Contents Operand 1	Contents Operand 2	Comment
AP TOTL(2),NG(2)	00 | 0C	45 | 0 | ④	A preceding PACK instruction packed a blank in NG, resulting in an invalid sign digit.
AP QTY,ZD	01 | 2C	F1 | F | ②	The second operand was not packed.
AP QTYP,PFIVE	01 | C | ②	5C	QTYP was packed twice.
AP SUM,P1	C1 | D2 | E | ⑤	1C	The first operand contains EBCDIC data.

E. Application of the AP Instruction: Performing Multiplication Through Repeated Addition

LABEL	OPERATION	OPERAND	COMMENTS
1	10 16		72
	AP	DBL,DBL	

Before   *After*

```
 1 2 | 3 C          2 4 | 6 C
```
DBL⌐   DBL⌐

This instruction effectively doubles the contents of the location called DBL. If the instruction were repeated again, the final result would be the same as multiplying the field DBL by 4. In many instances, this method is not only simple, but also an efficient means of multiplication.

SUMMARY OF THE ADD PACKED INSTRUCTION

1. The second operand is added to the first, one byte at a time, from low order to high order.
2. Both operands must contain packed-decimal data with valid signs, or else a data exception will occur.
3. The resulting sum is stored in the first operand in packed form; a positive result will contain a hex C in the sign position; a negative result will produce a hex D.
4. Length specifiers may be included in both operands or the length of the operation can be implied by the length of the first operand.
5. If the first operand is too small to contain all the significant digits of the addition, an overflow occurs and processing may terminate.
6. If the first operand is larger than the results produced, addition will take place normally.
7. A field may be added to itself, a process that doubles the contents of the field.

Self-Evaluating Quiz

1. In the Add Packed (AP) instruction, the sum replaces the (**first/second**) operand.
2. The positive integer '1' would occupy (**no.**) byte(s) in packed form and appear in storage as _____ .
3. A packed number representing −2000 would occupy (**no.**) bytes and appear in storage as _____ .
4. The AP instruction is classified as a(n) _____ type of instruction.
5. Within each operand, addition takes place from _____ to _____ .
6. Determine the results of the following AP instructions. The length of each data field is as illustrated. Note if a data exception or overflow results.

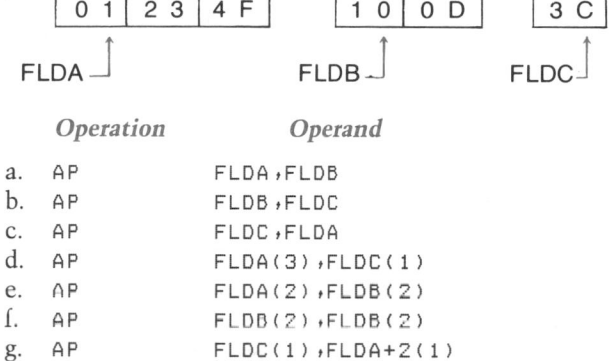

	Operation	*Operand*
a.	AP	FLDA,FLDB
b.	AP	FLDB,FLDC
c.	AP	FLDC,FLDA
d.	AP	FLDA(3),FLDC(1)
e.	AP	FLDA(2),FLDB(2)
f.	AP	FLDB(2),FLDB(2)
g.	AP	FLDC(1),FLDA+2(1)

In the last example, overlapping fields are permissible as long as a valid sign is involved. In other words, we simply added the 4F from FLDA to FLDC. Here is another example of this practice.

```
AP   FLDA(3),FLDA+2(1)
```

The result in FLDA would be | 0 1 | 2 3 | 8 C |

SOLUTIONS

1. First
2. 1; 1C
3. 3; | 02 | 00 | 0D |
4. Storage-to-storage
5. Right (low-order); left (high-order)
6. a. | 0 1 | 1 3 | 4 C | (in effect, subtraction occurs)
   b. | 0 9 | 7 D |
   c. Overflow
   d. | 0 1 | 2 3 | 7 C |
   e. Data exception (invalid sign for first operand)
   f. | 20 | 0D |
   g. | 7 C |

VI. THE UNPACK (UNPK) INSTRUCTION

You will recall from earlier in this chapter that zoned-decimal data was packed to perform decimal arithmetic. However, once the arithmetic operations are completed, the next step is to prepare the data for printing. It is necessary at this point to reverse the packing process and to convert the packed decimal data to its original zoned-decimal (EBCDIC) form so that it can be printed. The UNPK instruction is used for this purpose. Because the objective of **unpacking** is to prepare the data for printing, the defined output area is frequently used as the receiving field for the unpacked results.

The standard instructions to be performed for arithmetic operations include the following:

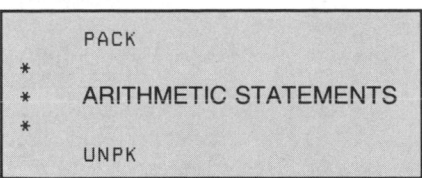

```
        PACK
*
*       ARITHMETIC STATEMENTS
*
        UNPK
```

Operation 10	Operand 16
UNPK	OP1,OP2

Instruction:	UNPK
Meaning:	Unpack a packed field so that it is converted to a zoned-decimal format.
Operand 1:	Receiving field should be described as zoned-decimal or "C" (character) field.
Operand 2:	Sending field must be in packed format.
Result:	The contents of the sending field are placed in the receiving field in an unpacked format. The sending field remains unchanged.
Limitations:	Make certain that the number of positions specified for the receiving field is large enough to accommodate results, otherwise truncation will occur. Sixteen-byte maximum for operands. Do not unpack a field into itself.

The following illustrates how the UNPK instruction operates.

Unpack (UNPK)

UNPK   OP1,OP2

Sending field [second operand]—packed-decimal

Receiving field [first operand]—zoned-decimal

Schematic

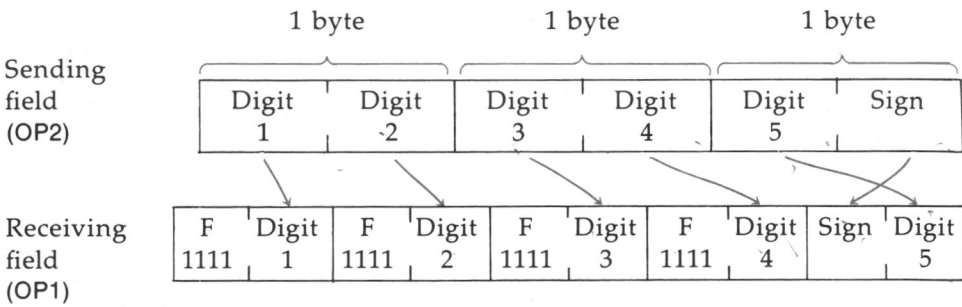

LABEL	OPERATION		OPERAND	COMMENTS	
1	10	16			72
	UNPK		NUMBOUT,PNUMB		
	.				
	.				
	.				
NUMBOUT	DS		CL3		
PNUMB	DC		PL2'123'		

Before Execution

(original contents of NUMBOUT do *not* affect UNPK)

```
PNUMB        | 12 | 3C |

                   X
                  / \
                 V   V
NUMBOUT      |    |    | C3 |         Step 1
```

```
PNUMB        | 12 | 3C |
                 |
                 V
NUMBOUT      |    | F2 | C3 |         Step 2
```

```
PNUMB        | 12 | C3 |
                /
               V
NUMBOUT      | F1 | F2 | C3 |         Step 3
```

After Execution

```
NUMBOUT — | F1 | F2 | C3 |          PNUMB — | 12 | 3C |
```

It should be noted that both operands reference the high-order positions of data in storage and that the instruction is of the storage-to-storage type. Neither operand may exceed 16 bytes which, we have already learned, is a general rule for decimal instructions. Notice in the example that the fields are processed from *right* to *left*, that is, from low-order to high-order. The receiving field, the first operand, is usually considerably longer than the sending field. To establish the minimum number of bytes required in the first operand, the following formula can be used.

CALCULATING THE LENGTH OF AN UNPACKED FIELD

Length (first operand) must be at least $2 \times$ Length (second operand) $- 1$

Therefore, as our example illustrates, the minimum length of NUMBOUT is calculated as follows:

$$\text{Length (NUMBOUT)} = 2 \times \text{length (PNUMB)} - 1$$
$$= 2 \times 2 - 1$$
$$= 3$$

Usually, as a precaution, the receiving field is *defined longer* than necessary. When this occurs, the high-order position(s) are filled with zoned zeros, represented in hex as F0. Zoned-zero characters will print as zeros and must be considered when planning the output layout.

The following example illustrates what happens if the receiving field is not large enough to accommodate the unpacked results.

LABEL	OPERATION	OPERAND	COMMENTS
	UNPK	SMALL(3),PAMT(3)	

Before Execution
PAMT

12	34	5C

After Execution
SMALL

F3	F4	C5

Note
High-order 12 in PAMT is truncated.

When the length specifiers are omitted, the length of the first operand determines the number of bytes to be unpacked. However, one or both operands may contain explicit length specifiers. We might, therefore, write an UNPK instruction in explicit form as follows.

LABEL	OPERATION	OPERAND	COMMENTS
	UNPK	HRSOUT(5),PHRS(2)	

Again, this method of controlling the lengths of both operands explicitly is recommended. Unpacking into the output area using implicit instead of explicit length specifiers often results in program errors. Consider the following.

LABEL	OPERATION	OPERAND	COMMENTS
	UNPK	OUTAREA,TOTAL	
	.		
	.		
	.		
OUTAREA	DS	CL132	

The first operand in this example *must* contain a length specifier or an attempt would be made to use the implied length of the defined storage area (132 bytes). Because both operands are limited to 16 bytes in an UNPK instruction, a syntax error would be indicated by the assembler for this instruction.

A problem exists with all of the unpacked fields shown in the preceding examples. If these fields were to be printed immediately after unpacking, the last byte in every instance would print as a letter. This is because the sign generated by decimal arithmetic is either a hex "C" (plus) or hex "D" (minus). After unpacking, the sign combines with a digit to produce a letter in the low-order byte. For example, the unpacking of positive digits 1 through 9 would result in the hex configuration C1 through C9, which would print as the letters A through I. See Table 7.1 for a listing of how low-order bytes of packed fields might print if signs were not stripped. The method used for stripping this sign is treated later on in the chapter.

Table 7.1 Possible Configurations in the Low-Order Byte of an Unpacked Field.

Actual Meaning	Character Printed	Hex Representation	Binary Representation	
+0	&	C0	1100	0000
+1	A	C1	1100	0001
+2	B	C2	1100	0010
+3	C	C3	1100	0011
+4	D	C4	1100	0100
+5	E	C5	1100	0101
+6	F	C6	1100	0110
+7	G	C7	1100	0111
+8	H	C8	1100	1000
+9	I	C9	1100	1001
-0	—	D0	1101	0000
-1	J	D1	1101	0001
-2	K	D2	1101	0010
-3	L	D3	1101	0011
-4	M	D4	1101	0100
-5	N	D5	1101	0101
-6	O	D6	1101	0110
-7	P	D7	1101	0111
-8	Q	D8	1101	1000
-9	R	D9	1101	1001

Recall, too, that a comparison of signed fields could produce illogical results. Consider the bit configuration for a −1, for example, which is a D1. This would result in a high condition when compared to +3, which is a C3 even though −1 is less than +3, as noted in the previous chapter. Hence, CLC instructions are not typically used for comparing signed numbers.

Self-Evaluating Quiz

1. The UNPK instruction is of the _____ type.
2. The first operand is the (**sending/receiving**) field while the second operand is the (**sending/receiving**) field.
3. Data in the second operand must be in _____ format.
4. The results of the UNPK instruction are found in the _____ operand in _____ form.
5. For unpacking a 4-byte packed-decimal field, the minimum length of the first operand must be (**no.**) bytes.
6. The maximum length of either operand is (**no.**) bytes.
7. The first operand is usually (**longer/shorter**) than the second.
8. The high-order digits may be lost when the (**first/second**) operand is too short.
9. When the first operand is longer than required, the high-order bytes are filled with (**zeros/zoned zeros/spaces**).

10. (T or F) The following is a valid set of instructions.

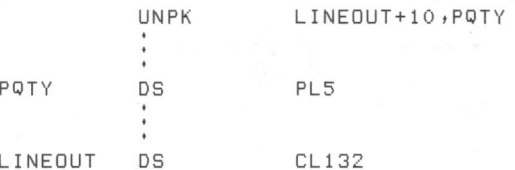

```
            UNPK        LINEOUT+10,PQTY
              .
              .
PQTY        DS          PL5
              .
              .
LINEOUT     DS          CL132
```

11. Indicate the contents of FLDB for each of the following instructions. Note when truncation will occur.
    FLDA is represented as:

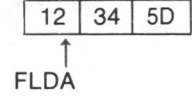

FLDA

a. UNPK   FLDB(5),FLDA
b. UNPK   FLDB(7),FLDA
c. UNPK   FLDB(4),FLDA(3)
d. UNPK   FLDB(1),FLDA+2(1)
e. UNPK   FLDB(5),FLDA+1(2)
f. UNPK   FLDB(3),FLDA(2)

12. Examine the program in Figure 7.1 and indicate the results that will print out. Use the data defined by the DC statements.

SOLUTIONS

1. Storage-to-storage
2. Receiving; sending
3. Packed-decimal
4. First; zoned-decimal (EBCDIC)
5. 7
6. 16
7. Longer (It is the receiving field)
8. First
9. Zoned zeros
10. F: The implied length is 122 bytes; LINEOUT+10 to LINEOUT+131
11. a. | F1 | F2 | F3 | F4 | D5 |
    b. | F0 | F0 | F1 | F2 | F3 | F4 | D5 |
    c. | F2 | F3 | F4 | D5 | (The high-order digit is dropped; truncation occurs)
    d. | D5 |
    e. | F0 | F0 | F3 | F4 | D5 |
    f. | F1 | F2 | 43 |; error condition, because 4 is not a valid sign
12. See Figure 7.2

V. OR LOGICAL IMMEDIATE

As previously illustrated, unless additional coding is supplied, the last byte of a field that has been unpacked will print as a letter. This is generally unacceptable because a numeric field should print with all numbers. Decimal arithmetic instructions generate a sign that is either a hex C or D but not the hex F required of numbers in EBCDIC or zoned-decimal format. To correct this problem, the sign in the last byte of an unpacked field must be changed to a

```
*                                                             *
*                              HOUSEKEEPING INSTRUCTIONS GO HERE  *
*                                                             *
ADD1      MVC       OUTAREA,SPACES
          AP        PAMT1,PAMT2
          UNPK      OUTAMT,PAMT1
          PUT       OUTFILE,OUTAREA
*
ADD2      MVC       OUTAREA,SPACES
          AP        PAMT3,PAMT2
          UNPK      OUTAMT,PAMT3
          PUT       OUTFILE,OUTAREA
*
ADD3      MVC       OUTAREA,SPACES
          AP        PAMT5,PAMT5
          UNPK      OUTAMT,PAMT5
          PUT       OUTFILE,OUTAREA
*
ADD4      MVC       OUTAREA,SPACES
          AP        PAMT8,=P'223'
          UNPK      OUTAMT,PAMT8
          PUT       OUTFILE,OUTAREA
*
ADD5      MVC       OUTAREA,SPACES
          PACK      PAMT6,AMT6
          PACK      PAMT7,AMT7
          AP        PAMT6,PAMT7
          UNPK      OUTAMT,PAMT6
          PUT       OUTFILE,OUTAREA
*                                                             *
*                              HOUSEKEEPING INSTRUCTIONS GO HERE  *
*                              ALONG W/DCB OR DTF MACRO FOR OUTFILE*
*                                                             *
SPACES    DC        CL1' '
OUTAREA   DS        0CL132
          DS        CL5
OUTAMT    DS        CL6
          DS        CL121
PAMT1     DC        P'1234'
PAMT2     DC        P'-226'
PAMT3     DC        P'-438'
PAMT4     DC        P'2387'
PAMT5     DC        P'4218'
AMT6      DC        C'197'
AMT7      DC        CL3'18N'          18N IN CHARACTER FORM IS -185
PAMT6     DS        PL2
PAMT7     DS        PL2
PAMT8     DC        P'992'
          END
```

Figure 7.1
Program for Question 12.

```
00100H
00066M
00843F
00121E
00001B
```

Figure 7.2
Solution to Question 12.

hex F. The Or Logical Immediate (OI) instruction, a storage-immediate (SI) type, can be used for this purpose. Consider the following:

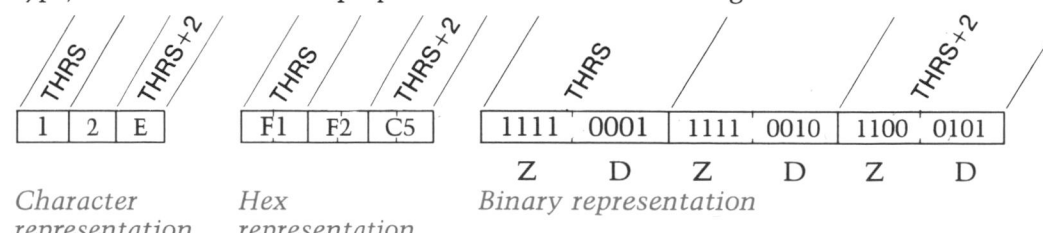

Character   *Hex*   *Binary representation*
representation   *representation*

To properly print the digit 5 contained in THRS+2, the programmer must change the *binary digits* or bits of the zone portion from 1100 (hex C), to 1111 (hex F). The bit pattern of the digit portion of the byte must remain unchanged. The OI instruction allows the programmer to set up a **binary pattern** or **mask** and perform "logical OR" operations between this pattern and the single byte to be modified, that is, THRS+2. The instruction may appear as follows:

LABEL	OPERATION		OPERAND	COMMENTS	
1	10	16			72
** METHOD ONE **					
*					
	OI		THRS+2,X'F0'		
*					
** METHOD TWO **					
*					
	OI		THRS+2,B'11110000'		

where the immediate operand X'F0' contains the binary pattern 1111 | 0000.

(handwritten margin note: COUNT UP TO / THE BYTE BEING CHANGED, BUT NOT THAT BYTE. ONE LESS THAN TOTAL LENGTH)

Before Execution	After Execution
F1 F2 C5	F1 F2 F5

The mask operates as follows:

> 1 in mask—Changes the corresponding bit in the receiving field to a 1.
> 0 in mask—Leaves the corresponding bit in the receiving field unchanged.

To change the sign bits of an unpacked field to 1111, and to leave the digit portion unchanged, we therefore use the mask '1111 0000'.

All arithmetic operations will thus contain the following sequence of instructions where fields are to be printed.

```
        PACK
*
*       ARITHMETIC OPERATIONS
*       ON PACKED FIELDS
*
        UNPK
        OI   OP1,X'F0'
```

Example 7.6   Suppose we wish to determine the total number of records read as input. We would add 1 to a TOTAL each time a record is read. When an end-of-job condition is reached and there are no more records to process, we would print out the value of TOTAL using the OI to replace the sign for printing purposes. See Figure 7.3 for a solution.

VI. LOOPING USING ARITHMETIC OPERATIONS FOR COUNTING

In the previous chapter we saw how the compare instructions, CLC and CLI, may be used to test for certain conditions.

```
*                                                                          *
*                                    HOUSEKEEPING INSTRUCTIONS GO HERE     *
*                                                                          *
          MVC     OUTAREA,SPACES
READ      GET     INFILE,RECORD
          AP      TOTAL,=P'1'
          B       READ
EOF       MVC     MESSAGE,=C'NUMBER OF RECORDS IS '
          UNPK    TOTOUT,TOTAL
          OI      TOTOUT+4,X'F0'       CHANGE SIGN FROM HEX C TO HEX F
          PUT     OUTFILE,OUTAREA
*                                                                          *
*                                    HOUSEKEEPING INSTRUCTIONS GO HERE     *
*                                    ALONG WITH DCB OR DTF MACROS          *
*                                                                          *
TOTAL     DC      PL5'00000'
RECORD    DS      CL80
SPACES    DC      CL1' '
OUTAREA   DS      0CL132
          DS      CL5
MESSAGE   DS      CL21
TOTOUT    DS      CL5
          DS      CL101
          END
```

Figure 7.3
Program to determine the number of records read as input.

One common application of such conditional statements is **looping,** which is the execution of a series of instructions a fixed number of times. Looping is typically performed as follows:

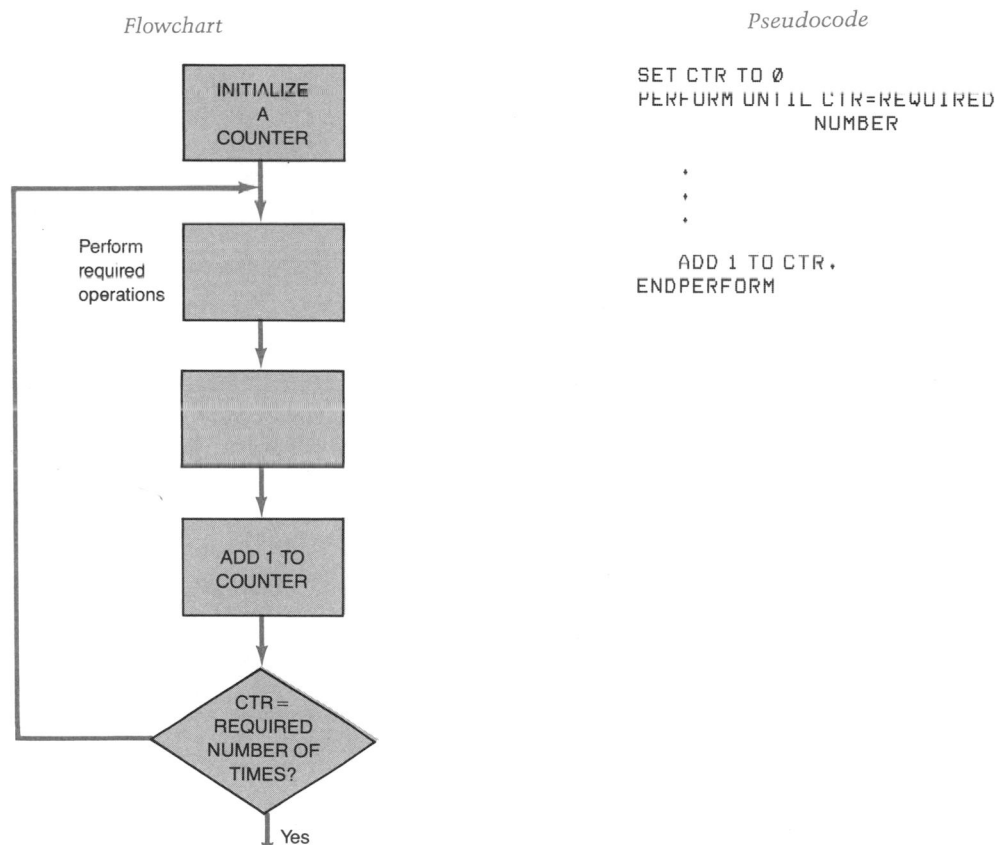

Flowchart

INITIALIZE A COUNTER

Perform required operations

ADD 1 TO COUNTER

CTR = REQUIRED NUMBER OF TIMES?

Yes

Pseudocode

```
SET CTR TO 0
PERFORM UNTIL CTR=REQUIRED
                    NUMBER
        .
        .
        .

        ADD 1 TO CTR.
ENDPERFORM
```

To perform looping, counters must be established, incremented each time through the loop, and compared to a fixed value to determine if the loop has been executed the required number of times.

Example 7.7 Suppose we wish to print 5 lines of output for an input record read. We could establish a field called CTR that is initialized at zero. Then we

1. Read the record.
2. Move the data to the output area.
3. Print a line.
4. Add 1 to counter.
5. If counter is less than 5, go to Step 3.

The routine could appear as follows:

```
        GET  INFILE,RECORD
        MVC  OUTREC,RECORD
LOOP    PUT  OUTFILE,OUTREC
        AP   CTR,ONE
        CLI  CTR,P'5'
        BL   LOOP
         .
         .
CTR     DC   P'0'
ONE     DC   P'1'
```

Example 7.8 Suppose we wish to multiply A by B, two positive numbers, using a series of successive additions. Assume that B is a signed, one-digit number. If 3 is added to itself 4 times, for example, the result is 12, which is the product of 3×4. We could code this as:

```
        PACK   PA,A
        PACK   PB,B
LOOP    AP     TOT,PA
        AP     CTR,ONE
        CLC    CTR,PB
        BNE    LOOP
         .
         .
CTR     DC     P'0'
ONE     DC     P'1'
PA      DS     PL2
PB      DS     PL1
TOT     DC     PL2'0'
```

Note that B would have a positive sign rather than being unsigned.

Example 7.9 Code a procedure that accomplishes the logic specified in the following flowchart and pseudocode excerpts.

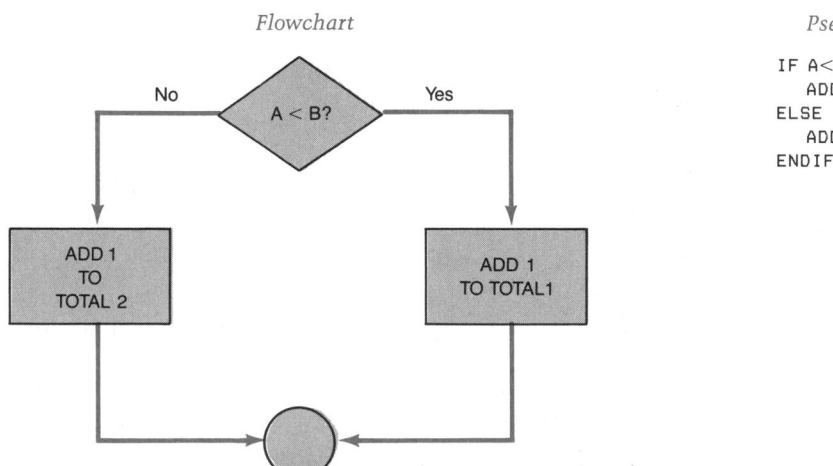

Flowchart

Pseudocode

```
IF A<B
    ADD 1 TO TOTAL1
ELSE
    ADD 1 TO TOTAL2
ENDIF
```

The coding is as follows:

```
         CLC   A,B
         BL    ADDIT
         AP    TOTAL2,=P'1'
         B     NEXT
ADDIT    AP    TOTAL1,=P'1'
         .
         .
         .
NEXT
```

The preceding examples illustrate how looping is performed. Later on, we will see that other versions of the compare instruction are better suited for comparing numeric fields.

Self-Evaluating Quiz

1. The Or Logical Immediate (OI) is a (SS/SI) type instruction.
2. When data is unpacked, the last byte will contain a hex _____ , hex _____ , or hex _____ , according to whether the data is positive, negative, or unsigned.
3. If a byte containing 1C were unpacked and printed, the letter _____ would appear in the output.
4. Each operand in the OI instruction is (no.) byte(s) in length.
5. The OI instruction sets up an immediate binary pattern called a(n) _____ against which the data in the first operand is processed.
6. When processing the mask, a bit in the first operand or receiving field will be changed if the corresponding bit in the mask contains a(n) _____ .
7. For a zoned-decimal (EBCDIC) digit to print correctly, the zone must contain a hex _____ or binary _____ .
8. Indicate the results of the following OI operations in both binary and hexadecimal form.

	DATA		MASK		RESULTS
	First Operand		Second Operand		First Operand
	Binary	Hex	Binary	Hex	
a.	1100 1001	C9	1111 0000	F0	
b.	1101 0111	D7	1111 0000	F0	
c.	0100 0000	40 (blank)	1111 0000	F0	
d.	1101 0011	D3	1111 0000	F0	
e.	1100 0001	C1	1111 0000	F0	

9. When using the OI instruction to correct for the sign, the second operand will always be _____ (in hex form) or _____ (in binary form).

SOLUTIONS

1. Storage immediate (SI)
2. C; D; F
3. A (hex C1)
4. 1
5. Mask
6. 1
7. F; 1111

8.

	Binary		*Hex*
a.	1111	1001	F9
b.	1111	0111	F7
c.	1111	0000	F0
d.	1111	0011	F3
e.	1111	0001	F1

9.   X'F0'; B'11110000'

Note

An equal sign is not used in the second operand of an OI instruction.

VII. AN ALTERNATE METHOD FOR REPLACING THE SIGN PORTION OF UNPACKED FIELDS WITH HEX F: THE MOVE ZONE INSTRUCTION (MVZ)

The Move Zone (MVZ) instruction serves the same purpose as the Or Immediate (OI); that is, it replaces the sign portion of unpacked numeric fields with the hex value F. As we have already learned, for the CPU to print unpacked numeric fields, the sign in the low-order byte must be changed to a hex F. Therefore, if a field contains a hex C or hex D resulting from decimal arithmetic, the sign must be changed to conform to the ordinary zoned-decimal format before it is printed. This method simply moves the zone from one of the high-order positions of the field that is an F to the low-order (sign) position of the same field. Let us consider that a field called (THRS) has just been unpacked, and an MVZ instruction is to be used to change the sign. The instruction and the unpacked area called THRS may appear as shown in the following example.

Example 7.10

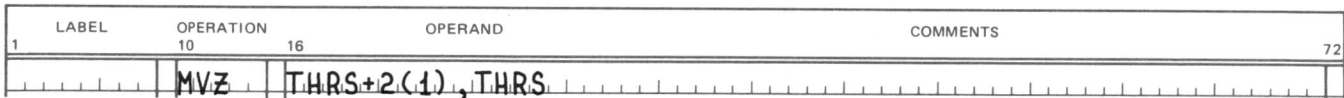

LABEL	OPERATION		OPERAND	COMMENTS	
1	10	16			72
	MVZ		THRS+2(1),THRS		

Before

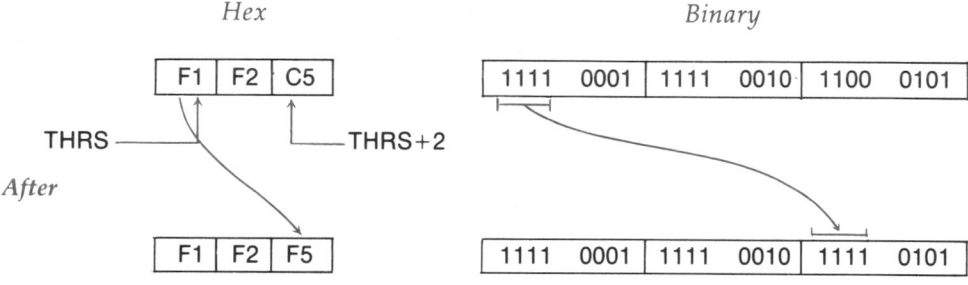

Example 7.11

```
MVZ     ZNUM+4(1),ZNUM+3
```
ZNUM references a 5-byte field.
Assume ZNUM is unpacked and is signed positive.

Before Execution

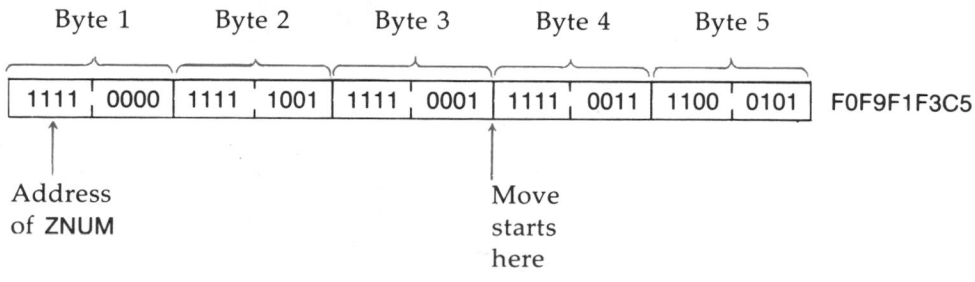

Result

Zone portion of byte 4 [ZNUM+3] is moved to zone portion of byte 5.

| 1111 | 0000 | 1111 | 1001 | 1111 | 0001 | 1111 | 0011 | 1111 | 0101 | F0F9F1F3F5 |

Note that the MVZ instruction moves *only* the zone portion (the four high-order bits) from one byte to another, while the numeric portion of the receiving field remains unchanged. The MVZ is another storage-to-storage instruction that is very similar in operation to the MVC. We will therefore briefly summarize its operation as follows.

SUMMARY OF MVZ

1. Meaning: Move Zone.
2. First operand: This is the receiving field; the contents of its zone portion will change.
3. Second operand: This is the sending field; it remains unchanged.
4. Zone portion is moved one byte at a time from left to right; digit portion remains unchanged.
5. To replace only one zone, use the explicit form specifying a (1) to denote that only a single zone is to be moved.
6. From 1 to 256 bytes may be referenced with a single MVZ instruction.
7. One or more zones of the first operand are replaced by the corresponding zone(s) of the second operand.
8. The number of zones in the first operand that are replaced depends on either
   a. the explicit length specified in the first operand, or
   b. the implicit length of the first operand.

Because we are only concerned with moving the zone from a nearby byte, the previous example could also be written

LABEL	OPERATION	OPERAND	COMMENTS	
	MVZ	THRS+2(1),THRS+1		

and the results produced would be identical to those of the previous example.

The MVZ is not, however, limited to changing the zone configuration of just one byte, as the following example illustrates.

LABEL	OPERATION	OPERAND	COMMENTS	
	MVZ	FLDA,FLDB		

Before

| 12 | 34 | 40 |
⌐FLDA

| F1 | F2 | F3 |
⌐FLDB

After

| F2 | F4 | F0 |
⌐FLDA

| F1 | F2 | F3 |
⌐FLDB

Self-Evaluating Quiz

1. The MVZ instruction moves the four (high/low)-order bits of each byte.
2. Once arithmetic operations are completed and a field is unpacked, the (high/low)-order byte will contain a hex C or hex D, depending on the sign.
3. The number of bytes affected by an MVZ instruction depends upon the length of the (first/second) operand or on a _____ .
4. From 1 to (no.) bytes may be referenced by a single MVZ statement.
5. Determine the results stored in FLDA for each of the following situations. Treat each situation independently.

    FLDA contains |11|22|33|44|55|

    FLBB contains |C6|FF|D8|F9|40|

    a. MVZ   FLDA,FLDB
    b. MVZ   FLDA+1(4),FLDB
    c. MVZ   FLDA+4(1),FLDB+1
    d. MVZ   FLDA(1),FLDB
    e. MVZ   FLDA+2(3),FLDB+1
6. (T or F) The Move Zone instruction is in the SI format.
7. (T or F) Overlapping fields are not permitted with the MVZ instruction.
8. When using the MVZ instruction on overlapped fields, the field(s) usually contain (packed/zoned-decimal) data.

SOLUTIONS

1. High (zone portion or 4 leftmost bits)
2. Low (rightmost)
3. First; length specifier in the first operand
4. 256
5. a. |C1|F2|D3|F4|45|
   b. |11|C2|F3|D4|F5|
   c. |11|22|33|44|F5|
   d. |C1|22|33|44|55|
   e. |11|22|F3|D4|F5|
6. F: storage-to-storage
7. F: they are used to change the sign
8. Zoned-decimal

VIII. DECIMAL SUBTRACTION: THE SUBTRACT PACKED INSTRUCTION (SP)

A. Format

Operation 10	Operand 16
SP	OP1,OP2

Instruction:	SP
Meaning:	Subtract Packed-Decimal Fields
Operands:	Both must be packed data fields (Operand 2 can be a packed self-defining constant)
	Both fields have a 16-byte limit
	Both fields can use implicit or explicit length specifiers
Result:	The second operand is subtracted from the first
	The result is placed in Operand 1
	Operand 2 remains unchanged
Limitations:	Make certain that the receiving field is large enough to accommodate the answer or an overflow will occur

The Subtract Packed (SP) instruction subtracts the contents of the second operand from the first operand. The arithmetic result is placed in the first operand. Once again, both operands must contain packed-decimal data and the rules for overflow, data exception, and field sizes are the same as presented under the Add Packed (AP) decimal instruction. Results of subtraction operations in general may need some review as subtracting signed numbers can sometimes be confusing. There is one basic rule to follow.

> RULE: Change the sign of the number to be subtracted (the second operand), and proceed as in addition.

Examples

1. $(+151) - (+51) = 151 + (-51) = +100$
2. $(+200) - (+400) = 200 + (-400) = -200$
3. $(-151) - (-51) = -151 + (+51) = -100$
4. $(-200) - (-100) = (-200) + (+100) = -100$

B. Examples

The following examples illustrate the SP instruction.

	Operation	Operand	Contents of FLDB (in decimal)	Contents of FLDA (in decimal)	Results in FLDB (in decimal)
a.	SP	FLDB,FLDA	00 78 9C	00 08 9C	00 70 0C (+)
b.	SP	FLDB(3),FLDA(2)	00 00 7C	01 3D	00 02 0C (+)
c.	SP	FLDB(2),FLDA(2)	00 7C	01 3C	00 6D (−)
d.	SP	FLDB(2),FLDA(2)	00 7D	99 9C	Overflow
e.	SP	FLDB(3),FLDA(1)	56 78 9C	9F	56 78 0C (+)
f.	SP	FLDB(2),FLDA(1)	56 78 9C	F9	Data exception

C. Subtraction Using Constants

Suppose we wish to subtract 100 from AMT1. We could code this as:

```
SP AMT1,=P'100'
```

To subtract AMT2 from 100, however, could *not* be coded as:

```
INVALID  SP = P'100',AMT2
```

because the self-defining constant can only appear as the sending field, that is, as the second operand. To subtract AMT2 from 100, we would need to use two packed data fields.

```
        SP TOTAL, AMT2
        ⋮
TOTAL DC P'100'
```

D. Overflow Conditions

Note that when the first operand is too small to contain the results, overflow occurs. If the first operand is of sufficient size, subtraction will take place normally provided that both operands contain valid signs.

CHAPTER SUMMARY

I. Storage-to-storage arithmetic uses symbolic storage locations for both Operand 1 and Operand 2

II. Data must be in packed-decimal format to be used in arithmetic operations

III. Typical Instruction Sequence:

PACK   (to put data into packed format)
Perform arithmetic
UNPK   (to put data back into EBCDIC form)
OI or MVZ   (to replace the sign in the low-order byte)

IV. The PACK instruction: Operand 1 will contain the packed equivalent

   A. Operand 2 is an EBCDIC field.
   B. The operation proceeds from right to left.
   C. The zone bits are "stripped" except for the low-order sign, which is placed in the low-order four bits of the rightmost byte.
   D. The packed operation can be implicit or explicit; 16 bytes is the maximum.
   E. Sizing:
      1. If the receiving field is longer than necessary, high-order unfilled bits are zero-filled.
      2. If the receiving field is shorter than necessary, truncation of high-order digit bits occurs.
   F. The Add Packed (AP) and Subtract Packed (SP) Instructions
      1. AP = Add Packed; SP = Subtract Packed.
      2. Both operands must be in packed format.
      3. Results are placed in the first operand.
      4. Operation can be implicit or explicit; 16 bytes is the maximum.
      5. Make certain that the receiving field (Operand 1) is large enough to accommodate the sum (AP) or difference (SP).
      6. Operand 2 may be a self-defining constant.
   G. The UNPK Instruction
      1. Converts a packed field to EBCDIC or zoned-decimal format.
      2. Results are placed in Operand 1, a character field.
      3. Operand 2 contains the packed version.
      4. Make certain that the receiving field (Operand 1) is large enough to accommodate the zoned-decimal equivalent of the packed field.
   H. Use OI (Or Immediate) or MVZ to replace the sign portion of a field that has been packed and used in arithmetic with a hex F.

CHAPTER SELF-EVALUATING QUIZ

For Questions 1–6, what, if anything, is wrong with the sequence of instructions indicated?

```
1.          SP   OP1,OP2
                 .
                 .
                 .
     OP1    DS   CL10
     OP2    DS   CL5
```

```
2.          SP   OP3,OP4
                 .
                 .
                 .
     OP3    DS   PL20
     OP4    DS   PL15
```

```
3.            SP  OP5,OP6
              .
              .
      OP5  DC  PL2'+826'
      OP6  DC  PL2'-335'
```

```
4.            SP  =P'100',OP7
```

```
5.            SP  OP8,=P'100'
              .
              .
      OP8  DC  PL3'000'
```

```
6.            S   OP9,OP10
              .
              .
      OP9   DS  PL4
      OP10  DS  PL3
```

For Questions 7–10, indicate the results of each of the instructions, using the following constants.

```
      FLD1  DC   PL3'+105'
      FLD2  DC   PL3'+250'
7.          SP   FLD1,FLD2
8.          SP   FLD1,FLD1
9.          SP   FLD2,FLD1
10.         SP   FLD2,FLD2
```

SOLUTIONS

		Page
1.	Character or zoned-decimal format for each DS is incorrect	192
2.	Operands cannot be more than 16 bytes.	192
3.	Result would be 826 − (−335) = +1161 but OP5 is not large enough to accommodate this result	193
4.	The first operand of SP instruction is receiving field; it cannot be a self-defining operand.	192
5.	Nothing wrong	192
6.	SP not S	192
7.	−145 (105 − 250)	193
8.	+0	193
9.	+145	193
10.	+0	193

PRACTICE PROGRAM

Consider the following problem definition.

a. Input Record Layout

LAST NAME	FIRST NAME	SALARY	
1 15	16 25	26 30	31 80

b. Printer Spacing Chart for Printed Output

H	6	EMPLOYEES WHO EARN OVER $15,000	
H	8	LAST NAME	FIRST NAME	SALARY
D	10	X————X	X———X	$X—X
T	15	NO. WHO EARN OVER $15,000 IS XXX	

c. Sample Input Data

```
BAGLEY        JOAN       14750
BREWSTER      WESLEY     38950
JOHNSON       SUSAN      21500
MARTIN        HAROLD     13925
WILLIAMS      JAMES      27950
```

d. Sample Output

```
                    EMPLOYEES WHO EARN OVER $15,000

        LAST NAME                    FIRST NAME              SALARY

        BREWSTER                     WESLEY                  $38950
        JOHNSON                      SUSAN                   $21500
        WILLIAMS                     JAMES                   $27950

    NO. WHO EARN OVER $15,000 IS 003
```

Write a program to produce the type of report shown. See Figure 7.4 for a solution.

KEY TERMS

Abend
Data exception
EBCDIC
Explicit length
Implicit length
Loop
Mask

Overflow
Packed-decimal format
Packing
Truncation
Unpacking
Zoned-decimal format

REVIEW QUESTIONS

1. What will be the resulting values in FLD1 and FLD2 after execution of the following instructions?

```
          SP    FLD2,FLD1
          AP    FLD2(3),FLD2(3)
          .
          .
FLD1      DC    P'-06531'
FLD2      DC    P'+09265'
```

```
*                                            HOUSEKEEPING INSTRUCTIONS GO HERE  *
*                                                                               *
*                                                                               *
          MVC    OUTAREA,SPACES
          MVC    OUTAREA+23(31),=C'EMPLOYEES WHO EARN OVER $15,000'
          PUT    OUTFILE,OUTAREA
          MVC    OUTAREA,SPACES
          PUT    OUTFILE,OUTAREA             PRINT BLANK LINE
          MVC    LNAME(9),=C'LAST NAME'
          MVC    FNAME(10),=C'FIRST NAME'
          MVC    SALOUT(6),=C'SALARY'
          PUT    OUTFILE,OUTAREA
          MVC    OUTAREA,SPACES
          PUT    OUTFILE,OUTAREA             PRINT BLANK LINE
READ      MVC    OUTAREA,SPACES
          GET    INFILE,RECORD
          CLC    SALARY,=C'15000'
          BNH    READ
          AP     COUNT,=P'1'
          MVC    LNAME,LAST
          MVC    FNAME,FIRST
          MVC    SALOUT,SALARY
          MVI    SALOUT-1,C'$'
          PUT    OUTFILE,OUTAREA
          B      READ
EOF       MVC    OUTAREA,SPACES
          PUT    OUTFILE,OUTAREA
          MVC    OUTAREA+1(29),=C'NO. WHO EARN OVER $15,000 IS '
          UNPK   OUTAREA+30(3),COUNT
          OI     OUTAREA+32,X'F0'
          PUT    OUTFILE,OUTAREA
```

```
*
                                       HOUSEKEEPING INSTRUCTIONS GO HERE  *
                                       ALONG WITH DCB OR DTF MACROS       *
                                                                          *
COUNT     DC     PL2'0'
RECORD    DS     0CL80                   INPUT FORMAT
LAST      DS     CL15                      *
FIRST     DS     CL10                      *
SALARY    DS     CL5                       *
          DS     CL50                      *
SPACES    DC     CL1' '
OUTAREA   DS     0CL132                  PRINT FORMAT
          DS     CL5                       *
LNAME     DS     CL15                      *
          DS     CL20                      *
FNAME     DS     CL10                      *
          DS     CL20                      *
SALOUT    DS     CL5                       *
          DS     CL57                      *
          END
```

**Figure 7.4
Solution to the Practice
Program.**

2. Indicate the errors, if any, in the following program excerpt.

LABEL	OPERATION	OPERAND	COMMENTS
	AP	SUM,=C'1'	
	AP	TOTAL,FLDA	
	UNPK	TOTAL,OUTAMT	
	.		
	.		
	.		
FLDA	DC	PL20'01'	
OUTAREA	DS	0CL132	
OUTAMT	DS	CL10	

3. Using the arithmetic operations AP and SP, compute the following:
   C = 4 × A − 2 × B

4. FIELD1 contains 92 43 9C, FIELD2 contains 00 00 01 32 4C. Would the instruction AP FIELD1,FIELD2 cause an overflow?

5. Indicate the results in the following:

```
          AP    TOTAL,TAX
          SP    TOTAL,=P'100'
          .
          .
TOTAL     DC    PL6'123456'
TAX       DC    PL3'2345'
```

6. Indicate the results in the following:

```
          AP    FIELD1,FIELD2
          AP    FIELD1,FIELD3
          UNPK  AMT,FIELD1
          MVZ   AMT+5(1),AMT+6
          .
          .
AMT       DS    CL7
FIELD1    DC    PL4'2231'
FIELD2    DC    PL4'-1230'
FIELD3    DC    PL4'+2235'
```

Write routines to perform the operations in Questions 7–10.

```
7.  PERFORM UNTIL CTR = 5
        READ
        ADD AMT TO TOTAL
        ADD 1 TO CTR
    ENDPERFORM
    WRITE TOTAL
```

```
8.  IF  A = B
        ADD 1 TO TOT1
    ELSE
        ADD 1 TO TOT2
    ENDIF
```

9.

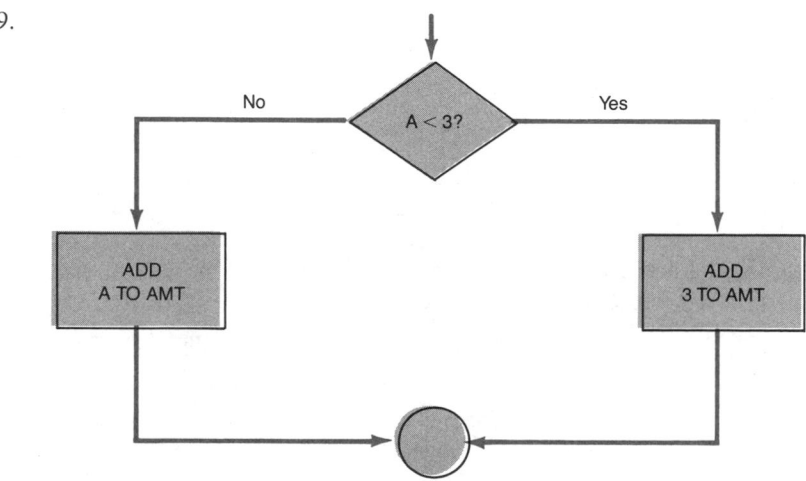

10.

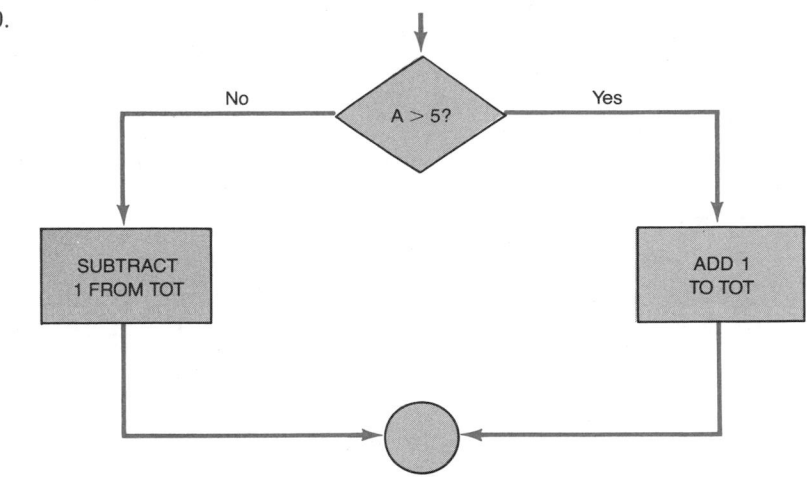

DEBUGGING EXERCISES

The following program excerpt calculates a new balance forward by using the equation:

`NEWBAL = OLDBAL + CHARGES - PAYMENT`

The printed output consists of the NAME, the OLD BALANCE, and the NEW BALANCE. The counter (CTR) serves to count the number of records processed. Identify the errors in the program by desk-checking and walking through the program.

```
*************************************************************
*        D E B U G   P R O G R A M   C H A P T E R   7
*************************************************************
         SP    CTR,CTR
CLEAR    MVZ   LINEOUT,SPACES
         GET   INFILE,RECORD
         AP    CTR,=P'1'
         MVC   NAMEO,NAME
         MVC   OLDBALO,OLDBAL
         PACK  AMTPAID,PAYMENT
         PACK  PCHARGES,CHARGES
         PACK  PBAL,OLDBAL
         AP    PBAL,CHARGES
         SP    PBAL,PAYMENT
         UNPAC NEWBALO,PBAL
         OI    NEWBALO,X'F0'
         PUT   OUTFILE,LINEOUT
         B     CLEAR
RECORD   DS    0CL80
NAME     DS    CL20
PAYMENT  DS    CL5
CHARGES  DS    CL5
OLDBAL   DS    CL7
*
SPACES   DS    CL1' '
LINEOUT  DS    0CL133
         DS    CL38
NAMEO    DS    CL20
         DS    CL10
OLDBALO  DS    CL7
         DS    CL13
NEWBALO  DS    CL7
REST     DS    CL38
*
AMTPAID  DS    PL3
PCHARGES DS    PL3
PBAL     DS    PL4
CTR      DS    PL2
```

SOLUTION

```
          SP     CTR,CTR            SHOULD CAUSE A DATA EXCEPTION
CTR       DC     PL2'0'            USE A DC AS SHOWN
CLEAR     MVZ    LINEOUT,SPACES    MVC NOT MVZ
*
          AP     PBAL,CHARGES      CHARGES IS UNPACKED-USE PCHARGES
*
          SP     PBAL,PAYMENT      PAYMENT IS UNPACKED-USE AMTPAID
*
          UNPAC  NEWBALO,PBAL      OP-CODE MUST BE UNPK
*
          OI     NEWBALO+6,X'F0'   CORRECT SIGN IN LAST BYTE
*
          DS     CL43              RECORD MUST CONTAIN 80 BYTES
                                   BUT ONLY CONTAINED 37
SPACES    DC     CL1' '            MUST BE DC, NOT DS
```

PROGRAMMING ASSIGNMENTS

1. Consider the following input.

Input Positions	Field
1–20	NAME
21–25	AMT1
26–30	AMT2
80	CODE

   a. If CODE=1, print NAME and the sum of AMT1 and AMT2.
   b. If CODE=2, print NAME and the difference of AMT1 − AMT2.
   c. If CODE ≠ 1 or 2, print NAME and 'ERROR'.

2. Consider the following input.

Input Positions	Field
1–20	NAME
21–25	SALESAMT
26–30	SALARY

   a. If SALESAMT is between $300 and $1000, print NAME and increased salary where

      Increased salary = SALARY + 150

   b. If SALESAMT is between $1001 and $5000, print NAME and increased salary where

      Increased salary = SALARY + 250

   c. If SALESAMT is greater than $5000, print NAME and extended salary where

      Increased salary = SALARY + 500

   d. If SALESAMT is less than $300, print NAME and reduced salary where

      Reduced salary = SALARY − 100.

3. Write a program to create a printed report from the following transaction records.

Input Positions	Field
1–5	Transaction number
6–20	Customer name
21–25	Amount 1
26–30	Amount 2
31–35	Amount of discount

The output format is as follows:

Print Positions	Field
1–15	Customer name
26–30	Transaction number
41–45	Total
56–60	Amount due
71–74	Date (month and year)
75–132	Not used

Notes:
a. Total = Amount 1 + Amount 2
b. Amount due = Total − Amount of discount
c. Place today's date in the date field.

4. Write a program to print the sum of the integers from 1 to 100.

5. Print the report depicted below including a title, column headings, detail lines, and total lines. The input record contains the following fields:

Input Record Layout

1–5	Customer Number
21–25	Amount of Daily Deposits
31–35	Amount of Daily Withdrawals
40	Transaction Code
	D if deposit
	W if withdrawal
	B if both
41–46	Old Balance

The following formulas are used.

DAILY CASH ON HAND = TOTAL DEPOSITS − TOTAL WITHDRAWALS
NEW BALANCE = OLD BALANCE + DEPOSITS − WITHDRAWALS

Printer Spacing Chart for Printed Output

8 Advanced Decimal Arithmetic Instructions

<table>
<tr><td>**OBJECTIVES**</td><td>*To familiarize you with:*
1. *The format and use of multiply and divide operations.*
2. *How the Zero and Add Packed (ZAP) instruction may be used to zero out fields and to test them for specified contents.*
3. *The use of the Compare Packed (CP) instruction and how it differs from the CLC instruction.*
4. *Examples of applications using loops and sequences of arithmetic operations.*</td></tr>
</table>

I. THE ZERO AND ADD PACKED (ZAP) INSTRUCTION

A. Format

Operation 10	Operand 16
ZAP	OP1,OP2

Instruction:	ZAP
Meaning:	Zero and Add Packed Decimal
	1. Sets the receiving field (first operand) to zero.
	2. Adds the packed-decimal contents of the sending field to the first operand.
Results:	The packed contents of the sending field is transmitted to the receiving field; high-order positions are zero-filled when the receiving field is longer than the sending field.
Operands:	The second operand must be in packed format or be a self-defining packed constant.
Length:	The length of the operation is determined by the first operand; length may be implicit or explicit; maximum length—16 bytes.

B. Purpose

The purpose of this instruction is to clear the receiving field and to move the packed contents of the sending field to it. You will recall that fields to be used as totals must be cleared prior to any accumulation. ZAP is frequently used for that purpose.

Illustration   Compute

    TOTAL = A + B - C

Assume all fields are in packed-format.

Without knowing the initial contents of TOTAL, the following routine would produce unpredictable, and thus incorrect, results.

LABEL	OPERATION 10	16	OPERAND	COMMENTS	72
	AP	TOTAL,A			
	AP	TOTAL,B			
	SP	TOTAL,C			

The following routine, which uses the ZAP instruction, will produce the correct results *regardless* of the initial contents of TOTAL.

LABEL	OPERATION 10	16	OPERAND	COMMENTS	72
	ZAP	TOTAL,A			
	AP	TOTAL,B			
	SP	TOTAL,C			

Example 8.1   Both operands are of the same length.

LABEL	OPERATION 10	16	OPERAND	COMMENTS	72
	ZAP	TOTAL,TRAN			

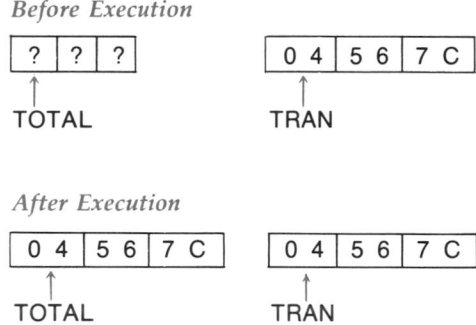

Before Execution

?	?	?
↑
TOTAL

0 4	5 6	7 C
↑
TRAN

After Execution

0 4	5 6	7 C
↑
TOTAL

0 4	5 6	7 C
↑
TRAN

Example 8.2   The first operand (receiving field) is longer than the second operand (sending field).

Result
High-order zeros fill the receiving field.

LABEL	OPERATION 10	16	OPERAND	COMMENTS	72
	ZAP	FLDA,TRAN			

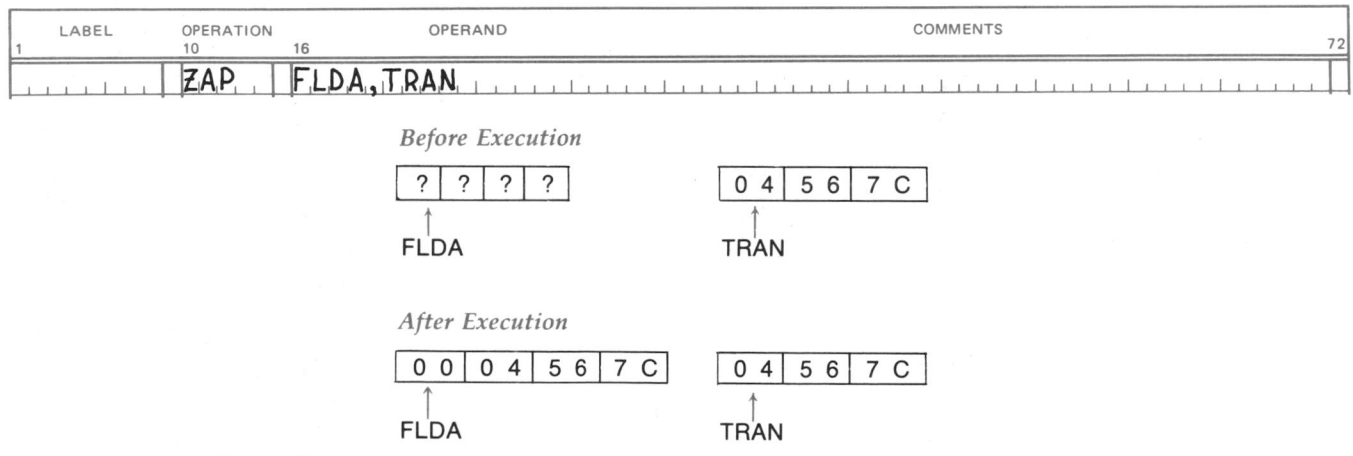

Before Execution

?	?	?	?
↑
FLDA

0 4	5 6	7 C
↑
TRAN

After Execution

0 0	0 4	5 6	7 C
↑
FLDA

0 4	5 6	7 C
↑
TRAN

Example 8.3   The first operand is too small to accommodate the packed contents of the second operand.

Result

a. Overflow condition occurs—condition code 3 is set. After a ZAP, the condition code can be tested with a BO (branch if overflow). For example:

```
ZAP   TOT,A
BO    ERROR
```

b. Abend condition occurs, that is, processing terminates (on many systems).

LABEL	OPERATION	OPERAND	COMMENTS
	ZAP	FLDB,TRAN	

Before Execution

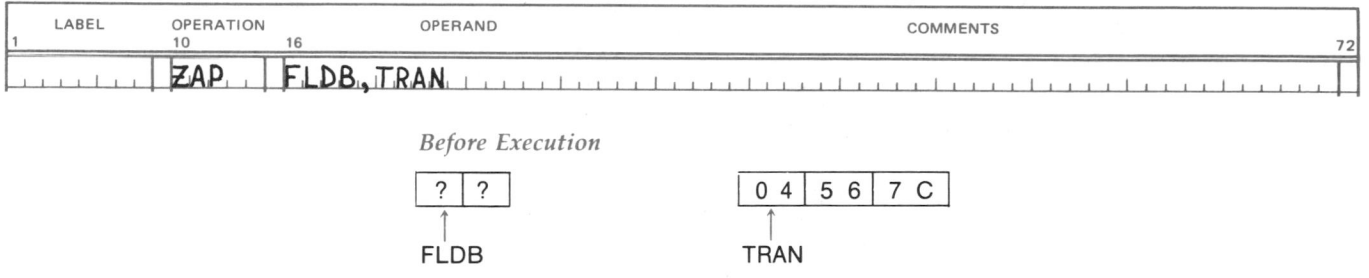

FLDB   TRAN

After Execution

| 5 6 | 7 C | (overflow) | 0 4 | 5 6 | 7 C |

FLDB   TRAN

The same rules apply if the second operand is a self-defining packed operand such as =P'04567':

LABEL	OPERATION	OPERAND	COMMENTS
*		EXAMPLES (1), (2) AND (3)	
*		USING SELF-DEFINING OPERANDS	
*			
	ZAP	TOTAL,=P'+04567'	
*			
	ZAP	FLDA,=P'+04567'	
*			
	ZAP	FLDB,=P'+04567'	

C. Alternate to ZAP

The following two excerpts produce the same result.

LABEL	OPERATION	OPERAND	COMMENTS
	ZAP	SUM,=P'0'	
	•		
	•		
	•		
SUM	DS	PL5	

LABEL	OPERATION	OPERAND	COMMENTS
	•		
	•		
	•		
	•		
SUM	DC	PL5'0'	

> NOTE: When SUM is a field to be cleared only at the start of the
> program, then the single DC entry in Method 2 will suffice.
> When SUM must be cleared for several different routines, the
> ZAP should be used.

D. ZAP in a Loop

Suppose we wish to accumulate a 5-digit AMT field on each of 5 input records
and then print the total. The pseudocode and assembler coding for this are as
follows.

Pseudocode

```
PERFORM UNTIL CTR = 5
    READ A RECORD
    ADD AMT TO TOTAL
    ADD 1 TO CTR
ENDPERFORM
    WRITE A LINE
```

Assembler Coding

```
GETIT     GET    IN,REC1
          PACK   AMT,AMT
          AP     TOTAL,AMT
          AP     CTR,ONE
          CP     CTR,=P'5'     COMPARE PACKED IS EXPLAINED LATER
          BL     GETIT                   IN THIS CHAPTER
UNPACK    UNPK   OUT+5,CTR
          OI     OUT+5,X'F0'
          UNPK   OUT+15(7),TOTAL(4)
          OI     OUT+21,X'F0'
PRINTIT   PUT    OUTFILE,OUT
            .
            .
            .
ONE       DC     PL1'1'
CTR       DC     P'0'
TOTAL     DC     PL4'0'
OUT       DS     0CL132
            .
            .
```

This program excerpt works properly if there is only 1 group of 5 records to
process. If we wish to repeat the procedure for numerous groups of 5 input
records, additional steps must be taken. Prior to GETIT, CTR and TOTAL must
be initialized to ensure they *always* begin at zero, not just initially. We could
use the ZAP for this purpose.

```
ZEROIT    ZAP    TOTAL,=P'0'   ZERO COUNTER AND RUNNING TOTALS
          ZAP    CTR,=P'0'     BEFORE ENTERING LOOP
GETIT     GET    IN,REC1
          PACK   AMT,AMT
          AP     TOTAL,AMT
          AP     CTR,ONE
          CP     CTR,=P'5'
          BL     GETIT
UNPACK    UNPK   OUT+5,CTR
          OI     OUT+5,X'F0'
          UNPK   OUT+15(7),TOTAL(4)
          OI     OUT+21,X'F0'
PRINTIT   PUT    OUTFILE,OUT
            .
            .
            .
ONE       DC     PL1'1'
CTR       DS     PL1
TOTAL     DS     PL4
OUT       DS     0CL132
            .
            .
```

E. ZAP **Compared to** MVC

Although an MVC will move the packed contents of one field to another, it produces the desired results only if the sending and receiving fields are exactly the same size. Otherwise, the MVC, which begins moving leftmost positions, will truncate differently or fail to fill with high-order zeros, depending on the size of the receiving field. In short, it is recommended that MVC's be avoided in transmitting packed fields. The MVC instruction is intended for moving data in zoned-decimal format. It should also be noted that the condition code is *not* set by the MVC instruction, although it is by the ZAP instruction.

F. Summary

The ZAP instruction clears a field by setting it to zero and then performs an add operation according to the same rules as defined for the AP instruction in Chapter 7.

ZERO AND ADD PACKED (ZAP) SUMMARY

1. The first operand is cleared to zero, and the contents of the second operand are added to the first, one byte at a time from *right* to *left*.
2. The *second operand* must contain valid packed-decimal data or a data exception will occur.
3. The result is stored in the first operand.
4. Length specifiers may be included in either or both operands.
5. If the first operand is too long, zeros will be filled in the high-order position(s).
6. If the first operand is not large enough to contain all of the significant digits of the first operand, overflow will result.
7. The second operand may be self-defining as long as the data is specified in the packed-decimal format.

Self-Evaluating Quiz   For Questions 1–3, indicate the results of the following instruction:

LABEL	OPERATION 10 16	OPERAND	COMMENTS	72
	ZAP	PAMT1,PAMT2		

Note that the original contents of PAMT1 do not affect the results.

For Questions 4–6, indicate the results of the following:

LABEL	OPERATION 10 16	OPERAND	COMMENTS	72
	ZAP	FLD1,=P'05'		

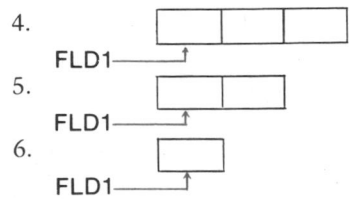

4.
FLD1

5.
FLD1

6.
FLD1

SOLUTIONS
1. | 0 | 0 | 1 | 2 | 2 | C |
2. | 2 | 3 | 3 | C | overflow occurs; condition code is set to 3
3. invalid; PAMT2 must be in packed form
4. | 0 | 0 | 0 | 0 | 5 | C |
5. | 0 | 0 | 5 | C |
6. | 5 | C | overflow occurs; condition code is set to 3

G. Helpful Hints

Using ZAP to test for *signed values.*

The ZAP instruction automatically sets a condition code as follows:

Condition Code	Meaning
0	Second operand is 0.
1	Second operand is negative.
2	Second operand is positive.
3	Second operand is larger than first—overflow.

Hence, you can ZAP a field into itself, which does not change any contents, and then test the condition code to determine if the value of the field is 0, negative or positive.

Conditions That Can Follow ZAP	
Instruction	Meaning
BZ	Branch on Zero
BM	Branch on Minus
BP	Branch on Positive
BO	Branch on Overflow

Example 8.4   Branch to NEGRTN if SUM is negative:

LABEL	OPERATION	OPERAND	COMMENTS
	ZAP	SUM,SUM	
	BM	NEGRTN	

II. MULTIPLYING PACKED FIELDS

A. Introduction

In this unit we will use the following example to demonstrate how multiplication is performed.

Example 8.5   An input record is defined as follows:

LABEL	OPERATION	OPERAND	COMMENTS	
1	10	16		72
RECIN	DS	ØCL8Ø		
NAME	DS	CL2Ø		
PRICE	DS	CL3		
QTY	DS	CL2		
	DS	CL55		

Operation to Be Performed	Terms	Sample Contents
PRICE	Multiplicand	999
x QTY	Multiplier	99
RESULT	Product	98901

Because all fields in the multiplication must contain packed data, we will establish the following storage areas.

LABEL	OPERATION	OPERAND	COMMENTS	
1	10	16		72
PRICEPKD	DS	PL2		
QTYPKD	DS	PL2		

We will then be able to pack the input fields PRICE and QTY into these areas before multiplication is performed. Notice that PRICEPKD is established as a 2-byte field because the input field PRICE contains 3 digits. You will recall that it requires 2 bytes to hold 3 digits and a sign in packed form. Similarly, QTYPKD is set up as a 2-byte field into which we can pack the field QTY. Two bytes are necessary to hold 2 digits plus a sign.

B. Steps to be Followed When Multiplying

MULTIPLICATION STEPS

1. Determine the size of the resultant field or **product.**
2. Move the **multiplicand** (number to be multiplied) to the first operand.
3. Multiply the multiplicand (first operand) by the **multiplier** (second operand), with the product replacing the first operand.

---

1. Determining the Size of the Resultant Field or Product

The number of bytes in the product field of a multiplication can be determined by adding the length of the bytes in the packed multiplicand (PRICE) to the length of the bytes in the packed multiplier (QTY).

Number of bytes in packed multiplicand	= 2
Number of bytes in packed multiplier	= 2
Number of bytes in the product	= 4

It is essential that the programmer establish a field large enough for the product of a multiplication. If the product field is too small to hold the results, an overflow condition will occur that may cause a program interrupt.

Length of product = Number of bytes in packed multiplier +
(in bytes)   number of bytes in packed multiplicand

Example 8.6   Consider the following.

```
UNITPR   DS   CL4
QTY      DS   CL3
```

If these fields are to be multiplied, UNITPR will be packed into a 3-byte field:

$$\frac{4 \text{ digits} + 1}{2} = 2.5$$

$$= 3 \text{ bytes}$$

QTY will be packed into a 2-byte field: $\frac{3 \text{ digits} + 1}{2} = 2 \text{ bytes}$

The product field will require 5 bytes: $3 + 2$.

Using the example where PRICE and QTY are to be multiplied with PRICE as a 3-digit field and QTY as a 2-digit field, PRICE would be packed into a 2-byte area and QTY into a 2-byte area as well. Hence, the field called RESULT that will contain the product must be defined as follows:

LABEL	OPERATION	OPERAND	COMMENTS
RESULT	DS	PL4	

2. The Multiplicand Must Be Packed and Moved to the First Operand

Data is read into the computer in zoned-decimal format and must be packed prior to any arithmetic operations. Before performing a multiplication operation, the packed multiplicand must be *moved* to a field large enough to accommodate the product. The field to which it is moved will be used as the first operand in the multiply operation. Note that we do *not* use an MVC to move the multiplicand to the resultant field. Rather, we use a ZAP that clears the resultant field first and then adds in the packed-decimal contents of the multiplicand.

3. Methods Used for Multiplication

a. Method 1

Before Execution

F 9	F 9	F 9		F 9	F 9		?	?		?	?		?	?	?	?

PRICE   QTY   PRICEPKD   QTYPKD   RESULT

LABEL	OPERATION	OPERAND	COMMENTS
	PACK	PRICEPKD,PRICE	
	PACK	QTYPKD,QTY	
	ZAP	RESULT,PRICEPKD	

After Execution

F 9	F 9	F 9		F 9	F 9		99	9F		09	9F		00	00	99	9C

PRICE   QTY   PRICEPKD   QTYPKD   RESULT
                                                            (add operation
                                                            generates + sign)

b. Method 2 (no need to establish PRICEPKD)

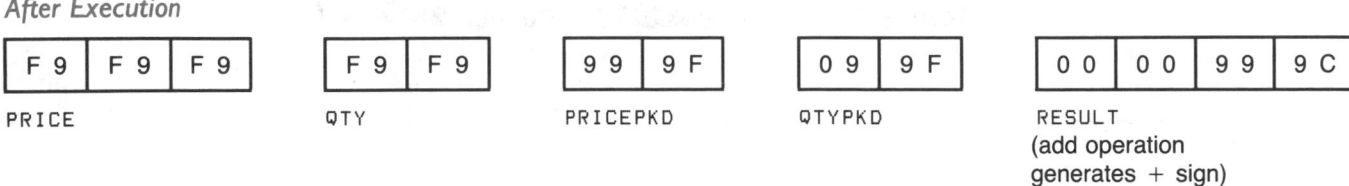

LABEL	OPERATION	OPERAND	COMMENTS
	PACK	QTYPKD,QTY	
	PACK	RESULT,PRICE	

In both cases, the multiplicand, PRICE, and the multiplier, QTY, are packed and the packed multiplicand is placed in the RESULT field. It is important to note that a PACK or ZAP instruction is used to put the multiplicand in the RESULT field. This will ensure that there will be *zeros* in the high-order positions of the first operand *before* multiplication is performed. If this requirement is not met, an interrupt or abend will occur.

4. Multiply Packed

Instruction:	MP
Meaning:	Multiply Packed Decimal
	1. The first operand contains the multiplicand in packed form.
	2. The second operand contains the multiplier in packed form.
Results:	The product replaces the multiplicand as the first operand in packed form; the second operand remains unchanged.
Operands:	The second operand may be a packed field or a self-defining packed constant.
Length:	1. The length of the second operand (multiplier) must not exceed 8 bytes—that is, 15 digits and a sign.
	2. The length of the multiplier must be less than the length of the first operand.
	3. The length of the first operand must be large enough to hold the product.
Limitations:	Use ZAP or PACK to place the multiplicand in the first operand. This ensures that zeros will be in the high-order positions of the first operand before multiplication.

C. Examples

The following 5 examples assume that PRICEPKD, a 2-byte packed field, was moved into RESULT and that QTY is a packed field.

			Before		After	Comment
			RESULT	QTY	RESULT	
Example 8.7 Error	MP	RESULT,QTY	00 90 0C	01 2C	10 80 0C	Three bytes are insufficient even though in this particular case, the result would fit: two bytes + two bytes require four bytes.
Example 8.8 Okay	MP	RESULT,QTY	00 00 90 0C	01 2C	00 10 80 0C	With four bytes, zeros are placed in high-order positions. RESULT *must* be four bytes or more.

Example 8.9 *Error*	MP	RESULT,QTY	90 0C	01 2C	80 0C	With two bytes, overflow occurs: condition code set to 3.
Example 8.10 *Okay*	MP	RESULT,QTY	00 00 08 89 0C	01 2C	00 01 06 68 0C	Five bytes in RESULT is fine.
Example 8.11 *Error*	MP	RESULT,QTY	00 00 99 9C	09 99 9C	99 89 00 1C	Because QTY is three bytes, four bytes are insufficient.

Example 8.12 Consider the following input.

LABEL	OPERATION	OPERAND	COMMENTS
STUDENTS	DS	0CL80	
NAME	DS	CL20	
CREDITS	DS	CL2	
RATEPER	DS	CL3	
	DS	CL55	

The following program excerpt computes tuition where

TUITION = RATEPER x CREDITS:

	LABEL	OPERATION	OPERAND	COMMENTS
1.		PACK	PRATE,RATEPER	
2.		PACK	PCREDITS,CREDITS	
3.		ZAP	TUITION,PRATE	
4.		MP	TUITION,PCREDITS	
	*			
	*			
	PRATE	DS	PL2	
	PCREDITS	DS	PL2	
	TUITION	DS	PL4 (2 + 2 BYTES)	

Sample Data

Before Execution

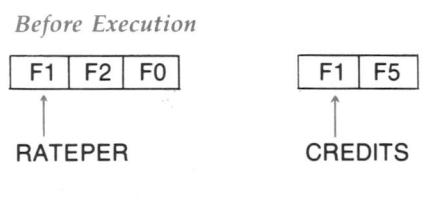

1.   PACK   PRATE,RATEPER

After Execution

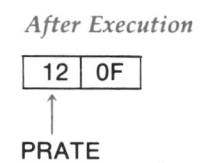

PRATE = 2 bytes

$$\frac{3 \text{ digits (RATE)} + 1}{2}$$

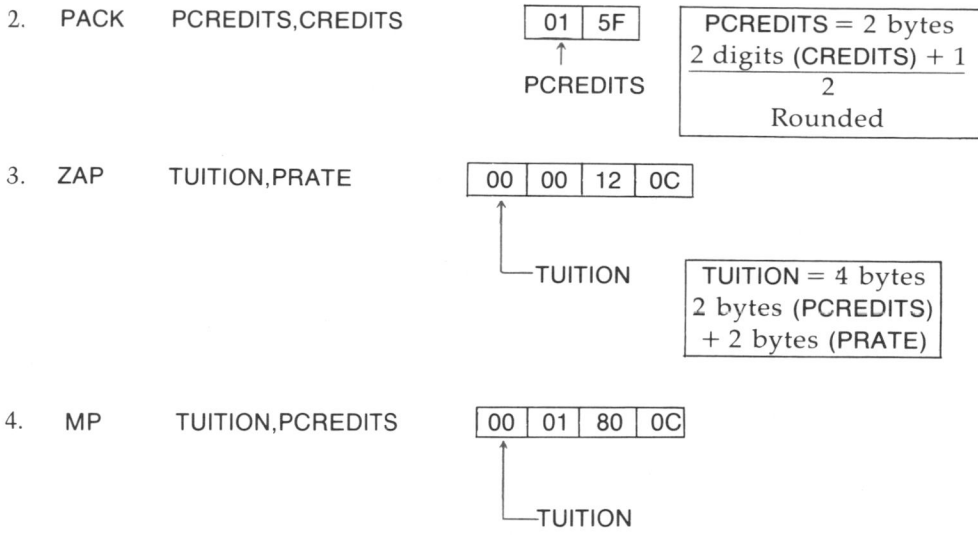

2. PACK   PCREDITS,CREDITS

01	5F

↑
PCREDITS

PCREDITS = 2 bytes
$$\frac{2 \text{ digits (CREDITS)} + 1}{2}$$
Rounded

3. ZAP   TUITION,PRATE

00	00	12	0C

└─TUITION

TUITION = 4 bytes
2 bytes (PCREDITS)
+ 2 bytes (PRATE)

4. MP   TUITION,PCREDITS

00	01	80	0C

└─TUITION

(TUITION will need to be unpacked and edited
before it is printed.)

Example 8.13   Consider the following input.

LABEL	OPERATION	OPERAND	COMMENTS
INREC	DS	ØCL8Ø	
NAME	DS	CL2Ø	
PRINC	DS	CL5	
RATE	DS	CL3	
	DS	CL52	

The following program excerpt computes INTEREST where

INTEREST = PRINC x RATE

	LABEL	OPERATION	OPERAND	COMMENTS
1.		PACK	PPRINC,PRINC	
2.		PACK	PRATE,RATE	
3.		ZAP	INTEREST,PPRINC	
4.		MP	INTEREST,PRATE	
*				
	PPRINC	DS	PL3	
	PRATE	DS	PL2	
	INTEREST	DS	PL5	

Sample Data   _Before Execution_

F1	F5	F0	F0	F0

↑
PRINC

F8	F1	F0

↑
RATE

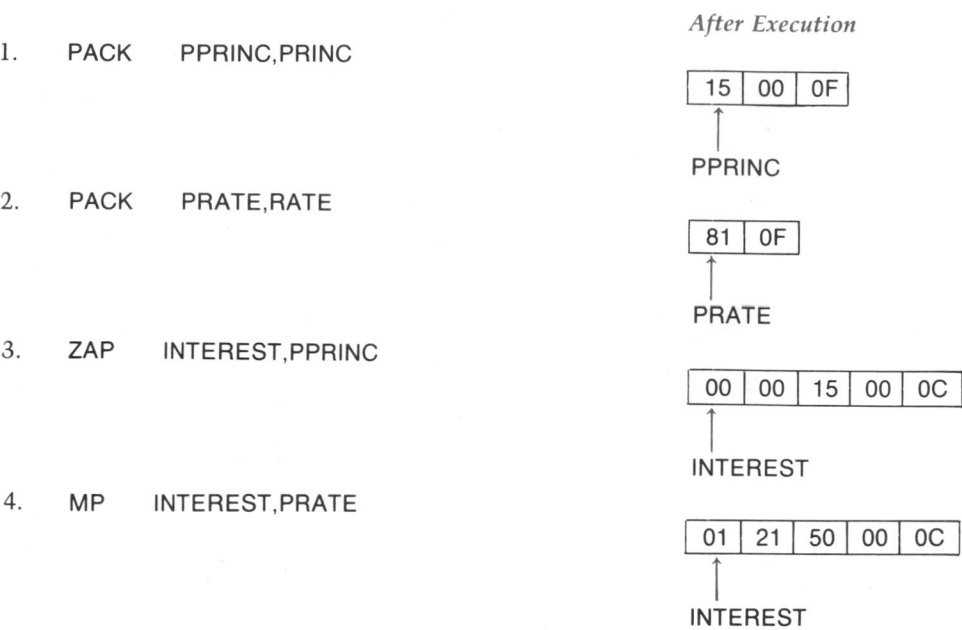

After Execution

1. PACK   PPRINC,PRINC

```
| 15 | 00 | 0F |
```
↑
PPRINC

2. PACK   PRATE,RATE

```
| 81 | 0F |
```
↑
PRATE

3. ZAP   INTEREST,PPRINC

```
| 00 | 00 | 15 | 00 | 0C |
```
↑
INTEREST

4. MP   INTEREST,PRATE

```
| 01 | 21 | 50 | 00 | 0C |
```
↑
INTEREST

Note

This problem is actually being used to multiply a principal of $15,000 by an interest rate that in reality is 8.10% or 0.0810. Hence, the answer indicated, 12150000, will print, when edited, as $1215.00. Edit procedures are considered in the next chapter.

SUMMARY OF MULTIPLY PACKED (MP)

1. Determine the size of the product field, the first operand, using the formula provided: Number of bytes in packed multiplier + number of bytes in packed multiplicand.
2. Place the multiplicand in the first operand (the number to be multiplied).
3. Both the multiplicand and multiplier must be in packed format. The product is in packed format.
4. The second operand (multiplier) may not exceed 15 digits and a sign (or 8 bytes), or a specification error and an abend condition will result.
5. The product (first operand after execution) is in packed format and is limited to 31 digits and the sign, or 16 bytes.
6. If the product field is incorrectly defined so that it is too small, an overflow condition will result.
7. When the product field is larger than necessary, normal multiplication will take place.

Self-Evaluating Quiz

1. A product is produced by multiplying the _____ by the _____ .
2. When a 5-digit number is multiplied by a 3-digit number, the product field should be **(no.)** bytes long.
3. Before we multiply, the _____ must be placed in the first operand.
4. The multiplier is referenced by the **(first/second)** operand.
5. After execution, the product is found in the **(first/second)** operand in the _____ format.
6. If both operands are not packed a(n) _____ will occur.

7. (T or F) Neither operand may exceed 8 bytes.
8. (T or F) If the product field is too small, the low-order (rightmost) digits will be truncated.
9. Write a routine to multiply A by B and place the answer in C where A and B are defined as follows:

```
A    DS    CL3
B    DS    CL3
```

10. Write a routine to multiply D by 154 and place the answer in E where D is defined as follows:

```
D    DS    CL5
```

11. Calculate a 7 percent sales tax for an input field called TOTAL defined as follows.

```
TOTAL    DS    CL7
```

SOLUTIONS

1. Multiplicand (number to be multiplied); multiplier
2. 5 [3 packed bytes + 2 packed bytes]
      (5 digits)   (3 digits)
3. Multiplicand—larger field
4. Second
5. First; packed
6. Data exception
7. F: the first operand may be 16 bytes in length.
8. F: the high-order digits are lost, and an overflow condition occurs.
9.

```
LABEL      OPERATION   OPERAND
           PACK        PACKA,A
           PACK        PACKB,B
           ZAP         C,PACKA
           MP          C,PACKB
*
PACKA      DS          PL2
PACKB      DS          PL2
C          DS          PL4
```

10.

```
LABEL      OPERATION   OPERAND
           PACK        PACKD,D
           ZAP         E,PACKD
           MP          E,=P'154'
*
PACKD      DS          PL3
E          DS          PL5   THE CONSTANT P'154' WOULD
*                            REQUIRE 2 BYTES: 2 + 3 = 5
```

11.

```
LABEL      OPERATION   OPERAND
           PACK        TAX,TOTAL
           MP          TAX,=P'7'
* NOTE: NO ATTENTION IS GIVEN HERE TO DECIMAL
* POINT ALIGNMENT. THIS IS CONSIDERED LATER
* ON IN THIS CHAPTER.
TAX        DS          PL5
```

III. DIVIDING PACKED FIELDS

A. Introduction

The divide procedure is analogous to the multiply procedure. Let us use the following example.

Example 8.14   An input record is defined as follows.

LABEL	OPERATION	OPERAND	COMMENTS
RECIN	DS	0CL80	
COURSE	DS	CL20	
TGRADES	DS	CL4	
PUPILS	DS	CL3	
	DS	CL53	

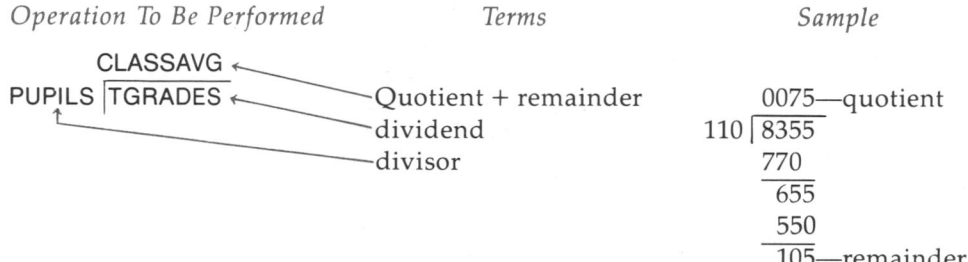

Operation To Be Performed	Terms	Sample
CLASSAVG ←	Quotient + remainder	0075 — quotient
PUPILS ⟌ TGRADES ←	dividend	110 ⟌ 8355
	divisor	770
		655
		550
		105 — remainder

Note
We will not illustrate solutions with decimal or fractional components until the next section.

B. Steps to be Followed When Dividing

The three facets to the divide operations are analogous to the multiply.

> **DIVIDE**
> 1. Determine the size of the field that will contain the result. This depends on both dividend and the divisor.
> 2. Move the packed dividend to the first operand, which is the result field.
> 3. Divide the packed dividend (first operand) by the packed divisor (second operand). The answer appears in the first operand.

1. Determine the Size of the Field That Will Contain the Result

The result field, which is the first operand in the divide operation, contains *both* the quotient and the remainder. The length of the field, then, is calculated as follows:

DETERMINE LENGTH OF RESULT

1. The length of the result field equals the length of the quotient plus the length of the **remainder.**
2. The length of the **quotient** will be equal to the length in bytes of the packed **dividend.** (4 digits in the example = 3 bytes.)
3. The length of the remainder will be equal to the length in bytes of the packed **divisor.** (3 digits in the example = 2 bytes.)

Both results—the quotient and remainder—are stored in *one* field. The quotient is stored in the high-order (leftmost) positions of this field, and the remainder is in the low-order (rightmost) positions. The quotient and the remainder each have their own signs. The length of the field is determined as follows.

1. Calculate the packed length of the quotient and the remainder. Remember, these are the same lengths as the dividend and divisor, respectively. The quotient will be 4 digits; hence 3 bytes are required. The remainder will be 3 digits; hence 2 bytes are required.
2. Number of bytes of first operand = number of bytes of the packed quotient + number of bytes of the packed remainder = 3 + 2 = 5

2. Move the Packed Dividend to the First Operand—the Result Field

As with multiplication, all fields must be packed. Either of the two alternative methods of coding may be used.

a. Method 1

LABEL	OPERATION	OPERAND	COMMENTS
	PACK	PGRADES,TGRADES	
	PACK	PPUPILS,PUPILS	
	ZAP	CLASSAVG,PGRADES	
*			
PGRADES	DS	PL3	
PPUPILS	DS	PL2	
CLASSAVG	DS	PL5	

b. Method 2

LABEL	OPERATION	OPERAND	COMMENTS
	PACK	PPUPILS,PUPILS	
	PACK	CLASSAVG,TGRADES	
*			
PPUPILS	DS	PL2	
CLASSAVG	DS	PL5	

The calculations indicate that a minimum of 5 bytes are necessary to contain the entire answer (both quotient and remainder) in our illustration. The first 3 bytes will store the quotient and the last 2 bytes will contain the remainder.

We recommend coding the Define Storage or DS instruction for this area as follows:

LABEL	OPERATION	OPERAND	COMMENTS
CLASSAVG	DS	ØPL5	
QUOTNT	DS	PL3	
RMDR	DS	PL2	

When division is completed, using the preceding designations you can directly reference both the quotient (QUOTNT) and remainder (RMDR) for unpacking purposes.[1]

If you define CLASSAVG as:

```
CLASSAVG   DS   PL5
```

then you must use relative addressing to access the quotient and remainder.

Relative Addressing

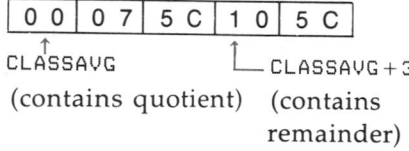

```
CLASSAVG   DS   PL5
```

If you define CLASSAVG as:

```
ANSWER    DS   ØPL5
QUOTNT    DS   PL3
RMDR      DS   PL2
```

then you can access both the quotient, QUOTNT, and the remainder, RMDR, directly.

Direct Addressing

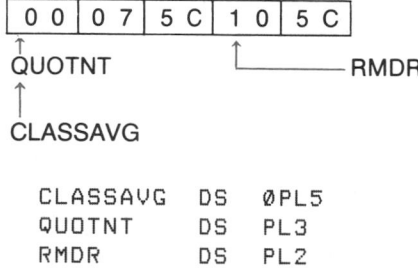

```
CLASSAVG   DS   ØPL5
QUOTNT     DS   PL3
RMDR       DS   PL2
```

Relative addressing length specifiers must be used if the area CLASSAVG is not subdivided. This initial planning is essential to use the Divide Packed (DP) instruction effectively.

---

[1]See Chapter 17 for instructions that can be used for rounding.

3. Divide Packed Format

Instruction:	DP
Meaning:	Divide Packed decimal
	1. The first operand contains the dividend in packed form.
	2. The second operand contains the divisor in packed form.
Results:	First operand:
	1. The high-order bytes (same size as packed dividend) contain the quotient with a sign.
	2. The low-order bytes (same size as packed divisor) contain the remainder with a sign.
	The second operand remains unchanged.
Operands:	The second operand may be a packed field or a self-defining packed constant.
Length:	The first operand may not exceed 16 bytes. The second operand may not exceed 8 bytes.
Limitations:	An effort to divide by zero (zero divisor) will cause an error.

C. Examples

Example 8.15 The following illustrates how the Divide Packed (DP) instruction operates.

LABEL	OPERATION	OPERAND	COMMENTS
1.	PACK	PGRADES,TGRADES	
2.	PACK	PPUPILS,PUPILS	
3.	ZAP	CLASSAVG,PGRADES	
4.	DP	CLASSAVG,PPUPILS	
*			
PGRADES	DS	PL3	
PPUPILS	DS	PL2	
CLASSAVG	DS	ØPL5	
QUOTNT	DS	PL3	
RMDR	DS	PL2	

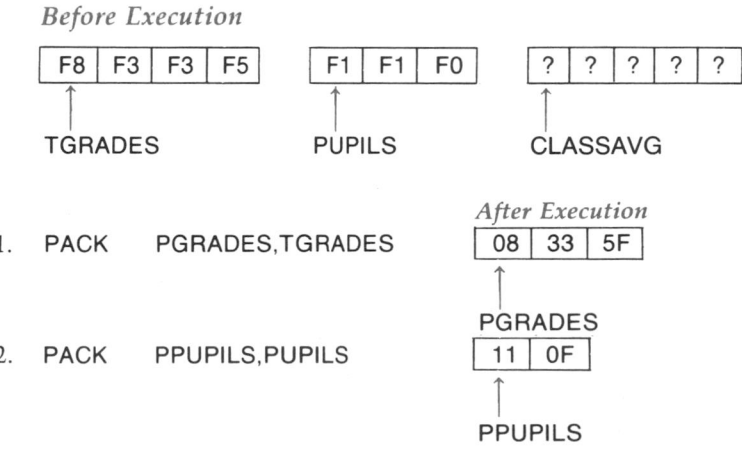

Before Execution

| F8 | F3 | F3 | F5 |
↑
TGRADES

| F1 | F1 | F0 |
↑
PUPILS

| ? | ? | ? | ? | ? |
↑
CLASSAVG

After Execution

1. PACK   PGRADES,TGRADES

| 08 | 33 | 5F |
↑
PGRADES

2. PACK   PPUPILS,PUPILS

| 11 | 0F |
↑
PPUPILS

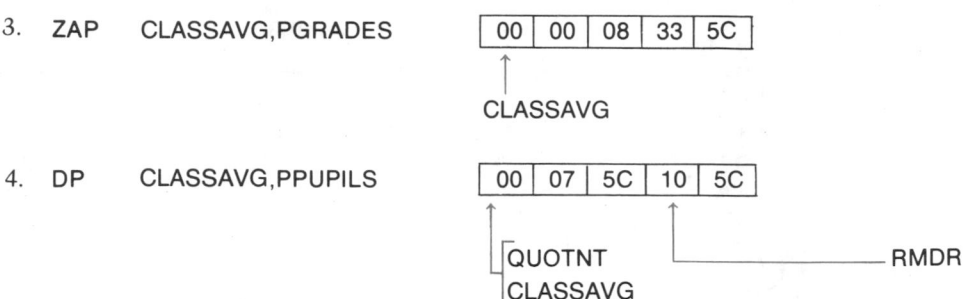

3. ZAP   CLASSAVG,PGRADES

| 00 | 00 | 08 | 33 | 5C |

↑
CLASSAVG

4. DP   CLASSAVG,PPUPILS

| 00 | 07 | 5C | 10 | 5C |

QUOTNT
CLASSAVG   RMDR

Notice that the dividend (PGRADES) was moved to the first operand (CLASS-AVG) by a ZAP instruction. After the division is performed, the first operand (CLASSAVG) contains a quotient (QUOTNT) of 00075, and a remainder (RMDR) of 105. *Both* the quotient and the remainder have signs included. Note that the remainder in this example will never exceed 3 digits. Similarly, had we divided by 1, we would produce the largest possible quotient (08335), which is the same number of bytes as the dividend.

In the next example, we will divide a 6-digit dividend (TSALES) by a 2-digit divisor (QTY). Our calculations indicate the following:

1. Quotient = 4 bytes
    Remainder = 2 bytes
2. Bytes in 1st operand = bytes in quotient + bytes in remainder = 4 + 2 = 6

The Define Storage instructions for the first operand would therefore be coded as follows:

LABEL	OPERATION	OPERAND	COMMENTS
UNITPR	DS	0PL6	
AVGSALE	DS	PL4	
RMDR	DS	PL2	

Example 8.16   The following illustrates how TSALES is packed and moved to the first operand UNITPR, and then divided by QTY to obtain a unit price.

	LABEL	OPERATION	OPERAND	COMMENTS
1.		PACK	PSALES,TSALES	
2.		PACK	PQTY,QTY	
3.		ZAP	UNITPR,PSALES	
4.		DP	UNITPR,PQTY	
	*			
	INREC	DS	0CL80	
	TSALES	DS	CL6	
	QTY	DS	CL2	
		DS	CL72	
	*			
	PSALES	DS	PL4	
	PQTY	DS	PL2	
	UNITPR	DS	0PL6	
	AVGSALE	DS	PL4	
	RMDR	DS	PL2	

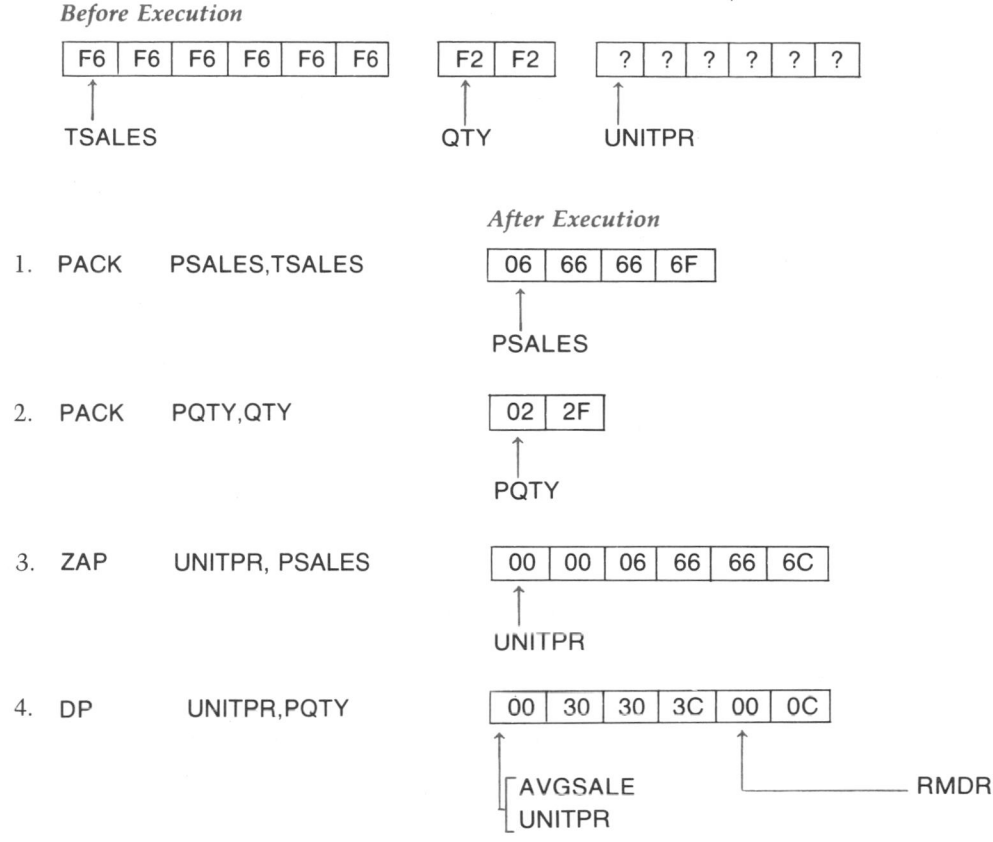

Before Execution

After Execution

1. PACK   PSALES,TSALES

2. PACK   PQTY,QTY

3. ZAP   UNITPR, PSALES

4. DP   UNITPR,PQTY

The quotient (AVGSALE) is equal to 30303 with a remainder of 0. These results could be unpacked and printed by referring to the storage areas named AVGSALE and RMDR.

If QTY were known to be 22, then the sample Divide Pack instruction could also have been written using a self-defining operand.

LABEL	OPERATION		OPERAND	COMMENTS	
1	10	16			72
	DP		UNITPR,=P'22'		

The results produced would be identical to those previously illustrated.

D. Errors Caused by Zero Divisors

If the divisor is 0, a **decimal divide exception** will occur. This problem may be avoided by using the ZAP instruction to set the condition code, and branching on a zero condition to an error routine called ZERODIV. The instructions necessary for this test are:

LABEL	OPERATION		OPERAND	COMMENTS	
1	10	16			72
	ZAP		DIVSOR,DIVSOR (DOES NOT CHANGE VALUE —		
*			JUST SETS CONDITION CODE)		
	BZ		ZERODIV		

The DP procedure will now be summarized. Note that many of its characteristics are similar to the MP (Multiply Pack) instruction.

SUMMARY OF DP INSTRUCTION

1. Determine the size of the quotient and remainder in bytes; this becomes the length of the first operand.
2. Both the dividend and divisor must be in packed format.
3. Place the packed dividend in the first operand.
4. The second operand may not exceed 8 bytes.
5. The first operand may not exceed 16 bytes.
6. The second operand may be self-defining.
7. The resulting quotient and remainder are in packed format.
8. A decimal divide exception will occur if:
   a. The first operand is too small to contain the quotient and the remainder (overflow).
   b. The second operand equals zero.

E. Helpful Hints

1. Obtaining a Percentage

Suppose we wish to obtain the percentage of students in a school who have taken an introductory data processing course. We discover that fifty (50) students of 500 have taken the course. How do we compute the percentage? The mathematical formula is as follows:

$$\frac{50}{500} = 500\overline{\smash{\big)}\,50.0}^{\,0.10} = 10\%$$

To use the divide instruction as described would produce the following:

$$500\overline{\smash{\big)}\,50}^{\,0}\quad\text{Quotient}$$
$$\underline{0}$$
$$50 \longleftarrow \text{Remainder}$$

The division does *not* produce any decimal or fractional results. Because we wish to obtain a percentage, we can do the following:

$$\% = 100 \times \text{decimal value}$$
[Example: 10% = 100 × .10]

$$\frac{\text{Dividend}}{\text{Divisor}} \times 100 = \%$$

$$\text{Example: } \frac{50}{500} \times 100 = \%$$

$$\frac{5000}{500} = 10\%$$

$$500\overline{\smash{\big)}\,5000}^{\,10} = 10\%$$

Hence to obtain a percentage when we divide, we must multiply the dividend by 100 *prior to* the division. The result will be integers that refer to the actual percentage.

2. Packed Decimal (P) Format in DS

Note that DS areas in storage, even those used in arithmetic operations, can be established in P or even C format. Because DS simply reserves space for a storage area, coding ANSWER, for example,

```
ANSWER    DS    CL5
```

or

```
ANSWER    DS    PL5
```

is really of no consequence. The P or the C is merely for documentation purposes. To use the field ANSWER in an arithmetic operation, however, it must contain *packed data only.*

3. Example

Figure 8.1 illustrates a program to read in cards with the following format and to produce the report shown. (The Xs indicate data that will be filled in by the computer, depending on the input processed.) Figure 8.2 shows the logic used.

a. Input Record Layout

LAST NAME	FIRST NAME	SALARY	

1   15 16   25 26   30 31   80

b. Printer Spacing Chart for Printed Output

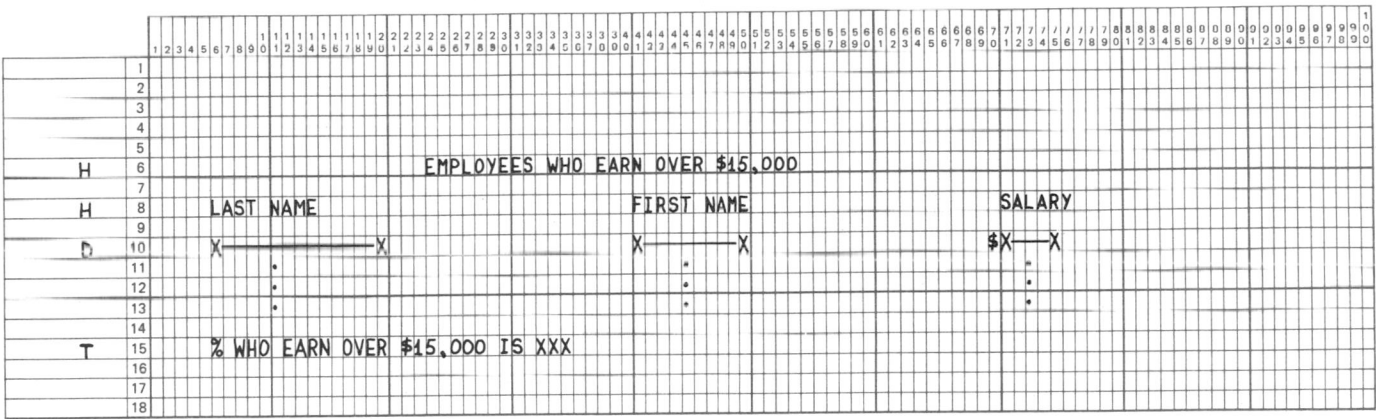

Notice that in the EOF routine, the UNPK instruction is:

```
UNPK    OUTAREA+27(3),HOLD+2(2)
```

HOLD is a 6-byte packed field that, after the DP instruction, will appear as follows.

```
         *                                                                    *
         *                                    HOUSEKEEPING INSTRUCTIONS GO HERE  *
         *                                                                    *
                 MVC    OUTAREA,SPACES
                 MVC    OUTAREA+23(31),=C'EMPLOYEES WHO EARN OVER $15,000'
                 PUT    OUTFILE,OUTAREA
                 MVC    OUTAREA,SPACES
                 PUT    OUTFILE,OUTAREA            PRINT BLANK LINE
                 MVC    LNAME(9),=C'LAST NAME'
                 MVC    FNAME(10),=C'FIRST NAME'
                 MVC    SALOUT(6),=C'SALARY'
                 PUT    OUTFILE,OUTAREA
                 MVC    OUTAREA,SPACES
                 PUT    OUTFILE,OUTAREA            PRINT BLANK LINE
         READ    MVC    OUTAREA,SPACES
                 GET    INFILE,RECORD
                 AP     TOTEMP,=P'1'
                 CLC    SALARY,=C'15000'
                 BNH    READ
                 AP     COUNT,=P'1'
                 MVC    LNAME,LAST
                 MVC    FNAME,FIRST
                 MVC    SALOUT,SALARY
                 MVI    SALOUT-1,C'$'
                 PUT    OUTFILE,OUTAREA
                 B      READ
         EOF     MVC    OUTAREA,SPACES
                 PUT    OUTFILE,OUTAREA
                 MVC    OUTAREA+5(27),=C'% WHO EARN OVER $15,000 IS '
                 ZAP    NUM,COUNT
                 MP     NUM,=P'100'
                 ZAP    HOLD,NUM
                 DP     HOLD,TOTEMP
                 UNPK   OUTAREA+32(3),HOLD+2(2)
                 OI     OUTAREA+34,X'F0'
                 PUT    OUTFILE,OUTAREA
         *                                                                    *
         *                                    HOUSEKEEPING INSTRUCTIONS GO HERE  *
         *                                    ALONG WITH DCB OR DTF MACROS       *
         *                                                                    *
         COUNT   DC     PL2'0'
         HOLD    DS     PL6
         TOTEMP  DC     PL2'0'
         NUM     DS     PL4
         RECORD  DS     0CL80                      INPUT FORMAT
         LAST    DS     CL15                          *
         FIRST   DS     CL10                          *
         SALARY  DS     CL5                           *
                 DS     CL50                          *
         SPACES  DC     CL1' '
         OUTAREA DS     0CL132                     PRINT FORMAT
                 DS     CL5                           *
         LNAME   DS     CL15                          *
                 DS     CL20                          *
         FNAME   DS     CL10                          *
                 DS     CL20                          *
         SALOUT  DS     CL5                           *
                 DS     CL57                          *
                 END
```

Figure 8.1
Program to list employees who
earn over $15,000.

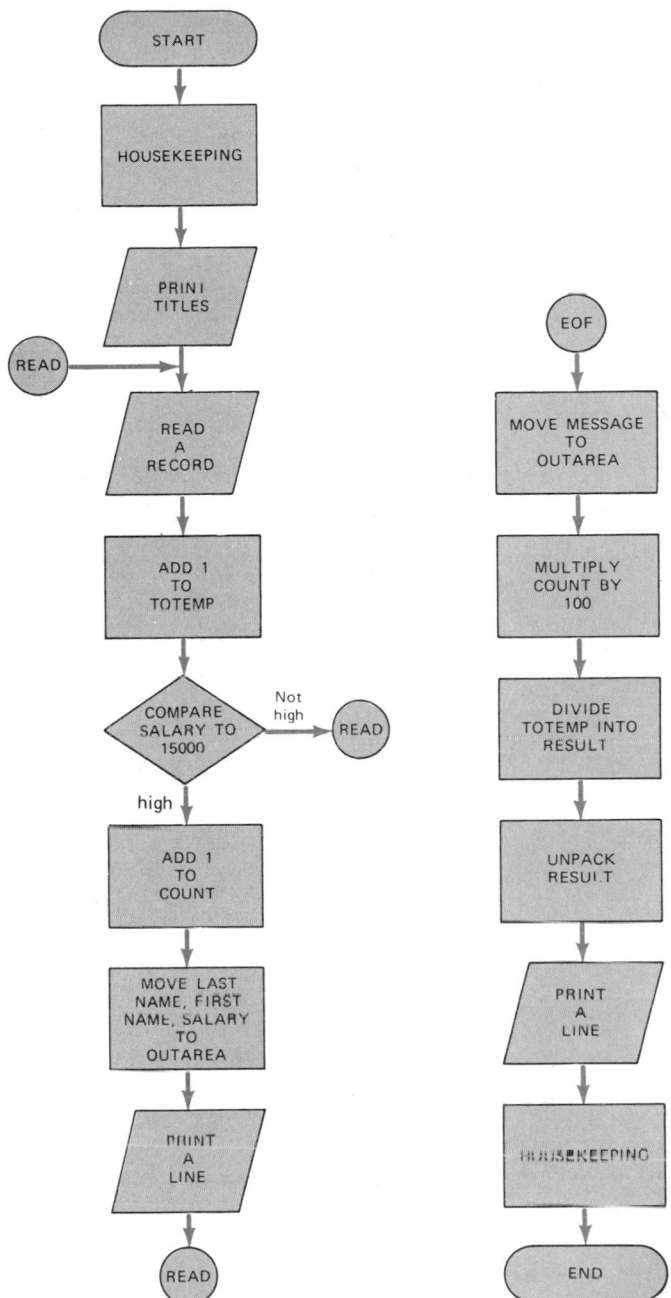

Figure 8.2
Flowchart for the program in
Figure 8.1.

Because we are finding a percentage, we know that the *maximum* amount in
HOLD will be 100 percent. This would be represented as follows.

00	00	10	0C	00	0C

HOLD   HOLD+2

You will recall that after the division operation, the quotient and the remainder each have their own sign—in this case, C for positive. Notice that the two
high-order bytes of HOLD are zero-filled. Consequently, when we unpack the
quotient, we can refer to HOLD+2(2) without losing any of the result.

Self-Evaluating Quiz

1. A quotient is the _____ of a divide operation.
2. Quotients are obtained by dividing a(n) _____ by a(n) _____ .
3. The length of the resultant field in a divide operation must be equal to the sum of the _____ and _____ .
4. The high-order bytes of the resultant field in a divide operation will contain the _____ and the lower-order bytes will contain the _____ .
5. An effort to divide by _____ will cause an error.
6. In a divide operation, the second operand may be a packed-decimal field or a(n) _____ .
7. Prior to the DP operation, the _____ is placed in the result field.
8. The quotient will be the same size as the _____ field, and the remainder will be the same size as the _____ field.

What, if anything, is wrong with the routines in Questions 9 and 10?

9. $A = B \neq C$

    3 bytes   2 bytes

Note
B and C are already packed.

LABEL	OPERATION	OPERAND	COMMENTS
	ZAP	A,C	
	DP	A,B	
*			
A	DS	PL5	

10. $D = \dfrac{E}{F}$ E = 4 bytes

        F = 3 bytes
        E and F are packed.

LABEL	OPERATION	OPERAND	COMMENTS
	ZAP	D,E	
	DP	D,F	
*			
D	DS	PL6	

11. Consider the following input areas.

LABEL	OPERATION	OPERAND	COMMENTS
SALESREC	DS	0CL80	
TOTALPR	DS	CL5	
QTY	DS	CL2	
	DS	CL73	

Write a routine to divide TOTALPR by QTY to obtain UNITPR.

12. Consider the following input areas.

LABEL	OPERATION	OPERAND	COMMENTS
STUDENTS	DS	ØCL8Ø	
NAME	DS	CL2Ø	
TUITION	DS	CL4	
RATE	DS	CL3	
	DS	CL53	

Write a routine to divide TUITION by RATE to obtain NOCREDS.

SOLUTIONS
1. Result
2. Dividend; divisor
3. Packed dividend in bytes; packed divisor in bytes
4. Quotient; remainder
5. Zero
6. Self-defining packed operand
7. Dividend
8. Dividend; divisor
9. Result obtained is A = C/B not B/C
10. D is not large enough to accommodate the results; it should be 7 bytes long (4 for quotient and 3 for remainder).

11.

LABEL	OPERATION	OPERAND	COMMENTS
	PACK	PACK1,TOTALPR	
	PACK	PACK2,QTY	
	ZAP	UNITPR,PACK1	
	DP	UNITPR,PACK2	
*			
PACK1	DS	PL3	
PACK2	DS	PL2	
UNITPR	DS	PL5 (ANSWER WILL BE IN 3 HIGH-ORDER BYTES)	

12.

LABEL	OPERATION	OPERAND	COMMENTS
	PACK	PTUITION,TUITION	
	PACK	PRATE,RATE	
	ZAP	NOCREDS,PTUITION	
	DP	NOCREDS,PRATE	
*			
PTUITION	DS	PL3	
PRATE	DS	PL2	
NOCREDS	DS	PL5	

IV. COMPARING PACKED FIELDS

A. Format

Operation 10	Operand 16
CP	OP1,OP2

Instruction:	CP
Meaning:	Compare Packed decimal.
	Sets condition code depending on the results of an algebraic comparison.
	First operand is compared to second operand.
Results:	Both operands are unchanged.
	Condition code is set to enable a branch on low, equal, or high.
	A BL (Branch Low) occurs, for example, if the first operand is less than the second operand.
Operands:	First operand must contain packed-decimal data. Second operand must either contain packed-decimal data, or be a self-defining packed constant.

B. Purpose

The CP instruction is used to compare two packed-decimal fields. The comparison is **algebraic,** meaning that the sign is included in the test, with the result that negative quantities have less value than positive quantities. The Compare Packed (CP) instruction is similar in many respects to the CLC instruction previously specified. A major difference, however, is that with the CP instruction the two operands are compared algebraically. That is, negative numbers are considered to have less value than positive numbers. The condition code is set depending on the relative value of the first operand as compared to the second operand. Neither operand is changed. The following instructions could be used to determine if an HRS field is greater than 40, and to branch to an overtime routine (OVERTIME) if it is. Both operands must be in packed-decimal format.

Flowchart

Pseudocode

```
IF HRS >40
   GO TO OVRTIME
ENDIF
```

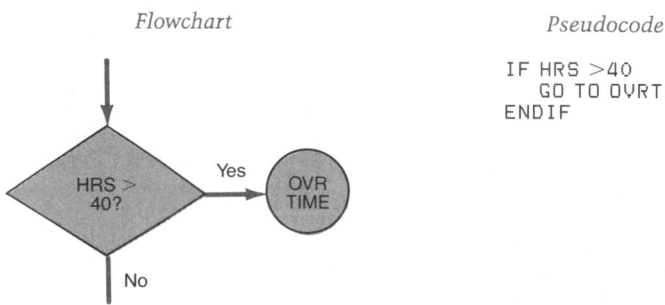

	LABEL	OPERATION 10	16	OPERAND	COMMENTS	72
1						
		CP	HRS,FORTY			
		BH	OVRTIME			
		.				
		.				
		.				
	FORTY	DC	P'40'			

C. Condition Code Settings

Let us review the condition code settings.

Relationship	Condition Code	Condition	Condition Met
First operand equals second operand.	0	Equal	BNH BNL BE
First operand is less than (<) second operand.	1	Low	BL BNH BNE
First operand is greater than (>) second operand.	2	High	BNL BH BNE

D. Examples

LABEL	OPERATION	OPERAND	COMMENTS
	CP	P1,P2	

	Contents of P1	Contents of P2	Result of Comparison
Example 8.17	123C	00123C	Equal (+123 — +00123)
Example 8.18	0C	123C	Low (0 < 123)
Example 8.19	456C	456D	High (+456 > −456)
Example 8.20	017C	018C	Low (17 < 18)
Example 8.21	022F	022C	Equal (022 = +022)
Example 8.22	1D	5D	High (−1 > −5)
Example 8.23	0C	0D	Equal (negative and positive zeros are considered equal)
Example 8.24	1F2F3F	01234C	Data exception (P1 is not a valid packed field)

The CP instructions could also be written using a self-defining operand as shown in the following example. Remember, however, that both operands must contain packed data.

LABEL	OPERATION	OPERAND	COMMENTS
	CP	HRS,=P'40'	
	BH	OVRTIME	

Because the CP compares packed data algebraically we need not worry about an illogical result. That is, with a CLC, 456C is less than 456D. This is because a CLC performs a bit-by-bit comparison while a CP compares algebraically.

The CP instruction is summarized as follows.

SUMMARY OF CP INSTRUCTION

1. The CP instruction is an algebraic compare; negative operands have a lesser value than positive operands.
2. Both operands in the packed format, or a data exception will occur.
3. The first operand is compared to the second operand.
4. When unequal fields are compared, the shorter field is extended with high-order zeros.
5. Plus zero (0C or 0F) and minus zero (0D) are considered equal.

V. APPLICATIONS

A. Looping Applications

Suppose we wish to compute a commission as 8 percent of sales for sales greater than $500. If the sales amount is $\leq$ $500, then the commission is 5 percent.

LABEL	OPERATION	OPERAND	COMMENTS
	PACK	PSALES,SALES	
	ZAP	COMMIS,PSALES	
	CP	PSALES,=P'500'	
	BH	COMMB	
	MP	COMMIS,=P'5'	
	B	WRITE	
COMMB	MP	COMMIS,=P'8'	
	B	WRITE	

B. Calculating Miles per Gallon

Each input record includes NMILES, for number of miles traveled, and GALS, for gallons used. Determine the MPG (miles per gallon) for each input record.

```
GET     IN,REC
PACK    PNMILES,NMILES
PACK    PGALS,GALS
ZAP     MPG,PNMILES
DP      MPG,PGALS
B       WRITE
```

C. Noting the Sequence of Steps to be Followed When Performing Arithmetic Operations

Perform the following sequence of steps to find an average AMT.

$$\frac{AMT1 + AMT2}{2} = (AMT1 + AMT2) / 2$$

Note that the division operation must be performed *after* the addition.

```
PACK    PAMT1,AMT1
PACK    PTOT,AMT2
AP      PTOT,PAMT1
DP      PTOT,=P'2'
```

CHAPTER SUMMARY

I. The Zero and Add Packed (ZAP) Instruction
   A. Used for clearing a field and replacing it with the packed contents of the sending field.
   B. Second operand must be a packed-decimal field or self-defining packed constant.
   C. Operand 1 is the receiving field and its contents are changed.
   D. The length of the operation may be implicit or explicit with a 16-byte maximum length.
   E. Be sure the receiving field is large enough to accommodate the results.
   F. The ZAP may be used to set the condition code.

II. The Multiply Packed (MP) Instruction
   A. Product field must be equal in length to the size of the multiplicand and the size of the multiplier.
   B. First move the multiplicand to Operand 1 using the ZAP.
   C. Multiply first operand that contains multiplicand by the second operand that contains multiplier.
   D. Product replaces the first operand.
   E. Both operands must be in packed format.
   F. The first operand cannot be larger than 16 bytes; the second operand cannot exceed eight bytes.

III. The Divide Packed (DP) Instruction
   A. Result field must be equal in length to the quotient plus the remainder.
   B. The value to be divided, the dividend, is moved to the first operand.
   C. The divisor is placed in the second operand.
   D. The divisor may be a self-defining constant.
   E. Both operands must contain packed-decimal data.
   F. When executed, the DP instruction places the quotient in the high-order bytes, and the remainder in the low-order bytes

QUOTIENT	REMAINDER

   G. The first operand may not exceed 16 bytes; the second may not exceed 8 bytes.
   H. Be sure the divisor is not zero; if it is, a divide exception error will occur and the computer will abend.

IV. The Compare Packed (CP) Instruction
   A. Two packed-decimal fields are compared.
   B. A condition code is set depending on the comparison; the condition code can be used in a subsequent instruction to cause a branch:

      BL   Operand 1 < Operand 2
      BH   Operand 1 > Operand 2
      BE   Operand 1 = Operand 2

      Similarly, BNL, BNH, BNE may be used.
   C. Operand 2 in the CP instruction may be a self-defining constant.
   D. Data is compared algebraically so that −456, for example, will compare "less than" +456.

CHAPTER SELF-EVALUATING QUIZ

1. (T or F) The CP instruction may be used to compare alphanumeric data.
2. (T or F) When executed, the CP instruction sets a condition code depending on the relationship of the first operand to the second.

3. The contents of (first/second/both/neither) operand(s) are changed when the CP instruction is carried out.

4. (T or F) The data referenced by both operands must be in the zoned-decimal format.

5. (T or F) A positive 0 has a greater value than a negative 0.

6. (T or F) The second operand of a CP statement can contain a self-defining operand.

7. Determine the values of AMT1, AMT2, and AMT3 after execution of the instructions indicated below. The three fields have the following initial values:

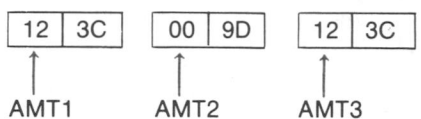

12	3C		00	9D		12	3C

AMT1   AMT2   AMT3

LABEL	OPERATION	OPERAND	COMMENTS
	AP	AMT1,AMT3	
	CP	AMT1,=P'+123'	
	BL	READRTN	
	AP	AMT1,AMT2	
	CP	AMT1,=P'+126'	
	BNH	READRTN	
	AP	AMT1,=P'+111'	

8. Compute 5 × A using the arithmetic operation AP only. Note that 5 × A = A + A + A + A + A. Use a loop for this routine. Assume A is in packed form.

9. Compute A × B using the arithmetic operation AP only. Note that A × B = A + A + ... + A. Assume A and B are both packed.
   └── B times ──┘

10. Compute N! where N is a 2-digit packed field.

    N! = N factorial = N × (N−1) × (N−2) × 1

11. Examine the program in Figure 8.3 that is supposed to determine the percentage of employees who earn under $29,000. Indicate any errors that exist.

    Indicate if the following instructions are valid or invalid using the data shown. The overflow condition is considered invalid.

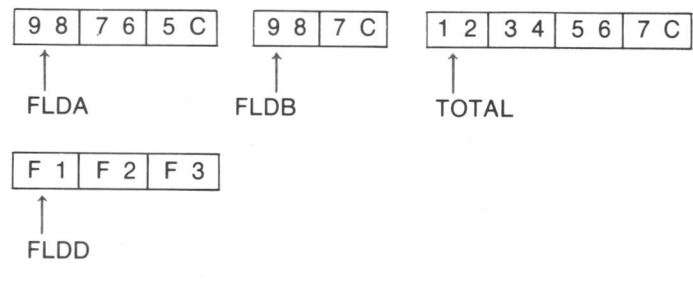

9 8	7 6	5 C		9 8	7 C		1 2	3 4	5 6	7 C

FLDA   FLDB   TOTAL

F 1	F 2	F 3

FLDD

(a) Valid   (b) Invalid

```
12.  PACK   FLDD,FLDD
13.  AP     TOTAL,FLDB
14.  CLC    FLDD,=C'000'
15.  AP     FLDA(3),FLDB(2)
16.  ZAP    TOTAL,FLDB(2)
17.  AP     TOTAL,TOTAL
18.  AP     FLDA,FLDD
19.  SP     FLDA,FLDB(1)
```

```
*                                                                       *
*                                  HOUSEKEEPING INSTRUCTIONS GO HERE     *
*                                                                       *
READ      GET     INFILE,RECORD
          A       TOTNUM,=P'1'
          CLC     SALARY,=C'29000'
          BNH     READ
          AP      TOTAL,=P'1'
          B       READ
EOF       MVC     OUTAREA+5(28),=C'% WHO EARN UNDER $29,000 IS '
          ZAP     CNT,TOTAL
          MP      CNT,=P'100'
          ZAP     RSLT,CNT
          DP      RSLT,TOTNUM
          UNPK    OUTAREA+32(4),RSLT
          OI      OUTAREA+34,X'F0'
          PUT     OUTFILE,OUTAREA
*                                                                       *
*                                  HOUSEKEEPING INSTRUCTIONS GO HERE     *
*                                  ALONG WITH DCB OR DTF MACROS          *
*                                                                       *
TOTAL     DC      PL2'0'
RSLT      DS      PL6
TOTNUM    DC      PL2'0'
CNT       DS      PL4
RECORD    DS      0CL80                   INPUT FORMAT
LAST      DS      CL15                         *
FIRST     DS      CL10                         *
SALARY    DS      CL5                          *
          DS      CL50                         *
SPACES    DC      CL1' '
OUTAREA   DS      CL132
          END
```

Figure 8.3
Program for Question 11.

```
20.  PACK    TOTAL,FLDA
21.  AP      FLDA,FLDD(1)
22.  AP      FLDB,=P'1'
23.  UNPACK  TOTAL,FLDA
24.  AP      FLDA,TOTAL
25.  UNPK    TOTAL,FLDB
26.  SP      FLDB,FLDD
27.  ZAP     FLDA,FLDD
```

SOLUTIONS

		Page
1.	F (only packed-decimal data)	228
2.	T	228
3.	Neither	228
4.	F (packed-decimal only)	228
5.	F (both are equal)	229
6.	T	228

7. | 34 | 8C | | 00 | 9D | | 12 | 3C | 229

     AMT1   AMT2   AMT3

8. 206

LABEL	OPERATION	OPERAND	COMMENTS
	ZAP	TOTAL,A	
LOOP	AP	CTR,=P'1'	
	CP	CTR,=P'5'	
	BE	FINISH	
	AP	TOTAL,A	
	B	LOOP	
*			
TOTAL	DS	PL5	
CTR	DC	P'0'	

9.

LABEL	OPERATION	OPERAND	COMMENTS
	ZAP	TOTAL,A	
LOOP	AP	CTR,=P'1'	
	CP	CTR,B	
	BE	FINISH	
	AP	TOTAL,A	
	B	LOOP	
*			
TOTAL	DS	PL5	
CTR	DC	PL2'∅'	

10.

LABEL	OPERATION	OPERAND	COMMENTS
	ZAP	ANSWER,N	
LOOP	SP	N,=P'1'	
	CP	N,=P'∅'	
	BE	PRINT	
	MP	ANSWER,N	
	B	LOOP	

11. See Figure 8.4.   224

12. Valid   172

13. Valid   178

14. Valid   138

15. Valid   178

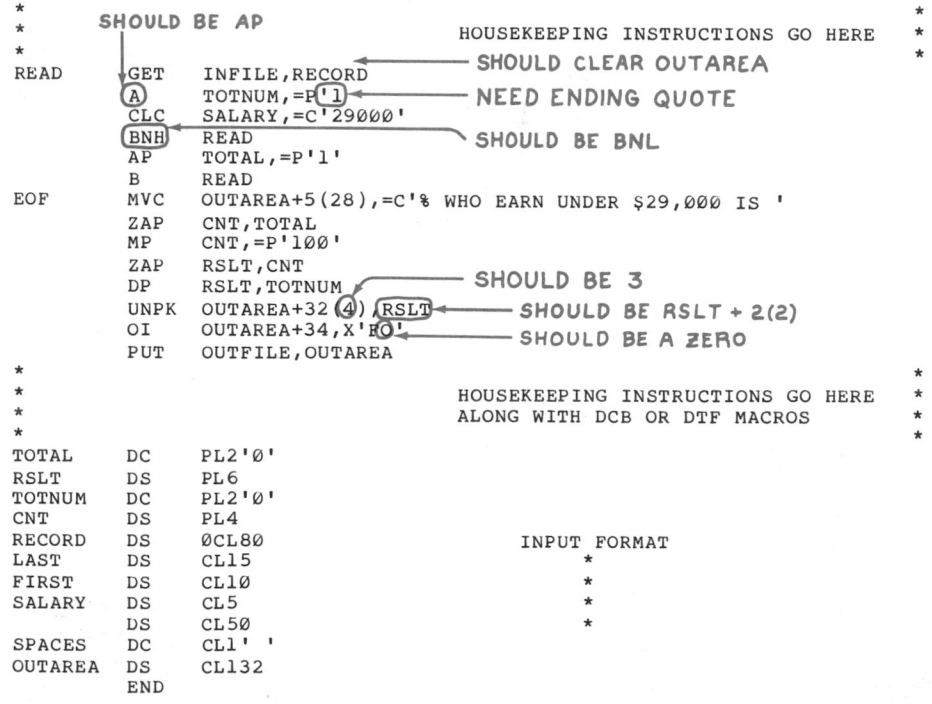

Figure 8.4
Solution to Question 11.

```
*                                                                      *
*             SHOULD BE AP              HOUSEKEEPING INSTRUCTIONS GO HERE  *
*                                                                      *
READ    GET    INFILE,RECORD    ←─── SHOULD CLEAR OUTAREA
        A      TOTNUM,=P'1      ←─── NEED ENDING QUOTE
        CLC    SALARY,=C'29000'
        BNH    READ             ←─── SHOULD BE BNL
        AP     TOTAL,=P'1'
        B      READ
EOF     MVC    OUTAREA+5(28),=C'% WHO EARN UNDER $29,000 IS '
        ZAP    CNT,TOTAL
        MP     CNT,=P'100'
        ZAP    RSLT,CNT
        DP     RSLT,TOTNUM      ←─── SHOULD BE 3
        UNPK   OUTAREA+32(4),RSLT  ←─── SHOULD BE RSLT + 2(2)
        OI     OUTAREA+34,X'FO'    ←─── SHOULD BE A ZERO
        PUT    OUTFILE,OUTAREA
*                                                                      *
*                                       HOUSEKEEPING INSTRUCTIONS GO HERE  *
*                                       ALONG WITH DCB OR DTF MACROS       *
*                                                                      *
TOTAL   DC     PL2'∅'
RSLT    DS     PL6
TOTNUM  DC     PL2'∅'
CNT     DS     PL4
RECORD  DS     ∅CL80                   INPUT FORMAT
LAST    DS     CL15                         *
FIRST   DS     CL10                         *
SALARY  DS     CL5                          *
        DS     CL50                         *
SPACES  DC     CL1' '
OUTAREA DS     CL132
        END
```

PRACTICE PROGRAM

Write a program that totals all the odd numbers from 1–99. See Figure 8.5 for the solution.

KEY TERMS

Algebraic comparison   Multiplier
Decimal divide exception   Product
Dividend   Quotient
Divisor   Remainder
Multiplicand

```
*                                                                        *
*                                     HOUSEKEEPING INSTRUCTIONS GO HERE   *
*                                                                        *
ODDRTN    AP      SUM,ODD
          AP      ODD,=P'2'
          CP      ODD,=P'101'
          BE      PRINT
          B       ODDRTN
PRINT     MVC     OUTAREA,SPACES
          MVC     MESSAGE,=C'TOTAL OF ODD NOS.1-99 IS '
          UNPK    SUMOUT,SUM
          OI      SUMOUT+4,X'F0'         CHANGE SIGN FROM HEX C TO HEX F
          PUT     OUTFILE,OUTAREA
*                                                                        *
*                                     HOUSEKEEPING INSTRUCTIONS GO HERE   *
*                                     ALONG W/DCB OR DTF MACRO FOR OUTFILE*
*                                                                        *
SPACES    DC      CL1' '
OUTAREA   DS      OCL132
          DS      CL5
MESSAGE   DS      CL25
SUMOUT    DS      CL5
          DS      CL97
SUM       DC      PL5'00000'
ODD       DC      PL2'01'
          END
```

Figure 8.5
Solution to the
Practice Program.

```
TOTAL OF ODD NOS.1-99 IS 02500
```

REVIEW QUESTIONS

For Questions 1 to 3, assume the following input record format:

LABEL	OPERATION	OPERAND	COMMENTS
RECIN	DS	0CL80	
A	DS	CL3	
B	DS	CL4	
C	DS	CL5	
D	DS	CL3	
	DS	CL65	

Compute the following, creating as many DSs as you need.

1. $X = A + B \times C$
2. $Y = D^2 (D^2 = D \times D)$
3. $Z = D \times A - B$
4. Compute Celsius temperature when Fahrenheit (F) is read in, in zoned-decimal format.

$$C = \frac{5}{9}(F - 32)$$

5. Write a routine to print the total of the amount fields for each group of 20 input records. Assume that the input records are entered in multiples of 20.
6. Compute TUITION from a field (zoned-decimal) called CREDITS:
   a. Tuition is $50/credit if the student is taking 12 credits or less.
   b. Tuition is $600 for students taking more than 12 credits.
7. Using a multiply operation, find the absolute value of A, a field read in as input. The absolute value of A, denoted as |A|, is calculated as follows:

   if $A < 0$ $|A| = -A = -1 * A$
   if $A \geq 0$ $|A| = A$

8. FICA, which is an abbreviation for Federal Insurance Compensation Act, is a Social Security tax computed at 7 percent of your salary up to $39,600. That is, you are not taxed on income above $39,600. Thus the maximum tax is 7% × 39,600. Write a routine to calculate FICA.
9. Code a routine that performs the following pseudocode operation.

```
SET COUNTER TO 0.
PERFORM UNTIL COUNTER = 10
    READ A RECORD
    ADD AMT TO TOTAL
    ADD 1 TO COUNTER
ENDPERFORM
WRITE TOTAL
```

10. Write a routine based on the following information to determine sales commissions.

    if SALES < 500   COMMIS = 2 percent of SALES
    if SALES is between 500 and 1000   COMMIS = 5 percent of SALES
    if SALES > 1000   COMMIS = 7 percent of SALES

11. For each input field called SALES calculate a PRICE that allows a 3 percent discount.
12. Two input fields are entered representing hours worked and hourly rate. Calculate and print total wages.
13. Using the preceding information, calculate total wages, allowing double time for overtime hours. Overtime hours are those over 40.

14. Input consists of 3 exam grades. Calculate an average of the 3, with 2 decimal places to the right. (*Hint* Multiply the sum by 100 before dividing by 3.)

DEBUGGING EXERCISES

The objective of the following program excerpt is to calculate the GROSS pay for each record as follows:

If the HOURS <= 40 then GROSS = RATE * HOURS
If the HOURS > 40 then GROSS = RATE * 40 + OT, where OT = RATE * (HOURS − 40) * 2

meaning that overtime is paid a premium rate equal to double-time. Perform a desk check and indicate the errors found in the program.

```
************************************************************************
*          D E B U G   P R O G R A M   C H A P T E R   8
************************************************************************
CLEARIT  MVC   LINEOUT,SPACES
         GET   INFILE,RECORD
PROCESS  PACK  PHRS,HRS
         PACK  PRATE,RATE
         CP    HRS,P'40'
         BH    OVERTIME
         ZAP   GROSS,=P'0'
         BLE   REG-PAY
OVERTIME ZAP   OT,PHRS
         SP    OT,=P'40'       CALCULATE OVERTIME HOURS.
         AP    OT,OT           DOUBLE OVERTIME HOURS AND
         MP    OT,PRATE          MULTIPLY BY RATE GIVING OT-PAY.
         ZAP   GROSS,PRATE
         MP    GROSS,=P'10'    CALCULATE REGULAR PAY FOR 40 HRS
         AP    GROSS,OT          AND ADD OT-PAY GIVING GROSS.
         B     PRINT
REG-PAY  ZAP   GROSS,PRATE     CALCULATE REG-PAY AS RATE TIMES
         MP    GROSS,PHRS                   HOURS
         B     PRINT
LINEOUT  DS    CL133
RECORD   DS    0CL80
NAME     DS    CL20
         DS    CL5
RATE     DS    CL3     FORMAT X.XX
         DS    CL2
HOURS    DS    CL2     FORMAT XX
         DS    CL48
*
SPACES   DC    C' '
*
OT       DS    PL3
GROSS    DS    PL3     NOTE 3 BYTES PACKED HOLDS 5 DIGITS
PRATE    DS    PL2
PHRS     DS    PL2
```

SOLUTIONS

1. LINEOUT must follow the DC defining SPACES.
2. HOURS of RECORD should be coded HRS.
3. The CP should be corrected to DP PHRS,=P'40' because HRS is not packed and the equal sign is missing.
4. REG-PAY is invalid and may be corrected to read REGPAY.
5. BLE does not exist as an extended mnemonic. Use BNH instead.
6. The ZAP GROSS,=P'0' resets the condition code causing the "BLE" to function illogically. There is no need to set GROSS to zero in the first place. The instruction should therefore be removed from the program. The branching instructions must immediately follow the compare.
7. GROSS and OT must be four bytes in length to accommodate the multiplication of two packed fields, each two bytes in length. Hence, the DS instructions must be corrected for GROSS and OT.

PROGRAMMING ASSIGNMENTS

1. Write a program to create a report from the following input records.

   1–20 Employee name
   21–22 Hours worked
   23–25 Rate
   26–80 Not used

   Output report:

   1–20 Employee name
   41–45 Gross pay

   Gross pay = reg hours × rate + overtime hours × rate × 2
   Overtime hours are those hours exceeding 40.

   Note
   Assume that rate is in dollars and cents.

2. Write a program to summarize accident records to obtain the following information:
   a. Percentage of drivers under 25.
   b. Percentage of drivers who are female.
   c. Percentage of drivers from New York.

   There is one input record for each driver involved in an accident in the past year.

   1–4 Driver number
      5 State code (1 for New York)
   6–9 Birth date (Month and Year)
     10 Sex (M for male, F for female)
   11–80 Not used

   Results should be printed with constants.

   ```
   % OF DRIVERS UNDER 25
   % OF DRIVERS FEMALE
   % OF DRIVERS FROM NY
   ```

   Hint
   Multiply the numerator of each fraction by 100 to obtain the corresponding percentage.

3. Write a program to read detail Bank Transaction records with the following format.

   1–19 Name of depositor
     20 Type 1—Previous balance, 2—Deposit, 3—Withdrawal
   21–25 Account number
   26–30 Amount xxxxx
   31–80 Not used

   The input is in sequence by account number. Type 1 records exist for each account number followed by Types 2 and 3, if they exist. Types 2 and 3 may be present for a given account number and may appear in any sequence.
      Print out the name of the depositor and his or her current balance (Previous Balance + Deposits − Withdrawals). Also print the heading BANK REPORT.

4. Write a program to read in records that each contain an exam grade. The number of input records is unknown. Calculate and print the average exam grade.

9 Print Options and Control Break Processing

OBJECTIVES

To familiarize you with:
1. *The major characteristics of printed output.*
2. *The types of editing that can be performed to make printed output user-friendly.*
3. *Criteria to use when designing printed reports.*
4. *Control break processing.*

I. SPECIAL FEATURES OF PRINTED OUTPUT

A. Introduction

When output is written on disk or tape, the following rules apply:

1. Data should be as concise as possible (e.g., use part numbers instead of item descriptions to identify parts stored in a warehouse).
2. Do not include "edit" symbols such as dollar signs or commas.
3. Use codes in place of long field names (e.g., 1, 2, 3, or "M", "S", "D" for marital status rather than "Married," "Single," "Divorced").

Disk and tape output are generally used for intermediate storage, with the stored data ultimately reentering the computer flow as input to another program. These types of output are created with efficiency in mind. Fields and records on these files are kept as concise as possible to make effective use of the computer and its storage capabilities. In some instances, numeric fields are stored in the packed-decimal format to further reduce the length of records.

Due to the fact that the printed report is designed with businesspeople or other users in mind, such forms must be clear, neat, and easy to interpret. Several features, not applicable to other forms of output, must be considered when preparing reports.

Computer-generated reports are printed on **continuous forms.** A continuous form is a series of perforated forms with each perforation indicating the end of an individual page. (After all continuous forms in a report have been generated, the individual pages must be **burst,** or separated, into single sheets.)

Unless the computer is instructed to do otherwise, it will treat the entire continuous form as one long sheet rather than as individual pages. That is, it will write each line and advance the paper, printing from one form to another and ignoring the fact that each is an individual page. At times, it may even print on the perforations, making the report very difficult to read.

Thus, even though printing is done from one continuous form to another, the computer must be instructed to observe page delineations. Consequently, printing requires the following considerations:

---

1. Each page should begin with a heading.
2. Lines containing data, commonly called **detail lines,** generally follow.
3. A test for the end of the form is performed. If the end of an individual form is reached, we need to skip to a new page and write the heading again.

---

1. Spacing of Forms

The lines on printed output must be properly spaced to allow for ease of reading. Certain lines must be single spaced, others double spaced. The printed output must have adequate margins at both the top and the bottom of each page. This requires the computer to be programmed to sense the end of a page and thus to transmit the next line of information to a new page.

2. Alignment of Data and the Printer Spacing Chart

Reports do not have fields of information placed adjacent to one another as is the practice with other forms of output. Printed output is more easily interpreted when data is spaced neatly and evenly across the page. Recall that the **Printer Spacing Chart** is used for planning the output design so that detail lines and heading lines are neatly spaced (see Figure 9.1). Note that the Printer Spacing Chart is used to designate the precise print positions in which data will be placed.

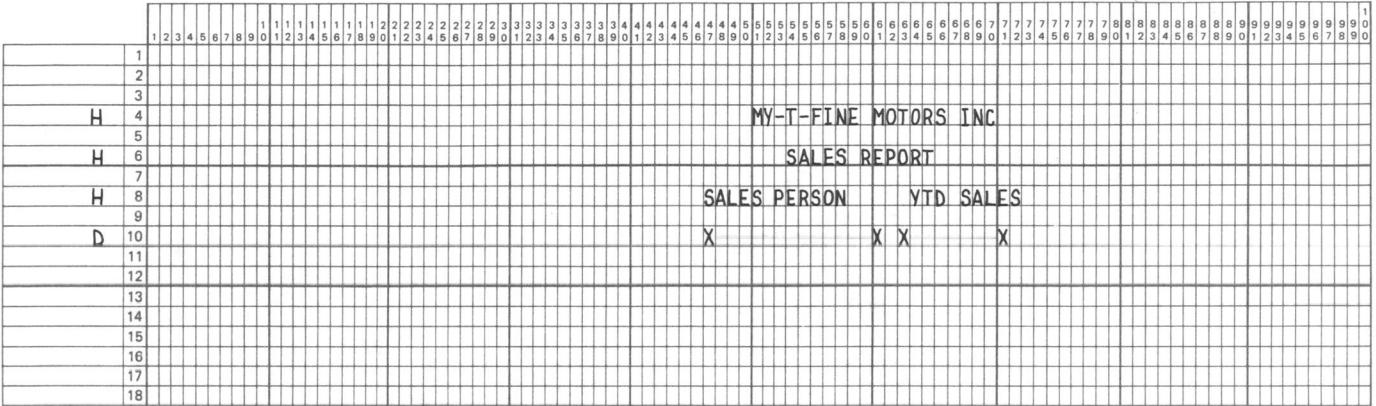

Figure 9.1
Sample Printer Spacing Chart.

"MY-T-FINE MOTORS INC" and "SALES REPORT" are called *report headings*. "SALES PERSON" and "YTD SALES" refer to the fields to be printed and are called *column headings*. The Xs indicate that *detail lines* are to be supplied. Sometimes we also include *total lines*.

The steps necessary to code the printing of the headings are illustrated in Figure 9.2. Note that the coding is simplified because we are using a Printer Spacing Chart, combined with the programming techniques of relative addressing. To place the M of MY-T-FINE MOTOR, INC, in print position 51, we refer to LINEOUT+50. It becomes a simple matter of determining what positions are to be used for headings once the Printer Spacing Chart is completed.

Figure 9.2
Sample instructions to print headings.

```
*                                                                    *
*               HEADING ROUTINE USING ASA CTLCHR                     *
*                                                                    *
HEADING   MVC    LINEOUT,SPACES
          MVC    LINEOUT+50(20),=C'MY-T-FINE MOTORS INC'
          MVI    LINEOUT,C'1'              ADVANCE TO TOP OF PAGE
          PUT    OUTFILE,LINEOUT
          MVC    LINEOUT,SPACES
          MVC    LINEOUT+53(12),=C'SALES REPORT'
          MVI    LINEOUT,C'0'              DOUBLE SPACE
          PUT    OUTFILE,LINEOUT
          MVC    LINEOUT,SPACES
          MVC    LINEOUT+46(12),=C'SALES PERSON'
          MVC    LINEOUT+63(9),=C'YTD SALES'
          MVI    LINEOUT,C' '              TRIPLE SPACE
          PUT    OUTFILE,LINEOUT
          MVC    LINEOUT,SPACES
          MVI    LINEOUT,C'0'              DOUBLE SPACE
          PUT    OUTFILE,LINEOUT
```

3. Printing of Headings

Heading information, which generally supplies job name, date, and field designations, is essential for a clear and meaningful presentation of printed information.

Figure 9.3 provides a schematic of how data may be printed. The output would print according to the specifications provided in the Printer Spacing Chart in Figure 9.1. Because printed information has characteristics different from other output, we will study the printed report as a separate, and rather special topic.

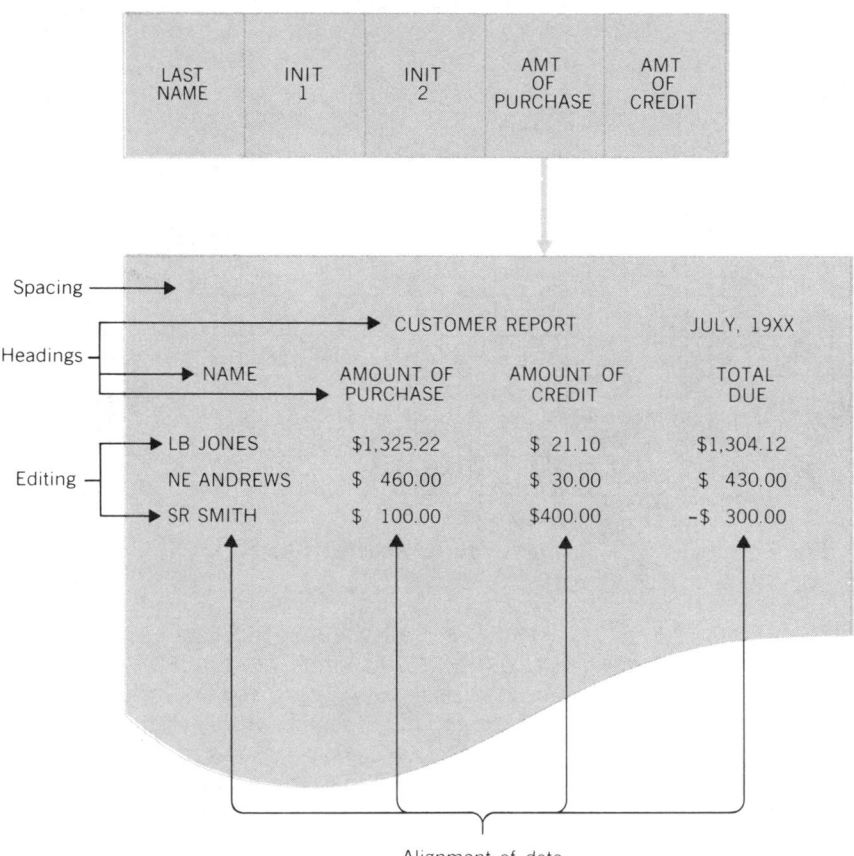

Figure 9.3
Schematic of how input data may be printed.

4. Edited Data

A disk, tape, or card may have two amount fields with the following data: 00450 and 3872658. Although these fields are acceptable on disk, tape, and cards, the printed report should contain this information in edited form to make it more meaningful to the user. For example, $450.00 and $38,726.58 are clearer methods of presenting the data.

Editing is defined as the manipulation of fields of data to make them clearer, neater, and more user-friendly. Editing of input data is a prime consideration when printing information. In this chapter, we will discuss the various types of editing that can be performed on numeric fields.

B. The Control ⟨CNTRL⟩ Macro for Proper Spacing of Forms

Two methods are typically used for spacing print lines on a report:

1. Leaving 1, 2, or 3 blank lines between each print line. This is called **spacing.**
2. **Skipping** to a specific line on the form.

Spacing and skipping can be achieved with a CNTRL macro.

1. Space Option (SP)

Unless otherwise indicated, a PUT statement will result in single spacing. With the CNTRL macro and a Space or SP option, we can also obtain double or triple spacing, that is, advancing the paper two or three lines.

2. Skip Option (SK)

The SK, or skip option is used to advance the paper to a designated line.
The general format for the CNTRL macro is as follows.

Operation 10	Operand 16
CNTRL	*File name, Option, n, m*

where

File name	is the name assigned to the DTFPR or the DCB for the print file
Option	SP for spacing, SK for skipping
n	denotes *immediate* spacing or skipping—that is, *before* printing
m	denotes *delayed* spacing or skipping—that is, *after* printing

The *n* and *m* parameters allow advancing before and after the print (PUT) statements. For the SP option, *n* and *m* must range in value from 1 to 3 corresponding to single, double, or triple spacing. For the SK option, *n* and *m* indicate the line to be skipped to.

3. Spacing Before and After Printing

The CNTRL macro allows us to space a form *both* before and after printing.

LABEL	OPERATION 10 16	OPERAND	COMMENTS	72
	CNTRL	OUTFILE,SP,2,3		
	PUT	OUTFILE,LINEOUT		

Causes

1. Triple spacing before printing (2 lines + standard single spacing).
2. A line to be printed.
3. Triple spacing after printing (the after-print option suppresses the standard single spacing).

4. DOS and OS Considerations When Using the CNTRL Macro

We can also use the CNTRL macro to skip to a specified line *both* before and after printing.

DOS CONSIDERATIONS WHEN USING THE CNTRL MACRO

The entry CONTROL = YES *must* be included in the DTFPR file description.
The entry CONTROL = YES *may* also be included in PRMOD macro, if PRMOD is included.[1]
CONTROL means "carriage control," which is the mechanism used for spacing forms.

---

[1]See Appendix E.

> OS CONSIDERATIONS WHEN USING THE CNTRL MACRO
> The entry $\boxed{\text{MACRF = PMC}}$ must be included in the DCB for the print file.

5. Advancing to Top of Page

LABEL	OPERATION	OPERAND	COMMENTS
	CNTRL	OUTFILE,SK,1	
	PUT	OUTFILE,LINEOUT	

The CNTRL macro directs the printer to skip immediately to the top of a form, typically to line 6. Before the PUT is executed, the paper is advanced. The PUT instruction prints the heading created in the output area defined as LINEOUT.

6. Immediate Spacing

LABEL	OPERATION	OPERAND	COMMENTS
	CNTRL	OUTFILE,SP,1	
	PUT	OUTFILE,LINEOUT	

The CNTRL macro causes the printer to advance immediately to the next line. The PUT statement then causes the printer to advance *another* line and print out the results. The net effect is that the printer has advanced 2 lines. The information printed out will thus be *double spaced*. See Figure 9.4.

LABEL	OPERATION	OPERAND	COMMENTS
	CNTRL	OUTFILE,SP,1	⟶ Single spacing
	PUT	OUTFILE,LINEOUT	⟶ Single spacing and printing

```
BROWN               LEROY              $22,234

MOSS                SAM                $21,212

GREENSPAN           ANDY               $23,888

DEAN                JAMES              $22,877

WHITE               FORREST            $22,555
```

Figure 9.4 How double spacing is achieved using the CNTRL macro.

Replacing the 1 with a 2 in the CNTRL macro, for example, will have a net effect of triple spacing.

7. Delayed Spacing

LABEL	OPERATION	OPERAND	COMMENTS
	CNTRL	OUTFILE,SP,,2	
	PUT	OUTFILE,LINEOUT	

This option permits spacing after the PUT or print instruction has been issued. Note that the CNTRL will cause the computer to space only *after* the PUT has been executed. The 2 commas indicate that *no* immediate spacing is required.

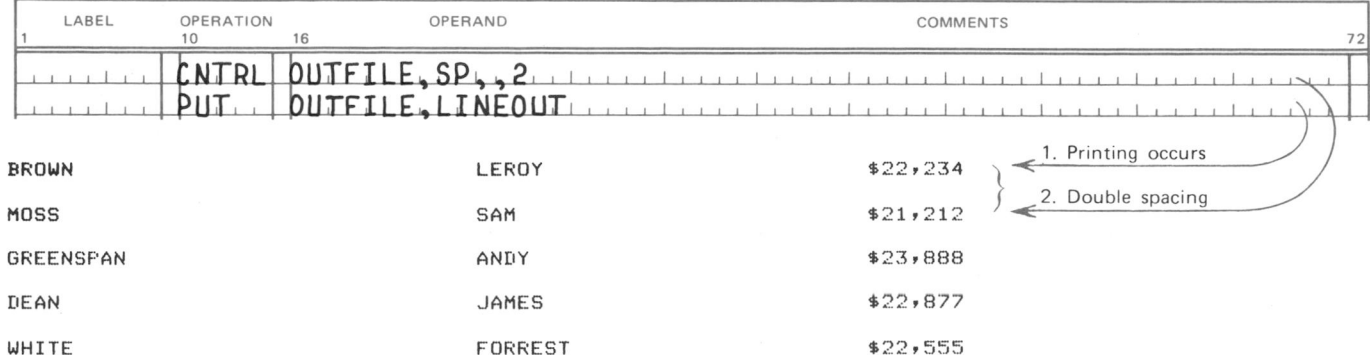

Figure 9.5
How delayed spacing is achieved using the CNTRL macro.

Note that the fourth parameter is coded by inserting an additional comma. *When delayed spacing is specified, the standard single spacing that usually takes place after the line is printed does not occur.* The preceding example would therefore cause 2 lines to be spaced *after* the PUT instruction has been issued, which will result in double spacing as shown in Figure 9.5.

$(n \stackrel{?}{=} operand)$

SUMMARY OF CNTRL MACRO

1. The CNTRL macro is used to control spacing or skipping to a specific line.
2. The file name reference by the macro must be the same symbolic name assigned in the DCB or DTF to the printer device.
3. The skip (SK) or space (SP) option must be specified with the CNTRL macro.
4. The third parameter (n) indicates the first line to contain printing if SK is used, or the number of lines to be spaced before printing. When used with the SP option, the result reflects the number of lines plus the standard single spacing that occurs when a print operation is performed. Therefore, when 1 is specified, double spacing will occur. The digits 1–3 are permissible for the SP option.
5. The fourth parameter (m) is used to provide spacing after the printing operation. From 1 to 3 lines may be spaced. Standard single spacing is eliminated when this option is used and, therefore, a 2 specified as the fourth parameter will cause double spacing.
6. The entries CONTROL = YES must be included in the DTFs and may be included in the PRMOD statements when using the CNTRL macro with DOS. With OS, the entry MACRF = PMC must be included in the DCB.

Self-Evaluating Quiz

1. Consider the Printer Spacing Chart in Figure 9.6. Write the series of statements that will print the header in the appropriate print positions.
2. Consider the following statement.

LABEL	OPERATION	OPERAND	COMMENTS
	CNTRL	OUTSIDE,SK,1	

OUTSIDE is the _____ that is specified in the _____ . The CNTRL macro is used, in general, for _____ . SK in the above causes _____ . The effect of the operation is to _____ .

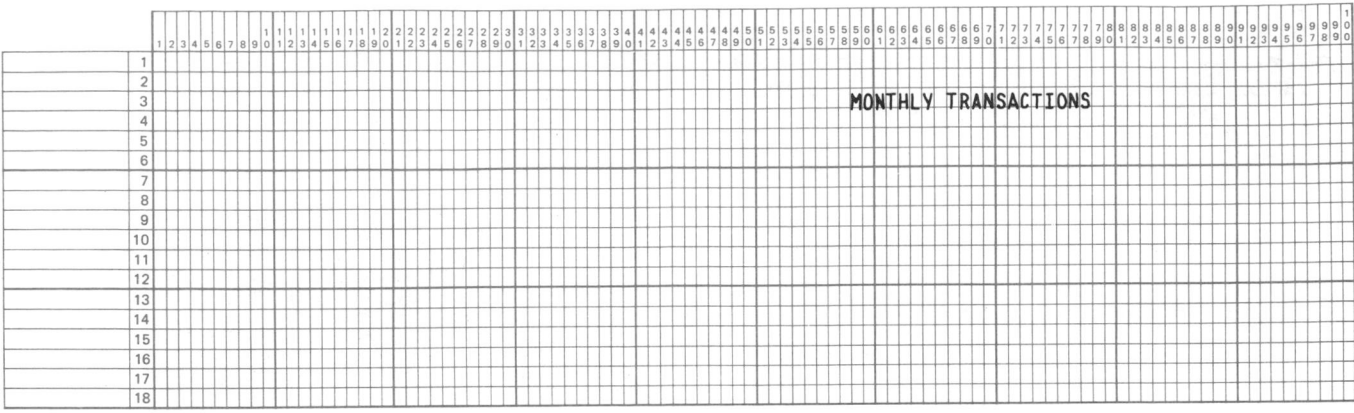

Figure 9.6 Printer Spacing Chart for Question 1.

3. What is the major difference between spacing and skipping?
4. Consider the following instructions.

LABEL	OPERATION	OPERAND	COMMENTS
1	10 16		72
	CNTRL	PRINTOUT,SP,3	
	PUT	PRINTOUT,LINEOUT	

PRINTOUT is assigned with a DTFPR or _____ . LINEOUT is defined with a(n) _____ . Printing occurs (before/after) spacing. The paper is spaced (no.) lines.

5. Write an instruction to advance the paper 2 lines before printing.
6. Write an instruction to advance the paper to the top of a new page after printing.

SOLUTIONS   1.

LABEL	OPERATION	OPERAND	COMMENTS
1	10 16		72
HEADING	MVC	LINEOUT,SPACES	
	MVC	LINEOUT+58,=C'MONTHLY TRANSACTIONS'	
	PUT	OUTFILE,LINEOUT	

2. File name; DTFPR or DCB; Spacing and skipping; Skipping to the first line of print or the top of a new page; Advance the paper to a new page *before* printing
3. Skipping causes the paper to skip to a specified line. Spacing means advancing the paper 1, 2, or 3 lines.
4. DCB; DS; After; 3
5. CNTRL OUTFILE,SP,2
6. CNTRL OUTFILE,SK,,1

C. Using ASA Control Characters: An Alternative Method of Advancing Without Using the CNTRL Macro

1. Introduction to ASA Characters

Most printers typically print either 120 or 132 print positions per line. In this text we assume that the printer prints 132 characters per line. American Standards Association (ASA) control characters may be used in a program to designate the spacing required. When ASA control characters are used, the output area will be defined as 133 bytes (*one more than necessary*) because the *first* print position is set aside for indicating the desired spacing. A **carriage control** character is placed in this first byte to designate the spacing requirements.

LABEL	OPERATION		OPERAND	COMMENTS	
1	10	16			72
LINEOUT	DS		CL133		

This means that the first position of the output area will *not* print. It is used to control skipping and spacing operations. Any of the following ASA carriage control characters can be placed in this first position of the print area for carriage control purposes.

ASA Control Character		Hex Representation	Carriage Control Operation
Blank	(space)	40	Normal single spacing
0	(zero)	F0	Double spacing
−	(minus)	60	Triple spacing
1	(one)	F1	Skip to top of new page
+	(plus)	4F	Suppress advancing

The last control character, which suppresses advancing of the paper, is used, for example, for printing underlines with headings.

An MVI (Move Immediate) instruction that moves one byte of data may be used to place the desired carriage control character in the first, or high-order position of the output. This should be performed *prior* to the print or PUT command.

This method, then, is an alternative to the CNTRL macro for advancing the paper *prior* to printing. It may *not* be used, however, for automatically advancing the paper *after* printing. That option is available only with the CNTRL macro.

Example 9.1   Print a line after double spacing.

LABEL	OPERATION		OPERAND	COMMENTS	
1	10	16			72
	MVI		LINEOUT,C'Ø'		
	PUT		OUTFILE,LINEOUT		

or

LABEL	OPERATION		OPERAND	COMMENTS	
1	10	16			72
	MVI		LINEOUT,X'FØ'		
	PUT		OUTFILE,LINEOUT		

Example 9.2   Print a line at the top of a new page.

LABEL	OPERATION		OPERAND	COMMENTS	
1	10	16			72
	MVI		LINEOUT,C'1'		
	PUT		OUTFILE,LINEOUT		

or

LABEL	OPERATION		OPERAND	COMMENTS	
1	10	16			72
	MVI		LINEOUT,X'F1'		
	PUT		OUTFILE,LINEOUT		

2. Comparing CNTRL with MVI and ASA Characters

Figure 9.7 illustrates an entire procedure for printing headings. This procedure relies on the MVI instruction and the use of ASA characters in the first print position. It performs the same spacing options as in Figure 9.8, which uses the CNTRL macro.

```
*                                                                          *
*               HEADING ROUTINE USING ASA CTLCHR                           *
*                                                                          *
HEADING   MVC    LINEOUT,SPACES
          MVC    LINEOUT+50(21),=C'MY-T-FINE MOTORS INC'
          MVI    LINEOUT,C'1'              ADVANCE TO TOP OF PAGE
          PUT    OUTFILE,LINEOUT
          MVC    LINEOUT,SPACES
          MVC    LINEOUT+53(12),=C'SALES REPORT'
          MVI    LINEOUT,C'0'             DOUBLE SPACE
          PUT    OUTFILE,LINEOUT
          MVC    LINEOUT,SPACES
          MVC    LINEOUT+46(21),=C'SALES PERSON'
          MVC    LINEOUT+63(9),=C'YTD SALES'
          MVI    LINEOUT,C'-'             TRIPLE SPACE
          PUT    OUTFILE,LINEOUT
          MVC    LINEOUT,SPACES
          MVI    LINEOUT,C'0'             DOUBLE SPACE
          PUT    OUTFILE,LINEOUT
```

Figure 9.7
Printing headings with the use of ASA characters.

Note that when using the ASA characters, the print line must be established as *133* characters, rather than 132, and that the first, or high-order position is used for carriage control and is *not* printed.

```
*                                                                          *
*               PRINT ROUTINE USING CNTRL MACRO                            *
*                                                                          *
HEADING   CNTRL  OUTFILE,SK,1             ADVANCE TO TOP OF PAGE
          MVC    LINEOUT,SPACES
          MVC    LINEOUT+50(21),=C'MY-T-FINE MOTORS INC'
          PUT    OUTFILE,LINEOUT
          CNTRL  OUTFILE,SP,1             DOUBLE SPACE
          MVC    LINEOUT,SPACES
          MVC    LINEOUT+53(12),=C'SALES REPORT'
          CNTRL  OUTFILE,SP,,3            TRIPLE SPACE AFTER PRINT
          PUT    OUTFILE,LINEOUT
          MVC    LINEOUT,SPACES
          MVC    LINEOUT+46(21),=C'SALES PERSON'
          MVC    LINEOUT+63(9),=C'YTD SALES'
          CNTRL  OUTFILE,SP,,3            TRIPLE SPACE AFTER PRINT
          PUT    OUTFILE,LINEOUT
```

Figure 9.8
Printing headings with the use of the CNTRL macro.

3. DOS and OS Considerations for Use of ASA Characters

DOS CONSIDERATIONS FOR USE OF ASA CHARACTERS

The DTF macro describing the print field must contain the following entry:

CTLCHR=ASA

CTLCHR is an abbreviation for control character. Blocksize (BLKSIZE) is also increased to 133 to allow for the carriage control position. The DTF would now appear as follows.

LABEL	OPERATION		OPERAND	COMMENTS	
1	10	16			72
OUTFILE	DTFPR		BLKSIZE=133,CTLCHR=ASA,DEVADDR=SYSLST,IOAREA1=BUFFROUT,		*
			WORKA=YES		

OS CONSIDERATIONS FOR USE OF ASA CHARACTERS

The DCB macro describing printed output changes. The blocksize and logical record length operands are each increased to 133 to allow for carriage control. The DCB would now appear as follows.

LABEL	OPERATION		OPERAND	COMMENTS	
1	10	16			72
OUTFILE	DCB		DDNAME=OUTFILE,MACRF=PM,BLKSIZE=133,LRECL=133,DSORG=PS		

Review of I/O Changes Required for Carriage Control

Method	Format	Use	DOS Changes Required for		OS Changes Required for DCB
			DTFPR	PRMOD	
CNTRL Macro	CNTRL File name, Option, *n, m* — Option—SP or SK *n*—immediate spacing or skipping *m*—after print spacing or skipping	Can be used for spacing or skipping before *and* after printing.	CONTROL= YES	CONTROL= YES	MACRF= PMC
ASA character placed in *high-order* byte of 133 character print area using MVI.	MVI PRINTOUT, C' ' b—single spacing 0—double spacing −—triple spacing 1—skip to top of page +—no advancing	Can be used for spacing or skipping *before* printing.	BLKSIZE=133, CTLCHR=ASA		BLKSIZE=133, LRECL=133

Note: ☐ = entries to be coded as part of program.

D. Skipping to a New Page

1. The Print Overflow (PRTOV) Macro: For Use with On-Line Printers

As noted, a computer will print lines of data without paying any attention to perforations between forms unless otherwise instructed. When printing data requires more than a single page of information, it is necessary to test for a

form overflow condition. The PRTOV macro, which is an abbreviation for print overflow, is used to test if the end of a page or form has been reached.

When a form overflow condition is reached, we usually instruct the computer to:

1. Advance the form to the top of the next page (skip to 1), or
2. Branch to a routine that produces a top-of-page heading, page numbers, date, and so on.

The format of the PRTOV instruction is:

Operation 10	Operand 16
PRTOV	*File name, n, Routine-name*

where:

File name is the name assigned to the DTFPR or the DCB for the print file.

n is the channel number used to indicate the end of the page. Channel 12, for instance, typically means the end of a form.

Routine-name is an optional entry used if a branch to a heading routine is desired. If this entry is omitted, PRTOV will cause the printer to skip to a new page automatically.

Example 9.3 After writing a detail line, test to see if an end-of-page has been reached. If so, skip to a new page. The number 12 is used below to test for the end of a form.

LABEL	OPERATION 10 16	OPERAND	COMMENTS 72
	PUT	OUTFILE,LINEOUT	
	PRTOV	OUTFILE,12	

In the instruction above, a form overflow condition is denoted by channel 12 of the carriage control mechanism. When an end-of-form condition is sensed, the printer advances to the top of the next page. Whether or not an overflow condition has been sensed, the computer will continue executing with the next sequential instruction.

Example 9.4 Branch to a heading routine when an end-of-page condition has been sensed.
In this example, when the end-of-page condition is sensed (denoted by channel 12), the printer should *not* automatically advance to the top of the next page. Instead, a branch to the routine called HEADING should occur.

LABEL	OPERATION 10 16	OPERAND	COMMENTS 72
	PUT	OUTFILE,LINEOUT	
	PRTOV	OUTFILE,12,HEADING	

Hence, in the program excerpt above, the program will proceed to the next sequential instruction *unless* an overflow has occurred; when an overflow occurs, a branch to HEADING is performed.

To use print overflow in the earlier programming example (MY-T-FINE MOTOR INC), Figure 9-1, we test for print overflow prior to branching to the read instruction. When overflow is detected, a branch to the routine called HEADING causes headings to be repeated on succeeding pages. See Figure 9.2 for the HEADING routine that has been previously illustrated.

DOS CONSIDERATIONS

The entry PRINTOV = YES *must* appear in the DTFPR file description.

The entry PRINTOV = YES *may* also be included in the PRMOD macro, discussed in Appendix E.

OS CONSIDERATIONS

Same as for CNTRL macro; that is, include the entry MACRF = PMC.

SUMMARY OF PRTOV MACRO

1. The PRTOV macro is used to detect the end-of-page condition.
2. The file name referenced must be the same symbolic name assigned in the DTFPR or DCB for the printer device.
3. The second operand (n) typically specifies 12 when a test for form overflow is to be performed.
4. When the third operand is omitted and the overflow condition is detected, the form automatically advances to the top of the next page.
5. When a routine name is given as the third operand and the form overflow condition is detected, a branch to that routine takes place.
6. The routine name specified as the third operand must appear in the NAME field of the program (starting in column 1).
7. The entry PRINTOV = YES must appear in the DTFPR and PRMOD statements when using the PRTOV macro with DOS. With OS, the entry MACRF = PMC must be included in the DCB.

---

2. Alternative Method for Testing for End-of-Page: Counting Lines

Counting lines is an alternative method for testing for form overflow. Its major advantage is that it does not rely on any carriage control mechanism and is therefore completely independent of the operating system (OS or DOS) and the printer.

A counter is established and intialized. The counter is incremented each time a line is printed. In this way, the counter serves as a total of the number of lines actually printed. The programmer then determines exactly how many print lines are desired per page. When the counter is equal to that desired number, the program branches to a HEADING routine where headings are printed at the top of the next page.

In this way, the programmer can build a routine into the program that prints exactly 25 double-spaced lines per page, or 50 single-spaced lines per page, or whatever variation is desired.

This method *must* be used for systems in which print operations are performed off-line. That is, data to be printed is *not* automatically transmitted to the printer on many systems because print operations are relatively slow. Instead, the data is **spooled** onto a medium such as disk in a high-speed operation. In this way, the relatively slow printing becomes a disk-to-print procedure that can be performed in an off-line mode. This frees the CPU to perform other functions while printing is being completed.

Example 9.5 Print 25 double-spaced detail lines per page.

LABEL	OPERATION	OPERAND	COMMENTS
	CNTRL	OUTFILE,SP,1	
	PUT	OUTFILE,LINEOUT	
	AP	CTR,=P'1'	
	CP	CTR,=PL2'25'	
	BE	HEADING	
	B	READ	
	.		
	.		
	.		
CTR	DC	PL2'00'	
	.		
	.		

In summary, to use a programmed line counter to achieve end-of-page control, we must use the following procedure.

PROGRAMMED LINE COUNTER

1. Determine the number of lines to be printed.
2. Establish a line counter field and initialize it at zero.
3. After each PUT statement, increment the line counter field by one. In this way, the number in the line counter field will be equal to the number of lines actually printed.
4. After each PUT statement, test the line counter to determine if it equals the number of lines we want printed per page. If it does, we print a heading on a new page. If it does not, we continue with the program.
5. If the line counter has reached the desired number, we perform a heading routine where the line counter is reinitialized at zero.

The programmed line counter should be used in all programs that produce a significant number of print lines and for which the possibility exists that more than one page of printing will be required. Without such a procedure, the printer will simply print one line after another, regardless of page delineations or perforations. Most programs that produce printed reports will generate more than one page and thus require end-of-page programming techniques.

Note

If one or more of the options discussed in this section is not available with your DOS system, see Appendix E, "Generating IOCS Modules for DOS Systems." (IOCS is an abbreviation for input-output control system.) Appendix E includes a discussion of PRMOD and CDMOD, and how the preceding options considered may be incorporated in your programs.

Self-Evaluating Quiz

1. Another name for an end-of-page condition is _____ .
2. PRTOV can cause the computer to either _____ or _____ .
3. (T or F) The alternative to the PRTOV (line counting) for testing for an end-of-page condition requires more programming but is independent of the carriage control mechanism.
4. Indicate the advantage of the alternative to the PRTOV option.
5. Using the PRTOV option, write a statement to skip to a new page.
6. Using the line counting method, write a routine to print 20 triple-spaced lines per page.

SOLUTIONS

1. Form overflow
2. Automatically skip to a new page; branch to a special routine (usually for the purpose of printing headings)
3. T
4. It is independent of any carriage control mechanism; it must be used when the printer is off-line.
5.

LABEL	OPERATION	OPERAND	COMMENTS
	PUT	OUTFILE,LINEOUT	
	PRTOV	OUTFILE,9	

6.

LABEL	OPERATION	OPERAND	COMMENTS
	CNTRL	OUTFILE,SP,2	
	PUT	OUTFILE,LINEOUT	
	AP	CTR,=PL1'1'	
	CP	CTR,=PL2'20'	
	BE	HEADING	
	.		
	.		
	.		
CTR	DC	PL2'0'	

E. Printing the Current Date

We frequently want the current date to appear in the heading of a report to indicate when the report was actually produced. The technique of retrieving the date from the system depends on if we are running the program under DOS or OS.

DOS With DOS, the date is stored in the first eight bytes of the communications region in the form mm/dd/yy, including the slashes. For example, January 15, 1987 is stored as 01/15/87. To access the date and move it to the print area, we use the following two instructions.

```
COMRG
MVC      DATEOUT(8),0(1)
```

The COMRG (Communications Region) macro causes the *address* of the communications region to be loaded into register 1. The MVC moves the date to the field called DATEOUT. The second operand of the MVC will be discussed in detail in Chapter 16.

OS With OS, the date can be obtained from the system through the TIME macro. This instruction causes the current date to be placed in register 1 in Julian date form. This format is as follows.

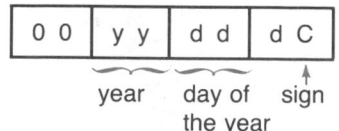

For example, January 15, 1987 is stored as 87015. Most computer centers have a catalogued subroutine to convert a Julian date into Gregorian format (e.g., 01/15/87).

Note
The following instruction can be used on some systems to retrieve directly the date in the form mm/dd/yy.

```
MVC    DATEO(8),=C'&SYSDATE'
```

II. EDITING PRINTED DATA

A. Types of Editing

Data on input media is usually in concise or condensed form. The printed output, however, must contain additional specifications, such as $, ., +, or − signs, to make the fields more readable.

Editing is considered the manipulation of data fields to make them clearer and neater for reporting purposes. The following are considered editing functions.

---

1. Suppressing high-order or leading zeros.
2. Printing decimal points where decimal alignment is implied.
3. Printing dollar signs and commas.
4. Printing a plus or minus sign to reflect the value of a field.

The Edit or ED instruction will *unpack* a field and edit it according to the specifications indicated. When using the ED, there is no need to unpack or to replace zones with an OI or MVZ instruction. Thus, the UNPK, OI, and MVZ are only used when *no* editing is required.

Figure 9.9 illustrates an unedited report. Figure 9.10 illustrates the same report with data in edited form. Without editing, the report is cumbersome. The suppression of leading zeros in the DEPENDENTS field and the use of the dollar sign, comma, and decimal point in the YTD (Year-to-Date) field greatly increase the readability of the report.

B. Steps in Editing Data

Editing requires the following three steps.

STEPS IN EDITING DATA

1. An edit pattern is established specifying the type of editing to be performed. The edit pattern is established as a Defined Constant (DC) or in a self-defining operand.
2. Using an MVC, the edit pattern is moved either to a work area or to the output area.
3. The data is edited by using the edit (ED) instruction.

DEPT	EMPLOYEE	DEPENDENTS	YTD GROS$
00050	BODAS MICHAEL	003	000870400
00100	BRINDLE CALVIN	004	000940800
00150	CARTER JOHN	007	000630400
00150	DUNCAN LEONARD	002	000313600
00200	ELLIS FORREST	004	000473600
00200	FINE ROBERT	006	001267200
00250	HUNTER PHILIP	007	000256000

Figure 9.9
Example of an unedited report.

DEPT	EMPLOYEE	DEPENDENTS	YTD GROSS
50	BODAS MICHAEL	3	$ 8,704.00
100	BRINDLE CALVIN	4	$ 9,408.00
150	CARTER JOHN	7	$ 6,304.00
150	DUNCAN LEONARD	2	$ 3,136.00
200	ELLIS FORREST	4	$ 4,736.00
200	FINE ROBERT	6	$12,672.00
250	HUNTER PHILIP	7	$ 2,560.00

Figure 9.10
Report showing data from
Figure 9.9 in edited form.

> NOTE: The edit pattern field is transmitted to the output area by an MVC instruction *prior* to the editing operation. This is because the edit pattern field is *destroyed* by each edit operation.

The data to be edited must be in *packed-decimal* form and is referenced as the second or sending operand in an ED instruction. The first operand always references a field containing a "pattern" of characters that controls the editing. After execution, the first operand contains the edited result in zoned-decimal format, the second operand remains unchanged. The instructions usually would be written in the following sequence:

LABEL	OPERATION	OPERAND	COMMENTS
	MVC	LINEOUT(6),PATTERN	
	ED	LINEOUT(6),PDATA	
	:		
PATTERN	DC		

where:

PATTERN   represents a 6-byte data pattern with special characters to be discussed
PDATA   is a 3-byte field containing 5 digits in packed form
LINEOUT   represents the output area

The packed field, PDATA, is 3 bytes in length and contains 5 digits. Therefore the edit pattern must accommodate the 5 digits and also provide for a starting fill character, usually a blank. Note that the edit pattern is 6 bytes in length.

The pattern field consists of special characters, each of which has a specific editing function. Unfortunately, many of these characters are not printable symbols and must be set up using a hexadecimal code, as in the following illustration.

LABEL	OPERATION	OPERAND	COMMENTS
	MVC	LINEOUT(6),PATTERN	
	ED	LINEOUT(6),PDATA	
	:		
PATTERN	DC	XL6'4020202020'	

or

LABEL	OPERATION	OPERAND	COMMENTS
	MVC	LINEOUT(6),=X'402020202020'	
	ED	LINEOUT(6),PDATA	

In our examples, reference characters are used to simplify the pattern. In our examples, D will signify digit and B will signify a blank when describing the characters to be edited by a pattern. During editing, the leftmost (high-order) byte of the pattern must contain a *fill character*. The pattern, therefore, is always at least *one byte longer* than the number of digits in the packed field. This is why, in the foregoing example, 5 digits were edited using a 6-byte pattern.

The following table will serve as a reference.

Character	Hex Code	Reference Used in Illustrations	Meaning
Digit Select	20	D for digit	Pattern is allowing for a digit.
Fill Character	40	B for blank	A blank is placed in pattern.

C. Interpreting Edit Characters

1. Suppression of Leading Zeros

Nonsignificant or leading zeros are zeros appearing in the leftmost positions of a field and having no significant value. For example, 00387 has two leading zeros that should be suppressed, or omitted, when printing. Note that the number 10,000 has no leading zeros. The entire number 10,000 should be printed because the zeros *follow* a significant digit.

To suppress leading zeros, we begin the edit pattern with a *fill character* indicating the specific symbol or character that should replace high-order zeros. For example, if blanks are to replace leading zeros, the fill character is a blank, or hex "40." Replacing leading zeros with blanks is called suppression of leading zeros.

If no other editing is to be performed, the edit pattern will contain the fill character and a hex "20" or digit select symbol for each character to be inserted from the sending field.

Using the previous illustration, we have:

LABEL	OPERATION	OPERAND	COMMENTS
	MVC	LINEOUT(6),=X'402020202020'	
	ED	LINEOUT(6),PDATA	

This will perform suppression on 5 decimal digits that are transmitted in packed format (3 bytes). In the following, D stands for digit select (digit to be transmitted with ED instruction), and B stands for blank.

Field	Hex Representation	Reference
PDATA	0 0 1 0 9 C	0 0 1 0 9 C
Edit Pattern	40 20 20 20 20 20	B D D D D D
LINEOUT (after execution of ED)	40 40 40 F1 F0 F9	B B B 1 0 9

Note

The zone bits of all significant digits are converted to 'F' by the ED instruction. Other examples using the BDDDDD edit pattern follow.

PDATA (Packed Decimal)	LINEOUT (Hex)	LINEOUT (Reference)
1 2 | 3 4 | 5 C	40 | F1 | F2 | F3 | F4 | F5	B12345
0 1 | 2 3 | 4 C	40 | 40 | F1 | F2 | F3 | F4	BB1234
0 0 | 5 6 | 7 C	40 | 40 | 40 | F5 | F6 | F7	BBB567
0 0 | 0 9 | 0 C	40 | 40 | 40 | 40 | F9 | F0	BBBB90
0 0 | 0 0 | 8 C	40 | 40 | 40 | 40 | 40 | F8	BBBBB8
0 0 | 0 0 | 0 C	40 | 40 | 40 | 40 | 40 | 40	BBBBBB
		B = blank

The fill character, then, is used in a pattern to replace high-order or leading zeros. When the fill character is a hex 40, then leading zeros are replaced with blanks. Any character may be used as the fill character, but the blank is the one most commonly used.

For the editing described, the number of characters in the edit pattern is *one* more than the number of digits to be edited. Also note that the number of digit select (D) characters appearing in the edit pattern must always be *odd* because packed fields always contain an odd number of digits. The following illustration will clarify this subject.

Packed Length in Bytes	Digits in Edit Pattern	Edit Pattern	Hex Pattern
1	1	B D	40 20
2	3	B D D D	40 20 20 20
3	5	B D D D D D	40 20 20 20 20 20

2. How Editing Is Actually Performed

Editing proceeds from *left* to *right*. All high-order zeros in the sending field are replaced with the fill character. Once a nonzero digit is transmitted, any zeros appearing to the right *will be printed*. In effect, an indicator within the CPU is turned on by a *nonzero digit* from the sending field. When the indicator is on, all remaining edit characters such as commas and zeros will appear in the output. This will be considered in detail shortly.

The fill character in an edit pattern may be an * in place of a blank. If the * is used as a fill character, 00025 will print as ***25. Whereas blanks in an amount field of a check can be altered by dishonest people, asterisks are frequently used because they reduce the feasibility of tampering with data. The asterisk (*) is called a **check protection symbol.** For example, an amount printed as `    547` can easily be changed to `99547` whereas `**547` is more difficult to change.

*Format for * as Fill Character*

Character	Representation	Hex Code Used in Pattern
Asterisk	*	5C

Using hex 5C in place of 40 as a fill character will result in leading zeros being replaced with *s.

The instruction for editing will be:

LABEL	OPERATION	OPERAND	COMMENTS
1	10 16		72
	MVC	LINEOUT(6),=X'5C202020202020'	
	ED	LINEOUT,PDATA	

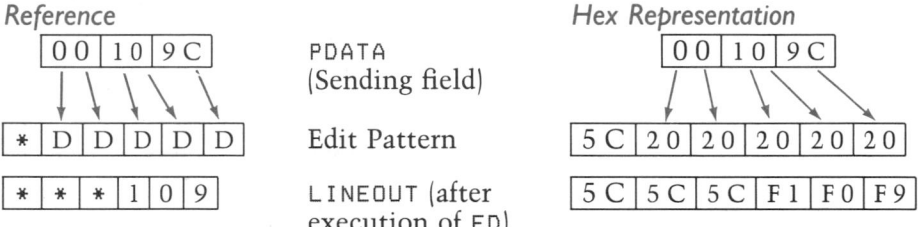

	Reference									*Hex Representation*					
	00	10	9C			PDATA (Sending field)			00	10	9C				
	*	D	D	D	D	D	Edit Pattern		5C	20	20	20	20	20	
	*	*	*	1	0	9	LINEOUT (after execution of ED)		5C	5C	5C	F1	F0	F9	

Other examples follow.

PDATA (Packed Decimal)			LINEOUT (hex)(after ED)						LINEOUT Actual Results
12	34	5C	5C	F1	F2	F3	F4	F5	*12345
01	23	4C	5C	5C	F1	F2	F3	F4	**1234
00	56	7C	5C	5C	5C	F5	F6	F7	***567
00	09	0C	5C	5C	5C	5C	F9	F0	****90
00	00	8C	5C	5C	5C	5C	5C	F8	*****8
00	00	0C	5C	5C	5C	5C	5C	5C	******

Self-Evaluating Quiz

1. The two instructions necessary to perform editing are _____ and _____ .
2. In the MVC instruction, the second operand is called the _____ field.
3. In the MVC and the ED instructions, the first operand refers to the (sending, receiving) field.
4. The data to be edited appears in the (first, second) operand of the (MVC,ED) instruction.
5. The data to be edited must be in _____ format.
6. Write a routine to print a 3-digit packed-decimal field called UNITS with zero suppression.
7. Write a routine to print a 4-byte packed-decimal field called TOTAL with asterisks (*) used as the zero suppression symbol.

SOLUTIONS

1. MVC; ED
2. Edit pattern field (established either as a constant or as a self-defining operand)
3. Receiving (usually located in the print area)

4. Second; ED
5. Packed-decimal
6.

LABEL	OPERATION	OPERAND	COMMENTS
	MVC	LINEOUT(4),=X'40202020'	
	ED	LINEOUT(4),UNITS	
	:		
UNITS	DS	PL2	

7. Recall that a 4-byte packed field contains 7 digits plus a sign.

LABEL	OPERATION	OPERAND	COMMENTS
	MVC	LINEOUT(9),=X'5C2020202020202020'	
	ED	LINEOUT(9),TOTAL	
	:		
TOTAL	DS	PL4	

3. Inserting Commas

Character	Representation	Hex Code Used in Pattern
Comma		6B

To insert a comma in an edit pattern we place the comma in the position desired. To print 0023456 as 23,456, for example, the edit pattern would appear as:

Edit Pattern	40	20	20	20	20	6B	20	20	20
Interpretation	B	D	D	D	D	,	D	D	D
	blank	digit	digit	digit	digit	comma	digit	digit	digit

|←——————————— 9 bytes ———————————→|

Note that a fill character in the edit pattern will suppress leading zeros and leading commas. Hence, if a field with value 0000245 were edited using the foregoing edit pattern, it would print as 245 *without* a comma. That is, the zero suppression character suppresses leading commas as well as leading zeros. The leftmost *six* positions are filled with blanks. Note that the field length specifier in the above is 9 bytes, which is the length of the pattern.

In the following examples, we will perform zero suppression and insert commas for clarity. The pattern necessary to accomplish this task will appear as:

B	D	D	,	D	D	D

The instructions to perform the editing are:

LABEL	OPERATION	OPERAND	COMMENTS
	MVC	LINEOUT(7),=X'402020 6B202020'	
	ED	LINEOUT(7),PDATA	

Note that in this case the field length specifier is 7.

Example 9.6

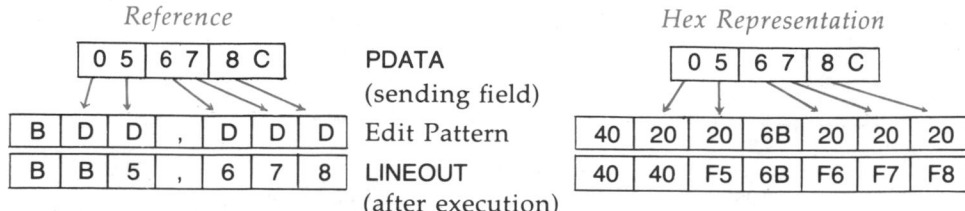

	Reference		*Hex Representation*

Note that the nonzero indicator that controls the printing or suppression of the comma is on because a nonzero digit precedes the comma. Therefore, all remaining edit characters will transmit without any suppression.

Other examples using the BDD,DDD edit pattern follow.

	PDATA	LINEOUT (Hex)	Reference
1.	12 | 34 | 5C	40 | F1 | F2 | 6B | F3 | F4 | F5	B12,345
2.	01 | 23 | 4C	40 | 40 | F1 | 6B | F2 | F3 | F4	BB1,234
3.	00 | 56 | 7C	40 | 40 | 40 | 40 | F5 | F6 | F7	BBBB567
4.	00 | 09 | 0C	40 | 40 | 40 | 40 | 40 | F9 | F0	BBBBB90
5.	00 | 00 | 8C	40 | 40 | 40 | 40 | 40 | 40 | F8	BBBBBB8
6.	00 | 00 | 0C	40 | 40 | 40 | 40 | 40 | 40 | 40	BBBBBBB

Note that a nonzero digit was *not* found before the comma in examples 3–6. Therefore, the nonzero indicator is off and the comma does *not* appear in the final result.

4. Inserting Decimal Points

Character	Representation	Hex Code
Decimal point	.	4B

The decimal point is commonly used in reports, typically in dollars and cents figures. When the program is designed, field sizes with *implied* decimal points are used for representing data in "raw" form. The programmer must know, however, where *actual* decimal points are to be inserted for printout purposes. In the following examples, we will assume that the desired results represent dollars and cents. The pattern used will be established so that a decimal point will be printed.

Pattern reference	B	D	D	D	.	D	D
Pattern (hex)	40	20	20	20	4B	20	20

Here are the instructions for editing.

LABEL	OPERATION	OPERAND	COMMENTS
	MVC	LINEOUT(7),=X'4020202004B2020'	
	ED	LINEOUT(7),PDATA	

Reference		Hex Representation

	0	5	6	7	8 C		PDATA (sending field)

	B	D	D	D	.	D	D	Edit Pattern

	B	B	5	6	.	7	8	LINEOUT (after execution)

Hex Representation:

0	5	6	7	8 C

40	20	20	20	4B	20	20

40	40	F5	F6	4B	F7	F8

Other examples using the BDDD.DD pattern include:

	PDATA			LINEOUT (Hex)							Reference
1.	12	34	5C	40	F1	F2	F3	4B	F4	F5	B 1 2 3 . 4 5
2.	01	23	4C	40	40	F1	F2	4B	F3	F4	B B 1 2 . 3 4
3.	00	56	7C	40	40	40	F5	4B	F6	F7	B B B 5 . 6 7
4.	00	09	0C	40	40	40	40	40	F9	F0	B B B B 9 0
5.	00	00	8C	40	40	40	40	40	40	F8	B B B B B 8
6.	00	00	00	40	40	40	40	40	40	40	B B B B B B B

In examples 1–3, the printed output is appropriate. There are, however, problems with examples 4–6.

Whenever a field contains all zeros, the fill character is the only item that prints, as in (6). Moreover, when the first significant or nonzero character *follows* the decimal point, as in (4) and (5), the decimal point does *not* print. To cause edit characters to print even if no significant digit has been sensed, we must use the *significant start character.* This character terminates the suppression of characters we always want to print, such as a decimal point.

5. Significant Start Character

Character	Representation	Hex
Significant start character	S	21

The significant start character functions like the digit select character in that it is replaced by:

1. A digit in the sending field when the nonzero indicator is on; that is, when a significant character has already been sensed; or
2. A fill character when the indicator is off.

However, the CPU indicator is *immediately turned on* when the significant start character has been reached. Therefore, all edit symbols and digits to the *right* of the significant start character will be transmitted to the pattern. In the previous examples, the best place to set up the significant start character is *directly before* the cents portion of the field. This is done to make certain that a decimal point prints even if there is no nonzero digit preceding it. The following, then, is used in place of the preceding pattern.

Pattern Reference	B	D	D	S		D	D
Pattern (hex)	40	20	20	21	4B	20	20

The editing instructions would be:

LABEL	OPERATION	OPERAND	COMMENTS
	MVC	LINEOUT(7),=X'4020202l4B2020'	
	ED	LINEOUT(7),PDATA	

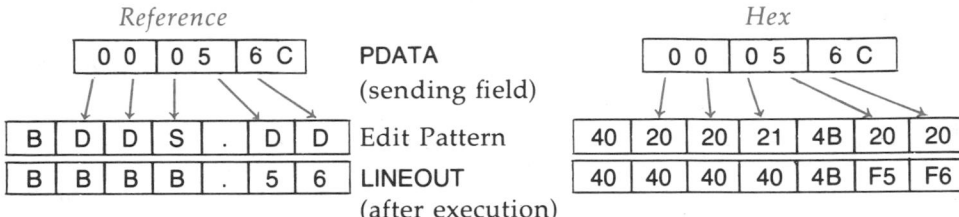

Note that the decimal point will print because the indicator was turned on by the significant start character. The significant start character (21), like the digit fill (20), is replaced by a digit or fill character.

Here are other examples using the BDDS.DD pattern.

PDATA	LINEOUT (Hex)	Reference
12 | 34 | 5C	40 | F1 | F2 | F3 | 4B | F4 | F5	B123.45
01 | 23 | 4C	40 | 40 | F1 | F2 | 4B | F3 | F4	BB12.34
00 | 56 | 7C	40 | 40 | 40 | F5 | 4B | F6 | F7	BBB5.67
00 | 09 | 0C	40 | 40 | 40 | 40 | 4B | F9 | F0	BBBB.90
00 | 00 | 8C	40 | 40 | 40 | 40 | 4B | F0 | F8	BBBB.08
00 | 00 | 0C	40 | 40 | 40 | 40 | 4B | F0 | F0	BBBB.00

6. Inserting a Dollar Sign

Character	Representation	Hex
Dollar sign	$	5B

To insert the dollar sign we use the MVI instruction. Recall that each pattern field is at least one byte longer than the number of digits contained in the sending field. In our examples, the high-order position typically will be a blank. We can then move the dollar sign to the high-order position of the field to be printed. With this method, all the dollar signs in a particular column will align. For example, the instruction could be written in either of the following ways.

LABEL	OPERATION	OPERAND	COMMENTS
	MVI	LINEOUT,X'5B'	

LABEL	OPERATION	OPERAND	COMMENTS
	MVI	LINEOUT,C'$'	

Using the preceding examples, the output when printed will appear as:

```
$ 1 2 3 . 4 5
$   1 2 . 3 4
$     5 . 6 7
$       . 9 0
$       . 0 8
$       . 0 0
```

The dollar signs will align in the same print position.

7. Combining Characters

In the following examples, the comma, decimal point, and dollar sign are used in combination. The pattern BDD,DDS.DD is used to unpack and edit a 4-byte, packed-decimal field that represents a dollars and cents figure. At this point, you should be sufficiently familiar with the editing process so that only the sending and result fields need be illustrated.

LABEL	OPERATION	OPERAND	COMMENTS
	MVC	LINEOUT(1Ø),=X'4Ø2Ø2Ø6B2Ø2Ø214B2Ø2Ø'	
	ED	LINEOUT(1Ø),PDATA	
	MVI	LINEOUT,C'$'	

PDATA	LINEOUT (Hex)	Reference
12 | 34 | 56 | 7C	5B | F1 | F2 | 6B | F3 | F4 | F5 | 4B | F6 | F7	$ 1 2 , 3 4 5 . 6 7
04 | 56 | 78 | 9C	5B | 40 | F4 | 6B | F5 | F6 | F7 | 4B | F8 | F9	$ B 4 , 5 6 7 . 8 9
00 | 23 | 45 | 6C	5B | 40 | 40 | 40 | F2 | F3 | F4 | 4B | F5 | F6	$ B B B 2 3 4 . 5 6
00 | 00 | 12 | 3C	5B | 40 | 40 | 40 | 40 | 40 | F1 | 4B | F2 | F3	$ B B B B B 1 . 2 3
00 | 00 | 02 | 6C	5B | 40 | 40 | 40 | 40 | 40 | 40 | 4B | F2 | F6	$ B B B B B B . 2 6

8. Printing a Sign

The ED operation automatically replaces the zone of the low-order byte with an F unless additional sign control is specified. The editing specified thus far, then, will print all fields as if they were positive. In effect, the low-order zone is ignored. Thus, the OI (Or Immediate) or MVZ (Move Zone) instructions are not needed to replace zones when the ED is used.

To print a minus sign for negative data fields, however, the rightmost position of the edit mask must contain a minus sign.

EDIT Mask

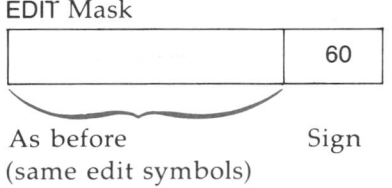

As before   Sign
(same edit symbols)

If the sending field is signed positive or unsigned, this rightmost position will be replaced with the fill character. If the sending field is signed negative, this rightmost position will print as a minus sign.

The following examples illustrate how an edit pattern with sign control operates.

Pattern Reference	B	D	D	D	Sign Control
Pattern (hex)	40	20	20	20	60

The editing instructions appear as:

LABEL	OPERATION	OPERAND	COMMENTS
	MVC	LINEOUT(5),=X'40202020 60'	
	ED	LINEOUT(5),PDATA	

PDATA	LINEOUT (Hex) (after Execution)	Reference
1 2 3 D	40 F1 F2 F3 60	B 1 2 3 −
1 2 3 F	40 F1 F2 F3 40	B 1 2 3 B
1 2 3 C	40 F1 F2 F3 40	B 1 2 3 B

The following table contains a review of the symbols that can be used in edit patterns.

Edit Code Summary

Hex Code Used in Mask	Meaning
20	Digit select: Used for each digit to be transmitted from packed sending field.
40	Blank fill: To replace leading zeros with blanks.
5C	Asterisk (∗) fill: To replace leading zeros with ∗.
6B	Comma: To insert commas.
4B	Decimal point: To insert a period.
21	Significant start character: To digit select and to turn on the indicator so that a decimal point will print even if no significant digit has been sensed.
60	Sign control: To print a minus sign for negative amounts.
5B (Not part of Mask. Inserted after ED.)	Dollar sign: Inserted in high-order position with MVI instruction.

SUMMARY: STEPS IN EDITING

For this example, let the packed-decimal field to be edited, PDATA, be 4 bytes long and contain dollars and cents.

1. First we determine the length of the packed decimal field to be edited. The field PDATA consists of 4 bytes.
   ```
   PDATA   DS  PL4
   ```
2. Remember, the number of digits contained in a packed field must *always* be odd. PDATA contains 7 digits represented in the edit pattern as follows:
   DDDDDDD
3. Next, include the B as the fill character because we intend to use zero suppression.
   BDDDDDDD
4. Include a comma and a decimal point.
   BDD,DDD.DD
5. In most business applications, zero balances are printed with the decimal point. Consequently, we change the D immediately preceding the decimal point to an S, the significant start character. Hence,
   BDD,DDS.DD
   represents a 10-byte edit pattern to be used in editing a 4-byte, packed-decimal field.
6. Convert the edit pattern to hexadecimal using the preceding Edit Code Summary. The following instructions correctly edit the field PDATA.
   ```
   MVC   LINEOUT+20(10),=X'4020206B2020204B2020'
   ED    LINEOUT+20(10),PDATA
   ```
7. Note the first operand in the MVC instruction is identical to the first operand in the edit instruction.

III. CONTROL BREAK PROCESSING

A. An Introduction to Control Break Processing

1. Detail and Group Printing: An Overview

Thus far, we have focused on the printing of individual lines for each input record read. When every input record is printed, we call this **detail printing.** Sometimes we wish to print total or summary lines for a group of records in place of, or in addition to, detail lines. This is called **group printing.** Figure 9.11 compares detail and group printing.

This section will consider group printing and will focus on a specific type that uses **control fields** to indicate when totals are to print. This procedure is called **control break processing.**

2. An Example of a Control Break Procedure

Consider the problem definition in Figure 9.12. A disk file consists of sales records, each with 3 input fields: a salesperson's department number, the salesperson's number, and the amount of sales accrued weekly by that sales-

```
                      SALES  REPORT
                    BY  ITEM  NUMBER              08/04/—

                                                 PAGE  1


         ITEM                    ITEM                 SALES
         NO,                  DESCRIPTION            AMOUNT

         587                   WIDGETS               142.38
         587                   WIDGETS               382.27
         763                   WAXED  PAPER          872.53
         763                   WAXED  PAPER          821.33
         763                   WAXED  PAPER          168.38
         923                   BALLOONS              858.21
         923                   BALLOONS              923.73
         923                   BALLOONS               15.82
         923                   BALLOONS               77.93
```

Detail report

```
                  SUMMARY  SALES  REPORT
                    BY  ITEM  NUMBER
                                                 08/04/—

                                                 PAGE  1


         ITEM                    ITEM                 SALES
         NO,                  DESCRIPTION            AMOUNT

         587                   WIDGETS              524.65*
         763                   WAXED  PAPER        1862.24*
         923                   BALLOONS            1875.69*
```

Group report

Figure 9.11
Comparison of detail and group printing.

person. There may be numerous sales records for DEPT 01, 02, and so on. That is, each department will contain records for several different salespeople. The output is a report that prints each salesperson's amount of sales and the total sales amount for each department.

The input file is in sequence by DEPT. Thus all records pertaining to salespeople in DEPT 01 are followed by all records pertaining to salespeople in DEPT 02, and so on.

For this problem, detail printing is required; that is, each input record is to be printed, as in previous examples. Summary lines indicating department totals must also print. Thus, group printing is required, where a total line is written for each department.

In summary, after all records for DEPT 01 have been read and printed, a total for DEPT 01 will print. Similarly, after all records for DEPT 02 have been read and printed, a total for DEPT 02 will print, and so on. This type of processing requires all DEPT 01 records to be entered and processed first, followed by the next DEPT's records, and so on.

Note that the file of input records *must be in sequence by department number.* Department totals will print correctly, one for each department, only if the input records are properly sorted into DEPT sequence. All salesperson records for DEPT 01 must be read first, followed by salesperson records for DEPT 02, etc; otherwise, it would not be possible to accumulate a total and

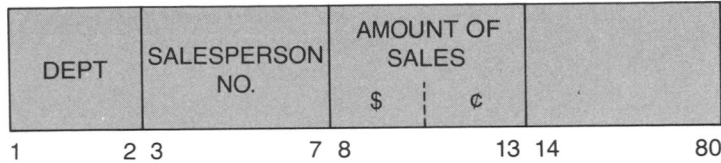

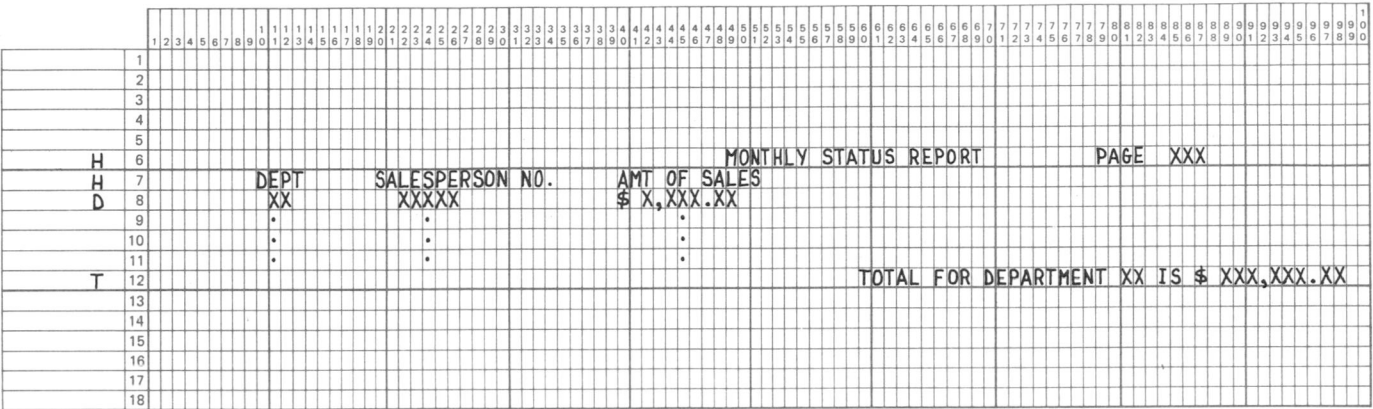

Figure 9.12
Problem definition for a control break procedure.

print it at the end of a group. Note that files can always be *sorted* into the desired sequence using a utility program.

Detail lines print, in the usual way, after each input record is read and processed. In addition, after each input record is read, the amount of sales is then added to a DEPT total. This department total will be printed whenever a change in DEPT occurs. Because a change in DEPT triggers the printing of a department total, we call DEPT the *control field*.

Thus all salesperson records for DEPT 01 will be read and printed, and a DEPT total accumulated. This processing continues until a salesperson record is read that contains a DEPT different from the previous one. When this record with a different DEPT is read, the totals for the previous department will be printed. Thus the first input record pertaining to a salesperson in DEPT 02 will cause a total for DEPT 01 to print. Because totals are printed *after* a change occurs in DEPT (the control field) we call this type of group processing *control break processing*.

This section provides you with some definitions related to control break processing and with an illustration of the output produced by a control break procedure. In the next section, we focus on one way this procedure is coded. You may wish to examine Figure 9.13 on pages 268–270 for the program that will perform the control break procedure. This program will be discussed in detail in the next section.

B. Program Requirements for Control Break Processing

1. A Single-Level Control Break

For each input record read for the problem previously outlined, two functions will always be performed.

1. Print a detail line.
2. Add the PAMT field to a department total that we call PDEPT.

```
*                                                                         *
*                                    HOUSEKEEPING INSTRUCTIONS GO HERE     *
*                                                                         *
*
            GET     INFILE,RECORD
            ZAP     PDEPT,=P'Ø'
            ZAP     PCTR,=P'Ø'
            MVC     FLAG,=C'Ø'
            MVC     FLAG2,=C'Ø'
HEADRTN     ZAP     LCTR,=P'1'
            AP      PCTR,=P'1'
            UNPK    PAGE,PCTR
            OI      PAGE+2,X'FØ'
            PUT     OUTFILE,OUTAREA1
            PUT     OUTFILE,OUTAREA2
            CLC     FLAG2,=C'1'
            BE      PRINT
NEWDEPT     MVC     CHECK,DEPTIN
            MVC     DEPTOUT,DEPTIN
            MVC     DEPTNO,DEPTIN
CONTROL     CLC     CHECK,DEPTIN
            BH      ERROR
            BL      BREAK
            MVC     SALESO,SALESI
            PACK    PAMT,AMTIN
            AP      PDEPT,PAMT
            MVC     AMTOUT(9),MASK1
            ED      AMTOUT(9),PAMT
            MVC     FLAG2,=C'1'
            AP      LCTR,=P'1'
            CP      LCTR,=P'25'
            BNL     HEADRTN
PRINT       PUT     OUTFILE,OUTAREA3
            MVC     FLAG2,=C'Ø'
            GET     INFILE,RECORD
            B       CONTROL
BREAK       MVC     TDEPT(11),MASK2
            ED      TDEPT(11),PDEPT
            PUT     OUTFILE,OUTAREA4
            CLC     FLAG,=C'1'
            BE      END
            ZAP     PDEPT,=P'Ø'
            B       NEWDEPT
ERROR       MVC     OUTAREA+1,SPACES
            MVC     OUTAREA+10,=C'TERMINATE RUN--BAD DATA'
            MVC     FLAG,=C'1'
            PUT     OUTFILE,OUTAREA
            B       END
```

Figure 9.13
Control break program with sample input and output (continued on pages 269 and 270).

In addition, a total line ("TOTAL FOR DEPARTMENT XX IS $XX,XXX.XX") will print only *after* the first record with the next DEPT is read. When this total prints, we set PDEPT to zero and process the new input record as before.

This is called a single-level control break because we have only one field, DEPT, that triggers the printing of totals. To perform single-level control break processing, the following steps must be coded after the standard initializing routines. Those initializing procedures include the opening of files, printing of headings, clearing of fields, and so on.[2] The following operations would then be coded.

---

1. Initialize a hold area with the contents of the first record's control field. This is performed in the main module after the initial read.

---

[2]We will discuss the use of the "switches" FLAG and FLAG2 later in this chapter.

```
EOF       MVC    FLAG,=C'1'
          B      BREAK
END       .                          HOUSEKEEPING INSTRUCTIONS GO HERE
          .                          ALONG WITH DCB OR DTF MACROS
          .
*
RECORD    DS     0CL80
DEPTIN    DS     CL2
SALESI    DS     CL5
AMTIN     DS     CL7
          DS     CL66
*
OUTAREA   DS     0CL133
CC        DC     CL1' '
          DS     CL132
*
OUTAREA1  DS     0CL133
C1        DC     CL1'1'
          DC     CL48' '
          DC     CL21'MONTHLY STATUS REPORT'
          DC     CL9' '
          DC     CL6'PAGE  '
PAGE      DS     CL3
          DC     CL45' '
*
OUTAREA2  DS     0CL133
C2        DC     CL1' '
          DC     CL9' '
          DC     CL4'DEPT'
          DC     CL6' '
          DC     CL15'SALESPERSON NO.'
          DC     CL5' '
          DC     CL13'AMT OF SALES'
          DC     CL80' '
*
OUTAREA3  DS     0CL133
C3        DC     CL1' '
          DC     CL10' '
DEPTOUT   DS     CL2
          DC     CL9' '
SALESO    DS     CL5
          DC     CL13' '
          DC     CL1'$'
AMTOUT    DS     CL8
          DC     CL84' '
*
OUTAREA4  DS     0CL133
C4        DC     CL1' '
          DC     CL59' '
          DC     CL21'TOTAL FOR DEPARTMENT '
DEPTNO    DS     CL2
          DC     CL5' IS $'
TDEPT     DS     CL10
          DC     CL35' '
*WORKAREAS
```

Figure 9.13 (continued)

The first input record is read and its control field, in this program DEPTIN, must be moved to a DS area to save it for comparison purposes. We will call the area CHECK. Thus, we have the following instructions:

```
GET    INFILE,RECORD
MVC    CHECK,DEPTIN
```

2. Process input records at CONTROL. Processing depends on whether or not the control field read in matches the one stored at CHECK.

We begin at CONTROL by comparing DEPTIN to CHECK. The first time through, CHECK and DEPTIN will be equal because we just moved DEPTIN to CHECK. For all subsequent passes through CONTROL, CHECK will contain the DEPTIN

```
FLAG      DS    CL1
FLAG2     DS    CL1
PCTR      DS    PL2
LCTR      DS    PL2
CHECK     DS    CL2
PDEPT     DS    PL5
PAMT      DS    PL4
SPACES    DC    CL132' '
MASK1     DC    X'4020682020214820 20'
MASK2     DC    X'402020206820 2021482020'
          END
```

Sample Input Data

```
01123450023154
01123460232152
01242120032542
02421520003254
02452120021453
02452320021452
02421230021453
02542320086532
03457740986523
03422110532452
04122210336520
04563250021203
05000015666532
06222320222457
09566660222454
09333330023325
```

Sample Printed Report

```
                                        MONTHLY STATUS REPORT          PAGE   001
DEPT       SALESPERSON NO.      AMT OF SALES
01         12345                $     23.15
01         12346                $    232.15
01         24212                $     32.54
                                              TOTAL FOR DEPARTMENT 01 IS $     287.84
02         42152                $      3.25
02         45212                $     21.45
02         45232                $     21.45
02         42123                $     21.45
02         54232                $     86.53
                                              TOTAL FOR DEPARTMENT 02 IS $     154.14
03         45774                $    986.52
03         42211                $    532.45
                                              TOTAL FOR DEPARTMENT 03 IS $   1,518.97
04         12221                $    336.52
04         56325                $     21.20
                                              TOTAL FOR DEPARTMENT 04 IS $     357.72
05         00001                $  5,666.53
                                              TOTAL FOR DEPARTMENT 05 IS $   5,666.53
06         22232                $    222.45
                                              TOTAL FOR DEPARTMENT 06 IS $     222.45
09         56666                $    222.45
09         33333                $     23.32
                                              TOTAL FOR DEPARTMENT 09 IS $     245.77
```

Figure 9.13 (continued)

of the previous record read. When CHECK and DEPTIN are equal, there is no control break and we perform three steps:

1. Move input data to a detail line and print.

```
MVC    SALESO,SALESI
MVC    AMTOUT(9),MASK1
ED     AMTOUT(9),PAMT
PUT    OUTFILE,OUTAREA3
```

Notice in Figure 9.13 that DEPTIN was already moved to DEPTOUT in the NEWDEPT routine.

2. Accumulate a department total.

```
PACK    PAMT,AMTIN
AP      PDEPT,PAMT
```

3. Read the next record.

```
GET     INFILE,RECORD
```

We then repeat the steps.

```
B       CONTROL
```

We continue processing input records in this way until the DEPTIN in an input record differs from the previous DEPTIN stored at CHECK. When they are different, a control break has occurred.

---

3. Group processing occurs in the BREAK procedure after a record is read that has a different value in the control field.

Each time DEPTIN is not equal to CHECK, the BREAK procedure is performed, where the accumulated department total is printed.

BREAK prints a total for the *previous* department. After the total is printed and reinitialized at zero, we proceed to NEWDEPT to process the *current* record.

---

4. Processing of the last department total occurs when the end-of-file condition has been reached.

Thus far we have seen how CONTROL is executed. When a record is read with the same DEPTIN as the previous one, it is printed and added to PDEPT.

When a change in DEPTIN occurs, DEPTIN and CHECK will be different and BREAK will be executed. At BREAK, we print a total line, reinitialize PDEPT at zero, and proceed to NEWDEPT to process the current input record. What remains is the processing of the very last control total when an end-of-file condition is reached.

Note that a control break printing of a department total occurs when a record with a *new* control field is read. The total for the last group of records, then, will have been accumulated but a control total will not have been printed because there is no subsequent record to trigger a change. Consider the following.

```
DEPTIN
  01
  01
  01
 ─────
  02      01 totals are printed when 02 is read
  02
  02
  02
 ─────
  03      02 totals are printed when 03 is read
  03
─────────
End of file  At this point, 03 totals must be "forced"
             after the end-of-file is reached
```

There must be a procedure to print the 03 totals. At the end, when there are no more records to process, we must force a printing of this final total. FLAG, which was initialized at zero, is used for this purpose. When the end-of-file condition is reached, control is transferred automatically to EOF. At EOF, FLAG is set to 1, and a branch is made to BREAK, where the last total is printed. Because FLAG is now equal to 1, a branch is made to the END routine, instead of back to NEWDEPT. At the END routine, the files are closed and the program is terminated.

The full program for processing a single-level control break with detail printing appears in Figure 9.13. Notice the following in the program:

1. A line counter, (LCTR), is used to determine when the bottom of a page has been reached and headings should be printed on the top of a new page.
2. A page counter (PCTR) is used to print out the page number as part of the headings.
3. The "switch" FLAG2, which is initialized at zero, serves the following purpose. In the CONTROL procedure, FLAG2 is set to 1. When the line counter (LCTR) reaches 25, a branch is made to HEADRTN. After the headings are printed, a branch is made back to PRINT, which is part of the CONTROL procedure, to resume processing instead of continuing with NEWDEPT.

The flowchart for this procedure is illustrated in Figure 9.14 on pages 273–274, and the pseudocode is shown in Figure 9.15.

2. Refinements to Improve the Quality of a Control Break Report

a. Printing a Final Total. Sometimes control break processing also requires the printing of a final total. This would be coded after the last control group has been printed.

The final total (FINTOT) may be accumulated by adding AMT for each record. This may be done by adding an AP instruction in the CONTROL routine of Figure 9.13:

```
AP    FINTOT,PAMT
```

Alternately, the FINTOT may be accumulated by adding each PDEPT to it, in the BREAK module. This means that FINTOT would be accumulated, *not* for each detail record, but only when a control break has occurred. This would be accomplished by coding the following before we clear PDEPT:

```
BREAK
      .
      .
      .
      AP  FINTOT,PDEPT
      ZAP PDEPT,=P'0'
```

Note that the second procedure is far more efficient than the first. Suppose we have 10,000 input records but only 20 department control breaks. If we added PAMT to FINTOT for each input record, we would be performing 10,000 additions. If instead, we added the PDEPT to FINTOT when each control break occurred, we would be performing the addition only 20 times. Thus, adding PDEPT to FINTOT would result in far fewer additions than adding PAMT for each sales record to FINTOT.

b. Starting a New Page After Each Control Break. It is likely that reports created with control breaks would be distributed to a variety of users. That

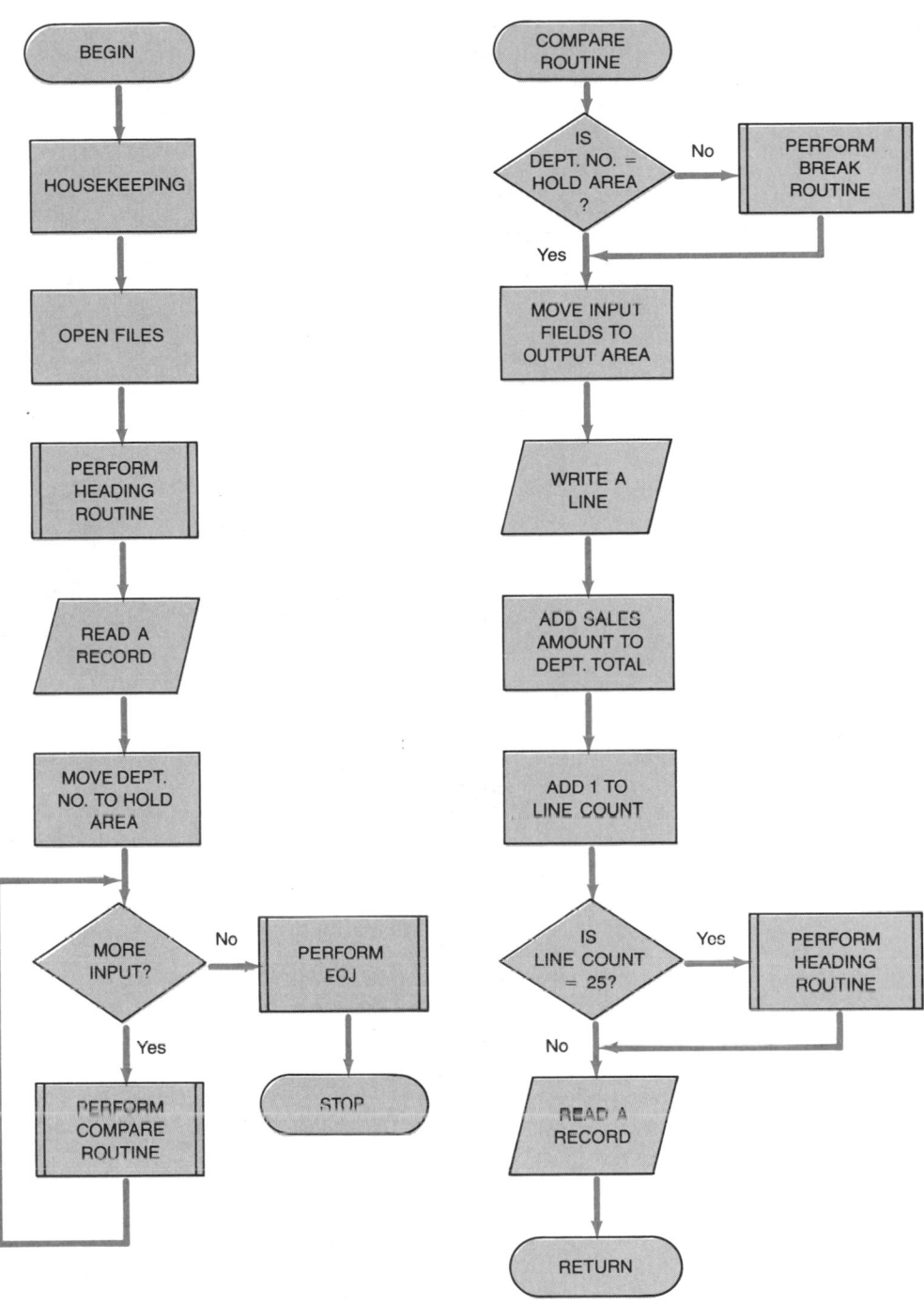

Figure 9.14
Flowchart for the sample control break program (continued on page 274).

is, the listing pertaining to DEPT 01 in the preceding illustration would be transmitted to that department; the listing for DEPT 02 would go to that department, and so on. In this situation, it is useful to have *each department's* data begin on a new page. Typically, then, a change in control fields should also include a statement to execute the heading routine to advance the paper to a new page.

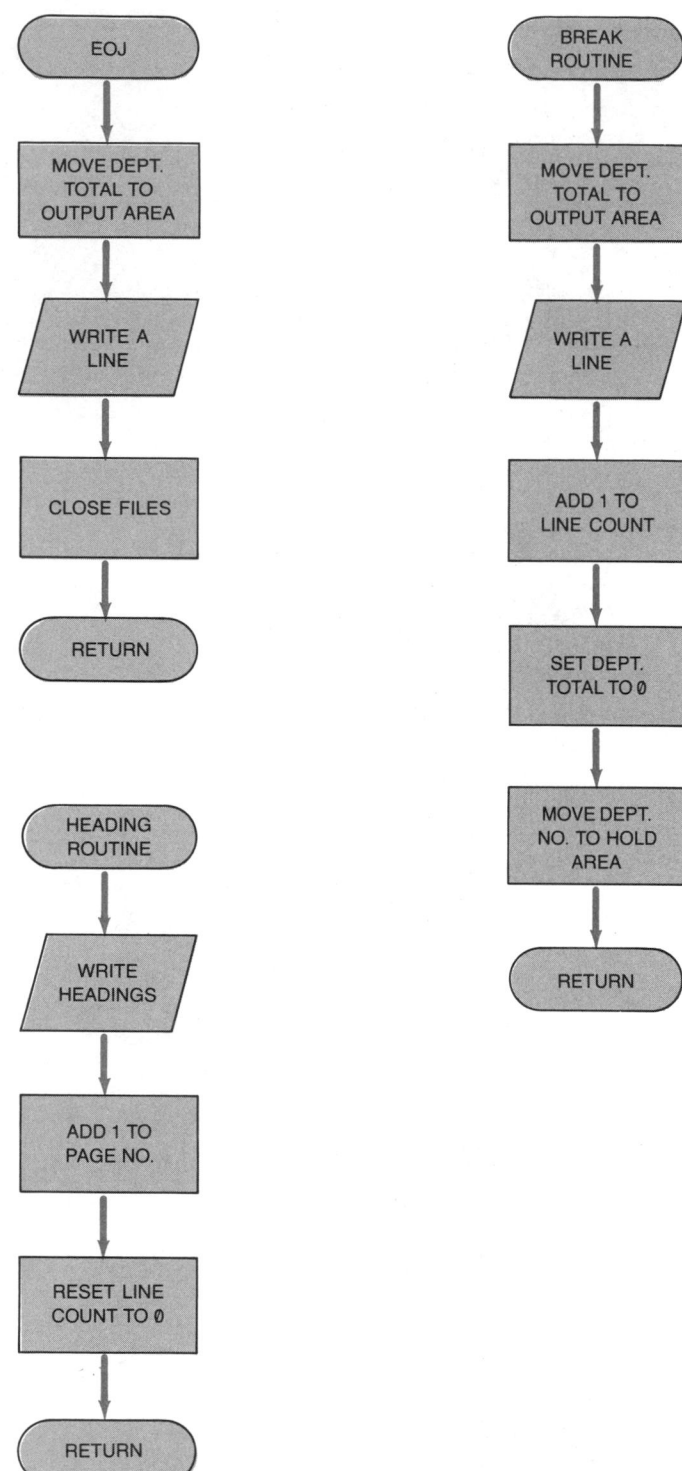

Figure 9.14 (continued)

```
Open the files
Write the heading
Read an input record
Move department to a hold area
PERFORM UNTIL no more data
    IF department is not equal to hold area
        Move fields to output area
        Write a group line
        Initialize all fields
    ENDIF
    Move detail data to output
    Write a line
    Add sales to department total
    Add 1 to line counter
    IF line counter > 25
        Write headings
        Initialize line counter
    ENDIF
    Read an input record
ENDPERFORM
Close the files
Stop run
```

Figure 9.15
Pseudocode for the sample
control break program.

In this instance it would be redundant to also print DEPT on each detail line. Rather, it would be more appropriate to print it once at the beginning of each page.

```
                        MONTHLY STATUS REPORT        PAGE xx   xx/xx/xx

    DEPT-01             SALESPERSON NO.              AMT OF SALES

                            12345                    $7,326.45

                            18724                    $9,264.55


                    TOTAL FOR DEPT IS   $16,591.00
```

c. Sequence-Checking: To Ensure That Input Data was Entered in the Correct Sequence.   For control break processing to proceed accurately, records must be in sequence by the control field. Consider the following sequence error.

```
DEPTIN
   01
   01
   02   ⟵ sequence error—DEPT 02 out of sequence
   01
   01
    .
    .
    .
```

Because it is always possible for input errors to occur, it would be useful to check to make certain, after each control break, that the current DEPTIN is greater than or equal to the previous one in CHECK. If a current DEPTIN is less than CHECK, then a sequence error has occurred and an error message should print. We may also wish to terminate processing in such a case. The systems analyst typically provides the programmer with the actions to be taken in case of specified error conditions.

CHAPTER SUMMARY

I. Printed output requires special handling not usually necessary with other forms of output.
   A. Forms must be spaced with top and bottom, and left and right margins.
   B. Headings are required.
II. Spacing and Skipping
   A. Space (SP) option may be used to space 1, 2, or 3 lines.
   B. Skip (SK) option may be used to advance to the top of a form.
   C. SP and SK may be programmed to occur immediately or after printing.
   D. SP and SK used with CNTRL macro.
   E. ASA characters may be used in place of CNTRL macro.
   F. To skip to a new page when an end-of-page is reached you may use a line counter.
III. Editing
   Packed fields are edited into zoned-decimal edited fields.

20	Digit select
40	Fills leading zeros with blanks
5C	Fills leading zeros with *
6B	Inserts commas
4B	Inserts decimal point
21	Significant start character: to turn on indicator so that a decimal point prints even if it is the first significant character.
60	Prints a minus sign for negative amounts
5B	Prints a dollar sign

   Note that the number of digit select characters in an edit pattern must always be odd, because packed fields always contain an odd number of digits.
IV. Control Break Processing
   A. Purpose: To print groups or totals based on specific control fields.
   B. Perform total routine until new record's control field is no longer equal to previous record's control field.
   C. If an unequal condition exists, print the total and clear all fields.
   D. At end, "force" a control break to print the last total.
   E. Control break printing is a form of group or summary printing.

CHAPTER SELF-EVALUATING QUIZ

1. Write the edit pattern necessary to obtain the desired results.

	Sending Field	Receiving Field
a.	0002354	2,354
b.	0267859	2,678.59
c.	0087546	**87,546

2. Consider the following edit pattern.

   40 20 20 6B 20 20 20

   If 00235 is to be edited, will 235 or ,235 print?

3. Write the statement necessary to have a $ print in problem 1b, assuming that the receiving field is located at LINEOUT+49.

4. Indicate the number of digits to be transmitted for each type of editing illustrated.
   a. 40 20 20 6B 20 20 20 4B 20 20
   b. 40 20 20 6B 20 20 20 4B 20 20 60
   c. 40 20 20 21 4B 20 20

5. Suppose the data to be edited in Question 4 is the following. Indicate the results.
   a. 0082654 (packed, 4 bytes)
   b. 0038726 (packed, 4 bytes)
   c. 00046   (packed, 3 bytes)

What, if anything, is wrong with the following program excerpts?

```
6.          MVC     LINEOUT(6),=X'40202020204B2020'
            ED      LINEOUT(6),PDATA
              ·
              ·
    PDATA   DS      PL4
```

```
7.          MVC     LINEOUT(4),X'40202020'
            ED      LINEOUT(4),PDATA
              ·
              ·
    PDATA   DS      PL2
```

```
8.          MVC     LINEOUT(5),=X'402020202020'
            ED      LINEOUT(5),PDATA
              ·
              ·
    PDATA   DS      CL4
```

```
9.          MVC     LINEOUT(9),=X'5C206B2020214B2020'
            ED      LINEOUT(9),PDATA
              ·
              ·
    PDATA   DS      PL3
```

```
10.         MVC     LINEOUT(7),=X'5B20204B202020'
            ED      OUTAREA(7),PDATA
              ·
              ·
    PDATA   DS   PL3
```

```
11.         MVC     LINEOUT(7),PATT
            ED      LINEOUT(7),PDATA
              ·
              ·
    PDATA   DS      PL3
    PATT    DC      X'5C20214B202020'
```

12. When each input record is printed, we call this _____ printing.

13. When groups of input records are summarized on one or more lines of printing, we call this _____ printing.

14. (T or F) In general, printing each individual record requires less processing time than summarizing the data.

Consider the following problem definition. Each input record includes a warehouse number where the item is stocked and the value of that item's stock on hand.

a. Input Record Layout

WAREHOUSE NO.	ITEM NO.	QUANTITY ON HAND	UNIT PRICE $ ¢	TOTAL VALUE $ ¢
1 2	3 5	6 9	10 14	15 23

b. Printer Spacing Chart for Printed Output

```
                                        WAREHOUSE REPORT    XX/XX/XX   PAGE XX

WAREHOUSE NO.    TOTAL NO. OF ITEMS STORED     TOTAL VALUE OF INVENTORY
    XX              X,XXX                      $XXX,XXX,XXX.XX
```

15. If the output report consists of each warehouse's total value of inventory, we would call this a(n) _____ report.

16. Because only total warehouse information prints, warehouse number would be called the _____ field.

17. The procedure used for printing the total inventory value for each warehouse is called a(n) _____ procedure.

18. To print warehouse totals using the format described in this chapter, input data must be in sequence by _____ .

19. Write the main module for this problem.

20. Assuming that you have called the detail module DETLRTN, code that module.

21. Assuming that you have called the control break module CONTROL, code that module.

				Page
SOLUTIONS	1.	a.	X'40206B2020206B202020'	264
		b.	X'4020206B2020204B2020'	264
		c.	X'5C2020214B2020'	264
	2.	235		259
	3.	MVI	LINEOUT+49,X'5B'	262
	4.	a.	seven digits (four bytes)	265
		b.	seven digits (four bytes)	265
		c.	five digits (three bytes); 21 also digit selects	265
	5.	a.	ᵬᵬᵬᵬ82,654	263
		b.	ᵬᵬᵬᵬ387.26	263
		c.	****.46	263
	6.	Pattern is too large for a 6-byte move; also, it contains an even number of digits.		265
	7.	Second operand in MVC is not a self-defining operand; it should be: =X'40202020'		256
	8.	PDATA must be in packed-decimal format and have a length of 3.		255
	9.	Self-defining operand must be as follows: =X'5C20206B2020214B2020' because PDATA accommodates 7 digits, not 6.		265
	10.	5B in a self-defining operand would generate $ as a zero suppression character; this is normally not intended.		256
	11.	Okay		265
	12.	Detail		265
	13.	Group or summary		265
	14.	F: in general, printing summary listings is faster than printing detail listings		266

19.
```
        *        HOUSEKEEPING AND OPEN INSTRUCTIONS GO HERE    268
        *
                 GET    INFILE,RECORD
        HEADRTN  ZAP    LCTR,=P'1'
                 AP     PCTR,=P'1'
                 MVC    DATEOUT,=C'&SYSDATE'
                 UNPK   PAGE,PCTR
                 OI     PAGE+1,X'F0'
                 PUT    OUTFILE,HEADING1
                 PUT    OUTFILE,HEADING2
                 CLC    FLAG2,=C'1'
                 BE     PRINT
        NEWWHSE  MVC    HOLD,WHSEIN
```

20.
```
        DETLRTN  CLC    HOLD,WHSEIN                              268
                 BNE    CONTROL
                 PACK   PVALUE,AMTIN
                 AP     ITEMS,=P'1'
                 AP     WHTOTAL,PVALUE
                 GET    INFILE,RECORD
                 B      DETLRTN
```

21.
```
        CONTROL  MVC    WHSEOUT,HOLD                            268
                 MVC    ITEMSOUT,EDITPAT1
                 ED     ITEMSOUT,ITEMS
                 MVC    TOTALOUT,EDITPAT2
                 ED     TOTALOUT,WHTOTAL
                 PUT    OUTFILE,LINEOUT
                 CLC    FLAG,=C'1'
                 BE     END
                 MVC    FLAG2,=C'1'
                 AP     LCTR,=P'1'
                 CP     LCTR,=P'25'
                 BNL    HEADRTN
        PRINT    MVC    FLAG2,=C'0'
                 ZAP    ITEMS,=P'0'
                 ZAP    WHTOTAL,=P'0'
                 B      NEWWHSE
```

PRACTICE PROGRAM

Consider the problem definition shown in Figure 9.16. Write a program that incorporates the CNTRL macro and editing to print the names and salaries of employees who earn more than $15,000. Print the percentage of employees who earn more than $15,000 at the end. See Figure 9.17 for a solution.

KEY TERMS

Burst	Editing
Carriage control	Form overflow condition
Check protection symbol (*)	Group printing
Continuous forms	Printer Spacing Chart
Control break processing	Skipping
Control field	Spacing
Detail line	Spooling
Detail printing	

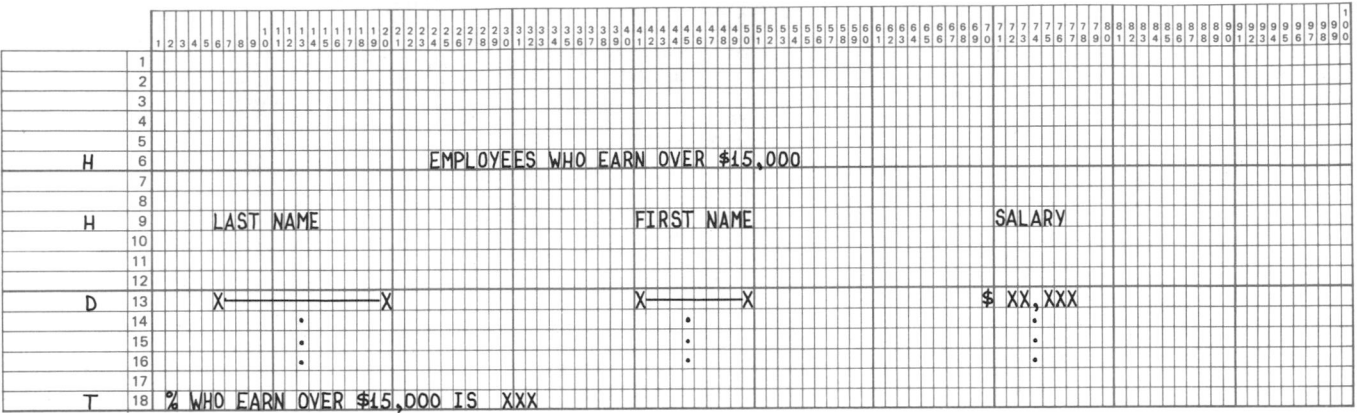

c. Sample Input Data

```
BAGLEY        JOAN       14750
BREWSTER      WESLEY     38950
JOHNSON       SUSAN      21500
MARTIN        HAROLD     13925
WILLIAMS      JAMES      27950
```

d. Sample Output

```
                    EMPLOYEES WHO EARN OVER $15,000


        LAST NAME                    FIRST NAME              SALARY


        BREWSTER                     WESLEY                $ 38,950
        JOHNSON                      SUSAN                 $ 21,500
        WILLIAMS                     JAMES                 $ 27,950

% WHO EARN OVER $15,000 IS     60
```

Figure 9.16
Problem definition for the
Practice Program.

REVIEW QUESTIONS

1. Explain the functions of the following HEADING routine in detail. Prepare a Printer Spacing Chart that illustrates how the headings will print, including spacing.

```
HEADING   MVC    LINEOUT,SPACES
          MVC    LINEOUT+50(20),=C'MY-T-FINE MOTORS INC'
          MVI    LINEOUT,C'1'
          PUT    OUTFILE,LINEOUT
          MVC    LINEOUT,SPACES
          MVC    LINEOUT+53(12),=C'SALES REPORT'
          MVI    LINEOUT,C'0'
          PUT    OUTFILE,LINEOUT
          MVC    LINEOUT,SPACES
          MVC    LINEOUT+46(12),=C'SALES PERSON'
          MVC    LINEOUT+63(9),=C'YTD SALES'
          MVI    LINEOUT,C' '
          PUT    OUTFILE,LINEOUT
```

```
        MVC    LINEOUT,SPACES
        MVI    LINEOUT,C'0'
        PUT    OUTFILE,LINEOUT
```

2. Indicate the purpose of the following routine. Explain an alternative method for achieving the same results.

```
        ZAP    LINES,=P'0'
READ    GET    INFILE,CARDIN
        MVC    LINEOUT,SPACES
        MVC    LINEOUT(80),CARDIN
        PUT    OUTFILE,LINEOUT
        AP     LINES,=P'1'
        CP     LINES,=P'10'
        BNL    HEADING
        B      READ
```

```
*                                                      *
*                        HOUSEKEEPING INSTRUCTIONS GO HERE  *
*                                                      *
        CNTRL OUTFILE,SK,1        ADVANCE TO TOP OF PAGE
        MVC    OUTAREA,SPACES
        MVC    OUTAREA+23(31),=C'EMPLOYEES WHO EARN OVER $15,000'
        PUT    OUTFILE,OUTAREA
        MVC    OUTAREA,SPACES
        MVC    LNAME(9),=C'LAST NAME'
        MVC    FNAME(10),=C'FIRST NAME'
        MVC    SALOUT(6),=C'SALARY'
        CNTRL OUTFILE,SP,1,3       DBLE SPACE BEFORE & TRPLE SPACE AFTER
        PUT    OUTFILE,OUTAREA
READ    MVC    OUTAREA,SPACES
        GET    INFILE,RECORD
        AP     TOTEMP,=P'1'
        CLC    SALARY,=C'15000'
        BNH    READ
        AP     COUNT,=P'1'
        MVC    LNAME,LAST
        MVC    FNAME,FIRST
        PACK   PKDSAL,SALARY
        MVC    SALOUT(7),=X'4020206B202020' EDIT WITH COMMA
        ED     SALOUT(7),PKDSAL
        MVI    SALOUT-1,C'$'
        PUT    OUTFILE,OUTAREA
        B      READ
EOFCD   MVC    OUTAREA,SPACES
        PUT    OUTFILE,OUTAREA
        MVC    OUTAREA+1(27),=C'% WHO EARN OVER $15,000 IS '
        ZAP    NUM,COUNT
        MP     NUM,=P'100'
        ZAP    HOLD,NUM
        DP     HOLD,TOTEMP
        MVC    OUTAREA+28(4),=X'40202020'
        ED     OUTAREA+28(4),HOLD+2
        PUT    OUTFILE,OUTAREA
*                                                      *
*                        HOUSEKEEPING INSTRUCTIONS GO HERE  *
*                        ALONG WITH DCB OR DTF MACROS        *
*                                                      *
PKDSAL  DS     PL3
COUNT   DC     PL2'0'
HOLD    DS     PL6
TOTEMP  DC     PL2'0'
NUM     DS     PL4
RECORD  DS     0CL80                 INPUT FORMAT
LAST    DS     CL15                        *
FIRST   DS     CL10                        *
SALARY  DS     CL5                         *
        DS     CL50                        *
SPACES  DC     CL1' '
OUTAREA DS     0CL132                PRINT FORMAT
        DS     CL5                         *
LNAME   DS     CL15                        *
        DS     CL20                        *
FNAME   DS     CL10                        *
        DS     CL20                        *
SALOUT  DS     CL5                         *
        DS     CL57                        *
        END
```

Figure 9.17
Solution to the
Practice Program.

3. State the purpose of each entry in the following printout.

```
INFILE    DTFCD BLKSIZE=80,RECFORM=FIXUNB,DEVADDR=SYSIPT,        *
                WORKA=YES,IOAREA1=BUFFRIN,EOFADDR=EOF
OUTFILE   DTFPR BLKSIZE=133,DEVADDR=SYSLST,IOAREA1=BUFFROUT,      *
                CTLCHR=ASA,WORKA=YES
```

4. (T or F) The sending field in the Edit instruction must be in packed format.
5. (T or F) Both alphanumeric and numeric data may be edited with the use of the Edit instruction.
6. (T or F) Using the Edit instruction, leading zeros are replaced by the fill character.

Consider the following instructions.

```
MVC    OUTAREA,PATTERN
ED     OUTAREA,PDATA
```

Indicate the results in OUTAREA in each of the following cases.

Before Execution

	Size of OUTAREA	PDATA			PATTERN								
7.	7 bytes	00	58	7C	5C	20	20	6B	20	20	20		
8.	9 bytes	00	67	8D	40	20	6B	20	20	21	4B	20	D0
9.	9 bytes	00	67	8C	40	20	6B	20	20	20	4B	20	D0
10.	10 bytes	00	00	00	7C	40	20	20	6B	20	20	20	4B	20	20
11.	10 bytes	00	00	00	7C	40	20	20	6B	20	20	21	4B	20	20
12.	6 bytes	00	00	5C	40	20	20	21	20	20			

13. (T or F) To utilize a control break procedure, input data must be in sequence by the control fields.
14. (T or F) Before a detail or calculation routine is initially executed, the control fields must be moved to hold areas.
15. (T or F) One method for minimizing errors in a control break procedure is to perform a sequence-check routine where you check that the control fields have been sorted properly.
16. (T or F) The control break module must always clear the total fields to zero.

DEBUGGING EXERCISES

The program excerpt below reads a record containing an employee name and year-to-date payroll figures for gross pay (YTDGROSS), Social Security (YTDFICA), and union dues (YTDUES). These numeric fields are to be edited and printed by the program. All figures represent dollars and cents and therefore contain decimal points, commas, and suppression of leading zeros. Identify the errors in the program excerpt by desk checking and walking through the coding.

```
******************************************************************
*        D E B U G   P R O G R A M   C H A P T E R   9
******************************************************************
CLEAR     MVC    LINEOUT,SPACES
          GET    INFILE,RECORD
          PACK   YTDGROSS,YTDGROSS
          PACK   YTDFICA,YTDFICA
          PACK   YTDUES,YTDUES
          MVC    GROSSO,PAT1
          MVC    FICAO,PAT2
          MVC    DUESO,PAT3
          ED     GROSSO(10),YTDGROSS+3
          ED     FICAO(9),YTDFICA+2
```

```
              ED      DUESO(7),YTDUES+1
              PUT     OUTFILE,LINEOUT
              B       CLEAR
*
RECORD    DS      0CL80
NAME      DS      CL20
YTDGROSS  DS      CL7
YTDFICA   DS      CL6
YTDDUES   DS      CL5
          DS      CL32
*
SPACES    DC      X'40'
LINEOUT   DS      0CL133
          DS      CL10
NAMEO     DS      CL20
          DS      CL10
GROSSO    DS      CL10
          DS      CL11
FICAO     DS      CL9
          DS      CL13
DUESO     DS      CL7
          DS      CL43
*
PAT1      DC      XL10'4020204B2020216B2020'
PAT2      DC      XL9'40204B2020216B2020'
PAT3      DC      XL7'402020216B2020'
```

SOLUTIONS
1. RECORD does not contain 80 bytes; change DS 32 to 42
2. Change YTDDUES of RECORD to YTDUES.
3. In all patterns, interchange 4B and 6B specifications; remember the decimal point is 4B and the comma is 6B.
4. PAT2 is incorrect because it contains an even number of digit specifications; use PAT1 and eliminate PAT2.
5. The edit instruction for FICAO then appears as:

   `ED FICAO(10),YTDFICA+2`

6. Increase the length of FICAO to 10 bytes:

   `FICAO DS CL10`

7. Decrease the length of LINEOUT by 1 byte to accommodate the change in FICAO:

   `DS CL42`

8. An MVC is required to move the NAME to NAMEO:

   `MVC NAMEO,NAME`

PROGRAMMING ASSIGNMENTS

1. Write a program to print an output report from the following input record format:

   1–5 Product number (control field)
   6–8 Quantity (may be negative in case of credit)
   9–13 Unit price (to be interpreted as having $ only)
   14–33 Product description
   34–36 Discount percent .xxx
   37–80 Not used

   Output: Print line

   3–7 Product number
   10–29 Description
   32–38 Unit price   zero suppress; print dollar sign
   40–43 Quantity   print minus sign, if present; zero suppress

48–58 Gross	print minus sign, if present; zero suppress; print $
60–71 Discount amount	print decimal point; zero suppress; print $
75–85 Net	zero suppress; decimal point; minus sign, if present; print $

Formulas

Gross = quantity × unit price
Discount amount = gross × discount percent
Net = gross − discount amount

Print heading PRODUCT LISTING on the top of the output page.

2. Write a program to print the total of the amount fields of groups of input records.

Input:

1–20 Name
21–25 Amount xxx.xx
26–80 Not used

Output: Print

11–30 Name
41–50 Total (edited with dollar sign, comma, decimal point, and check protection)

Note
The name is the same for each group of records. The number of records per group varies.

3. Consider the following input record format.

1–20 Customer name (1—initial 1, 2—initial 2)
21–25 Transaction amount for week 1   xxx.xx
26–30 Transaction amount for week 2   xxx.xx
31–35 Transaction amount for week 3   xxx.xx
36–40 Transaction amount for week 4   xxx.xx
41–46 Amount of credit   xxxx.xx
47–80 Not used

a. Print heading MONTHLY TRANSACTIONS
b. Print each data field edited
   (1) Two spaces between initials of name.
   (2) Print decimal point, dollar sign, − for negative transaction amount.
   (3) Print decimal point, comma, dollar sign, and * for credit amount.
   (4) For each card record, print a balance due (transaction amounts − credit), dollar sign, operational sign, and decimal point.

4. Using the following problem definition, write a program to print a sales total for each of 7 days.

a. Input Record Layout

DAY NO.	SALES-PERSON NO.	SALES AMOUNT $ ¢	

1   2   4 5   9 10   80

b. Printer Spacing Chart for Printed Output

b. Printer Spacing Chart for Printed Output

		Columns
H	6	SALES REPORT XX/XX/XX
H	8	DAY TOTAL SALES
T	10	MON $XX,XXX.XX
T	12	TUE $XX,XXX.XX
T	14	WED $XX,XXX.XX
T	16	THU $XX,XXX.XX
T	18	FRI $XX,XXX.XX

Notes

a. There is an input record for each sale made by a salesperson; thus, there are an undetermined number of input records.

b. Records are in sequence by day number, which ranges from 1 to 5 (Mon–Fri).

UNIT 3

THE ASSEMBLY PROCESS AND DEBUGGING

10 Understanding the Assembly Process

<table>
<tr><td>

OBJECTIVES

</td><td>

To familiarize you with:
1. *Reading and interpreting program listings.*
2. *The translation process.*
3. *The need for and techniques used for desk checking programs.*
4. *Interpreting and correcting syntax errors.*
5. *Finding and correcting logic errors.*

</td></tr>
</table>

I. TECHNIQUES USED TO MINIMIZE THE DEBUGGING EFFORT

By now you have probably coded and executed several assembler programs. You should have found that writing the program is only one phase in the process. Getting the program to work, or **debugging** it, can be an even more complex task. A good programmer not only writes efficient programs but is adept at finding and correcting errors as well.

There are several tasks that may be used to reduce debugging. In this chapter, we focus on basic debugging tools and suggestions for avoiding errors.

The following techniques are used to improve the coding of programs, and will help to decrease errors and the time required to debug programs.

A. Planning a Program

Programmers who take the time to plan the logic used in their programs find that the time it takes to debug a program is often reduced. Flowcharting a program or writing a pseudocode that outlines the logic will reduce the coding and debugging time necessary. Verifying program logic with the user and the systems analyst even before coding is begun will also help reduce the overall debugging time required.

B. Desk Checking a Program

After a program has been coded, it should be **desk checked** to ensure that there are no obvious errors or omissions. Similarly, after a program has been keyed using either a terminal, punched cards, or some other storage medium, it should be rechecked for typographical errors, omissions, and mistakes in logic.

Because of the availability of computer power at many organizations, programmers frequently believe it is better to have the computer find typographical errors during compilation and execution than to take the time to manually check the program. This approach, however, is not only wasteful, but it actually takes more time to find and correct major errors than if the programmer spent some time reviewing a keyed program *before* compiling it. Manual review of a program is called desk checking.

C. Structured Walkthroughs

A **structured walkthrough** is a manual procedure of stepping through the logic of your program with sample data to ensure that it will produce correct results.

Like desk checking, this technique will actually minimize debugging and computer time. It is a method of program verification that requires the programmer to spend time stepping through the logic before the program is even run.

D. Programmer Teams

When programmers work together in teams to analyze and review the logic of each coded program, they usually learn from each other. The end result is apt to be a more efficient program with fewer initial errors. Moreover, programmers will learn new and efficient techniques from working with each other in an open, cooperative environment.

II. INTRODUCTION TO THE ASSEMBLY PROCESS

A. The Assembly Process

Computer programs can be executed only if they are in absolute or actual machine language. An assembler language program must be translated, or assembled, into actual machine language before it can be executed or run.

The assembly process uses the programmer's assembler language program as input, the assembler or translator as the processor, and produces, as output, a machine-language equivalent.

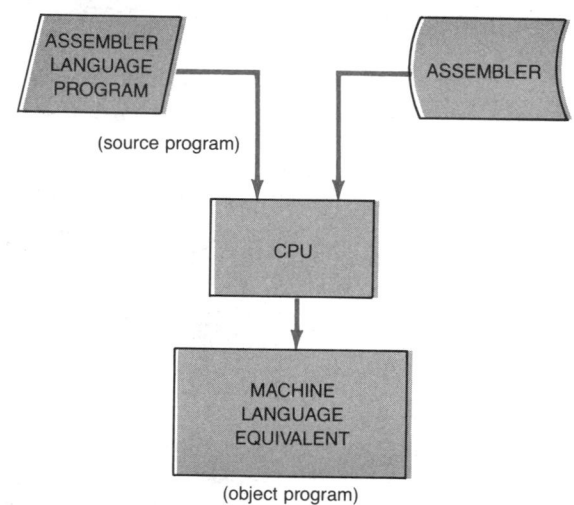

The assembler program is generally provided by the computer manufacturer or vendor. It is called into the Central Processing Unit (CPU), as needed, to translate *source programs* into *object programs*. Typically, the assembler is stored on a direct-access device such as a magnetic disk.

The three types of output of an assembler process generally consist of the following:

1. Object program.
   A machine-language equivalent of the source program.
   This can be stored on disk or tape for future processing.
2. Source program listing with associated cross-referenced printouts.
3. Listing of diagnostics, or violations of rules: these are called syntax errors.

Any rules that have been violated will cause the computer to print a syntax error message. If an Add Packed instruction is coded as A instead of AP, for example, an error message will print. Any major syntax error in the source program will result in an incomplete or erroneous object program that will not execute properly. In such cases the source program must be corrected and the translation process repeated. The object program created cannot be used because it contains errors. Most programs must be translated several times before they are free from syntax errors. Sample diagnostics describing syntax errors will be discussed in Section III of this chapter.

B. Execution Phase—Testing the Program

After a translation phase has been successfully completed so that no diagnostics are generated, the program's ability to execute properly must be tested. Although the program contains no syntax errors it may contain errors in logic that will cause inaccurate or incomplete processing. The Execution Phase is used to "debug" a program or to eliminate errors in it.

We run or execute a program with *test* or *sample* data. The programmer uses this sample data to test if the program executes properly. First, the expected results are computed manually by the programmer. Then the program is executed and the results obtained are compared against the manually produced results. If they match, then the program is executing properly. If they do not match, the cause of the error must be determined.

Test Data   Note that test data must be carefully prepared to incorporate all possible conditions for which the program tests. Every conceivable condition must be included. Only in this way can one be assured that future scheduled runs of the program will be error-free.

Test data is usually prepared by programmers. In a programming course, however, an instructor may provide it to ensure its completeness. Figure 10.1 illustrates both the assembly and the execution phase.

Before we learn how to debug a program, there are some machine concepts that must be introduced.

C. Interpreting Addresses

1. Definition of an Address

A computer's **memory** is subdivided into storage locations each of which is capable of holding a unit of information. Each storage location is called a **byte.** The byte consists of 8 **bits** (binary dig*its*) that can store a unit of information.

Communicating with the CPU so that both assembly and execution are achieved is a function of the Job Control Language (JCL). For students who

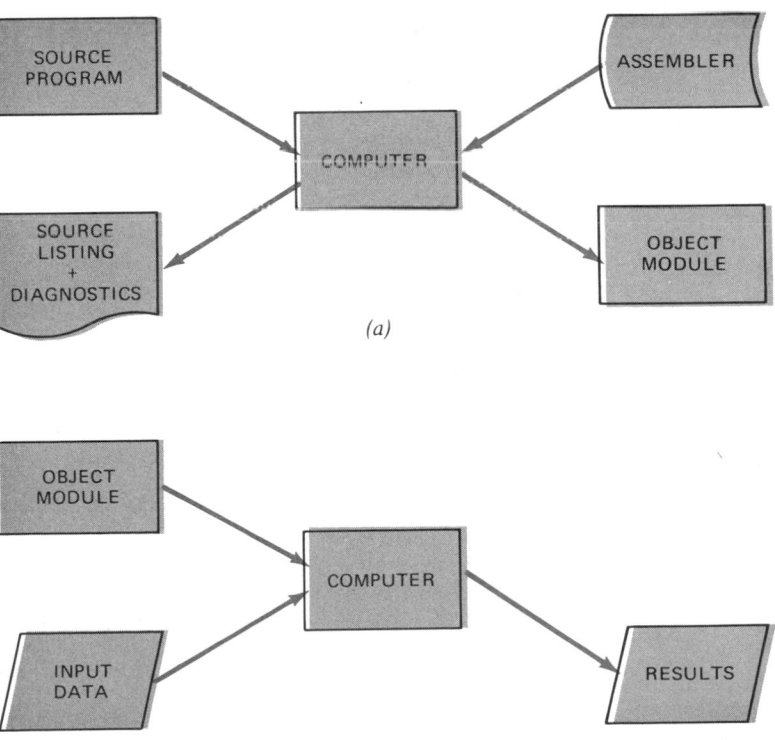

Figure 10.1
(a) Assembling a program.
(b) Executing a program.

have had no previous exposure to Job Control Language, see Appendix B "Communicating with the Operating System Using Job Control Language."

SUBDIVISIONS OF STORAGE

Memory	storage capacity
Byte	a single storage location
Bit	one of 8 subdivisions of a byte

The storage locations, or bytes, are said to be **addressable.** That is, storage locations can be accessed or referred to by a specific address. Every byte has a *unique* address, which means that no two storage addresses are the same. The concept is analogous to post office or safe deposit box numbers that are used to identify a single box. Such an address identifies a specific box number, *not* its contents.

2. How Addresses Are Specified

The address used to identify a storage location for most IBM and IBM–compatible computers consists of a 6-digit hexadecimal number. Thus storage locations can vary from 000000 to FFFFFF. This means that the maximum addressable byte is $16^6 = 2^{24} = 16,777,216_{10}$. Thus, a 6-digit hexadecimal number can represent storage addresses ranging, in decimal, from 0 to over 16 million. This latter number greatly exceeds the storage capacity of many computers, but a 6-digit representation was adopted by IBM as a standard to be used uniformly to identify storage locations of all its computers, regardless of size. Thus most IBM and IBM–compatible computer systems, large and small, use storage locations from 000000–FFFFFF.

3. Using Addresses

Consider the following instruction.

```
AP   TOTAL,AMT
```

When the program using this instruction is assembled, TOTAL and AMT are placed in actual storage locations. In machine language, these fields are accessible only by their actual storage addresses. Hence, when reading a storage dump, as we will later, we must be able to identify the actual address of a specified field to determine what is in that field.

It is important to note that the *instruction itself* is also placed in storage. To debug a program, you must be able to find specific instructions, as well as fields, in storage. To do this, you must access them by their addresses.

4. Base and Displacement

Most computers are capable of operating on programs in a **multiprogramming** environment; that is, several programs can be in computer storage simultaneously. To accomplish this, each program that is read into the system must be *relocatable.* That is, programs are assembled with assigned addresses ranging from 0–4095 in decimal, or 000–FFF in hexadecimal. These programs are then *relocated* by the computer to wherever, in storage, there is room.

Programs, then, are referenced in actual machine language by an address that consists of several parts. For purposes of **relocatability,** the address consists of a displacement and the contents of the base register.

a. Displacement. A relative address, ranging from 000–FFF in hexadecimal (0–4095 in decimal), indicates how far from the starting point of the program a particular instruction is located. This distance, in bytes, is referred to as the **displacement.**

b. Base Register. This is a general register, from 2–12, assigned by the programmer to contain the actual starting point of the program. This actual starting point is loaded into the base register just prior to execution and will vary depending on which partition in the CPU will store the program.

When the contents of the base register are added to the displacement, an *effective* or *actual machine address* is obtained.

Effective address = contents of base register + displacement

Each register consists of 4 bytes, but not all 4 bytes are needed to determine the effective address. Only the *3 low-order* bytes are used for this purpose. The high-order byte is ignored. Because storage locations are represented by a 6-digit hexadecimal number, only 3 bytes are necessary to specify them.

Let us amend the equation.

Effective address = contents of base register + displacement
(3 low-order bytes)   [dec 0–4095]
[hex 000–FFF]

Because each segment of a program is 4096 bytes in length, any program less than 4096 bytes can be written as one segment.

Consider, however, a program that requires 12,000 bytes. By sectioning it into 4096-byte modules, we would have 3 sections of our program with a base address and base register for each.

c. Why Use Base and Displacement? We have already indicated a major reason for the base and displacement concept—multiprogramming. There is an additional reason for utilizing this concept. Accessing an address in terms of a base register expressed as a single hex digit (0–F) and a 3-position displacement (000–FFF) uses two less digits than the standard IBM 6-digit address. Because typical programs consist of hundreds of instructions with dozens of storage addresses that need to be accessed, this savings is substantial and significant.

Example 10.1 How the Base-Displacement Concept Can Save Storage

Consider the following.

Op code	Address of Operand 1	Address of Operand 2

Without using base-displacement, each address would need to be specified in terms of a 6-digit or 3-byte field, that is,

Op code	01 2F 00	01 2F FF

If the op code were represented by a single byte, the above instruction might require 7 bytes of storage.

$$\frac{\text{Op code}}{1} + \frac{\text{Address of Operand 1}}{3} + \frac{\text{Address of Operand 2}}{3} = 7$$

(In actuality, instruction lengths will vary because additional elements must be considered.) Using the base-displacement concept, however, we can reduce the length of such an instruction.

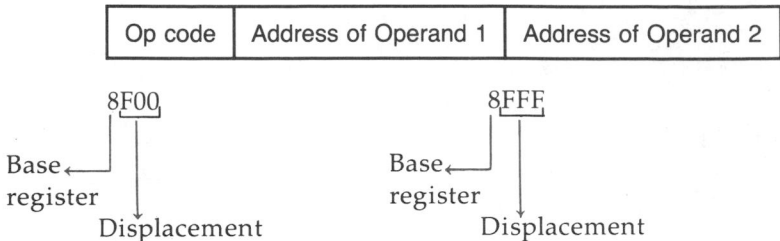

| Op code | Address of Operand 1 | Address of Operand 2 |

Using the base-displacement concept, we can reduce such an instruction by 2 bytes.

Op code   *Operand 1*   *Operand 2*

1 byte   +   2 bytes   +   2 bytes   = 5

In this example the base register would be register 8 and would contain the base address 01 20 00 to match the preceding problem.

Operand 1

```
01 20 00  Base
     F 00  Displacement
01 2F 00  Effective Address
```

Operand 2

```
01 20 00  Base
     F FF  Displacement
01 2F FF  Effective Address
```

SUMMARY

1. A program is a series of instructions stored in sequence. Each instruction is located a certain number of bytes from the starting point of the first instruction. This distance is referred to as displacement. All instructions and storage areas are referenced by addresses that indicate the displacement from the starting point.
2. When the program is ready to be loaded, the base register will point to a location in storage that will become the actual starting point of the program. This starting point is called the *program load address* or the *base address*.
3. Actual or effective storage addresses are obtained by adding the displacement value to the contents of a base register.
4. Each instruction contains the displacement in addition to the number of the general register that will be a base register.
5. Registers 2–12 may be used as a base register.
6. Only the 3 low-order bytes of the base register will contain the base address. The high-order byte is ignored.

Self-Evaluating Quiz

1. Assuming that the base register contains 5144 (decimal), the displacement for the absolute (decimal) location 9170 is _____ .
2. Any actual machine language address can be located by adding its _____ to the contents of _____ .
3. Suppose that a program was relocated so that it started at location 9192 and consisted of 3 modules or sections.

| Section 1 | Section 2 | Section 3 |

The base register for section 1 would contain 9192. The base register for section 2 would contain _____ . The base register for section 3 would contain _____ .

4. Using the above example, do the displacements change for instructions in sections 2 and 3?
5. The displacement range for any base is (no.) to (no.).
6. The base address is contained in the _____ .

SOLUTIONS
1. 4026_{10} (9170-5144)
2. Displacement; the base register
3. 13288 decimal (9192 + 4096); 17384 decimal (+4096)
4. No; the displacement in all 3 sections is given in terms of a starting address, which is independent of the base address.
5. $\left.\begin{array}{c}0 \\ 4095\end{array}\right\}$ decimal or $\left.\begin{array}{c}0 \\ \text{FFF}\end{array}\right\}$ hexadecimal
6. Base register

III. ELEMENTS OF AN ASSEMBLY PROCESS

The items that follow provide additional information about the assembly process.

---

1. The program becomes a series of instructions occupying consecutive bytes in storage.
2. Each symbolic address assigned in the source program is converted to an actual machine-language address.
3. An operation code, or **mnemonic,** is translated into an absolute machine-language code.
4. Areas of storage to be used as input, output, or work areas are assigned actual machine addresses.
5. Constants are also placed in actual storage locations.

A. The Location Counter

As we have already learned, a program is simply a series of instructions occupying consecutive bytes in storage. The purpose of the **Location Counter** is to keep track of the address or displacement of each instruction as it is being assembled. If each instruction were 1 byte in length, it would be a simple matter for the location counter to assign locations for each instruction in the program. As each instruction would be encountered by the assembler, a 1 would be added to the contents of the location counter. A program consisting of 100 instructions would therefore start at location 000 and end at location 064 hexadecimal or 100 decimal.

The length of an actual instruction is, however, *not* one byte but several bytes, depending upon the *format* of the instruction. Each instruction format, as indicated below, has a specific length.

Instruction Formats[1]

Description	Format	Length in Bytes
Register-to-Register	RR	2
Register-to-Indexed Storage	RX	4
Register-to-Storage	RS	4
Storage Immediate	SI	4
Storage-to-Storage	SS	6

[1]This topic is discussed in Chapter 14.

The location counter, therefore, is incremented according to the length of the instruction. If the instruction is a storage-to-storage instruction, the location counter would be incremented by 6. After each instruction is assembled, the location counter changes according to *the length of the instruction.* The assembler knows the length of each instruction by examining the operation code. Different op codes require different instruction lengths. These can vary from 2, 4, or 6 bytes.

When the op code is a Define Constant (DC) or Define Storage (DS), the assembler must examine the operand to determine the *length* of the field. The values of the location counter in a typical program are illustrated in Figure 10.2. Note that ① LOC references the location counter, which can vary from 000000-FFFFFF.

B. The Symbol Cross-Reference Table

Every time a symbolic name is encountered in the name field of an instruction, the setting of the location counter (displacement) and the symbolic name are placed in the *Symbol Table.* The symbol table also provides the programmer with additional data that will facilitate debugging. Figure 10.3 will illustrate these points.

ELEMENTS OF A SYMBOL CROSS-REFERENCE TABLE

1. SYMBOL: Symbolic names defined within the program.
2. LEN: The length in bytes specified as a decimal number.
3. VALUE: The relative address (displacement) established by the location counter.
4. DEFN: The statement number of the source instruction at which this symbol was defined.
5. REFERENCES: The statement numbers of the source instructions that reference the symbol in their operands.

ASSEMBLY PROCESS SUMMARY

1. The **assembler** is a program provided by the manufacturer or vendor to translate **source programs** into **object programs.**
2. The input to the assembler is the source program and output is an object program and a source listing. The source listing may contain diagnostic messages if syntax errors were detected in the program.
3. The **location counter** assigns storage locations to each instruction in the program.
4. The location counter is incremented 2, 4, or 6 bytes depending upon the type of instruction used.
5. Each name appearing in the name field of an instruction and its address are placed in the Symbol Table.

C. Understanding the Assembler Listing (See Figure 10.2)

LOC.   This column contains the hex displacement value assigned to each instruction by the location counter. The first executable instruction contains START as the op code and is customarily assigned location zero. All other instructions are displaced relative to this starting point.

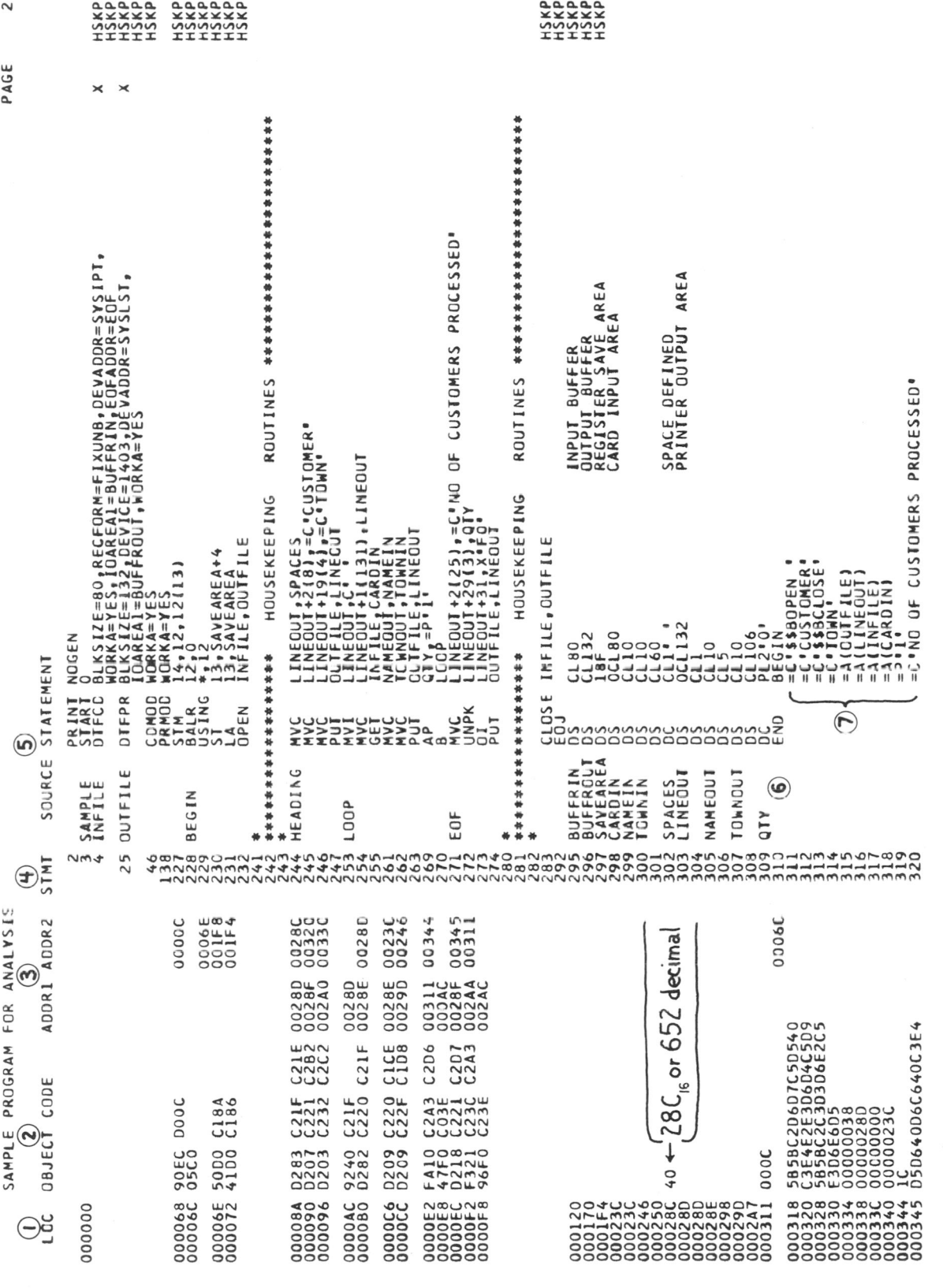

Figure 10.2
Program listing with values of the location counter.

① SYMBOL	② LEN	ID	③ VALUE	④ DEFN	⑤ REFERENCES								
BEGIN	00002	01	00006C	00228	0310								
BUFFRIN	00080	01	000120	00295	0018	0021							
BUFFROUT	00132	01	000170	00296	0039	0044							
CARDIN	00080	01	00023C	00298	0318								
EOF	00006	01	0000EC	00271	0020								
HEADING	00006	01	00008A	00244									
INFILE	00006	01	000000	00007	0238	0289	0317						
LINEOUT	00132	01	00028D	00303	0244	0245	0246	0253	0254	0254	0271	0272	0273	0316
LOOP	00004	01	0000AC	00253	0270								
NAMEIN	00010	01	00023C	00299	0261								
NAMEOUT	00010	01	00028E	00305	0261								
OUTFILE	00006	01	000038	00028	0239	0290	0315						
QTY	00002	01	000311	00309	0269	0272							
SAMPLE	00001	01	000000	00003	0137	0226							
SAVEAREA	00004	01	0001F4	00297	0230	0231							
SPACES	00001	01	00028C	00302	0244								
TOWNIN	00010	01	000246	00300	0262								
TOWNOUT	00010	01	00029C	00307	0262								

Figure 10.3 Sample symbol cross-reference table.

a. Note that the next addressable LOC on the sample listing is 00 00 68. The area between is reserved for assembler-generated instructions or I/O control. The DTFs are macros that generate a series of instructions that, in this case, use 68 (hex) bytes of storage.

```
LOC

000000




000068
00006C

00006E
000072




00008A
000090
    ⋮
    ⋮
```

b. The STM instruction begins in position 068, the BALR in 6C. That is, STM is a 4 byte instruction occupying positions 068, 069, 06A, 06B. Using the LOC field, we can determine: (1) the actual storage locations of instructions, and, (2) the length of instructions.

2. OBJECT CODE.   This field indicates the machine-language equivalant of instructions, each being a maximum of 6 bytes long (SS). Because each byte can be expressed as a 2-position hex number, the object code contains a maximum of 12 hex digits. Consider line 00 00 8A, which is the MVC instruction. It is a 6-byte instruction—12 hex digits. The minimum size for an instruction is 2 bytes (RR format). Hence the object code field can contain as few as 4 hex digits, 2 of them representing each byte. If the statement is a DC, then the object code contains the hex contents of each byte. Consider LOC 28C corresponding to the DC labeled SPACES. Note that it contains a hex 40, which is a blank.

```
OBJECT CODE
⋮

90EC D00C
05C0

50D0 C18A
41D0 C186

D283 C21F C21E
D207 C221 C2B2
⋮
```

Instructions will be analyzed in detail in a later chapter. All that is required at this point is that you become aware of the different instruction formats and the different lengths associated with each. Also, note that the first 2 hex digits of all executable instructions contain the operation code. For example, in the instruction identified as BEGIN the actual operation code of a BALR instruction is 05.

3. ADDR1 ADDR2.   These columns refer to the addresses of the first and second operands. When storage-to-storage instructions are used, these **addresses** reference the actual locations assigned to the symbolic names. Note that these addresses reference locations where the symbolic names are defined in the program.

```
ADDR1 ADDR2
⋮
0028D 0028C
0028F 00320
002A0 00330

0028D
0028E 0028D
⋮
```

The DC or DS instruction establishes an actual area in storage that is assigned a storage address. Each time the named field is used in the program, the computer substitutes the actual address in the ADDR fields.

4. STMT.   Each statement is assigned a STMT number by the computer. You will note that the numbers appear in ascending sequence. In some instances several numbers are skipped. This is because certain assembler language instructions coded by the programmer as *macro* instructions generate not one, but a series of actual machine language instructions. Only the instructions actually programmed are listed. Hence, INFILE DTFCD, which is referred to as Statement 4, generated a series of instructions. We know this because the next sequential instruction is not number 5, but 25. The DTF macro then, actually generated 21 individual assembly language instructions.

```
STMT

   2
   3
   4

  25

  46
 138
 227
  ⋮
```

The PRINT NOGEN statement is responsible for the suppression of macro-generated instructions. The use of this statement makes the program listing easier to read and decipher.

By removing the PRINT NOGEN statement, all macro-generated instructions will appear on the listing, and each will be identified by a plus (+) sign to the right of the statement number. In this case, all statement numbers would be consecutive and you would be able to see the actual machine-language instructions generated for each macro, as illustrated in the following example.

```
16          GET    INFILE,RECORD
17+         LA     1,INFILE
18+         LA     0,RECORD
19+         L      15,48(0,1)
20+         BALR   14,15
```

5. <u>SOURCE STATEMENT</u>. These are the source instructions coded by the programmer. Again in the sample presented, macro instructions generated by the computer will be suppressed and will not appear on the listing because PRINT NOGEN was used.

```
        SOURCE STATEMENT


          PRINT NOGEN
SAMPLE    START 0
            :
            :
```

6. <u>END BEGIN</u>. This statement indicates to the computer the first instruction to be *executed* once the assembly process has been completed. In the sample we are instructing the computer to begin execution at the BEGIN statement after the program has been assembled. All instructions prior to BEGIN are nonexecutable; that is, they are simply specifications to the computer. (An error would occur if we attempted to start executing at any instruction prior to the BEGIN statement.) A failure to include the proper operand in the END statement in our example will cause an error. If END is coded with *no* operand, the program will begin executing *at the first* instruction. If all DCBs (or DTFs), DCs, and DSs are defined at the end of the program and not at the beginning, then an END without an operand would function properly.

```
END    BEGIN
```

7. <u>Literal Pool.</u> The area following the END statement will usually contain the literals established by the programmer. These are easily identified because they begin with an equal sign within the operand. The assembler places literal data in an area called the *literal pool* at the end of the program. The storing of data in the literal pool is handled very efficiently by the CPU, which ensures that the space used is minimized and that proper boundary alignment is maintained.

```
=C'$$BOPEN '
=C'CUSTOMER'
=C'$$BCLOSE'
=C'TOWN'
=A(OUTFILE)
=A(LINEOUT)
=A(INFILE)
=A(CARDIN)
=P'1'
=C'NO OF CUSTOMERS PROCESSED'
```

D. The Linkage Editor Program

An **object module** is a program that has been assembled or compiled from a language such as assembler, COBOL, or PL/1. An object module(s) is the input to the *linkage editor program.* With large, complex programs the object module(s) may consist of a main program with several subprograms. These subprograms (subroutines) are independent CSECTs (control sections) frequently coded by different programmers working on a major project. The original source modules may have been coded in assembler, COBOL, PL/1, and so on. The resulting object modules are, however, in machine language. These programs are interrelated because data is passed back and forth between the main program and the subprograms, as well as interchanged between subprograms. This cross referencing of data is handled by the *linkage editor.* The main program and the subprograms may be assembled or compiled independently, but are linked together by the linkage editor. Similarly, if a program requires more than 4096 bytes, then 2 (or more) modules will be produced; these modules need to be link-edited before execution.

The output of the linkage editor is a program phase. See Figure 10.4. This program phase can be executed immediately, or it can be catalogued in the core image library for later execution. A *link edit map* is also produced that lists all the control sections (CSECTs) that make up the program phase. See Figure 10.5. The link edit map provides the following information for the programmer's use.

1. LABEL. Specifies the name of the program as declared in the START statement or a control section (CSECT) in the assembly. In this example, DEBUG is the name assigned.

2. LOADED. Indicates the hexadecimal starting position in storage where the program was loaded.

3. REL-FR. The relocation factor is used in reading storage dumps. The value of the REL-FR must be added to the relative address (displacement)

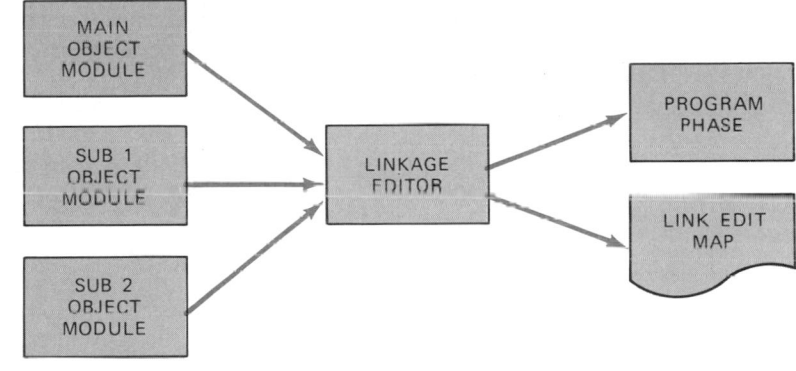

Figure 10.4
Output from the linkage editor program.

PHASE	XFR-AD	LOCORE	HICORE	DSK-AD	ESD TYPE	① LABEL	② LOADED	③ REL-FR	
PHASE***	0640E0	064078	064501	001 02 01	CSECT	DEBUG	064078	064078	RELOCATABLE
					CSECT	IJCFZIWO	0643E0	0643E0	
					CSECT	IJDFCPZW	064458	064458	
					* ENTRY	IJDFZPZW	064458		
					* ENTRY	IJDFZZZW	064458		
					* ENTRY	IJDFCZZW	064458		

Figure 10.5 Sample link-edit map.

to find a desired location in primary storage. (Because of instructions performed prior to assigning a base register, the relocation factor may be a few bytes different from the base address.)

Self-Evaluating Quiz

Consider the assembler listing in Figure 10.6.

1. What is the location of statement number 51?
2. How many bytes does statement number 51 actually contain?
3. (T or F) Statement numbers always appear in ascending sequence.
4. (T or F) Statement numbers are always consecutive.
5. (T or F) The programmer supplies the statement number that appears on the assembler listing.
6. Using statement number 48, find the storage locations of OUTAREA and SPACES.
7. LOC fields or displacements are always referenced as (no.) byte(s) or (no.) hexadecimal numbers.
8. (T or F) Omitting the PRINT NOGEN would cause an error.
9. (T or F) Omitting the label BEGIN in the END statement will cause an error.
10. (T or F) All literals are assembled at the end of the program.

SOLUTIONS

1. 00 00 7E
2. 4 bytes (7E, 7F, 80, 81)
3. T
4. F; actual machine-language equivalents of macros need not be listed.
5. F; it is generated by the computer.
6. OUTAREA—166; SPACES—165.
7. 3; 6
8. F; it would simply cause the generating of *all* machine language instructions including those derived from macros.
9. F
10. T

IV. A PROGRAMMER'S GUIDE TO DEBUGGING

A. Overview

Just as flowcharting prior to coding facilitates the writing of the program, so too does *desk checking* facilitate the debugging process.

First, if you enter your program on a terminal, you should examine it carefully for typographical as well as logic errors before assembling. If you enter your program using cards, it is recommended that an 80–80 list of the source program be generated *before* assembling, to take a final look at the coding. An 80–80 list is 80 columns printed as 80 print positions, one record per line. When the program is then viewed in its entirety, errors that may have gone unnoticed up to this point are frequently identifiable.

You should then compare the flowchart or pseudocode with the coding to ensure that logic flow is correct. When this initial desk checking of the program is complete, you are now ready to begin testing your program. We will discuss each of the three levels of errors that may occur in a program.

Levels of Errors

1. Syntax errors may occur producing diagnostic or error messages. These result when the rules of the language have been violated. The elimination of these errors is relatively straightforward and is the easiest problem to correct.
2. Errors may occur that are compensated for by the computer. That is, when certain errors occur, the computer automatically makes an assumption called a *default*. This default may or may not be what the

```
LOC      OBJECT CODE        ADDR1 ADDR2  STMT  SOURCE STATEMENT

                                           8   *                                                        SAM00080
                                           9   *        HOUSEKEEPING INSTRUCTIONS GO HERE               SAM00090
                                          10   *                                                        SAM00100
00000E                                    11        OPEN  (INFILE,INPUT,OUTFILE,OUTPUT)                  SAM00110
00002A                                    25   READ GET   INFILE,RECORD                                 SAM00130
000038   F224 C108 C128    0010E 0012E    30        PACK  PKDSAL,SALARY                                 SAM00140
000062   FA32 C10B C108    00111 0010E    46        AP    TOTAL,PKDSAL                                  SAM00160
000068   47F0 C024         0002A          47        B     READ                                          SAM00170
00006C   D283 C160 C15F    00166 00165    48   EOF  MVC   OUTAREA,SPACES                                SAM00180
000072   D218 C160 C2F2    00166 002F8    49        MVC   OUTAREA(25),=C'TOTAL ANNUAL SALARIES IS '     SAM00190
000078   F363 C179 C17F    0017F 00111    50        UNPK  OUTAREA+25(7),TOTAL                           SAM00200
00007E   96F0 C17F         00185          51        OI    OUTAREA+31,X'F0'                              SAM00210
000082                                    52        PUT   OUTFILE,OUTAREA                               SAM00220
000090                                    57        CLOSE (INFILE,,OUTFILE)                             SAM00230
                                         122   *                                                        SAM00270
                                         123   *        HOUSEKEEPING INSTRUCTIONS GO HERE               SAM00280
                                         124   *            ALONG WITH DCB MACROS                        SAM00290
                                         125   *                                                        SAM00300
00010E                                   129   PKDSAL  DS   PL3                                          SAM00340
000111   0000000C                        130   TOTAL   DC   PL4'0'                                      SAM00350
000115                                   131   RECORD  DS   OCL80          CARD FORMAT                  SAM00360
000115                                   132   LAST    DS   CL15                          *             SAM00370
000124                                   133   FIRST   DS   CL10                          *             SAM00380
00012E                                   134   SALARY  DS   CL5                           *             SAM00390
000133                                   135           DS   CL50                          *             SAM00400
000165   40                              136   SPACES  DC   CL1' '                                      SAM00410
000166                                   137   OUTAREA DS   OCL132         PRINT FORMAT                 SAM00420
000166                                   138           DS   CL5                           *             SAM00430
00016B                                   139   LNAME   DS   CL15                          *             SAM00440
00017A                                   140           DS   CL20                          *             SAM00450
00018E                                   141   FNAME   DS   CL10                          *             SAM00460
000198                                   142           DS   CL20                          *             SAM00470
0001AC                                   143   SALOUT  DS   CL5                           *             SAM00480
0001B1                                   144   BLANK   DS   CL57                          *             SAM00490
                                         254           END                                             SAM00540
```

Figure 10.6
Program for Self-Evaluating Quiz.

programmer actually intended. Such defaults may result in erroneous output if they are not what the program should be doing.

3. Errors in logic, as described in the previous section, may occur during execution of the program. These errors require us to identify the instruction causing the problem or "bug" in our program.

We will now discuss each of these areas in detail, applying them to packed-decimal instructions, and later utilize most of these concepts in debugging a sample program.

B. Assembler Diagnostics

The assembler checks each instruction for the following.

---

1. Valid symbolic names.
2. Valid operation codes.
3. Duplicate labels or symbolic names.
4. Correct operands (type) for the op code specified.

After each invalid statement is detected by the assembler, an error message will be printed. The error message may appear *after* the erroneous source statement, as follows:

```
LOC    OBJECT CODE      ADDR1  ADDR2  STMT   SOURCE STATEMENT

00007E D283 C0CA C131   00134  0019B   269            MVC   LINEOUT,SPACES
000084 0000 0000                       270            MVI   LINEOUT,=C'*'
       ***ERROR***
                                       271            MOVE  LINEOUT+1,LINEOUT
       ***ERROR***
                                       272            PUT   OUTFILE,LINEOUT
                                       278 READ       GET   INFILE,CARDIN
0000A8 FA10 C1E3 C316   0024C  00380   284            AP    NOFLDS,=P'2'
0000AE F224 C132 C192   0019C  001FC   285            PACK  PFLDA,FLDA
0000B4 F224 C135 C1DD   0019F  00247   286            PACK  PFLDB,FLDB
```

The assembler may print the error message within the listing itself, as in the foregoing example, or the diagnostic messages may appear altogether at the end of the program, or your system may provide both.

If the latter method of listing diagnostics or errors is provided, the statement number of the instruction and a message denoting the type of error are listed.

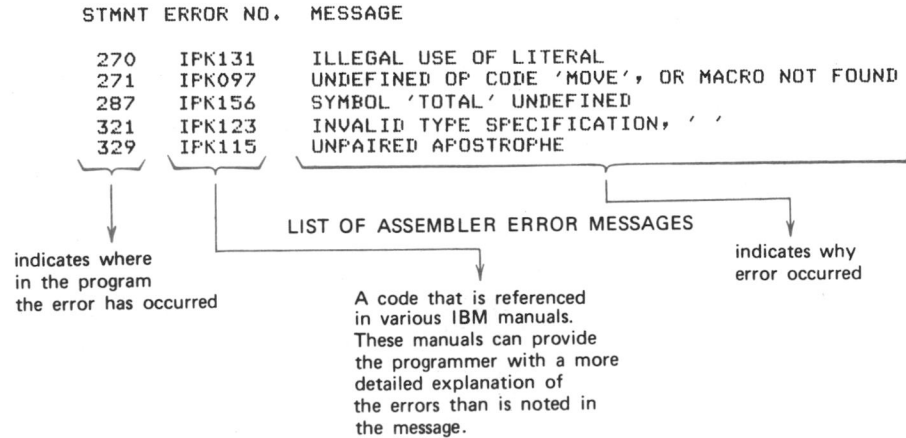

```
                               DIAGNOSTICS AND STATISTICS

     STMNT   ERROR NO.   MESSAGE

       270   IPK131      ILLEGAL USE OF LITERAL
       271   IPK097      UNDEFINED OP CODE 'MOVE', OR MACRO NOT FOUND
       287   IPK156      SYMBOL 'TOTAL' UNDEFINED
       321   IPK123      INVALID TYPE SPECIFICATION, ' '
       329   IPK115      UNPAIRED APOSTROPHE
```

LIST OF ASSEMBLER ERROR MESSAGES

indicates where in the program the error has occurred

A code that is referenced in various IBM manuals. These manuals can provide the programmer with a more detailed explanation of the errors than is noted in the message.

indicates why error occurred

Thus, a more detailed explanation of the problem can be obtained from the appropriate programmers' guide that provides an expanded version of each error by error number.

C. Types of Errors Not Detected by the Assembler

Finding and correcting syntax errors is a technique learned and refined through experience. However, there are typical mistakes. These can be avoided by carefully analyzing and desk checking the program. Following are five checks that can minimize syntax errors.

Hints

1. Check all Define Constants (`DC`s) to ensure that the contents of the locations are as specified and intended. The contents of each `DC` is listed in hex under the `OBJECT CODE` heading of the source program. For example:

```
LOC OBJECT CODE  ADDR1 ADDR2 STMT SOURCE STATEMENT
00019C                        350      DS      C'END OF JOB'
```

No object code—`DC` should have been specified instead of `DS`. `DC` would have generated some constant that would be specified under `OBJECT CODE`.

2. Inspect all Define Storage (`DS`) specifications to ensure that each field is of sufficient length to hold the largest result it is intended to contain. For example, consider the following.

```
FLDA     DS      CL7
  :
  :
PFLDA    DS      PL3
```

`PFLDA` is to hold the packed-decimal representation of `FLDA`. `PFLDA` is too small to hold the packed version of `FLDA`. Checking the program for such errors *before* it is executed may well save you hours of debugging later on.

3. When fields are subdivided, be sure that the total length of the subdivisions equals the length of the whole. For example, consider the following code.

```
INDATA   DS      0CL80  ⎫
NAME     DS      CL20   ⎬  Intended as the input area
STREET   DS      CL20   
TOWN     DS      CL15   ⎭

TOTAL1   DC      PL5'0' ⎫  Intermediate total areas
TOTAL2   DC      PL5'0' ⎭
MSSG     DC      CL25   }  Constant
```

This coding would cause the total fields to be destroyed when the first input record was read. That is, 80 positions will be loaded into the area beginning with `NAME`. Because of incorrect coding, input record position 56 will begin loading in `TOTAL1`, and so on. To avoid this type of error, the input data area *must* add up to the 80 positions defined by the `INDATA` instruction.

4. Be sure to code the Define Constant (`DC`) for `SPACES` immediately before the output area if the output area is to be properly cleared.

```
* INCORRECT CODING
LINEOUT  DS      CL132
  :
  :
SPACES   DC      X'40'
  :
```

```
* CORRECT CODING
SPACES    DC       X'40'
LINEOUT   DS       CL132
            ⋮
            ⋮
```

If the coding is not correct, the instruction MVC LINE-OUT(132),SPACES will not propagate blanks in the correct way.

5. Remember to properly open and close all input and output files.

These are just a few of the precautionary measures that should be taken during desk checking. In general, a careful review of your program after it has been coded could save you hours of debugging time as well as valuable computer time later on.

D. Execution Errors

1. Introduction

Execution errors fall into several categories, with the final result usually being an interrupt. In such a case, we say the program "bombs," or the run is "aborted," or an "abend" (*ab*normal *end*) has occurred. When this happens, the instruction causing the problem must be identified so that corrective action can be taken. The *type of interrupt* specified by the system serves as the first clue to finding the source of the problem. The type of interrupts typically encountered with decimal instructions include:

1. Data exceptions
2. Decimal overflow and divide exceptions
3. Specification exceptions.[2]

The following problems are often associated with interrupts involving the decimal instruction set.

2. Data Exceptions

With packed-decimal arithmetic instructions, recall that the CPU checks each digit as well as the sign in the low-order byte for validity.

When an invalid code is detected, a data exception occurs resulting in a program interrupt. The following problems may cause a data exception.

1. A numeric data field contains blanks or spaces in the low-order position. The PACK instruction will result in an invalid sign that will not itself cause the computer to abend. Rather, any packed-decimal operation such as AP, DP, CP, etc., performed on an invalid field will cause a data exception.
2. Failure to include the low-order byte when addressing a packed-decimal field. For example, consider the following.

```
                                        FLDB
                                         ↓
AP     TOTAL,FLDB(2)                 ┌────┬────┬────┐
                                     │ 12 │ 34 │ 5C │
                                     └────┴────┴────┘
                                       ‿‿‿‿‿‿
                                        FLDB(2)
```

This results in a sending field that contains an invalid low-order byte, one with no sign. This error frequently occurs when incorrectly referencing overlapped fields.

---

[2]Chapter 14 contains a full discussion of interrupts.

3. A data field containing EBCDIC or other data that fails to conform to the packed-decimal format. For example, when we add a field to TOTAL a data exception will occur.

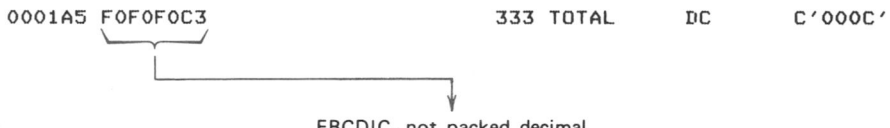

```
0001A5 F0F0F0C3                        333 TOTAL     DC      C'000C'
```

EBCDIC, not packed decimal

4. In decimal multiplication, the first operand must contain as many *bytes* of high-order zeros as there are bytes in the multiplier (second operand) or a data exception will again result.

Data exception error messages are listed on the last page of output in the following format.

```
OS03I PROGRAM CHECK INTERRUPTION - HEX LOCATION 1105EA
        - CONDITION CODE 2 - DATA EXCEPTION
OS00I JOB INST    CANCELED
```

Determining the instruction causing this problem is discussed in the sample programs appearing at the end of this chapter.

3. Decimal Overflow and Decimal Divide Exceptions

Decimal overflow may occur when using the AP, SP, ZAP, and the SRP (Shift and Round Packed)[3] instruction. Recall that when the receiving operand of a packed-decimal instruction is too small to contain all of the significant digits resulting from an arithmetic operation, a decimal overflow will result.

A similar error is the decimal divide exception. A decimal divide exception always occurs when we inadvertently attempt to divide by zero. It will also occur if the first operand is too small to hold the quotient and remainder resulting from the divide operation. The interrupt may appear as follows:

```
OS03I PROGRAM CHECK INTERRUPTION - HEX LOCATION 080634
        - CONDITION CODE 2 - DECIMAL DIVIDE EXCEPTION
OS00I JOB INST    CANCELED
```

4. Specification Exceptions

As discussed in the previous chapters, specification exceptions can occur in a variety of circumstances. Failure to adhere to one of the following rules will result in a specification exception.

1. In decimal multiplication, the length of the first operand must be greater than the length of the second operand.
2. In decimal multiplication, the multiplier must not exceed 8 bytes in length.
3. In decimal division, the length of the first operand must be greater than the length of the second operand.
4. The divisor must not be greater than 8 bytes.

These examples are typical of those encountered in programming with decimal instructions. They provide a general review of problems that are frequently and repeatedly found in programs.

A sample program will illustrate the techniques used in debugging. As we proceed step-by-step in correcting the sample problem, you will realize that the debugging procedure follows a systematic approach that can be improved with experience.

[3]See Chapter 17.

E. Illustrating the Debugging Process

1. The Problem

A data record contains two fields, FLDA and FLDB, in positions 1–5 and 76–80, respectively. The object of the program is to accumulate totals on both fields (TOTALA and TOTALB) and to count the number of fields (NOFLDA) processed. Once the last input record has been read, the totals (TOTALA, TOTALB) will then be added together to produce a final sum (SUM). We want to print on the right of the form an average of the SUM field dividing it by the number of fields processed, with two decimal places. To print 2 decimal places, we must shift SUM left 2 positions (we will call the field SHIFT2LT). We do this by multiplying by 100. The average (AVERAGE) is calculated and finally the output is produced. The format of the output is as follows.

```
XXXXX     XXXXX     XXX.XX
TOTALA    TOTALB    AVERAGE
```

Computer Run Number 1   The first assembly of the source program typically produces some syntax errors that are detected by the assembler program. The first step is to identify and correct these errors. Each instruction will be analyzed individually in sequence within the program.

The first assembly of the program produced the results indicated in Figure 10.7. There are additional pages with various tables that accompany this listing but, for now, let us confine our discussion to just the listing. Note that this is a DOS listing. We will, however, assume I/O is correct so as not to trouble OS readers with DOS conventions. The rest of the program is independent of specific DOS or OS considerations.

Error 1

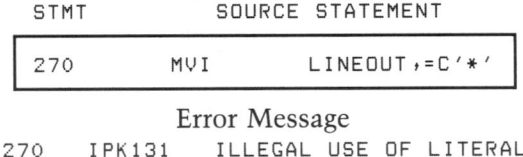

```
STMT              SOURCE STATEMENT

270      MVI       LINEOUT,=C'*'
```

Error Message

```
270    IPK131    ILLEGAL USE OF LITERAL
```

The second operand of the MVI instruction must contain 1 byte of immediate data. The equal sign is not permitted.

Correction 1

```
MVI       LINEOUT,C'*'
```

Error 2

```
STMT              SOURCE STATEMENT

271      MOVE              LINEOUT+1,LINEOUT
```

Error Message

```
271    IPK097    UNDEFINED OP CODE 'MOVE' OR MACRO NOT FOUND
```

The Move Character instruction was intended; however, an incorrect *mnemonic* (MOVE rather than MVC) was specified.

Correction 2

```
MVC       LINEOUT+1(131),LINEOUT
```

Note that we use the explicit form of the MVC when revising this instruction so as to avoid a potential logic problem when executing the program. If the

```
                                          DOS/VS ASSEMBLER REL 34.0  17.21                    PAGE  2

LOC     OBJECT CODE   ADDR1 ADDR2   STMT   SOURCE STATEMENT

000000                              1  DEBUG    PRINT NOGEN
                                    2  INFILE   START 0
                                    3  DTFCD    DTFCD BLKSIZE=80,RECFORM=FIXUNB,DEVADDR=SYSIPT,        X   HSKP
                                                      WORKA=YES,IOAREA1=BUFFRIN,EOFADDR=EOF               HSKP
                                   24  OUTFILE  DTFPR BLKSIZE=132,DEVICE=1403,DEVADDR=SYSLST,IOAREA1=BUFFROUT,X  HSKP
                                                      CONTROL=YES,PRINTOV=YES,WORKA=YES                    HSKP
                                   45           CDMOD WORKA=YES                                            HSKP
                                  137           PRMOD WORKA=YES,CONTROL=YES,PRINTOV=YES                    HSKP
000068  05C0                      257  BEGIN    BALR  12,0                                                 HSKP
                       0006A      258           USING *,12                                                 HSKP
                                  259           OPEN  INFILE,OUTFILE                                       HSKP


                                          DOS/VS ASSEMBLER REL 34.0  17.21                    PAGE  3

LOC     OBJECT CODE   ADDR1 ADDR2   STMT   SOURCE STATEMENT

00007E  D283 C0CE C133       0019D  269           MVC   LINEOUT,SPACES
000084  0000 0000                   270           MVI   LINEOUT,=C'*'     EQUAL SIGN ILLEGAL
        *** ERROR ***
                                    271  READ     MOVE  LINEOUT+1,LINEOUT   ILLEGAL OPERATION CODE
        *** ERROR ***
0000A8  FA10 C1E4 C31E 00244 00388  272           PUT   OUTFILE,LINEOUT
0000AE  F224 C134 C194 0019E 001FE  278           GET   INFILE,CARDIN
0000B4  F224 C137 C1DF 001A1 00249  284           PACK  NOFLDS,=P'2'
0000BA  0000 0000 0000              285           PACK  PFLDA,FLDA
        *** ERROR ***
                                    286           PACK  PFLDB,FLDB     BLANKS ARE NOT PERMITTED IN OPERAND
0000C0  FA22 C13E C137 001A8 001A1  287           AP    TOTAL A,PFLDA
0000C6  47F0 C02E       00098       288           AP    TOTALB,PFLDB
0000CA  D283 C0CE C133 001AB 0019D  289           B     READ
0000D0  FA23 C141 C13A 001A4 0014A  290  EOF      MVC   LINEOUT,SPACES
0000D6  D204 C0CE C138 00258 001A8  291           AP    SUM,TOTALA
0000DC  DE04 C0CE C13A 001A8 0014A  292           MVC   AOUT,PATTERN
0000E2  FA22 C141 C13E 001A4 00258  293           ED    AOUT,TOTALA
0000E8  D204 C0DD C147 001A8 00258  294           AP    SUM,TOTALB
0000EE  DE04 C0DD C141 00147 001A8  295           MVC   BOUT,PATTERN
0000F4  F842 C1E9 C141 00253 001A1  296           ED    BOUT,TOTALB
0000FA  FC42 C1E9 C1E6 00253 00250  297           ZAP   SHIFT2LT,SUM
000100  FD41 C1E9 C1E4 00253 00156  298           MP    SHIFT2LT,HUNDRED
000106  D208 C0EC C31F 00156 00389  299           DP    SHIFT2LT,NOFLDS
00010C  DE08 C0EC C1E9 00156 00253  300           MVC   AVERAGE,SHIFT2LT
                                    301           ED    AVERAGE,SHIFT2LT
                                    302           PUT   OUTFILE,LINEOUT
                                    308           CLOSE INFILE,OUTFILE
```

Figure 10.7
Sample program listing with syntax errors (continued on page 310).

```
                                                                              PAGE   4

000138             317 LINEOUT  EQU  OCL132
       *** ERROR ***
000138             320          DS   30
00013D             321          DS
000147             322 ADOT     DS   CL5
00014C             323 BJOT     DS   CL10
00015F             324          DS   CL10
                   325 AVERAGE  DS   CL10
                   326          DS   CL62
                   327 PACKI    DC   PL1' '          ILLEGAL DEFINE CONSTANT

00019D 40          329 SPACES   DC   CL1' '
       *** ERROR ***
00019E             330 PFLDA    DS   PL3
0001A1 F0F0F0C3    331 PFLDB    DS   PL3
0001A4             332 TOTALA   DC   C'0000C'         SHOULD BE X TYPE SPECIFICATION, NOT C
0001A8 00000C      333 TOTALB   DC   PL3'0'
0001AB             334 SUM      DS   PL3'0'           USE DC FOR INITIALIZING, NOT DS
0001AE             335 CARDIN   DS   CL80             ZERO MISSING FOR SUBDIVIDING DS
0001FE             336 FLDA     DS   CL5
000249             337 FLDB     DS   CL70
00024E 000C        338 FLDB     DS   CL5
000250 0010OC      339 NOFLDS   DC   PL2'0'
000253 402020202020 340 HUNDRED DC   PL3'100'
000258             341 SHIFT2LT DS   PL5
                   342 PATTERN  DC   X'402020202020'


LOC    OBJECT CODE      ADDR1 ADDR2  STMT  SOURCE STATEMENT              DOS/VS ASSEMBLER REL 34.0 17.21

00025E                        00068  344 BUFFKIN  DS   CL132
0002E2                               345 BUFFROUT DS   CL132
                                     346          END  BEGIN
000368 585BC2D6D7C5D540              347 =C'$$BOPEN '
000370 585BC2C3D3D6E2C5              348 =C'$$BCLOSE'
000378 00000038                      349 =A(OUTFILE)
00037C 00000138                      350 =A(LINEOUT)
000380 00000000                      351 =A(INFILE)
000384 000001AE                      352 =A(CARDIN)
000388 2C                            353 =P'2'
000389 40202020214B2020              354 =X'40202020214B2020'
```

Figure 10.7 (continued)

explicit specification were omitted, an extra asterisk would be moved to the area immediately following LINEOUT. This would present problems if that field were to be used for packed-decimal arithmetic operations.

Error 3

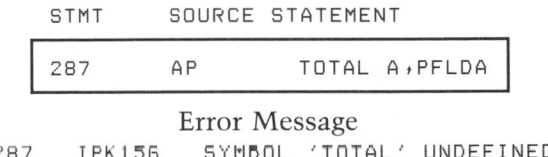

Error Message

287   IPK156   SYMBOL 'TOTAL' UNDEFINED

Examination of the instruction reveals that a space or blank was embedded in Operand 1. The assembler therefore assumed that everything after the space was a comment. Remember, the space is used as a field separator in this free-form language.

Correction 3

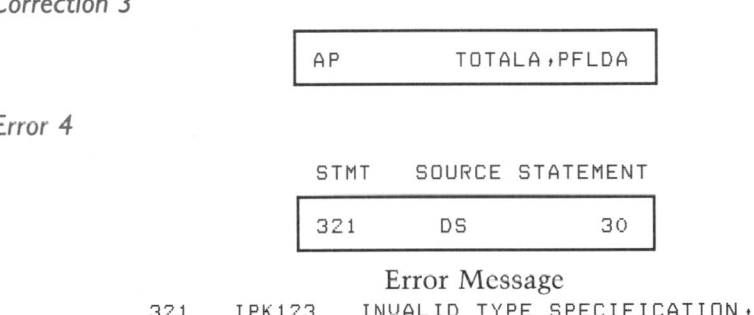

Error 4

STMT   SOURCE STATEMENT

321   DS   30

Error Message

321   IPK123   INVALID TYPE SPECIFICATION, ' '

The type of data to be stored in this define storage operation (X, C, P, F, H, etc.) was omitted in coding the instruction.

Correction 4

DS   CL30

Error 5

STMT   SOURCE STATEMENT

328   PACK1   DC   PL1' '

Error Message

328   IPK115   UNPAIRED APOSTROPHE

When a field is defined as packed-decimal, the assembler expects to find digits between the quotes. The space after the first apostrophe, then, would signal the end of the operand. Hence, the second apostrophe is ignored, as noted in the error message. Further inspection of the program logic reveals that this field is *not* referenced anywhere in the program. It could be that its inclusion is unnecessary or it could be that an instruction has been inadvertently omitted.

Correction 5

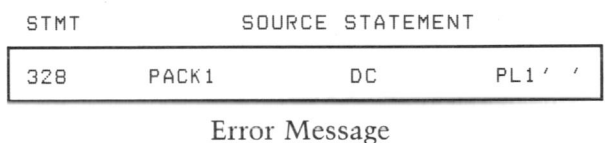

We will simply delete this instruction.

The meaning of the errors detected by the assembler for the most part are usually quite obvious once you become familiar with them; in some instances, however, certain syntax errors will require further interpretation.

At this point, you may be inclined to resubmit your corrected program immediately, believing that all the "errors" have been eliminated. It is, however, important to desk check your program again. In our example, several additional programming errors may be detected if you reexamine the program. Note that there are errors that have not been detected by the assembler.

2. Errors Not Detected by the Assembler

As a general rule, recall that you should check the hex contents of each Define Constant (DC). If you do this, you will find that the following errors exist.

Statement 332

```
TOTALA          DC              C'000C'
```

This instruction should initialize TOTAL at zero, but it does not. It incorrectly sets up zoned-decimal data (EBCDIC) because of the C-type specification. Note that this did *not* produce an error message. Rather, the computer used the C or character format and the contents *defaulted* to that specification.

Correction 6

```
TOTALA          DC              X'00000C'
```

Statement 334

```
SUM             DS              PL3'0'
```

SUM is not initialized at zero because a DS was used erroneously instead of a DC. This is a common error that is easily detected during desk checking.

Correction 7

```
SUM             DC              PL3'0'
```

Statement 335

```
CARDIN          DS              CL80
```

FLDA and FLDB were to be defined within CARDIN; however a zero did not precede the CL80 specification. References to FLDA or FLDB, then, as originally coded in the program would result in an error when the program was actually executed.

Correction 8

```
CARDIN          DS              0CL80
```

While desk checking the field subdivisions, we find the subdivisions of LINEOUT do not add up to 132 positions. Instead, they equal 131. This correction requires us to change an instruction.

```
DS              CL62
```
must be changed to

Correction 9

```
DS              CL63
```

In the next run, we have incorporated all of the corrections mentioned with *one* exception. We failed to change the contents of PACK1. Hence, it still contains a blank. We did this to show you what will happen. The error is referenced as Correction 10 in the revised program. We are now ready to proceed. Let us now consider the second computer run.

Computer Run Number 2 See Figure 10.8. (Cross-reference tables have *not* been included to facilitate the presentation.) Note that *no* syntax errors have occurred. Thus, the execution phase may begin.

A logic error has occurred that produced a program interrupt at hex location 110620. This interrupt is a result of a data exception.

```
OSOEI PROGRAM CHECK INTERRUPTION - HEX LOCATION 110620 - CONDITION CODE 2 -
      DATA EXCEPTION
```

We must now find the erroneous instruction. Referring to the linkage editor map, we find the load, or starting point of the program has a symbolic name DEBUG (defined in the START statement) and an actual address of 110520.

```
PHASE
      DEBUG          110520  110881    000000 000361       362         866
```

By subtracting the load point from the address of the interrupt, we are able to ascertain the displacement in the program where the error occurred.

$$\begin{array}{r} 110620 \\ -110520 \\ \hline 000100 \end{array} \begin{array}{l} \text{Address of error} \\ \text{Load point} \\ \text{Displacement} \end{array}$$

We find the instruction at LOC 100 to be the MP instruction.

```
LOC      SOURCE STATEMENT
100      MP          SHIFT2LT,HUNDRED
```

In analyzing the field sizes, we find the first operand does *not* contain a sufficient number of high order zeros. Remember, SUM was 3 bytes in length and HUNDRED is also 3 bytes. The product field should therefore be 6 bytes. To correct this problem, we simply enlarge the field size of the product.

```
SHIFT2LT          DS          CL6
```

Computer Run Number 3 See Figure 10.9. Success at last! Our program has finally generated output. Note, however, that we cannot assume that all of our problems are solved. We must compare the computer-produced results with our own manual calculations of what the results should be to be sure that there are no further logic errors. Suppose our input test data consisted of 4 records, as follows:

	FLDA	FLDB
Input Record 1:	200	400
Input Record 2:	100	200
Input Record 3:	50	100
Input Record 4:	50	100

Based on our calculations, AOUT, the total of the 4 FLDAs, should be 400; BOUT, the total of the 4 FLDBs, should be 800; and, average should be (400 + 800)/8 (number of fields) = 150.00.

Note that the correct average prints, but AOUT and BOUT print as 40 and 80 respectively, and they are off by a factor of 10. Hence, there is a logic error.

```
                                                         DOS/VS ASSEMBLER REL 34.0 17.24                    PAGE 2

LOC    OBJECT CODE   ADDR1 ADDR2   STMT  SOURCE STATEMENT

                                     1          PRINT NOGEN
                                     2  DEBUG   START 0
000000                               3  INFILE  DTFCD BLKSIZE=80,RECFORM=FIXUNB,DEVADDR=SYSIPT,          X
                                                       WORKA=YES,IOAREA1=BUFFKIN,EOFADDR=EOF                 HSKP
                                    24  OUTFILE DTFPR BLKSIZE=132,DEVICE=1403,DEVADDR=SYSLST,IOAREA1=BUFFROUT,X  HSKP
                                                       CONTROL=YES,PRINTOV=YES,WORKA=YES                     HSKP
                                    45          CDMOD WORKA=YES,CONTROL=YES,PRINTOV=YES                      HSKP
                                   137          PRMOD WORKA=YES                                              HSKP
000068 05C0                        257  BEGIN   BALR  12,0                                                   HSKP
                       0006A       258          USING *,12                                                   HSKP
                                   259          OPEN  INFILE,OUTFILE
```

```
                                                         DOS/VS ASSEMBLER REL 34.0 17.24                    PAGE 3

LOC     OBJECT CODE     ADDR1 ADDR2   STMT  SOURCE STATEMENT

00007E  D283 C0D3 C0D2  013D  013C    269          MVC   LINEOUT,SPACES
000084  925C C0D3       013D          271          MVI   LINEOUT+1(131),LINEOUT   CORRECTION 1
000088  D282 C0D4 C0D3  013E  013D    272          MVC   LINEOUT+1(131),LINEOUT   CORRECTION 2
                                      278  READ      GET   INFILE,CARDIN
0000AE  FA10 C1B6 C2EE  01C4  00358   284          PACK  NOFLDS,=P'2'
0000B4  F224 C157 C1B1  0157  001D0   285          PACK  PFLDA,FLDA
0000BA  F224 C15A C1B1  015A  0021B   286          PACK  PFLDB,FLDB
0000C0  FA22 C160 C157  01C7  001C1   287          AP    TOTALA,PFLDA
0000C6  FA22 C160 C15A  01CA  001C4   288          AP    TOTALB,PFLDB
0000CC  47F0 C034       0009E         289  EOF       B     READ
0000D0  D283 C0D3 C0D2  013D  013C    291          MVC   LINEOUT,SPACES
0000D6  FA22 C163 C15D  01C7  015B    292          MVC   SUM,TOTALA
0000DC  DE04 C0F1 C1C0  015B  01C0    293          ED    AOUT,PATTERN
0000E2  FA22 C163 C160  01CA  001CA   294          AP    SUM,TOTALB
0000E8  DE04 C100 C160  016A  001CA   295          MVC   BOUT,PATTERN
0000EE  DE04 C100 C163  016A  001CD   296          ED    BOUT,TOTALB
0000F4  F842 C100 C163  0225  001CD   297          ZAP   SHIFT2LT,SUM
0000FA  FC41 C1BB C1B8  0225  00222   298          MP    SHIFT2LT,=...
000106  FD41 C1BB C1B6  0225  00220   300          DP    SHIFT2LT,NOFLDS
00010C  D208 C10F C2EF  0179  00359   301          MVC   AVERAGE,=X'40202020202148B2020'
000112  DE08 C10F C1BB  0179  00225   302          ED    AVERAGE,SHIFT2LT
                                      308            PUT   OUTFILE,LINEOUT
                                                     CLOSE INFILE,OUTFILE
                                      317            EOJ
```

Figure 10.8
Sample program with a logic error (continued on pages 315 and 316).

```
                                                                                    PAGE   4

LOC                                                                    DOS/VS ASSEMBLER REL 34.0  17.24

00013C  40          320 SPACES    DC   CLL' '          CORRECTION 10  MUST PRECEDE LINEOUT
00013D              321 LINEOUT   DS   OCLL32          CORRECTION 4
00015B              322           DS   CLL30
000160              324 AOUT      DS   CL5
00016A              325 BOUT      DS   CLL0
00016F              326           DS   CLL0
000182              327 AVERAGE   DS   CL9
                    328 *         DS   CL63                           CORRECTION 9
                    329 ****           PACK1 NOT USED BY PROGRAM, THEREFORE REMOVED   CORR 5
0001C1              330 PFLDA     DS   PL3
0001C4  00000C      331 PFLDB     DS   PL3
0001C7  00000C      332 TOTALA    DC   X'00000C'       CORRECTION 6
0001CA  00000C      333 TOTALB    DC   PL3'0'
0001CD              334 SUM       DC   PL3'0'
0001D0              335 CARDIN    DS   OCL80
0001D5              336 FLDA      DS   CL5
                    337           DS   CL70
00021B              338 FLDB      DS   CL5
000220  000C        339 NOFLDS    DS   PL2'0'
000222  0100C       340 HUNDRED   DC   PL3'100.'       CORRECTION 7
000225              341 SHIFT2LT  DS   PL5             CORRECTION 8
00022A  40202020202020  342 PATTERN DC X'40202020202020'


LOC     OBJECT CODE       ADDR1  ADDR2  STMT   SOURCE STATEMENT

000230                                  344 BUFFRIN  DS   CLL32
0002B4                                  345 BUFFROUT DS   CLL32
                                C0068   346          END  BEGIN
000338  5B5BC2D6D7C5D540                347               =C'$$BOPEN '
000340  5B5BC2C3D3D6E2C5                348               =C'$$BCLOSE'
000348  00000038                        349               =A(OUTFILE)
00034C  00000130                        350               =A(LINEOUT)
000350  000001D0                        351               =A(INFILE)
000354                                  352               =A(CARDIN)
000358  2C                              353               =P'2'
000359  40202020214B20                  354               =X'40202020214B2020'
```

Figure 10.8 (continued)

PAGE   8

DIAGNOSTICS AND STATISTICS

NO ERRORS FOUND

THE FOLLOWING MACRO NAMES HAVE BEEN FOUND IN MACRO INSTRUCTIONS
    CDMOD   PKMOD   OPEN   PUT   GET   CLOSE   EOJ
    DTFCD   DTFPR

OPTIONS FOR THIS ASSEMBLY - ALIGN, LIST, XREF, LINK, NORLD, NODECK, NOEDECK

THE ASSEMBLER WAS RUN IN 65416 BYTES
END OF ASSEMBLY

EOP $3ASM
// EXEC LNKEDT

JOB INST   17.25.01 F-LE-E FAST-LINKAGE-EDITOR VM4.0   DOS/VS R34-0A G O A L   S Y S T E M S

ACTION TAKEN MAP CLEAR REL LINK
LIST PHASE MONITOR,ROOT
LIST INCLUDE ILFFEXIT
LIST AUTOLINK IJDFAPZZ
LIST PHASE STDPGM,*
LIST ENTRY

```
      PHASE-CSECT-ENTRY  LO-LNK HI-LNK  LO-REL HI-REL  LN-HEX  LN-DEC   XF-LNK  XF-REL   G O A L   S Y S T E M S

      LINK PARTITION = F3  110000 169FFF  000000 059FFF  5A000  368,640

ROOT  MONITOR            11007B 11051B  000000 0004A3   4A4   1,188   110076 00007B
      ILFFEXIT           110078 1103F9  000000 000381   382     898   110073 000000   RELOCATABLE
      I*EXIT             1100F4         000007C          11C     284
      IJDFAPZZ           110400 11051B  000388 0004A3
      * IJDFAZZZ                        000388

PHASE STDPGM            110520 1109A9  000000 000489   48A   1,162   110568 000068   RELOCATABLE
      DEBUG            110520 110881  000000 000361   362     866
      IJCFZIWO         110888 110DFF  000368 00030F    7D     120
      IJDFCPZW         110900 1109A9  0003E0 000489    AA     170
      * IJDFZPZW       110900         0003E0
      * IJDFZZZW       110900         0003E0
      * IJDFCZZW       110900         0003E0
```

NORMAL COMPLETION, BLOCKS AVAIL =   33+, USED IN EDIT =   4, PCIL=X'1C0', CYL=001, SERIAL=MORK01.

// EXEC
****

OS031 PROGRAM CHECK INTERRUPTION - HEX LOCATION 110620 - CONDITION CODE 2 - DATA EXCEPTION
OS001 JOB INST CANCELED

Figure 10.8 (continued)

```
LOC    OBJECT CODE   ADDR1 ADDR2  STMT  SOURCE STATEMENT        DOS/VS ASSEMBLER REL 34.0 17.27          PAGE 2

000000                               1         PRINT NOGEN
                                     2  DEBUG  START 0
                                     3  INFILE DTFCD BLKSIZE=80,RECFORM=FIXUNB,DEVADDR=SYSIPT,       X    HSKP
                                                     WORKA=YES,IOAREA1=BUFFRIN,EOFADDR=EOF                HSKP
                                                                                                          HSKP
                                    24  OUTFILE DTFPR BLKSIZE=132,DEVICE=1403,DEVADDR=SYSLST,IOAREA1=BUFFROUT,X  HSKP
                                                     CONTROL=YES,PRINTOV=YES,WORKA=YES                    HSKP
                                                                                                          HSKP
                                    45          CDMOD WORKA=YES                                           HSKP
                                   137          PRMOD WORKA=YES,CONTROL=YES,PRINTOV=YES                   HSKP
                                                                                                          HSKP
000068 05C0                        257  BEGIN   BALR 12,0
                            0006A   258          USING *,12
                                    259          OPEN  INFILE,OUTFILE


LOC    OBJECT CODE        ADDR1 ADDR2  STMT  SOURCE STATEMENT     DOS/VS ASSEMBLER REL 34.0 17.27         PAGE 3

00007E D283 C0D3 C0D3     0013C 0013C  269          MVC   LINEOUT,SPACES
000084 925C C0D3          0013D        270          MVI   LINEOUT,C'*'
000088 D282 C0D4 C0D3     0013E 0013D  271          MVC   LINEOUT+1(131),LINEOUT
                                       272          PUT   OUTFILE,LINEOUT
                                       278  READ    GET   INFILE,CARDIN
0000AE FA10 C1B6 C2F6     00220 00360  284          AP    NO=LDS,=P'2'
0000B4 F224 C157 C166     001C1 00166  285          PACK  PFLDA,FLDA
0000BA F224 C15A C15D     001CB 001C1  286          PACK  PFLDB,FLDB
0000C0 FA22 C15D C157     001C7 001CB  287          AP    TOTALA,PFLDA
0000C6 FA22 C160 C15A     001CA 001C4  288          AP    TOTALB,PFLDB
0000CC 47F0 C034          0009E        289          B     READ
0000D0 D283 C0D3 C0D3     0013C 0013C  290  EOF     MVC   LINEOUT,SPACES
0000D6 FA22 C163 C15D     001CD 001C7  291          AP    SUM,TOTALA
0000DC D204 C0F1 C15D     0015B 001C7  292          MVC   ACUT,PATTERN
0000E2 DE04 C0F1 C163     0015B 001CD  293          ED    ACUT,TOTALA
0000E8 FA22 C163 C160     001C7 001CA  294          AP    SUM,TOTALB
0000EE D204 C100 C1C1     0016A 001CA  295          MVC   BOUT,PATTERN
0000F4 DE04 C100 C160     0016A 001CA  296          ED    BOUT,TOTALB
0000FA F852 C1BB C163     00225 001CD  297          ZAP   SHIFT2LT,SUM
000100 FC52 C1BB C1B6     00225 00220  298          MP    SHIFT2LT,HUNDRED
000106 F051 C1BB C1BB     00225 00225  299          DP    SHIFT2LT,NOFLDS
00010C D208 C20F C2F7     00179 00361  300          MVC   AVERAGE,=X'40202020202021482020'
000112 DE08 C10F C1BB     00179 00225  301          ED    AVERAGE,SHIFT2LT
                                       302          PUT   OUTFILE,LINEOUT
                                       308          CLOSE INFILE,OUTFILE
```

Figure 10.9
Sample program with a logic error (continued on page 318).

PAGE 4

```
LOC      OBJECT CODE        ADDR1  ADDR2   STMT   SOURCE STATEMENT
                                           317   SPACES    EQU   40
00013C   40                                320   LINEOUT   DC    CL1' '
00013D                                     321             DS    0CL132
00015B                                     322             DS    CL30
000160                                     323   AOUT      DS    CL10
00016A                                     324             DS    CL5
00016F                                     325   BOUT      DS    CL10
000179                                     326             DS    CL10
000182                                     327   AVERAGE   DS    CL9
0001C1                                     328             DS    CL63
0001C4                                     329   PFLDA     DS    PL3
0001C7   00000C                            330   PFLDB     DS    PL3
0001CA   00000C                            331   TOTALA    DC    X'0000C'
0001CD                                     332   TOTALB    DC    PL3'0.'
0001D0                                     333   SUM       DC    PL3'0.'
0001D5                                     334   CARDIN    DS    0CL80
                                           335   FLDA      DS    CL5
                                           336             DS    CL70
00021B                                     337   FLDB      DS    CL5
000220   000C                              338   NOFLDS    DC    PL2'0.'
000222   0100C                             339   HUNDRED   DC    PL3'100'
000225                                     340   SHIFTZLT  DS    PL6
00022B   402020202020                      341   PATTERN   DC    X'402020202020'
                                                           CORRECTION   INCREASED FIELD SIZE
```

PAGE 8

DOS/VS ASSEMBLER REL 34.0 17.27

```
LOC      OBJECT CODE        ADDR1  ADDR2   STMT   SOURCE STATEMENT
000231                                     343   BUFFKIN   DS    CL132
0002B5                                     344   BUFFKOUT  DS    CL132
                                    00068  345   BEGIN     END

000340   5B5BC206D7C5D540                  346                   =C'$$BOPEN '
000348   5B5BC2C3D3D6E2C5                  347                   =C'$$BCLOSE'
000350   00000038                          348                   =A(OUTFILE)
000354   0000013D                          349                   =A(LINEOUT)
000358   00000000                          350                   =A(INFILE)
00035C   2C                                351                   =A(CARDIN)
000361   402020202021482020                352                   =P'2'
                                           353                   =X'402020202021482020'
```

DIAGNOSTICS AND STATISTICS

NO ERRORS FOUND

THE FOLLOWING MACRO NAMES HAVE BEEN FOUND IN MACRO INSTRUCTIONS
DTFCD   CDMOD   PRMOD   OPEN   PUT   GET   CLOSE   EOJ
DTFPR

OPTIONS FOR THIS ASSEMBLY - ALIGN, LIST, XREF, LINK, NORLD, NODECK, NOEDECK

THE ASSEMBLER WAS RUN IN 65416 BYTES
END OF ASSEMBLY

Figure 10.9 (continued)

First, we must check the keying of the test data to ensure that no errors occurred during the data entry process. Our check verifies that the input records were properly prepared. Therefore, the problem lies within the program. We must examine instructions that use TOTALA, TOTALB, AOUT, and BOUT as receiving fields. The instructions referencing these fields can be found in the Symbol Reference Table.

			CROSS-REFERENCE			
SYMBOL	LEN	IC	VALUE	DEFN	REFERENCES	
AOUT	00005	01	00015B	00323	0292	0293
AVERAGE	00009	01	000179	00327	0300	0301
BEGIN	00002	01	000068	00257	0345	
BOUT	00005	01	00016A	00325	0295	0296
BUFFRIN	00132	01	000231	00343	0017	0020
BUFFROUT	00132	01	0002B5	00344	0038	0043
CARDIN	00080	01	0001D0	00334	0351	
DEBUG	00001	01	000000	00002	0136	0256
EOF	00006	01	0000D0	00290	0019	
FLDA	00005	01	0001D0	00335	0285	
FLDB	00005	01	00021B	00337	0286	
HUNDRED	00003	01	000222	00339	0298	

As illustrated, the table is arranged in alphabetic sequence. AOUT will be the first field of our group to be checked.

Note that AOUT is referenced by instructions 292 and 293. At statement 292, the edit pattern is moved to AOUT.

In checking the field descriptions we find AOUT has a length of 5 bytes while PATTERN contains 6 bytes. The object code of the MVC instruction is now checked and we find a length of 5 bytes (04 + 1) specified by the move. This is our first problem. The failure to utilize an explicit MVC instruction has resulted in truncation of the edit pattern, as well as truncation of our results. We can correct this problem by redefining the areas AOUT and BOUT.

The program will now process the data correctly. Figure 10.10 is a correct listing of the program and its output.

Sometimes more elaborate test data should be prepared for the following tests:

1. Every branch performed by the program.
2. All possible combinations of data (to ensure that overflows do not occur).

As we have seen, there is a great deal of work involved in debugging programs correctly. The debugging process is more complex with assembler programs than with high-level programs because of the machine-like level and detail of the instructions involved.

We will see in Chapter 15 how a memory dump, or listing of the contents of main storage, can also be used to debug a program.

CHAPTER SUMMARY

I. Employ the following techniques to minimize errors.
   A. Plan a program thoroughly.
   B. Desk check it for data entry and logic errors.
   C. Perform structured walkthroughs, checking the logic with test data as you step through the program.

```
LOC    OBJECT CODE   ADDR1 ADDR2   STMT   SOURCE STATEMENT        DOS/VS ASSEMBLER REL 34.0  17.29      PAGE 2

                                     1     DEBUG   PRINT NOGEN
000000                               2     INFILE  START 0
                                     3             DTFCD BLKSIZE=80,RECFORM=FIXUNB,DEVADDR=SYSIPT,          X    HSKP
                                                         WORKA=YES,IOAREA1=BUFFKIN,EOFADDR=EOF,                  HSKP
                                    24     OUTFILE DTFPR BLKSIZE=132,DEVICE=1403,DEVADDR=SYSLST,IOAREA1=BUFFROUT,X  HSKP
                                                         PRINTOV=YES,WORKA=YES                                  HSKP
                                    45             CDMOD WORKA=YES                                             HSKP
                                   137             PRMOD WORKA=YES,CONTROL=YES,PRINTOV=YES                     HSKP
000068 05C0                        257     BEGIN   BALR 12,0                                                   HSKP
                                   258             USING *,12
                           0006A   259             OPEN  INFILE,OUTFILE
```

```
LOC    OBJECT CODE   COD2 COD3 COD4   ADDR1 ADDR2   STMT   SOURCE STATEMENT        DOS/VS ASSEMBLER REL 34.0  17.29      PAGE 3

00007E D283 COD2 COD3      0013D 0013C   269   READ   MVC   LINEOUT,SPACES
000084 925C COD3           0013D 0013D   270          MVC   LINEOUT,C'*'
000088 D282 COD4 COD3      0013E 0013D   271          MVC   LINEOUT+1(131),LINEOUT
                                         272                 PUT   OUTFILE,LINEOUT
                                         278          GET   INFILE,CARDIN
0000AE FA10 C1B6 C2F6      00220         284          AP    NOFLDS,=P'2'
0000B4 F224 C157 C166      001C1 00166   285          PACK  PFLDA,FLDA
0000BA F224 C15A C1B1      001C4 001D0   286          PACK  PFLDB,FLDB
0000C0 FA22 C160 C157      001CA 001C1   287          AP    TOTALA,PFLDA
0000C6 FA22 C160 C15A      001CA 001C4   288          AP    TOTALB,PFLDB
0000CC 47F0 C034           0009E         289          B     READ
0000D0 D283 C003 COD2      0013D 0013C   290   EOF    MVC   LINEOUT,SPACES
0000D6 FA22 C163 C15D      001CD 001C7   291          AP    SUM,TOTALA
0000DC D205 COF1 C150      001CD 00158   292          MVC   AOUT,PATTERN
0000E2 DE05 C0F1 C15B      001CD 00158   293          ED    AOUT,TOTALA
0000E8 FA22 C163 C160      001CD 001CA   294          AP    SUM,TOTALB
0000EE DE05 C101 C160      001CB 001CA   295          MVC   BOUT,PATTERN
0000F4 DE05 C101 C163      001CB 001CD   296          ED    BOUT,TOTALB
0000FA FC52 C1BB C163      00225 001CD   297          ZAP   SHIFT2LT,SUM
000100 FD51 C1BB C1B8      00225 00222   298          DP    SHIFT2LT,NOFLDS
000106 D208 C111 C1B6      00225 00220   299          MVC   AVERAGE,=X'40202020202148 2020'
00010C D208 C111 C1BB      0017B 00225   300          MVC   AVERAGE,SHIFT2LT
000112 DE08 C111 C1BB      0017B 00225   302          ED    OUTFILE,LINEOUT
                                         308                 PUT   OUTFILE,LINEOUT
                                         317   CLOSE  INFILE,OUTFILE
                                                      EOJ
```

Figure 10.10
Corrected sample program (continued on pages 321 and 322).

LOC	OBJECT CODE	STMT	SOURCE STATEMENT			
00013C	40	320	SPACES	DC	CL1' '	
00013D		321	LINEOUT	DS	CCL132	
00015B		322		DS	CL30	CORRECTION INCREASED FIELD SIZE
000161		323	AOUT	DS	CL6	
00016B		324		DS	CL10	CORRECTION INCREASED FIELD SIZE
000178		325	BOUT	DS	CL10	
000184		326		DS	CL9	
0001C1		327	AVERAGE	DS	CL61	
		328		DS	PL3	
		329	PFLDA	DS	PL3	
		330	PFLDB	DS	PL3	
0001C4	00000C	331	TOTALA	DC	X'00000C'	
0001C7	00000C	332	TOTALB	DC	FL3'0'	
0001CA	00000C	333	SUM	DC	FL3'0'	
0001CD		334	CARDIN	DS	CCL80	
0001D0		335	FLDA	DS	CL5	
0001D5		336		DS	CL70	
00021B		337	FLDB	DS	CL5	
000220	000C	338	NOFLDS	DC	FL2'0'	
000222	00100C	339	HUNDRED	DC	FL3'100'	
000225		340	SHIFTZLT	DS	FL6	
00022B	40202020202020	341	PATTERN	DC	X'402020202020'	

LOC	OBJECT CODE	ADDR1	ADDR2	STMT	SOURCE STATEMENT		
000231				343	BUFFRIN	DS	CL132
0002B5				344	BUFFROUT	DS	CL132
			00066	345		END	BEGIN
000340	5B5BC2D6D7C5D540			347			=C'$$BOPEN '
000348	5B5BC2C3D3D6E2C5			348			=C'$$BCLOSE'
000350	00000038			349			=A(OUTFILE)
000354	0000013D			350			=A(LINEOUT)
000358	00000000			351			=A(INFILE)
00035C	000001D0			352			=A(CARDIN)
000360	2C			353			=P'2'
000361	402020202021432020						=X'402020202021432020'

PAGE 4

DOS/VS ASSEMBLER REL 34.0 17.29

Figure 10.10 (continued)

PAGE 8

DIAGNOSTICS AND STATISTICS

NO ERRORS FOUND

THE FOLLOWING MACRO NAMES HAVE BEEN FOUND IN MACRO INSTRUCTIONS
DTFPR   CDMOD   PKMOD   OPEN   PUT   GET   CLOSE   EOJ

OPTIONS FOR THIS ASSEMBLY - ALIGN, LIST, XREF, LINK, NORLD, NODECK, NOEDECK

THE ASSEMBLER WAS RUN IN 65416 BYTES
END OF ASSEMBLY

EOP $3ASM
// EXEC LNKEDT

JOB INST   17.30.02 F-LE-E FAST-LINKAGE-EDITOR VM4.0   DOS/VS R34-0A GOAL SYSTEMS

ACTION TAKEN MAP CLEAR REL
LIST PHASE MONITOR,ROOT   LINK
LIST INCLUDE ILFFEXIT
LIST AUTOLINK IJDFAPZZ
LIST PHASE STDPGM,*
LIST ENTRY

PHASE-CSECT-ENTRY	LO-LNK	HI-LNK	LO-REL	HI-REL	LN-HEX	LN-DEC	XF-LNK	XF-REL	GOAL SYSTEMS
LINK PARTITION = F3	110000	169FFF	000000	059FFF	5A000	368,640	110078	000078	
ROOT MONITOR	110078	11051B	000000	0004A3	4A4	1,188	110078	000000	RELOCATABLE
ILFFEXIT	110078	1103F9	000000	000381	382	898			
*EXIT	1100F4	00007C							
IJDFAPZZ	110400	11051B	000388	0004A3	11C	284			
*IJDFAZZZ	110400		000388						
PHASE STDPGM	110520	1109B1	000000	000491	492	1,170	110588	000068	RELOCATABLE
DEBUG	110520	1108B9	000000	000369	36A	874			
IJCFZIWD	110890	110907	000370	0003E7	78	120			
IJDFCPZW	110908	1109B1	0003E8	000491	AA	170			
*IJDFZZZW	110908								
*IJDFZZZW	110908		0003E8						
*IJDFCZZW	110908		0003E8						

NORMAL COMPLETION, BLOCKS AVAIL = 334, USED IN EDIT = 4, PCIL=X'1C6', CYL=001, SERIAL=WORK01.

****
400   800   150.00

// EXEC
****

Figure 10.10 (continued)

D. Have programmer teams study the program and discuss its strengths and weaknesses.
II. Learn to understand common syntax errors, as listed by the assembly. These are called diagnostics.
III. Test the program with test data and compare the results you obtain manually with those the computer produces.
IV. Let the Location Counter and Symbol Cross Reference Table help you find where instructions and data are placed in storage. If you get a storage dump when an abend occurs, you can determine the actual contents of storage at the time of the interrupt.

CHAPTER SELF-EVALUATING QUIZ

1. Examine the partial assembly listing in Figure 10.11. Explain each of the errors.
2. Examine the assembly listing in Figure 10.12. Explain each of the errors. Note that when there is an error within a macro instruction, the particular instruction that is part of the macro is listed with a plus (+) sign next to the statement number.

SOLUTIONS

Statement Number	Explanation of Error	Page
46	NEXT-10 is an invalid label because of the hyphen.	12
54	There is a space after the comma.	12
55	The immediate data should be defined with a C for character, not an X.	113
61	NEXT-10 is an invalid label because of the hyphen.	12
69	SALARY should be defined as a DS. With a DC operation code, the assembler expects to find a constant defined in the operand. CL5 is not a valid operand for a DC.	59

Statement Number	Explanation of Error	
17	The error is in the OPEN macro (+ sign next to statement number). There is no DCB defined for OUTFILE. (Note that a DCB labeled PRTFILE appears in the program, but it is not referenced.)	300
21	The error is in the GET macro (+ sign next to statement number). CARDFILE is not described by a DCB. (Note that a DCB labeled INFILE appears in the program, but it is not referenced.)	300
25	LAST is not defined. Notice that RECORD is defined by DS 0CL80. The first 0 indicates that RECORD will be subdivided into fields. However, this was not done.	53
26	FIRST is not defined. (Same explanation as for statement 25.)	53
27	SALARY is not defined. (Same explanation as for statement 25.)	53
29	The error is in the PUT macro (+ sign next to statement number). There is no DCB for OUTFILE.	300
33	READRTN is not defined as a label or name of any instruction to which a branch can be made. (Notice that there is a label READ at the beginning of the loop.)	304
37	The error is in the CLOSE macro (+ sign next to statement number.) There is no DCB for OUTFILE.	300
51, 52, and 54	The errors are in the DCB macro. The continuation character was omitted on the first line of the DCB. The assembler thus interpreted the second line to be an independent instruction with an invalid operation code. It therefore indicated that the required operand DSORG was omitted from the first line of the DCB, because it did not treat the second line as a continuation.	72

```
LOC    OBJECT CODE      ADDR1 ADDR2  STMT  SOURCE STATEMENT

000080 D283 C102 C101   00108 00107   46 NEXT-10  MVC  OUTAREA,SPACES          SAM00230
       *** ERROR ***
000086                                47          GET  INFILE,RECORD           SAM00240
000094 D20E C107 C0B6   0010D 000BC   52          MVC  LNAME,LAST              SAM00250
00009A D209 C12A C0C5   00130 000CB   53          MVC  FNAME,FIRST             SAM00260
0000A0 0000 0000 0000   00000 00000   54          MVC  SALOUT, SALARY         SAM00270
       *** ERROR ***
0000A6 0000 0000        00000         55          MVI  SALOUT-1,X'$'          SAM00280
       *** ERROR ***
0000AA                                56          PUT  OUTFILE,OUTAREA        SAM00290
0000BB 0000 0000        00000         61          B    NEXT-10                SAM00300
       *** ERROR ***

0000BC                                66 RECORD   DS   0CL80      CARD FORMAT  SAM00350
0000BC                                67 LAST     DS   CL15            *        SAM00360
0000CB                                68 FIRST    DS   CL10            *        SAM00370
                                      69 SALARY   DC   CL5             *        SAM00380
       *** ERROR ***
0000D5                                70 SPACES   DS   CL50                     SAM00390
000107 40                             71          DC   CL1' '                   SAM00400
000108                                72 OUTAREA  DS   0CL132     PRINT FORMAT  SAM00410
000108                                73          DS   CL5             *        SAM00420
00010D                                74 LNAME    DS   CL15            *        SAM00430
00011C                                75          DS   CL20            *        SAM00440
000130                                76 FNAME    DS   CL10            *        SAM00450
00013A                                77          DS   CL20            *        SAM00460
00014E                                78 SALOUT   DS   CL5             *        SAM00470
000153                                79 BLANK    DS   CL57            *        SAM00480
```

Figure 10.11
Partial assembly listing for Question 1.

```
LOC    OBJECT CODE       ADDR1 ADDR2  STMT   SOURCE STATEMENT

                                        8  *                                                                    SAM00080
                                        9  *            HOUSEKEEPING INSTRUCTIONS GO HERE      *                 SAM00090
                                       10  *                                                  *                 SAM00100
00000E 000000                          11     OPEN  (INFILE,INPUT,OUTFILE,OUTPUT)                                SAM00110
000019 000000                          17+    DC    AL3(OUTFILE)              DCB ADDRESS
       *** ERROR ***
00001E D283 C057 C056 0005D 0005C      19  READ  MVC  OUTAREA,SPACES                                            SAM00120
000024 0000 0000                       20  GET        CARDFILE,RECORD                                           SAM00130
000024 0000 0000         00000         21+    LA    1,CARDFILE                LOAD PARAMETER REG 1
       *** ERROR ***
000032 0000 0000 0000 00000 00000      25     MVC   LNAME,LAST                                                  SAM00140
       *** ERROR ***
000038 0000 0000 0000 00000 00000      26     MVC   FNAME,FIRST                                                 SAM00150
       *** ERROR ***
00003E 0000 0000 0000 00000 00000      27     MVC   SALOUT,SALARY                                               SAM00160
       *** ERROR ***
000044                                 28     PUT   OUTFILE,OUTAREA                                             SAM00170
000044 0000 0000       00000           29+    LA    1,OUTFILE                 LOAD PARAMETER REG 1
       *** ERROR ***
000052 0000 0000                       33     B     READRTN                                                     SAM00180
       *** ERROR ***
000056                                 34  EOF  CLOSE  (INFILE,OUTFILE)                                         SAM00190
                                       37+12,*** IHB002  INVALID OPTION OPERAND SPECIFIED-OUTFILE
       *** MNOTE ***
                                       38  *
00005C                                 39  RECORD     DS  0CL80                                                 SAM00200
00005C 40                              40  SPACES     DC  CL1' '                                                SAM00210
00005D                                 41  OUTAREA    DS  0CL132                                                SAM00220
00005D                                 42             DS  CL5                                                   SAM00230
000062                                 43  LNAME      DS  CL15                                                  SAM00240
000071                                 44             DS  CL20                                                  SAM00250
000085                                 45  FNAME      DS  CL10                                                  SAM00260
00008F                                 46             DS  CL20                                                  SAM00270
0000A3                                 47  SALOUT     DS  CL5                                                    SAM00280
0000A8                                 48  BLANK      DS  CL50                                                   SAM00290
0000DC                                 49  SAVEAREA   DS  18F                                                   SAM00300
                                       50  INFILE     DCB DDNAME=INFILE,MACRF=GM,BLKSIZE=80,                    SAM00310
                                       51+12,*** IHB052  DSORG OMITTED
                                       52+12,*** IHB066  INCONSISTENT OPERAND                                   SAM00320
       *** MNOTE ***
       *** MNOTE ***
                                       54     LRECL=80,DSORG=FS,EODAD=EOF                                       SAM00330
000124                                 55  PRTFILE    DCB DDNAME=OUTFILE,MACRF=PM,BLKSIZE=132,LRECL=132,DSORG=FS  SAM00340
       *** ERROR ***
000124                                109     END
```

Figure 10.12
Assembly listing for Question 2.

KEY TERMS

Addressable location

Assembler

Assembly

Base register

Bit

Byte

CSECT

Debugging

Desk check

Displacement

Effective address

END statement

Instruction formats

Location counter

Memory

Mnemonic

Multiprogramming

Object module

Object program

PRINT NOGEN

Relocatability

Source program

Structured walkthrough

Symbol cross-reference table

Symbolic address

REVIEW QUESTIONS

1. Define and describe some of the planning tools used before a program is coded.

2. A(n) _____ is a procedure in which the programmer manually steps through the logic of a program with sample data to ensure correct results.

3. The _____ program translates source programs into _____ programs.

4. Define and describe the three types of output resulting from a translation process.

5. Define and describe the two types of errors that a program may have.

6. Each storage location in memory is called a(n) _____ .

7. Each storage location represents data using eight _____ , which is an abbreviation for _____ _____ .

8. A relative address ranges from 000–FFF in hexadecimal, which is 0 to (no.) in decimal. This relative address indicates how far from the starting point of a program a particular instruction is located. This distance is referred to as the _____ .

9. The _____ is a general register from 2 to 12 assigned by the programmer to contain the actual starting point of a program.

10. When the contents of the base register are added to the displacement, a(n) _____ address is obtained.

11. Indicate why the base and displacement concepts are used in programming.

12. Define and describe the following elements:
    a. Location counter
    b. Symbol cross-reference table

13. The _____ statement suppresses macro-generated instructions. The use of this statement makes the listing easier to read.

14. After the END statement, a group of entries listed with an equal sign within the operand typically appears on the source listing. These entries are referred to as the _____ .

15. Define and describe the linkage editor program.

Define and describe the following types of errors (Questions 16–18):

16. Data exception

17. Decimal overflow

18. Specification error

19. What is an abend?

20. (T or F) If a program has no syntax errors, then it will always run properly.

UNIT 4

REGISTERS AND BINARY OPERATIONS

Binary Operations Using RX-Format Instructions

	To familiarize you with:
OBJECTIVES	1. Registers.
	2. RX instructions.
	3. Procedures used in converting data from decimal to binary, and from binary to decimal.
	4. Boundary alignment.

In this section we will discuss operations that maximize efficient use of the computer.

Instructions operating on *binary* data are among the most efficient operations that a computer can perform. If a number is stored in decimal or hexadecimal form, it takes longer to execute an arithmetic operation using that number than if the data were stored in binary form.

Thus, to reduce the time required to perform calculations we operate on data in binary form. The use of the **general purpose registers** in arithmetic operations thereby maximizes the efficient use of the computer. But, general registers can be used in arithmetic operations only if data is entered in **binary form.**

I. GENERAL PURPOSE REGISTERS

A. An Overview

You will recall that there are 16 general-purpose registers, numbered 0–15. As a general rule only registers 2–12 should be used for arithmetic, because the other registers are used for special purposes.   *2 – 11   12 is base register*

1. General registers may be used as *accumulators* in add, subtract, multiply, and divide operations.
2. General registers may also be used as index registers.

    An **index register** is frequently used for processing tables and arrays, and in performing matrix operations. The index register contains an address that is modified during execution of the program. Therefore, data such as a tax table may be stored in consecutive locations of primary storage. By modifying the contents (or address) of the index register, the programmer can "look up" any desired tax schedule contained in the table. The use of index registers will be discussed in depth in Chapter 16.
3. General registers may be used for looping. Looping can be performed most efficiently through the use of registers, and is essential for handling repetitive information-processing operations. Scientific and mathematical problems often involve repetitive or *iterative* computational techniques as well.

The efficient programmer uses registers whenever possible to avoid the more time-consuming operations needed to manipulate data in primary storage.

B. Representing Data in Binary Form in Registers: A Review

Registers are each four-bytes or one **fullword** in length. Data is represented in registers in *binary* form. This is referred to as **fixed-point data.** The high-order **bit** of a 32-bit register (eight bits per byte × four bytes) is used for a sign bit: 0 for + and 1 for −. There are thus 31 bits that can be used to represent a number. The 32 bits of a general register are assigned values as in the following illustration, where S denotes the sign bit.

Positional value	S	2^{30}	......	2^2 2^1 2^0
Bits	0	1	......	31

For example, the number represented when the rightmost three bits are on is $+7$. That is, $7 = (4 + 2 + 1)$, or $2^3 - 1$. Similarly, the largest number that can be represented in a general register is $2^{31} - 1 = 2,147,483,647$. The smallest number that can be stored is $-(2^{31} - 1)$. Keep in mind that a register containing all 1s has the value -1 because negative numbers are stored as complements.

Example 11.1 $+5$ in a general register would be represented as follows.

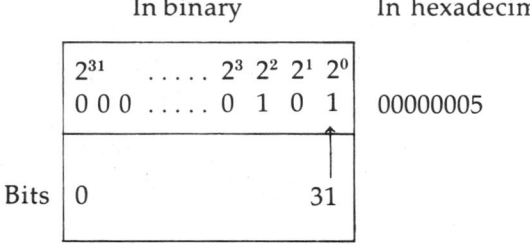

Example 11.2 -5 in a general register would be represented as follows.

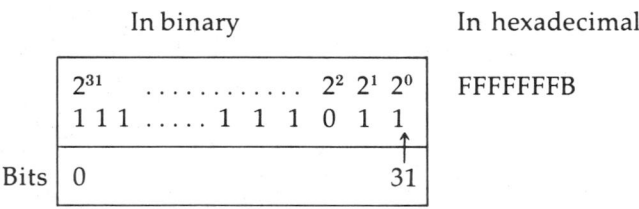

Recall that a negative number in binary is represented in *complement* form. To represent -5 in binary, we do the following.

1. Represent the number as a positive value.

    0000 0101
    ⏟ 32 bits

2. Complement the number. A 1 in the high-order bit position designates the field as negative. (A 0 designates the field as positive.)

    1111 1010
    ⏟ 32 bits

3. Add 1 to the result.

    1111 1011
    ⏟ 32 bits

To represent the number in hexadecimal, we group 4 consecutive bits together.

    1111   ....   1111 1011
      F F F F F F   F   B

REVIEW OF REGISTERS

1. Registers can function as accumulators.
2. A general purpose register may be used as an index register.
3. There are 16 general purpose registers, each 4 bytes (one fullword) in length.
4. Registers are numbered 0–15. Note, however, that the programmer is usually restricted to the use of registers 2–12 for arithmetic.
5. Data is represented in registers in *binary* form. This is referred to as fixed-point data. The leftmost or high-order bit is interpreted as an algebraic sign. For positive numbers, the sign bit is off (containing the digit 0).
6. Negative numbers are identified by the sign bit being on (containing the digit 1), and negative numbers are stored in *complement* form.
7. Arithmetic is performed 2–4 times faster in registers than in storage locations, depending upon the computer.
8. The largest positive and negative decimal numbers that can be stored in a fullword are $+2,147,483,647$ (decimal) and $-2,147,483,648$.

Self-Evaluating Quiz

1. Data is represented in registers in _____ form.
2. The general purpose registers are numbered (**no.**) through (**no.**).
3. The number of binary digits, including the sign, which can be used for storing a number in a register is _____ .
4. A 1 in the high-order position of a register identifies the number as (**positive, negative**).
5. A 0 in the high-order position of a register identifies the number as (**positive, negative**).
6. (T or F) The number 2 is a valid high-order digit in a register.
7. (T or F) Arithmetic operations can be performed more efficiently using general purpose registers.
8. (T or F) A general purpose register can be used as an index for table look-up operations.
9. Each register is (**no.**) bytes in length.
10. (T or F) 32 bits are equal to one fullword.

Questions 11–17 are designed to review binary and hexadecimal numbers that were discussed in Chapter 2.

11. $(1011001)_2 = (?)_{10}$
12. $(10A7)_{16} = (?)_{10}$
13. $(121)_{10} = (?)_2$
14. $(121)_{10} = (?)_{16}$
15. How is -6 represented in two bytes in binary?
16. How is $+7$ represented in two bytes in binary?
17. The following binary number is located in two bytes.

00000000	11111001
First byte	Second byte

    a. What is the number in base 10?
    b. What is the number in hexadecimal notation?

SOLUTIONS

1. Binary
2. 0–15
3. 32
4. Negative
5. Positive

6. F: 0 or 1 only
7. T
8. T
9. 4
10. T
11. 89 (1 + 8 + 16 + 64)
12. 4263 (1 × 7 + 10 × 16 + 1 × 4096)
13. 1111001
14. 79 (Four binary digits are grouped to form one hexadecimal digit: $[0111\ 1001]_2 =$ $[79]_{16}$. Notice that a high-order zero was added to make a group of four digits.)
15. 11111111   11111010
First byte   Second byte

   Two bytes consist of 16 bits (binary digits). Negative numbers are represented in binary in two's complement form. The following three steps illustrate the conversion process.

   1. Represent the number as a positive value.

      00000000   00000110
      First byte   Second byte

   2. Complement the number. Recall that a 1 in the high-order bit position designates the field as negative.

      11111111   11111001
      First byte   Second byte

   3. Add 1 to the result.

      11111111   11111010
      First byte   Second byte

16. 00000000   00000111
First byte   Second byte

   Recall that a 0 in the high-order bit position designates the field as positive.
17. a. +249 (High-order bit position is 0; therefore the number is positive.)
    b. +00F9

There are two classes of instructions that use registers.

Instructions That Use Registers

Type	Meaning	Type of Operands
RX	Register and indexed storage	One operand = register One operand = storage (+ indexing, only if applicable[a])
RR	Register-to-register	Both operands are registers

[a]Indexing will be discussed in Chapter 16.

In this chapter, we will discuss the basic RX instructions. The RR instructions will be presented in the next chapter.

II. REGISTER AND INDEXED STORAGE (RX) INSTRUCTIONS

A. An Overview

RX instructions perform operations using both registers and storage locations. Initially, we will assume that indexing is not performed.

The operands used with RX-format instructions must be fixed length, either on a halfword, fullword, or doubleword boundary. The data in storage, as well as the data in the registers, must be in *binary* form.

B. F , H , and D **Formats for Data in Storage**

You will recall that by assigning F for **fullword,** H for **halfword,** or D for **doubleword** to a DC or Define Constant statement, data will be entered into the field in binary form. A constant assigned, as follows

LABEL	OPERATION 10 16	OPERAND	COMMENTS	72
AMT	DC	F'Ø'		

assures that the result, which appears in AMT, is in binary form.

Using RX instructions, the address of the storage locations used as operands should begin on fullword, halfword, or sometimes doubleword boundaries. This **boundary alignment** is automatically assured when the F , H or D formats, respectively, are used in Define Constant (DC) and Define Storage (DS) statements.

In short, F , H , or D are used as field specifications for constants or work areas to be employed with RX instructions. If data to be operated on is entered as input and is in zoned-decimal or packed form, it must *first* be converted to binary form before an RX instruction can be executed.

SUMMARY

1. RX operations use operands of fixed length, which are:
   a. Fullword
   b. Halfword
      or
   c. Doubleword
2. The data in storage must be in binary format.
3. Fullword, halfword, or doubleword boundary alignment is necessary, and will be automatically maintained by the assembler.

C. Examples of RX Instructions

1. Load Instruction

The general format for the Load instruction is:

Operation 10	Operand 16
L	REG ,OPERAND

Instruction:	Load
Op code:	L
Operand 1:	Register (2–12)
Operand 2:	Four-byte storage area or self-defining fullword operand containing binary data
Purpose:	Data transmitted from storage to register
Limitations:	Operand 2 should be on a fullword boundary

The movement of data from a storage location to a register is called *loading.* The purpose of the load instruction is to provide the register with an initial value where necessary, and it is similar to the MVC instruction for character moves. The MVC instruction moves zoned-decimal data between storage locations; the load instruction moves four bytes of binary data from storage to a register.

The receiving field is the general purpose register identified in the first operand. Its contents change as a result of this instruction. The sending field is a fullword in storage and its contents do not change. An example of this instruction follows.

```
        L     8,NUMBER
              :
              :
NUMBER  DC    F'121'
```

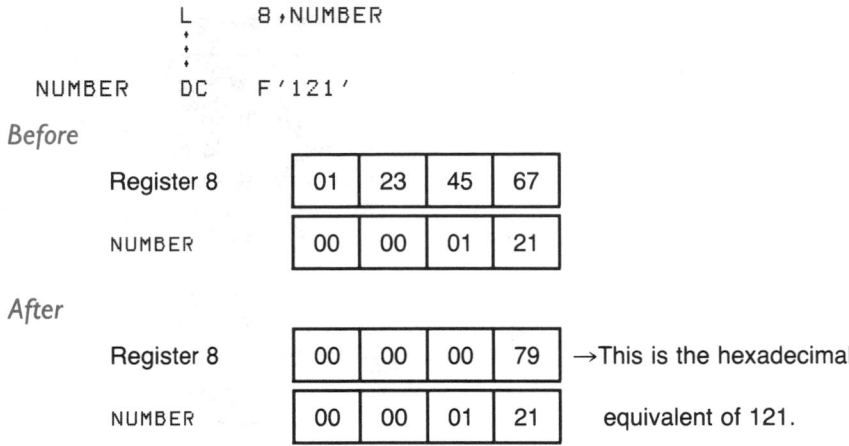

Before

Register 8

| 01 | 23 | 45 | 67 |

NUMBER

| 00 | 00 | 01 | 21 |

After

Register 8

| 00 | 00 | 00 | 79 | →This is the hexadecimal

NUMBER

| 00 | 00 | 01 | 21 | equivalent of 121.

In actuality, the number in register 8 is in a *binary* format. Internally, register 8 has the following bit configuration that represents the number 121:

00 . . . 001111001
⎵⎵⎵⎵⎵⎵⎵⎵⎵⎵⎵
  32 bits

Note that in storage dumps, the contents of a register are displayed as *8 hexadecimal digits*, because 4 binary digits are grouped together to form one hexadecimal digit. We will use 8 digits to represent the contents of registers, but these 8 digits from now on will be shown in *decimal* form rather than hexadecimal form. This approach is intended to simplify the illustrations and to make the results of the various operations easier to understand. Note, however, that when you debug an actual program and locate the contents of general registers, the contents will be displayed hexadecimally.[1] Register 8 would therefore contain | 00 | 00 | 00 | 79 | in hexadecimal, which simply is another means of representing decimal 121.

The load instruction can also be used with a self-defining operand or literal as follows:

LABEL	OPERATION		OPERAND	COMMENTS	
1	10	16			72
	L		8,=F'121'		

This instruction will produce the same results as the previous example.

The examples below illustrate what happens when the following instruction is used.

---

[1]The illustrations in this chapter demonstrate how instructions operate on data. For ease of reading, we have represented all numbers in decimal form. Some students, however, may have difficulty with the hexadecimal and/or binary representation of numbers. We have, therefore, included in the self-evaluating questions at the end of each unit, problems that illustrate and test the student's ability to understand instructions that operate on data in hexadecimal or binary form.

LABEL	OPERATION	OPERAND	COMMENTS	
1	10 16			72
	L	8,FULLWORD		

Register 8 Before Execution	Contents of FULLWORD	Register 8 After Execution	
	(decimal)	(decimal)	(binary)
+12 34 56 78	+00 00 01 51	+00 00 01 51	0 . . . 010010111
+12 34 56 78	−00 00 00 25	00 00 00 25	1 100111
+12 34 56 78	+00 00 00 50	+00 00 00 50	0 0110010

2. Store Instruction

The general format for a Store instruction is:

Operation 10	Operand 16
ST	REG,OPERAND

Instruction:	Store
Op code:	ST
Operand 1:	Register 2–12
Operand 2:	Storage area
Explanation:	Four bytes of binary data (fullword) transmitted from register to storage
	Note Movement is from the *first* operand to second operand
Limitations:	Operand 2 should be on a fullword boundary

The Store instruction produces the opposite results of the Load instruction. That is, the purpose of the Store instruction is to *move* data *from* a general purpose register to main storage. The entire contents of a register are moved into four bytes, that is, a fullword of main storage. The Store instruction is different from most instructions thus far encountered in that the *first* operand is the *sending* field, while the *second* operand is the *receiving* field. The first operand is a register, and the second operand is an area in storage that should be defined on a fullword boundary with specification F.

The register is the sending field and its contents *remain the same*. The storage location is the receiving field and its contents change. The operation of this instruction is shown in the following illustration.

```
          ST    8,NUMBER
                .
                .
                .
NUMBER    DS    F
```

Before Execution[2]   *After Execution*

Register 8	+00 00 01 21	Register 8		+00 00 01 21
NUMBER	+12 34 56 78	NUMBER	decimal	+00 00 01 21
			binary	00 . . . 01111001

[2]These contents are given in decimal form for purposes of clarification only.

Here are other examples using the ST instruction.

INSTRUCTION	Contents of Register 8	Contents of NUMBER Before Execution	Contents of NUMBER After Execution
ST 8,NUMBER	+00 00 00 03	+12 34 56 78	+00 00 00 03
	−00 00 04 00	+12 34 56 78	−00 00 04 00
	+05 00 00 00	+12 34 56 78	+05 00 00 00

Errors That May Occur with RX Instructions

1. If the actual address of Operand 2 is not a multiple of four (that is, not on a fullword boundary), a *specification exception* occurs.
2. If the actual address of Operand 2 is greater than any existing address for the computer, an *addressing exception* will occur.
3. If Operand 2 references an existing address, but is not within the area reserved for the program, a *protection error* occurs.

Self-Evaluating Quiz

1. In an RX instruction, the first operand refers to a(n) _____ and the second operand refers to a(n) _____ .
2. The data in both operands of an RX instruction must be in _____ form.
3. The instruction TOTAL DC F'0' establishes a field that is **(no.)** bytes long and that contains **(type)** data.
4. (T or F) Boundary requirements should be maintained when using an RX instruction.
5. (T or F) The use of an F or H format in Define Constant statements automatically assures proper boundary fullword and halfword alignment respectively.
6. The purpose of a Load (L) instruction is to _____ .
7. The Load (L) instruction moves **(no.)** bytes from storage to a register.
8. In a Load instruction, the first operand is the **(sending/receiving)** field while the second operand is the **(sending/receiving)** field.
9. The purpose of a Store (ST) instruction is to _____ .
10. In a Store instruction, the first operand is the **(sending/receiving)** field, whereas the second operand is the **(sending/receiving)** field.
11. (T or F) The contents of the first operand in a Load instruction remain unchanged after execution.
12. (T or F) The contents of the first operand in a Store instruction remain unchanged after execution.
13. Write an instruction to move the value 1234 into register 3.
14. Write an instruction to move the contents of register 8 into a field called STORE.

SOLUTIONS

1. Register; storage location
2. Binary
3. 4; binary
4. T
5. T
6. Provide a register with an initial value
7. 4
8. Receiving; sending
9. Move data from a register to storage
10. Sending; receiving
11. F: (The first operand, a register, is the *receiving* field)
12. T: (The first operand, a register, is the *sending* field)
13. L 3,=F'1234'
14. ST 8,STORE

3. Add Instruction: RX Format

The general format for the RX Add instruction is:

Operation 10	Operand 16
A	REG,OPERAND

Instruction:	Add
Op code:	A
Operand 1:	General register 2–12.
Operand 2:	Four-byte storage area or self-defining fullword operand containing binary data.
Explanation:	Binary contents of second operand added to contents of general register.
Limitation:	Operand 2 should be aligned on a fullword boundary.

The purpose of this Add instruction is to add the contents of a four-byte field (fullword) in storage to the contents of a general purpose register (2–12). As usual, the contents of the first operand are destroyed while the contents of the second operand remain the same. A sample instruction would appear as follows.

```
        A    8,TEN
        .
        .
TEN     DC   F'10'
```

Before Execution[3]   *After Execution*

	Decimal		*Decimal*	*Binary*
Register 8	+00 00 01 21	Register 8	+00 00 01 31	0 . . . 10000011
TEN	+00 00 00 10	TEN	+00 00 00 10	

The above could also be accomplished using a self-defining operand in the instruction:

LABEL	OPERATION 10 16	OPERAND	COMMENTS 72
	A	8,=F'10'	

Other examples of how the RX Add instruction operates include:

Instruction	Register 8 Before Execution	Contents of NO	Register 8 After Execution
A 8,NO	+00 00 56 78	+00 00 00 78	+00 00 57 56
	+00 00 00 75	+00 00 01 00	+00 00 01 75
	−00 00 01 25	+00 00 01 25	+00 00 00 00
	−00 00 02 50	−00 00 03 00	−00 00 05 50
	+00 00 07 85	−00 00 00 15	+00 00 07 70

[3]The contents are given in decimal form for purposes of clarification only.

4. Subtract Instruction: RX Format

The general format of the RX Subtract instruction appears as follows.

General Format

Operation 10	Operand 16
S	REG,OPERAND

where

S	denotes the arithmetic subtraction operation.
Register	is a number that refers to a general register (2–12).
Operand 2	is either the name of a 4-byte fullword storage location containing binary data or a self-defining binary operand.

Instruction:	Subtract
Op code:	S
Operand 1:	General register 2–12.
Operand 2:	Four-byte storage area or self-defining fullword operand containing binary data.
Explanation:	Contents of second operand are subtracted from first operand.
Limitation:	Second operand should be aligned on a fullword boundary.

The subtract instruction functions in a manner similar to the add instruction. However, it subtracts the contents of a four-byte (fullword) field in storage from the contents of a register. This instruction might appear as follows.

```
       S    8,NO
        .
        .
        .
NO     DC   F'20'
```

Before Execution[4]   *After Execution*

	Decimal		*Decimal*	*Binary*
Register 8	+00 00 02 70	Register 8	+00 00 02 50	0 . . . 011111010
NO	+00 00 00 20	NO	+00 00 00 20	

The instruction could also be written with a self-defining operand, as follows.

LABEL 1	OPERATION 10 16	OPERAND	COMMENTS 72
	S	8,=F'20'	

Other examples of the RX-type subtraction include:

Instruction	Register 8 Before Execution	Contents of NO	Register 8 After Execution
S 8,NO	+00 00 56 78	+00 00 00 78	+00 00 56 00
	+00 00 00 75	+00 00 01 00	−00 00 00 25
	−00 00 01 25	+00 00 01 25	−00 00 02 50
	−00 00 02 50	−00 00 03 00	+00 00 00 50
	+00 00 07 85	−00 00 00 15	+00 00 08 00

[4]The contents are given in decimal form for purposes of clarification only.

Self-Evaluating Quiz

1. Write a series of instructions to clear register 4, add AMT1 and AMT2 in register 4, and place the answer in a field called TOTAL. Assume all fields have been defined properly and that AMT1 and AMT2 are in binary form.

2. Write a series of instructions to subtract AMT3 from AMT4 and place the answer in DIFF. Use registers and assume all fields have been established properly and that AMT3 and AMT4 are in binary form.

3. Write a routine, using registers, to add AMT1 and AMT2, and to subtract AMT3, where AMT1, AMT2, and AMT3 have been defined as follows:

```
AMT1    DC    F'1234'
AMT2    DC    F'2680'
AMT3    DC    F'2222'
```

4. Redo Question 3 adding an instruction that will place the results in a field called HOLD.

5. In place of

```
L     4,AMT1
```

in Question 3, would the following serve just as well?

```
A     4,AMT1
```

6. Write another statement or series of statements to accomplish:

```
L     4,AMT1
```

7. Most instructions place results in the **(first/second)** operand. An exception to this is the _____ instruction.

8. After the following instructions are executed, what are the contents of registers 5 and 6? Show the results in binary as well as hexadecimal form.

```
L     6,=F'10'
L     5,=F'0'
A     5,=F'125'
S     6,=F'16'
```

SOLUTIONS

1.
```
    L     4,=F'0'
    A     4,AMT1
    A     4,AMT2
    ST    4,TOTAL
```

2.
```
    L     4,AMT4
    S     4,AMT3
    ST    4,DIFF
```

3.
```
    L     4,AMT1
    A     4,AMT2
    S     4,AMT3
```

4.
```
          ST    4,HOLD
    HOLD  DC    F
```

5. No; the add will not clear out the original contents of the register.

6.
```
    L     4,=F'0'
    A     4,AMT1
```

7. First; Store (ST)

8. Register 5:

$$\underbrace{0000 \ldots 01111101}_{\text{32 bits}} \qquad (0000007D)_{16} \qquad (125_{10})$$

Register 6:

$$\underbrace{1111 \ldots 11111010}_{\text{32 bits}} \qquad (FFFFFFFA)_{16} \qquad (-6)_{10}$$

5. Converting Input Data to Binary

You will recall that data must be in binary form to be operated upon in a register. The instruction that converts packed data into binary form has the following format.[5]

Operation 10	Operand 16
CVB	REG,OPERAND

Instruction:	Convert to binary.
Op code:	CVB
Operand 1:	Register 2–12 (receiving field).
Operand 2:	Storage location (sending field) 8 bytes long (doubleword).
Explanation:	Contents of doubleword packed data is converted to binary form and placed in general register.
Limitation:	Operand 2 should be on a doubleword boundary.

As we have seen, to use registers for calculations, the data must be in a binary format. Input data entered in the conventional zoned-decimal format must be converted to binary in two steps.

1. Pack the data in a doubleword.
2. Convert the packed-decimal data to binary and load in a register.

You are already familiar with the PACK instruction. The *ConVert to Binary* (CVB) is used to convert a **doubleword** of packed-decimal data to binary form and to store the results in a register.

A doubleword of packed-decimal data in the second operand is converted into a 32-bit binary number in the register specified as the first operand. If the contents of the packed field are positive, the sign of the binary result will be positive (high-order bit = 0). When the contents of the packed field are negative, the binary result will be negative (high-order bit = 1).

An example follows in which a zoned-decimal AMT field is packed and then converted to binary.

```
            PACK    AMTIN,AMT
            CVB     9,AMTIN
            .
            .
RECORD      DS      0CL80
AMT         DS      CL4
            DS      CL76
*
AMTIN       DS      D
```

---

[5]See Appendix K for the XDECI instruction that can be used with ASSIST assemblers.

Before Execution (PACK)   *After Execution* (PACK)

```
AMTIN  00 00 00 00 00 00 00 00      AMTIN  00 00 00 00 00 00 09 8C
AMT    F0 F0 F9 C8                  AMT    F0 F0 F9 C8
```

Before Execution[6] (CVB)   *After Execution* (CVB)

		Decimal	Binary
Register 9	+ 12 34 56 78	Register 9 + 00 00 00 98	0 . . . 01100010

```
AMTIN 00 00 00 00 00 00 09 8C     AMTIN 00 00 00 00 00 00 09 8C
```

Note the actual contents of register 9 are represented in binary, which in turn are displayed in hexadecimal when a storage dump occurs. Therefore, the 98 in decimal would appear as 62 in hexadecimal. In the following examples, assume AMTIN is already in packed form.

Instruction	Register 9 After Execution	AMTIN (Packed Decimal)
CVB 9,AMTIN	00 00 98 76	00 00 00 00 00 09 87 6C
	−00 00 01 51	00 00 00 00 00 00 15 1D
	00 00 00 00	00 00 00 00 00 00 00 0C
	01 23 45 67	00 00 00 00 12 34 56 7C

The largest number that can be converted is the maximum number that a register may hold (2,147,483,647). The storage location used with the CVB instruction should begin on a doubleword boundary. You will recall that we can define a doubleword with a D.

SUMMARIZING THE CVB INSTRUCTION

1. The CVB instruction converts a doubleword of packed-decimal data into binary and stores it in a register.
2. The second operand should contain packed-decimal data and be aligned on a doubleword boundary.
3. Invalid data in the second operand causes a data exception.
4. The first operand must be a register, and receives the converted data in binary form.
5. The magnitude of the numbers that may be converted is restricted to that of a 32-bit register: −2,147,483,648 to +2,147,483,647.

---

6. Converting Binary Data to Decimal

Fields that have been operated on in registers must be converted from binary to decimal, particularly if we wish to print them.

a. Format   The general format of the convert-to-decimal instruction follows.[7]

Operation 10	Operand 16
CVD	REG,OPERAND

---

[6]The contents are given in decimal form for purposes of clarification only.

[7]See Appendix K for the XDECO instruction that can be used with ASSIST assemblers.

where

CVD	instructs the computer to convert to decimal.
Operand 1	is a register (sending field) containing binary data.
Operand 2	is an 8-byte storage location on a doubleword boundary.

Instruction:	Convert to decimal.
Op code:	CVD
Operand 1:	Register 2–12 (sending field).
Operand 2:	Storage location (receiving field 8 bytes long).
Explanation:	Binary contents of register converted to decimal form and placed in doubleword storage location.
Limitation:	Operand 2 should be on a doubleword boundary.

Note
Operand 1 (register) is the sending field and Operand 2 (storage) is the receiving field.

The purpose of this instruction is to convert the binary contents of a register to packed-decimal format and place the result in a storage location.

This is necessary because binary data must first be converted to packed decimal, and then either unpacked or edited (ED) before the result can be printed. As with the *Store instruction*, the first operand of the convert-to-decimal (CVD) instruction is the *sending field* (register) and the second operand is the *receiving field* (storage location). The storage location should be a *doubleword* boundary or else a specification exception error may cause a program interrupt. If the contents of the register are positive, the sign bits of the resulting packed field will contain a hex C. If the contents of the register are negative, the sign bits will contain a hex D.

Example 11.3

LABEL	OPERATION	OPERAND	COMMENTS
1	10 16		72
	CVD	8,ANS	

Before Execution[8]

	Decimal	Binary
Register 8	00 00 07 89	0 . . . 01100010101
ANS	12 34 56 78 12 34 56 78	

After Execution

Register 8	00 00 07 89
ANS	00 00 00 00 00 00 78 9C
	(ANS in packed-decimal format)

After execution, register 8 will remain unchanged and ANS will contain the packed-decimal equivalent. The sign supplied in the packed field is a hex C. If the high-order bit of the register is 0, then C is the sign generated; if the high-order bit of the register is 1, then D is the sign generated. A few additional examples will clarify this concept.

---

[8]The contents are given in decimal form for purposes of clarification only.

Instruction	Register 8 (Binary)	ANS After Execution (Packed Decimal)
CVD 8,ANS	+00 00 98 76	00 00 00 00 00 09 87 6C
	−00 00 01 51	00 00 00 00 00 00 15 1D
	+00 00 00 00	00 00 00 00 00 00 00 0C
	−01 23 45 67	00 00 00 00 12 34 56 7D

ANS can be defined as a doubleword with the following instruction:

LABEL	OPERATION	OPERAND	COMMENTS
1	10 16		72
ANS	DS	D	

This will define ANS as an eight-byte area in storage and will align it on a doubleword boundary.

b. Printing Results   The following program excerpt allows us to print the results instead of simply storing the data in ANS. Note that ANS contains 15 decimal digits, and we are assuming that it is signed positive.

```
        CVD  9,ANS
        MVC  LINEOUT,SPACES
        MVC  LINEOUT+5(16),=X'402020202020202020202020202020'
        ED   LINEOUT+5(16),ANS
        PUT  OUTFILE,LINEOUT
          .
          .
          .
ANS     DS   D
SPACES  DC   C' '
LINEOUT DS   CL133
```

There are many times when we use RX format instructions to operate on data in registers and we know that the high-order bytes of the doubleword will be zero. If, for example, registers are used to perform arithmetic operations on 4-, 5-, or even 6-digit positive numbers, we can be reasonably certain that the result in ANS, when converted back to decimal, has zeros in the 4 high-order bytes. In such cases, the following coding may be used to edit the results.

```
        CVD  9,ANS
        MVC  LINEOUT,SPACES
        MVC  LINEOUT+5(8),=X'4020202020202020'
        ED   LINEOUT+5(8),RESULT
        PUT  OUTFILE,LINEOUT
          .
          .
          .
ANS     DS   0D
        DS   CL4
RESULT  DS   CL4
SPACES  DC   C' '
LINEOUT DS   CL133
```

We can assume for the purpose of this type of illustration that the result in ANS will contain at most 7 significant digits plus a sign (4 bytes rather than 8), with the remaining high-order positions filled with zeros. Note that the edit pattern contains a blank (40) as a fill character for zero suppression and 7 digit select characters (20). Note, too, that while ANS is 8 bytes long, the edit (ED) instruction edits only the low-order 4 bytes labeled RESULT. These four low-order bytes of RESULT, which are equivalent to ANS+4 through ANS+7, contain the seven significant digits plus a sign.

An alternative solution would have been to unpack ANS, as shown in the following example. Remember, the UNPK instruction operates from right to left. The high-order zeros would simply be truncated.

```
            CVD     9,ANS
            MVC     LINEOUT,SPACES
            UNPK    LINEOUT+5(7),ANS
            OI      LINEOUT+11,X'F0'
            PUT     OUTFILE,LINEOUT
            .
            .
            .
ANS         DS      D
SPACES      DC      C' '
LINEOUT     DS      CL133
```

D. A Review

When performing arithmetic operations with the use of registers, the following sequence of instructions is required for fields entered in zoned-decimal format.

```
      PACK          ZONED-DECIMAL FIELDS MUST BE PACKED
      CVB           PACKED FIELDS MUST BE CONVERTED TO BINARY
*
*     ARITHMETIC    RX OR RR FORMAT ARITHMETIC
*     OPERATIONS
*
      CVD           BINARY RESULTS MUST BE CONVERTED TO DECIMAL
      UNPK or ED    RESULTS ARE UNPACKED OR EDITED FOR
*                   READABILITY
```

CHAPTER SUMMARY

  I. RX Instructions
     A. Use general registers as Operand 1.
     B. Use storage addresses as Operand 2.
     C. Operate on data in binary form.
     D. Are, in general, more efficient for arithmetic operations.
 II. General registers
     A. There are 16, numbered 0–15.
     B. As a rule, only registers 2–12 are typically used for arithmetic and comparisons.
     C. Are 4-bytes or one fullword in length.
     D. Represent data in binary form.
III. Storage addresses
     A. Must be on a fullword, halfword, doubleword boundary depending on the instruction.
     B. Data must be in binary format.
 IV. Examples
     A. Load:
        1. L   REG,OPERAND2
        2. Moves 4 bytes of data from Operand 2, on a fullword boundary, to a register.
     B. Store:
        1. ST   REG,OPERAND2
        2. Moves 4 bytes of binary data from a register to a fullword of storage.
     C. Arithmetic operations:
        Receiving field—the register
        1. Add
           A   REG,OPERAND2
           A—a fullword is added to REG

2. Subtract

```
S   REG,OPERAND2
```

D. Converting packed-decimal data to binary

```
CVB  REG,OPERAND2
```

1. Operand 2 is a doubleword in packed format.
2. Contents of doubleword packed data are converted to binary form and placed in a general register.

E. Converting binary data to packed decimal

```
CVD  REG,OPERAND2
```

1. Operand 2 is a doubleword in binary form.
2. Binary contents of the register are converted to decimal and placed in the storage location.

CHAPTER SELF-EVALUATING QUIZ

1. The CVB instruction converts a <u>(fullword/doubleword)</u> of <u>(packed/binary)</u> data into <u>(packed/binary)</u> form.
2. The first operand in a CVB instruction is _____ .
3. (T or F) The following is a valid instruction.

```
CVB  FLDA,FLDB
```

4. What, if anything, is wrong with the following?

```
        CVB    FLDA,1
                :
                :
FLDA    DS     F
```

5. (T or F) The first operand in a CVD instruction is the sending field.
6. (T or F) The following is a valid instruction.

```
        CVD    2,HOLD
                :
                :
HOLD    DS     D
```

7. After using a CVD instruction to convert the binary contents of a register to packed-decimal format, we generally _____ or _____ the result before it is printed.

		Page
SOLUTIONS	1. Doubleword; packed; binary	340
	2. A general register	340
	3. F: the first operand must be a register	340
	4. In a CVB instruction, the first operand is a register (2–12), and the second operand is a doubleword in storage containing packed-decimal data.	341
	5. T	342
	6. T	342
	7. Unpack (UNPK); edit (ED)	343

KEY TERMS

Binary numbers	Fullword
Binary operations	General purpose registers
Binary representation	Halfword
Bit	Index register
Boundary alignment	Iterative

Doubleword
Fixed-point data

Loading

REVIEW QUESTIONS

1. Why are registers used?
2. How would the decimal number −127 be represented in a register in hexadecimal form?
3. How would the decimal number +127 be represented in a register in hexadecimal form?
4. Discuss what is meant by boundary alignment.
5. Discuss how data in registers can be printed.
6. Write a program to count the number of input records and print the result out with the message "THE NUMBER OF RECORDS IS." Use a register for the addition.
7. Write a program to read in records with the following format and print out each employee's name and salary with a $500 bonus added on.

   Hint
   Use a CVB to move the salary (after it is packed) to a register. Use an A instruction to add the bonus to that register.

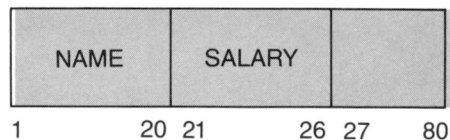

NAME	SALARY	
1 20	21 26	27 80

8. Write a program to read in records with the following format and print out for each record the amount fields, each reduced by five. HINT: Use a CVB to move each amount (after it is packed) to a different register. Use an S instruction to subtract five from each register.

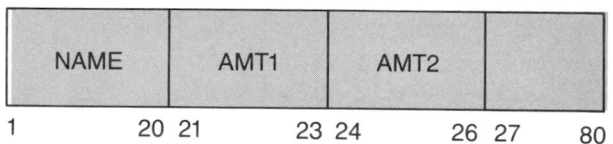

NAME	AMT1	AMT2	
1 20	21 23	24 26	27 80

9. Write a routine, using registers, to compute the following.

   C = D + E + 50 − F − 200

   Assume D, E and F are packed-decimal fields, four bytes in length. Print C, using the UNPK and OI instructions.

10. Write a routine, using registers, to compute the following. (Note that 4W = W added to itself three times.)

    X = 4W − 275 + Y

    Assume W and Y are zoned-decimal fields containing three digits. Print X with editing.

11. (T or F) The first operand of a load instruction must be a register.
12. (T or F) The contents of the first operand of a load instruction are replaced by the contents of the second operand.
13. (T or F) The second operand of an L instruction should begin on a halfword boundary.
14. (T or F) The load instruction moves data from main storage to a register.
15. (T or F) The first operand of a store instruction is always a register.

DEBUGGING EXERCISES

The purpose of the following program is to accumulate a running total of an amount field in a register. When the end-of-file is reached, the data is converted to packed decimal and listed. Find and correct any errors in the program.

```
**************************************************************
*          D E B U G    P R O G R A M     C H A P T E R    11
**************************************************************
           LH     7,=F'0'                     SET REGISTER TO ZERO
CLEAR      GET    INFILE,RECORD                TO ACCUMULATE TOTAL
           PACK   PAMOUNT,AMOUNT
           CVB    5,PAMOUNT
           AR     5,7
           B      CLEAR
EOF        CVB    7,PAMOUNT                    END-OF-FILE-ROUTINE
           MVC    LINEOUT+20(13),PATTERN
           ED     LINEOUT+20(13),PTOTAL
           PUT    OUTFILE,LINEOUT
           CLOSE  INFILE,OUTFILE
           EOJ
*
RECORD     DS     0CL32
SOCSEC#    DS     CL9
AMOUNT     DS     PL7
OTHER      DS     CL16
*
SPACES     DC     X'40'
LINEOUT    DS     CL133
*
PATTERN    DC     XL13'40206B2020206B2020214B2020'
PAMOUNT    DS     0CL8
           DS     CL4
PTOTAL     DS     PL4
```

SOLUTIONS

1.		MVC	LINEOUT,SPACES	LINEOUT MUST BE CLEARED
2.		LH	7,H'0'	HALFWORD CONSTANT REQUIRED
3.		AR	7,5	REG 7 ACCUMULATES TOTAL, NOT 5
4.	EOF	CVD	7,PAMOUNT	CONVERT TO DECIMAL, NOT BINARY
5.	PAMOUNT	DS	0D	DOUBLEWORD BOUNDARY IS REQUIRED
		DS	CL3	
6.	PTOTAL	DS	PL5	MUST ACCOMMODATE MORE THAN 7 DIGITS OR BE LARGER THAN 4 BYTES. THE NEXT LARGER PACKED FIELD IS 5 BYTES IN LENGTH AND CONTAINS 9 DIGITS.

7. Note that the instruction AMOUNT DS PL7 simply reserves or allocates seven bytes of storage, nothing more.

PROGRAMMING ASSIGNMENTS

1. Write a program to print a report from the following transaction card records.

   1–5   Employee number
   6–20 Employee name
   21–25 Pay xxx.xx
   26–80 Not used

   Each line of the report contains the following fields:

   1–15 Employee name
   36–40 Employee number
   61–67 Gross pay $xxx.xx

76–82 Net pay $xxx.xx
91–95 Date (month and year: xx/xx)

Notes
a. Gross pay = Pay + Bonus
b. Net pay = Gross pay − Bond deduction
c. Every employee gets the same Bonus and has the same Bond deduction. The
following constants are to be defined in binary and used for these amounts:
Bonus amount   200.00
Bond deduction   56.25
d. If net pay is negative, print "INPUT ERROR."
e. Place today's date in the Date field.
f. Use registers for performing the arithmetic operations.

2. Consider input transaction records with the following data.

1–20 Customer name
21 Type of transaction (1 = Master that contains previous balance)
                        (2 = Deposit)
                        (3 = Withdrawal)
22–26 Amount
27–31 Account number
32–80 Not used

All input records are in sequence by Account Number and by Type within Account Number. Write a program that will print the name of each depositor and the corresponding *number* of deposits and withdrawals. At the end of the report, print the number of customers processed. Keep in mind that there is only one Type 1 (previous balance) input record per account number, but there may be numerous deposit and withdrawal records. Use RX format instructions for all arithmetic operations.

3. Consider the following input insurance records.

1–20 Name
21 Sex (M = male, F = female)
22–25 Birth date (month and year)
26 Number of traffic violations in last 18 months
27–28 Number of accidents in last 18 months

Write a program to print:
a. Total number of drivers under 25.
b. Total number of female drivers.
c. Total number of drivers who have had more than two traffic violations in last 18 months.
d. Total number of drivers who have had one or more accidents in last 18 months.
e. Total number of drivers in the sample.

Use RX format instructions for arithmetic operations.

Register-to-Register Instructions (RR) and Additional RX Instructions

To familiarize you with:
1. *Register-to-register (RR) instructions.*
2. *Additional RX instructions.*
3. *Techniques for looping.*
4. *The use of registers for multiplying and dividing.*

I. RR FORMAT INSTRUCTIONS

A. An Overview

Register-to-Register instructions (RR type) are used to move data from one register to another and to perform arithmetic operations using only registers. These instructions function in a manner similar to the RX type, except that there are no storage locations used—only registers. The general format for these RR instructions is given below.

General Format for RR Instructions

Operation 10	Operand 16
OP	REG1,REG2

The operations to be discussed initially will be the following:

LR Load Register
AR Add Register
SR Subtract Register

REG1 is the receiving field and its contents change.
REG2 is the sending field and its contents remain unchanged.

B. The Load Register (LR) Instruction

Instruction:	LR
Meaning:	Load Register
Operands:	Both must be general registers.
	Both contain binary data.
Result:	Operand 1: Receiving field
	Operand 2: Sending field, remains unchanged.
	Contents of Operand 2 are loaded or moved to Operand 1.

Example 12.1

LABEL	OPERATION	OPERAND	COMMENTS
1	10 16		72
	LR	8,5	

Before Execution[1]

Register 5	00	00	12	34

Register 8	56	78	90	12

After Execution

Register 5	00	00	12	34

Register 8	00	00	12	34

Test your understanding of the LR instruction by following the next series of instructions carefully. Assume they are executed in sequence.

Examples of Load Register (LR)

Instruction	Contents of Registers			
	Register 5	Register 6	Register 7	Register 8
Before Execution	+00 00 01 23	+00 00 04 56	−00 00 01 00	+00 00 00 19
LR 8,5 LR 5,7 LR 7,6 LR 6,8	−00 00 01 00	+00 00 01 23	+00 00 04 56	+00 00 01 23
After Execution	−00 00 01 00	+00 00 01 23	+00 00 04 56	+00 00 01 23

C. The Add Register (AR) Instruction

The general format of the AR instruction is:

Operation 10	Operand 16
AR	REG1,REG2

Instruction:	AR
Meaning:	Add Register
Operands:	Both must be registers.
	Both contain binary data.
Result:	Contents of Operands 1 and 2 are added together.
	Result replaces contents of Operand 1.
	Operand 2 remains unchanged.

Example 12.2

LABEL	OPERATION 10 16	OPERAND	COMMENTS	72
	AR	8,5		

Before Execution[2]

Register 5	+00 00 01 50

Register 8	+00 00 02 00

After Execution

Register 5	+00 00 01 50

Register 8	+00 00 03 50

[1]The contents are given in decimal form for purposes of clarification only.
[2]The contents are given in decimal form for purposes of clarification only.

Review the following sequence of AR instructions.

Examples of Add Register (AR)

Instructions	Contents of Register			
	Register 5	Register 6	Register 7	Register 8
Before Execution	+00 00 01 23	+00 00 04 56	−00 00 01 00	+00 00 00 19
AR 8,5				+00 00 01 42
AR 5,7	+00 00 00 23			
AR 7,6			+00 00 03 56	
AR 6,8		+00 00 05 98		
AR 5,5	+00 00 00 46			
After Execution	+00 00 00 46	+00 00 05 98	+00 00 03 56	+00 00 01 42

In the last example notice that AR 5,5 has the effect of doubling or multiplying the contents of register 5 by 2. This is a simple method to accomplish multiplication, which we will see later becomes quite involved.

An example will illustrate how the AR instruction can be used in a program. Consider the following input record layout.

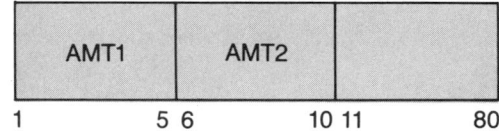

Problem
Add these two amount fields using registers.

Solution
```
        PACK    DWORD1,AMT1
        PACK    DWORD2,AMT2
        CVB     4,DWORD1
        CVB     3,DWORD2
        AR      4,3
         .
         .
         .
RECIN   DS      OCL80
AMT1    DS      CL5
AMT2    DS      CL5
        DS      CL70
DWORD1  DS      D
DWORD2  DS      D
```

D. The Subtract Register (SR) Instruction

The general format for the subtract register (SR) instruction follows.

Operation 10	Operand 16
SR	REG1,REG2

Instruction:	SR
Meaning:	Subtract Register
Operands:	Both must be registers.
	Both contain binary data.
Result:	Contents of Operand 2 are subtracted from Operand 1.
	Result replaces Operand 1.
	Operand 2 remains unchanged.

Example 12.3

LABEL	OPERATION	OPERAND	COMMENTS
	10 16		72
	SR	8,5	

Before Execution[3]	After Execution
Register 5 +00 00 01 50	Register 5 +00 00 01 50
Register 8 +00 00 02 00	Register 8 +00 00 00 50

The following sequence of SR instructions clarifies its use.

Examples of Subtract Register (SR)

Instruction	Contents of Register			
	Register 5	Register 6	Register 7	Register 8
Before Execution	+00 00 01 23	+00 00 04 56	−00 00 01 00	+00 00 00 19
SR 8,5				−00 00 01 04
SR 5,7	+00 00 02 23			
SR 7,6			−00 00 05 56	
SR 6,8		+00 00 05 60		
SR 5,5	+00 00 00 00			
After Execution	+00 00 00 00	+00 00 05 60	−00 00 05 56	−00 00 01 04

In the last example, register 5 was set to zero by subtracting the contents of the register from itself. Whenever it is necessary to initialize a register at zero, this method can be utilized.

The following review of the subtraction process will aid in your understanding of the results obtained in the preceding examples.

---

[3]The contents are given in decimal form for purposes of clarification only.

REVIEW OF RULES FOR SUBTRACTING SIGNED NUMBERS

1. Change the sign of the number to be subtracted (contents of second operand or register).
2. Proceed as in addition.

Examples

a. $+12 - (+13) = +12 + (-13) = -1$
b. $-5 - (-2) = -5 + (+2) = -3$
c. $-4 - (+2) = -4 + (-2) = -6$
d. $+12 - (-15) = +12 + (+15) = 27$

Self-Evaluating Quiz

Exercises 1–7 are designed to review how RR instructions operate. In addition, they are designed to review your ability to add and subtract in hexadecimal. Indicate the result in hex in each case. Treat each example independently *not* sequentially.

Note:
Each hex digit = 4 binary digits.

Instruction	Contents of Registers (in Hex)			
	Register 4	Register 5	Register 6	Register 7
	00 00 00 11 (17_{10})	00 00 00 7E (126_{10})	00 00 00 11 (17_{10})	FFFFFF7A (-134_{10})
1. AR 6,5				
2. SR 5,4				
3. SR 4,6				
4. SR 4,7				
5. LR 4,6				
6. L 4,=F'123'				
7. AR 4,6				
SR 4,7				

8. Write a routine to add the numbers 456 and 223 using registers.
9. Write an RX-type instruction to subtract 100 from the contents of register 5.
10. Code the above instruction using an RR-type instruction for the subtraction.

SOLUTIONS

1. Register 5: 00 00 00 7E   Register 6: 00 00 00 8F (143_{10})
2. Register 4: 00 00 00 11   Register 5: 00 00 00 6D (109_{10})
3. Register 6: 00 00 00 11   Register 4: 00 00 00 00 (0_{10})
4. Register 7: FFFFFF7A   Register 4: 00 00 00 97 (151_{10})
5. Register 6: 00 00 00 11   Register 4: 00 00 00 11 (17_{10})
6. Register 4: 00 00 00 7B   (This is an RX instruction that can have a self-defining operand.) (123_{10})
7. Register 6: 00 00 00 11   Register 7: FFFFFF7A
   Register 4: 00 00 00 A8   (00 00 00 11 + 00 00 00 11 − [FFFFFF7A]

```
8.  L    4,=F'223'
    L    5,=F'456'
    AR   4,5
9.  S    5,=F'100'
10. L    4,=F'100'
    SR   5,4
```

II. ADDITIONAL RR AND RX FORMAT INSTRUCTIONS

A. An Overview

Now that you understand the general format of RX- and RR-type instructions, we will consider the remaining instructions in pairs.

1. *Comparison:*

C	is an RX instruction
CR	is an RR instruction

2. *Multiplication:*

M	is an RX instruction
MR	is an RR instruction

3. *Division:*

D	is an RX instruction
DR	is an RR instruction

B. Binary or Fixed-Point Compare Instructions (C and CR)

Compare instructions are used to set the **condition code** so that conditional branching may take place. Many other instructions affect the condition code setting, as we will see in the next section. Thus, it is advisable to follow a compare instruction immediately with a branch instruction to ensure that another instruction does not alter the condition code setting.

The Compare Register (CR) and Compare (C) instructions perform an *algebraic* compare between the two operands. That is, the comparison is not bit-by-bit. It depends on the magnitude of the fields. Thus, positive values are considered greater than negative values as would be expected in an algebraic compare.

You may recall that the Compare Pack (CP) is also an algebraic comparison. The CR instruction is used to compare the contents of two registers and follows the general format.

1. The Compare Registers (CR) Instruction

Instruction:	Compare Registers
Op Code:	CR
Operand 1:	Register
Operand 2:	Register
Result:	The condition code will be set to low, equal, or high depending upon whether Operand 1 is <, =, or > Operand 2, respectively. Contents of registers are not affected by the comparison.

Operation 10	Operand 16
CR	REG1,REG2

where

CR   indicates a register-to-register comparison.

REG1   is the first operand and tests high, low, or equal with respect to REG2.

REG2   is the second operand and is a general register.

Neither operand is affected by the compare. Note that because we are dealing with an algebraic comparison, a negative value is considered lower than a positive value. (High-order 1 compares *low* to high-order 0.)

For a review of how condition codes are affected by operations discussed in this section, see the following table.

Instruction	Condition Code			
	0	1	2	3
CR Compare Register	=	First < second	First > second	Not set by compare
C Compare (RX)	=	First < second	First > second	Not set by compare
AR Add Register	= 0	<0	>0	Overflow
A Add (RX)	= 0	<0	>0	Overflow
SR Subtract Register	= 0	<0	>0	Overflow
S Subtract (RX)	= 0	<0	>0	Overflow

A few examples will illustrate how the instruction operates.[4]

Instruction	Contents of Register 5	Contents of Register 6	Condition Code Setting
CR 5,6	+00 00 01 25	+00 00 01 08	HIGH
	+00 00 02 58	+00 00 02 58	EQUAL
	−00 00 00 17	+00 00 00 00	LOW
	−00 00 00 15	−00 00 00 21	HIGH
	+00 00 00 07	+00 00 00 08	LOW

The following illustration shows how the CR instruction can be coded in a program.

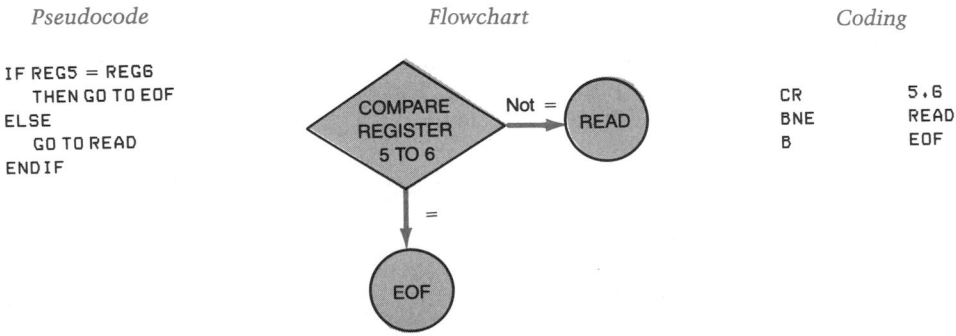

Pseudocode	*Flowchart*	*Coding*
IF REG5 = REG6		CR 5,6
THEN GO TO EOF		BNE READ
ELSE		B EOF
GO TO READ		
ENDIF		

_____
[4]The contents are shown in decimal form for purposes of clarification only.

2. The Compare Fullword (C) Instruction

Instruction:	Compare
Op Code:	C
Operand 1:	Register
Operand 2:	Four-byte storage area or self-defining fullword operand containing binary data
Result:	Condition code will be set to low, equal, or high depending on whether Operand 1 is <, =, or > Operand 2, respectively. Registers are not affected by the comparison.
Limitation:	The storage area should be on a fullword boundary.

The compare fullword (C) instruction is used to compare the contents of a storage location with the contents of a general register. Here is the general format.

Operation 10	Operand 16
C	REG,FULLWD

where

C	indicates a register-to-storage comparison.
REG	is the first operand and tests high, low, or equal with respect to FULLWD.
FULLWD	is the second operand and either a storage location or a self-defining operand of 4 bytes (fullword). The FULLWD operand should be on a fullword boundary.

Neither operand is affected by the execution of this instruction. As with the CR instruction, a negative value is considered less than a positive value. The following examples clearly illustrate this point.[5]

Instruction	Contents of Register 7	Contents of FULLWORD	Condition Code Setting
C 7,FULLWORD	+00 00 01 25	+00 00 01 18	HIGH
	+00 00 02 58	+00 00 02 58	EQUAL
	−00 00 00 17	+00 00 00 00	LOW
	−00 00 00 15	−00 00 00 21	HIGH
	+00 00 00 07	+00 00 00 08	LOW

The following illustration shows how the C instruction might be coded in a payroll program.

---

[5]The contents are given in decimal form for clarification purposes only.

Pseudocode	*Flowchart*	*Coding*

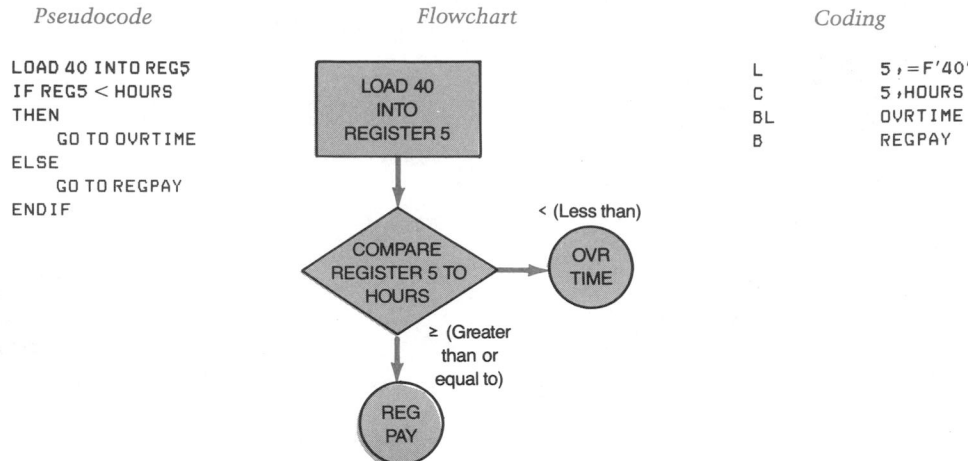

```
LOAD 40 INTO REG5                                    L      5,=F'40'
IF REG5 < HOURS                                      C      5,HOURS
THEN                                                 BL     OVRTIME
     GO TO OVRTIME                                   B      REGPAY
ELSE
     GO TO REGPAY
ENDIF
```

If the HOURS an employee has worked are greater than 40 (register 5 < HOURS), then we want to go to the OVRTIME routine; otherwise, we go to the REGPAY routine. If register 5 (contents 40) compares low to HOURS, that means that the employee has worked over 40 hours and is entitled to overtime pay.

SUMMARIZING C AND CR INSTRUCTIONS

1. The first operand of a Compare (C) or Compare Register (CR) instruction is always a register.
2. The condition code always refers to the status of the first operand (register) relative to the second operand and is set EQUAL, LOW, or HIGH.
3. The comparison is *algebraic,* meaning that positive numbers have a higher value than negative numbers.
4. The length of the comparison is 4 bytes.

Condition Code Tested After Arithmetic Operations   The **condition code** is set as a result of all arithmetic as well as comparison operations. After an arithmetic or compare instruction, a conditional branch can be coded that will alter the sequence of instructions to be executed if a given condition is met. This *conditional branch* tests the value of the condition code. The results of the *arithmetic* operations may be zero, negative (minus), positive, or overflow. After an arithmetic operation is performed, the conditional branch instructions may be coded as in the following table.

Conditional Branch Operation	Arithmetic Condition Tested	Actual Condition Code Setting (for Programmer's Information)
BZ	Zero result	0
BNZ	Not zero result	1, 2, or 3
BM	Minus (negative) result	1
BNM	Not minus	0, 2 or 3
BP	Positive result	2
BNP	Not positive result	0, 1 or 3
BO	Overflow	3

A few examples follow.

Example 12.4   Testing for Overflow

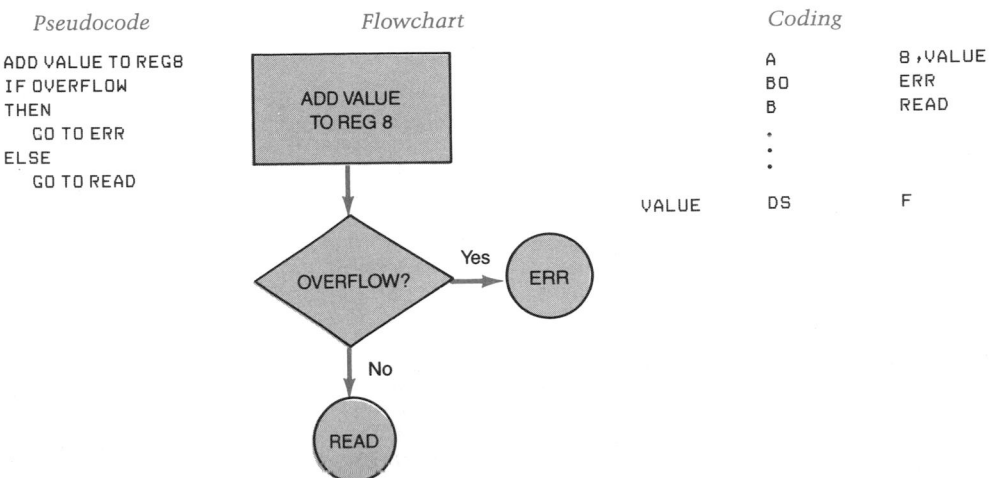

Pseudocode		Flowchart		Coding	
Pseudocode		*Flowchart*		*Coding*	

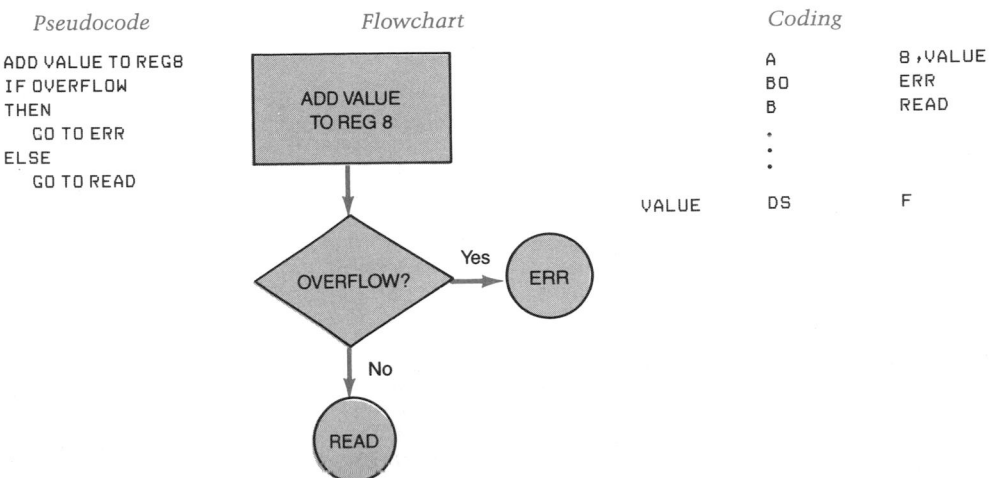

Register 8 is used as an accumulator and a test is made for an overflow condition. You will recall that overflow occurs in a register when the result is larger than the largest number that can be stored in a register. In a general register, the largest number that can be stored is 2,147,483,647. If this number were exceeded, an overflow would occur and the program would branch to the error routine labeled ERR. Similarly, a negative number less than −2,147,483,648 could not be stored in a register.

Example 12.5   Testing a Counter for Zero

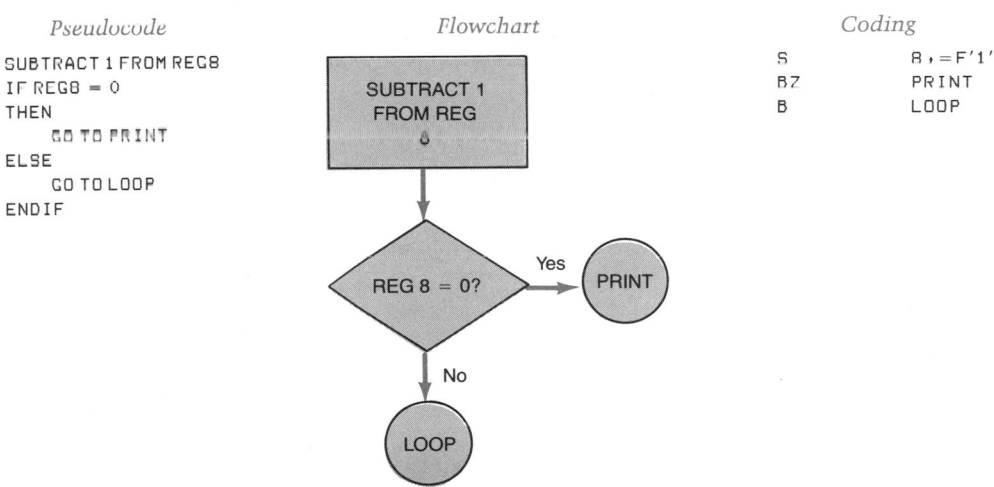

The register serves as a counter. With each pass through the loop, the counter is reduced by 1 until it reaches zero. When this condition occurs, the program will branch to the routine called PRINT.

Self-Evaluating Quiz Indicate the condition code setting after each instruction is executed.

Contents in Hex

Register 2:	00 00 26 E3
Register 3:	FF A2 2D 80
AMT1:	02 68 75 AC
AMT2:	FE 30 26 E3

1. CR 2,3
2. CR 3,2
3. C 2,AMT1
4. C 3,AMT2
5. C 2,AMT2
6. AR 3,2
7. S 2,AMT1
8. SR 3,3
9. AR 3,3
10. A 2,AMT2

SOLUTIONS

	Condition Code	Explanation
1.	High	Register 3 contains a negative amount.
2.	Low	
3.	Low	
4.	High	AMT2 is considered < register 3 because AMT2 has a larger negative amount.
5.	High	Positive number > negative number.
6.	Condition Code 1: Less than zero result	
7.	Condition Code 1: Less than zero result	
8.	Condition Code 0: Zero result	
9.	Condition Code 3: Overflow	
10.	Condition Code 1: Less than zero result	

3. **The Branch on Condition (BC) Instruction

What you have learned so far is called *extended mnemonics*; it enables you to utilize an operation code that tests a specific condition. The generalized format for a branch condition follows, one which may be used for *all* types of branches.

BC ⏞Mask Value , ⏞Label to be Branched to

Mask Value	Mask	Condition Code Settings	Result of Previous Operation if Comparison	Result of Previous Operation if Arithmetic
8	1000	0	OP1=OP2	=0 no overflow
4	0100	1	OP1<OP2	<0 no overflow
2	0010	2	OP1>OP2	>0 no overflow
12	1100	0,1	OP1≤OP2	≤0 no overflow

**This is an optional topic.

10	1010	0,2	OP1≥OP2	≥0 no overflow
6	0110	1,2	OP1≠OP2	≠0 no overflow
14	1110	0,1,2	All	no overflow
1	0001	3	None	overflow
9	1001	0,3	OP1−OP2	0 or overflow
5	0101	1,3	OP1<OP2	<0 or overflow
3	0011	2,3	OP1>OP2	>0 or overflow
13	1101	0,1,3	OP1≤OP2	≤0 or overflow
11	1011	0,2,3	OP1≥OP2	>0 or overflow
7	0111	1,2,3	OP1≠OP2	≠0 or overflow

Example 12.6	*Coding*		*Meaning*
	C	6,FLD1	Branch to RTN1 if register 6 = FLD1
	BC	8,RTN1	
Example 12.7	CR	6,9	Branch to STEP1 if register 6 ≤ register 9
	BC	12,STEP1	
Example 12.8	S	5,=F'1'	Subtract 1 from contents of register 5. Branch to LOOP1
	BC	7,LOOP1	if register 5 ≠ 0. Note that BC 6,LOOP1 is also acceptable.

The BC instruction is simply another method of coding the extended form of the branch.

BC and Extended Mnemonics

Extended Form		Ordinary Form		Meaning
BM	label	BC	4,label	Branch on minus
BZ	label	BC	8,label	Branch on zero
BNP	label	BC	13,label	Branch on not plus
BNM	label	BC	11,label	Branch on not minus
BNZ	label	BC	7,label	Branch on not zero
BO	label	BC	1,label	Branch on overflow

The following instructions, then, are equivalent.

```
1.  BM    STEP1      BC    4,STEP1
2.  BNZ   STEP4      BC    7,STEP4
```

C. Binary or Fixed-Point Multiplication

1. The Multiply (M) and Multiply Register (MR) Instructions

Recall the principles of multiplication that follow.

```
        123   multiplicand
    ×    45   multiplier
        615
       492
       5535   product
```

where the total number of digits in the final product cannot exceed the sum of the digits of the **multiplicand** and **multiplier.** This is an important consideration. The M and MR instructions use 4-byte or 32-bit operands. That is, both the first and second operands are 4 bytes long. When two 32-bit operands are multiplied, the product requires 64 bits. Obviously, the result is too large to be stored in a single register. Therefore, *two consecutive even-odd registers* are used to store the product. The registers must be *adjacent* and the odd-numbered register must be one greater than the even-numbered register. That is, registers 4 and 5 would be suitable, but register 5 and 6 would not (odd-numbered register not greater than even-numbered register). The steps necessary to multiply 123 by 45 follow.

```
L    5,=F'123'
M    4,=F'45'
```

See Figure 12.1 for a more detailed explanation.

Registers 4 and 5 will be used to store the final product. In principle, registers 4 and 5 serve as an 8-byte accumulator. The multiplicand is placed in the *rightmost* 4 bytes of the even–odd register pair; that is, in the odd register. (See the L instruction above.) The multiply instruction must reference the *even*-numbered register of the even–odd pair.

The general formats of the M and MR instructions follow.

Operation 10	Operand 16
M	EVEN REG, FULLWD
MR	EVEN REG, REG

Symbolic		Assembler Instruction	Register Contents[a]	
Register 4	Register 5		Register 4	Register 5
/////	MLTIPLCN	L 5,MLTIPLCN	/////	+00 00 01 23
└Contents ignored				
FINAL	PRODUCT	M 4,MLTPLR or M 4,=F'45'	+00 00 00 00	00 00 55 35
└Reference high-order position, register 4			└Final product in registers 4 and 5	

Figure 12.1
Finding the product of 123 × 45.

[a]*Note:* Data shown in decimal form for purposes of clarification only. MLTIPLCN will be set equal to 123. MLTPLR will be set equal to 45.

where

M and MR	indicate fullword multiplication.
EVEN REG	is the even register of an even–odd pair. Before execution its contents are ignored. After execution, the product is stored in the even–odd pair of registers.
REG	is a general register containing the multiplier.
FULLWD	is a fullword in storage containing the multiplier and should be aligned on a fullword boundary.

The only *valid* register pairs that may be used for multiplication are illustrated below. (See also Figure 12.2.)

Register Pair		Load Multiplicand in Register	First Operand in Multiply Instruction	Product Contained in Registers
Even Register	Odd Register			
2	3	3	2	2–3
4	5	5	4	4–5
6	7	7	6	6–7
8	9	9	8	8–9
10	11	11	10	10–11

A specification exception resulting in a program interrupt will occur if the even–odd pair is incorrectly referenced.

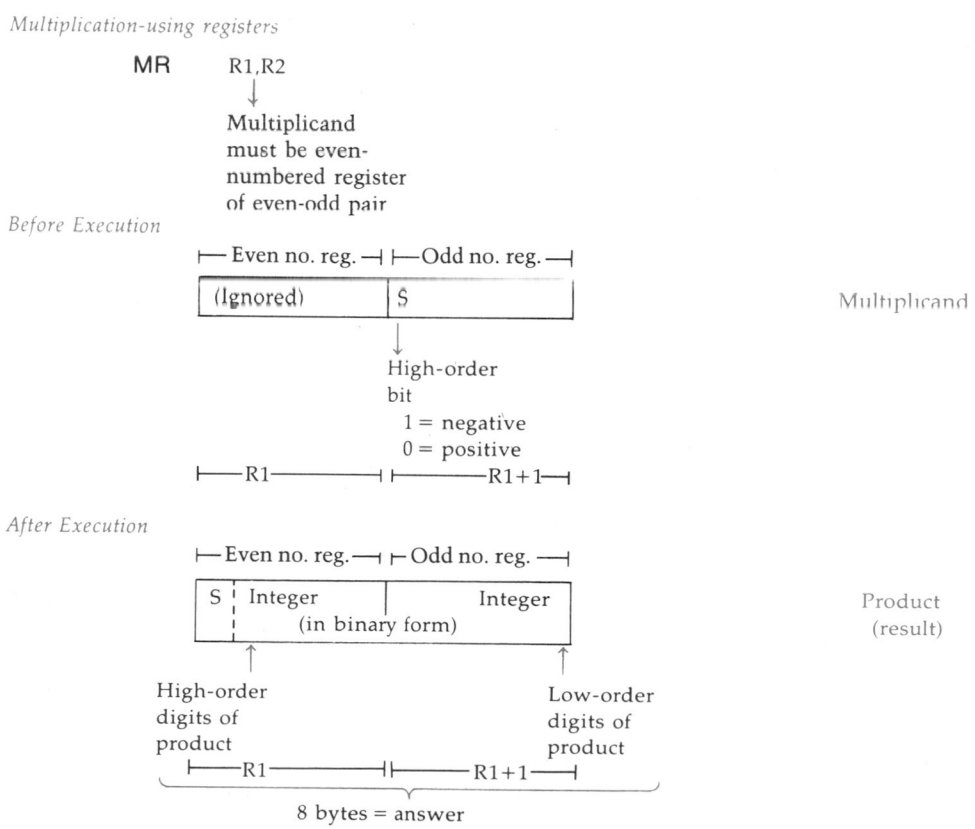

Figure 12.2
Schematic of the MR instruction.

2. Examples of the Multiply Instruction (M)

The multiply instruction is best illustrated with a few examples. For purposes of clarification, only 4 decimal digits will be used in the examples.

Multiply Instruction (M) Instruction

Instruction	Multiplicand Register 7	Fullword (MLTPLR)	Final Product Registers 6 and 7
M 6,MLTPLR	+00 78	+00 02	+01 56
	−02 50	+00 06	−15 00 (− × + = −)
	+07 12	−00 04	−28 48
	−03 00	−00 12	+36 00 (− × − = +)

Depending upon the values of the multiplier and multiplicand, the product may extend beyond register 7 and into register 6. However, if you are certain that the result or product can be stored in 4 bytes, you need only reference register 7 when using a CVD or ST instruction in preparation for printing the results.

3. Examples of the Multiply Register (MR) Instruction

Multiply Register (MR) Instruction

Instruction	Multiplicand Register 7 (Contents)	Register 9	Final Product Registers 6 and 7
MR 6,9	+12 34	+00 02	+24 68
	−00 17	+00 05	−00 85
	+07 50	−00 03	−22 50
	−06 12	−00 04	+24 48

Notice that the multiplicand must first be placed in register 7, the low-order register of an even-odd (6–7) pair.

SUMMARY M AND MR:
BINARY OR FIXED-POINT MULTIPLICATION

1. With binary multiplication, an even-odd pair of registers are linked together to form an 8-byte accumulator.
2. The even-odd register pair serves as the first operand of the multiply instruction.
3. The multiplicand is placed in the odd register of the even-odd pair.
4. Ignore the contents of the even register before multiplication takes place.
5. The second operand contains the multiplier and is either
   a. a general register (MR) or
   b. a fullword in storage (M) on a fullword boundary.
6. The multiply instruction always references the even register of the even-odd pair in the first operand.
7. The product is right justified in the even-odd register pair after execution.
8. Because two registers store the results, overflow cannot occur.
9. A specification exception will occur if the even-odd register pair is incorrectly referenced.

D. Binary or Fixed-Point Division

1. Divide (D) and Divide Register (DR) Instructions

Let us review the principles of division.

```
                                        126   Quotient
                        Quotient    121 |15268  Dividend
                Divisor |Dividend   Divisor 121
                                        316
                                        242
                                        748
                                        726
                                         22   Remainder
```

As with multiplication, binary division requires the use of an even-odd register pair. The **dividend** is loaded in the rightmost positions of the even-odd register pair. The divide instruction must reference the *even*-numbered register. The **divisor** is referenced by the second operand and is either

1. A fullword in storage using D as the op code, or
2. A general register using DR as the op code

Note that division produces two results, the **quotient** and the **remainder.** After division, the quotient and the remainder are stored in the even-odd register pair, as follows.

---

1. The even-numbered register contains the remainder.
2. The odd-numbered register contains the quotient.

See Figure 12.3 for a schematic of the DR instruction.

Because the dividend is loaded in the odd register of the even-odd pair, the *even* register must be set to *zero*. Remember, the divide instruction treats the even-odd pair as one large 8-byte accumulator that contains the dividend. The steps necessary to divide 15,268 by 121 are shown in Figure 12.4.

ERRORS

An error called a *fixed-point divide* occurs if
a. the quotient is too large to be stored in a register, or
b. the divisor is zero.

Under these circumstances, *no* division takes place and the even–odd registers remain unchanged.

The general format for binary division, then, is

Operation 10	Operand 16
D	EVEN REG, FULLWD
DR	EVEN REG, REG

Division—Using Registers

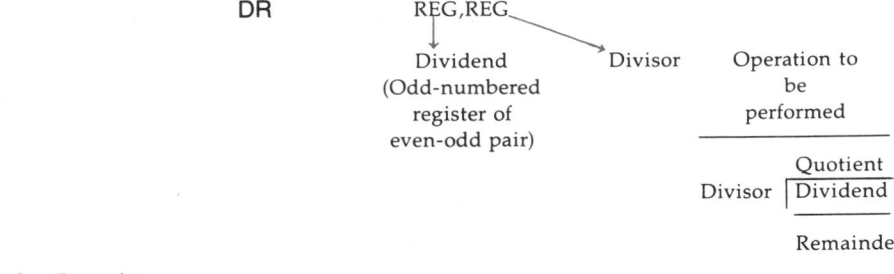

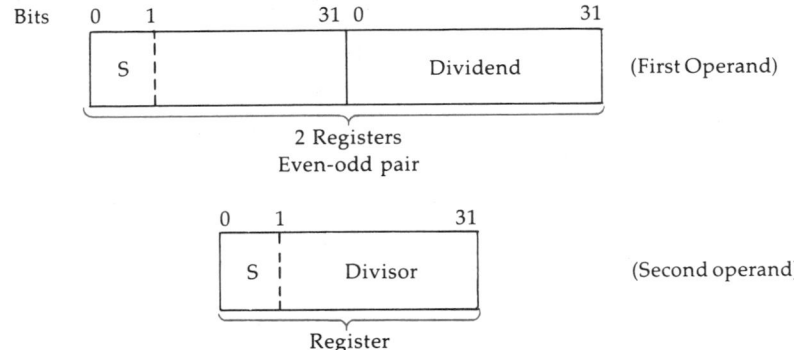

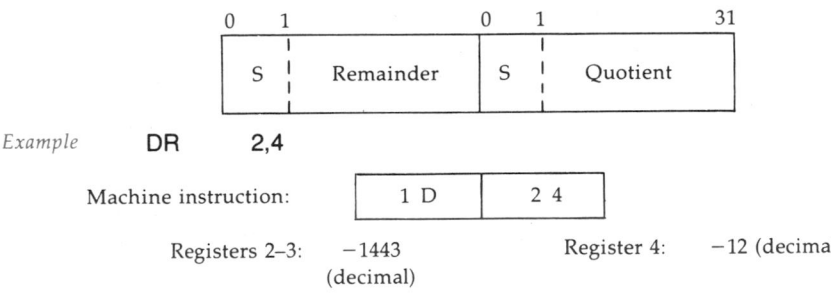

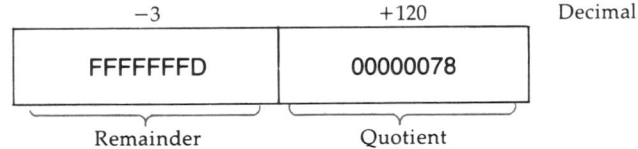

Figure 12.3
Schematic of the DR instruction.

	Symbolic			Contentsª	
Register 4	Register 5		Instruction	Register 4	Register 5
0....0	/////		SR 4,4	+00000000	+00099999
	DIVIDEND		L 5,DIVIDEND	+00000000	+00015268
Remainder	Quotient		D 4,DIVISOR	+00000022	+00000126

Figure 12.4
Using binary division to divide 15,268 by 121.

ª*Note:* Data shown in decimal form for purposes of clarification only.

where

D and DR	indicate fullword binary division.
EVEN REG	is the even register of an even–odd pair.
REG	is a general register containing the divisor.
FULLWD	is a fullword in storage containing the divisor. FULLWD should be aligned on a fullword boundary.

2. Examples

Because the D and DR are so similar, only examples of the D will be presented. The data is shown in decimal form only for purposes of clarification.

Instruction	Dividend: Register 6 and Register 7	Fullword in Storage (Divisor)	Remainder Register 6	Quotient Register 7
D 6,DIVISOR	+00 00 01 51	+00 00 00 12	+00 07	+00 12
	−00 00 01 09	+00 00 00 09	−00 01	−00 12
	−00 00 02 48	−00 00 00 06	−00 02	+00 41
	+00 00 24 68	−00 00 00 08	+00 04	−03 08

Note that the sign of the quotient depends on the signs of the divisor and dividend. When the signs are the same, the result is positive; when they are different, the result is negative. The remainder receives the sign of the dividend. Following is a summary of these rules.

Sign of Divisor	Sign of Dividend	Sign of Quotient	Sign of Remainder
+	+	+	+
+	−	−	−
−	+	−	+
−	+	+	−

SUMMARY—BINARY DIVISION

1. Binary division requires the use of an even–odd register pair that serves as the first operand. Usually, the even register is set to zero, and the dividend is loaded into the odd register.
2. When the dividend is less than 4 bytes (2,147,483,647 in decimal), the even register is set to zero. The dividend is then loaded into the odd or low-order register.
3. The second operand contains the divisor, and is either
   a. a fullword in storage (D), or
   b. a general register (DR)
4. The divide binary instructions always reference the *even* register in the first operand.
5. After division takes place, the even register contains the remainder, and the sign is the same as the dividend.
6. The odd register contains the quotient. The sign is negative only when the signs of the dividend and divisor are not alike.
7. A specification error will result if the even–odd register pair is incorrectly referenced.
8. A fixed-point divide error occurs when the divisor is zero, or the quotient is too large to be stored in a register.
9. When a fixed-point divide error occurs, division does not take place.

E. Halfword Binary Instructions

Halfword (16-bit) operands may be used in many instances in place of the fullword operands. The primary advantage of halfword instructions is their more efficient use of storage and faster performance. However, to preserve precision, the fullword instruction is recommended.

The largest decimal number that can be stored in a halfword is $+32,767$, while the smallest is $-32,768$. If the data falls within this range, the halfword instructions may be used. Operationally, halfword instructions function in a manner similar to fullword instructions. For example, when a halfword is loaded into a register, the halfword is *automatically* expanded to a fullword. This is accomplished by propagating the sign bit through the leftmost 16 bits in the register. The following examples illustrate how this operates.

Example 12.9

Decimal Number	Halfword Representation (in Hex)	Fullword Representation (in Hex)
$+10$	00 0A	00 00 00 0A
-10	FF F6	FF FF FF F6

In effect, the results are the same as if a fullword were used. The only limitation is that the numbers must range approximately between $\pm 32,767$. Halfword data should be located on halfword integral boundaries.

The general format for halfword (RX) instructions follows.

Operation 10	Operand 16
OP	REG,HLFWD

where

OP is any of the operations LH, AH, SH, MH, STH, CH.

The following instructions are halfword equivalents of all the instructions discussed in this chapter.

HALFWORD INSTRUCTIONS

LH:	Load Halfword
AH:	Add Halfword
SH:	Subtract Halfword
MH:	Multiply Halfword
STH:	Store Halfword
CH:	Compare Halfword

(Because of the limitations placed on the size of the operands, Divide Halfword is *not* an available option.)

REG   denotes the first operand is a general register.

HLFWD   is a location in storage, 2 bytes in length and is located on a halfword boundary.

F. Comparison of Fullword and Halfword Instructions

	Fullword Instruction	Corresponding Halfword Instruction	Differences
1.	L 8,FULLWD	LH 8,HLFWD	None
2.	A 8,FULLWD	AH 8,HLFWD	None
3.	S 8,FULLWD	SH 8,HLFWD	None
4.	M 8,FULLWD	MH 5,HLFWD	The product is stored in a *single* register. There is no need for even-odd pairs. The product cannot exceed ±2,147,483,647 (decimal). If an arithmetic overflow occurs, it is ignored. Thus, an arithmetic overflow will produce incorrect results.
5.	C 5,FULLWD	CH 5,HLFWD	The halfword operand is expanded to fullword for the comparison. Negative numbers have a lesser value than positive numbers.
6.	D 8,FULLWD	No halfword instruction exists.	
7.	ST 8,FULLWD	STH 8,HLFWD	The low-order 2 bytes of register 8 (16 bits) are placed in the storage location HLFWD.

Figure 12.5 illustrates a program to solve an equation using RX instructions. Figure 12.6 illustrates a program to solve the same equation using RR instructions.

```
*
*                 HOUSEKEEPING INSTRUCTIONS GO HERE
*
*         SOLVE THE EQUATION R = 8A - 4B + C + 3D + 15 USING RX TYPES
*
          LH      9,AA
          MH      9,=H'8'           8*A IN REG 9
          LH      3,BB
          MH      3,=H'4'           4*B IN REG3
          SR      9,3               8A - 4B
          AH      9,CC
          LH      3,DD
          MH      3,=H'3'
          AR      9,3               8A-4B+C+3D
          AH      9,=H'15'
          CVD     9,DBLE
          MVC     LINEOUT,SPACES
          MVC     LINEOUT+2(6),=X'402020202020'
          ED      LINEOUT+2(6),DATA+1
          PUT     OUTFILE,LINEOUT
*
*                 HOUSEKEEPING INSTRUCTIONS GO HERE
*                 ALONG WITH DTF OR DCB FOR OUTFILE
*
DBLE      DS      0D
          DS      CL4
DATA      DS      CL4
SPACES    DC      C' '
LINEOUT   DS      CL132
AA        DC      H'16'
BB        DC      H'12'
CC        DC      H'125'
DD        DC      H'250'
          END
```

Figure 12.5
Sample program using RX instructions.

```
*
*                     HOUSEKEEPING INSTRUCTIONS GO HERE
*
*          SOLVE THE EQUATION R = 8A - 4B + C + 3D + 15 USING RR TYPES
*
           L      4,A
           AR     4,4                      REG4 CONTAINS 2*A
           AR     4,4                           CONTAINS 4*A
           AR     4,4                           CONTAINS 8*A
           L      5,B
           A      5,B                      REG5 CONTAINS 2*B
           AR     5,5                                      4*B
           SR     4,5                      REG4 CONTAINS 8A-4B
           A      4,C                                     8A-4B+C
           L      5,D                      REG5 CONTAINS D
           A      5,D                                     2D
           A      5,D                                     3D
           AR     4,5                      REG4     8A-4B+C+3D
           L      5,=F'15'
           AR     4,5                      REG4     8A-4B+C+3D+15
           CVD    4,DBLE
           MVC    LINEOUT,SPACES
           MVC    LINEOUT+2(6),=X'402020202020'
           ED     LINEOUT+2(6),DATA+1
           PUT    OUTFILE,LINEOUT
*
*                     HOUSEKEEPING INSTRUCTIONS GO HERE
*                     ALONG WITH DTF OR DCB FOR OUTFILE
*
DBLE       DS     0D
           DS     CL4
DATA       DS     CL4
SPACES     DC     C' '
LINEOUT    DS     CL132
A          DC     F'16'
B          DC     F'12'
C          DC     F'125'
D          DC     F'250'
           END
```

Figure 12.6
Sample program using RR instructions.

CHAPTER SUMMARY

I. RR Format Instructions
    A. Both operands are registers.
        1. Registers contain negative values when the high-order bit contains a one.
        2. Negative numbers are stored as complements.
        3. The largest positive number is 2,147,483,647.
        4. A register containing all ones is equal to -1.
    B. In the following, Operand 1 is the receiving field and Operand 2 is the sending field.

```
LR   REG1,REG2   Load Register
AR   REG1,REG2   Add Register
SR   REG1,REG2   Subtract Register
```

II. Additional RR and RX Format Instructions
    A. Comparison

```
C    REG1,FULLWORD
CR   REG1,REG2
```

        1. Data is in binary fixed-point format.
        2. Comparison is algebraic, e.g., $+2$ is considered greater than -2.
        3. Condition code is set to low, high, or equal depending on whether Operand 1 is $<$, $>$, or $=$ Operand 2, respectively.

4. Neither operand is affected by the C or CR.
B. The Branch on Condition (BC) Instruction

    BC   MASK,LABEL

  1. Used to branch if Operand 1 >, <, =, ≥, ≤, ≠, Operand 2.
  2. Also used to branch if an overflow has occurred.
  3. Branch occurs depending on the value of the MASK.

    Example:

    C   6,FLD1
    BC 8,RTN1

    branches to

    RTN1 if register 6 = FLD1.

  4. Can use extended mnemonics.

    Example:

    C   6,FLD1
    BE RTN1

C. Multiplication

    M   EVEN REG,FULLWD
    MR EVEN REG,REG

  1. EVEN REG is the even register of an even-odd pair (e.g., 2–3, 4–5, etc.).
  2. The multiplicand is first placed in the odd register of the even-odd pair.
  3. The multiply instruction references the even register of the even-odd pair in the first operand.
  4. The product is right justified in the even-odd pair.
D. Division

    D   EVEN REG,FULLWD
    DR EVEN REG,REG

  1. EVEN REG is the even register of an even-odd pair.
  2. The dividend is loaded in the odd register of the even-odd pair.
  3. The even register must be set to zero.
  4. After the divide, the even-numbered register will contain the remainder and the odd-numbered register will contain the quotient.
E. Halfword RX Instructions
  1. OPCODE REG,HLFWD
  2. OPCODE may be:

    LH   Load Halfword
    AH   Add Halfword
    SH   Subtract Halfword
    MH   Multiply Halfword
    STH Store Halfword
    CH   Compare Halfword

  3. Operand 2 must be on a halfword boundary.

CHAPTER SELF-EVALUATING QUIZ

For Questions 1–5, indicate the result of each instruction and specify the field description of the operand.
  1. CVD   4,TOTAL
  2. LH   8,AMT

3. ST   6,ANS
4. M   8,CONST1
5. D   6,CONST2

6. Indicate two types of errors that can occur when a divide operation is executed.

Using binary operations, perform the calculations in Questions 7 and 8.

7. $A = \dfrac{(B - C)}{D}$

8. $E = F^2$

9. RX format instructions are instructions in which _____ .

10. RR format instructions are instructions in which _____ .

Page

SOLUTIONS

1. The contents of register 4 are placed in TOTAL in *packed-decimal* format.   342
   That is, the contents are converted from binary to packed decimal. TOTAL
   must be a doubleword.

   TOTAL   DS   D

2. The contents of AMT are loaded into register 8; AMT is a halfword.   368

   AMT   DS   H

3. The contents of register 6 are stored in the field called ANS, which should   335
   be on a fullword boundary.

4. CONST1 and the contents of register 9 are multiplied together; registers 8   362
   and 9 contain the results; CONST1 should be a fullword field, aligned on a
   fullword boundary.

5. CONST2 is the divisor; the contents of register 7 are divided by CONST2;   365
   The quotient is contained in register 7 and the remainder is in register 6.

6. Overflow; attempt to divide by 0   365

7. L   5,B   365
   S   5,C
   D   4,D
   ST   4,A
   ST   5,A+4

   Notice that the remainder is stored in the fullword at A and the quotient
   is stored in the fullword at A + 4.

8. L   5,F   362
   M   4,F
   ST   4,E
   ST   5,E+4

9. The first operand is a register and the second operand is a storage location.   333

10. Both operands are registers.   350

PRACTICE PROGRAM

Consider the problem definition shown in Figure 12.7. Write a program to print a profit
report with headings. See Figure 12.8 for a solution.

Notes
a. Profit = Cost − Selling Price
b. List the average profit at the end of the report.

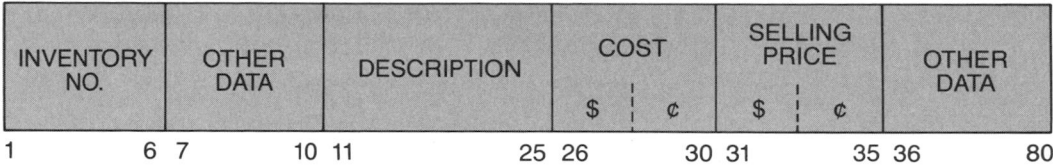

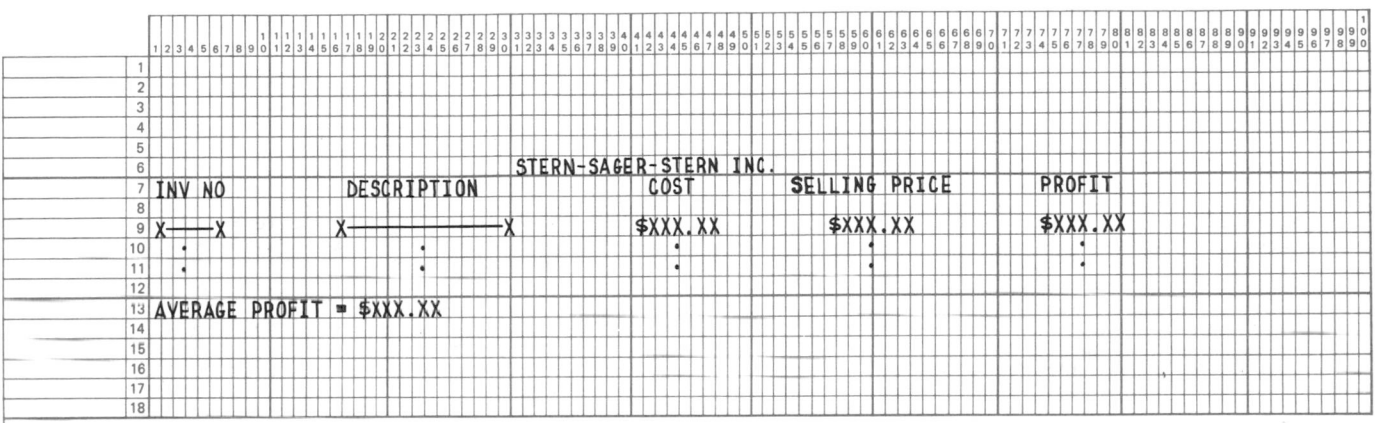

c. Sample Input Data

```
000001      ROLLER SKATES   0110001800
000002      ALUMINUM MAGNET0020000400
000003      MERCEDES MODEL  0130001600
000004      WATERFORD CRYS.0140002800
000005      THERMOS BOTTLE  0050001000
000006      PORTABLE TV     1660031200
000007      HOCKEY STICKS   0070001400
000008      ISLES JERSEYS   0480006600
000009      VITAMIN-HORMONE0090001800
000010      OLYMPIC WEIGHTS1100018900
```

d. Sample Output

```
                        STERN-SAGER-STERN INC.

INV NO          DESCRIPTION         COST        SELLING PRICE      PROFIT

000001          ROLLER SKATES     $ 11.00        $ 18.00         $   7.00
000002          ALUMINUM MAGNET   $  2.00        $  4.00         $   2.00
000003          MERCEDES MODEL    $ 13.00        $ 16.00         $   3.00
000004          WATERFORD CRYS.   $ 14.00        $ 28.00         $  14.00
000005          THERMOS BOTTLE    $  5.00        $ 10.00         $   5.00
000006          PORTABLE TV       $166.00        $312.00         $146.00
000007          HOCKEY STICKS     $  7.00        $ 14.00         $   7.00
000008          ISLES JERSEYS     $ 48.00        $ 66.00         $  18.00
000009          VITAMIN-HORMONE   $  9.00        $ 18.00         $   9.00
000010          OLYMPIC WEIGHTS   $110.00        $189.00         $  79.00

AVERAGE PROFIT = $ 29.00
```

Figure 12.7
Problem definition for the Practice Program.

```
  LOC   OBJECT CODE      ADDR1 ADDR2  STMT   SOURCE STATEMENT

                                        1            PRINT NOGEN
                                        2  ******************************
                                        3  *      START OF PROGRAM      *
                                        4  ******************************
000000                                  5  PRNTRPT  START 0
000000  90EC D00C        0000C          6           STM   14,12,12(13)
000004  05C0                            7           BALR  12,0
                         00006          8           USING *,12
000006  50D0 C492        00498          9           ST    13,SAVEAREA+4
00000A  41D0 C48E        00494         10           LA    13,SAVEAREA
                                       11           OPEN  (INFILE,INPUT)
                                       17           OPEN  (PRNTOUT,OUTPUT)
000026  D284 C25E C403   00264 00409   23           MVC   DETLINE,BLANKS
00002C  1B44                           24           SR    4,4           REG PAIR 4-5 IS USED
00002E  1B55                           25           SR    5,5           TO ACCUMULATE PROFITS.
000030  1B66                           26           SR    6,6           REG 6 COUNTS RECORDS.
                                       27  HEADRTN  PUT   PRNTOUT,BLANKS
                                       32           PUT   PRNTOUT,HEADING
                                       37           PUT   PRNTOUT,SUBHEAD
                                       42           PUT   PRNTOUT,BLANKS
00006A  F810 C3FA C488   00400 0048E   47           ZAP   LINECTR,ZERO
                                       48  ******************************
                                       49  *      MAIN PROCESSING       *
                                       50  ******************************
00007E                                 51  GETINFIL GET   INFILE,INREC
000084  D205 C25F C20E   00265 00214   56           MVC   DETLINE+1(6),ININVNO
00008A  D20E C26E C218   00274 0021E   57           MVC   DETLINE+16(15),INDESC
000090  F274 C3F2 C227   003F8 0022D   58           PACK  DBLE,INCOST        PACK INCOST
                         003F8         59           CVB   7,DBLE             MOVE TO REG 7 AND
000094  4F70 C3F2        003F8                                              
000094  D206 C286 C3FC   0028C 00402   60           MVC   DETLINE+40(7),EDPAT1  EDIT INTO DETAIL LINE
00009A  DE06 C286 C3F7   0028C 003FD   61           ED    DETLINE+40(7),PDATA
0000A0  925B C286        0028C         62           MVI   DETLINE+40,C'$'
0000A4  F274 C3F2 C22C   003F8 00232   63           PACK  DBLE,INSELPR
0000AA  4F80 C3F2        003F8         64           CVB   8,DBLE             PACK INSELPR
0000AE  D206 C297 C3FC   0029D 00402   65           MVC   DETLINE+57(7),EDPAT1  MOVE TO REG 8 AND
0000B4  DE06 C297 C3F7   0029D 003FD   66           ED    DETLINE+57(7),PDATA   EDIT INTO DETAIL LINE
0000BA  925B C297        0029D         67           MVI   DETLINE+57,C'$'
0000BE  1B87                           68           SR    8,7                CALCULATE PROFIT IN REG 8
0000C0  4E80 C3F2        003F8         69           CVD   8,DBLE             AND MOVE TO DETAIL LINE
0000C4  D206 C2A8 C3FC   002AE 00402   70           MVC   DETLINE+74(7),EDPAT1
0000CA  DE06 C2A8 C3F7   002AE 003FD   71           ED    DETLINE+74(7),PDATA
0000D0  925B C2A8        002AE         72           MVI   DETLINE+74,C'$'
0000D4  9240 C25E        00264         73  PUTLINE  MVI   DETLINE,C' '
                                       74           PUT   PRNTOUT,DETLINE
0000E6  FA10 C3FA C489   00400 0048F   79           AP    LINECTR,ONE
0000EC  5A60 C4DA        004E0         80  ACCUMTOT A     6,=F'1'            COUNT RECORDS PROCESSED.
0000F0  1A58                           81           AR    5,8                ACCUMULATE PROFITS IN
0000F2  F911 C3FA C48A   00400 00490   82           CP    LINECTR,FIFTY      REG 4-5 PAIR.
0000F8  47B0 C02C        00032         83           BNL   HEADRTN
0000FC  47F0 C06A        00070         84           B     GETINFIL
                                       85  ******************************
                                       86  *      END OF FILE ROUTINES   *
                                       87  ******************************
00010A                                 88  EOJ      CLOSE (INFILE)
00010A  D284 C25E C403   00264 00409   94           MVC   DETLINE,BLANKS
000110  1D46                           95           DR    4,6
000112  4E50 C3F2        003F8         96           CVD   5,DBLE
000116  D210 C25F C4DE   00265 004E4   97           MVC   DETLINE+1(17),=C'AVERAGE PROFIT = '
00011C  D206 C270 C3FC   00276 00402   98           MVC   DETLINE+18(7),EDPAT1
000122  DE06 C270 C3F7   00276 003FD   99           ED    DETLINE+18(7),PDATA
000128  925B C270        00276        100           MVI   DETLINE+18,C'$'
00012C  92F0 C25E        00264        101           MVI   DETLINE,C'0'
                                      102           PUT   PRNTOUT,DETLINE
                                      107           CLOSE (PRNTOUT)
00014A  58D0 C492        00498        113           L     13,SAVEAREA+4
00014E  98EC D00C        0000C        114           LM    14,12,12(13)
000152  07FE                         115           BR    14
                                      116  ******************************
                                      117  *      FILE SPECIFICATIONS    *
                                      118  ******************************
                                      119  INFILE   DCB   DDNAME=SYSIN,          *
                                                          MACRF=GM,             *
                                                          BLKSIZE=80,           *
                                                          LRECL=80,             *
                                                          DSORG=PS,             *
                                                          EODAD=EOJ
                                      173  PRNTOUT  DCB   DDNAME=SYSPRINT,       *
                                                          MACRF=PM,             *
                                                          BLKSIZE=133,          *
                                                          LRECL=133,            *
                                                          DSORG=PS
```

Figure 12.8
Solution to the Practice Program.

```
                          227 ****************************
                          228 *       INPUT RECORD        *
                          229 ****************************
000214                    230 INREC      DS     0CL80
000214                    231 ININVNO    DS     CL6
00021A                    232            DS     CL4
00021E                    233 INDESC     DS     CL15
00022D                    234 INCOST     DS     CL5
000232                    235 INSELPR    DS     CL5
000237                    236            DS     CL45
                          237 ****************************
                          238 *       OUTPUT RECORD       *
                          239 ****************************
000264                    240 DETLINE    DS     CL133
                          241 ****************************
                          242 *       HEADINGS        *
                          243 ****************************
0002E9                    244 HEADING    DS     0CL133
0002E9 F1                 245            DC     CL1'1'
0002EA 4040404040404040   246            DC     30CL1' '
000308 E2E3C5D9D560E2C1   247            DC     CL22'STERN-SAGER-STERN INC.'
00031E 4040404040404040   248            DC     80CL1' '
00036E                    249 SUBHEAD    DS     0CL133
00036E F0                 250            DC     CL1'0'
00036F C9D5E540D5D6        251            DC     CL6'INV NO.'
000375 4040404040404040   252            DC     10CL1' '
00037F C4C5E2C3D9C9D7E3   253            DC     CL11'DESCRIPTION'
00038A 4040404040404040   254            DC     14CL1' '
000398 C3D6E2E3           255            DC     CL4'COST'
00039C 4040404040404040   256            DC     8CL1' '
0003A4 E2C5D3D3C9D5C740   257            DC     CL13'SELLING PRICE'
0003B1 40404040404040     258            DC     7CL1' '
0003B8 D7D9D6C6C9E3       259            DC     CL6'PROFIT'
0003BE 4040404040404040   260            DC     53CL1' '
                          261 ****************************
                          262 *       WORK AREAS       *
                          263 ****************************
0003F8                    264 DBLE       DS     0D
0003F8                    265            DS     PL5
0003FD                    266 PDATA      DS     PL3
000400 050C               267 LINECTR    DC     PL2'50'
000402 402021204B2020     268 EDPAT1     DC     XL7'402021204B2020'
000409 4040404040404040   269 BLANKS     DC     133CL1' '
00048E 0C                 270 ZERO       DC     PL1'0'
00048F 1C                 271 ONE        DC     PL1'1'
000490 050C               272 FIFTY      DC     PL2'50'
000494                    273 SAVEAREA   DS     18F
                          274            END
0004E0 00000001           275                   =F'1'
0004E4 C1E5C5D9C1C7C540   276                   =C'AVERAGE PROFIT = '
```

Figure 12.8 (continued)

KEY TERMS

Condition code	Multiplicand
Dividend	Multiplier
Divisor	Product
Fullword	Quotient
Halfword	Remainder

REVIEW QUESTIONS

1. Using registers, write a routine to find the product of A and B where A is a number in register 3 and B is a number in register 6.
2. Using registers, write a routine to branch to OUT1 if AMT is between 100.3 and 207.5, inclusive.

3. Using registers, write a program to add all the even numbers from 2 to 100.

4. Using registers, write a routine to find the largest of each set of 3 fields A, B, and C read in. Each field is 5 positions long.

5. Given the following fields

```
BALANCE    DS    F
WITHDRWL   DS    F
DEPOSITS   DS    F
```

Write a routine, using registers, to compute

```
NEWBAL = BALANCE + DEPOSITS - WITHDRWL
```

If NEWBAL is zero, branch to ALERTRTN
If NEWBAL is negative, branch to OVERDRWN
If NEWBAL is positive, branch to PRINT

6. Write a routine using registers to compute

$$\text{RESULT} = A \times B - \frac{C + D}{F}$$

where A, B, C, D, and F are defined as fullwords and RESULT is to be a packed-decimal field.

7. Using registers, write a routine to convert Fahrenheit temperatures into Celsius using the formula

$$F = \frac{9}{5} C + 32$$

F and C are zoned-decimal fields.

8. Given three 5-digit amount fields in positions 1–15 (positions 1–5, positions 6–10, positions 11–15) of a record, write a routine to add these quantities using registers and to place the answer in a packed-decimal field called TOTAL. Branch to ERROR if TOTAL is negative.

9. Using registers, write a routine to compute

$$C = A^2 + B^2$$

Assume A and B are fullwords. C is a zoned-decimal field.

10. Using registers, compute WAGES where

```
WAGES = RATE × REGHRS + (1.5 × RATE × OVTHRS)
```

Two fields are supplied in zoned-decimal form as input: RATE (3 digits) and HRS (2 digits). OVTHRS is equal to the number of hours worked (HRS) in excess of 40, if the employee worked more than 40 hours. REGHRS = 40, if hours worked (HRS) is in excess of 40; otherwise, REGHRS = HRS.

Note:
RATE is to be interpreted as a dollars and cents figure.

DEBUGGING EXERCISES

The following program is designed to calculate a class average by accumulating student grades and counting the number of students processed. When the end-of-file condition is reached, the grade total is multiplied by 100 and then divided by the number of students to obtain a class average in the format XXX.XX. For example, if the student grades totaled 2630 and we multiply by 100, the result obtained equals 263,000. Then we divide by the number of students, 30, and obtain the class average of 87.66. Finally, the class average is listed. Find and correct any errors in the program. Remember to load the odd register, and reference the even register with both the multiply and the divide.

```
************************************************************
*        D E B U G    P R O G R A M    C H A P T E R    12
************************************************************
           LH    6,=H'O'              REG 6-COUNT THE STUDENTS
           SR    9,9                  REG 9-ACCUMULATE GRADES IN
SETUP      GET   INFILE,RECORD             REG 8-9 EVEN/ODD PAIR
           PACK  DWORD,GRADE
           CVB   7,GRADE
ACCUM      AR    9,7                  ACCUMULATE GRADES IN REG 9
           AH    6,ONE                ADD 1 TO STUDENT COUNT
           B     SETUP
EOF        MVC   LINEOUT,SPACES       END-OF-FILE-ROUTINE
           M     9,=F'100'            EXTEND ACCURACY
           DR    8,6                  DIVIDE BY NUMBER OF STUDENTS
           CVD   9,DWORD
           MVC   LINEOUT+50(7),=X'402020214B2020'
           ED    LINEOUT+50,DWORD+4
           MVC   LINEOUT+28(20),=C'THE CLASS AVERAGE IS'
           PUT   OUTFILE,LINEOUT
           CLOSE INFILE,OUTFILE
           EOJ
*
RECORD     DS    0CL30
NAME       DS    CL20
GRADE      DS    CL3
OTHER      DS    CL7
*
SPACES     DC    CL1' '
LINEOUT    DS    CL133
*
ONE        DS    H'1'
```

SOLUTIONS
```
1.         CVB   7,DWORD              DWORD, NOT GRADE
2.         M     8,=F'100'            REFERENCE REGISTER 8 OF THE 8-9
                                      EVEN-ODD PAIR.
3.         ED    LINEOUT+50(7),DWORD+5 EXPLICIT EDIT. ALSO NOTE A
                                      DISPLACEMENT OF 5 BYTES.
4. ONE     DC    H'1'                 MUST BE DC, NOT DS.
```

Note
Register 8 need not be set to zero since the multiply will do this for you. However, if the multiply was not present, then to divide correctly, it would be necessary to set register 8 to zero.

PROGRAMMING ASSIGNMENTS

1. Write a program using registers to print out each student's class average. The input is student class records with the following format.

    1–20 Student name
    21–23 Exam 1 score
    24–26 Exam 2 score
    27–29 Exam 3 score
    30–32 Exam 4 score
    33–80 Not used

    Each output line should contain student name and class average, spaced anywhere on the line.

    Note:
    First line should include heading: CLASS GRADES.

2. Write a program to compute compound interest from the following formula using the RR or RX format instructions.

    $$P_n = P_o(1 + r)^n$$

P_n = amount of principal after n periods of investment of P_o at rate r/period

The input is a file with the format

1–6   Principal P_o
7–8   Rate .xx r
9–80 Not used

Output is a printed report with compound interest calculated from periods 1 year to 10 years ($n = 1, 2, \ldots, 10$).

```
        PRINCIPAL-xxxxxx
                RATE-.xx
PERIODS         AMOUNT
   1            xxxxxx.xx
   2            xxxxxx.xx
   .
   .
  10            xxxxxx.xx
```

All amount fields must be edited.

3. Write a program using RR or RX format instructions to compute the arithmetic mean for an input file with the format

Record 1 for group: 1–5   Account number
                               6–7   Number of records in group
Remainder of records for group: 1–5   Account number
                               6–10   Amount

Print the account number and arithmetic mean for each group.

13 Branching and Looping With Registers

<table>
<tr><td>

OBJECTIVES

</td><td>

To familiarize you with:
1. *Branching using RX and RR instructions.*
2. *Looping using RX and RR instructions.*
3. *Methods to avoid infinite loops and abends caused by erroneous looping.*
4. *The load instructions of* LTR *(Load and Test Register) and* LA *(Load Address).*

</td></tr>
</table>

I. AN OVERVIEW OF BRANCHING OPERATIONS

Assembler language statements are executed in the order in which they appear, unless the computer is instructed to do otherwise with a *branch* instruction.

Thus far, we have learned the method used for unconditional branching.

```
B        LABEL
```

We have learned, as well, the method used for conditional branching.

```
⎡ BE  ⎤
⎢ BNE ⎥
⎢ BH  ⎥   LABEL
⎢ BL  ⎥
⎢ BNH ⎥
⎣ BNL ⎦
```

In this chapter, we will consider additional operation codes that may be used for altering the path of a program. These op codes are used for performing loops.

You will recall that a **loop** is a series of operations performed until a specific condition occurs. Every high-level programming language contains special looping instructions for sequence control, as shown in the following table.

Language	Instruction
BASIC	FOR/NEXT
FORTRAN	DO
COBOL	PERFORM . . . UNTIL
PL/1	DO

II. THE BRANCH ON COUNT (BCT) INSTRUCTION

A. Format

Instruction:	BCT
Meaning:	Branch on Count
Operand 1:	Register—contains the number of times the loop is to be performed.
Operand 2:	Contains the name or label of an instruction that is the beginning of a loop.

The Branch on Count (BCT) instruction provides you with loop control. The general format of this instruction follows.

Operation 10	Operand 16
BCT	REG,LABEL

where

BCT   signifies the branch on count loop routine.
REG   is a register and contains the number of times the loop is to be repeated.
LABEL   references a label appearing in the name field of an instruction. It is usually the first instruction of the loop.

The coding, flowchart, and pseudocode in Figure 13.1 indicate the logic contained in the BCT instruction.

Initially, the number of times the loop is to be repeated is placed in the register (REG). The CPU *automatically* subtracts one from the contents of the register (REG) each time the BCT instruction is executed. If, after subtraction, the contents of the register *are not zero,* the program branches to the routine named in the second operand. When the contents of the register reach zero, *no* branch occurs and the instruction *following* the Branch on Count instruction is then executed.

Note that if the preceding register had contents of zero initially, the logic would be incorrect. One is subtracted from the register *before* it is compared to zero. Hence an initial value of zero would be decreased by 1, making the contents −1, which is not equal to zero. Each additional pass through the routine decreases the register by another 1. The value of the register, then, becomes −1, −2, −3, . . . never reaching zero again. This condition would cause a program interrupt. To avoid it, you must make certain that the initial value of the register used in a BCT is not zero or a negative value.

We will now analyze a series of instructions using the BCT for loop control.

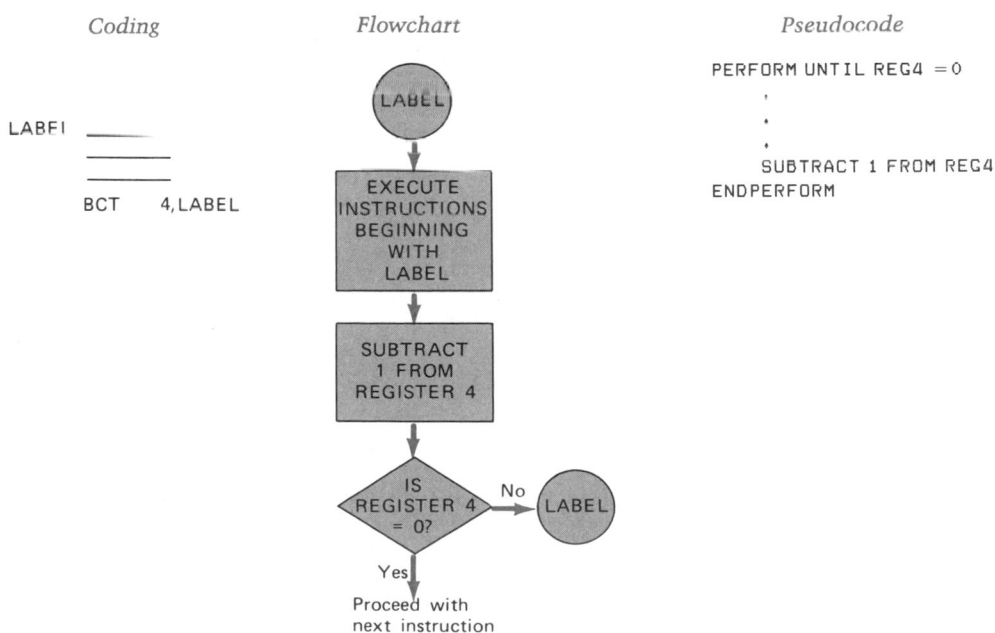

Figure 13.1
The coding, flowchart, and pseudocode for the BCT instruction.

B. Examples

Example 13.1 Calculate the product 5 × AVALUE using repeated addition rather than multiplication. Figure 13.2 illustrates the coding.

The Add instruction will be executed five times. As a result, register 8 will contain the answer, 5 × AVALUE. Note in the example that the BCT instruction references the label DO5X, which is the first instruction of the loop. When the loop is completed, register 2 will contain a zero because one was subtracted each time the BCT instruction was executed.

```
         L      8,=F'0'
         L      2,=F'5'
DO5X     A      8,AVALUE
         BCT    2,DO5X
         ST     8,ANSWER
         .
         .
         .
AVALUE   DC     F'100'
ANSWER   DS     F
```

Figure 13.2
Using repeated addition to perform multiplication.

Example 13.2 Write a routine to add all even numbers from 2 to 100 using the BCT. See Figure 13.3 for the solution.

```
         L      3,FIFTY      DO 50 TIMES
         L      5,ZEROS      ANSWER REGISTER
         L      2,TWO        EVEN NO.
LOOP     AR     5,2
         A      2,TWO
         BCT    3,LOOP
         ST     5,ANSWER
*
FIFTY    DC     F'50'
ZEROS    DC     F'0'
TWO      DC     F'2'
ANSWER   DS     F
```

Figure 13.3
Adding the even numbers from 2 to 100.

Example 13.3 Write a routine to find A^N, where A and N are binary input fields. Assume $N \geq 1$. See Figure 13.4 for the solution.

You must make sure that the loop is always entered from the top so that the control register is **initialized.** If, for some reason, this instruction is bypassed and you enter in the middle of the loop, you would have a logic error.

```
         L      3,N
         L      5,ONE
LOOP     M      4,A
         BCT    3,LOOP
         .
         .
         .
*
ONE      DC     F'1'
```

Figure 13.4
Finding A^N.

C. Structured Programming Using the BCT

You will recall that a structured program is designed to avoid the use of unconditional branches. If a series of instructions are to be executed a fixed number of times within a structured program, you should use a BCT rather than an unconditional branch.

Suppose we wish to add the amount fields of 100 records. We could use a BCT to achieve a structured approach.

```
            L      3,HUNDRED
PROCESS     GET    IN,REC
            PACK   PAMT,AMT
            AP     TOTAL,PAMT
            BCT    3,PROCESS
             .
             .
HUNDRED     DC     F'100'
```

This is equivalent to the PERFORM . . . UNTIL logical control structure used in pseudocode.

```
PERFORM . . . UNTIL 100 RECORDS PROCESSED
    READ
    ADD AMT TO TOTAL
ENDPERFORM
```

III. THE LOAD AND TEST REGISTER (LTR) INSTRUCTION

We noted previously that the register used in a BCT instruction should *not* have an initial value of zero or a negative number. This would cause the register to be decreased by one each time (−1, −2, −3, . . .), which would result in an infinite loop. The program would abend after a fixed period of time has elapsed, depending on a pre-established time limit set in the operating system.

You can avoid this problem by using a Load and Test Register (LTR) instruction, which sets the condition code. You would follow the LTR by any of the following conditional branches.

Conditional Branches that Can Be Used
After Arithmetic or LTR Instructions

Op Code	Meaning
BZ	Branch if Zero
BM	Branch if Minus
BP	Branch if Positive
BNZ	Branch if Not Zero
BNM	Branch if Not Minus
BNP	Branch if Not Positive

Instruction:	LTR
Meaning:	Load and Test Register
Operand 1:	General register
Operand 2:	General register (same as Operand 1)
Purpose:	Used for testing the contents of a register for −, +, or 0 value; usually followed by BM, BP, BZ.
Applications:	1. To avoid the possibility of BCT causing an infinite loop.
	2. To avoid the possibility of dividing by zero.
	3. In general, to test the sign of a register.

Note:
The contents of the general register used in the LTR instruction are not changed.

The LTR instruction is used in a manner similar to that described for the ZAP instruction. To determine if the *control register* (register 9, for example) contains a negative value, we simply add the following instructions to the loops (Figure 13.5).

Figure 13.5
Using the LTR to determine if a control register contains a negative value.

```
LTR    9,9
BM     ERROR
```

If register 9 inadvertently contained a negative number, the condition code would be set and the program would branch to a routine named ERROR. An abend condition would be avoided if register 9 were to be used in a BCT instruction.

An **infinite loop** resulting in an abend condition would also occur if the register inadvertently contained zero. We therefore include the following within the loop (Figure 13.6), which checks for both zero and negative values in register 9 with a BNP.

The coding in Figure 13.6 ensures that register 9 remains positive throughout the loop.

Figure 13.6
Using the LTR to determine if a control register contains a zero or negative value.

```
LOOP     .
         .
         .
         LTR    9,9
         BNP    ERROR
         BCT    9,LOOP
```

The LTR instruction may be used in a similar manner to prevent the computer from inadvertently dividing by zero. You will recall that a divisor of zero will cause a program interrupt when a divide instruction is executed. If the divisor is in a register, then the LTR instruction can be used prior to the divide (Figure 13.7).

Figure 13.7
Using the LTR to avoid division by zero.

```
LTR    5,5
BZ     ERROR
DR     2,5
```

In summary, whenever the sign of the contents of a register must be known, the LTR instruction can be used.

IV. THE BRANCH REGISTER (BR) AND LOAD ADDRESS (LA) INSTRUCTIONS

A. Formats

The Branch Register (BR) instruction causes a branch to the *address* stored in the referenced register.

Instruction:	BR
Meaning:	Branch to the address specified in the register in Operand 1.
Operands:	Use Operand 1 only; Operand 1 is a register that contains the address to be branched to.

The general format for the BR follows.

Operation 10	Operand 16
BR	REG

The BR is similar to the Branch (B) instruction. However, the general register in the BR instruction contains the *address of the instruction* to which we want to branch. For example, if register 9 contained the address of the instruction named LOOP, the program would branch to LOOP using either of the following.

B. Unconditional Branching to LOOP

LABEL	OPERATION 10 16	OPERAND	COMMENTS	72
	B	LOOP		

or

LABEL	OPERATION 10 16	OPERAND	COMMENTS	72
	BR	9		

The BR instruction provides the programmer with another means of unconditional branching. To use the BR instruction correctly, we place the address of an instruction (LOOP) in the register. The actual loading of an address into the register is performed with the Load Address (LA) instruction that follows.

C. The Load Address (LA) Instruction

The purpose of the Load Address (LA) instruction is to place an *address* of a reference point (label) into a register. This address then becomes the branch point for branching operations. The general format follows.

Operation 10	Operand 16
LA	REG,LABEL

where

LA   indicates the RX instruction Load Address.
REG   is a general register that receives the address of the instruction named in the second operand.
LABEL   identifies a labeled instruction or an entry point in the program.

For example, the following two sets of instructions would both cause an unconditional branch to the instruction named LOOP.

LABEL	OPERATION 10 16	OPERAND	COMMENTS	72
	B	LOOP		

LABEL	OPERATION 10 16	OPERAND	COMMENTS	72
	LA	9,LOOP		
	BR	9		

The Load Address instruction places the actual or effective address of LOOP in register 9. The BR instruction creates an unconditional branch to the *effective address* stored in register 9, which is the instruction identified as LOOP. If the instruction identified as LOOP were stored in the actual location 8C910, then the address 8C910 would be placed in register 9 when the LA instruction was executed.

The LA instruction can be used with a loop to perform string processing operations. That is, you can use an LA in conjunction with a loop to test a string of characters for specified values.

Example 13.4 Replace all commas in a text with blanks.

LABEL 1	OPERATION 10	OPERAND 16	COMMENTS	72
*				
START	LA	3,STRING	R3=ADDR OF 1ST BYTE OF STRING	
	LA	4,LENGTH	R4=LENGTH OF STRING	
*				
* SEARCH	FOR ALL COMMAS			
*				
COMPARE	CLI	Ø(3),C','	COMPARE CURRENT BYTE TO ','	
	BNE	NEXT		
	MVI	Ø(3),C' '	IF EQUAL REPLACE WITH SPACE	
NEXT	LA	3,1(3)	R3=ADDR OF NEXT BYTE IN STRING	
	BCT	4,COMPARE	DECR STRING LENGTH BY 1	
*			AND REPEAT	
STRING	DC	C'TOMORROW, AND TOMORROW, AND TOMW!'		
LENGTH	EQU	*-STRING	EQUATES LENGTH TO SIZE OF STRING	

V. THE BRANCH ON COUNT REGISTER (BCTR) INSTRUCTION

Instruction:	BCTR
Meaning:	Branch on Count Register
Operand 1:	Register that contains the number of times a loop is to be repeated.
Operand 2:	Register that contains the address of the first instruction of the loop.

Note:
An address must be loaded into Operand 2 *before* the BCTR is executed.

The BCTR, like the BCT instruction, is used to control the looping process. The difference, however, is that the second operand is a *register* in the BCTR instruction instead of a label. This register points to the entry point in the program where the loop begins. The address of the entry point (the beginning of the loop) must first be placed in a register using a Load Address (LA) instruction.

The general format for the BCTR follows.

Operation 10	Operand 16
BCTR	REG1,REG2

where

BCTR denotes a *Branch* on *Count Register* operation.
REG1 contains the number of times the loop is to be repeated.
REG2 contains the address of the beginning (first instruction) of the loop.

The number of times the loop is to be repeated is placed in the first operand (REG1). The *address of the first instruction* (the beginning of the loop) is loaded into the second operand (REG2). As with the BCT instruction, the contents of REG1 are reduced by one *automatically* with each pass through the loop. As long as the contents of REG1 are not zero, the program branches to the *address* stored in the second operand (REG2). When REG1 reaches zero, no branch occurs and the instruction following the BCTR instruction is executed next. A sample program will illustrate how the BCTR is used.

In the following example, multiplication will be performed by repeated addition. See Figure 13.8. Compare this example with that presented for the BCT instruction and note that the only differences are

1. the Load Address (LA) instruction is used, and
2. the BCT instruction is replaced by a BCTR.

```
            LA      5,DO5X
            L       2,=F'5'
   DO5X     A       8,AVALUE
            BCTR    2,5
            ST      8,ANSWER
            .
            .
            .
   AVALUE   DC      F'100'
   ANSWER   DS      F
```

Figure 13.8
Using the BCTR to perform repeated addition.

Another use of the BCTR instruction is to subtract one from any register at any time in the program. This occurs when the second operand is identified as *register zero*. For example, the instructions

LABEL	OPERATION	OPERAND	COMMENTS	
1	10 16			72
	BCTR	8,0		

LABEL	OPERATION	OPERAND	COMMENTS	
1	10 16			72
	S	8,=F'1'		

will both cause the contents of register 8 to be reduced by one.

Again, caution is advised in using both the BCT and BCTR instructions. If the initial count is zero, the first execution of the instruction (BCT or BCTR) will result in a -1 being stored in the first operand. This will cause a branch to occur because the count is not zero. If this happens, you will find your program in an infinite loop and an abend condition will occur eventually. In summary, note that the CPU does not check the contents of the count register until *after* it has subtracted one. An understanding of these concepts provides you with the powerful technique known as automatic loop control.

CHAPTER SUMMARY

I. Branching is used for logical control and looping

II. The Branch on Count (BCT) Instruction
   A. Similar to a DO in FORTRAN and a PERFORM . . . UNTIL in COBOL.
   B. Used extensively for looping.
   C. RX instruction: Operand 1 is a register, Operand 2 is a label.
   D. One is subtracted from the register; a branch to the label then occurs if the contents of the register are not zero.
   E. Make certain that the register in the BCT does not contain a zero initially.

III. The Load and Test Register (LTR) Instruction
   A. Used to test the contents of a register for plus, minus, or zero values.
   B. Used prior to BCT to ensure that an infinite loop does not occur.
   C. RR instruction: typically followed by a branch instruction.
   D. If both operands are the same, BP will cause a branch if the contents of the register are positive, BM will cause a branch if the contents of the register are negative, etc.

IV. The Branch Register (BR) Instruction
   A. Only one operand (a general register is used).
   B. An unconditional branch to the address stored in the general register occurs.

V. The Load Address (LA) Instruction
   A. For the BR instruction, a register must contain an address. The LA loads an address into a register.
   B. This is an RX instruction; Operand 2 is a label and Operand 1 is a register.
   C. The address specified by the label is loaded into the general register.

VI. The Branch on Count Register (BCTR) Instruction
   A. Functions like a BCT.
   B. Operand 2 is a register that contains the address to be branched to if the register in Operand 1 is not zero.
   C. Comparison of BCT and BCTR.
      1. The BCT and BCTR instructions are used for loop control.
      2. The first operand is always a register and contains the number of times the loop is to be repeated.
      3. Each time the loop is repeated, one is automatically subtracted from the contents of the first operand.
      4. If the contents of the first operand are not zero, a branch to the beginning of the loop occurs.
      5. When the first operand reaches zero, no branch occurs and the instruction following the BCT/BCTR is then executed.
      6. The Load and Test Register (LTR) instruction may be used to test the control register and ensure that its contents are not negative.
      7. The Load Address (LA) instruction is used to store the address of the first instruction of a loop in a register so that the BCTR may be used.

CHAPTER SELF-EVALUATING QUIZ

1. Sketch out a routine that performs a loop function 5 times.
2. Indicate the error in the following.

```
         L       5,=F'0'
LOOP
         ____
         ____
         ____
         ____
         BCT     5,LOOP
```

3. What sequence of steps may be used to ensure that an infinite loop will not occur?

Indicate what, if anything, is wrong with the instructions in Questions 4 and 5.

```
4.  RTN1      BCT       9,RTN1
5.  LOOP      L         9,=F'1'
              AR        6,5
              BCT       9,LOOP
```

6. Consider the following.

```
EAST          _____
              _____
              _____
              BCT       5,EAST
```

After proceeding through EAST the first time, the contents of register 5 are <u>increased/decreased</u> by one. Then, a(n) _____ is performed. If register 5 contains _____ , a branch to EAST occurs. If not, then _____ .

7. Code a single instruction that can be used in place of the following.

```
LA        7,LOOP1
BR        7
```

8. Using a BR instruction, code a branch to RTN5.

9. When is a BCTR instruction used in place of a BCT instruction?

10. Write a routine to sum all the odd integers from 1 to 101.

Page

SOLUTIONS

```
1.            L         5,=F'5'
     LOOP     _____
              _____
              _____
              BCT       5,LOOP
```
381

2. The result will be an infinite loop; because register 5 has an initial value of zero, BCT will decrease the register by 1 and then compare it to zero. Register 5 will become $-1, -2, -3, \ldots$, never reaching zero again.
381

```
3.  LTR       5,5
    BNP       ERROR
```
384

These instructions should directly precede the BCT instruction.

4. The label RTN1 should be on the first instruction of the loop.
382

5. The load instruction that initializes the control register should not be inside the loop. In addition, because a value of one is placed in the control register there is no need to set up a loop at all! These instructions are not intended to be repeated.
382

6. Decreased; test or comparison; any value other than zero; the next sequential instruction is executed
381

```
7.  B         LOOP1
```
385

```
8.  LA        6,RTN5
    BR        6
```
385

9. When the address of an instruction to be branched to is in a register.
386

```
    BCT       5,LOOP1
              or
    LA        9,LOOP1
              :
              :
    BCTR      5,9
```

```
10.           L         5,=F'50'
              L         3,=F'0'
              L         2,=F'1'
     LOOP     AR        3,2
              A         2,=F'2'
              BCT       5,LOOP
```
382

KEY TERMS

Infinite loop   Loop

REVIEW QUESTIONS

1. In a BCT instruction, the first operand is a(n) _____ that contains _____ . The second operand is a(n) _____ .
2. (T or F) The computer automatically subtracts one from the first operand of the BCT instruction every time it is executed.
3. Explain under what circumstances an infinite loop will occur with a BCT instruction.
4. Explain how to avoid the possibility of an infinite loop when using a BCT instruction.
5. Illustrate how the LA and BR instructions can be used to cause an unconditional branch.
6. Explain the difference between the BCT and BCTR instructions.

DEBUGGING EXERCISES

The following program is designed to calculate the sum of the series 5, 10, 15, 20, and so on until 100 is reached. The program utilizes a BCTR loop. A counter is established with register 3 and the running total of the counter values are stored in register 7. The LTR instruction is used to prevent an infinite loop. Perform a desk check and identify any errors you find in the program.

```
****************************************************************
*         D E B U G   P R O G R A M     C H A P T E R   13
****************************************************************
          L      4,TWENTY               REG 4-NO. OF PASSES
          SR     3,3                     REG 3-REPRESENTS CTR
          LA     5,DO20X                 REG 5-POINTS TO DO20X LABEL
DO20X     L      7,=F'0'                 REG 7-REPRESENTS TOTAL
          A      3,FIVE                  INCREMENT COUNTER
          AR     7,3                     ACCUMULATE CTR IN REG 7
          LTR    4,4
          BP     ERROR
          BCTR   4,5
*
          CVD    5,ANS
          MVC    LINEOUT+50(8),=X'4020202020202120'
          ED     LINEOUT+50(8),ANS
          MVC    LINEOUT+20(23),=C'THE SUM OF 5-100 BY 5 IS'
          PUT    OUTFILE,LINEOUT
          CLOSE  INFILE,OUTFILE
          EOJ
*
SPACES    DC     CL1' '
LINEOUT   DS     CL133
*
FIVE      DC     F'5'
DWORD     DS     0D
          DS     PL4
ANS       DS     PL4
TWENTY    DS     F'20'
```

SOLUTIONS
1. LINEOUT was not cleared.
2. Register 7 is reset to zero with each pass through the loop. Change to:

```
          L      7,=F'0'
DO20X     A      3,FIVE
```

3. Change `BP ERROR` to `BM ERROR`.
4. Change `CVD 5,ANS` to `CVD 5,DWORD`
5. The operation code is `DC`:

   ```
   TWENTY    DC    F'20'
   ```

6. The length of the move is 24 in

   ```
   MVC    LINEOUT+20(24),.....
   ```

PROGRAMMING ASSIGNMENTS

1. Write a program to determine N!, where $N! = N \times N - 1 \times N - 2 \times \ldots 1$. For example, $5! = 5 \times 4 \times 3 \times 2 \times 1$.

2. Given P_o, R, N, write a program to compute $P_N = P_o (1 + R)^N$ where

   P_o = principal
   R = rate .xx
   N = number of periods of investment of P_o at rate R per period
   P_N = principal after N periods of investment of P_o at rate R per period

3. Write a program to read in 20 records, each with a student name in positions 1–20 and a final exam grade in positions 21–23. Print the class average.

4. There are 15 salespeople in company ABC. For each salesperson, there are 5 input records, one for each day of the week.

   1–2 Salesperson number
     3 Day number (1–5)
   4–8 Amount of sales

   Prepare a report that prints for each salesperson the salesperson number and the weekly sales amount.

UNIT 5

DEBUGGING ASSEMBLER PROGRAMS

Using Instruction Formats and Interrupt Codes for Debugging Programs

OBJECTIVES

To familiarize you with:
1. *Techniques used to debug assembler language programs.*
2. *The machine-language object code.*
3. *How instructions are translated into machine language.*
4. *The program status word and how it is used for finding program errors.*
5. *The types of program interrupts that may occur.*

I. INSTRUCTION FORMATS

A. An Overview

The following table provides an overview of the five instruction types in assembler language and their lengths when translated into machine language.

Instruction Types

Description	Format	Instruction Length in Bytes
Register-to-Register (Both operands are registers)	RR	2
Register and Indexed Storage (Operand 1—register Operand 2—storage area)	RX	4
Register and Storage (Operand 1—register Operand 2—storage area)	RS	4
Storage Immediate (Operand 1—storage area Operand 2—one-byte constant defined within instruction)	SI	4
Storage-to-Storage (Both operands are storage areas)	SS	6

To read storage dumps and to understand how instructions actually appear in machine language, it is necessary to determine the format of each instruction and the number of bytes it utilizes.

From the above, we see that instruction formats can be specified in three lengths: 1, 2, or 3 halfwords (2, 4, or 6 bytes) depending on the general category and the specific operation code or mnemonic. Before discussing each instruction format, note these general rules.

General Rules
1. Each operation code is 1 byte long (two hexadecimal digits).
2. The first *2 bits* of each operation code specify the type of instruction, as in the following table.

Two High-Order Bits of Op Code Indicate
Instruction Type

High-Order Bits	Instruction Type	
00	RR	
01	RX	
10	RS	Note these have
10	SI	the same high-order bits
11	SS	

B. One Halfword Instructions: RR-Type

An RR instruction in which both operands are general registers is always 2 bytes, or one halfword, in length.

RR Format

OP CODE	FIRST OPERAND	SECOND OPERAND
OP	R1	R2

Machine language
equivalent   8 bits   4 bits   4 bits = 2 bytes

For RR-type instructions, as with most assembly language instructions, the first operand is the receiving field. The 4 bits used to represent R1 and the 4 bits used to represent R2 can contain 0000–1111 in binary, that is, 0–15 in decimal. Because general registers can be numbered from 0–15, this 4-bit representation suffices.

Example 14.1

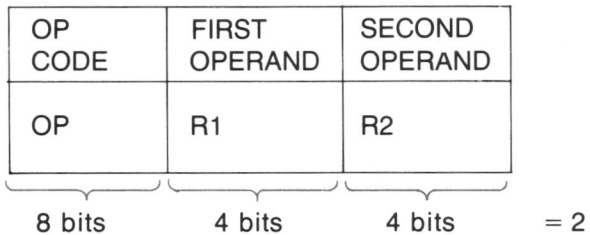

Assembly Instruction   *Machine Language Equivalent*
  AR 4,5   OP R1 R2

Binary | 0001 | 1010 | 0100 | 0101 |

Hex | 1 | A | 4 | 5 |

On the inside back cover of this text is a listing of the machine-language equivalent for each RR instruction discussed. This is a very handy guide when debugging programs. Figure 14.1 illustrates sample RR instructions.

Instruction	Op Code	Machine Language Equivalent
Add Registers	AR	1A
Branch and Link Registers	BALR	05
Branch on Condition	BCR	07
Branch on Count	BCTR	06
Compare Registers	CR	19
Divide Registers	DR	1D
Load Registers	LR	18
Multiply Registers	MR	1C
Subtract Registers	SR	1B

Figure 14.1
Sample RR instructions.

High-order Bits   Note that the first 2 bits of each operation code that utilizes two registers as its operands are *00*.

Suppose the AR instruction in the example is stored beginning in address 3001. Then, bytes 3001–3002, when printed as part of a dump, will appear as

   1   A   4   5

Notice that the operation code 1A begins with the bit pattern 0001, with the first 2 bits being 00.

C. Two Halfword Instructions: RX-, RS-, SI-Type

The two halfword instructions considered here are RX, RS, and SI. Instructions of this type have one operand that is defined as a storage location and another operand that is either a register or storage-immediate byte. These instructions are always two halfwords, or 4 bytes in length.

RX instructions (see Figure 14.2) are the following:

RX Format

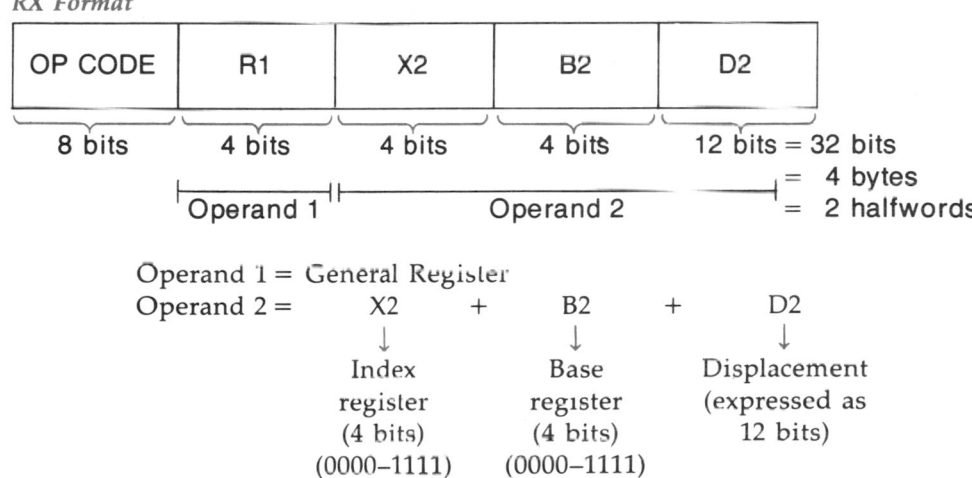

Instruction	Op Code	Machine Language Equivalent
Add	A	5A
Add Halfword	AH	4A
Branch and Link	BAL	45
Branch on Condition	BC	47
Branch on Count	BCT	46
Compare	C	59
Compare Halfword	CH	49
Convert to Binary	CVB	4F
Convert to Decimal	CVD	4E
Divide	D	5D
Load	L	58
Load Address	LA	41
Load Halfword	LH	48
Multiply	M	5C
Multiply Halfword	MH	4C
Store	ST	50
Store Halfword	STH	40
Subtract	S	5B
Subtract Halfword	SH	4B

Figure 14.2
Sample RX instructions.

B2 and D2   All effective addresses of storage areas are obtained by adding

1. A 12-bit displacement labeled D2 in the following examples. This is the absolute storage address from 0000–4095 in value.
2. The 24 lower-order bits of the base register labeled B2 in the examples. These bits are represented in the 3 low-order bytes of the instruction.

As we will see, all storage areas must be defined using this 36-bit representation—12 bits for the displacement and 24 bits for the base register.

X2   For RX-type instructions *only*, an additional specification is necessary to determine the effective address of the storage area, in this case the second operand. X2 refers to a general register that may be used for indexing, which is a form of address modification discussed in Chapter 16. If an RX format instruction is used without indexing, then X2 will contain 0000.

The "2" in B2, D2, and X2 indicates that we are referencing the *second* operand.

Example 14.2   An example of the RX-type Add instruction follows.

LABEL	OPERATION	OPERAND	COMMENTS
	A	2,TOTAL	

TOTAL is a storage area that, when converted to machine language, is specified with an index register X2, a base register, B2, and a displacement, D2. Hence, this Add may be represented as follows (the actual representation will depend on the address assigned to TOTAL).

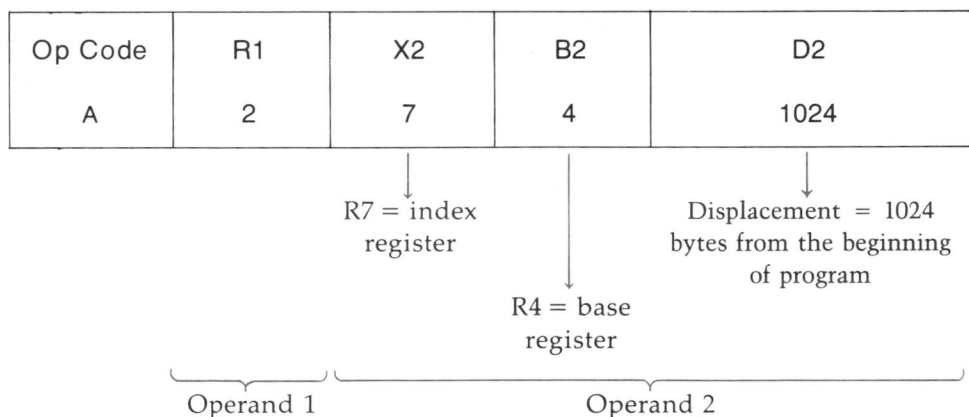

Op Code	R1	X2	B2	D2
A	2	7	4	1024

R7 = index register

R4 = base register

Displacement = 1024 bytes from the beginning of program

Operand 1   Operand 2

Operation—Add
Operand 1 = Contents of general register 2
Operand 2 = the effective address of TOTAL
= contents of register 7 + contents of register 4 + 1024
(X2)   (B2)   (D2)

Machine-Language Equivalent

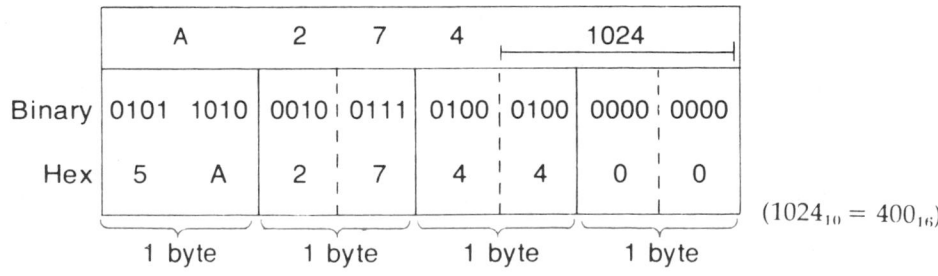

	A	2	7	4		1024	
Binary	0101 1010	0010	0111	0100	0100	0000	0000
Hex	5 A	2	7	4	4	0	0

$(1024_{10} = 400_{16})$

1 byte   1 byte   1 byte   1 byte

Note that all dumps will print in hex notation. Consequently, the preceding would be expressed in a storage dump as

```
5A  27  44  00
```

High-Order Bits   The machine-language equivalent of the Add (A) instruction had 01 in its first 2 high-order bits. As noted, *all* RX instructions have a 01 in the 2 high-order bits of the operation code.

Figure 14.3 illustrates sample RS instructions.

Instruction	Op Code	Machine Language Equivalent
Branch on Index High	BXH	86
Branch on Index Low or Equal	BXLE	87
Load Multiple	LM	98

Figure 14.3
Sample RS instructions.

The RS instructions, like the preceding RX type, are register and storage instructions. The RS type, however, does *not* have an indexing factor but may include a third element as part of the operand.

RS Format

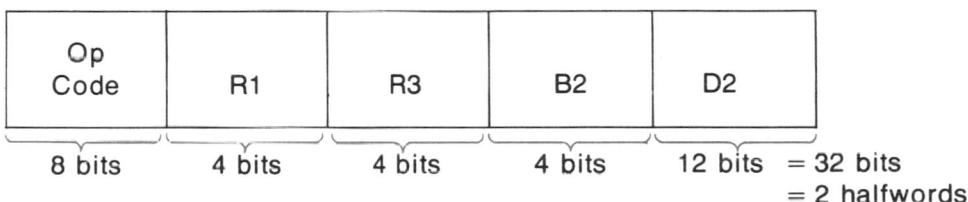

Op Code	R1	R3	B2	D2
8 bits	4 bits	4 bits	4 bits	12 bits = 32 bits = 2 halfwords

Example 14.3   An example of the Load Multiple Instruction, an RS-type instruction, follows.

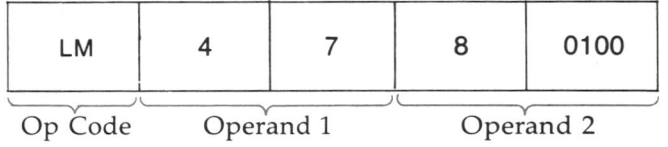

LABEL	OPERATION	OPERAND	COMMENTS
	10 16		72
	LM	4,7,TOTAL	LOADS TOTAL INTO R4-R7

This instruction requires TOTAL to be translated into some address that specifies a base register and a displacement, as follows.

LM	4	7	8	0100
Op Code	Operand 1		Operand 2	

Purpose of the Instruction
Contents of registers 4–7 are replaced by the contents of the storage locations beginning at Operand 2.

In the above, TOTAL, which is Operand 2, has an effective address of B2 (contents of the base register) plus D2 (displacement). That is, the contents of base register 8 are added to the displacement of 100 to obtain the effective address.

Machine-Language Equivalent

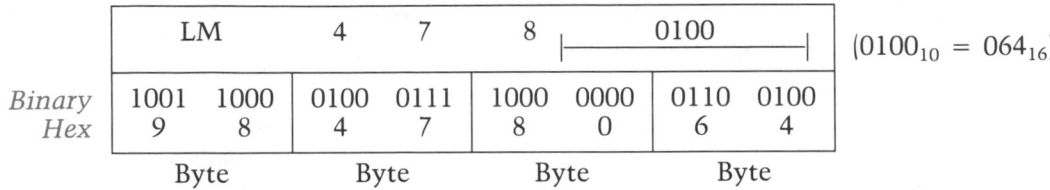

$(0100_{10} = 064_{16})$

	LM	4	7	8	0100	
Binary	1001 1000	0100 0111	1000 0000	0110 0100
Hex	9 8	4 7	8 0	6 4
	Byte	Byte	Byte	Byte

A dump would list this instruction as

9 8 4 7 8 0 6 4

High-Order Bits RS instructions all have 10 in the first 2 bits of the machine-language equivalent of the operation code.

3. SI Instructions

Figure 14.4 lists sample SI (Storage Immediate) instructions.

The SI format is used when the first operand is in main storage and the second is a self-defining operand.

Figure 14.4
Sample SI instructions.

Instruction	Op Code	Machine Language Equivalent
Compare Logical Immediate	CLI	95
Move Immediate	MVI	92

SI Format

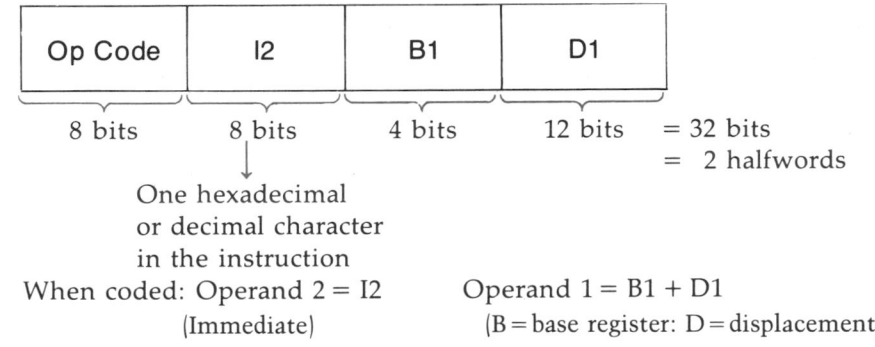

Op Code	I2	B1	D1
8 bits	8 bits	4 bits	12 bits = 32 bits
			= 2 halfwords

One hexadecimal
or decimal character
in the instruction
When coded: Operand 2 = I2   Operand 1 = B1 + D1
(Immediate)   (B = base register: D = displacement)

Note that the machine-language equivalent of SI instructions places the second operand, I2, in bits 8–15 and the first operand, which is B1 + D1, in bits 16–31. The order of the operands, then, is reversed during the conversion to machine language.

Example 14.4   An example of the Move Immediate (MVI) instruction follows.

LABEL	OPERATION	OPERAND	COMMENTS	
1	10 16			72
	MVI	HOLD,C'5'		

This MVI instruction may convert to the following, depending on the actual address of HOLD.

MVI	5	4	1000

Machine-Language Equivalent

MVI		5	4		1000	
1001	0010	1111	0101	0100	0011	1110	1000
9	2	F	5	4	3	E	8

Note
This is actually *coded* as the second operand but is assembled into machine language as indicated.

High-Order Bits   Like the RS format, SI instructions always have a 10 in the high-order bits of the operation code.

D. Three Halfword Instructions: SS-Type

Figure 14.5 illustrates sample SS instructions.

Instruction	Op Code	Machine Language Equivalent
Add Packed Decimal	AP	FA
Compare Packed Decimal	CP	F9
Divide Packed Decimal	DP	FD
Multiply Packed Decimal	MP	FC
Edit	ED	DE
Subtract Packed Decimal	SP	FB
Zero and Add Packed	ZAP	F8
Compare Logical	CLC	D5
Move Characters	MVC	D2
Pack	PACK	F2
Unpack	UNPK	F3

Figure 14.5
Sample SS instructions.

These instructions are sometimes called variable-length formats because the actual number of storage positions affected by the instruction is *not fixed* but, rather depends on the specific operation. The *length* of the instruction, however, is fixed.

SS Format

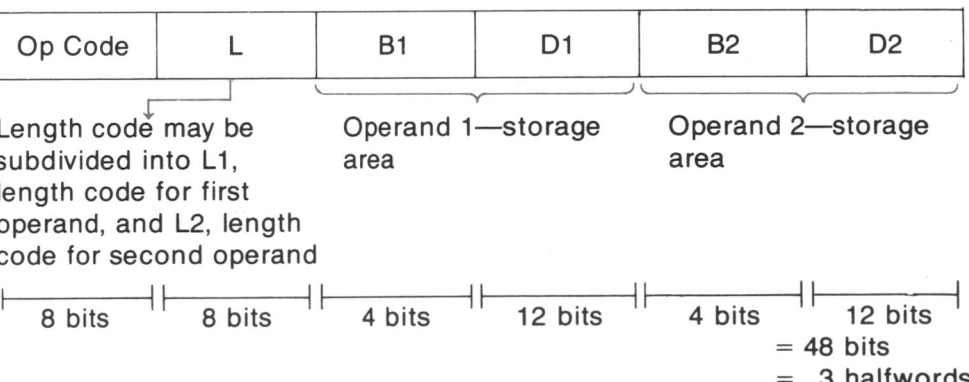

Length Code The length code specifies the number of bytes (*in excess of one*) that are to be processed. Hence, if a four-byte operand is to be operated on, the length code would contain 3. That is, 3 bytes in excess of 1 are to be processed.

Some instructions, such as move operations, require only one length code. One operand determines the length of the operation. Thus, only one explicit length may be indicated with move instructions. For other instructions, such as the Add, the length of *both* operands may be specified.

Example 14.5 An example of the Add Packed instruction follows.

LABEL	OPERATION	OPERAND	COMMENTS
1	10 16		72
	AP	TOTAL,AMT1	

The AP instruction converts TOTAL and AMT1 to actual machine addresses. The following represents a partial machine-language conversion.

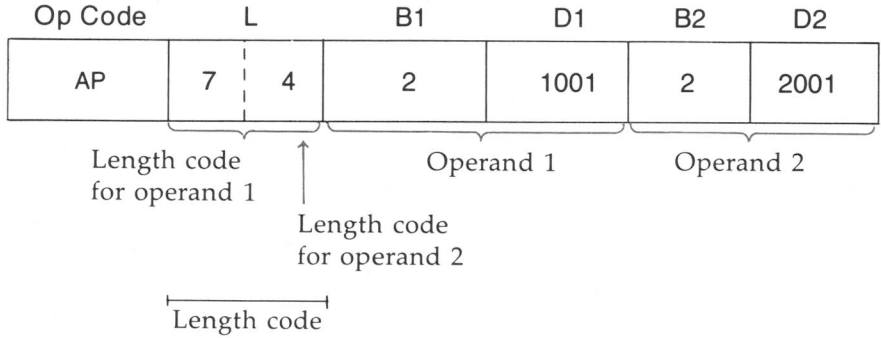

Suppose base register 2 contains 1000. Operand 1 would have an address of 2001 (1001 + 1000) while Operand 2 would have an address of 3001 (2001 + 1000). The length code of 7 means that 8 bytes of the first operand are operated on. The length code of 4 means that 5 bytes of the second operand are operated on.

Result

The foregoing operation would result in the addition of the contents of storage locations 3001–3005 to 2001–2008.

Machine-Language Equivalent

AP		7	4	2		1001		2		2001
1111	1010	0111	0100	0010	0011	1110	1001	0010	0111	1101	0001
F	A	7	4	2	3	E	9	2	7	D	1

|—Op Code—||——L——||—B1—||——D1——||—B2—||——D2——|

High-Order Bits For SS instructions, the first two bits of the operation code will contain 11.

Summary A table on the inside back cover of this text indicates

1. Every instruction discussed.
2. The format for each instruction.
3. The machine-language operation code.

This information will prove exceedingly useful in debugging programs. You can use this table to determine the machine-language equivalent of all instructions. Moreover, it can help you to read a dump and determine the meaning of each machine instruction.

Self-Evaluating Quiz

1. When instructions are assembled they may be (no.), (no.), or (no.) bytes in length. Hence, all instruction addresses are divisible by (no.).
2. The first part of every instruction is the _____ , which is (no.) bits long.
3. A program can be relocated in storage by changing the contents of the _____ register.
4. All storage addresses are obtained by adding the contents of the _____ to the _____ . RX-format instructions require an additional _____ register whose contents must also be added to obtain a storage address.
5. Each register is converted to a (no.)-bit representation.
6. The displacement is specified as a (no.)-bit field.
7. For the following operation codes expressed hexadecimally, indicate the bit configuration of the 2 high-order bits. From this configuration derive the length of the instruction in halfwords. Then look up the instruction in the table that appears on the inside back cover of this text.
   a. 1A
   b. 95
   c. FD
8. The displacement has a range, in decimal, from 0 to (no.) bytes.
9. Only general register (no.) through (no.) can be used as a base register.
10. Label the fields in the following formats. Also indicate the number of bits for each field.
    a. RR
    b. RX
    c. RS
    d. SI
    e. SS
11. For most assembler instructions, the results replace the (first/second) operand.
12. Only the _____ -type instruction uses an index register.
13. Only the _____ -type instruction requires a length code to indicate the number of bytes to be operated on.
14. In the SI format, the second operand (I2) is (no.) bytes long.
15. Given the following machine-language instructions, provide the equivalent assembler instructions. Assume the following storage definitions and base register 3.

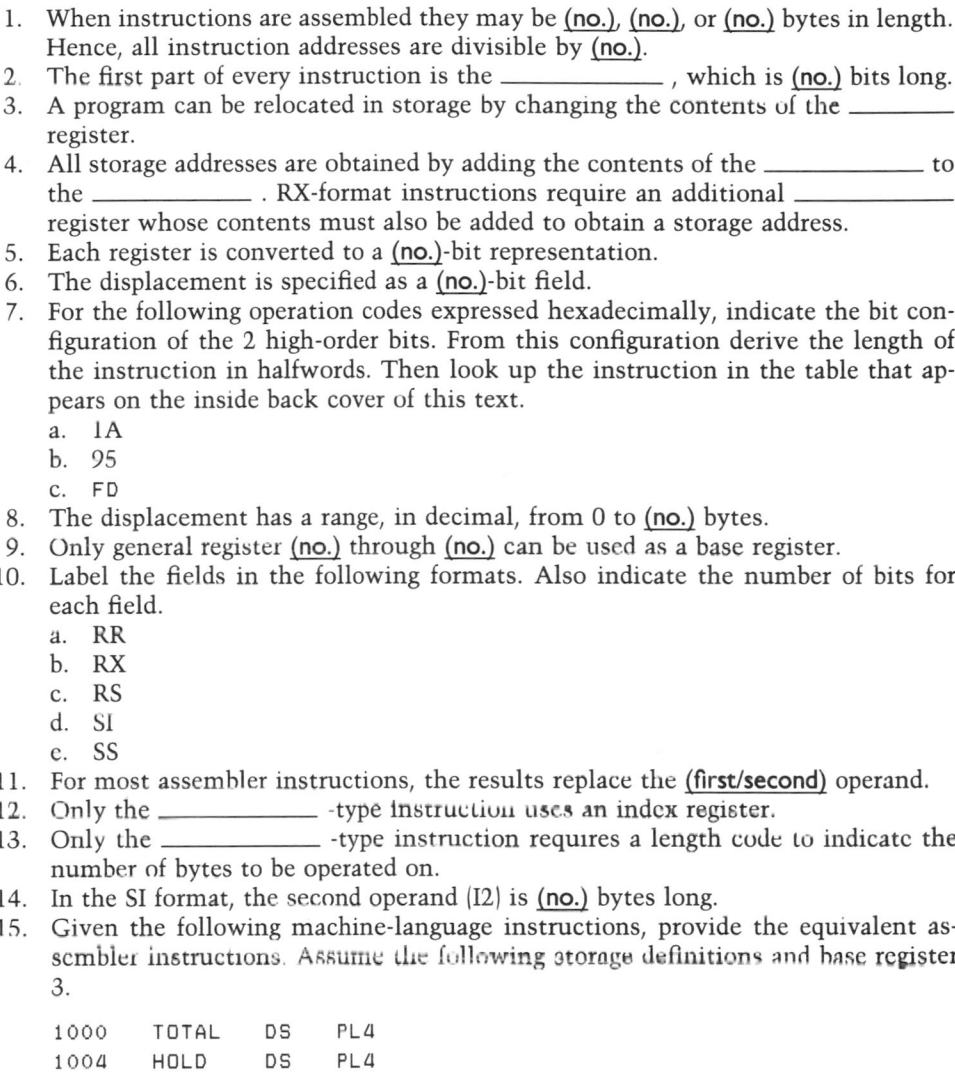

```
1000    TOTAL    DS    PL4
1004    HOLD     DS    PL4
```

a. | 1 9 | 5 3 |

b. | 1 8 | 7 9 |

c. | F 9 | 3 3 | 3 3 | E 8 | 3 3 | E C |

SOLUTIONS

1. 2; 4; 6; 2
2. Operation code; 8
3. Base
4. Base register; displacement; index
5. Four
6. 12

7. a. 1A

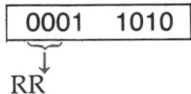

```
0001   1010
```
RR

one halfword
1A = AR instruction (Add Register)

b. 95

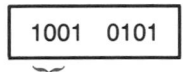

```
1001   0101
```
(RS or SI)
two halfwords
95 = CLI instruction (Compare Logical Immediate). Therefore, it is an SI-type instruction.

c. FD

```
1111   1101
```
SS

three halfwords
FD = DP instruction (Divide Packed Decimal)

8. 4095; this is the largest number that can be represented in 12 bits.

9. 2–12

10. a. RR

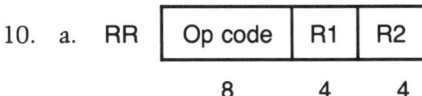

Op code	R1	R2
8	4	4

b. RX

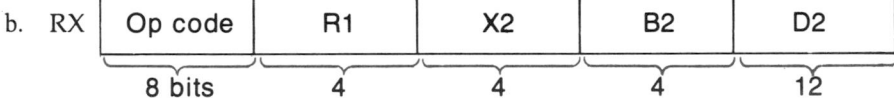

Op code	R1	X2	B2	D2
8 bits	4	4	4	12

c. RS

Op code	R1	R3	B2	D2
8	4	4	4	12

d. SI

Op code	I2	B1	D2
8	8	4	12

e. SS

Op code	Length		B1	D1	B2	D2
	L1	L2				
8	8		4	12	4	12

11. First
12. RX
13. SS
14. One
15. a. CR 5,3
    b. LR 7,9
    c. CP TOTAL,HOLD

II. PROGRAM INTERRUPTS AND PROGRAM STATUS WORDS

A. Introduction

On first- and second-generation computers any unanticipated problem would cause the computer to "hang up," that is, to stop processing. It was then the operator's job to determine the source of the problem, correct it if possible, or abort the job and move on to the next application. Such a procedure was exceedingly inefficient because the time required to resolve a problem while the computer was idle was very costly.

Third-and fourth-generation computers are designed to operate with minimum manual intervention and maximum automatic efficiency. The *supervisor* controls the operations of the computer in such a way that when unanticipated situations arise it can redirect the activities of the machine, resolve or bypass the source of the problem, or abort (abend) a job if necessary and read in the next job. The method used to handle problems is called an *automatic interrupt system*.

If you have actually run any programs, you are probably familiar with the procedure used by the computer to handle programming errors. This procedure is part of the **interrupt** system. If a major error has occurred in your program, the supervisor prints an error message, aborts the run, and automatically begins to process the next program.

B. Types of Interrupts

There are other types of interrupts in addition to those caused by program errors, as listed here.

TYPES OF INTERRUPTS

1. Conditions **external** to the system (for example, the interrupt key is depressed by an operator and the system is turned off)
2. **Input/output** problem
3. **Program error**
4. **Machine error**
5. **Supervisor call** (for example, the end of job results in an interrupt that returns control to the supervisor)

Note that every job ends with an interrupt. If the job has been processed with no execution errors, the interrupt that occurs is called a "supervisor call." This "supervisor call" interrupt returns control to the supervisor so that the next program may be processed. When **debugging** a program, you may find that other interrupts have caused your job to be aborted. Most often, a program error is responsible for these program interrupts. Keep in mind, however, that an abend condition can result from one of the other interrupts as well.

To determine the cause of an aborted run, the programmer must be able to read and decipher the **Program Status Word** (PSW), which provides valuable information on the status of a program at the time an interrupt has occurred. Learning how to interpret a PSW will not only enable you to find the actual type of interrupt and/or error that caused the problem, but will provide you with information on the contents of key fields when the interrupt occurred.

C. Program Status Words (PSW) and Interrupts

1. Old and New PSW

Each time an instruction is executed a Current PSW is generated. This is a doubleword of information on the status of that instruction. If any interrupt occurs (machine, program, supervisor, external, or I/O), the Current PSW is placed in a field called the Old PSW. The address of a routine used to patch or resolve such an interrupt is automatically loaded into the Current PSW by the supervisor. If the interrupt can be resolved by the interrupt-handling routine, then the Old PSW is loaded back into the Current PSW and the program continues.

When an interrupt occurs the following procedure is implemented.

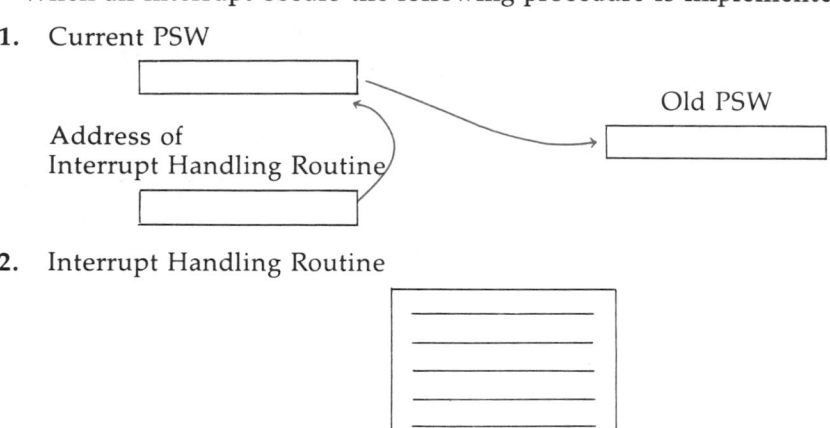

1. Current PSW

   Address of
   Interrupt Handling Routine

   Old PSW

2. Interrupt Handling Routine

   Load Old PSW

3. Old PSW

   Current PSW

2. An Example

Suppose a PUT instruction is executed that attempts to write a line on the printer. If there is no paper in the printer, an interrupt will occur. The Current PSW is loaded into the Old PSW. The supervisor calls in an interrupt-handling routine that prints a message on the console for the computer operator. Once the printer is ready, the interrupt-handling routine loads the Old PSW back into the Current PSW and the program continues executing.

Most often the interrupt-handling routine is part of the operating system. It is, however, possible for programmers to write their own interrupt-handling routines. However, such a procedure is considered beyond the scope of this text.

When an irresolvable program error or other interrupt has occurred, the computer simply prints the contents of the PSW, aborts the job, and reads in the next job. (If the interrupt that occurs is a result of a machine error, the computer may shut itself off completely.)

3. Contents of PSW

As an overview, note that the following elements are part of the doubleword PSW that provides the programmer with the status of a program at the time of an interrupt.

ELEMENTS OF THE PSW: AN OVERVIEW

1. Type of interrupt
2. Address of the next instruction to be executed
3. Length of the previous instruction
4. Condition code at the time of interrupt
5. The state of the CPU at the time of the interrupt—states are "stopped or operating," or "problem or supervisory"

We will *not* discuss the entire PSW in depth but only those elements that are likely to be of value when debugging a program. The other elements will be discussed only briefly.

4. Interrupt Code

You will recall that the PSW is a 64-bit, or doubleword, field with bits numbered 0–63. The **interrupt code** is in bits 16–31.

PSW

	Interrupt code	

0   16   31   63

Bits 16–23 of the interrupt code provide information on the exact type of interrupt that occurred. Because we are focusing our attention on program interrupts, we will not concern ourselves with the contents of bits 16–23. Bits 24–31, however, provide the programmer with the type of program error that caused the interrupt, as shown in the following table.

Interrupt Codes (Bits 24–31 of PSW)

Hexadecimal	Binary	Error Condition
01	0000 0001	Operation
02	0000 0010	Privileged operation
03	0000 0011	Execute
04	0000 0100	Protection
05	0000 0101	Addressing
06	0000 0110	Specification
07	0000 0111	Data
08	0000 1000	Fixed-point overflow
09	0000 1001	Fixed-point divide
0A	0000 1010	Decimal overflow
0B	0000 1011	Decimal divide
[a]0C	0000 1100	Exponent overflow
[a]0D	0000 1101	Exponent underflow
0E	0000 1110	Significance
[a]0F	0000 1111	Floating-point divide

[a]Error conditions discussed in Chapter 20.

Here are some examples of error conditions that cause interrupts.

5. More Examples

a. Specification Error (06).   A Specification Error (06) error code will occur when the following is executed.

LABEL	OPERATION	OPERAND	COMMENTS
	ZAP	TOTAL,AMT	
	•		
	•		
	•		
TOTAL	DS	PL6	
AMT	DC	CL5'12345'	

AMT is not a valid packed field. When the interrupt occurs and the PSW is printed, bits 24–31 will contain 00000110 (06), which denotes a specification error.

b. Decimal Divide Error (0B). A Decimal Divide Error (0B) error code will occur when the following is executed.

LABEL	OPERATION	OPERAND	COMMENTS
	DP	SALES,QTY	
	•		
	•		
	•		
SALES	DS	PL5	
QTY	DC	PL3'000'	

Recall that any attempt to divide by zero will produce a 0B interrupt. Similarly, a quotient too large to be stored in the receiving field will produce this interrupt.

The following table represents a more extensive explanation of the kinds of interrupts you may encounter. (The interrupts that occur in the case of more complex instructions have been omitted.)

Type of Interrupts

Interrupt Code	Definition	Meaning
1	Operation	Op code is illegal.
2	Privileged operation	Attempt was made to execute an instruction that can only be executed in a supervisor state.
4	Protection	Attempt was made to operate on data in storage protection area.
5	Addressing	Address used is outside the limits of storage available to the program.
6	Specification	Incorrect operand (i.e. if first operand (register) is odd in D, DR, M, and MR instruction, this error will result; incorrect boundary alignment will also cause this error).
7	Data	Operand does not contain valid digit and/or sign.
8	Fixed-point overflow	Binary operations that produce results are too large to be accommodated.
9	Fixed-point divide	Attempt was made to divide by zero, or a quotient was too large for the receiving field.

6. PSW: **Address of Next Instruction to Be Executed**

We will focus here on the following bits of the program status word.

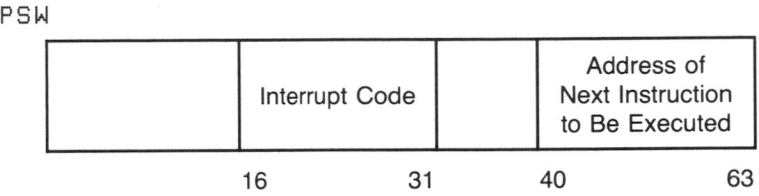

PSW

	Interrupt Code		Address of Next Instruction to Be Executed
	16	31	40 63

The low-order 24 bits of the doubleword PSW contain the address of the next instruction to be executed. Consider the following.

Storage Location		Instruction
2060	DP	HOLD,AMT
2066	AP	TOTAL,AMT

Suppose a program with the foregoing instructions was aborted and bits 40–63 of the PSW contained the address 2066. Then the instruction *prior* to the one at 2066, in this case the DP, caused the error.

In general, one would look at the instruction directly preceding the one specified in the PSW for an error. This cannot, however, be taken as a general rule. If an instruction that is branched to from several points in a program has its address indicated in the PSW, then the erroneous instruction could be any of the instructions prior to the branch. Consider the following instructions.

LABEL	OPERATION	OPERAND	COMMENTS
STEP1	AP	TOTAL,AMT1	
	B	STEP3	
STEP2	CP	HOLD,AMT2	
	BE	STEP3	
	B	STEP1	
STEP2A	MVI	LINEOUT+6,C'5'	
STEP3	.		
	.		
	.		

If the address of STEP3 were listed in the PSW, *any* of the instructions prior to the branch to STEP3 (AP, CP, MVI) could be in error.

The difficulty in debugging programs with numerous branch points is one reason why structured programming techniques that minimize unconditional branching are considered useful.

7. **Instruction Length Code**

PSW

	Interrupt Code	ILC		Instruction Address
	16 31	32 33		40 63

The ILC is interpreted as follows.

ILC

Binary Value of ILC	Decimal Value	Length of Last Instruction	Format of Last Instruction
01	1	1 halfword	RR
10	2	2 halfwords	RX, RS, SI
11	3	3 halfwords	SS

As indicated above, it is not always possible to determine the source of an error simply by knowing the address of the next instruction to be executed (bits 40–63). If that next instruction can be reached from several points, the exact cause of the error may not be obvious.

By using the **Instruction Length Code (ILC),** however, we can determine the *length* of the last instruction executed. This information, combined with knowledge of the next instruction to be executed, may be enough to determine the source of the error precisely.

If, in our previous illustration, the ILC were 10, we would know that the instruction in error was the MVI, not the AP or CP. The MVI, an SI instruction, has a 4-byte length whereas AP and CP, as SS instructions, are each 6 bytes in length.

8. Condition Code

Bits 34–35 of the PSW indicate the setting of the condition code at the time of the interrupt.

PSW

	Interrupt code	ILC	CC		Instruction address
0	16	31 32 33	34 35	40	63

Condition codes are affected by arithmetic and compare instructions, as shown in the following table.

Review of Condition Codes

ARITHMETIC Arithmetic Result	Condition Code	
	Binary	Hex
= 0	00	0
< 0	01	1
> 0	10	2
Overflow	11	3

COMPARISON	Condition Code	
	Binary	Hexa-decimal
=	00	0
Low	01	1
High	10	2

Note that a condition code remains set until another arithmetic or compare instruction resets it. Hence, if an Add instruction, for example, results in an overflow, the condition code of 11 may remain part of the PSW even if the interrupt occurs several instructions after the Add. Use of condition codes in debugging programs is helpful in determining the value of the last arithmetic or compare instruction executed.

9. State of CPU

There are 4 bits referred to as AMWP that are specified in bits 12–15 of the PSW.

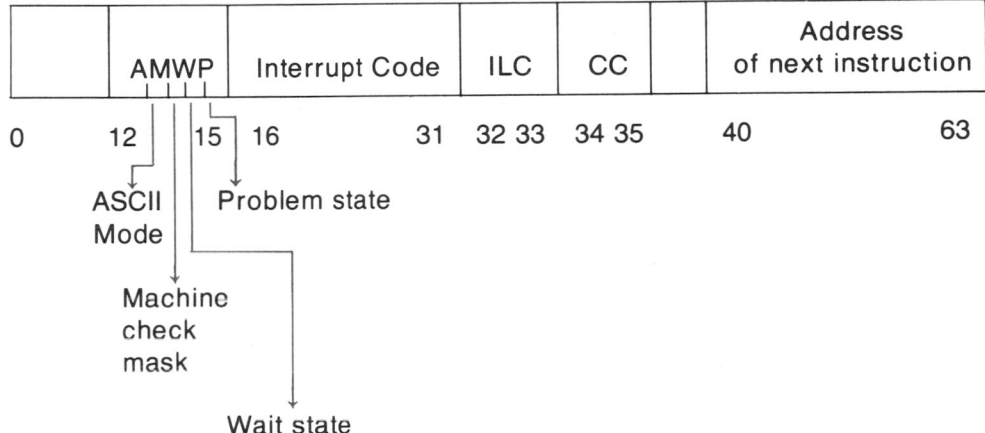

Each of these AMWP bits can contain a 0 or 1.

AMWP Bits (12–15)

Bit	Code	Meaning	Values		Standard Entry When Executing
			0	1	
12	A	Is mode ASCII or EBCDIC?	EBCDIC	ASCII	0
13	M	Should machine failure cause interrupt?	Mask or avoid interrupt	Machine check will cause interrupt	1
14	W	Is machine in wait or run state?	Run	Wait	0
15	P	Is machine in problem or supervisory state?	Supervisory state	Problem state	1

10. System Considerations

The remaining fields of the PSW usually are not of much significance to the student. We will list them here, but not provide an in-depth analysis.

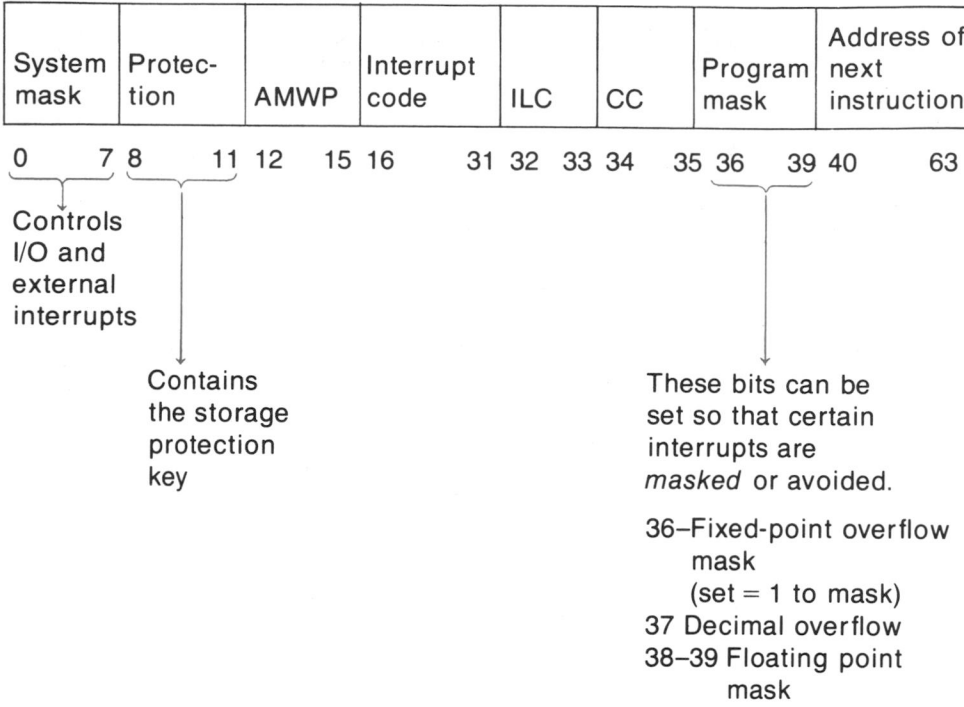

System mask	Protec-tion	AMWP	Interrupt code	ILC	CC	Program mask	Address of next instruction
0 7	8 11	12 15	16 31	32 33	34 35	36 39	40 63

Controls
I/O and
external
interrupts

Contains
the storage
protection
key

These bits can be
set so that certain
interrupts are
masked or avoided.

36–Fixed-point overflow
mask
(set = 1 to mask)
37 Decimal overflow
38–39 Floating point
mask

The program can use special instructions to **mask** interrupts. These change the contents of the Program Mask field of the PSW.

CHAPTER SUMMARY

I. Each operation code, regardless of the instruction format, is 1 byte long.
II. The 2 high-order bits of each operation code indicate the type of instruction to be used.

High-Order Bits	*Instruction Type*
00	RR
01	RX
10	RS or SI
11	SS

III. Instruction lengths are as follows:

Instruction Type	*Length of Instruction*
RR	2 bytes—one halfword
RX, RS, SI	4 bytes—two halfwords
SS	6 bytes—three halfwords

IV. There are 5 types of program interrupts.
   a. Machine
   b. Program
   c. I/O
   d. Supervisor call
   e. External
V. The program status word (PSW) is a doubleword of information on the status of

an instruction. By examining a PSW after a program interrupt has occurred, you can determine certain facts about the status of the last instruction executed.

Bits of PSW	Meaning
0–7	System mask (used for I/O and external interrupts).
8–11	Provides information on storage protection key.
12–15	Indicates status of
	12—ASCII mode
	13—Machine check mask
	14—Wait state
	15—Problem state
	(0 or 1 in bit is "no" or "yes")
16–31	Indicates which interrupt code caused the error.
32–33	Length of previous instruction executed.
34–35	Status of condition code. Condition codes are not affected by all instructions; the status may not be relevant for all instructions.
36–39	Used to mask or avoid certain types of interrupts.
40–63	Indicates the address of the last instruction executed.

CHAPTER SELF-EVALUATING QUIZ

1. PSW is an abbreviation for _____ .
2. The number of bits in a PSW is (no.).
3. When an interrupt occurs, the Current PSW is moved to the _____ PSW and a(n) _____ is moved to the Current PSW.
4. Indicate the types of interrupts that can occur.
5. When a program is finished, it signals the supervisor via a(n) _____ .
6. The location and type of the last instruction executed prior to the interrupt can be determined by examining the _____ PSW.
7. Provide a schematic of the PSW.
8. Which part of the PSW can actually be programmed?
9. A 1 in bit 14 of the PSW indicates _____ .
10. A 11 in bits 34–35 indicates that _____ .
11. (T or F) Knowing the instruction address of the next instruction to be executed will always provide you with the instruction that caused the interrupt.
12. If ILC contained a 11, the format of the instruction that caused the error is _____ .

SOLUTIONS

Page

1. Program status word — 405
2. 64 — 407
3. Old; interrupt-handling routine address — 406
4. Machine; program; I/O; external; supervisor — 405
5. Interrupt (supervisor call) — 405
6. Old — 406
7. — 412

System mask	Protection key	AMWP	Inter-rupt code	ILC		CC	Program mask	Instruc-tion address
0 7	8 11	12 15	16 31	32 33	34 35	36 39	40 63	

8. The program mask — 412
9. That the program is in the wait state — 411
10. An overflow condition has occurred. — 410

11. F: If the instruction were branched to from several points, we may not   409
     know definitely which instruction caused the error.

12. SS format   410

KEY TERMS

Debug	Masking
Execution phase	Program interrupt
External interrupts	Program Status Word (PSW)
Input/Output interrupts	Supervisor call interrupt
Instruction Length Code	System mask
Interrupt	Test data
Interrupt code	Translation phase
Machine check interrupt	Wait state

REVIEW QUESTIONS

Given the fact that the base register is 3, convert the following instructions to machine language. Assume the following storage assignments have been made by the computer.

Location

006	AMT	DS	PL4
00A	HOLD	DS	PL6
010	ONE	DS	CL1
011	TWO	DS	CL2

Location		*Instruction*	
1.	024	CLI	ONE,C'6'
2.	040	AP	HOLD,AMT
3.	060	AR	5,6
4.	080	MVC	ONE,TWO
5.	090	CP	HOLD,AMT

Indicate the assembler language equivalent of the following instructions.

	LOC	OBJECT CODE	
6.	000652	D283 B822	B821
7.	000666	9240 B821	
8.	00066A	D283 B822	B821
9.	000670	D208 B841	B74C
10.	000676	D500 B75B	B92B
11.	00067C	4780 B68C	
12.	000680	D500 B75B	B92C
13.	000686	4780 B6B4	
14.	000698	47F0 B648	
15.	00069C	D205 B863	B755
16.	0006B0	F275 B9B8	B755
17.	0006B6	4F80 B9B8	

18. Indicate the meaning of the following.

```
*
* --- PSW AT INTERRUPT   071D0007   8F3F06BE
*
```

Run-Time Debugging

To familiarize you with:
1. Additional methods used for debugging assembler programs.
2. The PDUMP and SNAP macros for displaying key fields.
3. Errors commonly encountered during program execution.

I. INTRODUCTION TO PDUMP AND SNAP

A. An Overview: The Need for Displaying Fields During Program Execution

During the testing of a program, errors frequently occur that are difficult to pinpoint. Sometimes programs "abend," which means that execution is aborted because of some error that the computer cannot resolve. Sometimes, the execution of a program produces erroneous output.

To make debugging easier, a tool is available to enable you to display data fields or intermediate work areas at various checkpoints. Thus, during a phase of a major calculation or after it, you can examine fields not normally printed as output. This will help you to ascertain if the calculations are being performed properly.

This debugging technique of displaying fields requires the programmer to determine the routines or instructions that require special attention. Sometimes this is done *after* an error has actually occurred, in which case the program is then modified to display the required fields. Sometimes programmers routinely incorporate display instructions during the debugging phase to facilitate the checking of specified segments of the programs.

To test a program adequately, the programmer manually performs the operations required and compares the results obtained with those produced by the computer. If a discrepancy exists, there is a logic error in the program. Displaying fields during the test phase enables the logic to be checked at various points in the program as needed. Once debugging has been completed, the instructions used for display purposes are no longer needed and are removed from the source program.

The methods used to display key fields are

```
PDUMP—DOS
SNAP —OS
```

We will discuss these two methods separately.[1]

Depending on your system's specifications and your job control language commands, you may get a dump of storage whenever the program bombs. This system dump provides you with a hexadecimal representation of *all* storage. Because such a listing, or memory dump, is very long, it is cumbersome to read and makes it difficult to pinpoint the fields you actually want to examine. The advantages of a SNAP or PDUMP are that

1. only specified areas are displayed, and

---

[1]See Appendix K for the XDUMP instruction that can be used with ASSIST assemblers.

2. a dump can be obtained during normal execution of a program, not just when an abend occurs.

B. A Note on the Organization of this Chapter

The PDUMP is coded for DOS systems and the SNAP is coded for OS systems. The procedures for reading storage dumps, whether generated by a PDUMP or a SNAP, are *exactly* the same. Hence, it is highly recommended that both DOS and OS users read this *entire* chapter, focusing on the problems provided and how one can interpret storage dumps. For DOS users, the rules specified for the SNAP macro may be viewed as fundamentally analogous to those for the PDUMP. Similarly, for OS users, the rules for the PDUMP macro may be viewed as fundamentally analogous to those for the SNAP.

II. PDUMP

A. The Format

The PDUMP instruction available under DOS enables you to obtain storage dumps of specified fields during the normal execution of the program. The format of the PDUMP instruction follows.

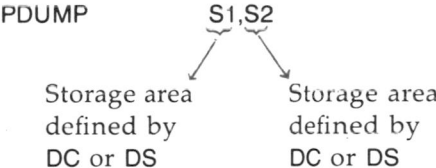

```
PDUMP          S1,S2
```

Storage area defined by DC or DS   Storage area defined by DC or DS

The computer will print all storage areas defined in the program, in sequence, beginning with S1 and ending with S2, but *not including* S2.

B. Examples

Example 15.1   Consider the following.

```
              ⋮
              ⋮
              PDUMP    CONST1,CONST5
              ⋮
              ⋮
CONST1   DS    CL5
CONST2   DS    PL3
CONST3   DS    CL6
CONST4   DS    PL2
CONST5   DS    F
```

Result:
Storage dumps of CONST1-CONST4 are provided when the PDUMP instruction is encountered.

Important Note
S1, the first operand in the PDUMP instruction (CONST1 in the example), must be defined by a DS or DC that *precedes* the definition of S2, the second operand in the PDUMP instruction (CONST2 in the example).

The PDUMP differs from dumps initiated by the operating system when an abend occurs, in that control is returned to the *next instruction* in your program after the PDUMP has been executed.

You will find the PDUMP to be a valuable asset in finding and correcting errors. Here is an example of using the PDUMP to display storage after a record is read.

```
                 ⋮
                 ⋮
         GET     INFILE,RECIN
         PDUMP   A,Z+4
                 ⋮
                 ⋮
A        DS      CL3
RECIN    DS      CL80
                 ⋮
                 ⋮
Z        DS      F
         END
```

Note
A displacement of 4 is necessary if the contents of the storage area Z are to be exhibited.

Helpful Hints
It is sometimes useful to establish blank areas between fields that will be dumped to make the dump more readable.

Example 15.2   Consider the following.

```
                 ⋮
                 ⋮
         PDUMP   CONST1,CONST5
                 ⋮
                 ⋮
CONST1   DS      CL5
         DC      CL4'      '
CONST2   DS      PL3
         DC      CL4'      '
CONST3   DS      CL6
         DC      CL4'      '
CONST4   DS      PL2
         DC      CL4'      '
CONST5   DS      F
```

The Storage Dump
The contents of the 16 general registers and main storage are displayed on the computer listing as a result of the PDUMP.

Consider a line that is dumped as in Figure 15.1. The format for storage dumps is fairly standard. In its most common form, the contents of storage are displayed in hex. Eight words of storage are printed on each line. Each word is separated from the next by several blanks to improve readability.

To the right we find the EBCDIC representation of the data contained on each line of the printout. Because data is often stored in binary or packed-decimal form, a great deal of the data is not in valid EBCDIC form and cannot

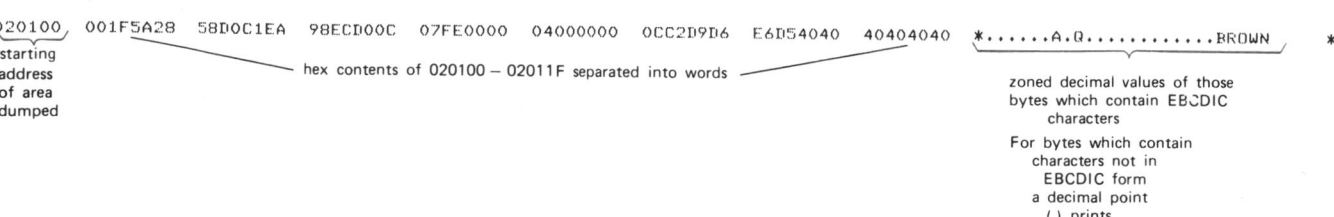

Figure 15.1
One line of a dump.

print as a recognizable character. Note that periods (.) are printed for these characters.

To the extreme left of each line is the address of the first byte of storage. See Figure 15.2.

Recall that 2 hex digits represent a byte of storage. Therefore, a 4-byte word is represented by 8 hex digits. Each line of the listing contains 20_{16} bytes or 32_{10} bytes (8 words). A brief look at the storage dump of 020120–2013F reveals that spaces (40) occupy bytes 020120–20123 and bytes 020129–2013F. The hex digits D3 C5 D9 D6 E8 occupy bytes 020124–020128. If you consult a conversion table you will find that these digits represent the word LEROY. Note that on the right-hand side of the listing the word LEROY prints.

Suppose it were necessary to inspect the contents of a 2-byte field beginning at location 020150. Because addresses are printed 20 hex bytes at a time, we would need to find location 020140 (020160 would be too late). We would then check the addresses printed to the left until we found 020140. By counting 16 bytes from the *zero position*, we arrive at 020150 ($020150 - 020140 = 10_{16} = 16_{10}$). Remember, the first byte of each line always contains a low-order zero. Therefore, 020150 would be the first byte of word 5. See Figure 15.3.

The contents of this location are 40 or a space. Again, 2 hex digits represent one byte.

Now that we are able to examine the contents of storage, let us show how this can assist us in debugging a sample program.

C. Sample Program I[2]

1. The Problem

Consider the program in Figure 15.4. Figure 15.5 indicates the results of the first run. Note that there were no diagnostics when the program was assembled and that no output was obtained except a dump. A PROGRAM CHECK INTERRUPTION occurred, however, at hex location 1105D6.

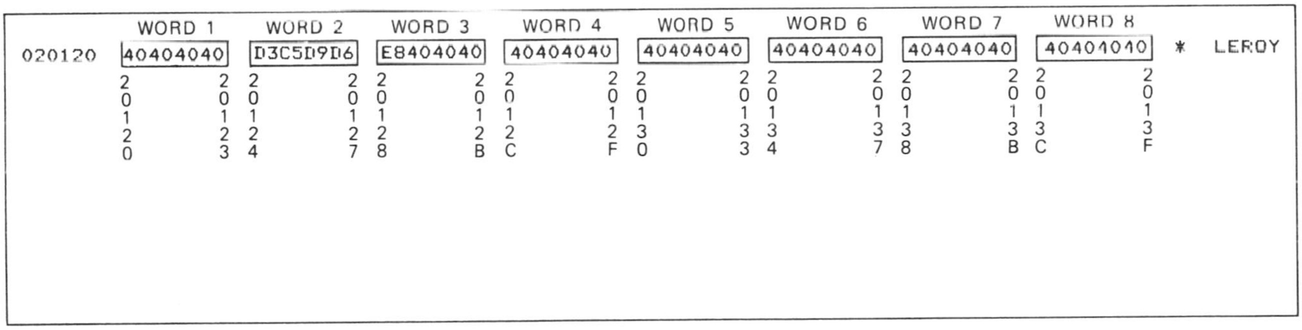

Note: Each byte is displayed in a dump as two hex digits.

Figure 15.2
Schematic of one line of a dump.

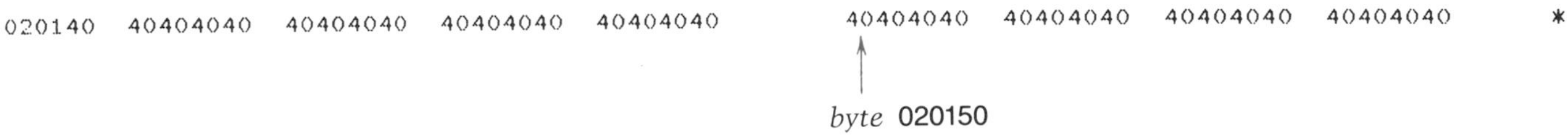

Figure 15.3
Finding a byte in a storage dump.

[2]Because this is a DOS listing, assume all of the I/O is correct. The rest of the program would be the same for DOS or OS runs. Thus, the program can be interpreted by both DOS and OS users.

```
                                                      DOS/VS ASSEMBLER REL 34.0 09.09            PAGE   2

LOC     OBJECT CODE   ADDR1 ADDR2   STMT  SOURCE STATEMENT

000000                               1            PRINT NOGEN
                                     2    DUMP    START 0
                                     3    INFILE  DTFCD BLKSIZE=80,RECFORM=FIXUNB,DEVADDR=SYSIPT,          X    HSKP
                                                        WORKA=YES,IOAREA1=BUFFRIN,EOFADDR=EOF                    HSKP
                                    24    OUTFILE DTFPR BLKSIZE=132,DEVICE=1403,DEVADDR=SYSLST,IOAREA1=BUFFROUT,X HSKP
                                                        CONTROL=YES,PRINTOV=YES,WORKA=YES
                                    45            CDMOD WORKA=YES,CONTROL=YES,PRINTOV=YES
                                   137            PRMOD WORKA=YES
000068 05C0                        257    BEGIN   BALR 12,0
       0006A                       258            USING *,12
                                   259            OPEN INFILE,OUTFILE


                                                      DOS/VS ASSEMBLER REL 34.0 09.09            PAGE   3

LOC     OBJECT CODE        ADDR1 ADDR2   STMT  SOURCE STATEMENT

00007E  D283 COE3 COE2     0014D 0014C   269  READ   MVC   LINEOUT,SPACES
000094  D20E C1CB C16B     00235 001D5   270         GET   INFILE,CARDIN
00009A  F232 C167 C17A     001D1 001E4   276         MVC   NAMEO,NAME
0000A0  FA33 C1BB C167     00225 001D1   277         PACK  COMM,SALES
0000A6  D202 C1E0 C17A     0024A 001E4   278         AP    TOTAL,COMM
                                         279         MVC   DOLLARS,SALES
0000B6  F921 C17A C33E     001E4 003A8   280         PDUMP CSUM,PATTRN3
0000BC  47B0 C08C 00F6             285         CP    SALES,=P'500'
                                         286         BNL   PREM
0000C0  FC31 C167 C1D1     001D1 003AA   287  REG    MP    CSUM,COMM
0000C6  FA33 C0D8 C167     00142 001D1   288         AP    COMMOUT,PATTRN
0000CC  D206 C1ED C1F4     00257 0025E   289  EDIT   MVC   COMMOUT,COMM+1
0000D2  DE06 C1ED C168     00257 001D2   290         ED    COMMOUT,C'$'
0000D8  925B C1C1          00257         291         MVI   OUTFILE[5],DETAIL
0000DC  D232 C0E3 C1C1     0014D 0022B   292         PUT   OUTFILE,LINEOUT
                                         293         PUT   READ
0000F2  47F0 C014          0007E         299         B     COMM,=P'18'
0000F6  FC31 C167          001D1         300  PREM   MVC   LINEOUT+54(3),=C'***'
0000FC  D202 C119          00183         301         B     EDIT
000102  47F0 C05C          003C6         302         MVC   LINEOUT+19(8),PATTRN2
000106  D207 COF6          00160         303  EOF    MVC   LINEOUT+19(8),TOTAL
00010C  DE07 COF6          00160         304         ED    LINEOUT+27(3),CENTS
000112  DE07 C1E3          00168         305         MVC   DIVIDE,CSUM
000118  F853 CODC          00146         306         ZAP   DIVIDE,NO
00011E  FD51 CODC          00146         307         DP    LINEOUT+32(7),PATTRN3
000124  D206 C103          0016D 00260   308         MVC   LINEOUT+32(8),AVERAGE+1
00012A  DE07 C103          0016D 00147   309         ED    OUTFILE,LINEOUT
                                         310         PUT
                                         316         EOJ
```

```
000142 0000000C    319 GSUM     DC  PL4'0'
000146             320 DIVIDE   DS  0PL6
000146             321 AVERAGE  DS  PL4
00014A             322 RMDR     DS  PL2
00014C 40          323 SPACES   DC  C' '
00014D             324 LINEOUT  DS  CL132
0001D1             325 COMM     DS  PL4
0001D5             326 CARDIN   DS  0CL80
0001D5             327 NAME     DS  CL15
0001E4             328 SALES    DS  CL15
0001E7             329          DS  CL62

000225 0000000C    331 TOTAL    DC  PL4'0'
000229 000C        332 NO       DC  PL2'0'
00022B             333 DETAIL   DS  0CL51
00022B             334          DS  CL10
000235             335 NAMEO    DS  CL15
                   336          DS  CL5
000244 40404040    337          DC  CL4' '
000248 5B40        338 DOLLARS  DC  CL2'$ '
00024A 4BF0F04040404040  339 CENTS    DC  CL10'.00'
00024D             340 COMMOUT  DS  CL7
000257 40202021 4B2020   341 PATTKN   DC  X'402020214B2020'
00025E 4020202020202021  342 PATTRN2  DC  X'4020202020202021'
000265 40202021 4B2020   343 PATTRN3  DC  X'402020214B2020'
00026D             344 BUFFRIN  DS  CL132
000274             345 BUFFROUT DS  CL132
0002F8             346          END BEGIN

00068

000380 5B5BC2D6D7C5D540   347 =CL8'$$BOPEN '
000388 5B5BC2D7C4E4D4D7   348 =CL8'$$BPDUMP'
000390 00000142 0000026D  349 =A(CSUM,PATTKN3)
000398 00000030           350 =A(INFILE)
00039C 000001D5           351 =A(CARDIN)
0003A0 00000038           352 =A(OUTFILE)
0003A4 0000014D           353 =A(LINEOUT)
0003A8 500C               354 =P'500'
0003AA 012C               355 =P'12'
0003AC 018C               356 =P'18'
0003AE 5C5C5C             357 =C'***'
```

Figure 15.4
Sample program 1.

```
                                                                              PAGE  7

DIAGNOSTICS AND STATISTICS

NO ERRORS FOUND

THE FOLLOWING MACRO NAMES HAVE BEEN FOUND IN MACRO INSTRUCTIONS
DTFCD    CDMOD    DTFPR    PRMOD    OPEN    GET    PUT    EOJ
                                            PDUMP

OPTIONS FOR THIS ASSEMBLY - ALIGN, LIST, XREF, LINK, NORLD, NODECK, NOEDECK

THE ASSEMBLER WAS RUN IN 65416 BYTES
END OF ASSEMBLY
EOP $3ASM
// EXEC LNKEDT

JOB INST    09.10.31    F-LE-E    FAST-LINKAGE-EDITOR    VM4.0    DOS/VS R34-OA GOAL SYSTEMS    PAGE 1

ACTION TAKEN MAP CLEAR
LIST PHASE MONITOR,ROOT    REL    LINK
LIST INCLUDE ILFFEXIT
LIST AUTOLINK IJDFAPZZ
LIST PHASE STDPGM,*
LIST ENTRY

     PHASE-CSECT-ENTRY  LO-LNK HI-LNK  LO-REL HI-REL  LN-HEX  LN-DEC   XF-LNK XF-REL   GOAL SYSTEMS

LINK PARTITION = F3      110000 169FFF  000000 059FFF  5A000   368,640  110078 000078

ROOT    MONITOR          110078 11051B  000000 0004A3  4A4     1,188    110078 000000   RELOCATABLE
      * ILFFEXIT         110078 1103F9  000000 000381  382       898
      * EXIT                    1100F4         00007C  11C       284
        IJDFAPZZ         110400 11051B  000388 0004A3
      * IJDFAZZZ         110400         000388

PHASE   STDPGM
        DUMP             110520 1108D0  000000 0004D9  4DA     1,242    110588 000068   RELOCATABLE
        IJCFZIWO         1108D8 11094F  000388 0003BD  381       945
        IJDFCPZW         110950 1109F9  000430 00042F  78        120
      * IJDFZPZW         110950         000430         AA        170
      * IJDFZZZW         110950         000430
      * IJDFCZZW         110950         000430

NORMAL COMPLETION, BLOCKS AVAIL = 334, USED IN EDIT = 4, PCIL=X'1C6', CYL=001, SERIAL=WORK01.

// EXEC INST

GR 0-7  00110880 001108A8 00169FFF 00001BB0  0000F416 80000035 80000035 00169FFF
GR 8-F  80112883 0A16180C 41100000 182F07F1  40110588A D4D6D5C9 80110584 0011080B
FP REG  42540000 00000000 0200FA80 00000000  00000000 00000000 00000000 00000000
CR 0-7  80400050 0200FA80 FFFF0000 00000000  00000000 00000000 EF000000 00000000
CR 8-F  00000000 00000000 00000000 00000000

110660  0A0E0000 000C0000 00000000 40404040  00000000 40404040 40404040 40404040  .........
110680  40404040 --SAME--
1106E0  40404040 F3F0F040 40404040 40404040  40000030 0FC8C1D9 D9C9D5C7 E3060540  .....HARRINGTON
110700  40404040 --SAME--
110720  40404040 40000030 0C000C00 00000000  00000000 00C8C1D9 D9C9D5C7 E3060540  .....HARRINGTON
110760  40404040 5B40F3F0 F04BF0F0 20202020  40404040 40404040 40004020   $ 300.00  ........
110780  20214820 20402020 21402020                                         300

OS031 PROGRAM CHECK INTERRUPTION - HEX LOCATION 1105D6 - CONDITION CODE 2 - DATA EXCEPTION
OS00I JOB INST CANCELED
```

Figure 15.5
Results of running sample program 1.

FINDING ERROR POINT

Subtract the load point (entry point) address from the interrupt address.[3]

LO-LINK for the program entitled DUMP contains the entry point, which is 110520.

1105D6	Interrupt point
− 110520	Load point
B6	Relative address (LOC) of instruction that caused the interrupt.

Looking at the source listing to find address B6, we see that the error occurred when the CP instruction was executed. If the error is not easily ascertained by desk checking, it is useful to dump fields to examine their contents prior to the interrupt. Sometimes it is useful to include PDUMP at strategic points in a program before any execution has been attempted. In this way, careful checking of program steps can be accomplished.

Examine the PDUMP illustrated in Figure 15.5 that accompanies the program.

2. Interpreting the Dump Locations

Note that a PDUMP instruction precedes the instruction in question. The contents of CSUM, the first operand at hex location 142, through PATTRN3 (but exclusive of PATTRN3), at location 26D, print just prior to the interrupt. Adding the actual load or entry point, or 110520, the PDUMP will provide a storage dump of 110662–11078D. (Note that all calculations are performed in hex.)

If you reexamine the storage dump in Figure 15.5 you will note that storage positions 110660–11078F are dumped. Because 8 words per line are provided, each line of a dump always begins on a doubleword boundary.

3. Determining the Contents of Fields Using Dumps

Note that the CP instruction that resulted in the interrupt has two operands. They are

```
SALES
P'500'
```

Upon examination of the ADDR1 field of the CP instruction, we find that SALES is located at relative address 1E4, which is within the limits of our PDUMP (142–26D). Adding the starting point 110520, we can locate the contents of SALES just prior to the CP when PDUMP was executed, at hex 110704.

The following is located between 110700 and 110720.

```
40404040 F3F0F040 40404040 40404040 40404040 40404040 40404040 40404040
         ‿‿‿‿‿
         SALES
```

Counting bytes, we find that F3F0F0 is contained within the field called SALES. You should realize that this is *not* a packed field and, hence, when used with a CP instruction will cause an interrupt. Reading up several lines in the program, we find that SALES was packed into COMM and hence COMM should have been the first operand in the CP instruction. Note that COMM at relative address 1D1 and effective address 1106F1 does indeed contain 300 in packed form.

```
40404040 40404040 40404040 40404040 40000030 0FC8C1D9 D9C9D5C7 E3D6D540
                                     ‿‿‿‿‿
                                     COMM
```

---

[3]For ASSIST users, it is not necessary to perform this subtraction; the system provides the relative address.

Inserting the following in place of the erroneous CP will produce the correct results.

```
CP    COMM,=P'500'
```

Note that once the program is error-free, we remove the PDUMP because it is a debugging tool and not normally a part of desired output.

D. Sample Program 2

Consider the sample program in Figure 15.6. The results of the assembly and execution of this program are indicated in Figure 15.7.

Note that this program has produced some output before it abended. An error occurred when executing the instruction at hex location 11063E. By subtracting the entry point 110520 for this program, we can determine the LOC of the instruction as 11E, which is the DP instruction. This should come as no surprise because the interrupt was caused by a DECIMAL DIVIDE EXCEPTION.

To find the error, we need to examine the contents of the two fields, DIVIDE and NO, which are operated on in the DP instruction.

Field	Displacement	Load Point	Effective Address
DIVIDE	146	110520	110666
NO	229	110520	110749

The PDUMP inserted prior to the divide lists all storage areas from CSUM, 142, to PATTRN3, 26D. That is, all areas from the effective address 110662 (110520 + 142) − 11078D (110520 + 26D) will print.

Checking this dump we note that

DIVIDE   contains 00 00 00 52 72 2C
NO   contains 00 0C

The error, then, is obvious. An attempt has been made to divide by zero. NO was never updated to contain a nonnegative value.

You can now begin to appreciate the advantages of using dumps in the debugging process. Nothing needs to be left to interpretation because the machine-language instructions and the contents of storage can be analyzed on a microscopic level.

PDUMPs, then, are debugging tools used to find errors by examining actual storage locations. All areas to be studied are simply specified as parameters.

With the use of the appropriate job control commands, the computer can be instructed to provide an automatic dump of all storage used by the program in case of an interrupt. Note, however, that this form of dump (1) only occurs in case of an interrupt, whereas a PDUMP will allow continuous execution of the program, and (2) it dumps *all* storage associated with the program, not just selected areas, such as those obtainable with the PDUMP.

E. PDUMPs and Fixed-Point Arithmetic

Another advantage of using the PDUMP is the display of the 16 general purpose registers. Because these registers are used in fixed-point arithmetic, their contents are usually a clue to pinpointing a program error. To illustrate this point, we will analyze a sample program, focusing our attention primarily on registers. The program is shown in Figure 15.8. Recall that each register contains 4 bytes, or a fullword. In addition, negative numbers are stored in complement form. Therefore, any register containing a digit 8 through F in the high-order hex position (1000_2–1111_2) contains a negative number in complement form.

In our sample problem, we use register 12 as the base register. Let us examine its contents. See Figure 15.9. We find register 12 contains a base address of 0960AA, which is, as we would expect, different from the load or entry point. In fact, the base address references the instruction labeled FIRST in our program. By subtracting the displacement of the instruction FIRST from the base address, we can calculate the load point or entry address.

0960AA	Base address
−00003 2	Address of FIRST
09607 8	Load point

This exercise is useful in that you can always double-check the load point in this manner. However, there is a more serious problem that resulted in an interrupt. The interrupt message indicates that a fixed-point overflow at location 0960D2 caused the termination of the program. We are again able to find the instruction causing the interrupt by subtracting the load or entry point (096078) from the location of the interrupt. This provides us with the displacement in our program of the erroneous instruction. The instruction in error is located at 00005A (0960D2–096078) and is coded

```
LOOP2           AR          8,9
```

Both operands are registers, and we find general register 9 correctly contains the hex equivalent of 1050_{10} or $41A_{16}$. See Figure 15.9. However, general register 8 contains a very large binary number, which leads us to believe that fixed-point overflow has occurred. When correctly programmed, the LOOP1 procedure would be performed five times whereas the LOOP2 procedure should be executed three times. Apparently LOOP1 was executed without any detectable problems and, thus, we will now turn our attention to LOOP2. The BCT instruction controls the loop by the value contained in register 7. Let us examine register 7. First, register 7 contains a negative value. How can this be?

Register 7 was given an initial value of 5 prior to entering the LOOP1 procedure. When LOOP2 was executed, however, register 7 contained the value zero. Therefore, from this point on, the BCT instruction continued to subtract 1 with each pass. Our correction is simple. We must initialize register 7 to 3 prior to entering the LOOP2 procedure.

```
LA          7,3             CORRECTION
```

Note that on the next run, a PDUMP (STMT 162 in Figure 15.8) is used to display the contents of the general registers (see Figure 15.10). The answer found in register 8 is correct. Register 8 contains 1FD6 in hex or 8150 in decimal. As expected, the loop counter has been decreased to zero as evidenced by the contents of register 7. When using fixed-point binary instructions, the contents of registers play an important role in debugging.

III. THE SNAP **MACRO**

A. Format

The SNAP macro enables the OS programmer to obtain storage dumps of specified fields during the normal execution of the program.

The general format of a SNAP instruction and the required additions to the program follows.

```
SNAP        DCB=XX,PDATA=(PSW,REGS),STORAGE=(S1,S2)
```

```
                              DOS/VS ASSEMBLER REL 34.0 09.12                                    PAGE  2

LOC     OBJECT CODE   ADDR1 ADDR2  STMT  SOURCE STATEMENT

000000                                 1 DUMP    PRINT NOGEN
                                       2 INFILE  START 0
                                       3         DTFCD BLKSIZE=80,RECFORM=FIXUNB,DEVADDR=SYSIPT,       X   HSKP
                                                       WORKA=YES,IOAREA1=BUFFRIN,EOFADDR=EOF              HSKP
                                      24 OUTFILE DTFPR BLKSIZE=132,DEVICE=1403,DEVADDR=SYSLST,IOAREA1=BUFFROUT,X
                                                       CONTROL=YES,PRINTOV=YES,WORKA=YES                  HSKP
                                     145         CDMOD WORKA=YES,CONTROL=YES,PRINTOV=YES
                                     137         PRMOD WORKA=YES,CONTROL=YES,PRINTOV=YES
000068  05C0                         257 BEGIN   BALR  12,0
000068                        0006A  258         USING *,12
                                     259         OPEN  INFILE,OUTFILE
0007E   D283 C0E3 C0E2  0014D 0014C  269 READ    MVC   LINEOUT,SPACES
00094   D20E C1C8 C167  00235 001D5  270         GET   INFILE,CARDIN
0009A   F232 C167 C17A  001D1 001E4  276         MVC   NAMEO,NAME
000A0   FA33 C1BB C1E0  00224 001E4  277         PACK  COMM,SALES
000A6   D202 C1E0 C167  001D1        278         AP    TOTAL,COMM
000AC   F931 C1E0 C33E  003A8        279         MVC   DOLLARS,SALES
000B2   47B0 C082       000EC        280         CP    COMM,=P'500'     CORRECTION 1
000B6   FC31 C167 C167  001D1 001D1  281         BNL   PREM
000BC   FA33 C0D8 C167  00142 001D1  282 REG     MP    COMM,=P'12'
000C2   D206 C1F4 C1E0  00257 001E4  283         AP    CSUM,COMM
000C8   DE06 C1ED C257  00257 00257  284         MVC   COMMOUT,PATTRN
000CE   925B C1ED       00257        285         ED    COMMOUT,COMM+1
000D2   D232 C1ED C14D  00257 0014D  286         MVI   COMMOUT,C'$'
                                     287         MVC   LINEOUT(51),DETAIL
                                     288         PUT   OUTFILE,LINEOUT
000E8   47F0 C014       0007E        294         B     READ
000EC   FC31 C167 C119  00183        295 PREM    MP    COMM,=P'18'
000F2   D202 C352 C344  003AC 003AE  296         MVC   LINEOUT+54(3),=C'***'
000F8   47F0 C0F6       00160        297         B     EDIT
000FC   D207 C0F6 C1BB  00160 00225  298 EOF     MVC   LINEOUT+19(8),PATTRN2
00102   DE07 C1E3 C168  00240 001D2  299         ED    LINEOUT+19(8),TOTAL
00108   D202 C0DC C146  00146 00142  300         MVC   LINEOUT+27(3),CENTS
0010E   F853 C0D8 C0E3  00147 00229  301         ZAP   DIVIDE,CSUM
0011E   FD51 C0DC C16D  00146 00147  302         PDUMP CSUM,PATTRN3
                                     307         DP    DIVIDE,NO
00124   D206 C103 C1D6  00147 0016D  308         MVC   LINEOUT+32(7),PATTRN3
0012A   DE07 C103 C103  00147 00147  309         ED    LINEOUT+32(8),AVERAGE+1
                                     310         PUT   OUTFILE,LINEOUT
                                     316         EOJ
00142   0000000C                     319 CSUM    DC    PL4'0'
00146                                320 DIVIDE  DS    0PL6
00146                                321 AVERAGE DS    PL4
0014A                                322 KMDR    DS    PL2
0014C   40                           323 SPACES  DC    C' '
0014D                                324 LINEOUT DS    CL132
001D1                                325 COMM    DS    0CL80
001D1                                326 CARDIN  DS    0CL80
001D5                                327 NAME    DS    CL15
001E4                                328 SALES   DS    CL3
                                     330 *
00225   0000000C                     331 TOTAL   DC    PL4'0'
00229   000C                         332 NO      DC    PL2'0'
0022B                                333 DETAIL  DS    0CL51
00235   40404040                     334         DC    CL10
00244   5B40                         335 NAMEO   DS    CL15
00248                                336         DC    CL4' '
0024D   4BF0F0404040404040           337 DOLLARS DS    CL4'$'
00257                                338 CENTS   DC    CL3
0025E   402020214B2020               339 COMMOUT DC    CL10'.00'
00266   402020202020021              341 PATTRN  DC    X'402020214B2020'
00274   402020214B2020               342 PATTRN2 DC    X'402020202020021'
002F8                                343 PATTRN3 DC    X'402020214B2020'
                                     345 BUFFRIN DS    CL132
                                     346 BUFFROUT DS   CL132
                              00068  347         END   BEGIN
00380   5B5BC2D6D7C5D540             348                =C'$$BOPEN'
00388   5B5BC2D7C4E4D4D7             349                =CL8'$$BPDUMP'
00390   000001420000026D             350                =A(CSUM,PATTRN3)
0039C   000001D5                     351                =A(INFILE)
003A0   00000038                     352                =A(CARDIN)
003A4   0000014D                     353                =A(OUTFILE)
003A8   500C                         354                =A(LINEOUT)
003AA   012C                         355                =P'500'
003AC   018C                         356                =P'12'
003AE   5C5C5C                       357                =P'18'
                                                        =C'***'
```

Figure 15.6
Sample program 2.

PAGE 1

DIAGNOSTICS AND STATISTICS

NO ERRORS FOUND

THE FOLLOWING MACRO NAMES HAVE BEEN FOUND IN MACRO INSTRUCTIONS
DTFCD   DTFPR   CDMOD   PRMOD   OPEN   GET   PUT   PDUMP   EOJ

OPTIONS FOR THIS ASSEMBLY - ALIGN, LIST, XREF, LINK, NORLD, NODECK, NOEDECK
THE ASSEMBLER WAS RUN IN 65416 BYTES
END OF ASSEMBLY

EOP $3ASM
// EXEC LNKEDT

JOB INST   09.12.45   F-LE-E   FAST-LINKAGE-EDITOR   VM4.0   DOS/VS R34-0A GOAL SYSTEMS

ACTION TAKEN MAP CLEAR REL   LINK
LIST PHASE MONITOR,ROOT
LIST INCLUDE ILFFEXIT
LIST AUTOLINK IJDFAPZZ
LIST PHASE STDPGM,*
LIST ENTRY

```
                                         XF-LNK  XF-REL    G O A L   S Y S T E M S
PHASE-CSECT-ENTRY  LO-LNK HI-LNK  LO-REL HI-REL  LN-HEX  LN-DEC
LINK PARTITION = F3 110000 169FFF  000000 059FFF  5A000   368,640

ROOT  MONITOR     1107E 11051B  000000 0004A3  4A4    1,188    110078 000000   RELOCATABLE
      ILFFEXIT    11007E 1103F9  000000 000381  382      898
      *EXIT       110F04 11051B  00007C 0004A3  11C      284
      IJDFAPZZ    110400 11051B  000388 0004A3
      * IJDFAZZZ  110400          000388

PHASE STDPGM      110528 1109F9  000000 0004D9  4DA    1,242    110588 000008   RELOCATABLE
      DUMP        110528 1108D0  000000 0003B0  3B1      945
      IJCFZIWO    1108CE 11094F  0003B0 00042F  78       120
      IJDFCPZW    11095C 1109F9  000430 0004D9  AA       170
      * IJDFZPZW  11950           000430
      * IJDFZZZW  11950           000430
      * IJDFCZZW  11950
```

NORMAL COMPLETION, BLOCKS AVAIL = 334, USED IN EDIT = 4, PCIL=X'1C6', CYL=001, SERIAL=WORKO1.

// EXEC INST
```
     HARRINGTON    $ 300.00
     MCNAMARA      $ 652.00
     SAGER         $  85.00    $ 36.00  ***
     THOMAS        $ -25.00    $117.72  ***
     WHITE         $ 456.00    $160.02
     VOSS          $ 800.00    $ 14.76      .... .VOSS
                               $ 54.72  ***
                               $144.00      ...... VOSS
```

```
INST                                                                              PAGE 1
GR 0-7  00110880 001108A8 00169FFF 000010B0  0000F416 80300035 80000035 00169FFF
GR 8-F  80112880 0A161B0C 40110C7A 182F07F1  4311058A D4D6D5C9 00110610 00110808
FP REG  42540300 00000000 41100C00 00000000  00000000 00000000 00000000 00000000
CR 0-7  80400000 0200FA80 FFFF0L0C 00000000  00000000 00000000 EF000000 00000000
CR 8-F  00000000 00000000 00000000 00000000

110660  0A0E0052 722C0000 00527220 4BF9FC40  0000F416 40404040 40404040 40404040
110680  40404040 F3F2F2F2 4BF9FC40 40404040  40404040 40404040 40404040 40404040
1106A0  40404040  -SAME-
1106E0  40404040 F8F0F040 40404040 40404040  40001440 0CE5D6E2 E2404040 40404040    .. .VOSS
110720  40404040  -SAME-
110740  40404040 40000322 2C000000 00000000  00000000 00E5D6E2 E2404040 40404040    ..... VOSS
110760  40404040 5B40F8F0 F04BF0F0 21402020  40404040 40404040 F1F4F44B F0F04020    $ 800.00 .
110780  20214B20 20402020 20202020
```

OS031 PROGRAM CHECK INTERRUPTION - HEX LOCATION 11063E - CONDITION CODE 2 - DECIMAL DIVIDE EXCEPTION
OS001 JOB INST CANCELED

Figure 15.7
Results of running sample program 2.

```
      LOC   OBJECT CODE    ADDR1 ADDR2  STMT    SOURCE STATEMENT

                                        144 *
                                        145 *              SOLVE  SUM = 5 * A  +  3 * B
                                        146 *
     000030 05C0                        147 BEGIN   BALR  12,0
                                 00032  148         USING *,12
     000032 5670 C042           00074   149 FIRST   D     7,MASK          USED TO ALLOW FIXED-POINT OVERFLOW
     000036 0470                         150         SPM   7              SINCE IT IS NORMALLY MASKED
     000038 4170 0005           00005   151         LA    7,5
     00003C 4180 0000           00000   152         LA    8,0
     000040 F872 C046 C04E 00078 00080  153         ZAP   DBLE,A(3)
     000046 4FA0 C046           00078   154         CVB   10,DBLE
     00004A 1A8A                         155 LOOP1   AR    8,10
     00004C 4670 C018           0004A   156         BCT   7,LOOP1
     000050 F872 C046 C051 00078 00083  157         ZAP   DBLE,B(3)
     000056 4F90 C046           00078   158         CVB   9,DBLE
     00005A 1A89                         159 LOOP2   AR    8,9
     00005C 4670 C028           0005A   160         BCT   7,LOOP2
     000060 5080 C03E           00070   161         ST    8,ANSWER
                                         162         PDUMP BEGIN,BUFFROUT
                                         167         EOJ
                                         170 *
                                         171 *
                                         172 *
                                         173 *
     000070                              174 ANSWER  DS    F
     000074 08000000                     175 MASK    DC    X'08000000'
     000078                              176 DBLE    DS    D
     000080 01000C                       177 A       DC    P'1000'
     000083 01050C                       178 B       DC    P'1050'
     000086                              179 BUFFRIN  DS   CL132
     00010A                              180 BUFFROUT DS   CL132
                                 00030  181         END   BEGIN
```

Figure 15.8
Sample program that uses fixed-point arithmetic.

```
      Register 8        Register 9         Register 12        Register 7                    PAGE   1

GR 0-F  00096078 000960A8 000E6FFF 0000EA40  C000EB82 80000035 80000035 FFE0CADF
        80000FC  0000041A 000003E8 182F07F1  400960AA 07C8C1E2 C55C5C5C 000E6FFF
```

Figure 15.9
Display of the general purpose registers.

```
         Register 8                              Register 7                     PAGE   1

GR 0-7  00084218 00084210 00095FFF 0000F9F8  C000EA3F 80000025 80000025 00000000
GR 8-F  00001FD6 0000041A 000003E8 182F07F1  4CC840AA 07C8C1E2 C55C5C5C 00095FFF
```

Figure 15.10
Display of the general purpose registers.

An explanation follows.

1. DCB=XX
    The SNAP instruction requires an additional DCB within the program, because we want to create a separate file for writing the contents of the storage dump. The DCB appears as follows.

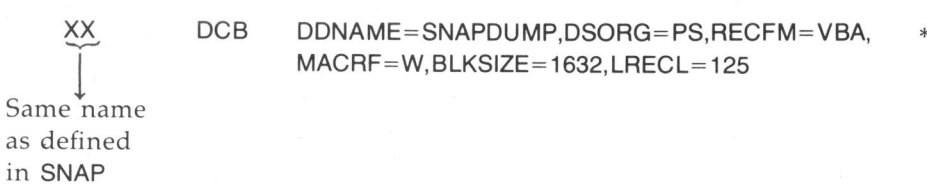

```
    XX        DCB    DDNAME=SNAPDUMP,DSORG=PS,RECFM=VBA,          *
                     MACRF=W,BLKSIZE=1632,LRECL=125
```

Same name
as defined
in SNAP

The DDNAME has been arbitrarily chosen as SNAPDUMP. Because an additional DCB macro is required with the SNAP to indicate that another form of output is to be produced, an additional DD line is required as part of job control. (See Appendix B for details on job control.)

```
//GO.SNAPDUMP       DD       SYSOUT=A
```

The RECFM operand indicates that the records will be variable in length (V) and blocked (B). The "A" indicates that ASA control characters are being used for carriage control.

The "W" in the MACRF operand indicates that we are using the SNAP macro to write out a file.

2. PDATA=(PSW,REGS)
   Execution of the SNAP instruction with this operand will display

   Program Status Word (PSW)
   general registers (REGS)

3. STORAGE=(S1,S2)

Indicates initial storage area to be dumped   Indicates storage area where dump is terminated

Because we added a DCB to the program to write out the dump, we must remember to OPEN and CLOSE this output file as we do any other file.

The following program excerpt illustrates the 4 instructions that must be added to an OS program when we want to use the SNAP.

```
*  ILLUSTRATION OF SNAP
       :
       :
          OPEN     (SNAP,OUTPUT)
       :
       :
          SNAP     DCB=SNAP,PDATA=(PSW,REGS),STORAGE=TOTAL1,TOTAL5
       :
       :
          CLOSE    (SNAP)
       :
       :
SNAP      DCB      DDNAME=SNAP,DSORG=PS,MACRF=(W),BLKSIZE=1632,      *
                   LRECL=125,RECFM=VBA
       :
       :
TOTAL1    DC       PL4'0'
TOTAL2    DC       PL4'0'
TOTAL3    DC       PL4'0'
TOTAL4    DC       PL4'0'
TOTAL5    DC       PL4'0'
```

Result   The PSW and the general registers will be displayed when the SNAP macro is executed.

Storage dumps of TOTAL1-TOTAL4 will also be provided.

Note that TOTAL5, the second delimiter of the storage areas to be printed, does *not* itself print. The dump is provided up to, but not including, TOTAL5.

Important Note
The first operand in the SNAP instruction (TOTAL1 in the example) must be defined by a DS or DC that precedes the definition of the second operand in the SNAP instruction (TOTAL5 in the example).

B. Sample Program 3

Figure 15.11 shows a program designed to sum the salary fields from each input record and to print a total. The program was assembled with *no* diagnostics or errors. Upon execution, however, an interrupt message appeared indicating that a DECIMAL DATA EXCEPTION OCCURRED AT 020032.

On the computer on which the program was executed, all programs start at hexadecimal address 020000. We know, therefore, that the interrupt occurred at relative address 000032 (020032–020000). By examining Figure 15.12, we see that the instruction at 000032 is AP TOTAL,PKDSAL.

To find the error, we must examine the contents of storage at the time of the interrupt. This is done by including the SNAP macro before the AP instruction, along with its associated DCB, OPEN, and CLOSE macros, as shown in Figure 15.13. We then execute the program again. Figure 15.14 shows the dump that is obtained.

To find why the AP instruction caused the interrupt, we need to examine the contents of the fields operated on in this instruction, that is, TOTAL and PKDSAL.

The address of TOTAL, a 4-byte field, is indicated in the AP instruction under ADDR1 (Figure 15.13), which refers to Operand 1 of the corresponding instruction. From this instruction, we find that the address of TOTAL is 000111. The address of TOTAL may also be found by examining the LOC (location) field of the DC labeled TOTAL. It, too, has an address of 000111.

The address of PKDSAL, the 3-byte sending field in the AP instruction, is listed under ADDR2 (Operand 2) of that instruction.

The address, 0010E, may also be found under ADDR1, or Operand 1, of the PACK instruction, or in the LOC field of the DC labeled PKDSAL.

By examining the dump in Figure 15.14, we discover that the contents of PKDSAL at the time of the interrupt is 000004. This is *not* a valid packed number, because the digit 4 is *not* a valid sign. Therefore, we look at the field that was packed into PKDSAL by the PACK instruction. That field is SALARY, a 5-byte field in the input record starting at address 00012E. By looking at the contents of these 5 bytes, we find that SALARY contains 4040404040, or 5 blanks. We have just located the cause of the interrupt. Because the SALARY field contains all *blanks*, this resulted in an invalid sign when the field was packed, as illustrated below.

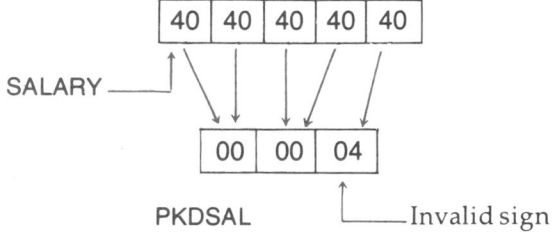

CHAPTER SUMMARY

I. The Debugging Process
   A. First, programs are translated.
      1. A source listing, object program (machine-language equivalent), and a listing of syntax errors are produced.
      2. Correct syntax errors before the program can be executed.
   B. After all syntax errors have been corrected, the program is run or executed.
      1. Use test data that includes all conditions for which the program tests.
      2. Check the computer results to make sure they are correct.
   C. Logic errors can occur.
      1. They can produce erroneous results.
      2. They can result in program interrupts (abnormal end of the program).

```
LOC      OBJECT CODE           ADDR1  ADDR2   STMT  SOURCE STATEMENT

000000E                                         8   *                                                       SAM00080
                                                9   *                                                       SAM00090
                                               10   *        HOUSEKEEPING INSTRUCTIONS GO HERE              SAM00100
00001E                                         11   READ  OPEN  (INFILE,INPUT,OUTFILE,OUTPUT)               SAM00110
00002C  F224 C072 C092  00078  00098           19         GET   INFILE,RECORD                               SAM00120
000032  FA32 C075 C072  0007B  00078           24         PACK  PKDSAL,SALARY                               SAM00130
000038  47F0 C018       0001E                  25         AP    TOTAL,PKDSAL                                SAM00140
00003C  D283 COCA COC9  000D0  000CF           26         B     READ                                        SAM00150
000042  D218 COCA C25A  000D0  00260           27   EOF   MVC   OUTAREA,SPACES                              SAM00160
000048  F363 COE3 C075  000E9  0007B           28         MVC   OUTAREA(25),=C'TOTAL ANNUAL SALARIES IS '   SAM00170
00004E  96F0 COE9       000EF                  29         UNPK  OUTAREA+25(7),TOTAL                         SAM00180
000052                                         30         OI    OUTAREA+31,X'F0'                            SAM00190
000060                                         31         PUT   OUTFILE,CUTAREA                             SAM00200
                                               36         CLOSE (INFILE,OUTFILE)                            SAM00210
                                               44   *                                                       SAM00220
                                               45   *        HOUSEKEEPING INSTRUCTIONS GO HERE              SAM00230
                                               46   *             ALONG WITH DCB MACROS                     SAM00240
                                               47   *                                                       SAM00250
000078                                         51   PKDSAL   DS   PL3                                       SAM00290
00007B  0000000C                               52   TOTAL    DC   PL4'0'                                    SAM00300
00007F                                         53   RECORD   DS   0CL80    CARD FORMAT                      SAM00310
00007F                                         54   LAST     DS   CL15           *                          SAM00320
00008E                                         55   FIRST    DS   CL10           *                          SAM00330
000098                                         56   SALARY   DS   CL5            *                          SAM00340
00009D                                         57            DS   CL50           *                          SAM00350
0000CF  40                                     58   SPACES   DC   CL1' '                                    SAM00360
0000D0                                         59   OUTAREA  DS   0CL132   PRINT FORMAT                     SAM00370
0000D0                                         60            DS   CL5            *                          SAM00380
0000D5                                         61   LNAME    DS   CL15           *                          SAM00390
0000E4                                         62            DS   CL20           *                          SAM00400
0000F8                                         63   FNAME    DS   CL10           *                          SAM00410
000102                                         64            DS   CL20           *                          SAM00420
000116                                         65   SALOUT   DS   CL5            *                          SAM00430
00011B                                         66   BLANK    DS   CL57           *                          SAM00440
                                              176            END                                           SAM00490
```

Figure 15.11
Program to add the salary fields from each input record.

```
LOC    OBJECT CODE      ADDR1 ADDR2  STMT  SOURCE STATEMENT

                                        8  *                                                    SAM00080
                                        9  *           HOUSEKEEPING INSTRUCTIONS GO HERE         SAM00090
                                       10  *                                                    SAM00100
00000E                                 11        OPEN  (INFILE,INPUT,OUTFILE,OUTPUT)             SAM00110
00001E                                 19 READ   GET   INFILE,RECORD                            SAM00120
00002C F224 C072 C092  00078 00098     24        PACK  PKDSAL,SALARY                            SAM00130
000032 FA32 C075 C072  0007B 00078     25        AP    TOTAL,PKDSAL                             SAM00140
000038 47F0 C018        0001E          26        B     READ                                     SAM00150
00003C D283 C0CA C0C9  000D0 000CF     27 EOF    MVC   OUTAREA,SPACES                           SAM00160
000042 D218 C0CA C25A  000D0 00260     28        MVC   OUTAREA(25),=C'TOTAL ANNUAL SALARIES IS ' SAM00170
000048 F363 C0E3 C075  000E9 0007B     29        UNPK  OUTAREA+25(7),TOTAL                      SAM00180
00004E 96F0 C0E9        000EF          30        OI    OUTAREA+31,X'F0'                         SAM00190
000052                                 31        PUT   OUTFILE,OUTAREA                          SAM00200
000060                                 36        CLOSE (INFILE,OUTFILE)                         SAM00210
                                       44  *                                                    SAM00220
                                       45  *           HOUSEKEEPING INSTRUCTIONS GO HERE         SAM00230
                                       46  *           ALONG WITH DCB MACROS                    SAM00240
                                       47  *                                                    SAM00250
                                                                                                SAM00290
000078                                 51 PKDSAL  DS    PL3                                      SAM00300
00007B 0000000C                        52 TOTAL   DC    PL4'0'                                   SAM00310
00007F                                 53 RECORD  DS    0CL80          CARD FORMAT              SAM00320
00007F                                 54 LAST    DS    CL15                                     SAM00330
00008E                                 55 FIRST   DS    CL10                                     SAM00340
000098                                 56 SALARY  DS    CL5                                      SAM00350
00009D                                 57         DS    CL50                                     SAM00360
0000CF                                 58 SPACES  DC    CL1' '                                   SAM00370
0000D0  40                             59 OUTAREA DS    0CL132         PRINT FORMAT             SAM00380
0000D0                                 60         DS    CL5                                      SAM00390
0000D5                                 61 LNAME   DS    CL15                                     SAM00400
0000E4                                 62         DS    CL20                                     SAM00410
0000F8                                 63 FNAME   DS    CL10                                     SAM00420
000102                                 64         DS    CL20                                     SAM00430
000116                                 65 SALOUT  DS    CL5                                      SAM00440
00011B                                 66 BLANK   DS    CL57                                     SAM00490
                                      176         END
```

Figure 15.12
Finding the instruction that caused a decimal data exception.

```
LOC      OBJECT CODE          ADDR1 ADDR2  STMT  SOURCE STATEMENT

                                              8   *                                                               * SAM00080
                                              9   *                                                               * SAM00090
                                             10   *                HOUSEKEEPING INSTRUCTIONS GO HERE              * SAM00100
00000E                                       11         OPEN   (INFILE,INPUT,OUTFILE,OUTPUT)                         SAM00110
00001E                                       19         OPEN   (SNAP,OUTPUT)                                        SAM00120
00002A                                       25  READ   GET    INFILE,RECORD                                        SAM00130
00003E   F224 C108 C128       0010E 0012E    30         PACK   PKDSAL,SALARY                                        SAM00140
                                             31         SNAP   DCB=SNAP,PDATA=(PSW),STORAGE=(PKDSAL,BLANK)          SAM00150
000062   FA32 C10B C108       00111 0010E    46         AP     TOTAL,PKDSAL                                         SAM00160
000068   47F0 C024                  0C02A    47         B      READ                                                 SAM00170
00006C   D283 C160 C15F       00166 00165    48  EOF    MVC    OUTAREA,SPACES                                       SAM00180
000072   D218 C160 C2F2       00166 002F8    49         MVC    OUTAREA(25),=C'TOTAL ANNUAL SALARIES IS '            SAM00190
000078   F363 C179 C10B       0017F 00111    50         UNPK   OUTAREA+25(7),TOTAL                                  SAM00200
00007E   96F0 C17F                  00185    51         OI     OUTAREA+31,X'F0'                                     SAM00210
000082                                       52         PUT    OUTFILE,OUTAREA                                      SAM00220
000090                                       57         CLOSE  (INFILE,,OUTFILE)                                    SAM00230
00009E                                       65         CLOSE  (SNAP)                                               SAM00240
0000AA                                       71  SNAP   DCB    DDNAME=SNAP,DSORG=PS,MACRF=(W),BLKSIZE=1632        * SAM00250
                                                                LRECL=125,RECFM=VBA                                 SAM00260
                                            122   *                                                               * SAM00270
                                            123   *                HOUSEKEEPING INSTRUCTIONS GO HERE              * SAM00280
                                            124   *                ALONG WITH DCB MACROS                         * SAM00290
                                            125   *                                                               * SAM00300
00010E                                      129  PKDSAL DS     PL3                                                  SAM00340
000111   0000000C                           130  TOTAL  DC     PL4'0'                                              SAM00350
000115                                      131  RECORD DS     0CL80                   CARD FORMAT                  SAM00360
000115                                      132  LAST   DS     CL15                                              * SAM00370
00012A                                      133  FIRST  DS     CL10                                              * SAM00380
00012E                                      134  SALARY DS     CL5                                               * SAM00390
000133                                      135  SPACES DS     CL50                                                SAM00400
000165   40                                 136  SPACES DC     CL1' '                                             SAM00410
000166                                      137  OUTAREA DS    0CL132                  PRINT FORMAT                 SAM00420
000166                                      138         DS     CL5                                               * SAM00430
00016B                                      139  LNAME  DS     CL15                                              * SAM00440
00017A                                      140         DS     CL20                                              * SAM00450
00018E                                      141  FNAME  DS     CL10                                              * SAM00460
000198                                      142         DS     CL20                                              * SAM00470
0001AC                                      143  SALOUT DS     CL5                                               * SAM00480
0001B1                                      144  BLANK  DS     CL57                                              * SAM00490
                                            254         END                                                        SAM00540
```

Figure 15.13

Using the SNAP macro to examine the contents of storage at the time of the interrupt.

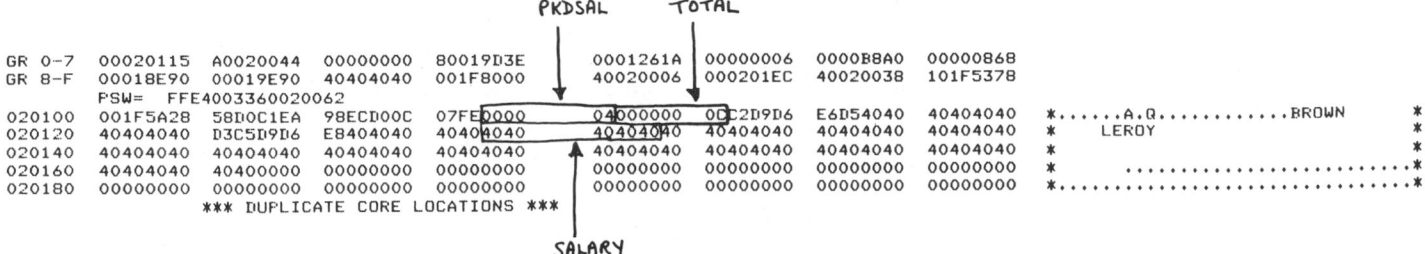

Figure 15.14 Dump obtained from the sample SNAP macro.

II. Debugging Aids for Detecting Logic Errors
    A. PDUMP and SNAP.
        1. PDUMP—for DOS.
        2. SNAP—for OS.
    B. PDUMP and SNAP are instructions that display the contents of key fields during program testing.
        1. These instructions are inserted during program testing and removed once the program runs properly.
        2. PDUMP and SNAP can display contents of storage, general registers, and program status words.
        3. Format:

```
PDUMP   S1,S2
```

        or

```
SNAP   DCB=XX,PDATA=(PSW,REGS),STORAGE=(S1,S2)
```

        When the instruction is encountered, all storage areas beginning with S1 and ending with S2, but *not including* S2, will be displayed.
        4. The program must define S1 *before* S2.
        5. It is useful to define a one-position blank between each storage area to be displayed. The one-position blank makes it easier to read the storage display (sometimes called a storage dump).

CHAPTER SELF-EVALUATING QUIZ

1. Explain the meaning of the following SNAP macro.

```
SNAP   DCB=SNAPDCB,PDATA=(PSW),STORAGE=(COUNT,BLANK)
```

2. What other instructions must be included in the program when the SNAP macro is utilized?

3. (T or F) The SNAP macro can be used to pinpoint syntax errors, that is, errors that violate the rules of the language.

4. Examine the program listing in Figure 15.15 and explain why a dump was not obtained, although a SNAP macro was included.

For Questions 5–7, examine the dump in Figure 15.16.

5. What data is located in the 15 bytes starting at $02016D_{16}$? Show the data in hexadecimal and zoned-decimal formats.

6. What data is located in the 10 bytes starting at $02017C_{16}$? Show the data in hexadecimal and zoned-decimal formats.

7. What data is located in the five bytes starting at 020186_{16}? Show the data in hexadecimal and zoned-decimal formats.

SOLUTIONS   1. The SNAP instruction requires a DCB macro, arbitrarily named SNAPDCB, to describe the file to be used for writing out the dump. The data to be displayed includes

Page
425

```
 LOC     OBJECT CODE        ADDR1 ADDR2  STMT         SOURCE STATEMENT

                                            8   *                                                               *  SAM00080
                                            9   *          HOUSEKEEPING INSTRUCTIONS GO HERE                     *  SAM00090
                                           10   *                                                               *  SAM00100
000000E                                    11        OPEN  (INFILE,INPUT,OUTFILE,OUTPUT)                            SAM00110
00001E                              READ   19        GET   INFILE,RECORD                                           SAM00120
00002C  F224 C0FC C11C  00102 00122        24        PACK  PKDSAL,SALARY                                           SAM00130
000032                                     25        SNAP  DCB=SNAF,PDATA=(PSW),STORAGE=(PKDSAL,BLANK)             SAM00140
000056  FA32 C0FF C0FC  00105 00102        40        AP    TOTAL,PKDSAL                                            SAM00150
00005C  47F0 C018       0001E              41        B     READ                                                    SAM00160
000060  D283 C154 C153  0015A 00159 EOF    42        MVC   OUTAREA,SPACES                                          SAM00170
000066  D218 C154 C2E2  0015A 002E8        43        MVC   OUTAREA(25),=C'TOTAL ANNUAL SALARIES IS '              SAM00180
00006C  F363 C16D C0FF  00173 00105        44        UNPK  OUTAREA+25(7),TOTAL                                     SAM00190
000072  96F0 C173       00179              45        OI    OUTAREA+31,X'F0'                                        SAM00200
000076                                     46        PUT   OUTFILE,OUTAREA                                         SAM00210
000084                                     51        CLOSE (INFILE,,OUTFILE)                                       SAM00220
000092                                     59        CLOSE (SNAP)                                                  SAM00230
00009E                              SNAF   65        DCB   DDNAME=SNAP,DSORG=PS,MACRF=(W),BLKSIZE=1632           * SAM00240
                                                           LRECL=125,RECFM=VBA                                     SAM00250
                                          116   *                                                               *  SAM00260
                                          117   *          HOUSEKEEPING INSTRUCTIONS GO HERE                     *  SAM00270
                                          118   *                ALONG WITH DCB MACROS                          *  SAM00280
                                          119   *                                                               *  SAM00290
000102                              PKDSAL 123        DS    PL3                                                     SAM00330
000105  0000000C                    TOTAL  124        DC    PL4'0'                                                  SAM00340
000109                              RECORD 125        DS    0CL80                                                   SAM00350
000109                              LAST   126        DS    CL15                CARD FORMAT                         SAM00360
000118                              FIRST  127        DS    CL10                              *                     SAM00370
000122                              SALARY 128        DS    CL5                               *                     SAM00380
000127                                     129        DS    CL50                              *                     SAM00390
000159  40                          SPACES 130        DC    CL1' '                                                  SAM00400
00015A                              OUTAREA 131       DS    0CL132              PRINT FORMAT                        SAM00410
00015A                                     132        DS    CL5                               *                     SAM00420
00015F                              LNAME  133        DS    CL15                              *                     SAM00430
00016E                                     134        DS    CL20                              *                     SAM00440
000182                              FNAME  135        DS    CL10                              *                     SAM00450
00018C                                     136        DS    CL20                              *                     SAM00460
0001A0                              SALOUT 137        DS    CL5                               *                     SAM00470
0001A5                              BLANK  138        DS    CL57                              *                     SAM00480
                                          248        END                                                           SAM00530
```

Figure 15.15
Program for Question 4.

```
GR 0-7  0002016D A002009C 00000000 80019D3E 0001261A 00000006 0000B8A0 00000868
GR 8-F  00018E90 00019E90 40404040 001F8000 40020006 00020244 40020090 101F5378
        PSW=  FFE40033600200BA
020160  98ECD00C 07FE1345 0F000000 0CC1C4C1 D4E24040 40404040 40404040 D1D6E8C3
020180  C5404040 4040F1F3 F4F5F040 40404040 40404040 40404040 40404040 40404040
0201A0  40404040 40404040 40404040 40404040 40404040 40404040 40404040 40404040
             *** DUPLICATE STORAGE LOCATIONS ***
```

Figure 15.16
Dump for Questions 5-7.

a. the Program Status Word (PSW), and
b. the contents of the storage areas starting with COUNT up to, but not including, BLANK.

2.   OPEN   (SNAPDCB,OUTPUT)   429
   SNAPDCB DCB   DDNAME=SNAPDUMP,DSORG=PS,MACRF=(W),   *
                    BLKSIZE;1632,LRECL=125,RECFM=VBA
            CLOSE   (SNAPDCB)

3. F: the SNAP is used to debug errors in *logic*.   416
4. The file for the SNAP was not opened.   429
5. C1 C4 C1 D4 E2 40 40 40 40 40 40 40 40 40 40   423
   A D A M S
6. D1 D6 E8 C3 C5 40 40 40 40 40   423
   J O Y C E
7. F1 F3 F4 F5 F0   423
   1 3 4 5 0

REVIEW QUESTIONS

1. The term _____ is used to designate the termination of a program resulting from a logic error.
2. (T or F) If a program is translated and no syntax errors occur, then the program will always execute properly.
3. If the execution of a program produces erroneous output, we call this a(n) _____ error.
4. (T or F) Debugging is the process of correcting *all* errors in a program—both syntax and logic.
5. (T or F) Packing a field that contains blanks will not result in any logic errors.
6. (T or F) Displaying fields during the test phase enables the programmer to check the logic at various points in the program as needed.
7. The command used for displaying key fields during program testing is _____ for DOS and _____ for OS.
8. Consider the following instruction.

   PDUMP FLD1,FLD8

   Storage dumps of _____ will be provided when the PDUMP instruction is encountered.
9. Abend is an abbreviation for _____ .
10. (T or F) It is sometimes useful to establish blank areas between fields that will be dumped to make the dump more readable.
11. (T or F) You can use the PDUMP instruction to display the contents of the 16 general registers.
12. (T or F) A SNAP instruction will be executed by the computer only if an abend occurs.
13. (T or F) You may use a SNAP or PDUMP to display the contents of the PSW.
14. If blanks mistakenly appear in a numeric field that is to be used in an arithmetic operation, a(n) _____ error will occur when the arithmetic is performed.

UNIT 6

ADVANCED CONCEPTS

16 Indexing

OBJECTIVES

To familiarize you with:
1. *The use of indexes.*
2. *Looping with the use of indexes.*
3. *Table-handling procedures.*
4. *The* EQU *statement.*

I. INTRODUCTION

A. Looping Redefined

You will recall that a loop is a sequence of instructions executed a fixed number of times. An example of a loop is a routine that reads in 5 input records and adds an AMT field from each record, to produce one TOTAL. In general, the sequence of steps necessary for looping includes the following.

B. Steps in a Loop

Example 16.1

1. Initialize all fields (including a counter (CTR) field).		ZAP	TOTAL,=P'0'
		ZAP	CTR,=P'0'
2. Perform the necessary operations.	LOOP	GET	INFILE,RECORD
3. Add 1 to CTR.		PACK	PAMT,AMT
4. Does CTR = desired number?		AP	TOTAL,PAMT
5. If yes, branch out.		AP	CTR,P'1'
6. If no, repeat from Step 2.		CP	CTR,=P'5'
		BE	OUT
		BNE	LOOP

Such a routine eliminates the need to code the three instructions beginning at LOOP 5 times, one for each record. Imagine the savings if we had 100 records to process in this way! Suppose, however, we wish to add 5, 4-byte amount fields that are in storage defined either as

```
ITEM1    DS    F
ITEM2    DS    F
ITEM3    DS    F
ITEM4    DS    F
ITEM5    DS    F
```

or more simply as:

```
ITEM    DS    5F
```

A simple loop will not suffice to add these fields because we are not operating on the *same* field repeatedly as in the previous looping example.

Indexing is a method that enables the programmer to increment the *address* of the fields to be operated on. Using indexing, we can code one looping routine that contains an add instruction and that also increments the address of the field to be added.

In the preceding example, we could perform the add operation and then increment the address of the field to be operated on by four.

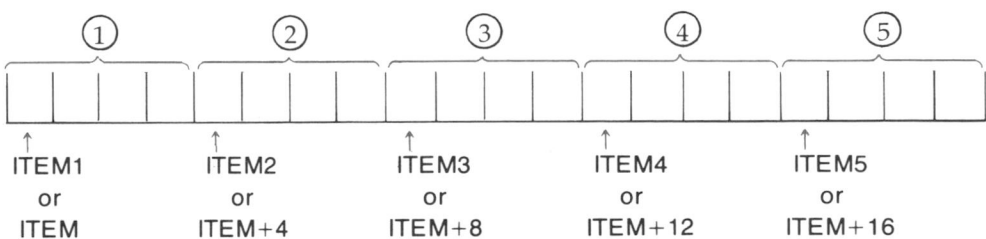

C. An Overview of Indexing

From the illustration, we see that relative addressing, as well as looping, is an integral part of indexing.

INDEXING

1. Performs a looping procedure.
2. Utilizes **relative addressing** (field to be operated on is changed within the loop).

Note that to utilize an index for incrementing the fields to be operated on, these fields must meet certain requirements.

REQUIREMENTS FOR FIELDS WHEN INDEXING

1. Fields must be located adjacent to one another in storage, that is, defined sequentially in the program. Or, the fields may be separated by some fixed number of bytes.
2. Fields must all be the same length.

The ITEM fields described above meet these requirements and can, therefore, be indexed.

D. Additional Applications of Indexing

Fields arranged in the preceding manner are sometimes referred to collectively, as a table, list, matrix, or array. A table, to use the most common term, consists of a series of items called *elements*. Indexing is the method used to process tables.

The specification

```
ITEM    DS    5F
```

for example, defines a 20-byte table of 5 elements, each 4 bytes long.

A table can be created in storage for the purpose of summing the elements, or producing a series of totals. A table can also be created for *look-up* purposes. A tax table, for example, may be read into storage with a STATE and COUNTY code and a corresponding SALESTAX rate for each state and county. Indexing, in this instance, is *not* used for totaling, but for "looking-up" a SALESTAX rate from the table. If input records have a STATE and COUNTY code, we can find the appropriate SALESTAX rate by a look-up procedure that uses the *indexing* technique.

E. Steps Involved in Indexing

Let us return to our example, where we have 5 ITEM fields that we want to add together using indexing to produce a TOTAL. Here are the steps involved.

```
                    STEPS INVOLVED IN INDEXING
     1.  Initialize TOTAL.
     2.  Establish a counter (CTR).
     3.  Establish an index register that will contain the address of ITEM.
     4.  Add ITEM, indexed, to TOTAL.
     5.  Add 4 to index to obtain the next ITEM (each ITEM is 4 bytes long).
     6.  Add 1 to CTR.
     7.  Test CTR for 5.
     8.  If −, branch out.
     9.  If not equal, branch to Step 4.
```

We can generalize these steps to apply to any indexing problem, as illustrated in Figure 16.1.

Indexing can be performed using RX or SS type instructions. We will examine RX instructions first.

II. INDEXING USING RX INSTRUCTIONS

A. Introduction

RX (Register and Indexed Storage) format instructions utilize a register in conjunction with storage areas. To perform indexing, we may use RX instructions for obtaining a TOTAL of the 5 ITEM fields. Steps 3–5, which include the indexing procedures, will be discussed in detail. Before discussing them, however, we must review and expand our understanding of RX instructions.

```
1.                  L       3,=F'0'              REG3=TOTAL
2.                  L       2,=F'0'              REG2=CTR
3.    *****                                              *****
4.    *****   INDEXING PROCEDURES STEPS 3-5      *****
5.    *****   (STEP4 IS LABELED LOOP)            *****
6.                  A       2,=F'1'
7.                  C       2,=F'5'
8.                  BE      OUT
9.                  B       LOOP
                            ¦
                            ¦
                            ¦
      ITEM1         DS      F
      ITEM2         DS      F
      ITEM3         DS      F
      ITEM4         DS      F
      ITEM5         DS      F
```

B. Expanded Version of RX Instructions

1. An Overview

You will recall that the actual or effective address of all storage locations is obtained by adding a **displacement** to a **base address,** where the base address is stored in a base register. This base address *cannot* be altered during the execution of the program.

When using the RX format, the programmer has the option of including another element for calculating the effective address. This third element is an additional displacement that is stored in **an index register.**

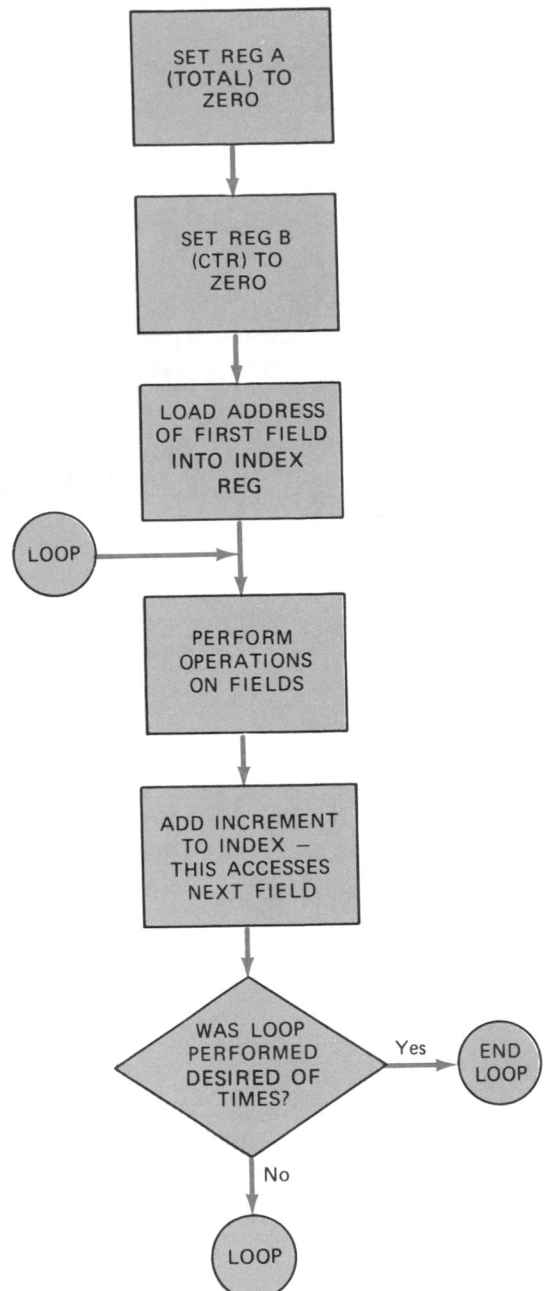

Figure 16.1
Basic logic used for RX
indexing.

Let us review the format for RX instructions.

Op code	R	X2	B2	D2

An index register is a general-purpose register that may be used to store an adjustment or displacement in a manner similar to the base register. However, the index register, unlike the base register, *may be altered* during the program's execution. When indexing is to be performed, the programmer must specify which general purpose register is to be used as the index register.

2. RX Format: Without Indexing

Consider the following RX instruction.

```
A    5,AMT
```

AMT is a symbolic name that is converted, during the assembly process, to an actual address expressed as X2 + B2 + D2. Because indexing is *not* being performed in the above, X2 will be given a value of 0. Hence, the effective address of AMT may, for example, have the following value.

BASE ADDRESS	8040
DISPLACEMENT	1024
INDEX VALUE	0
EFFECTIVE ADDRESS OF AMT	9064
(no indexing)	

Note that an index value of 0 does *not* mean register 0, but means that no indexing is being performed.

When an RX instruction contains an operand such as ITEM, which will be incremented, then the operand must be coded using a different format, one that includes the index register.

3. Expanded Format(s) for RX Instructions

1.

Operation 10	Operand 16
OP	REG,D(X,B)

where

  D = displacement
  X = index register
  B = base register

or

2.

Operation 10	Operand 16
OP	REG,D(X)

where the computer keeps track of the value of the base register.

In our example, let us use general register 4 as an index register. Suppose that the index register already contains the address of ITEM. The following instructions (Steps 4 and 5 on page 441) allow us to add each ITEM to TOTAL (register 3) and then to increment the index register by 4 so that the next ITEM is added.

---

4. A   3,0(4)   Add ITEM (no displacement) to register 3
                     (total).
5. A   4,=F'4'   Increment address (of ITEM) by 4.

The entire indexing procedure is then complete except for the instruction that loads the address of ITEM into index register 4. Figure 16.2 shows the entire

```
* INDEXING PROCEDURE
          L       3,=F'0'
          L       2,=F'0'
          LA      4,ITEM1
LOOP      A       3,0(4)
          A       4,=F'4'
          A       2,=F'1'
          C       2,=F'5'
          BE      OUT
          B       LOOP
          .
          .
          .
ITEM1     DS      F
ITEM2     DS      F
ITEM3     DS      F
ITEM4     DS      F
ITEM5     DS      F
```

Figure 16.2
Sample indexing procedure.

program. The LA or Load Address instruction (Step 3) will be explained in the next section.

SUMMARY

1. All RX-type instructions may include an index register if one is desired.
2. For RX-type instructions that are not processed for indexing, the machine-language equivalent includes a 0, denoting that *no* indexing is to be performed.

III. THE LA INSTRUCTION AND EXPLICIT ADDRESSING

A. Format

Instruction:	LA
Meaning:	Load Address
Operand 1:	Register
Operand 2:	Symbolic address or displacement with index and/or base register indicated in parentheses.
Result:	The effective address obtained by adding the displacement, index register contents, and base register contents is loaded into the first operand.

The primary function of the Load Address (LA) instruction is to place an actual or effective address specified in the second operand into the register specified as the first operand. The address, when contained in a register, can then be modified for indexing purposes. It is important to realize that the LA instruction does not load the *contents* of the location, just the address itself. Here is the general format for the LA instruction when used for explicit addressing.

Operation 10	Operand 16
LA	REG,D(X,B)
LA	REG,OP2

or

where

LA	denotes the operation Load Address.
REG	is a register and the first operand.
D	is a displacement.
X	specifies an index register.
B	specifies the base register.

D(X,B) is the second operand

The contents of the base register (B) and the contents of the index register (X) are added together. This sum is then added to the displacement to determine the actual or effective address.

An example will clarify this type of instruction.

```
LA    3,ITEM
```

This instruction loads the address of ITEM into register 3, the index register in this example.

We may now refer to register 3 to obtain the address of ITEM.

```
0(3) refers to ITEM1
4(3) refers to ITEM1 + 4 (ITEM2)
8(3) refers to ITEM1 + 8 (ITEM3)
12(3) refers to ITEM1 + 12 (ITEM4)
16(3) refers to ITEM1 + 16 (ITEM5)
```

Examine Figure 16.2 again to be sure you understand how indexing is performed using the LA instruction.

Self-Evaluating Quiz

1. (T or F) Assembler-language instructions may produce indexed results by using a base + displacement + index format, or by using a symbolic name + index.
2. Indicate the results of the following.
   a. LA   7,RECIN
   b. LA   7,RECIN(7)
   c. LA   6,200(5,4)
   d. LA   5,3(5)
3. Write a routine to add 30, 4-position numbers at TABLE into register 5. Assume that each 4-position number is in binary form.

SOLUTIONS

1. T
2. a. Address of RECIN loaded into register 7
   b. Register 7 = address of RECIN + previous contents of register 7
   c. Register 6 = 200 + contents of register 5 + contents of register 4
   d. Register 5 = 3 + previous contents of register 5
3.

```
        L     5,=F'0'     SET REG5 (TOTAL) TO ZERO
        L     6,=F'0'     SET REG6 (COUNTER) TO ZERO
        LA    3,TABLE     ADDRESS OF FIRST NUMBER
LOOP    A     5,0(3)      ADD NUMBER TO TOTAL
        A     6,=F'1'     ADD 1 TO COUNTER
        A     3,=F'4'     ADD 4 TO ADDRESS TO ACCESS NEXT NUMBER
        C     6,=F'30'    WAS ROUTINE PERFORMED 30 TIMES?
        BNE   LOOP        IF NOT, REPEAT
         •
         •
         •
TABLE   DS    30F
```

B. An In-depth Look at the Load Address Instruction

1. Uses

The LA instruction may be used in the following ways.

1. Using symbolic names
   LA   5,RECIN—This instruction loads the *address* of RECIN into register 5.
2. Using the base-displacement format

Operation 10	Operand 16
LA	5,200(3,4)

This instruction loads into register 5, 200 plus the contents of index register 3 plus the contents of base register 4.

Example 16.2

Before Execution	After Execution
Register 3 00 00 20 00	Register 3 00 00 20 00
Register 4 00 00 10 00	Register 4 00 00 10 00
Register 5 00 12 34 56	Register 5 00 00 32 00

Register 5 now contains the address, or storage location, 3200. The contents of register 3 and register 4 are added to a displacement of 200. Note that the displacement is coded in decimal and may range in value from 0 to 4095.

When either the base or index register is specified as 0, it means that these elements of the instruction are to be omitted. It does *not* mean that register 0 is to be used as an index register or base register. In addition, the 0 specification may be omitted from the instruction entirely. For example, the following three LA instructions all produce the same results.

Instruction	Register 3 Before Execution	Register 5 After Execution
LA 5,350(3,0)	2000	2350
LA 5,350(3)	2000	2350
LA 5,2350	2000	2350

The last example is interesting in that the decimal displacement (2350) is loaded into register 5. Because the base and index registers have been omitted, only the displacement value (2350) has been stored in register 5. The register makes *no* distinction between an address and the constants used in a program. The decimal value 2350 is converted to binary and stored in the register. The LA instruction, then, provides us with an additional means of giving a register a starting value.

In order to zero out register 5, we simply code LA 5,0. The value zero would then be placed in register 5.

2. Loading Constants with the LA Instruction

The following illustrations of the LA instruction will improve your understanding of explicit addressing and increase your efficiency as a programmer.

The effect of the instructions below is to add 4 to the contents of register 5.

LA 5,4(5)	or	A 5,=F'4'

(register 5 = 4 + register 5)
   = displacement of 4 + contents of register 5

The LA instruction, however, is more efficient, because a fullword containing a 4 was not required. The advantage of this approach is that it saves 4 bytes of storage each time a constant is added to a register. Whenever a register is to be initialized, the same approach may be taken. For example, to set a register to zero, any of the following instructions could be used.

Load Address	Load Halfword	Load Fullword
LA 8,0	LH 8,=H'0'	L 8,=F'0'

The most efficient method is to use the Load Address because the other instructions require either a halfword or fullword with value of zero. Consequently, 2 or 4 additional bytes of storage are needed if the other instructions are used.

C. Indexed Addressing and Symbolic Names

When an RX (Register and Indexed Storage) instruction refers to a storage location by name, the assembler converts the actual address of that storage location to the base-displacement format. When the index register is specified, it is used by the CPU to calculate the effective address. If storage areas were defined as follows

```
ITEM1    DC    F'15'
ITEM2    DC    F'7'
ITEM3    DC    F'91'
ITEM4    DC    F'11'
ITEM5    DC    F'82'
```

we would reference the data in these areas in several ways.

First, we could code the instruction

Operation 10	Operand 16
LA	3,ITEM1

to store the actual address of ITEM1 in register 3. If it were necessary to reference the other items we could now use any of the following alternatives in referencing ITEM1–ITEM5.

Using Symbolic Name	Relative Addressing	Explicit Addressing
ITEM1	ITEM1	0(3) Index register
ITEM2	ITEM1+4	4(3) [Contents of index register 3 (ITEM1) + 4]
ITEM3	ITEM1+8	8(3) [Contents of index register 3 (ITEM1) + 8]
ITEM4	ITEM1+12	12(3) [Contents of index register 3 (ITEM1) + 12]
ITEM5	ITEM1+16	16(3) [Contents of index register 3 (ITEM1) + 16]

Remember that register 3 contains the effective address of ITEM1. The displacement values are added to this address to arrive at the actual address. The following instructions would, then, all be equivalent.

A 9,ITEM5	A 9,ITEM1+16	LA 3,ITEM1
		A 9,16(3)

In addition, a fourth format may be used as follows, where the decimal value 16 is first loaded into register 5.

Operation 10	Operand 16
LA	5,16
A	9,ITEM1(5)

The base-displacement address of ITEM1 and the contents of register 5 are added to produce the effective address. If register 5 contained the decimal value 16, the second operand would reference ITEM5. However, if register 5 contained a zero, then the Add instruction would be referencing ITEM1.

Therefore, there are 2 formats to explicitly reference RX instructions, as illustrated in the following table.

Summary

Symbolic Address	Explicit Type 1 (may be coded this way)	Explicit Type 2 (may be coded this way)	Register 5 (in decimal)	Register 3
ITEM1	0(3)	ITEM1(5)	000	[Contains the address of ITEM1]
ITEM2	4(3)	ITEM1(5)	004	
ITEM3	8(3)	ITEM1(5)	008	
ITEM4	12(3)	ITEM1(5)	012	
ITEM5	16(3)	ITEM1(5)	016	

Example 16.3

Write a routine to sum the contents of 20 consecutive fullwords, the first of which is located at AMTS. We use the LA instruction in place of less efficient instructions. We count the number of times the routine is performed. When the count is equal to 20, we have added all 20 numbers.

```
* SOLUTION TO INDEXING EXAMPLE 16.3
          LA      6,0     SET REGISTER 6 (TOTAL) TO ZERO
          LA      7,0     SET REGISTER 7 (CTR) TO ZERO
          LA      5,AMTS  REGISTER 5 IS INDEX REGISTER
LOOP      A       6,0(5)  ADD AMT TO TOTAL
          LA      7,1(7)  ADD 1 TO CTR
          LA      5,4(5)  ADD 4 TO ADDRESS
          C       7,=F'20' WAS ROUTINE PERFORMED 20 TIMES?
          BNE     LOOP    IF NOT, REPEAT
          .
          .
          .
AMTS      DS      20F
```

Self-Evaluating Quiz

1. Question 3 in the previous section stated the following:
   Write a routine to add 30, 4-position numbers at TABLE into register 5. Assume that each 4-position number is in binary form. Code this same procedure using LA instructions.
2. Why is the LA instruction more efficient than the A or L instruction used in the previous section?
3. (T or F) The LA instruction loads into Operand 1 the contents of Operand 2, if Operand 2 is defined as a symbolic name.

SOLUTIONS 1.

```
            LA       5,0       SET REG 5(TOTAL) TO ZERO
            LA       6,0       SET REG 6(CTR) TO ZERO
            LA       3,TABLE   ADDRESS OF FIRST NUMBER
    LOOP    A        5,0(3)    ADD NUMBER TO TOTAL
            LA       6,1(6)    ADD 1 TO CTR
            LA       3,4(3)    ADD 4 TO ADDRESS TO GET NEXT NUMBER
            C        6,=F'0'   WAS ROUTINE PERFORMED 30 TIMES?
            BNE      LOOP      IF NOT, REPEAT
```

2. The A and L instructions require self-defining constants that use a fullword of storage; the instruction L 3,=F'0', for example, sets up a 4-byte constant of zero—unnecessary when using an LA instruction.

3. F: It loads in the *address* of Operand 2, not the contents, if Operand 2 is defined as a symbolic name.

D. Address Constants

In our routines so far, we have tested for the end of a loop by *counting* the number of times the loop has been performed. The logic has been basically as follows.

```
            LA       3,0       SET REGISTER 3 (COUNTER) TO ZERO
            .
    LOOP    .
            .
            LA       3,1(3)    ADD 1 TO COUNTER
            C        3,LIMIT   WAS ROUTINE PERFORMED LIMIT TIMES?
            BNE      LOOP      IF NOT, REPEAT
```

This test includes the following items.

> 1. Initialize a register as a counter.
> 2. Add 1 to the register every time we process LOOP.
> 3. Compare the register or counter to the desired number.
> 4. Branch back to LOOP if the desired number has not been reached.

Another method for testing for the end of a loop is to use an ADCON, which is an abbreviation for **address constant.** If, for example, we want to operate on RECIN until the appropriate register used for address modification is equal to RECIN+80, we can program it as follows.

```
            LA       5,RECIN
            .
    LOOP    .
            .
            C        5,=A(RECIN+80)
            BNE      LOOP
```

The operand = A(RECIN+80) indicates the *address of* RECIN+80. The Compare instruction thus compares the contents of register 5 (an address) with the address of RECIN+80.

By using an address constant, we need not establish a separate register as a counter. Similarly, we need not add 1 to the counter every time we pass through the loop. Figure 16.3 is an alternative method for coding the ITEM problem using an ADCON in place of a register as a counter.

Note, too, that if items are added to the table, the use of the address constant eliminates the need to alter the program.

```
* INDEXING PROCEDURE USING ADDRESS CONSTANT IN PLACE OF COUNTER
                LA      3,0
                LA      2,0
                LA      4,ITEM1
LOOP            A       3,0(4)
                LA      4,4(4)
                C       4,=A(ITEM1+20)
                BE      OUT
                B       LOOP
                .
                .
                .
ITEM1           DS      F
ITEM2           DS      F
ITEM3           DS      F
ITEM4           DS      F
ITEM5           DS      F
```

Figure 16.3
Indexing procedure using an
address constant in place of a
counter.

IV. INDEXING USING SS INSTRUCTIONS

A. Advantage of SS Indexing

Thus far, we have illustrated how indexing can be performed using RX instructions. Indexing is not, however, limited to RX instructions; it can also be performed on SS (storage-to-storage) instructions. An advantage of using SS instructions for indexing is that the length of each element of a stored table is not limited. Because RX instructions place results in a register, indexing is limited to 4 bytes. With SS indexing, each element of a table may contain from 1 to 256 bytes. This, of course, provides more flexibility.

B. Requirements of SS Indexing

Indexing of main storage requires that **explicit addresses** be used. An index register is referenced as part of the explicit address. It must *not* be the program's base register; that is, the register used for indexing may *not* be specified in the USING instruction.[1]

C. Expanded Format for SS Instructions

The symbolic format for explicit operands when using storage-to-storage (SS) operations is somewhat different from that discussed for RX operations.

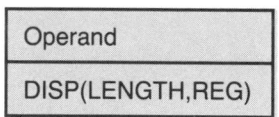

Operand
DISP(LENGTH,REG)

where

DISP	specifies a displacement. This displacement will be added to the contents of the register to arrive at an actual address. With indexing, this displacement is usually specified as 0.
LENGTH	refers to the length of the field to be operated on in bytes. With indexing, it will usually be the length of each element of the table.
REG	indicates a general register that contains the address of the first item to be indexed. This register will serve as an index register.

An LA or Load Address instruction is usually needed for loading the required address into the index register.

---

[1]See Appendix F for a discussion of how a base register is assigned.

D. Examples

Example 16.4 Consider the following.

```
L A         7,RECIN
M V C       LINEOUT + 10(80),0(7)
```

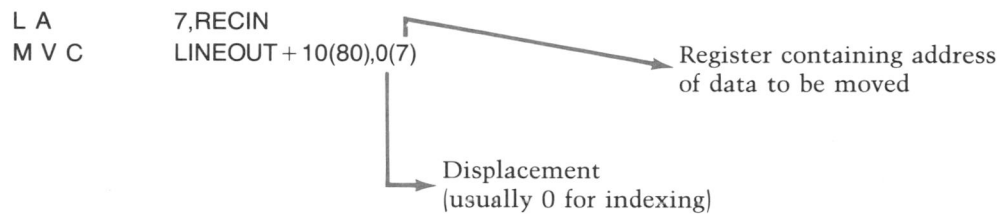

Register containing address
of data to be moved

Displacement
(usually 0 for indexing)

Note:
The length specification for an MVC instruction can only appear in the first operand.

Result
Eighty positions at RECIN are moved to LINEOUT. The following will also produce the same results.

```
MVC    LINEOUT+10(80),RECIN
```

If the programmer were also required to test record positions 79–80 for a state code such as NY, the following CLC instruction could be coded.

Operation 10	Operand 16
CLC	78(2,7),=C'NY'

The second operand is self-defining and contains the EBCDIC configuration for NY. The first operand is referencing RECIN+78, or position 79 of the input area. Recall that register 7 contains the *address* of RECIN whereas a displacement of 78 bytes from that point of reference has been prescribed. We are therefore referencing the 79th position of RECIN or position 79 of the input data record. The number of bytes to be compared has been specified as 2. Therefore, positions 79 and 80 of RECIN will be compared to the EBCDIC configuration of NY. When an equal condition occurs, we want to branch to a routine called BIGAPPLE where further processing will take place. This instruction would be coded as follows.

```
BE    BIGAPPLE
```

As we will see in the following examples, explicit addressing is a powerful tool for the programmer and is essential for storage-to-storage indexing.

Example 16.5 Suppose a population table consisting of 50 state population figures has been read into an area called STATE.

```
STATE   DS    50PL4
```

The preceding entry defines the storage area for the table. Data must be read from an input device and moved into this area. Later in this chapter we will discuss the routines necessary for reading and accumulating the table data. For now, let us assume that STATE contains all the data; that is, the 50 packed figures have been accumulated in this table and are now available for processing.

We want to write a routine to find the total population of 50 states and place the answer in register 3. Examine the following program excerpt.

```
* FIND TOTAL USA POPULATION USING INDEXING
1.              LA      3,0                 REG 3 = TOTAL
2.              LA      5,STATE             REG 5 = INDEX REGISTER
3.  LOOP        ZAP     DWORD,0(4,5)        STATE POPS ARE ADDED
4.              CVB     2,DWORD                         USING
5.              AR      3,2                 RR FORMAT ADDITIONS
6.              LA      5,4(5)              INDEX REGISTER INCREMENTED BY 4
7.              C       5,=A(STATE+200)     ARE WE FINISHED?
8.              BNE     LOOP                IF NOT, REPEAT
                .
                .
                .
    DWORD       DS      D
    STATE       DS      50PL4
```

EXPLANATION

1. The first instruction initializes register 3 at 0.
2. The second instruction loads the address of STATE into register 5.
3. Instruction 3 places the field specified in a doubleword, (DWORD DS D), initially STATE, then STATE+4, and so on.
4. Instruction 4 converts the field specified into binary and places the result in register 2.
5. Instruction 5 adds the binary field to register 3.
6. Instruction 6 increments register 5 by 4.
7. Instruction 7 tests to see if all fields have been added; if the address in register 5 is equal to STATE+200, we have completed the table.

The following illustration will clarify this.

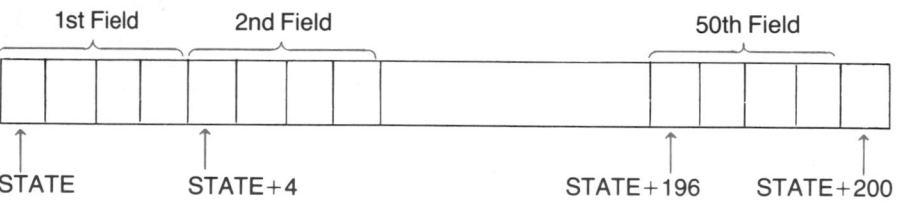

If the table has not been completely processed, a branch to LOOP occurs at instruction 8.

Example 16.6   Using the population table (STATE) referred to in Example 16.5, find the number of states with population figures in excess of 1,000,000.

```
* FIND THE NUMBER OF STATES WITH POPULATIONS IN EXCESS OF 1,000,000
*
             L       2,=F'1000000'
             LA      5,STATE
    LOOP     ZAP     DWORD,0(4,5)
             CVB     4,DWORD
             CR      2,4
             BNL     NOCOUNT
             AP      TOTAL,=P'1'
    NOCOUNT  LA      5,4(5)
             C       5,=A(STATE+200)
             BNE     LOOP
*
```

```
*  TOTAL NOW EQUALS THE NUMBER OF STATES WITH
*  POPULATIONS GREATER THAN 1,000,000
                    .
                    .
DWORD      DS    D
STATE      DS    50PL4
TOTAL      DC    PL2'0'
```

Let us use our population table again.

```
STATE      DS       50PL4
```

Note that if we are using SS-type instructions, each STATE field need not be restricted to 4 bytes. That is, the following table would be valid, if used with SS-type instructions.

```
STATE      DS    50PL6
```

To be consistent, however, we will use the original description of STATE (50PL4) for the following problems.

Example 16.7 Assuming that the state figures are in alphabetic sequence, write the instructions necessary to move the population of Alabama (1st state) and Wyoming (50th state) to output areas called POP1 and POP50, respectively.

```
UNPK    POP1,STATE(4)
UNPK    POP50,STATE+196(4)
```

Example 16.8 Write a routine to find the largest state population figure. Place this figure in an area called HOLD.

```
*  FIND THE LARGEST STATE POPULATION FIGURE
           LA    7,STATE
           ZAP   HOLD,STATE(4)
LOOP       CP    HOLD,0(4,7)
           BNL   NEXT
           ZAP   HOLD,0(4,7)
NEXT       A     7,4(7)
           C     7,=A(STATE+200)
           BNE   LOOP
*
*  HOLD NOW CONTAINS LARGEST STATE POPULATION FIGURE
*
                    .
                    .
HOLD       DS    PL4
STATE      DS    50PL4
```

Instruction 1 indicates that register 7 will be the index register. The address of STATE is loaded into register 7. Instruction 2 moves the first state field into HOLD. The LOOP compares HOLD to the first field. If HOLD is equal to or greater than the STATE figure, no operation is performed. If HOLD is less than the state figure, the new state figure is moved into HOLD. Register 7 is compared to the address of STATE+200 to determine if all fields in the table have been compared. If not, a branch to LOOP occurs. When the routine has been performed 50 times, HOLD will contain the largest state population figure.

Thus far in the example we have assumed that our population table (STATE) has been previously read in and accumulated in storage. Let us now consider the routine that will actually read in the data and accumulate it into the table.

Suppose there are 50 table records each with a 7-position population figure. We wish to accumulate these 50 figures in STATE for future processing. Note that the table data is *not* simply read and immediately processed, as is the convention with other forms of input. Rather, the table data is read and *stored* for future processing.

The input record format is as follows.

```
RECORD   DS   OCL80
POP      DS   CL7
         DS   CL73
```

We will read 50 such records and accumulate the data in the following area.

```
STATE    DS   50PL4
```

The following loop may be used.

```
         LA    7,STATE
LOOP     GET   INFILE,RECORD
         PACK  0(4,7),POP
         LA    7,4(7)
         C     7,=A(STATE+200)
         BNE   LOOP
          .
          .
          .
STATE    DS    50PL4
RECORD   DS    OCL80
POP      DS    CL7
         DS    CL73
```

Self-Evaluating Quiz

1. Explain the meaning of the following instruction.

   ```
   C    7,=A(INDATA+50)
   ```

2. What is a main advantage of storage-to-storage indexing as compared to indexing used with RX instructions?
3. (T or F) Indexing of main storage requires explicit addresses to be used.
4. Write the instructions necessary to move bytes 1–50 from INDATA to positions 11–60 of LINEOUT. Use explicit addressing.
5. Explain the meaning of the following instructions.

   ```
   LA    5,STATE
   ZAP   DWORD,0(4,5)
   ```

6. Write an LA instruction to add 4 to the contents of register 7.
7. If there are twenty 4-byte figures stored in TABLE, write an instruction to unpack the fifth entry in the table into TDATA.
8. (T or F) The instruction LA 9,ITEM usually indicates that register 9 will be an index register.
9. Using the state population table defined in this section, write a routine to find the total number of states with population figures less than 250,000.
10. Using the state population table defined in this section, write a routine to find the smallest state population figure and the *number* of that state.

SOLUTIONS

1. The instruction compares the contents of register 7 (an address) with the address of INDATA+50.
2. With SS instructions, each element of a stored table is not limited to 4 bytes as it is with RX instructions; with SS indexing, each element of a table may contain from 1 to 256 bytes.
3. T
4. ```
   LA    8,INDATA
   MVC   LINEOUT+10(50),0(8)
   ```
5. The address of STATE is loaded in register 5; then, we ZAP a field 4 bytes in length, starting at the address found in register 5.
6. ```
   LA    7,4(7)
   ```
7. ```
   UNPK  TDATA,TABLE+16(4)
   ```
   ```

8. T: the address of ITEM is loaded into register 9.

```
9.              L     2,=F'250000'
                LA    5,STATE
        LOOP    ZAP   DWORD,0(4,5)
                CVB   4,DWORD
                CR    2,4
                BNH   NOCOUNT
                AP    TOTAL,=P'1'
        NOCOUNT LA    5,4(5)
                C     5,=A(STATE+200)
                BNE   LOOP
        * TOTAL CONTAINS THE NUMBER OF STATES
        *    WITH POPULATION FIGURES LESS THAN 250,000
                        .
                        .
                        .
        DWORD   DS    D
        TOTAL   DC    PL2'0'
        STATE   DS    50PL4
10.             LA    7,STATE
                ZAP   CTR,=P'0'
                ZAP   HOLD,0(4,7)
        LOOP    CP    HOLD,0(4,7)
                BNH   NEXT
                ZAP   HOLD,0(4,7)
                ZAP   HOLDNO,CTR
        NEXT    A     7,4(7)
                AP    CTR,=P'1'
                C     7,=A(STATE+200)
                BNE   LOOP
        * HOLD CONTAINS SMALLEST STATE POPULATION FIGURE
        * HOLDNO CONTAINS STATE NUMBER WITH SMALLEST STATE POPULATION
                        .
                        .
                        .
        HOLD    DS    PL4
        HOLDNO  DS    PL2
        STATE   DS    50PL4
```

E. The Branch Index Low or Equal (BXLE) Instruction

With the RX instruction, a field length of 4 bytes is specified to increment or step through one storage location of a table to the next. However, with storage-to-storage (SS) instructions, the fields may vary from 1 to 256 bytes. As we have already learned, the indexing increment must match the length of each element of the table. For example, if each element were 6 bytes in length, it would be necessary to add a value of 6 to the index register with each pass through the loop. The BXLE instruction allows us to combine many of the steps presented in the previous indexing problem into one instruction. The symbolic form of the BXLE instruction is

Operation 10	Operand 16
BXLE	REG1,REG2,LABEL

where

BXLE   indicates Branch on Index, Low or Equal.
REG1   specifies the index register.
REG2   is an *even-numbered register* (of an even–odd pair) and contains the field length in bytes of each element.

REG3   (not coded) is an *implied odd register* numbered REG2 + 1 and contains the limit value to be used to end the loop.

LABEL   identifies the first instruction of the loop as in the BCT instruction.

The index register (REG1) identifies the element of the table to be processed. The register specified as REG2 contains the field length of each element and is the *even* register of an *even–odd* pair. The *odd* register contains the limit value used to end the loop. Let us review what operations this instruction performs.

REG1		REG2	REG2 + 1
Index value		Field length	Limit

The index value points to a different element in the table with each pass through the loop.

The field length is the increment added to the index register with each pass through the loop.

The limit controls the number of passes through the loop.

Each time the BXLE instruction is executed, the following steps occur in the sequence shown.

STEPS IN BXLE

1. The field length specified in REG2 is added to the contents of REG1. This allows us to reference the next element in the table.
2. The contents of REG1 (the current index value) are then compared to the contents of REG2 + 1 (the limit value).
3. If the index register is *low or equal*, the program branches to the label (first instruction of the loop) specified in the second operand.

In the previous examples, involving a population table called STATE, we used the following instructions to determine if the loop should be repeated. The loop is now performed 50 times, since there are fifty 4-byte fields to be processed. The address of the last field to be processed is STATE+196.

```
        LA      5,STATE              LOAD ADDRESS OF 1ST NO. INTO REG 5
        .
        .
LOOP    .
        .
        .
        LA      5,4(5)               INCREMENT REG 5 BY 4
        C       5,=A(STATE+200)      WAS LOOP PERFORMED REQUIRED NO. TIMES?
        BNE     LOOP                      IF NOT, REPEAT
```

By using the BXLE, we can replace these instructions with the following.

```
* ILLUSTRATION OF BXLE IN INDEXING
        LA      5,STATE     LOAD ADDRESS OF 1ST NO. INTO REG5
        L       6,=F'4'     LOAD FIELD LENGTH OF 4 INTO REG 6
LOOP    L       7,=A(STATE+196)   LOAD LIMIT INTO REG 7
        .
        .
        BXLE    5,6,LOOP
```

The limit value may be specified in two different ways.

SPECIFYING LIMIT VALUE

1. By specifying the address of the *last element* of the table. (The method used in the preceding examples.)
2. By specifying the *length of the table* in bytes and then *subtracting* one.

When the table length is specified, we are required to subtract 1. The reason for the subtraction is as follows. You will recall that the field length is *first* added to the index register and then a comparison of the index register to the limit value is made. An example illustrates this point.

Assume that a table consists of 5 elements, each 4 bytes in length, and that the limit value is set up as 20. When the entire table has been processed, the index value and the limit value will both have a value of 20. At this point in the program the loop should end. However, the program will incorrectly branch back to the first instruction of the loop, because the BXLE is designed to branch on a low or *equal* condition. To prevent this from occurring, 1 is always subtracted from the length of the table. In this way the BXLE will branch out when the table has been completely processed, that is, when the limit value of 19 is exceeded.

If the programmer establishes the limit by specifying the address of the last element of the table, a Load Address (LA) instruction is used. We will apply both these techniques again in finding the sum of 5 items, ITEM1-ITEM5, in the following examples.

Example 16.9   Specifying the limit as the length of the table minus one.

```
        LH      6,=H'0'         SET TOTAL TO ZERO
        LH      7,=H'0'         SET INDEX REGISTER TO ZERO
        LH      8,=H'4'         FIELD LENGTH OF 4 BYTES PLACED IN EVEN REG
        LH      9,=H'19'        TABLE LENGTH MINUS ONE PLACED IN ODD REG
DO5X    A       6,ITEM1(7)
        BXLE    7,8,DO5X        IF REG7+REG8 > REG 9 END LOOP
        CVD     6,RESULT
        :
```

Example 16.10   Specifying the limit as the address of the last element of the table.

```
        LA      6,0             SET TOTAL TO ZERO
        LA      7,ITEM1         STORE ADDRESS OF 1ST ELEMENT IN INDEX REG
        LA      8,4             FIELD LENGTH OF 4 PLACED IN REG 8
        LA      9,ITEM5         STORE ADDRESS OF LAST ELEMENT IN TABLE
DO5X    A       6,0(7)
        BXLE    7,8,DO5X
        CVD     6,RESULT
        :
```

The field specifications for both examples appear as follows.

```
ITEM1   DC      F'15'
ITEM2   DC      F'7'
ITEM3   DC      F'91'
ITEM4   DC      F'11'
ITEM5   DC      F'82'
RESULT  DS      D
```

There are many ways to assign initial values to the registers. In Example 16.9, we used the LH (Load Halfword) instruction and in Example 16.10 the LA (Load Address) instruction. Remember, the LA instruction is more efficient because a 2-byte halfword constant is unnecessary, and only wastes storage.

We also note that explicit (RX) addressing is used in Example 16.10. Notice that in this example, register 7 initially contained the address of ITEM1. The BXLE adds the field length contained in register 8 to the address stored in register 7 with each pass through the loop.

The values of the registers at the *completion* of each pass through the loop in Example 16.9 are as follows. These values are shown in decimal for the purpose of clarification.

BXLE 7,8,D05X

After Pass	(Total) Register 6	Index Register 7	(Field Length) Register 8	(Limit Value) Register 9
1	15	4	4	19
2	22	8	4	19
3	113	12	4	19
4	124	16	4	19
5	206	20	4	19

When the contents of register 7 are greater than the contents of register 9, the looping process is terminated and the instruction following the BXLE is executed.

Self-Evaluating Quiz

1. BXLE is an operation code that stands for _____ .
2. Consider the following instruction with the contents of registers 4, 6, and 7 as shown before execution.

   BXLE   4,6,LOOP
   Register 4 = +8
   Register 6 = +1
   Register 7 = +16

   When the BXLE instruction is executed, a branch to LOOP (will, **will not**) occur.
3. With the BXLE instruction, a branch only occurs when the sum of the first and second operands is (high/low/equal) or (high/low/equal) compared to the third operand.

   For Questions 4–6, assume the following hexadecimal values in the registers 2–7.

   R2: 00 00 00 0A
   R3: 00 00 00 2A
   R4: 00 00 00 0A
   R5: 00 00 00 08
   R6: 00 00 00 02
   R7: 00 00 00 0C

   Indicate whether or not a branch occurs.
4. BXLE   4,6,LOOP1
5. BXLE   4,2,LOOP2
6. BXLE   3,6,LOOP3

SOLUTIONS

1. Branch on index, low or equal
2. Will; the sum is less than contents of register 7.
3. Low or equal
4. A branch occurs; the limit is in register 7.

   A+2 = C = Reg7   branch occurs on an equal condition

5. A branch occurs; the limit is in register 3.

$A + A < 2A$ ($A_{16} + A_{16} = 20_{10}$; $2A_{16} = 42_{10}$)

6. A branch does not occur; the limit is in register 7.

$2A + 2 > C$ ($2A_{16} + 2_{16} = 44_{10}$; $C_{16} = 12_{10}$)

F. A Full Illustration of Storage-to-Storage Indexing

You will recall that storage-to-storage indexing permits a series of consecutive storage positions to be processed efficiently by a looping procedure that addresses the fields one at a time, in sequence. For example, let us assume that an input record contains 30 fields, each 2 positions in length. These 30 fields represent the temperatures for each day of the month of April: that is, positions 1–2 have the temperature for April 1, positions 3–4 the temperature for April 2, and so on. To calculate the average temperature for the month, it is necessary to sum the 30 temperatures and then divide by 30. Without indexing, 30 different symbolic names would be assigned to the 30 fields; moreover, 30 PACK and Add (AP) instructions would be required.

Indexing simplifies the solution to this problem. Figure 16.4 contains the coded program. The 30 temperatures occupy adjacent storage positions in the input area called RECORD. Therefore, the *address* of RECORD becomes a starting point and is placed in register 7 by the LA instruction, LA 7,RECORD. Effectively, register 7 now points to the area called RECORD and will serve as an index register. Each temperature is then processed one at a time simply by incrementing the contents of the index register.

Explicit addressing is used to reference each data field. Note that the first temperature can be referenced as 0(2,7), where, you will recall

0 refers to a zero displacement;
2 denotes a field length of 2 bytes; and,
7 is the general register serving as an index register.

```
*                                                                        *
*                                         HOUSEKEEPING INSTRUCTIONS GO HERE  *
*                                                                        *
          MVC    OUTAREA,SPACES
READ      GET    INFILE,RECORD
          ZAP    TOTAL,=P'0'
          LA     7,RECORD
          LA     5,RECORD+58
          LA     4,2
D030X     PACK   0(2,7),0(2,7)
          AP     TOTAL,0(2,7)
          BXLE   7,4,D030X
          ZAP    PROD,TOTAL
          MP     PROD,=P'100'
          ZAP    ANSWER,PROD+1(4)
          DP     ANSWER,=P'30'
          MVC    OUTAREA+10(9),=X'4020202020214B2020'
          ED     OUTAREA+10(9),QUOTNT
          PUT    OUTFILE,OUTAREA
*                                                                        *
*                                         HOUSEKEEPING INSTRUCTIONS GO HERE  *
*                                         ALONG WITH DTF OR DCB MACROS      *
*                                                                        *
RECORD    DS     CL80
SPACES    DC     CL1' '
OUTAREA   DS     CL132
ANSWER    DS     0CL6
QUOTNT    DS     CL4
REMDR     DS     CL2
TOTAL     DS     CL3
PROD      DS     CL5
          END
```

Figure 16.4
Illustration of storage-to-storage indexing.

Initially, the explicit address 0(2,7) points to RECORD and specifies the first field to be processed that consists of RECORD and RECORD+1. With each pass through the loop, the temperature will be packed and added to a field called TOTAL. The concept of indexing is illustrated in the schematic in Figure 16.5. Note that indexing is really a form of relative addressing. By adding 2 to the contents of the index register with each pass through the loop, the register will then point to the next temperature to be processed.

Clearly the advantages of indexing are the reduction in the number of instructions required to perform a particular task, and the resulting efficiency.

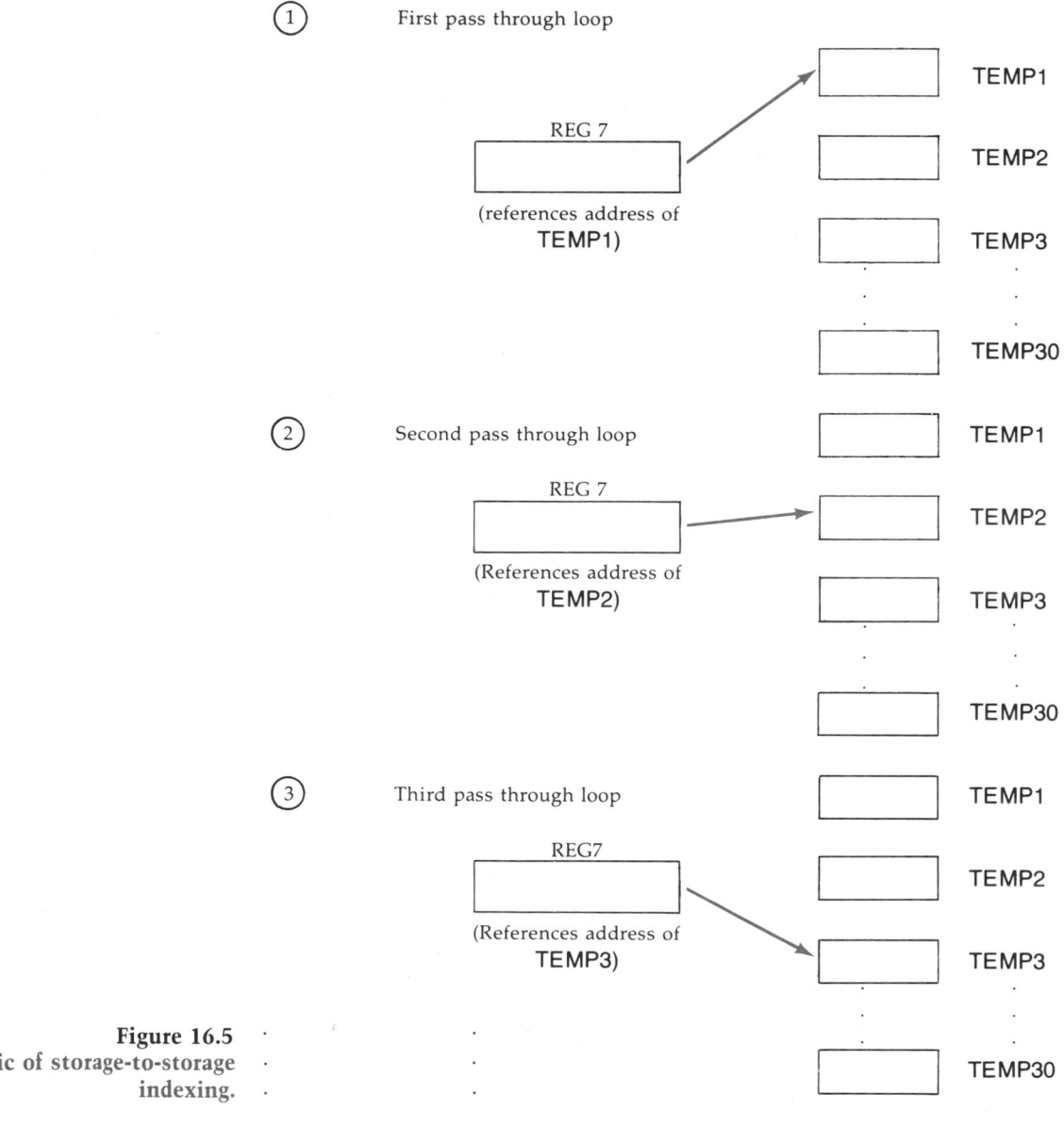

Figure 16.5
Schematic of storage-to-storage indexing.

> **SUMMARY**
>
> With storage-to-storage indexing note the following:
> 1. The address of the first field to be indexed is placed in an index register with an LA instruction.
> 2. The number of times the loop is to be executed is placed in a register that serves as a counter.
> 3. Explicit addressing must be used; it specifies
>   a. The index register
>   b. The length of the data field
> 4. The index register is incremented by the length of the data field with each pass through the loop.
> 5. Execution of the loop will cease when all fields have been processed.

Self-Evaluating Quiz

1. (T or F) With storage-to-storage indexing, the data fields to be indexed may be in consecutive positions or they may be randomly located.
2. The address of the starting point of the area to be indexed is placed in a(n) _____ .
3. The type of instruction used to place the starting point in the index register is a(n) _____ .
4. To perform indexing, (implicit/explicit) addressing must be used.
5. With explicit addressing, the instruction AP SUM,0(5,9) uses _____ as the index register. The length of the field to be added is (no.) bytes.
6. To perform indexing, addressing is performed within a procedure called a(n) _____ .
7. With each pass through the loop, the index register is incremented by the _____ .
8. The number of times the loop is to be executed is controlled by a(n) _____ .
9. The count register is initialized (before/after) the loop is executed.
10. (T or F) A single general register may be used as both an index register and a base register.

SOLUTIONS

1. F; they must be in consecutive positions.
2. Index register
3. LA (Load Address)
4. Explicit
5. Register 9; 5
6. Loop
7. Length of the element or data field
8. Register
9. Before
10. F; two separate registers must be used.

V. TABLE LOOK-UP USING INDEXING

A. An Overview

As we have seen, a **table** is simply a list of data, systematically organized to permit sequential reference to storage locations. One use of a table is to look up information. This function of table handling is commonly called a **table look-up** or *search*. Each item of data within the table is called an *element*.

The elements of a table to be searched consist of two components: the **argument** and the **function.**

Consider the following table.

Argument	Function
Wage Category	Percent Federal Tax
750.00	0.35
615.00	0.32
500.00	0.29
385.00	0.26
307.00	0.24
230.00	0.22
154.00	0.20
77.00	0.17
20.00	0.14
00.00	0.00

The table consists of *10* elements. The *argument* represents a weekly salary level whereas the *function* indicates the corresponding tax percentage to be used in calculating the federal tax deduction. The figure to be compared or "looked-up" in the table—in this case, weekly salary—is called the *argument.* The *function* is the figure sought from the table—in this case, the percent tax.

In summary, each element of the table contains a weekly wage, which will be defined as 3 packed bytes and the corresponding tax percentage, which will be defined as 2 packed bytes.

We will begin by assuming that the table has been defined within the program in the packed-decimal format.

```
***** TAX TABLE SPECIFICATIONS *****
TAXTBL    DS     0PL50
ARG1      DC     X'75000C'
FCN1      DC     X'035C'
ARG2      DC     X'61500C'
FCN2      DC     X'032C'
             .
             .
ARG9      DC     X'02000C'
FCN9      DC     X'014C'
ARG10     DC     X'00000C'
FCN10     DC     X'000C'

***** TAX TABLE SPECIFICATIONS: A SHORT-CUT *****
TAXTBL    DS     0PL50
          DC     X'75000C035C'
          DC     X'61500C032C'
             .
             .
          DC     X'02000C014C'
          DC     X'00000C000C'
```

The table consists of 10 elements, each 5 bytes in length, or a total of 50 bytes. Note that the placement of the decimal point is the programmer's responsibility and will be considered when the federal tax is edited. That is, decimal points are not part of the arithmetic operations to be performed.

After a PAY field has been read from an input record, the table will be searched to determine the correct tax percentage that applies to the PAY field. Starting at the first element of the table and proceeding through it sequentially, PAY is compared to each wage category (table argument). When PAY is greater than or equal to the wage category, the appropriate entry in the table has been found (see Figure 16.6). When PAY is greater than or equal to wage, the corresponding tax will be moved to an area called `TAXPCT` where it will be used in calculating the tax deduction. If, for example, `PAY` were equal to 400.00, the corresponding tax percentage of 0.26 would be moved to `TAXPCT` because 400.00 is greater than 385.00, but less than 500.00.

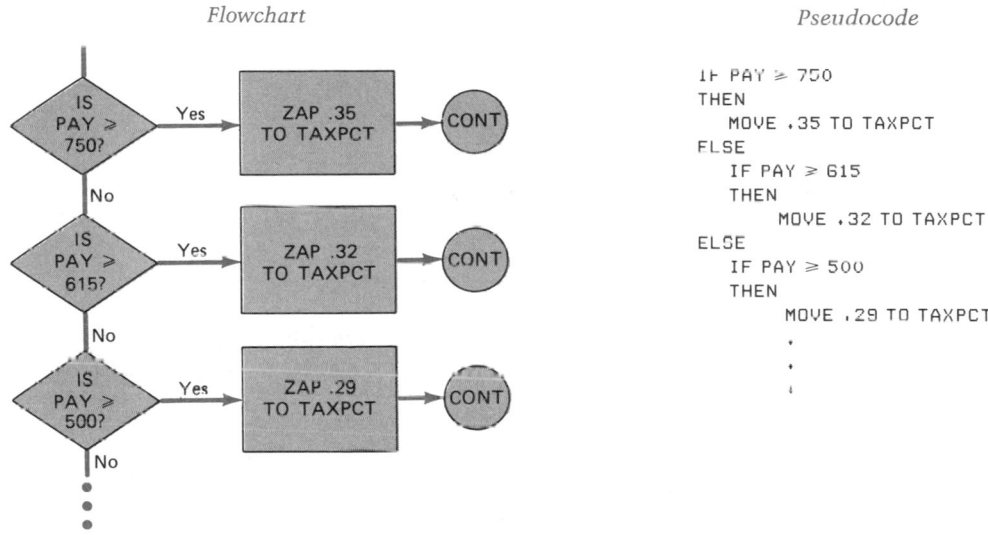

Figure 16.6
Example of a table search.

B. The Alternative to the Table Look-Up: Inefficiency

An alternative method of finding the percentage would be to code separate instructions to compare `PAY` to each wage category. The flowchart and pseudocode in Figure 16.7 illustrate this point.

Figure 16.7
Logic for a table look-up
without indexing.

Flowchart

Pseudocode

```
IF PAY ≥ 750
THEN
    MOVE .35 TO TAXPCT
ELSE
    IF PAY ≥ 615
    THEN
        MOVE .32 TO TAXPCT
ELSE
    IF PAY ≥ 500
    THEN
        MOVE .29 TO TAXPCT
```

Using this method, 10 compare and `ZAP` instructions would need to be coded. This method, however, is very inefficient and time-consuming. It also becomes increasingly impractical when the number of entries is greater than 10.

C. Programming a Table Look-Up

The flowchart in Figure 16.8 illustrates the logic we will use in our program.

`PAY` is input from a data record (positions 1–5) and must be converted to the packed-decimal format. The following instructions can be used for this purpose.

```
READ    GET     INFILE,RECIN
        PACK    PAY,PAY
```

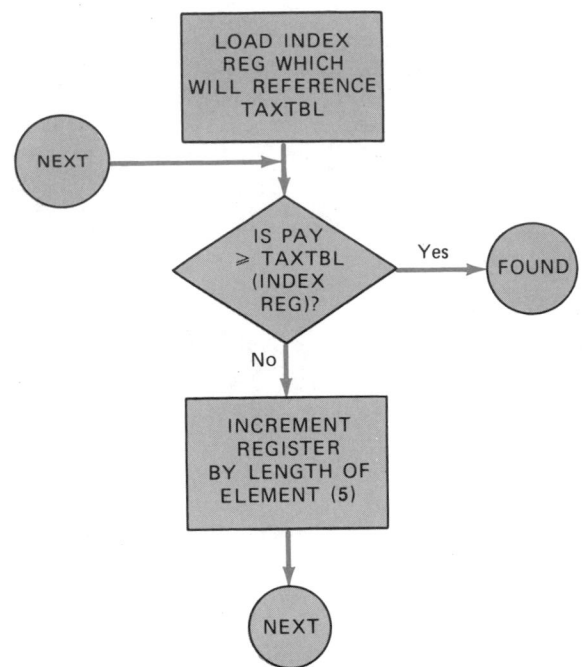

Figure 16.8
Logic for a table look-up with
indexing.

The coding necessary for the table look-up or search follows.

```
        LA      7,TAXTBL
NEXT    CP      PAY,0(3,7)      THREE BYTES OF ELEMENT
        BNL     FOUND
        LA      7,5(7)          ADD FIVE TO REG 7
        B       NEXT
```

The address of TAXTBL is placed in register 7. Register 7 then points to the area called TAXTBL. Remember each element consists of a 3-byte argument followed by a 2-byte function. The CP instruction compares the data field PAY with the table argument (wage category). An explicit length of 3 bytes has been specified as well as the use of index register 7. Consequently, the operand contains 0(3,7).

When the search condition is satisifed, the program branches to the routine called FOUND. If the condition is not met, the index register is incremented and the next table argument is compared. The process continues until the search condition is satisfied or the end of the table is reached. If the end of the table has been reached and no match has been found, we might want to print an error message. Our table has 000 as its last entry. Assuming PAY is positive, it will compare high (or equal) to this argument.

D. Referencing the Table Function at the Routine Labeled FOUND

Recall that each element of the table consists of a 3-byte argument followed by a 2-byte function. When the appropriate entry in the table has been found, the program branches to the routine called FOUND. At this point, register 7 contains the address of the desired element. However, we are interested in moving *only* the tax percentage of the element, not the entire element. We must again utilize explicit addressing. We want to skip the first 3 bytes of the element to reference the table function only (percent federal tax).

The following instruction serves this purpose.

```
FOUND       ZAP         TAXPCT,3(2,7)
```

Note that for the first time, the *displacement* portion of explicit addressing is put to use. That is, the displacement in this case is *not* 0, but 3.

The Practice Program at the end of this chapter illustrates the entire program to print NAME and PAY from each input record and TAXPCT as looked up in the table.

E. Creating a Table from Input

In the previous example, the TAXTBL was defined internally through the use of the Define Constant (DC). Tables that are subject to frequent change are often placed on data records and read into the program as variable data so that frequent changes to the programs are not required. The table data read into the input area would be in the following format.

Positions			
	1–5	Wage category 1	(Argument 1)
	6–7	Percent tax 1	(Function 1)
	8–12	Wage category 2	(Argument 2)
	13–14	Percent tax 2	(Function 2)

Notice that a 5-byte wage field is followed by a 2-byte percent field. The resulting table consists of elements each containing a 3-byte packed wage field followed by a 2 byte packed percent field.

It is therefore necessary to use 2 index registers—one for accessing the input data and one for loading data into the table. The following set of instructions would be coded immediately after the data record containing the table data was read. We begin by moving Percent Tax 1 into a 2-byte area in TAXTBL next to Wage Category 1.

```
          LA      6,10          SET COUNT REGISTER TO 10
          LA      7,REGIN       INITIALIZE INPUT INDEX REGISTER
          LA      8,TAXTBL      INITIALIZE TABLE INDEX REGISTER
*
SETUP     PACK    0(3,8),0(5,7)     PACK WAGE CATEGORY
          PACK    3(2,8),5(2,7)     PACK TAX PERCENT
          LA      7,7(7)            ADD 7 TO INPUT INDEX
          LA      8,5(8)            ADD 5 TO TABLE INDEX
          BCT     6,SETUP
```

The first pack instruction packs 5 bytes of data beginning with Wage Category 1 into a 3-byte area starting with TAXTBL.

The next instruction packs 2 bytes of data.

VI. **THE BRANCH ON INDEX HIGH (BXH) INSTRUCTION

This instruction is similar in format to the BXLE.

Operation 10	Operand 16
BXH	REG1,REG2,LABEL

where

REG1 is the index register.

REG2 contains the increment, which must be an even-numbered register (2, 4, 6, etc).

REG2 + 1 is an odd-numbered register (3, 5, 7, etc.) containing the limit value to be used to end the loop.

LABEL refers to the branch point.

**Two asterisks identify this as an optional topic.

FUNCTION OF THE BXH

1. The contents of REG2 are added to REG1.
2. If REG1 is greater than REG2 + 1, a branch is taken to the branch point.
3. If REG1 is less than or equal to REG2 + 1, the next sequential step is executed.

Example 16.11   BXH   7,4,BRANCH

Before		*After*	
REG 7:	00 00 00 02	REG 7:	00 00 00 06
REG 4:	00 00 00 04	REG 4:	00 00 00 04
REG 5:	00 00 00 20	REG 5:	00 00 00 20

Note
Branch does not occur (6 < 20).
Regardless of whether or not the branch occurs, the contents of register 4 are added to register 7 and the result is placed in register 7.

Example 16.12   BXH   7,4,LOOP

Before	
REG 7:	00 00 00 06
REG 4:	FF FF FF FF (−1)
REG 5:	00 00 00 00

The BXH will be executed 5 times with a branch to LOOP occurring. The sixth time the BXH is executed, register 7 will contain zero. (Remember that −1 will be added to register 7 *before* the compare.) Thus, the sixth time the BXH is executed, register 7 will equal register 5. Thus, a branch to LOOP will not occur because register 7 is no longer greater than register 5. In short, the sixth time BXH is executed, the next sequential instruction will be executed.

Comparing the BXH *to the* BXLE   You will note that the BXH is used exactly as the BXLE, only instead of branching if the index register is less than or equal to a quantity, we branch if the index register is greater than a specific quantity.

Let us examine the BXLE as used previously and adapt the problem using the BXH.

Previous Illustration Using BXLE*:*
Specifying the Limits as the Length of the Table Minus 1

```
        LH      6,=H'0'         SET TOTAL TO ZERO
        LH      7,=H'0'         SET INDEX REGISTER TO ZERO
        LH      8,=H'4'         FIELD LENGTH OF FOUR BYTES IN EVEN REG
        LH      9,=H'19'        TABLE LENGTH MINUS ONE IN ODD REGISTER
DO5X    A       6,ITEM1(7)
        BXLE    7,8,DO5X        IF REG 7 > REG 9 THEN END LOOP
        CVD     6,RESULT
          .
          .
          .
```

Same Problem, Using BXH

```
* THE USE OF BXH WITH INDEXING
        LH      6,=H'0'         SET TOTAL TO ZERO
        LH      7,=H'16'        SET INDEX REGISTER TO LAST ELEMENT IN TABLE
        LH      8,=H'-4'        INDEX REGISTER WILL BE INCREMENTED BY -4
        LH      9,=H'-4'        WHEN INDEX REGISTER = -4, TIME TO STOP
```

```
LOOP      A       6,ITEM1(7)
          BXH     7,8,LOOP        WILL BRANCH TO LOOP UNTIL XREG = -4
          CVD     6,RESULT
          .
          .
          .
```

VII. **ASSIGNING REGISTERS: THE EQUATE ⟨EQU⟩ STATEMENT

The EQU statement allows you to assign or equate a symbolic name to a register. It also serves to document the program. The general format of the EQU instruction is

Name	Operation	Operand
SYMNAME	EQU	REG

where

SYMNAME   is a name by which a register may be identified.
EQU   identifies the operation Equate.
REG   is the register to be referenced by the name.

Example 16.13

```
* PROGRAM EXCERPT USING EQU
          .
          .
          LA      INDEX,0
          A       TOTAL,=F'5'
          .
          .
          .
TOTAL     EQU     9
INDEX     EQU     8
```

Example 16.14

```
          USING   BEGIN,12
BEGIN     MVI     FLDA,C'A'
```

The symbolic names TOTAL and INDEX replace the numeric specifications of the registers, making the program easier to read and understand. There is, however, another advantage to utilizing the EQU instruction.

It sometimes happens, with very long or complex programs, that a programmer inadvertently uses the *same* register for more than one function. Correcting such an error can be quite cumbersome because it requires the programmer to examine carefully every source statement. If, instead, all registers used were equated to symbolic names, as in the following program, correcting the duplicate use of a register would be simplified.

```
TOTAL1    EQU     9
TOTAL2    EQU     8
X1        EQU     6
FINTOT    EQU     4
PROD      EQU     3
TOTAL3    EQU     6      (ERROR: DUPLICATE ASSIGNMENT)
```

Although instructions would use the symbolic name rather than the register number, all duplicate assignments could be corrected by simply revising the EQU statement. In the preceding example, for example, it would *not* be necessary to alter all instructions that use TOTAL3 the way it would if we had referenced register 6 throughout. Rather, we would simply write another EQU statement to correct the duplication.

```
TOTAL3    EQU     7
```

**This is an optional topic.

The EQU statement also establishes meaningful labels or reference points in a program. This improves program documentation. An asterisk is placed in the operand field of the EQU statement.

```
          BL      ERRMSG1
          :
          :
ERRMSG1   EQU     *
          MVC     LINEOUT+10(20),MSSG1
          :
          :
```

In this example, we assign the symbolic name ERRMSG1 to the next instruction, the MVC instruction. This serves to document the program, and permits the program to be written in segments, each with a specific purpose. This facilitates program segmentation and structured programming, which will be discussed in depth in Chapter 18.

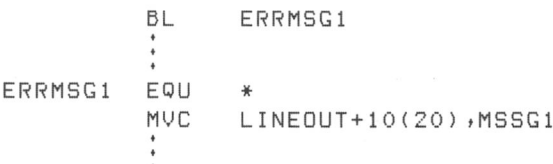

CHAPTER SUMMARY

I. Looping
  A. Purpose: to execute a series of steps in a program a fixed number of times.
  B. Steps in a loop.
    1. Initialize the counter field.
    2. Perform the required series of steps.
    3. Add 1 to the counter each time the series of steps is executed.
    4. Check to see if the counter is equal to the required number. (For example, if you want to execute a series of steps five times, add 1 to a counter each time you execute the steps; then check to see if the counter is equal to 5.)
    5. If the counter is equal to the required number, branch out; if it is not, repeat the series of steps.
II. Indexing
  A. Features
    1. Used to perform looping.
    2. Uses relative addressing to change the fields to be operated on within a loop.
  B. Requirements for fields to be used with indexing
    1. Fields must be located adjacent to one another in storage. This means they are defined in sequence, one after the other. Each field may also be separated by a fixed number of bytes.
    2. Each field used for indexing must be the same length.
  C. Fields that are indexed are sometimes referred to, collectively, as a table, list, matrix, or array.
III. Indexing Using RX Instructions
  A. When using the RX format, the programmer has the option of including an index register for additional displacement.

Op Code	Reg,D(X,B)

  where
    X = index register.
  B. For RX-type instructions that do not specify indexing, the machine-language equivalent for X is 0, denoting that no indexing is performed.
  C. The LA or Load Address Instruction
    1. The primary function is to place an actual or effective address specified in the second operand into the register specified as the first operand.
    2. The address, when contained in the register, can then be modified for indexing purposes.

3. Format:

```
LA    REG,D(X,B)
```

or

```
LA    REG,OP2
```

IV. Indexing Using SS Instructions
   A. Differences between indexing using RX instructions and indexing using SS instructions.
      1. Because RX instructions place results in a register, indexing is limited to four bytes.
      2. With SS indexing, each element to be indexed can be 256 bytes.
   B. The operand used in an SS indexing operation is defined as DISP(LENGTH,REG). The length is sometimes omitted; for example, the second operand in an MVC instruction does not include a length specification.
   C. Table look-ups are frequently performed using SS-type indexing.

CHAPTER SELF-EVALUATING QUIZ

1. A table occupies storage positions that are (consecutive/randomly placed).
2. Each element of a table consists of two components, the _____ followed by the _____ .
3. A table look-up or search begins with the _____ element of the table.
4. The elements of the table are searched (randomly/sequentially).
5. A table look-up requires (implicit/explicit) addressing as well as a procedure known as _____ so that the next element of the table will be processed when the tested condition is not satisfied.
6. When the search condition is satisifed, the loop is (terminated/continued).
7. The index register is initialized with a(n) _____ instruction.
8. With each pass through the loop, the index register is incremented by the length of the (table/argument/function/element).
9. Once the search condition is satisfied, the next step is to reference the (table/argument/function/element)
10. In referencing the function, a displacement must be used equal to the _____ .
11. Assume an element consisted of 10 bytes, with an argument of four bytes and a function of six bytes. Register 9 is serving as the index register. Write the instruction to move the function (indexed) to an area called STATED.

		Page
SOLUTIONS	1. Consecutive or adjacent	440
	2. Argument; function	462
	3. First	462
	4. Sequentially	462
	5. Explicit; looping	464
	6. Terminated	464
	7. LA (Load Address)	464
	8. Element	464
	9. Function	464
	10. Argument	464
	11. MVC STATED(6),4(9)	451

PRACTICE PROGRAM

The program in Figure 16.9 illustrates how a table look-up can be performed with indexing. The NAME and PAY from each input record are printed, along with TAXPCT, which is looked up in the table. Note that we edit PAY beginning at PAY+2. When we packed PAY we only needed three bytes. However, by packing PAY into itself, five bytes were used. Two high-order bytes of zeros resulted.

```
*  ILLUSTRATION OF A TABLE LOOK-UP USING INDEXING
*
*
READ        GET     INFILE,RECIN
            PACK    PAY,PAY
            LA      7,TAXTBL
NEXT        CP      PAY,0(3,7)
            BNL     FOUND
            LA      7,5(7)
            B       NEXT
FOUND       ZAP     TAXPCT,3(2,7)
            MVC     LINEOUT+5(20),NAME
            MVC     LINEOUT+30(7),=X'402020214B2020'
            ED      LINEOUT+30(7),PAY+2
            MVI     LINEOUT+30,C'$'
            MVC     LINEOUT+50(5),=X'40214B2020'
            ED      LINEOUT+50(5),TAXPCT
            PUT     OUTFILE,LINEOUT
            B       READ
                    .
                    .
                    .
LINEOUT     DS      CL132
TAXPCT      DS      PL2
RECIN       DS      0CL80
PAY         DS      CL5
NAME        DS      CL20
            DS      CL55
TAXTBL      DS      0PL50
            DC      X'75000C035C'
            DC      X'61500C032C'
                    .
                    .
                    .
            DC      X'02000C014C'
            DC      X'00000C000C'
```

Figure 16.9
Practice Program illustrating a table look-up with indexing.

KEY TERMS

Argument   Index register
Base address   Indexing
Base register   Relative addressing
Displacement   Table
Function   Table look-up

REVIEW QUESTIONS

1. Write a program using indexing to sum all of the odd numbers from 1 to 99.
2. Write a program using indexing to read in records with the following format. Print a report that lists for each student his or her name and average grade.

NAME	EXAM1	EXAM2	EXAM3	EXAM4	EXAM5	
1 20	21 23	24 26	27 29	30 32	33 35	

3. Write a program using indexing to read in records for each salesperson with sales figures (in dollars) for each day of the week. Print a report that lists for each salesperson his or her ID number and the average sales for the week.

SALES-PERSON ID	SALES MON	SALES TUES	SALES WED	SALES THURS	SALES FRI	SALES SAT	SALES SUN	
1 5	6 10	11 15	16 20	21 25	26 30	31 35	36 40	

4. Write the instructions necessary to create a table with the following format.

Argument (Number of Years Employed)	Function (Number of Weeks Vacation)
8	7
7	6
6	5
5	4
4	3
3	2
2	1

5. Using the table created in Question 4, write a program to do the following. Read input records with the format shown below and print, for each employee, his or her employee number and the number of weeks vacation to which he or she is entitled.

Employee Number	Number of Years Employed
1–7	8

PROGRAMMING ASSIGNMENTS

1. Input table entries have the following format.

    1–3   Warehouse number
    4–6   Product number
    7–11   Unit price xxx.xx
    12–80 Not used

    There are 250 of these table entries.
    The transaction input file that follows the table records has the following format.

    1–3   Product number
    4–7   Quantity
    8–20   Customer name
    21–80 Not used

    Create an output report containing product number, unit price, quantity, total amount, and customer name for each transaction record. Total amount is equal to unit price multiplied by quantity.

    Note that, for each transaction record, the product number must be found on the table file to obtain the corresponding unit price.

2. There are 20 salespeople in Company XYZ. Each sale that they have made is entered into a record with the following format.

1–2   Salesperson number (from 1 to 20)
3–17 Salesperson name
18–22 Amount of sale xxx.xx
23–80 Not used

The number of input records is unknown. Salesperson X may have 10 sales, Salesperson Y may have 5 sales, etc. The input is *not* in sequence.

Write a program to print the total amount of sales for each salesperson. Note that x number of input records will be read and that 20 total amounts are to be printed, one for each salesperson. All figures must be edited.

Print:

```
SALESPERSON        TOTAL AMOUNT

     1               XXXXX.XX
     .                  .
     .                  .
    20               XXXXX.XX
```

3. Write a program to print 12 transaction amounts, one for each month of the year and a yearly total. The input follows.

1–5   Transaction amount xxx.xx
6–30 Not used
31–32 Month number
33–80 Not used

Note that an undetermined number of records will serve as input, but only 12 totals are to be printed. All figures must be edited.

Note
The input is *not* in sequence.

Additional Considerations for Packed-Decimal Fields

<table>
<tr><td>

OBJECTIVES

</td><td>

To familiarize you with:
1. *Methods used for obtaining a specific number of digits in an arithmetic operation.*
2. *Methods used for rounding results.*
3. *Additional methods used for editing numeric results.*
4. *The use of* CR *and* DB *symbols.*
5. *The use of floating dollar signs.*

</td></tr>
</table>

I. THE NEED FOR SHIFTING

A. Shifting Packed-Decimal Fields to the Right

The following example illustrates how shifting packed-decimal fields to the right would be useful.

Purpose

To delete low-order digits when not needed in a decimal number.

Typical Application

Multiplication

You will recall that a multiplication operation results in a product that contains the same number of digits as the sum of the digits in the **multiplier** and **multiplicand.** To multiply 12.50 by 10.25, for example, we would need to provide for an 8-digit product, one with four integers and four decimal digits. If, however, only *2* decimal digits are required in the answer, we could *shift* the product *right, as soon as* the multiplication is completed, to eliminate two excess decimal places. This is discussed in Section II.

B. Shifting Packed-Decimal Fields to the Left

Purpose

To add low-order zeros for decimal alignment.

Applications

1. Addition and subtraction
2. Division

You will recall that decimal points are not part of arithmetic operations and that the computer does not automatically align data decimally. It is a programmer's responsibility to ensure that data is aligned decimally prior to any arithmetic operation so that the arithmetic is performed correctly.

Example 17.1   ***Add Operation Performed on Data with the Same Number of Decimal Places***
If 2.37 is to be used in an arithmetic operation, it will be entered as 237. If 1.16 is to be added to this field, then 116 would be entered, added, and 353 would represent the sum. The **edit** operation may then be used for printing

the result aligned decimally as 3.53. Hence, when operating on data with the same number of decimal positions, no special programming is required.

Example 17.2   *Arithmetic Operations Performed on Data with a Different Number of Decimal Places*
Suppose that 1.2 is to be added to 2.37. In this case, a problem could arise because they do *not*, as in the above example, have the same number of decimal places. Adding them without proper attention to decimal alignment will produce erroneous results.

237 + 12 = 249

However, 2.37 + 1.2 = 3.57.

Aligning Data by Shifting Left or Multiplying
It is the programmer's responsibility to align fields *before* addition or subtraction, where necessary, by **shifting** left or multiplying by a factor of 10. That is, by adding 237 to *120*, instead of 12 in the above, 357 would be the result or sum. When edited, 357 is the correct number. Note that multiplying 12 by 10 before addition would also produce decimal alignment. In general, one could shift left *or* multiply by a factor of 10 to achieve the same results.

Rules for Decimal Alignment
When the number of decimal positions in a field to be added or subtracted differs from the number of decimal positions in the other field(s) of the operation, shifting left will provide decimal alignment.

Example 17.3   *Shifting to Obtain Decimal Quotients After Division*
Suppose we wish to divide 15 by 30. Using normal rules for division, the answer would be .50. Using the divide operations (DP, D, DR), however, would produce a quotient of 00 and a remainder of 15. Division operations result in a quotient that contains the same number of digits as in the dividend. To produce the correct decimal (rather than integer) results, we would need to divide 1500 by 30 to obtain a result of 50 that, when edited, would print as .50. Here, again, we would need to *shift* the dividend *to the left* 2 positions before dividing. We could multiply the dividend by 100, or use a Move instruction that shifts digits to the left.

REVIEW

When Shifting May Be Required

A. SHIFT RIGHT: To delete decimal digits if not needed
    1. Multiplication
      Purpose: To eliminate excess decimal positions
      Example: $1.25 \times 1.35 = 1.6875$
      (decimal points not part of operation)
      If 1.68 is only required, shifting right two decimal places must be achieved.

B. SHIFT LEFT: To add zeros for decimal alignment
    1. Addition or Subtraction
      Purpose: To align decimal places
      Example: To add 1.65 + 1.3, 1.3 must be converted to 1.30. This is accomplished by shifting left a single position before adding.
    2. Division
      Purpose: To obtain decimal or fractional quotients
      Example: 25/100 would equal 0 unless 25 were shifted the desired number of decimal places to the left to produce a result that could then be converted to a decimal quotient.

II. SHIFTING PACKED-DECIMAL FIELDS RIGHT TO DELETE DIGITS

A. Using the Move Numeric (MVN) Instruction

The Move Numeric (MVN) instruction may be used after a decimal multiplication or other arithmetic operation, to truncate or delete low-order decimal positions.

Example 17.4

Suppose we want to multiply a tax percent by a purchase amount to obtain SALESTAX. Consider the following.

Tax % = 7%   Purchase Amt = 175.19

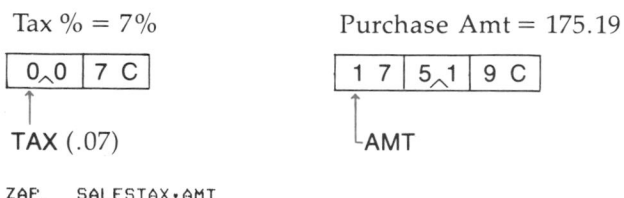

```
ZAP   SALESTAX,AMT
MP    SALESTAX,TAX
```

SALESTAX is 5 bytes long.

(Number of bytes in product = number of bytes in multiplier
                              + number of bytes in multiplicand)

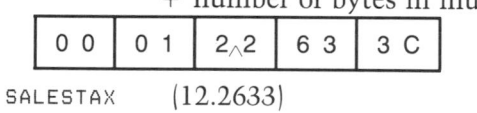

SALESTAX   (12.2633)

Because SALESTAX represents a field that is to be printed as dollars and cents, the two low-order decimal digits are unnecessary.

The MVN instruction is used to move data in the *low-order* 4 bits of a byte in the sending field to the low-order 4 bits of a byte in the receiving field.

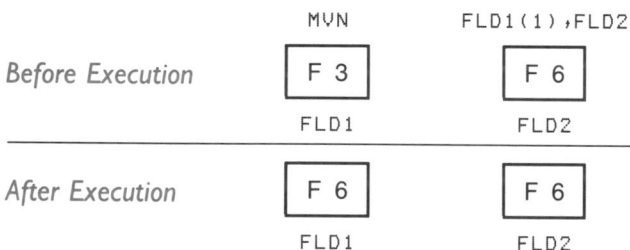

The MVN functions as a typical Move instruction. It operates, however, only on the low-order 4 bits of each byte. The MVN, then, is the converse of the MVZ instruction that is used to move the *high-order* 4 bits of each byte. The MVN may include an explicit length specifier or it may be implicit.

To truncate or delete the 2 low-order digits of SALESTAX so that it is reduced to 2 decimal positions instead of 4, we use the MVN.

```
MVN   SALESTAX+3(1),SALESTAX+4
```

Before Execution

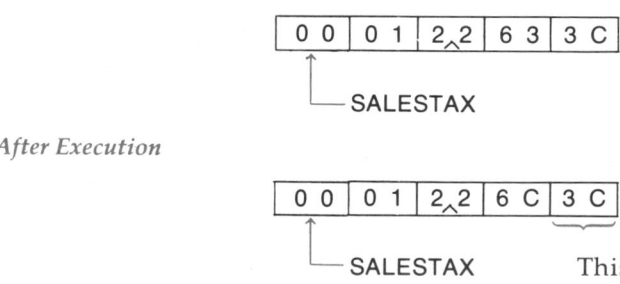

Using a Truncated Field After an MVN

By accessing SALESTAX(4), which contains 0001226C, we may

1. Perform additional calculations. For example;

   ```
   AP     TOTAL,SALESTAX(4)
   ```

2. Use the Edit instruction to print the results with only 2 decimal places.

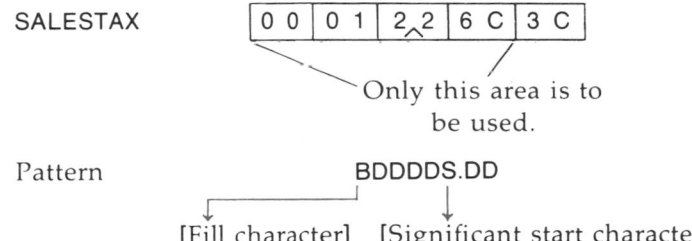

SALESTAX

Only this area is to be used.

Pattern   BDDDDS.DD

[Fill character]   [Significant start character]

Because the Edit instruction operates from left to right, we may shorten the edit pattern or mask to accept 7 digits instead of 9. In this way, truncation of rightmost digits will occur.

```
MVC    LINEOUT+25(9),=X'4020202020214B2020'
ED     LINEOUT+25(9),SALESTAX
```

This edit method is used only when further calculations are not required.

3. The preceding two methods require the programmer to use the truncated field SALESTAX cautiously so that the truncated byte does not enter into subsequent operations. We can, instead, reinitialize SALESTAX so that the low-order byte is *actually* truncated entirely. For this we use the ZAP instruction.

```
ZAP    SALESTAX,SALESTAX(4)
```

Before Execution

0 0	0 1	2∧2	6 C	3 C

After Execution

0 0	0 0	0 1	2∧2	6 C

Note again that shifting any field to the right can be accomplished by dividing by a multiple of 10.

B. Using the Move with Offset (MVO) Instruction

Note that using the MVN operation to truncate low-order digits is effective only if an *even* number of digits must be eliminated.

Example 17.5

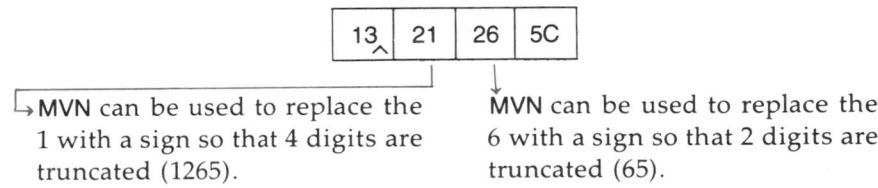

13∧	21	26	5C

↳MVN can be used to replace the 1 with a sign so that 4 digits are truncated (1265).

MVN can be used to replace the 6 with a sign so that 2 digits are truncated (65).

To truncate an *odd* number of digits, however, the replacement character (or digit to be replaced) would be in the *high-order* 4 bits of the byte. MVN cannot be used to achieve this result. Moreover, changing the high-order bits to a sign (using for example, the MVZ) will not enable the field to be used as a packed-decimal field. In short, additional programming is required if an *odd* number of digits is to be truncated.

Assume that the following is a TAX field resulting from an arithmetic operation. It has 5 decimal positions and is in packed-decimal form.

| 12 | 34 | 56 | 7C |

TAX (implied decimal)

We want to access this field as a dollars and cents figure, that is, with only two decimal places. Thus, we want to truncate, or shift right, 3 digits. This can be accomplished by dividing by 1000 or by using the MVO instruction.

Note that we cannot simply move TAX(2) to a storage area with an MVC because TAX(2) does not contain a sign that is required of all packed-decimal fields. The MVO:

1. Retains the contents of the low-order 4 bits of the receiving field.
2. Moves the sending field to the receiving field, the latter being filled with high-order zeros as required.

Example 17.6

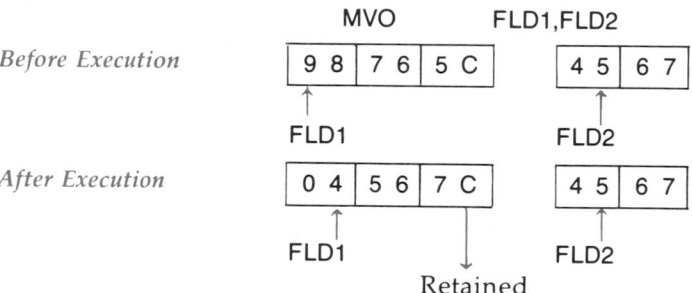

Because the low-order 4 bits of the receiving field contain a sign if the field is in **packed-decimal form,** the MVO may be used for truncating digits while retaining the sign. To do this, we must MVO a field into itself with the use of explicit addressing.

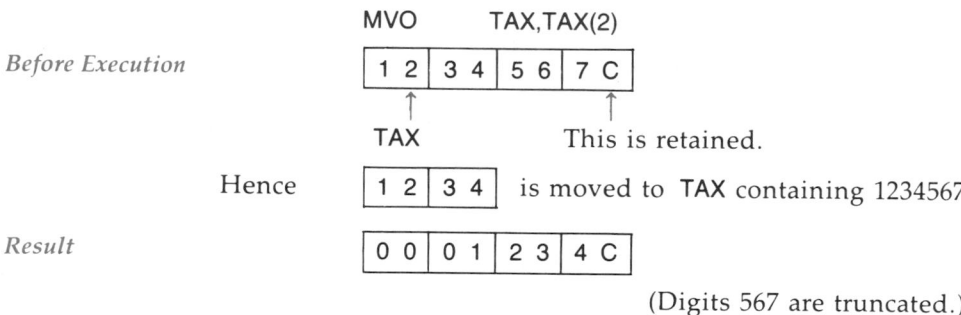

(Digits 567 are truncated.)

REVIEW OF RULES FOR TRUNCATING LOW-ORDER DIGITS

1. Even number of digits to be deleted or truncated: Use MVN.
2. Odd number of digits to be deleted or truncated: Use MVO.

Self-Evaluating Quiz

1. The shifting of packed-decimal fields is usually performed to align _____ .
2. Excess decimal positions resulting from multiplication can be truncated by shifting the field to the (right/left).

3. The instruction required to shift a field an *even* number of positions to the *right* is the _____ .

4. The purpose of the MVN instruction is to move the (**low-order/high-order**) bits of a byte.

5. Data fields used strictly for printed output employ the _____ instruction to truncate the excess low-order digits after an MVN has been executed.

6. To shift a field an *odd* number of positions to the right, the _____ instruction is used.

7. The MVO instruction processes the data from (**right/left**) to (**right/left**).

8. The first operand of the MVO and MVN is the (**sending/receiving**) field.

9. The contents of the first operand change in the MVO with the exception of the _____ bits in the _____ byte.

10. With packed-decimal data the low-order four bits always contain the _____ .

11. The MVO instruction is used to shift data an (**odd/even**) number of positions to the (**right/left**).

12. If the first operand is shorter than the second operand in an MVO instruction, truncation of (**high-order digits/high-order zeros**) results.

13. (T or F) Only packed-decimal data may be processed with the MVO instruction.

14. High-order zeros are inserted when an MVO instruction is executed if the (**first/ second**) operand is the longer.

15. Indicate the results in the first operand after execution of the following instructions. Treat the instructions independently.

    FLDA | 12 | 34 | 56 | 7 C |

    FLDB | 98 | 76 | 54 | 32 | 1 C |

    a. MVO   FLDB,FLDA
    b. MVO   FLDA,FLDA(3)
    c. MVO   FLDA,FLDB+1(3)
    d. MVO   FLDB(3),FLDA+2(2)
    e. MVN   FLDA+2(1),FLDA+3
    f. MVN   FLDB(4),FLDA

16. In each case indicate whether you would need to use the MVO or MVN to obtain the required results.

    a. | 12 | 3∧4 | 56 | 0 C |

        Truncate to 2 decimal places

    b. | 09 | 12 | 34 | 56 | 7 C |
              ∧

        Truncate to 1 decimal place

SOLUTIONS

1. Decimal points
2. Right
3. MVN
4. Low-order
5. Edit
6. MVO (Move with Offset)
7. Right to left (low-order to high-order)
8. Receiving
9. Low-order or rightmost 4; low-order or rightmost
10. Sign
11. Odd; right
12. High-order digits
13. F: no check is made on the data but usually the packed-decimal form is used.
14. First
15. a. FLDB | 01 | 23 | 45 | 67 | C C |
    b. FLDA | 01 | 23 | 45 | 6 C |
    c. FLDA | 07 | 65 | 43 | 2 C |
    d. FLDB | 05 | 67 | C 4 | 32 | 1 C |

e. FLDA | 1 2 | 3 4 | 5C | 7 C |

Presumably this byte will
no longer be used.

f. FLDB | 9 2 | 7 4 | 5 6 | 3 C | 1 C |

16. MVN; even number of digits to be truncated (60)
      MVN; even number of digits to be truncated (4567)

III. SHIFTING PACKED-DECIMAL FIELDS LEFT TO ADD ZEROS FOR DECIMAL ALIGNMENT

You will recall that shifting to the left is necessary to add low-order zeros to packed-decimal fields. Addition and subtraction operations may require this for decimal alignment.

Example 17.7

Adding 10.4 to 12.68 requires 10.4 to be shifted left. Thus $10_\wedge 40$ can be added decimally to $12_\wedge 68$.

Shifting left is also required for greater precision in divide operations.

Example 17.8

Dividing 120 by 240 will produce a quotient of 0 and a remainder of 120. To obtain 5 or 50, which can then be edited to print as .5 or .50, respectively, 120 must be shifted left one or two positions.

Moreover, shifting left can increase the decimal precision required even if a quotient contains integers.

Example 17.9

If the sum of the daily temperature for a month totaled 2630 and we divided it by 30, a result of 87 would be obtained. However, if further accuracy were required, the dividend could be shifted 2 places to the left (263000) to obtain a more accurate result.

Hence,

```
         87,66
    30 | 263000
         240
         ‾‾‾‾
         230
         210
         ‾‾‾‾
         200
         180
         ‾‾‾‾
         200
         180
         ‾‾‾‾
          20 ← remainder
```

The net result of shifting to the left 2 positions is the same as multiplying the dividend by 100. Again with shifting left, two different methods are used to accomplish a shift to the left: (1) for an even shift, and (2) for an odd number of positions.

A. Shifting Left an Even Number of Places

Example 17.10

Suppose we have a field called SUM that we want to shift left 2 places and move to DVDND, to serve as a dividend for a subsequent divide operation.

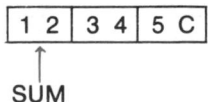

| 1 2 | 3 4 | 5 C |

SUM

We want DVDND to contain

| 1 2 | 3 4 | 5 0 | 0 C |

↑
DVDND

This can be accomplished in three stages.

1. MVC   DVDND(3),SUM
   Because DVDND is a 4-byte field, this operation will retain the original contents of the low-order byte.

Before Execution

| 9 9 | 9 9 | 9 9 | 9 D |

↑
DVDND

After Execution

| 1 2 | 3 4 | 5 C | 9 D |

↑
DVDND   (Low-order byte is retained.)

2. '5C' in DVDND+2 must be changed to '50'. (In general, DS must be changed to D0, where D = digit, S = sign.)
   We can establish a storage area with a 0 in the low-order four bits, and use the MVN to move it to DVDND+2.
   Or, we can use an *immediate* instruction, called AND IMMEDIATE (NI), to change the low-order 4 bits to that specified in the self-defining constant.

   NI   DVDND+2,X'F0'

Before Execution

| 1 2 | 3 4 | 5 C | 9 D |

After Execution

| 1 2 | 3 4 | 5 ⓪ | 9 D |

→Only this *1/2* byte (4 bits) is altered

3. To alter DVDND+3 from '9D' to '0C', use a simple MVC.

   MVC   DVDND+3(1),=X'0C'

Result

| 1 2 | 3 4 | 5 0 | 0 C |

Effect   Shift left 2 places.

The following illustration summarizes the above steps.

	DVDND				SUM			Comments
	9 9	9 9	9 9	9 D	1 2	3 4	5 C	Initial contents.
	1 2	3 4	5 C	9 D	1 2	3 4	5 C	Shift field to left.
MVC DVDND(3),SUM NI DVDND+2,X'F0' MVC DVDND+3(1),=X'0C'	1 2	3 4	5 0	9 D	1 2	3 4	5 C	Change C to zero.
	1 2	3 4	5 0	0 C	1 2	3 4	5 C	Add zero and sign.
	1 2	3 4	5 0	0 C	1 2	3 4	5 C	Result.

B. Shifting Left an Odd Number of Places

Assume it is necessary to perform a 3-position shift to the left. The first step taken would be to shift left 4 places. Once this is accomplished, an MVO instruction would adjust the field one position to the right. The result, as desired, is a 3-position shift to the left. See the following table for an example.

Instruction	DVDND	SUM
Before:	99 99 99 99 9D	12 34 5C
MVC DVDND(3),SUM	12 34 5C 99 9D	
NI DVDND+2,X'F0'	12 34 50 99 9D	
MVC DVDND+3(2),=X'000C'	12 34 50 00 0C	
MVO DVDND,DVDND(4)	01 23 45 00 0C	
After:	01 23 45 00 0C	12 34 5C

Requirements for Shifting Digits

A. Shifting to the right—deleting digits.
Commonly used after multiplication on packed-decimal fields.
PURPOSE: To eliminate excess decimal places resulting from multiplication.
METHODS: 1. Divide by 10 for each decimal place to be eliminated.
              2. Shift with
                 MVN. This eliminates an *even* number of digits.
                 MVO. This eliminates an *odd* number of digits.

B. Shifting to the left—adding zeros.
Commonly used before addition, subtraction, or division of packed-decimal fields.
PURPOSE: To add zeros for decimal alignment.
METHODS: 1. Multiply result by 10 for each shift required.
              2. Shift with
                 MVC, NI. This adds an *even* number of digits.
                 MVC, NI, MVO. This adds an *odd* number of digits.

Self-Evaluating Quiz

Indicate the results for Questions 1–3. Treat each question independently.

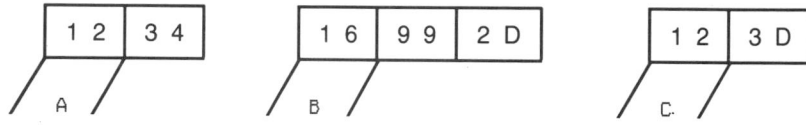

1. MVO   B,A
2. NI   B+2,X'F0'
3. MVC   C+1,=X'0C'
4. Write a sequence of steps to add three zeros to the following field.

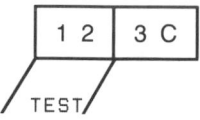

5. Write a sequence of steps to add two zeros to the following field.

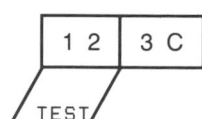

SOLUTIONS

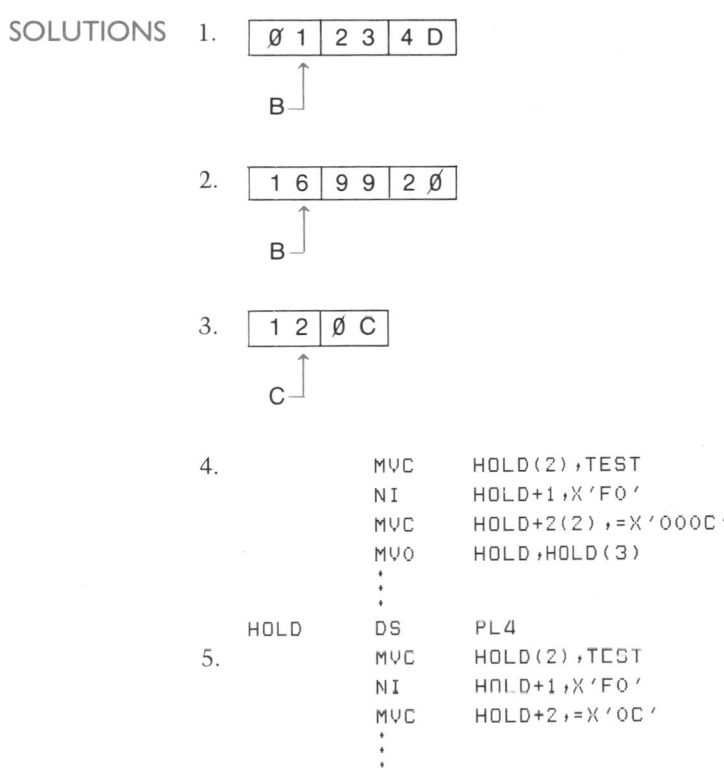

1. | Ø | 1 | 2 | 3 | 4 | D |

    B ↑

2. | 1 | 6 | 9 | 9 | 2 | Ø |

    B ↑

3. | 1 | 2 | Ø | C |

    C ↑

4.
```
          MVC    HOLD(2),TEST
          NI     HOLD+1,X'F0'
          MVC    HOLD+2(2),=X'000C'
          MVO    HOLD,HOLD(3)
            .
            .
            .
HOLD      DS     PL4
```
5.
```
          MVC    HOLD(2),TEST
          NI     HOLD+1,X'F0'
          MVC    HOLD+2,=X'0C'
            .
            .
            .
HOLD      DS     PL3
```

IV. ROUNDING

Consider the following example, where a caret $(\wedge)$ denotes an implied decimal point.

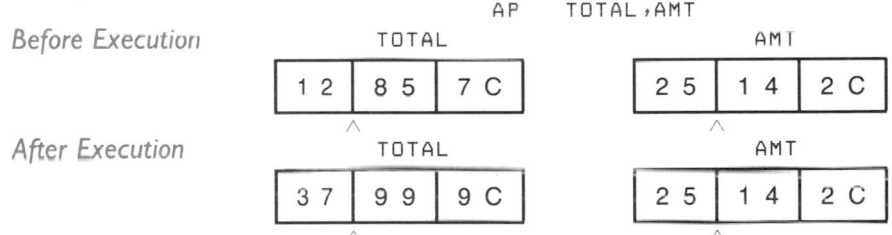

AP   TOTAL,AMT

Before Execution

TOTAL

| 1 2 | 8 5 | 7 C |
      ∧

AMT

| 2 5 | 1 4 | 2 C |
      ∧

After Execution

TOTAL

| 3 7 | 9 9 | 9 C |
      ∧

AMT

| 2 5 | 1 4 | 2 C |
      ∧

If we intend to print this result as a dollars and cents field, 37.99 would result. Note that two fields, each with 3 decimal positions, are added together, but the answer desired is valid to 2 decimal places. A more desirable result in this case would be 38.00. Results are more accurate if answers are **rounded** to the nearest decimal position.

RULE FOR ROUNDING

Add five to the leftmost or high-order digit to be truncated.

If the digit were originally equal to or greater than 5, rounding will add 1 to the result.

Example 17.11

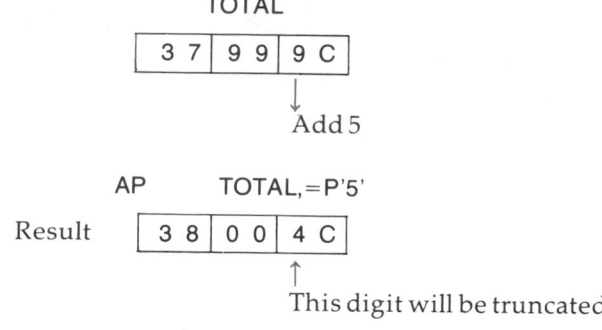

If the leftmost digit to be truncated were less than 5, adding 5 and then truncating would not cause an increment in the value of the number.

Example 17.12   HOLD has 4 decimal positions. We wish to truncate to 2 decimal positions. In this case, we add 5 to the third decimal position, which is the leftmost digit to be truncated.

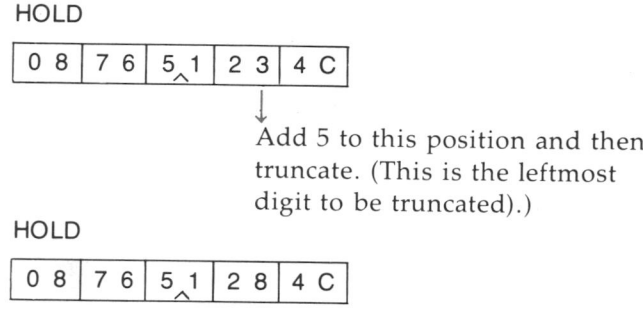

(Digits 84 are truncated.)

8765ˌ12 results

Adding 5 in the preceding examples is accomplished by

AP   HOLDˌ=P'50'

See Figures 17.1 and 17.2 for additional illustrations.

RULE FOR ROUNDING NEGATIVE FIELDS

Instead of *adding* 5 to the leftmost or high-order digit to be truncated, we must *subtract* 5.

Rounding and truncation

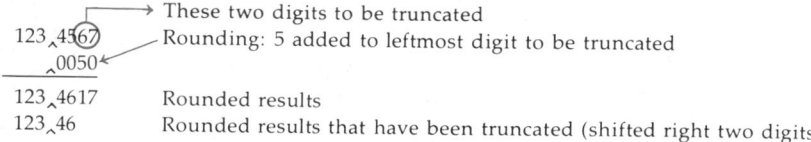

123ˌ4617   Rounded results
123ˌ46   Rounded results that have been truncated (shifted right two digits)

Rounding and truncation (rounding where results are unchanged)

765ˌ4321
 ˌ0050

765ˌ4371   Rounded
765ˌ43   Rounded and truncated

Figure 17.1
Illustration of rounding.

Correct method: Rounding to 2 decimal places

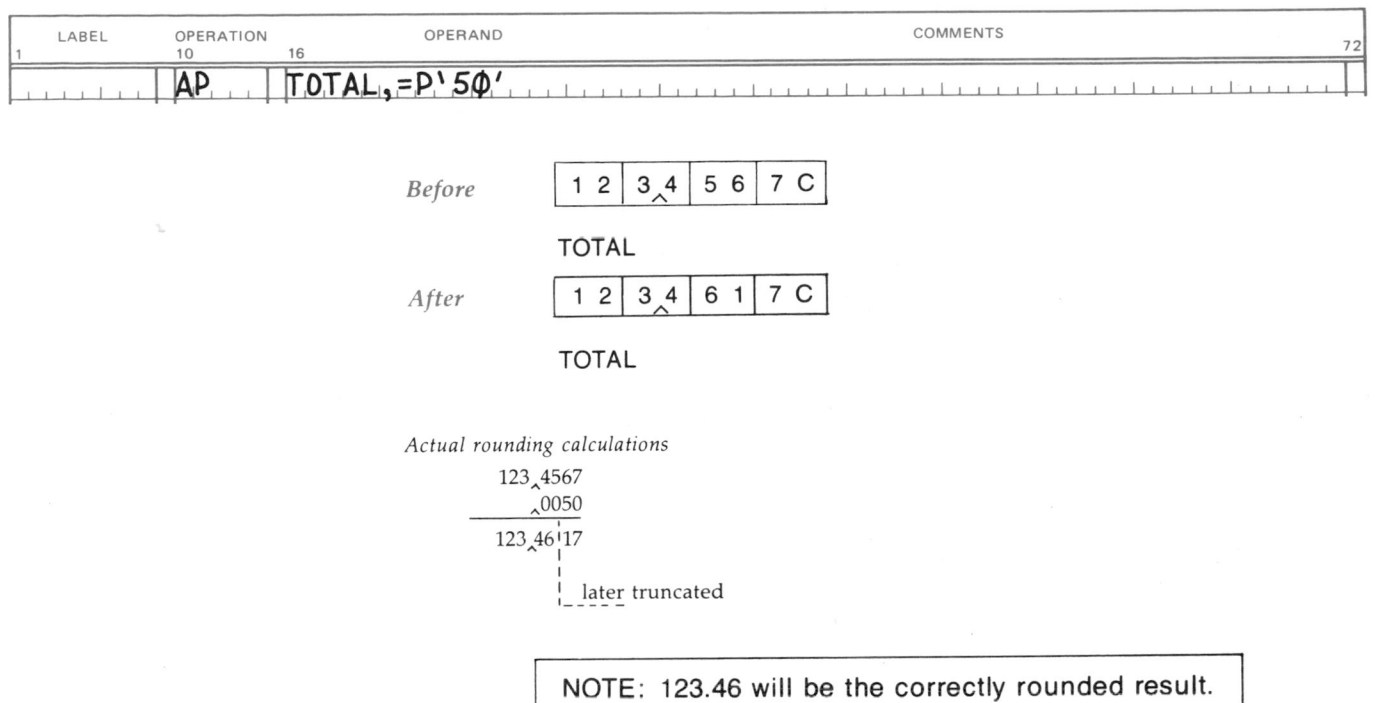

Actual rounding calculations

```
    123.4567
      .0050
   ─────────
    123.46 17
           │
           └─ later truncated
```

NOTE: 123.46 will be the correctly rounded result.

Incorrect method: Rounding to 2 decimal places .

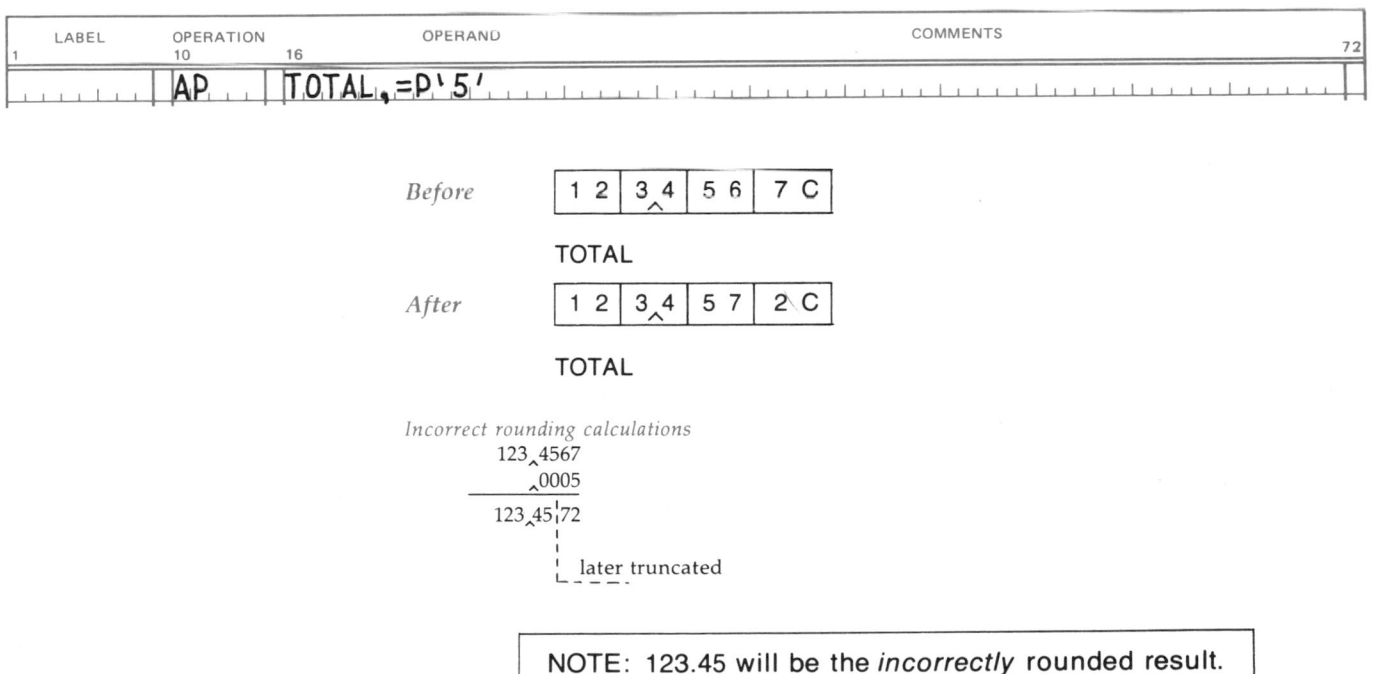

Incorrect rounding calculations

```
    123.4567
       .0005
   ─────────
    123.45 72
           │
           └─ later truncated
```

NOTE: 123.45 will be the *incorrectly* rounded result.

Figure 17.2
Correct and incorrect methods of rounding.

Example 17.13

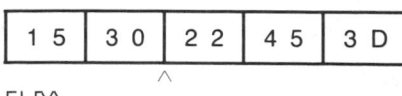

FLDA

Note that FLDA is negative. To round to 2 decimal places in this case, we wish to subtract 5, or add −5, to the high-order bits of FLDA+3 (the digit 4).

Result

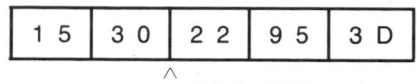

(digits 953 are truncated)

1530ᴧ22 results

If we added 5 in the above case, subtraction would have occurred, which would not have provided the correct answer. See Figure 17.3.

Incorrect method: Adding 5 to a negative number

```
      1978ᴧ876  −
          ᴧ005  +
    ─────────────
    − 1978ᴧ871        Rounded incorrectly
    − 1978ᴧ87         Later truncated
```

Correct method: Adding −5 to a negative number

```
      1978ᴧ876  −
          ᴧ005  −
    ─────────────
    − 1978ᴧ881        Rounded correctly
    − 1978ᴧ88         Later truncated
```

Figure 17.3
Correct and incorrect methods of rounding negative fields.

If there is a *possibility* that a field contains a negative amount, rounding must be performed, as follows.

---

1. Move sign of field to the sign of a constant containing a "5".

```
            MVN     CON,TOTAL+2     ← Sign of TOTAL moved to CON.
              ⋮
CON         DC      P'5'            ← 5C is generated.
TOTAL       DS      PL3             ← Field to be rounded to 2
                                      decimal places.
```

---

2. Add and truncate.

```
AP      TOTAL,CON
MVO     TOTAL,TOTAL(2)      Eliminate low-order byte.
```

Note
This procedure should be performed if there is a possibility that the field to be rounded is negative.

See Figure 17.4 for additional examples.

Recall that to **truncate** or shift right an even number of places, we can divide by 10^n where n is the number of places to be truncated. Or, we can use an MVN and ZAP.

Rounding and truncating (shifting right) one digit.

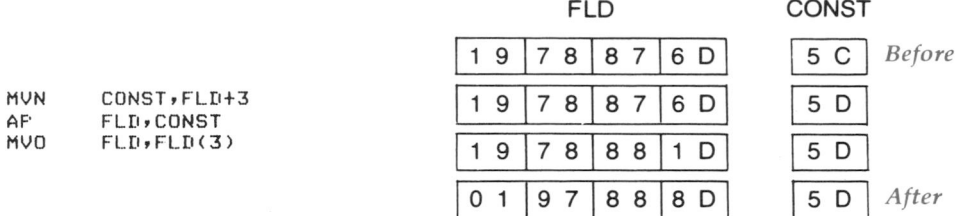

		FLD					CONST	
		1 9	7 8	8 7	6 D		5 C	*Before*
MVN	CONST,FLD+3	1 9	7 8	8 7	6 D		5 D	
AP	FLD,CONST	1 9	7 8	8 8	1 D		5 D	
MVO	FLD,FLD(3)	0 1	9 7	8 8	8 D		5 D	*After*

Rounding and truncating (shifting right) two digits.

Figure 17.4
Examples of rounding and truncating.

		FLD				CONST		
		0 1	2 3	4 5	6 C	0 5	0 C	*Before*
MVN	CONST+1(1),FLD+3	0 1	2 3	4 5	6 C	0 5	0 C	
AP	FLD,CONST	0 1	2 3	5 0	6 C	0 5	0 C	
MVN	FLD+2(1),FLD+3	0 1	2 3	5 C	6 C	0 5	0 C	
ZAP	FLD,FLD(3)	0 0	0 1	2 3	5 C	0 5	0 C	*After*

If, for example, FLD contained $12_\wedge3456$ and we wanted to round and truncate the results so that it prints as a dollars and cents field, the following coding could be used.

Before Execution

		FLD				CON	
		0 1	2 3	4 5	6 C	0 5	0 C

Instruction

MVN	CON+1(1),FLD+3	0 1	2 3	4 5	6 C	0 5	0 C
AP	FLD,CON	0 1	2 3	5 0	6 C		
MVN	FLD+2(1),FLD+3	0 1	2 3	5 C	6 C		
ZAP	FLD,FLD(3)	0 0	0 1	2 3	5 C		

After Execution

		FLD				CON	
		0 0	0 1	2 3	5 C	0 5	0 C

SUMMARY OF ROUNDING

1. Add 5 to the high-order or leftmost digit to be truncated.
2. If the field may be negative, move the sign of the field to the constant (5). Adding this constant then achieves normal addition for positive fields and subtraction for negative ones.

Self-Evaluating Quiz

Round the following fields as indicated.

1. $99_\wedge987$ to 2 decimal places
2. $123_\wedge5863$ to 1 decimal place
3. $67_\wedge1925$ to 2 decimal places
4. $-23_\wedge6835$ to 2 decimal places

5.

9 8	7 6	4 C

↑
TOTAL

Write the instructions to round to *2* decimal places.

6.

9 8	7 6	4 C

↑
TOTAL

Write the instructions to round to *1* decimal place.

SOLUTIONS

1.
```
   99∧987
        5
   99∧992
```

2.
```
  123∧5863
         5
  123∧6363
```

3.
```
   67∧1925
         5
   67∧1975
```

4.
```
  −23∧6835
        −5
  −23∧6885
```

5.
```
AP    TOTAL,=P'5'
MVO   TOTAL,TOTAL(2)
```

6.
```
AP    TOTAL=P'50'
NI    TOTAL+1,X'F0'
MVC   TOTAL+2,=X'0C'
```

Combining the Shift and Rounding Operations Using a Single Instruction on Some Computers The methods presented so far for rounding and truncating are somewhat cumbersome. There is an instruction available on some computers that facilitates this process. Its format differs somewhat from instructions thus far encountered.

Instruction:	SRP
Meaning:	Shift and Round Packed
Operation:	1. *Can shift left:* multiplies by factors of 10—no rounding necessary.
	2. *Can shift right:* divides by factors of 10 thereby truncating low-order digits—with or without rounding.

Format:	SRP Field, n_1,n_2
Field:	Field to be operated on
n_1:	A number that indicates both the direction (left or right) and number of digits to be shifted.
n_2:	Rounding factor (usually 5) (used with *right shift only*).

n_1 can be any of the values given in the following table.

n_1	Meaning
	Left Shift
0	0
1	.
2	.
3	.
.	.
.	.
.	.
.	.
.	.
31	31
	Right Shift
32	32
33	31
34	30
.	.
.	.
61	3
62	2
63	1
64	0

Example 17.14

$n_1 = 5$ left shift 5
$n_1 = 61$ right shift 3

     SRP   HOLD ,61 ,5

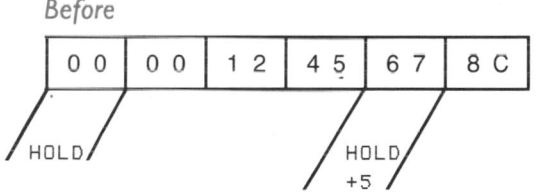
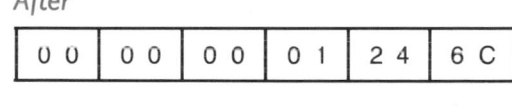

Before

| 0 0 | 0 0 | 1 2 | 4 5 | 6 7 | 8 C |

After

| 0 0 | 0 0 | 0 0 | 0 1 | 2 4 | 6 C |

HOLD   HOLD
                         +5

Packed digits in HOLD are shifted 3 digits to the right. The '6' has a 5 added to it before the low-order 3 digits are truncated.

Example 17.15

     SRP   AMT ,3 ,0

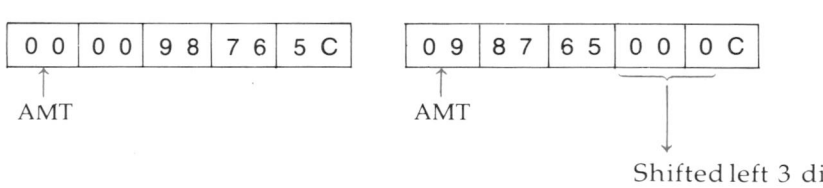

Before   *After*

| 0 0 | 0 0 | 9 8 | 7 6 | 5 C |

| 0 9 | 8 7 | 6 5 | 0 0 | 0 C |

AMT   AMT

                                      Shifted left 3 digits

No rounding.
Sign remains unchanged.

V. TESTING FOR VALID NUMERIC DATA

If input fields are to be used in arithmetic operations, as a precautionary measure it is frequently necessary to test them for validity. Suppose, for example, that AMT is an input field that is to be packed and then added to TOTAL. If AMT were incorrectly coded, or contained blanks instead of valid numeric characters, the instruction to PACK AMT would cause the following.

Instruction: PACK HOLD,AMT

Before Execution

Invalid numeric data (3 blanks)

4 0	4 0	4 0

AMT   PACK   HOLD,AMT

After Execution

0 0	0 0	0 4

HOLD

The low-order or rightmost character in the packed field is a 4, which should represent the sign of a packed field. This is invalid because C, D, or F are the only valid signs. Thus, a data exception would result and the job would terminate when an arithmetic operation is performed on HOLD.

It is important to include instructions in a program to avoid the abnormal termination of a program because of errors in numeric data fields. We can, for example, test these fields *prior* to performing any arithmetic operations on them to ensure that the data is valid.

TEST FOR VALID UNPACKED NUMERIC DATA

Make certain that the high-order bits of each byte contain a valid zone portion (usually F).

Let us restrict our discussion to unsigned numeric fields that are entered as input. The zone portion of each character, then, must be 'F'.

We use the MVN instruction in conjunction with the CLC to test numeric data for validity.

TEST

1. Use MVN to change the digit portion of each byte to zero.
2. Use CLC to perform a bit-by-bit comparison, which compares the changed field to zeros in zoned-decimal form (F0F0 . . .).

Our valid numeric field will contain

NUM
F D	F D	F D

F = 1111 in the zone portion of a byte
D = any digit

Change each D to 0 using the MVN.

If the field is valid, the following will result.

Hex	F 0	F 0	F 0
Binary	11110000	11110000	11110000

Compare this changed field, bit-by-bit, to C'000'.
C'000' converts to F0F0F0 in **zoned-decimal format.**

NUM after MVN (valid field)	11110000	11110000	11110000
Self-defining constant used in compare	11110000	11110000	11110000

The two fields will be equal if the original numeric field were valid. If the zone portion were *not* 1111 for each digit, then this would signal an error. That is, the original numeric input was not valid.

Because the original numeric field itself should *not* be cleared to zeros with an MVN, it must first be moved to a storage area of the same length before it is operated on.

```
          MVC     HOLD,NUM
          MVN     HOLD,=C'000'
          CLC     HOLD,=C'000'
          BNE     ERROR
                  .
                  .
HOLD      DS      CL3
```

Example 17.16   Valid Data in QTY

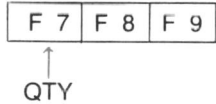

QTY

QTY refers to a 3-position zoned-decimal field.

```
MVC     TEST,QTY
MVN     TEST,=C'000'
CLC     TEST,=C'000'
BL      ERROR1
```

TEST			Second Operand		
F 7	F 8	F 9	F 7	F 8	F 9
F 0	F 0	F 0	F 0	F 0	F 0
F 0	F 0	F 0	F 0	F 0	F 0

"Equal" condition indicates valid data; no branch to ERROR1.

Example 17.17   Invalid Data in QTY

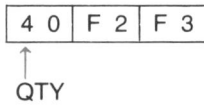

QTY

Note the blank in the high-order byte.

```
MVC     TEST,QTY
MVN     TEST,=C'000'
CLC     TEST,=C'000'
BL      ERROR1
```

	TEST				Second Operand		
	40	F2	F3		40	F2	F3
	40	F0	F0		F0	F0	F0
	40	F0	F0		F0	F0	F0

"Low" condition indicates invalid data; a branch to ERROR1 occurs.

If, in addition, the possibility exists that the numeric field were entered as a signed-positive or signed-negative number, the low-order byte would need to be compared to +0 (C0) and −0 (D0) because these, too, would be valid characters.

Self-Evaluating Quiz

Indicate which of the following represent valid numeric data in zoned-decimal format. Also indicate the value of each valid field.

1. | F0 | F1 | C3 |
   |---|---|---|
2. | C0 | C3 | C5 |
   |---|---|---|
3. | F0 | F2 | D6 |
   |---|---|---|
4. | F3 | F4 | F5 |
   |---|---|---|
5. | F0 | F0 | 40 |
   |---|---|---|
6. | E6 | E3 | E2 |
   |---|---|---|

7. Write a routine to test TAX to ensure that it contains valid numeric data. (TAX is a zoned-decimal 4-byte field.)

SOLUTIONS

1. Valid; +013
2. Invalid; sign C would appear only in a low-order byte.
3. Valid; −026
4. Valid; 345
5. Invalid; 40 (blank) is *not* a valid numeric character.
6. Invalid; E in zone portion is invalid.
7.
```
        MVC     HOLD,TAX
        MVN     HOLD,C'0000'  SETS LOW-ORDER BITS OF EACH BYTE TO 0
        CLC     HOLD,C'0000'
        BNE     ERROR
          .
          .
HOLD    DS      CL4
```

VI. SIGN CONTROL WHEN EDITING NUMERIC FIELDS

In Chapter 9 we discussed the edit symbol used to print a minus sign for negative fields. See the following for a review of some examples.

```
MVC     LINEOUT(5),=X'4020202060'
ED      LINEOUT(5),FLD
```

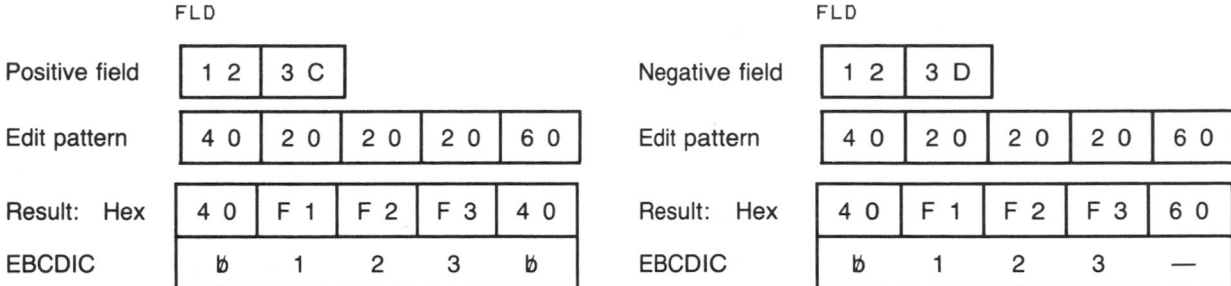

Examples of editing using sign control in ED instruction.

It is possible to print a sign indicator, instead of a minus sign, to indicate that a field is signed negative. These indicators include CR and DB. In accounting applications specifically, but in other applications as well, CR, which means credit, or DB, which means debit, may be the manner in which we wish to represent a negative amount.

In the following, for example, the AMT field associated with ITEM3 is negative. All other fields are positive. A report may include the following output.

```
                STATUS REPORT
       ITEM                AMT
       ITEM1        $    110.43
       ITEM2        $     25.68
       ITEM3        $  5,875.26 CR
```

Similarly, in the following report, TOTAL is negative for CUST3. In that report, DB, or debit, means a negative balance.

```
                  REPORT 586
        CUSTOMER            TOTAL
          CUST1       $  387.25
          CUST2       $  682.25
          CUST3       $   25.30 DB
```

How* CR *and* DB *are Printed as Edit Symbols The actual sign indicators to be printed, either C R or D B , are included in the edit pattern. When the field to be printed is positive, the CR or DB is suppressed and replaced by the fill character (the first character of the edit pattern). See Figure 17.5.

Note that the letters CR (or DB) are transmitted only when the field to be edited contains a negative amount. When the field is positive, as in Example 1 in Figure 17.5, the fill character (hex 40 or ƀ) replaces the *three* extra positions to the right.

In Examples 3 and 4 when the field is positive, the low-order characters in the edit pattern are replaced by the fill character (5C). Also recognize that a negative field transmits the characters precisely as they appear in the pattern. A final example of sign control appears in Figure 17.6.

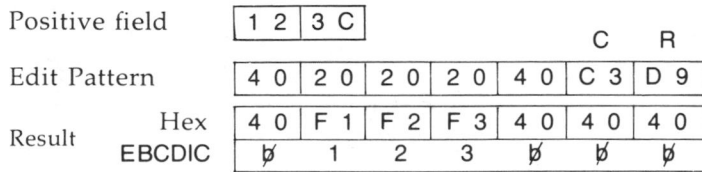

Example 1

Positive field

1 2	3 C

Edit Pattern

					C	R
4 0	2 0	2 0	2 0	4 0	C 3	D 9

Result — Hex

4 0	F 1	F 2	F 3	4 0	4 0	4 0

EBCDIC

ø	1	2	3	ø	ø	ø

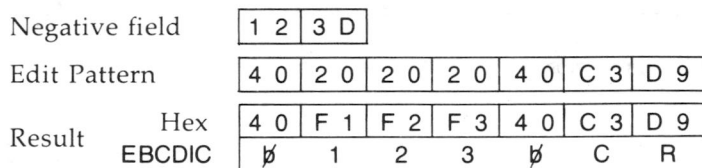

Example 2

Negative field

1 2	3 D

Edit Pattern

4 0	2 0	2 0	2 0	4 0	C 3	D 9

Result — Hex

4 0	F 1	F 2	F 3	4 0	C 3	D 9

EBCDIC

ø	1	2	3	ø	C	R

Example 3

Positive field

1 2	5 7	5 C

Edit Pattern

							D	B
5 C	2 0	2 0	2 0	4 B	2 0	2 0	4 0	C 4	C 2

Result — Hex

5 C	F 1	F 2	F 5	4 B	F 7	F 5	5 C	5 C	5 C

EBCDIC

*	1	2	5		7	5	*	*	*

Example 4

Negative field

1 2	5 7	5 D

Edit Pattern

5 C	2 0	2 0	2 0	4 B	2 0	2 0	4 0	C 4	C 2

Result — Hex

5 C	F 1	F 2	F 5	4 B	F 7	F 5	4 0	C 4	C 2

EBCDIC

*	1	2	5	.	7	5	ø	D	B

Figure 17.5
Use of CR and DB symbols.

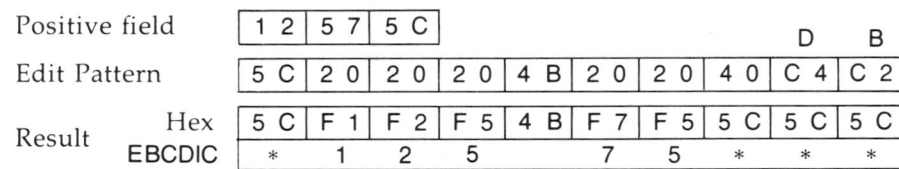

```
MVC    OUTFLD(13),=C'4020206B2020214B202040C3D9'
ED     OUTFLD(13),PFLD
```

Before Edit	After Edit
PFLD	OUTFLD
0 1 2 3 4 5 6 C	ø ø 1 , 2 3 4 . 5 6 ø ø ø
0 0 7 8 9 0 1 D	ø ø ø ø 7 8 9 . 0 1 ø C R
0 0 0 4 5 6 7 C	ø ø ø ø ø 4 5 . 6 7 ø ø ø
0 0 0 0 2 3 4 D	ø ø ø ø ø ø 2 . 3 4 ø C R
0 0 0 0 0 9 9 C	ø ø ø ø ø ø ø . 9 9 ø ø ø
0 0 0 0 0 0 8 D	ø ø ø ø ø ø ø . 0 8 ø C R

Figure 17.6
Examples of sign control.

A summary of the use of sign control follows.

SUMMARY

1. The editing of negative fields transmits the extra pattern characters to the receiving field unchanged; that is, they will appear in the receiving field precisely as they appear in the pattern.
2. The editing of positive fields will cause these characters to be replaced by the fill character of the pattern.

Self-Evaluating Quiz

Edit the following fields as indicated.

1. AMT is 3 bytes. Print
   a. With zero-suppress (with blanks).
   b. Decimal point for dollars and cents figure.
   c. $ in the high-order position.
   d. CR if negative; print the CR directly after rightmost digit.
2. TOTAL is 4 bytes. Print
   a. With zero-suppress (use ×).
   b. Decimal point and comma for dollars and cents figure.
   c. $ in the high-order position.
   d. DB if the number is negative (leave two blanks between the low-order digit and DB).

Indicate the results in each of the following.

```
MVC    LINEOUT+10(10),=X'402020214B202040C3D9'
ED     LINEOUT+10(10),HOLD
```

3. HOLD

0 1	9 9	3 D

4. HOLD

0 0	9 6	2 C

SOLUTIONS

1.
```
MVC    LINEOUT+10,=X'402020214B202040C3D9'
ED     LINEOUT+10(10),AMT
MVI    LINEOUT+10,X'5B'
```
2.
```
MVC    LINEOUT+10,=X'5C2020GB2020214B20204040L4C2'
ED     LINEOUT+10(14),HOLD
MVI    LINEOUT+10,X'5B'
```
3. ᵬᵬ19.93ᵬCR
4. ᵬᵬᵬ9.62ᵬᵬᵬ

VII. EDIT AND MARK INSTRUCTION AND FLOATING DOLLAR SIGNS

Examine the following sample output.

CUSTOMER NAME	QTY SOLD	AMT
J. JONES	5,000	$38,725.67
A. SMITH	2	$ 3.00

Although the fields are edited properly, the format is flawed in one respect. The dollar sign of AMT on the second detail line appears several spaces to the left of the first numeric character. This is a consequence of the editing in which the fill character (in this case, a blank) has been used to replace 0s.

The pattern must contain enough characters (20) to accommodate the entire sending field. If, however, the sending field has many nonsignificant zeros (for example, 0000300C), an appreciable number of blanks will appear between the dollar sign and the first significant digit. This may be inappropriate, particularly when printing checks. Unscrupulous people could easily alter the amount fields.

A dollar sign may be made to appear in the position *directly preceding* the first significant digit with the use of a **floating dollar sign.** That is, the $ may be made to "float" with the field. A floating dollar sign will cause suppression of leading zeros and, at the same time, force the $ to appear in the position directly to the left of the first significant digit.

Consider the following examples of floating dollar signs.

EXAMPLES OF THE FLOATING DOLLAR SIGN

$12,345.67
$8,901.23
$456.78
$90.12
$3.45
$.67
$.09

Note that the dollar sign appears in different positions depending on the length and content of the edited field.

The Edit and Mark instruction (EDMK) is used in place of the Edit (ED) instruction to allow dollar signs to float.

There are two essential parts to this process.

1. Establishing the address where the dollar sign is to be placed.
2. Editing the data.

Example 17.18 Illustration of EDMK (Edit and Mark instruction) in preparation for printing a floating dollar sign.

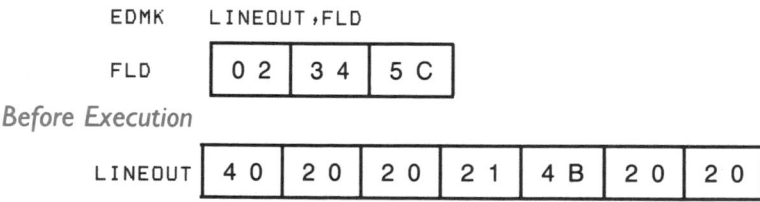

Before Execution

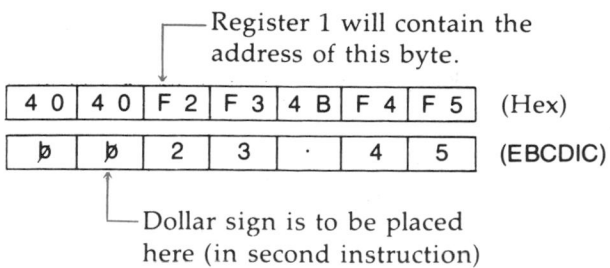

After Execution

Thus, the illustrated EDMK achieves the exact editing as previously discussed. How, then, do we get the dollar sign to float?

Note that the EDMK operation *automatically* places the *address* of the first significant digit in general register 1. Register 1, then, contains the address of the leftmost non-zero digit in the resulting area. In the above illustration, register 1 would contain the address of LINEOUT+2, because this position contains the first significant digit.

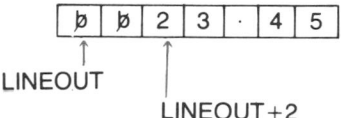

We need to print a \$ in the position that is *one less than* the contents of general register 1, that is, in LINEOUT+1 in this example. The necessary coding follows.

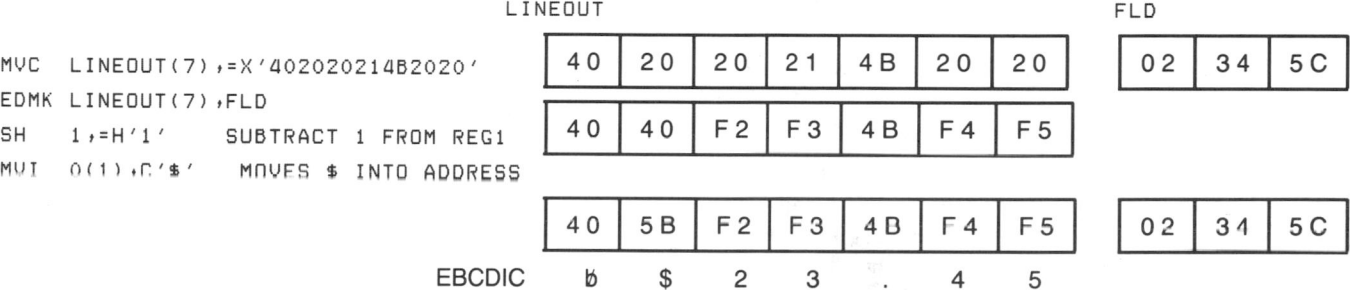

```
MVC   LINEOUT(7),=X'402020214B2020'
EDMK  LINEOUT(7),FLD
SH    1,=H'1'      SUBTRACT 1 FROM REG1
MVI   0(1),C'$'    MOVES $ INTO ADDRESS
```

The EDMK (Edit and Mark) instruction to print a floating dollar sign.

The address of the first significant digit is *automatically* placed in register 1 by the CPU. To determine the address of the position immediately to the left (where the dollar sign is to be located), we subtract 1 from register 1 with the Subtract Halfword instruction (or we could use the S instruction). Now, register 1 points to the precise location where the dollar sign is to be inserted.

Using explicit addressing, with the Move Immediate (MVI), we insert the dollar sign into the edited result. Recall that the operand 0(1) references the address contained in register 1, with a zero displacement.

Additional Coding   There is, however, one potential problem with this coding. When the significant start digit (hex 21) is used to force the editing of the pattern character (to the right of the decimal) *nothing* will be placed in register 1. That is, when there are no non-zero digits before the significant start character that forces printing, register 1 will *not* contain the desired results. Therefore, before the EDMK is executed, the address of the *decimal point* must be placed in register 1 by the programmer with an LA instruction. If the contents of register 1 are unchanged because significance is forced, the dollar sign will correctly appear immediately to the left of the decimal point because we first loaded the address of the decimal point into register 1.

The Load Address instruction is added to our coding sequence to store the address of the decimal point in the output field LINEOUT.

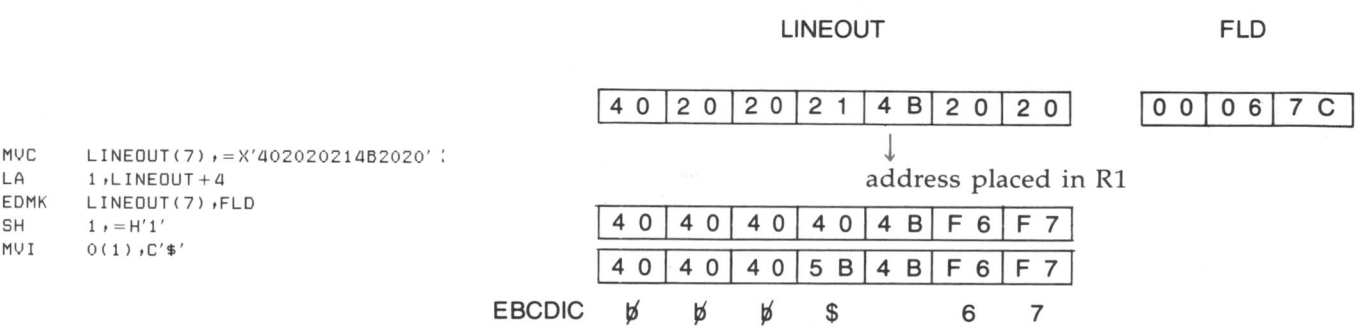

```
MVC   LINEOUT(7),=X'402020214B2020'
LA    1,LINEOUT+4
EDMK  LINEOUT(7),FLD
SH    1,=H'1'
MVI   0(1),C'$'
```

This represents the full routine using the EDMK (Edit and Mark) instruction to float the dollar sign.

The decimal point is located at LINEOUT+4, and this address is placed in register 1 as a form of protection. Remember, when significance is forced, nothing is placed in register 1 by the computer. However, we are also aware that when significance is forced, the output field (LINEOUT) will only contain digits in the cents portion of the field. When this situation exists, the dollar sign will be correctly positioned to the left of the decimal point as a result of the LA (Load Address) instruction.

CHAPTER SUMMARY

I. Types of Shifting
   A. Shifting packed-decimal fields to the right.
      1. To delete low-order digits when they are not needed in a decimal number.
      2. Used frequently to truncate decimal digits after a multiplication.
   B. Shifting packed-decimal fields to the left.
      1. To add low-order zeros for decimal alignment.
      2. Used with addition and subtraction so that all data has the same number of decimal places.
      3. Used in conjunction with division to obtain decimal quotients.
II. Shifting Right to Delete Digits
   A. Using the Move Numeric (MVN) instruction.
      1. To delete an even number of digits.
      2. Operates only on the low-order 4 bits of each byte.
      3. Operates like a typical Move in all other ways.
   B. Using the Move with Offset (MVO) instruction.
      1. To delete an odd number of digits.
      2. For this, the replacement digit is in the high-order bits of the byte.
      3. Retains the contents of the low-order 4 bits of the receiving field.
      4. Moves the sending field to the receiving field, the latter being filled with high-order zeros as required.
III. Rounding
   A. Rule: Add five to the leftmost or high-order digit to be truncated.
   B. If the field to be rounded may be negative, move the sign to the rounding constant 5. Adding this constant then achieves normal addition for positive fields and subtraction for negative ones.
IV. Testing for Valid Numeric Data
   A. Make certain that the high-order bits of each unpacked byte contain a valid zone.
   B. Method:
      1. Use MVN to change the digit portion of each byte to zero.
      2. Use CLC to perform a bit-by-bit comparison.
V. Sign Control When Editing Numeric Fields
   A. CR or DB is included in the edit pattern. CR or DB will print for any negative number.
   B. CR or DB is suppressed for positive numbers.
VI. Edit and Mark Instruction (EDMK) for Floating Dollar Signs
   A. Purpose: To print the $ adjacent to the first significant digit.
   B. Method:
      1. Establish the address where the $ is to appear.
      2. Edit the data.

CHAPTER SELF-EVALUATING QUIZ

Indicate the results in each of the cases (Questions 1–8) if the following instructions were executed.

```
        MVC     OUT(13),PATTRN
        LA      1,OUT+7
        EDMK    OUT,FLD
        SH      1,=H'1'
        MVI     0(1),C'$'
        .
        .
        .
PATTRN  DC      X'4020206B2020214B202040C3D9'
* PATTRN = BDD,DDS,DDBCR
```

FLD

1. | 12 | 34 | 56 | 7C |
2. | 01 | 23 | 45 | 6D |
3. | 00 | 12 | 34 | 5C |
4. | 00 | 01 | 23 | 4D |
5. | 00 | 00 | 12 | 3C |
6. | 00 | 00 | 01 | 2D |
7. | 00 | 00 | 00 | 1C |
8. | 00 | 00 | 00 | 0C |

9. (T or F) There is nothing the ED instruction can do that the EDMK instruction cannot do.

10. What is the difference between the ED and EDMK?

SOLUTIONS

		Page
1.	$12,345.67	497
2.	$1,234.56 CR	497
3.	$123.45	497
4.	$12.34 CR	497
5.	$1.23	497
6.	$.12 CR	497
7.	$.01	497
8.	$.00	497
9.	T	496

10. The EDMK instruction causes the address of the first significant digit of the result to be placed in general register 1. — 497

PRACTICE PROGRAM

Consider the problem definition shown in Figure 17.7. Write a program to produce the desired results. See Figure 17.8 for a solution.

a. Input Record Layout

EMPLOYEE NAME	EMPLOYEE NUMBER	OTHER DATA	HOURLY RATE $ ¢	HOURS WORKED	OTHER DATA
1 20	21 25	26 30	31 34	35 37	38 80

b. Printer Spacing Chart for Printed Output

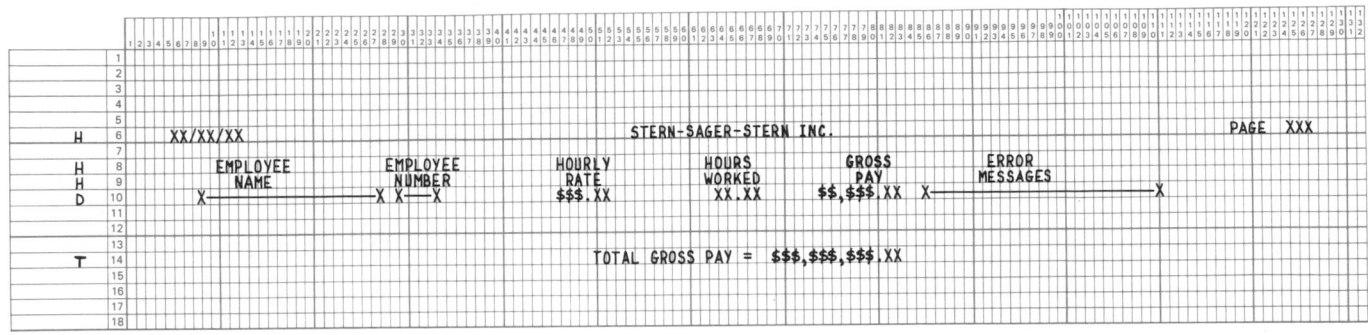

c. Sample Input Data

```
ABRAMSON BILL        00001    0100010
BUSSY MICHAEL        00002    02A0020
CARTMELL JOHN        00003    030003B
KALLUR ANDERS        00004    04C004D
FLATLY PATRICK       00005    0500050
FORTGANG NANCY       00006    0600060
GILLIES CLARK        00007    0700070
HAMILTON ALDEN       00008    0800080
HRUDEY KELLY         00009    0900090
HUNT MICHAEL         00010    1000100
```

d. Sample Output

```
04/02/85                          STERN-SAGER-STERN INC.                              PAGE   001

    EMPLOYEE          EMPLOYEE         HOURLY          HOURS           GROSS           ERROR
      NAME            NUMBER           RATE            WORKED          PAY             MESSAGES
  ABRAMSON BILL       00001           $1.00           1.0             $1.00
  BUSSY MICHAEL       00002           02A0            020                             RATE NOT NUMERIC
  CARTMELL JOHN       00003           0300            03B                             HOURS NOT NUMERIC
  KALLUR ANDERS       00004           04C0            04D                             RATE AND HOURS NOT NUMERIC
  FLATLY PATRICK      00005           $5.00           5.0             $25.00
  FORTGANG NANCY      00006           $6.00           6.0             $36.00
  GILLIES CLARK       00007           $7.00           7.0             $49.00
  HAMILTON ALDEN      00008           $8.00           8.0             $64.00
  HRUDEY KELLY        00009           $9.00           9.0             $81.00
  HUNT MICHAEL        00010           $10.00          10.0            $100.00


                            TOTAL GROSS PAY =                        $356.00
```

Figure 17.7
Problem definition for the Practice Program.

```
 LOC    OBJECT CODE      ADDR1 ADDR2  STMT    SOURCE STATEMENT

                                        1              PRINT NOGEN
                                        2      ****************************
                                        3      *       START OF PROGRAM        *
                                        4      ****************************
000000                                  5  PRNTRPT  START 0
000000 90EC D00C         0000C          6           STM   14,12,12(13)
000004 05C0                             7           BALR  12,0
                                00006   8           USING *,12
000006 50D0 C4AA         004B0          9           ST    13,SAVEAREA+4
00000A 41D0 C4A6         004AC         10           LA    13,SAVEAREA
                                       11           OPEN  (INFILE,INPUT)
                                       17           OPEN  (PRNTOUT,OUTPUT)
000026 F850 C45D C49E    00463 004A4   23           ZAP   TOTGROSS,ZERO
00002C D284 C347 C346    0034D 0034C   24  HEADRTN  MVC   DETLINE,BLANKS
000032 92F1 C347         0034D         25           MVI   DETLINE,C'1'
                                       26           MVC   DETLINE+6(8),=C'&SYSDATE'
00003C D215 C37E C56E    00384 00574   28           MVC   DETLINE+55(22),=C'STERN-SAGER-STERN INC.'
000042 D203 C3BE C54A    003C4 00550   29           MVC   DETLINE+119(4),=C'PAGE'
000048 FA10 C465 C5A0    0046B 005A6   30           AP    PAGECTR,=P'1'
00004E F321 C3C4 C465    003CA 0046B   31           UNPK  DETLINE+125(3),PAGECTR
000054 96F0 C3C6         003CC         32           OI    DETLINE+127,X'F0'
                                       33           PUT   PRNTOUT,DETLINE
000066 D284 C347 C346    0034D 0034C   38           MVC   DETLINE,BLANKS
00006C 92F0 C347         0034D         39           MVI   DETLINE,C'0'
000070 D219 C352 C584    00358 0058A   40           MVC   DETLINE+11(26),=C'EMPLOYEE          EMPLOYEE'
000076 D214 C376 C5A1    0037C 005A7   41           MVC   DETLINE+47(21),=C'HOURLY          HOURS'
00007C D213 C395 C54E    0039B 00554   42           MVC   DETLINE+78(20),=C'GROSS          ERROR'
                                       43  METHOD1  PUT   PRNTOUT,DETLINE
                                       48  METHOD2  PUT   PRNTOUT,SUBHEAD
00009E F810 C463 C5B6    00469 005BC   53           ZAP   LINECTR,=P'0'
                                       54      ****************************
                                       55      *       MAIN PROCESSING       *
                                       56      ****************************
                                       57  GETINFIL GET   INFILE,INREC
0000B2 D284 C347 C346    0034D 0034C   62           MVC   DETLINE,BLANKS
0000B8 D213 C350 C2F6    00356 002FC   63           MVC   DETLINE+9(20),INNAME
0000BE D204 C365 C30A    0036B 00310   64           MVC   DETLINE+30(5),INNUMBER
0000C4 F870 C46A C49E    00470 004A4   65           ZAP   ERRORCTR,ZERO
0000CA D203 C475 C314    0047B 0031A   66  CHECK1   MVC   HOLD4,INRATE
0000D0 D103 C475 C562    0047B 00568   67  RATE     MVN   HOLD4,=C'0000'
0000D6 D503 C475 C562    0047B 00568   68           CLC   HOLD4,=C'0000'
0000DC 4780 C0E0         000E6         69           BE    CHECK2
0000E0 FA70 C46A C49F    00470 004A5   70           AP    ERRORCTR,ONE
0000E6 D202 C472 C318    00478 0031E   71  CHECK2   MVC   HOLD3,INHOURS
0000EC D102 C472 C5B7    00478 005BD   72  HOURS    MVN   HOLD3,=C'000'
0000F2 D502 C472 C5B7    00478 005BD   73           CLC   HOLD3,=C'000'
0000F8 4780 C0FC         00102         74           BE    CK4ERRS
0000FC FA70 C46A C4A0    00470 004A6   75           AP    ERRORCTR,TWO
000102 F970 C46A C49E    00470 004A4   76  CK4ERRS  CP    ERRORCTR,ZERO
000108 4780 C130         00136         77           BE    PROCESS
00010C D203 C378 C314    0037E 0031A   78  ERRORTN  MVC   DETLINE+49(4),INRATE
000112 D202 C388 C318    0038E 0031E   79           MVC   DETLINE+65(3),INHOURS
000118 4130 C4EE         004F4         80           LA    3,ERRTABLE
00011C FB70 C46A C5A0    00470 005A6   81           SP    ERRORCTR,=P'1'
000122 4F50 C46A         00470         82           CVB   5,ERRORCTR
000126 5C40 C566         0056C         83           M     4,=F'26'
00012A 1A35                            84           AR    3,5
00012C D219 C39E 3000    003A4 00000   85           MVC   DETLINE+87(26),0(3)
000132 47F0 C1BE         001C4         86           B     PUTLINE
000136 F223 C453 C314    00459 0031A   87  PROCESS  PACK  PACKRATE,INRATE
00013C F212 C456 C318    0045C 0031E   88           PACK  PACKHOUR,INHOURS
000142 F842 C458 C453    0045E 00459   89           ZAP   PACKGROS,PACKRATE
000148 FC41 C458 C456    0045E 0045C   90           MP    PACKGROS,PACKHOUR
00014E FA40 C458 C5BA    0045E 005C0   91           AP    PACKGROS,=P'5'
000154 F143 C458 C458    0045E 0045E   92           MVO   PACKGROS,PACKGROS(4)
00015A FA54 C45D C463    00463 0045E   93           AP    TOTGROSS,PACKGROS
000160 D206 C375 C479    0037B 0047F   94           MVC   DETLINE+46(7),EDPAT1
000166 4110 C378         0037E         95           LA    1,DETLINE+49
00016A DF06 C375 C453    0037B 00459   96           EDMK  DETLINE+46(7),PACKRATE
000170 5B10 C56A         00570         97           S     1,=F'1'
000174 925B 1000         00000         98           MVI   0(1),C'$'
000178 D204 C386 C480    0038C 00486   99           MVC   DETLINE+63(5),EDPAT2
00017E DE04 C386 C456    0038C 0045C  100           ED    DETLINE+63(5),PACKHOUR
000184 D209 C391 C485    0039B 0048B  101           MVC   DETLINE+74(10),EDPAT3
00018A 4110 C397         0039D        102           LA    1,DETLINE+80
00018E DF09 C391 C459    0039B 0045F  103           EDMK  DETLINE+74(10),PACKGROS+1
000194 5B10 C56A         00570        104           S     1,=F'1'
000198 925B 1000         00000        105           MVI   0(1),C'$'
00019C 47F0 C1BE         001C4        106           B     PUTLINE
```

Figure 17.8
Solution to the Practice Program. (continued on pages 502 and 503)

```
0001A0  D206 C375 C479  0037B 0047F   107 FILLLINE  MVC    DETLINE+46(7),EDPAT1
0001A6  DE06 C375 C453  0037B 00459   108           ED     DETLINE+46(7),PACKRATE
0001AC  D204 C386 C480  0038C 00486   109           MVC    DETLINE+63(5),EDPAT2
0001B2  DE04 C386 C456  0038C 0045C   110           ED     DETLINE+63(5),PACKHOUR
0001B8  D209 C391 C485  00397 0048B   111           MVC    DETLINE+74(10),EDPAT3
0001BE  DE09 C391 C459  00397 0045F   112           ED     DETLINE+74(10),PACKGROS+1
0001C4  9240 C347       0034D         113 PUTLINE   MVI    DETLINE,C' '
                                      114           PUT    PRNTOUT,DETLINE

0001D6  FA10 C463 C49F  00469 004A5   119           AP     LINECTR,ONE
0001DC  F911 C463 C59E  00469 005A4   120           CP     LINECTR,=P'25'
0001E2  4780 C026       0002C         121           BE     HEADRTN
0001E6  47F0 C09E       000A4         122           B      GETINFIL
                                      123 ************************************
                                      124 *    END OF FILE ROUTINES       *
                                      125 ************************************
                                      126 EOJ       CLOSE  (INFILE)
0001F6  D284 C347 C346  0034D 0034C   132           MVC    DETLINE,BLANKS
0001FC  9260 C347       0034D         133           MVI    DETLINE,C'-'
000200  D210 C37A C5BB  00380 005C1   134           MVC    DETLINE+51(17),=C'TOTAL GROSS PAY ='
000206  D20E C38C C48F  00392 00495   135           MVC    DETLINE+69(15),EDPAT4
00020C  DF0E C38C C45D  00392 00463   136           EDMK   DETLINE+69(15),TOTGROSS
000212  5B10 C56A       00570         137           S      1,=F'1'
000216  925B 1000       00000         138           MVI    0(1),C'$'
                                      139           PUT    PRNTOUT,DETLINE
                                      144           CLOSE  (PRNTOUT)
000232  58D0 C4AA       004B0         150           L      13,SAVEAREA+4
000236  98EC D00C       0000C         151           LM     14,12,12(13)
00023A  07FE                          152           BR     14
                                      153 ************************************
                                      154 *    FILE SPECIFICATIONS        *
                                      155 ************************************
                                      156 INFILE    DCB    DDNAME=SYSIN,
                                                           MACRF=GM,
                                                           BLKSIZE=80,
                                                           LRECL=80,
                                                           DSORG=PS,
                                                           EODAD=EOJ
                                      210 PRNTOUT   DCB    DDNAME=SYSPRINT,
                                                           MACRF=PM,
                                                           BLKSIZE=133,
                                                           LRECL=133,
                                                           DSORG=PS
                                      264 ************************
                                      265 *    INPUT RECORD     *
                                      266 ************************
0002FC                                267 INREC     DS     0CL80
0002FC                                268 INNAME    DS     CL20
000310                                269 INNUMBER  DS     CL5
000315                                270           DS     CL5
00031A                                271 INRATE    DS     CL4
00031E                                272 INHOURS   DS     CL3
000321                                273           DS     CL43
                                      274 ************************
                                      275 *    OUTPUT RECORD    *
                                      276 ************************
00034C  40                            277 BLANKS    DC     CL1' '
00034D                                278 DETLINE   DS     CL133
                                      279 ********************
                                      280 *    HEADINGS        *
                                      281 ********************
0003D2                                282 SUBHEAD   DS     0CL133
0003D2  40                            283           DC     CL1' '
0003D3  4040404040404040              284           DC     12CL1' '
0003DF  D5C1D4C5                      285           DC     CL4'NAME'
0003E3  4040404040404040              286           DC     13CL1' '
0003F0  D5E4D4C2C5D9                  287           DC     CL6'NUMBER'
0003F6  4040404040404040              288           DC     12CL1' '
000402  D9C1E3C5                      289           DC     CL4'RATE'
000406  4040404040404040              290           DC     11CL1' '
000411  E6D6D9D2C5C4                  291           DC     CL6'WORKED'
000417  4040404040404040              292           DC     10CL1' '
000421  D7C1E8                        293           DC     CL3'PAY'
000424  4040404040404040              294           DC     10CL1' '
00042E  D4C5E2E2C1C7C5E2              295           DC     CL8'MESSAGES'
000436  4040404040404040              296           DC     35CL1' '
                                      297 ********************
                                      298 *    WORK AREAS      *
                                      299 ********************
```

Figure 17.8 (continued)

```
000459                       300 PACKRATE  DS    PL3
00045C                       301 PACKHOUR  DS    PL2
00045E                       302 PACKGROS  DS    PL5
000463                       303 TOTGROSS  DS    PL6
000469                       304 LINECTR   DS    PL2
00046B  000C                 305 PAGECTR   DC    PL2'0'
000470                       306 ERRORCTR  DS    D
000478                       307 HOLD3     DS    CL3
00047B                       308 HOLD4     DS    CL4
00047F  402021204B2020       309 EDPAT1    DC    XL7'402021204B2020'
000486  4021204B20           310 EDPAT2    DC    XL5'4021204B20'
00048B  402020206B2021204B   311 EDPAT3    DC    XL10'402020206B2021204B2020'
000495  402020206B202020     312 EDPAT4    DC    XL15'402020206B2020206B2021204B2020'
0004A4  0C                   313 ZERO      DC    PL1'0'
0004A5  1C                   314 ONE       DC    PL1'1'
0004A6  2C                   315 TWO       DC    PL1'2'
0004A7  050C                 316 FIFTY     DC    PL2'50'
0004AC                       317 SAVEAREA  DS    18F
0004F4                       318 ERRTABLE  DS    0CL78
0004F4  D9C1E3C540D5D6E3     319           DC    CL26'RATE NOT NUMERIC          '
00050E  C8D6E4D9E240D5D6     320           DC    CL26'HOURS NOT NUMERIC         '
000528  D9C1E3C540C1D5C4     321           DC    CL26'RATE AND HOURS NOT NUMERIC'
                             322           END
000548  F0F461F0F261F8F5     323                 =C'04/02/85'
000550  D7C1C7C5             324                 =C'PAGE'
000554  C7D9D6E2E2404040     325                 =C'GROSS          ERROR'
000568  F0F0F0F0             326                 =C'0000'
00056C  0000001A             327                 =F'26'
000570  00000001             328                 =F'1'
000574  E2E3C5D9D560E2C1     329                 =C'STERN-SAGER-STERN INC.'
00058A  C5D4D7D3D6E8C5C5     330                 =C'EMPLOYEE          EMPLOYEE'
0005A4  025C                 331                 =P'25'
0005A6  1C                   332                 =P'1'
0005A7  C8D6E4D9D3E84040     333                 =C'HOURLY          HOURS'
0005BC  0C                   334                 =P'0'
0005BD  F0F0F0               335                 =C'000'
0005C0  5C                   336                 =P'5'
0005C1  E3D6E3C1D340C7D9     337                 =C'TOTAL GROSS PAY ='
```

Figure 17.8 (continued)

KEY TERMS

Editing
Floating dollar sign
High-order
Low-order
Multiplicand
Multiplier

Packed-decimal form
Rounding
Shifting
Sign control
Truncation
Zoned-decimal form

REVIEW QUESTIONS

1. Write the appropriate edit instruction and pattern that will result with the following types of editing.
   a. Zero suppression—replaced by blanks.
      $
      ,
      . (two decimal digits)
      CR, if negative, two positions after last digit
      Field to be edited is `DD DD DD DS`
   b. Zero suppression—replaced by *.
      DB, if negative, two positions after last digit
      Field to be edited `DD DS`

2. Use an Edit and Mark sequence to achieve floating dollar signs in the preceding editing processes.

3. Shift the following fields left or right, as indicated.

   a. D D D S   Shift left two digits.
   b. D D D D D S   Shift right two digits.
   c. D D D D D S   Shift left three digits.
   d. D D D D D S   Shift right three digits.

4. Given the following, what is the result in QUOTIENT after the instructions are executed?

   FLD1 | D 1 | D 2 | D 3 | D 4 |

   QUOTIENT | F 0 | F 0 | F 0 | F 0 | (before)

   MVN   QUOTIENT,FLD1

5. Assume that the following is executed.

   ```
              MP    TOTAL,AMT
              .
              .
              .
   TOTAL   DS    PL4
   AMT     DS    PL2
   ```

   a. Write a routine to shift TOTAL right two places.
   b. Write a routine to shift TOTAL right one place.

6. Round the results in the previous examples before truncating.

7. Consider the following field.

   ```
   DVDND   DS    PL8
   ```

   a. Write a routine to add two zeros in preparation for dividing.
   b. Write a routine to add three zeros in preparation for dividing.

8. Indicate the pattern in each of the following cases.

DS	Contents	Edited Results
a. PL3	0 0 1 2 3 C	$ 1.23
b. PL3	0 0 1 2 3 D	$ 1.23
c. PL3	0 0 1 2 3 D	$ 1.23 CR
d. PL3	0 0 1 2 3 D	$ 1.23-

PROGRAMMING ASSIGNMENTS

1. **Input Record Format**

   1–5   Customer number
   6–7   Number of items bought (in 100s)
   8–10 Cost of each item x.xx
   11–80 Not used

   Output: Printed report (edited) with floating dollar signs

   1–5   Customer number
   16–25 Total charge xx,xxx.xx

   Notes
   a. Total charge = number of items (total) × cost per item.
   b. If customer number is a multiple of 10 (i.e., 00010, 00150), then the customer has a credit rating of A—allow two percent discount on total charge for these customers.

2. **Input Record Format**

    1–20 Name of employee
       21 Code 1—wages, 2—salary, 3—commission
    22–26 Amt1   xxx.xx
    27–31 Amt2   xxx.xx
    32–80 Not used

    Output: Print name and earned amount edited with a floating dollar sign

    Notes
    a. If wages (code = 1) multiply Amt1 by Amt2 to obtain earned amount.
    b. If salary (code = 2) earned amount is equal to Amt1.
    c. If Commission (Code = 3) multiply Amt1 by Amt2 and add on an additional 8 percent.
    d. Round all results.

Structured Programming in Assembler Language

OBJECTIVES

To familiarize you with:
1. *The advantages of structured programming.*
2. *Structured programming techniques.*
3. *Linkages, subroutines, and CALL statements.*

I. INTRODUCTION

Structured programming, as we have already indicated, is a coding technique that involves designing programs with a limited number of control structures or branching functions. It is a technique that results in a more efficient program regardless of the language utilized. Structured programming is an effort to modularize or segment programs into independent sections or modules. Here is a list of some of the objectives of this technique.

OBJECTIVES OF STRUCTURED PROGRAMMING

1. Simplify debugging.
2. Facilitate the coding of long and complex problems.
3. Make programs more efficient.
4. Make programs easier to read and understand.

II. STRUCTURED PROGRAMMING TECHNIQUES

Most nonstructured programs include numerous branch points. Consequently, it often becomes difficult to follow the logic and to debug a program when an error occurs. A major purpose of structured programming is to reduce the number of entry and exit points in a program. For that reason, structured programming is sometimes referred to as "GO TO-less" programming, where a "GO TO" statement is the high-level equivalent of a branch. Using the techniques of structured programming, the GO TO or branch statement becomes unnecessary. In COBOL, this means writing programs where sequences are controlled by PERFORM statements. In FORTRAN, this means writing programs where sequences are controlled by DO statements and subroutines. In assembler language, this means writing programs where most sequences are controlled by BALR and BAL statements.

With this technique, we can handle each section of a program independently without too much concern for where it enters the logic flow and what must be coded after that section has been completed. The modularized concept makes it possible for different programmers to code different sections of a large and complex program with only minimal concern for the interrelationships among the sections. Moreover, each module can be evaluated independently.

III. TOP-DOWN APPROACH

A structured technique that makes programs easier to read and debug is called **"top-down" programming.** As the term implies, efficient programs are written in modules with the first, or main, module followed by subsequent modules in decreasing order of significance. The first module coded is the most comprehensive and is followed by the other major modules, which are then followed by minor modules. To use this approach effectively, we make use of subroutines.

A. The Subroutine and Modular Concepts

The **subroutine** is a sequence of instructions, or a block, that performs a particular function. It is called into the main program as needed but is coded as a separate entity. Sometimes the same series of instructions is required at different places in a program or in different programs. It is possible to code these series of instructions *only once* as a subroutine and call it into a single program at several points as needed or call it into different programs as needed. An error printout routine, for example, may be required at different points of a program depending upon the type of error that has occurred. A single subroutine may be written and called into the program at the various error points.

IV. TYPES OF SUBROUTINES

A. External Subroutines

Subroutines may be totally independent of a program and written for a wide variety of applications. **External subroutines** are stored in a library and called into a program as needed. These subroutines have their own base register, are relocatable, and have a "stand-alone" capability. An edit routine, for example, that performs limit tests, validity checks and so on, may be written as a subroutine and called into individual programs as required. We will *not* discuss external subroutines in depth in this chapter but will consider them briefly in Appendix D.

B. Internal Subroutines

Internal subroutines are written in modular fashion and called into the main body of the program as required. When a subroutine is to be executed, a call from the main program is issued.

The subroutine's first instruction, called the **entry point,** is then executed as are all instructions in sequence. Upon completing the last instruction in the subroutine, we return to the main program, which continues executing in sequence from the **return address**—the next instruction in the main program after the subroutine is called.

An illustration of this process is presented in Figure 18.1. The routine HDGRTN identifies a block of code that is separate from the main program. The main program branches to the subroutine, and the subroutine is then executed. When the subroutine is completed, a branch to the *return address* in the main program occurs. In this example the return address references the instruction CLEAR LINEOUT.

The subroutine may be referenced at any time and from any point in the main program. See Figure 18.2 for an illustration.

Again, when the subroutine is completed, it will return to the instruction that follows the CALL. In this instance, the return address will be the instruction ADD 1 TO LINES.

C. Advantages of Subroutines

The major advantage of subroutines is that they are coded only once, but may be referenced frequently from different points in the program. In addition, subroutines allow you the flexibility of segmenting the program into modules. Even though a subroutine may be executed only once by the program, the sectioning of the program into modules is advantageous because it lends itself to top-down structured programming. It also assists in debugging, because each section or module can be debugged independently.

Flowchart   *Pseudocode*

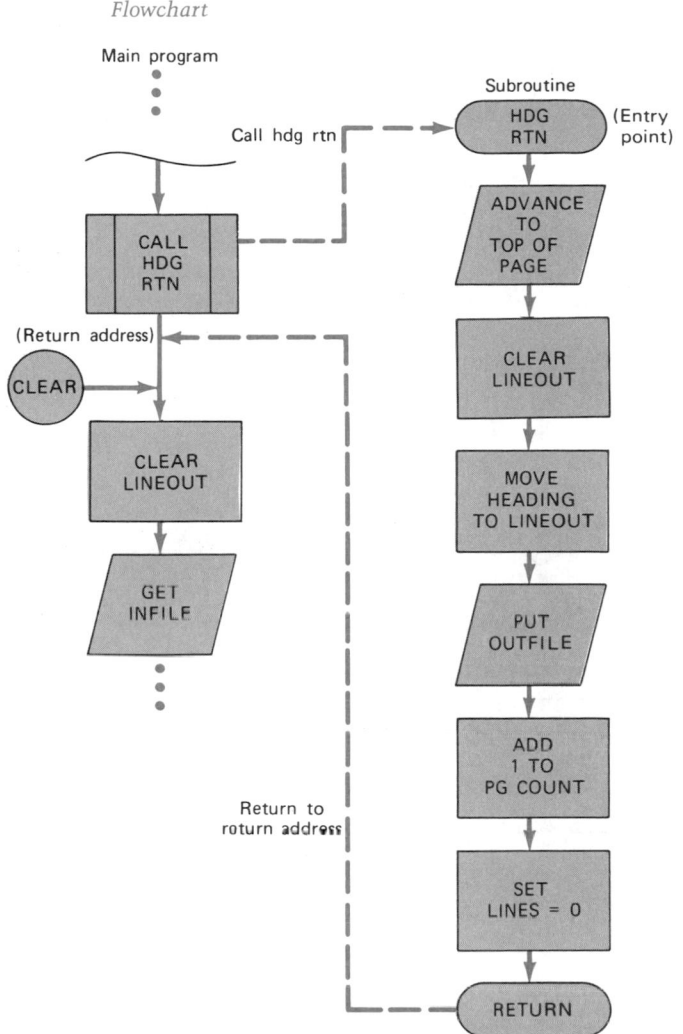

```
PERFORM HDG RTN
    ADVANCE TO TOP OF PAGE
    CLEAR LINEOUT
    MOVE HEADING TO LINEOUT
    PUT OUTFILE
    ADD 1 TO PG COUNT
    SET LINES TO 0
CLEAR LINEOUT
GET INFILE
    .
    .
```

Figure 18.1
A subroutine interfacing with a main module.

An additional advantage of segmentation is the ease of incorporating program changes when the program requirements of the job are subsequently modified. As students, you rarely encounter this maintenance problem in the classroom environment. In industry, however, changes become a normal part of program maintenance.

V. LINKAGE TO SUBROUTINES

To utilize subroutines, a **linkage** must be established.

1. The address of the *entry point* in the subroutine must be stored so that a branch to it may be executed.
2. The *return address* in the main program must be stored so that the subroutine may branch back to the main program.

This linkage is performed with a Branch and Link (BAL) instruction.

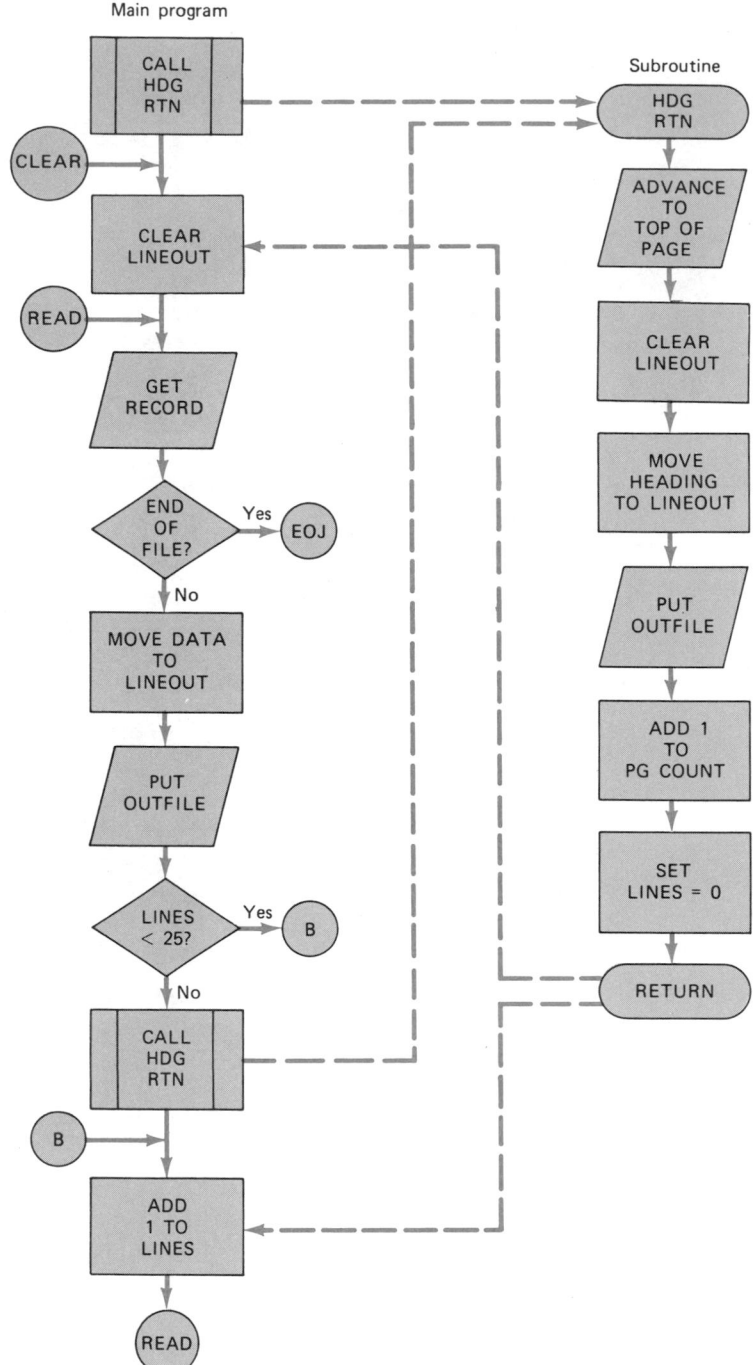

Figure 18.2
A subroutine interfacing with a main module from two points.

```
                              FORMAT
                    ┌─────────────────┬─────────────────┐
                    │ Operation       │ Operand         │
                    │ 10              │ 16              │
                    ├─────────────────┼─────────────────┤
                    │ BAL             │ REG,SUBRTN      │
                    └─────────────────┴─────────────────┘
```

Operation Code: BAL
Meaning: Branch and Link
Operand 1:   General register
As a result of the BAL, Operand 1 will contain the address of the next sequential instruction (in the main program) to be executed.
Operand 2:   Label or symbolic address
Entry point (of subroutine)—address to be branched to

As its name implies, the Branch and Link performs two separate functions.

1. It stores the address of the next instruction in the main program to be executed.
2. It branches to a routine.

Example 18.1

```
LABEL        OPERATION    OPERAND                                    COMMENTS
1            10      16                                                                      72
* MAIN PROGRAM
             .
             .
             .
             BAL     5,HDGRTN
             AP      LINES,=P'1'
             .
             .
             .
```

These instructions illustrate how the second CALL in Figure 18.2 can be coded. The address of the AP instruction is stored in register 5. The program branches to HDGRTN. In this way, linkage to the subroutine has been accomplished.

As we will see next, an additional instruction is required in the subroutine HDGRTN to branch back to the return address in the main program after the subroutine has been executed.

A. THE BRANCH REGISTER (BR) INSTRUCTION

FORMAT

Operation 10	Operand 16
BR	REG

Operation Code: BR
Meaning: Branch Register
Operand 1:   General register
Result: A branch to the address contained in the register will occur.

To complete the linkage with our subroutine we have the following:

LABEL	OPERATION 10	16 OPERAND	COMMENTS 72
* MAIN PROGRAM			
	.		
	.		
	.		
	BAL	5,HDGRTN	
	AP	LINES,=P'1'	
	.		
	.		
	.		
* SUBROUTINE			
HDGRTN	CNTRL	OUTFILE,SK,1	ADVANCE TO TOP OF PAGE
	.		
	.		
	.		
	BR	5	

Thus, when a call is made to the subroutine HDGRTN, the address of the next instruction in the main program, the AP, is stored in register 5. At the end of the subroutine, the BR instruction causes a branch to the address contained in register 5, which is the address of the AP instruction. The main program thus continues with the next sequential instruction *after* the CALL.

To review, linkage is accomplished

1. By storing in a register the address of the next instruction of the main program when branching to the subroutine (BAL).
2. By branching to the address of the next sequential instruction in the main program (BR) after executing the subroutine.

Note that a Load Address instruction followed by an unconditional branch may be coded instead.

```
 LABEL    OPERATION        OPERAND                              COMMENTS
1          10       16                                                                    72
* MAIN PROGRAM
          .
          .
          .
          LA       5,ADD
          B        HDGRTN
ADD       AP       LINES,=P'1'
          .
          .
* SUBROUTINE
HDGRTN    CNTRL    OUTFILE,SK,1  ADVANCE TO TOP OF PAGE
          .
          .
          .
          BR       5
```

The LA instruction loads the address of the AP instruction into register 5. Notice that a label, ADD, was put on the AP instruction so that it could be referenced in the LA instruction. If we wish to branch to the subroutine HDGRTN again at some later point, we may include another BAL instruction, as follows.

```
 LABEL    OPERATION        OPERAND                              COMMENTS
1          10       16                                                                    72
* MAIN PROGRAM
          .
          .
          .
          BAL      5,HDGRTN
          AP       LINES,=P'1'
          .
          .
          BAL      5,HDGRTN
          AP       TOTAL,AMT
* SUBROUTINE
HDGRTN    CNTRL    OUTFILE,SK,1  ADVANCE TO TOP OF PAGE
          .
          .
          BR       5
```

VI. LINKING SUBROUTINES TO SUBROUTINES

It is a common practice in programming to have subroutines call other subroutines. In Figure 18.3, we see that the subroutine DETLINE (*Det*ail *Line*) calls, or links to, the subroutine HDGRTN.

It is important to note that when subroutine one calls subroutine two, the former acts as the **calling program,** just as the main program did in the previous example. A different register must be used for proper linkage. The following will thus produce the correct results.

LABEL	OPERATION 10	OPERAND 16	COMMENTS
* MAIN PROGRAM			
	.		
	.		
	.		
	BAL	5,DETLINE	
	AP	TOTAL,=P'1'	
	.		
	.		
	.		
* SUBROUTINE ONE			
DETLINE	CP	LINES,=P'25'	
	BL	SKIP	
	BAL	4,HDGRTN	
SKIP	MVC	LINEOUT,SPACES	
	.		
	.		
	.		
	BR	5	
* SUBROUTINE TWO			
HDGRTN	CNTRL	OUTFILE,SK,1	ADVANCE TO TOP OF PAGE
	.		
	.		
	.		
	BR	4	

In the main program, a call is made to the subroutine DETLINE, with register 5 being used to store the return address to the main program. The subroutine DETLINE, in turn, calls the subroutine HDGRTN, with register 4 being used to store the return address to the subroutine DETLINE.

If the *same* register were used in the program, an error would occur. See Figure 18.4.

Register 5 would initially contain the return address in the main program. However, when executing the routine DETLINE, a new return address would be placed in register 5, destroying its original contents. When BR 5 in DETLINE is executed, an error will occur. That is, an infinite loop in the DETLINE routine would result because register 5 would still point to the entry point within DETLINE, the MVC instruction.

We can avoid this problem by using different registers, although this may become problematic if registers are required for normal processing within these subroutines. However, to avoid this problem, we save the contents of register 5 in a storage area for later reference. When we are ready to return to the calling program, the register is reloaded with its original contents and the linkage is then completed. The Store Register (ST) and Load (L) instructions are used for the purpose of saving and restoring the register.

A. Review of Store Register (ST) Instruction

Operation 10	Operand 16
ST	REG,FULLWD

where

ST	denotes storing data from a register.
REG	is a general purpose register and the sending field.

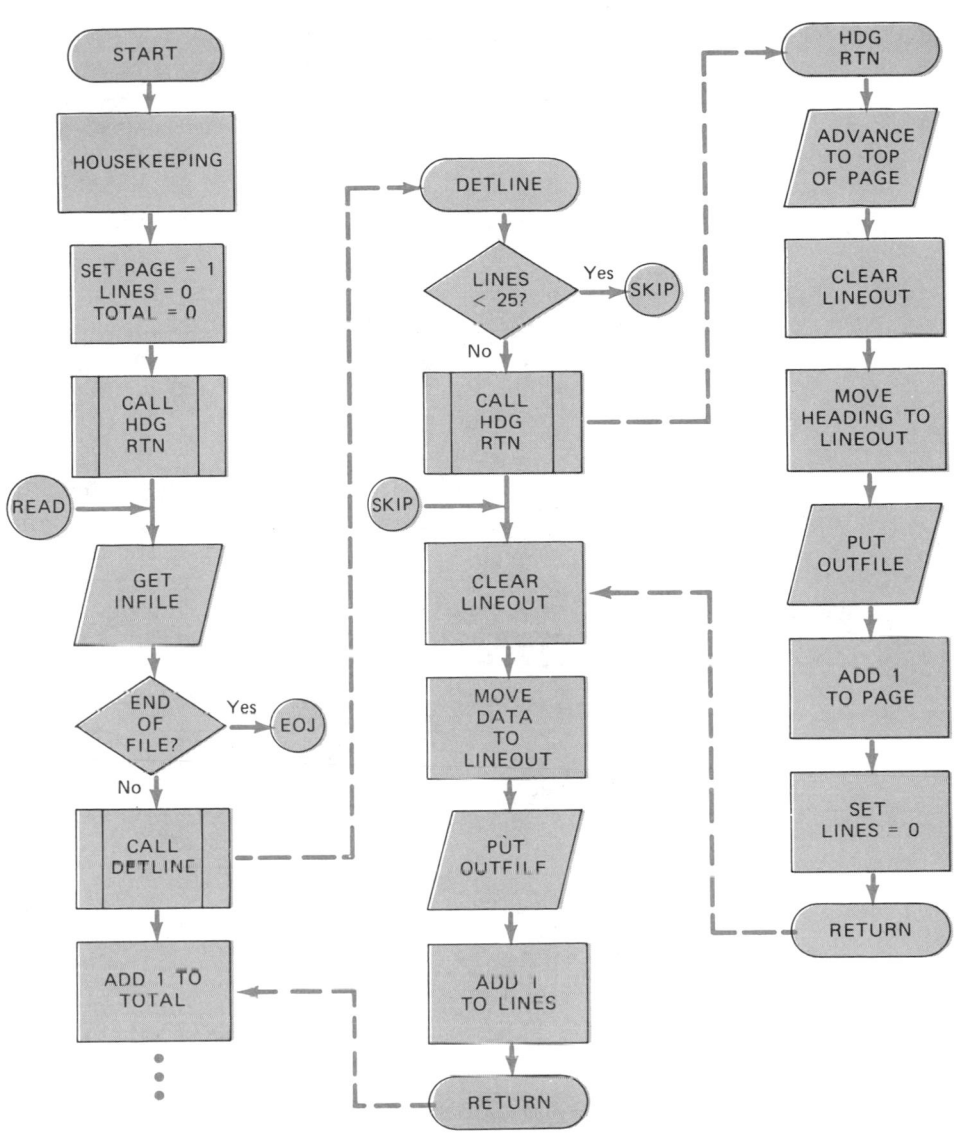

Figure 18.3
Illustration of a subroutine
that calls in a subroutine.

FULLWD   is a storage location, 4 bytes in length and located on a
          fullword boundary. Usually, it is defined by a DS
          instruction and an operand of F.

Result   Contents of REG are moved to FULLWD.

Example 18.2

LABEL	OPERATION	OPERAND	COMMENTS
	ST	3,SAVE	
	ST	4,HOLD1	
	ST	5,HOLD2	
	.		
	.		
	.		
SAVE	DS	F	
HOLD1	DS	F	
HOLD2	DS	F	

Before Execution

Registers		Storage	
Register	Contents	Name	Contents
3	00 00 56 78	SAVE	?
4	00 12 34 56	HOLD1	?
5	00 00 03 45	HOLD2	?

After Execution

Registers		Storage	
Register	Contents	Name	Contents
3	00 00 56 78	SAVE	00 00 56 78
4	00 12 34 56	HOLD1	00 12 34 56
5	00 00 03 45	HOLD2	00 00 03 45

The contents of registers 3, 4, and 5 are stored in the storage locations named SAVE, HOLD1, and HOLD2, respectively. Remember, the register is the sending field and the storage location is the receiving field.

We will see that for subroutine linkage, the contents of the register holding the return address will be stored in a fullword storage area.

B. Review of Load (L) Instruction

Operation 10	Operand 16
L	REG,FWD

where

L   denotes a load operation.
REG   is a general register and the receiving field.
FWD   is a 4-byte storage location (aligned on a fullword boundary).
The second operand is the sending field.

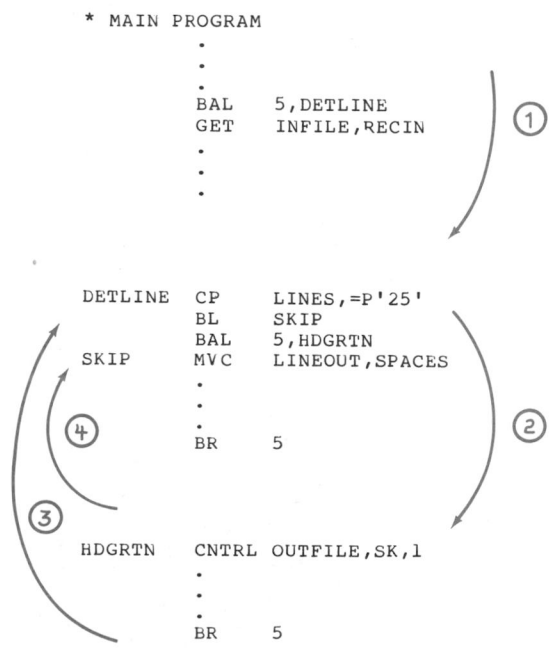

Figure 18.4
Incorrect use of a single register for linkage in two subroutines.

```
* MAIN PROGRAM
         .
         .
         .
         BAL    5,DETLINE
         GET    INFILE,RECIN          ①
         .
         .
         .


DETLINE  CP     LINES,=P'25'
         BL     SKIP
         BAL    5,HDGRTN
SKIP     MVC    LINEOUT,SPACES        ②
         .
         .
    ④   .
         BR     5


③   HDGRTN   CNTRL  OUTFILE,SK,1
         .
         .
         BR     5
```

Result   The contents of the fullword storage area are loaded into a register. See the following example.

LABEL	OPERATION	OPERAND	COMMENTS
	L	6,SAVE	CONTENTS OF SAVE MOVED TO REGISTER 6
	L	7,TEMP1	CONTENTS OF TEMP1 MOVED TO REGISTER 7
	L	8,TEMP2	CONTENTS OF TEMP2 MOVED TO REGISTER 8
	.		
	.		
	.		
SAVE	DS	F	
TEMP1	DS	F	
TEMP2	DS	F	

The contents of the storage locations SAVE, TEMP1, and TEMP2 are placed in the general registers 6, 7, and 8, respectively.

VII. LINKAGE OF INTERNAL SUBROUTINES

To use the *same* register for storing a return address for two or more subroutines the following must be done:

1. The original contents of the register, which holds the return address for subroutine 1, must be stored (ST) in a fullword storage area.
2. After subroutine 2 (or more) is executed, the contents of this storage area will be loaded (L) back into the register.

We will utilize the Load (L) and Store (ST) instructions in completing the subroutine linkages. Figure 18.5 shows the logic of a subroutine calling in a subroutine with the necessary linkage. Figure 18.6 illustrates the correct coding of this linkage.

1. Main Program.   The BAL instruction in the main program stores the return address (AP instruction) in register 5. Then, a branch to DETLINE takes place.

2. DETLINE.   Upon entering the routine DETLINE, the return address to the main program is stored in a save area (SAVE1) by the Store instruction. This frees register 5 for other programming tasks.

3. DETLINE.   The BAL instruction then saves the address of the MVC instruction in register 5 and the program branches to HDGRTN.

4. HDGRTN.   Upon entering HDGRTN, the return address to the calling program (DETLINE) is immediately stored in a save area (SAVE2) by the Store instruction. It is best to follow a consistent set of rules. Even though we are not using registers, we still free register 5 by saving its contents in the save area.

5. HDGRTN.   The Load (L) instruction restores register 5 with its original contents, the return address to DETLINE.

6. HDGRTN.   The Branch Register (BR) returns control to the MVC instruction in DETLINE.

7. DETLINE.   The Load (L) instruction restores register 5 with the return address to the AP instruction in the MAIN program. The main program is again ready to continue processing.

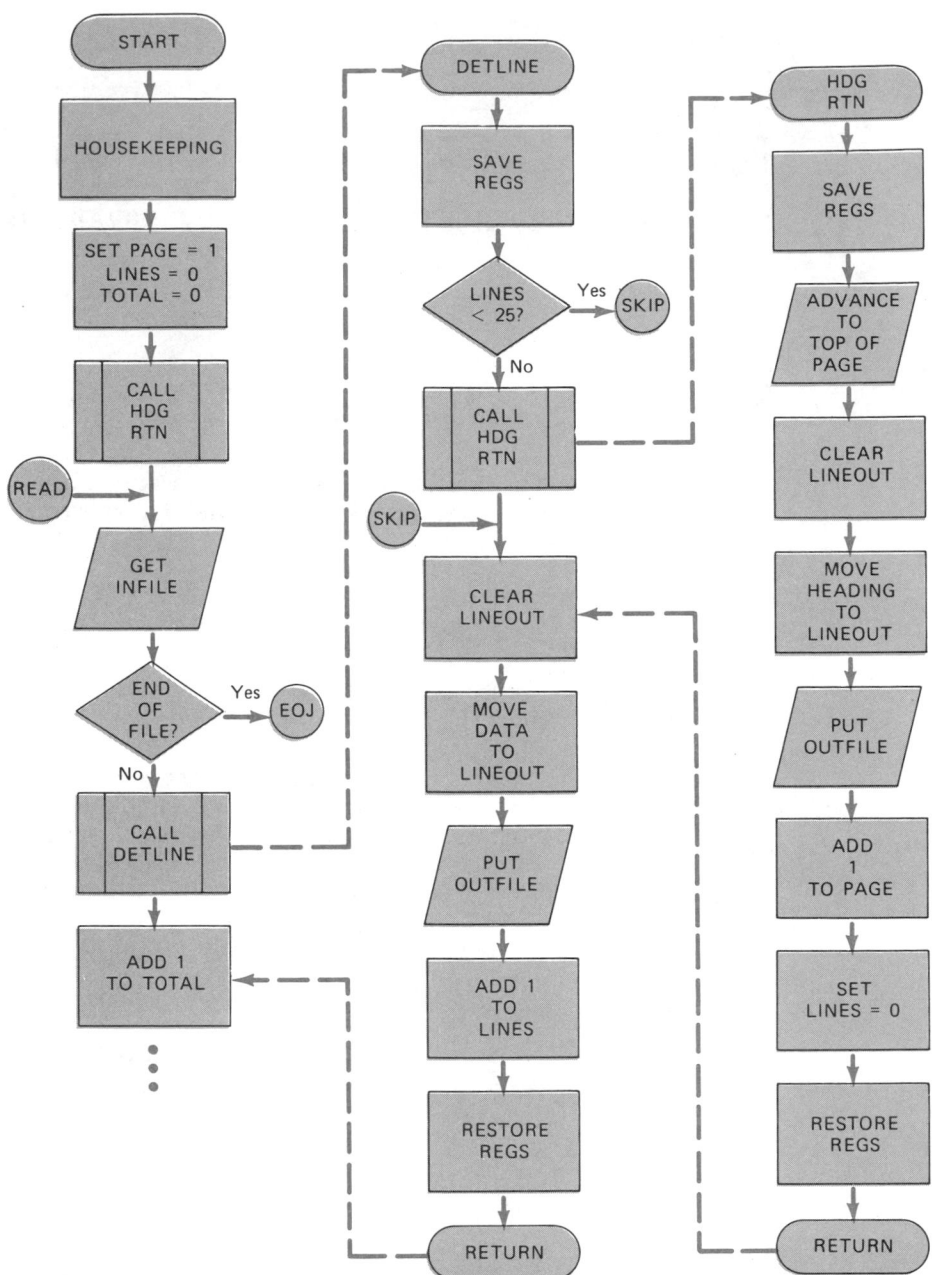

Figure 18.5
Logic of a subroutine calling in a subroutine.

The example in Figure 18.7 illustrates a full program that uses structured programming modules or subroutines.

A. Explanation of Changes

1. Note that DETLINE begins by processing the first record. When the first record has been completely processed, we insert a GET in DETLINE that reads another record. Hence, DETLINE is an independent routine that, if executed indefinitely, would be a complete routine for processing all records.

2. To execute DETLINE indefinitely we want the

```
BAL    5,DETLINE
```

in the main routine executed indefinitely. Under normal circumstances,

```
* MAIN PROGRAM
          .
          .
          .
          BAL     5,DETLINE
          AP      TOTAL,=P'1'
          .
          .
          .
* SUBROUTINE ONE
DETLINE   ST      5,SAVE1
          .
          .
          .
          BAL     5,HDGRTN
          MVC     LINEOUT,SPACES
          .
          .
          .
          L       5,SAVE1
          BR      5
* SUBROUTINE TWO
HDGRTN    ST      5,SAVE2
          .
          .
          .
          L       5,SAVE2
          BR      5
```

Figure 18.6
Correct use of a single register
for linkage in two subroutines.

the BR 5 in the DETLINE subroutine will take us back to the main routine, to the step *after* the BAL. To execute the BAL again, we subtract 4 (the length of the BAL instruction) prior to BR 5 in DETLINE subroutine. The BR 5 then would take us back to the main routine to the BAL 5,DETLINE that executes the subroutine again. This process will continue until EOF is executed. In this way we can write our main routine so that it contains *no* branches.

VIII. ALTERNATIVE METHOD OF LINKING TO A SUBROUTINE: THE BRANCH AND LINK REGISTER INSTRUCTION (BALR)

The Branch and Link Register (BALR) instruction is the Register-to-Register version of the Branch and Link (BAL). It serves the same purpose as the BAL instruction but is of the RR type.

Operation 10	Operand 16
BALR	REG1,REG2

where

BALR	indicates the Branch and Link Register instruction.
REG1	is a general register and contains the address of the next sequential instruction.
REG2	is a general register that contains the *address* of a routine that is branched to.

Result The address of the next sequential instruction of the calling program is loaded into REG1 and a branch to the address in REG2 is executed.

For example,

LABEL	OPERATION		OPERAND	COMMENTS	
1	10	16			72
	LA		5,RTN1		
	BALR		4,5		
NEXT	MVC		FIELDA,FIELDB		

is the same as

LABEL	OPERATION		OPERAND	COMMENTS	
1	10	16			72
	BAL		4,RTN1		
NEXT	MVC		FIELDA,FIELDB		

Initially, the address of RTN1 is placed in register 5 with an LA instruction. The BALR instruction results in the following.

1. It places the address of the MVC instruction in register 4.
2. It causes a branch to RTN1 to take place.

```
*                                                            *
*                          HOUSEKEEPING INSTRUCTIONS GO HERE *
*                                                            *
          BAL    5,HDGRTN
READ      GET    INFILE,RECIN
          BAL    5,DETLINE
HDGRTN    ST     5,SAVE1
          CNTRL  OUTFILE,SK,1
          MVC    LINEOUT,SPACES
          MVC    LINEOUT+45(27),=C'MY-T-FINE AUTO SUPPLY CORP.'
          MVC    LINEOUT+95(5),=C'PAGE '
          UNPK   LINEOUT+100(3),PAGE
          OI     LINEOUT+102,X'F0'
          CNTRL  OUTFILE,SP,,3
          PUT    OUTFILE,LINEOUT
          AP     PAGE,=P'1'
          ZAP    LINES,=P'0'
          L      5,SAVE1
          BR     5
DETLINE   ST     5,SAVE2
          CP     LINES,=P'25'
          BL     SKIP
          BAL    5,HDGRTN
SKIP      MVC    LINEOUT,SPACES
          MVC    PARTO,PART
          MVC    DESCO,DESC
          PUT    OUTFILE,LINEOUT
          AP     LINES,=P'1'
          GET    INFILE,RECIN
          L      5,SAVE2
          S      5,F'4'
          BR     5
*                                                            *
*                          HOUSEKEEPING INSTRUCTIONS GO HERE *
*                          ALONG WITH DTF OR DCB MACROS       *
*                                                            *
SAVE1     DS     F
SAVE2     DS     F
PAGE      DC     PL2'1'
LINES     DC     PL2'0'
SPACES    DC     CL1' '
LINEOUT   DS     0CL132
          DS     CL46
PARTO     DS     CL4
          DS     CL6
DESCO     DS     CL20
          DS     CL56
RECIN     DS     0CL80
PART      DS     CL4
DESC      DS     CL20
          DS     CL56
          END
```

Figure 18.7
Program illustrating structured
programming modules.

CHAPTER SUMMARY

I. Structured Programming
   A. Objectives
      1. To simplify coding and debugging.
      2. To make programs more efficient and easier to read, modify, and evaluate.
   B. Techniques
      1. Avoid the use of GO TOs.
      2. Use BALR and BAL instructions to control sequences.
II. Top-Down Programming
   A. The first set of instructions or module is the main one, and the one from which all other modules are executed.
   B. The other modules are coded in decreasing order of importance.
   C. Each module is treated as a subroutine.
III. Types of Subroutines
   A. External subroutines
      1. Written for numerous applications.
      2. Independent of a program.
      3. Called into a program as needed from a library.
      4. Each subroutine has its own base register.
   B. Internal subroutines
      1. Coded as a module and called into the main body of a program as needed.
      2. The first instruction of a subroutine is the *entry point.*
      3. After the last instruction in a subroutine is executed, we return to the main program by branching to the *return address* in the main program.
IV. Linkages to Subroutines
   A. Branch and Link (BAL) instruction
      1. Example: BAL 5,DETLINE
      2. Stores the address of the next instruction (in the main program) to be executed. This is stored in a register (e.g., register 5).
      3. Branches to a routine (e.g., DETLINE).
   B. The Branch Register (BR) instruction
      1. Executed as the last instruction in the subroutine.
      2. Includes the register number indicated in the BAL that contains the address in the main module to be branched to.
V. Other Instructions Used for Linking
   A. The Store (ST) Instruction
   B. The Load (L) Instruction
   C. The Branch and Link Register (BALR) Instruction
      1. Format: BALR REG1,REG2
      2. REG1 is a general register that contains the address of the next sequential instruction.
      3. REG2 is a general register that contains the address of a routine that is branched to.

CHAPTER SELF-EVALUATING QUIZ

1. A major purpose of structured programming is to reduce the number of _____ in a program.
2. A subroutine is a(n) _____ .
3. There are two types of subroutines: _____ and _____ .
4. An entry point is the _____ in a subroutine.
5. When the last instruction in a subroutine is completed, a(n) _____ is made to the main program, where execution continues with _____ .

6. Explain what is meant by the following instruction.

   ```
   BAL    6,BONUS
   ```

7. Write the necessary linkage instructions using the BAL and BR instructions to call in a subroutine PREMIUM, and then return to the main program when the subroutine is executed. The first instruction in PREMIUM clears OUTAREA.

8. (T or F) Only one register has to be used for linkage when a main program calls a subroutine that, in turn, calls another subroutine.

9. Write the linkage instruction(s) for Question 7 using the BALR instruction.

10. Are the following instructions a correct solution for Question 9?

    ```
    L      6,PREMIUM
    BALR   5,6
    ```

SOLUTIONS

Page

1. Entry and exit points (branches) — 507
2. Sequence of instructions that performs a particular function — 508
3. External; internal — 508
4. First instruction — 508
5. Return; the next instruction after the subroutine is called — 508
6. The address of the next instruction is stored in register 6. Then, a branch is made to the routine whose first instruction has a label or name of BONUS. — 511
7. — 512

   ```
              BAL    6,PREMIUM
                .
                .
   PREMIUM    MVC    OUTAREA,SPACES
                .
                .
              BR     6
   ```

8. T: the ST and L instructions can be used to save return addresses — 514
9. — 520

   ```
   LA     6,PREMIUM
   BALR   5,6
   ```

10. No: the first instruction loads the contents of PREMIUM, not the *address* of the subroutine to be branched to. An LA instruction must be used: — 516

    ```
    LA     6,PREMIUM
    ```

KEY TERMS

Calling program
Entry point
External subroutines
Internal subroutines
Linkage

Modular programming
Return address
Structured programming
Subroutines
Top-down programming

REVIEW QUESTIONS

1. Explain the major objectives of structured programming.
2. What are the differences between internal and external subroutines?
3. Explain how the necessary linkage between the main program and a subroutine is accomplished with the BAL and BR instructions.
4. Explain what instructions can be used for linkage when a subroutine calls another subroutine.

PROGRAMMING ASSIGNMENTS

Rewrite the programs at the end of Chapter 16 using the structured approach discussed in this chapter.

Macros

OBJECTIVES

OBJECTIVES

1. *To study the purpose and advantages of macro programming.*
2. *To study the basic components of a macro and the purpose of* MACRO, *prototype, body, and* MEND *instructions.*
3. *To provide an understanding of logical control procedures.*
4. *To become familiar with macro terminology, including* MEXIT, MNOTE, AGO, AIF, SYSNDX, LCL, *and* GBL.
5. *To develop an understanding of positional and keyword parameters.*
6. *To develop the ability to code simple macros.*

I. INTRODUCTION

A **macro** is a "symbolic" operation code that causes a series of instructions to be inserted in the object program.

GET and PUT are examples of macros that are system-defined so that they can be used by all source programs. If you check a program listing, you will see that a GET or PUT macro is assembled as a *series* of input/output instructions that access records, perform blocking or deblocking functions, and so on. Thus, a macro provides assembler language with a feature that is similar to that of high-level symbolic languages: a single programmed code that generates numerous machine-language instructions.

In addition to using system-defined macros such as GET and PUT, you may write your own macros. If a set of instructions is to be used at different times in a program, then they may be included within a macro. Macros may be used as needed by a program or may be called into different programs. This capability has many advantages.

ADVANTAGES OF USING MACROS

1. Reduces the risk of coding errors.
2. Facilitates debugging.
3. Helps to standardize programs.
4. Reduces the risk of errors made during program modification.
5. Enables you to write the program as a set of modules, where each module can be called in as a macro.

This last advantage of macros facilitates the processing of structured programs.

In summary, the features of macros include the following:

FEATURES OF MACROS

1. Enables assembly language to have high-level capabilities—one instruction generates numerous machine-language instructions.
2. Enables a series of steps to be defined once as a module and called into programs as needed.

Before a programmer-defined macro can be used, it must be defined. This definition may be included in a macro library and called by each program that needs it, or it may be contained within an individual source program. See Figure 19.1.

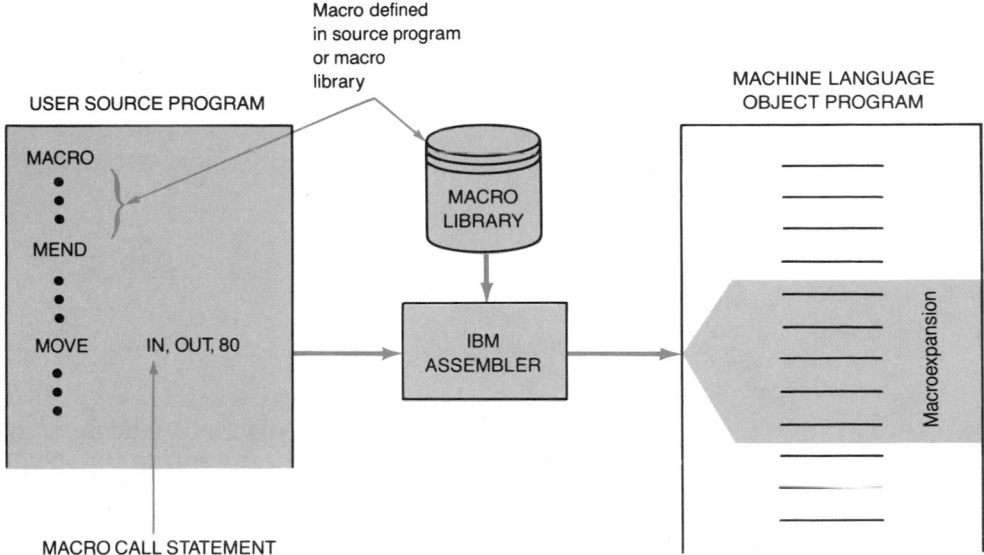

Figure 19.1

A programmer-defined macro must be defined in the source program or macro library.

The macro (MNAME) is invoked by a source statement as follows.

```
MNAME      , , .
```

The stored set of instructions that will be executed when MNAME is called has the following form:

```
MACRO  ←——— Denotes beginning of macro
MNAME ...,... ←——— Name of macro
             } Instructions
MEND   ←——————— Denotes end of macro
```

The MACRO command and its corresponding instructions are stored either in the source program or in a macro library. Each time your program is to access or "invoke" it, you code:

```
MNAME      ...
```

The dots (...) denote that additional parameters may be used. For now, keep in mind that simply coding MNAME as an operation code will access or invoke the macro or set of instructions defined by that name.

II. DEFINING A MACRO

A macro definition consists of the following four parts.

1. The MACRO statement, which simply states that a macro definition is to follow.
2. A prototype statement that names the macro and describes the variables used to pass data between the macro and the source program.
3. The body, consisting of a series of instructions that specify the set of procedures in the macro.
4. The MEND or Macro End statement, which signals the end of the macro.

Macro Instructions   *Macroscopic Flowchart*

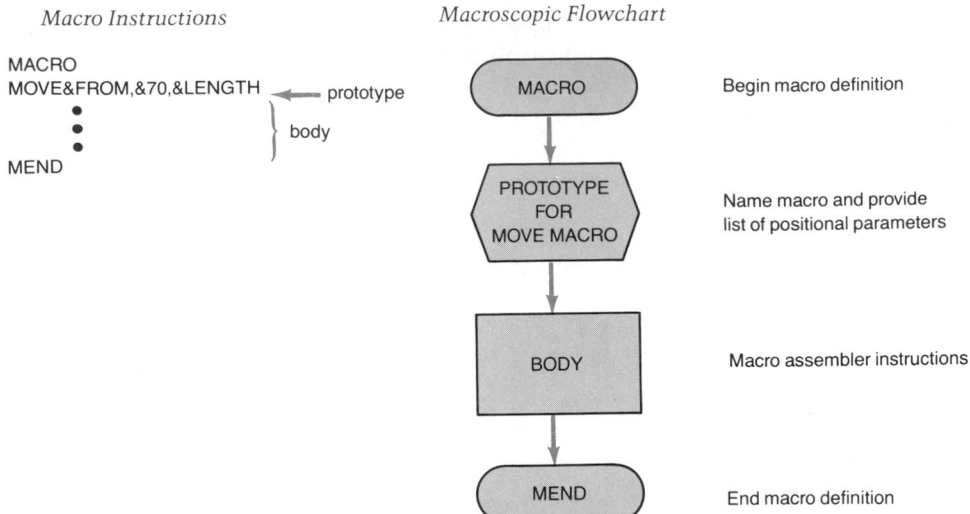

Figure 19.2
Example of a macro in
schematic form.

Figure 19.2 illustrates a macro in schematic form. Note that the MACRO and MEND statements must always appear as operation codes. No other data is permitted on these lines.

The **prototype statement** illustrates the format used in calling the macro. The following example shows the relationship between the prototype statement and the instruction required to call the macro named MOVE.

Source Statement

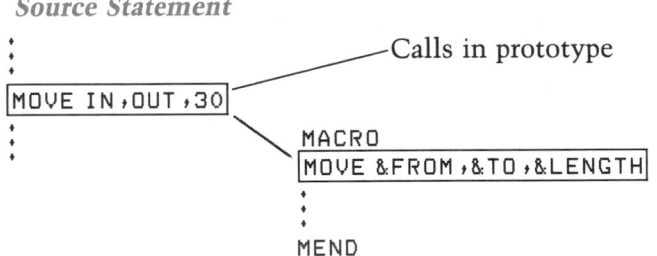

Notice that the name of the MACRO is MOVE. The operation code on the line following MACRO in the library defines the name. The symbolic names used in the prototype describe the variables to be used. These variables always begin with an ampersand (&). The rules for creating these variables or parameters follow.

RULES FOR CREATING VARIABLES

1. May contain from 2 to 8 characters.
2. First character must be an ampersand (&).
3. Second character must be a letter (A–Z).
4. Remaining characters may be letters or digits.
5. Cannot begin with &SYS because that combination is reserved *solely* for system macros.

In the example presented, the assembler will correlate the variables in the source statement with those in the prototype, and then make the following substitutions.

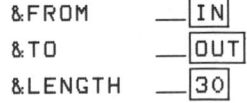

Once these substitutions are made, the instructions within the body of the macro would be executed resulting in the macro expansion.

We will now examine a macro designed to perform a simple register-to-indexed storage addition of two fields. It is important to note that the sum or result will be placed in the second operand, namely &RX2. The substitutions for the symbolic names are positional, that is, in the same relative positions of both the call statement and prototype, so they are referred to as **positional parameters.**

	Source Program		*Defined in the Program or in a Macro Library*	
	:		MACRO	
	RXADD	FWD1,FWD2	RXADD	&RX1,&RX2
	:		L	9,&RX1
FWD1	DC	F'100'	A	9,&RX2
FWD2	DC	F'150'	ST	9,&RX2
			MEND	

The execution of the macro RXADD will cause the assembler to make the following substitutions for the positional parameters.

```
L    9,&RX1          L    9,FWD1
A    9,&RX2          A    9,FWD2
ST   9,&RX2          ST   9,FWD2
```

The values of 100 in FWD1 and 150 in FWD2 are used in the RXADD macro in the Load, Add, and Store instructions. They are substituted for RX1 and RX2 prior to execution. After the macro RXADD is executed, FWD2 will have new contents generated as a result of the three instructions.

As the result of execution, the contents of FWD2 will contain 250, the sum of FWD1 (equated to RX1) and FWD2 (equated to RX2). FWD1 will remain unchanged.

Thus, a parameter list of a MACRO may include variables to be equated to those in the source program. **Keyword parameters** may also be used, which define constants that are to be used in the set of instructions defined by the macro. A keyword parameter uses a variable name beginning with &, immediately followed by an = sign.

Example 19.1

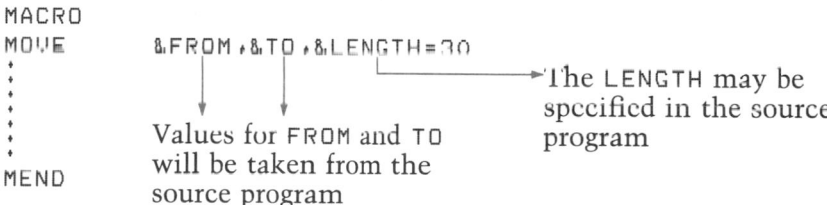

&LENGTH is called a keyword parameter, and &FROM and &TO are positional parameters that derive their values when the macro is invoked as shown in the following example.

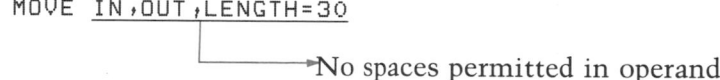

The value of IN would be equated to &FROM; the value of OUT would be equated to &TO; &LENGTH would be assigned a value of 30.

The ampersand (&) is omitted when the macro is invoked or called. LENGTH is used to specify the length of the move, not &LENGTH. Thus, when keyword parameters are used by a macro, the ampersand (&) is *always* omitted when calling the macro.

Keyword parameters do not necessarily have to be specified in the source (calling) program. In this instance, the keyword parameter defaults to whatever value was set up in the prototype statement. If no value was specified in the prototype statement for &LENGTH, the system would substitute a null value.

However, if you had decided to restrict the use of the MOVE macro to simply moving error messages in the program, and the shortest error message contained 10 bytes, then the default option for the length of the move could be established for 10 bytes. An example follows.

Source Program

```
MACRO                                    :
MOVE &FROM,&TO,&LENGTH=10        MOVE IN,OUT
  :                                      :
  :
MEND
```

In this example, if the keyword parameter LENGTH is omitted when the MOVE macro is referenced, by *default* a value of 10 will be assigned to LENGTH. However, remember that when the LENGTH is included, the specified value is substituted for the keyword parameter.

It is important to note that although both positional and keyword parameters may be used in a single prototype statement, the positional operands must appear *first*, followed by the keyword operands.

III. LOCAL AND GLOBAL SET SYMBOLS

A. Assigning Values to Macro Variables

The symbolic variables used in macros are assigned values in two ways. First, the macro prototype statement specifies a list of variables that are assigned values when the macro is called. For example,

```
MACRO
RXADD     &RX1,&RX2
  :
```

The symbolic variables &RX1 and &RX2 are replaced with the parameter list in the source statement. The second means of assigning values is by using SET *instructions*, which can be used to define all other variables found in the macro. Basically, there are three different types of SET variables used by the programmer.

Name	Op Code	Operand
variable symbol	SETA	Arithmetic expression
.	SETB	Boolean expression
.	SETC	Character string

Example 19.2

	Op Code	Operand	Meaning
&W	SETA	&W+4	4 is added to the current value of &W
&A	SETB	&V EQ &Z	&A will have the *binary value* 1 if &V = &Z, and the value 0 if &V ≠ &Z
&Q	SETC	'ABC'	&Q will contain the value ABC

However, before SET instructions can be used, the variable symbols defined in the name field of the SET must be declared with local directives (LCL) or global directives (GBL). Local SET symbols only affect the macro in which they are used. Each time a **local directive** (LCL) is declared at the beginning of the macro, the variables named are initialized as shown in the following display.

	Type	*Initial Value of Variable Symbol (Prior to* SET *)*
Arithmetic (SETA)		0
Boolean (SETB)		0
Character (SETC)		0

The LCL directive must precede the SET. In general, LCLx is used for initializing values for SETx. That is, LCLA initializes variables for SETA, LCLB initializes variables for SETB, and LCLC initializes variables for SETC.

Op Code	*Operand*	*Meaning*
LCLA	&A ,&B	Local arithmetic variables &A and &B are initialized to 0.
LCLB	&C	Local Boolean variable &C is set to 0.
LCLC	&D ,&E ,&F	Local character variables &D, &E, and &F are set to length of 0.

It is possible for a macro to invoke or access another macro. In such a case, we would want to have *common variables* that retain their value when passed from one macro to another. To pass data from one macro to another, we use the **global directive** (GBL) in place of the local directive LCL. The format of the global directives follows.

GBLA &G	Global arithmetic variable &G is set to 0.
GBLB &H ,&J	Global Boolean variables &H and &J are initialized at zero.
GBLC &K	Global character variable &K is given an initial null value.

Local LCL and global GBL directives immediately follow the prototype statement in the macro.

The choice of SETA, SETB, and SETC must be consistent with the initial declarations of the variables in the LCL / GBL statements. For example, a variable specified in a LCLA instruction can only be altered using the SETA directive, as illustrated in the following example.

```
        MACRO
        EQREG
        LCLA &X
         .
         .
&X      SETA &X+1
```

B. The SETA Directive

SETA directives are used to perform arithmetic operations with variable symbols. The result of these calculations is always an integer, without leading zeros or a sign. The value zero is converted to a single 0. The expression is evaluated in the same manner as expressions found in BASIC and FORTRAN. The arithmetic operators include the *, /, +, and - sign to denote multiplication, division, addition, and subtraction, respectively. Multiplication and division are performed before addition and subtraction. If there is more than one operation of the same level, the arithmetic is performed from left to right. Parentheses are used to alter the order in which the expression is evaluated. To illustrate, let &X = 12.

	Name	*Op Code*	*Operand*	*Meaning*
THEN	&Y	SETA	&X*10-15	&Y = 105
	&Z	SETA	&Y/10	&Z = 10
	&R	SETA	&R+1	&R = 1

Recall that SETA variables are initialized to zero and that integer arithmetic calculations result in truncation.

C. The SETB Directive

SETB symbols can have only two possible values: 0 or 1. The assembler performs the logical evaluation. If the expression proves true, a value of 1 is assigned to the parameter; if the statement is false a value of 0 is assigned to the parameter. To relate expressions, Boolean expressions may contain the logical operators EQ, NE, GT, LT, GE, LE, AND, as well as OR. The expressions may be either arithmetic or character as shown in the following example. The expressions are always enclosed in parentheses and the operators are always preceded by and followed by a blank.

Example 19.3

Let &N = *10*   &LEN = *'ABC'*

```
&A      SETB    (&N LT 100)                          &A = 1
&B      SETB    ('&LEN' EQ ' ')                      &B = 0
&C      SETB    ((&N GT 5) AND ('&LEN' EQ 'ABC'))    &C = 1
&D      SETB    ((&N EQ 5) OR ('&LEN' NE 'ABC'))     &D = 0
```

D. The SETC Directive

You may assign a character string to a symbolic variable using literals enclosed in quotes. The character string may be up to 255 characters. However, the initial value of the string may consist of no characters or a null value when none are specified. The instruction,

```
&CORP    SETC    'ALDEN RESEARCH'
```

assigns the 14-byte character string 'ALDEN RESEARCH' to the symbolic variable &CORP. Therefore, every time the symbolic variable &CORP is encountered in the macro, the character string will be substituted. The character string can also be changed by providing another SETC instruction. If Alden Research decided to change its name, for instance, you could modify the macro by changing the SETC instruction, as follows.

```
&CORP    SETC    'GLOBAL INFO SYSTEMS'
```

This would prove useful if macros were used to print business headings on reports or if different headings were sometimes necessary.

If a macro is included in a source program, it must be defined before the first CSECT or START command in the corresponding module. If the macro is in a separate library, the file in which it appears must be specified in a job control statement.

Example 19.4

```
         MACRO
         HEADR
         GBLC    &CORP,&D,&C
         GBLA    &PAGE
&PAGE SETA    &PAGE+1
&CORP SETC    'ALDEN RESEARCH'
&D    SETC    'TODAY IS &SYSDATE'
&T    SETC    'TIME IS SYSTIME'
         TITLE   'PAGE&PAGE &CORP &D&T'
         MEND
           .
           .
           .
NEWPG MVC     LINEOUT,SPACES
         HEADR
```

Self-Evaluating Quiz

1. Macro definitions may be included in the _____ or the _____ .
2. Macros always begin with a(n) _____ instruction and terminate with a(n) _____ .

3. The macro name is assigned by the _____ instruction, which always follows the _____ instruction.
4. Identify the invalid macro variable names and the reason they are invalid.
   a. &V
   b. NOGO
   c. &7UP
   d. $VAR
   e. &TOOLONG
   f. &SYMP
5. A macro named SWITCH is called with the statement SWITCH A,TEMP. The variables A and TEMP are called _____ .
6. The prototype for a macro named SWITCH appears as SWITCH &A,&B. If the macro was invoked by SWITCH A,TEMP, then the value contained in _____ would be substituted for &B.
7. The source statement ASDCB EODAD=EOF calls a macro and also specifies a(n) _____ parameter.
8. In the following prototype statement, ASDCB &EODAD=EOF, if the keyword parameter is not specified, then the default for this parameter is _____ .
9. When specifying keyword parameters in a "call instruction," the _____ is omitted or eliminated.
10. When values are to be passed from one macro to another, then a (local/global) directive would be used.
11. The SETA and SETC directives are used for _____ and _____ , respectively.
12. Identify the invalid prototype instructions.
    a. DOIT &A,&B
    b. TRYIT &X,Y=
    c. AGAIN &A, &B, &C
    d. FLIP &X=,&Y,&Z
    e. REF ENDIT &LAST

SOLUTIONS
1. Macro or system library; source program
2. MACRO; MEND
3. Prototype; macro
4. a. Valid
   b. Must begin with &
   c. Second character must be a letter.
   d. Must begin with &
   e. More than 8 characters
   f. Valid
5. Positional parameters
6. TEMP
7. KEYWORD
8. EOF
9. Ampersand (&)
10. Global
11. Arithmetic operations with variable symbols; assign character strings to variable symbols.
12. a. Valid
    b. Y is invalid: must be &Y
    c. Spaces not permitted in operand.
    d. Positional parameters must precede keyword parameters.
    e. Valid: REF is simply a label.

IV. CONDITIONAL ASSEMBLY INSTRUCTIONS

Conditional assembly instructions enable the sequence of instructions in a source program to be altered. They enable the assembler to branch and loop in macros. We will consider the most common of these.

A. Example Using the Equate Register Macro

The EQU assembler directive is frequently used to equate or associate a fixed value with a symbol. You will see that special assembler directives are used within macros. At many installations, it is standard practice to equate the symbolic names R0-R15 to the general registers 0–15. The macro named EQREG is designed to meet this need. The flowchart depicted in Figure 19.3 illustrates conditional branching, using the assembler IF (AIF), as well as the incrementing of the counter (&X). An assembler ANOP performs no operation—it is used to establish an entry point called .DO16X. The logical flow of the macro is best understood by examining the flowchart.

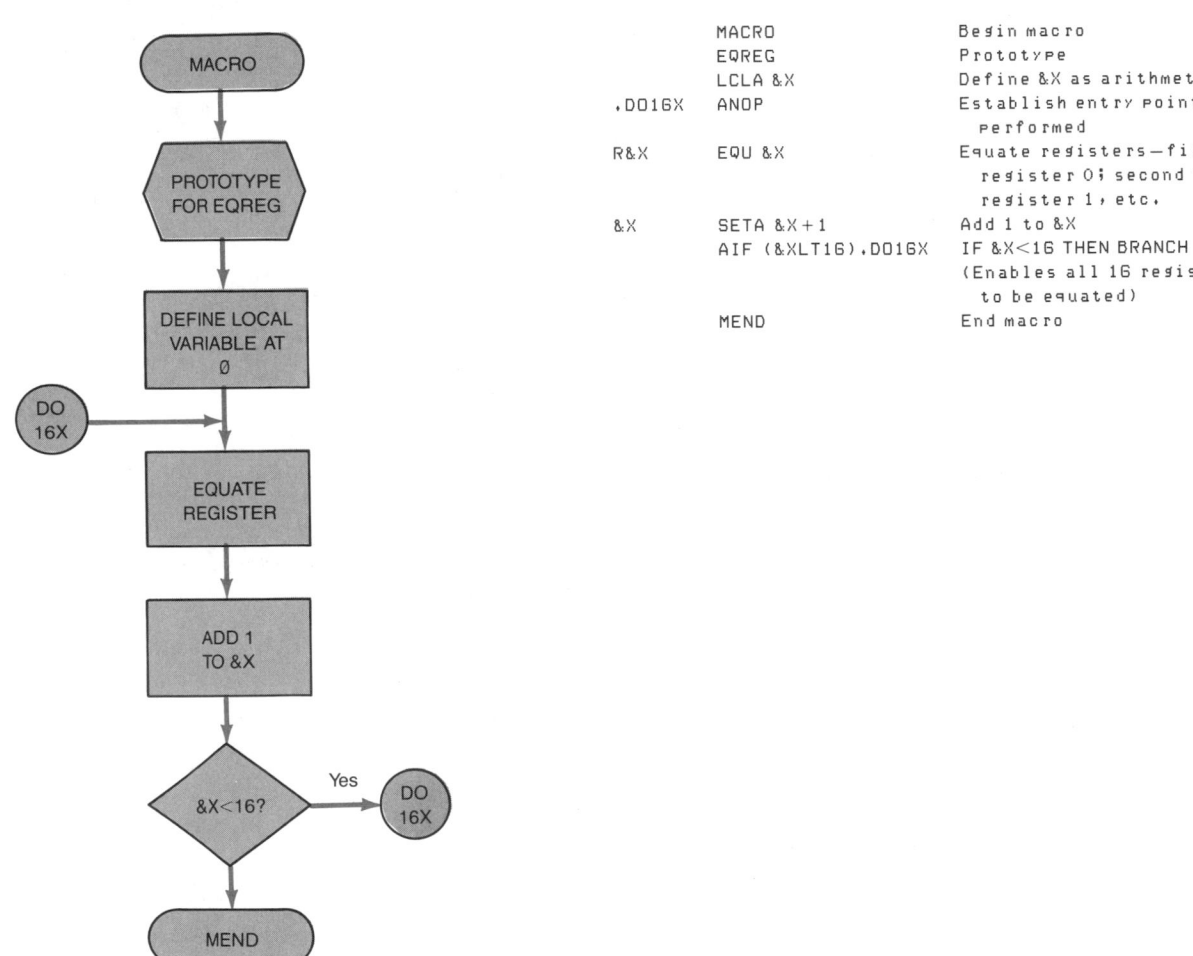

```
               MACRO               Begin macro
               EQREG               Prototype
               LCLA &X             Define &X as arithmetic (value 0)
      .DO16X   ANOP                Establish entry point—no operation
                                     performed
      R&X      EQU &X              Equate registers—first time R0=
                                     register 0; second time R1=
                                     register 1, etc.
      &X       SETA &X+1           Add 1 to &X
               AIF (&XLT16).DO16X  IF &X<16 THEN BRANCH TO .DO16X—
                                     (Enables all 16 registers (0-15)
                                     to be equated)
               MEND                End macro
```

Figure 19.3
The EQREG macro.

The EQREG macro generates the 16 consecutive EQU instructions necessary to equate the registers 0–15. The variable &X is initialized by the assembler to zero when the macro is executed. The loop in the macro will be performed 16 times. However, once register 15 is equated, the counter (&X) is incremented to 16, and the AIF will not branch back to the label .DO16X because the expression is no longer true. As a result, the next instruction in the sequence will be executed thereby ending the macro. To further assist your understanding of the EQREG macro, examine the following table.

Macro Vocabulary Summary

Op Code Entries Beginning in Position 10	Meaning in the Macro
MACRO	Begin the macro definition
MEND	Define the end of the macro
Additional op codes include:	
MEXIT	Terminates processing; has the same meaning as GO TO MEND
MNOTE	Used to generate messages in the assembler listing
ANOP	Establishes entry points (macro labels) in the body of the macro; indicates no operation and is similar to EQU *, which labels the next instruction
AGO	Unconditional branch or the GO TO type of instruction
AIF	Conditional branch; typically, the IF–THEN type of instruction

Name Field Entries Beginning in Position 1	Meaning in the Macro
.LABEL	Defines an entry point in the macro to be referenced when branching
.*	Used for comments and macro documentation; these statements will not appear in the source listing
*	These comments will be printed on the source listing and may be used to issue warnings or errors

B. AIF and AGO **Macro Instructions**

The conditional (AIF) and unconditional (AGO) branching instructions necessitate entry points to be established in the macro. These macro labels (or sequence symbols as they are sometimes called) must be unique and may be coded as follows.

RULES FOR MACRO LABELS

1. Column 1 must contain a period.
2. Column 2 must contain a letter (A–Z).
3. Up to 8 characters permitted.
4. Columns 3–8 may contain letters and digits.

The conditional branch AGO functions as a simple GO TO instruction and branches to the label or name field specified in the operand. The following examples will assist you in correctly coding the AGO instruction.

Valid			*Invalid*			*Reason*
.LABEL	AGO	.NEXT	.HERE	AGO	.HERE	Cannot branch to itself
	AGO	.JAIL		AGO	.7UP	Invalid label
	AGO	.B9		GOTO	.WHERE	Invalid op code
.ONE	AGO	.TWO		AGO	JAIL	Invalid label

AIF, or conditional branches, are executed in the same manner as those found in high-level languages. Typically, if the expression enclosed in parentheses is true, then the branch is executed. However, if the expression is false, then the next sequential instruction in the macro is performed. The arithmetic/logical operators follow.

```
                    ARITHMETIC/LOGICAL OPERATORS USED
                           IN AIF INSTRUCTIONS
      NE    not equal         LE      less than or equal to
      EQ    equal             GE      greater than or equal to
      LT    less than         GT      greater than
      AND   logical and       AND NOT logical and not
      OR    logical or        OR NOT  logical or not
```

The arithmetic/logical operators may be used in AIF instructions as shown in the following examples. Note that the operators are always preceded by and followed by a blank. This is unusual because blanks are not normally permitted in operands.

	Source Statement	*Meaning*

Example 19.5	Arithmetic AIF
	`AIF   (&STATE EQ 50).ENDIT`
	`AGO   .AGAIN`
		If &STATE = 50, then branch to .ENDIT; else go to .AGAIN

Example 19.6	Character String AIF `AIF   ('&CHAR' NE 'BIG APPLE').ISLES`	If the string contained in &CHAR is not equal to 'BIG APPLE' then branch to the instruction labeled .ISLES
Example 19.7	Logical And `AIF ((&STATE EQ 43) AND (&TAX LT 500)).JAIL`	If both conditions are true, branch to .JAIL
Example 19.8	Logical Or `AIF ((&AGE GT 50) OR ('NAME' EQ 'VENUS')).MOON`	If either condition is true, branch to .MOON

The programming of conditional and unconditional branches, loops, and so on appears very similar to programming in a high-level language. In fact, macros can be in a program in a manner similar to subroutines. Note the instructions generated by the following EQREG macro.

```
15              EQREG
16+R0           EQU     0
17+R1           EQU     1
18+R2           EQU     2
19+R3           EQU     3
20+R4           EQU     4
21+R5           EQU     5
22+R6           EQU     6
23+R7           EQU     7
24+R8           EQU     8
25+R9           EQU     9
26+R10          EQU     10
27+R11          EQU     11
28+R12          EQU     12
29+R13          EQU     13
30+R14          EQU     14
31+R15          EQU     15
```

Self-Evaluating Quiz

1. The _____ instruction represents the macro conditional branch.
2. The unconditional branch in a macro is coded as a(n) _____ operation.
3. Entry points in macro must begin with a(n) _____ .
4. (T or F) When a warning or error message is to be printed in the source program, the programmer may specify an MNOTE or a statement beginning with an *.
5. Identify the arithmetic/logical operations that may be used in a macro.
6. A global variable called &X is used as a counter in a program. Code the global and SET instructions to initialize &X to 1.
7. A local variable named &CHAR is to contain the character string ***ERROR***. Code the local and SET instructions.
8. Compare a macro variable named &STG to the character string 'BOSSY' and if an equal condition results, branch to the entry point .SCORE.

SOLUTIONS

1. AIF
2. AGO
3. Period (.)
4. T
5. LT GT EQ NE GE LE
   AND OR AND NOT OR NOT
6.   GBLA &X
   &X SETA &X+1
7.   LCLC &CHAR
   &CHAR SETC '***ERROR***'
8. AIF ('&STG' EQ 'BOSSY').SCORE

V. CONCATENATION

A character expression may consist of a character string or a combination of two or more strings. Combining two or more strings is called **concatenation.** For example,

If &TYPE = 'R'	then C&TYPE = 'CR'
If &TYPE = 'H'	then C&TYPE = 'CH'
If &TYPE = 'L'	then &TYPE.R = 'LR'

In the first example, the value R is added to C producing CR.

The period in the last example serves as a delimiter or separator. Whenever a symbolic variable appears *before* other characters that are to be concatenated, a period *must* be used to separate the variable name from the remaining characters. The following examples will further clarify concatenation. The contents of the symbolic variables are as follows.

| &DATE = '04/17/86' | 8–byte character string |
| &STRG = '**RUN DATE**' | 12–byte character string |

Expression	Concatenated String	Meaning
&DATE.&STRG	'04/17/86**RUN DATE**'	Character strings are substituted
&DATE&STRG	'04/17/86**RUN DATE**'	Period may be omitted when two or more symbolic variables are used
&DATE &STRG	'04/17/86 **RUN DATE**'	Embedded blank in the expression appears in string

```
&DATE.(XYZ)        '04/17/86(XYZ)'
```
A period *must* be included in this case; without it the other symbols (XYZ) would be considered part of the variable &DATE

```
(XYZ)&STRG         '(XYZ)**RUN DATE**'
```
Character strings are substituted again

The variables used for concatenation may also be Boolean and/or arithmetic variables. Boolean variables have the value "1" or "0" whereas arithmetic variables are represented numerically as integers with the leading zeros and signs removed. In the following examples, let the following values apply.

```
&B = 1             Boolean Variable
&N = 1234          Arithmetic Variable
&C = STRING        Character Variable
```

Expression	*Concatenated String*	*Meaning*
&C&B	STRING1	The value of each variable is replaced with the respective strings
&C&N	STRING1234	Simple substitution is performed
&B&C&N	1STRING1234	Simple substitution is performed
&C..&N	STRING.1234	The first period separates the variables; the second period is actually included in the string
&N + 3	1234 + 3	The result is a concatenated value; an arithmetic operation is *not* performed
&C + 3	STRING + 3	Embedded blanks may appear in the string

A. RXMVE **Macro**

The RXMVE macro is designed to move a fullword of data from one storage position to another. The contents of register 5 are saved and restored at the completion of the move. The calling instruction used by the source program to execute the macro would appear as

```
GO   RXMVE   A,B
```

where GO is the label, RXMVE is the macro name, and A and B are positional parameters.

			Macro Expansion (in library or
	MACRO		*prior to CSECT)*
&REF	RXMVE	&TO,&FROM	
	LCLC	&PREFIX	
&PREFIX	SETC	'FWORD'	
&REF	ST	5,SAVEAREA	GO ST 5,SAVEAREA
	L	5,PREFIX&FROM	L 5,FWORDB
	ST	5,&PREFIX&TO	ST 5,FWORDA
	L	5,SAVEAREA	L 5,SAVEAREA
	MEND		

Note in this example, the SETC instruction assigns the character string 'FWORD' to the symbolic variable &PREFIX. Therefore, &PREFIX is replaced with the string 'FWORD'. &FROM and &TO are also replaced with A and B and generate FWORDA and FWORDB in the second operand of the Load and Store instructions.

B. MOVE **Macro**

The flowchart in Figure 19.4 depicts the logic used to develop a storage-to-storage MOVE macro. If the length is specified, an explicit move will be performed. However, if the length parameter is omitted, then an implicit move will occur.

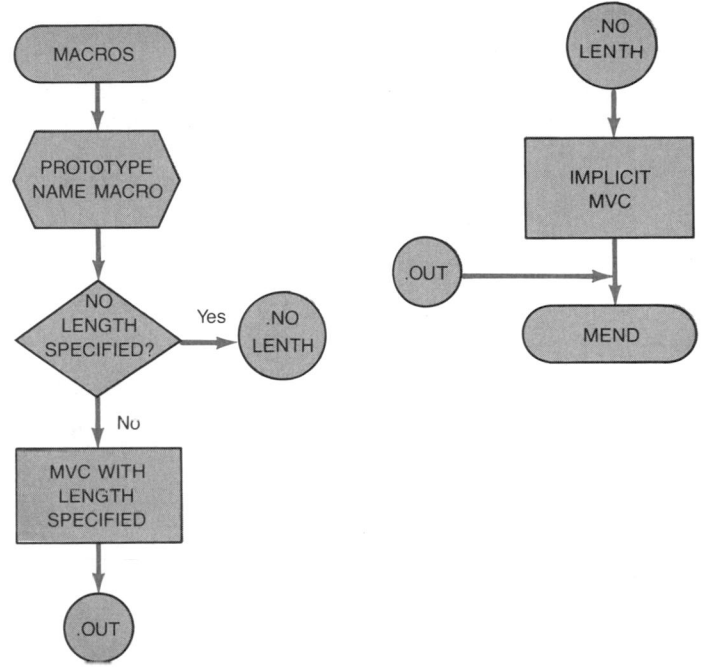

Figure 19.4
Logic used in developing a storage-to-storage MOVE macro.

```
          MACRO
          MOVE    &FROM,&TO,&LENGTH
.*
.* NOTE: IF LENGTH IS NOT SPECIFIED, THEN A NULL VALUE RESULTS
.*
          AIF    ('&LENGTH' EQ '').NOLENTH
          MVC    &TO.(&LENGTH),&FROM             EXPLICIT MOVE
          AGO    .OUT
.*
.* NOTE: IMPLICIT MOVE ROUTINE
.*
.NOLENTH ANOP                           ENTRY POINT
          MVC &TO,&FROM
.OUT      ANOP
          MEND
```

Note the period in the operand of the explicit move instruction. To correctly concatenate the characters in the operand, this period must be present. In addition, the two apostrophes, '', in the AIF statement test for a null condition, the result of omitting any specification for the LENGTH parameter. Also note that .* comments will not appear in the macro expansion. However, if the * is placed in position one, then the comment will appear in the macro.

VI. LOCAL SYSTEM SYMBOLIC VARIABLES

The three local system symbolic variables are &SYSND, &SYSLIST, and &SYSECT. Only &SYSNDX, the most widely used system variable, will be discussed in this section. The &SYSNDX symbol may not be declared in GBL or LCL instructions, nor may &SYSNDX be referenced with a SETA instruction. Furthermore, the SYSNDX directive must always appear in a macro when the macro is used more than once. It is typically used in the following manner.

Suppose a macro defined a storage area called SAVE and the macro was executed only once. Only one definition of SAVE would exist and we would not encounter any problems. However, if the macro were executed several times, then several definitions of the area called SAVE would be generated and, as a consequence, program errors would occur. The same problem is encountered with labels, because duplicate labels are not permitted in an assembler program.

The &SYSNDX command automatically numbers variables, labels, etc., each time the macro is called. The system macro &SYSNDX generates a 4-digit sequence number in the form 0001–9999 that is usually concatenated to other characters, thereby creating unique variable names and/or labels. For example, if a macro were to contain N&SYSNDX, then the first time the macro was executed the assembler would generate the string N0001. Each time the macro is executed, the &SYSNDX number or value is incremented by one. The following sample macro will assist in clarifying this point.

Example 19.9

```
          MACRO
          MAKE
          STM     R12,R13,N&SYSNDX
            :
            :
N&SYSNDX  DS      2F
          MEND
```

The macro MAKE is referenced anywhere in the program by the instruction

```
MAKE
```

The 10th time this macro is processed, the following code will be generated.

```
      STM   R12,R13,N0010
        :
        :
N10   DS    2F
```

Consequently, each execution of MAKE results in *different* labels so that there are no confusions. N&SYSNDX is necessary only if MAKE is executed more than once in the program.

The objective of the next example is to develop an automatic looping procedure similar to the DO, FOR/NEXT or PERFORM found in high-level languages. For the sake of simplicity, we will perform the loop a fixed number of times and the number of passes will be specified by a keyword parameter. In actuality, two macros are required—one to begin the loop and another to establish the end of the loop. The following illustration depicts an overview of the DOIT/ENDIT looping sequence.

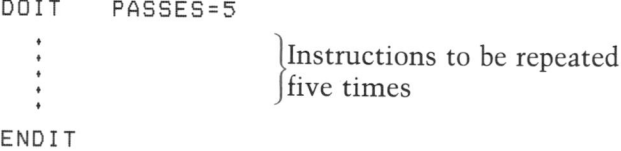

```
      DOIT    PASSES=5
        :                      ⎫Instructions to be repeated
        :                      ⎬five times
        :                      ⎭
      ENDIT
```

The GBL directive also provides for the passing of values from one macro to another. The branch on index high (BXH) instruction provides the control of the loop. The following example provides a brief review of this instruction.

Example 19.10

```
BXH  3,4,NEXT
```

REG3   Contents are incremented by the contents of REG4 and compared to the limit contained in REG5. If the result of the compare is high, then a branch to NEXT occurs that ends the loop. Otherwise, looping is continued.

REG4   Contains the increment 1 in this example.
REG5   Implied; contains the limit or number of passes to be performed.
NEXT   The label to which the BXH branches to terminate the loop.

The flowchart in Figure 19.5 depicts the logic used by the DOIT/ENDIT macro pair.

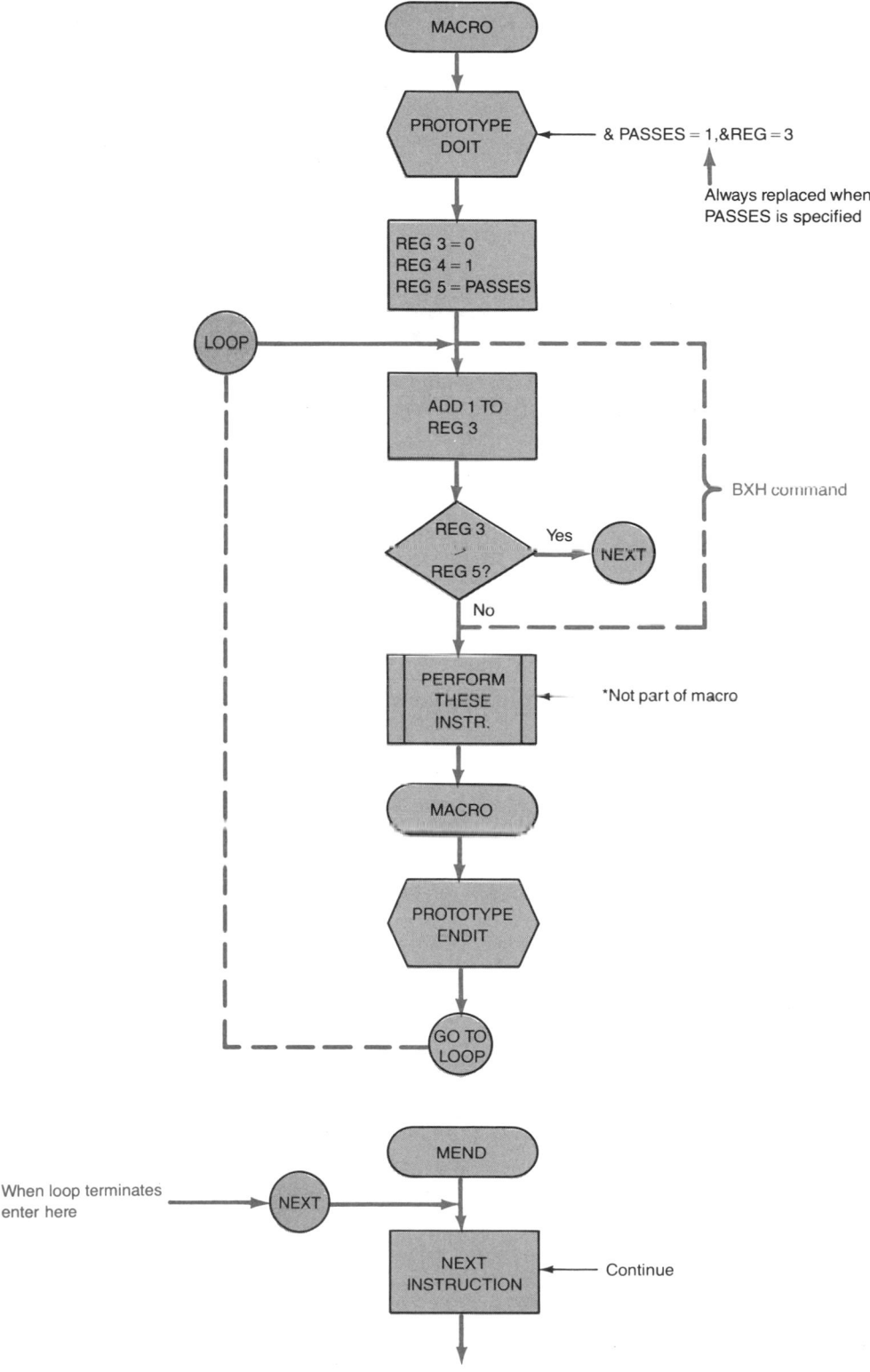

Figure 19.5
Logic used by the sample macros DOIT and ENDIT.

The macro may be called or executed using the following commands.

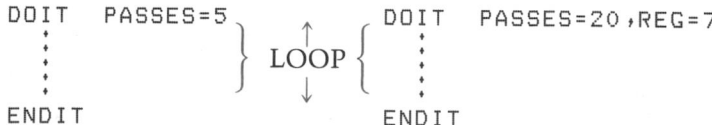

The macro is coded as shown in Figure 19.6. Note in particular that the keyword variable &REG=3 in the macro prototype statement provides a default option. When REG is not specified in the call statement, then registers 3, 4, and 5 are used to control the BXH. However, by coding REG=7 in the macro call (recall the & is always omitted), the use of registers 7, 8, and 9 would be invoked instead of 3, 4, and 5.

```
            MACRO
&REF        DOIT    &PASSES=1,&REG=3
            GBLC    &LOOP,&NEXT
&LOOP       SETC    'L&SYSNDX'
&NEXT       SETC    'N&SYSNDX'
&REF        LA      &REG,0              SET TO ZERO
            LA      &REG+1,1           INCREMENT BY ONE
            L       &REG+2,=A(&PASSES)  SET NUMBER OF PASSES
.***
.***  A TYPE CONSTANTS ARE USED IN PLACE OF F-TYPE CONSTANTS.
.***  FOR EXAMPLE, A(10) WILL GENERATE THE SAME VALUES AS F'10'.
.***  HOWEVER, EXPRESSIONS MAY BE ENCLOSED WITHIN THE PARENTEHESES
.***  THEREBY EXTENDING MACRO FLEXIBILITY.
.***
&LOOP       BXH     &REG,&REG+1,&NEXT
.***
.***     LOOP UNTIL LIMIT IS REACHED AND THEN TRANSFER OUT
.***
            MEND
```

Figure 19.6
Coding of the DOIT and ENDIT macros.

```
            MACRO
            ENDIT
            GBLC    &LOOP,&NEXT
            B       &LOOP              GO TO DOIT-BXH-STATEMENT.
&NEXT       DS      0H                 TAG NEXT INSTRUCTION
            MEND
```

The label &LOOP will be replaced by L0001 the first time the DOIT/ENDIT macro pair is expanded. Similarly, &NEXT is replaced by N0002. Each time the &SYSNDX is encountered, the system increments the number associated with the system variable. Consequently, it generates unique labels regardless of how many times the macro is executed. Recall that in this way there are no duplicate labels to cause program errors.

In addition to being replaced by character strings, the &LOOP and &NEXT labels are also specified as global GBLs. This allows the values of &LOOP and &NEXT to be made available to both macros.

The ENDIT macro functions as an unconditional GO TO and transfers control to the BXH instruction in the DOIT macro. The ENDIT macro also contains &NEXT DS 0H. Remember that when a field is subdivided, the next instruction is assigned the same address. Hence, the branch from the BXH instruction at the completion of the loop passes control to the NEXT instruction, namely the instruction immediately following ENDIT.

In summary, subroutines and macros appear functionally to accomplish the same tasks. Both enable certain sequences of instructions to be used more than once throughout the development of assembler programs. Subroutines may be either open—included in the program, or closed—meaning that the subroutine resides on an external device such as a disk. The open subroutine more closely resembles the macro because the actual expansion of instructions takes place at assembler time and the expanded code is inserted into the source module. The subroutine, however, is invoked at execution time and requires a transfer of control from the source program to the subroutine as well as a return. This exit and return from the source program requires control linkages to be established, and measures to be taken to pass parameters. With macros these problems are avoided because the expansion of the macro is included in the source program.

VII. ADVANCED CONDITIONAL ASSEMBLIES

Parameter Sublists   Positional and keyword parameters can be referenced by specifying a *parameter sublist.* A sublist is one or more entries separated by commas and *enclosed in parentheses* within the macro calling statement. Each element in the sublist is referenced in the macro as a subscript. For example, if a macro named ADDFW (Figure 19.7) was used to accumulate a variable number of fullword integers, the fields to be added could be passed to the macro as a parameter sublist, as follows.

| *Macro Call* | *Macro Definition* |

```
ADDFW   (WORD1,WORD2,WORD3),.....        MACRO
                                         ADDFW     &ARG,.....
                                            :
                                            :
```

The ADDFW macro will equate the sublist with the variable &ARG in the following way.

```
&ARG(1)  = WORD1
&ARG(2)  = WORD2
&ARG(3)  = WORD3
```

```
          MACRO
&LABEL    ADDFW    &ARG,&RESULT,&SAVE
          LCLA     &NUMBER
&NUMBER   SETA     1
          AIF      (T'&SAVE EQ 'O').SKIP1
&LABEL    ST       5,&SAVE                    SAVE CONTENTS OF
          L        5,&ARG(1)                  REGISTER 5
          AGO      .LOOP
.SKIP1    ANOP
&LABEL    L        5,&ARG1
.LOOP     AIF      (&NUMBER GE N'&ARG).OUT    SUBLIST FINISHED?
&NUMBER   SETA     &NUMBER+1
          A        5,&ARG(&NUMBER)            ADD NEXT FULLWORD
          AGO      .LOOP
.OUT      ST       5,&RESULT                  SAVE TOTAL
          AIF      (T'&SAVE EQ 'O').SKIP2
          L        5,&SAVE                    RESTORE REG. 5
.SKIP2    ANOP
          MEND
```

Figure 19.7
Macro designed to accumulate a variable number of fullword integers.

Hence, subscript 1 is used to reference the first item in the sublist, subscript 2 references the second item, and so on. Therefore, statements in the macro can refer to items in the sublist by means of subscripts. The ability to pass a *variable number* of arguments to a macro is a powerful tool when used for conditional assemblies.

Attributes   For each assembler instruction, constant, or area, the assembler assigns attributes such as field length, type of data (packed data or character data), and so on. By specifying attributes in conditional assembly instructions, you will be better able to establish more sophisticated logic and control of the instructions generated by the macro. The attributes and their main purpose are shown in the following table.

Attribute Summary

Attribute	Purpose	Main Uses
Number	Gives the number of sublist entries in a macro-instruction operand sublist	For scanning sublists; as a counter to test for end of sublist
Type	Provides a letter that identifies the type of data	In macros, to find missing operand; differentiate between data types; for value substitution
Count	Gives the number of characters in a macro-instruction operand	Scanning of character strings; indexes in substring notation
Scaling	Locates decimal point in fixed- and floating-point constants	Testing decimal point position; substitution into scale modifier
Integer	A function of the length and scaling attributes of decimal fixed- and floating-point constants	Keeps track of significant integer digits
Length	Gives number of bytes occupied by data in storage	For substitution into length fields; to calculate storage requirements

The following attributes are utilized by the ADDFW macro.

Type Attribute The type attribute refers to the type of instruction, DS, DC, or data definition. The type attribute has the value of a single letter that indicates the type of data represented. Several types are included in the following list.

Type Attributes

A	A-type address	G	Fixed-point	S	S-type address
B	Binary	H	Halfword	V	V-type address
C	Character	I	Machine instruction	W	CCW instruction
D	Long float	M	Macro instruction	X	Hexadecimal
E	Short float	O	Operand omitted	Y	Y-type address
F	Fullword	P	Packed-decimal	Z	Zoned-decimal

The type attribute can be referenced using SET and AIF instructions. To reference the type attribute of the variable &ARG, we code T'&ARG.

Note in the ADDFW macro the type attribute is used to determine if a positional parameter was specified for &SAVE. If this parameter was omitted, then the AIF test for the letter O would be true and a branch to .SKIP would occur.

Number Attribute The number attribute refers to the number of entries in a macro parameter sublist. Again referring to the macro ADDFW, we find reference to N'&ARG—the number of fullwords to be accumulated in register 5.

The looping procedure to add each fullword specified in the sublist is controlled by the counter (N'&ARG). Hence, if the macro call appeared as

```
EXAMPLE1 ADDFW (WORD1,WORD2,WORD3),SUM
```

then N'&ARG would have the value 3, meaning the sublist contains three arguments.

Conditional Assembly Using Attributes The macro in Figure 19.7 is designed to add or accumulate a variable number of fullwords and store the resulting sum in a specified area. Register 5 is used by the macro to accumulate the sum. If it is necessary to save the contents of register 5, a save area is specified in the macro call statement as shown below in Example 2.

In Example 1, the optional save area is not specified, and the original contents of register 5 will not be restored. The macro will add three fullwords and store the result in SUM. The macro call statement

```
EXAMPLE1 ADDFW (WORD1,WORD2,WORD3),SUM
```

would generate the following code:

```
EXAMPLE1 L    5,WORD1
         A    5,WORD2
         A    5,WORD3
         ST   5,SUM
```

Example 2, however, will utilize a save area so that register 5 will be restored with its original contents. The specified save area (HOLD) must be defined as a fullword in the program using a Define Storage (DS) instruction. The macro call statement

```
EXAMPLE2 ADDFW (WORD1,WORD2,WORD3),SUM,HOLD
```

would generate the following code:

```
EXAMPLE2 ST   5,HOLD
         L    5,WORD1
         A    5,WORD2
         A    5,WORD3
         ST   5,SUM
         L    5,HOLD
```

Again, note that by including the third positional parameter, HOLD, the contents of register 5 were restored to its original contents.

CHAPTER SUMMARY

    I. A macro is an operation code that provides assembler language with a high-level language capability—namely, a single programmed instruction generates numerous machine-language instructions.

   II. Although a macro is written once, it may be used to generate a desired set of instructions as many times as needed in the source program.

 III. Macro definitions may be stored in the macro library or included in the source program. However, if a macro is cataloged in a library, it may be accessed by many users.

 IV. The four basic components of a macro include:

MACRO	Beginning of macro
PROTOTYPE	Names macro and identifies parameters
BODY	Macro instructions to be executed
MEND	End of macro

  V. Parameters: Passing data to a macro

POSITIONAL	Symbolic variable names are replaced according to their relative positions in a list.
KEYWORD	Symbolic variable names are replaced according to specified keywords. When called, the ampersand (&) is omitted in the symbolic name. If the keyword is omitted, the default option is substituted.

 VI. Types of symbolic variables

LOCAL	Definition is restricted to the macro where it is defined
GLOBAL	Used when data is to be passed between macros

VII. Variable names referenced by SET symbols must be previously defined as Local or Global.

SETA   Arithmetic
SETB   Boolean
SETC   Character

VIII. Macro labels
  A. begin with a period (.) and are followed by a letter
  B. have remaining characters, if desired, that are letters or digits
  C. contain up to 8 characters
IX. Macro variables
  A. begin with an ampersand (&) and are followed by a letter
  B. have remaining characters that are letters or digits
  C. contain up to 8 characters
X. Branching instructions

AGO   Unconditional branch
AIF   Conditional branch

XI. Comments

.*   Comment not found in expansion
*   Comment appears in expansion

XII. Character strings may be combined using a technique called concatenation
XIII. The local symbolic variable, &SYSNDX, is used to define storage areas and labels. A 4-digit integer is concatenated to a variable to produce unique definitions. The variable is automatically updated by the system.

CHAPTER SELF-EVALUATING QUIZ

1. How does a macro definition differ from a macro call?
2. In assembler what is the difference between an AGO and a B instruction?
3. Define the four major components of a macro.
4. The _____ command automatically numbers variables and storage areas.
5. Conditional and unconditional branching is accomplished with the _____ and _____ macro instructions.
6. What is the problem with defining storage areas from within a macro?
7. In the DOIT macro in Figure 19.6, why doesn't the label identified &LOOP begin with a period?

SOLUTIONS

Page

1. The macro definition defines a set of macro instructions that are executed each time the macro is called. The calling of a macro is analogous to the calling of a subroutine.   525

2. The B instruction is an unconditional branch in assembler. The AGO is also unconditional, but its use is limited to macros.   533

3. MACRO; prototype; body; MEND   525

4. SYSNDX   538

5. AIF; AGO   533

6. Duplication; this is the reason the SYSNDX is used.   538

7. Because the macro DOIT may be executed many times, the address is set up as a variable. The variable &LOOP changes each time the macro is called.   526

PRACTICE PROGRAM

The program in Figure 19.8 incorporates the use of the macros developed in this chapter. The purpose of the program is to produce a mailing list by printing each record three times. Figure 19.9 illustrates sample data. Sample output is shown in Figure 19.10.

The macros ASLNK and ASDCB shown in Figure 19.11 provide for the housekeeping routines and utilize the concepts presented in Chapter 4.

```
LOC   OBJECT CODE       ADDR1 ADDR2  STMT    SOURCE STATEMENT

                                      3  ***********************************************************
                                      4  *   THIS OS PROGRAM UTILIZES THE MACROS DEVELOPED IN CHAPTER 19.   *
                                      5  *   THE ASLNK MACRO AND ASDCB MACROS ARE LISTED BELOW. NOTE THAT   *
                                      6  *   ASA CONTROL CHARACTERS ARE USED FOR CARRIAGE CONTROL. ALSO     *
                                      7  *   THE PROGRAM REFERENCES THE CURRENT GREGORIAN DATE.             *
                                      8  ***********************************************************
                                      9              ASLNK                        MACRO USAGE-LINKAGE
                                     23              EQREG                        MACRO USAGE-EQUATE REG
00001E D283 C223 C222 00229 00228    40              MVC     OUTAREA,SPACES
00002A D224 C232 C2B2 00238 002B8    41              MVC     OUTAREA+60(8),=C'&SYSDATE'
                                     43              MVC     OUTAREA+15(37),=C'THIS IS A SAMPLE MACRO-USAGE-PROGRAM'
000030 92F1 C223          00229      44              MVI     OUTAREA,C'1'
                                     45              PUT     OUTFILE,OUTAREA
000042 D283 C223 C222 00229 00228    50              MVC     OUTAREA,SPACES
000048 9260 C223          00229      51              MVI     OUTAREA,C'-'
00004C D222 C237 C2DA 0023D 002E0    52              MVC     OUTAREA+20(35),=C'M A I L I N G   L A B E L   L I S T'
                                     53              PUT     OUTFILE,OUTAREA
000060 D283 C223 C222 00229 00228    58  CLEAR       MVC     OUTAREA,SPACES
000066 92F0 C223          00229      59              MVI     OUTAREA,C'0'
                                     60              GET     INFILE,RECORD
                                     65              MOVE    NAME,NAMEO,15            MACRO USAGE-MOVE
                                     67              MOVE    ADDRESS,ADDRESSO
                                     70              MOVE    TOWN,TOWNO,20
                                     72              DOIT    PASSES=3                 MACRO USAGE-PERFORM
0000A8 9240 C223          00229      77              PUT     OUTFILE,OUTAREA          PRINT 3 COPIES OF LABEL
                                     82              MVI     OUTAREA,C' '
                                     83              ENDIT                            MACRO USAGE-END LOOP
0000B0 47F0 C05A          00060      86              B       CLEAR
                                     87  EOFCD       CLOSE   (INFILE,,OUTFILE)
                                     95  ***************************
                                     96              ASDCB            *              MACRO USAGE-DEFINE DCB'S
                                    208  ***************************
0001D8                              209  RECORD      DS      0CL80
0001D8                              210  NAME        DS      CL15
0001E7                              211  ADDRESS     DS      CL20
0001FB                              212  TOWN        DS      CL20
00020F                              213              DS      CL25
000228 40                           214  SPACES      DC      CL1' '
000229                              215  OUTAREA     DS      0CL132
000229                              216              DS      CL5
00022E                              217  NAMEO       DS      CL15
00023D                              218              DS      CL5
000242                              219  ADDRESSO    DS      CL20
000256                              220              DS      CL5
00025B                              221  TOWNO       DS      CL20
00026F                              222              DS      CL62
                                    223              END
0002B0 F0F361F0F661F8F5             224                      =C'03/06/85'
0002B8 E3C8C9E240C9E240             225                      =C'THIS IS A SAMPLE MACRO-USAGE-PROGRAM'
0002DC 00000003                     226                      =A(3)
0002E0 D440C140C940D340             227                      =C'M A I L I N G   L A B E L   L I S T'
```

Figure 19.8
Sample program with programmer-defined macros.

```
SMITH FRED        123 MARLBOROUGH RD.  SYOSSET,NY
JONES LEE         23-45 SKILLMAN LANE  HAUPPAUGE,NY
BROWN LES         34 BROWER PLACE      LYNBROOKE,NJ
GREEN JOE         12 STEELER ST        PITTSBURGH,PA
BOSSY MIKE        22 HATTRICK LA       UNIONDALE,NY
PACILIO JOE       129 FIRST AVE        BELLPORT,NY
```

Figure 19.9
Sample input data for the program in Figure 19.8.

```
                      THIS IS A SAMPLE MACRO-USAGE-PROGRAM          03/06/85


                           M A I L I N G   L A B E L   L I S T

           SMITH FRED            123 MARLBOROUGH RD.        SYOSSET,NY
           SMITH FRED            123 MARLBOROUGH RD.        SYOSSET,NY
           SMITH FRED            123 MARLBOROUGH RD.        SYOSSET,NY

           JONES LEE             23-45 SKILLMAN LANE        HAUPPAUGE,NY
           JONES LEE             23-45 SKILLMAN LANE        HAUPPAUGE,NY
           JONES LEE             23-45 SKILLMAN LANE        HAUPPAUGE,NY

           BROWN LES             34 BROWER PLACE            LYNBROOKE,NJ
           BROWN LES             34 BROWER PLACE            LYNBROOKE,NJ
           BROWN LES             34 BROWER PLACE            LYNBROOKE,NJ

           GREEN JOE             12 STEELER ST              PITTSBURGH,PA
           GREEN JOE             12 STEELER ST              PITTSBURGH,PA
           GREEN JOE             12 STEELER ST              PITTSBURGH,PA

           BOSSY MIKE            22 HATTRICK LA             UNIONDALE,NY
           BOSSY MIKE            22 HATTRICK LA             UNIONDALE,NY
           BOSSY MIKE            22 HATTRICK LA             UNIONDALE,NY

           PACILIO JOE           129 FIRST AVE              BELLPORT,NY
           PACILIO JOE           129 FIRST AVE              BELLPORT,NY
           PACILIO JOE           129 FIRST AVE              BELLPORT,NY
```

Figure 19.10
Sample output produced from the program in Figure 19.8.

```
          MACRO
          ASLNK
          CSECT
          STM     14,12,12(13)
          BALR    12,0
a         USING   *,12
          ST      13,SAVEAREA+4
          LA      13,SAVEAREA
          OPEN    (INFILE,(INPUT),OUTFILE,(OUTPUT))
          MEND



          MACRO
          ASDCB
          L       13,4(0,13)
          RETURN  (14,12),T
b OUTFILE DCB     DDNAME=SYSPRINT,MACRF=(PM),DSORG=PS,
                  LRECL=133,BLKSIZE=133,RECFM=FA
  INFILE  DCB     DDNAME=SYSIN,MACRF=(GM),DSORG=PS,
                  LRECL=80,BLKSIZE=80,RECFM=F,EODAD=EOFCD
  SAVEAREA DC     18F'0'
          MEND
```

Figure 19.11
The macros ASLNK and ASDCB used in Figure 19.8.

KEY TERMS

Concatenation	Local directive (LCL)
Conditional assembly instructions	Macro
Global directive (GBL)	Positional parameter
Keyword parameter	Prototype statement

REVIEW QUESTIONS

1. List the advantages of using macros.
2. Define a macro and describe how it is executed.

3. What advantages are derived by placing a macro in a macro library?
4. Define and explain the four basic components of a macro.
5. How are comments included in a macro for purposes of documentation?
6. What methods are available to print error or warning messages from a macro?
7. Delineate the rules used to create a macro symbolic name or variable.
8. What are the differences between a programmer-defined macro and a system macro?
9. Differentiate between a positional parameter and a keyword parameter.
10. What is the purpose of using conditional assemblies?
11. Define concatenation and give an example.

PROGRAMMING ASSIGNMENTS

1. Define a MOVE macro that issues a warning when an implicit move is used. Use the MOVE in this chapter as a guide and recall that when a positional parameter is not specified, a null condition results.
2. Define a macro called SWITCH that will interchange the contents of two fullwords in storage.
3. Code a macro to generate the following six constants.

```
PO     DC     PL1'0'
P1     DC     PL1'1'
P2     DC     PL1'2'
P3     DC     PL1'3'
P4     DC     PL1'4'
P5     DC     PL1'5'
```

4. Program a BEGIN macro to establish a base register for your program and to define storage for 18 fullwords to be used as a save area. Use keyword parameters for REG—the base register, and SAVE—the define storage.
5. Define a macro to generate the necessary DCBs or DTFs at your school's installation.
6. Remove the PRINT NOGEN from a working program and analyze the PUT and GET macros. How can these macros be streamlined or made more efficient at your school's installation?

Advanced Topics: An Overview

OBJECTIVES

To familiarize you with:
1. *Floating-point concepts and floating-point instructions.*
2. *The Translate (TR) and Translate and Test (TRT) instructions.*
3. *The Test Under Mask (TM) instruction.*
4. *The Execute (EX) instruction.*

I. FLOATING-POINT CONCEPTS

A. Scientific Notation:
A Preview to Floating-Point Representation

Using scientific notation, any number is represented as

$D \times 10^N$

1. D is a positive or negative decimal number that may have a fractional component. It is most typically between 0 and 10. D is called the **mantissa.**
2. N is a positive or negative integer (1, 2, 3, . . .), or zero. N is called the **characteristic.**
3. 10 is called the **base;** thus, scientific notation uses base 10, or decimal, numbers.

Consider the following decimal numbers and their representations using scientific notation.

Decimal Number	Scientific Notation
230	2.3×10^2
14	1.4×10^1
2.7	2.7×10^0
.13	1.3×10^{-1}

We select a mantissa between 0 and 10 for standardization purposes. Note however that 230, for example, can also be represented as 23×10^1 or 230×10^0.

You may recall that any number raised to the zero power is equal to 1. Thus $10^0 = 1$. Any number raised to a negative power or characteristic is represented as follows.

$$10^{-1} = \frac{1}{10}$$

$$10^{-2} = \frac{1}{10^2}$$

$$10^{-N} = \frac{1}{10^N}$$

In scientific notation, the characteristic, or power of 10, indicates where the decimal point in the mantissa is to be placed.

234×10^2 means add *two* zeros = 23400
        (move decimal point to the right 2 places)
114×10^3 means add *three* zeros = 114000
        (move decimal point to the right 3 places)

When the characteristic is negative, we multiply the mantissa by a fraction, which has the effect of moving the decimal point to the left. Thus,

$$1.2 \times 10^{-1} = 1.2 \times \frac{1}{10} = .12$$

(move decimal point to the left 1 place)

$$114 \times 10^{-2} = 114 \times \frac{1}{10^2} = 1.14$$

(move decimal point to the left 2 places)

Why Scientific Notation The use of scientific notation is very handy for performing arithmetic operations, particularly if large numbers are involved. In fact "scientific notation" is so named because scientists and engineers are the people most likely to perform arithmetic operations on large numbers.

Addition Using Scientific Notation To add numbers in scientific notation, if the numbers have the same characteristic, you simply add the mantissas. This rule simplifies addition in scientific notation.

Example 20.1

$$1.2 \times 10^3 + 2.7 \times 10^3 = 3.9 \times 10^3$$

mantissas have been added   same base and characteristic

Check
$$1.2 \times 10^3 = 1200$$
$$2.7 \times 10^3 = \underline{2700}$$
$$3900 = 3.9 \times 10^3$$

If the numbers to be added do not have the same characteristic, simply change the representation of one or more of the numbers so that the characteristics are identical.

Example 20.2

$$1.6 \times 10^2 + 2.3 \times 10^3 =$$
$$1.6 \times 10^2 + 23 + 10^2 =$$
$$24.6 \times 10^2$$

mantissas have been added   base and characteristic are unchanged

Check
$$1.6 \times 10^2 = 160$$
$$2.3 \times 10^3 = \underline{2300}$$
$$2460 = 24.6 \times 10^2$$

Subtraction Using Scientific Notation Subtraction of two numbers in scientific notation follows the same rules. That is, once the characteristic of both numbers is the same (that is, 10^N) simply subtract one mantissa from the other. The result, or difference, is the mantissa multiplied by 10^N.

Example 20.3

$$1.2 \times 10^2 - 1.1 \times 10^2 = .1 \times 10^2$$

Check
$$1.2 \times 10^2 = 120$$
$$1.1 \times 10^2 = \underline{110}$$
$$10 = .1 \times 10^2$$

Example 20.4

$$2.5 \times 10^3 - 1.3 \times 10^2 = 2.5 \times 10^3 - .13 \times 10^3 = 2.37 \times 10^3$$

Check
$$2.5 \times 10^3 = 2500$$
$$1.3 \times 10^2 = \underline{130}$$
$$2370 = 2.37 \times 10^3$$

Multiplication Using Scientific Notation Multiplication is a little different. To multiply two numbers using scientific notation, simply multiply the mantissas and add the characteristics.

Example 20.5 (mantissa × characteristic) × (mantissa × characteristic)

$$(2.6 \times 10^{②}) \times (3.1 \times 10^{③})$$

$$= (2.6 \times 3.1) \times 10^{(2+3)}$$

$$= 8.06 \times 10^{5}$$

Check

$2.6 \times 10^{2} = \quad 260$

$\phantom{2.6 \times 10^{2} = \quad} \times$

$3.1 \times 10^{3} = \quad \underline{3100}$

$\phantom{3.1 \times 10^{3} = \quad} \overline{806000} = 8.06 \times 10^{5}$

Division Using Scientific Notation Division is similar. You divide mantissas and *subtract* characteristics.

Example 20.6 (mantissa × characteristic) ÷ (mantissa × characteristic)

$$15 \times 10^{3} \div 3 \times 10^{2} = 5 \times 10^{1}$$

Check

$$15000 \div 300 = 5 \times 10^{1}$$

Self-Evaluating Quiz

1. Using _____ notation any number can be represented as $D \times 10^{N}$.
2. In Question 1, D is called the _____ and can be any _____ number.
3. In Question 1, N is called the _____ and can be any _____ number.
4. 10 is referred to as the _____ .

Indicate the value of the following.

5. 10^{1}
6. 10^{2}
7. 10^{3}
8. 10^{0}
9. 10^{-1}
10. 10^{-2}

Represent the following decimal numbers using scientific notation (where D is a number between 0 and 10).

11. 682
12. 38
13. 14
14. 4.6
15. .17
16. .012

Perform the following arithmetic operations. Check your answers.

17. $2.6 \times 10^{2} + 1.4 \times 10^{2}$
18. $3.7 \times 10^{2} + 1.6 \times 10^{3}$
19. $(1.1 \times 10^{2}) \times (2.3 \times 10^{3})$
20. $2.6 \times 10^{2} - 1.4 \times 10^{2}$

SOLUTIONS
1. Scientific
2. Mantissa; positive or negative decimal number (may have a fractional component; usually represented as a decimal number between 0 and 10)
3. Characteristic; zero, positive, or negative integer
4. Base
5. 10
6. 100
7. 1000
8. 1 (any number to the 0 power = 1)
9. .1
10. .01
11. 6.82×10^2
12. 3.8×10^1
13. 1.4×10^1
14. 4.6×10^0
15. 1.7×10^{-1}
16. 1.2×10^{-2}
17. $(2.6 \times 1.4) \times 10^2 = 4.0 \times 10^2$

Check
$$
\begin{array}{r}
260 \\
+ \ 140 \\
\hline
400 = 4 \times 10^2
\end{array}
$$

18. $(.37 + 1.6) \times 10^3 = 1.97 \times 10^3$
Note: $3.7 \times 10^2 = .37 \times 10^3$

Check
$$
\begin{array}{r}
370 \\
+ \ 1600 \\
\hline
1970 = 1.97 \times 10^3
\end{array}
$$

19. $(1.1 \times 2.3) \times 10^5 = 2.53 \times 10^5$

Check
$110 \times 2300 = 25300 = 2.53 \times 10^5$

20. $(2.6 - 1.4) \times 10^2 = 1.2 \times 10^2$

Check
$260 - 140 = 120 = 1.2 \times 10^2$

B. Floating-Point Notation: A Hexadecimal Version of Scientific Notation

IBM and IBM–compatible computers do not operate on data in decimal form. Rather, they use hexadecimal or base-16 numbers. **Floating-point notation** is a method of representing computer data in a format similar to scientific notation.

Although the base of numbers in scientific notation is 10, the base of floating-point numbers is 16. Thus, where scientific notation is used to represent any number as $D \times 10^N$, floating-point numbers are represented as $H \times 16^K$, where

1. H is a hexadecimal fraction between 0 and 1, rather than a decimal number between 0 and 10. It is called the *mantissa*.
2. K is a positive or negative integer (1, 2, 3, . . .), or zero. It is called the *characteristic*.
3. 16 is the base.

Consider the following examples.

Decimal System	*Floating-Point Notation*
	Note: Base is 16

1.0 0.1×16^1

Note: $0.1_{16} = 1 \times 16^{-1}$

$1 \times 16^{-1} \times 16^1 = 1$

2.0 0.2×16^1

0.5 0.8×16^0

Note: $0.8_{16} = 8 \times 16^{-1}$

1.225×10^1 $0.C4 \times 16^1$

Note: $0.C4 = 12 \times 16^{-1} + 4 \times 16^{-2}$

$$= \frac{12}{16} + \frac{4}{16 \times 16} = \frac{192 + 4}{16 \times 16}$$

$$= \frac{196}{256} = \frac{49}{64}$$

$$0.C4 \times 16^1 = \frac{49}{64} \times 16$$

$$0.C4 \times 16^1 = \frac{49}{4}$$

$$0.C4 \times 16^1 = 12 + \frac{1}{4}$$

$$= 1.225 \times 10^1$$

Floating-point numbers are represented in *normalized* form as $\pm H \times 16^K$, where H is a hexadecimal fraction between 0 and 1. Thus, 0.1×16^1 is a normalized floating-point number, whereas 10×16^3 is not.

As you may have observed from the above examples, converting decimal numbers to floating-point form is cumbersome. Thus, the computer performs the conversion using hexadecimal numbers in normalized form. This conversion may require truncation of digits. Consequently, floating-point numbers typically approximate the decimal numbers to be represented.

Example 20.7 $0.1_{10} = 0.1999\ldots$

$$= 1 \times 16^{-1} + 9 \times 16^{-2} - 9 \times 16^{-3} + \ldots$$

Floating-point numbers are typically represented in 32 bits. The exponent or characteristic of floating-point numbers can range from -64 to 63. Because the mantissa is a hexadecimal number in normalized form (between 0 and 1 for positive numbers, and -1 and 0 for negative numbers) this means that floating-point numbers can range from 16^{-65} to 16^{63} for positive numbers and from -16^{-65} to -16^{63} for negative numbers. In addition, **double-precision** or 64-bit, floating-point numbers can also be represented. This increases the range of numbers from 16^{-64} to 16^{63}, or from 10^{-78} to 10^{75}. Double precision means that the number is more precise because it is represented using 64 bits rather than 32 bits.

Floating-point representation, then, provides the ability for representing very large and very small numbers. This is a primary reason for their use. Another reason is that, as with scientific notation, arithmetic operations on very large and very small numbers can be efficiently performed on floating-point numbers.

C. Machine Language Representation of Floating-Point Numbers

Recall that a floating-point number is represented as $\pm H \times 16^K$. Three lengths are available to represent floating-point numbers.

Type of Format	Number of Bits	Type of Precision
Short format	32 bits (4 bytes)	Single precision
Long format	64 bits (8 bytes)	Double precision
Extended format	128 bits (16 bytes)	Extended precision

Short and long formats are available on all IBM and IBM–compatible computers. Extended format is available on most (not, however, on some of the older computers such as IBM's 360 series). The long and extended formats allow for greater precision. The numbers represented using this notation are more accurate than those represented when the single precision format is used.

Let us focus on single precision, keeping in mind that the representation is the same for double and extended but that more fractional numbers are available. Thus, data is represented the same in all three, but the long and extended formats allow for greater accuracy.

Format

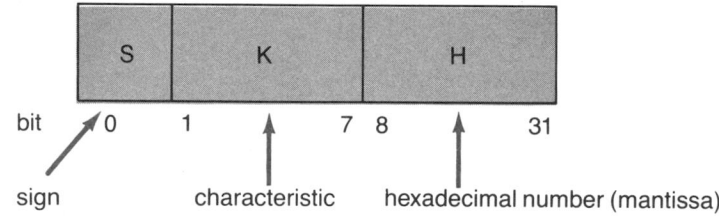

The left-most bit (bit 0) is the sign bit. If it is 0, the floating-point number is positive; if it is 1, the floating-point number is negative.

K, the characteristic, is represented within the computer using *excess-64 binary notation*. This means that the binary number K is *64 more than the true value of the exponent*. Because K is a binary number, the leftmost position (bit 0) represents the sign (0 for positive; 1 for negative). 10000000, for example, is a negative number because the leftmost bit is 1. All 0s indicate that the true value of K is −64, since 0 is 64 more than the true value of −64. K may vary from −64 to +63 and be represented as follows:

Decimal Value of K	Binary Value of Excess-64 K	Hex Equivalent of K (Represented in Two Full Bytes)
−64	0000000	00 | 0000 | 0000 |
−63	0000001	01 | 0000 | 0001 |
−62	0000010	02 | 0000 | 0010 |
⋮	⋮	⋮
−1	0111111	3F
0	1000000	40
+1	1000001	41
+2	1000010	42
⋮	⋮	⋮
+62	1111110	7E
+63	1111111	7F

Consider several examples where the characteristic and mantissa are represented in hex form for ease of reading.

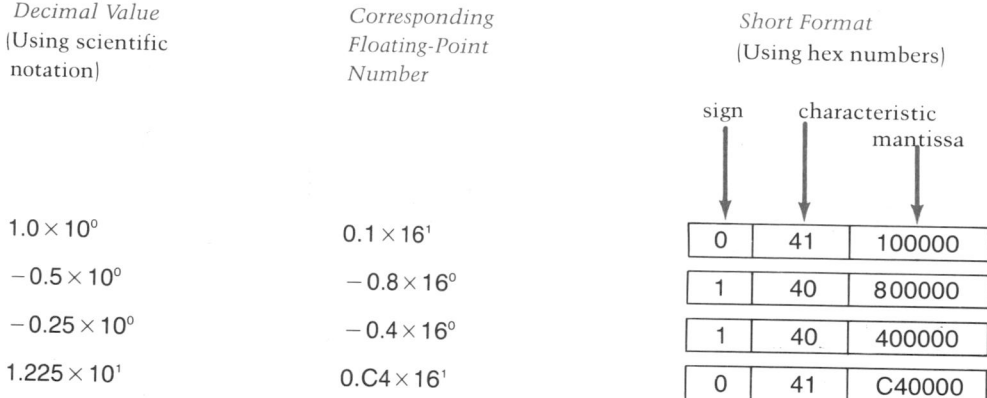

Decimal Value (Using scientific notation)	Corresponding Floating-Point Number	Short Format (Using hex numbers)		
		sign	characteristic	mantissa
1.0×10^0	0.1×16^1	0	41	100000
-0.5×10^0	-0.8×16^0	1	40	800000
-0.25×10^0	-0.4×16^0	1	40	400000
1.225×10^1	$0.C4 \times 16^1$	0	41	C40000

The preceding short format represents numbers in hex form. Actually, each of the numbers uses 32 bits in short form. Thus, 0.1×16^1 is represented in binary as

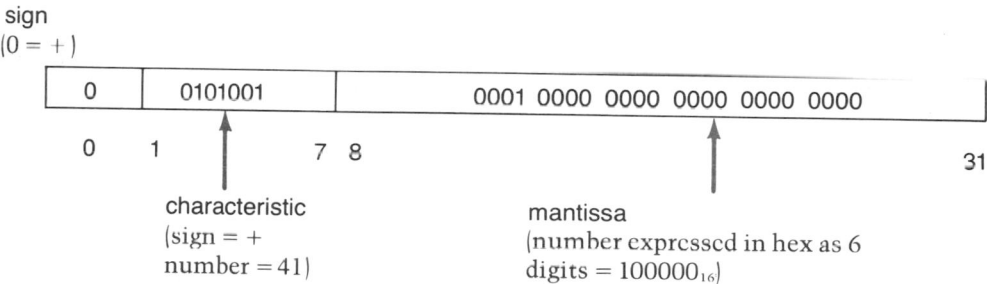

When using the long format, 14 hex digits (56 binary digits) are used to represent the characteristic. When using the extended form, 28 hex digits are used to represent the characteristic.

Conversion from long to short or to extended format is relatively simple. On the other hand, conversion from decimal notation to floating-point and vice-versa usually requires a subroutine.

D. Representing Floating-Point Numbers in Assembler Language

To define any constant or literal in assembler language you use a DC. Floating-point constants are also defined using DCs. You can indicate that the number is a floating-point constant by including the following type in the operand field prior to the number enclosed in quotes.

E = short format (single precision)
D = long format (double precision)
L = extended format (extended precision)

Consider the following.

Object Code

```
41100000          DC    E'1.0'          (ACTUALLY = .1 × 16¹ = 1)
41100000
```

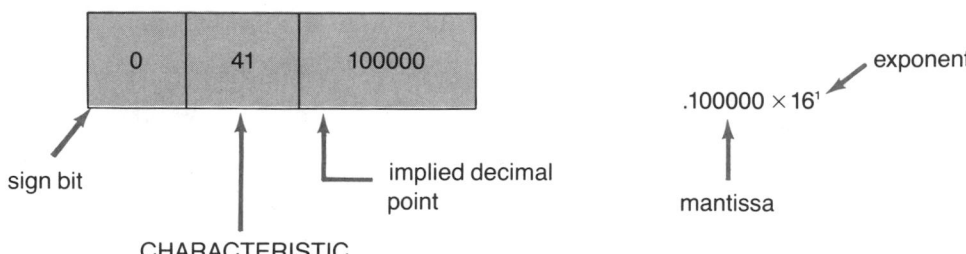

Note that greater precision can be achieved by specifying DC D'1.0'.

For the short format, alignment is always on a fullword boundary. For long and extended format, it is always on a doubleword boundary.

We may also reserve storage for floating-point numbers by using a DS, along with E, D, and L respectively.

FP1	DS	4E	Reserves space for four floating-point numbers in the short format. The number is correctly aligned on a fullword boundary.
FP2	DS	6D	Reserves space for six floating-point numbers each on a doubleword boundary.
FP3	DS	L	Reserves space for an extended-precision floating-point number.

E. Floating-Point Instructions

Floating-point instructions are of the RX or RR type. They consist of the following 51 instructions:

1. 22 instructions that process short format numbers.
2. 22 corresponding instructions that process long format numbers.
3. 7 instructions that process extended-format numbers (available on most, but not all IBM–compatible computers)

Figure 20.1 indicates the floating-point instructions and the corresponding integer or fixed-point instructions. Two instructions in the figure—HALVE and ROUND—have no equivalent when using integer instructions.

Because floating-point instructions are either of the RX or RR type, they all require the use of registers, each of which is 64 bits long. Registers 0, 2, 4, and 6 are used as floating-point registers. Note the following:

1. Short-format numbers
   a. Any of the 4 floating-point registers may be used.
   b. Short-format numbers represented as 32 bits are manipulated in the high-order 32 bits of the floating-point register.
2. Long-format numbers
   a. Any of the 4 floating-point registers may be used.
   b. The entire 64-bit floating-point register is used to manipulate the number.

	Name	Type	Integer Instructions			Floating-point Instructions		
						Short Format	Long Format	Extended Format
Load into Registers	Load	RX	L	LH	LM	LE	LD	
	Load Registers	RR	LR			LER	LDR	
Store into Memory	Store	RX	ST	STH	STM	STE	STD	
Compare or Test	Compare	RX	C	CH		CE	CD	
	Compare Registers	RR	CR			CER	CDR	
	Load and Test	RR	LTR			LTER	LTDR	
Sign	Load Complement	RR	LCR			LCER	LCDR	
	Load Negative	RR	LNR			LNER	LNDR	
	Load Positive	RR	LPR			LPER	LPDR	
Arithmetic Operations	Add	RX	A AL	AH		AE AU	AD AW	
	Add Registers	RR	AR ALR			AER AUR	ADR AWR	AXR
	Subtract	RX	S SL	SH		SE SU	SD SW	
	Subtract Registers	RR	SR SLR			SER SUR	SDR SWR	SXR
	Multiply	RX	M	MH		ME	MD	MXD
	Multiply Registers	RR	MR			MER	MDR	MXR MXDR
	Divide	RX	D			DE	DD	
	Divide Registers	RR	DR			DER	DDR	
	Halve	RR				HER	HDR	
	Round	RR						LRER LRDR

Figure 20.1
Floating-point instructions with the corresponding integer or fixed-point instructions. (Courtesy IBM.)

3. Extended-format numbers
   a. Two consecutive floating-point registers are used to represent the number (that is, registers 0 and 2, 2 and 4, 4 and 6).
   b. When using 0 and 2, register 0 is designated; when using 2 and 4, register 2 is designated; and so on.

When using RX-type instructions, the first operand must designate an appropriate floating-point register address. When using RR-type instructions, both operands must designate appropriate floating-point register addresses.

Consider the following instructions.

Instruction	Meaning
LER 2,4	Contents of register 4 are moved to the high-order 32 bits of register 2.
LE 2,FP1	Contents of FP1 are moved to the high-order 32 bits of register 2.
LDR 4,6	Contents of register 6 are moved to register 4.

Add and subtract instructions are available for both normalized numbers (AE, AER, and SE and SER) and un-normalized numbers (AU, AUR, and SU, SUR). Multiply and divide instructions must always operate on normalized numbers. The ME and MER multiply instructions generate double-precision products.

The HALVE instruction means to divide a number by two. The ROUND instruction automatically causes rounding. For further details, see the summary of arithmetic operations in Figure 20.2.

II. TR (TRANSLATE) and TRT (TRANSLATE AND TEST)

The Translate (TR) and Translate and Test (TRT) instructions are used to reduce the size and running time of programs that perform string operations. The TR and TRT result in the following.

Instruction	Meaning
TR	Replaces some or all bytes in a string with another byte or character.
TRT	Searches a string from left to right for the first occurrence of a specific character.

TR and TRT are SS-type instructions. Operand 1 is a field to be compared against a constant designated in Operand 2. Operand 1, the field to be tested, is called the **argument.** Operand 2 contains the values for testing or replacing and is called the **function.**

A. TR Instruction

The following are typical applications of TR instructions.

1. Changing data entered using ASCII code to EBCDIC. Although IBM and IBM-compatible computers use the EBCDIC code, other computers use ASCII code, an abbreviation for *American Standard Code for Information Interchange.* To translate data entered on disk or tape in ASCII code to EBCDIC, use the TR instruction.
2. Changing data erroneously packed into an acceptable form. Suppose an incoming 3-position amount field to be used in arithmetic actually contained asterisks rather than numbers. The field entered as X'5C5C5C', when packed, would be X'CCC5'. If an arithmetic operation is performed on this packed field, a data exception error would occur because the packed field does not contain valid characters. A TR can be used to avoid this data exception error.
3. Reading a string of characters from a terminal and translating them into a compact form that can be operated upon.
4. Translating uppercase letters to lowercase letters and vice versa.

1. Function String

With a TR instruction we must first select a **function string** to be compared to Operand 1, the argument. This function string must be coded so that if a selected byte in the argument contains a specified value, it is replaced by a corresponding byte in the function string.

1. Operand 1 references the address of the argument (256-byte maximum).
2. Operand 2 references a function string.
3. The operation begins by comparing the first or high-order byte of the argument and continues the comparison one byte at a time from left to right.
4. The value of the argument determines which byte in the function string will replace it.

2. Size of Function

If the argument byte being translated contains a 3A, for example, then the address of the function byte selected for comparison is 3A bytes from the beginning of the function string. If the argument byte is X'00', then the *first* byte in the function string is selected. If the argument byte is X'01', then the *second* byte in the function string is selected, and so on.

The function string typically consists of 256 characters. This accommodates the largest possible value in the argument byte, which would be X'FF'. If the argument byte contains X'FF' then the function byte selected would be 255 positions from the beginning, that is, the 256th byte. It is always advisable, therefore, to make the function string 256 bytes.

3. Characters in the Function String

Sometimes, you might want certain characters in the argument to be changed depending on their value. To perform this, a 256-byte character string is defined such that each argument byte's contents will point to the replacement character wanted in the function string

Example 20.8   Replacement illustration
Consider the following contents in a field called ARGUMENT.

```
ARGUMENT   DS   CL4
```

Assume the contents of ARGUMENT are X'02090C0C'.
Suppose we perform the following operation:

```
TR   ARGUMENT,TABLE
```

The replacements that will occur are as follows:

1. The contents of TABLE+2 will replace the first byte (leftmost) in ARGUMENT. This is because the first byte in ARGUMENT has a value of X'02'.
2. The contents of TABLE+9 will replace the second byte in ARGUMENT. This is because the second byte in argument has a value of X'09'.
3. The contents of TABLE+12 will replace the third byte. This is because the third byte in ARGUMENT contains a value of X'0C', which is a 12. Similarly, the contents of TABLE+12 will replace the fourth byte.

Suppose we want ARGUMENT to be replaced by corresponding letters. If ARGUMENT has a byte equal to 01, for example, it should be replaced with A; a byte of 02 should be replaced by B, and so on. To accomplish this, define the function as

```
TABLE   DC   C' ABCDEFGHIJKLMNOPQRSTUVWXYZ'
```

The first byte should be a blank because it would be used for replacement only if the argument byte equaled X'00'. X'01' would be replaced by TABLE+1, and so on. Hence, the translation of the argument X'02090C0C' would result in "BILL."

	Mnemonic Opcode	Instruction Type		Possible Errors					Condition Code
		RX	RR	Exponent Overflow	Exponent Underflow	Significance	Divide by Zero	Specification	
Single-Precision Instructions									
Except for ME and MER, these all operate on short-format numbers and produce short-format results.									
Add normalized	AE	X		X	X	X		X	X
	AER		X	X	X	X		X	X
Add unnormalized	AU	X		X		X		X	X
	AUR		X	X		X		X	X
Subtract normalized	SE	X		X	X	X		X	X
	SER		X	X	X	X		X	X
Subtract unnormalized	SU	X		X		X		X	X
	SUR		X	X		X		X	X
Multiply (short to long format)	ME	X		X	X			X	
(short to long format)	MER		X	X	X			X	
Divide	DE	X		X	X		X	X	
	DER		X	X	X		X	X	
Halve	HER		X		X			X	
Double-Precision Instructions									
All these operate on long-format numbers and produce long-format results									
Add normalized	AD	X		X	X	X		X	X
	ADR		X	X	X	X		X	X
Add unnormalized	AW	X		X		X		X	X
	AWR		X	X		X		X	X
Subract normalized	SD	X		X	X	X		X	X
	SDR		X	X	X	X		X	X
Subtract unnormalized	SW	X		X		X		X	X
	SWR		X	X		X		X	X
Multiply	MD	X		X	X			X	
	MDR		X	X	X			X	
Divide	DD	X		X	X		X	X	
	DDR		X	X	X		X	X	
Halve	HDR		X		X			X	

Figure 20.2
Summary of floating-point arithmetic instructions (continued on next page) (Courtesy IBM.)

	Operand	Result	Extended-Precision Instructions							
Add	extended	extended	AXR		X	X	X	X		X	X
Subtract	extended	extended	SXR		X	X	X	X		X	X
Multiply	extended	extended	MXR		X	X	X			X	
	long	extended	MXD	X		X	X			X	
	long	extended	MXDR		X	X	X			X	
Round	long	short	LRER		X	X				X	
	extended	long	LRDR		X	X				X	

Note:

The condition code is set by all add and subtract instructions as follows

0 = mantissa of result is zero
1 = result negative, mantissa $\neq$ zero
2 = result positive, mantissa $\neq$ zero

Figure 20-2
(continued)

Example 20.9 Replace lowercase letters in an argument with uppercase letters

Assume the argument is 30 characters and can have any value. If you check an EBCDIC conversion chart, you will find that lowercase letters are represented as follows:

a–i	X'81'–X'89'
j–r	X'D1'–X'D9'
s–z	X'E1'–X'E9'

X'81'–X'89' would be the 130–138th bytes in a character string. Because 81_{16} = 129_{10} a value of X'81' in an argument byte would be replaced by the byte in the high-order byte of a function + 129. This would be the 130th byte of a function. Similarly, an argument value of X'82' would be replaced by the 131st byte in a function string, and so on.

Consider the following.

Argument Byte	Position in Function that Would Serve as Replacement	Hex Value
a–i	130–139	X'81'–X'89'
j–r	146–154	X'D1'–X'D9'
s–z	163–170	X'E1'–X'E9'

To obtain uppercase replacement establish a character string such that

Byte Location in Function	Contents
130	A
.	.
138	I
146	J
.	.
154	R
163	S
.	.
170	Z

All other bytes in the function should contain values corresponding to their positions.

The instruction would be

```
TR   ARG1(30),FN1
```

ARG1(30) indicates that the number of bytes to be translated in ARG1 is 30. The following would result based on ARG1's initial contents.

Before execution: ARG1   DC   C' this is a 30-character string'
After execution: ARG1   DC   C' THIS IS A 30-CHARACTER STRING'

B. TRT **Instruction**

A TRT is typically used to scan or check a field for invalid characters. Replacements do not occur because it is just a scanning operation. It is also used for finding a string delimiter, that is, an ending value that indicates the precise termination point. This instruction is particularly useful in

1. Scanning for blanks;
2. Checking for positive or negative numbers; and,
3. Determining the length of a variable-length record.

A condition code is set depending on the results of the TRT. The condition code is then used for branching.

Although TRT scans and does not replace, it performs the following operations that are similar to TR.

1. Operand 1 references the address of an argument (256-byte maximum).
2. Operand 2 references a function string.
3. The operation begins with the first or high-order byte of the argument and continues one byte at a time.

TRT differs from TR, as follows.

1. If the value of the corresponding function byte is 0, TRT continues with the next argument byte. That is, no specific operation is performed.
2. If the value of the corresponding function byte is non-zero, TRT inserts the address of the argument into register 1 in bits 8–31 (bits 0–7 are unchanged) and inserts the contents of the function into register 2 in bits 24–31 (bits 0–23 are unchanged).
3. Condition codes are set as follows.

Code	Meaning
0	All corresponding function bytes were zero.
1	A non-zero function byte was found but not at the end of an argument.
2	A non-zero function was found at the end of the argument.

Application: Scanning for a Blank The following procedure can be used for testing for blanks in a last name field. If a blank is found, the routine inserts a comma, first initial, and a period to the right of the last name. This technique could prove useful if we entered data in a string format from a terminal and wish to store it in a more compact form for processing.

```
SCAN       TRT     LASTNME,TRTABLE
           BZ      NOBLANK
FOUND      MVI     0(1),C','          MOVE COMMA TO 1ST BLANK FOUND
           MVC     2(1,1),INITIAL     MOVE INITIAL
           MVC     3(1,1),=C'.'       END WITH PERIOD
           MVI     INITIAL,C' '       CLEAR INITIAL
           MVC     NAMEO(20),NAMEIN   MOVE AND WRITE
           PUT     OUTFILE,LINEOUT    MODIFIED NAME
                     .
                     .
                     .
TRTABLE    DS      0XL256
NULL       DC      64X'00'
BLANK      DC      X'40'
REST       DC      191X'00'
                     .
                     .
                     .
NAMEIN     DS      0CL20
LASTNME    DS      CL18
           DS      CL1
INITIAL    DS      CL1
                     .
                     .
                     .
*********************************************************************
*
* THE NAME HAMILTON----------A WOULD APPEAR HAMILTON, A.
*
*********************************************************************
```

The scan function table contains all hex zeros except for one in a blank (hex '40') position. TRT scans the last name for a blank. If a blank is found, the routine uses the address in register 1 to insert the commas, initial, and period. If a blank is not found, the routine exits. The assumption would be that the surname fills all available characters in its field.

Note that register 1 points to the first blank (X'40') in the string.

REGISTER 1

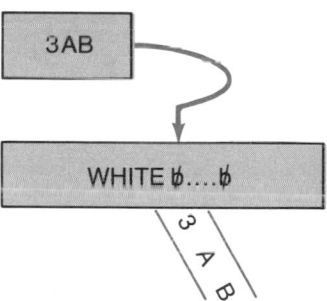

Self-Evaluating Quiz

1. TR is an abbreviation for _____ , and TRT is an abbreviation for _____ .
2. Both of the preceding instructions are _____ -type instructions.
3. In TR and TRT instructions, Operand (no.) is a field to be compared against, and Operand (no.) is a constant.
4. Operand 1 is called the _____ and Operand 2 is called the _____ .
5. The _____ instruction replaces some or all bytes in a string with another byte or character.
6. The _____ instruction searches a string from left to right for the first occurrence of a specific character.
7. In a TR instruction, a(n) _____ is the second operand such that if a selected byte in the argument contains a specified value it is replaced by a corresponding byte in this second operand.

8. If an argument byte being translated contains an 05, then the address of the function byte selected for comparison is <u>(no.)</u> bytes from the beginning of the function string.
9. The _____ instruction is used typically to scan or check a field for invalid characters.
10. (T or F) With the TRT instruction, replacements do not occur.

SOLUTIONS
1. Translate; Translate and Test
2. SS
3. 1; 2
4. Argument; function
5. TR
6. TRT
7. Function string
8. 05
9. TRT
10. T

III. TM (TEST UNDER MASK)

The Test Under Mask (TM) instruction is a Storage Immediate (SI) instruction that can be used to test the values of specific bits in a particular byte of storage. Operand 1 refers to one byte in storage containing the bits to be tested. Operand 2 contains an 8-bit immediate byte called a **mask.** The 1 bits in this mask indicate which bits to test in Operand 1.

All bits with a value of 1 in the immediate byte or mask are compared to the corresponding bits in the storage byte. If, for example, bits 0 and 1 in the immediate byte or mask are the only ones equal to 1, then only bits 0 and 1 in the storage byte will be tested. Those bits in storage that correspond to a mask of 0 are not tested. The format of the instruction follows.

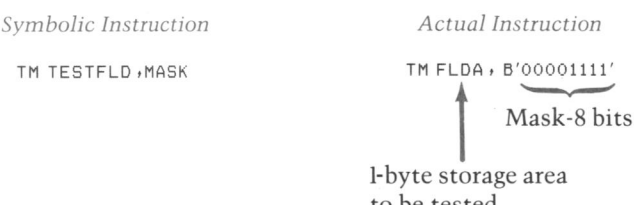

Symbolic Instruction   *Actual Instruction*

TM TESTFLD,MASK   TM FLDA,B'00001111'

Selected bits in TESTFLD are those corresponding to a 1 in the mask.

Test Under Mask	Condition Code	Typical Branches Performed
Selected bits in TESTFLD = 0	0	BZ (branch if all bits = 0) BNZ (branch if all bits ≠ 0)
Selected bits in TESTFLD = 1	3	BO (branch if all bits = 1) BNO (branch if all bits are ≠ 1)
Selected bits in TESTFLD are mixed (some are 0, some are 1)	1	BM (branch if bits are mixed) BNM (branch if bits are not mixed; that is, bits are all 0 or all 1)

Suppose you are testing to determine if the selected bits in TESTFLD = 0; then you would typically test for BZ or BNZ. If you are testing to determine if the selected bits in TESTFLD = 1, then you would typically branch using a BO or BNO. If the selected bits are expected to be mixed, you could branch using a BM or BNM.

Consider the following.

```
TM   FLAG,B'00000001'
```

The bits in the mask are numbered 0 through 7 from left to right. Only the low-order bit, typically numbered bit 7, in the storage byte called FLAG will be tested. This is because the immediate byte or mask only contains a 1 in the low-order or rightmost position.

Example 20.10   Suppose a storage byte called FLAG contains 00001111. The contents of FLAG, then, are equivalent to X'0F'.

```
                                    FLAG
FLAG = X'0F'             0 0 0 0 | 1 1 1 1
                   bit   0                 7
```

Consider the following.

Instruction 1:
```
TM   FLAG,B'10010000'
```

1. The instruction tests only the bits in the immediate byte that are equal to 1. This means only bits 0 and 3 in FLAG are tested.
2. Bit 0 in FLAG = 0.
   Bit 3 in FLAG = 0.
3. Because bits 0 and 3 in FLAG are both equal to 0, the condition code is set equal to 0. BZ or BNZ would typically be used for conditional branching.

Instruction 2:
```
TM   FLAG,B'10001000'
```

1. The instruction tests only the bits in the immediate byte that are equal to 1. This means bits 0 and 4 in FLAG are tested.
2. Bit 0 in FLAG = 0.
   Bit 4 in FLAG = 1.
3. Thus, the condition code is set equal to 1 (both bits are *not* equal to 1 and both are *not* equal to 0). BM, Branch if Mixed, or BNM, Branch if Not Mixed, would typically be used for branching.

Instruction 3:
```
TM   FLAG,B'00001110'
```

1. The instruction tests only the bits in the immediate byte that are equal to 1. This means bits 4–6 in FLAG are tested.
2. Bits 4–6 in FLAG are all "on" bits.

3. The condition code is set equal to 3 because all bits tested in FLAG are equal to 1. The BO instruction will cause a branch to occur.

Note that the binary format for representing the immediate byte is not the only one that may be used. The following is equivalent to Instruction 3.

```
TM  FLAG,X'0E'   or   TM  FLAG,B'00001110'
```

This is because X'0E' is equivalent to B'00001110'.

The TM, like the Compare, does not alter the contents of bits being tested.

In summary, the possible conditional branch instructions that may be executed after the TM instruction include

BO	(Branch if all tested bits = 1)
BZ	(Branch if all tested bits = 0)
BM	(Branch if some tested bits = 1, and some tested bits = 0)
BNO	(Branch if not all tested bits = 1; that is, some or all tested bits = 0)
BNZ	(Branch if not all tested bits = 0)
BNM	(Branch if not mixed; that is, all are 1 or all are 0)

Consider the following.

```
TM  FLAG, B'10010000'
BZ  NEXT
```

If FLAG has contents of X'0F', a branch to NEXT will occur because all tested bits (bit 0 and bit 3) equal 0.

The most common use of the TM instruction is testing for flag bits. Each of several bits in a storage byte can serve as a flag. Different procedures can be executed depending on the configurations of the bits in the byte. In this sense, the storage byte acts as an internal switch. This is particularly useful for testing for errors in indexed file processing. See Chapter 22.

The TM is one of the few instructions that tests bits rather than full or half bytes. The TM tests a string of bits and should not be confused with byte-comparison instructions such as CLC or CLI.

Self-Evaluating Quiz

1. TM is an abbreviation for _____ .
2. TM is a(n) _____ type of instruction.

Consider the following.

```
TM  FLAG,X'05'
```

What will be the setting of the condition code in each of the following and what branch instructions will typically be used for branching?

```
    FLAG
```

3. 00000101
4. 00000000
5. 00000011
6. 11111111
7. Will a branch to OUT occur if SSX has a hex content of F3?

```
TM  SSX,B'11110011'
BO  OUT
```

SOLUTIONS

1. Test Under Mask
2. Storage Immediate

3.	3	BO or BNO
4.	0	BZ or BNZ
5.	1	BM or BNM

6. 3

7. Yes

BO or BNO (on-bits in storage that do not correspond to on-bits in the immediate byte do *not* affect the comparison)

IV. THE EXECUTE (EX) INSTRUCTION

The Execute (EX) instruction is an RX instruction. During execution, it causes the computer to perform another instruction called the **target instruction.** The target instruction is located at the address given in the second operand.

The format of the EX instruction follows.

EX R1,D2(X2,B2)   or   EX R1,LABEL

This is the address of the target instruction

After the EX instruction causes the target instruction to be executed, the instruction following the EX is performed. The EX, then, is like a PERFORM in high-level languages, or a subroutine with the limitation that only one instruction is executed with it.

Note the following.

1. An EX cannot have another EX instruction as its target instruction.
2. If the target instruction is an unconditional branch instruction, the branch is performed and control will *not* return to the instruction following the EX.
3. The target instruction may be a conditional branch instruction: (a) if the condition is met, the branch is performed, and control will *not* return to the instruction following the EX, and (b) if the condition is not met the instruction after the EX is executed next.
4. If the target instruction is a BALR, control will return to the instruction after the EX.

When the EX is executed, the low-order 8 bits of the register used in the EX are used to change bits 8–15 of the target instruction. We say the bits in the register are *ORed* with the bits in the target instruction. The result of this OR actually becomes part of the target instruction. The result of an OR is as follows for each bit.

Results of an OR

Bit in Register of EX Instruction	Corresponding Bit in Target Instruction	New Result in Corresponding Bit in Target Instruction (After EX)
0	0	0
1	0	1
0	1	1
1	1	1

Note that if a bit in the target instruction is initially 0, it is *replaced* by 0 or 1, whichever is in the corresponding bit in the register of the EX instruction. Typically the target instruction is coded so that bits 8–15 will in fact begin as zero to allow this simple replacement.

Note the overall results of an OR. After the EX, each of bits 8–15 of the target instruction will always contain a 1 unless they were originally 0 and the corresponding bit in the register of the EX was also zero. The actual effect of this depends on the type of instruction being performed.

Because EX can perform any type of instruction (RR, RX, SS, SI), it can be used to

1. Modify immediate operands in SI instructions;
2. Test conditions to cause branching; and,
3. Identify actual registers to be used as operands in RR instructions.

Suppose we want to move a string of characters from Z to Y, where the length of the move is determined by the contents of a register. For example, let us use register 8. Note that to obtain a five-character move, register 8 should actually contain one less, or 4. This is because the computer begins counting from zero. We may code the following within the program as the target instruction.

```
VARLEN MVC Y(0),Z
```

Whenever we want an MVC performed where the length of characters moved from Z to Y is determined by the contents of register 8, we code

```
EX 8,VARLEN
```

In this way, the contents of register 8 will determine the number of characters moved. At one point register 8 may contain 8 characters, in which case 9 characters (one more than the contents of register 8) are moved from Z to Y; in another instance 6 characters may be moved from Z to Y if register 8 contains a 5 when EX is executed.

The instruction VARLEN is set off from the main sequence of the program so that it is only executed when the EX is performed.

```
      ⋮
      ⋮
      EX 8,VARLEN
      ⋮
      ⋮
      BR 14 ←——————— unconditional branch
VARLEN MVC Y(0),Z ←—— can only be executed from EX
```

After the MVC is executed, control returns to the instruction following the EX.

The MVC is an SS-type instruction that is assembled as follows:

Op Code		Length		Operand 1 Address		Operand 2 Address	
0	7	8	15	16	31	32	47

The EX will not only execute or perform the MVC, it will determine the length of the move. Because the MVC is translated as an explicit move with Operand 1 as Y(0), the length begins as all zeros. Whatever is in the 8 low-order bits of register 8 will be ORed with this length of zero. ORing bits where the receiving set of bits is all zeros, as in this case, is the same as replacing the receiving set. That is, 1 ORed with 0 is 1, and 0 ORed with 0 is 0. Thus, if register 8 contained 6 in the 8 low-order bits, then 6 would replace the length in the MVC, as follows.

Low-Order 6 Bits OR of Register 8	*Bits 8–15 (Length) of* MVC *Instruction*	*New Contents of Bits 8–15 of* MVC *(After* EX*)*
00000110	00000000	00000110

The EX 8,VARLEN then performs the instruction at VARLEN and determines the length of the MVC at VARLEN as well. The contents of the low-order 8 bits of register 8 replace the length code, which was initially zero. The above then results in a 7-character move.

The EX instruction is a useful structured programming tool that may be used for performing an instruction from different points in the program.

CHAPTER SUMMARY

I. Floating-Point Numbers and Instructions
  A. Floating-point numbers are hexadecimal versions of scientific notation.
    1. Makes it easier for performing arithmetic if all numbers use a mantissa and characteristic.
    2. Floating-point numbers are represented as $\pm H \times 16^K$ where H is a hexadecimal fraction between 0 and 1.
    3. Floating-point numbers are typically represented in 32 bits. The exponent or characteristic can range from -64 to 63, with the mantissa being between 0 and 1 for positive numbers and -1 and 0 for negative numbers.
    4. Thus, floating-point numbers range from 16^{-65} to 16^{63} for positive numbers, and -16^{-65} to -16^{63} for negative numbers.
    5. Double-precision or 64-bit floating-point numbers can also be represented.
  B. Figure 20.1 lists floating-point instructions and the corresponding integer or fixed-point instructions.
    1. Floating-point instructions are either of the RR or RX type.
    2. HALVE and ROUND have no corresponding integer instructions.
II. The Translate (TR) and Translate and Test (TRT) Instructions
  A. Meaning
    1. The TR replaces some or all bytes in a string with another byte or character.
    2. The TRT searches a string from left to right for the first occurrence of a specified character.
  B. Features
    1. Both instructions are used to reduce the size and run time of programs that perform string operations.
    2. Both are SS-type instructions.
  C. Uses for the TR instruction
    1. To change data entered as ASCII to EBCDIC.
    2. To translate uppercase letters to lowercase and vice versa.
  D. Uses for TRT instructions
    1. Searching for blanks.
    2. Checking for positive or negative numbers.
III. The Test Under Mask (TM) Instruction
  A. Tests the values of specific bits in a particular byte of storage.
  B. The TM is an SI instruction with Operand 2 containing an 8-bit immediate byte called a mask.
IV. The Execute (EX) Instruction
  A. Causes the computer to perform another instruction called the target instruction.
  B. After the EX instruction causes the target instruction to be executed, the instruction following the EX is performed.
  C. When the EX is executed, the low-order 8 bits of the register used in the EX instruction are ORed with bits 8–15 of the target instruction.

KEY TERMS

Argument

Function

Function string

Mask

REVIEW QUESTIONS

Assume that using scientific notation any number can be represented as $D \times 10^N$.

1. D is typically any positive or negative number, with or without a decimal component, with a value between _____ and _____ .

2. In the above, D is called the _____ .

3. N is a positive or negative integer or zero. It is called the _____ .

4. In the above, 10 is called the _____ .

5. Using scientific notation, 270 is represented as _____ .

6. Using scientific notation, 5387 is represented as _____ .

7. Any number raised to the zero power is _____ .

8. State the reasons why scientific notation is used with computers.

9. In addition, if numbers have the same characteristic, you simply add the _____ .

10. In subtraction, if the characteristic of both numbers is the same, subtract the first _____ from the second.

11. To multiply two numbers using scientific notation, multiply the _____ and add the _____ .

12. IBM and IBM-compatible mainframes represent data using _____ or base _____ numbers.

13. Although scientific notation is used to represent any number as $D \times 10^N$, _____ numbers are represented as $H \times 16^K$ where H is a number between 0 and 1 and K is a positive integer.

14. Using floating-point notation, 2.0 is represented as _____ .

15. Double precision means that a number is more precise because it is represented using (no.) bits.

16. To define any number, constant, or literal in assembler language, we use a(n) _____ .

17. For the short format or single precision, alignment is always on a(n) _____ boundary.

18. For the long or extended format, alignment is always on a _____ boundary.

19. The specification

```
XX   DS   4E
```

reserves space for (no.) floating-point numbers in short form.

20. (T or F) Floating-point instructions are of the RX or RR type.

21. (T or F) All floating-point instructions use registers.

22. The _____ instruction replaces some or all bytes in a string with another byte or character.

23. The _____ instruction searches from left to right for the first occurrence of a specific character.

24. (T or F) The TR instruction can be used for replacing uppercase letters with lowercase letters and vice versa.

25. (T or F) A scan or check operation to check a field for invalid characters may be performed with a TRT operation.

26. The TM is a(n) (type) instruction.

27. TM is an abbreviation for _____ .

28. In a TM operation, Operand 2 contains an 8-bit immediate byte called a(n) _____ .

29. (T or F) One common use of the TM instruction is testing for flag bits.

30. (T or F) The TM tests full or half bytes, not individual bits.

UNIT 7

DISK
AND TAPE
PROGRAMMING

Sequential File Processing Using Disk and Tape

To familiarize you with:
1. *Tape and disk concepts.*
2. *Sequential update procedures using disk or tape as a master file.*

I. MAGNETIC TAPE CONCEPTS: AN OVERVIEW

A magnetic tape, like a magnetic disk, is a high-speed medium that can serve as input to or output from a computer. Like disk, it is frequently used for storing files.

A magnetic tape drive (see Figure 21.1) is the device that can either read a tape or write onto a tape. It has *one* read/write head for either reading or writing.

A typical magnetic tape is generally from 2400 to 3600 feet long and ½ inch wide. The tape is made of plastic with an iron-oxide coating that can be magnetized to represent data.[1] It can store data in EBCDIC form with anywhere from 800–6250 characters per inch of tape depending on the system. The number of characters per inch is referred to as the *tape density*.

Tapes have the following advantages:

1. Large storage capacity: Tape can store millions of characters, that is, hundreds of thousands of records.
2. High speed: Data can be read from or written on tape very quickly.
3. Records can be any size. Moreover, they can be either fixed or variable in length.
4. Tapes, like cassettes used with home cassette recorders, can be rewritten when the stored data is no longer needed.

**Figure 21.1
Magnetic tapes and tape
drives. (Courtesy McNeil Pharmaceuticals.)**

[1]We will see in the next section how magnetized bits are used to represent characters.

Tapes also have some disadvantages:

1. You cannot read from a tape and write back onto the tape in a single procedure. Thus, to change a file stored on tape, you must create a new file that incorporates the changes.
2. Tapes must be read sequentially. You cannot write a program that instructs the computer to go to the middle of a tape, for example, even though you know that a specific record to be read is in the middle.

Magnetic disk does not have the limitations described above. Hence, magnetic disks tend to be used for large-volume files more frequently than tape.

II. MAGNETIC DISK CONCEPTS: AN OVERVIEW

In this chapter we focus on disk concepts as well as on sequential file processing that can be performed using either tapes or disks. In the next chapter we focus on file processing that can make use of a disk's random-access capability. Before considering the various file processing techniques, we will consider magnetic disk concepts. If you are already familiar with disk concepts, skip to Section III of this chapter.

A. Features of Magnetic Disk

1. Physical Characteristics

Magnetic disk is a high-speed medium that can serve as either input to, or output from, a computer system. See Figure 21.2 for an illustration of a disk. Like tape, a disk has an iron-oxide coating that can store hundreds of millions of characters of data. The magnetic **disk drive** is used both for recording information onto the disk and for reading information from it. A disk drive is the major form of direct-access storage device used at installations today.

The standard magnetic disk is actually a disk pack that consists of a series of platters or disks arranged in a vertical stack and connected by a central shaft. The concept is similar to a group of phonograph records stacked on a spindle. The number of disk platters in a pack varies with the unit. Figure 21.3 illustrates a disk pack with 11 platters.

Data may be recorded on *both* sides of each disk platter. There are, however, typically only 20 recording surfaces for an 11-disk unit because the top surface of the first disk and the bottom surface of the last disk do not contain data. Those two surfaces tend to collect dust and, therefore, are not viable for data storage. Some permanently enclosed disk packs, however, allow for recording data on all surfaces.

If we have an 11-disk pack with 20 recording surfaces, the disk drive would have 10 access arms, each with two read/write heads that are used for reading and writing data on the surface above and below, as in Figure 21.4. Recall that a tape drive has only one read/write head. One reason why access time for a disk is considerably shorter than for a tape is that disk drives have more than one read/write head. This is a primary reason why tape processing is being replaced with disk processing in many organizations.

Each disk surface stores data as magnetized bits on concentric circles called **tracks** (see Figure 21.5). There are usually from 200 to 600 tracks per surface depending on the unit. Each track can store thousands of characters of data. Although the surface area of tracks near the center is smaller than the surface area of outer tracks, all tracks store precisely the same number of characters. This is because data stored in innermost tracks is stored more densely. (This is true of phonograph records as well.)

Each concentric circle on all surfaces form a 3-dimensional cylinder. As you will see in Figure 21.6, all concentric circles on all surfaces are jointly called

Figure 21.2

a **cylinder.** The number-1 cylinder, for example, consists of all number-1 tracks on all surfaces, treated as a single unit.

Disks vary widely in storage capacity and specifications. Individual records on most disks, however, can be addressed by the following method.

ADDRESSING DISK RECORDS

1. Surface number (0 to 19 for our illustration).
2. Track or cylinder number (0 to 199 for our illustration).
3. Sector number (for some disks).
    Note that surface, track or cylinder, and sector numbers begin at 0.

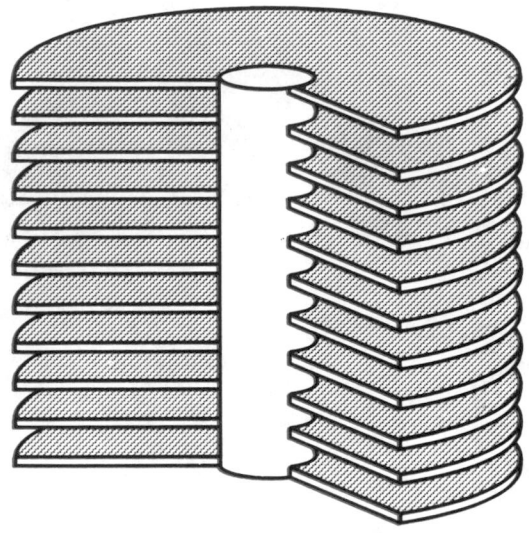

Figure 21.3
Cross-sectional view of a typical disk pack.

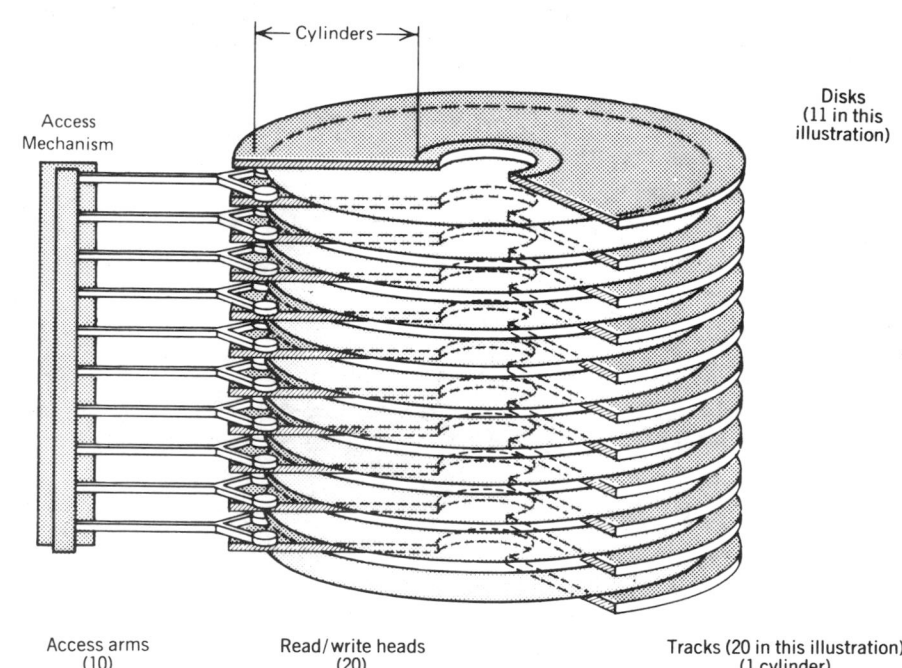

Figure 21.4
How data is accessed from a disk pack. Each read/write head accesses a specific surface. The read/write heads move in and out together as a function of the access mechanism.

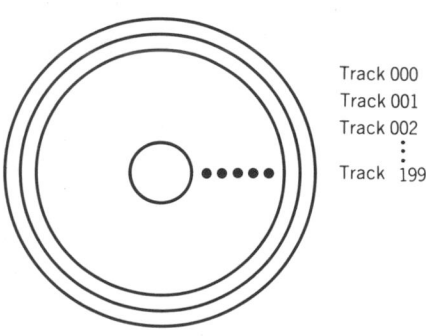

Figure 21.5
Tracks on a disk surface.

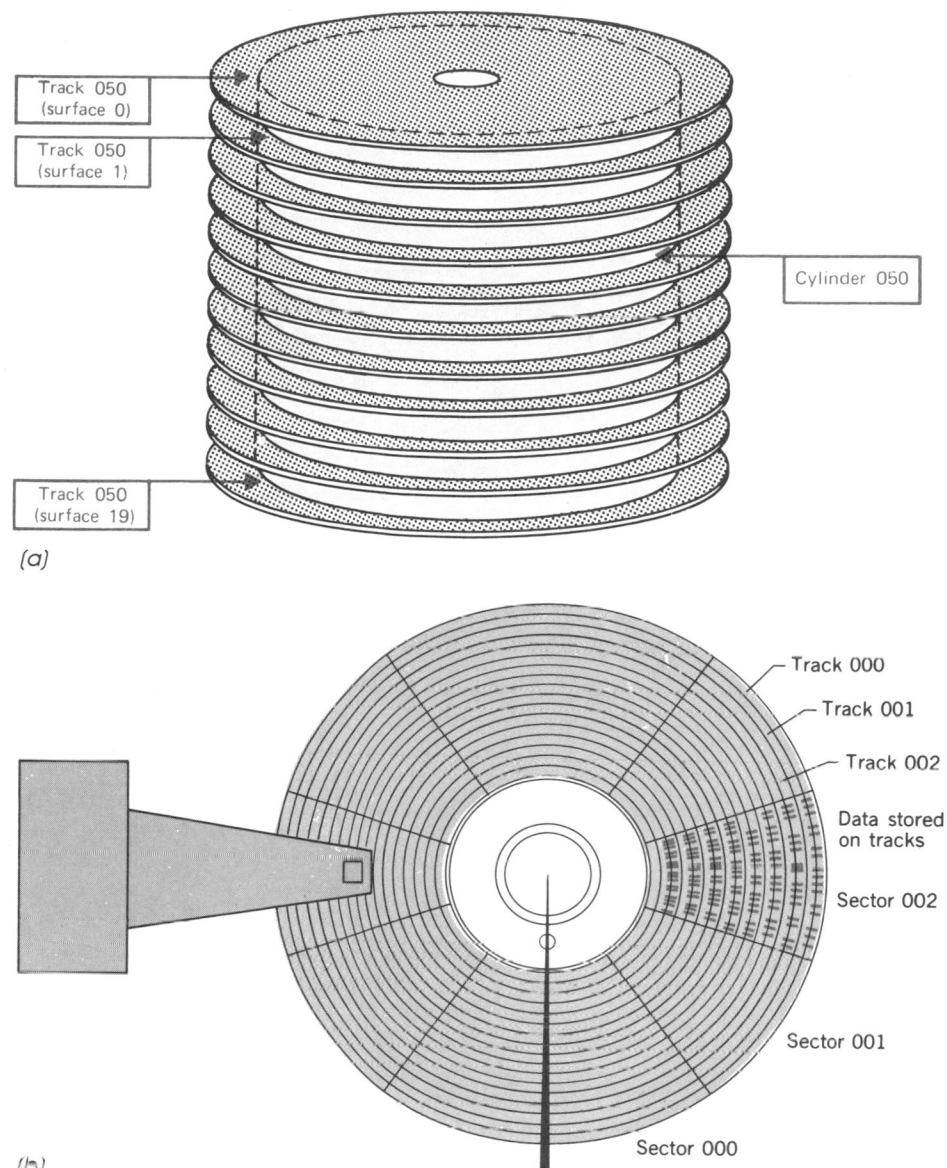

Figure 21.6
(a) The cylinder concept on a magnetic disk. (b) The sector concept on a magnetic disk.

The maximum capacities of several commonly used disks follow.

Device	Storage Capacity in Megabytes
IBM 3340	70
IBM 3350	317.5
IBM 3370	571.4
IBM 3380	1260.5

2. Representation of Data on a Magnetic Disk

Data is represented on many disks using the 9-bit EBCDIC code, the same code used to represent data internally in an IBM or IBM-compatible computer. Tapes store data in EBCDIC form, too. Each byte or character is represented longitudinally along a disk track by a 9-bit configuration. See Figure 21.7.

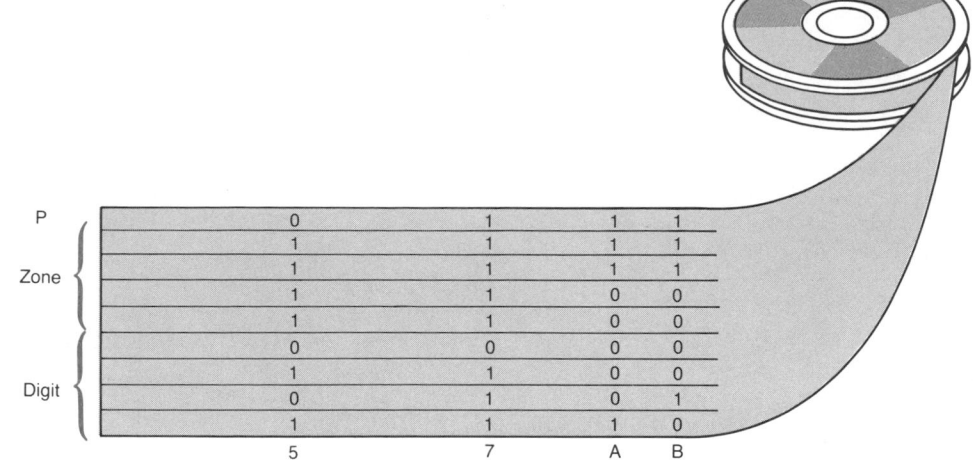

Figure 21.7
Example of how data is stored in EBCDIC form on a 9-track tape.

		0		1		1	1
P		1		1		1	1
Zone		1		1		1	1
		1		1		0	0
		1		1		0	0
		0		0		0	0
Digit		1		1		0	0
		0		1		0	1
		1		1		1	0
		5		7		A	B

3. Recording Data on a Magnetic Disk

There are two methods used to record data on a disk.

a. Magnetic Disk Drive. A program can be written to read data from an input device such as a terminal, and to produce a magnetic disk record using a magnetic disk drive as an output device.

b. Key-to-Disk Encoder or Key-to-Disk System. An operator may key data from a source document onto a magnetic disk using a terminal or other key-to-disk device.

4. Specifying Disk (and Tape) Records

a. Size of Records. As previously noted, a disk or tape can have any record size; it is not restricted, like a punched card or a line entered on a terminal, to an 80-column format. Moreover, all disk and tape records within a given file need not have the same length. That is, they can store (1) **fixed-length records,** where all records are the same size, or (2) **variable-length records,** where the lengths differ. We focus on fixed-length records in this text because they are easier to process and they are far more prevalent in industry.

b. Interblock Gap. Between physical disk and tape records the computer automatically reserves a fraction of an inch of blank area called an **interblock gap (IBG).** Thus, when a disk or tape is created as computer output, it is created as indicated in Figure 21.8, with interblock gaps between physical records.

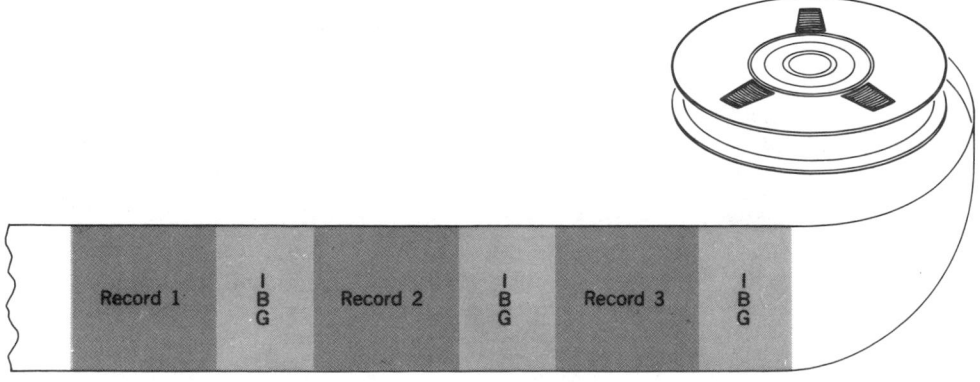

Figure 21.8
Physical records separated by interblock gaps (IBGs).

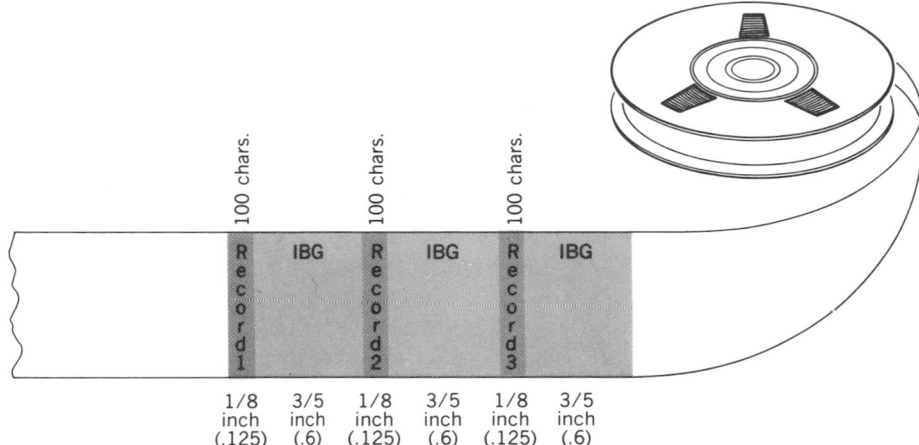

Figure 21.9
Example of how interblock gaps can result in inefficient use of a disk or tape.

Because a disk or tape record is read at high speeds, it takes a fraction of a second for the drive to stop physically when it senses the end of the record. This delay is analogous to what happens when the brakes are applied on a car: it takes several feet before the automobile physically comes to a halt. The interblock gap (IBG) is created so that, when a record is read, the mechanism will not pass over data from the next record in the time it takes to stop.

This interblock gap ranges up to $^6/_{10}$ of an inch on some systems. Thus, if small record sizes are used, there will be a significant amount of unused disk or tape between each actual record. See Figure 21.9 for an illustration of how interblock gaps can result in inefficient use of a disk or tape.

c. Blocking Records to Minimize Wasted Space and To Save Time. To minimize wasted space and save access time, disk and tape records are frequently **blocked** so that several actual or logical records are grouped together in a block, as in Figure 21.10. Blocking of logical records maximizes the use of the disk or tape by increasing the speed at which data is transferred to or from the CPU.

In assembler, it is relatively easy to instruct the computer that there are, for example, 90-character logical records that are blocked 10.

The DTF (Define the File) for a sequential disk is DTFSD; the DTF for a magnetic tape is DTFMT. We may use the following coding in a DTF to indicate that records are blocked.

```
DTFSD    BLKSIZE=900
            :
            :
         RECSIZE=90
```

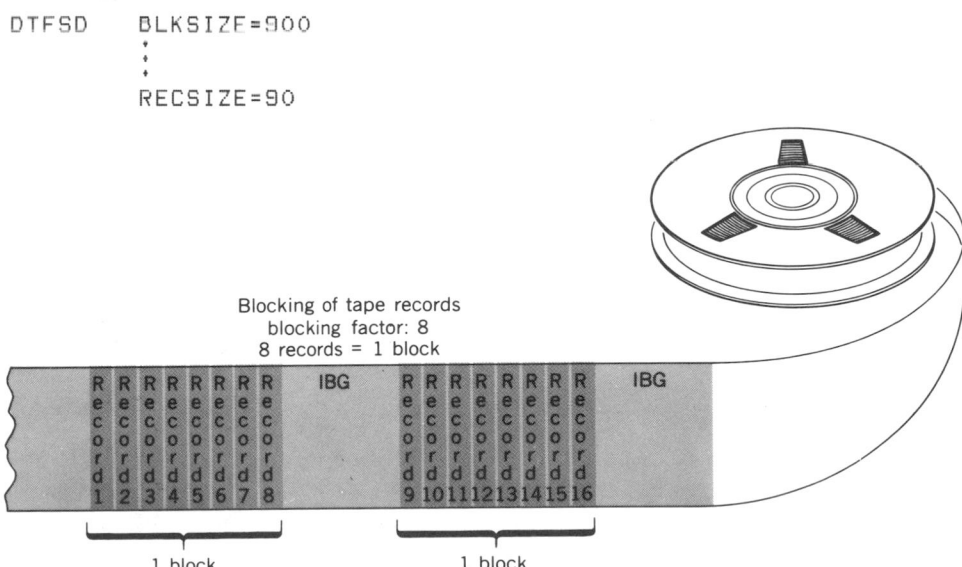

Blocking of tape records
blocking factor: 8
8 records = 1 block

1 block   1 block

Figure 21.10
Blocking of records.

If this is an input file, the computer will read in a block of 900 characters (90 × 10), processing each logical record within the block in sequence. The computer knows that the size of each logical record is 90; thus, there are 10 records per block.

In short, blocking makes for efficient use of computer time; moreover, the handling of blocked disk and tape files is relatively easy for the assembler language programmer.

d. Programming Standard Labels on Disk and Tape. Because data is represented on disk and tape as magnetized bits, it is not manually readable. Hence, disk and tape identification can be a problem. Consequently, to help identify disk and tape files, most programs include a built-in routine that creates a disk or tape label record on each output file. This label, which uses magnetized bits, is produced as the first disk or tape record. When the file is entered as input at some later date, this first label record, called a **header label,** is checked by the program to determine if the correct disk or tape is being used.

Thus, the header labels are created on output disks and tapes and subsequently checked on input disks and tapes. This label creation for output and label checking for input is a standard procedure in most programs. Because the computer verifies that the correct files are being used, the danger of errors resulting from carelessness is reduced.

To perform standard label routines in assembler as part of a disk or tape DTF, code

```
⎡ DTFMT ⎤
⎢  or  ⎥
⎣ DTFSD ⎦
     ⋮
     ⋮
  FILABL=STD
```

e. Density. Density is one entry required in a DTFMT but not in a DTFSD. Tape densities vary from 800 to 6250 characters per inch. In your DTFMT, you would code the actual DENSITY as follows:

```
DTFMT
  ⋮
  ⋮
DENSITY=800
```

B. Characteristics of Magnetic Disk Drives for Mainframes

Magnetic disk drives are direct-access devices designed to minimize the access time required to locate specific records. Each drive has a series of access arms that can locate records on specific surfaces. For disk drives with 10 access arms, as indicated in our illustration, the time needed to locate records that are not in sequence will be much less than that required by a tape drive with only one read/write mechanism.

There are several types of disk mechanisms.

1. Moving-Head and Fixed-Head Magnetic Disks

In a **moving-head magnetic disk,** all read/write heads are attached to a single movable access mechanism. As specified by the computer, the access mechanism moves directly to the specific track or cylinder on the disk. However, this type of mechanism has a relatively slow access rate as compared to fixed-head disks because all the read/write heads move together to locate a record.

Because disks are generally used for high-speed access of records from a file (for example, an airline reservation file), any method that can reduce the time to access an individual record directly is beneficial. **Fixed-head magnetic disks** were developed to decrease access time substantially. These devices do *not* have a movable access arm. Instead, each track has its own read/write mechanism that accesses a record as it rotates past the arm. The disks in this device are not, however, removable. Moreover, the capacity of each disk is somewhat less than with other types of disks, although the access time is significantly reduced.

2. Removable and Nonremovable Disk Packs

On some systems, the disks may be removed from the pack. On other systems, the disk pack is sealed and the disks are nonremovable.

IBM drives with removable disk packs include models 2314, 3330, and 3340. IBM drives with nonremovable disk packs include models 3344, 3350, 3375, and 3380.

C. Advantages of Magnetic Disk Processing

1. Disks (and Tapes) Are Ideally Suited for High-Volume Files

Because magnetic disks and tapes can be processed very quickly and can store large amounts of data, they are frequently used for high-volume files. A **master file,** which is the major collection of data for an application, is most frequently stored on disk (or tape). Thus, accounts receivable master files, and payroll master files, etc. are apt to be on disk or tape.

2. Disks May Be Used for Either Random-Access or Sequential Processing

A main advantage of disk processing, as compared to tape, is the ability to access records directly. Because most disk packs have many addressable recording surfaces and multiple read/write heads, records on a disk file can be accessed directly without searching through an entire file. If we knew a record was on surface 3, for example, it would *not* be necessary to start looking for the record at the beginning of the file.

There are three common methods of accessing data on disks.

1. Sequential
2. Indexed—ISAM and VSAM
3. Direct

In this chapter sequential files are described; in the next chapter indexed files are discussed in depth; direct files are only briefly explained because they are less frequently used

3. Disk Files May Be Easily Accessed and Modified as Needed

Disk files have the added advantage over tape files of permitting updates or changes to existing records *in the same disk location*. A new disk file does not have to be created to incorporate current changes, as is usually required with tape processing. That is, the *same* disk record may be used as *both* input and output in the same program. We can read a record from a disk, make changes to that record, and rewrite it at *the same disk location*. We can also add and delete records from the disk file. This is referred to as "updating in place."

Frequently, however, a new disk file is created and the old disk file maintained intact as a means of backup. This is a good security precaution.

D. Maintaining Disk Files

Disks, like tapes, cannot be read by the human eye. Consequently, there is a need for appropriate controls to handle disk files properly. Some of the commonly used types of controls include

1. An external label placed on the disk packs for visual identification;
2. A programmed header label created as the initial record on a disk file that can be checked each time the disk file is used. It ensures that the correct file is being processed; and,
3. A librarian or media specialist hired by a company to control access to disk packs.

Disks, however, have an added control problem associated with updating records in place. This problem never affects tape processing because tapes cannot be used as input and output during the same procedure. Each tape update always results in both a new tape and an old one, where the old can be used as **backup** if necessary. When new disk files are created and the old ones are retained, these disk backups are available just like tape backups. But, when changes are made directly to an existing disk file, the update procedure writes over previous file data. As a result, there is no automatic backup file created. To prevent the loss of master data resulting from erroneous processing, sabotage, or a natural disaster such as a fire, lightning strikes, or power outages, disk files should be copied onto a tape for backup purposes. Thus, a separate backup procedure is wise and necessary after disks have been processed in this way.

The following is a general summary of tape and disk concepts.

SUMMARY

1. To store high-volume files, like master files.
2. For auxiliary or secondary storage.

Common Features of Tape and Disk

1. Tapes and disks can be used as either input or output.
2. Tape and disk drives can read and write data very quickly using their read/write heads.
3. Tapes and disks can store millions of characters of data.
4. Tapes and disks can store records of almost any size.
5. Tapes and disks store data as magnetized bits.
6. Tape and disk records may be blocked to maximize efficient use of the storage medium.
7. Tape and disk files are identified with header labels.
8. Tape and disk files may be created by key-to-storage systems, that is, either key-to-tape or key-to-disk systems.

Distinctions Between Tape and Disk

1. Access mode
   a. Tapes must be processed sequentially.
   b. Disks can be processed either sequentially or randomly.
   For random-access capability, disk files are typically organized as indexed, relative, or direct.
2. Updating
   a. Changes may not be made directly to a tape—for updating, an entirely new tape must be created.
   b. Changes may be made directly to a disk; that is, disk records may be rewritten in place.

> ### Physical Characteristics of Magnetic Tape
>
> 1. 2400–3600 feet long, ½-inch wide, plastic tape with an iron-oxide coating.
> 2. Tape density is from 800–6250 characters per inch.
>
> ### Physical Characteristics of Magnetic Disk
>
> 1. Surfaces on a disk pack also have an iron-oxide coating.
> 2. A disk pack consists of a series of platters arranged in a vertical stack.
> 3. Each platter—except for the top and bottom—has two recording surfaces.
> 4. Address of a disk record consists of a surface and track or cylinder number, and sometimes a sector number.

III. PROCESSING OF SEQUENTIAL FILES

A. Systems Overview of Sequential File Processing

In this section we will focus on concepts applicable to sequential file processing regardless of whether the file is stored on tape or disk.

B. What is a Master File?

A **master file** is the major collection of data pertaining to a specific application. Typically, companies will have master files in the following application areas as well as many others.

1. Payroll.
2. Accounts receivable.
3. Accounts payable.
4. Production.
5. Sales.
6. Inventory.

In most installations, a master file will be stored on either a magnetic disk or a magnetic tape. There are several features of disk and tape that make them ideally suited for storing master file data.

> ### FEATURES OF DISK AND TAPE
>
> 1. Can store hundreds of thousands of records or more on a single tape or disk unit.
> 2. Can process records at very high speeds.
> 3. Can store records of any size.
> 4. Disk and tape drives can be used either to read or to record data.

C. Disk and Tape Master Files

Whether a master file is stored on disk or on tape depends on the needs of the company and on how the master file is to be accessed. There are two main reasons why a disk might be the primary storage medium for a master file.

REASONS WHY DISKS ARE PREFERRED FOR MASTER FILES

1. When records must be processed randomly—that is, in a sequence other than the one in which they are stored, disk files are used. Tapes can only be processed sequentially.
2. When immediate or direct access of records is required, as with a reservation system, disk files are used.
3. Data transmission rates are faster with disk than with tape.

When records are processed in sequence and direct accessing is not required, the master file can be stored sequentially on *either* disk or tape. Thus, a disk can be used either for random or direct access, or for sequential access. However, a tape is used almost exclusively for files that are processed sequentially. Because disk has more advantages than tape, many organizations have begun to phase out tape and to use disk for all master files.

File maintenance procedures are discussed in two chapters. These procedures are different for sequential and random processing, as follows:

1. *Sequential file processing* can be employed when disk or tape is used for storing the master file. This chapter focuses on sequential file processing.
2. *Random processing* is used with disk files *only*. Tapes can only be processed sequentially. The next chapter includes a discussion of how a disk file can be organized and processed using various random-access techniques.

D. Typical Master File Procedures

We will now focus on procedures typically used for handling master files, regardless of whether they are stored on disk or tape. These procedures include creating a master file, creating a transaction file of change records, updating the master file, and reporting from the master file.

1. Creating a Master File

When a new system is implemented, a master file must be created. This procedure can be performed by entering all master file data from a terminal or other data-entry device. The data is then recorded on a tape or disk and becomes the master file. This creation process is a one-time procedure. Once it is created, changes to the master file are made by using a different program.

The primary objective of a program that creates a master file is ensuring *data integrity*. A master file is useful only if it contains valid and reliable data; hence, a creation program must be designed so that it minimizes input errors. Validating procedures are *imperative* when creating a master file. A listing should also be produced that indicates the new master file data as well as whatever control totals are deemed necessary. This control listing is verified by personnel in the user department as an additional verification technique.

Creating a Sequential File Under DOS   The DOS file definition macro that defines a sequential file follows.

Magnetic tape	DTFMT
Sequential disk	DTFSD

The entries are quite similar to DTFCD, DTFPR, and DTFDI discussed throughout this book. The same macros are used for I/O processing.

I/O Macros to Create Sequential Disk or Tape

```
OPEN
CLOSE
PUT
```

PUT creates a sequential disk or tape file. We will see later that GET accesses this file. An I/O delay to check for errors is required to synchronize instructions properly when using a PUT or a GET. The instruction CHECK may be required after each PUT or GET to cause this delay with some systems. If so, the DTF or DCB must include an address to branch to if a synchronization error occurs. This is denoted as SYNAD = ERRORTN. At ERRORTN, you would indicate precisely what is to be done if a synchronization error occurs (for example, terminate the run, print a message, etc.).

The computer's input/output control system (IOCS) handles all label processing, blocking and deblocking, wrong length record checks, and so on.

Figure 21.11 illustrates a program that reads input records and writes them onto a sequential tape using DOS.

1. Records from INFILE are read into RECIN.
2. They are moved to the tape work area called TWORK.
3. The work area is then written onto the output file called OUTFILE with a PUT instruction.
4. When there is no more input, EOJRTN is executed, files are closed, and the run is terminated.

A brief review of DTF entries for the output file OUTFILE follows.

BLKSIZE=400	This indicates the size of a physical record. Because each logical record is 80 bytes there must be five logical records per block. The blocking factor, then, is 5.
DEVADDR=XXXXX	System-dependent entry.
FILABL=STD	Indicates that the tape file has standard labels.
IOAREA1=BUFFROUT	This is an I/O area that may be used as a buffer.
RECFORM=FIXBLK	Output records are fixed length and blocked.
RECSIZE=80	Each logical record is 80 characters.
TYPEFLE=OUTPUT	The file type is output.
WORKA=YES	Indicates that the program will process output records in the work area.
DENSITY=800	Indicates that the tape has a density of 800 characters per inch.

```
*                                                                        *
*                               HOUSEKEEPING INSTRUCTIONS GO HERE        *
*                                                                        *
CREATE    OPEN   INFILE,OUTFILE
          GET    INFILE,RECIN
          MVC    ACCTOUT,ACCTIN
          MVC    AMTOUT,AMTIN
          PUT    OUTFILE,RECOUT
          B      CREATE
EOJRTN    CLOSE  INFILE,OUTFILE
          EOJ
INFILE    DTFCD  DEVADDR=SYSIPT,BLKSIZE=80,RECFORM=FIXUNB,              *
                 IOAREA1=BUFFRIN,WORKA=YES,DEVICE=2501,                 *
                 TYPEFLE=INPUT,EOFADDR=EOJRTN
OUTFILE   DTFMT  BLKSIZE=400,DEVADDR=SYS012,FILABL=STD,                 *
                 IOAREA1=BUFFROUT,RECFORM=FIXBLK,RECSIZE=80,            *
                 TYPEFLE=OUTPUT,WORKA=YES,DENSITY=800
BUFFRIN   DS     CL80
BUFFROUT  DS     CL400
RECIN     DS     0CL80
ACCTIN    DS     CL5
AMTIN     DS     CL5
          DS     CL70
TWORK     DS     0CL80
ACCTOUT   DS     CL5
AMTOUT    DS     CL5
          DC     CL70' '
          END
```

Figure 21.11
DOS program that reads input records and writes them onto a sequential tape.

The major changes required in the DOS sequential file create program if output is on a sequential disk rather than tape are

```
DTFSD    BLKSIZE=408
         DEVADDR=XXXXX
            .
            .
         VERIFY=YES
```

Note, too, that the DENSITY entry is not required for sequential disk.

1. BLKSIZE=408
   An extra eight bytes are added to all disk blocks as a count field.
2. DEVADDR=xxxxx
   This is a device-dependent entry. Use the disk number, that is, 3330, 3340, and so on.
3. VERIFY=YES
   VERIFY ensures that disk output is created correctly.

The changes needed for the program in Figure 21.11 to create a sequential disk file appear in Figure 21.12.

Figure 21.12

Changes needed for the program in Figure 21.1 to create a sequential disk file under DOS.

```
OUTFILE  DTFSD BLKSIZE=408,DEVADDR=SYS010,FILABL=STD,            *
               IOAREA1=BUFFROUT,RECFORM=FIXBLK,RECSIZE=80,       *
               TYPEFLE=OUTPUT,WORKA=YES,DEVICE=3340,VERIFY=YES
            .
            .
            .
BUFFROUT DS    CL408
```

Figure 21.13 shows sample DCBs that can be used for OS creation of a sequential tape file. Figure 21.14 shows sample DCBs that can be used for OS creation of a sequential disk file.

Figure 21.13

Sample DCBs for an OS program to create a sequential tape file.

```
INFILE   DCB  DDNAME=FILEIN,MACRF=GM,LRECL=80,                   *
              DSORG=PS,EODAD=EOJRTN
OUTFILE  DCB  DDNAME=TAPEOUT,MACRF=PM,LRECL=80,DSORG=PS
```

Figure 21.14

Sample DCBs for an OS program to create a sequential disk file.

```
INFILE   DCB  DDNAME=FILEIN,MACRF=GM,LRECL=80,                   *
              DSORG=PS,EODAD=EOJRTN
OUTFILE  DCB  DDNAME=DISKOUT,MACRF=PM,LRECL=80,DSORG=PS
```

2. Creating a Transaction File of Change Records

After a master file is created, a procedure must be developed to make changes to it. Typically, change records are created and stored in a separate file referred to as a **transaction file.** Changes to an accounts receivable master file, for example, may consist of sales records and credit records. Changes to a payroll master file may consist of name changes, salary changes, and so on. Typically, the transaction file is edited first to ensure data integrity. Just as with master file creation, validating transaction data will minimize the risk of errors. The procedures for creating a transaction file are the same as for a master file.

3. Updating a Master File

Updating is the process of making a master file current. The master file is updated or made current by incorporating changes specified in the transaction records. This chapter will provide techniques used to perform *sequential up-*

dates for master files on disk or tape. The next chapter will focus on techniques used to perform *random-access updates,* where the master file must be on disk.

4. Reporting from the Master File

The purpose of maintaining a master file is to store data that will be used to provide meaningful output to both management and operating staff. This output is referred to as *reporting.* Reports or output can be *scheduled* so that they are prepared on a regular basis. Sales reports, bills, and payroll checks are examples of output from master files that would be prepared on a scheduled basis.

Reports can also be prepared *on demand.* That is, they are requested when needed. Such reports tend to have varied output requirements. Indeed, it is sometimes difficult to predict the needs of a user for an on-demand output report. Hence, such reports are usually provided through terminals.

The preparation of regularly scheduled reports using detail printing and group printing techniques are considered in Chapter 9.

E. Sequential File Updating

1. The Files Required

Both disk and tape can be used for storing sequential master files. The only difference in an assembler program between specifying a sequential file on disk and a file on tape is in the DTFs (DOS) or DCBs (OS). Later on, we will see that sequential disk files can be updated as described here, and can also be updated by rewriting records (that is, updating records in place).

Recall that an update procedure is one used to make a file current. To update a sequential master file—disk or tape—we typically use *three* files. An additional print file that provides a control listing for checking purposes is also required frequently.

a. Input Master File. This is the master file that is current through the previous updating period. That is, if updates are performed weekly, the input master file is the file that was created as the master during the previous week. We will call this file OLDMAST because it does not contain current changes.

b. Input Transaction File. The transaction file is the file that contains data to be used for updating the master file called OLDMAST. That is, the input transaction file contains all changes that have occurred as a result of business transactions since OLDMAST was created. We will call this file TRANS and use it to update the OLDMAST file.

c. Output Master File. The output master file is the file that will become the new master as a result of the updating procedure. The output master file will integrate data from the OLDMAST and the TRANS files. We will call this file NEWMAST. Note that for the next update run, this NEWMAST will become OLDMAST.

For our sample update procedure, we will assume that the input and output master files are on disk. The transaction file could be stored on floppy disks, cassette tapes, punched cards, magnetic disks, or magnetic tapes. But, for purposes of illustration, we will assume that the transaction file is on sequential disk. The systems flowchart in Figure 21.15, then, will summarize the files used in an update procedure.

A print file, called a control listing, is often created as output during a sequential file update. This print file would list changes made to the master file, errors encountered during processing, and totals to be used for control and checking purposes.

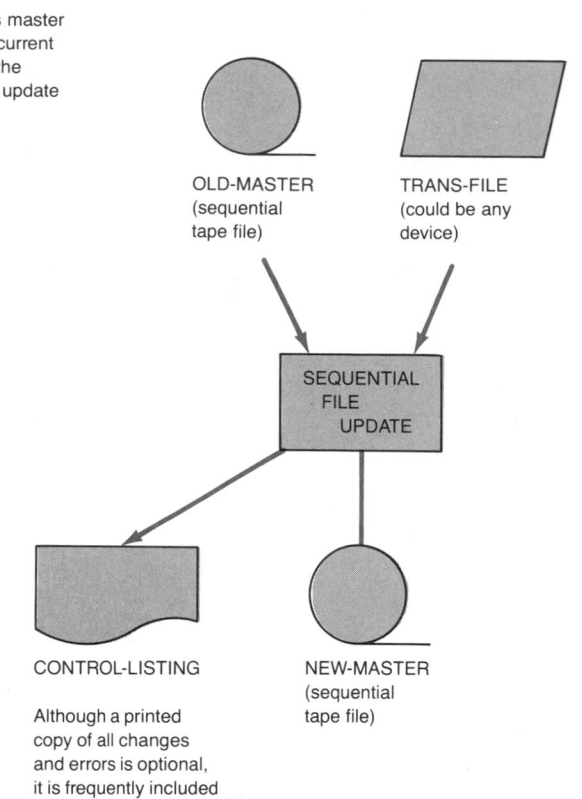

Contains master records current through the previous update cycle.

Contains changes to the master — must be the same sequence — as the master file.

OLD-MASTER (sequential tape file)

TRANS-FILE (could be any device)

SEQUENTIAL FILE UPDATE

CONTROL-LISTING

NEW-MASTER (sequential tape file)

Contains master information that has been updated with changes that have occurred since the previous update cycle.

Although a printed copy of all changes and errors is optional, it is frequently included for control purposes.

Figure 21.15
Systems flowchart that summarizes the files used in a sequential file update.

2. The Sequence of Records for Sequential Updates

In summary, OLDMAST contains all master information that was complete and current through the previous updating cycle. The TRANS file contains all transactions or changes that have occurred since the previous updating cycle. These transactions or changes must be incorporated into the master file to make it current. The TRANS file can be on any computer medium including disk, tape, cards, floppy disk, and so on. The NEWMAST will include all OLDMAST data in addition to the changes in the TRANS file that have been generated since the last update. The NEWMAST will always be on the same medium as the OLDMAST because the current NEWMAST becomes the OLDMAST during the next update cycle.

In a sequential master file, all records are in sequence by a specific **key field** such as account number, social security number, part number, and so on, depending on the type of master file. This key field uniquely identifies each master record. To update records in a sequential master file, the transaction file containing the change records must also be in sequence by the same key field.

3. The Procedures to Use for Sequential Updates

Let us consider the updating of a sequential accounts receivable master file. The key field used to identify records in the master file is account number, identified as MACCTNO, for master account number. All records in the OLDMAST accounts receivable file are in sequence by MACCTNO.

The transaction file contains all transactions to be posted to each master account. These transactions have all occurred since the previous update. This transaction file also has an account number as a key field, called TACCTNO for transaction account number. Records in the TRANS are in sequence by TACCTNO.

The formats for the two input files are

OLDREC
(in sequence by MACCTNO)

1–5   MACCTNO
6–10 MAMT
11–80 Not used

TRANSREC
(in sequence by TACCTNO)

1–5   TACCTNO
6–10 TAMT
11–80 Not used

NEWMAST becomes the current accounts receivable master file after the up-date procedure. It must, therefore, have the same format as the OLDMAST. The fields are described as follows.

NEWREC

1–5   NACCT
6–10 NAMT
11–80 Not used

At the end of the next updating cycle, the NEWMAST becomes the OLDMAST and is updated with transactions that have occurred during that cycle. In this way, we always have a backup in case some mishap occurs to NEWMAST.

Keep in mind that records within OLDMAST are in sequence by MACCTNO and that records within TRANS are in sequence by TACCTNO. The NEWMAST file, then, will also be created in account-number sequence.

Figure 21.16 illustrates a flowchart of the procedures to be coded in this update program. Figure 21.17 illustrates the pseudocode for this program. Figure 21.18 illustrates the full OS program. We will consider each procedure in detail.

a. An Overview.   The program opens all files, reads a record from both the master and the transaction files, and performs a COMPRTN until all records are processed. After all files have been processed, they are closed, and the run is terminated.

b. The Comparison Routine (COMPRTN).   A record has been obtained from both the OLDMAST and the TRANS files in the main module. COMPRTN compares the account numbers, MACCTNO of OLDREC and TACCTNO of TRANSREC. Because both files are in sequence by their respective account numbers, a comparison of MACCTNO to TACCTNO will determine the next procedure to be performed. Three possible conditions may occur when comparing MACCTNO to TACCTNO.

1. TACCTNO is equal to MACCTNO.   This means that a transaction record exists with the same account number as in the master file. If this condition is met, we perform a procedure called UPDATE. In this instance, the OLDREC is to be updated; that is, the transaction data is to be posted to the master record and the NEWREC is to contain the previous MAMT plus the TAMT of the transaction record. After a NEWREC is written, another record from both OLDMAST and TRANS file is read.

2. TACCTNO is greater than MACCTNO.   This means that there is a master record with an account number lower than the account number in the transaction file. Because both files are in sequence by account number, this condition indicates that a master record exists for which there is no

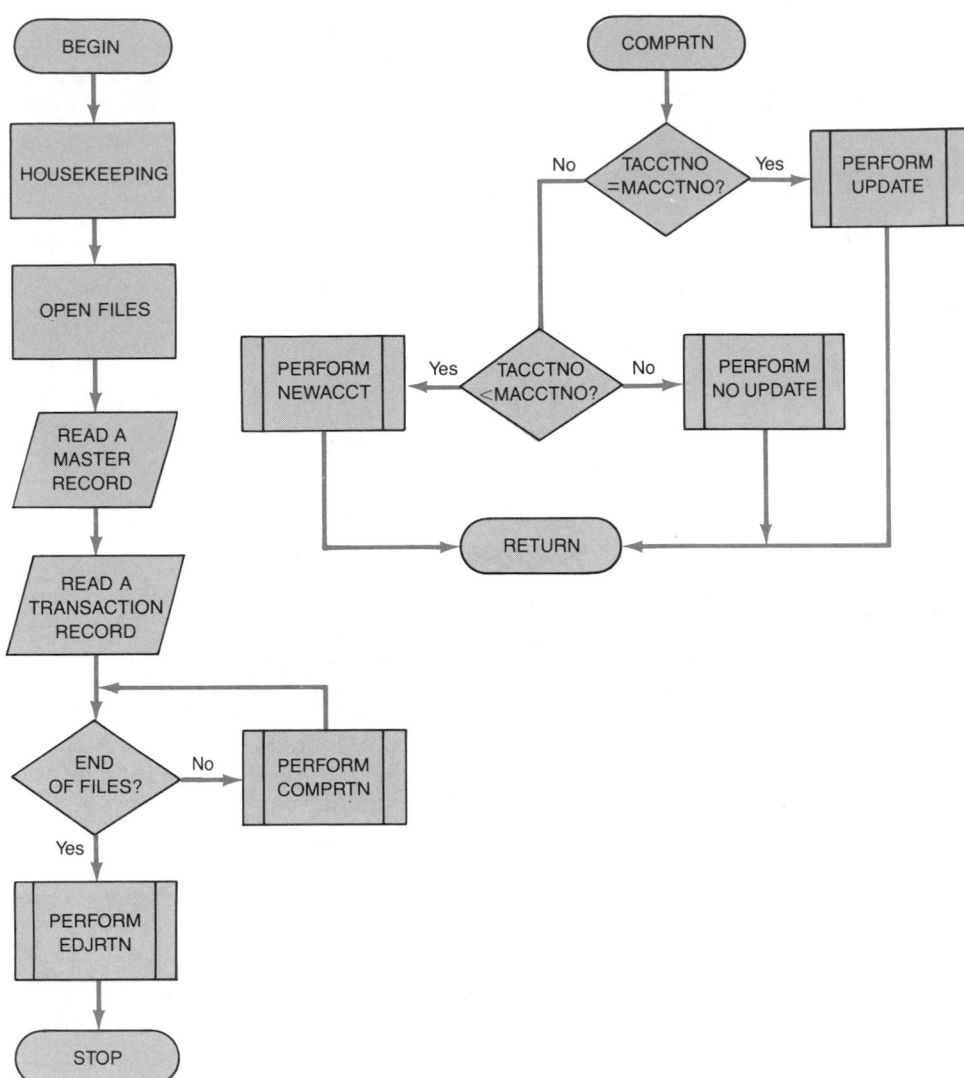

Figure 21.16
Flowchart of procedures to be coded in the sequential update program.

Figure 21.17
Pseudocode for the procedures to be coded in the sequential update program.

```
Open the files
Read master file
Read transaction file
If there are input records
    PERFORM until no more input
        IF TACCTNO = MACCTNO
            update the master record
        ELSE
            IF TACCTNO < MACCTNO
                add a new record
            ELSE
                write new master from old master
            ENDIF
        ENDIF
ENDPERFORM
Close the files
Stop
```

```
*                     HOUSEKEEPING INSTRUCTIONS GO HERE
*
             OPEN    (TRANS,INPUT)
             OPEN    (OLDMAST,INPUT)
             OPEN    (NEWMAST,INPUT)
FIRSTIME GET         TRANS,TRANSREC
         GET         OLDMAST,OLDREC
COMPRTN  CLC         TACCTNO,MACCTNO
         BL          NEWACCT
         BE          UPDATE
         BH          NOUPDATE
NEWACCT  MVC         NACCT,TACCTNO
         MVC         NAMT,TAMT
         PUT         NEWMAST,NEWREC
         GET         TRANS,TRANSREC
         B           COMPRTN
UPDATE   MVC         NACT,TACCTNO
         PACK        HOLDTAMT,TAMT
         PACK        HOLDMBD,NAMT
         AP          HOLDMBD,HOLDTAMT
         UNPK        NAMT,HOLDMBD
         OI          NAMT+4,X'FØ'
         PUT         NEWMAST,NEWREC
         GET         TRANS,TRANSREC
         GET         OLDMAST,OLDREC
         B           COMPRTN
NOUPDATE MVC         NEWREC,OLDREC
         PUT         NEWMAST,NEWREC
         GET         OLDMAST,OLDREC
         B           COMPRTN
EOJ2     CLC         MFLAG,=C'1'
         BE          CLOSEALL
         MVI         TFLAG,C'1'
         CLC         NACCT,MACCTNO
         BE          GETMSTR
FINISHM  MVC         NACCT,MACCTNO
         MVC         NAMT,MAMT
         PUT         NEWMAST,NEWREC
GETMSTR  GET         OLDMAST,OLDREC
         B           FINISHM
EOJ1     CLC         TFLAG,=C'1'
         BE          CLOSEALL
         MVI         MFLAG,C'1'
         CLC         NACCT,TACCTNO
         BE          GETTRANS
FINISHT  MVC         NACCT,TACCTNO
         MVC         NAMT,TAMT
         PUT         NEWMAST,NEWREC
GETTRANS GET         TRANS,TRANSREC
         B           FINISHT
CLOSEALL CLOSE       (TRANS)
         CLOSE       (OLDMAST)
         CLOSE       (NEWMAST)
*
*                     HOUSEKEEPING INSTRUCTIONS GO HERE
TRANS    DCB         DDNAME=TRANS,MACRF=GM,BLKSIZE=80,
                     LRECL=80,DSORG=PS,EODAD=EOJ2
OLDMAST  DCB         DDNAME=OMAST,MACRF=GM,BLKSIZE=80,
                     LRECL=80,DSORG=PS,EODAD=EOJ1
NEWMAST  DCB         DDNAME=NMAST,MACRF=PM,BLKSIZE=80,
                     LRECL=80,DSORG=PS
TRANSREC DS          ØCL80
TACCTNO  DS          CL5
TAMT     DS          CL5
         DS          CL70
OLDREC   DS          ØCL80
MACCTNO  DS          CL5
MAMT     DS          CL5
         DS          CL70
NEWREC   DS          ØCL80
NACCT    DS          CL5
NAMT     DS          CL5
         DS          CL70
HOLDTAMT DS          PL3
HOLDMBD  DS          PL3
TFLAG    DC          CL1'Ø'
MFLAG    DC          CL1'Ø'
         END
```

Figure 21.18
Sequential update program.

corresponding transaction record. That is, the master record has had no activity or changes occurring during the current update cycle and should be written onto the NEWMAST file *as is*. We call this procedure NOUPDATE.

At NOUPDATE, we write the NEWREC from the OLDREC and read another record from OLDMAST. Because we have not yet processed the transaction record that caused TACCTNO to compare greater than the MACCTNO of the OLDMAST, there is no need to read another transaction record at the NOUPDATE procedure. Consider the following example, which illustrates the processing to be performed if MACCTNO is less than TACCTNO.

MACCTNO	TACCTNO	
00001	00001	Update master record.
00002	00003	00002 is put on the NEWMAST as is; the next master record is read; TACCTNO 00003 has not yet been processed.

3. TACCTNO is less than MACCTNO.   Because both files are in sequence by account number, this condition means that a transaction record exists for which there is no corresponding master record. Depending on the type of update procedure being performed, this could mean either a new account is to be processed from the TRANS file, or an error has occurred—that is, the TACCTNO is wrong. In our illustration, we will assume that when a TACCTNO is less than an MACCTNO, this is a new account. First, however, let us consider the full range of procedures that could be executed if TACCTNO is less than MACCTNO.

(a) A New Account If TACCTNO is Less Than MACCTNO. As noted, for some applications, a transaction record with no corresponding master record means a new account. We call this procedure NEWACCT in our program. In this instance, a new master record is created entirely from the transaction record. Then the next transaction record is read. We do *not* read another record from OLDMAST at this time because we have not yet processed the master record that compared greater than TACCTNO.

(b) An Error Condition If TACCTNO is Less Than MACCTNO. For some applications, all account numbers on the transaction file *must* have corresponding master records with the same account numbers. For these applications, new accounts are handled by a different program and are *not* part of the update procedure.

In such an instance, an MACCTNO greater than TACCTNO would cause an ERRORRTN to be processed. Typically, the error routine would print out the transaction record that has a non-matching account number and then read the next transaction record.

In summary, in our main routine, a master and a transaction record are read. Then COMPRTN is executed where the account numbers are compared. Based on the comparison, UPDATE, NOUPDATE, or NEWACCT will be executed. COMPRTN is then repeated until there are no more records to process.

(c) The Procedures to be Performed Depending on How MACCTNO Compares with TACCTNO. The following examples illustrate the routines to be performed depending on the account numbers read.

MACCTNO	TACCTNO	Action
00001	00001	Regular Update Add TAMT to MAMT Write a master record Read a master record Read a transaction record
00002	00004	No Update Write a master record Read a master record
00003	00004	No Update Write a master record Read a master record
00005	00004	New Account Write a master record Read a transaction record
00005	00005	Regular Update Add TAMT to MAMT Write a master record Read a master record Read a transaction record

4. End-of-Job Routines

Suppose there are fewer TRANS records than OLDMAST records. When the TRANS file has been completely processed, the remaining OLDMAST records must be written onto NEWMAST in the NOUPDATE procedure. Similarly, if the OLDMAST file has been completely processed first, then the remaining TRANS records must be put onto NEWMAST as new accounts.

Suppose TRANS records are exhausted first. EOJ2 would be executed because the EODAD for TRANS has been set to EOJ2. At EOJ2 we first test to see if MFLAG is equal to a 1. This will happen only when we run out of OLDMAST records as well. The first procedure at EOJ2, then, is to determine if we have already finished processing the OLDMAST file. If we had, we would terminate the run. Because we have not, we process OLDMAST records until those are also exhausted. When OLDMAST records are completely processed, EOJ1 will be executed. We must set TFLAG equal to a 1 at EOJ2 so that when EOJ1 is executed, we have a way of indicating that *both* files are exhausted. Thus at EOJ1 we test to see if TFLAG is equal to a 1. The procedure at EOJ1, then, is the OLDMAST end-of-job routine. It performs the following:

1. Tests to see if there are more TRANS records to process. If not, the program is terminated.
2. If there are TRANS records to process, MFLAG, the end-of-OLDMAST indicator, is set before processing TRANS records.
3. Processing of TRANS records continues until that file is exhausted.

Similarly, the procedure at EOJ2 is the TRANS end-of-job routine. It performs the following:

1. Tests to see if there are more OLDMAST records to process. If not, the program is terminated.
2. If there are OLDMAST records to process, TFLAG, the end-of-TRANS indicator, is set to 1.
3. Processing of OLDMAST records continues until that file is exhausted.

Note that this update procedure assumes that there is only *one* transaction record for each master record. There are numerous applications where there may be multiple transaction records with the same account number that are to be used to update a particular master record. All of these transactions would need to be combined into a single transaction record if this procedure were to be used.

F. Validity Checking in Update Procedures

We have focused on the procedures necessary to perform a sequential master file update. Note, however, that numerous data validation techniques would typically be incorporated in an update procedure to minimize errors. Because updating involves the use of master files, it is imperative that errors be kept to a minimum.

Let us consider some common validity checking routines.

1. Checking for New Accounts

You will recall that there are two types of procedures commonly used if MACCTNO is greater than TACCTNO, that is, if there is a transaction record for which there is no corresponding master record. For some applications, transaction records should always have corresponding master records. Hence, if MACCTNO is greater than TACCTNO, it means that an error has occurred.

For other applications, MACCTNO greater than TACCTNO means that the transaction record could be a new account to be added to the new master file. To add this transaction record to the new master file without any additional checking, however, would be dangerous because the possibility exists that TACCTNO was coded incorrectly and that the transaction record is, in fact, *not* a new account.

To verify that a TRANSREC is a new account, we usually include a coded field in the TRANSREC itself. Hence, a more complete format for TRANSREC is needed, as follows.

```
TRANSREC

    1-5     TACCTNO
    6-10    NAMT
    11-79   Not used
    80      CODE
                1—NEWACCT
                2—UPDATE
```

Thus, if MACCTNO is greater than TACCTNO, this means that the transaction record is a new account *only if* it also contains a 1 in CODE. The procedure at NEWACCT, then, should be modified to validate the data being entered.

```
NEWACCT     CLI     CODE,C'1'
            BNE     ERROR
```

Similarly, CODE may be used to validate transaction data processed at UPDATE.

```
UPDATE      CLI     CODE,C'2'
            BNE     ERROR
```

2. Deleting Records from a Sequential Master File

Deleting master records is one type of update function not considered in our previous illustrations. Due to the fact that accounts may need to be deactivated if customers give up their account or have not paid bills, there must be some provision to eliminate specific records from the master file. We may use the technique of a coded transaction field as previously described to accomplish this. We could add a code of "3" to indicate that a record is to be deleted.

```
TRANSREC

  1-5     TACCTNO
  6-10    TAMT
 11-79    Not used
 80       CODE
              1—NEWACCT
              2—UPDATE
              3—DELETE
```

The procedure at UPDATE might be revised, as follows.

```
UPDATE    CLI    CODE,C'3'
          BE     GETNEXT
          CLI    CODE,C'2'
          BNE    ERROR2
          ⋮
          ⋮
GETNEXT   GET    TRANS,AREAIN2
          ⋮
          ⋮
```

Note that UPDATE is performed only if TACCTNO is equal to MACCTNO. Hence, at the end of UPDATE, we should retrieve one record from each file. If CODE is equal to 3, the OLDMAST is *not* written onto the new file. It is, in effect, deleted by not re-creating the corresponding master record in the new master file. Thus, if CODE is a 3, we branch around the routine that updates the master record; that is, we branch to the procedure that gets two new records.

3. Checking for Sequence Errors

Note that in an update program the sequence of the records in the transaction and master files is critical. If one or more records in the transaction or master file has been sequenced incorrectly, the entire production run could produce erroneous results. Hence, it is necessary to detect such errors either before or during the update procedure. Consider the following.

	TRANS TACCTNO	OLDMAST MACCTNO	
	00006	00006	
	00009	00009	
Incorrectly ⟶	00118	00014	All these records would
sequenced	00015	00015	be incorrectly processed
record	00016	00016	because the 00118 record
	.	00017	in TRANS is out of place.
	.	.	
	.	.	
	.	.	

A sequence error in the TRANS file causes the preceding files to be processed incorrectly.

If the possibility for a sequence error exists, it is advisable to include a sequence check in your program.

```
    LABEL      OPERATION        OPERAND                                    COMMENTS                                    72
1               10        16
            OPEN     . . .
            .
            .
            .
            MVC      THOLD,TACCTNO
            .
            .
COMPRTN     CLC      THOLD,TACCTNO
            BNH      SEQERR
            MVC      THOLD,TACCTNO
```

At SEQERR, you may want to simply print a message indicating that a sequence error has occurred, stop the run, or count the number of such errors and abort the run if the count exceeds a predetermined limit.

Alternative Method for Sequence Checking Aborting a run, resequencing transaction records, and then reupdating the master file would usually be a lengthy and costly procedure. A better alternative is to create the TRANS file on tape or disk, if it is not already on these media, and to sort the files. With a computer-generated sort, a procedure typically available in a library of routines that may be accessed by the operating system, we can be relatively certain that the sorted file is properly sequenced.

G. Updating Sequential Disk Records in Place

As we have noted, both disk and tape can be organized sequentially and can use a sequential-update procedure as the one described in this chapter.

Disks, however, have the added feature of being able to serve as both input and ouput *during the same run.* Thus, it is possible to read a disk record, make changes directly to that record, and rewrite it or update it in place. Using this capability of disks, we need only two files.

Open as	Name of File	Open Instruction
UPDATE	MASTER	OPEN MASTER,UPDATE
INPUT	TRANS	OPEN TRANS,INPUT

A disk file, then, can be opened for direct updating, which means records from the disk will be both accessed and written.

After each disk record is read, we make the changes directly to the MASTER record and rewrite it using a PUTX instruction (OS) or a PUT instruction (DOS). This procedure is not emphasized here because the previous method has the advantage of maintaining an automatic backup. By using three files for updating, an OLDMAST and a separate NEWMAST always exist. Hence, NEWMAST can be recreated if the need arises.

Note the Following for OS

1. Records to be updated—use PUTX.
2. Records to be added—use PUT.

A Note About Debugging When creating a tape or disk as output, you will need to examine the records created when you debug the program. You can do this by printing the record as well as creating it on tape or disk. Most computer systems also have a job control command such as /PRINT filename that allows you to print the entire file created as output.

CHAPTER SUMMARY

I. Techniques Used in Update Programs
 A. All files to be processed must be in sequence by the same key field—that is, ACCTNO, SOCSECNO, and so on.
 B. A record is read from each file and specified routines are performed depending on whether or not there are matching records.
 C. A conditional is usually used to determine which of a series of specified routines is to be performed. One of the following conditions must be met:
  1. "equal" or matching condition
   (Key field of record from first or master file = key field of record from second or transaction file.)
  2. "less than" condition
   (Key field of record from first file is less than key field of record from second file.)
   Actions:
   Process record from the first file.
   Read a record from the first file.
  3. "greater than" condition
   (Key field of record from first file is greater than key field of record from second file.)
   Actions:
   Process record from the second file.
   Read a record from the second file.

CHAPTER SELF-EVALUATING QUIZ

1. A(n) _____ is the major collection of data pertaining to a specific application.
2. (T or F) A tape or disk drive can be used for either reading or recording data on a tape or disk.
3. (T or F) Tapes and disks may be used for sequential storage of master files.
4. (T or F) A disk file can be created so that it may be accessed either sequentially or randomly.
5. Changes to a sequential master file are placed in a separate file typically referred to as a(n) _____ file.
6. The process of making a master file current is referred to as _____ .
7. In a sequential update procedure, three files are needed: they are _____ , _____ , and _____ .
8. (T or F) In a sequential update procedure, all files must be in sequence by the same key field.
9. In a master file sequential update procedure, the key field in the transaction file is compared to the key field in the _____ .
10. In Question 9, if the key fields are equal, a(n) _____ procedure is performed. Describe this procedure.
11. In Question 9, if the transaction key field is greater than the master key field, a(n) _____ procedure is performed. Describe this procedure.
12. In Question 9, if the transaction key field is less than the master key field, a(n) _____ procedure is performed. Describe this procedure.

SOLUTIONS

		Page
1.	Master file	583
2.	T	582
3.	T	582
4.	T	582
5.	Transaction	587
6.	Updating	587
7.	The old master file (current through the previous updating cycle); the transaction file; the new master file (incorporates the old master data along with the transaction data)	587
8.	T	588
9.	Old master file	589
10.	Regular update (transaction data is added to the master data, a new master record is written, and records from the old master and the transaction file are read)	589
11.	No update (a new master record is created directly from the old master record and a record from the old master file is read)	589
12.	New account or error (if new account, move transaction data to the new master and write; if error, print error message. In either case, a transaction record is then read)	592

KEY TERMS

Block	Interblock gap (IBG)
Cylinder	Key field
Disk drive	Master file
Disk pack	Moving-head magnetic disk
Fixed-head magnetic disk	Transaction file
Fixed-length records	Updating
Header labels	Variable-length records

REVIEW QUESTIONS

True–False Questions

1. (T or F) Updating is the process of making a file current.
2. (T or F) Exactly two files are always required for tape or sequential disk updating.
3. (T or F) Records on a disk or tape can be any length.
4. (T or F) Tapes may be processed randomly or sequentially.
5. (T or F) Files must be in sequence by key field in a typical update routine.
6. (T or F) When any input file has been completely read and processed during a sequential disk or tape update procedure, the program should be terminated.
7. (T or F) A transaction record with no corresponding master record always means an error.
8. (T or F) Sequential disk records can be rewritten in place.
9. (T or F) It is not necessary to perform a sequence check on transaction or master files.
10. (T or F) Transaction records that are to designate "new accounts" are typically coded to verify that they are really new accounts.

General Questions
1. Provide program flowcharts and pseudocodes for the following routines.
   a. Update
   b. Sequence-check
2. In an update, describe three different ways that a transaction record might be processed if it is "less than" a master record.
3. Indicate the major advantages of disk and tape processing.
4. Indicate the major disadvantages of tape processing as compared to disk processing.

Define the following (5–10).

5. "On demand" output
6. Scheduled output
7. Updating a disk in place
8. Master file processing
9. Key field
10. Sequential file processing

PROGRAMMING ASSIGNMENTS

1. Write a program to update a sales file. The problem definition is shown in Figure 21.19.

   Notes
   a. SALES and UPDSALES are sequential disk files.
   b. For a transaction record that has a corresponding master record (match on salesperson number), add the transaction figures for sales and commission to the corresponding year-to-date figures and the current period figures.
   c. For a transaction record that has no corresponding master record, print the transaction record. Do not put the transaction record on the master file.
   d. Both files are in salesperson number sequence.

2. Write a program to update a payroll file. The problem definition is shown in Figure 21.20.

   Notes
   a. Both files are in sequence by employee number.
   b. For master tape records without corresponding transaction records (no match on employee number), create an output record from the input tape.
   c. For transaction records with no corresponding tape records, create an output record from the input disk.
   d. For a master tape record with a corresponding transaction record, take the annual salary from the disk record and all other data from the tape record.
   e. Print all updated records for control purposes.

3. Develop a program to create a master file. The master record contains the following:

1–5	Student number
11–25	Student name
26–40	Street address
41–55	Town
56	Code, where F = full-time
	P = part-time
60–62	Credits completed
63	Major where C = Computer Science
	M = Math
	B = Business

(Continued on page 602.)

a. Systems Flowchart

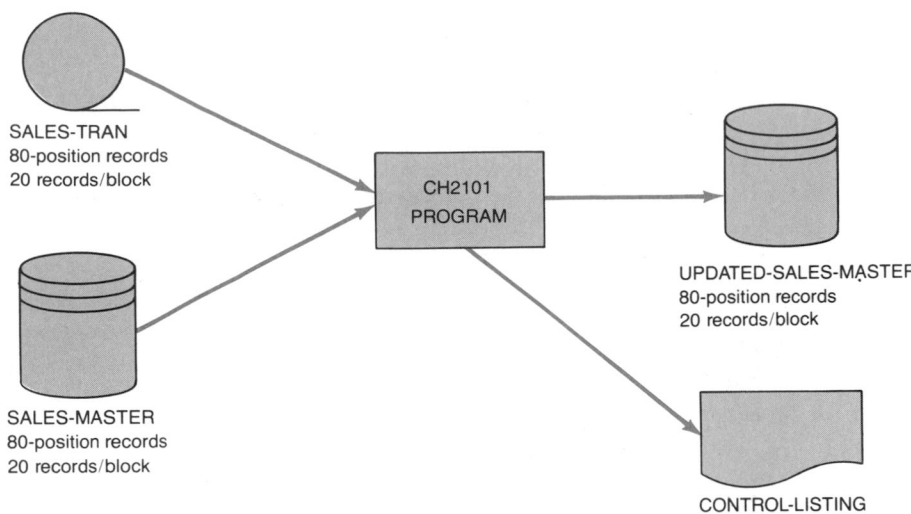

SALES-TRAN
80-position records
20 records/block

CH2101
PROGRAM

UPDATED-SALES-MASTER
80-position records
20 records/block

SALES-MASTER
80-position records
20 records/block

CONTROL-LISTING

b. Record Layout for SALES-MASTER and UPDATED-SALES-MASTER

SALESPERSON NO.	OTHER DATA	YEAR-TO-DATE FIGURES		OTHER DATA	CURRENT PERIOD FIGURES		OTHER DATA	
		SALES $ ¢	COMMISSION $ ¢		SALES $ ¢	COMMISSION $ ¢		
1 5	6 37	38 43	44 49	50 55	56 61	62 67	68 70	71 80

c. SALES-TRAN Record Layout

SALESPERSON NO.	SALES $ ¢	COMMISSION $ ¢	
1 5	6 11	12 17	18 80

d. CONTROL-LISTING Printer Spacing Chart

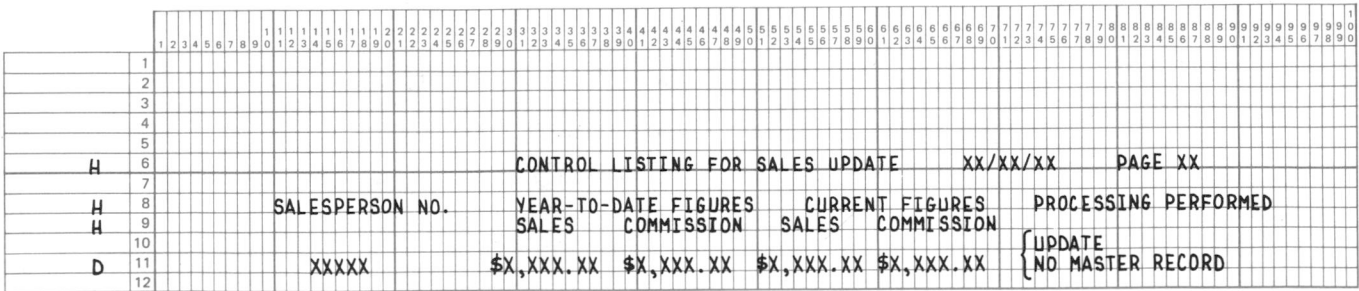

Figure 21.19
Problem definition for Programming Assignment 1.

a. Systems Flowchart

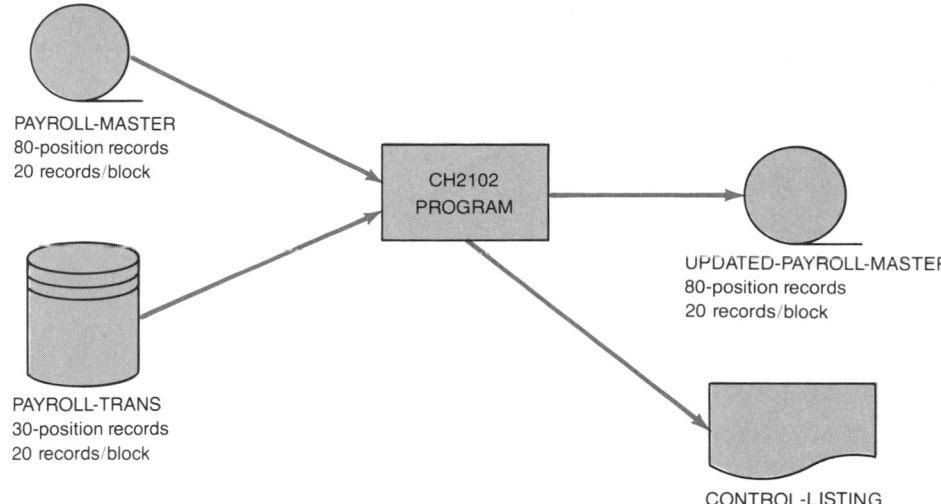

PAYROLL-MASTER
80-position records
20 records/block

CH2102
PROGRAM

UPDATED-PAYROLL-MASTER
80-position records
20 records/block

PAYROLL-TRANS
30-position records
20 records/block

CONTROL-LISTING

b. Record Layout for PAYROLL-MASTER and UPDATED-PAYROLL-MASTER

EMPLOYEE NO.	OTHER DATA	ANNUAL SALARY (in $)	OTHER DATA	
1 5	6 29	30 35	36 70	71 80

c. PAYROLL-TRANS Record Layout

EMPLOYEE NO.	OTHER DATA	NEW ANNUAL SALARY (in $)	OTHER DATA	
1 5	6 29	30 35	36 70	71 80

d. CONTROL-LISTING Printer Spacing Chart

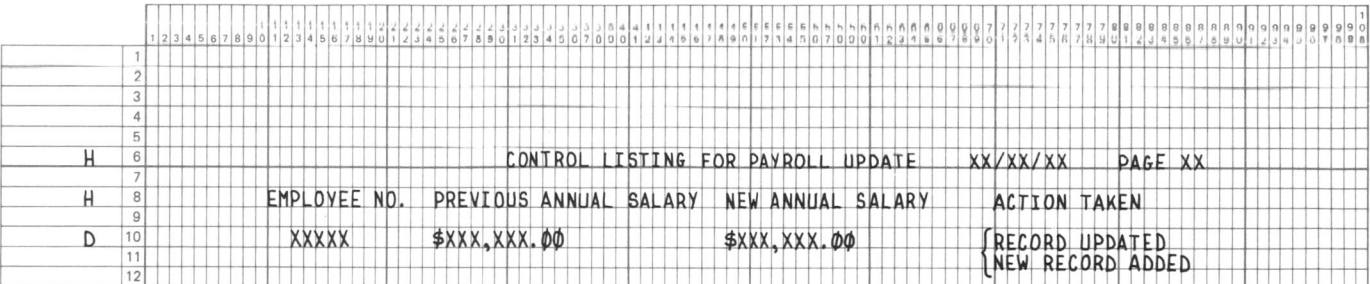

Figure 21.20
Problem definition for Programming Assignment 2.

64–66 Credits required for degree, where C = 127
M = 127
B = 120

71–75 ZIP code

Validate that numeric fields contain numeric data and credits completed are less than credits required for degree. Depending on student's major, place the correct number of credits required in 64–66. Also, perform a sequence check and print an exception report.

4. Code a program to generate a transaction file to update the master file of the preceding problem. The transaction record contains the following:

1–5 Student number
11–25 Student name
26–27 Credits completed this semester

The maximum number of credits completed in one semester is limited to 20. Perform a sequence check and list all transactions noting any records containing credits completed greater than 20.

5. Write a sequential update program using the master and transaction files developed in the previous problems. List the student's name, credits completed this semester and total credits for each updated record. Also add the message "GRADUATION" to all print records where the credits completed are greater than or equal to credits required.

Indexed File Processing: ISAM and VSAM

To familiarize you with:
1. *How to process disk files randomly.*
2. *The major features of indexed disk files.*
3. *How to delete records from, add records to, and update records in ISAM and VSAM files.*

I. METHODS OF FILE ORGANIZATION ON DISK

The term *file* refers to a collection of related records for a given application. We speak of an accounts receivable file, for example, as the collection of all records of customers who owe money to the company. We will now discuss how files can be stored on a disk storage unit.

There are generally three different ways in which information can be organized on a magnetic disk: sequential, indexed (ISAM and VSAM), and direct. We briefly consider each of these in the following sections.

A. Sequential File Organization

As indicated in the previous chapter, the simplest type of disk file organization is sequential. Sequential files are processed in the same way regardless of whether they are stored on tape or disk. Typically, the records to be stored in a sequential file are first sorted into sequence by a key field such as customer number, part number, employee number, and so on. With this key field as a guide, it is then relatively easy to locate a given record in the file. The record with employee number 00986, for example, would be physically located between records with employee numbers 00985 and 00987. Thus, to access that record the computer must read past the first 985 records.

We have already seen that a master sequential file can be updated in two ways: (1) by creating a new master that incorporates all the changes (disk and tape can be processed this way), and (2) by reading a master record and updating it in place (feasible only with disks that can serve as both input and output for a given procedure).

Other methods, considered in the following sections, focus on the use of disk for random access.

B. Indexed File Organization

An *indexed file* is a file that has an index for looking up locations of records on a disk. There are two methods of accessing indexed disk files: ISAM and VSAM.

1. Indexed Sequential (ISAM) File Organization

An indexed file enables the user to randomly access disk files. The term **ISAM** stands for *Indexed Sequential Access Method. Indexes,* or reference tables, are created on the disk at the same time that the data is recorded on the disk. These indexes store a record's key field and the corresponding disk address of that record.

With an ISAM file records can be accessed either sequentially or randomly, depending on the user's needs. The term "random access" implies that records are to be processed or accessed in an order other than the one in which they were physically written on the disk.

2. Virtual Storage (VSAM) File Organization

VSAM, an acronym for *Virtual Storage Access Method,* is very similar to ISAM in concept and in design. It is, in fact, an enhancement of ISAM for use on virtual storage computers. One main feature of VSAM is that it enables the user to access records using **alternate key** fields. We discuss it here because it is widely used in business.

With alternate keys, records can be accessed in many different ways. Suppose, for example, that an employee record contains both a Social Security number and an employee number. With a VSAM file, *either* can be used to access records. Suppose a user wishes to access an ISAM employee record that has Social Security number as its key field. If the user does not know the Social Security number for the employee record desired, it cannot be directly accessed. With a VSAM file, however, both employee number and Social Security number can be designated as key fields. Thus, if the user knows the employee number but not the Social Security number, the record is still directly accessible. Another advantage of VSAM over ISAM is that it is easier to establish variable-length records within a file. Moreover, records may be added to a VSAM file far more efficiently than they can be added to an ISAM file, as we will see later.

C. Direct File Organization: A Brief Overview

Another method of disk organization is called *direct file organization*. In this type of file, records are accessed by a key field that, through some calculations, reduces to the actual address (surface and track numbers) of the record. With the direct method, there is no need for an index.

To determine the record location for a direct file, a *randomizing* or *hashing technique* is used to convert the actual record key's value to a valid record location.

Hashing Technique for Direct Files

1. Compute the largest odd number not ending in 5 that is less than the total number of tracks available.
2. Divide the record key by this odd number.
3. The remainder becomes the track number.

Example
Suppose we allot 1000 tracks for a given disk file. The key field is social security number. Suppose we have a social security number of 072–38–7821.

1. Compute the largest odd number not ending in 5 that is less than the total number of tracks available.
   999 is the number.
2. Divide the record key by this number.

```
             72460
999 | 072387821
      6993
      2457
      1998
       4598
       3996
        6022
        5994
         281  ← remainder
```
281 is the track number.

Note that several records may be placed in the same track because this method of conversion does not result in unique track numbers. Because a track can typically store thousands of characters, this may not cause a problem. If, however, too many records result in the same computer track number, there may be a need for overflow areas.

Thus, no table is required from which the actual address is searched. Instead, calculations are performed by the computer according to programmer-supplied formulas that yield the disk address of each record.

Direct organization can result in fast access of specific records because there is no need to "look up" an address from an index. In practice, however, there are several factors that must be considered before this type of organization is adopted.

1. More programming effort is required with direct files because it is necessary for the programmer to develop and program the formula for converting the key fields into actual addresses. It should be noted that the preceding example used an extremely simple formula to determine the address. In reality, very complex formulas are often necessary. This is usually the case because programmers can only use specified areas of the disk for their files. The remaining areas may be either filled with other data or have a "dedicated" use. Consequently, the task of finding formulas to refer to only addresses of records in the file can sometimes be very cumbersome. Moreover, this type of organization makes it very difficult to distribute records evenly on a disk file to allow the file to make effective use of the available disk space.
2. In addition to increased programming effort, complex formulas can sometimes increase access time. Depending on the calculations, it might require more time for the computer to perform the calculations to find the address than to look up the address in an index.
3. Accessing a direct file sequentially is rather inefficient and impractical because records with sequential key fields are rarely adjacent to one another as they would be with other types of randomly accessed files.

In fact, direct files are best used when the files are accessed randomly (that is, rarely in sequence) and there is only infrequent need to add to the file. Because of the aforementioned considerations, direct files are not as commonly used as indexed files in business applications.

II. AN INTRODUCTION TO ISAM PROCESSING IN ASSEMBLER

A. Types of Indexed File Processing

In this section, we focus on indexed disk files. These are files organized using either the indexed sequential access method (ISAM) or the virtual storage access method (VSAM). With indexed files, we are able to perform random as well as sequential processing.

We will first consider ISAM files and then consider VSAM files. Although processing details for DOS and OS ISAM files differ somewhat, the basic concepts are the same.

B. ISAM Files

When an *indexed file* is created using the indexed sequential access method (ISAM), each record is placed on the disk in ascending sequence. At the same time, the computer establishes an index on the disk that keeps track of where each record is physically located. If, at some later time, you wish to access any record randomly, the computer "looks up" the address of the index and goes directly to that location to find the record. The index, then, operates exactly like a book index. To locate data, you "look up" the address in the index.

When creating an indexed file, the programmer must designate a field in the record as a *key field* that uniquely identifies the record to the computer. This key field is used to form the index. The index, then, contains each record's key field and the disk address assigned to that record. For a payroll file, the key field may be Social Security number; for an inventory file, the key field may be part number; for an accounts receivable file, the key field may be customer number.

In the index, the computer stores the key field and the actual address where the corresponding record is located. The actual address may be specified in terms of surface number and cylinder number. Although there may be several records with the same surface and cylinder number, this address significantly reduces the access time for a particular record.

In summary, indexed files are created sequentially with each record placed on the file as it is read in, and, at the same time, an index is created associating an actual address with each record's key field.

After the indexed file is created, it may be accessed both sequentially and randomly. The following is a list of typical procedures using sequential or random access.

Sequential Access

1. An indexed file is typically read sequentially to produce scheduled reports.
2. Records on an indexed file may be updated sequentially on occasions where high file activity exists. That is, if most of the records on a file are to be updated, it is most efficient to update the file sequentially.

Random Access

1. Records may be accessed randomly when random inquiries must be answered.
2. Files may be updated randomly as changes or transactions occur.

C. Physically Creating Indexes for ISAM Files

1. Track and Cylinder Indexes

An indexed file is physically located on a disk, which is a type of Direct Access Storage Device (DASD). A *cylinder index* is used to point the operating system to the correct cylinder containing the record for which we are searching. The cylinder index contains the highest key for each cylinder. Similarly, track zero (surface 0) of each cylinder also contains an index called a *track index* (see Figure 22.1). The track index points to the surface containing the record. For example, if the track index of cylinder 13 were searched for a customer number key of 555, the index would reference track or surface 11. This would occur because the highest record contained on track or surface 10 is 551, which is too low, and the highest record contained on track or surface 11 is 570. Note that the term "track" as used here is similar to "surface."

In summary, if a record with customer number 555 were to be retrieved, the following steps would occur.

1. The operating system searches the cylinder index first to locate the cylinder containing the record. The high key entries of the index are compared to the search key (555). The first entry equal to or greater than the search key is found at cylinder 13.
2. Next, the track index for cylinder 13 is read into storage. Again, the high key entries are compared to the search key. The high key entry (570) for track or surface 11 is greater than or equal to the search key. This indicates that the record we are searching for is stored on track or surface 11.

3. Surface 11 of cylinder 13 will be searched for record 555. The operating system then reads the record into a buffer and finally transfers the record to the ISAM input area.

	Track or Surface Number	_Highest Key_
	0	* Track "0" contains track index
	⋮	⋮
	8	501
	9	533
SEARCH	10	551
KEY →	11	570
555	12	588
	13	601
	14	643

Figure 22.1
Sample track index for
cylinder 13.

The cylinder index as well as the track index are stored on the disk along with the file. Consequently, the operating system must read the appropriate indexes into primary storage when random access of the file is required. The cylinder and track address must be found prior to physically retrieving a particular record; this increases access time. For most applications, however, the relative ease with which ISAM files are processed more than compensates for this slight reduction in response time.

2. Overflow Areas

All data records are initially stored during the file creation procedure in the disk's prime or main data area in ascending key sequence. As records are added to the indexed file during the update procedure, they force records contained on the specific surface to be moved or bumped into the overflow area. This feature permits records to be added without rewriting the entire file.

Two types of overflow areas may be specified by the programmer; a cylinder overflow area and an independent overflow area. See Figure 22.2 for an illustration.

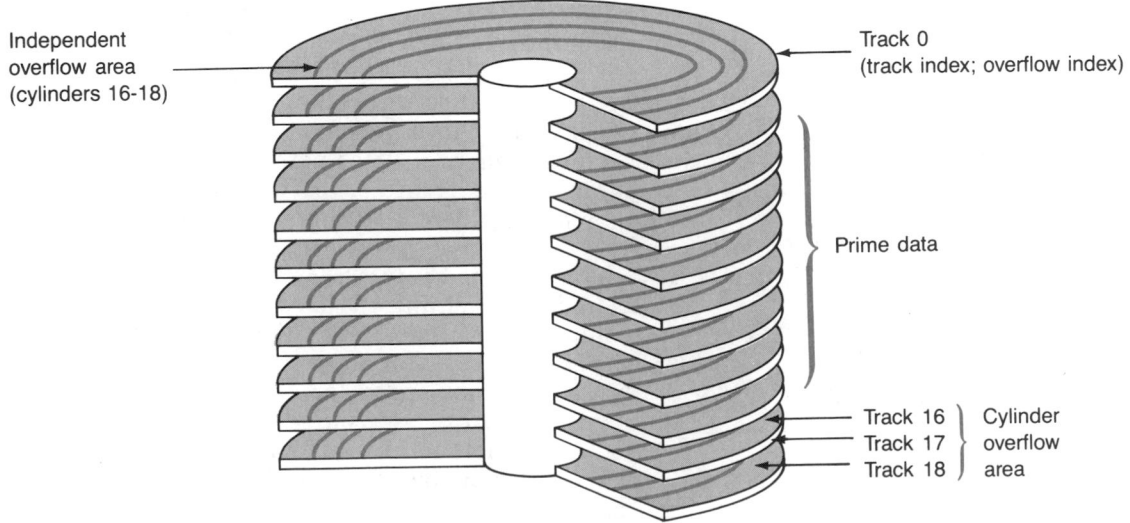

Figure 22.2
Cylinder overflow area and independent overflow area.

With many computer systems, the records in the overflow area are not in sequence. Consequently, when many records are forced into the overflow area during an update, the search time increases and processing efficiency decreases. The file must be reorganized periodically to reduce this inefficiency. That is, the records must be removed from the overflow area and placed in their proper sequence in the prime data area. This can be performed easily by a procedure that reads the indexed file sequentially by key field and creates a new indexed disk file that is in physical sequence.

D. Creating a DOS ISAM File

In this section we will begin by considering a DOS procedure that creates an ISAM file. Then we will consider a similar OS procedure. Note that although some processing rules differ, the basic concepts for DOS ISAM and OS ISAM processing are similar.

1. Sample Program

The sample program illustrates an application in which an indexed-sequential student master file is created. The input is a sorted sequential file that could be stored on any sequential medium such as disk, tape, or cards. The key field—the student number—is located in record positions 1–5. Indexed files are created in sequence by key field. The systems flowchart for this procedure appears in Figure 22.3.

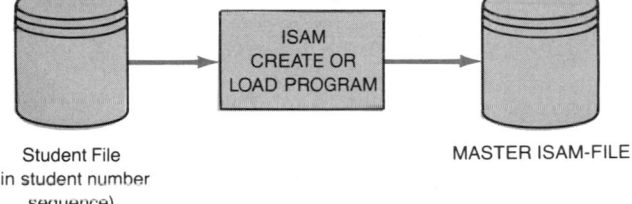

Figure 22.3
Systems flowchart for the sample program.

Student File
(in student number sequence)

ISAM
CREATE OR
LOAD PROGRAM

MASTER ISAM-FILE

Note that the standard OPEN and CLOSE macros are used to activate and deactivate the indexed file. In addition, new macros and instructions, as noted in the following table, are needed by the sample program.

Macro	*Purpose*
SETFL ISDISK	Initializes and formats the disk file named ISDISK; SETFL stands for "set file load."
WRITE ISDISK,NEWKEY reserved word	Writes a record onto disk (ISDISK) and creates an index. NEWKEY is the key field in the record; an index is created that associates an actual disk address with each record's key field. NEWKEY is a reserved word and must be used in the WRITE statement to create the record and add its key to the index.
ENDFL ISDISK	Performs final operations on the indexed disk; ENDFL stands for "end file load."
ISDISK DTFIS (parameters)	Defines the ISAM file's characteristics. The filename, called ISDISK here, is limited to 7 characters, not the usual 8. This filename, when combined with the letter C, is a special I/O name for an area set up by the operating system to test for I/O errors.

The SETFL macro immediately follows the OPEN macro and sets up the file for "file create" mode. ENDFL terminates this file create macro and must directly precede the CLOSE. Note that the usual PUT is replaced by a WRITE macro to create each new record in an indexed file. The WRITE instruction must be located between a SETFL macro and an ENDFL macro. Note that the WRITE macro consists of two operands; the first references the ISAM filename defined by the DTFIS, and the second references the macro named NEWKEY that is used for creating the index. Therefore, NEWKEY must always be specified when creating or loading an ISAM file under DOS.

Figure 22.4 illustrates a DOS program that will create an indexed file using ISAM. The input is in sequence by the key field.

2. The DTFIS Entries

There are 13 entries in the DTFIS of the sample program. The first 10 always have the same format for a specific ISAM file. The last three vary depending on whether the file is being used as input or output and whether it is being accessed sequentially or randomly. The entries are as follows.

CYLOFL=1	This operand must be included if cylinder overflow areas are reserved for a file. Enter the specific number of surfaces to be reserved on each cylinder. The maximum number of surfaces that can be reserved is device-dependent. See Figure 22.5.
DEVICE=3340	This entry specifies the unit or device that contains the prime data areas or overflow areas for the logical file. If not specified, the default option is disk device 2311. The DEVICE option is specified when (1) you are using a device other than 2311, or (2) when it is useful to put the entries for prime data areas and overflow areas on separate units.
DSKXTNT=2	This entry specifies the number of disk extent areas you will be using. An *extent* is a disk area assigned to an ISAM file. The minimum number that can be specified by this entry is 2, that is, one extent for a prime data area and one extent for a cylinder index.
HINDEX=3340	This entry specifies the unit or device containing the highest index for the file. If omitted, 2311 is the default. This option is specified when (1) you are using a device other than 2311, or (2) it is useful to put the highest index on a separate physical device.
KEYLEN=5	The length of the key must *always* be specified and may range from 1 to 255 bytes.
KEYLOC=1	This entry references the starting position of the key within the record. For the ISDISK file, the key field begins in position 1; that is, the key is the first field in the record. Typically, a key field is the first field in an ISAM record. This entry, like KEYLEN, is required.
NRECDS=2	This entry indicates the *number* of *records* per block. For unblocked records, code NRECDS=1.
RECFORM=FIXBLK	This entry indicates that records are blocked and of fixed length. The record format RECFORM is specified as fixed and blocked by coding FIXBLK. FIXUNB would be used for unblocked fixed-length records.
RECSIZE=80	This entry specifies the length of each logical record. In the sample program, we have specified 80 bytes per record.
VERIFY=YES	This entry is used to check disk records after they are written to ensure that an I/O error has not occurred.

IOREAL=ISBUFFER	When loading records, an output area (ISBUFFER) must be defined by a DS in the program. The minimum length of this area is computed through the following formula.

$$\text{Length} = 8 + \text{KEYLEN} + (\text{NRECDS} \times \text{RECSIZE})$$

	where the 8 denotes a count area. This area is used by the operating system to ensure that each physical record fits on the surface specified. The length of the buffer is, then, the block size plus 8 for a count area plus the length of the key. Thus, when defining ISBUFFER as a DS be sure you make it large enough.
IOROUT=LOAD	Notifies the assembler to create or LOAD an ISAM file. LOAD is used for creating an (output) ISAM file. Later on, we will see that RETRVE is used for reading (input) ISAM files.
WORKL=RECORD	Specifies the name of the work area for loading the file. In this case, it is RECORD. With blocked records, the size of the WORKL area must be the same as the record size, RECSIZE. However, if the records are unblocked then,

WORKL = RECSIZE + KEYLEN

That is, the KEYLEN only affects the size of WORKL if records are unblocked. In our sample program we blocked the records and simply used the input record area for WORKL. The DS for RECORD, like the DS for ISBUFFER, must reflect these length considerations.

The program to create an ISAM file sequentially contains the following commands and options.

OPEN	INFILE,ISDISK,OUTFILE	INFILE is used to create ISDISK; OUTFILE is a copy of the file that is printed for control purposes. Typically, a user will check this printout to ensure that the file created on disk is valid.
SETFL	ISDISK	This "set file load" instruction is required when creating ISAM files.
READ GET	INFILE,RECORD	Reads INFILE and places the indexed record in the ISAM work area called RECORD. The record must be in the WORKL field called RECORD before a write can be executed. Any processing required, including the transmission of input to output areas, will be coded between the GET and the WRITE.
WRITE	ISDISK,NEWKEY	Creates an ISAM record and the appropriate index. (The DTFIS for ISDISK tells the computer that the KEYLOC begins in the first position and that the length of the key, KEYLEN, is 5 characters.)
WAITF	ISDISK	Causes an I/O delay whenever an I/O error occurs. If you do not code for this delay and an I/O error occurs, the program could abend.
TM	ISDISKC,X'FF'	ISDISKC is a single byte that could have "on" bits in specified bit locations to indicate if an I/O error has occurred; comparing ISDISKC to a mask with all bits "on" tests for *all* I/O error conditions. See the next section for a full explanation of I/O errors.
BNZ	ERROR	A branch to ERROR occurs if any ISDISKC bit is a 1, indicating that an I/O error has occurred. The error routine tests for all possible types of I/O errors.

	B	READ					Continues the reading and processing of records if no I/O errors have occurred.

EOF	ENDFL	ISDISK					Terminates processing of the ISAM file.
	CLOSE						Closes all files.
	EOJ						Terminates the run.

The following will clarify those options and commands that are new to this discussion of ISAM files.

The Relationship Between Work Areas and I/O Areas. When you create an ISAM record with a valid key, each individual record is moved from the work area. In this case, RECORD is moved to the I/O area ISBUFFER where it is available for the transfer to disk.

```
LOC      OBJECT CODE      ADDR1 ADDR2    STMT    SOURCE STATEMENT

                                          1                PRINT  NOGEN
000000                                    2  ISAM          START
000000 05C0                               3  CREATE        BALR   12,0
                                00002     4                USING  *,12
                                          5  ****************************************************************
                                          6  *  O P E N   F I L E S   &   F O R M A T   I S A M   D I S K  *
                                          7  ****************************************************************
                                          8                OPEN   INFILE,ISDISK,OUTFILE
                                         18                SETFL  ISDISK
                                         24  ********************************************
                                         25  *         M A I N   P R O G R A M          *
                                         26  ********************************************
                                         27  READ          GET    INFILE,RECORD
000036 F222 C461 C461 00463 00463        33                PACK   CREDITS,CREDITS
                                         34                COMRG
000042 D207 C46B 1000 0046D 00000        38                MVC    DATE,0(1)
                                         39  COPY          WRITE  ISDISK,NEWKEY
000054 91FF C18C      0018E              44                TM     ISDISKC,X'FF'
000058 4770 C096      00098              45                BNZ    ERROR
00005C 47F0 C024      00026              46                B      READ
                                         47  ****************************************************************
                                         48  *  C L O S E   F I L E S   &   E O F   O F   I S A M  *
                                         49  ****************************************************************
                                         50  EOF           ENDFL  ISDISK
                                         62                CLOSE  INFILE,ISDISK,OUTFILE
                                         72                EOJ
                                         75  ****************************************************************
                                         76  *          E R R O R   R E C O V E R Y   R O U T I N E S       *
                                         77  ****************************************************************
000098 9139 C18C      0018E             78  ERROR         TM     ISDISKC,X'39'
00009C 4780 C0AC      000AE             79                BZ     CONT1
0000A0 D21D C493 C572 00495 00574       80                MVC    MSSG,=CL30'INSUFFICIENT DISK SPACE'
0000A6 45A0 C112           00114        81                BAL    10,PRINT
0000AA 47F0 C05E      00060             82                B      EOF
0000AE 9180 C18C      0018E             83  CONT1         TM     ISDISKC,X'80'
0000B2 4780 C0C2      000C4             84                BZ     CONT2
0000B6 D21D C493 C590 00495 00592       85                MVC    MSSG,=C'UNCORRECTABLE OUTPUT ERROR'
0000BC 45A0 C112           00114        86                BAL    10,PRINT
0000C0 47F0 C05E      00060             87                B      EOF
0000C4 9104 C18C      0018E             88  CONT2         TM     ISDISKC,X'04'
0000C8 4780 C0D8      000DA             89                BZ     CONT3
0000CC D21D C493 C5AA 00495 005AC       90                MVC    MSSG,=CL30'DUPLICATE RECORD IGNORED'
0000D2 45A0 C112           00114        91                BAL    10,PRINT
0000D6 47F0 C024      00026             92                B      READ
0000DA 9102 C18C      0018E             93  CONT3         TM     ISDISKC,X'02'
0000DE 4780 C0EE      000F0             94                BZ     CONT4
0000E2 D21D C493 C5C8 00495 005CA       95                MVC    MSSG,=CL30'OUT OF SEQUENCE RECORD IGNORED'
0000E8 45A0 C112           00114        96                BAL    10,PRINT
0000EC 47F0 C024      00026             97                B      READ
0000F0 9140 C18C      0018E             98  CONT4         TM     ISDISKC,X'40'
0000F4 4780 C104      00106             99                BZ     CONT5
0000F8 D21D C493 C5E6 00495 005E8      100                MVC    MSSG,=CL30'WRONG LENGTH RECORD CHECK SPEC'
0000FE 45A0 C112           00114       101                BAL    10,PRINT
000102 47F0 C05E      00060            102                B      EOF
000106 D21D C493 C604 00495 00606      103  CONT5         MVC    MSSG,=CL30'INVALID ERROR-CHECK PROGRAM'
00010C 45A0 C112           00114       104                BAL    10,PRINT
000110 47F0 C05E      00060            105                B      EOF
000114 D284 C4B2 C4B1 004B4 004B3      106  PRINT         MVC    OUTAREA,SPACES
00011A D284 C4B2 C622 004B4 00624      107                MVC    OUTAREA,=C'  JOB ABORTED FOR ERROR SHOWN  *** '
000120 D21D C40A C493 004DC 00495      108                MVC    OUTAREA+40(30),MSSG
                                       109                PUT    OUTFILE,OUTAREA
000136 07FA                            115                BR     10
```

Figure 22.4

DOS program to create an indexed file using ISAM (continued on next page).

```
                116 ************************************************************
                117 *          F I L E   S P E C I F I C A T I O N S
                118 ************************************************************
                119 INFILE    DTFCD DEVADDR=SYSIPT,BLKSIZE=80,RECFORM=FIXUNB,      *
                              IOAREA1=BUFFRIN,WORKA=YES,DEVICE=2501,TYPEFLE=INPUT, *
                              EOFADDR=EOF
                140           COMOD WORKA=YES,DEVICE=2501
                292 ISDISK    DTFIS CYLOFL=1,DEVICE=3340,DSKXTNT=2,HINDEX=3340,KEYLEN=5, *
                              KEYLOC=1,NRECDS=2,RECFORM=FIXBLK,RECSIZE=80,VERIFY=YES, *
                              IOAREAL=ISBUFFER,IOROUT=LOAD,WORKL=RECORD
                341 OUTFILE   DTFPR DEVADDR=SYSLST,IOAREA1=BUFFROUT,BLKSIZE=133,    *
                              WORKA=YES,DEVICE=3203,CTLCHR=ASA
                362           PRMOD WORKA=YES,DEVICE=3203
                452 ************************************************************
                453 *          D E F I N E   S T O R A G E   &   C O N S T A N T S
                454 ************************************************************
0002A8          455 BUFFRIN   DS    CL80
0002F8          456 ISBUFFER  DS    CL200
0003C0          457 BUFFROUT  DS    CL133
000445          458 RECORD    DS    0CL80
000445          459 KEYIN     DS    CL5
00044A          460           DS    CL5
00044F          461 NAME      DS    CL15
00045E          462           DS    CL5
000463          463 CREDITS   DS    CL3
000466          464           DS    CL7
00046D          465 DATE      DS    CL8
000475          466 OTHER     DS    CL32
000495          467 MSSG      DS    CL30
0004B3 40       468 SPACES    DC    C' '
0004B4          469 OUTAREA   DS    CL133
        00000   470           END   CREATE
000540 5B5BC2D6D7C5D540  471        =C'$$BOPEN '
000548 5B5BC2E2C5E3C6D3  472        =C'$$BSETFL'
000550 5B5BC2C5D5C4C6D3  473        =C'$$BENDFL'
000558 5B5BC2C3D3D6E2C5  474        =C'$$BCLOSE'
000560 00000170          475        =A(ISDISK)
000564 00000138          476        =A(INFILE)
000568 00000445          477        =A(RECORD)
00056C 00000278          478        =A(OUTFILE)
000570 000004B4          479        =A(OUTAREA)
000574 C9D5E2E4C6C6C9C3  480        =CL30'INSUFFICIENT DISK SPACE'
000592 E4D5C3D6D9D9C5C3  481        =C'UNCORRECTABLE OUTPUT ERROR'
0005AC C4E4D7D3C9C3C1E3  482        =CL30'DUPLICATE RECORD IGNORED'
0005CA D6E4E340D6C640E2  483        =C'OUT OF SEQUENCE RECORD IGNORED'
0005E8 E6D9D6D5C740D3C5  484        =CL30'WRONG LENGTH RECORD CHECK SPEC'
000606 C9D5E5C1D3C9C440  485        =CL30'INVALID ERROR-CHECK PROGRAM'
000624 4040D1D6C240C1C2  486        =C'  JOB ABORTED FOR ERROR SHOWN  *** '
```

Figure 22.4
(continued)

Disk Device	Maximum Number of Surfaces
2311	8
2314,2319,2321	18
3330,3333	17
3340	10

The WAITF *Instruction After a* WRITE.   In DOS, I/O delays are performed automatically by the operating system following a GET or PUT macro. A WAITF macro, however, must follow a READ or WRITE to cause the required delay. WAITF is used with ISAM files. Note that a similar command, CHECK, is used with sequential files and OS ISAM retrieval.

A complete list of declarative macros for Load And Random retrieval and Sequential retrieval is found in Figure 22.6.

3. Error Recovery

You may use ISAM macros to detect certain error conditions. After every ISAM I/O execution of a macro, the operating system places the condition or status of the operation in a one-byte field referenced as the 7-character ISAM filename, followed by the letter C. In the sample program the DTFIS is called

ISDISK; by referencing ISDISKC, then, I/O error information relating to ISDISK is available. If an I/O error occurs, one or more bits of the aforementioned byte will be set to 1 by the operating system. The meaning of the on bits for a file-creation routine where IOROUT is set equal to LOAD appears in Figure 22.7.

Applies to						
Ran. Rtvl.	Seq. Rtvl.	Load	Add			
X	X	X	X	M	DSKXTNT = n	Maximum number of extents specified for this file
X	X	X	X	M	IOROUT = xxxxxx	(LOAD, ADD, RETRVE, or ADDRTR)
X	X	X	X	M	KEYLEN = nnn	Number of bytes in record key (maximum is 255)
X	X	X	X	M	NRECDS = nnn	Number of records in a block. Specify for blocked records only; if unblocked, 1 is assumed.
X	X	X	X	M	RECFORM = xxxxxx	(FIXUNB or FIXBLK)
X	X	X	X	M	RECSIZE = nnnn	Number of characters in logical record.
X	X	X	X	O	CYLOFL = nn	Number of tracks for each cylinder overflow area. Maximum = 8 for 2311, 18 for 2314 and 2321, 17 for 3330 and 3333, 10 for 3340
X	X	X	X	O	DEVICE = nnnn	(2311, 2314, 2321, 3330, 3340). If omitted, 2311 is assumed.
X	X	X	X	O	ERREXT = YES	Non data-transfer error returns and ERET desired.
X	X	X	X	O	HINDEX = nnnn	(2311, 2314, 2321, 3330, 3340). Unit containing highest level index. If omitted, 2311 is assumed.
X	X		X	O	HOLD = YES	Track hold function is desired
X			X	O	INDAREA = xxxxxxxx	Symbolic name of cylinder index area
X			X	O	INDSKIP = YES	Index skip feature is to be used
X			X	O	INDSIZE = nnnnn	Number of bytes required for the cylinder index area
		X	X	O	IOAREAL = xxxxxxxx	Name of I/O area
X				O	IOAREAR = xxxxxxxx	
	X			O	IOAREAS = xxxxxxxx	
		X	X	O	IOAREA2 = xxxxxxxx	Name of second I/O area
X	X			O	IOREG = (nn)	Register number. Omit if WORKA or WORKS is specified

M = Mandatory; O = Optional

Figure 22.6
Declarative macros for Load And Random retrieval and Sequential retrieval. (Courtesy IBM.)

Bit	Cause	Explanation
0	DASD error	An uncorrectable DASD error has occurred (except wrong length record).
1	Wrong length record	A wrong length record has been detected during an I/O operation.
2	Prime data area full	The next to the last track of the prime data area has been filled during the load or extension of the file. You should issue the ENDFL macro, then do a load extend on the file with new extents given.
3	Cylinder Index area full	The Cylinder Index area is not large enough to contain all entries needed to index each cylinder specified for the prime data area. This condition can occur during the execution of the SETFL. You must extend the upper limit of the cylinder index by using a new extent card.
4	Master Index full	The Master Index area is not large enough to contain all the entries needed to index each track of the Cylinder Index. This condition can occur during SETFL. You must extend the upper limit, if you are creating the file, by using an extent card. Or, you must reorganize the file and assign a larger area.
5	Duplicate record	The record being loaded is a duplicate of the previous record.
6	Sequence check	The record being loaded is not in the sequential order required for loading.
7	Prime data area overflow	There is not enough space in the prime data area to write an EOF record. This condition can occur during the execution of the ENDFL macro.

Figure 22.7
Meaning of the on bits for a file creation routine where IOROUT is set to LOAD.
(Courtesy IBM.)

The TM (Test Under Mask) instruction is used here to test for specific I/O errors. This instruction is explained in detail in Chapter 20.

Look again at the program in Figure 22.5. The TM instruction compares the byte designated as ISDISKC to a hex mask of X'80'. A bit configuration of 10000000 (X'80') in ISDISKC would mean an uncorrectable disk (DASD) output error. If such an error occurred, then a branch to an error routine would follow.

BNZ (Branch if Not Zero) will cause a branch if the bit in ISDISKC corresponding to the mask 10000000 (X'80') is on. If the first or zero-bit in ISDISKC contains a "1", an error routine is executed. In this error routine, a message is printed describing the error and the run is terminated.

The hex mask used for the various program checks is determined by analyzing the error byte as in Figure 22.8. Again note in Figure 22.7 that the zero bit is set only when an uncorrectable disk (DASD) error is detected.

Suppose we wish to test for the possibility of insufficient disk space. There are several conditions that could result in insufficient disk space.

Contents of ISDISKC	*Meaning*
X'20'	Prime data area is full
X'10'	Cylinder index area is full
X'08'	Master index is full
X'01'	Prime data area overflow has occurred

	BIT POSITIONS	0 1 2 3	4 5 6 7
	BINARY CONTENTS OF ISDISKC	1 0 0 0	0 0 0 0

Figure 22.8
Analyzing the error byte to determine the hex mask to be used for program checks.

HEX. CONTENTS OF ISDISKC   8   0

We can use a *single* test for determining if any one of these conditions has occurred. The TM will test all those bits in ISDISKC that correspond to a "1" in the mask. Suppose we compare ISDISKC to X'39'. X'39' includes all four of the conditions indicated in Figure 22.7.

Hex Notation	*Bit Configuration*	*Meaning*
X'20'	00100000	Prime data area is full
X'10'	00010000	Cylinder index area is full
X'08'	00001000	Master index is full
X'01'	00000001	Prime data area overflow has occurred
X'39'	00111001 0 7 bit bit	Collectively accounts for all of the above

If we use a TM to compare ISDISKC to X'39' we could then branch on not zero (BNZ) to an error routine. This means if any of the bits 2, 3, 4, or 7 are set to 1, an error message indicating insufficient disk space is printed and the job is terminated. In effect, we are using a logical OR to test for any one of several conditions.

Invalid Key. Before records are created, the ISAM control system performs the following major checks on key fields.

1. Sequence check—Ensures that records are being created sequentially by key field.
2. Duplicate key check—Ensures that there is no more than one record created with the same key.

In a similar manner all I/O error conditions may also be tested. See Figure 22.9 for a summary.

Figure 22.9
Summary of I/O error conditions.

Test Byte	*Problem*	*Action*
X'39'	Insufficient disk space	Print message—terminate run
X'80'	Uncorrectable DASD error	Print message—terminate run
X'04'	Duplicate record	Print message—continue run
X'02'	Sequence error	Print message—continue run
X'40'	Incorrect record length	Print message—terminate run

In summary, to create a DOS ISAM file you must do the following:

1. Make certain that input records are in sequence by the key field.
2. Include the appropriate DTFIS entries.
3. Process input and write the ISAM file in the usual way.
4. Use a TM to test for any I/O error condition that may have occurred when you wrote a record onto the disk.

E. Creating an OS ISAM File

The processing of ISAM files under OS is very similar to that of DOS. For this reason only the necessary changes required to convert from DOS to OS will be discussed. Under OS, ISAM provides the *option* of using a delete code in the first byte. If the delete code contains "FF" (or *high values*), the operating system will automatically delete or deactivate the record when required.

The macros that *must* be employed in creating or loading an ISAM file under OS include OPEN, CLOSE, PUT, and DCB. The SETFL and ENDFL macros of DOS are not used and are therefore omitted in the OS create program. The WRITE instruction used to load the file in the DOS program is replaced with the PUT command in OS.

DOS   OS

```
┌────────────────────────────────┐   ┌────────────────────────────────┐
│ COPY  WRITE  ISDISK,NEWKEY      │   │ COPY  PUT  ISDISK,RECORD        │
└────────────────────────────────┘   └────────────────────────────────┘
```
                                                           ↑
                                            NEWKEY is not used; instead
                                            write from record area

The DTF entries of DOS are replaced with the following DCB entries for OS.

DDNAME=ISDISK	Data set name
CYLOFL=1	Number of overflow tracks per cylinder
KEYLEN=5	Length of key
LRECL=80	Length of each record
BLKSIZE=160	Length of block
RECFM=FB	FB denotes fixed-length, blocked records
	F denotes fixed-length, unblocked records
DSORG=IS	Indexed sequential organization
MACRF=PM	Macro format uses PUT in the move mode
OPTCD=YW	I specifies independent overflow areas
	L denotes delete option is to be used
	M denotes master index is to be created
	Y denotes cylinder overflow areas
	W specifies write verification after each write operation
RKP=0	Key begins in the first byte, byte "0"
SYNAD=ERRORTN	Specifies error routine to be executed when I/O synchronization errors occur

The DCB would appear:

```
ISDISK   DCB   DDNAME=ISDISK,CYLOFL=1,KEYLEN=5,LRECL=80,    *
               BLKSIZE=160,RECFM=FB,DSORG=IS,MACRF=PM,       *
               OPTCD=YW,RKP=0,SYNDAD=ERRORTN
```

Error Checking. As with DOS, checking for I/O errors in an OS program is an essential aspect of programming ISAM because the programmer is required to code error-checking routines. The data control block operand (DCB) may be coded with an entry SYNAD=ERRORTN, where ERRORTN is a programmer-defined name used to reference the error routine. The SYNAD=ERRORTN entry informs the operating system to branch to ERRORTN when I/O synchronization errors occur. This is similar in concept to EODAD=EOF, which causes the operating system to transfer control to the EOF routine when the end-of-file condition occurs. In OS, the operating system establishes the 81st and 82nd bytes of the DCB for error codes. In our example, this would mean ISDISK+80 and ISDISK+81. As with DOS, the error bytes are checked using the TM instruction. It is recommended that the following error conditions be checked in ERRORTN.

Reference Byte	*Reference Bit*	*Hex Code*	*Error Condition*
ISDISK+80	2	'20'	Overflow area filled
ISDISK+80	5	'04'	Uncorrectable I/O error
ISDISK+81	0	'80'	Duplicate record
ISDISK+81	1	'40'	Record out of sequence

A partial listing of the OS create program appears in Figure 22.10.

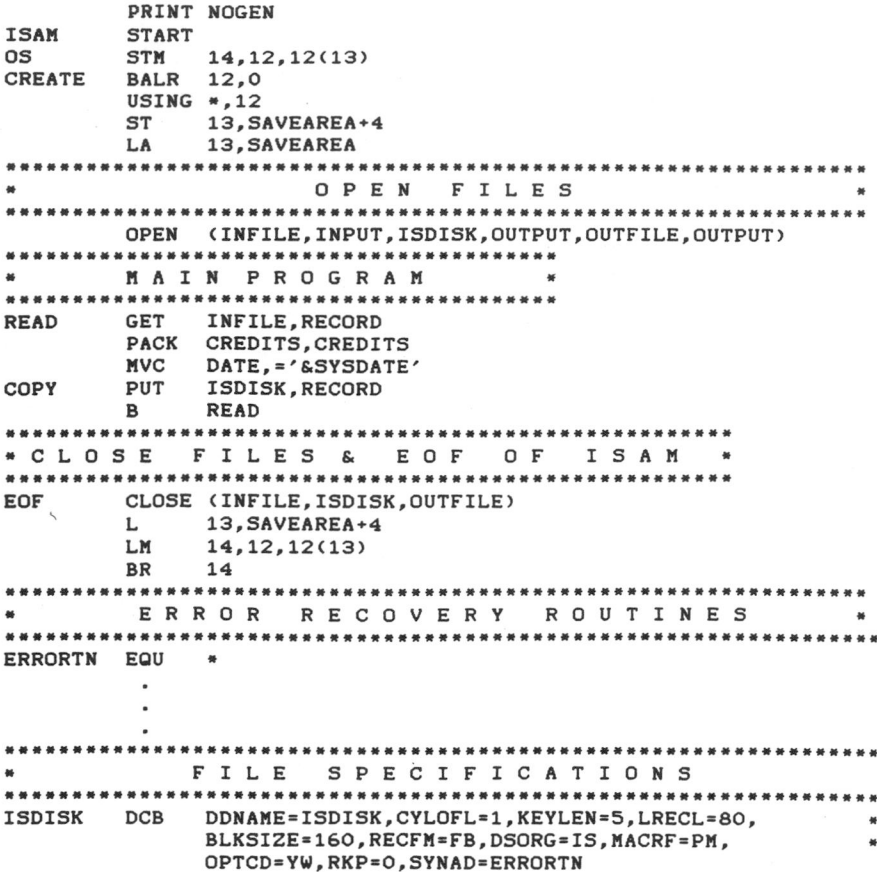

```
                    PRINT  NOGEN
ISAM        START
OS          STM    14,12,12(13)
CREATE      BALR   12,0
            USING  *,12
            ST     13,SAVEAREA+4
            LA     13,SAVEAREA
*************************************************************
*                    O P E N   F I L E S                    *
*************************************************************
            OPEN   (INFILE,INPUT,ISDISK,OUTPUT,OUTFILE,OUTPUT)
*************************************************************
*           M A I N   P R O G R A M           *
*************************************************************
READ        GET    INFILE,RECORD
            PACK   CREDITS,CREDITS
            MVC    DATE,='&SYSDATE'
COPY        PUT    ISDISK,RECORD
            B      READ
*************************************************************
* C L O S E   F I L E S  &  E O F   O F   I S A M  *
*************************************************************
EOF         CLOSE  (INFILE,ISDISK,OUTFILE)
            L      13,SAVEAREA+4
            LM     14,12,12(13)
            BR     14
*************************************************************
*           E R R O R   R E C O V E R Y   R O U T I N E S   *
*************************************************************
ERRORTN     EQU    *
            .
            .
            .
*************************************************************
*           F I L E   S P E C I F I C A T I O N S           *
*************************************************************
ISDISK      DCB    DDNAME=ISDISK,CYLOFL=1,KEYLEN=5,LRECL=80,      *
                   BLKSIZE=160,RECFM=FB,DSORG=IS,MACRF=PM,        *
                   OPTCD=YW,RKP=0,SYNAD=ERRORTN
```

Figure 22.10
Partial listing of an OS ISAM
create program.

F. Updating an ISAM File Randomly

You will recall that updating a sequential tape or disk file required *three* files, each in sequence by a specific key field.

1. OLDMAST, which contains master file information current through the previous updating cycle;
2. TRANS, which contains change records or records required to make the OLDMAST current; and,
3. NEWMAST, which combines TRANS data and OLDMAST data to form one updated master file.

One advantage of disk processing is that master records can be updated directly without having to create an entirely new file. Thus, only *two* files are needed for updating an ISAM file. They are the transaction file, which serves as input, and the master file, which serves as *both* input and output. The ISAM disk file may be accessed randomly, so there is no need to sort the transaction file into record-key sequence.

To update ISAM files *randomly*, we typically have a transaction file on disk, tape, or floppy disk, or transaction data that is entered with a keyboard terminal. This transaction data will specify which ISAM records we want to read or access for updating purposes. To access a record in the master file, we enter the field corresponding to the record key on the disk. For example, suppose we wish to access records that have PARTNO as the key field in an ISAM inventory file. We must read in transaction records containing the actual PARTNOs to be accessed. We move a transaction part number to the ISAM key field and then read the corresponding ISAM record.

UPDATING AN ISAM MASTER FILE

1. Read a transaction record.
2. Move the transaction record's key field to the master record key field and read from the master file. (At this point, in storage we have the transaction record and a corresponding master record that needs to be updated.)
3. Make the changes to the master record directly by moving transaction data to the master I/O record area.
4. Write the master record. This rewrites the updated disk record.

When coding an ISAM disk file, it is possible to perform all three of the following types of update procedures depending on the contents of the transaction file.

1. Change existing records. For example, you could use a payroll transaction file to incorporate promotions, salary increases, and transfers into a payroll master file.
2. Create new records. For example, you could add new hires to a payroll file. If a program's objective is to enable a transaction file to add new records to a master ISAM file, a coded field would typically appear in each transaction record. A separate code, then, could designate a transaction record as a new account. In our case, it would not be necessary to look up a master disk record when a transaction record designates a new account.
3. Delete some existing records. For example, resignations could be deleted from a payroll file. To do so, we look up the corresponding ISAM master records to be deleted and use special delete codes in the key fields to deactivate the records.

1. Illustrating a Random Update Procedure for an ISAM DOS File

Problem Definition. Assume that a master indexed disk file contains student data with a student number as a key field. The transaction file contains student number and the number of credits taken during the current semester. The transaction data is to be used to change or update the corresponding disk record, where the key field for the ISAM disk is its student number.

Our sample ISAM update program reads transaction records in random sequence and adds the credits completed by the student during the past semester to the ISAM Student Master (ISDISK). The transaction record, SEMREC, contains the key field (KEYIN) that is used to identify the ISAM record to be updated. An overview of the systems flowchart is depicted in Figure 22.11.

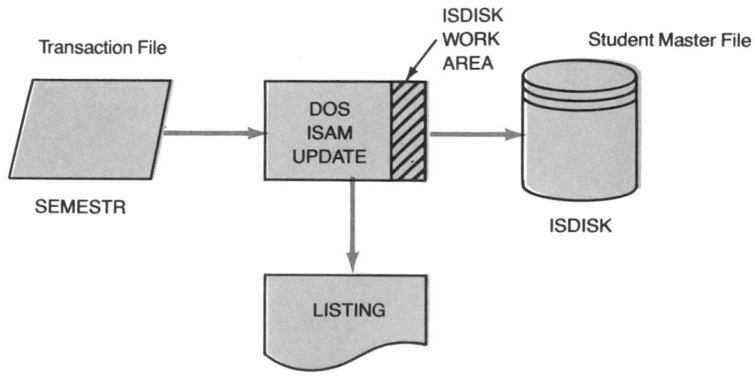

Figure 22.11
Systems flowchart of a random update procedure for an ISAM DOS file.

DOS ISAM Update. The sample DOS ISAM update program with random access appears in Figure 22.12. The result of a successful look-up is the reading of the ISAM record into the work area defined by the WORKR parameter (R for retrieve) in the DTFIS. That is, the WORKR area will contain the ISAM record with the same student number as SEMREC. We use R with WORK in the DTFIS to indicate that we are retrieving this ISAM file, rather than creating or loading it.

We will see in the sample update program that the entry WORKR=ISREC places the master record in the ISREC area, where it can be changed or updated. The updated record is then rewritten to the master with a WRITE ISDISK,KEY instruction. As in the create program, the WAITF macro is used to complete I/O operations and to detect errors in reading or writing the ISAM file. However, the error conditions have a different meaning when performing retrieval than when initially creating or loading the file. See Figure 22.13 for an illustration of the meaning of error codes when randomly accessing an ISAM file.

```
LOC     OBJECT CODE      ADDR1 ADDR2   STMT    SOURCE STATEMENT
                                        1               PRINT NOGEN
000000                                  2  ISAM         START
000000 05C0                             3  UPDATE       BALR  12,0
                                00002   4               USING *,12
                                        5               OPEN  SEMESTR,ISDISK,PRNTFLE
                                       15  ***********************************************
                                       16  *          M A I N   P R O C E S S I N G
                                       17  ***********************************************
00001A D284 C504 C503 00506 00505      18  GETREC       MVC   OUTAREA,SPACES
                                       19               GET   SEMESTR,SEMREC
000030 D204 C316 C2C6 00318 002C8      25               MVC   ISKEY,KEYIN
                                       26  RDISAM       READ  ISDISK,KEY
                                       31               WAITF ISDISK
00004E 91D3 C17C      0017E            36               TM    ISDISKC,X'D3'
000052 4770 C0CA      000CC            37               BNZ   READERR
000056 F222 C2E4 C2E4 002E6 002E6      38  PROCESS      PACK  NEWCRED,NEWCRED
00005C FA22 C334 C2E4 00336 002E6      39               AP    ISCRED,NEWCRED
                                       40               COMRG
000068 D207 C33E 1000 00340 00000      44               MVC   ISDATE,0(1)
                                       45  WRITEIS      WRITE ISDISK,KEY
                                       50               WAITF ISDISK
000086 91C0 C17C      0017E            55               TM    ISDISKC,X'C0'
00008A 4770 C0FC      000FE            56               BNZ   WRITERR
00008E D204 C505 C316 00507 00318      57  PRINTRTN     MVC   KEYOUT,ISKEY
000094 D20E C50F C320 00511 00322      58               MVC   NAMEO,ISNAME
00009A D207 C523 C33E 00525 00340      59               MVC   DATEO,ISDATE
0000A0 D203 C530 C58B 00532 0058D      60               MVC   CREDO,PAT1
0000A6 D203 C539 C58B 0053B 0058D      61               MVC   TOTCREDO,PAT1
0000AC DE03 C530 C2E5 00532 002E7      62               ED    CREDO,NEWCRED+1
0000B2 DE03 C539 C335 0053B 00337      63               ED    TOTCREDO,ISCRED+1
                                       64               PUT   PRNTFLE,OUTAREA
0000C8 47F0 C018      0001A            70               B     GETREC
                                       71  ************************************************************
                                       72  *          E R R O R   R E C O V E R Y   R O U T I N E S    *
                                       73  ************************************************************
                                000CC  74  READERR      EQU   *
0000CC D24F C505 C2C6 00507 002C8      75               MVC   KEYOUT(80),SEMREC
0000D2 9110 C17C      0017E            76               TM    ISDISKC,X'10'
0000D6 4770 C0E2      000E4            77               BNZ   NOREC
0000DA D228 C542 C5BA 00544 005BC      78               MVC   MSSG,=CL41'***RECORD CAUSED READ ERROR-CHECK DATA***'
0000E0 47F0 C0E8      000EA            79               B     PRNTMSSG
0000E4 D228 C542 C5E3 00544 005E5      80  NOREC        MVC   MSSG,=CL41'***RECORD NOT FOUND ON ISAM-CHECK DATA***'
                                       81  PRNTMSSG     PUT   PRNTFLE,OUTAREA
0000FA 47F0 C10C      0010E            87               B     EOF
                                000FE  88  WRITERR      EQU   *
0000FE D24F C505 C2C6 00507 002C8      89               MVC   KEYOUT(80),SEMREC
000104 D228 C542 C60C 00544 0060E      90               MVC   MSSG,=CL41'***WRITE ERROR OCCURRED WITH ISAM FILE***'
00010A 47F0 C0E8      000EA            91               B     PRNTMSSG
                                       92  ************************************************************
                                       93  *          E N D   O F   F I L E   R O U T I N E           *
                                       94  ************************************************************
                                0010E  95  EOF          EQU   *
                                       96               CLOSE SEMESTR,ISDISK,PRNTFLE
                                      106               EOJ
```

Figure 22.12
Sample DOS ISAM update program with random access. (continued on next page).

```
                        109 ***************************************************************
                        110 *          F I L E   S P E C I F I C A T I O N S              *
                        111 ***************************************************************
                        112 SEMESTR  DTFCD DEVADDR=SYSIPT,BLKSIZE=80,RECFORM=FIXUNB,        *
                                           IOAREA1=BUFFRIN,WORKA=YES,DEVICE=2501,TYPEFLE=INPUT,  *
                                           EOFADDR=EOF
                        133          CDMOD WORKA=YES,DEVICE=2501
                        285 ISDISK   DTFIS CYLOFL=1,DEVICE=3340,DSKXTNT=2,HINDEX=3340,KEYLEN=5, *
                                           KEYLOC=1,NRECDS=2,RECFORM=FIXBLK,RECSIZE=80,VERIFY=YES, *
                                           IOAREAR=ISBUFFER,IOROUT=RETRVE,WORKR=ISREC,KEYARG=ISKEY,*
                                           TYPEFLE=RANDOM
                        367 PRNTFLE  DTFPR DEVADDR=SYSLST,IOAREA1=BUFFROUT,BLKSIZE=133,       *
                                           WORKA=YES,DEVICE=3203,CTLCHR=ASA
                        388          PRMOD WORKA=YES,DEVICE=3203
                        478 ***************************************************************
                        479 *    T R A N S A C T I O N   R E C O R D
                        480 ***************************************************************
0002C8                  481 SEMREC   DS    OCL80
0002C8                  482 KEYIN    DS    CL5
0002CD                  483          DS    CL5
0002D2                  484 NAME     DS    CL15
0002E1                  485          DS    CL5
0002E6                  486 NEWCRED  DS    CL3
0002E9                  487 OTHER    DS    CL47
                        488 ***************************************************************
                        489 *               I S A M   D I S K   R E C O R D              *
                        490 ***************************************************************
000318                  491 ISREC    DS    OCL80
000318                  492 ISKEY    DS    CL5
00031D                  493          DS    CL5
000322                  494 ISNAME   DS    CL15
000331                  495          DS    CL5
000336                  496 ISCRED   DS    PL3
000339                  497          DS    CL7
000340                  498 ISDATE   DS    CL8
000348                  499 ISDATA   DS    CL32
                        500 ******************************************************
                        501 *         I S A M   B U F F E R                 *
                        502 ******************************************************
000368                  503 ISBUFFER DS    CL200
000430                  504 BUFFROUT DS    CL133
0004B5                  505 BUFFRIN  DS    CL80
000505 40               506 SPACES   DC    C' '
                        507 ********************************************************
                        508 *    D E T A I L   P R I N T   L I N E      *
                        509 ********************************************************
000506                  510 OUTAREA  DS    OCL133
000506                  511 CC       DS    CL1
000507                  512 KEYOUT   DS    CL5
00050C                  513          DS    CL5
000511                  514 NAMEO    DS    CL15
000520                  515          DS    CL5
000525                  516 DATEO    DS    CL8
00052D                  517          DS    CL5
000532                  518 CREDO    DS    CL4
000536                  519          DS    CL5

00053B                  520 TOTCREDO DS    CL4
00053F                  521          DS    CL5
000544                  522 MSSG     DS    CL41
00056D                  523          DS    CL32
                        524 ******************************
                        525 *   E D I T   P A T T E R N  *
                        526 ******************************
000580 40202120         527 PAT1     DC    XL4'40202120'
               00000    528          END   UPDATE
000598 5B5BC2D6D7C5D540 529                =C'$$BOPEN '
0005A0 5B5BC2C3D3D6E2C5 530                =C'$$BCLOSE'
0005A8 00000128         531                =A(SEMESTR)
0005AC 000002C8         532                =A(SEMREC)
0005B0 00000160         533                =A(ISDISK)
0005B4 00000298         534                =A(PRNTFLE)
0005B8 00000506         535                =A(OUTAREA)
0005BC 5C5C5CD9C5C3D6D9 536                =CL41'***RECORD CAUSED READ ERROR-CHECK DATA***'
0005E5 5C5C5CD9C5C3D6D9 537                =CL41'***RECORD NOT FOUND ON ISAM-CHECK DATA***'
00060E 5C5C5CE6D9C9E3C5 538                =CL41'***WRITE ERROR OCCURRED WITH ISAM FILE***'
```

Figure 22.12
(continued)

Bit	Cause	Explanation
0	DASD error	Any uncorrectable DASD error has occurred (except wrong length record).
1	Wrong length record	A wrong length record has been detected during an I/O operation.
2	End of file	The EOF condition has been encountered during execution of the sequential retrieval function.
3	No record found	The record to be retrieved has not been found in the file. This applies to Random (RANSEQ) and to SETL in SEQNTL (RANSEQ) when KEY is specified, or after GKEY.
4	Invalid ID specified	The ID specified to the SETL in SEQNTL (RANSEQ) is outside the prime file limits.
5	Duplicate record	The record to be added to the file has a duplicate record key of another record in the file.
6	Overflow area full	An overflow area in a cylinder is full, and no independent overflow area has been specified; or an independent overflow area is full, and the addition cannot be made. You should assign an independent overflow area or extend the limit.
7	Overflow	The record being processed in one of the retrieval functions (RANDOM/SEQNTL) is an overflow record.

Figure 22.13
Summary of error codes when randomly accessing an ISAM file. (Courtesy IBM.)

The DTFIS MACRO. Note that the first two lines of the DTFIS (the first 10 entries) have a similar format to those in the create program. We will not discuss these but focus instead on the DTF entries that differ from those in the ISAM create program.

IOAREAR=ISBUFFER — This entry has the same meaning as IOAREAL in the program that creates the ISAM file. IOAREAR is an I/O area to be retrieved (whereas in the create we used IOAREAL to load or create the I/O area). ISBUFFER is the name assigned to this I/O area.

IOROUT=RETRVE — When creating an ISAM file we included IOROUT=LOAD. Here, we must include IOROUT=RETRVE to retrieve records from an ISAM file. This specification is used for updating the file as well as for random or sequential processing of it.

WORKR=ISREC — WORKR is used when retrieving a file. WORKL is used when creating a file. When records are processed in random order, the READ and WRITE macros move the logical record in or out of this work area. This entry specifies that the data in the I/O area, previously defined as ISBUFFER, is to be moved to ISREC when reading the ISAM file. Similarly, the contents of ISREC will be moved from ISREC to the I/O area when rewriting or updating the ISAM file.

KEYARG=ISKEY — KEYARG is a required entry for random retrieval of records. It specifies the symbolic name of the key field. The search key, which is called KEYIN in the program, must be moved to ISKEY to access the corresponding record from the ISAM file.

TYPEFLE=RANDOM   This entry specifies random processing of the ISAM file. SEQNTL is used for sequential access of an existing ISAM file whereas RANSEQ is used when both random and sequential processing is required within one program.

The first 10 DTF entries are similar for all ISAM processing, regardless of whether we are creating or reading from an ISAM file. The other entries differ depending on whether the ISAM file is used as input or output, and whether random or sequential processing is required.

The macros used for random retrieval are shown in the following display.

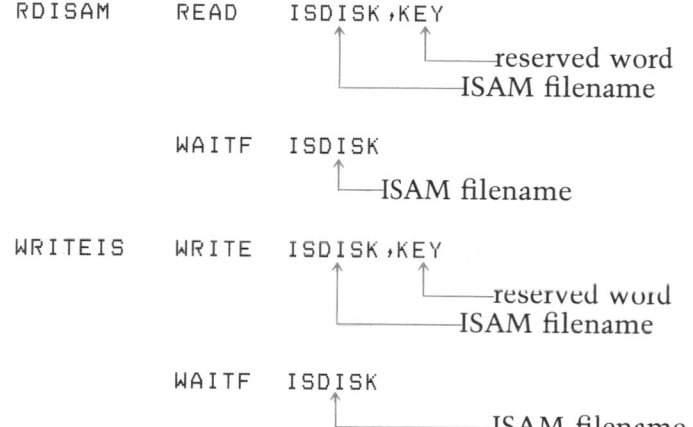

Recall that a transaction record used to update an ISAM file is read into storage in the usual way. In our example, when a transaction record with a student number is read, we wish to read the corresponding ISAM student record.

We call the student number on the transaction record a *search key* because it will be used to look up the corresponding record on the disk with that same number. Once the address of that corresponding ISAM record is found from the index, the record will be read directly into storage.

To accomplish this READ, we must first move the search key from the transaction record to the field referenced in the DTFIS as the KEYARG field. Because KEYARG=ISKEY appears in the DTFIS, we must move the transaction's student number to ISKEY before we read from the ISAM file. The following instruction transmits the search key to ISKEY.

        MVC   ISKEY,KEYIN

Now we may read from the ISAM file. READ ISDISK,KEY causes the operating system to retrieve the specified record from the ISAM file and place it in the I/O area referenced by the DTFIS (ISBUFFER). The computer then moves the record to the ISAM work area referenced in the DTFIS as WORKR=ISREC. Note that the first operand of the READ instruction references the ISAM filename, whereas the second must always specify the reserved word 'KEY'.

The ISAM record with the same student number as on the transaction record is now available for updating. The semester credits from the transaction record can be added to the accumulated credits. Upon completion of the update procedure, the WRITE macro is invoked to transfer the record from storage to the ISAM file. This, in effect, *rewrites* the record. Again, the first operand of the WRITE command references the ISAM filename, and the second must contain the word KEY.

The WAITF instruction is required after writing or reading from an ISAM file. This WAITF instruction causes an I/O delay whenever an I/O error has occurred.

Handling Invalid Keys. If we attempt to read an indexed record and bit 3 in ISDISKC is turned on, an invalid key condition has occurred. A branch to READERR is performed where an error message is displayed. This means that a record on the ISAM file with a key equal to the transaction key field does not exist.

Another review of the sample program is recommended at this point because the new instructions for this update procedure have been highlighted. I/O error conditions are handled in this program exactly as in the create program even though the actual errors detected differ. Refer to Figure 22.13 again for an overview of I/O errors that may be detected when accessing an ISAM file. The intention of this sample program is to present a relatively simple update procedure. Other possible update procedures may include

1. Changing a student's name.
2. Establishing a field for student status, where P denotes part-time and F denotes full-time.
3. Establishing a student activity field where A means active, G denotes graduated, and I identifies an inactive student.
4. Defining a field containing the required credits for graduation. The program would then compare the accumulated credits in the ISAM record with the credits required to graduate and list the students scheduled to be awarded a degree.

By using special coded fields, these additional procedures and considerations could be added to this update program.

2. Illustrating a Random Update Procedure for an ISAM OS File

***a. The Dummy* READ.** In OS programming, BISAM, the Basic Indexed Sequential Access Method, is used for direct access whereas QISAM, the Queued Index Sequential Access Method, is used to access and process an ISAM file sequentially. For BISAM to access records randomly, a 28-byte storage area is allocated and linked to the file's DCB. This storage area is referred to as a DECB (Data Event Control Block). The programmer may code the parameters for the DECB, but it is far easier to have the system generate the DECB automatically for your program. For the system to generate the DECB, a dummy READ statement is placed in the program. The reason this READ instruction is referred to as a "dummy read" is that it is placed after the last DS or DC in the program and hence, will be assembled but not executed. Once the DECB is assembled, it may be referenced by other read/write instructions. Two forms of the READ/WRITE macros should be considered. They are the execute form and list form. The dummy READ is of the list type and will be discussed first.

Dummy READ Instruction
```
READ    ISDECB,KU,ISDISK,'S','S',KEYIN,MF=L
```
where the positional parameters include the following.

ISDECB	Name of data event control block (programmer-defined name).
KU	Denotes accessed record is to be updated. Other READ options use the letter K in place of KU to denote that the record will be read but not updated.
ISDISK	The programmer-defined name of the DCB used to identify the ISAM file.
'S'	Buffer address generated by ISAM at execution time. This is referred to as dynamic buffering. The buffer area may be defined by the programmer using a DS statement. However, the length of the buffer must be equal to the blocksize plus 16. Be sure to include apostrophes as shown.
'S'	Length of buffer. For blocked records the S must be specified. Again, include apostrophes as shown.

| KEYIN | The location of the KEY in the transaction record. KEYIN is a programmer-defined name. |
| MF=L | Denotes the list form of the macro. The execute form is MF=E. |

Again, the dummy READ is used only to create the DECB named ISDECB in the sample program. Once this is accomplished, all other read and write statements will reference the defined DECB and will specify the MF=E type because the format is shorter and easier to use.

b. Data Event Control Block. The data event control block is created with a dummy READ instruction and is formatted as follows.

Word 1	Condition code	
Word 2	Type macro	Buffer length
Word 3	DCB address	
Word 4	Buffer address	
Word 5	Logical record address	
Word 6	Key address	
Word 7	Error codes	Not used

Condition code in first byte denotes successful completion or error

When records are updated, the record is changed in the buffer area and rewritten to disk from this area. The address of the logical record in the buffer area is stored in the data event control block. Word 3 of the DECB references the DCB name. The data control block (DCB) must contain a MACRF entry that indicates whether a CHECK or WAIT macro is to be used for I/O synchronization, regardless of whether the records are to be added and/or updated. The following is a summary of MACRF entries and an example to be used in the program.

MACRF Entries

Macro Operation	WAIT, dynamic	WAIT, direct	CHECK dynamic	CHECK direct
READ only	RS	R	RSC	RC
WRITE only	—	WA	—	WAC
Update records	RUS,WU	RU,WU	RUSC,WUC	RUC,WUC
Update/Add records	RUS,WUA	RU,WUA	RUSC,WUAC	RUC,WUAD

where

R denotes read, W denotes write.
S specifies dynamic buffering for READ macro.
U specifies updating.
A denotes adding records.

For example,

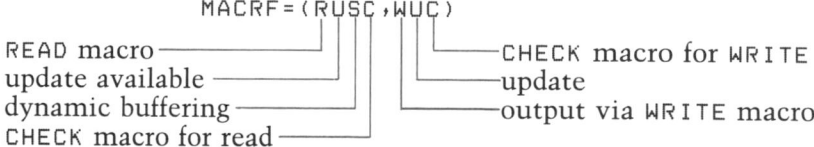

The DCB for the sample OS program would replace the DTF and appear as follows.

```
ISDISK  DCB  DSORG=IS,DDNAME=ISDISK,BUFNO=1  *
             MACRF(RUSC,WUC),SYNAD=ERRORTN
```

When dynamic buffering is specified, the DCB macro should include the entry BUFNO=1. This entry will inform the operating system that only one ISAM buffer area is required, and the programmer need not allocate space for the buffer.

c. OS Updating of Records.   The READ instruction may appear as

```
READ   ISDECB,K,...         read only
READ   ISDECB,KU,...        update available
```

When updating, the WRITE instruction must reference the same DECB and must follow a READ KU. When adding records, KN is used. However, dynamic buffering cannot be specified when records are added.

```
WRITE   ISDECB,K,...        update records
WRITE   ISDECB,KN,...       add records
```

Note that we are reading and writing from the same buffer area using the same data event control blocks. Recall that the dummy READ using the *list* format, MF=L, creates a macro expansion for the data event control block (DECB). Once created, this expansion can be referenced as follows providing the same DECB is always referenced.

Read/Write Summary

```
READ    ISDECB,K ,MF=E      Read only
READ    ISDECB,KU,MF=E      Read and update with WRITE K
WRITE   ISDECB,K ,MF=E      Update
WRITE   ISDECB,KN,MF=E      Add records
```

At run time, the execute format (MF=E) is processed using those parameters defined by the DECB.

The program changes to the READ/WRITE instructions are shown in the following displays.

DOS READ

```
RDISAM READ ISDISK,KEY
```

OS READ

```
RDISAM READ ISDECB,KU
```

DOS WRITE

```
WRITEIS WRITE ISDISK,KEY
```

OS WRITE

```
WRITEIS WRITE ISDECB,K,MF=E
```

d. ISAM WAIT and CHECK Macros.   As previously mentioned, the WAIT macro allows for completion of I/O operations and synchronizes processing to ensure that the record has been read (input) and is available for processing, or has been written (output) and transferred accurately to disk. The WAIT macro instructions would simply replace the WAITF macros found in DOS. The required coding follows.

```
WAIT   ECB=ISDECB
```
└─programmer-defined name to reference DECB

As with DOS, the programmer uses the TM instruction for testing. The error code is stored in the DECB with a displacement of 24 bytes. Hence, we reference the byte to be tested with the TM instruction as ISDECB+24.

The error codes for the WAIT macro follow.

Bit	Error Condition
0	Record not found
1	Incorrect record length
2	Insufficient space for new record
3	Dynamic-buffering request invalid
4	Uncorrectable I/O data-transfer error
5	Blocking error
6	Record read from overflow area
7	Record with duplicate key to be added to file

If bit 6 is set, it means that an error has not occurred but, rather, the data was found in the overflow area. Therefore, it is not recommended that this position be tested.

Also, the bits in position 0 and 7 need not cause a termination of the job. If bits 0 and 7 are set on, the program should print an appropriate error message and then continue processing the job. Hence, the bit positions 0, 6, and 7 would not be included in a test for an abend. The bit configuration of 01111100 or hex 7C would be coded as follows to test for an abnormal ending.

```
TM   ISDECB+24,X'7C'
BNZ  ABEND
```

Therefore, if the WAIT macro were used by the program, the following coding is necessary to convert from DOS to OS.

DOS Coding			OS Coding		
WRITEIS	WRITE	ISDISK,KEY	WRITEIS	WRITE	ISDECB,K,MF=E
	WAITF	ISDISK		WAIT	ECB=ISDECB
	TM	ISDISKC,X'C0'		TM	ISDECB+24,X'7C'
	BNZ	WRITERR		BNZ	ABEND

The error-recovery routines would also have to be recoded to meet the error conditions specified. Note that with the WAIT and WAITF macros, the operating system returns control to the instruction that immediately follows the WAIT macro regardless of whether or not any errors have been found. This is not the situation with the CHECK macro. When a READ instruction is executed and the end-of-data condition is reached, control is transferred to the EODAD address. Similarly, if an I/O error is detected by the CHECK macro, control is transferred to the address specified by the synchronization error address (SYNAD) of the DCB. However, if no errors are found, the operating system returns control to the instruction following the CHECK.

The format of the CHECK macro to be used in the OS update is

```
CHECK   ISDECB,DSORG=IS
```

where ISDECB is a programmer-defined name of the DECB. The DCB, called ISDISK, must contain an entry SYNAD=ERRORTN to check the status of the error flags set by the operating system in the data event control block, DECB. The DSORG=IS identifies that the disk file organization is indexed sequential.

The following list summarizes the changes necessary to convert from DOS to OS.

1. Place the dummy READ after the PAT1 DC statement at the end of the program to define the DECB called ISDECB.

```
PAT1   DC     XL4'40202120'
       READ   ISDECB,KU,ISDISK,'S','S',KEYIN,MF=L
```

2. The CHECK macro will be used; therefore, the SYNAD=ERRORTN will be added to the DCB identified as ISDISK.

```
ISDISK  DCB   DSORG=IS,DDNAME=ISDISK,BUFNO=1      *
              MACRF(RUSC,WUC),SYNAD=ERRORTN
```

The ISDISK DCB replaces the ISDISK DTF of the DOS program.
3. Replace DOS OPEN/CLOSE macros with OS OPEN/CLOSE.
4. Replace DOS READ and WRITE with OS counterparts.

DOS Coding			*OS Coding*		
RDISAM	READ	ISDISK,KEY	RDISAM	READ	ISDECB,KU,MF=E
	WAITF	ISDISK		CHECK	ISDECB,DSORG=IS
	⋮			⋮	
WRITEIS	WRITE	ISDISK,KEY	WRITEIS	WRITE	ISDECB,K,MF=E
	WAITF	ISDISK		CHECK	ISDECB,DSORG=IS
	⋮			⋮	

5. The OS error-recovery routine, ERRORTN, will have to be coded to print the appropriate error message.

A partial listing reflecting these changes follows.

```
            PRINT NOGEN
ISAM        START
OS          STM   14,12,12(13)
UPDATE      BALR  12,0
            USING *,12
            ST    13,SAVEAREA+4
            LA    13,SAVEAREA
*****************************************************************
*                      O P E N   F I L E S                     *
*****************************************************************
            OPEN  (SEMESTR,INPUT,PRNTFLE,OUTPUT)
            OPEN  (ISDISK)
****************************************************
*       M A I N   P R O G R A M        *
****************************************************
GETREC      MVC   OUTAREA,SPACES
            GET   SEMESTR,SEMREC
            MVC   ISKEY,KEYIN
RDISAM      READ  ISDECB,KU,MF=E
            CHECK ISDECB,DSORG=IS
PROCESS     PACK  NEWCRED,NEWCRED
            AP    ISCRED,NEWCRED
            MVC   ISDATE,='&SYSDATE'
WRITEIS     WRITE ISDECB,K,MF=E
            CHECK ISDECB,DSORG=IS
            B     GETREC
****************************************************
* C L O S E   F I L E S  &  E O F   O F   I S A M  *
****************************************************
EOF         CLOSE (SEMESTR,ISDISK,PRNTFLE)
            L     13,SAVEAREA+4
            LM    14,12,12(13)
            BR    14
*****************************************************************
*           E R R O R   R E C O V E R Y   R O U T I N E S      *
*****************************************************************
ERRORTN     EQU   *
              .
              .
              .
*****************************************************************
*    I S A M     F I L E   S P E C I F I C A T I O N    *
*****************************************************************
ISDISK      DCB   DSORG=IS,DDNAME=ISDISK,BUFNO=1,            *
                  MACRF=(RUSC,WUC),SYNAD=ERRORTN
```

```
*******************************
*      E D I T   P A T T E R N      *
*******************************
PAT1      DC     XL4'40202120'
********************************************************
*  D U M M Y   R E A D   T O   C R E A T E   D E C B    *
********************************************************
          READ   ISDECB,KU,ISDISK,'S','S',KEYIN,MF=L
```

G. Other Procedures That Access an ISAM File

1. Accessing or Reading From an ISAM File for Reporting Purposes

An ISAM file may be read from, or accessed, either sequentially or randomly for reporting purposes. Suppose, for example, that we have a payroll ISAM file that is in sequence by Social Security number and contains the name and salary for each employee. We could access the file through the methods described in the following sections.

a. Accessing an Indexed File Sequentially.   We may print a weekly status report that is also in sequence by Social Security number, which means that we would read or access the disk sequentially. We would begin reading the first record on the disk, process it, then read the next, and so on.

Note that processing the payroll file is exactly the same regardless of whether it is an ISAM file that is accessed sequentially or a standard sequential file. The only changes as we will see are in the SET, GET, and ESETL instructions.

If we wished to print payroll checks from a payroll file in ascending alphabetic sequence by NAME, we could *still* use sequential processing even though the file is not initially in sequence by NAME. First, we would copy the file and sort the copied file into alphabetic sequence by NAME using a utility program; then, we would print the checks.

DOS ISAM Sequential Processing.   Reading a DOS ISAM file sequentially involves the execution of the following macros.

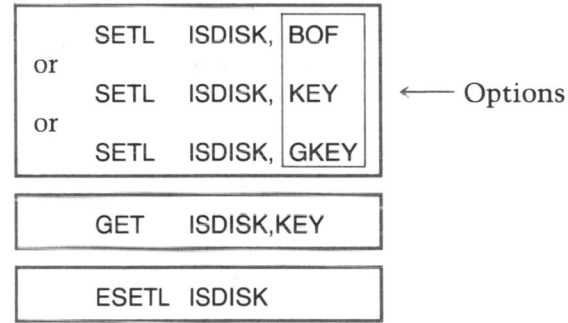

Consider the SETL ISDISK,option instruction. The following chart shows the options that can be used here.

Option	*Meaning*
BOF	Begin processing with the first record
KEY	Begin processing with the specified key, which must first be moved to the KEYARG area, ISKEY, as in the update program
GKEY	Begin processing with a key greater than or equal to the specified key called GKEY, which must be moved to the KEYARG area, ISKEY, as in the update program

The SETL (Set Limits) macro indicates that the ISAM file will be processed sequentially. The second operand determines where processing is to begin.

When the KEY option is used, the key must be supplied to the field referenced in the KEYARG operand. As noted, BOF indicates that we wish to start at the *Beginning Of the File*.

The ESETL (Endset Limit) ends sequential processing initiated by the SETL macro. The statement references the ISAM filename as the first operand. When records are blocked, the ESETL writes the last block to this ISAM file.

The sequence of instructions for processing an ISAM file sequentially follows.

```
OPEN
  ⋮
SETL
  ⋮
GET
  ⋮
ESETL
  ⋮
CLOSE
```

The changes to the DTFIS include the following.

> TYPEFLE = SEQNTL,IOROUT = RETRVE,IOAREAS = BUFFERIN

b. Accessing an Indexed File Randomly. Indexed files may also be read randomly. That is, if a manager wishes to examine an employee's record, we may want to access or read the ISAM record with the corresponding employee or Social Security number from the disk directly. In this case, we would be accessing the disk file randomly and inquiring about the status of the record. Because managerial inquiries are *not* entered in any specific employee or Social Security number sequence, we would access the disk randomly. Typically, making such inquiries about the status of records is performed randomly.

Accessing a disk randomly was illustrated in Figure 22.12 when we updated the indexed file. Similar programs can be coded that simply make random inquiries about the status of master disk records but do *not* update a file.

c. Accessing an ISAM File Both Randomly and Sequentially in the Same Program. Suppose we wish to update an ISAM file randomly and then print it in sequence. We may be able to access an ISAM file both randomly and sequentially *in the same program* by using the preceding macros. We update the disk randomly first and then provide a sequential report using SETL and ESETL instructions for sequential access. TYPEFLE would equal RANSEQ for this type of processing, indicating that both random and sequential processing are required.

2. Adding Records to an ISAM File as Part of an Update Procedure

The update program in Figure 22.12 enables us to access ISAM records randomly, to make changes, and to write them on disk again. Sometimes a transaction record is also used to add a record to the master file. The transaction record should have a code to designate it as a new account, that is, a record to be added. The transaction record in our student program could be modified in the manner that follows.

Positions	Field
1–5	Student number
6–25	Name
26–28	Number of credits
29	Code (1 for add record for new student; 2 for update existing record; 3 for delete record)

If the code is a 1, a new routine is coded which

1. Moves transaction data to the output area.
2. Uses WRITE with NEWKEY in Operand 2.

Several changes are required to the DTFIS to enable the ISAM file to *add* new records as well as to update existing ones.

DTFIS *Macro Additions for Adding to an ISAM File as well as Updating Existing Records*

1. IOROUT=ADDRTR enables you to add records as well as to retrieve them.
2. Both IOAREAL and IOAREAR are required. To add records, place them in the IOAREAL area and use a PUT command. To retrieve and update existing records, use IOAREAR for records read with READ and written with WRITE.
3. Similarly, WORKL and WORKR are required. WORKL is used for transaction records to be added to the ISAM master and WORKR is used for records that are retrieved from the ISAM master.

3. Deleting Records From an ISAM File as Part of an Update Procedure

Records are typically not deleted from an ISAM file *per se;* rather, they are deactivated. You may deactivate an ISAM record by placing a byte of X'FF' in the leftmost or high-order position of the record and then executing a WRITE. Thus, if a transaction record is entered with a coded field that indicates that the corresponding record is to be deleted from the ISAM file, your program should

1. Retrieve the corresponding ISAM record;
2. Move X'FF' to the high-order byte of that record; and,
3. Write the record back onto disk.

The ISAM record will still exist on the disk, but it will no longer be available for random processing.

To delete or add records from an ISAM file, use a coded field in the transaction file to indicate the type of update to be performed.

Summary. The following table may prove helpful in writing programs using ISAM files.

Random Access	Sequential Access	R/O	Clause	Meaning
		(R = required; O = optional)		
X	X	R	DSKXTNT=n	Maximum number of extents needed for the file
X	X	R	IOROUT=xxx	LOAD, to create, or RETRVE, to access
X	X	R	KEYLEN=nnn	Number of bytes in the record key (maximum is 255)
X	X	R	NRECDS=nnn	Number of records in a block
X	X	R	RECFORM=xxxxxx	FIXUNB for fixed unblocked or FIXBLK for fixed blocked
X	X	R	RECSIZE=nnn	Number of characters in a logical record

(Continued on next page)

Random Access	Sequential Access	R/O	Clause	Meaning
			(R = required; O = optional)	
X	X	O	CYLOFL=nn	Number of tracks for each cylinder overflow area. Maximums are: 8 for 2311, 18 for 2314 and 2321, 17 for 3300 and 3333, 10 for 3340
X	X	O	DEVICE=nnnn	Device number. Can use 2311, 2314, 2321, 3330, 3340; if omitted, 2311 is assumed
X	X	O	HINDEX=nnnn	Indicates device containing highest level index. Can use 2311, 2314, 2321, 3330, 3340. If omitted, 2311 is assumed
	X	O	IOAREAL=xxxxxx	Name of I/O area
X		O	IOAREAR=xxxxxx	Name of I/O area
X	X	O	KEYARG=xxxxxx	Name of key field in storage for random access or key to start at for sequential access
X	X	O	TYPEFLE=xxxxx	RANDOM, SEQNTL, or RANSEQ
X	X	O	VERIFY=YES	Check disk records after they are written
X			WORKL=xxxxxx	Name of work area for loading or adding to a file
	X		WORKR=xxxxxx	Name of work area for random retrieval

Summary of ISAM Processing Using DOS and OS

1. Loading or extending an ISAM file under DOS:

   Macros

   ```
   SETFL    filename
   WRITE    filename,NEWKEY
   ENDFL    filename
   ```

2. Random retrieval of an ISAM file under DOS:

   Macros

   ```
   READ     filename,KEY
   WAITF    filename
   WRITE    filename,KEY
   ```

3. Sequential retrieval of an ISAM file under DOS:

   Macros

   ```
   SETL     filename,BOF or KEY or GKEY
   GET      filename,KEY
   ESETL    filename
   ```

4. Loading an ISAM file under OS:

Macros

OPEN	filename
PUT	filename,record area
CLOSE	filename

5. For OS processing, DCB operands are:

Operand	*Entry*
BUFNO	Number of buffers to be assigned in the program
DDNAME	Name of the data set
DSORG	IS for indexed sequential
MACRF	R, RS, RUS, WU, RU, WU. Add A and/or C for add and check macros
BLKSIZE	Length of each block
CYLOFL	Number of overflow tracks per cylinder
KEYLEN	Length of the key area
LRECL	Length of each record
NTM	Number of tracks for master index, if any
OPTCD	Options required. For example, in MYLU, M establishes a master index (or omit M); Y and R control use of cylinder overflow and independent areas; L is the delete code, which results in the bypassing of records with X'FF' in the first byte; and, U (for fixed-length only) establishes the track index in main storage
RECFM	Record format for fixed/variable and unblocked/blocked: F, FB, V, VB
SYNAD	Address of I/O synchronization error routine

6. Macros used for sequential retrieval and update of an ISAM file under OS:

Under OS, sequential retrieval and update involves the OPEN, SETL, GET, PUTX, ESETL, and CLOSE macros. Once the data set has been created with standard labels, many DCB entries are no longer required. DDNAME and DSORG=IS are still used, and the following macros are applicable.

MACRF = (entry)	(GM) or (GL) for input only; (PM) or (PL) for output only; (GM,SK,PU) if read and rewrite in place, where S = use of SETL, K = key or key-class used, PU = use of PUTX macro
EODAD = eofaddress	For input, if reading to the end of the file
SYNAD = address	Optional error checking

The SETL Macro. SETL (Set Low address) establishes the first sequential record to be processed. It is used because a programmer may want to start anywhere in a data set, that is, at some location other than the beginning. The general format for the SETL macro follows.

```
SETL   dcb-name,start-position,address
```

The "start-position" operand has a number of options.

Option	*Meaning*
B	Begin with the first record in the data set (omit Operand 3 for B or BD)
K	Begin with the record with the key in the Operand 3 address

KC   Begin with the first record of the key class in Operand 3; if the first record is deleted, begin with the next non-deleted record (A key class is any group of keys beginning with a common value, such as all keys 287XXXX)

I   Begin with the record at the actual device address in Operand 3

BD, KD, KDH, KCD cause retrieval of only the data portion of a record.

Following are some examples of SETL to set the first record in an ISAM file called ISDISK, using a 6-character key.

Clause	*Meaning*
SETL ISDISK,B	Begin with the first record of the data set
SETL ISDISK,K,KEYADD1	Begin with key 012644 in data set
SETL ISDISK,KC,KEYADD2	Begin with first record that begins with key 012
KEYADD1 DC C'012644'	6-character key
KEYADD2 DC C'012',XL3'00'	3-character key followed by 3 bytes of hex zeros

Figure 22.14 illustrates a sequential retrieval of an OS ISAM file.

III. AN INTRODUCTION TO VSAM PROCESSING IN ASSEMBLER

A. Advantages of VSAM

The primary advantages of VSAM follow.

ADVANTAGES OF VSAM

1. The ability to use alternate keys for accessing records.
2. The ability to establish a file with variable-length records.
3. More efficient performance and data organization.

B. Physical Differences Between ISAM and VSAM

1. Index Structure

The index structure of VSAM files is based on an operating system concept referred to as **virtual storage.** The use of indexes with virtual storage is far more efficient than with main storage.

2. Overflow Areas

When primary locations on a disk are no longer available and data records need to be added, ISAM files store them in *overflow areas*. This requires the ISAM file to be periodically reorganized to allow records in overflow areas to be moved to their proper physical locations on the disk. Reorganization is absolutely necessary when frequent updating is performed. If it is not done in a timely fashion, then access time can be adversely affected. VSAM reduces this particular problem by initially leaving blank space in a newly created indexed file so that additional records can be placed in their proper location. This reduces the need for overflow areas. There are procedures such as using *multiple indexes* that can be performed using VSAM that are not always available using ISAM.

```
****************************************************************
*            LIST ALL STUDENTS THAT GRADUATED SINCE 1975       *
****************************************************************
          PRINT NOGEN
ISAM      START
OS        STM   14,12,12(13)
RETRVL    BALR  12,0
          USING *,12
          ST    13,SAVEAREA+4
          LA    13,SAVEAREA
****************************************************************
*                  O P E N   F I L E S                         *
****************************************************************
          OPEN  (ISDISK,INPUT,OUTFILE,OUTPUT)
****************************************************************
*              P R I N T   H E A D I N G S                     *
****************************************************************
HEADNGS   EQU   *
             .
             .
             .
********************************************
*      M A I N   P R O G R A M       *
********************************************
          SETL  ISDISK,B                    BEGIN WITH 1ST RECORD
READ      MVC   OUTAREA,SPACES
          GET   ISDISK,ISRECORD
          PACK  YRCK,ISYR
          CP    YRCK,=P'75'
          BL    READ
GRADS     MVC   NAMEO,ISNAME
          MVC   CREDO,PATTERN
          ED    CREDO,ISCRED
          MVC   YROUT,ISYR
          PUT   OUTFILE,OUTAREA
          B     READ
************************************
* C L O S E   F I L E S  *
************************************
EOF       ESETL ISDISK                      END SETL
          CLOSE (ISDISK,OUTAREA)
          L     13,SAVEAREA+4
          LM    14,12,12(13)
          BR    14
****************************************************************
*   I S A M     F I L E   S P E C I F I C A T I O N     *
****************************************************************
ISDISK    DCB   DSORG=IS,DDNAME=ISDISK,EODAD=EOF,MACRF=(GM,S)
************************************
*       E D I T   P A T T E R N        *
************************************
PATTERN   DC    XL4'40202120'
```

Figure 22.14
Sequential retrieval of an OS
ISAM file.

3. Multiple Indexes

A VSAM file can have more than one master index. Thus, a student file can have multiple key fields, such as student number *and* student name.

The main elements of VSAM are outlined in the following section. The similarities and differences with ISAM are indicated.

C. VSAM Concepts

1. Introduction

VSAM (virtual storage access method) is another access method developed by IBM for processing indexed files. It may be used for random and/or sequential processing of fixed and variable-length records on direct-access storage devices that have established indexes for records.

The following capabilities make VSAM more flexible than ISAM.

1. Allows creation of records with multiple keys, which means that records can be accessed in different ways.

2. Gives more efficient performance.
3. Provides better data integrity and improved data organization.
4. Permits processing of variable-length records.
5. Allows the specification of alternate keys with duplicates and thus facilitates data base processing. For example, it is possible to access all records directly with DEPT equal to 02, where DEPT is one key field. In this case, DEPT would not be a unique field because several records could have the same DEPT.

ISAM files may be converted to VSAM files by using the method described in the following IBM manuals.

G320-6029   *VSAM Tuning and ISAM to VSAM Conversion Guide*
G320-5774   *VSAM Primer and Reference*

Refer to "Using ISAM for VSAM Applications" at the end of the chapter for more details on this subject.

The records in a VSAM file are usually arranged in logical sequence by a key field. Like an ISAM file, the VSAM file has an index that allows records to be processed either sequentially or randomly. The key field uniquely identifies each record in the file. The key may be located anywhere within the record and may vary in length from 1 to 255 bytes. In addition, the key may be numeric or alphanumeric but must be arranged in ascending sequence. As with ISAM files, in VSAM files duplicate keys are not permitted as the primary key. Numerous keys are, however, permitted; that is, duplicate keys are allowed as alternate key fields.

A major advantage of VSAM is that *alternate keys* may be specified for a simple data file. Therefore, you do not need multiple files that contain the same information organized differently for various applications. If a VSAM file has been created with two keys (for example, EMPNO and NAME), it is possible to access a record directly from that file if either the EMPNO or the NAME is known. This is *not* the case with ISAM processing. Only one key is used with ISAM, so it would not be possible to access a record directly without knowing the specific key.

2. Types of Data Sets

VSAM is comprised of three types of data sets: **key-sequenced, entry-sequenced,** and **relative-record data sets.** The primary difference between them is the sequence in which data records are loaded or created.

Records are loaded into a key-sequenced data set (KSDS) in the order of a primary key. Each record has a unique key field and KSDS functions are very similar to keyed ISAM.

Records are loaded into an entry-sequenced data set (ESDS) without regard to a record's contents. This is a sequential file created in the sequence the records are entered.

Records are loaded into a relative-record data set (RRDS) by the relative position of each record. The data set consists of fixed-length slots, each identified by its relative position. When a new record is added, the programmer may assign the relative position, or VSAM may assign the record to the next available position at the end of the data set.

When a VSAM data set is created, it is defined as a **cluster.** A cluster may be a key-sequenced data set consisting of a data component and an index component (key), or it may be an entry-sequenced data set or a relative-record data set, which simply consist of a data component.

The total space of a data set is divided into a set of areas called **control areas,** which are further subdivided into **control intervals.** VSAM addresses a point in the data set by its *displacement*, a number indicating its distance from the position of byte 0, which is its **relative byte address** (RBA). For example, the first record of a data set has an RBA of 0, the second has an RBA

<u>KEY SEQUENCED DATA SET</u>	<u>ENTRY SEQUENCED DATA SET</u>	<u>RELATIVE RECORD DATA SET</u>
Records in order by key field	Records in order as entered	Records in relative record number sequence
Access via key field or relative byte address (RBA)	Access sequential in order of RBA	Access by relative record number which serves as key
Records inserted by using free space	Records added to end of file	Records inserted into empty slots or added to end of file
Free space reclaimed when records are deleted	Deleted record space reused by other records	Deleted record space can be reused

Figure 22.15
Comparison of the three types of VSAM data sets.

equal to the length of the first record, and so on. Typically, ESDS records are accessed in ascending RBA order.

The chart in Figure 22.15 compares the three types of VSAM data sets.

3. Data Organization

When a key-sequenced VSAM file is created, certain segments of the disk can be left empty. This means that **free space** is available to be distributed throughout the file. The free space may be distributed equally as a percentage of the space used by the file, or allocated in accordance with the job requirements. This free space is used by the system when inserting new records or enlarging existing records. Free space eliminates the need for overflow chaining, an operation that decreases the efficiency of ISAM files. Therefore, VSAM files are more efficient because access time is not adversely affected by the addition of records to the file. A disadvantage of ISAM is that ISAM files require the system to chain to overflow areas when records are added to the file. This increases access time, resulting in a corresponding loss of performance. Additionally, VSAM files do not require reorganization as frequently as ISAM files because additions to a VSAM file can use the available free space. VSAM also *reclaims* space when a record is deleted or shortened. This space becomes additional free space.

Figure 22.16 illustrates the logical organization of the data and index search used by VSAM. Data is grouped into control areas that are subdivided further into control intervals. Note that the control areas contain free space as illustrated.

The logic used in processing records is very similar to that of ISAM in that the *highest* keys for the data areas are stored in the area index. The highest key for each interval is similarly stored in the interval index. To access a record, the interval index is searched (see Figure 22.17).

If the key to be found is *less than* or equal to the index key, then control is transferred to the next lower subdivision. Finally, the control interval is searched sequentially until the record is found.

If a record is to be added, it is inserted in the control interval where it logically belongs, thereby making use of the free space available. This movement of records is done in primary storage before any writing takes place. Record movement for insertions, deletions, and updating takes place in primary storage before any actual input/output operations are performed, thereby improving data integrity and efficiency.

The fact that files can be moved from one DOS/VS system to another or from a DOS/VS system to an OS/VS system is another significant feature of VSAM. This is possible because the data formats of the files are identical.

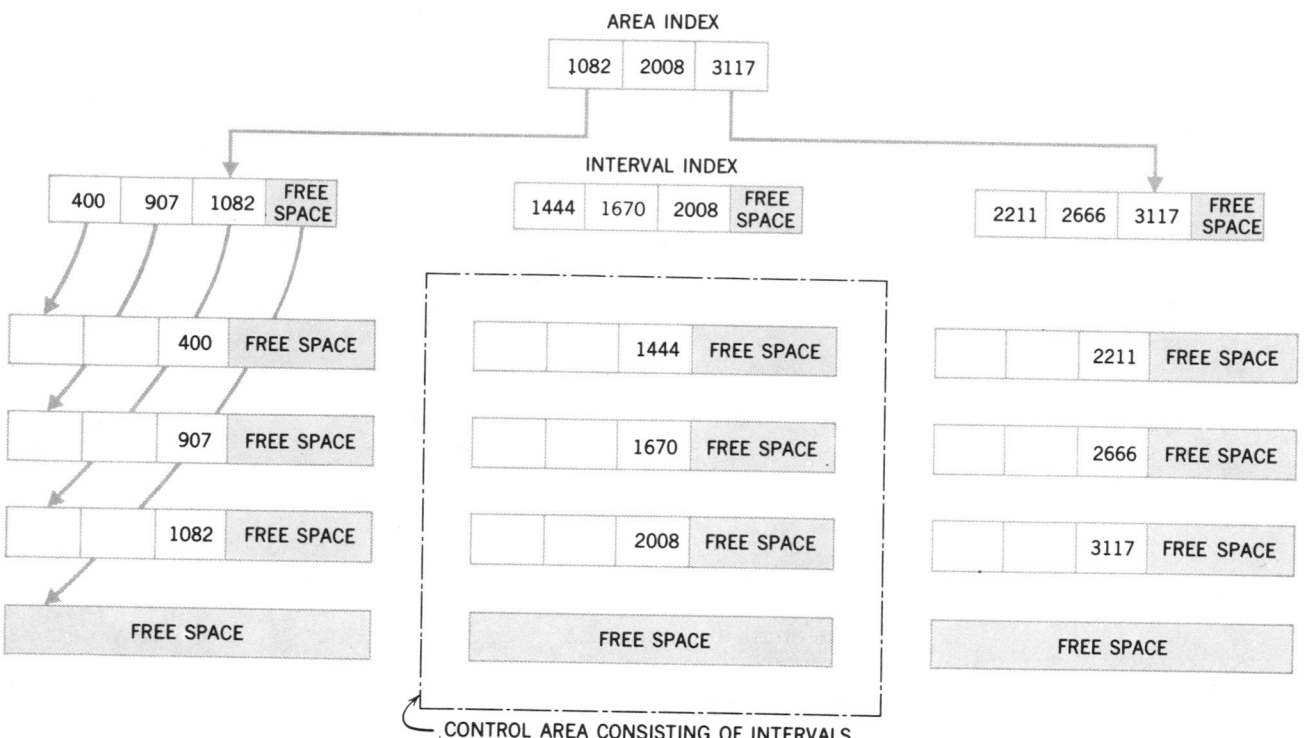

Figure 22.16
Illustration of the logical organizaton of the data and index search used by VSAM.

Note that VSAM is most widely used under DOS and OS systems.

VSAM files can be processed sequentially, randomly, or both sequentially and randomly. Processing a VSAM file during a single run as both a random and a sequential file is called **dynamic processing.** Dynamic processing provides the most flexibility because the capabilities of both sequential and random processing are supported at the same time. Processing can be switched from sequential to random and vice–versa as many times as is necessary. For example, dynamic processing would be extremely efficient if a VSAM file was to be updated randomly and then printed out sequentially.

The primary advantages of VSAM files are listed in the following summary.

SUMMARY: ADVANTAGES OF VSAM FILES

1. Improved performance for additions to the file.
2. Reorganization required less frequently.
3. Multiple keys eliminate the need for duplicate files.
4. Cross-system compatibility (OS/DOS).
5. Better system integrity.

D. VSAM Programming

1. An Overview

A description of how to program VSAM applications would require an entire text. The following presentation, therefore, is only intended as an introduction

Schematic

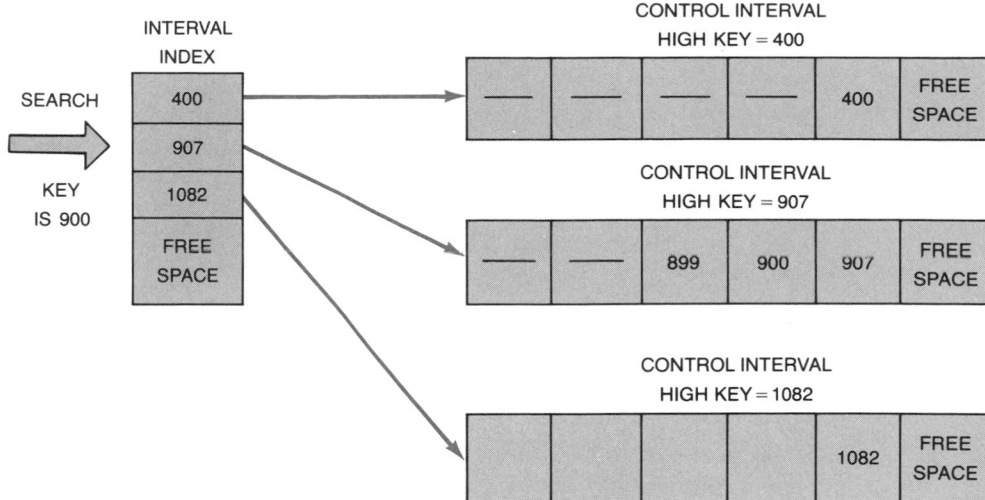

Flowchart

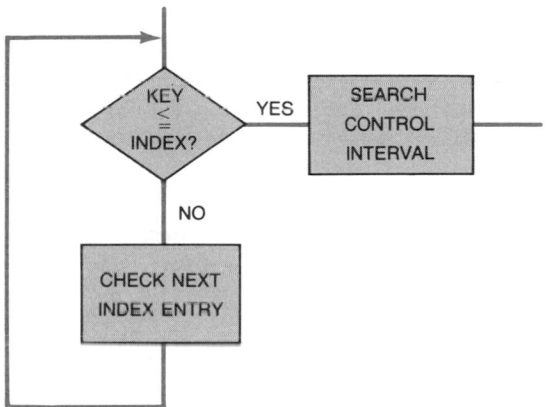

Figure 22.17
Searching the interval index.

to VSAM programming. The goal is to present a basic understanding of concepts, familiarize you with VSAM's technical vocabulary, introduce you to many of the macros used in VSAM programming, and provide sufficient material so that you may program elementary applications. Once familiar with the elementary aspects of VSAM, you may progress to more advanced applications through formal training and/or the assistance of reference manuals.

VSAM programming in assembler language is different from programming in most other languages because of the extensive use of systems macros. The macros used by VSAM include control block macros and request macros. Some of these are

1. ACB, which is used to build an **access method control block** at assembly time.
2. RPL, which is used to build a **request parameter list** at assembly time.
3. GENCB, which is used to build an access method control block, an **exit list,** or a request parameter list at execution time.

The macros used to modify, display, and test the contents of control blocks include

1. MODCB, which is used to modify an access method control block, an exit list, or a request parameter list at execution time.
2. SHOWCB, which is used to display fields in an access method control block, an exit list, or a request parameter list at execution time.
3. TESTCB, which is used to test the contents of fields in an access method control block, an exit list, or a request parameter list at execution time.

The macros used to store, retrieve, and delete records, to position VSAM in a data set, to suspend processing, and to terminate requests include

1. GET, which is used to retrieve a record.
2. PUT, which is used to store a record.
3. ERASE, which is used to delete a record.
4. POINT, which is used to position VSAM at a specific record.
5. CHECK, which is used to suspend processing.
6. ENDREQ, which is used to terminate a request.

Only those macros necessary to provide you with minimal skills in VSAM programming are included in this chapter.

A utility program named **Access Method Services** (AMS) provides commands used to establish and maintain data sets as well as to copy and print data sets. An integral part of VSAM programming is the use of the AMS utility program.

2. Request and Control Block Macros

To create or load the VSAM data set, the I/O programming is accomplished through macros in a manner similar to the use of macros in ISAM programming. Two unique and dependent macros exist that are used for VSAM: request macros (Request Parameter List or RPL) and control block macros (Access Control Blocks or ACB). Request macros or RPLs are used at execution time and relate to opening or closing a data set (OPEN, CLOSE), and retrieving and updating records with the GET and PUT instructions.

The control block macros (ACBs) have a purpose similar to the DTF and DCB macros. The ACBs provide the operating system with keyword parameters that establish the detail specifications of the data set.

When opening or closing a VSAM data set, the ACB is referenced. The ACB macro also references the DD or the DLBL job control statement and thereby identifies the VSAM data set as illustrated in Figure 22.18.

Other ACB options that may be specified include space requirements for buffers and the address of the exit list macro (EXLST) that provides for the error-handling routines of the ACB. When needed, a password may also be employed so that only authorized users have access.

The RPL macro is referenced when GET, PUT, and ERASE commands are issued. Again, refer to the PUT instruction in Figure 22.18. If RPL1, RPL2, and RPL3 were symbolic names assigned to RPL statements, then the following instructions would be valid.

```
GET     RPL=RPL1
PUT     RPL=RPL2
ERASE   RPL=RPL3
```

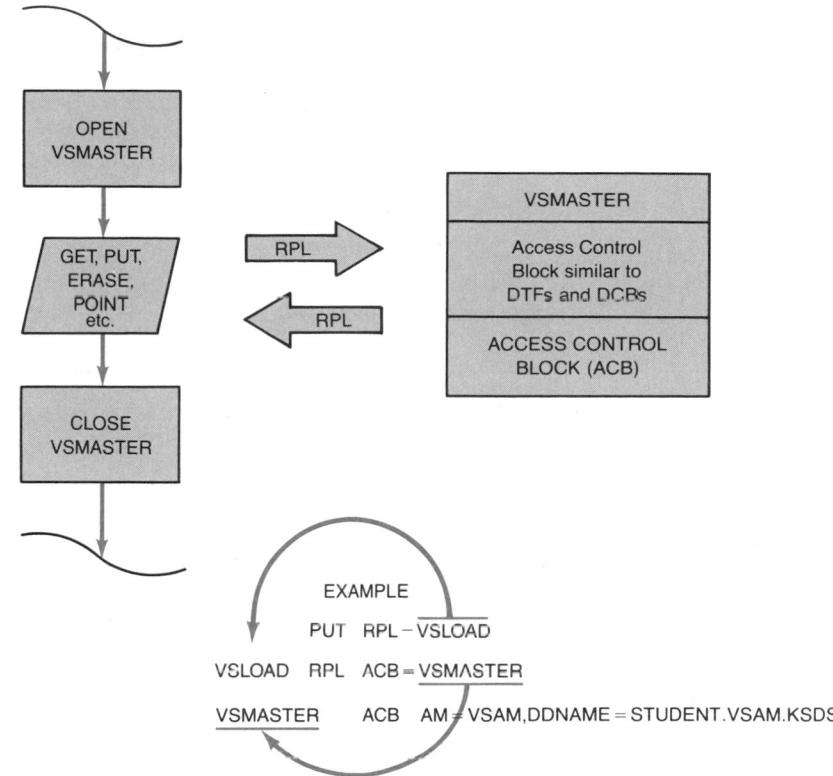

Figure 22.18
Use of the ACB macro to identify the VSAM data set.

Every `RPL` statement must reference an `ACB` instruction as shown in the following example.

```
RPL1    RPL    ACB=VSFLE,,,,
VSFLE   ACB    DDNAME=VSCRTE,,,,
```

Other options specified by the `RPL` include

1. I/O work area specifications.
2. Primary key length.
3. Method of access.
4. Address of the search key for direct access.
5. The ability to update or not update records.

The `ACB` and `RPL` macros are always required to process a VSAM file. However, before a data set can be referenced, it must be defined. This is accomplished with the AMS utility program.

3. Access Method Services

a. Purpose. Access Method Services (AMS) is a multi-function service program used to

1. Define and load VSAM data sets, and allocate space for them.
2. Convert indexed-sequential data sets to key-sequenced data sets (KSDS).
3. Create backup copies of data sets.
4. Build alternate indexes.
5. Print the contents of VSAM catalogs and data sets.

AMS provides macros that permit you to (1) name the VSAM data set, (2) describe the organization type, (3) specify the primary key location and the key length, and (4) describe other details required by VSAM. A VSAM data set is catalogued using an AMS program called IDCAMS as shown in the following example.

```
// STEP EXEC  PGM=IDCAMS     For OS
// EXEC IDCAMS,SIZE=AUTO      For DOS
```

To create a new catalog, use the AMS command DEFINE. There are several variations of the DEFINE statement, as shown in Figure 22.19.

Full DEFINE Command	Abbreviated Command	Description of the DEFINE Command
DEFINE MASTERCATALOG	DEF MCAT	Allocates space for the master catalog.
DEFINE USERCATALOG	DEF UCAT	Allocates space for the user catalog.
DEFINE SPACE	DEF SPC	Allocates space shared by all clusters & alternate indexes defined in catalog.
DEFINE CLUSTER	DEF CL	Requests space for a cluster.
DEFINE ALTERNATEINDEX	DEF AIX	Requests space for an alternate key index.

Figure 22.19 DEFINE commands.

The rules for coding AMS entries include

1. Entries are coded in columns 2 through 72.
2. A hyphen follows each entry to continue to the next line.
3. A blank or space serves as delimiter between command, parameter words, and values.

In the following discussion, the most commonly used DEFINE CLUSTER entries of AMS are presented.

b. The DEFINE CLUSTER Macro. The DEFINE CLUSTER general format is as follows.

```
DEFINE CLUSTER    ( list cluster options )
       DATA       ( list data options )
       INDEX      ( list index options )
       CATALOG    ( list catalog options )
```

The following DEFINE CLUSTER instruction is used in the VSAM create or load program. Other available options are also discussed.

```
DEFINE CLUSTER ( NAME (STUDENT.VSAM.KSDS)       -
                 FILE (VSCRTE1)                  -
                 RECORDS (50 10)                 -
                 FSPC (20 10)                    -
                 KEYS (5 0)                      -
                 VOL (VSPACK)                    -
                 RECSZ (22 22)                   -
          DATA ( NAME (STUDENT.VSAM.KSDS.DAT) ) -
          INDEX ( NAME (STUDENT.VSAM.KSDS.NDX) )
```

where

NAME (STUDENT.VSAM.KSDS)	Identifies the cluster. Up to 44 characters may be specified with periods separating each group of 8 or fewer characters.
FILE (VSCRTE1)	References the DDNAME or DLBL linked to the cluster via JCL.
RECORDS (50 10)	Specifies the number of primary records (50) the file is to contain. After these are used, secondary allocations in groups of 10 will be assigned. Other options include CYL and TRACK.
FSPC (20 10)	Specifies free space in percentages for the control interval (20) and control area (10) for KSDS files only. When the data set is created, 20 percent of the space allocated for the control interval is to be left empty. These specifications are usually provided by the VSAM administrator or systems personnel responsible for the installation.
KEYS (5 0)	Designates a primary key length of 5 bytes with the key location being a displacement beginning with zero, meaning the key occupies the first 5 bytes of the record.
VOL (VSPACK)	Designates a serial number or other DASD identification.
RECSZ (22 22)	Denotes the average and maximum record lengths. For fixed-length records both entries are the same. With variable-length records, the entries would differ.

The DATA entry specifies the name of the data cluster.

```
DATA ( NAME (STUDENT.VSAM.KSDS.DAT) )
```

The INDEX entry specifies the name of the index cluster.

```
INDEX ( NAME (STUDENT.VSAM.KSDS.NDX) )
```

Other entries include NONINDEXED for ESDS, INDEXED for KSDS, or NUMBERED for RRDS. If this entry is omitted, then INDEXED is assumed. In other words INDEXED is the default option.

The DEFINE CLUSTER and the necessary JCL to create or load the VSAM file are illustrated in Figure 22.20. Review the entries carefully to be sure you understand the purpose of each.

4. Program 1—VSAM Creation of a Key-Sequenced Data Set (KSDS)

a. The REPRO *Macro.* The **AMS REPRO command** is frequently used to load or to create a VSAM data set. Typically, the parameters for the data set are programmed using the DEFINE CLUSTER instruction, as shown. A sequential file is then created and converted to VSAM with the REPRO command. The REPRO macro is also capable of copying catalogs and clusters. Further information concerning these options is available in the AMS manuals at your computer center. To create or load the VSAM data set, your program should

1. Establish the characteristics of the data set with the DEFINE CLUSTER.
2. Create a sequential file using terminal input, "ditto," or some other utility program. In the example, the name of the sequential file is AMSD1.
3. Invoke the REPRO command to load or to create the VSAM file as illustrated in Figure 22.21.

b. The PRINT *Macro.* The reason that the REPRO macro is used frequently is its obvious simplicity. Once created, the contents of the file should be checked. To validate the contents of the VSAM file the PRINT instruction is used. The file data will be displayed in both hex and EBCDIC. This is especially advantageous when data in packed-decimal format is to be checked and verified. Both the JCL and printed output are illustrated in Figure 22.22.

```
// DLBL IJSYSUC,'USERCAT1',,VSAM
// DLBL VSCRTE1,'STUDENT.VSAM.KSDS',,VSAM
// EXEC IDCAMS,SIZE=AUTO



IDCAMS  SYSTEM SERVICES

DEFINE CLUSTER ( NAME (STUDENT.VSAM.KSDS)      -
                 FILE (VSCRTE1)                -
                 RECORDS (50 10)               -
                 FSPC (20 10)                  -
                 KEYS (5 0)                    -
                 VOL (VSPACK)                  -
                 RECSZ (22 22) )               -
          DATA ( NAME (STUDENT.VSAM.KSDS.DAT) ) -
          INDEX ( NAME (STUDENT.VSAM.KSDS.NDX) )

IDC0001I FUNCTION COMPLETED, HIGHEST CONDITION CODE WAS 0


IDC0002I IDCAMS PROCESSING COMPLETE. MAXIMUM CONDITION CODE WAS 0
```

Figure 22.20
The DEFINE CLUSTER and necessary JCL to create or load a VSAM file.

```
// DLBL IJSYSUC,'USERCAT1',,VSAM
// DLBL VSCRTE1,'STUDENT.VSAM.KSDS',,VSAM
// ASSGN SYS020,DISK,VOL=VSPACK,SHR
1T20I  SYS020 HAS BEEN ASSIGNED TO X'3EF'
// DLBL SDFLE,'AMSD1',0
// EXTENT SYS020,VSPACK,1,0,7272,5
// EXEC IDCAMS,SIZE=AUTO



IDCAMS  SYSTEM SERVICES

REPRO INFILE (SDFLE,ENV (RECFM(F),BLKSZ(22)))     -
      OUTFILE (VSCRTE1)

IDC0005I NUMBER OF RECORDS PROCESSED WAS 7

IDC0001I FUNCTION COMPLETED, HIGHEST CONDITION CODE WAS 0


IDC0002I IDCAMS PROCESSING COMPLETE. MAXIMUM CONDITION CODE WAS 0
```

Figure 22.21
Use of the REPRO command to load or create a VSAM file.

```
// DLBL IJSYSUC,'USERCAT1',,VSAM
// DLBL VSCRTE1,'STUDENT.VSAM.KSDS',,VSAM ←——— JOB CONTROL
// EXEC IDCAMS,SIZE=AUTO


    PRINT INFILE (VSCRTE1) ←——————— PRINT COMMAND


IDCAMS  SYSTEM SERVICES                          TIME: 13:55:08      04/02/85    PAGE    2
                        ←——————————OUTPUT LISTING
LISTING OF DATA SET -STUDENT.VSAM.KSDS                                EBCDIC EQUIVALENT

KEY OF RECORD - F1F1F1F1F1 ←———RECORD KEY IN HEX   ┌PACKED DATA IN HEX            ╱
 0000  F1F1F1F1 F1D1D6C8 D540E6C8 C9E3C540     40404040 140C              *11111JOHN WHITE      ..


KEY OF RECORD - F2F2F2F2F2
 0000  F2F2F2F2 F2D6E2C3 C1D94DD1 D6C8D5D2     C5404040 040C              *22222OSCAR JOHNKE    ..


KEY OF RECORD - F3F3F3F3F3
 0000  F3F3F3F3 F3C6C5D3 C9E74DE2 E3C5D9D5     40404040 034C              *33333FELIX STERN     .<


KEY OF RECORD - F4F4F4F4F4
 0000  F4F4F4F4 F4C1D3C4 C5D540E2 C1C7C5D9     F0D5C940 056C              *44444ALDEN SAGERONI .%


KEY OF RECORD - F5F5F5F5F5
 0000  F5F5F5F5 F5D3C5D9 D6E84DC2 C9E2E2D6     D5404040 121C              *55555LEROY BISSON    ..


KEY OF RECORD - F6F6F6F6F6
 0000  F6F6F6F6 F6D1C5E3 C8D9D640 E2C1C7C5     D9404040 152C              *66666JETHRO SAGER    ..


KEY OF RECORD - F7F7F7F7F7
 0000  F7F7F7F7 F7D5C1D5 C3E84DE2 E3C1D9D9     40404040 147C              *77777NANCY STARR     .a


IDC0005I NUMBER OF RECORDS PROCESSED WAS 7

IDC0001I FUNCTION COMPLETED, HIGHEST CONDITION CODE WAS 0
```

Figure 22.22
Printed display of a VSAM file.

5. Access Method Control Block (ACB)

The ACB is similar to a DTF or DCB in that it identifies the file to be processed. However, a great deal of information, such as key and record data, are specified in the DEFINE command of AMS. These specifications then reside in the VSAM catalog and are brought into virtual storage when the ACB is opened. The name of the ACB macro provides the symbolic address of the ACB and, if the DDNAME entry is omitted, the ACB name also serves as the DLBL filename.

   The ACB entries may be in any sequence, with each entry separated by a comma. As with a DCB or DTF, a continuation character is placed in column 72. The ACB used by the update program is illustrated in the following example:

```
VSFLE  ACB  AM=VSAM,                                                  X
            DDNAME=VSCRTE1,                                           X
            MACRF=(KEY,DIR,OUT)
```

where

VSFLE   Designates the name assigned to the Access Control
                          Block.

AM=VSAM	Specifies a VSAM control block. This entry is only required if your installation also uses VTAM.
DDNAME=VSCRTE1	Specifies a data name consisting of up to 7 characters that identifies the data set that is to be processed. This name is the same as the filename in the DLBL or DD job control statement.

The macro formats of MACRF are as follows:

KEY	Indicates keyed access for key-sequenced data set (KSDS) or relative-record data set. Another option is ADR (addressed sequential access) for KSDS or ESDS, entry-sequenced data sets.
DIR	Means direct processing. Other options include SEQ (sequential processing) and SKP (skip sequential processing).
OUT	Denotes retrieve, insert, update, and add records to the end of the file. Another option includes IN, for record retrieval only.

Other MACRF entries are NRM (the filename in the DDNAME operand is to be processed by normal means) and AIX (an alternate index is to be used). The default options for the MACRF operand include KEY, SEQ, IN, and NRM.

Additional ACB specifications include EXLST=EXITS and STRNO=1. EXITS is a programmer-defined name that identifies a list of user exit routines. Typically, an end-of-file exit for reading input sequentially would be provided. If, however, no exit routines are programmed, this entry is omitted. STRNO=1 indicates the number of concurrent RPLs that VSAM will handle. The default is one. Several requests with the corresponding RPLs referencing the same ACB can be active at the same time. Hence, VSAM can access different parts of a file simultaneously, using different accessing methods such as keyed, sequential, and so on.

There are entries in the ACB to specify buffer space; however, VSAM allocates buffers automatically very efficiently and we recommend that the standard defaults be used.

6. The Request Parameter List Macro or RPL

It is only necessary to include the RPL options that affect the processing of your particular program. In the VSAM update program, the following RPL is defined under the note VSAM DEFINITIONS.

```
UPDTE   RPL   OPTCD=(KEY,DIR,UPD,KEQ,FKS,MVE),         X
              ACB=VSFLE,                               X
              ARG=CDKEY,                               X
              KEYLEN=5,                                X
              AREA=VSREC,                              X
              AREALEN=22
```

where

UPDTE	Name assigned to the RPL for reference.
OPTCD	References various options for run-time processing where:
	KEY Denotes keyed-access. Other options include ADR (addressed) and CNV (control interval access).
	DIR Means direct- or random-access. Other options include SEQ (sequential) and SKP (skip sequential).
	UPD Denotes updating of records. Other options include NUP (no update) and NSP (note sequential position).

KEQ   Used for KSDS only (find key equal to search key). Another option is KGE (find key equal to or greater than search key).

FKS   Means full search key to be used. Another option is GEN (use generic key).

MVE   Denotes move mode. Another option is LOC (locate mode).

ACB=VSFLE	Identifies the name of the ACB block used.
ARG=CDKEY	Identifies the search key field name.
KEYLEN=5	Defines the length of the primary key.
AREA=VSREC	Specifies the logical record work area when using the MVE mode.
AREALEN=22	Specifies the length of the work area or logical record.

The RPL is referenced in the program with the GET instruction:

```
GET     RPL=UPDTE
```

7. VSAM Macro Instructions

a. OPEN *and* CLOSE.   The OPEN macro calls the open routine, which verifies that the user program has authority to process the file. The OPEN macro constructs VSAM control blocks and loads VSAM routines into your partition. VSAM routines, unlike other access methods, are not link-edited with the processing program. The OPEN instruction consists of two formats.

```
OPEN VSFLE  or  LA      9,VSFLE
                OPEN  (9)
```

Up to 16 filenames may be specified in the operand field, which may include ACBs, DTFs, or DCBs. However, to facilitate debugging we recommend that each ACB be opened initially with a separate OPEN instruction. A return code is set in register 15 to indicate whether the ACBs were opened successfully. As with ISAM files, the TM instruction may be used to check for error return codes. The meaning of the return codes follows.

Code	*Meaning*
X'00'	Successful open
X'04'	ACB opened but a warning exists
X'08'	ACB not opened due to errors

The CLOSE routine completes any I/O operations outstanding when the program issues the CLOSE macro instruction. Any output buffers containing data that has not been stored are written and the catalog entries are updated. CLOSE restores the ACB to its status before the file was opened. Register 15 again receives a return code.

Code	*Meaning*
X'00'	Successful CLOSE
X'04'	One or more ACBs not closed successfully
X'08'	Insufficient virtual storage space for CLOSE routine or the module could not be found

b. GET, PUT, *and* ERASE.   Register 15 is set with a return code by VSAM to indicate the success or failure of the macro's operation.

Code	*Meaning*
X'00'	Operation successful
X'04'	Too many requests of the same RPL; request not accepted; also results if an end-of-file condition has occurred
X'08'	Check error code in the RPL for logical error
X'0C'	Error code in RPL caused uncorrectable I/O errors

Errors resulting from GET, PUT, and ERASE also produce an error code in the FDBK field of the corresponding RPL macro. You may use the SHOWCB macro to determine further the precise cause of the error.

The GET is used to retrieve an existing record, whereas the PUT is used to create, update, add, or insert records. The ERASE macro is used with KSDS files to delete records.

Previous to issuing a PUT command to update records, a GET macro must be used to access the record. The ERASE macro also has the same limitation in that it *must be* preceded by the GET. Under these circumstances the GET is called a GET-for-update. Similarly, the PUT is referred to as a PUT-for-update. An RPL entry for the OPTCD parameters is used to specify whether a record is to be updated, "UPD," or not updated, "NUP." The GET may be used in the **move mode,** "MVE," meaning that the logical record is moved by VSAM to and from a work area specified by the AREA parameter of the RPL. **Locate mode** means that the address of the record in the I/O area is placed in the fullword referenced by the area parameter. However, because the move mode is easier to use and understand, the locate mode will not be discussed further. Hence, the following OPTCDs may be coded in RPLs regardless of whether the file is key- or entry-sequenced.

OPTCD	MACRO	PURPOSE
NUP,MVE	GET	Retrieve record
UPD,MVE	PUT	Update record
UPD,MVE	ERASE	Delete record
NUP	PUT	Add record

The move mode also requires the AREALEN parameter to be specified.

c. EXLST. An EXLST (*exit list*) operand must be coded if your ACB contains an EXLST entry. The EXLST macro identifies exit routines used to analyze errors and provide for end-of-file conditions. The EXLST operands, all of which are optional, include

1. EODAD, which specifies the address of the end-of-data routine; it is named ENDIT in our example.
2. LERAD, which specifies that the logical error routine is located at LOGERR; these are errors other than I/O errors, such as an invalid request.
3. SYNAD, which specifies that the physical-error routine is located at IOERR.

When VSAM encounters an uncorrectable I/O error, the physical-error routine IOERR is entered.

The name of the EXLST routine is EXITS.

```
EXITS     EXLST        AM=VSAM,                      X
                       EODAD=ENDIT,                  X
                       LERAD=LOGERR,                 X
                       SYNAD=IOERR
              .
              .
              .
ENDIT     EQU    *     EODAD ROUTINE
              .
              .
LOGERR    EQU    *     LERAD ROUTINE
              .
              .
IOERR     EQU    *     SYNAD ROUTINE
              .
              .
```

d. SHOWCB. The SHOWCB macro is a debugging tool that is used to display fields in an exit list (EXLST), an ACB, or an RPL. The control blocks from which information is retrieved must be indicated by one of the following parameters: EXLST=EXLST address, ACB=ACB address, or RPL=RPL address. The address identifies the location of the control block. The SHOWCB should be coded immediately following a VSAM macro that contains errors to be diagnosed.

The formats of the SHOWCB for EXLST and RPL follow. Note that the RPL option is used in the update program and hence, the EXLST SHOWCB will be explained in general terms.

EXLST SHOWCB

```
name      SHOWCB    EXLST = address,                          X
                    AREA = work-area,                         X
                    LENGTH = number of bytes,                 X
                    FIELDS = EODAD or LERAD or SYNAD
```

where

EXLST	Specifies the address of the exit-list fields to be displayed.
AREA	Specifies the address of the work area. VSAM displays the contents of fields specified in the FIELD operand. AREA must begin on a fullword boundary.
LENGTH	Specifes the byte length of the work area AREA. Each exit list requires a fullword boundary.

RPL SHOWCB

```
SHOWCB    RPL=UPDTE,                                          X
          FIELDS=(FDBK),                                      X
          AREA=FLESTS,                                        X
          LENGTH=4
```

where

RPL=UPDTE	Identifies the request parameter list; RPL contains the fields to be displayed.
FIELDS=(FDBK)	Obtains an error code that is placed in the RPL by VSAM; other options include RBA, which provides the relative byte address of the last logical record processed, and RECLEN, which specifies the length of the last logical record processed.
AREA=FLESTS	Provides VSAM with a work area to display the contents of the FIELDS operand.
LENGTH=4	Specifies the length of the work area referenced by AREA; each RPL requires a fullword.

8. Program 2—Random Update

Key-sequenced data sets can be accessed sequentially or randomly. When processing records randomly, a key field is used to find the record to be updated. This key field or search key provides direct access to the file. If, however, the record is not found, VSAM returns an error code in register 15. Figure 22.23 illustrates a program to randomly update a VSAM file.

You should check the program by analyzing the VSAM coding and reviewing the entries.

E. Using ISAM for VSAM Applications

An **ISAM interface** program enables a program that processes an indexed-sequential data set to process a VSAM key-sequenced data set. The key-sequenced data set may have been organized originally as an indexed or sequential file. The create or loading program may have been coded under ISAM, using the conventional ISAM macros. This means that records can be loaded or added to a newly defined VSAM key-sequenced data set with an ISAM program.

There are a few minor restrictions in using the interface program. They are described in the IBM publication entitled "Restrictions in the Use of the ISAM Interface."

```
 LOC    OBJECT CODE      ADDR1 ADDR2  STMT   SOURCE STATEMENT

000000                                  1 AMVSUP   START O
                                        2          PRINT NOGEN
000000 05C0                             3          BALR  12,0
                            00002        4          USING *,12
000002 41D0 C58E            00590        5          LA    13,SAVE
                                        6          OPEN  VSFLE
                                       14 ***********************************************************
                                       15 *                 TEST FOR SUCCESSFUL OPEN                 *
                                       16 ***********************************************************
000016 12FF                            17          LTR   15,15
000018 4770 C5D6      005D8            18          BNZ   OPNERR
                                       19          OPEN  PRFLE
                                       27 ***********************************************************
                                       28 *                     HEADINGS                            *
                                       29 ***********************************************************
                                       30          COMRG
000030 D207 C36F 1000 00371 00000      34          MVC   HD1DAT,0(1)
                                       35          PUT   PRFLE,HD1
                                       41          PUT   PRFLE,HD2
                                       47          PUT   PRFLE,HD3
                            00066       53 NXTTRN   EQU   *
                                       54 ***********************************************************
                                       55 *              REGISTER 3 WILL BE USED TO RETURN CONTROL   *
                                       56 *         TO THE CORRECT ROUTINE AFTER PROCESSING A VSAM ERROR *
                                       57 *         THE RETURN CODE PLACED IN REGISTER 15 IS EXAMINED BY  *
                                       58 *                 VSAM AFTER EVERY VSAM REQUEST            *
                                       59 ***********************************************************
000066 4130 C064          00066       60          LA    3,NXTTRN
                                       61 ***********************************************************
                                       62 *              READ A TRANSACTION RECORD                  *
                                       63 ***********************************************************
                                       64          GET   CDFLE,CDREC
                                       70 ***********************************************************
                                       71 * A DIRECT READ ON A KSDS IS ACCOMPLISHED VIA THE ARG PARAMETER *
                                       72 * OF THE RPL (REQUEST PARAMETER LIST) AND OPTCD=(DIR).    *
                                       73 * SINCE ARG=CDKEY IS SPECIFIED IN THE RPL WE WILL ATTEMPT TO READ*
                                       74 * THE VSAM RECORD CORRESPONDING TO THE CURRENT DETAIL RECORD.  *
                                       75 * OPTCD=(UPD) MUST BE SPECIFIED IN THE RPL IN ORDER TO ALLOW   *
                                       76 * THE UPDATED RECORD TO BE REWRITTEN.                     *
                                       77 ***********************************************************
                                       78          GET   RPL=UPDTE
                                       85 ***********************************************************
                                       86 * TEST FOR SUCCESSFUL READ. VSAM WILL ALWAYS RETURN CONTROL TO *
                                       87 * THE NEXT SEQUENTIAL INSTRUCTION REGARDLESS OF WHETHER OR NOT  *
                                       88 * THE OPERATION FAILED.  A RETURN CODE WILL BE PLACED IN REG 15. *
                                       89 ***********************************************************
00008C 12FF                            90          LTR   15,15
00008E 4770 C5E4      005E6            91          BNZ   LOGERR
000092 D203 C4DA C575 004DC 00577      92          MVC   PROCRED,VCREDMSK
000098 DE03 C4DA C20E 004DC 00210      93          ED    PROCRED,VSCRED
00009E FA21 C566 C20E 00568 00210      94          AP    TOTOCRED,VSCRED            ACCUMULATE OLD CREDITS
                                       95 ***********************************************************
                                       96 * UPDATE THE VSAM RECORD BY ADDING THE NEW CREDITS TO THE OLD, *
                                       97 * THEN REWRITE THE NEW VSAM RECORD AND PRINT THE DATA.    *
                                       98 ***********************************************************
0000A4 F222 C51B C51B 0051D 0051D      99          PACK  CDCRED,CDCRED
0000AA D205 C4EB C56F 004ED 00571     100          MVC   PRNCRED,CREDMSK
0000B0 DE05 C4EB C51B 004ED 0051D     101          ED    PRNCRED,CDCRED
0000B6 FA12 C20E C51B 00210 0051D     102          AP    VSCRED,CDCRED
0000BC FA21 C56C C20E 0056E 00210     103          AP    TOTCRED,VSCRED            ACCUMULATE UPDATED CREDITS
0000C2 D203 C4FE C575 00500 00577     104          MVC   PRCRED,VCREDMSK
0000C8 DE03 C4FE C20E 00500 00210     105          ED    PRCRED,VSCRED
                                      106          PUT   RPL=UPDTE
0000E0 FA20 C579 C6F8 0057B 006FA     113          AP    TOTRECS,=P'1'             COUNT SUCCESSFUL UPDATES
0000E6 FA22 C569 C51B 0056B 0051D     114          AP    TOTNCRED,CDCRED           ACCUMULATE NEW CREDITS
                                      115 ***********************************************************
                                      116 * CREATE THE REST OF THE PRINT RECORD AND JOURNEY THE TRANSACTION*
                                      117 ***********************************************************
0000EC D204 C480 C1FA 00482 001FC     118          MVC   PRACCT,VSACCT
0000F2 D20E C48F C1FF 004C1 00201     119          MVC   PRNAME,VSNAME
                                      120          PUT   PRFLE,DETAIL
000108 47F0 C064          00066       126          B     NXTTRN
                            0010C     127 TOTS     EQU   *
                                      128 ***********************************************************
                                      129 *                  PRINT TOTAL LINE                       *
                                      130 ***********************************************************
```

Figure 22.23
Sample program to randomly update a VSAM file.

```
00010C 9260 C491       00493    131        MVI    DETAIL,C'-'
000110 D205 C4D8 C56F 004DA 00571 132      MVC    PROCRED-2(6),CREDMSK
000116 DE05 C4D8 C566 004DA 00568 133      ED     PROCRED-2(6),TOTOCRED
00011C D205 C4EB C56F 004ED 00571 134      MVC    PRNCRED,CREDMSK
000122 DE05 C4EB C569 004ED 0056B 135      ED     PRNCRED,TOTNCRED
000128 D205 C4FC C56F 004FE 00571 136      MVC    PRCRED-2(6),CREDMSK
00012E DE05 C4FC C56C 004FE 0056E 137      ED     PRCRED-2(6),TOTCRED
000134 D204 C4B0 C6F9 004B2 006FB 138      MVC    PRACCT,=CL5' '
00013A D205 C4B0 C6F2 004B2 006F4 139      MVC    PRACCT(6),=C'TOTALS'
000140 D205 C4BF C57C 004C1 0057E 140      MVC    PRNAME(6),TOTMSK
000146 DE05 C4BF C579 004C1 0057B 141      ED     PRNAME(6),TOTRECS
00014C D20C C4C5 C6FE 004C7 00700 142      MVC    PRNAME+6(13),=C' RECORDS READ'
                                  143        PUT    PRFLE,DETAIL
                                  149 ****************************************************************
                                  150 * FAILURE TO CLOSE A  VSAM FILE MAY CAUSE THE FILE TO BE INACCESS-
                                  151 * ABLE TO SUBSEQUENT PROGRAMS. THE FILE MUST THEN BE VERIFIED.   *
                                  152 ****************************************************************
                                  153        CLOSE VSFLE
                                  161        CLOSE PRFLE
000182 0A0E                       169        SVC   14
                                  170 ****************************************************************
                                  171 *                    VSAM DEFINITIONS                          *
                                  172 ****************************************************************
                                  173 VSFLE   ACB    AM=VSAM,                                         X
                                                     DDNAME=VSCRTE1,                                  X
                                                     MACRF=(KEY,DIR,OUT)
                                  205 UPDTE   RPL    OPTCD=(KEY,DIR,UPD,KEQ,FKS,MVE),                 X
                                                     ACB=VSFLE,                                       X
                                                     ARG=CDKEY,                                       X
                                                     KEYLEN=5,                                        X
                                                     AREA=VSREC,                                      X
                                                     AREALEN=22                                       X
0001FC                            234 VSREC   DS     0CL22
0001FC                            235 VSACCT  DS     CL5
000201                            236 VSNAME  DS     CL15
000210                            237 VSCRED  DS     PL2
                                  238 ****************************************************************
                                  239 *                    UNIT RECORD FILES                         *
                                  240 ****************************************************************
                                  241        PRMOD WORKA=YES,                                         X
                                                    DEVICE=3203
                                  331 PRFLE   DTFPR DEVADDR=SYSLST,                                   X
                                                    BLKSIZE=133,                                      X
                                                    CTLCHR=ASA,                                       X
                                                    DEVICE=3203,                                      X
                                                    IOAREA1=PRREC,                                    X
                                                    WORKA=YES
                                  352 CDFLE   DTFCD DEVADDR=SYSIPT,                                   X
                                                    WORKA=YES,                                        X
                                                    DEVICE=2501,                                      X
                                                    IOAREA1=CDREC,                                    X
                                                    EOFADDR=TOTS                                      X
                                  373        CDMOD WORKA=YES,DEVICE=2501
                                  525 ****************************************************************
                                  526 *                    PRINT RECORDS                             *
                                  527 ****************************************************************
00027A                            528 PRREC   DS     CL133
0002FF                            529 HD1     DS     0CL133
0002FF F1                         530        DC     C'1'
000300 4040404040404040           531        DC     CL52' '
000334 E2C1D407D3C540E5           532        DC     CL26'SAMPLE VSAM UPDATE PROGRAM'
00034E 4040404040404040           533        DC     CL35' '
000371                            534 HD1DAT  DS     CL8
000379 4040404040404040           535        DC     CL11' '
000384                            536 HD2     DS     0CL133
000384 40                         537        DC     C' '
000385 4040404040404040           538        DC     CL53' '
0003BA D5C1E2C8E4C140C3           539        DC     CL29'NASHUA COMMUNITY COLLEGE'
0003D7 4040404040404040           540        DC     CL55' '
00040E                            541 HD3     DS     0CL133
00040E F0                         542        DC     C'0'
00040F 4040404040404040           543        DC     CL26' '
000429 C1C3C3D6E4D5E340           544        DC     CL14'ACCOUNT NUMBER'
000437 4040404040                 545        DC     CL5' '
00043C D5C1D4C540404040           546        DC     CL15'NAME'
00044B 4040404040404040           547        DC     CL7' '
000452 D6D3C440C3D9C5C4           548        DC     CL11'OLD CREDITS'
00045D 4040404040404040           549        DC     CL7' '
```

Figure 22.23
(continued)

```
000464  C3E4D909C5D5E340        550           DC     CL15'CURRENT CREDITS'
000473  404J404040              551           DC     CL5' '
000478  D5C5E640E3D6E3C1        552           DC     CL10'NEW TOTAL'
000482  40404040404040040       553           DC     CL17' '
000493                          554  DETAIL   DS     0CL133
000493  40404040404040040       555           DC     CL31' '
0004B2                          556  PRACCT   DS     CL5
0004B7  40404040404040040       557           DC     CL10' '
0004C1                          558  PRNAME   DS     CL15
0004D0  40404040404040040       559           DC     CL12' '
0004DC                          560  PROCRED  DS     CL4
0004E0  40404040404040040       561           DC     CL13' '
0004ED                          562  PRNCRED  DS     CL6
0004F3  40404040404040040       563           DC     CL13' '
000500                          564  PRCRED   DS     CL4
000504  40404040404040040       565           DC     CL20' '
                                566  ***************************************************************
                                567  *                   TRANSACTION RECORD                       *
                                568  ***************************************************************
000518                          569  CDREC    DS     0CL80
J00518                          570  CDKEY    DS     CL5
00051D                          571  CDCRED   DS     CL3
000520                          572           DS     CL72
                                573  ***************************************************************
                                574  *                     WORK AREAS                             *
                                575  ***************************************************************
000568  00000C                  576  TOTOCRED DC     PL3'0'
00056B  00000C                  577  TOTNCRED DC     PL3'0'
00056E  00000C                  578  TOTCRED  DC     PL3'0'
000571  402020202120            579  CREDMSK  DC     X'402020202120'
000577  40202120                580  VCREDMSK DC     X'40202120'
00057B  00000C                  581  TOTRECS  DC     PL3'0'
00057E  402020202120            582  TOTMSK   DC     X'402020202120'
000584                          583  FLESTS   DS     F
000588                          584  DBL      DS     D
                                585  ***************************************************************
                                586  * THE SAVE AREA IS REQUIRED IN ORDER TO ISSUE A SHOWCB MACRO. THE  *
                                587  * ADDRESS OF THIS SAVE AREA MUST BE IN REG. 13 WHEN MACRO IS CALLED*
                                588  ***************************************************************
000590                          589  SAVE     DS     18F
                                590  ***************************************************************
                                591  * ERROR HANDLING ROUTINES.  CONTROL IS PASSED TO THESE ROUTINES    *
                                592  * WHEN THE RETURN CODE IN REG. 15 IS NOT X'00' AFTER VSAM REQUEST.*
                                593  ***************************************************************
                        005D8   594  OPNERR   EQU    *
0005D8 D284 C278 C70B 0027A 0070D 595         MVC    PRREC,=CL133' VSAM OPEN ERROR.'
0005DE 4130 C6A6          006A8 596           LA     3,EOJ
0005E2 47F0 C5EA          005EC 597           B      RETCOD
                        J05E6   598  LOGERR   EQU    *
0005E6 D284 C278 C790 0027A 00792 599         MVC    PRREC,=CL133' VSAM I/O ERROR.'
                        005EC   600  RETCOD   EQU    *
                                601           PUT    PRFLE,PRREC
0005FC D284 C278 C815 0027A 00817 607         MVC    PRREC,=CL133' RETURN CODE = '
                                608  ***************************************************************
                                609  * SHOWCB MACRO-USED TO PLACE CERTAIN STATISTICS IN USER-DEFINED-  *
                                610  * AREAS. IN THIS CASE WE WISH TO PRINT THE RETURN CODE FROM A VSAM*
                                611  * OPERATION WHICH IS FOUND IN THE LOW ORDER BYTE OF THE FDBK FIELD*
                                612  ***************************************************************
                                613           SHOWCB RPL=UPDTE,                               X
                                                    AM=VSAM,                                  X
                                                    OBJECT=DATA,                              X
                                                    FIELDS=(FDBK),                            X
                                                    AREA=FLESTS,                              X
                                                    LENGTH=4
000684 5820 C582          J0584 665           L      2,FLESTS
000688 4E20 C586          00588 666           CVD    2,DBL
00068C F321 C288 C58C 0028A 0058E 667         UNPK   PRREC+16(3),DBL+6(2)
000692 96F0 C28A          0028C 668           OI     PRREC+18,X'F0'
                                669           PUT    PRFLE,PRREC
0006A6 07F3                    675           BR     3
                        006A8   676  EOJ      EQU    *
                                677           CLOSE  CDFLE
0006B6 0A0E                    685           SVC    14
                                686           END
0006B8 5B5BC2D6D7C5D540        687                  =C'$$BOPEN '
0006C0 5B5BC2C303D6E2C5        688                  =C'$$BCLOSE'
0006C8 C9D2D8E5E3D4E240        689                  =CL8'IKQVTMS'
0006D0 00000218                690                  =A(PRFLE)
0006D4 000002FF                691                  =A(HD1)
0006D8 00000384                692                  =A(HD2)
0006DC 0000040E                693                  =A(HD3)
0006E0 00000248                694                  =A(CDFLE)
0006E4 00000518                695                  =A(CDREC)
```

Figure 22.23
(continued)

```
0006E8  000001C8                    696              =A(UPDTE)
0006EC  00000493                    697              =A(DETAIL)
0006F0  0000027A                    698              =A(PRREC)
0006F4  E3D6E3C1D3E2                699              =C'TOTALS'
0006FA  1C                          700              =P'1'
0006FB  4040404040                  701              =CL5' '
000700  40D9C5C3D6D9C4E2            702              =C' RECORDS READ'
00070D  40E5E2C1D440D6D7            703              =CL133' VSAM OPEN ERROR.'
000792  40E5E2C1D440C961            704              =CL133' VSAM I/O ERROR.'
000817  40D9C5E3E4D9D540            705              =CL133' RETURN CODE = '
```

<pre>
                        SAMPLE VSAM UPDATE PROGRAM   04/02/85
                        NASHUA COMMUNITY COLLEGE

ACCOUNT NUMBER   NAME   OLD CREDITS   CURRENT CREDITS   NEW TOTAL
    11111   JOHN WHITE   180   20   200
    22222   OSCAR JOHNKE   80   20   100
    33333   FELIX STERN   58   12   70
    44444   ALDEN SAGERONI   92   18   110
    55555   LEROY BISSON   143   11   154
    66666   JETHRO SAGER   180   14   194
    77777   NANCY STARR   171   12   183

    TOTALS   7 RECORDS READ   904   107   1011
</pre>

Figure 22.23
(continued)

Figure 22.24 shows the interrelationship of the ISAM/VSAM interface. When a program written for ISAM issues an OPEN command to a VSAM data set, the ISAM interface program (IIP) serves to

1. Construct the control blocks required by VSAM.
2. Load the ISAM interface routines into virtual storage.
3. Modify the DCB or DTF so that the interface can respond to the ISAM requests.
4. Interpret error return codes via filename C or the DCB exit.

The IIP intercepts an ISAM request, analyzes the request to determine the equivalent VSAM request, translates the request to an RPL (Request Parameter List), and executes the request. The ISAM interface program also receives VSAM error codes and translates these errors to the corresponding ISAM errors. The error codes are then returned to the ISAM program. For unrecoverable errors that cannot be posted in filename C or the DECB, the IIP issues an error message, closes the VSAM file, and terminates the job.

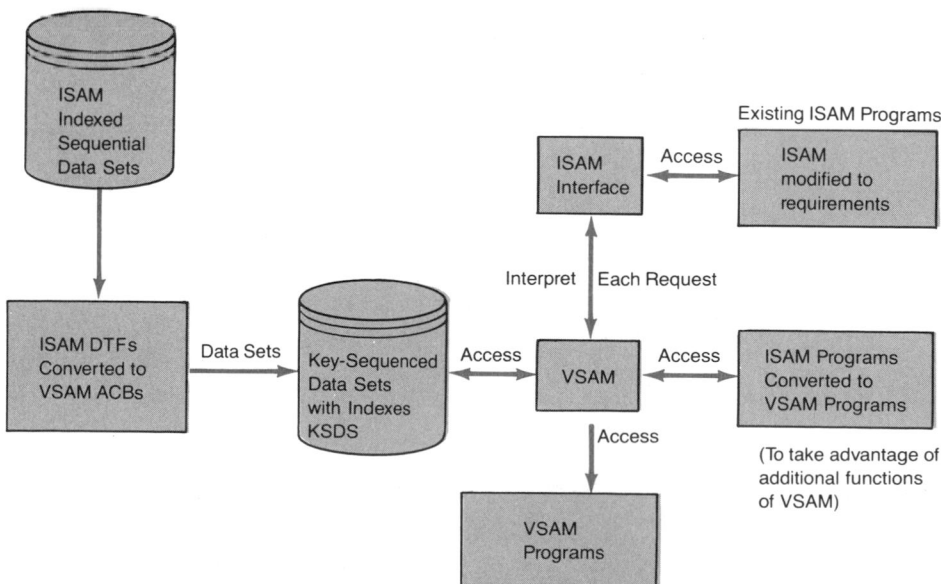

Figure 22.24
The interrelationships of the
ISAM/VSAM interface.

I. Indexed Sequential Access Method
   A. ISAM files permit data to be accessed either randomly or sequentially, according to the users' needs.
      1. Updating
         a. When only a small percentage of the records in a file are to be updated, a random update procedure will prove efficient because the transaction records do not have to be sorted first.
         b. When a large number of records require change, then a sequential file update procedure is recommended. However, the transaction records must be sorted first.
      2. Retrieval
         a. Inquiries require random retrieval but provide the ability to interrogate files at a moment's notice.
         b. Exception reports and related business reporting is usually organized sequentially as illustrated by typical control break procedures.
   B. Each record in an ISAM file is uniquely identified by a key field that may be numeric or alphanumeric and up to 255 bytes in length.
   C. When an ISAM file is created, the operating system establishes an index table that locates the records according to the search key. The physical location of the record is identified by the cylinder and track (surface) numbers.
   D. When ISAM files are created, the records must be in ascending (key) order.
   E. The operating system allocates space for the cylinder index area (track zero), the prime data area, and the independent overflow area according to the job control statements provided.
   F. When records are added to an ISAM file, they are placed in their logically correct position. As a result, because the track might be full already, a record might be "bumped" into the overflow area.
   G. An option is available in OS processing wherein the first byte of the record is reserved for a delete-flag byte. If this byte contains high values, that is X'FF', then it is ignored by the operating system.
   H. When too many records are placed in the overflow area the efficiency of the system may be impaired or system "degradation" may occur. Response time becomes excessive and, for this reason, periodic reorganization is necessary. Recall that reorganization of the ISAM file places all of the records in the prime data area.
   I. Typical problems encountered in processing ISAM files include
      1. Duplicate or out-of-sequence records that cause abend conditions when creating an ISAM file.
      2. An invalid key condition occurs when attempting to update or delete a record and the record cannot be found in the file.
      3. An invalid key condition results when attempting to add a record to an ISAM file and the record already exists.
II. Virtual Storage Access Method
   A. The primary advantage of VSAM briefly stated includes
      1. Better integrity and reliability.
      2. Use of multiple keys.
   B. Due to the wide use of macros used by VSAM processing, review the key terms presented in the chapter.

CHAPTER SELF-EVALUATING QUIZ

1. The two methods of accessing indexed disk files are _____ and _____ .

2. (T or F) One feature that is common to both ISAM and VSAM files is the ability to access records using alternate key fields.

3. (T or F) Direct files are not as commonly used as indexed files for business applications.

4. When creating an indexed file, the programmer must designate a field in the record as a(n) _____ field that uniquely identifies the record.

5. The _____ instruction is used to test for specific I/O errors.

6. (T or F) VSAM files are more useful than ISAM files for data base processing.

7. (T or F) VSAM files do not require reorganization as frequently as ISAM files.

8. Processing a VSAM file during a single run as both a random and a sequential file is called _____ .

9. When an indexed file is created under ISAM, each record is placed on the disk in ascending/descending/random sequence.

10. (T or F) The ACB (Access Control Block) and RPL (Request Program List) macros are always required to process a VSAM file.

SOLUTIONS

		Page
1.	ISAM; VSAM	604
2.	F: This feature is available only for VSAM files.	605
3.	T	606
4.	Key	606
5.	TM (Test Under Mask)	615
6.	T: VSAM files allow the specification of alternate keys with duplicates.	636
7.	T	637
8.	Dynamic processing	638
9.	Ascending	606
10.	T	641

KEY TERMS

Access-method services

Alternate keys

Cluster

Control areas

Control intervals

Entry-sequenced data set

ISAM

ISAM interface

Key-sequenced data set

Relative byte address

Relative record data set

Virtual storage

VSAM

REVIEW QUESTIONS

1. Explain the major advantages of VSAM processing over ISAM processing.

2. For DOS ISAM processing, explain how the TM (Test Under Mask) instruction can be used to test for specific I/O errors.

3. For OS ISAM processing, explain how the TM (Test Under Mask) instruction can be used to test for specific I/O errors.

4. In a random update procedure for an OS ISAM file, what is the purpose of a dummy READ statement?

5. Explain how records are deleted from an ISAM file as part of an update procedure.

6. Explain what is meant by a VSAM key-sequenced data set.

7. Explain why VSAM files do not require reorganization as frequently as ISAM files.

8. What is meant by dynamic processing of a VSAM file?

9. Explain the major functions that can be accomplished with the Access Method Services (AMS) utility program.

PROGRAMMING ASSIGNMENTS

1. Modify the ISAM create program provided in this chapter to
    a. Include a sequence check of student number.
    b. Incorporate tests to eliminate duplicate records.
    c. Provide a field to contain the number of credits required for graduation. Use positions 34–36 of the student record.
    d. Establish a STATUS field to indicate if the student is actively attending courses (A), has graduated (G), or has dropped out of school or is otherwise inactive (I). The STATUS field is to be located in position 40 of the record.
2. Rewrite the ISAM update program provided in this chapter to include
    a. Change of name due to marriage, divorce, etc.
    b. Change of status.
    c. Updating of records by adding credits completed this semester. Also, provide a list of all students scheduled to graduate by comparing the credits completed to the credits required for graduation.
3. Modify the ISAM update program to include additions and deletions.
4. Recode the VSAM program provided in this chapter to meet the requirements outlined in Problem 1.
5. Incorporate the changes delineated in Problem 2 to modify the VSAM update program.
6. Write a program to create an indexed master file from records with the following layout:

Positions	Description
1–5	Account number (key field)
6–30	Customer name
31–38	Balance forward (XXX,XXX.XX)
45–51	Credit limit (XX,XXX.XX)
55–80	Street address
81–100	Town,state,zip
101–108	Current gregorian date (XX/XX/XX)

Notes:
a. Check the sequence or ascending order of each input record to be placed in the file. If a record is out of sequence, do not add it to the file, but issue the message 'OUT OF SEQUENCE' instead. Also, for checking purposes, list the data contained in positions 1 to 100 of the record.
b. Validate that the rightmost position, position 5, of the account number contains a valid check digit. This means that calculations are performed on the first four digits and the result of these computations produces a check digit that appears in the fifth position. Assuming the account number is represented by the letters ABCDE, then the check digit E is calculated by

$$E = 60 + B + D - ((A + C) * 2)$$

Therefore, the account number 4567? would yield

$$
\begin{aligned}
E &= 60 + 5 + 7 - ((4 + 6) * 2) \\
&= \quad 72 \quad - \quad\quad 20 \\
&= 52, \text{ where only the low-order or rightmost} \\
&\qquad \text{digit is considered. Thus, 2 is the} \\
&\qquad \text{check digit and the account number} \\
&\qquad \text{would be 45672.}
\end{aligned}
$$

If a digit other than 2 appeared in the check-digit position, then the account number would be invalid and flagged by the program. Again, if the check digit proves invalid, issue the error message 'INVALID CHECK DIGIT' as well as listing the record. Also, do not add the record to the master file.
c. If duplicate records are found, issue an appropriate error message such as 'DUPLICATE RECORD' and do not write the record on the file.
d. Once the file is completed, list the contents for purposes of verification.

APPENDIXES

 **Glossary**

A

Abend. The termination or interruption of a program because of an error; abbreviation for *ab*normal *end*.

Access method services. A multifunction service program used to define VSAM data sets and allocate space for them, convert indexed-sequential data sets to key-sequenced data sets, modify data set attributes in the catalog, reorganize data sets, create backup copies of data sets, list the records of data sets and catalogs, and define and build alternate indexes.

Address. The number that uniquely identifies a particular storage location or byte.

Addressable location. A storage position that can be accessed or referred to by a specific address.

Algebraic comparison. A comparison in which negative numbers are considered to have less value than positive numbers despite the bit configuration.

Alternate index. A collection of index entries organized by the alternate keys of its associated base data records; provides an alternate means of locating records in the data component of a cluster on which the alternate index is based.

Alternate key. One or more consecutive characters taken from a data record and used to build an alternate index or to locate one or more base data records via an alternate index. See also *generic key, key,* and *key field.*

Argument. An item in a table that is compared to a variable data field for "lookup" or search purposes.

Assembler (Assembly). The translator (process) that produces an absolute or actual machine-language equivalent of an assembler language program.

ASSIST. An assembler that is used at many colleges and universities; an acronym for Assembler System for Student Instruction and Systems Teaching.

B

Base address. The actual starting address of a program.

Base register. A general register from 2–12 assigned by the programmer that contains the actual starting point of the program; when the contents of this register are added to the displacement, an effective, or actual, machine address is obtained.

Binary instructions. Instructions that operate on data that is in registers.

Binary numbering system. A numbering system that uses a combination of 0s and 1s; ideally suited for use in computers, where 0 represents the "off" state and 1 represents the "on" state.

Binary numbers. See *binary representation.*

Binary representation. The representation of data or numbers by a combination of 0s and 1s; ideally suited for use in computers, where 0 represents the "off" state and 1 represents the "on" state.

Bit. A contraction for *binary dig*it; refers to the representation of data in binary form, as a series of on–off or 1–0 digits.

Block. A group of several logical records combined into one physical record.

Block size (BLKSIZE). The number of characters in a physical record. Because tape and disk records are frequently "blocked," where several logical records are grouped into one physical record, BLKSIZE for tape and disk will vary. Cards have a BLKSIZE of 80 and print records typically have a BLKSIZE of 132 (or 133).

Boundary alignment. Some instructions require storage operands to be aligned on addresses that are evenly divisible by 2, 4, or 8 depending on the instruction. Those addresses are the *boundaries*.

Branching. Changing the sequence of instructions to be executed; see *conditional* and *unconditional branches*. Conditional branches require *two* assembler instructions, one that compares one field to another and another that branches depending on the condition code.

Buffer. A second input or output area reserved for overlapped I/O processing.

Bursting. Separating a continuous form into single sheets of paper.

Byte. A single storage position; consists of 8 bits.

C

Calling program. The program that calls in a subroutine.

Carriage control. Used for skipping to a specific print line or testing for a specific line.

Central Processing Unit (CPU). The computer unit that controls the actual operations of the computer system; a CPU consists of primary or main storage, an arithmetic-logic unit, and a control unit.

Character. A letter, number, or special symbol such as a $ or *.

Check protection symbol (*). An asterisk (*), or check protection symbol, is frequently used to replace leading zeros. This symbol is used to ensure that checks are not tampered with.

Cluster. A named structure consisting of a group of related components, for example, a data component with its index component; may also consist of a single component.

Coding sheet. A form used to prepare a program that contains the specific columns in which entries are required in a particular programming language.

Compiler (Compilation). The translator (process) that produces an actual machine-language equivalent of a high-level symbolic program such as one written in COBOL, BASIC, FORTRAN, and so on.

Complementation. The method used to represent negative numbers in binary form and to perform subtraction on binary numbers; all zeros are replaced by ones and all ones are replaced by zeros.

Complementation and end-around-carry. A method of performing subtraction on binary numbers.

Component. A named, cataloged collection of stored records. A component, the lowest member of the hierarchy of data structures that can be cataloged, contains no named subsets.

Computer system. An integrated series of components consisting of a central processing unit, input, and output devices.

Concatenation. The process of joining several fields together to form one field; a method of linking and grouping records, fields, or characters into one entity.

Condition code. A special code set as a result of arithmetic and compare operations; conditional branches may be coded by testing the results of the condition code.

Conditional assembly instructions. Enable the sequence of instructions in a source program to be altered; they also enable the assembler to branch and loop in macros.

Conditional branch. An instruction that causes a change in the sequence of instructions to be executed *only* if a specific condition is met; contrast with unconditional branch.

Conditional statement. Any statement that tests for the existence of some condition; usually followed by a conditional branch.

Constant. A fixed value used in a program.

Continuous forms. Computer-produced output forms that are perforated at regular intervals and where each perforation indicates the end of an individual page. After all continuous forms in a report have been generated, the individual pages must be burst, or separated along the perforations, into single sheets.

Control area. A group of control intervals used as a unit to format a data set before adding records to it.

Control break processing. The use of a control field to cause groups of records to be processed as one unit.

Control field. A control field is used in control break processing to indicate when totals are to print.

Control interval. A fixed-length area of auxiliary-storage space in which VSAM stores records; the unit of information transmitted to or from auxiliary storage by VSAM.

Control section. See *CSECT*.

CSECT. The statement that defines the beginning of a control section or subroutine.

Cylinder. A series of vertical tracks on a magnetic disk pack that is used for storing data; records on a disk are frequently accessed by their cylinder number.

D

Data exception. An error condition that occurs if field specifications are invalid. An add operation performed on a zoned-decimal or unpacked field, for example, would result in such an error.

Data set. The major unit of data storage and retrieval in the operating system, consisting of data arranged in a prescribed arrangement.

Data space. A storage area for the exclusive use of VSAM that is defined in the volume table of contents of a direct-access volume and is used to store data sets, indexes, and catalogs.

Debug. To eliminate errors from a program.

Decimal divide exception. Occurs when the divisor in a division operation is zero; also occurs when Operand 1 is too small to hold the quotient and the remainder resulting from a division operation.

Decimal instructions. Instructions that operate on data in main or primary storage.

Desk checking. A method of debugging programs by checking manually for typographic, keying, and other errors prior to an assembly or a compilation.

Detail line. A print line that contains the data from an individual input record.

Detail printing. The printing of one or more lines for each input record read.

Diagnostic. A listing and explanation of a syntax error.

Direct access. The method of processing data independent of the actual location of that data.

Disk drive. A direct-access device designed to minimize the access time required to locate specific records; ideally suited for on-line or immediate processing.

Disk operating system. See *DOS*.

Disk pack. A storage medium that consists of a series of platters or disks arranged in a vertical stack and connected by a central shaft.

Displacement. A relative address from 000–FFF that indicates how far from the starting point of the program a particular instruction is located.

Distributed free space. Space reserved within the control intervals of a key-sequenced data set for inserting new records into the data set in key sequence.

Dividend. The field to be divided; for example, in A/B = C, A is the dividend.

Divisor. The field one divides by; for example, in A/B = C, B is the divisor.

DOS. An abbreviation for Disk Operating System; refers to an intermediate-level operating system where programs are accessed from a disk. Contrast with *OS.*

Doubleword. Eight bytes in length; some instructions must begin on a doubleword boundary, which means that the address of the instruction must be divisible by eight.

E

EBCDIC (pronounced eb-ce-dick). A computer code used to represent characters; an abbreviation for Extended Binary Coded Decimal Interchange Code.

Editing. A technique involving the insertion of special characters such as $, ., and , in fields of data to make them clearer and neater for their specific purpose.

Effective address. A location of an instruction, determined by adding the contents of the base register to the displacement.

Entry point. The first instruction to be executed in a subroutine.

Entry sequence. The order in which data records are physically arranged in auxiliary storage, without respect to their contents.

Entry-sequenced data set. A data set in which records are loaded without respect to their contents; records are retrieved and stored by addressed access, and new records are added at the end of the data set.

Even parity. The use of an internal check bit to ensure that an even number of bits are "on" in any given storage position.

Exclusive comparison. A test that does not include endpoints.

Execution phase. The actual running of a program that has been translated into machine language.

Explicit length. Where the number of bytes involved in an operation is specifically indicated in an operand. Contrast with *implicit length.*

Explicit operation. An operation containing a length specifier that indicates the precise number of bytes involved.

External interrupt. A halt in execution caused by an operator depressing the interrupt key on the console; also caused by the external timer going from a positive to negative state; normally indicates that the system is to be shut down.

External subroutine. A subroutine that is *not* part of the program but is called in from a library as needed.

F

Field. A group of consecutive positions used to represent an item of data. In a record or a control block, a specified area used for a particular category of data or control information.

File. A collection of individual records that are treated as one unit. See *master file* and *transaction file.*

Fixed-head magnetic disk. A disk that does not use a movable access arm; each track has its own read/write mechanism that accesses a record as it rotates past the arm.

Fixed-length records. Records within a file that are all the same length.

Fixed-point data. Data for which the programmer must establish or fix where the decimal point falls; typically refers to binary data.

Floating dollar sign. A dollar sign that prints directly to the left of the first significant digit rather than printing in a fixed position that could be several spaces away from the first significant digit.

Flowchart. A planning tool that is a pictorial representation of the logic to be used in a program.

Form overflow condition. Occurs when the pre-determined limit on the number of lines to be printed on a single page has been reached. We test for a form overflow in a program to ensure that an adequate margin is left at the bottom of a page and that the printer will skip to the top of a new form.

Fullword. Four bytes in length; some instructions must begin on a *fullword boundary,* which means that the address of the instruction must be divisible by four.

Function. The item in a table that is actually "looked up" or searched.

G

General purpose registers. Registers 0–15; used as accumulators and for holding addresses.

Generic key. A high-order portion of a key, containing characters that identify those records that are significant for a certain application.

Global directive. Used to pass data from one macro to another.

Group printing. Printing one line of output for groups of input records; usually used to summarize data; also called summary printing.

H

Halfword. Two bytes in length; some instructions must begin on a *halfword boundary,* which means that the address of the instruction must be divisible by two.

Header label. The first record recorded on a tape or disk; used for identification purposes.

Hexadecimal numbering system. Base-16, positional-numbering system.

High-level language. A symbolic programming language that is relatively easy for the programmer to code, is least like the machine's internal code, and requires a complex translation process.

High-order position. The leftmost position of a field.

Housekeeping instructions. Those entries (mostly I/O macros) that are required in all programs and which contribute to efficient assembly and execution. They have been precoded in this text.

I

Identification sequence. An optional field specified as positions 73–80 of the assembler coding sheet; used to code a value that identifies the program and provides some sort of numbering. An edit program, for example, may have a source program with instructions containing `EDIT0010`, `EDIT0020`, `EDIT0030`, etc. in the identification-sequence field.

Immediate instructions. Those instructions that operate on only *one* byte of data.

Implicit length. Where the length of an operation is strictly determined by the length of the first operand. Contrast with *explicit length.*

Implicit operations. Instructions in which the length of the operation is strictly determined by the length of the first operand.

Inclusive comparison. A test or comparison that includes endpoints.

Index. An ordered collection of pairs, each consisting of a key and a pointer, used by VSAM to sequence and locate the records of a key-sequenced data set.

Index register. When the address in a register is systematically modified during the execution of a program, it is used as an index register. This feature is frequently used in processing tables or performing repetitive operations on consecutive fields.

Infinite loop. A sequence of instructions executed repeatedly and endlessly because a programmed branch point does not exist. This is usually the result of an incorrectly coded procedure.

Input/output interrupt. A halt in the execution of a program; commonly caused when channels communicate an error status or the completion of I/O operations to the supervisor.

Instruction formats. Classification schemes for instructions in assembler language; each format differs in length as well as in type.

Instruction length code. The part of the PSW that indicates the length of the last program instruction executed.

Interblock gap (IBG). An area of a tape or disk that separates physical records.

Internal subroutine. A subroutine that is part of the program but which is executed as a module.

Interrupt. Automatic interruption of program execution; the five classes include (1) external, (2) I/O, (3) program, (4) machine, and (5) supervisor call.

Interrupt code. The part of the PSW that indicates the type of interrupt.

IOCS. An abbreviation for Input–Output Control System; the part of the operating system that contains a series of routines, options, and macros available to the programmer for facilitating I/O processing.

ISAM. An abbreviation for Indexed Sequential Access Method; an access method in which a record's key field is used for locating the disk record by looking up the address in an index.

ISAM interface. A set of routines that allow a program coded to use ISAM (indexed-sequential access method) to gain access to a key-sequenced data set.

Iteration. The repeated execution of a routine or routines.

J

JCL (Job Control Language). The language used by the programmer or user to communicate job requirements to the supervisor; specifications include the type of translation desired, input/output equipment and macros to be used, start of data and end of data indicators, and so on.

Job. The program or application that constitutes a unit for computer processing.

Job catalog. A catalog made available for a job by means of the JOBCAT DD statement.

K

Key. One or more characters within an item of data that are used to identify it or control its use; one or more consecutive characters taken from a data record, used to identify the record and establish its order with respect to other records.

Key field. A field located in the same position in each record of a data set, whose contents are used for the key of a record.

Key sequence. The collating sequence of data records, determined by the value of the key field in each of the data records.

Key-sequenced data set. A data set whose records are loaded in key sequence and controlled by an index. Records are retrieved and stored by keyed access or by addressed access, and new records are inserted in the data set in key sequence by means of distributed free space.

Keyed-direct access. Retrieving or storing a data record through either an index that relates the record's key to its relative location in the data set or a relative record number.

Keyed-sequential access. Retrieving or storing a data record through its key or relative record sequence relative to the previously retrieved or stored record, as defined by the sequence set of an index.

Keyword parameters. Define constants that are to be used in the set of instructions defined by a macro.

L

Label. A name or symbolic address associated with a specific instruction, usually assigned so that the program can branch to that instruction.

Linkage. The process of linking subroutines to the main program.

Linkage editor (LNKEDT). The name of the program that is loaded in from the operating system to test and execute the programmer-supplied job.

Loading. A term used to describe the transfer of data from storage to a general register.

Local directive. Used to affect only the macro in which it is used.

Location counter. A counter that keeps track of the relative addresses of instructions to be assembled.

Logic error. An error that can occur from a mistake in the sequencing of instructions as well as from an improperly coded instruction that does not accomplish what was intended. Contrast with *syntax error.*

Logical record. The actual size of the record created as an independent unit for processing.

Loop. A sequence of steps in a program to be executed a fixed number of times or until a specified condition exists.

Low-level language. A programming language that most closely resembles actual machine language; it is somewhat more difficult to code than a high-level language and requires a relatively simple translation process. Assembler language is a low-level language.

Low-order position. The rightmost position of a field.

M

Machine check interrupt. A halt in execution of a program that indicates a malfunction of the computer system.

Machine language. The language into which programs must be translated before they can be executed.

Macro. An instruction that, when assembled, requires the assembler to generate many machine-language statements. Most I/O instructions in assembler language are coded as macros.

Mainframe. The traditional computer system used in most medium and large business organizations for (1) information processing in a centralized or distributed mode, and (2) data communications applications where terminals at remote locations transmit data to a central processing unit.

Masking. The ability to override interrupts. Some masking can only be performed by the supervisor; others can be programmed.

Master catalog. A catalog containing extensive data set and volume information that VSAM requires to locate data sets, to allocate and free storage space, to verify the authorization of a program or operator to gain access to a data set, and to accumulate usage statistics for data sets.

Master file. The major collection of data pertaining to a specific application.

Megabyte. Approximately one million bytes.

Memory size. The storage capacity of a computer system.

Mnemonics. Operation codes coded in assembler language.

Modular programming. See *structured programming.*

Module. A section, routing, procedure, or paragraph in a structured program.

Moving-head magnetic disk. A disk that has all read/write heads attached to a single movable-access mechanism. All read/write heads move in concert to locate a specific record.

Multiplicand. One of the numbers used in a multiplication operation. In assembler language, it must be the *larger* of the two numbers. In A $\times$ B = C, for example, A is the multiplicand if it is larger than B.

Multiplier. One of the numbers used in a multiplication operation. In assembler language, it must be the *smaller* of the two numbers. In A $\times$ B = C, for example, B is the multiplier if it is smaller than A.

Multiprogramming. The ability of a computer system to execute two or more programs simultaneously; a common feature of time-sharing and data communications systems.

MUSIC. An operating system that facilitates the use of terminals to enter and/ or modify programs; an acronym for McGill University System for Interactive Computing.

O

Object module. See *object program.*

Object program. A machine-language equivalent of a source program; output from an assembly process.

Octal numbering system. Base-8, positional-numbering system.

Odd parity. The use of an internal check bit that ensures that an odd number of on-bits are on in a given storage position.

One-to-many conversion process. The translation of a symbolic instruction into many machine-language instructions.

One-to-one conversion process. The translation of a symbolic instruction into one machine-language instruction.

Operands. The fields or storage areas to be operated on or branched to in each assembler language instruction. For example, in the instruction A 4,TOTAL, which adds the contents of TOTAL to register 4, TOTAL and 4 are operands.

Operating system (OS). A series of control programs that enables a computer to handle tasks automatically that would otherwise require manual intervention. These tasks include compilation, scheduling input/output control, and so on. See *OS* and *DOS*. Assembler language programs will vary slightly depending on whether they are to be run under OS or DOS.

Operation code. The item or verb that instructs the computer as to the operation to be performed. For example, in the instruction A 4,TOTAL, which adds the contents of TOTAL to register 4, A is the operation code.

OS. An abbreviation for Operating System; refers to a more elaborate or sophisticated form of operating system than DOS (Disk Operating System).

Overflow. Occurs when an arithmetic operation produces a result that is too large for the receiving field; such a condition may be tested within the program.

Overlapped fields. Describes two or more adjacent fields in storage that, usually inadvertently, contain overlapped results due to an operation that did not explicitly indicate the length of the fields to be operated on. Sometimes, however, this is a useful method of processing, particularly in clearing the print area.

P

Packed-decimal format. Results when numeric data is represented in storage so that each byte of a field contains two digits, except for the low-order byte, which contains a digit and a sign. To perform storage-to-storage arithmetic, numeric data must be packed.

Packing (pack). The operation of converting zoned-decimal data to packed format to allow arithmetic or compare instructions to be executed.

Parity. A system used to check that bits have not been lost or added within the computer during transmission; see *odd parity* and *even parity*.

Password. A unique string of characters stored in a catalog that a program, a computer operator, or a terminal user must supply to meet security requirements before being allowed access to a data set.

Path. A named, logical entity composed of one or more clusters (an alternate index and its base cluster, for example).

Physical record. A physical unit of recording on a medium; the size of the block of logical records. If 10 records of 50 characters each are blocked, for example, the size of the physical record or block is 500 characters.

Pointer. An address or other indicator of location. For example, a relative byte address (RBA) is a pointer that gives the relative location of a data record or a control interval in the data set to which it belongs.

Portability. The ability to use VSAM data sets with different operating systems. Volumes whose data sets are in one user catalog can be unmounted from storage devices on one system, moved to another system, and mounted on the storage devices of that system. Individual data sets can be transported between operating systems using the access method services program.

Positional numbering system. A numbering system in which the place value of each digit has significance.

Positional parameters. Refers to a macro, where the substitutions for the symbolic names are positional, that is, in the same relative positions in both the call and prototype statements.

Prime index. The index component of a key-sequenced data set that has one or more alternate indexes.

Print layout sheet. See *Printer Spacing Chart.*

PRINT NOGEN. The statement responsible for the suppression of macro-generated instructions; its use makes the program listing easier to read and decipher.

Printer Spacing Chart. A tool used to map out the spacing of output in a printed report.

Problem state. Occurs when the computer is executing a specific program, as opposed to waiting for something or being in the supervisory state.

Product. The result of a multiplication operation; in A × B = C, for example, C is the product.

Program. A set of instructions that reads input data, processes it, and produces output information.

Program flowchart. See *flowchart.*

Program interrupt. A halt in the execution of a program that is a result of a programming error.

Program sheet. See *coding sheet.*

Program Status Word (PSW). Contains status information about the program at the time of an interrupt.

Program walkthrough. The process of checking a program manually to see if it will produce the results desired.

Propagation. The repeated movement of data through storage; is usually a result of an implicit move.

Prototype statement. Names a macro and describes the variables used to pass data between the macro and the source program.

Pseudocode. A planning tool that uses English-like expressions rather than diagrams to depict the logic in a structured program.

PWS. See *Program Status Word.*

Q

Quotient. The result in a divide operation. In A/B = C, for example, C is the quotient.

R

RBA (relative byte address). The displacement (expressed as a fullword binary integer) of a data record or a control interval from the beginning of the data set to which it belongs.

Receiving field. The first operand in a move instruction; the field that will receive the results. In a move, data is transmitted from the sending field to the receiving field.

Record. A unit of information; a record may represent, for example, an employee's time card, or payroll information; records consist of fields of data.

Register. Serves as an accumulator or temporary storage area; greatly facilitates the processing of data by the computer. There are 16 general registers, numbered 0–15.

Register and Indexed Storage (RX) instruction. An assembler language instruction in which the first operand is a register and the second operand is a storage area that may or may not be indexed.

Register-to-register (RR) instruction. Assembler-language instruction in which both operands are registers.

Relative addressing. A method for referencing data in storage that does not contain a symbolic name. The nearest symbolic name is used; count the number of bytes needed to reach the desired storage location from that point.

Relative byte address. See *RBA.*

Relative record data set. A data set whose records are loaded into fixed-length slots by the relative position of each record.

Relative record number. A number that identifies not only the slot, or data space, in a relative record data set but also the record occupying the slot.

Used as the key for keyed access to a relative record data set.

Relocatability. Concept that enables several programs to be executed simultaneously. Relocatable programs are assembled independent of actual storage locations and then assigned such locations at execution time.

Remainder. The remaining numbers after an integer value is obtained for the quotient in a divide operation.

Remainder method. A technique used to convert a decimal number to a number in any other numbering system.

Return address. Address of the next sequential instruction in the main program to be executed *after* a subroutine is performed.

Reusable data set. A VSAM data set that can be reused as a work file, regardless of its old contents.

Rounding. To adjust the decimal value of a field either by truncating or by adding one (1), depending on whether the least significant digit was less than five, or greater than or equal to five.

Routine. A series of instructions that performs a specified sequence or task.

S

Search. See *table look-up*.

Self-defining operand. A constant that is part of an executable instruction; the use of a self-defining operand eliminates the need to establish a DC (Define Constant).

Sending field. The second operand in a move instruction, and whose data will be transmitted to the receiving field.

Shared resources. A set of functions that permits the sharing of a pool of I/O-related control blocks, channel programs, and buffers among several VSAM data sets that are open simultaneously.

Shifting. A technique used for decimal alignment of packed-decimal fields; shifting may be to the right or left depending on the application.

Sign control. An editing feature that enables the programmer to print a minus sign for negative quantities or a plus sign for positive quantities.

Simple conditional. A condition test that tests only a *single* condition.

Skipping. Refers to the spacing of a form so that the paper advances to a specific line.

Source program. A program written in a symbolic programming language; source programs must be translated before they can be executed.

Spacing of forms. Forms, unlike other types of output, must be properly spaced for ease of reading; certain entries must be single-spaced, double-spaced, or triple-spaced.

Spanned record. A logical record whose length exceeds the control interval length, and as a result, crosses, or spans, one or more control interval boundaries within a single control area.

Spooling. The process of performing an input or output operation at high speeds using a tape or disk in an off-line operation; for example, output to be printed might be spooled onto disk in a high-speed operation and then printed on the printer off-line.

Storage dump. A list of the contents of storage during a particular run.

Storage Immediate (SI) instruction. An assembler language instruction in which the first operand is a storage area and the second operand is an immediate, 1-byte constant.

Storage-to-storage (SS) instruction. An assembler-language instruction in which both operands are data fields in storage.

Stored-program concept. The use of main memory for temporarily storing programs as well as data.

Structured programming. A technique for coding programs in modules or separate blocks, each treated as independent entities for ease of reading and debugging.

Structured walkthrough. See *program walkthrough*.

Subroutine. An independent sequence of instructions that may be coded as part of a program or be called in from a library.

Supervisor. A program that is part of the operating system but resides in the CPU for the purpose of controlling the operations of the entire system.

Supervisor-call interrupt. A halt in the execution of a program that causes control to be returned to the supervisor.

Symbol cross-reference table. A cross-reference of all symbols used in the program and the statements in which they are used.

Symbolic address. A programmer-supplied name denoting an address in the source program; converted to an actual machine-language address during the assembly process.

Symbolic programming language. A programming language that is relatively easy for a programmer to learn but that requires a translation process before a program can be run.

Syntax error. An error caused by a violation of a programming rule.

System mask. A mask that can be used to override I/O or external interrupts. Part of PSW.

T

Table. A series of consecutive items, all with the same format, used to look up or match against an item read in or computed by the program.

Table look-up. The process of systematically searching through a table to find a specific entry or entries; requires indexing and the use of a loop.

Test data. Sample data used to test or debug a program.

Top-down programming. See *structured programming.*

Transaction file. A file containing data used to update a master file.

Translation phase. An assembly or compilation process used to convert a source program to an object program.

Translator. A program used to convert a source program into machine language; types of translators include compilers, interpreters, and assemblers.

Truncation. A loss or elimination of positions of a field when the resulting operand is not large enough.

U

Unconditional branch. A branch or transfer in a program that occurs regardless of any existing condition; contrast with *conditional branch.*

Unpacking. The conversion of packed data to an unpacked or zoned-decimal format so that it can be printed.

Updating. The process of putting current information in a master file.

V

Variable data. Data that changes during the execution of the program; input and output areas, for example, consist of variable data.

Variable-length records. Records in a file that have different lengths.

Virtual storage. The dynamic interaction between primary storage and auxiliary storage in such a way that the CPU appears to have more storage than it actually has; involves breaking a program up into segments or pages, and, one-at-a-time, bringing each part into the CPU.

VSAM. An abbreviation for Virtual Storage Access Method; an efficient method of organizing data on a disk so that on-line processing is facilitated, multiple keys may be used, and variable-length records can be processed.

W

Wait state. Occurs when a computer is not executing a problem but waiting for further instructions. The PSW indicates if the computer is in a wait state.

XYZ

Zoned-decimal format. The standard way for representing character data using the EBCDIC code; each byte contains a zone and a digit portion.

Communicating with the Operating System Using Job Control Language

I. WHAT IS AN OPERATING SYSTEM?

Because computers can operate on data far more quickly than people, computer systems have been designed to minimize the degree of human intervention. An **operating system** is a sophisticated control system that enables a computer to handle many tasks automatically that have previously required time-consuming manual intervention by a computer operator. Examples of such tasks are listed below.

SAMPLE FUNCTIONS OF AN OPERATING SYSTEM

1. Automatic logging in of date, time, cost, and other details relating to each program.
   Savings. Operator not needed to maintain this information for each program.
2. Automatic maintenance and easy access of compilers, assemblers, and other special programs usually supplied by the manufacturer.
   Savings: Less operation time needed to load programs from off-line devices.
3. Automatic procedures for terminating jobs even if errors have occurred; automatic restart procedures that can read new jobs so that they can be batched.
   Savings: Operator not needed to watch for programming errors or input errors that may cause the computer to halt; operator not needed to clear our malfunctioning program or to load in each program as needed.
4. Automatic communication of requirements from computer to operator and from operator to computer via a console.
   Savings: Operator can determine the status and requirements of each program easily and efficiently.
5. Automatic operations permitting terminal, real-time and time-sharing functions that would otherwise be impossible.

II. HOW OPERATING SYSTEM INTERFACES WITH COMPUTER

A major program providing the operating system with much of its capability and flexibility is the **supervisor.** The supervisor, sometimes called a **monitor,** controls the functions of the operating system, which is typically stored on a high-speed, direct-access medium such as magnetic disk. The supervisor must be *loaded* into storage each day prior to any processing, unless the computer operates on a 24-hour basis, in which case it permanently resides in storage. This control program calls in each user program for execution and extracts items, routines, or programs, as needed, from the system.

SAMPLE CONTROL FUNCTIONS PERFORMED BY SUPERVISOR

1. Calls in assembler, input/output macros, etc., as required by the program.
2. Calls in special interrupt routines in case of error.

III. EXAMPLE OF SUPERVISORY FUNCTIONS CALLED FOR BY PROGRAMMER

A programmer who writes a program in assembler language must, for example, instruct the supervisor to do the following:

1. Call in the assembly program from the operating system.
2. Release control to the assembler for translation.
3. Call in the appropriate subroutines that will supply a source listing, diagnostic messages, storage maps, and any other features deemed appropriate.
4. Abort the run if major errors have occurred.
5. Load the object program into main storage for execution.
6. Release control to the object program for execution.
7. At the end of the job, read in a new program.

Programmers communicate their job requirements to the supervisor in a special instruction format called **job control language.** Job control languages are dependent on the type of operating system under which one is running.

IV. TYPES OF OPERATING SYSTEMS

The type of operating system employed with a computer depends on its size and processing requirements. The three most common types of operating systems are

---

TYPES OF IBM OPERATING SYSTEMS

1. **DOS—Disk Operating System**
2. **OS—(Full) Operating System**
3. **VS—Virtual Storage Operating System**

These operating systems reside on direct-access devices such as disk and are called in, as needed, by the supervisor. A DOS system is somewhat less comprehensive and sophisticated than an OS or VS system.[1] The job control language, that is, the method of communicating with the supervisor, differs somewhat depending on which operating system is used.

V. JOB CONTROL LANGUAGE (JCL)

MAIN PURPOSE OF JOB CONTROL LANGUAGE

1. To communicate the programmer's needs to the supervisor.
2. To access features of the operating system required by the programmer.

Every programmer must become familiar with job control specifications. We would like to supply them in their entirety as part of this text but, unfortunately, there are numerous options and entries to be coded that are dependent on the requirements of each computer installation. Hence the JCL utilized at one data processing center will differ, if only slightly, from that used at another center. We will consider JCL for several IBM and UNIVAC systems. Before providing specific rules for each of these systems, let us consider some generalizations. The actual sequence of JCL commands discussed is considered in the next section.

A. Coding Rules

Coding rules must be followed *precisely.*

If a command requires // JOB in columns 1–6, for example, with a blank in column 3, then *no* variations are permitted.

1. JOB **Command (IBM) or** LOGON **Command (UNIVAC)**

A JOB or LOGON command indicates to the supervisor that a new job is being entered. Such a command normally specifies identifying information such as programmer name, job name, and date. Sometimes a JOB command must have a code or password that is known only to authorized users.

JOB name—usually 1 to 8 alphanumeric characters,
          with the first being alphabetic

2. OPTION **or** PARAM **Command**

This is a JCL command that specifies the options or parameters required for the specific run. There are numerous options that may be called for in a program. See Figures B.1 and B.5 for a listing of the more common ones.

---

[1]It should be noted that with a virtual storage computer, it is possible to have a DOS/VS system or an OS/VS system. See Appendix H for additional information on virtual storage.

PARAM or OPTION Coded	Meaning
LOG	Log control statements on SYSLST (printer) are desired.
NOLOG	Suppress LOG option.
DUMP	DUMP registers and storage if an interrupt occurs.
NODUMP	Suppress DUMP option.
LINK	Write the output of the language translator.
NOLINK	Suppress LINK.
LIST	Produce output listing of source statements on SYSLST.
NOLIST	Suppress LIST.
LISTX	Produce output listing of object program on SYSLST (usually printer).
NOLISTX	Suppress LISTX.
XREF	Produce symbolic cross-reference list on SYSLST.
NOXREF	Suppress XREF.
ERRS	Produce listing of errors in source program on SYSLST.
NOERRS	Suppress ERRS.

Figure B.1
Sample options.

Note: The order indicated above is usually the one required. Hence if LOG, XREF, and ERRS are required, they must be coded in that sequence.
Note: Remember to check the defaults of your system to see which options are automatically provided.

Each computer system sets up its operating system to supply some of these options automatically, without even the need to call for them with a JCL command. In such cases, the JCL OPTION or PARAM command can be used to *suppress* the option.

SUMMARY OF OPTION OR PARAM COMMAND

1. Determine which options are provided as a standard.
2. Use the OPTION or PARAM command to call for additional options not provided automatically.
3. Use the OPTION or PARAM command to suppress options not needed.

---

3. EXEC Command

This JCL command specifies the program or routine to be executed. Because assembler language programs require translation, linkage, and execution, usually three EXEC commands are included in a run.

a. Translation of Assembler Program. The first EXEC command calls for execution of the assembler—using your program as input and creating an object program as output. This object program may then be executed.

b. EXEC LNKEDT. Prior to the execution of an object program, that program must be loaded into an appropriate area of main storage and prepared for the run. These processes are placed under control of the **linkage editor** and must be executed *before* the object program can be run.

c. Execution of Assembler Program. The third EXEC command calls for execution of the object program.

4. Data Definition Commands (ASSGN or DD)

For every device utilized in a program, a device specification command is required, indicating the device classification, unit number, features of the file type, and so on. Sometimes a terminal is designated as the system's input device and a printer as the system's output device, so these devices do not require data definition commands. For all other file types, however, such as tape and disk, data definition commands are required.

5. /∗ Command

This JCL command is used to denote the end of a file. It is the *last* command of a *source program*, signaling the assembler that there are no more instructions to be assembled. It is also used as an end-of-file record. A /∗ command is automatically interpreted to mean there are no more records to be processed.

6. // (IBM) or /LOGOFF (UNIVAC)

This JCL command indicates the end of the run. It returns control to the supervisor, which automatically loads in the next job.

VI. JOB CONTROL—IBM DOS

Figure B.2 illustrates sample JCL coding for assembler language programs run on IBM DOS systems.

NOTE: Uppercase letters—required entries.
Lowercase letters—programmer-supplied.
Phrases in parentheses are optional or system-dependent.
Required entries must be coded in the precise positions indicated.

	LABEL	OPERATION	OPERAND	COMMENTS
1.	// JOB	job name		
2.	// OPTION	option1,option2,···		
3.	// ASSGN	SYSnnn,X'cuu'(optional specifications may also be included)		
4.	// EXEC	ASSEMBLY		
	(source program inserted at this point)			
5.	/∗			
6.	// EXEC	LNKEDT		
7.	// EXEC			
	(test data, if on cards, is entered here)			
8.	/∗			
9.	/&			

Figure B.2
Sample JCL coding for DOS assembler programs.

A. Review of Functions of JCL for IBM DOS

1. JOB command
   JOB name—Programmer-supplied.
     —Name by which computer will refer to program.
     —1 to 8 alphanumeric characters.
   Other identifying information such as programmer name and password may be required at specific installations.
2. OPTION command
   See Figure B.1 for an illustration of possible entries. Each system establishes its own **defaults,** options that are automatically supplied. The programmer, then, need only include options that are different from defaults.
3. ASSGN command
   SYSnnn—The symbolic name for the device(s) used in the program.
   SYSnnn—May be any number SYS000-244. Sometimes
        SYS001-SYS004 are reserved.
   SYSIPT—System input device.
   SYSRDR—System's input device for reading control messages.
   SYSLST—System's main output device; usually printer.
   SYSLOG—Console typewriter.
   SYSRES—System-resident disk unit.
   SYSLNK—Disk unit used by linkage editor.

   The symbolic device assignment is made by each individual computer installation.

   Note
   An assign statement is *only* required for each device used by the program.

   X'cuu'—address of physical unit used only for tapes or disk
        c—channel number
        uu—device number

   Check installation for exact specification.
4. // EXEC ASSEMBLY command
   Assembly program called in; must be followed by source program.
5. /* command
   Signals the end of source program.
6. // EXEC LNKEDT command
   Links object module in preparation for execution.
7. // EXEC command
   Executes the object program; followed by test data.
8. /* command
   Signals the end of test data (only included if test data is on cards).
9. /& command
   Signals the end of the run.

VII. JOB CONTROL—IBM OS OR OS/VS

The illustration in Figure B.3 includes the job control used with assembler language programs in IBM OS systems.

> NOTE: Uppercase letters—required entries.
>   Lowercase letters—programmer-supplied.
>   Phrases in parentheses are optional or system-dependent.
>   Required entries must be coded in the precise positions indicated or directly following programmer-supplied entry.

LABEL	OPERATION	OPERAND	COMMENTS

```
1. //jobname  JOB (password),programmer name
2. // EXEC ASMFCLG
3. // ASM.SYSIN DD *
   (source program follows)
4. /*
5. //GO.SYSPRINT DD SYSOUT=A
6. //GO.SYSIN    DD *
   (test data entered here)
7. /*
8. //
```

Figure B.3
Sample JCL coding for OS assembler programs.

1. JOB command
   JOB name—1 to 8 characters, placed directly after //.
   Other identifying data following JOB may be required by your specific system.
2. // EXEC ASMFCLG
   This is followed by the source program. ASMFCLG is the name of the assembler procedure for assembling, linkage editing, and executing the program. If an assembly process—but *no* execution—is desired, then ASMFC is the name used.
3. // ASM.SYSIN DD * command
   Notifies the assembler that the source program is on punched cards.
4. /* command
   Signals the end of the source program.
5. // GO.SYSPRINT DD SYSOUT=A command
   Indicates that all output from execution of program will be on printer.
6. // GO.SYSIN DD * command followed by test data.
   Indicates that test data for execution of the program is on cards.
7. /* command
   Indicates the end of test data.
8. //
   Indicates end of run.

To change an option, we use the PARM parameter with the EXEC command in OS.

```
// EXEC ASMFCLG,PARM.ASM='option 1,option 2, . . .'
```

VIII. JOB CONTROL—UNIVAC

See Figure B.4.

LABEL	OPERATION		OPERAND	COMMENTS	
1	10	16			72

```
1. /LOGON user id.,A (account no.)
2. /OPTION DUMP=YES
3. /PARAM option1=NO, option2=NO, ....
              YES          YES
4. /EXEC ASSEMB
   (source program entered here)
5. /*
6. /EXEC LNKEDT
7. /EXEC
   (test data entered here)
8. /*
9. /LOGOFF
```

Figure B.4
Sample JCL coding for UNIVAC assembler programs.

NOTE: Uppercase letters—required entries.
Lowercase letters—programmer-supplied (phrases in parentheses are optional).
Required entries must be coded in the precise positions indicated.

A. Review of UNIVAC JCL

1. /LOGON command
   Identifies the program to the system.
2. /OPTION command
   If a dump is required when a program is aborted, then /OPTION DUMP = YES must be coded.
3. /PARAM command
   Specifies the options that may be included.
   Figure B.5 specifies some UNIVAC options.
4. /EXEC ASSEMB command is followed by the source program.
   This statement calls in the assembler program, which will translate the source program into an object program.
5. /* command
   Indicates the end of the source program.
6. /EXEC LNKEDT command
   Indicates that the object module is to be linked in preparation for execution.
7. EXEC command, followed by test data.
   Executes the object program.

Parameter	Meaning
LIST $\begin{cases} = \text{YES} \\ = \text{NO}* \end{cases}$	indicates whether a source program listing is to be included.
MAP $\begin{cases} = \text{YES}* \\ = \text{NO} \end{cases}$	indicates whether the program's object summary and storage maps are to be printed.
DISC $\begin{cases} = \text{YES}* \\ = \text{NO} \end{cases}$	indicates whether an object module is to be generated.
DEBUG $\begin{cases} = \text{YES} \\ = \text{NO}* \end{cases}$	indicates that object time diagnostics from the debug routine contain source statement line numbers generated by the compiler.

Figure B.5

Sample UNIVAC options.   *An asterisk denotes the default that is automatically included.

8. /* command
   Indicates the end of the test data.
9. /LOGOFF command
   Indicates the end of the run.

Instruction Formats and Other Specifications

I. INSTRUCTION FORMATS

Type	Length	Contents of Two High-Order Bits of Op Code	Format
A. One halfword RR	2 bytes	00	**First operand** → R1, **Second operand** → R2. Op Code (8) · R1 (4) · R2 (4)
B. Two halfwords RX	4 bytes	01	**First operand** → R1, **Second operand** → X2, B2, D2. Op Code (8) · R1 (4) · X2 (4) · B2 (4) · D2 (12)
RS	4 bytes	10	**First operand** → R1, R3, **Second operand** → B2, D2. Op Code (8) · R1 (4) · R3 (4) · B2 (4) · D2 (12)
SI	4 bytes	10	**Second operand** → 12, **First operand** → B1, D1. Op Code (8) · 12 (8) · B1 (4) · D1 (12)
C. Three halfwords SS	6 bytes	11	**Length** → Length L1 ⋮ L2, **First operand** → B1, D1, **Second operand** → B2, D2. Op Code (8) · Length L1/L2 (8) · B1 (4) · D1 (12) · B2 (4) · D2 (12)

II. ASSEMBLER AND MACRO INSTRUCTIONS

	Chapter
CLOSE	4
CNTRL	9
DC	3
DC (Address Constants)	16
DCB	4
DS	3
DTF	4
END	4
EOJ	4
GET	4
PRTOV	9
PUT	4
START	4
USING	4

III. EXTENDED MNEMONICS

Extended Code		Machine Instruction		Meaning
Unconditional Branches				
B	D2(X2,B2)	BC	15,D2(X2,B2)	Unconditional branch
BR	R2	BCR	15,R2	Unconditional branch
After Compare (Operand 1 to Operand 2)				
BH	D2(X2,B2)	BC	2,D2(X2,B2)	Branch if Operand 1 is high
BL	D2(X2,B2)	BC	4,D2(X2,B2)	Branch if Operand 1 is low
BE	D2(X2,B2)	BC	8,D2(X2,B2)	Branch if operands are equal
BNH	D2(X2,B2)	BC	13,D2(X2,B2)	Branch if Operand 1 is not high
BNL	D2(X2,B2)	BC	11,D2(X2,B2)	Branch if Operand 1 is not low
BNE	D2(X2,B2)	BC	7,D2(X2,B2)	Branch if operands are not equal
After Arithmetic Instructions				
BO	D2(X2,B2)	BC	1,D2(X2,B2)	Branch on overflow
BP	D2(X2,B2)	BC	2,D2(X2,B2)	Branch if plus
BM	D2(X2,B2)	BC	4,D2(X2,B2)	Branch if minus
BZ	D2(X2,B2)	BC	8,D2(X2,B2)	Branch on zero
BNP	D2(X2,B2)	BC	13,D2(X2,B2)	Branch if not plus
BNM	D2(X2,B2)	BC	11,D2(X2,B2)	Branch if not minus
BNZ	D2(X2,B2)	BC	7,D2(X2,B2)	Branch if not zero

IV. CONDITION CODES

Instructions Not Affecting Condition Codes

Op Code	Meaning
BALR	Branch and link register
BR	Branch to register
CVB	Convert to binary
CVD	Convert to decimal
D	Divide
DR	Divide register
L	Load
LA	Load address

(continued)

Instructions Not Affecting Condition Codes

Op Code	Meaning
LH	Load halfword
LR	Load register
M	Multiply
MH	Multiply halfword
MR	Multiply register
MVC	Move character
PACK	Pack
ST	Store
STH	Store halfword
UNPK	Unpack

V. CONDITION CODES SET

Op Code	Meaning	Condition Code 0	1	2	3
A	Add	$=0$	<0	>0	Overflow
AP	Add packed	$=0$	<0	>0	Overflow
AR	Add register	$=0$	<0	>0	Overflow
C	Compare	$=$	First $<$ second	First $>$ second	
CP	Compare packed	$=$	First $<$ second	First $>$ second	
CR	Compare register	$=$	First $<$ second	First $>$ second	
S	Subtract	0	<0	>0	Overflow
SP	Subtract packed	0	<0	>0	Overflow
SR	Subtract register	0	<0	>0	Overflow

VI. EDIT AND MARK SYMBOLS

Symbol	Meaning
Hex 40	Blank
Hex 21	Significant start character
Hex 22	Field separator character
Hex 20	Digit select character

VII. SPECIFICATIONS FOR CONSTANTS

Code	Type	Meaning	Example	
			Coding	Representation
C	Character or Zoned-decimal	8-bit code for each specification	C'1'	F 1 `1111` `0001`
			C'A'	`1100` `0001` C 1
			Coding	Representation
X	Hexadecimal	4-bit code for each specification	X'F1'	`1111` `0001`
			X'C1'	`1100` `0001`
			Coding	Representation
B	Binary	Binary digits represented as 0s and 1s	B'11110001'	`1111` `0001`
			B'11000001'	`1100` `0001`
			Coding	Representation
P	Packed-decimal	4 bits per digit plus sign	P'1'	`0001` `1111` 1 F
			Coding	Representation
F	Fixed-point fullword	Signed, fixed-point binary format, fullword	F'1'	0 . . . . . 0001 32 bits– 4 bytes
			Coding	Representation
H	Fixed-point halfword	Signed, fixed-point binary format, halfword	H'1'	0 . . . 0001 16 bits 2 bytes
			Coding	Representation
D	Fixed-point doubleword	Signed, fixed-point binary format, doubleword	D'1'	00 . . . . 0001 64 bits 8 bytes

VIII. PROGRAM STATUS WORD (PSW)

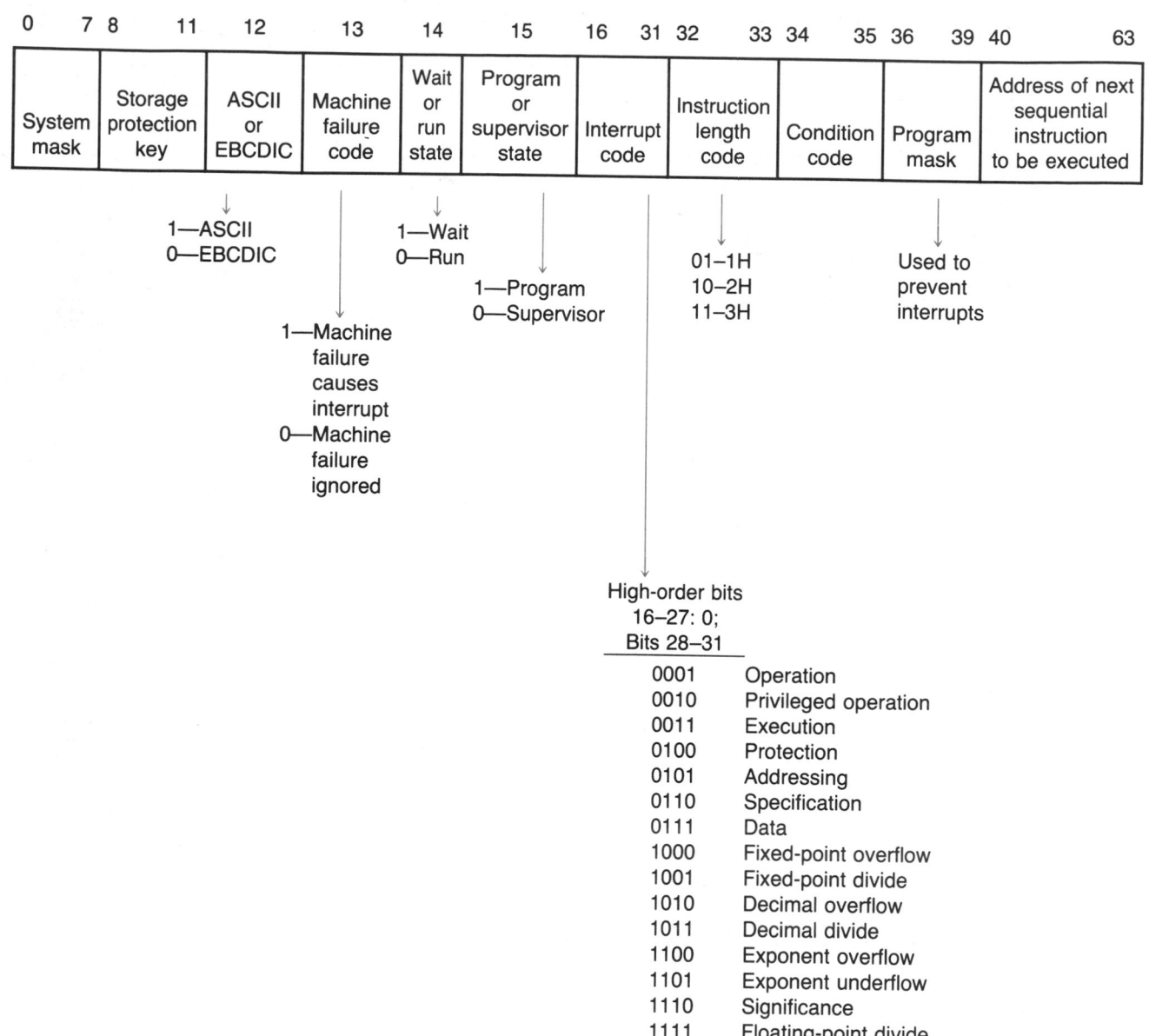

0 7	8 11	12	13	14	15	16 31	32 33	34 35	36 39	40 63
System mask	Storage protection key	ASCII or EBCDIC	Machine failure code	Wait or run state	Program or supervisor state	Interrupt code	Instruction length code	Condition code	Program mask	Address of next sequential instruction to be executed

1—ASCII
0—EBCDIC

1—Wait
0—Run

1—Program
0—Supervisor

01—1H
10—2H
11—3H

Used to prevent interrupts

1—Machine failure causes interrupt
0—Machine failure ignored

High-order bits
16–27: 0;
Bits 28–31

0001	Operation
0010	Privileged operation
0011	Execution
0100	Protection
0101	Addressing
0110	Specification
0111	Data
1000	Fixed-point overflow
1001	Fixed-point divide
1010	Decimal overflow
1011	Decimal divide
1100	Exponent overflow
1101	Exponent underflow
1110	Significance
1111	Floating-point divide

 **External Subroutines and Linkage Considerations**

An external subroutine is stored as an independent set of procedures in a library. It is then called into the main program as needed. In this way, external subroutines may be shared by many different users. The linkage procedure, that of linking the external subroutine to the main program, is the most difficult aspect of this process. Efforts have been made by IBM and other manufacturers to standardize linkage procedures. A fixed set of rules may be used, which

1. simplify the coding of subroutines
2. reduce the possibility of errors

These rules, when adapted to your system's requirements, will facilitate linkage. It is possible to deviate from standard conventions but then you must face the risk of writing programs that may not correctly interface with the operating system. To avoid this problem, it is strongly recommended that the consistent set of rules developed in this section be followed.

You will recall that the linking of internal subroutines to a main program required the following steps.

REVIEW

Main Program

1. Using a BAL instruction, place the address of the next instruction (to be branched to after execution of the subroutine) in a register. This is called the return address.
2. Branch to the entry point in the subroutine.

Subroutine

1. Store the contents of the register containing the return address in a save area.
2. Restore (Load) the register with the return address immediately prior to branching back to the main program.
3. Branch to the return address in the main program.

Along with these elements, there are several additional requirements that must be used for linking *external* subroutines.

I. LINKAGE

1. The main program and subroutine are *completely independent* blocks of code that are *relocatable*. Therefore, each module must establish addressability through a base register.
2. A subroutine *must* restore the registers to their original status prior to returning to the calling program (the main program in this instance). This requires us to temporarily store the contents of the registers in a save area and then to restore them later. This is similar to the procedure used with internal subroutines. However, *all* of the registers will be saved, not just the one used for linking.

A. The Save Area

The standard size for the register save area is 18 fullwords. In our main program, we can define the register save area as follows.

LABEL	OPERATION		OPERAND	COMMENTS	
1	10	16			72
SAVMAIN	DS		18F		

Using the standard established, registers are saved in the following order—14,15,0,1,2, . . . 12, starting with the fourth word of the save area.

SAVE AREA

SAVMAIN

Contents Reg 14
Contents Reg 15 Contents Reg 0
Contents Reg 12

The first three words will be discussed later as they are needed.

The save area is not filled with the registers' contents until the subroutine is entered. That is, the first instruction executed in the subroutine will save the contents of the registers in a save area in the main program. This means that the address of the save area in the main program (SAVMAIN) must be passed to the subroutine or the subroutine will be unable to restore the registers. Standard linkage procedures use register 13 for this purpose. We will now examine the steps necessary in the main program (MAIN) to establish linkage to the subroutine (SUB1).

B. The Main Program

The registers in the main program are programmed to contain the following data immediately before the subroutine is called.

Register	Use
13	Address of save area (SAVMAIN)
14	Return address in MAIN
15	Entry address in called subroutine (SUB1)

The instructions needed to properly load registers 13, 14, and 15 are shown in Figure D.1.

```
              LA      13,SAVMAIN
              L       15,=V(SUB1)
                 .
                 .
                 .
              BALR    14,15
      GO      MVC
                 .
                 .
                 .
      SAVMAIN DS      18F
```

Figure D.1
Instructions to load registers 13, 14, and 15.

The circled numbers in Figure D.2 are used to illustrate the effect of each of the preceding instructions on general registers 13–15.

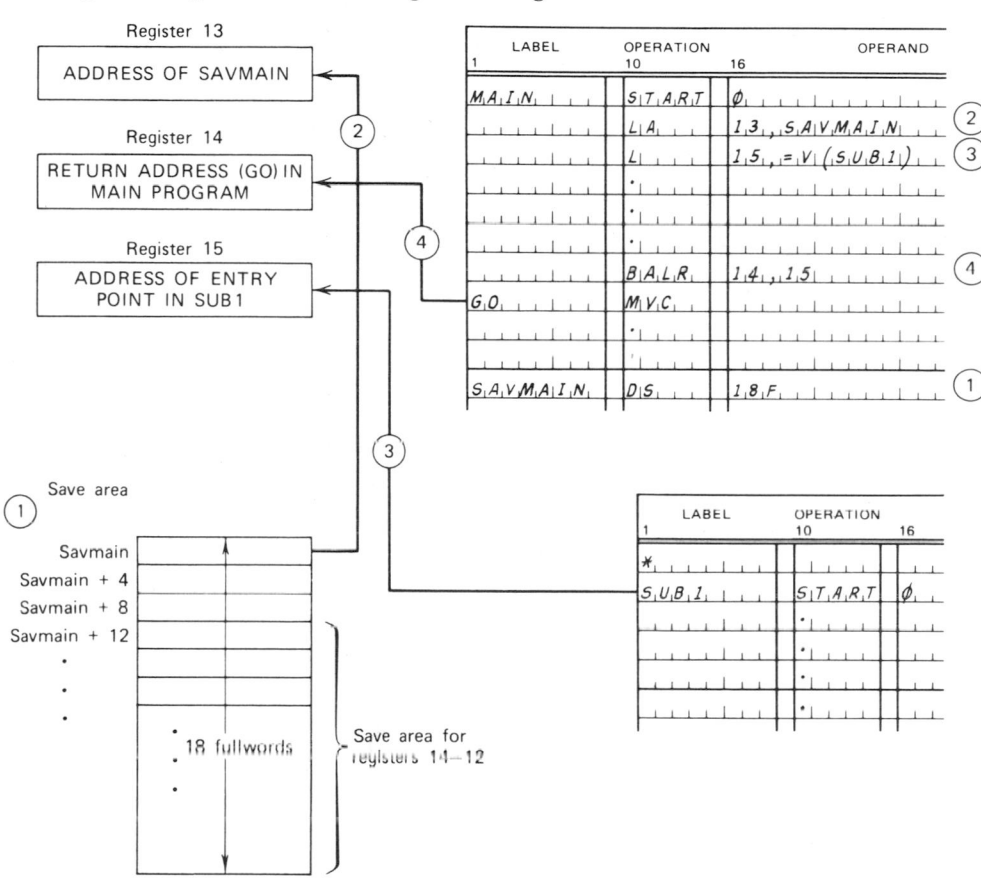

Figure D.2
Schematic of how registers 13, 14, and 15 are loaded.

<hr>

SUMMARY

1. The save area (SAVMAIN) is defined with a DS statement, and consists of 18 fullwords, each aligned on fullword boundaries.
2. The address of the save area (SAVMAIN) is loaded into register 13.
3. The V-type address is used to reference an external routine. This will be discussed later in this Appendix. For now, this instruction sets up the entry point in the subroutine (SUB1).
4. The BALR instruction saves the address of the next instruction (labeled GO) in register 14. This address is the return address. The program then branches to the address contained in register 15, the routine SUB1.

C. The Subroutine (SUB1)

Upon entering the subroutine (SUB1), the present status of the program is as illustrated in Figure D.2. As the instructions in the subroutine are executed, the changes that take place are described in the following paragraphs. Figure D.3 shows the instructions in the subroutine.

```
5. SUB1       START  0   .
6.            STM    14,12,12(13)
              BALR   12,0
7.            USING  *,12
8.            ST     13,SAVSUB1+4
9.            LA     13,SAVSUB1
                     .
                     .
                     .
10.           L      13,SAVSUB1+4
11.           LM     14,12,12(13)
12.           BR     14
              END
```

Figure D.3
Sample subroutine.

The following explanations will clarify the purpose of each of the above instructions.

(5) The subroutine is assigned the symbolic name SUB1 with the START instruction.

(6) The STM instruction saves the status of the registers in the save area of the MAIN program. The contents of registers 14, 15, 0, ..., 12 are transmitted to the storage area beginning with storage location 12(13). Recall that a displacement of 12 is added to the address stored in register 13. This address therefore references the *fourth* word in the area called SAVMAIN.

(7) Establishes the base register.

(8) The address of the main save area (SAVMAIN) is placed in the *second word* of the subroutine save area (SAVSUB1). (SAVSUB1 is defined as DS 18F in the subroutine.) This is the *key* to accessing the save area of the main program later and restoring the registers to their original status.

(9) In case another subroutine is called, the address of the save area in SUB1 is loaded into register 13 in accordance with the linkage conventions established by IBM.

(10) Once the subroutine is completed, the address of the main save area (SAVMAIN) (the key to returning the registers to their original status) is loaded into register 13.

(11) Starting with the fourth word in SAVMAIN, all of the general registers with the exception of register 13 are restored to their original status by the LM instruction.

(12) The BR instruction returns control to the entry point in MAIN. Remember, register 14 originally contained the return address, and it was restored to this status.

In summary, here are the steps taken thus far in both the main program and the subroutine.

Main Program

1. Establish an 18-word save area.
2. Load the address of the save area (SAVMAIN) into register 13.

3. Load the entry point of the subroutine into register 15.
4. Load the return address into register 14 and branch to the subroutine.

Subroutine

1. Store the contents of the registers in the save area of the calling program.
2. Save the address of the main (or calling program) in the second word of the subroutine's save area (SAVSUB1).
3. Load the subroutine's save area address in register 13 in case another subroutine is called from SUB1.
4. Upon completing the subroutine, restore register 13 with the address of the main save area (SAVMAIN).
5. Restore registers 14, 15, 0, 1, 2, . . ., 12.
6. Return to the entry point contained in register 14.

D. OS Linkage Conventions

With OS (Operating System) and VS (Virtual Storage), the main program is treated as if it were a subroutine of the supervisor. All of the steps outlined in the preceding section for subroutines are utilized in the *main program*. Notice that the housekeeping routines prescribed in Chapter 4 for OS are *identical* to those developed in this Appendix.

E. DOS Standard Linkage Conventions

In Disk Operating Systems (DOS), the main program is not treated as a subroutine, but is handled differently. Actually, the DOS linkage conventions are simpler than those of OS and require the *removal* of a few instructions. The STM and LM instructions at the beginning of the program, for example, are unnecessary and *must* be omitted. The BR 14 instruction is replaced with the EOJ macro instruction. It is to be noted that the housekeeping routines specified in Chapter 4 incorporate all of the instructions necessary to set up a main program in DOS.

Figure D.4 illustrates the instructions to be added to a DOS main program to call a subroutine. Figure D.5 illustrates the instructions to be added to the DOS *subroutine*. Notice that the instructions in Figure D.5 are the same as the ones we have used in an OS *main* program.

LABEL	OPERATION 10	OPERAND 16	COMMENTS
* DOS MAIN PROGRAM SHELL FOR CALLING A SUBROUTINE			
MAIN	START	0	
	BALR	12,0	
	USING	*,12	
*			
	LA	13,SAVMAIN	CALLING PROGRAM SUBROUTINE LINKAGE
	L	15,=V(HDGRTN)	POINT REG 13 TO SAVE AREA
	LA	14,RETRNPT	LOAD EXTERNAL ENTRY POINTS
	BAL	14,15	SET UP RETURN ADDRESS
			CALL HDGRTN
*			
RETRNPT	•		
	•		
	EOJ		
*			
SAVMAIN	DS	18F	

Figure D.4
Instructions to be added to a DOS main program to call a subroutine.

```
  LABEL    OPERATION          OPERAND                              COMMENTS
1           10       16                                                                            72
*  OS AND DOS  SUBROUTINE SHELL
*
HDGRTN   START  0
         STM    14,12,12(13)   SAVE REGISTERS IN SAVMAIN
         BALR   12,0
         USING  *,12
         ST     13,SAVSUB1+4   SAVE KEY TO SAVMAIN
           .
           .
           .
         L      13,SAVSUB1+4   FETCH KEY
         LM     14,12,12(13)   RESTORE REGISTERS
         BR     14             RETURN
SAVSUB1  DS     18F
           .
           .
           .
         END
```

Figure D.5
Instructions to be added to a DOS subroutine.

F. External References

In our program, we coded L 15,=V(SUB1) to store the entry address of SUB1 in register 15. The following setup shows several other possibilities.

```
    LA    15,SUB1  or        LA    15,SUB
                                     .
                                     .
                             SUB DC   A(SUB1)
```

The second example you will recall is an A-type of address or ADCON. In both of these examples, the address of SUB1 must be available within the program. By definition, external subroutines are not part of the main program, but are separate entities. The entry address of a subroutine represents an external symbol since it is not addressable within our main program. The linkage editor resolves the addresses of the object modules at execution time. This means that V-type addresses signal the linkage editor that an external address (SUB1) is to be located and made available to the main program.

Figure D.6 illustrates an entire DOS main program that calls in an external subroutine (Figure D.7).

```
*                                                                              *
*                                   HOUSEKEEPING INSTRUCTIONS GO HERE    *
*                                                                              *
         BALR   12,0
         USING  *,12
         OPEN   INFILE,OUTFILE
         LA     13,SAVMAIN      POINT REG 13 TO SAVE AREA
         LA     14,READ         SET UP RETURN ADDRESS
         L      15,=V(HDGRTN)   LOAD EXTERNAL ENTRY
         BALR   14,15              CALL HEADING ROUTINE
READ     GET    INFILE,CARDIN
         BAL    5,DETLINE
         B      READ
DETLINE  ST     5,SAVE2
         CP     LINES,=P'25'
```

Figure D.6
Sample program that calls in an external subroutine. (continued on next page)

```
                 BL      SKIP
                 LA      13,SAVMAIN      POINT REG 13 TO SAVE AREA
                 LA      14,ZERO         SET UP RETURN ADDRESS
                 L       15,=V(HDGRTN)      LOAD EXTERNAL ENTRY
                 BALR    14,15              CALL HEADING ROUTINE
        ZERO     ZAP     LINES,=P'0'
        SKIP     MVC     LINEOUT,SPACES
                 MVC     PARTO,PART
                 MVC     DESCO,DESC
                 PUT     OUTFILE,LINEOUT
                 AP      LINES,=P'1'
                 L       5,SAVE2
                 BR      5
        EOF      CLOSE   INFILE,OUTFILE
                 EOJ
        *                                                           *
        *                                  DTF MACROS & IOAREA DS'S GO HERE   *
        *                                                           *
        SAVMAIN  DS      18F
        SAVE2    DS      F
        LINES    DC      PL2'0'
        SPACES   DC      CL1' '
        LINEOUT  DS      0CL132
                 DS      CL46
        PARTO    DS      CL4
                 DS      CL6
        DESCO    DS      CL20
                 DS      CL56
        CARDIN   DS      0CL80
        PART     DS      CL4
        DESC     DS      CL20
                 DS      CL56
                 END
```

Figure D.6
(continued).

```
        HDGRTN   START   0
                 PRINT   NOGEN
                 STM     14,12,12(13)    SAVE REGISTERS IN MAIN PROGRAM
                 BALR    12,0
                 USING   *,12
                 ST      13,SAVSUB1+4    SAVE KEY TO SAVMAIN
                 OPEN    OUTFILE
                 CNTRL   OUTFILE,SK,1
                 MVC     LINEOUT,SPACES
                 MVC     LINEOUT+45(27),=C'MY-T-FINE AUTO SUPPLY CORP.'
                 CNTRL   OUTFILE,SP,,3
                 PUT     OUTFILE,LINEOUT
                 CLOSE   OUTFILE
                 L       13,SAVSUB1+4    FETCH KEY
                 LM      14,12,12(13)    RESTORE REGISTERS
                 BR      14              RETURN TO MAIN
        SPACES   DC      C' '
        LINEOUT  DS      CL132
        SAVSUB1  DS      18F
        *                                                           *
        *                                  OUTFILE DTF & IOAREA1 DS GO HERE    *
        *                                                           *
                 END
```

Figure D.7
External subroutine called in
by the program in Figure D.6.

 **Generating IOCS Modules for DOS Systems**

In a DOS system, there are several hundred IOCS (Input/Output Control System) routines and options available to the programmer. In its relocatable library, each installation will catalog those routines frequently used by its programming personnel. These input–output routines are therefore available and automatically incorporated in the module being assembled and executed.

However, if a routine is not commonly used and is therefore not available in the relocatable library, an error message will be issued by the "link edit" program, indicating an unresolved external reference.

If your system does not include any desired IOCS routine, it can be generated by including an XXMOD macro in your program, where XX = CD or PR. The macros CDMOD (card module) and PRMOD (print module) will generate the appropriate IOCS routines for the corresponding DTF. The modules in the following section are described, and the default options are underlined. When an operand is omitted, the default option is automatically assumed by the system.

I. PRMOD

The operands are

$$RECFORM = \begin{bmatrix} FIXUNB \\ VARUNB \\ UNDEF \end{bmatrix}$$

$$CTLCHR = \begin{bmatrix} YES \\ ASA \end{bmatrix}$$

CONTROL = YES
PRINTOV = YES
IOAREA2 = YES
WORKA = YES

The options selected cause the generation of a module that will correctly support the specified DTFPR. The print module is referenced by a code, IJDabcde, and listed in the External Symbol Dictionary where the following are substituted for abcde.

a = F, V, or U, depending on RECFORM
b = Y if CTLCHR=YES; A if CTLCHR=ASA; C if CONTROL=YES; and Z if neither is specified
c = P for PRINTOV; Z without PRINTOV
d = I for IOAREA2; Z without it
e = W for WORKA; Z without it

Thus, a module listed in the External Symbol Dictionary as IJDFCPZW, for example, supports a DTFPR specifying fixed-length records, use of the control (CNTRL) and print overflow (PRINTOV) macros, and a work area.

The print module would be specified in the program as

LABEL	OPERATION	OPERAND	COMMENTS
1	10 16		72
	PRMOD	CONTROL=YES,PRINTOV=YES,WORKA=YES	

In a similar manner, the card module is defined as follows.

$$
\text{RECFORM} = \begin{bmatrix} \underline{\text{FIXUNB}} \\ \text{VARUNB} \\ \text{UNDEF} \end{bmatrix}
$$

$$
\text{CTLCHR} = \begin{bmatrix} \text{YES} \\ \text{ASA} \end{bmatrix}
$$

$$
\text{CONTROL} = \text{YES}
$$

$$
\text{TYPEFLE} = \begin{bmatrix} \underline{\text{INPUT}} \\ \text{OUTPUT} \\ \text{CMBND} \end{bmatrix}
$$

$$
\text{WORKA} = \text{YES}
$$

$$
\text{IOAREA2} = \text{YES}
$$

$$
\text{DEVICE} = \begin{bmatrix} \underline{2540} \\ 1442 \\ 2501 \\ 2520 \end{bmatrix}
$$

$$
\text{CRDERR} = \text{RETRY}
$$

The card module is referenced by a code IJCabcde where the following are substituted for abcde.

a = F, V, or U depending on RECFORM
b = Y if CTLCHR=YES; A if CTLCHR=ASA; C if CONTROL=YES; and Z if neither is specified
c = I, O, or C, depending on TYPEFLE
d = W for WORKA; I for IOAREA2; B for both; and Z for neither
e = 0 for 2540; 1 for 1442; 2 for 2520; 3 for 2501; 4 for 2540 and CRDERR; 5 for 2520 and CRDERR.

A module listed in the External Symbol Dictionary as IJCFZIWO, for example, supports a DTFCD specifying fixed-length records, an input type of file, a 2540 card reader, and a work area.

The card module would be specified as

LABEL	OPERATION	OPERAND	COMMENTS
1	10 16		72
	CDMOD	WORKA=YES	

Additional Explanations of Housekeeping Routines

I. THE BALR INSTRUCTION

The BALR (Branch and Link Register) instruction is frequently used to load the base register. When establishing a base register, the branch to the address contained in the second operand is to be eliminated. This is done by specifying zero as the second operand. For example, the instruction,

LABEL	OPERATION		OPERAND	COMMENTS	
1	10	16			72
	BALR		12,0		

causes the address of the next instruction to be placed in register 12. However, *no* branch will occur because the second operand contains a zero. We are still able to continue with the next sequential instruction. When establishing a base register, the USING instruction immediately follows the BALR.

II. THE USING INSTRUCTION

The USING instruction is used to indicate the base register to the assembler. It is a nonexecutable instruction. This means that it does not appear in the object program, *but only provides information to the assembler.* The USING instruction

1. Identifies the register to be used as a base register (the second operand).
2. Specifies a storage location that is to be the starting point (the first operand).

The general format of the USING instruction is as follows.

Operation 10	Operand 16
USING	LOC,REG

where

USING   is a nonexecutable instruction necessary to set up a base register

LOC   denotes a storage location to be used as the base address or starting point of the program

REG   is a general register (2–12) identified as the base register

For example, the following USING instruction

```
        USING BEGIN,12
BEGIN   MVI   FLDA,C'A'
```

specifies register 12 as the base register, and the instruction labeled BEGIN as the first executable instruction in the program.

Recall that a block or module of 4096 bytes is serviced by one register. When a program is longer than 4096 bytes, more than one base register must be specified.

The instruction USING*,12 simply points to the next sequential instruction, as well as establishing 12 as the base register. To establish two base registers, each for one module of 4096 bytes, we may use the following.

LABEL	OPERATION		OPERAND	COMMENTS	
1	10	16			72
	USING		BEGIN,12,11		

Note that register 11 must be set up to contain BEGIN plus 4096. This is accomplished with the coding in Figure F.1.

Figure F.1
Coding to set up register 11 as a second base register.

```
          USING BEGIN,12,11
BEGIN     LR    11,12
          A     11,=F'4096'
```

We add 4096 to the base address contained in register 12. If the program exceeded 8192 bytes, then another register would be specified as in Figure F.2.

The address stored in register 10 is BEGIN plus 8192. Remember, the USING instruction merely informs the assembler of the base address or starting point. The programmer must load the value of BEGIN, the first instruction in our example, into the base register.

Figure F.2
Coding to establish three base registers.

```
          USING BEGIN,12,11,10
BEGIN     LR    11,12
          A     11,=F'4096'
          LR    10,12
          A     10,=F'8192'
```

III. SETTING UP THE BASE REGISTER

To load the base register and identify it to the assembler, two instructions are necessary at the beginning of the program, as in Figure F.3.

The BALR instruction stores the address of the next instruction in register 12. A branch does not occur because of the zero specified in the second operand. Because the USING instruction does *not* occupy space in the object program, the address of the BEGIN instruction is stored in register 12 when the program is ready to be executed.

From this point on, all addresses assigned by the assembler will utilize the base address as well as the displacements resulting from the instructions. At execution time, the BALR instruction takes the actual address of the store instruction in the above example and places that address in the base register. The actual address depends on where the program was loaded by the system.

Remember, programs are relocatable. The system may decide to locate the program at location 4000 one time and at 8000 another. This does not present a problem, because the BALR instruction will store the *actual address* of the next instruction in the base register.

The BALR instruction has an RR format and is thus 2 bytes long. Consequently, in the above example, the address placed in register 12 will be the starting address plus 2.

Figure F.3
Coding to load the base register and identify it to the assembler.

```
          BALR  12,0
          USING BEGIN,12
BEGIN     ST    13,SAVEAREA+4
```

Example F.1 Starting address: 4000   Base register: 4002

Example F.2 Starting address: 8000   Base register: 8002

Our starting address and base address are not the same. This sometimes causes confusion in reading dumps, because students tend to confuse the two. It is the starting point (load-point) that is most frequently utilized in reading dumps.

In summary, the designation and assignment of base registers are house-keeping operations that must be carried out so that a program can be relocated and addressed by the computer.

IV. LOAD MULTIPLE (LM)

The LM instruction is an extension of the Load (L) instruction. However, with the Load Multiple, up to 16 fullwords of consecutive storage may be loaded into all 16 registers.

Operation 10	Operand 16
LM	REG1,REG2,LOC

where

LM	indicates a Load Multiple operation
REG1	is the first register to be loaded
REG2	is the last register to be loaded
LOC	identifies the storage area where loading is to start

The storage areas must be consecutive fields, each being a fullword in length.

```
        LM      5,8,FLD1
                .
                .
                .
FLD1    DC      F'1'
FLD2    DC      F'2'
FLD3    DC      F'3'
FLD4    DC      F'4'
```

Figure F.4
Sample LM instruction.

For example, the instruction in Figure F.4 produces the following results.

Before Execution		After Execution	
Register	Contents	Register	Contents
5	?	5	00 00 00 01
6	?	6	00 00 00 02
7	?	7	00 00 00 03
8	?	8	00 00 00 04

Note that registers from 5 through 8 inclusively are loaded from consecutive locations with this single instruction.

An important consideration of this instruction is the wraparound feature. This means that the registers are arranged in ascending sequence (0,1,2, . . ., 15), with register 0 following register 15. Therefore, the instruction

LABEL	OPERATION 10 16	OPERAND	COMMENTS 72
	LM	14,2,FLWD	

would load the five registers 14, 15, 0, 1, 2.

Most important,

LABEL	OPERATION	OPERAND	COMMENTS
1	10 16		72
	LM	14,12,SAVE	

would load 15 registers, beginning with register 14. A block of 15 fullwords would be loaded starting from the storage location called SAVE. All of the general registers would be loaded with this instruction, with the exception of register 13.

V. STORE MULTIPLE INSTRUCTION (STM)

The Store Multiple (STM) instruction reverses the process of the Load Multiple (LM) instruction. The contents of the sending registers are transmitted to consecutive locations in main storage. As with the Store (ST) instruction the first operand is the *sending* field, and the second operand is the receiving field.

We may store the contents of as many as 16 registers in consecutive fullwords in main storage with one STM instruction.

Example F.3

LABEL	OPERATION	OPERAND	COMMENTS
1	10 16		72
	STM	5,8,SAVE	

Register	Contents	Storage Before Execution		Storage After Execution	
5	00 00 00 01	SAVE	01 23 34 56	SAVE	00 00 00 01
6	00 00 00 02	SAVE+4	06 54 32 10	SAVE+4	00 00 00 02
7	00 00 00 03	SAVE+8	01 35 78 98	SAVE+8	00 00 00 03
8	00 00 00 04	SAVE+12	08 34 56 75	SAVE+12	00 00 00 04

The wraparound feature described in the LM instruction is an available option when using the STM. For external subroutine linkages, the STM and LM are used extensively. The STM is used to place the contents of registers in a storage area. Later, the registers are restored to their original status with the LM instruction.

Shells for DOS and OS Programs

I. SHELL FOR DOS PROGRAM

LABEL	OPERATION	OPERAND	COMMENTS
	PRINT	NOGEN	
	START	[PLACE NAME OF PROGRAM IN COLS. 1-8]	
	BALR	12,Ø	
	USING	*,12	
	OPEN	INFILE,OUTFILE	
CLEAR	MVC	OUTAREA,SPACES	
	GET	INFILE,RECORD	
** LOGIC	GOES	HERE	
**	:		
	PUT	OUTFILE,OUTAREA	
	B	CLEAR	
** INCLUDE END-OF-JOB ROUTINES HERE, THEN CLOSE. IF NO EOJ ROUTINE INCL:			
EOF	CLOSE	INFILE,OUTFILE	
	EOJ		
INFILE	DTFCD	DEVADDR=SYSIPT,BLKSIZE=8Ø,IOAREA1=BUFFRIN,WORKA=YES,	*
		DEVICE=25Ø1,TYPEFLE=INPUT,EOFADDR=EOF	
OUTFILE	DTFPR	DEVADDR=SYSLST,BLKSIZE=132,IOAREA1=BUFFROUT,WORKA=YES,	*
		DEVICE=32Ø3	
BUFFRIN	DS	CL8Ø	
BUFFROUT	DS	CL132	
RECORD	DS	ØCL8Ø	
** PLACE	DS'S FOR FIELDS IN INPUT RECORD HERE		
SPACES	DC	CL`` '	
OUTAREA	DS	ØCL132	
** PLACE DS'S FOR FIELDS IN OUTPUT RECORD HERE—INCLUDING BLANK AREAS			
** ALL OTHER DS'S AND DC'S NECESSARY FOR PROCESSING GO HERE			
	END		

II. SHELL FOR OS PROGRAM

LABEL	OPERATION	OPERAND	COMMENTS	
	PRINT	NOGEN		
	START	[PLACE NAME OF PROGRAM IN COLS 1-8]		
	STM	14,12,12(13)		
	BALR	12,∅		
	USING	*,12		
	ST	13,SAVEAREA+4		
	LA	13,SAVEAREA		
	OPEN	(INFILE,INPUT,OUTFILE,OUTPUT)		
CLEAR	MVC	OUTAREA,SPACES		
	GET	INFILE,RECORD		
** LOGIC	GOES	HERE		
**	:			
	PUT	OUTFILE,OUTAREA		
	B	CLEAR		
** INCLUDE END-OF-JOB ROUTINES HERE THEN CLOSE;IF NO EOJ ROUTINE INCL:				
EOF	CLOSE	(INFILE,,OUTFILE)		
	L	13,SAVEAREA+4		
	LM	14,12,12(13)		
	BR	14		
SAVEAREA	DS	18F		
RECORD	DS	∅CL8∅		
** PLACE	DS'S	FOR FIELDS IN INPUT RECORD HERE		
SPACES	DC	CL1` '		
OUTAREA	DS	∅CL132		
** PLACE	DS'S	FOR FIELDS IN OUTPUT RECORD HERE-INCLUDING BLANK AREAS		
INFILE	DCB	DDNAME=INFILE,MACRF=GM,BLKSIZE=8∅,LRECL=8∅,DSORG=PS,		*
		EODAD=EOF		
OUTFILE	DCB	DDNAME=OUTFILE,MACRF=PM,BLKSIZE=132,LRECL=132,DSORG=PS		
	END			

Features of Operating Systems

The differences between OS and DOS have been presented throughout the text. It should be noted, however, that due to the development of virtual storage (VS) systems, a particular computer may actually be running under DOS/VS or OS/VS. The following discussion introduces the concept of virtual storage and suggests ways to write more efficient assembler language programs when VS is available.

Virtual storage involves the dynamic interaction between primary storage of the CPU and auxiliary storage on a direct-access device such as magnetic disk. As a consequence of this interaction, it is possible to treat the computer as if it has more primary storage than it actually does. Thus, for example, a computer with a CPU capacity of 256,000 bytes can be made to appear as if it has, instead, several million bytes.

The basic idea of a virtual storage system is that when a program is written, it is broken into various segments. Each segment, sometimes referred to as a *page*, is then transferred from auxiliary storage into the CPU, one at a time. After a page has been executed, the next page to be executed is transferred into the CPU, thereby overlaying the previous page, which then is no longer needed. It is this efficient management of the allocation and use of storage within the CPU that allows a virtual storage system to appear larger than it really is.

Here are some of the advantages of virtual storage.

1. Very large programs can be run more easily. On systems that do not utilize virtual storage, it is sometimes difficult to fit a large program in its entirety into a relatively small CPU. You will recall that part of the CPU always has a supervisor program in it to control the operations of the system. In addition, there may be other programs in the CPU if the system has multiprogramming capability. Thus, without virtual storage, it is sometimes necessary to expend much effort in trying to reduce the size of a program so that it is manageable.
2. On-line systems can handle many more terminals because more efficient management of primary storage is possible with virtual storage.
3. It is possible, in general, for a high-priority job to be started without seriously disrupting any jobs that are running.

The question arises as to whether or not a virtual storage system affects programming logic when writing a program in assembler language. The answer is yes and no. It is possible to program in assembler language without paying any attention at all to the virtual storage feature of most computers. What is sacrificed by this approach is efficiency.

If an assembler language programmer wishes to maximize both the efficiency of the program and the virtual storage capability of the computer, then certain techniques may be employed when writing the program.

One suggestion is to segment your program so that fields in storage operated on by particular instructions are defined near those instructions. In this way, accessing data will be made easier because these instructions and the corresponding data being referenced will be contained within the same page in the CPU.

Similarly, if your program requires an external subroutine that is relatively short and that is used only a few times during execution, it should be coded within the main program. In this manner, it is possible to have contained within one page all the necessary logic for processing a particular phase of the program.

It is recommended that you check the reference manual for the particular operating system on your computer for further details on how you can take full advantage of the virtual storage concept.

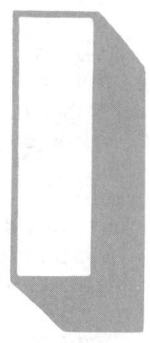

Reference Summary for IBM Computers[1]

MACHINE INSTRUCTIONS

②

NAME	MNEMONIC	OP CODE	FORMAT	OPERANDS
Add (c)	AR	1A	RR	R1,R2
Add (c)	A	5A	RX	R1,D2(X2,B2)
Add Decimal (c)	AP	FA	SS	D1(L1,B1),D2(L2,B2)
Add Halfword (c)	AH	4A	RX	R1,D2(X2,B2)
Add Logical (c)	ALR	1E	RR	R1,R2
Add Logical (c)	AL	5E	RX	R1,D2(X2,B2)
AND (c)	NR	14	RR	R1,R2
AND (c)	N	54	RX	R1,D2(X2,B2)
AND (c)	NI	94	SI	D1(B1),I2
AND (c)	NC	D4	SS	D1(L,B1),D2(B2)
Branch and Link	BALR	05	RR	R1,R2
Branch and Link	BAL	45	RX	R1,D2(X2,B2)
Branch on Condition	BCR	07	RR	M1,R2
Branch on Condition	BC	47	RX	M1,D2(X2,B2)
Branch on Count	BCTR	06	RR	R1,R2
Branch on Count	BCT	46	RX	R1,D2(X2,B2)
Branch on Index High	BXH	86	RS	R1,R3,D2(B2)
Branch on Index Low or Equal	BXLE	87	RS	R1,R3,D2(B2)
Clear I/O (c,p)	CLRIO	9D01	S	D2(B2)
Compare (c)	CR	19	RR	R1,R2
Compare (c)	C	59	RX	R1,D2(X2,B2)
Compare and Swap (c)	CS	BA	RS	R1,R3,D2(B2)
Compare Decimal (c)	CP	F9	SS	D1(L1,B1),D2(L2,B2)
Compare Double and Swap (c)	CDS	BB	RS	R1,R3,D2(B2)
Compare Halfword (c)	CH	49	RX	R1,D2(X2,B2)
Compare Logical (c)	CLR	15	RR	R1,R2
Compare Logical (c)	CL	55	RX	R1,D2(X2,B2)
Compare Logical (c)	CLC	D5	SS	D1(L,B1),D2(B2)
Compare Logical (c)	CLI	95	SI	D1(B1),I2
Compare Logical Characters under Mask (c)	CLM	BD	RS	R1,M3,D2(B2)
Compare Logical Long (c)	CLCL	0F	RR	R1,R2
Convert to Binary	CVB	4F	RX	R1,D2(X2,B2)
Convert to Decimal	CVD	4E	RX	R1,D2(X2,B2)
Diagnose (p)		83		Model-dependent
Divide	DR	1D	RR	R1,R2
Divide	D	5D	RX	R1,D2(X2,B2)
Divide Decimal	DP	FD	SS	D1(L1,B1),D2(L2,B2)
Edit (c)	ED	DE	SS	D1(L,B1),D2(B2)
Edit and Mark (c)	EDMK	DF	SS	D1(L,B1),D2(B2)
Exclusive OR (c)	XR	17	RR	R1,R2
Exclusive OR (c)	X	57	RX	R1,D2(X2,B2)
Exclusive OR (c)	XI	97	SI	D1(B1),I2
Exclusive OR (c)	XC	D7	SS	D1(L,B1),D2(B2)
Execute	EX	44	RX	R1,D2(X2,B2)
Halt I/O (c,p)	HIO	9E00	S	D2(B2)
Halt Device (c,p)	HDV	9E01	S	D2(B2)
Insert Character	IC	43	RX	R1,D2(X2,B2)
Insert Characters under Mask (c)	ICM	BF	RS	R1,M3,D2(B2)
Insert PSW Key (p)	IPK	B20B	S	
Insert Storage Key (p)	ISK	09	RR	R1,R2
Load	LR	18	RR	R1,R2
Load	L	58	RX	R1,D2(X2,B2)
Load Address	LA	41	RX	R1,D2(X2,B2)
Load and Test (c)	LTR	12	RR	R1,R2
Load Complement (c)	LCR	13	RR	R1,R2
Load Control (p)	LCTL	B7	RS	R1,R3,D2(B2)
Load Halfword	LH	48	RX	R1,D2(X2,B2)
Load Multiple	LM	98	RS	R1,R3,D2(B2)
Load Negative (c)	LNR	11	RR	R1,R2
Load Positive (c)	LPR	10	RR	R1,R2
Load PSW (n,p)	LPSW	82	S	D2(B2)
Load Real Address (c,p)	LRA	B1	RX	R1,D2(X2,B2)
Monitor Call	MC	AF	SI	D1(B1),I2
Move	MVI	92	SI	D1(B1),I2
Move	MVC	D2	SS	D1(L,B1),D2(B2)
Move Long (c)	MVCL	0E	RR	R1,R2
Move Numerics	MVN	D1	SS	D1(L,B1),D2(B2)
Move with Offset	MVO	F1	SS	D1(L1,B1),D2(L2,B2)
Move Zones	MVZ	D3	SS	D1(L,B1),D2(B2)
Multiply	MR	1C	RR	R1,R2
Multiply	M	5C	RX	R1,D2(X2,B2)
Multiply Decimal	MP	FC	SS	D1(L1,B1),D2(L2,B2)
Multiply Halfword	MH	4C	RX	R1,D2(X2,B2)
OR (c)	OR	16	RR	R1,R2

[1]Reprinted by permission of International Business Machines Corporation.

MACHINE INSTRUCTIONS (Contd) ③

NAME	MNEMONIC	OP CODE	FORMAT	OPERANDS
OR (c)	O	56	RX	R1,D2(X2,B2)
OR (c)	OI	96	SI	D1(B1),I2
OR (c)	OC	D6	SS	D1(L,B1),D2(B2)
Pack	PACK	F2	SS	D1(L1,B1),D2(L2,B2)
Purge TLB (p)	PTLB	B20D	S	
Read Direct (p)	RDD	85	SI	D1(B1),I2
Reset Reference Bit (c,p)	RRB	B213	S	D2(B2)
Set Clock (c,p)	SCK	B204	S	D2(B2)
Set Clock Comparator (p)	SCKC	B206	S	D2(B2)
Set CPU Timer (p)	SPT	B208	S	D2(B2)
Set Prefix (p)	SPX	B210	S	D2(B2)
Set Program Mask (n)	SPM	04	RR	R1
Set PSW Key from Address (p)	SPKA	B20A	S	D2(B2)
Set Storage Key (p)	SSK	08	RR	R1,R2
Set System Mask (p)	SSM	80	S	D2(B2)
Shift and Round Decimal (c)	SRP	F0	SS	D1(L1,B1),D2(B2),I3
Shift Left Double (c)	SLDA	8F	RS	R1,D2(B2)
Shift Left Double Logical	SLDL	8D	RS	R1,D2(B2)
Shift Left Single (c)	SLA	8B	RS	R1,D2(B2)
Shift Left Single Logical	SLL	89	RS	R1,D2(B2)
Shift Right Double (c)	SRDA	8E	RS	R1,D2(B2)
Shift Right Double Logical	SRDL	8C	RS	R1,D2(B2)
Shift Right Single (c)	SRA	8A	RS	R1,D2(B2)
Shift Right Single Logical	SRL	88	RS	R1,D2(B2)
Signal Processor (c,p)	SIGP	AE	RS	R1,R3,D2(B2)
Start I/O (c,p)	SIO	9C00	S	D2(B2)
Start I/O Fast Release (c,p)	SIOF	9C01	S	D2(B2)
Store	ST	50	RX	R1,D2(X2,B2)
Store Channel ID (c,p)	STIDC	B203	S	D2(B2)
Store Character	STC	42	RX	R1,D2(X2,B2)
Store Characters under Mask	STCM	BE	RS	R1,M3,D2(B2)
Store Clock (c)	STCK	B205	S	D2(B2)
Store Clock Comparator (p)	STCKC	B207	S	D2(B2)
Store Control (p)	STCTL	B6	RS	R1,R3,D2(B2)
Store CPU Address (p)	STAP	B212	S	D2(B2)
Store CPU ID (p)	STIDP	B202	S	D2(B2)
Store CPU Timer (p)	STPT	B209	S	D2(B2)
Store Halfword	STH	40	RX	R1,D2(X2,B2)
Store Multiple	STM	90	RS	R1,R3,D2(B2)
Store Prefix (p)	STPX	B211	S	D2(B2)
Store Then AND System Mask (p)	STNSM	AC	SI	D1(B1),I2
Store Then OR System Mask (p)	STOSM	AD	SI	D1(B1),I2
Subtract (c)	SR	1B	RR	R1,R2
Subtract (c)	S	5B	RX	R1,D2(X2,B2)
Subtract Decimal (c)	SP	FB	SS	D1(L1,B1),D2(L2,B2)
Subtract Halfword (c)	SH	4B	RX	R1,D2(X2,B2)
Subtract Logical (c)	SLR	1F	RR	R1,R2
Subtract Logical (c)	SL	5F	RX	R1,D2(X2,B2)
Supervisor Call	SVC	0A	RR	I
Test and Set (c)	TS	93	S	D2(B2)
Test Channel (c,p)	TCH	9F00	S	D2(B2)
Test I/O (c,p)	TIO	9D00	S	D2(B2)
Test under Mask (c)	TM	91	SI	D1(B1),I2
Translate	TR	DC	SS	D1(L,B1),D2(B2)
Translate and Test (c)	TRT	DD	SS	D1(L,B1),D2(B2)
Unpack	UNPK	F3	SS	D1(L1,B1),D2(L2,B2)
Write Direct (p)	WRD	84	SI	D1(B1),I2
Zero and Add Decimal (c)	ZAP	F8	SS	D1(L1,B1),D2(L2,B2)

Floating-Point Instructions

NAME	MNEMONIC	OP CODE	FORMAT	OPERANDS
Add Normalized, Extended (c,x)	AXR	36	RR	R1,R2
Add Normalized, Long (c)	ADR	2A	RR	R1,R2
Add Normalized, Long (c)	AD	6A	RX	R1,D2(X2,B2)
Add Normalized, Short (c)	AER	3A	RR	R1,R2
Add Normalized, Short (c)	AE	7A	RX	R1,D2(X2,B2)
Add Unnormalized, Long (c)	AWR	2E	RR	R1,R2
Add Unnormalized, Long (c)	AW	6E	RX	R1,D2(X2,B2)
Add Unnormalized, Short (c)	AUR	3E	RR	R1,R2
Add Unnormalized, Short (c)	AU	7E	RX	R1,D2(X2,B2)

c. Condition code is set.
n. New condition code is loaded.

p. Privileged instruction.
x. Extended precision floating-point.

Floating-Point Instructions (Contd) ④

NAME	MNEMONIC	OP CODE	FORMAT	OPERANDS
Compare, Long (c)	CDR	29	RR	R1,R2
Compare, Long (c)	CD	69	RX	R1,D2(X2,B2)
Compare, Short (c)	CER	39	RR	R1,R2
Compare, Short (c)	CE	79	RX	R1,D2(X2,B2)
Divide, Long	DDR	2D	RR	R1,R2
Divide, Long	DD	6D	RX	R1,D2(X2,B2)
Divide, Short	DER	3D	RR	R1,R2
Divide, Short	DE	7D	RX	R1,D2(X2,B2)
Halve, Long	HDR	24	RR	R1,R2
Halve, Short	HER	34	RR	R1,R2
Load and Test, Long (c)	LTDR	22	RR	R1,R2
Load and Test, Short (c)	LTER	32	RR	R1,R2
Load Complement, Long (c)	LCDR	23	RR	R1,R2
Load Complement, Short (c)	LCER	33	RR	R1,R2
Load, Long	LDR	28	RR	R1,R2
Load, Long	LD	68	RX	R1,D2(X2,B2)
Load Negative, Long (c)	LNDR	21	RR	R1,R2
Load Negative, Short (c)	LNER	31	RR	R1,R2
Load Positive, Long (c)	LPDR	20	RR	R1,R2
Load Positive, Short (c)	LPER	30	RR	R1,R2
Load Rounded, Extended to Long (x)	LRDR	25	RR	R1,R2
Load Rounded, Long to Short (x)	LRER	35	RR	R1,R2
Load, Short	LER	38	RR	R1,R2
Load, Short	LE	78	RX	R1,D2(X2,B2)
Multiply, Extended (x)	MXR	26	RR	R1,R2
Multiply, Long	MDR	2C	RR	R1,R2
Multiply, Long	MD	6C	RX	R1,D2(X2,B2)
Multiply, Long/Extended (x)	MXDR	27	RR	R1,R2
Multiply, Long/Extended (x)	MXD	67	RX	R1,D2(X2,B2)
Multiply, Short	MER	3C	RR	R1,R2
Multiply, Short	ME	7C	RX	R1,D2(X2,B2)
Store, Long	STD	60	RX	R1,D2(X2,B2)
Store, Short	STE	70	RX	R1,D2(X2,B2)
Subtract Normalized, Extended (c,x)	SXR	37	RR	R1,R2
Subtract Normalized, Long (c)	SDR	2B	RR	R1,R2
Subtract Normalized, Long (c)	SD	6B	RX	R1,D2(X2,B2)
Subtract Normalized, Short (c)	SER	3B	RR	R1,R2
Subtract Normalized, Short (c)	SE	7B	RX	R1,D2(X2,B2)
Subtract Unnormalized, Long (c)	SWR	2F	RR	R1,R2
Subtract Unnormalized, Long (c)	SW	6F	RX	R1,D2(X2,B2)
Subtract Unnormalized, Short (c)	SUR	3F	RR	R1,R2
Subtract Unnormalized, Short (c)	SU	7F	RX	R1,D2(X2,B2)

EXTENDED MNEMONIC INSTRUCTIONS†

Use	Extended Code* (RX or RR)	Meaning	Machine Instr.* (RX or RR)
General	B or BR	Unconditional Branch	BC or BCR 15,
	NOP or NOPR	No Operation	BC or BCR 0,
After	BH or BHR	Branch on A High	BC or BCR 2,
Compare	BL or BLR	Branch on A Low	BC or BCR 4,
Instructions	BE or BER	Branch on A Equal B	BC or BCR 8,
(A:B)	BNH or BNHR	Branch on A Not High	BC or BCR 13,
	BNL or BNLR	Branch on A Not Low	BC or BCR 11,
	BNE or BNER	Branch on A Not Equal B	BC or BCR 7,
After	BO or BOR	Branch on Overflow	BC or BCR 1,
Arithmetic	BP or BPR	Branch on Plus	BC or BCR 2,
Instructions	BM or BMR	Branch on Minus	BC or BCR 4,
	BNP or BNPR	Branch on Not Plus	BC or BCR 13,
	BNM or BNMR	Branch on Not Minus	BC or BCR 11,
	BNZ or BNZR	Branch on Not Zero	BC or BCR 7,
	BZ or BZR	Branch on Zero	BC or BCR 8,
After Test	BO or BOR	Branch if Ones	BC or BCR 1,
under Mask	BM or BMR	Branch if Mixed	BC or BCR 4,
Instruction	BZ or BZR	Branch if Zeros	BC or BCR 8,
	BNO or BNOR	Branch if Not Ones	BC or BCR 14,

†Source: GC33-4010; for OS/VS, VM/370 and DOS/VS.

*Second operand, not shown, is D2(X2,B2) for RX format and R2 for RR format.

SOME EDIT AND EDMK PATTERN CHARACTERS (in hex)

20—digit selector	40—blank	5C—asterisk
21—start of significance	4B—period	6B—comma
22—field separator	5B—dollar sign	C3D9—CR

CONDITION CODES ⑤

Condition Code Setting	0	1	2	3
Mask Bit Value	8	4	2	1

General Instructions

Add, Add Halfword	zero	<zero	>zero	overflow
Add Logical	zero, no carry	not zero, no carry	zero, carry	not zero, carry
AND	zero	not zero	—	—
Compare, Compare Halfword	equal	1st op low	1st op high	—
Compare and Swap/Double	equal	not equal	—	—
Compare Logical	equal	1st op low	1st op high	—
Exclusive OR	zero	not zero	—	—
Insert Characters under Mask	all zero	1st bit one	1st bit zero	—
Load and Test	zero	<zero	>zero	—
Load Complement	zero	<zero	>zero	overflow
Load Negative	zero	<zero	—	—
Load Positive	zero	—	>zero	overflow
Move Long	count equal	count low	count high	overlap
OR	zero	not zero	—	—
Shift Left Double/Single	zero	<zero	>zero	overflow
Shift Right Double/Single	zero	<zero	>zero	—
Store Clock	set	not set	error	not oper
Subtract, Subtract Halfword	zero	<zero	>zero	overflow
Subtract Logical	—	not zero, no carry	zero, carry	not zero, carry
Test and Set	zero	one	—	—
Test under Mask	zero	mixed	—	ones
Translate and Test	zero	incomplete	complete	—

Decimal Instructions

Add Decimal	zero	<zero	>zero	overflow
Compare Decimal	equal	1st op low	1st op high	—
Edit, Edit and Mark	zero	<zero	>zero	—
Shift and Round Decimal	zero	<zero	>zero	overflow
Subtract Decimal	zero	<zero	>zero	overflow
Zero and Add	zero	<zero	>zero	overflow

Floating-Point Instructions

Add Normalized	zero	<zero	>zero	—
Add Unnormalized	zero	<zero	>zero	—
Compare	equal	1st op low	1st op high	—
Load and Test	zero	<zero	>zero	—
Load Complement	zero	<zero	>zero	—
Load Negative	zero	<zero	—	—
Load Positive	zero	—	>zero	—
Subtract Normalized	zero	<zero	>zero	—
Subtract Unnormalized	zero	<zero	>zero	—

Input/Output Instructions

Clear I/O	no oper in progress	CSW stored	chan busy	not oper
Halt Device	interruption pending	CSW stored	channel working	not oper
Halt I/O	interruption pending	CSW stored	burst op stopped	not oper
Start I/O, SIOF	successful	CSW stored	busy	not oper
Store Channel ID	ID stored	CSW stored	busy	not oper
Test Channel	available	interruption pending	burst mode	not oper
Test I/O	available	CSW stored	busy	not oper

System Control Instructions

Load Real Address	translation available	ST entry invalid	PT entry invalid	length violation
Reset Reference Bit	R=0, C=0	R=0, C=1	R=1, C=0	R=1, C=1
Set Clock	set	secure	—	not oper
Signal Processor	accepted	stat stored	busy	not oper

CNOP ALIGNMENT

DOUBLEWORD							
WORD				WORD			
HALFWORD		HALFWORD		HALFWORD		HALFWORD	
BYTE	BYTE	BYTE	BYTE	BYTE	BYTE	BYTE	BYTE
0,4 0,8		2,4 2,8		0,4 4,8		2,4 6,8	

ASSEMBLER INSTRUCTIONS† ⑥

Function	Mnemonic	Meaning
Data definition	DC	Define constant
	DS	Define storage
	CCW	Define channel command word
Program sectioning and linking	START	Start assembly
	CSECT	Identify control section
	DSECT	Identify dummy section
	DXD*	Define external dummy section
	CXD*	Cumulative length of external dummy section
	COM	Identify blank common control section
	ENTRY	Identify entry-point symbol
	EXTRN	Identify external symbol
	WXTRN	Identify weak external symbol
Base register assignment	USING	Use base address register
	DROP	Drop base address register
Control of listings	TITLE	Identify assembly output
	EJECT	Start new page
	SPACE	Space listing
	PRINT	Print optional data
Program Control	ICTL	Input format control
	ISEQ	Input sequence checking
	PUNCH	Punch a card
	REPRO	Reproduce following card
	ORG	Set location counter
	EQU	Equate symbol
	OPSYN*	Equate operation code
	PUSH	Save current PRINT or USING status
	POP	Restore PRINT or USING status
	LTORG	Begin literal pool
	CNOP	Conditional no operation
	COPY	Copy predefined source coding
	END	End assembly
Macro definition	MACRO	Macro definition header
	MNOTE	Request for error message
	MEXIT	Macro definition exit
	MEND	Macro definition trailer
Conditional assembly	ACTR	Conditional assembly loop counter
	AGO	Unconditional branch
	AIF	Conditional branch
	ANOP	Assembly no operation
	GBLA	Define global SETA symbol
	GBLB	Define global SETB symbol
	GBLC	Define global SETC symbol
	LCLA	Define local SETA symbol
	LCLB	Define local SETB symbol
	LCLC	Define local SETC symbol
	SETA	Set arithmetic variable symbol
	SETB	Set binary variable symbol
	SETC	Set character variable symbol

SUMMARY OF CONSTANTS†

TYPE	IMPLIED LENGTH, BYTES	ALIGNMENT	FORMAT	TRUNCATION/PADDING
C	–	byte	characters	right
X	–	byte	hexadecimal digits	left
B	–	byte	binary digits	left
F	4	word	fixed-point binary	left
H	2	halfword	fixed-point binary	left
E	4	word	short floating-point	right
D	8	doubleword	long floating-point	right
L	16	doubleword	extended floating-point	right
P	–	byte	packed decimal	left
Z	–	byte	zoned decimal	left
A	4	word	value of address	left
Y	2	halfword	value of address	left
S	2	halfword	address in base-displacement form	–
V	4	word	externally defined address value	left
Q*	4	word	symbol naming a DXD or DSECT	left

†Source: GC33-4010; for OS/VS, VM/370, and DOS/VS.
*OS/VS and VM/370 only.

CODE TRANSLATION TABLE (9)

Dec.	Hex	Instruction (RR)	BCDIC	EBCDIC(1)	ASCII	7-Track Tape BCDIC(2)	Card Code EBCDIC	Binary
0	00			NUL	NUL		12-0-1-8-9	0000 0000
1	01			SOH	SOH		12-1-9	0000 0001
2	02			STX	STX		12-2-9	0000 0010
3	03			ETX	ETX		12-3-9	0000 0011
4	04	SPM		PF	EOT		12-4-9	0000 0100
5	05	BALR		HT	ENQ		12-5-9	0000 0101
6	06	BCTR		LC	ACK		12-6-9	0000 0110
7	07	BCR		DEL	BEL		12-7-9	0000 0111
8	08	SSK		GE	BS		12-8-9	0000 1000
9	09	ISK		RLF	HT		12-1-8-9	0000 1001
10	0A	SVC		SMM	LF		12-2-8-9	0000 1010
11	0B			VT	VT		12-3-8-9	0000 1011
12	0C			FF	FF		12-4-8-9	0000 1100
13	0D			CR	CR		12-5-8-9	0000 1101
14	0E	MVCL		SO	SO		12-6-8-9	0000 1110
15	0F	CLCL		SI	SI		12-7-8-9	0000 1111
16	10	LPR		DLE	DLE		12-11-1-8-9	0001 0000
17	11	LNR		DC1	DC1		11-1-9	0001 0001
18	12	LTR		DC2	DC2		11-2-9	0001 0010
19	13	LCR		TM	DC3		11-3-9	0001 0011
20	14	NR		RES	DC4		11-4-9	0001 0100
21	15	CLR		NL	NAK		11-5-9	0001 0101
22	16	OR		BS	SYN		11-6-9	0001 0110
23	17	XR		IL	ETB		11-7-9	0001 0111
24	18	LR		CAN	CAN		11-8-9	0001 1000
25	19	CR		EM	EM		11-1-8-9	0001 1001
26	1A	AR		CC	SUB		11-2-8-9	0001 1010
27	1B	SR		CU1	ESC		11-3-8-9	0001 1011
28	1C	MR		IFS	FS		11-4-8-9	0001 1100
29	1D	DR		IGS	GS		11-5-8-9	0001 1101
30	1E	ALR		IRS	RS		11-6-8-9	0001 1110
31	1F	SLR		IUS	US		11-7-8-9	0001 1111
32	20	LPDR		DS	SP		11-0-1-8-9	0010 0000
33	21	LNDR		SOS	!		0-1-9	0010 0001
34	22	LTDR		FS	"		0-2-9	0010 0010
35	23	LCDR			#		0-3-9	0010 0011
36	24	HDR		BYP	$		0-4-9	0010 0100
37	25	LRDR		LF	%		0-5-9	0010 0101
38	26	MXR		ETB	&		0-6-9	0010 0110
39	27	MXDR		ESC	'		0-7-9	0010 0111
40	28	LDR			(		0-8-9	0010 1000
41	29	CDR			)		0-1-8-9	0010 1001
42	2A	ADR		SM	*		0-2-8-9	0010 1010
43	2B	SDR		CU2	+		0-3-8-9	0010 1011
44	2C	MDR			,		0-4-8-9	0010 1100
45	2D	DDR		ENQ	-		0-5-8-9	0010 1101
46	2E	AWR		ACK	.		0-6-8-9	0010 1110
47	2F	SWR		BEL	/		0-7-8-9	0010 1111
48	30	LPER			0		12-11-0-1-8-9	0011 0000
49	31	LNER			1		1-9	0011 0001
50	32	LTER		SYN	2		2-9	0011 0010
51	33	LCER			3		3-9	0011 0011
52	34	HER		PN	4		4-9	0011 0100
53	35	LRER		RS	5		5-9	0011 0101
54	36	AXR		UC	6		6-9	0011 0110
55	37	SXR		EOT	7		7-9	0011 0111
56	38	IFR			8		8-9	0011 1000
57	39	CER			9		1-8-9	0011 1001
58	3A	AER			:		2-8-9	0011 1010
59	3B	SER		CU3	;		3-8-9	0011 1011
60	3C	MER		DC4	<		4-8-9	0011 1100
61	3D	DER		NAK	=		5-8-9	0011 1101
62	3E	AUR			>		6-8-9	0011 1110
63	3F	SUR		SUB	?		7-8-9	0011 1111

CODE TRANSLATION TABLE (Contd) (10)

Dec.	Hex	Instruction (RX)	BCDIC	EBCDIC(1)	ASCII	7-Track Tape BCDIC(2)	Card Code EBCDIC	Binary
64	40	STH		Sp Sp	@	(3)	no punches	0100 0000
65	41	LA			A		12-0-1-9	0100 0001
66	42	STC			B		12-0-2-9	0100 0010
67	43	IC			C		12-0-3-9	0100 0011
68	44	EX			D		12-0-4-9	0100 0100
69	45	BAL			E		12-0-5-9	0100 0101
70	46	BCT			F		12-0-6-9	0100 0110
71	47	BC			G		12-0-7-9	0100 0111
72	48	LH			H		12-0-8-9	0100 1000
73	49	CH			I		12-1-8	0100 1001
74	4A	AH		¢ ¢	J		12-2-8	0100 1010
75	4B	SH	.	. .	K	B A 8 2 1	12-3-8	0100 1011
76	4C	MH	□)	< <	L	B A 8 4	12-4-8	0100 1100
77	4D		[	((	M	B A 8 4 1	12-5-8	0100 1101
78	4E	CVD	<	+ +	N	B A 8 4 2	12-6-8	0100 1110
79	4F	CVB	‡	| |	O	B A 8 4 2 1	12-7-8	0100 1111
80	50	ST	& +	& &	P	B A	12	0101 0000
81	51				Q		12-11-1-9	0101 0001
82	52				R		12-11-2-9	0101 0010
83	53				S		12-11-3-9	0101 0011
84	54	N			T		12-11-4-9	0101 0100
85	55	CL			U		12-11-5-9	0101 0101
86	56	O			V		12-11-6-9	0101 0110
87	57	X			W		12-11-7-9	0101 0111
88	58	L			X		12-11-8-9	0101 1000
89	59	C			Y		11-1-8	0101 1001
90	5A	A		! !	Z		11-2-8	0101 1010
91	5B	S	$	$ $	[	B 8 2 1	11-3-8	0101 1011
92	5C	M	*	* *	\	B 8 4	11-4-8	0101 1100
93	5D	D	]	))	]	B 8 4 1	11-5-8	0101 1101
94	5E	AL	;	; ;	¬ ^	B 8 4 2	11-6-8	0101 1110
95	5F	SL	Δ	¬ ¬	_	B 8 4 2 1	11-7-8	0101 1111
96	60	STD	-	- -	`	B	11	0110 0000
97	61		/	/ /	a	A 1	0-1	0110 0001
98	62				b		11-0-2-9	0110 0010
99	63				c		11-0-3-9	0110 0011
100	64				d		11-0-4-9	0110 0100
101	65				e		11-0-5-9	0110 0101
102	66				f		11-0-6-9	0110 0110
103	67	MXD			g		11-0-7-9	0110 0111
104	68	LD			h		11-0-8-9	0110 1000
105	69	CD			i		0-1-8	0110 1001
106	6A	AD		| |	j		12-11	0110 1010
107	6B	SD	,	, ,	k	A 8 2 1	0-3-8	0110 1011
108	6C	MD	% (	% %	l	A 8 4	0-4-8	0110 1100
109	6D	DD	γ	_ _	m	A 8 4 1	0-5-8	0110 1101
110	6E	AW	\	> >	n	A 8 4 2	0-6-8	0110 1110
111	6F	SW	⧧	? ?	o	A 8 4 2 1	0-7-8	0110 1111
112	70	STE			p		12-11-0	0111 0000
113	71				q		12-11-0-1-9	0111 0001
114	72				r		12-11-0-2-9	0111 0010
115	73				s		12-11-0-3-9	0111 0011
116	74				t		12-11-0-4-9	0111 0100
117	75				u		12-11-0-5-9	0111 0101
118	76				v		12-11-0-6-9	0111 0110
119	77				w		12-11-0-7-9	0111 0111
120	78	LE			x		12-11-0-8-9	0111 1000
121	79	CE		`	y		1-8	0111 1001
122	7A	AE	□	: :	z	A	2-8	0111 1010
123	7B	SE	# ≡	# #	{	8 2 1	3-8	0111 1011
124	7C	ME	@ '	@ @	|	8 4	4-8	0111 1100
125	7D	DE	'	' '	}	8 4 1	5-8	0111 1101
126	7E	AU	>	= =	~	8 4 2	6-8	0111 1110
127	7F	SU	√	" "	DEL	8 4 2 1	7-8	0111 1111

1. Two columns of EBCDIC graphics are shown. The first gives IBM standard U.S. bit pattern assignments. The second shows the T-11 and TN text printing chains (120 graphics).
2. Add C (check bit) for odd or even parity as needed, except as noted.
3. For even parity use CA.

TWO-CHARACTER BSC DATA LINK CONTROLS

Function	EBCDIC	ASCII
ACK-0	DLE,X'70'	DLE,0
ACK-1	DLE,X'61'	DLE,1
WACK	DLE,X'6B'	DLE, ;
RVI	DLE,X'7C'	DLE,<

CODE TRANSLATION TABLE (Contd) ⑪

Dec.	Hex	Instruction and Format	BCDIC	EBCDIC(1)	ASCII	7-Track Tape BCDIC(2)	Card Code EBCDIC	Binary
128	80	SSM -S					12-0-1-8	1000 0000
129	81		a	a			12-0-1	1000 0001
130	82	LPSW -S	b	b			12-0-2	1000 0010
131	83	Diagnose	c	c			12-0-3	1000 0011
132	84	WRD ⎫SI	d	d			12-0-4	1000 0100
133	85	RDD ⎭	e	e			12-0-5	1000 0101
134	86	BXH	f	f			12-0-6	1000 0110
135	87	BXLE	g	g			12-0-7	1000 0111
136	88	SRL	h	h			12-0-8	1000 1000
137	89	SLL	i	i			12-0-9	1000 1001
138	8A	SRA					12-0-2-8	1000 1010
139	8B	SLA ⎱RS			{		12-0-3-8	1000 1011
140	8C	SRDL			≤		12-0-4-8	1000 1100
141	8D	SLDL			(		12-0-5-8	1000 1101
142	8E	SRDA			+		12-0-6-8	1000 1110
143	8F	SLDA			+		12-0-7-8	1000 1111
144	90	STM					12-11-1-8	1001 0000
145	91	TM ⎫SI	j	j			12-11-1	1001 0001
146	92	MVI ⎬	k	k			12-11-2	1001 0010
147	93	TS -S	l	l			12-11-3	1001 0011
148	94	NI	m	m			12-11-4	1001 0100
149	95	CLI ⎬SI	n	n			12-11-5	1001 0101
150	96	OI	o	o			12-11-6	1001 0110
151	97	XI	p	p			12-11-7	1001 0111
152	98	LM -RS	q	q			12-11-8	1001 1000
153	99		r	r			12-11-9	1001 1001
154	9A						12-11-2-8	1001 1010
155	9B				}		12-11-3-8	1001 1011
156	9C	SIO, SIOF			□		12-11-4-8	1001 1100
157	9D	TIO, CLRIO ⎫S			)		12-11-5-8	1001 1101
158	9E	HIO, HDV ⎬			±		12-11-6-8	1001 1110
159	9F	TCH ⎭			■		12-11-7-8	1001 1111
160	A0				–		11-0-1-8	1010 0000
161	A1		~	°			11-0-1	1010 0001
162	A2		s	s			11-0-2	1010 0010
163	A3		t	t			11-0-3	1010 0011
164	A4		u	u			11-0-4	1010 0100
165	A5		v	v			11-0-5	1010 0101
166	A6		w	w			11-0-6	1010 0110
167	A7		x	x			11-0-7	1010 0111
168	A8		y	y			11-0-8	1010 1000
169	A9		z	z			11-0-9	1010 1001
170	AA						11-0-2-8	1010 1010
171	AB				∟		11-0-3-8	1010 1011
172	AC	STNSM ⎫SI			⌐		11-0-4-8	1010 1100
173	AD	STOSM ⎭			[		11-0-5-8	1010 1101
174	AE	SIGP -RS			≥		11-0-6-8	1010 1110
175	AF	MC -SI			●		11-0-7-8	1010 1111
176	B0				0		12-11-0-1-8	1011 0000
177	B1	LRA -RX			1		12-11-0-1	1011 0001
178	B2	See below			2		12-11-0-2	1011 0010
179	B3				3		12-11-0-3	1011 0011
180	B4				4		12-11-0-4	1011 0100
181	B5				5		12-11-0-5	1011 0101
182	B6	STCTL ⎫RS			6		12-11-0-6	1011 0110
183	B7	LCTL ⎭			7		12-11-0-7	1011 0111
184	B8				8		12-11-0-8	1011 1000
185	B9				9		12-11-0-9	1011 1001
186	BA	CS ⎫RS					12-11-0-2-8	1011 1010
187	BB	CDS ⎭			⌐		12-11-0-3-8	1011 1011
188	BC				¬		12-11-0-4-8	1011 1100
189	BD	CLM ⎫			]		12-11-0-5-8	1011 1101
190	BE	STCM ⎬RS			≠		12-11-0-6-8	1011 1110
191	BF	ICM ⎭			—		12-11-0-7-8	1011 1111

Op code (S format)

B202 - STIDP	B207 - STCKC	B20D - PTLB
B203 - STIDC	B208 - SPT	B210 - SPX
B204 - SCK	B209 - STPT	B211 - STPX
B205 - STCK	B20A - SPKA	B212 - STAP
B206 - SCKC	B20B - IPK	B213 - RRB

CODE TRANSLATION TABLE (Contd) ⑫

Dec.	Hex	Instruction (SS)	BCDIC	EBCDIC(1)	ASCII	7-Track Tape BCDIC(2)	Card Code EBCDIC	Binary
192	C0		?	{		BA8 2	12-0	1100 0000
193	C1		A	A	A	BA 1	12-1	1100 0001
194	C2		B	B	B	BA 2	12-2	1100 0010
195	C3		C	C	C	BA 21	12-3	1100 0011
196	C4		D	D	D	BA 4	12-4	1100 0100
197	C5		E	E	E	BA 4 1	12-5	1100 0101
198	C6		F	F	F	BA 42	12-6	1100 0110
199	C7		G	G	G	BA 421	12-7	1100 0111
200	C8		H	H	H	BA8	12-8	1100 1000
201	C9		I	I	I	BA8 1	12-9	1100 1001
202	CA						12-0-2-8-9	1100 1010
203	CB						12-0-3-8-9	1100 1011
204	CC			∫			12-0-4-8-9	1100 1100
205	CD						12-0-5-8-9	1100 1101
206	CE			Ч			12-0-6-8-9	1100 1110
207	CF						12-0-7-8-9	1100 1111
208	D0		!	}		B 8 2	11-0	1101 0000
209	D1	MVN	J	J	J	B 1	11-1	1101 0001
210	D2	MVC	K	K	K	B 2	11-2	1101 0010
211	D3	MVZ	L	L	L	B 21	11-3	1101 0011
212	D4	NC	M	M	M	B 4	11-4	1101 0100
213	D5	CLC	N	N	N	B 4 1	11-5	1101 0101
214	D6	OC	O	O	O	B 42	11-6	1101 0110
215	D7	XC	P	P	P	B 421	11-7	1101 0111
216	D8		Q	Q	Q	B 8	11-8	1101 1000
217	D9		R	R	R	B 8 1	11-9	1101 1001
218	DA						12-11-2-8-9	1101 1010
219	DB						12-11-3-8-9	1101 1011
220	DC	TR					12-11-4-8-9	1101 1100
221	DD	TRT					12-11-5-8-9	1101 1101
222	DE	ED					12-11-6-8-9	1101 1110
223	DF	EDMK					12-11-7-8-9	1101 1111
224	E0		∓	\		A8 2	0-2-8	1110 0000
225	E1						11-0-1-9	1110 0001
226	E2		S	S	S	A 2	0-2	1110 0010
227	E3		T	T	T	A 21	0-3	1110 0011
228	E4		U	U	U	A 4	0-4	1110 0100
229	E5		V	V	V	A 4 1	0-5	1110 0101
230	E6		W	W	W	A 42	0-6	1110 0110
231	E7		X	X	X	A 421	0-7	1110 0111
232	E8		Y	Y	Y	A8	0-8	1110 1000
233	E9		Z	Z	Z	A8 1	0-9	1110 1001
234	EA						11-0-2-8-9	1110 1010
235	EB						11-0-3-8-9	1110 1011
236	EC			⊣			11-0-4-8-9	1110 1100
237	ED						11-0-5-8-9	1110 1101
238	EE						11-0-6-8-9	1110 1110
239	EF						11-0-7-8-9	1110 1111
240	F0	SRP	0	0	0	8 2	0	1111 0000
241	F1	MVO	1	1	1	1	1	1111 0001
242	F2	PACK	2	2	2	2	2	1111 0010
243	F3	UNPK	3	3	3	21	3	1111 0011
244	F4		4	4	4	4	4	1111 0100
245	F5		5	5	5	4 1	5	1111 0101
246	F6		6	6	6	42	6	1111 0110
247	F7		7	7	7	421	7	1111 0111
248	F8	ZAP	8	8	8	8	8	1111 1000
249	F9	CP	9	9	9	8 1	9	1111 1001
250	FA	AP					12-11-0-2-8-9	1111 1010
251	FB	SP					12-11-0-3-8-9	1111 1011
252	FC	MP					12-11-0-4-8-9	1111 1100
253	FD	DP					12-11-0-5-8-9	1111 1101
254	FE						12-11-0-6-8-9	1111 1110
255	FF			EO			12-11-0-7-8-9	1111 1111

ANSI-DEFINED PRINTER CONTROL CHARACTERS
(A in RECFM field of DCB)

Code	Action before printing record
blank	Space 1 line
0	Space 2 lines
–	Space 3 lines
+	Suppress space
1	Skip to line 1 on new page

MACHINE INSTRUCTION FORMATS ⑬

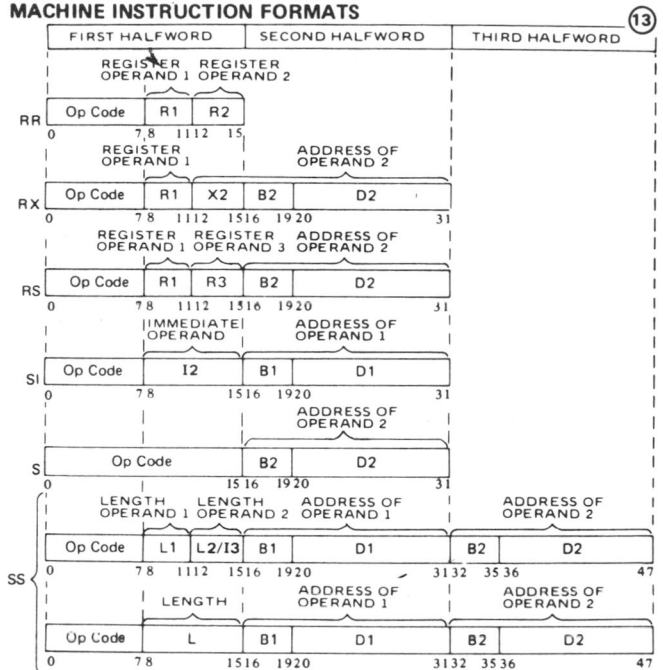

CONTROL REGISTERS

CR	Bits	Name of field	Associated with	Init.
0	0	Block-multiplex'g control	Block multiplex'g	0
	1	SSM suppression control	SSM instruction	0
	2	TOD clock sync control	Multiprocessing	0
	8-9	Page size control		0
	10	Unassigned (must be zero)	Dynamic addr. transl.	0
	11-12	Segment size control		0
	16	Malfunction alert mask		0
	17	Emergency signal mask		0
	18	External call mask	Multiprocessing	0
	19	TOD clock sync check mask		0
	20	Clock comparator mask	Clock comparator	0
	21	CPU timer mask	CPU timer	0
	24	Interval timer mask	Interval timer	1
	25	Interrupt key mask	Interrupt key	1
	26	External signal mask	External signal	1
1	0-7	Segment table length	Dynamic addr. transl.	0
	8-25	Segment table address		0
2	0-31	Channel masks	Channels	1
8	16-31	Monitor masks	Monitoring	0
9	0	Successful branching event mask		0
	1	Instruction fetching event mask		0
	2	Storage alteration event mask	Program-event record'g	0
	3	GR alteration event mask		0
	16-31	PER general register masks		0
10	8-31	PER starting address	Program-event record'g	0
11	8-31	PER ending address	Program-event record'g	0
14	0	Check-stop control		1
	1	Synch. MCEL control	Machine-check handling	1
	2	I/O extended logout control	I/O extended logout	0
	4	Recovery report mask		0
	5	Degradation report mask		0
	6	Ext. damage report mask	Machine-check handling	1
	7	Warning mask		0
	8	Asynch. MCEL control		0
	9	Asynch. fixed log control		0
15	8-28	MCEL address	Machine-check handling	512

PROGRAM STATUS WORD (BC Mode) ⑭

Channel masks	E	Protect'n key	CMWP	Interruption code
0 6	7 8 11	12 15	16 23 24 31

ILC	CC	Program mask	Instruction address
32 34 36 39	40 47	48 63

0-5 Channel 0 to 5 masks
6 Mask for channel 6 and up
7 (E) External mask
12 (C=0) Basic control mode
13 (M) Machine-check mask
14 (W=1) Wait state
15 (P=1) Problem state

32-33 (ILC) Instruction length code
34-35 (CC) Condition code
36 Fixed-point overflow mask
37 Decimal overflow mask
38 Exponent underflow mask
39 Significance mask

PROGRAM STATUS WORD (EC Mode)

0R00 0TIE	Protect'n key	CMWP	00	CC	Program mask	0000 0000
0 7 8 11	12 15	16 18	20 23 24			31

0000 0000	Instruction address
32 39 40 47	48 55 56 63

1 (R) Program event recording mask
5 (T=1) Translation mode
6 (I) Input/output mask
7 (E) External mask
12 (C=1) Extended control mode
13 (M) Machine-check mask
14 (W=1) Wait state

15 (P=1) Problem state
18-19 (CC) Condition code
20 Fixed-point overflow mask
21 Decimal overflow mask
22 Exponent underflow mask
23 Significance mask

CHANNEL COMMAND WORD

Command code	Data address
0 7 8	15 16 23 24 31

Flags	00	/////	Byte count
32 37 38 40		47 48	55 56 63

CD—bit 32 (80) causes use of address portion of next CCW.
CC—bit 33 (40) causes use of command code and data address of next CCW.
SLI—bit 34 (20) causes suppression of possible incorrect length indication.
Skip—bit 35 (10) suppresses transfer of information to main storage.
PCI—bit 36 (08) causes a channel program controlled interruption.
IDA—bit 37 (04) causes bits 8-31 of CCW to specify location of first IDAW.

CHANNEL STATUS WORD (hex 40)

Key	0	L	CC	CCW address
0 3	4	5	6 7 8	15 16 23 24 31

Unit status	Channel status	Byte count
32 39 40	47 48	55 56 63

5 Logout pending
6-7 Deferred condition code
32 (80) Attention
33 (40) Status modifier
34 (20) Control unit end
35 (10) Busy
36 (08) Channel end
37 (04) Device end
38 (02) Unit check
39 (01) Unit exception

40 (80) Program-controlled interruption
41 (40) Incorrect length
42 (20) Program check
43 (10) Protection check
44 (08) Channel data check
45 (04) Channel control check
46 (02) Interface control check
47 (01) Chaining check
48-63 Residual byte count for the last CCW used

PROGRAM INTERRUPTION CODES

0001	Operation exception	000C	Exponent overflow excp
0002	Privileged operation excp	000D	Exponent underflow excp
0003	Execute exception	000E	Significance exception
0004	Protection exception	000F	Floating-point divide excp
0005	Addressing exception	0010	Segment translation excp
0006	Specification exception	0011	Page translation exception
0007	Data exception	0012	Translation specification excp
0008	Fixed-point overflow excp	0013	Special operation exception
0009	Fixed-point divide excp	0040	Monitor event
000A	Decimal overflow exception	0080	Program event (code may be
000B	Decimal divide exception		combined with another code)

FIXED STORAGE LOCATIONS (15)

Area, dec.	Hex addr	EC only	Function
0- 7	0		Initial program loading PSW, restart new PSW
8- 15	8		Initial program loading CCW1, restart old PSW
16- 23	10		Initial program loading CCW2
24- 31	18		External old PSW
32- 39	20		Supervisor Call old PSW
40- 47	28		Program old PSW
48- 55	30		Machine-check old PSW
56- 63	38		Input/output old PSW
64- 71	40		Channel status word (see diagram)
72- 75	48		Channel address word [0-3 key, 4-7 zeros, 8-31 CCW address]
80- 83	50		Interval timer
88- 95	58		External new PSW
96-103	60		Supervisor Call new PSW
104-111	68		Program new PSW
112-119	70		Machine-check new PSW
120-127	78		Input/output new PSW
132-133	84		CPU address assoc'd with external interruption, or unchanged
132-133	84	X	CPU address assoc'd with external interruption, or zeros
134-135	86	X	External interruption code
136-139	88	X	SVC interruption [0-12 zeros, 13-14 ILC, 15:0, 16-31 code]
140-143	8C	X	Program interrupt. [0-12 zeros, 13-14 ILC, 15:0, 16-31 code]
144-147	90	X	Translation exception address [0-7 zeros, 8-31 address]
148-149	94		Monitor class [0-7 zeros, 8-15 class number]
150-151	96	X	PER interruption code [0-3 code, 4-15 zeros]
152-155	98	X	PER address [0-7 zeros, 8-31 address]
156-159	9C		Monitor code [0-7 zeros, 8-31 monitor code]
168-171	A8		Channel ID [0-3 type, 4-15 model, 16-31 max. IOEL length]
172-175	AC		I/O extended logout address [0-7 unused, 8-31 address]
176-179	B0		Limited channel logout (see diagram)
185-187	B9	X	I/O address [0-7 zeros, 8-23 address]
216-223	D8		CPU timer save area
224-231	E0		Clock comparator save area
232-239	E8		Machine-check interruption code (see diagram)
248-251	F8		Failing processor storage address [0-7 zeros, 8-31 address]
252-255	FC		Region code*
256-351	100		Fixed logout area*
352-383	160		Floating-point register save area
384-447	180		General register save area
448-511	1C0		Control register save area
512†	200		CPU extended logout area (size varies)

*May vary among models; see system library manuals for specific model.
†Location may be changed by programming (bits 8-28 of CR 15 specify address).

LIMITED CHANNEL LOGOUT (hex B0)

0	SCU id	Detect	Source	000	Field validity flags	TT	00	A	Seq.
0	1 3	4 7	8 12	13 15	16 23	24 26	28	29	31

4 CPU
5 Channel
6 Main storage control
7 Main storage
8 CPU
9 Channel
10 Main storage control
11 Main storage

12 Control unit
16 Interface address
17-18 Reserved (00)
19 Sequence code
20 Unit status
21 Cmd. addr. and key
22 Channel address
23 Device address

24-25 Type of termination
00 Interface disconnect
01 Stop, stack or normal
10 Selective reset
11 System reset
28(A) I/O error alert
29-31 Sequence code

MACHINE-CHECK INTERRUPTION CODE (hex E8)

MC conditions	000	00	Time	Stg. error	0	Validity indicators
0	8 9		13 14	16 18	19	20 31

0000	0000	0000	00	Val.	MCEL length
32 39	40	45 46		48	55 56 63

0 System damage
1 Instr. proc'g damage
2 System recovery
3 Timer damage
4 Timing facil. damage
5 External damage
6 Not assigned (0)
7 Degradation
8 Warning

14 Backed-up
15 Delayed
16 Uncorrected
17 Corrected
18 Key uncorrected
20 PSW bits 12-15
21 PSW masks and key
22 Prog. mask and CC
23 Instruction address

24 Failing stg. address
25 Region code
27 Floating-pt registers
28 General registers
29 Control registers
30 CPU ext'd logout
31 Storage logical
46 CPU timer
47 Clock comparator

DYNAMIC ADDRESS TRANSLATION (16)

VIRTUAL (LOGICAL) ADDRESS FORMAT

Segment Size	Page Size		Segment Index	Page Index	Byte Index
64K	4K	Bits	8 - 15	16 - 19	20 - 31
64K	2K	0 - 7	8 - 15	16 - 20	21 - 31
1M	4K	are	8 - 11	12 - 19	20 - 31
1M	2K	ignored	8 - 11	12 - 20	21 - 31

SEGMENT TABLE ENTRY

PT length	0000*	Page table address	00*	I
0 3	4 7	8 28	29	31

*Normally zeros; ignored on some models.   31 (I) Segment-invalid bit.

PAGE TABLE ENTRY (4K)

Page address	I	00	
0 11	12	13	15

12 (I) Page-invalid bit.

PAGE TABLE ENTRY (2K)

Page address	I	0	
0 12	13	14	15

13 (I) Page-invalid bit.

HEXADECIMAL AND DECIMAL CONVERSION

From hex: locate each hex digit in its corresponding column position and note the decimal equivalents. Add these to obtain the decimal value.

From decimal: (1) locate the largest decimal value in the table that will fit into the decimal number to be converted, and (2) note its hex equivalent and hex column position. (3) Find the decimal remainder. Repeat the process on this and subsequent remainders.

Note: Decimal, hexadecimal, (and binary) equivalents of all numbers from 0 to 255 are listed on panels 9 – 12.

HEXADECIMAL COLUMNS

	6		5		4		3		2		1
HEX	= DEC	HEX	= DEC	HEX	= DEC	HEX	= DEC	HEX	= DEC	HEX	= DEC
0	0	0	0	0	0	0	0	0	0	0	0
1	1,048,576	1	65,536	1	4,096	1	256	1	16	1	1
2	2,097,152	2	131,072	2	8,192	2	512	2	32	2	2
3	3,145,728	3	196,608	3	12,288	3	768	3	48	3	3
4	4,194,304	4	262,144	4	16,384	4	1,024	4	64	4	4
5	5,242,880	5	327,680	5	20,480	5	1,280	5	80	5	5
6	6,291,456	6	393,216	6	24,576	6	1,536	6	96	6	6
7	7,340,032	7	458,752	7	28,672	7	1,792	7	112	7	7
8	8,388,608	8	524,288	8	32,768	8	2,048	8	128	8	8
9	9,437,184	9	589,824	9	36,864	9	2,304	9	144	9	9
A	10,485,760	A	655,360	A	40,960	A	2,560	A	160	A	10
B	11,534,336	B	720,896	B	45,056	B	2,816	B	176	B	11
C	12,582,912	C	786,432	C	49,152	C	3,072	C	192	C	12
D	13,631,488	D	851,968	D	53,248	D	3,328	D	208	D	13
E	14,680,064	E	917,504	E	57,344	E	3,584	E	224	E	14
F	15,728,640	F	983,040	F	61,440	F	3,840	F	240	F	15
	0 1 2 3		4 5 6 7		0 1 2 3		4 5 6 7		0 1 2 3		4 5 6 7
	BYTE				BYTE				BYTE		

POWERS OF 2

2^n	n
256	8
512	9
1 024	10
2 048	11
4 096	12
8 192	13
16 384	14
32 768	15
65 536	16
131 072	17
262 144	18
524 288	19
1 048 576	20
2 097 152	21
4 194 304	22
8 388 608	23
16 777 216	24

$2^0 = 16^0$	
$2^4 = 16^1$	
$2^8 = 16^2$	
$2^{12} = 16^3$	
$2^{16} = 16^4$	
$2^{20} = 16^5$	
$2^{24} = 16^6$	
$2^{28} = 16^7$	
$2^{32} = 16^8$	
$2^{36} = 16^9$	
$2^{40} = 16^{10}$	
$2^{44} = 16^{11}$	
$2^{48} = 16^{12}$	
$2^{52} = 16^{13}$	
$2^{56} = 16^{14}$	
$2^{60} = 16^{15}$	

POWERS OF 16

16^n	n
1	0
16	1
256	2
4 096	3
65 536	4
1 048 576	5
16 777 216	6
268 435 456	7
4 294 967 296	8
68 719 476 736	9
1 099 511 627 776	10
17 592 186 044 416	11
281 474 976 710 656	12
4 503 599 627 370 496	13
72 057 594 037 927 936	14
1 152 921 504 606 846 976	15

A Review of Flowcharts, Pseudocode, and Structured Programming Concepts

I. FLOWCHARTS

A. Introduction

A useful tool for analyzing the necessary logic in a program is called a *flowchart*. A flowchart is a diagram, or pictorial representation, of the logic flow of a program; it is a program planning tool drawn *before* the problem is coded. It is similar to a blueprint an architect prepares before a house is built. Through the use of a flowchart, the programmer can organize and verify the logic that will be employed in the program.

This section is designed to illustrate the elements of program flowcharting. The examples illustrate the *structured* approach to programming. Using the method of flowcharting presented here will enable you to code an assembler language program directly from a flowchart, and to incorporate the structured approach, described later on, in your programs.

B. Illustrations

Consider the flowchart in Figure J.1. This is a simple chart that reads disk records and prints the data contained in them.

FLOWCHART RULES

1. A logic flow in a flowchart is read from top to bottom unless a specific condition alters the path.
2. Different symbols are used for different functions.
3. All symbols have explanatory notes indicating the specific operations to be performed. The reasoning behind this is that a symbol denotes a major class of functions such as input–output or processing.

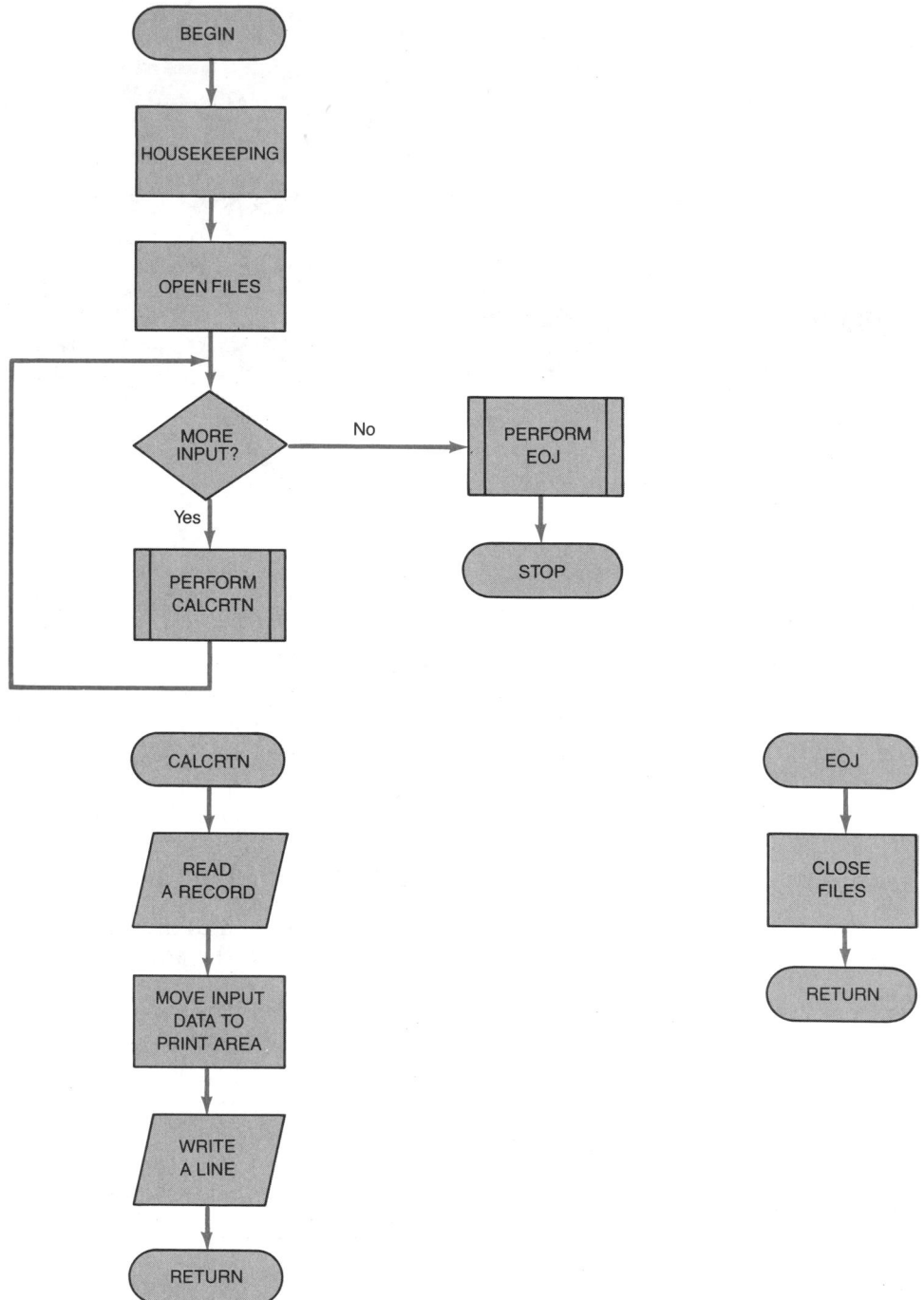

Figure J.1
Flowchart to read disk records and print the data contained in them.

You will note that there are three separate sequences or modules indicated in this flowchart. The main routine, which begins with a symbol labeled BEGIN, performs the following operations:

---

1. Housekeeping instructions are executed.
2. Files are opened or prepared for processing.
3. If there are no input records left to be processed, an end-of-job (EOJ) routine is executed.
4. A separate routine called CALCRTN is executed repeatedly until there are no more input records to process.

CALCRTN is the sequence or set of steps that performs the required operations for each record. At CALCRTN, we have the following sequence of steps:

---

1. An input record is read.
2. The input data is moved from the input area to the print area.
3. A line is written.
4. The sequence of steps at CALCRTN is repeated until an end-of-file condition occurs. When an end-of-file condition occurs, the sequence is terminated and control is transferred to the routine labeled EOJ where files are closed and the job is terminated.

Consider now the program flowchart indicated in Figure J.2.

This flowchart depicts the logic flow used to print salary checks for all salespeople in a company. If a salesperson has made over $100 in sales, the commission is 10 percent of sales, which is added to the salesperson's salary. If a salesperson has made $100 or less in sales, then the commission is only 5 percent or .05 of sales.

Here again, there are three sequences: one begins with BEGIN, one with CALCRTN, and one with EOJ. Note that the BEGIN sequence has the exact same set of instructions as the previous illustration. The major difference in this flowchart is the actual operations to be performed on input records, as indicated at CALCRTN.

If sales are greater than $100, 10 percent of sales is used to determine the commission; otherwise, 5 percent is used. After the commission has been determined, the amount of each check is calculated, and a check is written with name and amount. Another salesperson's record is read and CALCRTN is repeated until there is no more input. When an end-of-file condition exists, control is transferred to EOJ where files are closed and the run is terminated.

The flowchart excerpt that compares sales to 100.00 is referred to as an IFTHENELSE sequence and has the following general format.

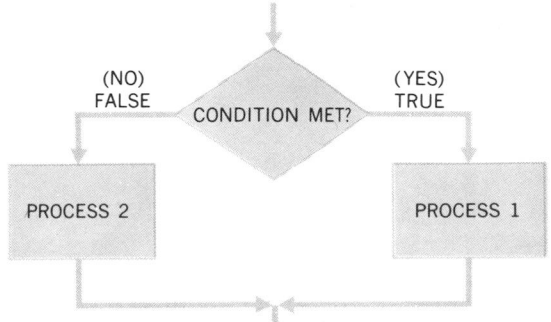

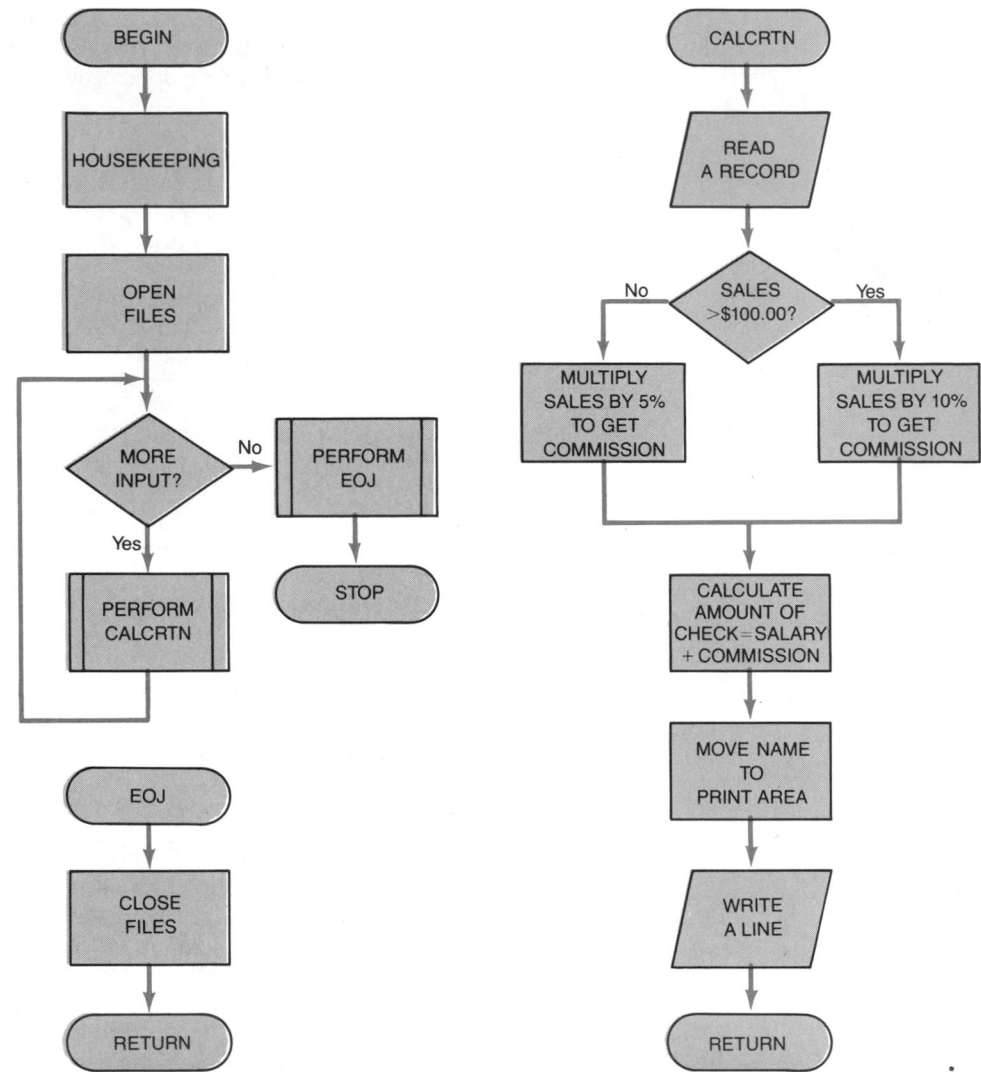

Figure J.2
Flowchart to print salary checks.

C. Describing Symbols Used in Flowcharts

The following symbols are the ones most frequently used in program flowcharts.

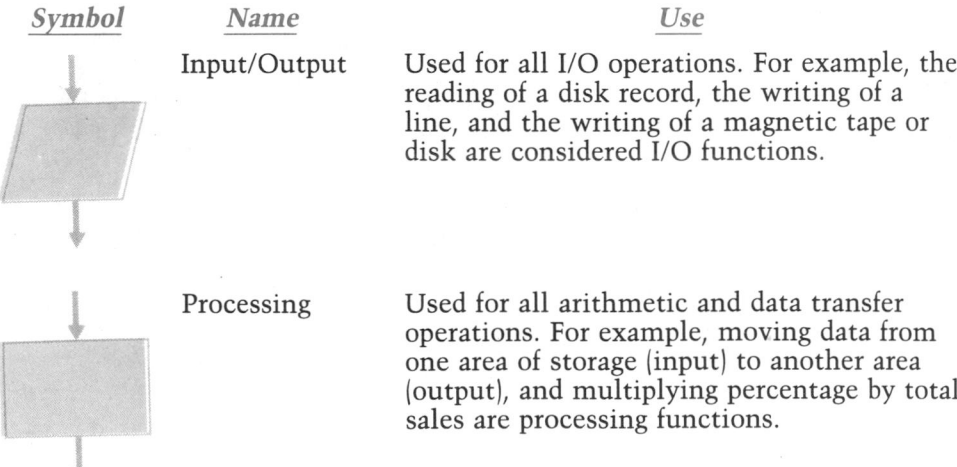

Symbol	Name	Use
	Input/Output	Used for all I/O operations. For example, the reading of a disk record, the writing of a line, and the writing of a magnetic tape or disk are considered I/O functions.
	Processing	Used for all arithmetic and data transfer operations. For example, moving data from one area of storage (input) to another area (output), and multiplying percentage by total sales are processing functions.

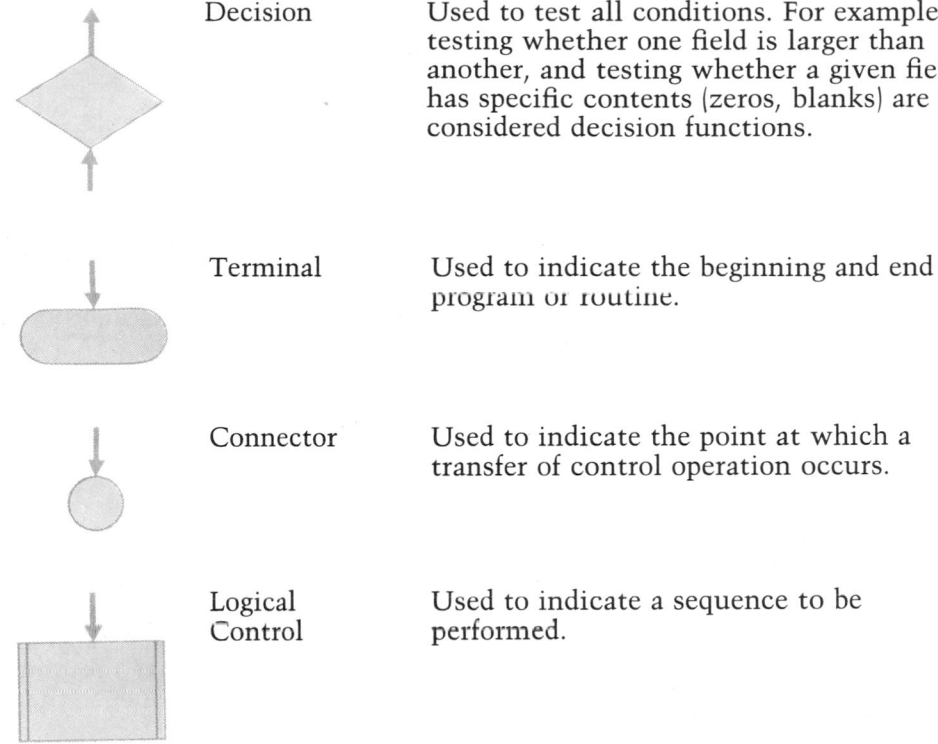

Decision — Used to test all conditions. For example, testing whether one field is larger than another, and testing whether a given field has specific contents (zeros, blanks) are considered decision functions.

Terminal — Used to indicate the beginning and end of a program or routine.

Connector — Used to indicate the point at which a transfer of control operation occurs.

Logical Control — Used to indicate a sequence to be performed.

D. Logical Control Sequences

The full range of logical control sequences follows.

1. Sequence

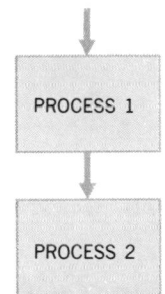

Instructions are executed in sequence.

2. IFTHENELSE

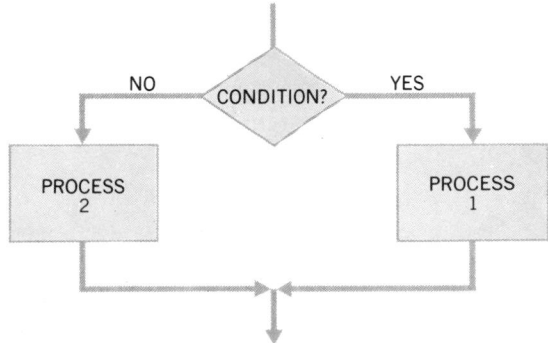

In assembler language programs, IFTHENELSE sequences are executed by using compare and branch instructions.

3. PERFORM

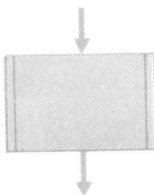

Control is passed to a different module. After that module is executed, control returns to the next instruction after the one that called the module.

In assembler language, control is passed to other modules using a branch and link (BAL) instruction or a branch and link register (BALR) instruction. As indicated in Chapter 18, these instructions are typically used to code PERFORM structures in a structured program.

4. PERFORM . . . UNTIL

Most assembler routines that are executed until an end-of-file condition exists can be flowcharted as a PERFORM . . . UNTIL structure. That is, CALCRTN is executed until there are no more records to process. The DTF or DCB for the input file indicates the sequence to execute when an end-of-file condition exists. A flowchart for the PERFORM . . . UNTIL sequence follows. Note that the processing symbol with two parallel bars is used to denote a sequence that is to be performed.

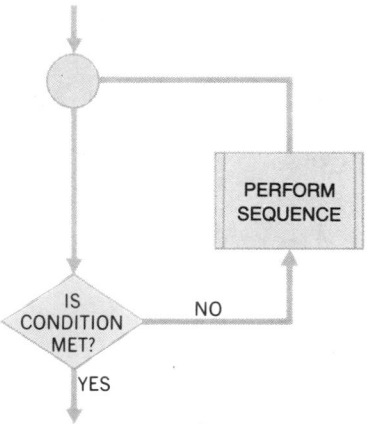

E. Additional Illustrations

Let us consider another illustration. From the following record format, we wish to print the names of (1) all blue-eyed, blonde males, and (2) all brown-eyed, brunette females.

1–20	Name
21	Sex
	M—male
	F—female
22	Color of eyes
	1—Blue
	2—Brown
	3—Other
23	Color of hair
	1—Brunette
	2—Blonde
	3—Other
24–80	Not used

The flowchart for this problem is illustrated in Figure J.3.

Note that drawing detailed flowcharts may be a difficult task at first. Elementary level flowcharts, however, are relatively simple to code. For intermediate-level programs, where the logic flow is often complex, a flowchart can be even more helpful, but more difficult to draw. At this stage, however, we will familiarize you with flowcharts by drawing on numerous examples. We suggest that even when the logic is not complex, you should draw flowcharts to document exactly what you will do in the program.

Self-Evaluating Quiz

1. A flowchart is used for analyzing the _____ necessary in a program.
2. A flowchart is drawn **(before/after)** the problem is coded.
3. A program flowchart is read from _____ to _____ .
4. Different _____ are used to denote different functions.
5. The input/output symbol is coded as _____ .
6. A processing symbol is coded as _____ .

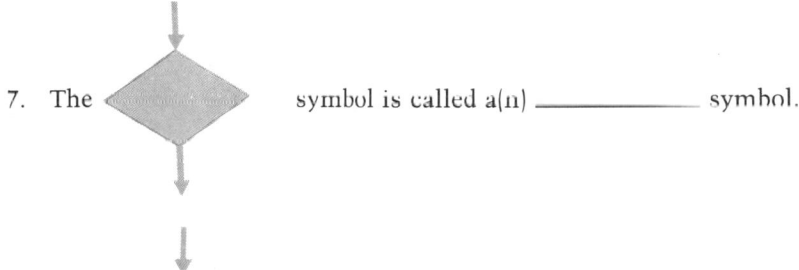

7. The [diamond symbol] symbol is called a(n) _____ symbol.

8. The [circle symbol] symbol is used to denote a(n) _____ .

9. After a transfer of control is executed, the logic flow continues with _____ .
10. All symbols have _____ indicating the specific operations to be performed.

SOLUTIONS

1. Logic
2. Before
3. Top; bottom
4. Symbols
5.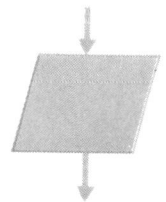

6.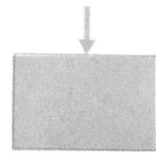

7. Decision
8. Branch or transfer of control
9. The next sequential statement (after the transfer)
10. Explanatory notes

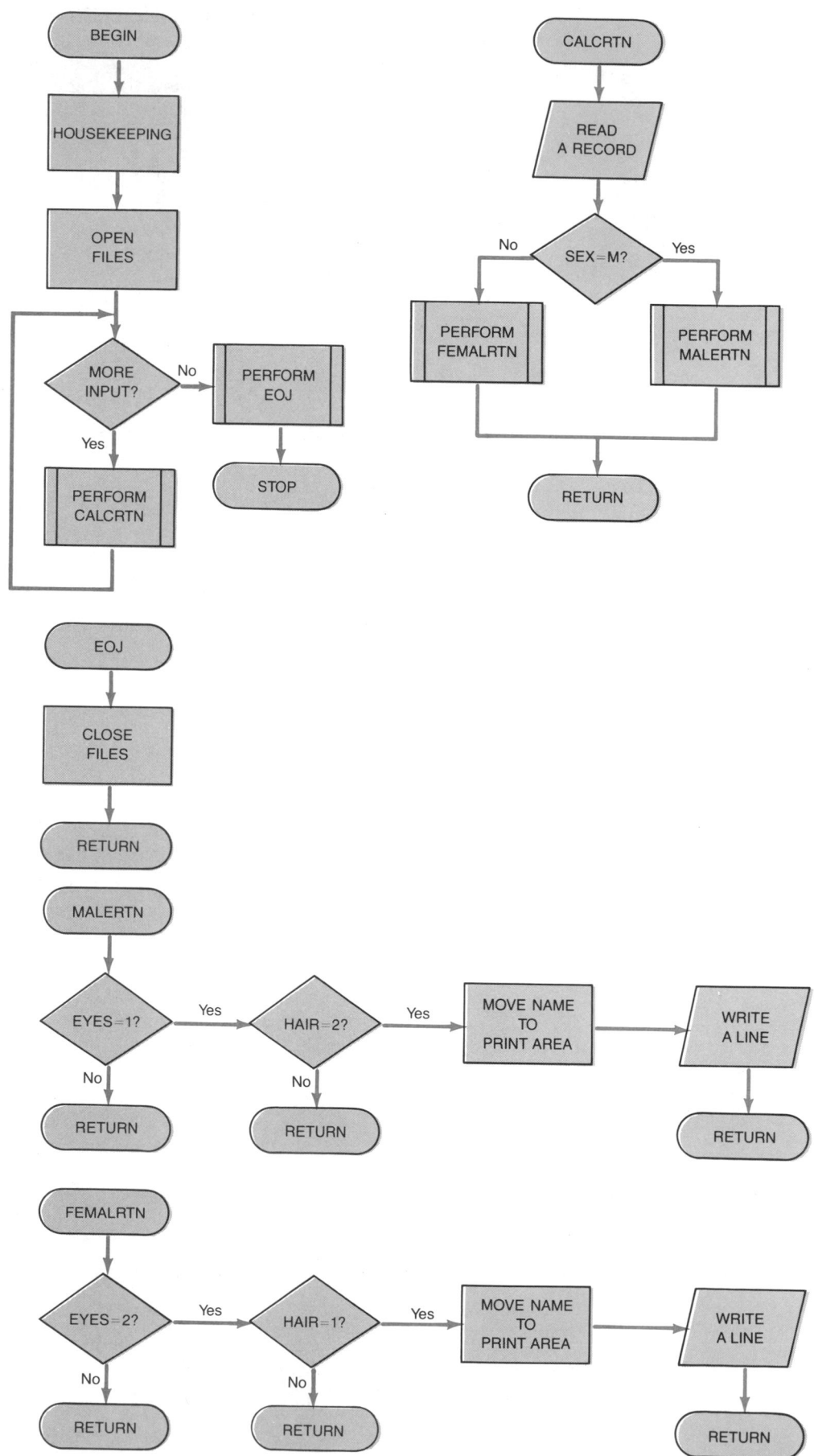

Figure J.3
Flowchart to print the names
of people who meet certain
conditions.

II. STRUCTURED PROGRAMMING

We have noted many times in this text that one of the main problems with computerization is the lack of established standards. Programming is one area in which the need for standards is particularly great.

Until recently, each program was viewed by both programmers and their managers as a unique, individual creation. This perspective made it very difficult to assess the competence of individual programmers, to evaluate their work, or to make modifications to existing programs. As a result, many leaders in the field have been arguing for a less "ego-oriented" approach to programming, one that would be more standardized.

Structured programming is one method to standardize and improve programs so that they are easier to evaluate, debug, and modify. The structured technique consists of modularizing or segmenting each program into distinct blocks. These modules or blocks

1. Can be written in a standardized way;
2. Enable one program to be written and debugged by a team of programmers;
3. May be used in discussion groups where a team of programmers evaluates the program using a "structured walk-through" of the modules; and
4. Can be used or copied in several programs.

To enable each module to function as a stand-alone entity, branches, called "GO TO" instructions in many languages, are to be minimized. Thus, structured programming is sometimes referred to as *GO TO-less programming*. PERFORM . . . UNTIL (end-of-job) is easily handled in assembler. Other structured programming techniques are explained in Chapter 18.

III. PSEUDOCODE

In the first section of this Appendix, we demonstrated how flowcharts may be used for depicting the logic flow coded in programs. Such flowcharts have been the traditional tool of the programmer for planning the sequence of necessary steps.

In recent years, however, flowcharts have been widely criticized for being cumbersome and difficult to follow. Moreover, the techniques of structured programming do not entirely lend themselves to simplified representation by flowcharts. An alternative method for depicting the logic flow in a program has, therefore, been developed and is called *pseudocode*. The name implies that the representation is a *code*, like that used in a program; the term "pseudo" implies that although this code is similar to that used in a program, it is merely a representation, not a language itself.

Pseudocode has been designed to easily represent a structured approach. Each processing or input–output step is denoted by a line of pseudocode. Just as with flowcharts, the pseudocode need not indicate all the processing details; abbreviations are permissible.

The logical control instructions are indicated by

1. PERFORM statements, and
2. IFTHENELSE specifications that are used to test specific conditions.

A. PERFORM Statements

The structure of a PERFORM is as follows.

```
PERFORM
        ____ ⎫
        ____ ⎬  Instructions to be performed
        ____ ⎭  (indented for ease of reading)

ENDPERFORM
```

The indented statements would be those under the control of a PERFORM. We can also use a PERFORM . . . UNTIL this way. See the pseudocode for Flowchart J.1 (Figure J.4), which illustrates the use of a PERFORM.

```
Housekeeping Operations
Open Files
PERFORM CALCRTN Until No More Data
    Read an Input Record
    Move Input Data to Print Area
    Write a Line
ENDPERFORM
Close Files
Stop
```

Figure J.4
Pseudocode for Flowchart J.1.

As noted, PERFORM . . . UNTIL (end-of-job) is a common structure used in assembler language programs. Most main routines are executed until an end-of-file condition exists. The DTF or DCB for the input file specifies the sequence to be executed when there is no more input.

PERFORM structures are executed in assembler using a branch and link (BAL) instruction or a branch and link register (BALR) instruction. See Chapter 18.

B. IFTHENELSE Specifications

To indicate the testing of conditions, the following format is used.

IF	(condition)
THEN	(operation to be performed)
ELSE	(operation to be performed if condition is not met)
ENDIF	

See the pseudocode for Flowchart J.2 (Figure J.5) for an illustration.

```
Housekeeping Operations
Open Files
PERFORM CALCRTN Until No More Data
    Read an Input Record
    IF Sales Greater Than 100.00
    THEN
        Multiply Sales by 10% (.10) Giving Commission
    ELSE
        Multiply Sales by 5% (.05) Giving Commission
    ENDIF
    Calculate Amount of Check = Salary + Commission
    Move Name to Print Area
    Write a Line
ENDPERFORM
Close Files
Stop
```

Figure J.5
Pseudocode for Flowchart J.2.

Pseudocodes are being used for structured programs with increasing frequency both for documenting and for assisting the programmer in providing the most efficient and accurate logic flow necessary.

IFTHENELSE sequences are handled easily in assembler with compare and branch instructions.

Self-Evaluating Quiz

1. Pseudocodes have been used with increasing frequency in place of _____ to represent the logical flow to be used in a program.
2. Pseudocodes are used for depicting the _____ of a program.
3. The transfer of control or decision specifications are denoted by a(n) _____ and _____, respectively.
4. The last step in a PERFORM sequence is _____ .
5. The last step in an IF sequence is _____ .

SOLUTIONS

1. Flowcharts
2. Logic
3. PERFORM; IFTHENELSE
4. ENDPERFORM
5. ENDIF

REVIEW QUESTIONS

1. Give four examples of input/output functions.
2. Give four examples of processing functions.
3. Give two examples of decision functions.
4. (T or F) A program flowchart is required before any programs are written.
5. Consider the flowchart in Figure J.6. With the following input records, what will be the contents of TOTAL at the end of all operations?

Record No.	Contents of Record Position 18	Contents of Record Position 19
1	1	2
2	1	3
3	1	2
4	1	0
5	(blank)	(blank)
6	(blank)	1
7	1	(blank)
8	1	2
9	1	2
10	(blank)	2

6. Use the flowchart in Figure J.7 to answer the following questions. Input is in 15 records. Codes in the 15 records (in position 1) are:

    1, 2, 3, 2, 1, 1, 2, 2, 3, 3, 1, 2, 3, 1, 2

    (a) How many records will be read?
    (b) What is the value of SWITCH when the program is finished?
    (c) What is the value of ACCUM when the program is finished?
    (d) How many records would have been read if ACCUM was originally set to 1 instead of 0?

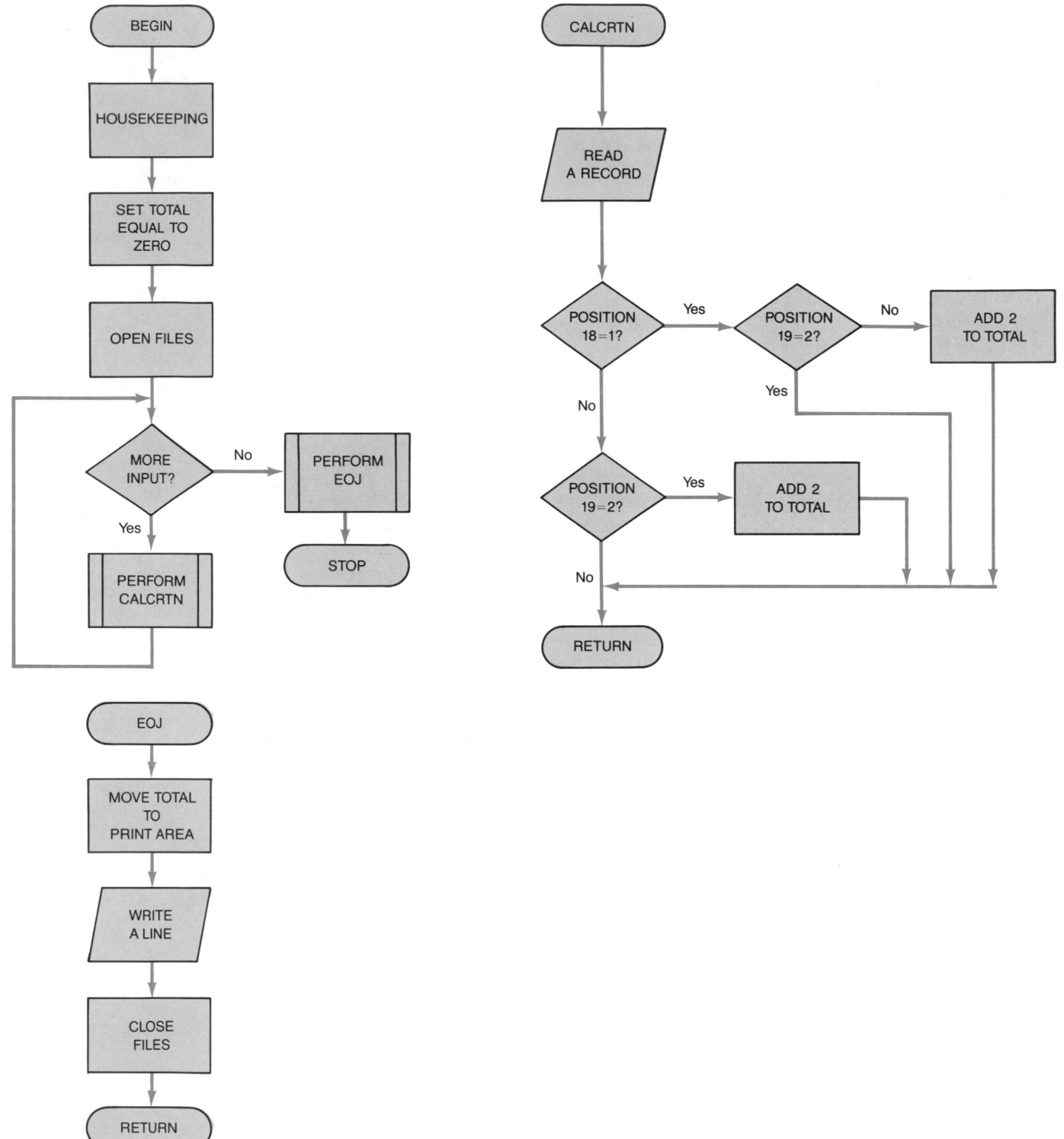

Figure J.6
Flowchart for Programming Assignment 1.

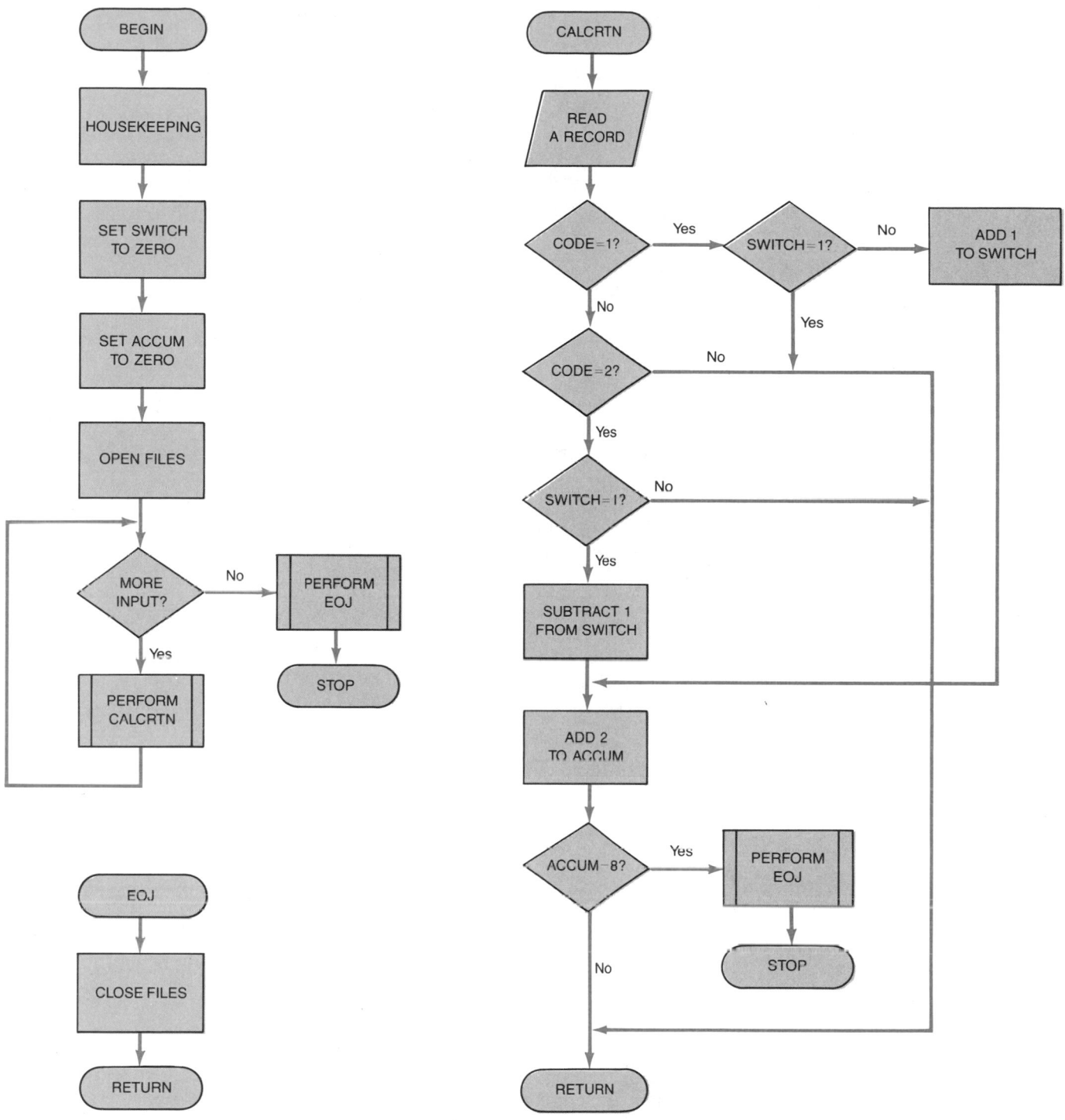

Figure J.7
Flowchart for Programming Assignment 2.

Programming With ASSIST and MUSIC

I. THE ASSIST ASSEMBLER

The ASSIST assembler is discussed in Chapter 4 and throughout the book. The major pseudo-instructions or macros are briefly reviewed here.

I. XREAD

This instruction is used to read punched-card data records. An example of the XREAD instruction follows.

```
XREAD     RECORD,80
```

where

RECORD   is the area in storage where the data will be temporarily stored
80   is the length of the record to be read

When the XREAD instruction is executed, the condition code is set as follows:

0—A card was read
1—The end-of-file condition was reached

2. XPRNT

This instruction is used to print a line. An example of the XPRNT instruction follows.

```
XPRNT     LINEOUT,133
```

where

LINEOUT   is the area in storage from which a line will be printed
133   is the number of bytes to be printed

3. XDECI

The purpose of this instruction is to convert a number in zoned-decimal or character form into binary form for use in a general-purpose register. An example of the XDECI instruction follows.

```
XDECI     5,AMOUNT
```

where

5   is the register into which the binary form of the number is to be placed
AMOUNT   is the address of the number in zoned-decimal or character form

When an XDECI instruction is executed, the condition code is set as follows:

0—The number converted was zero
1—The number converted was negative
2—The number converted was positive
3—The number could not be converted because it was not a valid number

4. XDECO

The purpose of this instruction is to convert a binary number in a general-purpose register into zoned-decimal or character form so that it can be printed. The converted number will be 12 bytes in length. An example of the XDECO instruction follows.

```
XDECO    5,AMTOUT
```

where

5   is the register that contains the binary number to be converted
AMTOUT   is the address of a 12-byte area in storage into which the zoned-decimal or character form of the number is to be placed

Note that the number will be right-justified in the field in storage, with high-order, non-significant zeros replaced with blanks. If the number is negative, a minus sign will print to the left of the first significant digit.

5. XDUMP

The XDUMP instruction can be used to display the contents of a particular field, as shown in the following example.

```
XDUMP    AMTOUT,12
```

where

AMTOUT   is the address of the field to be displayed
12   is the number of bytes to be displayed

If no operands are included with the XDUMP instruction, then the contents of the 16 general-purpose registers will be displayed.

II. THE MUSIC OPERATING SYSTEM

The use of the MUSIC operating system is discussed in Chapter 4. Under MUSIC, alternative macros are used in place of the standard access, I/O and DCB macros to provide more efficient utilization of the system. The instructions that make up each of the alternative macros are shown in the following figures.

Standard Macro	Alternative Macro	Figure
OPEN	MOPEN	K.1
CLOSE	MCLOSE	K.2
GET	MGET	K.3
PUT	MPUT	K.4
DCB (for input)	MDCBIN	K.5
DCB (for printed output)	MDCBOUT	K.6

Note that the MDCBIN macro is designed for 80-byte input records.

```
LOC   OBJECT CODE    ADDR1 ADDR2 STMT   SOURCE STATEMENT
                                  2 *
                                  3 *         M U S I C   I/O   M A C R O  -----> MOPEN
                                  4 *
                                  5         MACRO
                                  6         MOPEN &LIST
                                  7 .*                          OPEN  (FILENAME,(OPTION))
                                  8 .*                            OPTION=INPUT OR OUTPUT
                                  9         AIF   ('&LIST(2)' EQ '(INPUT)').IN
                                 10         AIF   ('&LIST(2)' EQ '(OUTPUT)').OUT
                                 11         MNOTE 9,'*****INCORRECT I/O OPTION. OPTION CHOSEN = &LIST(2).'
                                 12         MEXIT
                                 13 .IN     ANOP
                                 14         CNOP  0,4
                                 15         BAL   1,*+8
                                 16         DC    AL1(128)
                                 17         DC    AL3(&LIST(1).)
                                 18         SVC   19
                                 19         MEXIT
                                 20 .OUT    ANOP
                                 21         CNOP  0,4
                                 22         BAL   1,*+8
                                 23         DC    AL1(143)
                                 24         DC    AL3(&LIST(1).)
                                 25         SVC   19
                                 26         MEND
```

Figure K.1
Sample MUSIC MOPEN macro

```
LOC   OBJECT CODE    ADDR1 ADDR2 STMT   SOURCE STATEMENT
                                  2 *
                                  3 *         M U S I C   I/O   M A C R O  -----> MGET
                                  4 *
                                  5         MACRO
                                  6 &MGET   MGET  &INFILE,&RECORD
                                  7 &MGET   LA    1,&INFILE
                                  8         LA    0,&RECORD
                                  9         L     15,48(0,1)
                                 10         BALR  14,15
                                 11         MEND
```

Figure K.2
Sample MUSIC MCLOSE macro.

```
LOC   OBJECT CODE    ADDR1 ADDR2 STMT   SOURCE STATEMENT
                                  2 *         M U S I C   I/O   M A C R O  -----> MCLOSE
                                  3 *
                                  4         MACRO
                                  5 &MCL    MCLOSE &FILE
                                  6 .*                          CLOSE (FILENAME)
                                  7 &MCL    BCR   0,0
                                  8         CNOP  0,4
                                  9         BAL   1,*+8
                                 10         DC    AL1(128)
                                 11         DC    AL3&FILE
                                 12         SVC   20
                                 13         MEND
```

Figure K.3
Sample MUSIC MGET macro.

```
LOC   OBJECT CODE    ADDR1 ADDR2 STMT   SOURCE STATEMENT
                                  2 *
                                  3 *          M U S I C  I/O  M A C R O -----> MPUT
                                  4 *
                                  5            MACRO
                                  6 &MPUT      MPUT    &OUTFILE,&OUTAREA
                                  7 &MPUT      LA      1,&OUTFILE
                                  8            LA      0,&OUTAREA
                                  9            L       15,48(0,1)
                                 10            BALR    14,15
                                 11            MEND
```

Figure K.4
Sample MUSIC MPUT macro.

```
              MACRO
NAME          MDCBIN &EOF=
*                               INFILE    DCB    DDNAME=SYSIN,
*                                                MACRF=GM,
*                                                BLKSIZE=80,
*                                                LRECL=80,
*                                                DSORG=PS,
*                                                EODAD=&EOF
NAME          DC     0F'0'
              DC     BL16'0'
              DC     A(0)
              DC     AL1(0)
              DC     AL3(1)
              DC     AL2(0)
              DC     BL2'0100000000000000'
              DC     A(1)
              DC     BL1'00000000'
              DC     AL3(&EOF)
              DC     BL1'00000000'
              DC     AL3(0)
              DC     CL8'SYSIN'
              DC     BL1'00000010'
              DC     BL1'00000000'
              DC     BL2'0101000000000000'
              DC     BL1'00000000'
              DC     AL3(1)
              DC     A(1)
              DC     H'0'
              DC     AL2(80)
              DC     F'0'
              DC     A(1)
              DC     AL1(0)
              DC     AL3(1)
              DC     A(1)
              DC     H'0'
              DC     AL2(80)
              DC     BL1'00000000'
              DC     AL3(1)
              DC     F'0'
              DC     A(1)
              DC     X'E3E5C4'
              MEND
```

Figure K.5
Sample MUSIC MDCBIN macro.

```
                    MACRO
        &NAME1      MDCBOUT
        .*
        .*                      OUTFILE   DCB    DDNAME=SYSPRINT,
        .*                                       MACRF=(PM),
        .*                                       BLKSIZE=133,
        .*                                       LRECL=133,
        .*                                       DSORG=PS
        &NAME1      DC     0F'0'
                    DC     BL16'0'
                    DC     A(0)
                    DC     AL1(0)
                    DC     AL3(1)
                    DC     AL2(0)
                    DC     BL2'0100000000000000'
                    DC     A(1)
                    DC     BL1'00000000'
                    DC     AL3(1)
                    DC     BL1'00000000'
                    DC     AL3(0)
                    DC     CL8'SYSPRINT'
                    DC     BL1'00000010'
                    DC     BL1'00000000'
                    DC     BL2'0000000001010000'
                    DC     BL1'00000000'
                    DC     AL3(1)
                    DC     A(1)
                    DC     H'0'
                    DC     AL2(133)
                    DC     F'0'
                    DC     A(1)
                    DC     AL1(0)
                    DC     AL3(1)
                    DC     A(1)
                    DC     H'0'
                    DC     AL2(133)
                    DC     BL1'00000000'
                    DC     AL3(1)
                    DC     F'0'
                    DC     A(1)
                    MEND
```

Figure K.6
Sample MUSIC MDCBOUT macro.

Index

LABEL	OPERATION	OPERAND	COMMENTS
1	10	16	72

LABEL	OPERATION	OPERAND	COMMENTS

LABEL	OPERATION	OPERAND	COMMENTS

LABEL	OPERATION	OPERAND	COMMENTS
1	10	16	72

LABEL	OPERATION	OPERAND	COMMENTS
1	10	16	72

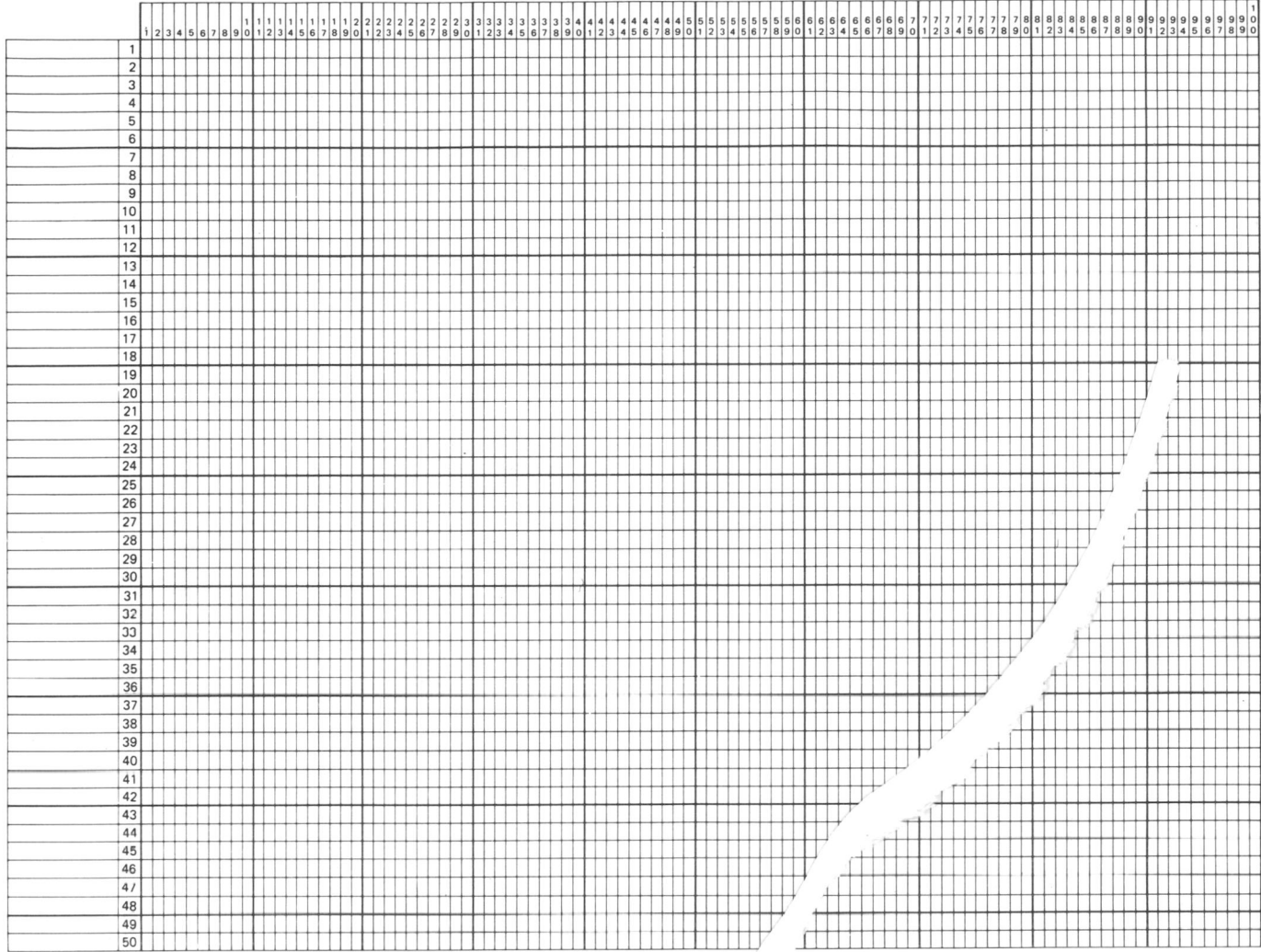